CYRUS HALL McCORMICK

Cyrus Hall McCormick
From a pastel by Lawton S. G. Parker

CYRUS HALL McCORMICK

HARVEST, 1856-1884

WILLIAM T. HUTCHINSON
Associate Professor of History, The University of Chicago

ILLUSTRATED WITH PHOTOGRAPHS,
CHARTS, AND MAPS

D. APPLETON-CENTURY COMPANY
INCORPORATED
NEW YORK   1935   LONDON

HD 9486
.U4
M35
v.2

PREFACE

Cyrus Hall McCormick: Seed-Time, 1809-1856, published by The Century Company five years ago, traces the life of the inventor of the first practical grain reaper until the eve of the Civil War when he was established in Chicago with fame and fortune assured. The present volume completes the story of his career. In this sequel the history of the harvesting-machine industry is carried forward to 1885, but much space is necessarily allotted to McCormick's philanthropies and his rôle in the Presbyterian Church, the Democratic Party, and important railroad and mining companies.

Although articles in contemporary newspapers and magazines have been frequently consulted in writing this biography, chief reliance has been placed upon the voluminous files of letters in the libraries of the McCormick Historical Association and the Nettie F. McCormick Biographical Association in Chicago. To these organizations, and to their members individually, I am indebted for the privilege of freely examining this correspondence, for most of the illustrations in this volume, and for cordial coöperation at every stage of the work.

Eight years of research in the rich collection of the McCormick Historical Association have placed me under heavy obligation to Mr. Herbert A. Kellar, the librarian, for much assistance and many courtesies. I am grateful to Miss Virginia Roderick, the librarian of the Nettie F. McCormick Biographical Association, for aid in exploring the valuable source

v

materials under her charge. My sincere thanks are also due to other members of the staffs of these libraries—Miss Loraine Weber, Miss Portia Cheal, Miss Rose Oenning, Miss Marie Succo, Mr. Charles E. O'Connor, and particularly to Mrs. Herbert A. Kellar who has helped me so often on special problems.

Professor William E. Dodd first aroused my interest in the life of Cyrus Hall McCormick and my debt to him has been an increasing one. Portions of the manuscript have benefited from the suggestions of Professor Wood Gray of The George Washington University, and of my colleagues, Professor Andrew C. McLaughlin, Professor Avery O. Craven, and Professor William L. Eagleton. I wish also to express my appreciation for the time and counsel generously given by Professor Marcus W. Jernegan, Professor Bessie L. Pierce, and Professor Einar Joranson when I have gone to them with matters relating to this study.

My indebtedness to my wife, Frances R. Hutchinson, for help with the typing and proof-reading, and for unfailing encouragement at all times, is greater than any acknowledgment here can express.

WILLIAM T. HUTCHINSON.

New Brunswick, N. J.

CONTENTS

vii

ILLUSTRATIONS

CYRUS HALL McCORMICK

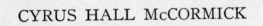

CYRUS HALL McCORMICK

CHAPTER I

CYRUS McCORMICK AND THE PRESBYTERIAN CAUSE, 1855-1865

A NEW chapter in the life of Cyrus McCormick began as the last decade before the Civil War drew to its close. By then he was fifty years of age, and since 1840 his attention had been almost exclusively devoted to the improvement and sale of his reaper. This concentration of effort had brought him both wealth and renown. He had plowed deep but in a single furrow, and his eyes had seldom been lifted from the task. In the opinion of those who had felt his power when they tried to block his course, he was a man of iron. To fight and not to compromise had been his formula of success, and appropriately enough, *"Sine Timore"* was the motto on the ancient coat-of-arms of his family. In 1858, as lawsuits and other business connected with his factory obliged him to hurry from city to city of the North and West, men who did not share his confidence would have scorned to believe that he could alter his way of life, or that he was even then preparing a program of action which would make that year a turning point in his career.

Doubtless his marriage in January, 1858, to young Nancy (Nettie) Fowler was a most important, if not the decisive, factor in widening his horizon. The range of her interests was as broad as his was narrow. She drew him into society and he was gratified to find that persons of distinction who first welcomed him because of his wealth and his reputation

3

as an inventor, soon listened with respect to his views upon
the issues of the day. He discovered that he had something
of interest to say about matters unrelated to his business,
and under her tactful guidance the courtesy and hospitality
of his native state of Virginia were transferred to northern
soil. Both enjoyed music and he often accompanied her on
his violin or sang with her the hymns and folk melodies
loved since his youth. The Presbyterian Church was a mutual bond, and a Bible went with them on all their trips
together.[1] After his marriage, "Business before pleasure" replaced the "All business" rule of the earlier years.

Mrs. McCormick was his only master and she conquered
him by bending to his will. From the outset of their life together, he made her his business confidante and, probably
to her surprise, she quickly came to share his enthusiasm
for his work and brought to his problems a hitherto unsus-
pected talent for giving wise counsel. His letters rarely credit
a decision to her influence, but without doubt as he grew older
he came more and more to rely upon her advice. She was his
mainstay and he seldom took an important step without first
gaining her approval. Although proud of his victories, she
valued them the more because the wealth that they brought
could be used to help those who were less fortunate. To her,
this opportunity was the supreme justification of her husband's inflexibility and his determination to work and win
as long as his strength permitted. He came to share her point
of view and during the last twenty-five years of his life he
devoted large sums of money to the service of others. As he
wrote to his former slave, "Jo" Anderson, in 1870, "Increased
means and success in a business life bring with them usually,
as in my own case, an increase of cares and responsibility;
while the . . . means I find to counteract *injurious* effects

[1] C. H. McCormick, from Eureka Springs, Ark., to C. H. McCormick,
Jr., May 21, 1882.

therefrom are . . . in being also actively employed in works of benevolence." [2] On another occasion he assured an old friend in Virginia, "I am in favor of using means while one lives, rather than leave all to be lost or squandered, as it *may be,* after death." [3]

McCormick's conservatism and his early life in Virginia go far toward explaining why he was always a Presbyterian of the Old School and a stanch "stand pat" member of the Democratic Party. Innovations in methods of harvesting grain account for his fame and his fortune by the eve of the Civil War, but he willingly devoted both to the maintenance of "sound principles" hallowed by long usage in church and state. He prided himself upon his adherence to the old, and was the more convinced of the correctness of his beliefs when he saw new ideas threaten the unity of his denomination and the nation. In his opinion the Presbyterian Church (O.S.) and the Democratic Party, with their many members in both the slave and the free states, were two of the chief, if not the chief, ties which held the Union together between 1845 and 1860. He regretted the doctrinal schism of 1837 which had set apart the New School Presbyterians as a separate church. The Old School Presbyterian Church, however, was still national in its membership and it would not break in twain over the slavery question if he could prevent it. His policy in relation to his party and his church from 1856 to 1861 was shaped by his determination that the Union should be preserved. After this hope failed with Sumter and the Old School denomination divided, he bent his efforts for the next ten years and more, at the cost of much popularity, to reknit

[2] C. H. McCormick to "Jo" Anderson, Greenville, Va., Jan. 19, 1870.
[3] ‡C. H. McCormick to T. J. Massie, Aug. 6, 1866. The "‡" here and elsewhere in this volume indicates that the letter is a part of the manuscript collection of the Nettie F. McCormick Biographical Association. All other documents cited, unless otherwise noted, are in the library of the McCormick Historical Association.

the church bond. Only by doing so, in his opinion, would the country again be truly united. For these reasons, patriotism, party loyalty, and religious faith were often but slightly differentiated in McCormick's mind. On several occasions after the Civil War, friends felt obliged to remind him that all conservative Old School Presbyterians were not Democrats and that all supporters of Andrew Johnson and his reconstruction policy were not equally "sound" in matters of religion.[4] He found it difficult to understand how a true conservative could fail to be both.

Although his course in politics and in religion was pursued toward a single objective, he insisted that the unity of his church would be broken if the General Assembly took a stand upon political questions in its "deliverances." By "politics" in the 1850's McCormick and many other Presbyterians (O.S.), remembering the unhappy experiences of the Methodists and Baptists a few years before, meant the agitation within their ranks of the issues of slavery and slavery–extension. To an increasing number of northern Old School Presbyterians (although far from a majority of the denomination as late as 1860), refusal to modify the "non-interference" deliverance of the General Assembly of 1845 on the subject of slavery and to return to the positive antislavery position of 1818, was in reality taking a stand in politics with a vengeance.[5] By the time of the Kansas-Nebraska Bill and the Dred Scott decision, the members of the Old School Church, reflecting the political conflicts of the times, were classed as "radicals" or "conservatives," depending upon whether or not they opposed or upheld the deliverance of 1845.

[4] *Post,* Chap. II.
[5] In 1845 the General Assembly of the O. S. Presbyterian Church declared that "since Christ and his inspired Apostles did not make the holding of slaves a bar to communion, we, as a court of Christ, have no authority to do so; since they did not attempt to remove it from the Church by legislation, we have no authority to legislate on the subject."

The southern Presbyterians were almost without exception within the conservative camp on this question, and many of the most influential northern members, including McCormick, were willing to support them.

It perhaps need not be added that the New School Presbyterians of the North had also experienced, although to a lesser degree, the impact of the same issues, and were divided. In fact, by 1860 doctrinal differences between individual members of these two branches of the church often seemed unimportant when compared with the cleavage within their ranks on the subject of slavery. An Old School and a New School Presbyterian might feel a closer community of interest if they thought alike upon the absorbing political topics of the day, than either did with a member of his own group who viewed these same issues in another light. There were many New School Presbyterians whose theological beliefs squared in all essentials with Old School tenets. In short, the distinction between these two wings of the same denomination, although fixed by twenty-five years of practice, was often an academic one.

Not so, however, to McCormick or to most of the influential Old School Presbyterians who lived in the South. The inventor read his Bible devoutly, made a close study of the dogmas of his denomination on the subjects of free will, election, imputation, and grace, and was convinced that the "standards" of the Old School Church could not without real loss be twisted to harmonize with those of the seceders of 1837. For the sake of peace he outwardly yielded a little to the New School position in the early 1870's, but with slight exaggeration it may be said that the maintenance of "good old" Presbyterianism against assaults by heretic or unbeliever was one of the consuming interests of the last twenty-five years of his life. He was often willing to defer decision upon important business matters during this period if the needs of his denomination seemed to require his whole attention.

Because of his residence in Chicago after 1847, and the rapid growth of the Northwest, he naturally felt that the chief opportunity of the Old School Presbyterian Church lay in his own section of the country. He had noted many evidences of infidelity along the Ohio River during his first visit there in behalf of his reaper in 1845, and he saw more clearly as years went by that the advancing West was a challenge to his denomination to keep step. Other churches must not be permitted to preëmpt the new field. With this jealous regard for the spread of sound Presbyterianism, went hand in hand a firm belief by 1858 that the fate of the Union would be decided by the stand taken by the Northwest upon the questions of the day. Thus the welfare of his country as well as of his church was in the balance, and the future of each would be assured if the Northwest remained sanely conservative. On these issues McCormick was no longer the hard man of business, coldly calculating financial profit and loss, but an idealist ready to break a lance in behalf of a cause which some historians, wise after the event, believe to have been doomed to failure from the outset.

McCormick appreciated the influence of the pulpit upon public opinion, and by 1856 was grieved to find that his own minister in Chicago, among others, was leaning toward abolitionism. This, in the inventor's view, was both unorthodox and dangerous to the public peace. Thus far the leading seminaries of his faith in the North, Princeton, Union, and Western (Allegheny, Pa.), had remained true to the deliverance of 1845, but the little institution at New Albany, Indiana, largely on account of the same question, was fairly upon the rocks. It was high time to halt the menacing radicalism for the sake of his party, his church, and his country.

With these convictions, and with perhaps a million dollars in his pocket, McCormick in 1859 put in train several projects which significantly suggest the methods used by Stephen Doug-

Mrs. Cyrus Hall McCormick

From a photograph by Koehne, Chicago, about 1880

las in his rise to political eminence,—a newspaper to champion Democracy, a religious magazine to disseminate conservative Old School Presbyterianism, a Seminary to teach the same principles, and its professors and graduates, by advancing the cause of the denomination in the Northwest through their pulpits in Chicago and elsewhere, to hold this pivotal region from radicalism. The political phase of this plan will be separately considered in the next chapter.

A master mind seemed providentially ready at hand among the clergy of the West to be McCormick's executive. Dr. Nathan L. Rice, a pastor and the editor of a Presbyterian journal in St. Louis, had been known for over twenty years as one of the ablest controversialists in the church. His career had been a stormy one, but whether battling Catholics at Bardstown, Campbellites at Lexington, Universalists at Cincinnati, or Abolitionists everywhere, he had held his own in debate and was early counted among the giants of the Old School Church. He denied that he was a proponent of slavery, although he was ready to demonstrate by chapter and verse that slaveholding as practiced in the South was not a sin, and that it was not the duty of the church to preach against it.[6] McCormick first met him at Cincinnati in 1845, and at that time expressed his admiration in a letter to his brother. Here an acquaintance began which soon ripened into a friendship of large moment in the lives of both men for the next twenty-five years.

Shortly after coming to Chicago to live, McCormick helped to organize a little Presbyterian Church (O.S.) which was familiarly known as the "North Church." The congregation prospered and outgrew two buildings within a decade.[7] Here

[6] "Chicago Daily Press," Oct. 30, and Nov. 7, 1857, letter of N. L. Rice, printed in both issues.
[7] In 1857 the North Church was located at the corner of Illinois and Wolcott sts.

the inventor made many new friends but perhaps none of more significance in the life of Chicago Presbyterianism than Charles A. Spring, superintendent of the Sunday-school for several years, and brother of the famous Dr. Gardiner Spring of the Brick Presbyterian Church of New York City.[8]

Charles Spring, McCormick, and others were dissatisfied with the preaching of the Rev. R. H. Richardson, and by 1854 were planning to organize a new and more orthodox O.S. Church further south in what one day would be called the "Loop." Rice was to be their pastor if he could be secured. McCormick wrote to his friend:

There does seem to us to be a striking providence in this matter when *all* eyes and hearts are at once turned toward you as the man for the place and the work. . . . We do think the cause for which you have been so successfully laboring would be promoted by the change. We believe our whole church throughout the country is now sensible of the great importance of securing its proper influence at this point, and the proper exercise of that influence upon the vast interests extending throughout the great N. Western country of which Chicago must be the principal City and commercial emporium. . . . It is but reasonable to calculate that the magnitude of the work to be undertaken will demand a vigorous effort on the part of the church with the "right man" as its pastor.

It is thought that for the publication of your paper, too, this is *quite as suitable* a point as is St. Louis and that in this opinion you probably concur, having yourself proposed to issue it from both places.

We have secured a very commodious and suitable hall in which to commence operations. Presbytery is to meet about the 22nd inst. to organize the new Church.[9]

[8] C. A. Spring, Sr., to C. H. McCormick, Jr., Dec. 1, 1884. Spring states that he assumed charge of the Sunday-school because Cyrus McCormick urged it. McCormick's friendship for Spring ripened but slowly. C. H. to W. S. McCormick, Dec. 9, 1857 and July 15, 1858. Here he calls Spring a "silly man," and "a weak brother." "He, good man, has need to be held up to the point of firmness."

[9] C. H. McCormick to N. L. Rice, Dec. 3, 1854. McCormick here intimates that he had written him two years before upon the same subject.

Thus, so far as records show, McCormick somewhat vaguely first gave written expression to the "cause" which he had in mind.

These great expectations came to naught when Rice declined to leave St. Louis, and for almost three years the project hung fire for want of a suitable pastor. McCormick's patent business and lawsuits obliged him to live in Washington for long periods. Here he became a well-known figure in the congregation of the eminent Dr. Phineas Gurley, who one day would number Lincoln among his parishioners and be at his bedside when he died.

Between 1854 and 1857 Spring and a few others kept alive the plan for a South Church in Chicago, and in late 1855 secured for their pastor the youthful Rev. R. W. Henry of Pittsburgh. McCormick at once showed his interest by joining the new congregation and contributing liberally to its support. Without his donation the church building could not have been erected on his lot. He loaned money to Mr. Henry and rented him a house at one half the usual rate.[10] Soon, however, it was learned that the clergyman had voted for the presidential candidate of the Republican Party in the autumn of 1856, and rumor persisted that he was "tainted" on the slavery issue.[11] He refrained from discussing the questions of the day from his pulpit, but McCormick was convinced that he was not the man to advance the "great cause" in the Northwest.[12] By good fortune, the minister of the North Church resigned in the summer of 1857, and with Mr. Henry's cooperation, McCormick at once held out such tempting induce-

[10] C. H. McCormick in the "Chicago Daily Press" of Jan. 20, 1858, states that he paid one half of Mr. Henry's salary until about Sept., 1857.

[11] C. H. to W. S. McCormick, Oct. 7, 1856, Jan. 13, and 28, 1857.

[12] *Idem* to *idem,* n. d., but in 1857, prior to Sept. 1: "The present *Church* is but a circumstance; and I possibly *could* build a Church, and rent the pews, if *necessary* to carry out a *Great Church enterprise,* which has been my object throughout."

ments to the debt-burdened Dr. Rice that he could no longer afford to decline.[13]

Although the manufacturer announced his intention of joining Rice's congregation, it was understood that this change would not affect the fortunes of the South Church, since he would continue his financial arrangement with Mr. Henry, and donate the church lot, then estimated to be worth $30,000. The two ministers would be, in fact, co-pastors, frequently exchanging pulpits and working hand in hand for the advancement of Old School Presbyterianism in Chicago. This was the more necessary since the North Church building was inconveniently located and too small to accommodate the crowds who would doubtless wish to hear the distinguished divine from St. Louis. When this plan of interchurch coöperation was first suggested, Mr. Henry tentatively acquiesced, but he changed his mind before Dr. Rice arrived in Chicago in early October. By that time the smoldering discontent of the South Church congregation had become an open blaze.

The forces giving rise to the South Church schism were constants in the history of Chicago Presbyterianism for the next ten years. Most of the elders were conservative men of comfortable fortune who had attended the church at its birth and were well aware that it could hardly continue to live without their aid. Mr. Henry was not an able preacher, and although he prudently confined his sermons to non-controversial subjects, his discretion deserted him when he left the

[13] C. H. McCormick to N. L. Rice, Aug. 17, 1857. Rice would receive $3000 a year from his congregation and McCormick would add to it $2300 annually for five years. He would also send him $1000 for moving expenses and assume on easy terms the $5000 debt Rice owed in St. Louis. Rice would not need to pay interest to McCormick on this sum unless his paper yielded profits, and if Rice should die before the principal was discharged, the balance due would be cancelled. As early as March, 1857, McCormick had urged Rice to locate in Chicago, suggesting that a third church might be organized for him. C. H. to W. S. McCormick, Mch. 28, 1857. "Chicago Daily Democrat," Sept. 18 and Oct. 10, 1857.

pulpit. Although he had joined in the call sent to Dr. Rice, he doubtless anticipated with little pleasure the coming of a colleague with whom he could not compete. Spring and one other elder, of their own volition, admonished him privately to spend more time in his study. They, like McCormick, were eager to be of Dr. Rice's flock, but unlike him, they could not leave a substantial peace-offering upon their departure. Mr. Henry, who had no wish to stay where he was not wanted, tendered his resignation, but the congregation gave him an almost unanimous vote of confidence and refused to let him go. The discontented elders and trustees were virtually ejected from their positions and left the Church. Peace and poverty thus descended upon the congregation in the midst of the Panic of 1857.

Mr. Henry, perhaps emboldened by this evidence of loyalty, spoke with less reserve upon the subject of slavery, and the eager Republican press, contrary to his wishes, expanded his remarks into essays which placed him squarely at odds with the redoubtable Dr. Rice.[14] To add to the trouble, Cyrus McCormick now withdrew his aid from the South Church, pressed its needy pastor for payment of his debt, and cut off his supply of free coal from the factory yard.[15] But most serious of all, he declined to donate the lot to the Church on the grounds that there was no longer any possibility of coöperation between the two congregations, that the position of Henry on slavery was unorthodox, and that the property was too

[14] "Chicago Daily Tribune," Oct. 13, 1857. "Chicago Daily Press," Oct. 15, 30; Nov. 7, 1857. "Daily Chicago Times," Oct. 30, 1857.

[15] Mr. Henry, with C. A. Spring as his endorser, borrowed about $1400 of McCormick. In 1865, Spring wrote bitterly that Henry had left him with this debt to pay. It is probable that McCormick at that time released his friend from the obligation. C. H. to W. S. McCormick, Sept. 12, 1857; Apr. 3, July 17, 1858. L.P.C.B. No. 9, pp. 99-100, W. S. to J. B. McCormick, Oct. 8, 1857. ‡C. A. Spring to C. H. McCormick, Nov. 2, 1865. "L.P.C.B." here, and wherever used in this volume, stands for "Letter Press Copy Book."

valuable to give to an organization in so precarious a condition that its continued existence was a matter of grave
doubt.[16]

Although McCormick was willing that the South Church
building should remain on his lot until he needed it for other
purposes, the little congregation of less than one hundred
members bravely determined to throw off its dependence upon
the generosity of a man, who in its opinion, had treated Mr.
Henry unjustly and violated his pledge. The "Chicago Press
and Tribune" complimented this resolve and denounced Mc-
Cormick as the self-appointed "lay-bishop" of Presbyterianism
who "has an ambition to hold in fee simple a Church and a
pastor. . . . The opening on Wabash Avenue, at the corner
of Congress Street [site of South Church], is a good one for
any clergyman who happens to be for sale." [17] McCormick
released his interest in the South Church building and it was
sold to Lutherans. The congregation worshipped in the Railroad Chapel near the station of the Michigan Southern Railroad until its new edifice was completed. War issues darkened
its history for the next four years, and for thrice that long it
was severely harassed by debt.[18]

"It is glorious," wrote Cyrus McCormick to his brother
William S., on September 1, 1857, when he heard that Dr.
Rice would move his large family and his paper to Chicago.
At last the inventor's ambitious plan was fairly launched and
he was immediately accused of subsidizing the preaching of
pro-slavery principles in the free Northwest.[19] Since Dr. Rice

[16] "Chicago Daily Press," Oct. 31, Dec. 29, 1857; Jan. 20, 21, 22, 1858.
[17] "Chicago Daily Press and Tribune," July 31, Aug. 2, 1858.
[18] C. H. McCormick to J. Wilson and R. J. Hamilton, Dec. 10, 1857.
L.P.C.B. No. 9, pp. 878-9; C. H. to W. S. McCormick, Dec. 4, 5, and 29,
1857. Article by C. H. McCormick in "Chicago Daily Press," Jan. 20,
1858. ‡J. Forsythe to C. H. McCormick, Mch. 14, 1869.
[19] "Richmond (Va.) Examiner," September 25, 1857, quoting an article
by Horace Greeley in the "New York Daily Tribune." "The South" (Richmond), Sept. 3, 1857. Dr. Rice preached his first sermon in North Church

and Mr. Henry were soon crossing swords over the issue in the Chicago press, the suspicions of those hostile to McCormick were confirmed. Dissension within the ranks of the Chicago Old School Presbyterians increased in bitterness as the Lincoln-Douglas debates fanned the flame, but although the North Church was enlarged,[20] the forceful sermons of Dr. Rice soon overcrowded it with listeners. Money was difficult to raise in those hard times and it was early 1861 before the congregation was ready to dedicate its new, large, heavily mortgaged, brick edifice at the corner of Cass and Indiana streets. From the outset, McCormick had been anxious that a "handsome" structure should be erected with all speed. His $10,000 headed the subscription list, and although court decisions at that time were going strongly against him, he was prepared to give more if need should arise.[21] Little wonder that his enemies soon called the building "Mr. McCormick's Church." [22]

on Oct. 11, 1857. "Chicago Daily Press," Oct. 3, 10, Dec. 29, 1857; Jan. 18, 20, 21, 22, 1858. "Chicago Daily Tribune," Dec. 10, 1857 ff. Strangely enough, Rice was not a Democrat. See letter of C. H. McCormick in "Chicago Daily Press" of Jan. 20, 1858.

20 "Chicago Daily Press and Tribune," Aug. 2, 1858. At this time, while its building was being enlarged, the North Church congregation held services in old St. James' Church, on Cass St. The erection of the "new and beautiful" church was delayed for financial reasons until 1859.

21 Letters to Nettie F. McCormick of Amanda J. Adams, Mch. 13, 1858; Henrietta M. McCormick, Mch. 17, 1858; and of Mary Ann McCormick, Sept. 1, 1858, and Feb. 17, 1861. L.P.C.B. No. 11, pp. 399, 503 ff., No. 12, p. 152, letters of W. S. to C. H. McCormick, Mch. 27, Apr. 2, and June 4, 1858. C. H. to W. S. McCormick, Mch. (?), Apr. 9, 19, May 3, 26, and 31, 1858. W. S. to J. B. McCormick, Mch. 29, 1858. In a letter of June 10, 1858, to C. H. McCormick, W. S. Johnston, Jr., offered to sell the lot at the corner of Cass and Indiana sts. for $15,000.

22 H. A. Hurlbut to C. H. McCormick, Feb. 14, 1861. At this time, the new North Church was still unfinished, and Hurlbut hoped that McCormick would find some way to provide $1500 so that the job could be completed. See also, W. S. to C. H. McCormick, July 9, 1862, and ‡H. A. Hurlbut to C. H. McCormick, Jan. 31, 1866. These letters show that the church was mortgaged for $12,000 to C. H. McCormick, Wesley Munger, and E. S.

In the meantime, Dr. Rice transferred his monthly "St. Louis Presbyterian" to Chicago. Although the number of its subscribers increased, it was never self-supporting. Because the entire financial burden of the periodical was necessarily shouldered by McCormick, it was, in fact, his property. During its career of less than two years, the "Presbyterian Expositor," as it was soon called, represented a further contribution of over $6,000 by the inventor to "the cause" in the Northwest.[23] He had been sanguine that it would pay its way. Its failure to do so, coupled with his costly publication venture in the secular field at this time, made him hesitate a decade later when the establishment of a new religious magazine seemed to be desirable.[24]

But the prime instrument for the accomplishment of McCormick's design was to be an Old School Presbyterian seminary in Chicago. From this institution as a focus, with each professor holding a pastoral charge in the city and contributing sermons and articles *gratis* to the "Expositor," conservative influences and sound theology would radiate to more and more homes in the Northwest.[25] Each alumnus would reflect

Wadsworth. C. H. McCormick to H. A. Hurlbut, Dec. 3, 1866. "Chicago Evening Post," Dec. 2, 1868.

[23] When the "Presbyterian Expositor" was established in Jan. 1860, McCormick understood that he, the North, and the South Church, should each bear one-third of its running expenses. The South Church under Mr. Henry would not, and the North Church could not, pay their quotas. C. H. to W. S. McCormick, Dec. 9, 1857. A final settlement between McCormick and Dr. Rice, given in L.P.C.B. No. 40, p. 592, Apr. 6, 1861, indicates that the "Expositor" cost the inventor over $7,000. The amount is given as $6,282.06 in #C. A. Spring, Jr., to C. H. McCormick, Aug. 27, 1866. In letters to H. A. Boardman, July 8, 1866, and to the faculty of the Presby. Theo. Sem. of the NW., Jan. ?, 1874, C. H. McCormick mentions $8,000 as his loss from Rice's paper. "Chicago Times," Jan. 24, 1875, states $8,000-$10,000.

[24] *Post*, pp. 43 ff.

[25] C. H. McCormick to B. M. Smith, July 14, 1865: "In what was done by me for the 'Presbyterian Theological Seminary of the Northwest' one important object designed to be secured was the establishment of such an

from his pulpit the principles he had learned as a student. As early as the autumn of 1856, McCormick expressed an interest in the news that the little seminary at New Albany, unable longer to compete with Danville across the Ohio River, was obliged to move or die.[26] The board of directors of the Indiana institution, controlled by the seven Old School Presbyterian synods in the Northwest, convened in Chicago in November to take counsel with leading churchmen there. The outcome of this meeting was the appointment of six members of the North and South Churches as the trustees of a "Presbyterian Theological Seminary of the Northwest," as yet unlocated and without endowment.[27] On the first of the following month, McCormick wrote to his brother that he proposed to use his

institution in the great West . . . with a view to strengthen the national religious influence there, as opposed to the sectional, or radical influence, and thus so far to promote the stability of the Union."

[26] C. H. to W. S. McCormick, Oct. 24, 1856. The New Albany Seminary was an outgrowth of a log-cabin academy founded by Dr. John F. Crowe at Hanover, Ind., in 1827. From this academy came Hanover College in 1833. In 1840, to secure the benefits of a gift, the theological school was moved to New Albany, on the Ohio River. With Lyman Beecher at Lane Seminary (N. S.), a short distance to the eastward, and Robert L. Breckinridge at Danville Seminary (O. S.) after 1853, it is not surprising that the ability of the school at New Albany to survive was in doubt. The faculty there attempted to maintain neutrality on the question of slavery, but the antislavery students drifted to Lane, and those from the South, to Danville. See J. G. McClure, "The Story of the Life and Work of the Presbyterian Theological Seminary, Chicago, founded by Cyrus H. McCormick" (Chicago, 1929) ; W. W. Moore, "Halsey's History of McCormick Seminary," in "Presbyterian Quarterly" (Charlotte, N. C.), Jan. 1, 1894; Alfred Nevin, "Encyclopædia of the Presbyterian Church in the United States of America" (Phila., 1884), p. 303; Pamphlet, "1829-1929, Presbyterian Theological Seminary, Chicago" (Chicago, 1929). This states, without giving its authority, that in 1855 Dr. J. G. Monfort of Cincinnati suggested that McCormick should be approached on the question of moving the seminary to Chicago. If this is true, Monfort later had good cause to regret his suggestion.

[27] The act of incorporation by the legislature was dated Feb. 16, 1857. "McClure," pp. 31-32; Pamphlet, "Constitution and Charter of the Presbyterian Theological Seminary of the Northwest" (Chicago, 1872).

influence and his money to secure the transfer of the school
from New Albany to Chicago, since it would be of "importance to our cause." [28] Dr. Rice prepared a pamphlet in support
of the project and it also received considerable notice in the
newspapers of the city.[29]

The Panic of 1857, coupled with acute differences of opinion
between radical and conservative Old School leaders in the
Northwest, made it impossible to go forward during the next
two years. Until 1858 it was planned to establish the seminary
in Hyde Park, just south of Chicago, where Paul Cornell and
others promised to give land, but definite action was delayed
both by the hard times and because the members of the board
of directors failed to agree whether the institution should remain under synodical control or be transferred to the supervision of the General Assembly of the whole church. Since the
churches of the Northwest were becoming more antislavery
in outlook, this issue was of far more importance than a mere
question of administration.[30] In the meantime, the seminary at
New Albany was unable to survive the financial storm, and the
closing of its doors after Commencement in 1857 signified that
whenever the new institution should commence instruction, it

[28] C. H. to W. S. McCormick, Dec. 1, 1856.

[29] "Chicago Daily Press," Nov. 20, 1857.

[30] *Ibid.*, Nov. 21, 1857. At a meeting of the board of directors at this
time it was decided to remain under synodical control for the time being.
Among the directors were C. A. Spring, Paul Cornell, A. B. Newkirk, and
Jesse L. Williams. An unsigned and undated memo. in the papers of the
N. F. McCormick Biog. Asso. states that between 1856 and May, 1859,
this synodical board did little except run up expenses. Its agent spent more
than the contributions received, and employed an architect, at a fee of
$1,600, to design a seminary building to cost $200,000! The board was
replaced by a new body of forty directors in May, 1859, when the seminary
passed under the control of the General Assembly of the national Church.
On Dec. 15, 1857, Wm. Houston of Rockbridge Cy., Va., wrote to
W. S. and C. H. McCormick that he had read in the "New York Observer"
of Cyrus's "munificent offer of land and money for a Theological Seminary
in connection with the name of Professor R[ice]." I have not found in the
McCormick MSS. any mention of an offer being made at this time.

would be in only a nominal sense a continuation of the old.[31] McCormick's interest did not lag during these troublous times, and he found a loyal ally in Charles Spring.[32]

By 1859, conditions were more favorable for a resumption of the campaign for an endowment of land and money. Shortly before the Lincoln-Douglas debates, Dr. Rice and Dr. Erasmus D. MacMaster, able defender of the growing antislavery group within the Old School Church, fought an indecisive duel of words over the issue of the day.[33] Rice wished to be, and MacMaster had been and hoped to be again, a member of the faculty of the seminary, and the matter in controversy between them was the same question which had hitherto made coöperation impossible among the friends of that institution. Naturally, the opposing groups in the General Assembly at Indianapolis in May, 1859, rallied around one or the other of these leaders. If the antislavery forces should carry out their program of reëstablishing the seminary at Indianapolis with MacMaster as senior professor, McCormick's "grand design" would be defeated.[34] But several days before the Assembly convened, McCormick placed in the hands of Charles Spring, a delegate from the Chicago Presbytery, a weapon so power-

[31] "Report of the Minority of the Board of Directors to the Committee of Inquiry of the General Assembly, May 15, 1869." Article by Rev. D. X. Junkin, "The Presbyterian Banner" (Pittsburgh), Mch. 24, 1869. Dr. Junkin was one of the directors.

[32] C. H. to W. S. McCormick, Sept. 12, 1857. C. H. McCormick to C. A. Spring, Sr., Mch. 7, 1872: "You the most aged and experienced of us all, and to whom I was myself indebted for the original suggestion and advice to make the donation to this cause [the seminary] in 1859." C. A. Spring to C. H. McCormick, Jr., Nov. 26, 1884. W. H. Neff, in his "Reminiscences of the Second Presbyterian Church, Cincinnati" (Cin., 1898), states that Rev. Thos. H. Skinner was largely responsible for inducing C. H. McCormick to make his gift. I have found no confirmation of this.

[33] C. H. to W. S. McCormick, Nov. 19, 1857.

[34] Dr. MacMaster, who will enter this story on several occasions, was fifty-three years of age in 1859. He had been President both of Hanover College and Miami University. He was an able scholar, and it was said that he could fill with distinction any chair in a theological seminary.

ful that the issue was not long in doubt. On May 13, 1859, the inventor, then in Washington, drafted a proposal to endow four professorships in the seminary with $25,000 each, provided that the Assembly took over the control of the institution from the seven synods of the Northwest and located it in Chicago. McCormick added that he regarded "this proposed enterprise as of the greatest importance not only to the religious, but also the general interests of the country." [85] Faced with the offer of a gift larger, so it is said, than any made to a theological seminary up to that time, and also promised a liberal donation of land,[36] the Assembly declined the bid by the MacMasterites of $10,000 and ten acres, and emphasized its preference for Chicago by a vote of 251 to 71. Nor could Dr. MacMaster prevent the election of Dr. Rice to the Chair of Didactic and Polemic Theology. In view of the future, it was also significant that Dr. Willis Lord was selected for the Chair of Biblical and Ecclesiastical History

[35] C. H. McCormick to C. D. Drake, n.d., but 1869: "My opinion then was that the peace of the Country was greatly threatened by the agitation of that question [slavery]; and that, to keep that *agitation out of the Church* so far as possible was an important means for the preservation of the *Union,* as well as for the peace of the Church." "Daily Chicago Times," May 27 and June 8, 1859.

[36] "Minutes of the General Assembly of the Presbyterian Church in the United States of America," 1859-1864 (Phila. n.d.), p. 25. Here it is stated that forty-five acres of land had been promised in Chicago. The present writer is unable to particularize more than thirty-one acres. Twenty-five of these were the "North Side" property on which the seminary was finally located in 1864. Twenty acres there were given by Wm. B. Ogden and his partner J. E. Sheffield of New Haven, Conn., with the proviso that a building costing a stipulated sum should be erected on it within two years (by May, 1861). Adjoining this land, Lill & Diversey, brewers, gave five acres. Thos. H. Beebe was chiefly instrumental in securing the gift from Ogden, and Charles Spring in gaining the donation from Lill & Diversey. In June, 1859, Chas. Macalister of Philadelphia gave, or promised to give, six acres in the West Division at the corner of Taylor and Rucker sts. "Chicago Daily Press and Tribune," June 25, 1859. C. A. Spring, Sr., to C. H. McCormick, Jr., Dec. 20, 1884.

and Dr. Leroy J. Halsey for the Chair of Historical and Pastoral Theology.[37] McCormick had won the day.

Probably few gifts have brought a philanthropist more trouble, and ultimately more satisfaction, than McCormick's pledge to the Presbyterian Seminary of the Northwest. Less than two years after the first students assembled about their professors in the temporary class-rooms in a Chicago hotel in the autumn of 1859,[38] the opening of the Civil War brought to a head the growing dissension within the Old School Church over the question of slavery. McCormick's donation had not been an unconditional one. As he wrote later: "When my offer of the endowment was before the Assembly of 1859, it was well understood to have been made in connection with the position then held by the Genl. Assembly of the O. School P. Church on the Slavery question, as represented by Dr. Rice, in the Deliverance of the Assembly on that question in 1845." [39] In other words, there were *implied* qualifications at-

[37] "McClure," p. 43. "Minutes of the General Assembly," *op. cit.* pp. 1-40, C. A. Spring was a member of the first board of directors, composed of twenty ministers and twenty ruling elders. In his old age he affirmed that "delicacy prevented" C. H. McCormick from going as a delegate to Indianapolis. C. A. Spring, Sr., to C. H. McCormick, Jr., Dec. 19, 1884. A letter written by ‡Dr. B. M. Smith to C. H. McCormick, May 12, 1866, leaves little doubt that McCormick, although not a delegate, was at Indianapolis during the meeting of the General Assembly of 1859. "Chicago Daily Press and Tribune," May 25 and 27, 1859.

[38] "McClure," pp. 46, 55. The hotel was at the west corner of Clark and Harrison sts. Classes were also held in buildings at the corner of Illinois and Pine sts., and in the basement of North Church.

[39] C. H. McCormick to C. D. Drake, n.d., but late 1869. C. H. McCormick to W. Lord, Jan. 6, 1869: "The written conditions of my bond were not the only ones. There were also *understood and implied* pledges and one was that the Seminary should be the exponent of sound scriptural and conservative views." D. X. Junkin stated in "The Presbyterian Banner," Mch. 24, 1869, that there was, in 1859, a *"very explicit understanding* . . . in regard to the type of theology that was to prevail in it." "Minutes of the General Assembly," 1865-1869, p. 507: "It is historically true that he [McCormick] and the great majority of that Assembly [1859] were agreed as to the

tached to the gift. McCormick was later to argue that if the seminary faculty departed from the doctrines of their denomination as held in 1859, he would be released from his obligations. In his view, the question of freedom of speech was not involved, since this was a theological seminary and not a university. The faculty were naturally expected to teach the orthodox doctrines of their denomination. What these doctrines were at the time of his gift, there could be no question.

The rather small minority of the delegates to the General Assembly of 1859 in favor of the Indianapolis location did not accurately represent the strength of the midwestern antislavery group within the church.[40] It was soon made clear that the new institution could expect little or no financial support from most of the synods of the Northwest, and without the substantial and continued aid of McCormick and the members of the North Church, the enterprise would quickly fail.[41] Thus a seminary which was intended to be the regional focus of a large denomination, soon became the instrument of a conservative group, chiefly residing in one city. The political drift of the Northwest beween 1859 and 1861 augured ill for the success of an institution dedicated in part to the task of pre-

impropriety of agitating the slavery question in the judicatories of the church. . . ."

[40] The history of the Old and New School Presbyterian Churches during these years is admirably told by Lewis C. VanderVelde in "The Presbyterian Churches and the Federal Union, 1861-1869" (Cambridge, Mass., 1932).

[41] ‡Copy from the "Original Endowment Book of the First Financial Agency of the Pres. Theological Seminary of the Northwest," written in 1887 by C. A. Spring. This shows that up to Feb. 25, 1860, about 140 people had contributed or pledged $132,918. Of this amount, McCormick's was $100,000. C. H. McCormick to C. D. Drake, n.d., but 1869. Besides the contributions from the Chicago group, and small donations from friends at Galena and Rockford, Ill., the funds raised for the seminary during the war came chiefly from New York City. The depressed state of agriculture in the Northwest on the eve of the Civil War also hampered the raising of funds for the seminary.

serving the *status quo* upon a question that had made much history since 1845. McCormick's participation in politics drew his opponents' fire upon "his" seminary, and many wished to believe that he had established a "fortress of slavery" in their midst.[42] This was a damaging charge in days when nice distinctions were forgotten, and northerners who worked for peace and compromise were labelled "pro-slavery" by their foes.[43]

As Cyrus McCormick surveyed the general situation in April, 1861, he must have felt that his efforts had brought very small return. His "castle," as one of his enemies sneeringly termed it later, had fallen in ruins.[44] The land donated for the seminary was an expanse of "grass pastures and cabbage patches" with the turf still unbroken for the erection of a building. The seminary in 1861 graduated eleven students who had received their instruction in makeshift class-rooms about the city. For want of a dormitory, some had been sheltered in the homes of the professors. Dr. William M. Scott, the Professor of Biblical Literature and Exegesis, was on his death-bed, and Dr. Rice in impaired health and tired of braving the rising radicalism of Chicago, "felt himself called by Providence to resign his Chair" in order to accept the pastorate of the Fifth Avenue Presbyterian Church in New York City.[45] Only Dr.

42 "McClure," p. 48.
43 N. L. Rice to C. H. McCormick, Jan. 4, 1869: "I never had any intimation that you desired the Professors of the Theological Seminary to take any ground on slavery other than that which the Presbyterian Church had ever occupied. . . . While I was a Professor at the Seminary I never knew you to inquire into the opinion of the Professors in regard to slavery."
44 "Chicago Evening Post," Dec. 2, 1858.
45 "Minutes of the General Assembly," 1859-1864, *op. cit.*, p. 153. McCormick's order of preference for a successor of Dr. Rice was Dr. H. A. Boardman of Philadelphia, Dr. T. V. Moore of Richmond, and Dr. P. Gurley of Washington. See, #C. H. McCormick to Rev. T. V. Moore, Richmond, Va., Apr. 13, 1861: "I may remark that the health of Dr. Rice has not been good, while he has labored under some embarrassments in other respects."

Halsey and Dr. Lord were left of the original faculty, and while Halsey remained true to the Old School position of 1845, he was a timid fighter and shunned all controversy. The "wanton war spirit" and inefficient office management brought the "Presbyterian Expositor" low, and since it had failed in its purpose, it was abandoned in order to save useless expense.[46] Conservatism in church or state was now akin to disloyalty. War had come and Lincoln's election had been made possible by the vote of the Northwest.

With war excitement at white heat, the Old School Presbyterian General Assembly convened at Philadelphia in mid-May, 1861. For the first time in over twenty years the conservatives were unable to control its deliberations. After prolonged and bitter debate, with Dr. Charles Hodge and the Princeton group leading the opposition, the Gardiner A. Spring Resolutions were adopted. In these it was affirmed that "this General Assembly . . . do hereby acknowledge and declare our obligations to promote and perpetuate, so far as in us lies, the integrity of these United States, and to strengthen, uphold, and encourage the Federal Government in the exercise of all its functions under our noble Constitution; and to this Constitution, in all its provisions, requirements, and principles, we profess our unabated loyalty." This judgment upon a political question was accepted by the southerners who comprised at least one-third of the membership of the Old School Presbyterian Church as a sentence of banishment.[47] Allegiance to the Constitution was thereby made a test of membership in the

[46] ‡J. M. Faris to C. H. McCormick, Apr. 20, 1861.

[47] "Minutes of the General Assembly," 1859-1864, op. cit., pp. 138 ff. McCormick believed that Lincoln, when his opinion was asked, advised the General Assembly not to pass the Spring Resolutions. See, C. H. McCormick to B. M. Smith, July 14, 1865. McCormick's view of these measures is summarized in his letter to W. S. Plumer on Jan. 5, 1864: "I have never believed in the policy of the Gen'l. Assembly at Phila. . . . in cutting off the Church South, and thus severing the strongest cord of sympathy and communication between the North and the South."

denomination and, in fact, an evidence of godliness. Among those who voted in the affirmative were Rev. Willis Lord and Charles Spring.

When members of the Assembly who like Cyrus McCormick viewed their church as a safe-guard of the Union, protested that this action was a "national calamity," they were reminded that "there are occasions when *political* questions *rise into the sphere of morals and religion*. . . . Would you [they] have us recognize, as good Presbyterians, men whom our own government, with the approval of Christendom, may soon execute as traitors?" [48] Dr. Lord and Jesse L. Williams, who for many years was prominent in the affairs of the Chicago Seminary, were members of the committee which framed this reply. By 1862, the General Assembly, on the motion of Dr. R. J. Breckinridge, declared that treason and rebellion were sinful. In 1863, following the Emancipation Proclamation, it decided that slavery was contrary to the will of God. Thus, until the mid-year of the war, the church expanded its definition of sin to keep step with Lincoln and his policy. For three years thereafter, it left the President and his followers far behind. Thaddeus Stevens could hardly have surpassed the vituperative language of its resolutions.

In such fashion did the Old School Church desert Cyrus McCormick and those of like mind in the crisis of 1861-1865. At a time when, in his opinion, it could have performed a notable service for the whole country, it spurned its opportunity, descended into the political arena, and drove out a large portion of its membership. The Spring Resolutions were, in effect, an official repudiation of the purpose McCormick had in view when he pledged $100,000 to the seminary. With an aroused public sentiment and a depleted faculty, which could only be brought to full strength again by the action of the radical General Assembly, the chief patron of the institu-

[48] "Minutes of the General Assembly," 1859-1864, *op. cit.*, p. 173.

tion saw his own money used to promote doctrines believed by him to be both unscriptural and unwise. He could either submit or resist, and as always when faced by this alternative, he had but one choice. For ten years he fought. During the first nine he lost almost every skirmish. In the tenth he won substantially all for which he had contended. Doubtless he was helped to this long-delayed victory by the gradual abatement of party and sectional bitterness following the Civil War. His contest against radicalism in his denomination portrays in miniature the struggle which simultaneously gave direction to the history of the nation between 1861 and 1871.

Following the death of Dr. Scott, Drs. Halsey and Lord, with some little tutorial assistance in Hebrew, carried the entire teaching load at the seminary for the rest of the war. Rising prices and reduced salaries added to the difficulty of their position.[49] The student body was very small and the uncertainty of the times handicapped the efforts of the efficient agents of the seminary, C. A. Spring and his successor, Fielding N. Ewing, to raise money for a building. Fortunately, those who had donated land in 1859 with the stipulation that a building should be begun within two years, generously granted a period of grace.[50] By 1863 sufficient money had been

[49] "McClure," pp. 49-50. MS. "Facts and Allegations as to Dr. Lord." Dr. Rice had received no salary as Professor of Theology at the seminary, but had been content with his income as pastor of the North Church and editor of the "Presbyterian Expositor." The release of this $1500, supplemented by a few small gifts, allowed each of the other three professors a salary of $3,000 a year. Drs. Lord and Halsey received this amount until 1863 when their stipend was reduced to $2500. Thereafter they were unable to meet expenses. In 1861 the professors protested that they were being paid in "stump tail" currency, then so common in the Northwest. See, L.P.C.B. No. 41, pp. 749-754, W. S. and L. J. McCormick to Mr. Munger, May 17, 1861; #W. S. to C. H. McCormick, May 2, 1861.

[50] "Cook County (Ill.) Deed Book," No. 270, p. 472, Deed of Jos. E. Sheffield, Wm. B. Ogden, et al, conveying twenty acres of land on May 1, 1863, to the trustees of the seminary, provided that within forty days a building should be begun—to cost at least $15,000. This land could not be sold by the seminary for twenty-five years.

found to begin the erection of a three-story structure of general utility known as Ewing Hall.[51]

Besides his will to fight, McCormick had one weapon of considerable effectiveness to use against his foes. By the terms of his gift, $25,000 were to be paid in each of the first four years following the opening of the seminary. Each instalment represented the endowment of one Chair, and until the full sum was turned over, he promised to pay six per cent interest on the balance due. In this way, salaries would be provided for the four members of the faculty from the outset, although the seminary would not gain control of the entire principal for several years.

When the first instalment came due in September, 1860, McCormick met it promptly. At that time his friends controlled the seminary and the impending revolution was not foreseen. Before another year had elapsed, however, the entire situation had changed and the national church to which McCormick had pledged the money no longer existed. For this reason the autumn and winter of 1861-1862 went by with the second instalment still withheld. By the spring of 1862 the institution was in a "delicate and critical situation" but McCormick was unwilling as yet to assume the responsibility of forcing its closure for lack of funds.[52] Thereupon, in May,

[51] Ewing Hall was opened in February, 1864. See, Pamphlet, "Theological Seminary of the Northwest; A Brief Statement of its Condition and Prospects; together with the Annual Report of the Board of Trustees" (Chicago, 1867). Dr. Rice secured from his rich parishioners in New York the money to erect Ewing Hall. See, N. L. Rice to C. H. McCormick, Jan. 4, 1869; Mary C. Shields to Nettie F. McCormick, Sept. 1, 1863, and Amanda Adams to Nettie F. McCormick, Aug. 20, 1863. "Minutes of the General Assembly," 1859-1864, pp. 292 ff.

[52] The quoted phrase is from the minutes of the General Assembly of 1862. See, ibid., p. 225. This Assembly adopted a "hands-off" policy toward the seminary, and allowed the board of directors to act as it deemed best. McCormick attended the sessions of the Assembly at Columbus, O. The critical situation of the seminary may be implied from the copy of a telegram sent by C. H. McCormick to Dr. Gurley on Apr. 5, 1862, and found

he paid the second instalment, and the trustees agreed not to call upon him for the remaining $50,000, or interest upon it, unless the two vacant professorships were filled. Since it was understood that the General Assembly should not be pressed by the board of directors of the seminary to make new appointments to its faculty, the payment of the last two instalments thus seemed to be deferred indefinitely into the future.[53]

McCormick was abroad for two years beginning in the summer of 1862, and learned to his surprise that the General Assembly of 1863, at the request of the board of directors, appointed Rev. Charles Elliott, D.D., of Oxford, Ohio, to the Chair of Biblical Literature and Exegesis. When the inventor protested that this was both unjust to him and unwise in view of the need for retrenchment, F. N. Ewing answered that "he thought Vallandigham would be elected governor (!) and the Republican rule overthrown." [54] But, as McCormick wrote, "I want the Seminary to go forward and prosper notwithstanding the excision" of the southern churches, and he consented to advance the interest on the third instalment for Elliott's support, although he insisted that he did not thereby acknowledge their right to demand it, since in his opinion the agreement of 1859 had been violated. Shortly thereafter he directed his brother, William S., to pay the principal.[55]

on the inside front cover of L.P.C.B. No. 47, "Seminary continued another year with the two Professors without election."

[53] MS. agreement between C. H. McCormick and the trustees, dated Apr. 22, 1862. The principal of the second instalment was paid on May 2, 1862. Memo. in the papers of the N. F. McCormick Biog. Asso., Seminary File for 1862. See also W. Lord to McCormick, Dec. 19, 1868.

[54] This is a striking illustration of the close connection between the fortunes of war and the church. Clement Vallandigham of Ohio was probably the oustanding Copperhead of the Middle West. Ewing meant that if this element gained control, the war would probably be brought to a speedy close and better days would then come to the seminary.

[55] MS. Receipt dated Aug. 2, 1864. He met the third instalment in two payments of $12,500 each. The second payment was made Oct. 31, 1864.

The improved situation at the seminary doubtless accounts in some measure for McCormick's decision to come to its assistance. By 1864 the trustees could report to the General Assembly "a decided financial advance" and an increase in student enrollment.[56] Danville Seminary was in the theater of the war, and its distress had been Chicago's gain. Although one of the major reasons for the establishment of the Seminary of the Northwest had been defeated by the secession of the southern states, there still remained the work of spreading Old School Presbyterianism throughout the upper Mississippi Valley, not, to be sure, the brand represented by the radical majority in the General Assemblies, but the conservative doctrines which might again come into their own with the peace.

Thus, by the close of the Civil War, McCormick had paid all except $25,000 of the sum pledged to the seminary six years before. The remaining instalment was for the endowment of the Chair of Theology, unfilled since Dr. Rice's resignation in 1861. Of the four professorships, this one was the senior in rank and interested McCormick the most keenly. The Chair bore his name and its incumbent would have the maintenance of orthodoxy among the students principally in his charge. There was a real danger that the General Assembly would elevate Dr. Lord to the position since he was in tune with its wartime deliverances on secession and slavery, and had taught

Memo. in N. F. McCormick B.A., Seminary File, 1864. #C. H. McCormick to F. N. Ewing, April 1, 1864. C. H. McCormick to Wm. S. Plumer, Jan. 5, 1864. From this letter it is evident that the plea of his friend, Dr. Halsey, had also been an important factor in persuading McCormick to come to Dr. Elliott's aid. The letter continues: "The first question is, whether the results of the present fearful war will make it advisable yet to extend it [the seminary] to its original dimensions; and second, if so, that it should be done as originally designed—so *far* as to have *preachers* for professors. This was the original calculation with Dr. Rice and myself, with a view to Church extension in the City, by supplying pastors for several churches."

[56] "Minutes of the General Assembly," 1859-1864, pp. 365 ff.

theology at the seminary after Dr. Rice left. Quite apart from considerations of personal hostility, McCormick believed that Dr. Lord's theological views were unsound. Lord had entered the Old School Church through the door of Congregationalism and was at least tolerant of the advanced ideas of the New School Presbyterians.[57] For this reason McCormick agreed heartily with the suggestion of John M. Faris, the new agent of the seminary, that the Chair should remain temporarily vacant because no suitable candidate could be found "who would be acceptable to conservative men and at the same time not encounter such violent opposition from radicals as would probably prevent his election" by the General Assembly.[58] If this were done and a proper person were finally secured for the position, McCormick was willing to increase considerably the endowment of each Chair,—a proposal the more tempting since the interest on $25,000 no longer paid the living expenses of a professor.[59] By good fortune the General Assembly of 1865 adjourned without making an appointment to the vacant place.

The Lord-McCormick opposition following the Civil War cannot be understood without a review of the history of the North Church in Chicago between 1861 and 1865. When Dr. Lord left his Brooklyn pastorate and joined, with hesitation as he afterward remembered, the faculty of the little seminary by the Lake, he had the endorsement of Dr. Rice. This was sufficient to win him favor in the eyes of Cyrus McCormick. He made friends easily and he lacked neither ability nor ambition. But he veered with the political wind, and although he

[57] ‡On Jan. 5, 1864, he wrote W. S. Plumer: "But I do feel I should be entitled to some consideration and that if I carry out my part [i.e., pay the instalments still due], Dr. Lord should resign. He has been no friend of mine, nor of the great conservative cause I had in view when the Seminary was established."

[58] J. M. Faris to C. H. McCormick, Feb. 28, and Mch. 1, 1865.

[59] ‡C. H. McCormick to J. M. Faris, Mch. 26, 1865.

could endorse Dr. Rice's articles in the "Expositor" opposing
secession in the winter of 1860-1861,[60] he could not approve
his lectures against Abolitionism and Congregationalism delivered at about the same time.[61] He dropped from the list of contributors to the paper and refused to sign an address of friendship to the South drafted by Dr. Scott at McCormick's suggestion during the same critical months.[62] While keeping on
good terms with the kindly Dr. Halsey, he sought the companionship of men who supported a policy of coercion toward
the seceding states, notably Dr. Robert ("Scotch") Patterson
of the First Reformed Presbyterian Church of Chicago, and
Mr. Jesse L. Williams, a rich civil engineer of Fort Wayne
who had assisted the seminary with money. Lord's alignment
with the radical group in the General Assembly of 1861 and
McCormick's growing distrust of the Doctor's theology, have
already been mentioned.[63]

After Dr. Rice shifted his field of labor to New York City,
McCormick endeavored to secure Dr. T. V. Moore of Richmond, Va., as pastor of the North Church. Dr. Lord worked
to defeat this election on the grounds that Moore was a disunionist.[64] McCormick believed, although Lord later denied

[60] N. L. Rice to C. H. McCormick, Jan. 4, 1869. Shortly after the fall
of Sumter, Dr. Lord prepared an article for the "Presbyterian Expositor"
on the duties of Christian citizens in the crisis. McCormick refused to allow
it to appear. Dr. Lord to C. H. McCormick, Dec. 19, 1868.

[61] Letters of W. S. McCormick in L.P.C.B. No. 29, p. 500, to J. C.
Walker, Jan. 25, 1860; and in No. 30, pp. 678, 690, to W. A. Braxton,
Mch. 3, 1860; and W. T. Rush, Mch. 5, 1860: "The Old School Church
is *weak* where there is so much *abolitionism.*"

[62] N. L. Rice to C. H. McCormick, Jan. 4, 1869; W. Lord to C. H.
McCormick, Dec. 19, 1868.

[63] *Supra,* pp. 25, 30.

[64] ‡C. H. McCormick to T. V. Moore, Richmond, Va., Apr. 13, 1861.
McCormick offered him $5,000 as a joint salary for preaching and teach-
ing theology at the seminary. Dr. Halsey urged McCormick to secure
Moore. C. H. McCormick to W. Lord, Jan. 16, 1869; W. Lord to C. H.
McCormick, Dec. 19, 1868; T. V. Moore to W. Lord, March 5, 1869. In
this letter, Moore denied that he had been a disunionist in 1861.

the charge, that his opposition was in some measure due to his wish to secure the appointment for himself.[65] If this were so, he failed to gratify his ambition. Although the radical antislavery members of the congregation were in a majority, the conservatives had to be relied upon for most of the minister's salary. McCormick then worked in vain to prevent the congregation from inviting the young Rev. David Swing.[66] He wished Dr. Stuart Robinson of Louisville to be called so that the seminary and North Church might both benefit. When Robinson came to Chicago to speak, however, he was barred from the church building.[67] Swing occupied the pulpit during most of the summer of 1862 after McCormick sailed for Europe but he found the war-torn congregation no inducement to remain.[68]

Thereupon, the North Church called the Rev. J. B. Stewart

[65] McCormick persuaded the congregation to call Dr. Gurley, but to McCormick's chagrin, the offer was declined, "leaving us at *sea* whence we were unable to get back to land!" #C. H. McCormick to W. S. Plumer, Jan. 5, 1864. At a meeting of the congregation in the late summer or early autumn of 1861, Dr. Lord apparently attacked C. H. McCormick for his attitude toward the war. See C. H. McCormick to W. Lord, Jan. 16, 1869. Dr. Lord told Rev. E. Erskine that if McCormick's ideas in regard to the seminary had been followed, a mob would have quickly pulled down its walls. #E. Erskine to C. H. McCormick, Nov. 25, 1868. Dr. Lord later denied that he had denounced C. H. McCormick before the congregation in this manner. Dr. Lord to C. H. McCormick, Dec. 19, 1868.

[66] #C. H. McCormick to the "Moderator of To-Night's Meeting of the Congregation of North Church," June 18, 1862. C. H. McCormick opposed the call of Mr. Swing on the grounds that he did not have the ability to teach in the seminary; he was too young and never had had a pastoral charge; and because his delivery was awkward and his voice unpleasant. In this letter McCormick chided the congregation for not better supporting the seminary.

[67] W. S. to C. H. McCormick, July 30, 1862. #C. H. McCormick to Wm. S. Plumer, Jan. 5, 1864.

[68] W. S. to C. H. McCormick, June 13, Sept. 28, 1862. Rev. R. H. Richardson preached in North Church for at least two Sundays in August. L.P.C.B. No. 49, p. 869, C. A. Spring, Jr., to C. H. McCormick, Aug. 25, 1862. C. H. McCormick to Dr. Lord, Jan. 16, 1869.

of Ohio.[69] According to Mary Ann McCormick he delivered on Thanksgiving Day "the worst abolition sermon ever preached in the Church. . . . Thought the proclamation [of Emancipation] did not go far enough and favored arming the negro or in any other way aid them to insurrection, and every other mean thing a *devilish heart* could devise." [70] She and her husband, William S. McCormick, no longer attended church,[71] being unable to endure the antislavery sermons and the applause of the congregation when the minister denounced the South. As early as mid-May, 1861, William wrote to a cousin who lived in St. Louis: "Do you clap your Preachers on Sunday? They do it here *loud* and *long*. I believe they pray substantially that every devil of you down south shall be *killed* (not die) in his sins. They don't pray that your eyes shall be opened to see the glorious light of the everlasting patron-

[69] W. S. to C. H. McCormick, Oct. 12, 1862: "I hear Armour of Munger & A. says C. H. McCormick & Dr. Rice did more than any other two men to make the troubles in the country!! Stewart elected Pastor *unanimously* I hear." Mr. Stewart was never installed as pastor, although he preached in the North Church for over a year.

[70] Mary Ann McCormick to Nettie F. McCormick, Dec. 7, 1862. Amanda Adams to Nettie F. McCormick, Aug. 20, 1863. L. J. and Wm. S. McCormick formally left the North Church in Feb., 1863, and L. J. McCormick took a pew in the South Church. Apparently Mary Caroline Shields, the sister, retained her membership in, and continued to attend, the North Church. See W. S. to C. H. McCormick, Feb. 15, 1863, and Mary Caroline Shields to Nettie F. McCormick, Sept. 1, 1863. C. H. McCormick had not contributed to the support of the North Church for some time but he still paid pew rent there.

[71] W. S. to C. H. McCormick, Oct. 3, 1862: "I do not myself feel like going to Church here and whether I am a skeptic or not I don't know. I have not much confidence in anything I see connected with the church *here* certainly. I some times think I will leave it absolutely and while I conceal these feelings from my family, I know to my sorrow that there are no church influences *here* that are of any service whatever to my family. There has not been a man here that you could even regard as a friend —I mean preacher—and *who* as Elder or Member can you confide in?" Mary Ann McCormick expressed the same thought in a letter to Nettie F. McCormick on Mch. 5, 1864.

Saints of the North, but rather that you may in your darkened understanding, plod along up to the cannon's mouth. I never had any sympathy for secession . . . but I fear the remedy is to be far worse than the disease." [72]

Dr. Lord approved of Mr. Stewart and assisted him in the pulpit on his first Sunday in the North Church.[73] But the new pastor was in poor health and many did not like his sermons.[74] Church attendance dwindled during 1863, and by the close of the year some of the discouraged conservatives of his congregation were of a mind to withdraw and establish a new church.[75] Much to their relief, Stewart resigned before the winter was over.[76] An evening in early March was appointed for the election of a new pastor. Owing to the extreme inclemency of the weather, only a few members of the congregation assembled at the designated hour. They resolved to ask Dr. Lord to be their clergyman. Many of the radicals, how-

[72] L.P.C.B. No. 41, p. 609, W. S. to J. B. McCormick, May 14, 1861. On Oct. 5, 1862, he wrote to C. H. and L. J. McCormick in the same vein: "Even our religious people would deal out death and destruction—extermination—of men women and children at the hand of the Slave or other midnight assassin. The cry is *not* (as it seems) 'God be merciful to us miserable sinners.' But help us to destroy these southern wretches—all of them—without mercy. Should we buy specie or remove to Europe?" See also, L.P.C.B. No. 58, p. 119, W. S. McCormick to C. A. Spring, Sr., Mch. 21, 1863.

[73] ‡C. H. McCormick wrote to W. S. Plumer on Jan. 5, 1864, that he had hoped the professors at the seminary would be pastors: "calculating myself to have the benefit of *one* so provided, while, as matters now stand, *I* and my friends are without a preacher, unable to support the present abolitionist *Stuart* [*sic*] of the *North Church.*"

[74] Amanda Adams to Nettie F. McCormick, Aug. 20, 1863; Mary Ann McCormick to Nettie F. McCormick, Oct. 21-22, 1863.

[75] Mary C. Shields to Nettie F. McCormick, Sept. 1, 1863; ‡C. H. McCormick to W. S. Plumer, Jan. 5, 1864. At this time, C. H. McCormick hoped that Dr. Lord would leave the seminary, if the North Church radicals could be persuaded to choose him as their pastor. Then a new church could be formed and some eminent conservative, preferably Dr. Stuart Robinson or Dr. Gurley, might be called to its pulpit and the Chair of Theology at the seminary.

[76] In May, 1864, Mr. Stewart accepted a call to the 5th Presbyterian Church of Cincinnati. "Daily Chicago Times," May 25, 1864.

ever, although they agreed with the Professor's views, did not wish him for their minister. Faced by the opposition of a majority of the congregation, made up of an unnatural alliance of members from both camps, Dr. Lord declined the call. His friends at once seceded and with Dr. Lord as their temporary pastor, organized the Central Presbyterian Church, its building located within one hundred yards of their former meeting-house.[77] These events were reported in due time to Cyrus McCormick, who was about to return to Chicago from London. They confirmed him in his opinion that Dr. Lord must be kept from the Chair of Theology, and if possible, be forced to resign from the seminary altogether.

The withdrawal of Dr. Lord's adherents left the conservatives in control of the North Church. They at once called Dr. David C. Junkin to be their leader. His recent service as a chaplain in the Navy well prepared him to bid defiance to the charges of disloyalty launched against him and his congregation by the Chicago Presbytery. He was not a persuasive speaker, however, and he was in poor health.[78] Upon his installation the members of the McCormick clan once more returned to their pews. William S. and Mary Ann McCormick, who had heard but one sermon since Dr. Rice left Chicago, attended a church sociable in December, 1864, and furnished the ice-cream and cake.[79]

[77] "Daily Chicago Times," Apr. 13, 1864. In 1868, Dr. Lord wrote C. H. McCormick (letter of Dec. 19) that he had tried his best to prevent this schism. The Central Presbyterian Church lasted a little over two years, and then most of its members returned to the North Church. Mary C. Shields to N. F. McCormick, Jan. 3, 1865. Mary Ann McCormick to Nettie F. McCormick, March 5, 1864, and Apr. 16, 1866. L. J. McCormick to C. H. McCormick, Apr. 17, 1866. C. H. McCormick to H. A. Hurlbut, Dec. 3, 1866.

[78] When C. H. McCormick learned of Dr. Junkin's appointment, he prophesied that he would not last long. See, ‡C. A. Spring, Jr., to C. H. McCormick, Apr. 17, 1866.

[79] Letters to Nettie F. McCormick of Mary Ann McCormick, Dec. 27, 1864, and Mary C. Shields, Jan. 3, 1865. During the war, the South Presbyterian Church, in the charge of Dr. W. W. Harsha (1862-69), experi-

Cyrus McCormick always personalized the forces against which he contended. His beloved Old School Presbyterianism had run after strange gods for five years and had worked injustice to him and to the South. No one man better epitomized the whole church and seminary issue than Dr. Willis Lord. Although his salary was made possible by McCormick's endowment, he had led in the policy of proscription. If he could be ousted, McCormick would be ready to believe that a better day had dawned for his church and his country. The story of his long fight to achieve his purpose throws light upon the history of Presbyterianism in both the North and South during the early years of the Reconstruction Era.

enced much the same troubles as the North Church. The South Church owed $5,400 and since its creditors were radicals they threatened to foreclose unless the interest were promptly paid. Finally the church decided to sell its lot in order to meet some of its most pressing obligations. With Cyrus McCormick's consent it moved its building in late 1865 to its old site on his property at Wabash and Congress sts., rent free. At the same time he leased Dr. Harsha a house at about half the usual charge and helped to pay the interest on the church debt. ‡C. H. McCormick to H. N. Waller, Mch. 29, 1865. Receipt of T. Armstrong, Trustee, to C. H. McCormick, June 7, 1862. Letters to C. H. McCormick of ‡W. W. Harsha, Feb. 25, Apr. 7, 1865; ‡H. N. Waller, Mch. 4, 1865; ‡D. X. Junkin, Mch. 6, 1865; C. A. Spring, Jr., Feb. 22, 1866; ‡Mrs. J. C. Partridge, Apr. 9, 1866; and of ‡C. A. Spring, Sr., Apr. 6, 1865 and Feb. 23, 1866. In his letter of Apr. 6, 1865, Mr. Spring, Sr., told the inventor that by his generosity he was heaping coals of fire upon the heads of some members of the South Church, who during Mr. Henry's pastorate had treated him so unjustly.

CHAPTER II

CYRUS McCORMICK AND THE CIVIL WAR

THOSE who followed the earlier career of Cyrus Mc-
Cormick could have predicted with reasonable assurance
his course in the political crisis of 1860 and 1861. His birth
and long residence in Virginia, his close association for fifteen years with Chicago and the farmers of the Middle West,
and his long journeys in the interest of his business throughout the whole of the North with the exception of New
England, gave him a national outlook and a fixed belief that
the utmost concession to the South was preferable to a dis-
solution of the Union and Civil War. Viewed from the narrow standpoint of his economic interests, his growing emphasis
upon the need of expanding his southern market would alone
account for his opposition to the program of the new Republican Party. By inheritance and by conviction he was a Democrat. His conservatism increased with his wealth, and his
faith in the principles of his party was strengthened by the
belief that upon its success in the elections of 1856 and 1860
depended the continued life of the nation.

Virginia, perhaps more than any other state, enjoys the enduring affection of her sons, even after they have made new
homes beyond her borders. McCormick was no exception to
the rule.[1] Strong ties of blood and of friendship led him, when

[1] "Daily Chicago Times," July 5, 1866. In February, 1880, C. H. McCormick was elected the first President of the Virginia Society of Chicago.
At a banquet of the society that month, he said: "We may say that the
love of our country as one great whole, is a noble virtue of the mind, while
the love of our native State is a pure affection of the heart. . . . I may

37

all plans of compromise failed, to prefer a peaceful separation of the South from the North to a war in which the Old Dominion would be the principal battle-ground.[2] His opposition to the use of force after Lincoln's first inauguration was in harmony with the "union at any cost" principle which shaped his entire political course between 1856 and 1865.

His attitude toward slavery was doubtless moulded by his southern upbringing, but it was in harmony with the view of many Northerners who had never owned negroes. Because his three or four slaves refused to leave Virginia, he was unable under the law of that state to emancipate them when he moved to Chicago. He hired them out for service to neighbors in the Valley and in 1860 they were still his property. They were old, however, and their small value, when compared with his large fortune, certainly did not determine his position on the issues of the day. As a Jeffersonian, he was antislavery in principle, but he held that the Constitution sanctioned human bondage and that the Union should not be endangered by agitating the issue of immediate emancipation. In common with many others in the North, he blamed the Abolitionists for the uncompromising pro-slavery feeling of the South by 1850. Twenty years earlier, so he believed, the willingness of the border states to inaugurate a program of gradual enfranchisement had been stifled by the tactics of William Lloyd Garrison and his fellow-radicals. If the country had been spared abolitionism, an antislavery movement in the South would have been well under way by 1860.

say of Virginia, as David said of the city of his love: 'If I forget thee, O Jerusalem, let my right hand forget her cunning.'" "The Daily Inter Ocean" (Chicago), Feb. 24, 1880; G. Garnett to C. H. McCormick, Feb. 12, 1880; ‡J. E. Cooke, Millwood, Va., to C. H. McCormick, July 18, 1880.

[2] L.P.C.B. No. 41, p. 52, W. S. McCormick to N. Chandler, Apr. 18, 1861; No. 41, p. 377, to J. B. McCormick, May 3, 1861; No. 42, p. 40, to W. T. Rush, May 22, 1861.

Except for his support of a compromise as the most practical method of dealing with the problems of slavery and slavery-extension, McCormick seems never to have formulated a plan whereby the institution could eventually be abolished in the United States. Slavery handicapped the South economically, but the Bible was proof enough to him that human bondage was not an offense against God or man. Horace Greeley was mistaken when he chided McCormick for supporting a system of forced labor which blocked the extensive sale of his machines in the South.[3] McCormick did not champion slavery, except in the sense that he believed immediate emancipation by federal action without compensation would be an invasion of States' rights and individual rights, and a remedy worse than the disease. In several letters he emphasized that slavery should be treated as a "national" rather than a "sectional" evil, and that Southerners should be asked in a friendly spirit to coöperate through the central government in preparing the slaves for ultimate freedom.[4] He urged that men of the North ought in fairness to admit that their fathers for their own profit had carried the negroes from Africa, and therefore, they were as much at fault as were the slave-owners.

Political differences of opinion, however, were no bar to his friendship, and in his estimation his services to his party were always subordinate in importance to his work for his church. A surprising number of his warmest friends, lawyers, and office employees, were of the Presbyterian faith, but many of them voted the Republican ticket and were outspoken in their opposition to slavery.[5] To draw the obvious conclusion

[3] "Richmond Examiner," Sept. 25, 1857, quoting from the "New York Daily Tribune," C. H. to W. S. McCormick, Sept. 10, 22, 1857.

[4] ‡MS. of C. H. McCormick, n.d., but about Jan. 16, 1869. ‡C. H. McCormick to Ed., "Chicago Times," Apr. 11, 1864; to Ed., "New York World," June 20, 1864.

[5] L.P.C.B. No. 39, p. 205, J. T. Griffin to E. Healy, Feb. 25, 1861: "The writer as well as all of those in the office (except W. S. McC.) are

from this fact would probably be unwarranted since no letter remains to indicate that he ever applied a religious test when choosing a helper. The Church was his chief social focus and acquaintanceships formed there were naturally carried over into his business life without a conscious purpose of excluding members of other denominations.

Nevertheless, as has already been indicated, he believed that the Democratic Party and the Presbyterian Church were of the utmost importance as cohesive forces within the nation. Acting upon this assumption, his policy toward the one was so closely akin to his program for the other that his enemies were unable clearly to disassociate the two in their attacks upon him. They accused him of sacrilege in using religion to further his political ends, and called him the "Presbyterian Pope" because he made so little distinction in practice between the issues of church and state.

Personal ambition unquestionably helped to lead McCormick into the forum in 1860. He was one of the first manufacturers of the modern type who sought a political crown for a successful business career. At one time or another between 1860 and 1880 he looked with favor upon the offices of mayor, governor, congressman, senator, vice-president, and ambassador. Some friends told him that his wealth, influence, and ability should make him President of the United States.[6]

republicans and supporters of Lincoln." L.P.C.B. No. 93, p. 772, C. A. Spring, Jr., to A. McCoy, Nov. 22, 1866: "I have never known any difference made by him [C. H. McCormick] in business matters on account of politics."

[6] T. J. Paterson, Rochester, N. Y., to C. H. McCormick, July 5, 1860: "I should have thought a few years since that nothing short of a miracle could work so great a change [in you], but . . . now that you are afloat on the political waves, with your indomitable will, means, & abilities, I shall be supprised [sic] at nothing you may accomplish, & shall expect to see you yet a candidate for the Presidency. When Pierce, Buchanan, Douglas, & Linclon [sic] & Co. can accomplish so much, you have no reason to dispare [sic]."

Republicans charged that he succumbed to the flattery of Democratic leaders who wished the benefit of his wealth at election time.[7] His participation in politics was doubtless expensive, and if McCormick viewed it as an investment, it was a singularly unprofitable one. The Democratic Party was in eclipse during the twenty-five years of his active interest in its welfare, and he was not spared to witness its triumph in the autumn of 1884. He was Chairman of the Democratic State Central Committee during two presidential election contests, and a member of the National Committee at the same time, but he never held an office as the result of an election or by appointment of a national or state administration. He once said that he could not stay out of political life because there were principles at stake which deserved to be defended. He believed in the utility of action against a rival, whether in business, politics, or the church. This gives a singular unity to his career. In his opinion, life without competition would merely be an existence.

His executive ability fitted him for public office, but his brusque forthrightness and his refusal to conciliate or to use "weasel words" greatly reduced his chances of obtaining it. He sought to transfer to political life his code of success in business and found that subduing his competitor and gaining the favor of an electorate called for different techniques. The loyalty of the buying public could be held by the quality of performance of his reaper, but voters demanded more oratory and smooth promises than he was prepared to supply. His southern birth was always a political handicap in northern Illinois, and his refusal to delegate to a subordinate his manifold business problems during an election campaign made it

---

[7] Article by "Long John" Wentworth in "The Daily Inter Ocean," May 14, 1884: "Whenever the Democrats wanted money in their campaigns they would always try to get Cyrus in to bleed him." Wentworth and McCormick were at opposite poles in politics but they were good friends.

impossible for him to devote more than a part of his time and energy to the game of politics.

In 1856 McCormick urged his two brothers to become citizens of Chicago, so that they might vote for Buchanan [8] in the autumn election. This advice was superfluous. They were both stanch Democrats and William, at least, believed that if Buchanan won, he would bring back better times and stifle Abolitionism.[9] Cyrus McCormick was doubtful of the outcome, but he was willing to contribute $1,000 to the cause, if a Democratic victory in Illinois could thereby be rendered more certain.[10] Should Fremont win, the Patent Office officials at Washington would probably view applications for patent-extensions from prominent Democrats with an unfriendly eye.

Because "Long John" Wentworth and his "Chicago Democrat" deserted Stephen Douglas in 1854, the Illinois Senator later in the same year set up the "Chicago Daily Times," with Isaac Cook as publisher and Daniel Cameron and James W. Sheahan as editors, to champion his policies. Cook refused to follow Douglas when he broke with Buchanan in 1858, and left the "Times" in order to establish the "Chicago Daily Herald" as an administration organ.[11] McCormick rejoiced because of Douglas's defeat of Lincoln for the United States

[8] C. H. to W. S. McCormick, from Balto., Oct. 1, 1856. L.P.C.B. No. 2, pp. 95, 122½, J. L. Wilson to J. B. McCormick, June 6, 1856, and to D. Zimmerman, June 9, 1856.

[9] *Ibid.*, No. 3, pp. 471, 480, 595, 689-690; W. S. McCormick to J. L. Myer, Oct. 1, 1856; to T. J. Paterson, Oct. 1, 1856; and Messrs. Fairbanks, Concord, Ill., Oct. 16, 1856: "If we succeed in electing James Buckhanan [*sic*] I think Reapers & every other interest will be *right side up* & that is just what I think we shall do." *Ibid.*, No. 4, pp. 215-216, 219, W. S. McCormick to T. Berry, Cline's Mills, Va., Nov. 12, 1856. W. S. McCormick was in Va. at election time and lost his vote.

[10] C. H. to W. S. McCormick, from Phila., Oct. 7, 14, 1856.

[11] The first issue of the "Chicago Daily Herald" was on July 25, 1858. See "Chicago Daily Press and Tribune," July 27, 1858.

Senate that autumn,[12] but he continued to support the policy of Buchanan. Although Douglas and McCormick remained good friends, their political views were no longer in accord, and the statesman opposed in Congress the inventor's efforts to secure an extension of his patents.[13] McCormick believed that unless the discordant wings of the Democratic Party could be reconciled, the "abolitionist" Republicans would win in 1860, and endanger the Union by their victory.

To him, John Brown's raid was the first fruit of the new radicalism and a foretaste of what would become the rule if the Republicans gained control. For this reason the Harpers Ferry outrage was a call to action. He determined to do what he could in his own section to reunite his party, combat Garrisonian doctrines, and foster a tolerance of the "peculiar institution" of the South. The immediate practical steps to be taken was to halt the bickering between the "Herald" and "Times" of Chicago, and combine them so that they could more effectively fight that "dirty sheet," as he called the "Tribune." [14]

On February 17, 1860, he bought for $2,000 a half-interest from Isaac Cook in the "Chicago Herald." By the terms of the purchase he was given control of its policy "as fully as if he was the sole owner." E. W. McComas, an able Virginia lawyer then living in the city, was to be its political editor. "It is agreed that the paper shall be devoted to no party except the democratic party. Nor shall it . . . advocate the claims of

[12] L.P.C.B. No. 16, p. 514, W. S. McCormick to J. G. Hamilton, Nov. 4, 1858.

[13] "Congressional Globe," 34th Cong. 1st Sess. (July 14, 1856), p. 1601. Douglas highly complimented McCormick's services as an inventor but opposed extension of his patent by a special act of Congress, for constitutional reasons. See W. T. Hutchinson, "Cyrus Hall McCormick: Seedtime" (New York, 1930), p. 295. Hereafter cited as "Hutchinson, I."

[14] C. H. to W. S. McCormick, from Washington, Aug. 2, 1858: "Stop [my subscription to] the dirty sheet, instantly."

any aspirant or person for the presidency until after the nomination of the National Democratic Convention at Charleston." [15] In the early winter McCormick failed to receive the Democratic mayoralty nomination, but his successful rival in the convention was roundly beaten in the March election by "Long John" Wentworth, a Republican.[16]

Due to the withdrawal of many southern delegates from the Charleston convention in April, 1860, no nomination of candidates could there be made, and it was resolved to reassemble at Baltimore in mid-June.[17] Thither McCormick journeyed, not as a delegate, but as one who hoped that his influence with southern members might help to heal the schism.[18] He wrote of the result of his efforts as follows: [19]

I did my best here to the last to effect a Compromise between D.[ouglas] & the South in *some* way, but his leading frds. would hear nothing. . . .

It seems to me *now* that it is scarcely possible to prevent Lincoln from being elected by the *people,* while, if that be possible, it would seem to be best . . . that Douglas should carry Ill, and run as well as possible at the North. The election might thus go to the House of

[15] MS. Agreement dated Feb. 17, 1860, between Isaac Cook and C. H. McCormick. The "Herald's" slavery-in-territories platform which it urged upon the Democratic national convention, was unacceptable to Douglas.

[16] L.P.C.B. No. 30, p. 736, W. S. to J. B. McCormick, Mch. 7, 1860. Douglas Democrats were charged with "knifing" C. H. McCormick at the last moment when his nomination seemed to be assured.

[17] In view of Isaac Cook's association with McCormick, it is interesting to note that he led an Illinois "Danite" (anti-Douglas) delegation to the Charleston convention, but it was refused admission.

[18] *Ibid.,* No. 32, pp. 241, 545, 591, J. T. Griffin to J. B. McCormick, May 23, 1860; W. S. to J. B. McCormick, June 2, 1860; W. S. McCormick to W. T. Rush, June 4, 1860.

[19] C. H. McCormick to E. W. McComas, dated "Baltimore 1860," and doubtless written in late June. "Squatter Sovereignty must be crushed out. . . . The South must continue to be the great body of *the Democratic party,* as agst. the *Northern Republican party.* The South demanding *equal rights* in the Territories—the North demanding that the South shall be excluded therefrom! This is the issue that is before the country and must be met."

Baltimore   1860

Hon. E. W. McComas
        Dear Sir.

I have only time now to write a line to say that I am not yet prepared to advise you as to your future course.

I saw Douglas before the committee, also gave the most positive assurances that could be given that he had disapproved the course of the *Times* in regard to us throughout — preferred my nomination to Guthrie's — could not communicate any confidential matter to Sheahan &c

I need not say more of this now. I did my best here & to the last to effect a Compromise between D. & the South in some way, but his leading friends would hear nothing   I

Facsimile of a Letter Written by Cyrus Hall McCormick in 1860

Facsimile of a Letter Written by Cyrus Hall McCormick in 1860

Rep. It may thus be better to have no Breck.[inridge] electoral ticket in Ill. of which I can better determine at Washington *tomorrow.* . . . If this cannot be done, and if Douglas cannot be induced to *decline an acceptance* of the nomination—nor both he & B.[reckinridge]—then I think it, *at present,* extremely doubtful whether all our labor would not be lost to continue the contest further.

The Southern position is now, without doubt, *sound & just,* and I think they are determined to maintain it. *They can't now* recede unless Douglas does; . . .

Squatter sovereignty is in my judgment *dead.* Douglas cannot possibly, in my judgment, carry in this contest *more* than three or four states . . . while I repeat that it must be very doubtful whether he can carry a single one.

From the tenor of this letter it might be expected that henceforward the "Chicago Herald" would work for Douglas, not because its proprietor favored his principles, but in order to forestall a Lincoln victory by throwing the choice of a president into the House of Representatives with its Democratic majority.[20] Jefferson Davis was working toward the same end. Although the plan does credit to McCormick's political acumen, it was rendered impracticable by the inability of southern and western Democrats to unite upon a third candidate in case Breckinridge and Douglas should withdraw. Consequently, sound political strategy demanded that McCormick champion Douglas. His honest conviction, however, counseled him to support Breckinridge, but to do this in Illinois would merely work to Lincoln's advantage by weakening Douglas. Faced by this dilemma, the "Chicago Herald" carried the name of neither candidate at the head of its editorial column

[20] L.P.C.B. No. 33, p. 606, W. S. McCormick to Jas. Campbell, Aug. 18, 1860: "Expect to vote for Douglas though not my *choice* by a good deal." The "Chicago Press and Tribune" on Aug. 16, 1860, called the "Chicago Times" "tamely pro-Douglas, but fiercely pro-slavery." During the campaign, Douglas called the Breckinridge Democrats "disunionists," but the "Chicago Times" denied that this label was deserved.

but continued to defend the Buchanan administration.[21] This was more helpful to Breckinridge than to Douglas, since many "Danites," as the Buchanan supporters in Illinois were known, seemed willing to resign themselves to the election of Lincoln, if Douglas could thereby be defeated.

In late July, 1860, McCormick bought out Cook's remaining interest in the "Herald"[22] and also paid James W. Sheahan and Abner Price about $10,000 for the "Chicago Daily Times."[23] Perhaps one strong Democratic paper could be made by combining two weak ones. The "Daily Chicago Times," as the new journal was soon called, was edited by E. W. McComas with the assistance of Daniel Cameron. Sheahan, always a faithful Douglas man, late in the same year established the "Morning Post."[24] McCormick scanned the

[21] "Principles—Not Men," was its motto. T. J. Paterson, Rochester, N. Y., to C. H. McCormick, July 5, 1860: "I see the Herald goes for the nominee of the Baltimore Democratick Convention & places no name at the head of its columns. As there were two Conventions at Baltimore claiming to be Democratick I consider you are in the fog yet, & are in doubt which was the Simon Pure Democratick Convention. I trust you will not renounce the Religion & Politicks of your fathers to embrace that miserable heresy of Douglass [sic] Squatter Sovereignty." "New York World," Aug. 5, 1860. "Chicago Press and Tribune," July 30, 1860.

[22] #Receipt of I. Cook, July 28, 1860. At this time it was reported that McCormick would run for Congress in the autumn. "Chicago Daily Democrat," July 23, 1860.

[23] C. H. McCormick to H. A. Boardman, July 8, 1866: "I bo't out the *Times* (Chicago) for opposition to the election of Old Abe." The bill of sale was drawn on July 25, 1860, and the new paper made its first appearance as the "Chicago Times-Herald," on July 31. Shortly thereafter, the name was changed to the "Daily Chicago Times." "Chicago Press and Tribune," Feb. 14, 15, July 30, Aug. 16, 1860. According to this paper, McCormick purchased the "Times" because Sheahan had defeated his candidacy for the mayoralty nomination earlier in the year. McCormick bought up the debts of the paper and thus forced its sale. "Scientific American" (N. Y.), Aug. 25, 1860.

[24] "New York World," Aug. 5, 1860. It was rumored in 1860 that McCormick had obliged Sheahan to promise that he would not publish another political paper in Chicago. "Chicago Daily Democrat," Mch. 19, 1861. If Douglas felt that he had any chance of winning the election, he would

copy for his paper as closely as he did the material submitted for the "Presbyterian Expositor," and his blue pencil, according to the recollection of his friend Judge Murray F. Tuley, sometimes made McComas writhe.[25] The desecration of the Sabbath by work in the newspaper office was avoided by issuing the Sunday edition on Saturday evening. All articles or advertisements calculated to corrupt the morals of its subscribers were barred. "Nothing will be allowed in its columns that will cause a blush to the most rigidly pure." [26] While McCormick was its owner, the daily circulation of the "Times" was not over 2,000 or 3,000, and it was far from self-sustaining. Probably no complete file of the paper for the period from July 1860 to June 1861 now exists.

By mid-September, McCormick was the chairman of the Cook County Central Committee of his party. He most probably voted for Douglas on Election Day. His worst fears were realized when the final returns were announced and a convention in South Carolina adopted an ordinance of secession. Henceforward, McCormick shelved his disagreement with the "Little Giant" over the proper position of the national government on the issue of slavery-extension in the territories, and worked with him in behalf of any compromise which might preserve the Union.[27] In late December he urged Doug-

hardly have permitted Sheahan to sell out to McCormick during the campaign. Letter of J. W. Sheahan in "Chicago Press and Tribune," Aug. 17, 1860. ‡D. Cameron to C. H. McCormick, n.d., but probably Dec., 1860.

[25] MS. Reminiscences of C. H. McCormick by Judge Murray F. Tuley, undated, but after May, 1884. In view of McCormick's frequent absences from Chicago during this period, Tuley's statement must be accepted with reservations.

[26] MS. Sketch of C. H. McCormick by D. Cameron, Sept. 8, 1870. In the "Daily Chicago Times" of Dec. 8, 1860, McComas assured his readers: "Vulgarity and licentious details of every description will be wholly excluded from its columns. Not one sentiment will be uttered that could bring a blush to the cheek of virtue, or a rebuke from the strictest moralist."

[27] The "Chicago Times" of Oct. 30, 1864, states that McCormick voted for Douglas in 1860. ‡An undated MS., probably written by C. H. McCor-

las to support the Crittenden Plan, believing that under his lead the entire northwestern democracy and enough Republicans would rally around it to carry it through Congress. To make certain in this crisis that Douglas and he should act in harmony, he waited upon the word of the Illinois Senator before committing the "Times" to any measure. "Of course," he wrote, "it requires *true greatness* to be able to accommodate such differences so as to strike the line that will carry the cause, and save the Union."[28] He was convinced that attempts to conciliate the South would be futile without Republican aid, but he hoped that his friend William H. Seward would lead the more conservative leaders of his party along the path of peace.[29]

On the wisdom of preventing secession by reaching a peaceful agreement with the South, all leading Democrats in Chicago were as one, but they were not unanimous on the question whether coercion should be used in case persuasion failed

mick in 1869, suggests, but does not positively state, that he voted for Douglas in 1860. He attended a Douglas rally in Chicago in early October of that year. L.P.C.B. No. 35, p. 396, W. S. to J. B. McCormick, Sept. 26, 1860; No. 41, p. 414, W. S. McCormick to A. Steele, New Orleans, May 6, 1861. In the issue of "Daily Chicago Times" for Dec. 8, 1860, its editor affirmed: "It will stand to the Union as long as a shred holds it together, and struggle earnestly to reconstruct it if it falls asunder." On this same day, Chas. H. Lanphier, an influential Douglasite and editor at Springfield, warned his chief that the "Daily Chicago Times" was still as much pro-Buchanan as pro-Douglas. "Has not McCormick's application," continued Lanphier, "for a renewal of his reaper patent got something to do with the 'Times' seeming go-between course? Such renewal would amply pay him for fifty or seventy-five thousand sunk in a daily newspaper." This letter is one of the Douglas MSS. at the University of Chicago. A "Chicago Daily Tribune" editorial on Oct. 27, 1860, charged McCormick with planning to supplant Douglas in the U. S. Senate.

[28] C. H. McCormick to S. Douglas, Dec. 28, 1860: "We aim to leave the subject open . . . for your final decision as to what is best." Thereafter, Douglas worked in the U. S. Senate to have McCormick's patent of 1847 extended.

[29] L.P.C.B. No. 38, p. 144, C. H. McCormick to P. H. Watson, Jan. 8, 1861.

to hold the southern states under the flag. The necessity of facing this issue became more apparent with every passing day, since Republican spokesmen, voicing the will of Lincoln at Springfield, showed their determination to stand firm upon their platform of 1860.

Although McCormick from the outset declared that a union worthy of the name could not be preserved by the use of force, he admitted as early as January 8, 1861, that counsels of peace, in the event of the failure of compromise, would go unheeded, and that the secession of the South would bring "all the horrors of a civil war." [30] Douglas, on the other hand, was prepared to support a policy of coercion if the issue could not be avoided.[31] At a meeting called to order by the inventor in North Market Hall, Chicago, in mid-January, to elect delegates to a convention at Springfield, the "McCormick Party," as the "Tribune" called it, was in the majority, and resolved that "it would be unwise and impolitic to seek by war to compel an unwilling Union." [32]

From this time until the close of the first week in April, McCormick refused to abandon hope of a compromise.[33] He

[30] *Ibid.,* No. 38, p. 144, C. H. McCormick to P. H. Watson, Jan. 8, 1861. W. S. McCormick concisely stated the McCormick position in a letter on Jan. 30, 1861, to T. H. Silvez of Newark, N. J. (*Ibid.,* No. 39, p. 557) : *"We* are with the Democratic party of the Northwest. *First the Union as it is, if possible by peace, compromise,* but *in any event peace, & no war,* even if that peace is only attainable by a separation. If a compromise is offered that will satisfy the Border States, I believe the Union will be safe."

[31] "Congressional Globe," Jan. 9, 1861; "Chicago Daily Tribune," May 2, 1861.

[32] L.P.C.B. No. 38, p. 336, W. S. McCormick to J. Henry, Jan. 15, 1861. "Chicago Daily Tribune," Jan 16, 23, 1861. This paper believed that McCormick would fail to swing the Cook County Democracy away from Douglas to support a policy of peace at any cost. "We think it safe to say, that in undertaking to swallow the Democracy of Cook, McCormick overestimated his power of deglutition and underestimated the size of the pill."

[33] L.P.C.B. No. 38, pp. 180, 394, 422, W. S. McCormick to T. Berry, Jan. 9, 18, 20, 1861: "We think the black Republicans will yield tho

remarked with satisfaction that those Republicans who advocated no concessions faced a mutiny within their own ranks, and that Seward, who spoke more softly now that the crisis had come, seemed destined to guide the policy of the Lincoln administration. McCormick believed that secession was both unconstitutional and the worst of folly, and that the will of the people, if ascertained through the medium of a convention called in both North and South, would be for peace and union. In his view, the nation had been brought to its sorry pass by a few designing politicians of both North and South who were ready to sacrifice their country to advance their own selfish ends. Many agreed with him, and the Peace Democrats of the North throughout the war reaffirmed on many occasions their opinion that the conflict could be ended and the Union restored, if a convention "fresh from the people" were called. Nor did McCormick during the rest of his life change his opinion that the war might have been avoided by the same method.

McCormick's peace-at-any-cost position brought down upon his head the fury of the "Chicago Tribune." He was denounced as a "rebel" and a "slave-driver." [34] For a few days

they curse us. Many Republicans here yesterday (17th) signed our petition for the Crittenden Compromise." *Ibid.*, p. 714, W. S. McCormick to J. Churchman, Feb. 6, 1861: "Just now we feel encouraged at the apparent prospect of returning reason on the part of our Politicians. . . . Our *ranting* Republicans here are being sorely exercised at the present position of Seward, Cameron, Kellogg (of Ills.) and others of their leaders. . . . We rejoice that conservative Republicans are fast coming to our position against coercion & for compromise." *Ibid.*, No. 39, p. 599, J. T. Griffin to J. T. Higgins, Mch. 11, 1861: "We trust that our political troubles are drawing to an end." *Ibid.*, No. 40, p. 317, Wm. S. to J. B. McCormick, Mch. 28, 1861: "The pulse of the 'Blood and Thunder' Republicans of this latitude is coming *down.*" *Ibid.*, No. 40, p. 731, J. T. Griffin to J. B. McCormick, Apr. 11, 1861: "News from the South looks *warlike,* and we now look daily for the conflict."

[34] "Chicago Daily Tribune," Feb. 12, 1861. L.P.C.B. No. 39, p. 161, W. S. McCormick to A. B. Tanqueray, Lexington, Va., Feb. 23, 1861. W. S. McCormick sent him a copy of the "Tribune" to show "a sample of the *Devils* we have to oppose here." *Ibid.*, No. 39, p. 205, J. T. Griffin to E. Healy, Feb. 25, 1861.

in mid-February, 1861, he considered the advisability of suing this newspaper for libel, but his own editors reminded him that the "Times" was equally unsparing in its attacks upon abolitionists.[35] Since McCormick was at this time in Washington on patent business, his brothers rushed to his defense in a public letter, comparing the value of the services rendered by the "Tribune" with those of the reaper factory to the city and the entire Northwest, and pointing out that because of the national scope of his business, among other reasons, the inventor was the most ardent of unionists. "Cyrus H. McCormick is interested in saving a Union," they wrote, "not in saving a party. Is it not possible that the 'Chicago Tribune' might lose more by the breaking of its party than the breaking of the government?" With this shrewd question, the letter closed.[36]

But Washington's Birthday parades by Conservatives in Chicago,[37] peace-convention deliberations and the maneuvers of Seward at Washington served rather to increase the tension than to furnish the solution which McCormick so eagerly sought. The enthusiastic outburst in the North which greeted the news of the Fort Sumter bombardment made it imperative for him publicly to declare his position in the conflict. Those who work for peace on the eve of war become suspect as soon as the first gun is fired. Rumors were abroad that McCormick was disloyal, and there was danger that the office of the

[35] Mary Ann McCormick to Nettie F. McCormick, Feb. 17(?), 1861.

[36] L.P.C.B. No. 39, pp. 84-93, Joint letter of W. S. and L. J. McCormick, Feb. 19(?), 1861: "A more Demon like production [than the "Tribune" article of Feb. 12] could not be hatched this side the infernal regions." Ibid., No. 39, p. 343, W. S. McCormick to Jas. Henry, Mch. 2, 1861: "We have helped to build this city by hundreds of thousands & these Editors though strong politically are without body or soul substantially. . . . We are not secessionists by a good deal but we are for the South having her rights."

[37] Ibid., No. 39, p. 165, W. S. McCormick to T. Berry, Feb. 23, 1861: "I regretted much I did not think of having a fine reaper in the procession behind four elegant horses & followed by our 300 men from the office & Factory."

"Chicago Times" would be demolished by a "patriotic" mob.[38] Under these circumstances, in late April, 1861, an editorial over his signature appeared in that journal. It read in part:

I have deemed it a duty which I owe alike to myself and to the public, to make known as the proprietor of the paper, my views on the present war, in such explicit terms as to put all doubts forever at rest.

It is not necessary for me to enter into any explanation of my past course. It is known to all, that to the extent of my humble ability, my utmost efforts were directed to the maintenance of peace, believing, as I did, that the best interests of the country would be thereby promoted. For having occupied that position in the past, I have no regrets to express or apologies to offer. . . .

Born and reared in the South, I would disgrace my manhood did I not say that my heart sickens at the prospect of the conflict which must ensue. Yet while I regard the war as a great calamity, I am fully aware that there are greater calamities even than war, and the loss of National honor is one of them. Though a native of the South, I am a citizen of Illinois, and of the United States, and as such shall bear true allegiance to the Government. That allegiance I shall never violate or disregard. I am and ever shall be on the side of my country in war—without considering whether my country is right or wrong.

Although this article left those who read it in no doubt of the side McCormick would support, it did not commit him to cease striving for peace. Probably, however, its references to "loss of national honor" and "my country . . . right or wrong" reflect the emotion aroused by the guns of Sumter and not its author's considered opinion.[39] At this time Dr. Lord sub-

[38] L.P.C.B. No. 38, p. 714, W. S. McCormick to J. Churchman, Feb. 6, 1861. W. S. to J. B. McCormick, May 7, 1861. L.P.C.B. No. 41, p. 804, W. S. McCormick to T. Berry, May 21, 1861: "Most deeply have we been interested in *maintaining* the *Union in peace* and to that end did we struggle as long as we *dare* do so & almost beyond the point of safety."

[39] *Ibid.*, No. 40, p. 862, J. T. Griffin to P. H. Watson, Apr. 16, 1861: *"War War War!"* is now the only topic of conversation. Our people are all for the Stars and Stripes and for the *Union* and the 'Administration.' There is as you say no party now . . . the people of the North West are as

mitted an editorial entitled "The Crisis" to the "Presbyterian Expositor," in which he called the southerners "traitors" and the rebellion "an outrageous conspiracy." The closing sentence ran as follows: "At whatever cost, it must be crushed. This is demanded by truth and righteousness,—by Liberty and Religion." [40] This represented a length to which McCormick would not go, and Dr. Lord's fulmination was never published.

The commencement of hostilities signified that the "Daily Chicago Times" had failed in its purpose. There was little prospect that the embattled nation would be in a mood to listen to counsels of peace in the near future. So far as McCormick was concerned, the paper's reason for being no longer existed, and he was eager to get clear of an enterprise that had returned him little except expense and criticism. [41] As early as April 2, 1861, a notice appeared to the effect that he had transferred to his brother-in-law, Elbridge M. Fowler, "all my right and interest in, and all accounts due the 'Chicago Times' to the present date." [42] This was misleading, since the inventor

one in defense of the national government." *Ibid.*, No. 41, p. 50, W. S. McCormick to W. T. Rush, Steele's Tavern, Va., Apr. 18, 1861. He rejoiced that Va's. ordinance of secession had failed of adoption. "I am as much opposed to 'Abolitionism' as anybody but let us not have the *Union* broken up *yet*. If secession be persisted in I believe we shall *all* be disgraced in the eyes of the world and *all* ruined." *Ibid.*, No. 41, p. 54. On Apr. 18, he also wrote James Henry of Steele's Tavern: "I hope even yet that 'nobody may be hurt.'"

[40] MS. article by Dr. Lord, n.d., but probably written in late April, 1861, and certainly after the Baltimore Riot of the 19th.

[41] ‡C. A. Spring, Jr., to C. H. McCormick, Aug. 27, 1866. McCormick's loss from the "Herald" and "Times" is here shown as $28,357.35.

[42] ‡E. M. Fowler to C. H. McCormick, May 20, 1861: "I have reduced the liabilities [of the "Times"] from $1500 to $18.00 since the first of the month,—in most part by using second class currency from the Factory. The amount due to this [the "Times"] office is fully as much as when you left, —for the past week I have not dared to collect anything, as our currency is in such bad shape that it was not safe to take it, and a large share is today worth only 50 or 60 cents on the dollar." ‡C. C. Copeland to C. H.

continued to be the proprietor of the journal for two months thereafter.[43]

By mid-May, however, he was negotiating with Wilbur F. Storey of the "Detroit Free Press" for the purchase of the "Times." [44] On June 1, the bill of sale was drawn and signed. Storey sold his Detroit paper to Alosh H. Walker of Ann Arbor, Michigan, but retained a mortgage on the plant until the new owner could pay the full sum due. Storey assigned this lien to McCormick as security that he would carry out his agreement in regard to the "Chicago Times." The sum that McCormick eventually received from Storey for this journal is not known, but it seems to have been about $13,000.[45] On June 8, 1861, the paper began its hectic but prosperous career under Storey's able editorship. Within less than a year its opposition to the war made it notorious, and in early June, 1863, it was suppressed for a few days by General Burnside's order.[46] Many people still associated it with the inventor and

McCormick, Apr. 8, 1864: "I've long ago realized all that can be had from the old *Times* claims except $150 due from the Democratic German Paper here. It is prosperous and will soon pay up."

[43] Mary Ann McCormick to Nettie F. McCormick, Feb. 17th (?), 1861.

[44] ‡Telegram of W. F. Storey to C. H. McCormick, May 20, 1861. ‡E. M. Fowler to C. H. McCormick, May 20, 1861. C. H. McCormick was in Washington during most of May, 1861, after the 6th. L.P.C.B. No. 41, pp. 429, 609, W. S. to J. B. McCormick, May 7, 14, 1861.

[45] Indenture of June 1, 1861, between A. H. Walker and W. F. Storey. Agreement of June 1, 1861, between C. H. McCormick and W. F. Storey. S. T. Douglass to C. H. McCormick, June 5, 1861, and May 27, 1862. S. T. Douglass to E. M. Fowler, July 15, 1861. In a letter dated July 17, 1872, to D. Cameron, C. H. McCormick wrote: "You know I lost fully $20,000 by *my experiment* in political papers!" Judge Murray F. Tuley in a MS. giving his impression of his friend C. H. McCormick, stated that after the inventor sold the "Times," he "sunk" twelve or fifteen thousand dollars in the "Post," the paper of the Chicago War Democrats edited by J. W. Sheahan. I have found no contemporary evidence supporting this reminiscence.

[46] D. B. Sanger, "The Chicago Times and the Civil War," in the "Mississippi Valley Historical Review," Vol. XVII, No. 4 (Mch. 1931), pp. 557-580. "Chicago Daily Tribune," June 3, 4, 1863. Mary Ann McCor-

almost to the close of the war the "Chicago Tribune," for political purposes of its own, called it "Mr. McCormick's paper." [47] Thus the erroneous belief was fostered that McCormick was still its owner and sponsored the views advanced by Storey in his editorials.

Whether Cyrus McCormick was, or was not, a Copperhead during the Civil War depends entirely upon the inclusiveness given to that opprobrious term. Those persons who advocated war without stint and no peace until the South was completely subjugated, were prone to label as Copperheads all who were not equally belligerent. By 1863 too vigorous opposition to Lincoln's Emancipation Proclamation might lead an annoyed Abolitionist to place the recalcitrant in the same category. All would agree that advocates of immediate peace on the basis of an independent Confederacy deserved the title, but what of those who believed that the war should stop because it blocked, rather than promoted, a restoration of the Union? Let an armistice be arranged, or, if needs be, negotiations attempted without a cessation of hostilities in order to ascertain whether the South would come back with a guarantee that slavery should not be disturbed. If the Confederacy rejected this proposal, then let the conflict continue to the bitter end, not however to compel emancipation, but to achieve the highest of all ends, the preservation of an united nation. If advocates of this view were Copperheads, then McCormick was one of them. In his opinion, Stephen Douglas, if he had lived, would

mick to Nettie F. McCormick, Jan. 1, 1863: "Yesterday there was a move on the Board of Trade to expel from it the commercial reporter of the Times, & the Journal in the afternoon wrote a dirty article about it & the Times replies this morning. . . . The Times is very bold I tell you. . . . It is said the Tribune will be torn down if the Times reporter is not again admitted etc. I somehow dread the morrow lest something evil crosses our path."

[47] "Chicago Daily Tribune," Nov. 7, 1864. According to an editorial in this paper on Oct. 30, 1862, the "lodge room" of the "treasonable" Knights of the Golden Circle was in the McCormick Block.

have been found in the same camp because his sanction of coercion was to prevent secession and not to deprive men of their property by force and without compensation. The inventor was a pall-bearer at his funeral.

As early as the summer of 1861, William S. McCormick, who was usually more pessimistic and always less vocal than his elder brother on political questions arising from the war, thought that it was time to inquire whether the conflict was being waged for motives of patriotism or to advance the fortunes of Republicans and Abolitionists. "I love the Union of these States as much as any man that lives," he added, "but . . . can we save this Union by *blood?*" [48] Cyrus McCormick was soon asking himself the same question, and in a letter written to the "Daily Chicago Times" in the spring of 1864, he suggested that his departure for England almost two years before was prompted in a measure by his realization that "the Negro policy of the *ultra* half of the Cabinet at Washington [seemed] likely to prevail." [49] The chief purpose of his two years' residence abroad was to promote the sale of his reapers, but when he left the United States he carried with him a letter of introduction from Horace Greeley to William L. Dayton, the United States Ambassador to France. The wording of this brief note suggests that McCormick hoped that Napoleon III could be induced to intervene in behalf of peace.[50]

[48] L.P.C.B. No. 44, p. 760, W. S. McCormick to M. Forney, Balto., Md., Aug. 9, 1861.

[49] W. A. Richardson, M. C., to C. H. McCormick, Apr. 11, 1862: "I fear the Abolitionists have us hook line bob and sinker in this Congress. We shall give them a hard fight however."

[50] H. Greeley to W. L. Dayton, July 14, 1862: "Reared in Virginia, a resident of Illinois, he aims to be a 'Peace' man in our civil contest, and may give you some ideas of this slave evil from his peculiar stand-point. His visit to Europe is mainly one of business, but he will proceed to Paris with other views; and I commend him to your kind consideration as a citizen of lofty character and eminent usefulness." In L.P.C.B. No. 47, Opp. p. 355, is the notation: "The leaves torn out here contained a letter written

He was surprised to remark during his stay in Europe that there was a general opinion, in sharp contrast to what he had heard there in 1851 and 1855, that democratic governments were everywhere doomed to failure.[51]

McCormick remained overseas until the early summer of 1864, "plodding along in the pursuit of business . . . but watching with the deepest concern the progress of events at home." [52] William S. McCormick and Charles C. Copeland kept him in touch with events in Chicago. The temper of that city, as well as the skilful handling of his business interests by his brother, left him small inducement to hasten his return.[53] He believed that the Emancipation Proclamation was issued by Lincoln in order to permit the enlistment of negroes, and that by thus making the confiscation of private property one of the chief objectives of the war, the preservation of the Union by force of arms became an even more chimerical hope than before. In his view, the Proclamation would drive the Confederacy to fight with desperation, and the North might well be assured that its foe was confident of success as long as it found it unnecessary to free and arm the slaves. If that day should come, England and France, in exchange for the emancipation of the negroes, would intervene in the war and recognize the independence of the Confederacy. Logically, according to McCormick, Lincoln should have recognized the sovereignty of the Richmond government on the day that his

by Mr. C. H. McC. to J. E. Thompson, & torn out by C. H.'s order April 15th, 1862." Thompson, an ex-member of Buchanan's cabinet, was associated with the Canadian activities of the Confederacy. This is the only evidence which indicates that McCormick destroyed any of his Civil War correspondence. The scarcity of manuscript material dealing with his political course during the conflict is noticeable, but may be accounted for by the fact of his two years' residence in England.

[51] ‡C. H. McCormick to the Ed., "Chicago Times," Apr. 11, 1864.
[52] C. H. McCormick to the Ed., "New York World," June 20, 1864.
[53] W. S. to C. H. McCormick, Sept. 27, 1862; ‡C. C. Copeland to C. H. McCormick, Apr. 8, 1864.

Emancipation Proclamation was issued, for by that stroke he made northern victory impossible.

Nevertheless, McCormick was confident that the South would prefer reunion with slavery to independence without it, and on this basis he believed that the Confederacy would be willing to make peace. So why should the war continue until both sides were ruined and utterly exhausted, and more white men sacrificed than the number of negroes then held in bondage? Many northern Democrats agreed with McCormick's ideas or had others quite similar to them. He would not admit that the South was weakening; he failed to realize the significance of the northern victories during the last five months of 1864, and with a strange persistence he held to his opinion until the eve of Appomattox.

In April, 1864, while still in London, he was unable longer to remain silent, and expressed his views at length in a letter to W. F. Storey. He felt "that it becomes every one who has interests to be protected, or a patriotic pulse beating for the welfare of his country, to apply his shoulder to the wheel . . . to say what he thinks, and do what he can." He was now determined to come home for the purpose of winning the Democratic Party in the approaching presidential election to a support of his policy. *"Stop the war,"* he urged, "declare an armistice—call a convention, and consider *terms of peace*. . . . May the *Democratic party* then not falter at this stupendous crisis! . . . Another Republican President elected and the country—*the Union is lost*. The Democratic Party only can— and *it can if it will*—save it. Will it not to the rescue? The ballot box is the only remedy." [54] By thus charging that the war was a failure and urging the call of a convention, he

---

[54] ‡C. H. McCormick to the Ed., "Chicago Times," from London, Apr. 11, 1864. Apparently this letter was never published in the "Times," but it appeared in substantially the same form in the "New York World," July 10, 1864.

anticipated by four months the platform to be adopted by the Democratic Party at its national convention.[55]

In September, 1864, he consented to be the Democratic candidate for Congress from the 1st district of Illinois.[56] "Long John" Wentworth was his opponent, and McCormick realized that he had very small chance of success.[57] The bitterness of the campaign is well illustrated by the following paragraph from the "Chicago Daily Tribune :" [58]

The Democracy of Cook County could not have nominated another man so well calculated to cement the loyalty of the people, and excite every lover of the Union to unwonted exertions for his defeat, as C. H. McCormick. Mr. McCormick has not an instinct that is not in sympathy with the rebellion. Like all poor white trash of Virginia, he left the State a better friend of slavery than the slaveholders themselves, and the prejudices of his youth have built upon a defective education, a perfect monomania in behalf of man-stealing. His intrigues against Douglas and in favor of Breckinridge in 1860, will doubtless commend him to the mass of the party hereabouts. He has been nominated avowedly for his money . . . and we trust that he may be made to bleed as freely as his

[55] C. H. McCormick to Rev. L. Cumming, London, Mch. 23, 1864: "What is yet to result from the war is only known to the Great Ruler above but my opinion still is that the South will never be *subjugated* by the North." ‡C. H. McCormick to F. Ewing, from London, Apr. 1, 1864: "The war has been conducted in a manner neither calculated to restore the Union nor to protect the property interests of the country, but to lead in the end to bankruptcy & ruin,—individual and national."

[56] "Daily Chicago Times," Sept. 17, 1864.

[57] "Prairie Farmer" (Chicago), Sept. 24, 1864. L.P.C.B. No. 75, p. 207, W. S. McCormick to D. Zimmerman, Oct. 6, 1864. *Ibid.,* No. 76, p. 51, C. A. Spring to J. T. Griffin, Nov. 9, 1864.

[58] "Chicago Daily Tribune," Sept. 18, 19, 21, 22, 23, Oct. 27, 28, 29, and Nov. 7, 1864. On Oct. 25, 1864, in an article over two columns in length, this paper told of the "General Explosion of McCormick's Pretended Inventions. His Piracies and his Fictitious Claims." O. Hussey was the chief hero of this article as he was also of the ones of Sept. 21 and 23. On Oct. 25 the "Tribune" insinuated that McCormick had purchased Confederate bonds while in Europe, although contributing not a penny to the Union cause. On Oct. 27 and 28 it charged him with oppressing his factory employees.

most greedy supporter can desire. But all the wealth which he has
extorted from the loyal farmers of the West will not elect him.
. . . Mr. McCormick will be beaten by a majority which will
stifle his political ambition for the rest of his natural life.

Libels of this kind doubtless helped to defeat McCormick,
but "Long John" was a very popular political veteran and the
outcome of the elections throughout the land was mainly determined by the victories of Sherman in Georgia and Sheridan
in the Shenandoah Valley.[59] McCormick conceded on November 12 that it was a "Waterloo defeat," but he believed the
result had been due to "power and patronage" and the skill of
the Republicans in misleading the people to associate the
Democrats with disunion.[60] He refused to admit that the election returns signified a repudiation by the people of true Democratic principles. Although many of his colleagues were apa-
thetic and some talked of disbanding the party altogether, he
was never more active politically than between November,
1864, and March, 1865.[61] "We (the Democrats) must pick

[59] McCormick received one vote to Wentworth's three. The inventor
loaned $20,000 to the Illinois Democratic State Central Committee in this
election. James C. Robinson, the candidate of the Democratic Party for
Governor of Illinois, was sufficiently acceptable to Jacob Thompson, the
Confederate Agent in Canada, to secure from him a subsidy of $40,000. One
half of this was used to reimburse McCormick. The inventor was appar-
ently unaware of the source of this windfall. See, J. B. Castleman, "On
Active Service" (Louisville, Ky., 1917), pp. 144-148. F. G. Smyth, Madison,
Wis., to Co., Nov. 7, 1868. In a suit brought by the McCormick Co. to
collect a debt from a farmer, the defendant's lawyer told the jury that
C. H. McCormick had given Jefferson Davis $17,500 to carry on the war.
Perhaps the incident mentioned in Castleman's book accounts for this story.
If the "Chicago Tribune" of Oct. 25, 1864, can be believed, C. H. McCor-
mick contributed at least $15,000 to the Democratic campaign fund in 1864.

[60] Letter of C. H. McCormick, dated Nov. 12, 1864, in "New York
World," Nov. 22, 1864, and in "Daily Chicago Times," Nov. 16, 1864.
MS. article by C. H. McCormick, entitled "The *Tribune* is the War," n.d.,
but written after the election in the autumn of 1864.

[61] Letter of C. H. McCormick called "A New Way to Peace," Nov. 12,
1864, addressed to the Editor of the "New York World," and published in
that paper on Nov. 22.

our flints and try again," counseled the inventor, ". . . while the object for which we have labored is the restoration of the Union . . . we must not become weary in well doing; but, on the contrary, with our views of the situation, while sunk in humility, we should rise in devotion and patriòtic effort with the greatness of the emergency."

As has been noted earlier in this chapter, McCormick did not realize that the Confederacy was on the verge of collapse, and he believed that if the common people of both North and South could be reached, they were as ready now as they always had been to speak for an immediate peace with union and slavery. The reëlection of Lincoln had made the South more determined than ever not to yield, and doubtless when necessity arose, Jefferson Davis would free the three or four million slaves and put them in the field. If so, the northern cause would be hopeless. Therefore, argued McCormick, the Democratic National Convention should reassemble, and with Lincoln's sanction, open negotiations with the South. Lincoln had often said that he stood above party and was concerned first of all about the welfare of the nation. Since the Confederacy refused to negotiate with him, let him demonstrate his sincerity and patriotism by sanctioning an effort by the Democratic Party representing the North, to draw the southerners into a peace conference. This is the "last chance" to save the Union, warned McCormick, and the North must realize that they have only the choice of an united country with slavery or an independent Confederacy without slavery.

These suggestions were received with little favor even by the Democrats.[62] Storey felt that it would be "an extraordinary step" and "end in humiliating failure" for a vanquished

---

[62] C. H. McCormick to the Editors of the "New York World," Dec. 7, 1864. "Chicago Tribune," Nov. 17, 1864. This paper professed to believe that McCormick was more concerned about preserving slavery than the Union.

party to ask the victors to adopt its policy.[63] But that something must be done at once, McCormick strongly believed. He now considered the possibility of purchasing the "National Intelligencer" in order to use it to advance his views and the cause of Democracy at Washington.[64] He wrote President Lincoln asking that he "with or without an accompanying friend as your Excellency may determine, be permitted to go to Richmond for the purpose of such conferences with Confederates as might be obtained, that might be useful." [65] He drafted resolutions incorporating his ideas of the way to make peace and hoped that they might be adopted by the Democrats in Congress.[66] All of these efforts were fruitless, but as late as March, 1865, McCormick was still writing of his desire to visit the Confederate Capital, and was taking counsel with Horace Greeley upon the best plan to bring peace.[67]

The news of the surrender of Lee must have come to McCormick as a distinct surprise.[68] It demonstrated that he had overestimated the strength of the Confederacy. The Union had been preserved and slavery was no more, although he had repeatedly asserted that these objectives could not together be achieved. He was glad that slavery was gone, but he ab-

[63] W. F. Storey, Chicago, to C. H. McCormick, Dec. 17, 1864: "For the present, in my judgment we have no alternative to watching and waiting."

[64] ‡J. T. Coyle, Washington, to C. H. McCormick, Dec. 15, 1864.

[65] ‡C. H. McCormick to A. Lincoln, from Washington, Dec. 19, 1864: "My former residence in the South, and acquaintance with the people there might be rather favorable to the object than otherwise."

[66] MS. draft, in McCormick's hand, of resolutions for introduction in the 38th Congress.

[67] H. Greeley to C. H. McCormick, Jan. 27, Feb. 14, and Apr. 26, 1865, and to ‡Gen'l N. P. Banks, Mch. 24, 1865. W. S. to C. H. McCormick, Mch. 9, 1865. In the Nettie Fowler McCormick Biog. Asso. Files is the following receipt written by C. H. McCormick: "Rec'd Feb. 18th '65 of C. H. McCormick Fifty Dollars bal. in full for services in connection with trip to Canada & expenses." (Signed) Henry S. Nettleton. No other reference has been found to this mission.

[68] Few letters of McCormick on any topic, and none bearing upon politics, survive from the period March-July, 1865.

horred the arbitrary method employed to abolish it. Conciliation must now be the key-note of the policies adopted at
Washington and by his church toward the South, and he hoped
that "the noble administration" of President Johnson would
attain the success that its magnanimity merited.[69]

Now that, in the Providence of God, we have passed the terrible ordeal of a protracted civil war, unparalleled in destructive-
ness and all that makes war horrible, and are again without controversy the United States, with yet a glorious future in prospect,
religiously as well as politically should wise counsels prevail, it
would afford me the greatest satisfaction if, by any humble means
in my power, I could contribute anything toward the consummation of that universal harmony between all parts of our country,
which is only necessary now soon to make it the most powerful and
influential of all countries of the World.[70]

With this spirit of optimism and desire for service, Mc-
Cormick turned to face the new problems of the Reconstruction Era.

[69] C. H. McCormick to C. C. Baldwin, Aug. 14, 1866, R. H. Glass,
Lynchburg, Va., Aug. 9, 1866, and #Wm. Brown, Richmond, Va., Oct. 6,
1865. In the last of these he writes: "Reunion & Restoration seem now to
be the great conservative [Democratic] principles of the day—led in good
faith I trust by President Johnson, and which I trust will be met by as
full a response as possible from the South in its broadest application, religiously as well as politically & commercially. This I think *right,* and especially the interest of the South."

[70] C. H. McCormick to B. M. Smith, July 14, 1865.

CHAPTER III

THE REAPER IN YEARS OF DEPRESSION AND
CIVIL WAR

B Y 1855 the manufacture of harvesting machinery, although still on a small scale, had gained a firm foothold among the industries of the nation. The focus of grain production in the United States had crossed the Alleghenies and was moving quite rapidly westward into the prairie belt. In this area the central location of Chicago, with its unrivaled transportation facilities both by land and lake, made it the outlet for much of the crop of the Middle West and a natural distributing point for reapers and mowers. Here, in the heart of the city, on North Water Street, hard by the mouth of the Chicago River, was the factory of Cyrus McCormick, employing about two hundred men and boys, and manufacturing some twenty-five hundred machines a year.

He no longer enjoyed a virtual monopoly of sales in the grain-fields of the West. His success during the preceding decade, and the lapse of his original patent, had drawn rival firms into the field, both in his own neighborhood and in the states east of the Appalachians. Machine production was already showing a tendency to concentrate in the Genesee Valley, central Ohio, and northern Illinois.

The new industry depended for its prosperity in large degree upon conditions fostered by its own output. Its advancement was obviously a result of the well-being of the farmer and the increase of small-grain culture in the United States. That these arose in some measure from the use of reapers and

mowers had ever been a chief talking-point of Cyrus Mc-
Cormick, and the testimony of many witnesses could be cited
in his support.

After 1845, large numbers of immigrants from northern
Europe, together with settlers who were native born, pushed
the frontier west and north into Iowa, Kansas, Wisconsin
and Minnesota. Wherever they went, soil and climate invited
the cultivation of wheat. Railroads, reapers, and an enlarging
domestic market kept pace with their advance. Currency inflation attending the influx of gold from California, and a
heightened demand for American grain in Europe during the
Crimean War, gradually raised the price of wheat to $1.75 a
bushel in Chicago by May, 1855. Not a few landowners, especially in Illinois, used their credit to extend their holdings in
order to raise more grain. It was too early, however, for farmers and manufacturers of harvesting machinery to talk of a
permanent prosperity.

Beginning in that year and continuing for the next decade,
the number of foreigners seeking homes in the United States
sharply declined. The war in Europe was soon over and the
export market collapsed. Wheat was selling for eighty cents a
bushel by the late autumn of 1856, and one year later fell off
another twenty cents. On the few occasions between 1856
and 1862 when it commanded above $1.25 a bushel in Chicago,
a corner on grain was largely responsible and the farmer derived but little benefit.[1] At all times he received a much smaller
sum for his crop at the wharf or railhead than the price per
bushel quoted in the newspapers of the city.[2]

[1] James E. Boyle, "Chicago Wheat Prices for Eighty-One Years, 1841-
1921" (Ithaca, N. Y., 1922).
[2] O. Klug, Davenport, Ia., to Co., Dec. 10, 1857: Barley is 25-40¢ a bu.
here and 45 to 50¢ in Chicago. C. B. Griffin, Newark, O., to Co., June 13,
1858: Wheat is bought for 45¢ a bushel. M. M. McNair, Brodhead, Wis.,
to Co., Feb. 19, and Apr. 29, 1858: Farmers purchased machines when
wheat was at $1.50 a bu. and now it is 45¢. The big farmers are the most

If, due to a drop in the market-price or other causes, the real value of the cash received by a farmer from the sale of his wheat was too small to yield him a reasonable margin of profit, he could apply one or more of several remedies. He might endeavor to increase his yield per acre by the use of fertilizers or a crop-rotation system. Most probably, however, in the Middle West he would seed more wheat on more land so that the net profit from a large crop would equal the income gained from his smaller output in the day of better prices.[3] To garner his increased harvest and to reduce his labor costs demanded the use of a reaper. Perhaps he preferred to turn from the small grains to hay and stock. In the diversified farming belt of the Middle West this was quite possible, and was often advisable both to relieve exhausted land of its one crop burden and to take advantage of a more favorable market for those commodities when compared with wheat and rye. In this case, he would need a mower, and the manufacturer of harvesting machinery again benefited as well as the farmer. Low prices for grain, therefore, did not necessarily mean that reaper and mower companies would suffer, unless the general level of prices for all the staple agricultural products was so depressed that the ordinary farmer could not make ends meet even by using machinery. Otherwise, in hard times, a manufacturer's insistence that reapers and mowers were a farmer's only salvation, carried a wide appeal. The implements were of peculiar efficacy both in fair weather and foul.

This being true, it is not surprising that McCormick's sales

in debt for they have been adding farm to farm or building largely. I never saw such blue times in Wisconsin. J. Brumaugh, Mt. Pleasant, Ia., to Co., May 31, 1858: Wheat sells here @ 35¢; corn @ 15-20¢; and potatoes @ 20¢ per bushel.

[3] L.P.C.B. No. 10, p. 532, Co. to T. Carter, Bloomington, Ind., Feb. 2, 1858. Following a general failure of winter wheat in the prairie belt between 1847 and 1853, many farmers in Ia., Wis., and northern Ill. turned to the cultivation of spring wheat. Ranked in order, Ill., Ind., Wis., and Ohio were the leading wheat states in the Union in 1860.

jumped from twenty-five hundred in 1855 to over four thousand in the next season, and did not drop below that figure during the depression on the eve of the Civil War. He was unable to supply the demand. Other builders showed as large or a greater increase, and most of the 125,000 or more reapers and mowers in use by 1861 had been purchased during the preceding five years. Evidently low prices and the short harvests of 1858 and 1859 do not explain why some builders of harvesting machinery were driven into bankruptcy, or why others, more fortunate, believed they were weathering the "hardest years" they had even known.[4]

Currency troubles were chronic in the Middle West. Ohio Valley farmers had regarded the second National Bank of the United States as a "monster," but since its downfall in the day of President Jackson, "fly-by-night" bankers, "free" and state banks had brought troubles of another kind. State banking laws were lax and the worth of the note issues of many of these institutions was most uncertain. Manufacturers of harvesting machinery first began to complain of the handicap of poor currency about 1854. Agents were furnished with bank-note detectors and were ordered to receive no money from purchasers of reapers which could not be exchanged for a sight draft on New York or Philadelphia for less than a five per cent discount.[5] This was often impossible to procure. The small amounts of specie and sound bank-notes in the rural districts were hoarded or quickly returned to the cities to meet the adverse balance of trade. Money scarcity was a common complaint throughout the Middle West by 1856.[6]

[4] *Ibid.,* No. 17, p. 679, W. S. to C. H. McCormick, Jan. 21, 1859. *Ibid.,* No. 21, p. 73, Co. to G. Hagerman & Co., May 4, 1859. *Ibid.,* No. 29, p. 765, Co. to A. G. Foster, Ottawa Creek, K. Terr., Feb. 3, 1860.

[5] *Ibid.,* No. 9, p. 57, Co. to J. B. Erb, Durlach, Pa., Oct. 3, 1857. No. 10, p. 547, to G. M. Gault, Annapolis, O., Apr. 3, 1858. No. 38, p. 387, to W. H. Page, Reed's Mills, O., Jan. 18, 1861.

[6] Short crops in the East in 1854 and 1855 caused money scarcity there. Farming areas in the Middle West often had no specie except the little

The severe cold of the open winter of 1856-1857 killed much wheat. Spring and harvest came about a month late. Although the crop in central Illinois and in the eastern states was very short, the general yield throughout the land was of average size and Cyrus McCormick sold his entire stock of machines without difficulty. Following the harvest, the price of wheat fell over fifty per cent in five months and the farmers withheld their grain from market. Because corn and pork were also selling at a low figure, reaper agents reported that their clients could not pay their notes when they fell due on December 1. The financial panic which swept through the North and West that autumn added to the distress. Produce men and country merchants had no money to offer for grain and were refused credit by the city correspondents from whom they had customarily purchased their stock in trade.[7] Banks throughout the country suspended specie payments or went to the wall. Municipalities and individual business men in the Mississippi Valley added to the welter of depreciated or worthless currency by issuing scrip of doubtful value. Iowa and Minnesota were particularly hard hit. Gold was at a twelve per cent premium in Davenport by December, 1857, and St. Paul business men were obliged to send food and clothing to destitute farmers in their neighborhood.[8]

brought in by immigrants. See, L.P.C.B. No. 43, p. 276, W. S. to C. H. McCormick, June 26, 1861: "We occasionally now get from a dutchman $130 in gold for a reaper." Bankruptcies in the Middle West made it impossible to borrow on western paper in the eastern money markets. *"The West at present has a bad name,"* wrote J. Campbell, Westons, N. J., to W. S. McCormick, on Sept. 6, 1858. See also his letters to W. S. McCormick of Oct. 7, 11, and Nov. 9, 1858.

[7] Letters to the Co. of D. Zimmerman, Oquawka, Ill., Jan. 3, 1858, J. Campbell, Balto., Nov. 15, 1857, and J. B. Erb, Durlach, Pa., Jan. 16, 1858.

[8] Letters to the Co. of O. Klug, Davenport, Ia., Dec. 9, 1857; D. Zimmerman, Rock Island, Ill., Jan. 29, 1858; L. Westergaard, Winona, Minn. Terr., May 24, 1858; Constans & Stevenson, St. Paul, Minn., Mch. 16, 1858; and T. Chapman, Spring Valley, Minn. Terr., May 26, and Dec. 24, 1857: My father-in-law has about 1000 bushels of oats and wheat, and 30 acres of corn, and can't sell enough to pay his taxes.

The following winter was mild, but an exceptionally wet spring made the roads so muddy that farmers could not get their grain to miller or commission merchant, and agents were delayed in their canvass for money and orders.[9] As late as mid-June some sections reported that not one half of their corn had been planted.[10] The hot, soggy summer brought rust in the wheat. Central and northern Illinois was once again a principal sufferer. Discouraged, debt-laden farmers listened to Lincoln debate with Douglas in August and September, after harvesting their meager crops. Probably the hope of relief from "the curse of the Almighty" sent many into the ranks of the Republican Party between 1856 and 1860.[11] Conditions were not much better anywhere in the Northwest, except in southern Illinois where McCormick's representatives noted that men were more conservative, refused to buy unless they could pay cash, and had not rashly extended their holdings earlier in the decade.[12]

Although bad weather and pests caused crop failures in some localities in the Northwest during these years, the prairie

[9] Ward & Waller, Portsmouth, O., to the Co., Feb. 6, 1858. L.P.C.B. No. 12, p. 237, W. S. McCormick to T. Berry, June 7, 1858: "Some one who kept count says it rained 35 days last month."

[10] W. B. Silver, Sugar Valley, O., and C. Wright, Vallonia, Ind., to the Co., June 5, 1858. L.P.C.B., No. 12, p. 327, W. S. McCormick to A. D. Hager, June 11, 1858.

[11] Letters to the Co. of H. S. Champlin, Courtland, Ill., July 12, 1858; I. Kirkpatrick, Freeland, Ill., Oct. 19, 1858; and W. C. Leyburn, Galesburg, Ill., Apr. 6, May 15, 27, June 7, 17 and July 3, 1858. Frost injured southern grain in 1860, and the spring of that year in the Middle West was very dry. But the McCormicks, although they sold over 4000 machines, needed 500 or a 1000 more to fill the demand. See L.P.C.B. No. 31, p. 786, W. S. McCormick to J. Henry, May 9, 1860, and No. 34, passim.

[12] Ibid., No. 22, p. 439, the Co. to F. W. Smith, Woodstock, Ill., June 8, 1859: "In these northern counties [of Illinois] the risk is fifty per cent greater in selling any machinery to the general run of customers than it is in the South half of the State." T. J. Walker & Co., Belleville, Ill., to the Co., Feb. 8, 1858. Southern Illinois farmers were more hesitant than others in putting aside hand-rake reapers for self-rakes. See L.P.C.B. No. 78, p. 616, the Co. to N. W. Jones, Griggsville, Ill., May 9, 1865.

farmer's inability to shake off his load of debt because of low prices and worthless currency was the chief reason why he complained that times had never been so hard since 1837.[13] He was obliged to crave the indulgence of his creditors and take refuge behind the stay laws of his state. Taxes went unpaid. Many acres seized for their nonpayment in Tama County, Iowa, in the summer of 1858 were offered for sale, but not a one-hundredth part of them was bid in because money was so scarce.[14] Except for its unusually faulty spelling, the following letter to the company is characteristic of many others:

Sir I 'hant got your mony for your Reeper and it is out of my power to git it on a Count of the storm of hale that wee had a bout a month agoe it destroyed every bit of my Corn and the biger part of my wheat I hev a nof wheat to bread and seed mee and for Corn I heav too by to keep my stock over tel spring I have $150 dollars doo mee which i 'alowed for to paid you out of but the man is in the same fix that i em my self and Cant gitit. Mr. C. h. McCormick ser if you plees i want you to let this fifty dollars run over tel nex september i shud not hev asked you to a waited if the storm hedent destroyed every thing that ihed.[15]

These same graingrowers wished to buy reapers and mowers in order to save their crops. Very few resembled those described by an agent in Virginia who found that penniless farmers refused to take his handbills for fear lest they might be tempted to buy.[16] To sell was the easiest duty required of the agent. To avoid selling to an insolvent farmer required more care, and to collect after a sale was the most difficult task of all. McCormick was better prepared to extend credit

[13] D. R. Burt, Dunleith, Ill., to the Co., Oct. 13, 1857.
[14] J. Ramsdell, Eureka, Ia., to the Co., July 10, 1858: I can't raise $50 to pay you although I have broken 100 acres of my fine farm and have good stock. I have my last year's wheat but can't sell it. I only owe $14 besides what is due you. L. Westergaard, Decatur, Wis., to the Co., Jan. 18, 1858.
[15] G. Preston, Mazon, Ill., to the Co., Sept. 1, 1858.
[16] T. Berry, Cline's Mills, Va., to W. S. McCormick, Mch. 23, 1858.

than were most of his competitors. For several years during this period his income from sales was scarcely equal to the cost of the materials needed for his next season's supply of machines. His agents often had so little cash in their possession that he was obliged to advance them money to pay the freight on their consignments until they could collect from the purchasers.[17] By the close of 1860 the farmers of the Northwest, and particularly those of Illinois, owed the firm over a million dollars.[18] Other manufacturers were in a similar plight, and those who could not ride out the depression on borrowed capital were forced to suspend business. The elimination of some of his rivals by bankruptcy was one consoling aspect of the hard times.[19] The solid credit of Cyrus McCormick was his chief business asset between 1857 and 1861.

Faith in the farmers of the Northwest led McCormick to continue selling them machines even when they were unable to pay.[20] Being a business man, however, he buttressed his faith with certain safe-guards. He agreed with his brother that the note of a good farmer was worth more than an unsold reaper or depreciated currency, but he insisted that his agents should not sell to any one to whom they would refuse to loan

[17] L.P.C.B. No. 29, p. 719, W. S. McCormick to N. W. Jones, Griggsville, Ill., Feb. 4, 1860: It is "the *fact* that we have not collected on last year's sales money enough to pay the *manufacturer's cost* on *one* fourth of the sales of the year." *Ibid.*, No. 31, p. 316, the Co. to W. A. Polk, Oak Station, Ind., Apr. 24, 1860: "Collections for the past winter & thus far this Spring have been *very poor,* more especially *North* & *West* of Chicago."

[18] Business Statement, dated Nov. 23, 1860, in *Ibid.*, No. 36, p. 857. Between Aug. 1, 1856 and this date, $1,479,041.38 had been collected and $1,162,619.09 were still outstanding in farmers' notes. Kansas farmers suffered severely from drought in 1860 and C. H. McCormick joined with other Chicago citizens to send aid. "Chicago Daily Tribune," Dec. 18, 1860.

[19] L.P.C.B. No. 10, p. 50, the Co. to D. W. Stier, Steubenville, O., Dec. 24, 1857. *Ibid.*, No. 18, pp. 92-93, W. S. to C. H. McCormick, Feb. 1, 1859.

[20] *Ibid.*, No. 10, p. 360, W. McCormick to D. Williams, Jan. 20, 1858.

their own money.[21] To drive this lesson home, they were obliged to wait for the greater part of their commission on each sale until the purchaser had paid for his machine. They should beware of a homesteader who had not yet acquired a title to his holding, and of a renter unless he could secure the endorsement of a substantial landowner on his reaper note. These rules were sometimes relaxed for the benefit of German and Norwegian settlers. They had a higher reputation for honesty and thrift than the native born, who sometimes forgot to pay their debts before they moved to a new steading or joined in the gold rush to Colorado.[22]

The clerks in the factory office believed that farmers relied upon Cyrus McCormick's indulgence not to sue.[23] Because of his distance from the delinquent debtor and the necessity of depending for collections upon an agent who might well be the friend of the purchaser, he doubtless did not press for his due as vigorously or successfully as did the country storekeepers. He disliked to sue for debts during the spring selling sea-

[21] *Ibid.*, No. 10, p. 215, the Co. to Wm. Marshall & Son, Cordova, Ill., Jan. 11, 1858. *Ibid.*, No. 37, pp. 129, 134, 137, the Co. to W. T. Scott, Bainbridge, Ind.; to J. B. Fairbank & Sons, Lincoln, Ill.; and to G. C. Hoyt, Franklin, O., Nov. 30, 1860.

[22] M. M. McNair, Dunleith, Ill., to the Co., Jan. 27, 1858. L.P.C.B. No. 5, p. 730, the Co. to O. Ashley, Fox Lake, Wis., Mch. 23, 1857; and No. 18, p. 33, to T. J. Walker & Co., Belleville, Ill., Jan. 29, 1859: "I trust the Pikes Peak fun will take away many persons that may as *well be* spared from any community." For a later manifestation of the same feeling see, W. F. Carr, Freeport, Ill., to Co., Oct. 31, 1873: "Iowa will soon be blessed with all our scallawags—God forbid that I should ever have to live in that State." It is interesting to recall that Timothy Dwight sixty years earlier was of the same opinion about those who were leaving Conn. for the Old Northwest. See quotation from Dwight's "Travels," in F. J. Turner, "Rise of the New West" (N. Y. 1906), pp. 20-21, L.P.C.B. No. 17, p. 94, W. S. to C. H. McCormick, Feb. 1, 1859.

[23] M. Cummings, Winfield Scott Co., Ia., to W. Marshall & Sons, Cordova, Ill., Jan. 3, 1858. J. B. Fairbank, Concord, Ill., to the Co., Jan. 22, 1858. L.P.C.B. No. 10, p. 439, the Co. to Patrick & Co., Urbana, O., Jan. 25, 1858.

son; his agents were too busy during the summer, and in the autumn farmers could not be expected to have money until their grain was threshed and their pork sold. Even where a judge in these hard times was willing to entertain a suit for recovery of debt, a favorable verdict would bring McCormick only unpopularity in the debtor's neighborhood and an award of real or personal property which could not be turned readily into cash.[24]

He sued more frequently, however, during the period 1857-1861 than ever before. "I shall proceed to make you both trouble and expense if you don't pay the note at once," is the warning so often found in the letters of these years. Those farmers who would not sell their grain or stock because of low prices, notwithstanding his advice to them that the market was bound to decline still further, were sometimes brought before the court to serve as a salutary example to their fellow-debtors.[25] Several states, of which Texas was a good example, enacted legislation so favorable to those who could not meet their obligations that it was perilous to sell there except for cash.[26] Homesteads were everywhere beyond the grasp of the

[24] T. J. Walker & Co., Belleville, Ill., to the Co., Apr. 10, 1858. L. T. Ball, Keithsburg, Ill., to the Co., Nov. 3, 1858.

[25] C. H. to W. S. McCormick, Nov. 13, Dec. 16, and 21, 1857: *"Collections, Collections! Rogues, roughs. Are the agents going to just absorb everything? . . . Must you not sue a good deal. . . . If we can get on without taking produce of any kind, of course better. . . . If men won't give notes & security, then it would seem they should be sued. . . . This as I said is now the great point in the business. It is useless to sell machines & get nothing for them!"*

[26] L.P.C.B. No. 12, p. 538, the Co. to I. G. Porter & Co., Decatur, Wis., June 18, 1858: "We have yet to see what depth of infamy is yet to be exhibited by your Law Makers. The laws of a State clearly exhibit the character & moral tone of its people. . . . We believe your legislature are composed of a set of swindling naves & demagogs & the sooner you allow them to retire into private life the better it will be for the reputation of the people.—There is one redeeming feature however,—they can not pass ex post facto Laws—or Laws affecting existing contracts." 1933 was still in the future! A. Z. Rumsey, Houston, Texas, to the Co., Dec. 29, 1857.

creditor, as well as an amount of personal property varying in value from state to state.

The manufacturer was obliged to choose his customers with a good deal of care. An attractive discount was offered for cash, but even in the best of times very few reapers could be sold unless credit were extended to the purchaser. Those who were unquestionably honest and able to buy, were sometimes allowed two years in which to pay for their reaper.[27] Where competition was keen and there was likelihood that the season would close before all machines had been sold, agents were authorized to disregard the printed price list, if necessary, in order to dispose of their stock.[28] McCormick usually demanded cash on delivery equal to about one-third of the price of the implement. On the balance due after the first payment, he required that six per cent interest should be paid, and if the notes were not met on time and the usury laws of a state allowed it, they were renewed at ten per cent secured by a mortgage on the farm or personal property. Since his financial standing generally enabled him to borrow at six per cent or seven per cent in New York,[29] the money owed to him by farmers represented a fair investment, although it might have

[27] L.P.C.B. No. 6, p. 102, the Co. to John Ott, Rockville, Ind., Apr. 7, 1857; and No. 30, p. 78, the Co. to Fiske & Eliot, Iowa City, Ia., Feb. 11, 1860: "As times are, it will hardly answer to take a *report* for the solvency of any man, and we trust that . . . [you] in all cases *probe* to the bottom."

[28] *Ibid.*, No. 22, p. 43, the Co. to W. H. B. Warren, Wabash, Ind., May 27, 1859; and No. 19, pp. 469, 595, the Co. to M. M. McNair, Madison, Wis., Apr. 18, 1859, and to S. Brandt, New Guilford, Pa., Apr. 22, 1859. Variations from the list prices were particularly numerous in 1859 because of the "unusual and discouraging times."

[29] As a rule, farmers were obliged to pay more than 10% for a loan. Sixty per cent a year (one report says 200%) was not uncommon in Minnesota. McCormick was sometimes willing to agree that if a farmer bought a reaper and his crop failed, he need not pay interest on his note for the first year. *Ibid.*, No. 31, p. 829, W. S. McCormick to T. J. Massie, Lovingston, Va., May 10, 1860.

been used much more profitably for speculations in Chicago real estate.[30]

When a machine was sold by mistake to "a hard case" and McCormick had the alternative of losing the entire amount of the sale or of taking depreciated bank-notes which would not pass current in Chicago, he of course received the "wild cat" or "stump tail," as they were known, and authorized his agent either to loan them out at two per cent a month to a farmer or to use them for the purchase of grain or stock. The horses and buggies that were often supplied to the general agents to aid them in canvassing were sometimes secured in this way.[31] By 1858 the McCormicks organized and financed the commission house of C. H. McCormick & Co. of Chicago for their brother-in-law, Hugh Adams, and this company handled these commodities as well as other payments in kind that were made for machines.[32] But between 1856 and 1861, prices of agricultural products were usually declining and the factory office refused to accept wheat or cattle except as a last resort.[33]

Because country banks were unsafe, McCormick's agents often held large sums of his money in their possession until exchange rates were favorable or until they could come to

[30] *Ibid.*, No. 5, p. 824; No. 6, p. 304, W. S. to C. H. McCormick, Mch. 27, and Apr. 16, 1857.

[31] *Ibid.*, No. 5, p. 561; No. 6, p. 112, W. S. to C. H. McCormick, Mch. 14, and Apr. 7, 1857. Short-term loans in Chicago at this time were often made at 2% a month interest. *Ibid.*, No. 32, p. 385, the Co. to H. E. Griffin, Zanesville, O., May 28, 1860; No. 31, pp. 334, 409, the Co. to L. Perkins, Tiskilwa, Ill., Apr. 24, 1860.

[32] *Ibid.*, No. 6, p. 304, W. S. to C. H. McCormick, Apr. 16, 1857; No. 8, pp. 534, 654, W. S. McCormick to Hugh Adams, Aug. 21, 1857; to J. B. McCormick, Sept. 5, 1857; C. H. to W. S. McCormick, Sept. 12, 1857.

[33] C. H. to W. S. McCormick, Oct. 7, 1857; Oct. 30, and Nov. 30, 1858. L.P.C.B. No. 30, p. 787, the Co. to W. C. Leyburn, Galesburg, Ill., Mch. 9, 1860: You may take shelled corn on reaper notes at an exchange rate that will permit it to be delivered in Chicago at not over 45¢ a bus.

Chicago to settle their accounts. Most of them were engaged in other businesses and they were watched carefully by his traveling representatives to see that they resisted the temptation to use his funds for their own purposes.[34] There were few defalcations, but to such districts as the one centering at Cordova, Illinois, where the agent held nearly $200,000 in unpaid notes, it was necessary to despatch a man from the factory to guard its interests.[35]

Competition increased from year to year, and honest agents with mechanical skill and persuasive tongues were at a premium among reaper manufacturers. High-pressure methods of salesmanship, aided by brightly colored posters from the home office, probably led many farmers to buy who could not use a machine with profit.[36] It may be doubted whether a landowner with two or three in his family to help him, and with less than thirty-five acres of grain, could cut his crop as inexpensively with a reaper as with cradle-scythes. Horse-drawn harvesting implements worked to the advantage of the man with a large farm, and small holders were the more ready to increase their acreage because they were available for their use.

The troublous times in the Northwest in the late 1850's led Cyrus McCormick to give more attention than ever before to the East and South as a selling field.[37] For a dozen years his

[34] C. H. to W. S. McCormick, May 21, and Sept. 1, 1857. In view of the weakened condition of many banks, he believed it would probably be safer to leave in the hands of farmers all monies due, rather than to let the agents collect.

[35] L.P.C.B. No. 11, p. 3, W. S. McCormick to T. J. Paterson, Rochester, N. Y., Mch. 4, 1858, and in No. 15, p. 69, to C. H. McCormick, Nov. 29, 1858.

[36] The first advertising pamphlet of C. H. McCormick was issued in the harvest of 1859. He had earlier prepared several of them for distribution at fairs abroad.

[37] *Ibid.*, No. 22, p. 618, the Co. to W. S. McCormick, June 13, 1859. Compared with the other states of the Middle West, except Michigan, Ohio was always a poor sales territory for McCormick machines. This was

cousin, J. B. McCormick, had canvassed Missouri, Kentucky, and Tennessee in the interest of the reaper, but now for the sake of efficiency he was obliged, over his protest, to be satisfied with a smaller territory. He established a commission business in St. Louis, and was allowed to sell his kinsman's machines in a small district around that city. He asked too large a fee for forwarding the implements to purchasers further down the Mississippi, and Cyrus McCormick soon put that business in the charge of agents at Cairo, Louisville, Nashville, and New Orleans.[38] Reports from the South indicated that planters were placing greater emphasis upon the culture of wheat and oats, but farms in the areas best fitted for the growth of these cereals were too often dotted with stumps. Nor could reapers operate in a grain-field where a planter had neglected to pull up the tough stalks of his last season's cotton plants.[39]

Agents whose homes were in the Old Northwest felt that they were in a foreign land as soon as they crossed the southern border of Kentucky or Mason and Dixon's line. A new selling technique was necessary there. Suspicion of all "Yankee wares" was met everywhere. "The very name of Chicago in some parts of the South is like presenting cold water in a case of Hydrophobia. It is considered as a den of negroe [sic]

largely due to the many large reaper factories there by 1858. *Ibid.,* No. 29, pp. 10, 41, 46, the Co. to W. W. Campbell, Hopkinsville, Ky., Jan. 6, 1860; R. H. Powell, Lewisburg, Tenn., and to Cable & Co., Shelbyville, Tenn., Jan. 7, 1860.

[38] *Ibid.,* No. 15, p. 759; No. 17, pp. 86 and 689, W. S. to C. H. McCormick, Dec. 21, 1858, Jan. 4 and 21, 1859. *Ibid.,* No. 20, p. 58, the Co. to Northup & Howland, St. Louis, Mch. 5, 1859; No. 20, pp. 60, 142, W. S. to J. B. McCormick, Mch. 5 and 8, 1859. By 1863, J. B. McCormick's selling territory was confined to St. Louis and St. Charles Cy., Mo. See *Ibid.,* No. 56, p. 424, the Co. to F. R. Baker, St. Louis, Jan. 24, 1863.

[39] J. Stuart, Summerville, Ga., to the Co., Sept. 9, 1856; Feb. 16, and May 15, 1857. F. R. Marshall, Natchez, Miss., to C. H. McCormick, May 5 and July 27, 1857. J. B. McCormick, St. Louis, to W. S. McCormick, Apr. 8, 1858.

thieves." [40] Enticing posters and glib sales talk repelled the planter because they reminded him of his northern creditor, or at least of hard business efficiency out of tune with his way of life. Leisurely conversation over a glass of apple-jack sometimes effected a sale, if the agent did not insult his prospect by presenting him with a "judgment note" to sign, or ask him to vary his usual practice of settling his accounts once a year.[41] For these reasons Miller, Wingate & Co., a firm manufacturing reapers and mowers at Louisville, which was deemed to be a southern city, had a large advantage in the planter trade. The agents of McCormick, however, stressed the southern birth of the inventor of the "Virginia Reaper" to their patrons, and the factory office sent copies of the "Chicago Times" and Dr. Rice's "Presbyterian Expositor" to remind the planters that their employer was "right" on the slavery question.[42]

Prejudice was not so sharp in Texas, and McCormick enjoyed a brisk trade there by the opening of the Civil War. Agents ordering machines from the forwarding house of Graham & Boyle of New Orleans supplied customers in the Red River Valley and the country about Houston, Dallas, and

[40] J. B. to W. S. McCormick from Versailles, Ky., May 24, 1858. *Cornelius Aultman vs Henry C. Holley and Edwin H. Fittz, in Equity, United States Circuit Court, in and for the Southern District of New York* (N. Y. 1870), p. 417. Hereafter cited as *Aultman vs Holley and Fittz.*

[41] A "judgment note" was appended to the reaper order blank and expressed the willingness of the purchaser to be sued by the company in case he did not pay his note when due. J. T. Griffin from Nashville and Knoxville, Tenn., to W. S. McCormick, Dec. 13, and 17, 1858. Townes, Orgill & Co., Memphis, to the Co., May 26, 1858. J. B. McCormick, Versailles, Ky., to W. S. McCormick, Apr. 5, 1858.

[42] L.P.C.B. No. 30, pp. 108, 677, 786, the Co. to T. Berry, Staunton, Va., Feb. 13, 1860; and to W. A. Braxton and J. Henry, both of Va., Mch. 3, 1860: "Our *latitude* may be a drawback & I send you some numbers of Dr. Rice's paper which you can refer to. We don't hesitate to make war *here* upon Abolitionism." *Ibid.,* No. 37, p. 672, the Co. to E. A. McNair, Clarksville, Tenn., Dec. 21, 1860.

Fort Worth.[43] State laws for the protection of debtors compelled McCormick to demand upon delivery a large down payment. Inadequate transportation facilities away from the navigable streams was another principal drawback to trade in Texas. Machines were sometimes freighted as much as two hundred miles by ox-team.[44] The amount of business done by McCormick in the South did not come up to his expectations. The border states suffered from the depression and wheat there was severely damaged by late frosts in 1860.[45]

Ever since McCormick moved to Chicago in 1847, he had endeavored with slight success to build up a market in the middle states of the eastern seaboard. High freight charges, late deliveries, inability in some seasons to supply the demand of the Middle West, and the development of a machine that was better adapted to the level prairies than to hillside farms, are some of the reasons why he had not realized his hopes.[46] Between 1856 and 1861, he advertised to sell for Chicago prices at Philadelphia and Baltimore. Since the rough finish and the weight of his reapers displeased both agents and farmers, he improved their appearance with blue or brown paint,

[43] Reapers were carried by steamboat from Cairo to New Orleans for $5.00. This included the Cairo transfer charge of $1.00. *Ibid.,* No. 20, pp. 178, 251, 385, the Co. to N. W. Graham & Co., Cairo, Mch. 9, 1859, and to I. McKay, Ferguson, Texas, Mch. 11, and 17, 1859; No. 26, p. 506, to B. W. Musgrove, Bright Star, Texas, Dec. 21, 1859: "I now regard Texas as one of the most inviting fields which I can occupy and am naturally anxious for a more extended introduction."

[44] A. K. Ellet, Clarksville, Texas, to the Co., July 24, 1856. A. Z. Rumsey, Westfield, Texas to the Co., Oct. 22, 1857.

[45] L.P.C.B. No. 26, p. 441 and *passim,* letters of the spring of 1860; No. 30, pp. 736, 743, W. S. to J. B. McCormick, Mch. 7, 1860; No. 30, p. 147, the Co. to Robins & Brogham, White Oak, Tenn., Feb. 14, 1860.

[46] *Ibid.,* No. 20, pp. 52, 155, the Co. to Gen'l. Fght. Agts. of the Fort Wayne RR., Mch. 4, 1859, and of the Pa. Central RR., Mch. 8, 1859. By 1860, thanks to the increase of rwy. competition, McCormick could ship a reaper to Balto. for about $6.00 freight. The cost had been nearly $17.00 in 1854. *Ibid.,* No. 41, p. 692, the Co. to G. Walker, Shoreham, Vt., May 16, 1861.

and built a light two-horse machine for small landowners who were not prepared to use his standard four-horse type.[47] Most important of all, his two brothers, aided by his suggestions, developed an excellent mower by 1860.[48] A succession of poor crop years in the Middle States, and the preference of grain-growers for implements manufactured near their own homes, were barriers to eastern sales which McCormick could not surmount. At all times the factory office viewed the Atlantic seaboard principally as an outlet for surplus machines.[49]

By good fortune, a considerable trade with California and Oregon was opened up during these years, and reapers and mowers unsold in the East were collected at New York or Boston for transfer in clipper-ships around Cape Horn to San Francisco. The "Golden Fleece" and the "Westward Ho" sometimes returned with letters from far-western consignees protesting that they had been sent damaged second-hand machines "dating as far back as 1850." This was not news to McCormick, for he had designed the Pacific Coast trade to serve as a market for outmoded reapers. For three years following 1860, California was said to be overstocked with agricultural machinery and shipments thither virtually ceased. Beginning in 1865, Oregon supplanted California for a few years as the best sales territory in the Far West.[50]

[47] *Ibid.*, No. 19, pp. 5, 11, W. S. McCormick to J. T. Griffin, and to G. A. Walker, Portsmouth, O., Apr. 5, 1859. The two-horse machine cut a 5½-foot swath and was priced @ $140, and the four-house @ $155.

[48] L.P.C.B. No. 16, p. 83, W. S. to C. H. McCormick, Oct. 8, 1858; and in No. 19, pp. 263, 550, to J. B. McCormick, Apr 13 and 21, 1859. W. S. to C. H. McCormick, June 27, and July 6, 1859.

[49] Treadwell & Co. of Boston purchased reapers @ $153 each for sale in California. This firm bought about 125 McCormick machines a year between 1859 and 1861. L.P.C.B. No. 24, pp. 46, 47; No. 33, p. 64; the Co. to Treadwell & Co., Oct. 12, 1859 and July 24, 1860.

[50] R. T. Elkinton, Phila., Pa., to C. H. McCormick, Nov. 26, and Dec. 1, 1856; L.P.C.B. No. 64, p. 227, the Co. to O. Ames & Son, Boston, Sept. 10, 1863; No. 65, p. 545, to Wakeman, Dimon & Co., N. Y., Nov. 10, 1863; No. 85, pp. 52-54, to Knapp, Burrall & Co., Portland, Ore., Oct. 18, 1865.

Skies brightened somewhat for the grain-grower during 1860. For the first time in several years there was a brisk foreign demand for wheat, and about one-third of the total crop was sent abroad.[51] McCormick's supply of reapers and mowers was again too small, but western currency was still unsound, and the prairie farmer did not give expression to his reviving optimism by paying his reaper notes. "Times *very* hard in the western cities & country," commented William S. McCormick in May of that year, "everything flat. We have to *sell* on long time to a great extent & it will take good crops to bring us out. Rents here [Chicago] are *down* but our cities are *built* & our railroads are *made* & though the majority of those who built *them* may have to give up to others, the whole country must ultimately derive great benefit therefrom & this must be a great country." [52] This is a good example of the spirit to which Chicagoans credit the surprising growth of their city.

Doubt replaced hope as the year grew older. Ten thousand printed dunning letters, each accompanied by a stamped return-envelop as a new departure in business practice, failed to induce many farmers to pay their debts.[53] The election of Lincoln, the secession of South Carolina, and a short-lived money panic in the North, made "the times . . . look rather gloomy" to the McCormicks. The factory, however, was going full blast in an effort to build five thousand machines for

[51] The wheat crop of the United States in 1860 was 173,104,924 bus. Estimating a barrel of flour as equivalent to six bushels of grain, the export of wheat between June 30, 1860, and June 30, 1861, was equal to about 1/3 of the crop. In how far this export total included wheat held over from previous harvests is not clear. 1/5, 1/4, 1/5, 1/10th of the crops of 1855 to 1858, respectively, had been exported during the fiscal year following each of these harvests.

[52] *Ibid.*, No. 31, p. 786, W. S. McCormick to J. Henry. May 9, 1860.

[53] *Ibid.*, No. 45, p. 14, the Co. to W. H. Warren, Marshallville, O., Aug. 17, 1861. By the close of the harvest of 1861, over 20,000 farmers owed money to McCormick.

the harvest of 1861.[54] William S. McCormick hesitated to believe that the Union would be broken or that war would follow a failure to reach a compromise.[55]

No matter how earnestly the company sought to keep politics and business distinct, Cyrus McCormick's active rôle in the campaign of 1860 and the crisis which followed, obliged the men in his factory office for a time to ride two horses going full speed in opposite directions. Before the bombardment of Fort Sumter, it was good business, as well as the truth, to remind salesmen in Virginia that "our heart still yields allegiance to the 'Old Dominion' and we claim a place as the representatives of your interests." [56] Agents in the North were assured that the Confederate flag did not fly over the Chicago factory, that its owner opposed secession, and would stand by the "Stars and Stripes," first, last, and all the time.[57]

[54] Ibid., No. 36, p. 749, the Co. to G. H. Cook & Co., New Haven, Conn., Nov. 13, 1860; No. 38, p. 557, W. S. McCormick to T. H. Silvez, Newark, N. J., Jan. 30, 1861. W. S. McCormick wished to send Silvez as an agent to Va., but first of all demanded assurance that his political views would be acceptable to his clientele.

[55] Ibid., No. 40, pp. 83, 117, 313, the Co. to S. M. Swenson, Austin, Texas, Mch. 21, 1861; to Magraw & Koons, Balto., Mch. 22, and to W. Ward, Varis Valley, Ga., Mch. 29, 1861; No. 41, p. 25, the Co. to R. B. Norwall, Huntsville, Ga., Apr. 17, 1861, and p. 146, to A. Chapman, New York City, Apr. 23, 1861. In mid-March, sixteen reapers were shipped to Texas, and a car-load to Balto. for sale in Virginia. At this time the Co. was still ready to grant credit to southern buyers, but cash was required after the fall of Fort Sumter.

[56] Ibid., No. 37 (Nov. 1860-Jan. 1861) passim; No. 38, pp. 22, 164, the Co. to Tipton & Alvord, Lexington, Ky., Jan. 3, 1861, and to P. W. Margaren, New Providence, Tenn., Jan. 9, 1861; No. 40, p. 497, the Co. to J. McCormick, Augusta, Ga., Apr. 3, 1861.

[57] Ibid., No. 39, p. 205, the Co. to E. Healy, Earlville, Ia., Feb. 25, 1861: "All our interests are with the Union,—not a part—but the whole." Ibid., No. 41, p. 771, the Co. to J. Rodermel, Freeport, Ill., May 18, 1861: "We wish you to bear in mind that the 'Times' office & the Reaper office are separate and distinct." Ibid., No. 42, p. 615, the Co. to J. Hoffman, Crown Point, Ind., June 10, 1861. Rival agents were telling farmers that the McCormicks were disloyal.

Because of plans carefully laid and the fine outlook of crops everywhere in 1861, the firm was loath to abandon its southern market.[58] By April, unpaid reaper-notes and unsold machines stored in the South represented a property value of at least $75,000, and steps were taken to realize upon these before it was too late.[59] In fact, for six weeks after Sumter the McCormicks were ready to sell to planters for cash even as far south as Georgia. They sought in vain to evade the Virginia blockade by freighting reapers in wagons through Harpers Ferry into the Valley. Machines were concentrated at Cairo and Cincinnati to ship to Arkansas and Tennessee if opportunity should offer.[60] Fully aware of the immediate seriousness of the situation, as southern agents resigned one by one, they refused for long to believe that a northern army would invade the South, or that business could not go on as usual by 1862, either with a restored Union or with the new Confederacy.[61] When it was clear that no shipments could be made south of the line in 1861, special agents were sent into Virginia and Tennessee, not to collect or to sell, since notes of Confederate banks were virtually worthless in the North, but to secure the promissory notes of old purchasers, pledging pay-

[58] *Ibid.*, No. 40, p. 31, the Co. to N. P. Thomas, Bowling Green, Tenn., Mch. 19, 1861: "Providence seems to be lavishing blessings on all sections of the country alike to teach us our common brotherhood, and we hope we may not be slow to learn this great truth."

[59] This comprised about $35,000 in Va., $35,000 in Texas, and $5,000 elsewhere in the South. There were about 200 machines unaccounted for. *Ibid.*, No. 40, pp. 784, 811, the Co. to J. J. McBride, New Orleans, Apr. 15, 1861, and to J. McKay, Farmington, Texas, Apr. 15, 1861; No. 41, p. 465, to S. S. Sykes, Jackson, Tenn., May 9, 1861; No. 42, p. 10, W. S. McCormick to W. T. Rush, Staunton, Va., May 22, 1861.

[60] *Ibid.*, No. 41, pp. 251, 793, the Co. to W. Cartmell, Nashville, Tenn., Apr. 25, 1861, and to Magraw & Koons, Balto., May 20, 1861; No. 42, pp. 262, 483, to M. W. Forney, Balto., May 29, and June 5, 1861.

[61] *Ibid.*, No. 41, p. 370, the Co. to Pennywit, Scott & Co., Van Buren, Ark., May 3, 1861; No. 46, p. 88, to P. Mohan, Louisville, Ky., Oct. 3, 1861.

ment when the crisis was past.[62] Long after the organization of the Confederacy was completed, mail was received by the company from many parts of the South, forwarded by special arrangement from commission house to commission house, and finally across the Ohio River at Louisville.[63]

The year 1861 was near its close before the McCormicks were convinced that watchful waiting could be their only policy. Southern patriots paid their northern debts into the Confederate treasury and unsold reapers were confiscated as contraband of war.[64] Throughout the conflict McCormicks' agents, in company with canvassers for other northern factories, were camp-followers of every Union Army which tapped the grain lands of the Confederacy.[65] The company quickly made up for the loss of its southern market by keeping step with the railroads and steamboat lines as they pushed farther and farther into the North and West. MacGregor,

[62] *Ibid.*, No. 41, pp. 440, 769, the Co. to E. A. McNair, Haydensville, Ky., May 8, and to W. Cartmell, Lebanon, Tenn., May 18, 1861; No. 42, p. 721, Co. to M. W. Forney, Balto., June 13, 1861: We wish to send an envoy to Va. to collect all reaper notes held by our agents. We don't fear that the planters will not eventually pay us, but we worry lest our agents defraud us in the South.

[63] The U. S. postal service in the South was officially suspended on May 31, 1861. After that time, some of the business houses which relayed letters were Graham & Boyle, New Orleans, Fisher, Wheeless & Co., Nashville, and Moore, Wheeler & Robinson of Louisville. *Ibid.*, No. 55, p. 632, the Co. to P. Mohan, Louisville, Ky., Dec. 22, 1862; Mary Ann McCormick to Nettie F. McCormick, Feb. 17, 1863; ‡P. Calhoun, Houma, Terre Bonne Pas, La., to C. H. McCormick, Feb. 6, 1865.

[64] L.P.C.B. No. 44, p. 815, the Co. to M. W. Forney, Balto., Aug. 13, 1861; No. 53, p. 688, to L. Farrell, Port Tobacco, Md., Nov. 13, 1862.

[65] *Ibid.*, No. 47, pp. 260, 768, the Co. to Spear Bros., Balto., Md., Mch. 27, 1862, and to Magraw & Koons, Balto., Apr. 18, 1862; No. 57, p. 440, to J. N. Keller, Elm Grove, Va., Mch. 3, 1863; No. 65, p. 431, to P. Mohan, Louisville, Ky., Nov. 4, 1863; No. 66, p. 383, to W. Cartmell, Gallatin, Tenn., Jan. 25, 1864. Civil War in Mo. hindered sales there during much of the war, but it was deemed safe to sell north of the Missouri River in that State by 1863. Except for a brief period in 1861, Ky. was a good market for machines during the entire conflict since money was unusually plentiful there.

Iowa, St. Joseph, Missouri, and Fort Leavenworth, Kansas, were important distributing points for this trade.[66]

Meanwhile, in the spring of 1861, the McCormicks looked forward without confidence to the northern harvest. Over five thousand machines were almost finished and the excellent crop outlook signified a brisk demand. But the farmers, carried away by the first war excitement, seemed to forget that their grain was ripening for the reaper. Orders came in with unprecedented slowness.[67] By May, which was ordinarily the height of the selling season, agents were resigning without warning in order to enlist, western bank-notes reached a new "low," and farm produce showed no sign of advancing in price.[68] So desperate did the situation become, that the firm ordered its representatives to dispose of machines on almost any terms and devote their principal attention to collecting or securing old debts. Hardly had these instructions gone out, than with bewildering suddenness the spell cast by Sumter was broken and orders poured in upon the company as never before. By late June angry farmers were told that McCormick's supply of reapers and mowers was exhausted, and agents were ordered to sell only for cash. After the harvest was over

[66] Sales in Kansas and Minnesota particularly increased, and a beginning was made in Nebraska Terr. In 1863, 170 machines were sold in Kansas and Nebraska, but they were too few to meet the demand. In 1864 a special circular was printed in three languages for the Minnesota trade. *Ibid.*, No. 37, p. 302, the Co. to E. S. Hawley, Nebraska City, Neb., Dec. 6, 1860; No. 47, p. 43, to I. C. Hoagland, St. Joseph, Mo., Mch. 15, 1862; No. 60, p. 202, to Grant & Prest, Leavenworth, Kan., May 22, 1863. J. O. Henning, Fort Leavenworth, Kan., to the Co., Sept. 22, and Dec. 3, 1864. Kansas was an excellent market for mowers since farmers there produced much hay for sale to the government.

[67] So little money was collected from farmers in the early summer of 1861, that the McCormicks for three weeks were unable to pay their factory hands. See letters in *Ibid.*, No. 41, pp. 145, 244; No. 42, pp. 322, 421; No. 43, pp. 610, 640, 805.

[68] ‡W. S. to C. H. McCormick, May 2, 1861. See Co. letters in L.P.C.B. No. 41, pp. 171, 774; No. 42, pp. 40, 470, 605; No. 43, p. 792; No. 44, p. 704, covering the months May-Aug., 1861. Because of low prices, some wheat-fields in Iowa were left to the hogs.

the firm estimated that two thousand more machines could have been disposed of for ready money if they had been available.[69] The currency situation in the Northwest improved by late summer and record quantities of grain began to move toward the seaboard as prices tended upward.[70]

In the late autumn, fear that a blockade by and war with England would result from the Trent Affair, momentarily depressed the price of wheat. In general, however, farmers during the Civil War had much reason to be happy. The McCormicks oversold about five hundred machines in the harvest of 1862. Shortage of flat cars and the inability of the factory to keep pace with the call for reapers, obliged them to insist that a farmer upon signing an order blank should waive his right to sue for breach of contract in case the machine could not be delivered in time for harvest.[71] Extremely low water in the Mississippi River and raids by Confederates in the border states, combined to lose sales for the McCormicks in the summer of 1863.[72] Drought and poor crops in parts of the

[69] The rush of orders began in late May. W. S. wrote to C. H. McCormick on June 26: "The demand for machines *beats all.*"

[70] L.P.C.B. No. 42, p. 521, W. S. to J. B. McCormick, June 6, 1861: "Our prospects are good for *large* sales but whether we will ever collect or not I can't tell. Stump tail is the order of the day & I suppose no tail at all will come next." But on Oct. 8, 1861, he could write (No. 46, p. 204): "Grain is coming into Chicago beyond all account, and wheat is bringing a still better price. Most of my agents are beginning to send money quite freely." The change from doubt to optimism in regard to the currency is first noticeable in the letters of late Aug., but the low price of pork and grain was believed to be hindering collections as late as the new year.

[71] On the expected effect of the Trent Affair on the reaper business, see letters of W. S. McCormick during the last week of Dec., 1861, in *ibid.,* No. 54, pp. 124, 293. L.P.C.B. No. 48, p. 205, the Co. to T. Thomson, National, Ia., May 1, 1862; No. 50, pp. 188, 219, to J. L. Briggs, Geneseo, Ill., and to L. Perkins, Tiskilwa, Ill., June 17, 1862.

[72] *Ibid.,* No. 61, p. 346, the Co. to Grant & Prest, Leavenworth, Kan., June 18, 1863. The Co. had reduced its output by 20% in this harvest through fear of depreciated currency and Confederate raids into the border states. No. 64, p. 567, the Co. to C. Etheridge, Hastings, Minn., Sept. 26, 1863. The weather during the winter of 1862-1863 was very mild.

Middle West left them with a surplus of two thousand machines at the close of the next harvest.[73] Due, also, to a widening market and the depreciation of the currency, wheat gradually rose in price to $2.25 a bushel in Chicago by July, 1864, although it sharply dropped to $1.18 by the following May.[74] The unwillingness of farmers to buy machines in 1865 was caused by their uncertainty concerning the effect of the war's close upon prices, and the unusually wet summer which made many grain-fields so muddy that reapers could not be employed.[75]

At no previous time in its history did the firm select its salesmen and the purchasers of its reapers with more care. Canvassers were required to post a $3,000 bond, and William S. McCormick often complained of the "moral slackness" and degeneracy of the times. Hundreds of orders were rejected every season because, in the judgment of the general agent or the factory office, they were given by farmers who could not be relied upon to pay their debts. A landowner of known probity and too old to go to war was the ideal client. Although, by early 1865, "farmers [were] . . . generally out of debt & there . . . [was] less danger of losing by them than at most any former period," [76] the great majority of machines were still sold on credit. Collections were deemed to be excellent during the war, but "excellent" was a highly relative term, and meant that about sixty-five per cent of the reaper notes were paid when they were due.[77] In the spring of 1863 there was still a million dollars' worth of paper outstanding,

[73] W. S. to C. H. McCormick, Apr. 13, 1865.

[74] According to Boyle's study, *op. cit.*, the $2.25 price was due in part to a wheat corner. Catalog of C. H. McCormick & Bros., 1864, p. 2.

[75] L.P.C.B. No. 81, p. 288, the Co. to J. B. McCormick, St. Louis, June 20, 1865: "We never saw such apathy among buyers and bewilderment as to plans among agents."

[76] ‡C. A. Spring, Jr., to C. H. McCormick, Jan. 2, 1865.

[77] W. S. to C. H. McCormick, July 19, 1863; L.P.C.B. No. 67, pp. 491-492, the Co. to Bass & Elmendorf, McGregor, Ia., Mch. 11, 1864.

and about $775,000 at the close of the next year. As for the currency situation, the company office could write as late as April, 1864: "The banks of this city *reject* all banknotes of Pennsylvania, New Jersey, Maryland, Michigan. Also notes of Ohio & Indiana except the issue of State Banks of those States. It will be well to confine collections as much as possible to Treasury Notes & National Bank Bills as all other currency is being gradually superseded here by them." [78] Up to the autumn of 1863, William S. McCormick was often of the opinion that the "uncertainties of the times" made advisable a suspension of manufacturing until the close of the war.[79]

Lumber more than doubled and pig-iron and coal almost tripled in price between 1861 and the summer of 1864.[80] Good mechanics and iron-finishers were hard to find, wages mounted, and the company officials found it difficult to compete with the free whiskey dispensed by the recruiting stations and the lure of Canada when a draft was to be drawn.[81] Firms were obliged to bid against the government for the services of mechanics. Apparently the country was being industrialized

[78] *Ibid.,* No. 68, p. 814, the Co. to L. G. Dudley, Apr. 20, 1864.

[79] W. S. to C. H. McCormick, Oct. 19, and Nov. 9, 1862. The Democratic victories in the by-elections of this autumn appear to have been chiefly responsible for his change from gloom to hope.

[80] The Co. purchased 3 inc. ash plank for $12.50 per M. in Sept., 1860, $28 in Dec., 1863, $30 in Feb., 1864, and $26 in Aug. 1865. Pig-iron was $20 a ton in Aug., 1861, $29 in May, 1862, $45 in Apr., 1863, $48 in Feb., 1864, and $55 in Oct., 1865. Coal was purchased for $3.45 a ton in Aug., 1861, $5.73 in Sept., 1862, $6.00 in June, 1863, $7.58 in Oct., 1863, $9 in July, 1864, and at about the same price one year later. *Ibid.,* No. 45-No. 75, *passim.*

[81] *Ibid.,* No. 49, p. 866, the Co. to W. S. McCormick, Aug. 21, 1862; No. 61, pp. 691, 715, to E. Brinckman, Cassville, Wis., June 26, 1863, and to W. C. Stacey, Sigel, Ia., June 27, 1863; No. 73, pp. 477-479, to E. A. McNair, Davenport, Ia., July 19, 1864. W. S. to C. H. McCormick, Sept. 28, 1862, Apr. 8, and June 7, 1863; L. J. to C. H. McCormick, Apr. 7, Nov. 22 and Dec. 6, 1863. In Aug., 1862, the Co. paid unskilled factory hands $1.25 a day, and stevedores 40¢ an hour. Fifteen months later, ordinary laborers received $1.50 a day, carpenters $2.00, and moulders doing piecework were making between $2.75 and $5 a day.

too rapidly for skilled labor to keep up with the demand. For the first time in the history of the McCormick Company, unions and strikes find mention in its correspondence. "Green and obstreperous" hands were blamed for mistakes in machine construction and for the costly delay in finishing the supply of reapers and mowers in 1863. "We may incidentally mention," wrote an office scribe in April, 1864, "our moulders are going on their fourth Strike for an advance of wages since last fall. They now want 25% more!!! Manufacturers will have to shut up Shop if things go much farther in this line." [82] Even the clerks were restless and several scorned to work for $1,000 or $1,500 a year while speculative ventures invited a much larger return. If an experienced agent were drafted, the company paid one-half or more of the hire of a substitute. Income taxes and taxes on raw materials were heavy, and by 1863 the national government also required five per cent of the gross sales money, with no deduction allowed when farmers failed to complete payments for their reapers.[83]

High transportation charges on agricultural implements

[82] L.P.C.B. No. 68, p. 568, the Co. to G. Monser, Wenona, Ill., Apr. 11, 1864. Wages probably did not advance as rapidly as prices, and this was due in part to the introduction of cheap foreign labor by such concerns as the United States Land and Immigration Co. of No. 7 Broadway, New York City. Chicago manufacturers using iron, including W. S. McCormick, met on Mch. 14, 1863, and resolved that they would not pay moulders over $2.00 a day. "Chicago Daily Tribune," Mch. 15 and May 31, 1863. Mary Ann McCormick wrote to Nettie F., on Oct. 21-22, 1863: "The prices of *every-thing* is so high, & increasing all the time, that I don't see how it can hold out so. The poor must do without many of the necessaries of life."

[83] D. M. Osborne, from Phila., to C. H. McCormick, Apr. 12, 1862; W. S. to C. H. McCormick, Nov. 22, 1863. L.P.C.B. No. 47, pp. 232, 259, 300, 376, 637, the Co. letters of Mch. and Apr. 1862; No. 71, p. 756, the Co. to W. R. Selleck, Milwaukee, Jan. 2, 1864; No. 69, pp. 183, 351, 498, 523, the Co. to T. R. Robinson, Wauseon, O., Apr. 28, 1864, and to C. Wellman, Defiance, O., May 4, 1864; No. 75, p. 143, the Co. to N. M. Lester, Elmwood, Ill., Oct. 4, 1864. By 1865 the federal tax was 6% upon manufacturing and 6% upon each sale. *Ibid.,* No. 86, p. 435, the Co. to N. Hornaday, West Elkton, O., Dec. 21, 1865.

were a grievance of farmers and manufacturers alike from the time that railroads and reapers first came to the Middle West. With the closing of the Mississippi River by the Confederate Army, railroad freight rates greatly increased on grain and reapers moving east. Steamboat companies on the Great Lakes boosted their charges and irritated the McCormicks by their indifference when asked to condescend enough to carry reapers and mowers from Chicago to Cleveland and Buffalo.[84] Canal-boats as well as freight cars were commandeered for war use, and the government's need for them reached a maximum each year at the very time when harvesting machinery was ready for distribution to the agents.[85] Railway officials turned deaf ears to the plea that farm implements were essential to the winning of the war and merited preferential treatment because they produced return freights in the form of grain and hay.[86] Although the McCormicks, as long as the contest lasted, were never certain that they could get their entire output to their consignees in time for harvest, they somewhat remedied their embarrassment in this regard after 1862 by working a full force of men at their factory all the year around so that shipments could be made

[84] *Ibid.*, No. 57, p. 502, the Co. to W. H. Stewart, Mch. 4, 1863; No. 42, p. 753, the Co. to U. C. Van Tyne, Cleveland, O., June 14, 1861.

[85] *Ibid.*, No. 60, p. 471, the Co. to G. Monser, Wenona, Ill., May 29, 1863: "We *cannot* get cars . . . oh for two weeks more in which to do our shipping—Wish we could like Joshua make the sun stand still!" *Ibid.*, No. 67, p. 432; No. 70, pp. 430, 733; No. 72, p. 436, the Co. to P. Mohan, Louisville, Mch. 9, 1864, to E. A. McNair, Davenport, Ia., to G. Plahn & Co., Beardstown, Ill., July 2, 1864, and to J. B. Fairbank & Sons, Concord, Ill., June 3, 1864, respectively. In 1864, the freight rates on eastern shipments were in many cases 100% higher than in 1863. The Co., in order to get cars, often had to guarantee that they would be unloaded within twelve hours after reaching their destination.

[86] *Ibid.*, No. 57, pp. 500, 749, the Co. to J. I. Houston, Mch. 4, 1863, and to H. E. Sargent, Mch. 14, 1863; No. 67, pp. 508, 631, the Co. to Rwy. Freight Agents, Mch. 12, and 16, 1864.

in late winter or early spring before the military campaigns opened.[87]

Midwestern farmers in early 1863 justified their insistent demand that the Confederate Army should be speedily driven from the Mississippi line upon the ground of "the impossibility of bringing to the markets of the world a very large proportion of their surplus agricultural production. No avenue of transit now open to them has one-half the capacity to afford the necessary transportation." [88] They had come to rely more and more upon freight cars to carry their crops to market, but they wished the alternative water route to be available for their use as a salutary check upon high railway tariffs. It was at this time that General John A. McClernand, eager to supplant Grant in command of the Army of the Mississippi, warned Lincoln of the growing secession sentiment among the farmers of the prairie belt because one of their principal outlets of trade was still in the hands of the enemy.[89] Politics and personal ambition doubtless influenced McClernand's attitude, but it was grounded upon a real economic grievance, particularly among the farmers of northern Missouri and southern Illinois. As early as 1862, a farmers' association at Geneseo, Illinois, foreshadowing the day of the Grangers, protested

[87] *Ibid.*, No. 64, p. 814, the Co. to Graff, Bennett & Co., Pittsburgh, Oct. 9, 1863.

[88] "Transactions of the Illinois State Agricultural Society" (Springfield, Ill.), V (1861-1864), p. 82; H. K. Beale, ed., "The Diary of Edward Bates, 1859-1866," in "Annual Report of the American Historical Association, 1930" (Wash., 1933), Vol. IV, pp. 20, 70, 169, 192.

[89] J. A. McClernand to Secy. of War, E. Stanton, Nov. 10, 1862, in "The War of the Rebellion. A Compilation of the Official Records of the Union and Confederate Armies" (Wash. 1882), Ser. I, Vol. XVII, pt. 2, pp. 332-334. The "Chicago Times" in late Dec. was sounding the same note. L.P.C.B. No. 47, p. 265, the Co. to D. B. Young, Richland City, Wis., Mch. 27, 1862: "Should we be favored with a few more Federal victories, and the Mississippi River be opened to the Gulf, farmers will feel more like buying."

against the exorbitant transportation charges.[90] Grain-growers were often unable to take advantage of a favorable market because of their inability to find cars to carry their wheat to the cities. Manufacturers of harvesting machinery shifted most of the transportation costs to their patrons, but they did their best to make the burden as light as possible.

In view of the rising prices of grain and factory raw materials, it is surprising, and an indication of the bitterness of the competition, that McCormick reapers were sold at their pre-war figure up to 1864, and then at an increase of less than fifteen per cent. This course would have been suicidal if the profit on each sale before the war had not been so large that the cost of production could greatly increase and still leave a small margin of profit.[91]

Following the harvest of 1862, reaper- and mower-makers in the East agreed to advance prices ten per cent and transfer manufacturers' taxes to the farmers.[92] Although the McCormicks announced that they would abide by this resolution, there was much undercutting, and by summer the new schedule was abandoned.[93] The Manny, "Buckeye," and Osborne firms which made hand-rake reapers, could not be held in line, and companies that were endeavoring to introduce the self-rake type, found that their innovation carried little appeal if it were accompanied by a large advance in price. In December, 1863, the Esterlys of Wisconsin and the McCormicks took the initiative. Meeting at Chicago with other harvesting-machinery manufacturers, a verbal pact was made to yield to "impera-

[90] L.P.C.B. No. 47, p. 637, the Co. to L. Briggs, Geneseo, Ill., Apr. 16, 1862.

[91] W. S. to C. H. McCormick, Sept. 28 and Oct. 5, 1862. Here W. S. McCormick believed no profit could be made on reapers sold at the old price, if the premium on gold went above 20%. In view of the next two harvests, this would appear to have been an error.

[92] "Prairie Farmer," Nov. 1, 1862, p. 280.

[93] L.P.C.B. No. 55, pp. 784-785, the Co. to W. H. B. Warren, Wabash, Ind., Jan. 5, 1863; W. S. to C. H. McCormick, Apr. 8, 1863.

tive necessity" and sell for a ten per cent increase of price in 1864.[94] Despite continued charges and counter-charges of violations by the agents, the Chicago partners stood by their agreement and declared at the close of the harvest that they would sell for a further advance of fifty per cent in 1865. "We think it is high time that we all looked to our interests in this question," wrote William S. McCormick in September, 1864, ". . . when a pound of iron costs as much as a pound of sugar used to cost." [95] He felt, however, that an inter-company compact to reduce output and to sell for cash or near-cash terms exclusively, was as important as an agreement to raise prices. These three propositions dovetailed, and each depended for its success upon the faithful carrying out of the other two. If full payment upon delivery were made the rule, and the price were raised, doubtless many farmers in the Middle West would be unable to buy. This being so, common sense dictated that the output should be curtailed, since otherwise a manufacturer who was faced with the prospect of holding over a large number of unsold machines, would slash his prices in order to dispose of his stock.[96] Nor were the McCormicks ready to pledge themselves to sell in the harvest of 1865 at quotations determined upon months ahead of time. The political outlook and the premium on gold, "a good deal like mercury in the thermometer—never at rest," were too uncertain to determine a price schedule so long in advance.[97] They were more anxious to advocate a reduction in the number of new machines to be

[94] *Ibid.*, No. 71, pp. 437-39, 514, 552, 668, 678, the Co. to W. H. B. Warren, Lafayette, Ind., Dec. 17 and 21, 1863; to D. S. Morgan, Dec. 22, 1863; to W. A. Wood, Dec. 29, 1863; No. 66, p. 113, the Co. to Whiteley, Fassler & Kelly, Jan. 16, 1864.

[95] *Ibid.*, No. 74, p. 801, the Co. to Emerson & Co., Rockford, Ill., Sept. 22, 1864; p. 842, to W. H. B. Warren, Sept. 26, 1864; No. 73, pp. 135, 163, the Co. to R. R. S. Marshall, Elmwood, Ill., Aug. 12, 1864.

[96] *Ibid.*, No. 76, pp. 821, 824, the Co. to Emerson & Co., Rockford, Ill., and to Walter A. Wood, Hoosick Falls, N. Y., Dec. 21, 1864.

[97] *Ibid.*, No. 75, p. 532, the Co. to J. Ackerman, Oct. 19, 1864.

manufactured for 1865, since they had two thousand left over from the harvest of the preceding summer. These would not be covered by a price-fixing agreement, and could be used for "fighting" purposes in case any competitor was so incautious as to run amuck.

Eastern manufacturers supported the McCormicks' desire to sell only for cash, but other midwestern firms would not agree, urging with much truth that few prairie farmers could buy unless credit were extended.[98] A Cleveland meeting in September, 1864, accomplished nothing, and when a new conference was called three months later at Buffalo, the Chicago partners declined to attend. This assembly, presuming to speak for about fifty manufacturers, established a price list for machines of the 1865 model, passed an innocuous resolution to sell for "as near cash as possible," and refused to restrict the annual output.[99] The McCormicks for several months tried to abide by the figures set by this convention. It was good business for them to keep up the price of their new reapers and mowers until they could dispose of their last year's surplus at the price level of 1864 to angry farmers who believed the new schedule highly unreasonable. By April, events on the field of battle and the condition of the money market, when combined with the difficulty of effecting sales, determined the McCormicks to steal a march on their competitors and reduce prices. Farmers would give their favor to the company which led the retreat, and "we expect it will prove a heavy blow on rival machines who cannot afford the loss as well as we can." This was on May 1, and they pushed down their selling list almost to its level in the 1864 harvest.[100] Nearly a month later

[98] *Ibid.,* No. 76, p. 155, the Co. to W. A. Knowlton, Rockford, Ill., Nov. 14, 1864.

[99] *Ibid.,* No. 79, pp. 302-3, the Co. to Agents, Mch. 24, 1865.

[100] *Ibid.,* No. 78, p. 452, the Co. to J. Rhodes, Hastings, Minn., May 3, 1865; No. 78, pp. 246, 388, the Co. to W. C. Stacey, Washington, Ind., Apr. 24, and to Seymour, Morgan & Allen, Apr. 29, 1865. The McCormick two-

representatives of other firms met at Cleveland and of necessity followed the McCormicks' lead. Thus the partners played the game as it was played, and probably echoed the general sentiment of harvesting machinery manufacturers when they wrote, on the eve of the Cleveland session: "We . . . don't mean to be bound by any further conventions or meetings, either to raise or lower. We found out there was tricking about it. . . . We must watch these fellows closely that they don't cut under us in price and we are most determined not to let them." [101]

Well might they assure the farmer that reapers were the cheapest commodity on the market, and urge their purchase, whether needed or not, as a good investment looking ahead to the return of normalcy.[102] Whenever an advance in price was announced, the grain-growers knew their cue; boycotted the machine in question, and talked of joining forces to cut the grain of their neighborhood with one or two old machines. Under these circumstances, agents warned the company that a rival would gain the patronage of a district hitherto loyal to the McCormicks unless the old price schedule were restored. This plea was usually effective although the clerks in the factory office seemed to derive some consolation from reminding the salesmen that "Farmers as a class will *grumble* whether prices are high or low; crops good or bad," and that a threat to stop buying reapers was merely "bluff."

All these economical intentions about fitting up old broken down, far gone and consumptive machines, or the clubbing of men to cut horse self-rake reaper sold for $168 cash in 1862 and $190 cash in 1864 and 1865.

[101] *Ibid.*, No. 80, p. 8, the Co. to W. C. Stacey, Lancaster, O., May 17, 1865. The Cleveland meeting was on May 25.

[102] *Ibid.*, No. 66, p. 676; No. 67, pp. 551-2, the Co. to G. Smith, Burnett, Wis., Feb. 8, 1864, and to P. Mohan, Louisville, Ky., Mch. 14, 1864, respectively. In its advertising circular for 1865, the McC. Co. emphasized that in spite of the rise in machine prices, fewer bushels of wheat were needed to buy a reaper in 1865, than in 1862.

each others grain in succession, is all just *moonshine,* and will vanish before the stern fact that John Doe's crop *won't wait* until Richard Roe's and his neighbors' crops are cut, and John will lose his patience and get a machine himself. When a woman gets 'a love of a bonnet,' you know all her acquaintances must get as good a hat if they can worry their husbands out of the dimes, and men act pretty much the same way.[103]

The McCormicks were aware that their implements were helping the Union cause and that every sale of a self-rake reaper potentially released two or three farm hands for service in each summer campaign.[104] Even during the dark months between the election of Lincoln and the first Battle of Bull Run, they derived some comfort from the knowledge that grain would have to be grown and that the labor shortage resulting from a prolonged war would work to their advantage.[105] Agricultural associations in the Middle West reminded farmers that famine had usually accompanied domestic strife and urged them to double their acreage of grain. Thus the Executive Committee of the Illinois State Agricultural Society issued the following appeal in the spring of 1861:

[103] *Ibid.,* No. 67, p. 500, the Co. to D. N. Barnhill, Salem, Ill., Mch. 2, 1864; No. 69, p. 650, to J. L. Briggs, Iowa City, Ia., May 14, 1864.

[104] *Ibid.,* No. 41, p. 699, W. S. McCormick to D. Zimmerman, Cordova, Ill., May 16, 1861: "Let us see if we can sell out our stock of reapers & enable the Farmers to act their part by furnishing plenty of bread for the Army & everybody else." The McCormicks had a few experimental self-rake reapers in the harvest of 1861; 200 in 1862, 2000 in 1863, 4000 in 1864, and 4750 in 1865. Iowa furnished over 40,000 soldiers to the northern armies and Illinois over 100,000.

[105] *Ibid.,* No. 37, p. 276, the Co. to I. Goon, Marshallville, O., Dec. 5, 1860: "Then you know that if we *fight,* bread will be in demand & Reapers will sell." No. 37, p. 686, W. S. McCormick to J. Henry, Dec. 18, 1860: "At all events we must work & eat & the Farmers must buy reapers." No. 38, p. 180, W. S. McCormick to T. Berry, Jan. 9, 1861; No. 41, p. 115, the Co. to H. G. Grattan, Pittsburgh, Pa., Apr. 20, 1861. Harvest hands by 1864 commanded a daily wage of from $3 to $5. Ibid., No. 73, pp. 477-79, the Co. to E. A. McNair, Davenport, Ia., July 19, 1864.

Let us exhort you to till this year every productive acre of your soil. Let no excitement, no interest in the stirring events of the day interrupt the operations of the farm. . . . Your market is certain, and all history is a lie if it shall not be remunerative.

We urge you then to strain every nerve; your interest financially cannot fail to be promoted by it, while your country and the cause of humanity alike demand it.[106]

As early as 1861 the letters, and soon the advertisements, of the McCormicks equated machines and soldiers. The two hundred and fifty thousand reapers and mowers sold during the war, when added to those in use at the outset of the struggle, were equivalent to many men in the harvest fields.[107] In 1863, the secretary of the State Agricultural Society of Iowa deemed it to be "a fact worthy of attention that, while all other crops show a deficiency, the wheat crop has increased fifty per cent the past three years." [108] "Don't be so blue over the prospects," a reaper agent at Concord, Illinois, was told by his employer in May, 1864, "Remember 20,000 militia have to leave this

[106] "Transactions of the Illinois State Agricultural Society" V (1861-1864), pp. 10-11; Broadside (no place, but dated Apr. 29, 1861), beginning "War, and Famine—*Plant Double Your Usual Amount of Land*," cited on pp. 8-9 of Catalog, No. 54, Argosy Book Stores, Inc., New York City.

[107] The McCormick Co. sold 5550 in 1861; 5050 in 1862; 3933 in 1863; 5000 in 1864. ‡A printed leaflet, entitled "Harvester Builders, 1864," lists 203 makers of reapers and mowers in the United States and estimates that they produced over 87,000 machines. It is significant that very few of them had largely increased their annual output since 1861, and even less were making more each year than the McCormicks. Of the 203, 17 were in New England, 59 in N. Y., 6 in N. J., 10 in Del. and Md., 40 in Pa., 28 in Ohio, 18 in Ill., 17 in Wis., 3 in Mich., and 1 each in Ky., Mo., and Iowa. In the "Annual Report of the Massachusetts Board of Agriculture" (Boston), Vol. XXI (1873-1874), pp. 32-37, it is stated that in 1864 there were 187 reaper and mower factories, employing over 60,000 people, and annually producing about 100,000 machines, worth over $15,000,000.

[108] "Ninth Report of the Secretary of the State Agricultural Society to the Governor of the State for the Year 1863" (Des Moines, Ia., 1864), p. 7; "Proceedings of the Wisconsin State Historical Society" (Madison, Wis.), 1908, p. 255.

state for 100 days, and these men will have to come, many or a large share of them, from the farms." [109]

High prices, patriotism, favoring weather, and appeals similar to the one just cited, stimulated small-grain production in the United States during the Civil War. All of these incentives would have been of little avail if grain-growers, handicapped by a curtailed labor supply, had still been depending upon the cradle-scythe to cut their harvest. The domestic demand for grain was satisfied and a much larger surplus than ever before was available for export.[110] England and Russia suffered from poor harvests for several years during the Civil War period. French crops were very light in 1861 and those of the Danube Valley were equally so in 1863 and 1865.[111] "The cotton of the South is doubtless very important to the interests of the Districts referred to in M. Thouvenel's Despatch," the United States Ambassador to France informed W. H. Seward in November, 1861, "but the bread of the North and West is an *absolute necessity*. Cut off from it just now and a month would not pass without the danger of a terrible revolution in France." [112] In how far the dependence of England and

[109] L.P.C.B. No. 69, p. 367, the Co. to J. B. Fairbank & Son, Concord, Ill., May 4, 1864; No. 69, p. 133, to Goetschius & Holtz, Ottawa, O., Apr. 26, 1864. See also, the catalogs of the McCormick Co. for 1863 and 1864.

[110] The value of the total agr'l. exports of the U. S. in 1860 was approximately $91,000,000, of which southern ports sent out about $20,000,000 worth. In 1861, with a million men under arms and few southern exports, the total value reached $137,000,000. In 1862, with a million men changed from producers to consumers (perhaps one-half from the farms), $155,000,000. "Genesee Farmer" (Rochester, N. Y.), Sept. 1863, p. 290.

[111] "Scientific American," Oct. 4, 1862, p. 215. Grain crops were light in England in every year between 1861 and 1867 (both inc.) except 1863.

[112] W. L. Dayton to W. H. Seward, Nov. 25, 1861, Archives of U. S. State Department, Diplomatic Correspondence, 1861-1863, France, MS. Dispatch, No. 86. See also, MS. Dispatch No. 75, "Confidential," W. H. Seward to W. L. Dayton, Oct. 30, 1861. For different views of the influence of grain upon the official attitude of England and France toward the Civil War, see L. B. Schmidt, "The Influence of Wheat and Cotton on Anglo-American Relations During the Civil War," in "The Iowa Journal of His-

France upon grain from the United States was a factor in restraining those nations from recognizing the independence of the Confederacy, is a question which probably admits of no certain answer. It is perhaps significant, however, that their need for foreign wheat was the greatest in the early years of the war when the North had the most reason to fear that they would intervene.

The stirring events in forum and field were almost unmentioned in the thousands of letters mailed annually by the McCormick factory office between 1861 and 1865. Fredericksburg signified that the premium on gold might rise, and Lee's march to Gettysburg that fewer reaper sales might be expected in Maryland and Pennsylvania. Judging from the silence of this correspondence, there was no Emancipation Proclamation, the siege of Vicksburg and Petersburg are myths, Lee did not surrender, and Lincoln was never assassinated. Business did not go on as usual, but it was all-absorbing.[113]

tory and Politics" (Iowa City), July, 1918, pp. 400-439; Wm. Trimble, "Historical Aspects of the Surplus Food Production of the United States, 1862-1902," in "Annual Report of the American Historical Association," 1918 (Wash., 1921), I, pp. 223-239; E. D. Adams, "Great Britain and the American Civil War" (N. Y., 1925), II, p. 13.

[113] L.P.C.B. No. 55, p. 516, W. S. to J. B. McCormick, Dec. 15, 1862; No. 61, p. 234, the Co. to I. Dickey & Co., Pittsburgh, Pa., June 16, 1863.

CHAPTER IV

BUILDING A FORTUNE DURING YEARS OF DEPRESSION AND CIVIL WAR

THE first ten years of manufacturing reapers and mowers in Chicago made Cyrus McCormick a millionaire. At the close of the harvest of 1856 he was told that his profits for the season would probably total $300,000, and by then he had little more than sampled the immense field of sale in the Mississippi Valley.[1] In the main, his money had come from the farmers who had purchased his machines, rather than from patent fees or damages won in suits for infringements. A not inconsiderable item, however, was the value of his factory site with its three hundred feet of river frontage near the heart of the busy city. Purchased for about $25,000, this plot of ground was now conservatively estimated to be worth at least four times as much.[2] Hitherto he had put back much of his profits into the business, erecting new buildings, installing additional machinery, and improving his dock.[3] To continue to concentrate his fortune upon a single enterprise was inadvisable in view of the threatening economic situation in the Middle West by 1857. His wealth, beyond the needs of his factory, demanded prudent investment in days of financial depression and civil war. How to conserve and to employ it wisely came gradually to occupy more of his attention than his plant in Chicago.

[1] L.P.C.B. No. 5, p. 561, W. S. to C. H. McCormick, Mch. 14, 1857.
[2] MS. "Diary of Greenlee Davidson," entry of Sept. 19, 1856.
[3] "Lexington Gazette" (Lexington, Va.), Apr. 28, 1859.

Fortunately for him, by the time he was ready to widen his financial interests, his two brothers were prepared to stand in his stead in the office and construction department of his factory. He could be away for a large part of each year with the confident knowledge that he was ably represented there. William S. McCormick was his chief reliance, and until 1865 loyally shouldered many of his responsibilities, shrewdly investing large amounts of his funds and acting as a buffer for him when times were tense in the early days of the Civil War.

Although William S. had much business acumen, he disliked the confinement of the office and was happiest when at his "home" in Virginia or in a harvest field near Chicago experimenting with some new device.[4] He was unjust to himself when he claimed that he lacked mechanical talent, for the development of a good mower between 1854 and 1860 was due in no small measure to his skill. Like his older brother, he did not know how to relax. He carried his business worries with him on his annual hunting and fishing trips to northern Wisconsin or Minnesota, and often made an office of his home after the day's work at the factory was over.[5] His letters reveal him toiling long hours at his desk, and after a sleepless night, arising be-times to hurry without breakfast to the country to test a mower while the dew was on the grass.[6]

He derived little pleasure from the company of those who were endeavoring to make a "fashionable" Chicago society, although he naturally was pleased to note that his rapid rise

[4] L.P.C.B. No. 1, pp. 338, 365, W. S. to C. H. McCormick, May 7, 8, 1856. Mary Ann to Nettie F. McCormick, July 9 and Sept. 1, 1858.

[5] L.P.C.B. No. 31, p. 829, W. S. McCormick to T. J. Massie, Lovingston, Va., May 10, 1860; No. 42, p. 403, the McCormick Co. to J. Rhodes, Hastings, Minn., June 3, 1861. As a rule, railroads which carried McCormick machines were willing to transport W. S. McCormick, his hunting party, his tents, wagons, etc., without charge. Ibid., No. 62, p. 400, the McCormick Co. to G. C. Dunlap, Supt. of N. Western RR., July 10, 1863.

[6] Mary Ann to Nettie F. McCormick, Sept. 1, 1858. L.P.C.B. No. 14, p. 439, W. S. McCormick to T. Berry, Christian's Creek, Va., Aug. 28, 1858.

won him recognition from its inner circle. Success in business was the "open sesame" to the homes of the great of Chicago and few men there were among the élite at an evening "affair" who could not be found at their desks early the next morning. William came to be enough of a Chicagoan to have great faith in the future of his city and to write frequently to friends of the ease with which money could be made there.[7] In spirit, however, he remained the southern farmer, dreaming of the time when he could live the year around amid the simple neighborliness of his Virginia country-side.[8] His devoted wife, Mary Ann Grigsby, whose brother was to don a Confederate uniform, shared his longing for her native valley. After ten years in Chicago she could still write: "What a pity this [Illinois] wasn't a slave state because so easily cultivated." [9]

William S. McCormick's dislike of indoor work was intensified after 1856 by ill health. Probably with justice he attributed his dyspepsia to nervous exhaustion and lack of exercise. But he confessed that he had "been a hearty eater of everything eatable almost," and while this habit brought no penalty during his youthful years at "Walnut Grove," it was unsuited to his more sedentary life in the city. By 1859 under doctor's orders, he was accustoming himself with difficulty to a regimen of stale bread, eggs, milk and vegetables.[10] On his saddle horse, or by an evening's rivalry with his kinsfolk and church friends in the gymnasium of his new house in Chicago, he tried without success to recapture the physical well-being

[7] *Ibid.,* No. 1, p. 398, W. S. McCormick to A. D. Hager, Proctorsville, Vt., May 9, 1856, and in No. 5, p. 322, to J. M. Lilley, Greenville, Va., Feb. 25, 1857.

[8] L.P.C.B. No. 31, pp. 759-762, W. S. McCormick to A. Leyburn, Lexington, Va., May 8, 1860.

[9] Mary A. McCormick to L. P. Grigsby, Hickory Hill, Va., Aug. 10, 1858.

[10] L.P.C.B. No. 24, p. 167, W. S. McCormick to Dr. G. R. Woods, Phila., Oct. 18 and 19, 1859.

he had known in Virginia.[11] His business judgment remained as keen as ever, but he was aware that he had paid a heavy price for his small fortune.

Shortly after William and his brother, Leander, came to Chicago to live, they began to invest in real estate the small surplus left each year from their salaries.[12] Soon with the consent of their elder brother, they borrowed in advance of wages due, whenever a favorable opportunity to purchase property presented itself.[13] So alluring were the prospects of a large return that William tried for a half-dozen years to find a buyer for the old home of the family in Virginia in order to have additional capital for his speculations in Chicago.[14] Memories of his youth, awakened by a long visit to the farm in the summer of 1859, weakened his determination to raise money by selling the homestead to a stranger.[15] Thereafter, he planted a new orchard, repaired the fences, and drained the fields.[16] When the war came and the plantation was threatened with sequestration by the state as the property of an alien enemy,

[11] *Ibid.,* No. 29, p. 569; No. 30, pp. 246-248, 739, W. S. McCormick to L. G. Hamilton, Fancy Hill, Va., Jan. 27, 1860; to L. Grigsby, Feb. 18, 1860, and to J. B. McCormick, Mch. 7, 1860.

[12] *Ibid.,* No. 5, p. 132, W. S. to C. H. McCormick, Feb. 6, 1857; No. 6, p. 196, to J. Shields, Apr. 11, 1857.

[13] C. H. to W. S. McCormick, Sept. 12, 1857. L.P.C.B. No. 5, pp. 561, 824; No. 6, pp. 112, 304, W. S. to C. H. McCormick, Mch. 14, 27, Apr. 7, 16, 1857; No. 28, p. 738, to L. G. Hamilton, Fancy Hill, Va., Apr. 9, 1860. No. 11, pp. 217 ff. According to this financial statement of Feb. 27, 1858, W. S. owed C. H. McCormick over $21,000; Hugh Adams owed him over $14,000, and J. Shields, about $5,000.

[14] C. H. to W. S. McCormick, Feb. 7 and 12, 1857. L.P.C.B. No. 10, pp. 662, 860, W. S. McCormick to T. Berry, Feb. 8, 1858; to R. T. Elkinton, Phila., Mch. 1, 1858; No. 11, p. 127, to J. Campbell, Westons, N. J., Mch. 11, 1858.

[15] Mary Ann to Nettie F. McCormick, Jan. 17, 1859. W. S. to C. H. McCormick, July 6, 1859. L.P.C.B. No. 33, p. 606, W. S. McCormick to J. Campbell, Westons, N. J., Aug. 18, 1860. He would still sell "Walnut Grove" for $20,000.

[16] *Ibid.,* No. 35, p. 720, W. S. McCormick to J. Murdock, Pittsburgh, Pa., Oct. 12, 1860.

he transferred it to his sister-in-law in the Valley, in discharge of what was said to be a *bona fide* debt of about $7,000.[17]

Little shrewdness was needed in order to make money in Chicago in the early 1850's. A "neat" two-story frame dwelling could be built for $5,000 and rented for $700 or $800 a year, or sold upon its completion at an advance of at least twenty per cent over the first cost. To purchase a lot and hold it for a rise in value was equally remunerative. The brothers prospered, and like others who were also "on the make," they migrated as often within the restricted area of the "North Side" as pioneers who were ever seeking a new frontier. To build a house, live in it for a time, sell out at a profit, and then move to another dwelling where the process could be repeated, was the formula whereby both Leander and William attained a modest competence during their first ten years in Chicago.[18] On the eve of the Civil War they had risen both economically and socially to the class which could afford to have a permanent residence, while continuing to keep their money active by the purchase and sale of desirable properties.[19] The residential district north of the Chicago River was probably the most exclusive in the city. Here, by 1859, the four families of the McCormick clan had gathered, each in its own home, with a broad, shaded lawn over-looking the lake and several, at least, with their cows in the stable behind the

[17] *MS., Defense by J. G. Davidson and Emma Grigsby vs. J. G. Slack, Confederate Receiver, before Judge J. W. Brockenbrough of the District Ct. of the Confed. States, Western Dist. of Va.* The property was saved and by 1865, at least, was occupied by J. G. Hamilton as a tenant of W. S. McCormick. W. S. to C. H. McCormick, Mch. 9, 1865; J. G. Davidson to J. G. Hamilton, Feb. 23, 1866.

[18] Letters from W. S. McCormick in L.P.C.B. No. 1, p. 365, to C. H. McCormick, May 8, 1856; No. 9, p. 700, to J. B. McCormick, Dec. 3, 1857, No. 10, p. 141, to Emma Grigsby, Jan. 4, 1858; No. 19, p. 865, to Jacqueline Grigsby, Apr. 30, 1859.

[19] In fact, L. J. McCormick built a new residence "as handsome as any in the City" for a home in 1863. Mary Ann to Nettie F. McCormick, Oct. 21-22, 1863.

house.[20] Friends from the Old Dominion came to marvel at their rise. One of them was moved to confide to his diary: "A man with money at his command is a fool to stay in Virginia. With judicious management he can make his fortune here in 10 years. . . . The go-a-headitiveness of the people exceeds anything I ever conceived of. It is one continuous rush & hurry." [21]

Cyrus McCormick began to purchase residence lots in Chicago at least as early as 1854, but owing to the attractiveness of other investments and the financial demands of his business during the several years when collections from sales were very light, it is probable that his holdings by 1860, exclusive of the factory and its site, were not as valuable as those of either William or Leander.[22] The coming of the Panic of 1857 and its four years' aftermath of low rents and real estate values— particularly of business properties—led him and others who were confident of Chicago's great future to extend their purchases.[23] As the most important of these deals, in 1860 he acquired the Revere House, which had been the first five-story brick building in the city at the time of its erection by Isaac Cook seven years before.[24]

[20] L.P.C.B. No. 40, p. 103, W. S. McCormick to H. S. Champlin, Mch. 22, 1861.

[21] MS. "Diary of Greenlee Davidson," entry of Sept. 16, 1856.

[22] "Democratic Press" (Chicago), Dec. 4, 1854; J. Forsythe, Chicago, to C. H. McCormick, Nov. 24, 1855; C. H. to W. S. McCormick, Oct. 1, 1856; L.P.C.B. No. 11, pp. 217 ff., W. S. to C. H. McCormick, Feb. 11, 1858. W. S. believed that his brother's land in Chicago, including the factory site, was worth about $100,000. The factory buildings and its machinery were valued at $50,000, and materials on hand, $60,000.

[23] C. H. to W. S. McCormick, Sept. 1, 5, Oct. 7, 1857. L.P.C.B. No. 11, p. 806, W. S. McCormick to J. T. Griffin, Apr. 16, 1858, and No. 20, p. 334, to C. H. McCormick, Mch. 16, 1859.

[24] The Revere House at the corner of Randolph and Dearborn sts. was formerly the Young America Hotel. In 1860, C. H. McCormick had it pulled down to make way for his McCormick Block. Several years later the partners acquired the old Foster House at the corner of Clark and Kinzie sts. After remodeling it at a cost of about $33,000, they opened it

As an investment, iron and lumber were purchased at low prices for factory use in advance of need. During this period McCormick joined with J. Watson Webb of the "New York Courier and Inquirer" to secure coal-mining rights in the Laurel Hill property of about 1700 acres on the Guyandotte River in western Virginia. When Webb was unable to repay a loan made to him by McCormick, he transferred his interest in this concession to the inventor.[25]

McCormick declined to enter the private banking business although money borrowed in New York at seven or eight per cent a year could be loaned in Chicago on short term and with good real estate security at from one and one-half to two per cent a month. Nevertheless, William S., with his more intimate knowledge of the financial opportunities of his city, braved his brother's displeasure by using in this way some of the money sent in by reaper agents during 1857.[26] Although Cyrus was unwilling to launch upon an enterprise with which he was wholly unfamiliar, he was attracted by the profits made annually by the Marine Bank in Chicago. When he heard that some of the most solid men of the city, including George Armour, William Ogden, and Wesley Munger, were about to open a new financial institution to be called the Merchants' Savings Loan and Trust Company, he purchased $20,000 worth of its stock.[27] It was an excellent investment, although the bank did not fulfill his early hopes of permitting him to

in the spring of 1864 under the name of the Revere House. C. H. Mc-Cormick purchased the original Revere House for about $60,000. See also, *post,* ftn. 82.

[25] C. H. to W. S. McCormick, May 30, 1857. ‡J. W. Webb to C. H. Mc-Cormick, Oct. 3, 1859 and Mch. 31, 1870. ‡L.P.C.B., No. 1, 2nd ser., p. 118, C. H. McCormick to J. W. Webb, June 6, 1870. McCormick here stated that his deed for this property was destroyed when his luggage was burned in Mch. 1862. See, *post,* p. 756.

[26] C. H. to W. S. McCormick, Apr. 20, 1857. W. S. had a power of attorney from C. H. McCormick.

[27] *Idem* to *Idem,* Apr. 9, 15, 17, 1857.

borrow on easy terms.[28] He continued to look to New York City when loans were needed, and the Importers' and Traders' National Bank there was for many years his principal place of deposit.

Strongly believing in family solidarity, and wishing his two sisters to share in his prosperity, he persuaded Hugh Adams and his wife, Amanda McCormick, to exchange Virginia for Chicago as a home. Mrs. Adams was glad to be relieved of "the care and responsibility of a family of collored [sic] people" and her husband with the aid of the McCormick name and money was soon established as a commission merchant, using a part of a factory building as his warehouse.[29] This promised to be better than storekeeping and farming in the Valley, particularly since he handled all grain taken in exchange for reapers.[30] In like manner, but without

[28] *Idem* to *Idem*, Dec. 16, 1857. McCormick was a trustee of this bank for about ten years, although he attended few, if any, meetings of the board. In 1866 he declined to exercise his option as a stock-holder, to purchase 250 more shares of stock, but by 1871 his investment in the bank had increased to $25,000. L.P.C.B. No. 91, p. 486, C. H. McCormick to L. J. Gage, Aug. 1, 1866; No. 95, p. 612, C. A. Spring to C. H. McCormick, Feb. 18, 1867; No. 121, p. 420, C. A. Spring, Jr., to C. H. McCormick, Sept. 5, 1870. As late as 1882, the Merchants' Savings Loan and Trust Co. handled the Chicago account of the McCormick Harvesting Machine Company, and C. H. McCormick, Jr., was then one of its board of trustees. In 1873, the elder McCormick was a director of the Security Savings Bank, located in his Reaper Block in Chicago.

[29] L.P.C.B. No. 8, pp. 534, 654, W. S. McCormick to H. Adams, Aug. 21, 1857, and to J. B. McCormick, Sept. 5, 1857. "Daily Chicago Times," May 17, 1859. Amanda J. Adams to Nettie F. McCormick, Mch. 13, 1858. This was the commission house of C. H. McCormick & Co. H. Adams received a salary from the McCormick brothers, and they apparently supplied all the capital used by this Co. until 1866. In that year its office was moved to La Salle St.: "on account of the river being so unhealthy & at times unbearable from the dreadful odors." Mary Adams to Nettie F. McCormick, May 20, 1866. ♯L. J. to C. H. McCormick, Mch. 3, 1866.

[30] During the war, C. H. McCormick & Co. was "handling the pork of some very heavy pork men on the Miss. River." L.P.C.B. No. 65, p. 823, W. S. McCormick to B. Mills, LaCrescent, Minn., Nov. 24, 1863.

success, the McCormicks sought to provide their other brother-in-law, James Shields, with a lumber business and guarantee him from loss.[31] But Shields was a minister and his poor health and unwillingness to enter trade [32] held him on his little living in the mountains of Pennsylvania until his death in 1862, while on a hunting trip with William S. McCormick. Thereafter his widow, Mary Caroline McCormick, moved with her two children to Chicago.[33]

Cyrus McCormick was aware that his wealth had come more directly from his success as a manufacturer than from his possession of several important patents. His brothers also stressed the fact that without their aid his large profits during the 1850's would not have been possible. They felt that they had done most of the work and by their ingenuity had kept the McCormick reaper and mower in step with the progress of the art, while their brother spent the larger part of each year in the East. He wrote to them from Philadelphia and Washington, from ocean resorts, and the springs of New York, Virginia, and Vermont, and told them confidentially of his dinners and carriage-drives with the Commissioner of Patents while he was trying to secure an extension or reissue

[31] L.P.C.B. No. 6, pp. 196, 304, W. S. McCormick to J. Shields, Apr. 11, 1857; to C. H. McCormick, Apr. 16, 1857; No. 8, pp. 521, 816, to Caroline Shields, Aug. 21, 1857, and to C. H. McCormick, Sept. 19, 1857.

[32] Shields, through W. S. McCormick, had purchased at least one house in Chicago. In 1860-61, it was occupied by Dr. Rice. *Ibid.*, No. 49, p. 577, W. S. McCormick to J. Shields, June 4, 1862.

[33] *Ibid.*, No. 60, p. 290, the Co. to S. Cuthbert & Sons, Juniata, Pa., May 25, 1863. The Shields' 52-acre farm at Mexico, Pa., was offered @ $100 an acre, and 200 acres in the Western Reserve of Ohio @ $20 an acre, cash. Following her husband's death, Mrs. Shields lived in W. S. McCormick's home in Chicago until the autumn of 1865, when she moved to a house on Rush St. C. A. Spring, Jr., to C. H. McCormick, Oct. 26, 1865. She moved several times during the next three years and L. J. McCormick aided her with money. Finally in 1868, L. J. and C. H. McCormick agreed to contribute ⅓rd and ⅔rds of the cost, respectively, to the erection of houses for both her and Amanda Adams. Mary Caroline McCormick died on Mch. 18, 1888, and Amanda Adams on Oct. 12, 1891.

of his monopolies. Now and again he would take a hurried trip to Chicago to talk about family affairs, but he came mainly, it seemed, to have a financial accounting and to make sure of their devotion to his interests at the factory.[34] They knew how much money he was making each year and how very small their own salaries seemed by comparison. Mary Ann McCormick, worried by the strenuous routine of her husband, told a long story in a single sentence when she wrote to her brother, "C. H. is the picture of health, he takes it easy and thinks after all he does the hardest of the work." This verdict was unjust but it was not an unnatural one.[35]

In early 1857 William S. McCormick bluntly told his elder brother that he "calculated upon something considerable more than a salery [sic] out of the business." [36] Soon Leander threatened to resign unless he were better provided for. "As I have said to you I have done *not a little* for the machine and I am resolved not to be satisfied without a pretty strong interest if I remain in the business." [37] The brothers were financially unprepared to purchase an interest in the factory, but on the other hand Cyrus McCormick realized that their skill and experience made their services invaluable to him. Finally, near the close of 1859, a firm was organized under a twelve years' agreement. Its style was C. H. McCormick & Bros., and the inventor was to supply all the needed capital at eight per cent interest. He agreed to furnish new factory machinery at cost and to rent the plant to the company for $10,000 a year. The brothers should each receive an annual

[34] *Ibid.*, No. 8, p. 495, W. S. to J. B. McCormick, Aug. 17, 1857; C. H. to W. S. McCormick, Oct. 30, 1858.

[35] Mary Ann McCormick to L. P. Grigsby, Aug. 10, 1858.

[36] L.P.C.B. No. 6, p. 112, W. S. to C. H. McCormick, Apr. 7, 1857.

[37] L. J. to W. S. McCormick, July 1, 1859. L. J. had evidently written in a similar vein in 1858. C. H. to W. S. McCormick, Oct. 30, 1858: "I think he [L. J. McCormick] regretted the course he took with me, and [I] have no idea it would be his *interest* to leave the business."

salary of $5,000 and each was allotted one-fourth of the net
profits. They guaranteed that they would not manufacture
harvesting machinery elsewhere or work for another reaper-
builder during the life of the contract. On his part Cyrus also
pledged that he would not erect a branch factory although he
reserved the right to license others under his patents. It was
emphasized that "no actual partnership" existed, probably because the eldest brother assumed all the financial risk and furnished the entire capital.[38] That same autumn he moved with
his wife and son, who had been born in May of that year at
Washington, to 230 North Dearborn Street, Chicago. There
was a lull in his patent and lawsuit business in the East and
he had been eager for several years to settle down and make
a real home.[39] He at once surprised his brothers by taking
more interest than was his wont in the details of factory operation and management. "Bro. C. H. is having a say so in
almost everything now-a-days," wrote William, with perhaps
a tinge of regret because his word was no longer law in the
routine affairs of the plant.[40] William's health improved, now
that he was receiving a return commensurate with the value
of his services.[41]

By 1860, however, politics, the new seminary, a newspaper,
a religious journal, and his effort to secure an extension of

[38] This is a summary of two agreements, one made on Nov. 1, 1859, and
the other on Jan. 1, 1860. It is interesting to note that even at this late
date W. S. McCormick was not certain that he would long remain in the
business. L.P.C.B. No. 26, p. 444, W. S. McCormick to L. J. Hamilton,
Fancy Hill, Va., Dec. 17, 1859.

[39] Cyrus Rice McCormick was born on May 16, 1859. About 1870, his
name was changed to Cyrus Hall McCormick. In "Nettie F. McCormick
B. A." files is an envelop dated May 24, 1869, and marked Cyrus Rice
McCormick. In a letter to W. S. McCormick on Jan. 12, 1858, C. H. Mc-
Cormick expressed his regret that his long absences from Chicago had
allowed him to make few close friends there. L.P.C.B. No. 29, p. 489.

[40] Ibid., No. 24, p. 516, W. S. McCormick to G. Walker, Ann Arbor,
Mich., Nov. 4, 1859.

[41] Ibid., No. 26, p. 78, W. S. McCormick to J. Shields, Dec. 3, 1859.

his patent of 1847 kept the inventor too occupied to give much thought to his factory. Since he was abroad during the two most critical years of the conflict, the task of investing the company's funds fell largely upon the shoulders of William. Suffering in mind and in body, and unsympathetic toward the objectives of the war, he viewed his work without enthusiasm. The bright future in store for the Northwest, Chicago, and the McCormick factory, were the only articles of his old faith which seemed to him worth preserving during the crisis. Former values were swept away, close friendships broken, and to use his own words, "a good deal of humility has had to be endured on account of our position." [42]

Now our hearts sicken at the spectacle that is presented [he confided to a friend in Virginia]. We are attending closely to our *business*. We see few people on the streets & corners & say but little & hope & pray that an all wise Providence may overrule all the evil, that is now so much in the ascendent, for good. We *expect* our relations & friends & acquaintances for whom we have a high regard will be slain in this war—We think & talk much about it. Our little circle meet very often to think & talk of what is going on & can hardly realize the condition of things in & around our native State & the Home of our Fathers & Mothers.[43]

To him, and to others in the company office who reflected his opinion, it would have been better "if old Buck had remained President for a dozen years longer." [44] "All is treason that is not fanaticism," and "with stamp duty, taxes, conscription, paper trash, and bastiles, we begin to feel respect for the more liberal and moderate laws of Russia and Austria." [45]

[42] W. S. to C. H. McCormick, Mch. 6, 1864.
[43] L.P.C.B. No. 42, p. 40, W. S. McCormick to W. T. Rush, May 22, 1861; No. 41, p. 377, to J. B. McCormick, May 3, 1861.
[44] *Ibid.,* No. 44, p. 28, W. S. to J. B. McCormick, July 15, 1861: "These are most glorious Lincoln Republican times to be sure. . . . Verily Democratic sins are *nothing* to the Sins of these Times."
[45] *Ibid.,* No. 58, p. 249, W. J. Hanna to W. A. Polk, Oak Station, Ind., Mch. 26, 1863.

In this atmosphere of dissent the McCormick reaper business was carried on from 1861 to 1865. The prosperity of northern manufacturer and farmer during the Civil War has often been emphasized. Mill-owners became millionaires. Grain-growers paid their old debts and in many instances contracted new ones before the struggle was over. Little attention, however, has been given by writers to the puzzling problems arising daily for solution by a manufacturer whose wealth could not increase rapidly unless the farmers enjoyed "flush times." The experiences of the harvest of 1861, with its changes in outlook so unexpected that the most careful planning was of no avail, were duplicated a hundred-fold during the next four years. They partially explain why men who were growing rich beyond their fondest dreams, became old before their time, and prayed for the war to end despite its heavy yield of prosperity. A Federal defeat, a new tax law, a quick rise or fall in the premium on gold, appeared to signify all the difference between large profits and bankruptcy. Looking back upon these years, it would now appear that more gain or less gain, not ruin or riches, hinged upon the choice of one or another of the several investment projects so often under consideration.

At the outset of the struggle, when prices were still low and agents were unable to collect for the reapers and mowers sold, the McCormicks gloomily predicted that the situation would not improve until peace came. They talked much about economizing, reducing the force in field and factory, and sailing under bare poles as long as the hurricane lasted.[46] It would

[46] L.P.C.B. No. 44, p. 730, W. S. McCormick to D. Zimmerman, Cordova, Ill., Aug. 8, 1861: "If this war is to be waged indefinitely, I believe we shall all be nearly ruined. We just now begin to see the veil lifted. We shall be *burdened* with *taxes* & low prices & I *ask* the *question,* is there at the end of this war the *gold* that is to compensate us for the *blood* & *treasure* that our Rulers are so lavishly pouring out. I love the Union but will our *Rulers* save it so as to be a *blessing?*" Emphasis on economizing

perhaps be better, in their opinion, to cease manufacturing altogether, for the enormous crop of 1861 and the closure of the southern market for grain, signified that farmers would have no money to spend for reapers.[47] But when times improved in the autumn of 1861, the chief question was no longer where money might be borrowed to keep the wheels turning, but how to invest safely the cash that was flowing to the factory office from the farms of the Northwest. The cash, however, had no certain value and the improvement of the currency situation in the Middle West by late 1861 was largely counteracted by measures of the national government during the next ten years. The greenbacks issued in 1862 and thereafter, added to the confusion although the McCormicks foresaw as early as December of the previous year that gold would probably go to a heavy premium.[48] The National Banking Act of 1863 had a depressing effect upon state bank-note issues, the only circulating medium that was current in many rural districts of the Old Northwest. To invest in those uncertain times meant not only to make the difficult choice of a reasonably safe project that would probably yield an attractive return upon the sum ventured, but also to decide wisely in haste before the funds available had further depreciated.

The more cheerful note of the factory correspondence in the autumn of 1861 was replaced by hysteria in late December when the crisis over the Trent Affair led William S. McCormick to telegraph his New York bankers to convert all company funds into gold and express the metal to Chicago as

continued throughout the war. See, W. S. to C. H. McCormick, Mch. 15, 1863.

[47] L.P.C.B. No. 44, p. 28, No. 45, p. 300, W. S. to J. B. McCormick, July 15 and Sept. 2, 1861. As late as mid-Oct., 1861, the firm had not begun to manufacture for 1862. See, Ibid., No. 46, p. 434, the Co. to S. H. Mitchell, Concord, Ill., Oct. 16, 1861. W. S. McCormick did not foresee the large foreign market for northern grain.

[48] Ibid., No. 54, p. 110, W. S. to C. H. McCormick, Dec. 24, 1861.

a safeguard against the anticipated bombardment of the eastern metropolis by English warships.[49] With this danger averted and grain once again resuming its upward trend,[50] optimism returned for a few months.

But the failure of the military campaigns of 1862 to end the war, the issuance of the Emancipation Proclamation, and the realization that Lincoln would not change his policy in spite of his rebuff by many voters in the by-elections of that year, reduced William McCormick to despair.[51] Ill health and overwork doubtless helped to determine his outlook. For eleven months following the Federal rout at the second battle of Manassas in August, 1862, he saw no light.[52] He, and those in the company office during that anxious time, wrote often of "the fiery ordeal through which we shall have to pass," and of "the big smash-up which seems to be peeping around the corners of the future."[53] William's letters are filled with references to the over-extension of government credits, the probable repudiation of the national debt, the imminent "commercial revolution," and of two hundred thousand dissatisfied Union soldiers marching home before long under

[49] *Ibid.*, No. 54, p. 107, *Idem* to *idem*, Dec. 23, 1861.

[50] *Ibid.*, No. 54, p. 293, the Co. to J. Rodermel, Freeport, Ill., Dec. 31, 1861.

[51] W.S. to C. H. McCormick, Sept. 28, 1862. In this letter, he wondered whether, in view of possible anarchy in the North, it might not be wise to transfer their fortune and factory to Europe. *Idem* to *idem*, Oct. 5, 1862, "I feel our ship is sinking. . . . Things look black as midnight." See also his letters to C. H. McCormick, Sept. 25, Oct. 19, Nov. 9, 1862, and Mch. 1, 1863.

[52] From the northern victories at Vicksburg and Gettysburg until 1865, his general opinion as to the military outcome of the war is summarized in the following sentence from a letter to C. H. McCormick on July 2, 1863. "It would seem that by numbers & brute force the South must gradually be crushed." C. H. McCormick did not agree with this prophecy. See, *supra*, pp. 57, 61.

[53] L.P.C.B. No. 57, pp. 208, 216, the Co. to E. A. McNair, Davenport, Ia., and to Bass & Elmendorf, McGregor, Ia., Feb. 21, 1863.

the lead of "a Jacobin." [54] In his opinion a civil war might possibly be avoided in the North if the government were shrewd enough to pledge a fifty per cent redemption of its enormous debt. To pay it dollar for dollar was unthinkable.[55]

"I assure you," he wrote his elder brother, "I *think* enough upon the various questions I have to act upon to make a man grey." [56] But Cyrus McCormick had no encouraging word to send him from England, and in fact did little more than to criticize the investments which his brother made after so much tortured study. Both in building reapers at the factory and in using the money of the firm, "be cautious," was the burden of the inventor's letters during his two years abroad. He was advised by Junius Morgan and Charles Francis Adams to avoid borrowing for purposes of investment, to place surplus funds in land, and to contract business as much as possible.

That the revulsion must come is considered *certain*. The N. W. has not yet felt this tremendous war. The stimulant of gov't credit has so far been equal to the draught upon the patient, but already the dose has to be increased $32\frac{1}{2}\%$ to keep up the effect, and soon the whole thing must *fail*, when reaction must set in and "down, down, down" must go everything. We feel we can understand from here better than you can in Chicago. . . . I am opposed to speculation now with the prospect of revulsion, depression, and ruin ahead. . . . The collapse is inevitable, . . . the only question is when? [57]

[54] W. S. to C. H. McCormick, Jan. 19 and May 31, 1863.

[55] *Idem* to *idem,* Dec. 11, 1862.

[56] *Idem* to *idem,* Nov. 23, Dec. 31, 1862, and Jan. 4, 1863: "You would be so puzzled you would throw up a copper to know what to do."

[57] C. H. to W. S. McCormick, Dec. 2, 1862. L.P.C.B. No. 49, p. 856, C. A. Spring to W. S. McCormick, Aug. 12, 1862. C. H. McCormick hoped to gain a perspective abroad which would enable him better to judge of the proper investments to make at home. ‡Jas. Buell, the cashier of the Importers' and Traders' Bank, probably comforted him but little when he reminded him in a letter of Dec. 5, 1863, that Bank of England notes during the Napoleonic Wars were within ten points of being as low in relation to gold, as were greenbacks in that month.

Thus McCormick, in December, 1862, confirmed from London, after talking with a financier and his country's ambassador, the fears for the future which plagued his brother in Chicago.

William had a power of attorney from the inventor, but he was expected to ask his advice and consent before investing the profits of the firm. He did so in long, revealing letters which he rightly supposed "would be a curiosity among many others after this war shall have ended." [58] Nevertheless, the kaleidoscopic changes in the financial situation from day to day [59] and the failure of his brother to answer his many questions either fully or promptly, obliged him to act upon his own responsibility and report his course after it had been taken. Thereby he risked the censure and even the refusal of Cyrus McCormick to abide by his decision, in so far as the latter's share in the venture was concerned.

The largest amounts of money reached the company office during the darkest period of the war, for it was then that currency was the most depreciated and farmers were able and ready to cancel debts which in many cases had been incurred four or five years before the conflict opened. This fact also helped to shape the financial policy of the company, since at a time when William McCormick was the most pessimistic he was obliged to handle sums of money dwarfing any in his previous career. He brought no wide experience to his task except an expert knowledge of Chicago real estate and farm values.

To dispose of greenbacks quickly and to forecast accurately the amount they would depreciate between January, when reaper prices were announced, and the selling season of the following summer, were two of the most serious and usual

[58] W. S. to C. H. McCormick, Mch. 15, 1863.
[59] *Idem* to *idem*, Mch. 29, 1863: "We don't think *worth while now* to report little events such as an advance or decline of only forty per cent in gold." See also *idem* to *idem*, Jan. 24, 1864.

problems of the war period.[60] Since the value of the paper
money in relation to gold was in a considerable degree determined by the fortunes of the northern armies, and since significant victories or defeats chiefly occurred during the summer campaigns, the currency was most unstable in the months
when harvesting machinery was sold. With the price of reaper
raw materials—wood and iron—increasing faster after 1862
than the rate of greenback depreciation, more than human wisdom was required to fix terms of sale one winter that would
pay without question for the cost of machine reproduction the
next, and yield a fair profit.[61] Nevertheless, prices once advertised were never raised, although the purchaser of a reaper
was expected either to pay cash upon delivery so that the paper
could be invested at once before further depreciation took
place, or, since this was usually impracticable, to sign notes
extending in the future for three to five years, with the hope
that when they fell due, greenbacks would be at a parity with
gold.[62] Although a plan in the late autumn of 1862 to sell
reapers only for wheat was never carried out,[63] grain and

[60] *Idem* to *idem*, July 4, 1862: "You have not seemed to *fear* as I have
this *depreciation* in paper money. I am for investing somehow without delay.
. . . Farming lands or lots or anything sooner than paper money these times
in Bank." He wondered how his elder brother could even think of going
abroad before an investment policy was decided upon.

[61] L.P.C.B. No. 73, p. 482, the Co. to J. Fisher, Liberty Mills, Ind., July
19, 1864. Here the Co. insisted that it was making no profit on its 1864 sales,
since the cost of all factory raw materials had so much advanced after it
had issued its machine price list earlier in the year.

[62] Letters from the Co. in *Ibid.*, No. 49, p. 869, to W. S. McCormick,
Aug. 25, 1862; No. 55, pp. 784-5, 844, to W. H. B. Warren, Wabash, Ind.,
Jan. 5, 1863, and to J. B. McCormick, Jan. 6, 1863; No. 57, pp. 216, 505,
to Bass & Elmendorf, McGregor, Ia., Feb. 21, 1863, and to G. Smith,
Burnett Station, Wis., Mch. 5, 1863.

[63] He proposed to take wheat in exchange for reapers at its average price
in Chicago during the past four or five years (86½¢ a bu.) and even to
make the interest on reaper notes payable in wheat. The idea was abandoned
by Jan., 1863. Early in the autumn of 1862, he considered the advisability
of building grain elevators in Chicago, borrowing $200,000 in N. Y. for

stock were occasionally received for machines; the grain sold through the commission house of C. H. McCormick & Co.; the cattle quickly taken by the city packers who had for long made the Chicago River run red with blood; and the horses and buggies held during the winter on the several stock farms of the firm for apportionment among the three hundred agents when the spring canvass opened.[64]

Two normal avenues of investment were closed to William S. McCormick. He had no acquaintance with the stock market and declined to gain it during the uncertain times of the Civil War.[65] Because of his determination to "play safe," his fear that the federal government would repudiate its enormous debt, and perhaps also because of his lack of sympathy for the policy of coercion, United States bonds were not included in his portfolio of investments.[66] In fact, he believed that any man wishing to borrow money or to sell a farm would prefer McCormick's reaper notes to greenbacks. It was a fine conceit to assume that a private partnership was more solvent than the

investment in wheat, and holding it through the winter for shipment in 1863 to Europe. Possibly word from his brother that the depredations of Confederate cruisers would probably boost ocean freight rates, made him less ready to go forward with this plan, as well as the one mentioned in the text. *Ibid.*, No. 52, W. S. McCormick to L. Hopkins, Oct. 17, 1862; No. 55, the Co. to F. Cuddington, Dixon, Ill., Dec. 20, 1862. C. H. to W. S. McCormick, Dec. 19-20, 1862; W. S. to C. H. McCormick, Aug. 3, Oct. 19, Dec. 28, 1862. On Oct. 19, he wrote: "There isn't room now in Chicago, to hold the grain pouring in despite the short crop." Statistics do not support his judgment that the crop was light.

[64] *Ibid.*, No. 54, pp. 725-727. In Jan., 1862, the Cordova, Ill., agency had 65 horses, 15 cows, 2 oxen, 1 mule, and a variety of farm wagons, etc., taken in payment of reaper notes. Other McCormick depots of this kind were at Concord, Courtland and Tiskilwa, Ill.

[65] W. S. to C. H. McCormick, Nov. 22, 1863.

[66] *Idem* to *idem*, Oct. 19, 1862. Apparently C. H. McCormick invested $16,000 in U. S. bonds in Jan., 1863, but this is an exception to the rule. L.P.C.B. No. 56, p. 111, the Co. to J. Buell, Importers' and Traders' Bank, N. Y., Jan. 12, 1863; W. S. to C. H. McCormick, Jan. 31 and Feb. 21, 1864. C. H. McCormick still owned some U. S. 6% gold bonds in 1868. C. H. McCormick to C. A. Spring, Jr., July 17, 1868.

national government, but at least he was able to loan many thousand dollars' worth of company paper at interest rates of from seven to ten per cent.[67] These notes paid six per cent interest to the holder, were guaranteed by the firm, and were said to be negotiable and stable in value, although the borrowers seem to have overlooked the fact that they would be cancelled eventually in depreciated currency, either by the farmer who first signed them on the delivery of his reaper, or by the company as endorser. However, every note so loaned saved the firm the cost of its collection and lessened the quantity of paper money which it was obliged to handle.[68]

By the summer of 1862, William McCormick realized that the war years would be a debtors' paradise. He was obliged to give a receipt in full when farmers sent him cheap legal tender of a face value equal to the old reaper obligations, totaling well over a million dollars and incurred when a dollar was a dollar. Consequently, he understood why "creditors were running away from debtors who pursued them in triumph and paid them without mercy."[69] If reaper purchasers could do

[67] L.P.C.B. No. 53, pp. 455, 476, the Co. to H. S. Champlin, Courtland, Ill., and to E. Healy, Earlville, Ia., Nov. 6, 1862. To combine portions from each letter: "There must be a demand for capital with you. If there is, then *why* should not our *good Solvent* Reaper notes be as available as other paper. . . . Currency may depreciate but *this* paper will not, the farmer can keep it, as it bears interest, and collect along just as he needs the money. We are satisfied with the paper, but we wish to concentrate our means, and make investments on long time." By Dec., 1864, at least $185,000 in notes and money had been loaned. W. S. to C. H. McCormick, Dec. 10, 1864.

[68] L.P.C.B. No. 52, pp. 848-852, 889, a form letter of the Co. to its agents, Oct. 20, 1862. In this, it proposed to sell and loan reaper notes, loan money, and buy farm lands with notes or greenbacks. *Ibid.,* No. 55, p. 66, the Co. to W. C. Leyburn, Sparta, Wis., Nov. 24, 1862; and p. 806, to W. H. Brazier, Salem, Ill., Jan. 5, 1863.

[69] W. S. to C. H. McCormick, July 9, 1862; Jan. 25, 1863, "I have told you long ago that legal tender would in the end be a good Bankrupt law. 'Money' *may* be bought by the bushel to pay debts to us. This legal tender law is to be a *great leveler.* It will enable the Creditor to pay up his honest debts with scraps of paper."

this, why could not the company borrow large amounts of greenbacks, invest them at once, and pay back the loans when the paper was still further depreciated? Big profits were made in this way. At one time the partners owed almost $225,000, and a considerable portion of this debt was cancelled in the winter of 1863-1864 before the currency reflected the Federal victories around Richmond and Atlanta.[70] Fortunately for the success of this plan, there was never a time during the war when the McCormicks could not borrow large sums at from six per cent to eight per cent interest, with the date of repayment, in most cases, at their option.[71]

In addition to the ante-bellum reaper notes, which most farmers, spurning the shelter afforded by the stay laws, were now able and anxious to cancel, the annual sale of about five thousand machines brought to the company treasury more than three-quarters of a million dollars in greenbacks during the autumn and winter months. To hold them was to lose money, and quick decisions had to be made, often involving as much as fifty thousand dollars a week. Factory raw materials were purchased two years in advance of need and paper currency was loaned to farmers at from six per cent to ten

[70] *Idem* to *idem,* Oct. 14, 1862, and Nov. 22, 1863. In Nov., 1863, the firm owed $222,000, but to W. S. McCormick's regret, $99,000 was about due to be paid.

[71] *Idem* to *idem,* Oct. 12, 19, 26, 1862. L.P.C.B. No. 52, W. S. McCormick to L. Hopkins, N. Y., Oct. 17, 1862. An interesting illustration of the financial advantage enjoyed by a big firm over a smaller competitor is furnished by C. H. McCormick & Bros'. practice of overdrawing its account at the Importers' & Traders' Bank, sometimes as much as $80,000. Of course it paid interest on the amount of its overdraft, and its special specie account was considered security, but it was none the less a convenient and elastic way of borrowing. *Ibid.,* No. 69, p. 377; No. 76, p. 77, C. A. Spring, Jr., to J. Buell, May 5 and Nov. 10, 1864. Nevertheless, in 1867, this bank called a halt upon this practice. Thereupon C. H. McCormick transferred his funds for a time to the Park National Bank of N. Y., which offered him easier accommodations. ‡J. Buell to C. H. McCormick, Jan. 27, 1867; L.P.C.B. No. 95, C. A. Spring, Jr., to C. H. McCormick, Jan. 29, 1867; ‡C. A. Spring, Jr., to C. H. McCormick, Feb. 5, 16, 1867.

per cent interest for a seven- to ten-year term, with the hope
that the date for repayment would find greenbacks at par.[72]

Whether to place surplus funds in gold or in real estate was
always one of the most puzzling problems that faced William
McCormick. His opinion as to the relative profit to be expected
from these two modes of investment changed time and again
during the war, and at its close he was still in a quandary about
them. He admitted in 1864 that city property had not advanced in value as much as he had anticipated two years
before, but on the other hand, gold paid no interest to its
holder. In the summer of 1862 he favored gold over real
estate, regretted his change of heart in the spring of 1863,
was again cheering for city property in preference to specie by
December of that year, and by February, 1864, repented that
he had not purchased more metal.[73] Whichever alternative he
followed, his brother usually was sorry that he had not made
the opposite choice.[74] The McCormick hoard never exceeded
$200,000, and apparently was largest in the autumn of 1862
and the winter of 1863-1864. At the latter time Cyrus trans-

[72] W. S. to C. H. McCormick, Apr. 11, 1863. By this date over $100,000
had been loaned for from five to ten years, and in the next Sept., the total
was half again as large. About one-third of the total, however, consisted
of reaper notes rather than money. Curiously enough, the firm would only
loan money on improved farm land security, "not desiring [to have] the
care and attention that city or town securities impose." L.P.C.B. No. 56,
p. 495. Probably the preference for loans to farmers arose also from the fact
that, unlike city dwellers, their security "can't be burned or destroyed by
mobs." W. S. to C. H. McCormick, Mch. 29, 1863. *Idem* to *idem*, Oct. 14,
and Nov. 23, 1862. The Co. had invested $246,313 in raw materials, and in
July, 1864, the sum tied up in this way was equally large. Pig-iron was
piled like cord wood all over the factory yard.

[73] *Idem* to *idem*, July 9, Nov. 9, 1862; Mch. 1, Dec. 13, 1863; Feb. 28,
1864.

[74] *Idem* to *idem*, Jan. 24, 1864. In this letter W. S. McCormick opposed
his brother's suggestion that the firm should buy $300,000 in gold and ship
it to Europe for investment. William argued that gold was worth more in
the U. S. than abroad, that it could only be loaned @ 4% interest overseas,
while investments in Chicago real estate yielded 10% a year.

ferred $75,000 in specie from his New York account to London for investment, and although his holdings thereafter were not very large, the purchase and sale of gold are mentioned in his correspondence until the close of 1866.[75]

By far the largest proportion of the surplus money of the firm was invested in real estate. Here a choice had to be made between city property, subject to heavy taxes and insurance charges, and farm lands—both wild and improved—which could be held at small cost until railroads and the coming of more settlers advanced their value. Attractive bargains in both city and country were available throughout the conflict, and the depreciation of the currency affected real estate values but slowly.[76] Increasing faith in Chicago made the decision an easier one as the war dragged on and the city boomed as never before. *"Chicago must* be a success if any city in this country will be,"* wrote William McCormick in October, 1863. "The best men and capital are here and coming here. There *are not* enough stores to do the business." [77] Leander, fresh from London, believed his home city had larger crowds than the English metropolis, while Mary Ann McCormick was astonished at "the indifference manifested by the loss of life" in the war. "The idea is with everybody to go ahead, & see how much you can *swindle* out of everybody while this thing lasts." [78] Crime kept pace with the city's growth; even the

[75] ‡Naylor & Co., N. Y., to C. H. McCormick, Feb. 19, 1864; W. S. to C. H. McCormick, Oct. 14, 1862, and Feb. 7, 1864. At the earlier date, C. H. McCormick had $104,791 in gold and W. S. McCormick $35,000. In Feb. 1864, C. H. McCormick held $105,701, and about half that amount by autumn.

[76] L.P.C.B. No. 55, p. 60, the Co. to B. G. Fitzhugh, Frederick, Md., Nov. 24, 1862: "Real estate is low, very cheap; the general inflation has not affected that yet; we can invest our money in real estate at bargains. . . . Real estate must feel the depreciation, and rise in value."

[77] W. S. to C. H. McCormick, Oct. 4, 1863. As early as the spring of 1862, Chicago merchants were agreed that business was better than at any time since before the Panic of 1857.

[78] Mary Ann to Nettie F. McCormick, Oct. 21, 22, 1863, and Mch. 5, 1864.

main streets were unsafe after dark. Cyrus McCormick's home was ransacked by burglars, and thereafter, until it was rented, a clerk from the factory office slept in the house with a Colt revolver under his pillow and threads running from all the doors and windows to a bell at the head of his bed.[79]

In the autumn of 1862, William McCormick wished the firm to invest a million dollars in Chicago real estate.[80] Cyrus demurred, but by the close of the war the value of the partners' properties in the city was almost that much, and were returning about $100,000 a year in rents.[81] Their hotel, the Revere House, was a money-maker after they had widely advertised it among their agents in 1863.[82] About a dozen stores were erected and as many more were purchased. The McCormicks were the largest landlords of Chicago and William might well

[79] C. A. Spring, Jr., to Nettie F. McCormick, July 29, 1862; Feb. 7, and May 23, 1863. L.P.C.B. No. 65, p. 595, the Co. to W. J. Beebe, Kankakee, Ill., Nov. 12, 1863; No. 80, p. 143, to P. Mohan, Louisville, Ky., May 20, 1865.

[80] W. S. to C. H. McCormick, Nov. 20, Dec. 11, 1862.

[81] ‡C. A. Spring, Jr., to C. H. McCormick, Feb. 22, 1865. Annual rents paid to C. H. McCormick totaled about $40,000, while $60,000 more came in from properties owned by the firm. In July of that year, C. H. McCormick's real estate in Chicago, including the factory, was valued at over $600,000, an increase of more than $200,000 since the previous summer. W. S. to C. H. McCormick, Mch. 29, 1863. Land for which the firm had paid $40,000 was renting @ $3,600 a year, while two stores on Lake St., costing $22,000, returned $2,700 a year. The heaviest purchases of city real estate were made during the winter of 1862-1863, and by Mch., 1863, the partners had invested $355,000 in this way. In September of this year, the firm had $500,000 in city property, $42,000 in farm lands, $157,311 loaned to farmers, $85,000 in gold, etc. *Idem* to *idem,* Sept. 27, 1863.

[82] *Idem* to *idem,* Feb. 15, 1863. The McCormicks distributed 100,000 circulars through their agents who "will work for & fill our Hotel with customers we think." L.P.C.B. No. 67, p. 2, W. S. McCormick to S. C. Johnson, Kenosha, Wis., Feb. 19, 1864; No. 69, p. 111, the firm made over $20,000 from the hotel during its first year of operation, W. S. to C. H. McCormick, Apr. 6, 1865. "Chicago Times," Apr. 8, 1864. In 1868, following the death of Wm. S. McCormick and the division of the properties owned jointly by the partners, this hotel passed into the possession of Leander. It was destroyed in the fire of 1871, but two years later a new Revere House was opened a half-block further north.

write to Cyrus, "We even command the respect of the Abolitionists for doing so much for the City." [83] Only the commission house of C. H. McCormick & Co. failed to yield a profit. William wished his elder brother to enable Hugh Adams to improve both his social and financial standing by being "rid of [grain] gamblers for associates" and join the "quiet, gentlemanly capitalists" engaged in the wholesale dry goods business.[84] This Cyrus refused to do, and he also declined a golden opportunity to enter a partnership with the young and able Marshall Field in the same type of enterprise.[85]

With several hundred agents in all parts of the Northwest the firm had unusual opportunity to hear of bargains in farm lands.[86] Rural real estate was expected to decline in value after the war, but William McCormick judged that it would be al-

[83] W. S. to C. H. McCormick, Dec. 13, 1863; "Chicago Times," May 8, 13, 1864. "Chicago Daily Tribune," Oct. 8, 1863, May 20 and July 21, 1864.
[84] W. S. to C. H. McCormick, Oct. 4, 1863, Feb. 28, and Dec. 14, 1864. W. S. McCormick to H. Adams, July 21, 1865; H. Adams to C. H. McCormick, Jan. 31, 1866; C. H. McCormick to H. Adams, Mch. 27, 1877. Following the war, Adams continued in the commission business but was no longer paid a salary by the reaper firm. The concern prospered (L. J. to C. H. McCormick, Jan. 10, 1866; L.P.C.B. No. 89, p. 262, C. A. Spring, Jr., to H. Adams, Apr. 14, 1866). In the winter of 1873-1874, Adams admitted his eldest son, Cyrus Hall, to the firm and its name was changed to McCormick, Adams & Co. By 1877 it was one of the largest of its kind in Chicago, and its profits for 1876 were said to have been between $65,000 and $75,000. Hugh Adams died on Mch. 10, 1880, at the age of 60, but the business was continued.
[85] *Ibid.*, No. 76, p. 383, W. S. McCormick to M. Field, Nov. 29, 1864. W. S. to C. H. McCormick, Jan. 31, Dec. 10, 14, 26, 31, 1864. W. S. advised that C. H. McCormick or the firm should put $200,000 into the venture. Field, who was a member of Farwell, Field & Co., was negotiating also with Potter Palmer. In 1865, Field and his partner, L. Z. Leiter, purchased the retail dry goods business of Palmer.
[86] L.P.C.B. No. 53, p. 16, the Co. to H. G. Grattan, Oct. 22, 1862: "We learn thru one of our agents that owners of farming lands find it very difficult to get tenants owing in a measure to the great drafts of men for the war. This is calculated to lessen the price of lands." *Ibid.*, No. 57, p. 884, W. S. McCormick to C. A. Spring, Sr., Mch. 19, 1863: "There is a great deal of land in market low, and for cash, *very* low."

most tax-exempt as long as the farmers held the whip-hand
in the state legislatures, and that at least a three per cent or
four per cent return could be counted upon annually from
rents.[87] Compared with the large purchases of city property,
the $100,000 used to buy over 11,000 acres outside of Chicago
seems quite small. These holdings were scattered through
more than fifty counties in six states of the Northwest.[88] Because of the agricultural collapse a few years after the close
of the war, this investment was probably unwise, but as late
as 1867 the firm believed that these properties were worth
over half as much again as they cost.[89]

William McCormick could truthfully assert when giving an
account of his stewardship to his brother in 1864, that no
company funds entrusted to his care had been lost and that
the profits of the firm would have been much larger if a less
cautious course had been run. To find the safest rather than
the most remunerative investment, and to divide financial risks
as much as possible, were two considerations always uppermost in his mind.[90] Buildings and land, gold, grain, pig-iron,
and wood attracted most of the McCormick money during the
Civil War and helped to place the inventor's name at the head

[87] W. S. to C. H. McCormick, Oct. 19, 1862: We can buy farms under
cultivation for $20 an acre, lease them for a rental that will return us 3%
annually on our investment, and we can probably sell them "on time" at the
close of the war for $15 an acre, the notes paying us 10% interest. Some
farm property was purchased with reaper notes. L.P.C.B. No. 52, pp. 331,
359, the Co. to S. H. Mitchell, St. Francisville, Mo., Sept. 30, 1862, and
to C. W. Battell, Paris, Ill., Oct. 1, 1862; No. 55, p. 256, to W. S. Beebe,
Kankakee, Ill., Dec. 4, 1862.

[88] Of this total, 7,318 acres were in Ill., 2,791 in Ia., 600 in Minn., 360
in Wis., 120 in Ind., and 40 in Mich. The largest county acreage was in
Rock Island and Pike Cys., Ill., where the Co. owned 1520 and 905 acres,
respectively. Ibid., No. 157, p. 807, Co. to J. Edgar, Rochester, Minn.,
May 11, 1875: We would like to sell all of our country real estate.

[89] Financial Statements of C. H. McCormick, and C. H. McCormick &
Bros., 1867. C. H. McCormick also invested $46,000 in farm lands.

[90] W. S. to C. H. McCormick, Mch. 16, 1864; Jan. 19, Mch. 1, May 31,
1865.

of the income tax list of Chicago by 1868.[91] "Buying and investing in advance of rising prices" was William McCormick's terse formula of success. Because competition kept the price of reapers at a low level while the cost of their production almost doubled, it is evident that the prosperity of at least one war-time industry was not due to the exploitation of the consumer. The McCormick Company made much money, but its history during these four years does not harmonize with the usual story of war-profiteering and industrial expansion. Shrewd investment of the funds received from reaper sales, and not large profits from those sales, explain why the partners were much richer in 1865 than they had been at the opening of the conflict.

The firm balanced its accounts on August 1 of each year, but its investments had been made in such a way that hard feeling between the three brothers was almost inevitable if the time should ever come when each must be allocated his proper share of the profits. Cyrus had not collected his moiety, and by the close of the war the company owed him over half a million dollars.[92] He believed that his two brothers had used more than their percentage of the profits for their own speculations; investments had been made contrary to his advice, and if he wished to assert his rights he could demand his due at any time in cash. But much of his portion had been used to buy real estate which could not readily be turned into money except at a loss.[93] He had complained that Leander had sub-

[91] "Chicago Evening Journal," May 28, 1869. C. H. McCormick's net income for tax purposes in 1868 was $231,667.

[92] W. S. to C. H. McCormick, Dec. 14, 1864.

[93] According to the agreement of 1859, C. H. McCormick was obliged to furnish the money needed by the firm for manufacturing machines. But his two brothers used Cyrus's share of the undivided profits as well as their own, to purchase real estate and insisted that they were entitled to a 50% interest in this property. For the sake of peace, C. H. McCormick agreed, although a strict interpretation of the contract placed him under no obligation to do so. C. A. Spring, Sr., to C. H. McCormick, Sept. 28, 1866.

jected him to "cruel treatment" by not finishing as many machines as were needed for the European market, and he further angered his youngest brother by advising him not to forget his work at the factory while he was building his new residence.[94]

When Cyrus McCormick returned from Europe in the summer of 1864, a new business agreement between the brothers was urgently needed. This was concluded in mid-November of that year. The name of the firm and the portion of the profits to be enjoyed by each brother remained unchanged, but thereafter they were associated into a true partnership and Leander and William were each obliged to furnish one-fourth of the capital. Each of these two was to receive a salary of $6,000 a year, while Cyrus was guaranteed at least $1,000 annually as well as a bonus of $25,000 from the assets of the old firm. All matters in disagreement connected with the former business were to be submitted for decision to three arbitrators. Of significance for the future were the provisions that certain patents owned by Cyrus McCormick should be purchased by the firm, and that all patents held by any one of the brothers could be used without charge by the partnership.[95]

With this contract closed and Illinois politics no longer requiring his presence in Chicago, Cyrus McCormick hurried to the seaboard to work for peace between the warring sections and to meet his wife and children upon their return from Europe.[96] He hoped that his stay might be a brief one, since he had recently purchased a residence on Michigan Avenue and

[94] L. J. to C. H. McCormick, Aug. 8 and Dec. 6, 1863.

[95] This agreement was made for a seven-year term on Nov. 18, 1864, and was to date from the first of that month. The partnership assumed all the assets and liabilities of the old firm. C. H. McCormick was to receive about $11,000 a year rent for the plant, and proportionately more if the annual production of machines exceeded 4,000. He agreed to supply all new machinery required by the factory.

[96] *Supra,* pp. 60 ff.

longed to occupy it with his family.[97] The call of business, however, once again determined his course. The Fifth Avenue Hotel in New York City was his address until November, 1866, when he purchased a near-by residence for $80,000. While living at the hotel in late 1864, his three children were stricken with scarlet fever, and the youngest, Robert Fowler, succumbed to the disease.[98]

Word now came from Chicago that William S. McCormick was again broken in health and suffering "from *nervous* headaches, *low spirits,* & general debility—about as he was some years ago." [99] Electrical treatments, a stay of almost two months at a hydropathic institute in New York, and ten days at Dr. Seely's "water cure" at Cleveland failed to bring relief. By the close of the summer his case was desperate.[100] His

[97] This was No. 128 Michigan Ave., and is often called the Burch house in the correspondence. Its fruit orchard and "grapery" especially appealed to its owner, as did the greenhouse and flowers of his Dearborn Street home, now rented to Mr. J. Lombard. ‡C. A. Spring, Jr., to C. H. McCormick, May 30, July 10, 13, Nov. 8, and Dec. 23, 1865. W. S. to C. H. McCormick, Apr. 10, 11, 1865. L.P.C.B. No. 84, p. 637, C. A. Spring, Jr., to Mr. Lombard, Oct. 9, 1865; No. 86, pp. 167, 355, C. A. Spring, Jr., to C. H. McCormick, Dec. 7, 1865. Because McCormick refused to give a year's lease, thinking he might soon return to Chicago to live, the Michigan Ave. house remained unrented until the spring of 1866.

[98] Robert McCormick was a year and three months old at the time of his death on Jan. 6, 1865. "New York Daily Tribune," Jan. 7, 1865. Letters to Nettie F. McCormick from Mary C. Shields, Jan. 3, 9, 1865; Mary Ann McCormick, Jan. 11, 1865, and Henrietta McCormick, Jan. 7, 1865. Mary Virginia McCormick was born in Chicago on May 5, 1861. The residence at 40 5th Ave. was purchased of Murray F. Smith. C. H. McCormick wrote to his friend J. D. Davidson on Mch. 18, 1867, that he found it necessary to "have a stopping place in this great centre of the country, & prospective centre of the *world.*"

[99] Mary Ann to Nettie F. McCormick, Jan. 31, 1865.

[100] W. S. to C. H. McCormick, Apr. 19, 22, 25, 28, 1865. L.P.C.B. No. 80, p. 50, C. A. Spring, Jr., to Dr. H. Brown, South Pass, Ill., May 18, 1865; No. 83, pp. 400, 564, the Co. to J. B. McCormick, Aug. 9, 1865. C. A. Spring, Sr., to C. H. McCormick, Aug. 8, 1865; Mary Shields to Nettie F. McCormick, Aug. 22, 1865; ‡B. M. Smith to W. S. McCormick, Aug. 22, 1865.

William Sanderson McCormick
From a photograph in the possession of the Nettie Fowler McCormick Biographical Association

physical condition, religious doubts, and business cares preyed upon his mind, and in late August he was taken to Jacksonville, Illinois, to live for a time in the home of Dr. Andrew McFarland, the Superintendent of the State Hospital for the Insane. Dysentery was epidemic in that town, and when Cyrus visited his brother two weeks later, he vainly urged that the patient should be brought back to Chicago.[101] Under Dr. McFarland's care, William's mental condition improved and his dyspepsia was apparently yielding to treatment. In mid-September, however, he was attacked by "dysentery of a typhoid character—very little under the control of medical measures." [102] Before the end came on the twenty-seventh, he regained his peace of mind, and with almost his last breath urged his brothers to realize the folly of money-making and to "forbear one another in love!" [103] To Cyrus McCormick the death of William was an irreparable loss.[104] Their differences of opinion were never of a personal nature and they had worked together since the reaper was in its infancy. William

[101] C. H. McCormick to Dr. A. Leyburn, Oct. 9, 1865, and to C. A. Spring, Sr., Oct. 18, 1865. C. A. Spring, Sr., to C. A. Spring, Jr., Aug. 27, 1865. Mr. Spring, Sr., attended William during his long illness. The patient's mind was intermittently clear, and he was then consulted on matters of business. He desired to go to Jacksonville because he feared "his mind may be deranged if he does not have the best of treatment." L.P.C.B. No. 83, p. 718, C. A. Spring, Jr., to Dr. H. Brown, Aug. 25, 1865. Dr. McFarland diagnosed his affliction as "softening of the brain" and believed that general paralysis would follow. No. 83, p. 879, C. A. Spring to J. B. McCormick, Sept. 2, 1865. C. H. McCormick visited his brother in Jacksonville in mid-September but was at Avon Springs, N. Y., at the time of his death and funeral. Burial was at Graceland Cemetery, Chicago, on Nov. 15, 1865.

[102] A. McFarland to C. A. Spring, Sept. 30, 1865; Mary Ann McCormick, to Nettie F. McCormick, Sept. 5, 1865. L.P.C.B. No. 84, p. 250, C. A. Spring, Jr., to L. J. McCormick, Sept. 17, 1865. #C. H. McCormick to the Editor of "The Herald," New York, Oct. 6, 1865.

[103] C. A. Spring, Sr., to C. A. Spring, Jr., Sept. 1, and 7, 1865; Letters to C. H. McCormick of Mary C. Shields, Oct. 5, 1865, and of Mary Ann McCormick, Dec. 12, 1865.

[104] C. H. McCormick to C. A. Spring, Sr., Oct. 18, 1865.

had conducted the business of the firm through the years of panic and civil war with great skill.

A new partnership arrangement between Cyrus and Leander was now necessary, and in June, 1866, they agreed to continue the interest of William's heirs in the business until 1871, or until such time prior to that date when Leander, as administrator of his deceased brother's estate and guardian of the minor heirs, should see fit to withdraw it. Cyrus was released from his obligation to furnish machinery for the factory at his own expense, and Charles A. Spring, Jr., as his representative, together with Leander, was entrusted with the general superintendence and management of the firm's business.[105] Although this contract declared that most of the old matters at issue between the partners were now passed into oblivion, the pact was concluded in an atmosphere of ill will, created mainly by disagreement over the title to certain mower patents.[106] Henceforward, William S. McCormick would be sorely missed as a peacemaker between his two brothers.

During his last illness, he had implored Cyrus and Leander

[105] MS. Agreement of June 16, 1866, between C. H. and L. J. McCormick, revising the contract of Nov. 18, 1864. C. H. McCormick furnished Leander's security, as administrator.

[106] *Post,* p. 520. C. A. Spring, Jr., to C. H. McCormick, June 18, 1866: "He [Leander] feels sore and says little. . . . I advised him to forget it and he agreed with me." Leander submitted to his brother's view of the mower patent question by Feb., 1867, but upon Cyrus's return from Europe a year later, an old issue, involving the obligation of the firm to pay for certain patents which the inventor had purchased in the later 1850's, caused a new rift. As in several other instances during his lifetime, Cyrus stood upon the spirit of, and the implied obligations in, a contract—in this case the 1859 agreement between the brothers—while Leander insisted upon an observance of its letter. The amount of money in question was about $25,000. After much bickering and many threats of suit, a compromise was reached, which was chiefly in accord with L. J. McCormick's position. C. H. to L. J. McCormick, Apr. 11, ‡Nov. 12, 1868. L. J. to C. H. McCormick, Apr. 23, 1868. ‡J. N. Jewett to C. H. McCormick, Apr. 22, June 4, July 8, and Sept. 9, 1868.

to work together in harmony, but by a strange whim of Fate the real estate investments made by him for the firm were now to lead to their further estrangement. As administrator, Leander was naturally anxious that his brother's estate should be settled as soon as possible, and he early decided that the heirs should withdraw their interest from the reaper company.[107] To effect this, the value of all the farms and city property held jointly by the partnership had to be appraised in order that an equitable division might be made. This was a tedious matter, and Cyrus McCormick, who wished both to go to Europe in 1867 and to be on hand when the apportionment was made, was annoyed by Leander's determination to press ahead with all speed.[108] The inventor doubted the wisdom of removing William's investment from a profitable business, although he realized that to do so would save much confusion in the future

[107] The judge of the Probate Court had been loath to agree that William's money should remain tied up in the reaper business. He finally acquiesced, but with the express understanding that any losses should be borne by the administrator and guardian. This probably goes far to explain why Leander, so shortly after the contract of June 16th, determined to withdraw William's interest from the firm. C. A. Spring, Jr., to C. H. McCormick, July 12, 1866. For a time in the spring of 1867, relations between Leander and Cyrus were cordial, but the statement in the text is generally true. C. H. to L. J. McCormick, Feb. 19, 1867: "I desire nothing but *peace with all men,* if that can be had on *honorable terms;* and much more especially do I desire 'peace & goodwill' toward my 'kindred according to the flesh' if that can be on *proper* terms." L. J. to C. H. McCormick, Feb. 25, 1867: "Let all differences between us be of the past from this time forward."

[108] ‡C. A. Spring, Jr., to C. H. McCormick, Oct. 31, 1866, Sept. 19 and Mch. 16, 1867. Spring agreed with Leander and believed that the division of the real estate should be made at once and that the interest of William's heirs should be taken out of the business. At the time of his death, W. S. McCormick owned fourteen houses in Chicago and several more jointly with one or another of his brothers, in addition to his one-fourth interest in the large holdings of the firm. L.P.C.B. No. 96, p. 645, C. A. Spring to C. H. McCormick, Mch. 22, 1867. C. H. McCormick was relieved to learn that even though he should be in Europe at the time the division was made, he would be allowed five years in which to file an appeal in case he deemed it to be unfair. C. H. to L. J. McCormick, Mch. 26, 1867.

and give him a dominant voice in the policy of the firm.[109] On the other hand, farm values were declining, and the partners would be unable to unload their country property as long as the slow work of arriving at a just division was in progress.[110] Even though William's share were drawn out, his estate could not be settled, for his five children were all minors and one of them would not reach her majority until 1881.[111]

The division of the firm's property was not completed until 1869.[112] Fortunately, the commissioners made the allotments so fairly that no one of the three parties in interest had just cause for complaint.[113] Thereafter, for the next twenty years, the company gradually sold its country real estate as favorable opportunities appeared. The firm of C. H. McCormick & Bro., in which Cyrus and Leander had a two-thirds and one-third interest respectively, agreed to give the heirs of William $400,000 for their share in the business.[114] This large payment, and the need for each surviving partner to invest more money in the company, called for a financial outlay which neither brother was prepared to meet. Leander was particularly embarrassed, and after trying various expedients which need not be described here, Cyrus McCormick borrowed

[109] As long as W. S. McCormick's heirs retained a share in the partnership, Leander could speak for them as well as for himself. He and his deceased brother each had a one-fourth interest. Thus his opinion was now equal in weight to that of his elder brother.

[110] L.P.C.B. No. 95, p. 565, the Co. to D. W. Fairbanks, Concord, Ill., Feb. 16, 1867.

[111] L.P.C.B. No. 161, pp. 364-365, L. J. McCormick to J. S. Waterman, Sycamore, Ill., Aug. 12, 1875.

[112] The court order for the division of the real estate was not issued until Sept., 1868. ‡C. A. Spring, Jr., to C. H. McCormick, Sept. 28, 1868. L.P.C.B. No. 105, p. 679, the Co. to Dr. H. Brown, South Pass, Ill, June 18, 1868; No. 108, C. A. Spring, Jr., to D. W. Cobb, Marshalltown, Ia., Oct. 24, 1868; C. H. McCormick to C. A. Spring, Jr., Oct. 22, 1868.

[113] ‡C. A. Spring, Jr., to C. H. McCormick, Dec. 5 and 19, 1868. C. H. McCormick to C. A. Spring, Jr., Dec. 9, 1868.

[114] ‡C. A. Spring, Jr., to C. H. McCormick, Dec. 30, 1868.

$200,000 of the Connecticut Mutual Life Insurance Co. and loaned one half of it to his brother on real estate security. The interest to be paid by Leander on this sum was soon in dispute, although for a time the relations between the partners were generally cordial.[115]

In 1867, the real estate of Cyrus McCormick, both in and outside of Chicago, was worth almost twice as much as he had paid for it. His annual income from rents was $95,000, and of this total about one-third was derived from his two principal groups of stores, known as the McCormick and Larmon Blocks. In addition to this sum, the reaper company collected each year from its own tenants over $130,000, of which the senior partner was entitled to one-half.[116] To put the matter differently, a decade after the inventor began to invest heavily in real estate, his annual rents amounted to about one-third of the profits from the sale of reapers and mowers. Thanks to the expert management of Charles A. Spring, Jr., assisted by his father during the rush of the spring leasing season, these properties demanded but little of the inventor's time and thought. Speculations at this time in mines and railroads required more of his attention but brought him a smaller return.

[115] *Idem* to *idem,* June 1 and Aug. 30, 1867; Apr. 28 and 30, 1868; Mch. 17, 19, Apr. 19, 22 and 23, 1870; May 13, June 15, Aug. 7, and 8, 1871. ‡L.P.C.B., No. 1, 2nd ser., pp. 34, 58, 82, C. H. McCormick to C. A. Spring, Jr., Apr. 20, and 28, 1870, and to the McCormick Co., Apr. 19, 1870. At this time, C. H. McCormick had advanced the firm more money than he was obliged to do under the contract. He desired to use these funds for other purposes, and called upon Leander to contribute his due share to the factory's treasury. C. H. McCormick repaid $100,000 of his loan from the Insurance Co., in July, 1871. See, *ibid.,* No. 127, p. 581, C. A. Spring, Jr., to the Conn. Mutual Life Ins. Co., Hartford, Conn., June 29, 1871. C. H. McCormick's heavy borrowings at this time were also due to his large loans to the Union Pacific Railroad Co. *Post,* p. 137.

[116] The value of McCormick's real estate in 1867 was said to be $1,347,522. This represented an investment by him of $718,479. About 7% of his rents were derived from farm lands. The firm had farm properties valued at $150,000, and about 4% of its total rents came from this source.

CHAPTER V

RAILROADS AND MINES

CYRUS McCORMICK, the conservative in politics and religion, the innovator in methods of manufacturing and harvesting, the investor in gilt-edge Chicago real estate, was also fascinated by speculative risks, offering remote chances of large profits. He relished a new financial adventure and enjoyed it as long as it was exciting and not too expensive. Participation in hazardous schemes afforded him a release from the humdrum affairs of every day. He shared the spirit of the rich and would-be rich of his generation, men who thought of progress in terms of rapid exploitation of natural resources. To subdue a continent was to confer a public benefit, and in his opinion no instrument was better adapted to achieve this end than the railroad.

In the summer of 1865 George Francis Train, "a splendid, dashing-looking fellow, with a head like Apollo's, a voice full of music, a hand with an electric thrill in its grasp," was taking a "water cure" at the Hydropathic Institute in New York City. Here Cyrus McCormick met him and was regaled with a rosy account of the Union Pacific Railroad and the Crédit Mobilier. Soon the inventor's heavy purchases of stock in both of these companies led Train to congratulate him upon his admission to the "Pacific Board of Brothers." [1]

[1] A. C. Cole, "The Irrepressible Conflict, 1850-1865" (N. Y. 1934), p. 11. U.P.R.R. Co., N. Y., to C. H. McCormick, Sept. 5, 1865. This letter makes clear that McCormick had purchased 250 shares of Crédit Mobilier stock for $50,000. See also, #Receipt of H. C. Crane, Asst. Treas. of C. M., to C. H. McCormick, Nov. 20, 1865. By the close of 1866, McCormick owned

The Credit Mobilier [continued Train], is made up of wealthy men; and owning the the [*sic*] Pacific Contract [2]—Someday will be the Grandest Financial Institution in the world. What other Banking concern ever had $100,000,000 Government Bonds and 20,-000,000 acres of Land for a Base? . . . You are just the man to be interested in the World's Highway—*Paris to Pekin in Thirty Days, by Two Ocean Ferry Boats and Continental Railway.*

Your $50,000 interest, in five years, I believe will be worth $500,000. . . .

I want you to know Gen'l Dix and Mr. Cisco—as well as your Brother Contractors. You will find Durant a live man—This is the project of his life, and he succeeds in Everything he undertakes. I hope you will try that Yacht of his before you leave the City.[3]

"To oblige two or three wealthy parties," the capital of the Crédit Mobilier was enlarged and care was taken to admit a few Democrats to its benefits, "for we have too many Republicans now." [4] On this score too, McCormick qualified, and by October he was also a director of the Union Pacific Railroad Company.[5]

Some who were prominent in this enterprise and were Crédit Mobilier stock-holders as well, were aware of still another opportunity to make large profits. With Train as its president,

945 shares of C. M. stock and 1251 shares of U. P. stock. L.P.C.B. No. 96, p. 330, C. A. Spring, Jr., to C. H. McCormick, May 12, 1867. C. H. McCormick's earliest purchase of railroad securities was in 1858 when he invested $600 in the stock of the Galena & Chicago R.R. In 1865 he also purchased 550 shares of the Chicago & Rock Island R.R.

[2] The "Pacific Contract" was the Hoxie Contract of 1864, to build about 250 miles of the railroad for over $12,000,000. The obligations and benefits of this agreement were assumed by the Crédit Mobilier Co. in the spring of 1865.

[3] ‡G. F. Train to C. H. McCormick, Aug. 28, 1865. John A. Dix was president of the U.P.R.R. Co., and John J. Cisco was treasurer. Thomas C. Durant was president of the Crédit Mobilier and vice-pres. of the Union Pacific.

[4] *Idem* to *idem*, Sept. 29, 1865.

[5] U.P.R.R. Co., N. Y., to C. H. McCormick, Oct. 5, 1865. He was also a member of the Finance Committee of the Board.

and George P. Bemis, secretary, the Crédit Foncier, or Pacific Cottage and Land Company, was organized under a charter from Nebraska Territory.[6] It was described in its prospectus as "a wheel within a wheel," and its sponsors felt no scruples in referring to its membership as a "Ring."[7] Although "entirely independent of the Pacific and Crédit Mobilier," its identity of personnel with these gave it "the advantage of knowing where Station Buildings and Towns will be built" along the railroad.[8] Profiting by their advance information, the concern planned to buy land and erect houses for the workmen along the right of way. "As towns will be started at every station on the U.P., the idea [behind the Crédit Foncier] is but in its infancy, and by reinvesting the profits every forty miles where the station is built & town started, leaving the alternate lots of land to increase in value, the man who puts down his one thousand dollars now can judge of the harvest he will reap."[9]

McCormick took his allotted share in this grandiose enterprise and was made one of the seven directors. It soon attracted to its subscription list members of Congress and well-known business men such as George M. Pullman and Ben

[6] The act of incorporation was passed on Feb. 15, 1866, over the governor's veto. The capital might be increased to $1,000,000, but at the outset it was $100,000, divided into 100 shares. "It will be a new idea in American Finance, to see a *special co-partnership* of Millionaires, where no one risks but *One Thousand Dollars,* which may indirectly represent a *Thousand Millions.*"

[7] *Prospectus* of Crédit Foncier of America, 1866. In this, the plan was said to be based on "Péreire's system" of Crédit Mobilier and Crédit Foncier, sponsored by Napoleon III, "the best statesman in Europe, and the best financier in the world." G. F. Train to C. H. McCormick, Sept. 29, 1865.

[8] *Ibid.* Each subscriber to the Crédit Mobilier stock was given the option of purchasing one share in Crédit Foncier.

[9] G. P. Bemis to C. H. McCormick, Feb. 1, 1866. In its prospectus, the Crédit Foncier group frankly stated that it proposed "to own the towns and cities at every station on the line of the Pacific Railway."

Holladay of the Overland Stage Company.[10] Except for a purchase of eighty acres of land at Omaha and the erection of a few houses there, its dream was never realized. It remains, however, an excellent illustration of the business "temper" of the times and the close tie-up between politics and private enterprise.[11]

For about five years, McCormick's investments in the Crédit Mobilier brought him a golden return. A fifty per cent dividend was declared in the summer of 1866 and by the close of 1868 profits in the form of cash and Union Pacific stocks and bonds totaled several times the amount of his subscription.[12] Crédit Mobilier stock "skyrocketed" and the company's undivided profits were then very large. This rich harvest resulted from the assignment by the Ames brothers to the Crédit Mobilier of their 1867 contract with the Union Pacific to build the line west of the 100th meridian.[13]

As a director and big stock-holder of the railroad company, McCormick was afforded the opportunity to loan it large sums of money on short term at high rates of interest. On every

[10] Other members of the Crédit Foncier were T. C. Durant, J. A. Dix, J. J. Cisco, H. S. McComb, H. Clews, Simon Cameron, P. H. Smith (vice-pres. of the N.W.R.R.), C. H. Ray (of "Chicago Tribune"), W. G. Fargo, C. A. Seward (late Asst. Secy. of State), G. T. Brown (Sergeant-At-Arms of the U.S. Senate), J. W. Forney (Secy. of the Senate), Senator S. C. Pomeroy, and the following members of the House of Representatives, W. D. Kelley, H. T. Blow, W. B. Allison, O. Ames, and R. T. Van Horn.

[11] ‡Letters to C. H. McCormick of G. P. Bemis, Nov. 1, 1866, G. F. Train, Mch. 30, 1867, and H. M. Taber, N. Y., Jan. 8, 1873.

[12] Letters to C. H. McCormick, from John Duff, Sept. 21, 1866, and S. L. M. Barlow, Jan. 7, 1868. C. H. Adams for C. H. McCormick to C. A. Spring, Jr., July 3 and Nov. 25, 1868, and Jan. 7, 1869. During 1868 McCormick received dividends of 155% from his C. M. investment and on Jan. 6, 1869, a 200% dividend. C. H. McCormick's financial balance-sheet for Jan. 1, 1869, shows his C. M. profit as $565,687.25, or almost 600% on his investment.

[13] A construction agreement was, as a rule, not made directly with the Crédit Mobilier, but with an individual who assigned it to certain stockholders of that concern.

sum advanced, he also received a brokerage fee of one or two per cent. These loans were so remunerative that he borrowed heavily from banks and insurance companies in order to be able to make them.[14] On his motion in the spring of 1867, the directors of the Union Pacific appropriated $10,000 to use in advertising its stocks and bonds in Europe in connection with the Paris Exposition and to make known "the size and importance of the U.P.Rd." He, Samuel B. Ruggles who was the Commissioner of the United States at the Fair, and John A. Dix the Ambassador of the United States to France, were appointed a committee to spend this money.[15] The inventor

[14] Thus on June 15, 1867, he wrote to his broker, S. L. M. Barlow, of N. Y.: ". . . they allow say 14½% per cent int. on so much as I have in the P.[acific] R.R. for 4 *mos* (with "commissions") *like others.*" This letter is in Room No. 400, 606 S. Michigan Ave., Chicago. Soon however, the railroad co. refused to pay more than 7% (plus 1% commission) on its loans, but McCormick continued to advance large sums ($100,000 to $200,000 at various times), especially in 1868. See, C. H. McCormick to C. A. Spring, Jr., ‡Apr. 1, ‡May 30, ‡June 8, and Oct. 22, 1868; C. A. Spring, Jr., to C. H. McCormick, Nov. 12, 1867; L.P.C.B. No. 101, p. 738, C. A. Spring, Jr., to C. H. McCormick, Oct. 29, 1867. C. H. Adams, for C. H. McCormick, to C. A. Spring, Jr., Jan. 14, 1869. In this letter it is stated that C. H. McCormick had loaned $100,000 to the U.P. and wished to double it "immediately in order to secure a large rate of interest & commission which is paid to the members of the Co. only." Although the road was not generous in issuing passes, McCormick secured several for ministers whom he wished to befriend. ‡J. Duff to C. H. McCormick, June 5, and 17, 1869; C. H. McCormick to C. A. Spring, Jr., June 28, 1869, and to J. Duff, June 10, 1869. ‡B. M. Smith, Hampden Sidney, Va., to C. H. McCormick, June 16, 1869.

[15] Letters to C. H. McCormick from Oliver Ames, Mch. 1, 1867, ‡Louis D. Combe, Paris, Jan. 5, 1868, and ‡J. A. Dix, Paris, Apr. 17, 1868. Dix wrote: "I should certainly have been very agreeable to remain at the head of the Co. until it met the Central [Pacific], but it is no doubt best as it is. I have purchased $30,000 of the first mortgage Bonds, and, of course, feel deeply interested in the prosperity of the Company." ‡C. R. Norton of Norton & Co., Bankers, Paris, to C. H. McCormick, June 9, 1868. He asked C. H. McCormick to use his influence to gain the appointment of his firm as financial agent in Europe of the U.P. He believed that he could sell $4,000,000 worth of the bonds in Europe. "These bonds would be very popular in Germany." He advised that the U.P. Co. should issue land mortgage bonds of small denomination, each to bear a coupon, which when

believed that his contribution to the enterprise was of service to the public and should be given consideration in estimating his qualifications for admittance to the French Legion of Honor.[16]

In that same year, he and John Duff of Boston were named trustees of the lands granted by the national government to the road.[17] With this property as security, ten $1,000 bonds were issued for each mile of track laid. Many of these were turned over to the Crédit Mobilier in part payment for its construction work. The two trustees were obliged to sign every bond, and McCormick wrote his name on about ten thousand of them. For this purpose he was expected to go to the Boston office of the Union Pacific Company whenever a new issue was made, but most often he required the annoyed treasurer to send the securities by special messenger to his home in New York or Richfield Springs.[18] Although he asked to be paid one dollar for every bond that he signed, the Union Pacific Company refused to agree that his autograph was so valuable, and he eventually consented to accept $5,000 in full payment for his services.[19]

detached would entitle the holder to a passage to Omaha where he might settle along the line of the road. C. H. McCormick to C. R. Norton, July 29, 1868. McCormick thought that the bonds were selling too well in the U.S., to try to market them abroad.

[16] C. H. McCormick to J. T. Griffin, Apr. 25, 1867, and to M. Chevalier, Paris, Sept. 12, 1868: "The U. Pacific is going forward very fast & the stock in *our* Crédit Mobilier in connection with it is now 4 to one advanced. . . . In fact nothing is lacking to see our great country advancing to front rank among nations, but the overthrow of the present Radical rule, wh. *I Hope* is soon to be realized. I hope Gen'l Dix is not for Grant for Pres."

[17] MS. Indenture between the U.P.R.R. Co., C. H. McCormick, and John Duff, Apr. 16, 1867. C. Tuttle to C. H. McCormick, Mch. 28, 1867.

[18] ‡Oliver Ames to C. H. McCormick, Jan. 20, 1869, and ‡J. M. S. Williams to him on June 15, 25, July 16, Aug. 20, 31, and Sept. 2, 1869: "As the mountain couldn't come to the mole hill, we must go to the mountain, with our Bonds."

[19] Letters to C. H. McCormick of ‡J. Duff, Dec. 2, 1874, S. Dillon, Jan. 8, 1876, and H. Day, ‡June 17, 1876, Mch. 31, Apr. 10, ‡May 5, and July 14, 1877; ‡F. H. Matthews to H. Day, Apr. 4, 1877. ‡L.P.C.B. No. 4, 2nd ser., p. 89, C. H. McCormick to F. H. Matthews, Nov. 25, 1877.

The directors of the Union Pacific were not a harmonious "band of brothers." Personal jealousies and differences on matters of policy served to divide them. The Durant faction wished to build the line as inexpensively as possible so as to have for its own pockets a large surplus from the government subsidies, while the Ames group believed the construction work should be done with more care, since it optimistically expected that the road would operate at a profit as soon as it was ready for use. By 1867 a *modus vivendi* had been arranged, but Oliver and Oakes Ames were in the ascendancy.[20] At this time McCormick, who had favored their position, left for a long stay abroad. On his return in the spring of 1868 he learned that he had been dropped from the board of directors. Why he was displaced is by no means clear because his relations with the Ameses remained cordial, and he was restored to the board in the following year.[21] In any event his absence in Europe was a stroke of good fortune. While there, Oakes Ames, who feared that the legality of the contract made by the Union Pacific with the Crédit Mobilier might be challenged, sold on favorable terms to certain members of Con-

[20] In Aug., 1867, the board of directors, including Durant, accepted the proposal of Oakes Ames that he should build the road west of the 100th meridian and receive his pay in the stocks and bonds of the U.P. It was known that Ames would assign to the Crédit Mobilier. Oliver Ames wrote to C. H. McCormick on Aug. 23: "I think the Dr. [Durant] found that he was getting in a position where he would be deprived of all power in the Road and is now anxious to make friends in the Board. This Contract will give a large amt. of Stock to Cr. Mobr. We are getting on Splendidly with the Road. . . . We are selling our Bonds Rapidly and our Finances are in first rate condition. . . . Your investment in the road looks as though it would pay 100 per cent this year. Our only Trouble now is with the Indians." Oliver Ames to C. H. McCormick, July 18, 1867: "Durant's Injunction don't stop us. But he is annoying us every sort of way and we want a strong body of the Stockholding Directors at our next meeting who are too honest to lend themselves to plunder."

[21] ‡J. M. S. Williams to C. H. McCormick, May 22, 1869; C. H. McCormick to J. M. S. Williams, May 24, 1869; ‡C. A. Spring, Jr., to C. H. McCormick, May 26, 1869.

gress whose friendship was desired, stock of the construction company, and thereby prepared the way for the scandal of 1872. Cyrus McCormick, at least, would have a convincing alibi.

By May, 1869, when the simple and impressive ceremony at Promontory Point in Utah marked the completion of the first transcontinental railroad, the Union Pacific Company was under heavy fire. James Fisk and others of the Wall Street crowd were convinced that as stock-holders they had not received their due share of the profits. They secured from pliable judges in New York City a court order to restrain the road from disposing of its assets, pending an investigation of its financial management.[22] At this time Cyrus McCormick was owed about $250,000 by the company and held its land grant and first mortgage bonds to the amount of $275,000 as his security. On the evening of April 26, a bailiff appeared at the door of his Fifth Avenue residence with a process designed to prevent him from disposing of these securities. Luck favored the inventor, since the paper was made out in the name of "Charles H. McCormick" and he refused to accept it. As soon as the embarrassed deputy had left, McCormick penned a hasty note to Oliver Ames, the president of the road. "A hint is said to be sufficient for the wise," he wrote, "and I concluded it better no longer to hold any of these Bonds as collaterals." He took the securities for his own in payment of his

[22] ‡J. Duff, Washington, to C. H. McCormick, Mch. 20, 1869: "I understand that the Erie Ring and the Central Pacific are working against us but I hope we shall get something that will releive [sic] us from the Judiciary of New York City." C. H. McCormick to C. A. Spring, Jr., Apr. (?), 1869: "There will be perhaps a great demand here latter part next week for money—in connection with Pa. R.R. investigation (disgraceful) by a scoundrel Fisk. I have been told to have money ready by that time, if possible, as *important* results may be secured by it. . . . Could you send me $50,000 as soon as you get this?" ‡C. A. Spring, Jr., to C. H. McCormick, Apr. 27, 1869: I borrowed the $50,000 from the Bank for you @ 8%.

loan, sending to Ames on the same evening a check for $25,-
000 and the canceled "I'O'U'S" of the Union Pacific.[23]

By this time, however, McCormick was also convinced that
the management of the company was dishonest and that he had
not received all of the profits that were rightfully his due.
"While others have got Bonds largely," he complained to its
treasurer, "I have not—nor have I yet sold a dollar of them—
not wishing like others to keep the *price down* by keeping the
market glutted, &c! H—— says B—— is $400,000 behind!
. . . We all [the Directors at yesterday's meeting] feel that
there has been large *stealing* in this business, while I have not
an *equal chance* at that." [24]

He admitted that he was "entirely *too slow* for this
game," [25] and therafter refused to loan the road as liberally
as before until the "vast whirlpool somewhere that swallows
up [money] faster than it can be supplied" was revealed.[26]

Although the company was in a very shaky financial condition, its officials deluded themselves with the belief that

[23] C. H. McCormick to Oliver Ames, Apr. 26, 1869. A. C. Rogers for
C. H. McCormick to C. A. Spring, Jr., May 1, 1869. The Fisk group
petitioned that the U.P.R.R. should be declared bankrupt, and a N.Y. judge
appointed "Boss" Tweed's son, receiver of the Co's. assets. But the officials
of the road managed to remove most of its securities and cash from the
jurisdiction of the court. The story is told in dramatic fashion by Robert H.
Fuller in his "Jubilee Jim" (N.Y., 1928), pp. 215 ff.

[24] C. H. McCormick to J. M. S. Williams, June 26, 1869. From a letter
to Williams on Aug. 3, it is evident that McCormick meant Cornelius S.
Bushnell by "B." Who "H" was, is not certain, although probably Springer
Harbaugh or Rowland Hazard. ‡Undated letter in C. H. McCormick's hand,
probably written in 1869 to J. M. S. Williams: "There is little doubt I
suppose that there has been enormous stealing in some way in connection
with the *building* of the Road! Where *has* [*sic*] all the proceeds of the
Govt & Mortgage Bonds—with the Capital of the Stockholders—gone to?
Of course you know I have not been in a position to know any thing about
the practical details of this business."

[25] C. H. McCormick to J. M. S. Williams, Aug. 3, 1869.

[26] ‡*Idem* to *idem*, Aug. 2, 1869: "$600,000 & over rec'd from Govt. again—
where all gone to?"

prosperity would return as soon as the national government placed its seal of approval upon the completed road and paid the amount due under its contract. To secure this approval, John Duff, Cornelius Bushnell, and others, exerted pressure upon prominent members of Congress.

"Wade & Conklin(g) are enthusiastic about the road," wrote Duff, "& have telegraphed Cox and the President that it is the best road they ever rode on and its equipment & buildings are Superior to any in the United States—they examined everything thoroughly & will speak understandingly— Wade says he will go to Washington & tell Grant that we have built the best road in the world & that you can ride fifty miles per hour as safely as twenty."[27]

But Congress moved slowly and Union Pacific securities steadily declined. In an effort to sustain their market value, big stock-holders of the company were urged not to unload their paper while the price was low.[28]

McCormick was willing to coöperate with his associates to this end as long as all loyally played the game, but it was patent that a few men were violating their pledges to their own profit and to his loss. In the autumn of 1870, he refused longer to stand passively by while Union Pacific stocks and bonds fell lower and lower. During the following year, he released almost $250,000 worth of this stock at sacrifice prices.[29]

[27] J. M. S. Williams to C. H. McCormick, July 10, 1869, quoting a letter written to him by J. Duff on July 5.

[28] ‡Circular Letter of the U.P.R.R. Co. to its Stock-holders, Aug. 11, 1869.

[29] C. H. McCormick to R. Welsh, July 4, 1870; ‡F. D. Cobb & Co. to C. H. McCormick, Oct. 5, 1870; ‡C. A. Spring, Jr., to C. H. McCormick, Sept. 30 and Oct. 8, 1870; C. H. McCormick to C. A. Spring, Jr., May 9, 1871. On May 8, McCormick sold 6200 shares of U.P. stock @ about 32. He had sold 500 shares in the preceding Oct. @ 27½. By 1877 he held only 11 shares. In order that his disposal of the stock might not he known, his shares were sold in the name of W. H. Taylor, an employee of his brokers.

According to his balance-sheet of August 1, 1871, his remaining shares of stock in this company and his Crédit Mobilier securities with a face value of $111,000 and $95,000 respectively, were of little value.[30] Two years later he ordered his broker to sell most of his Union Pacific bonds, and shortly thereafter he resigned as trustee of the land grant bonds.[31]

Thus McCormick's official connection with the Union Pacific Railroad Company ended in 1873, although he was still a large stock-holder in the Crédit Mobilier. Since the summer of the preceding year, the affairs of this construction company had been the talk of America. In 1868, Henry S. McComb of Wilmington, Delaware, brought suit to compel the Crédit Mobilier to deliver to him 375 shares of its stock for which he claimed to have subscribed. He charged that Oakes Ames had been given most of these securities to distribute at Washington "where they will do most good." [32] This court action reached its climax in the late summer of 1872, when the Democrats and Liberal Republicans endeavored to discredit some of the "Stalwarts" in the presidential election campaign by pointing with disgust to the revelations made in the published Ames-McComb correspondence.[33] Cyrus McCormick was directing the campaign of his party in Illinois that autumn, but if the Crédit Mobilier scandal disturbed him, at least no reference to it is found in his correspondence. He had had no part in the transactions that were under fire and his name was rarely mentioned either in the testimony given be-

[30] C. H. McCormick's Balance Sheet, Aug. 1, 1871. He also owned at this time over $73,000 of U.P. first mortgage bonds, over $163,000 of its income bonds, and about $26,000 of its land grant bonds.

[31] Lord, Day & Lord, N. Y., to C. A. Spring, Jr., Feb. 24 and 27, 1873. C. H. McCormick resigned as trustee on June 28, 1873 (#C. H. McCormick to J. Duff, June 28, 1873), but his resignation was not accepted until Oct. 15, 1873 (E. H. Rollins, Boston, to C. H. McCormick, Oct. 28, 1873).

[32] Oakes Ames to H. S. McComb, Jan. 25, 1868, printed on pp. 104-105 of J. B. Crawford, "The Crédit Mobilier of America" (Boston, 1880).

[33] "New York Sun," Sept. 4, 1872.

fore the Poland Investigation Committee of Congress or in the several monographs that have been since written on the history of the Crédit Mobilier. He was aware that the course of some of its officials had been a sinuous one, but he believed that the company had performed a great public service and that its profits had not been excessive in view of the large risks involved.[34]

The work of the Crédit Mobilier was finished in 1869 and its officials, in order to avoid paying state taxes longer than was necessary, wished to surrender its charter as soon as the McComb suit was settled.[35] Following the Panic of 1873, however, Jay Gould gained control of the Union Pacific Railroad Company and certain of its stock-holders threatened to hale the Crédit Mobilier before a court in order to compel it to return all of its "profits and Dividends." Oakes Ames was dead, but his brother, Oliver, was still a director of the railroad and hoped that there were enough Crédit Mobilier men on the board "to settle the whole matter (without suit) and release us from all future Liability." Although he admitted that if action were brought it would be "very dangerous," he believed that the Crédit Mobilier had a rightful claim against the Union Pacific for an amount of money about equal to the sum which the disgruntled railroad stock-holders expected to compel the construction company to disgorge.[36]

[34] C. H. McCormick to H. Day, July 7, 1877. Henry K. White, "The Building and Cost of the Union Pacific," in William Z. Ripley, ed., "Railway Problems" (Boston, 1907), p. 97. White, after a careful analysis of the records available, estimates that the total profit gained from building the Union Pacific was "slightly above 27½ per cent of the cost of the road. Considering the character of the undertaking and the time when it was carried through, this does not seem an immoderate profit." Interview with C. H. McCormick about Crédit Mobilier, in "Chicago Times" of May 28, 1873.

[35] ‡B. F. Ham, N. Y., to C. H. McCormick, May 6, 1872.

[36] Letters to C. H. McCormick of O. Ames, Aug. 24, 1875, June 14 and 17, 1876, F. H. Janvier, Oct. 14, 1875, and H. Day, June 21, 1876. Day reported that the Crédit Mobilier had a claim of $2,263,620.13 against the

McCormick was no longer on cordial terms with the leading spirits of the Crédit Mobilier. He had refused to contribute money to its defense in an action brought against it by the United States.[37] After resuming his residence in Chicago in 1871, he was unable to talk with big railroad men almost daily in the lobbies of the Fifth Avenue Hotel. If any more profit could be realized from his Crédit Mobilier stock he wished to have it.[38] He asked his New York friend and counsel, Henry Day, to investigate and tell him what to do. Day first advised that because of the apparent intention of the Union Pacific stock-holders to sue, "it would be discreet to be satisfied with what you have received from the C. M. & take a release from them [the U.P.] of all further claims & give up the Stock [of the Créd. Mobr.] to them." [39] The following day, however, after talking to Durant and McComb, he hastened to assure the inventor that the old Crédit Mobilier group, still owning many shares of Union Pacific stock, could probably dominate the stock-holders' meeting of the road as well as its board of directors. If this proved to be the case, not only could court action be prevented, but some of the alleged claims of the Union Pacific against the Crédit Mobilier would be shelved. Should this happen, the board of directors of the railroad would probably recognize the validity of the Crédit Mobilier's bill of about two and a half millions of dollars

U. P., and that this road had claims against the C. M. of $2,516,348.09. #MS. entitled "Arrangement, as proposed by H. S. McComb, for collection of the Union Pacific's $2,000,000 note due to the Crédit Mobilier of America."

[37] S. Dillon to C. H. McCormick, Jan 8 and #Nov. 13, 1876. #B. F. Ham, to C. H. McCormick, July 13, 1876. This suit had been won by the C. M. at a cost of $22,500 in counsel fees. #L.P.C.B., June 1876—Apr. 1878, p. 57, F. H. Matthews to H. Day, Apr. 4, 1877, C. H. McCormick did not help pay the cost of this suit because the U.P.R.R. had not compensated him for his services as trustee of the land grant bonds.

[38] H. Day to C. H. McCormick, June 21, 1876.

[39] Idem to idem, June 21, 1876.

against the road. In this event, the stock of the construction company, now worthless, could be canceled for about sixty-five per cent of its par value. To Cyrus McCormick this would mean an unexpected windfall of approximately $60,000.[40]

That the Crédit Mobilier, when on its deathbed, might be able in this way still further to "bleed" the stock-holders of the Union Pacific Railroad, was highly improbable. Most of the prominent members of the construction company, fearing the outcome if a suit were brought against them by the Union Pacific, made haste to turn in their Crédit Mobilier stock to the road and receive a release from all future claims.[41] Not so, however, Cyrus McCormick, Henry S. McComb, and Rowland G. Hazard. They met in conference in July, 1877, and decided that the Crédit Mobilier's bill against the Union Pacific could be collected.[42] By this time Day had once again changed his opinion, and was now certain that McCormick was taking a big risk. "I should not want to have you sued by Mr. Gould or any other of these gentlemen on a/c of the C. M. It would be a long, ugly & troublesome affair depending very much upon evidence under their own control." [43] Pressed from all sides by those who urged him to close this chapter of his financial career, the inventor finally yielded in December, 1877, and relinquished his 945 shares of Crédit Mobilier stock to the Union Pacific.[44]

[40] *Idem* to *idem*, June 22, 1876.

[41] Oliver Ames to C. H. McCormick, June 14 and 17, 1876. He urges C. H. to send in his Crédit Mobilier stock "& a power of Atty. to sign your name to the paper exempting you from Liability to U.P.R.R. or any Stockholder thereof on a/c of any Div'd. recd. that rightfully belonged to the U.P. I think Senator Grimes' widow of Iowa but a few days since sent in a paper of this kind with her Cr. Mobr. Stock."

[42] C. H. McCormick to R. G. Hazard, Peace Dale, R. I., Aug. 1, 1877. H. S. McComb to C. H. McCormick, Sept. 21, 1877.

[43] H. Day to C. H. McCormick, July 14 and Apr. 10, 1877. ‡L.P.C.B., June 1876—Apr. 1878, pp. 57, 59, F. H. Matthews to H. Day, Apr. 4, 1877.

[44] C. H. McCormick's long delay in surrendering this stock was due, in a measure, to his insistence that as a partial *quid pro quo* he should be com-

During the fifteen years following the Civil War, McCormick was associated as a stock-holder with several of the Union Pacific leaders already mentioned, and with John I. Blair and C. E. Vail, in building railroads in Iowa and Nebraska with the aid of government subsidies. These half-dozen enterprises stemmed back to the original Iowa Railway Construction Company in which McCormick invested $50,000 during 1866.[45] After paying in four-fifths of his subscription, the balance due was transferred to the Sioux City & Pacific Railway Company, while his dividends from the Iowa Company were in the form of bonds of the Cedar Rapids & Missouri River Railroad.[46] This is merely a sample of the confused interlocking of the securities of these lines and several others. By 1879 the farthest west strand of this tangled web was forty miles up the Elkhorn Valley from Wisner, Nebraska.[47] These roads were for the most part pushed too

pensated for his services as trustee of the land grant bonds. See, *supra*, p. 139. H. Day to C. H. McCormick, Dec. 7, 1877 and Sept. 18, 1879. Two telegrams of S. Dillon to C. H. McCormick, Dec. 14, 1877. ‡C. H. McCormick, Jr., to C. H. McCormick, Oct. 29, 1882.

[45] C. H. McCormick to J. M. Williams, Aug. 20, 1866. ‡MS. Account-book of C. H. McCormick called "Journal A" and begun in Nov., 1866, pp. 91-94. ‡C. E. Vail to C. H. McCormick, May 9, June 3, 1868, and Feb. 24, 1870. John I. Blair was a leading Presbyterian and a benefactor of Blair Academy, Lafayette College, and Princeton College.

[46] ‡J. M. Williams, Boston, to C. H. McCormick, Sept. 26, 1866, and ‡C. E. Vail to him on May 15, 1868.

[47] C. H. McCormick invested $40,000 in the Iowa Railway Contracting Co., and when this concern settled up its affairs he received $30,000 in the bonds of the Cedar Rapids & Mo. River Rwy. (a unit of Chicago & Northwestern), and 470 shares ($47,000 @ par) of its stock. In 1871, he estimated that these bonds were worth one-half of their face value. He invested $14,000 in Sioux City & Pacific Railroad Co. bonds in 1868 and also received a like amount of its stock. This Co. consolidated with the Northern Nebraska Air Line Railroad in 1869, and three years later leased the Fremont, Elkhorn & Missouri Valley R. R., in which McCormick owned 70 shares of stock. He also held $15,834 of stock in the Sioux City Railroad Contracting Co. When this concern finished building the Iowa Falls & Sioux City R.R. (a unit of the Ill. Central) this investment was transmuted into

rapidly into uninviting, treeless, and sparsely settled country.[48] Although the many stocks and bonds of these companies, owned by McCormick, had a face value of almost $150,000, their market price was far below par, and dividends were small or omitted altogether. Because of these investments he was occasionally given the opportunity to buy land along the track for two dollars an acre, but apparently he never availed himself of the privilege.[49]

The Southern Railroad Association was another enterprise of these years which brought C. H. McCormick an impressive amount of paper securities but a large ultimate loss.[50] In 1868 he, with nine other men of whom Henry S. McComb and Grenville M. Dodge are still remembered to-day, formed the Southern Railroad Association with a capital of $1,500,000. The inventor subscribed $125,000 to its stock, while McComb, the largest share-holder, risked nearly four times as

stocks and bonds of this road. Letters to C. H. McCormick from ‡C. E. Vail, June 6, 1867, July 1, 1868, and Feb. 18, 1871; ‡J. M. Williams, July 28 and 30, 1870; and ‡D. P. Kimball, Boston, Sept. 20, 1879. ‡J. I. Blair to Stock-holders, Sioux City R.R. Ctg. Co., Feb. 15, 1870. ‡L.P.C.B. No. 1, 2nd ser., p. 300, C. H. McCormick to McCormick Co., Oct. 27, 1870.

[48] ‡Circular to the Stock-holders of the Cedar Rapids and Mo. R.R. Co., the Iowa Land Co., and the Sioux City and Pacific R.R. Co., Apr. 13, 1870. These three concerns owned over 1,200,000 acres and deemed it wise to divide them into 160-acre farms and sell them as quickly as possible. They estimated that, in normal times, each farm would pay annually to the road an average of $2 an acre in freights.

[49] L.P.C.B. No. 169, p. 494, F. H. Matthews to Greenbaum Bro. & Co., N. Y., Dec. 18, 1877. H. Williams to C. H. McCormick, Feb. 10, 1873. In 1881, C. H. McCormick received $1175 in dividends on his stock in the Cedar Rapids & Mo. R.R. Co., and Iowa Land Co. See, ‡C. H. McCormick to D. P. Kimball, Boston, Apr. 28, 1881. At the time of McCormick's death in 1884, he had 80 bonds of the Cedar Rapids & Mo. R.R., Fremont, Elkhorn & Mo. Valley R.R., Iowa Falls & Sioux City R.R., and Sioux City & Pacific R.R., listed as worth $74,000. If this sum were ever realized from them, the estate received back a little more than the amount of the original investments.

[50] According to C. H. McCormick's annual financial balance-sheets of Aug. 1, 1870, and Aug. 1, 1871, he had paid in $95,871 to the S.R. Asso.

much.[51] The company leased for sixteen years the 230 miles of the Mississippi Central Railroad, and agreed to extend it north from Jackson, Tennessee, to Paducah, Kentucky, where it would connect with the Memphis & Ohio Railroad. The securities of the Mississippi Central were selling at a very low figure, and the association, in accord with its original purpose, used much of its capital to buy them in, and thus became owners of the road.[52] Title to the line carried with it the obligation of paying a debt of about a million and a third dollars to the state of Tennessee, but the associates shrewdly purchased the bonds of this commonwealth at about 50 and used them at par to discharge the obligation.[53]

Until the mid-1870's the association seemed to be prosperous, although its members had not received any dividends on their investments.[54] For $60,000 McCormick purchased 2,000 shares of stock (worth $200,000 at par) in the New Orleans, Jackson & Great Northern Railroad, of which McComb was

[51] Pamphlet entitled "The Southern Railroad Association, Articles of Association, with Minutes of a Meeting of Its Share-holders, June 25, 1868" (Wilmington, Del., 1868). By 1870, the capital stock of the Asso. had been increased to $2,000,000. McComb, Eben D. Jordan, McCormick, and H. Winthrop Gray were the largest stock-holders of the ten. McCormick was a director of the Asso. after Sept. 1, 1869. #S. H. Edgar to C. H. McCormick, Sept. 15, 1869.

[52] Pamphlet entitled "The Southern Railroad Association, Lease of the Mississippi Central Railroad. Agreement for Milan Extension, and Articles of Agreement Between the Trustees" (Wilmington, 1868). The Asso. paid $500,000 for the lease of the road. It was obligated by the terms of the lease to extend the line for twenty-one miles north from Jackson, Tenn., to Milan. The Asso. had a Tenn. charter at first but by the summer of 1870 was incorporated under the laws of Miss. #H. S. McComb to C. H. McCormick, Jan. 12, 1869. #J. B. Alexander, N. Y., to C. H. McCormick, July 28, 1870.

[53] Letters to C. H. McCormick from J. L. King, Treas. S.R.A., Feb. (?), 1870, #H. Day, Nov. 19, 1873, and #J. M. Rodney, Sept. 16, 1873.

[54] E. Norton, N. Y., to C. H. McCormick, Feb. 21, 1870. At this time the S. R. Asso. proposed to give $25,000 and 4000 shares of its stock to the Paducah & Gulf R.R. in exchange for a 4/5ths control of that road. J. L. King, to C. H. McCormick, June 5, 1871: "Due to yellow fever, floods, and our heavy expenditures for rolling stock and the paper of the Miss. Central R.R., the S. R. Asso. is bare of funds."

president. This line, together with the Mississippi Central and Illinois Central, agreed in 1871 to lay down a track from Jackson, Tennessee, to Cairo, Illinois, and thus make an unbroken rail connection between Chicago and New Orleans. To help in this project, the Illinois Central loaned the association a million dollars.[55] McCormick also, in the early 1870's, advanced large sums to the association and to the New Orleans, Jackson & Great Northern Railroad at twelve per cent interest. These were repaid when due, and since these transactions were only possible because of his large interest in both enterprises, the profits gained from them should probably be taken into account when estimating his net loss from the entire venture.[56]

One sample of the financial manipulations of the Southern Railroad Association must suffice. In 1873 it determined to retire its first mortgage bonds by levying a pro rata assessment upon its stock-holders. McCormick's share was about $66,000 and in exchange for the payment of this sum he received an equivalent value in the seven per cent gold bonds of the Mississippi Central Railroad, as well as $166,700 in income and equipment bonds of the same road.[57] In the following year he exchanged a thousand shares of the New

[55] ‡D. Lord to H. Day, Dec. 14, 1871: Because of this arrangement with the Ill. Central R.R., the S. R. Asso. is "exceedingly prosperous." ‡H. S. McComb to C. H. McCormick, Dec. 2, 1871, and May 29, 1872. L.P.C.B. No. 131, pp. 106-107, C. H. McCormick to "My dear Sir," Dec. 8, 1871. The line between Jackson and Cairo was ready for use by late 1873.

[56] ‡H. S. McComb to J. H. Day, Aug. 9, 1872. L.P.C.B. No. 137, p. 442, telegram of C. H. McCormick to H. Day, Sept. 4, 1872; No. 138, p. 346, C. A. Spring, Jr., to Lord, Day & Lord, Oct. 30, 1872. It is interesting to note that C. H. McCormick was able to make these loans totaling $125,000 at a time when he was under very heavy expenses in Chicago because of the Great Fire there; L.P.C.B. No. 141, p. 313, C. H. McCormick to H. S. McComb, May 3, 1873. ‡H. Day to C. H. McCormick, Sept. 11, 1872. Letters to C. H. McCormick from ‡J. M. Rodney, Dec. 6 and 20, 1872, ‡H. S. McComb, Dec. 26, 1872, and May 12, 1873, and ‡D. Lord, Jr., Jan. 4, 1873.

[57] ‡J. M. Rodney to C. H. McCormick, Sept. 11, 1873. L.P.C.B. No. 150, p. 445, C. H. McCormick to Lord, Day & Lord, May 25, 1874. W. Calhoun, N. Y., to C. H. McCormick, May 23, 1874 and Sept. 17, 1875.

Orleans, Jackson & Great Northern Railroad stock, which had cost him $30,000, for one thousand more Mississippi Central income and equipment bonds worth $75,000 at par. Thus, by 1874, from an investment of about $222,000 he held railroad paper of over $400,000 face value, not including the worth, whatever it might be, of his 1667 shares of Southern Railroad Association stock.[58] All in all, this was McCormick's largest venture outside of his reaper factory and Chicago real estate.

By now, the New Orleans, Jackson & Great Northern Railroad and the Mississippi Central had consolidated, and the northern extension, making contact with the Illinois Central, had been completed. The Southern Railroad Association had more than doubled its length of track, but each mile represented $37,000 of debt.[59] Although this load was not unusually large, it could not be carried since the freight and passenger traffic on the road did not come up to expectations. The Mississippi Central was bankrupt by 1877, and in the reorganization which followed McCormick was obliged to exchange the seven per cent gold bonds of this road as well as his stock in the New Orleans, Jackson & Great Northern, for bonds and stock in the new company which rose upon the

[58] For his 1667 shares of S. R. Asso. stock, McCormick between 1868 and 1873 paid in various assessments totaling $162,551. The $66,000 mentioned in this paragraph was the last of these. To this total should be added the $60,000 paid for 2,000 shares of N.O., J., & G.N. stock. For these payments, McCormick owned by 1874,—$308,380 in Miss. Central R.R. bonds, 1000 shares in N. O., J. & G. N. stock (par value $100,000) and 1667 shares of S. R. Asso. stock. Letters in L.P.C.B. No. 151, pp. 590-591, W. J. Hanna to H. Day, June 22, 1874, and pp. 668-671, to J. S. McComb, June 25, 1874; No. 152, p. 29, C. H. McCormick to Lord, Day & Lord, June 29, 1874 and pp. 461-462, W. J. Hanna to H. Day, July 8, 1874; No. 168, p. 296, F. H. Matthews to C. H. McCormick, Sept. 23, 1876. ‡H. Day to C. H. McCormick, July 28, 1874.

[59] H. S. McComb to C. H. McCormick, June 30, 1874. W. Calhoun to C. H. McCormick, Sept. 17, 1875. The consolidated road was 560 miles long.

ruins.[60] His large holding of Mississippi Central income and
equipment bonds was written off as a total loss. As soon as the
market was favorable, McCormick unloaded his new securities
for about $126,000.[61] This was in 1882, and he still had the
Southern Railroad Association stock to salvage.

Since 1877 he had considered this to be worthless, but some
of the share-holders of the association believed that Henry S.
McComb had mismanaged its affairs and that an investigation
would probably reveal some hidden assets.[62] McComb died in
1882, and his widow, left with the tangled residue of her husband's Crédit Mobilier and Southern Railroad Association
interests, employed Wayne McVeagh as her counsel. Faced
by the prospect of a long and probably embarrassing suit by
several of the association's share-holders, she wrote to Mc-
Cormick: "I wish to be at peace over my husband's name and
grave, and not to renew the misery, nor perpetuate the memory, of what was to him the most disastrous of all his enterprises." [63] To settle the matter forever she offered to buy the
inventor's shares in the association for $7.50 a share. He tried
for several months to induce her to give $10, but eventually

[60] W. H. Osborn to H. Day, Aug. 7, 1877; Stuyvesant Fish, Ill. Central
R.R. Co., to C. H. McCormick, Oct. 3, 1877. The new railroad company
was known as the Chicago, St. Louis & New Orleans. It was virtually
owned by the Ill. Central. McCormick was assessed $1320 at the time this
reorganization took place. C. H. McCormick to H. Day, Aug. 16, 1877 and
‡Jan. 8, 1881.

[61] L.P.C.B. No. 221, p. 394, C. H. McCormick to H. L. Horton & Co.,
Mch. 2, 1882, ‡W. R. Selleck to C. H. McCormick, Jr., Sept. 20, 1882.
‡C. H. McCormick, Jr., to C. H. McCormick, May 13, 1882.

[62] H. Day to C. H. McCormick, ‡Sept. 11, 1879, Dec. 14, 1880, and Apr.
26, 1883. ‡C. H. McCormick to H. Day, Nov. 23, 1875.

[63] ‡Elizabeth P. McComb to "My dear Sir," Oct. 22, 1883: "My compensation will be in the peace and satisfaction which all who have ever been
concerned in protracted and bitter litigation must have learned to appreciate." ‡A. P. Whitehead and M. Storey to the President and Directors
of the S. R.R. Asso., Oct. 9, 1883. Circular Letter of Whitehead and Storey
to the Stock-holders of the S. R. Asso., Oct. 10, 1883.

accepted her original offer.[64] If the sum of about $12,500 received for this stock is added to the $126,000 realized from the sale of securities in 1882, McCormick's net loss from the Southern Railroad Association was about $85,000.

To aid his native state recover from the effects of the Civil War, McCormick accepted a directorship in the Virginia International Land, Loan & Trust Company. This firm was closely affiliated with the Norfolk & Great Western Railroad. Although it was organized for profit, its members also desired to confer benefit upon their commonwealth by promoting viticulture and the sugarbeet industry there, to encourage immigration to their lands along the railroad, and to make clear to the outside world that the Old Dominion was a safe place in which to invest capital. This praiseworthy program was never carried out, and the company dissolved in 1870 after less than two years of life.[65]

[64] H. Day to C. H. McCormick, Dec. 28, 1883, and Jan. 5, 1884. #Telegram of C. H. McCormick to H. Day, Nov. 6, 1883. #C. H. McCormick, Jr., to C. H. McCormick, Nov. 1, 5, and Dec. 1, 1883. C. H. McCormick received $12,386 from Mrs. McComb on Jan. 29, 1884.

[65] "Minutes" of the Directors of the Va. International Land Co., Oct. 13, 1869. #Act of Incorporation of the Va. International Land, Loan & Trust Co., Mch. 23, 1870. By its charter it was permitted to increase its capital to $1,000,000 and to lay out towns, but by 1880 it should not own over 10,000 acres in any one county, or more than 1000 acres after 1900. J. McKaye was its president in 1870, J. D. Imboden, vice-president, and R. H. Maury, its treasurer. #Maj. Gen'l. Sam Jones, C.S.A., Amelia Cy., Va., Feb. 28, 1870, to C. H. McCormick. He applied for the position of land agent for the Co. and added: "My brother, the Chief Engineer of that Road (Norfolk & Great Western), could give me valuable information in regard to the Country through which the road will pass, which would enable me to purchase or sell to advantage." #E. DeLeon, N. Y., to C. H. McCormick, Nov. 3, 1870. At this time, C. H. McCormick was also interested in W. Va. coal lands and secured an option from R. H. Maury to buy over 40,000 acres on Gauley Creek and elsewhere in that state. McCormick then sent a mining engineer to estimate the value of this property, as well as the holding near Lewisburg of Jas. G. Paxton of Lexington, Va. Mainly because of the inaccessibility of the Maury lands the report was unfavorable, and McCormick thereupon waived his option. #Letters of J. D. Imboden, Richmond, Va., to C. H. McCormick, Oct. 20, Nov. 22, and Dec. 28, 1869, Feb. 4,

Later in this decade the Shenandoah Valley Railroad and
the James River Valley Railroad (the Richmond & Allegheny)
were rivals for the financial favor of C. H. McCormick, each
basing its claim for assistance upon the plea that its track
would rest upon the soil of his native county of Rockbridge.
Somewhat to the annoyance of the "Lexington Gazette and
Citizen," McCormick was made a director and bought the
stock of the Richmond & Allegheny.[66] This company hoped to
tap the coal lands of West Virginia and by a tie-up with Ohio
railroads eventually to complete a short "sea level" line from
Chicago to tidewater.[67] Control was secured of the old James
River and Kanawha County Canal, one of George Washington's favorite projects, and much dependence was placed upon
James G. Blaine to give assistance over any political hurdles
that might bar its way.[68] By the autumn of 1880, when the
first train was ready to move along its tracks, C. H. Mc-
Cormick, Jr., had also invested in its stocks and bonds.[69] Due

and Mch. 2, 1870. ‡Letters of C. E. Detmold, R. P. Rothwell, and J. G.
Paxton to C. H. McCormick and to each other, dating between Apr. 18.
1870 and Mch. 17, 1871.
   [66] "The Lexington Gazette and Citizen," Feb. 15, 1878. ‡Letters to C. H.
McCormick from T. F. Randolph, Washington, D. C., June 19, July 19 and
29, 1879; J. S. Wells, Dec. 12, 1879; E. R. Leland, Dec. 13, 1880; H. C.
Parsons, Dec. 24, 1879, and Jan. 18, 1880. ‡C. H. McCormick to E. R.
Leland, N. Y., Dec. 21, 1880. Parsons, who was a good friend of Mc-
Cormick, was the vice-president of the road. Hugh McCulloch and W. L.
Scott were also directors.
   [67] ‡H. C. Parsons to C. H. McCormick, Jan. 25, 1880, and Feb. 19, 1881,
and to C. H. McCormick, Jr., Mch. 20, 1881. C. H. McCormick was also a
member of the Richmond & Allegheny Coal and Iron Co., formed to buy
mineral properties along the R. & A. R.R. track. Its leading spirits were
directors of this road.
   [68] ‡H. C. Parsons's telegram to C. H. McCormick of Feb. 4, and letters
of Feb. 10, 21, Mch. 8, and 18, 1880, Mch. 4, 1881, and May 27, 1882.
‡Telegram of C. H. McCormick to H. C. Parsons, Mch. 5, 1880. ‡H. C.
Parsons to C. H. McCormick, Jr., Nov. 23, 1881. ‡C. C. Copeland to C. H.
McCormick, Jr., June 1, 1882.
   [69] ‡H. C. Parsons to C. H. McCormick, Jr., Sept. 1, 1880, and May 1,
1881, and telegram of Nov. 9, 1880. ‡G. MacNeill to C. H. McCormick, Jr.,
Nov. 6, 1882. ‡C. H. McCormick, Jr., to H. C. Parsons, Nov. 26, 1881.

to inefficient management, so it was said, the road failed to secure profitable connections with West Virginian and northwestern lines.[70] The second mortgage bond-holders forced the company into the hands of a receiver, and for several years thereafter the McCormicks gained no return from their investments.[71]

Soon after the close of the Civil War McCormick became interested in promoting closer communications between the United States and foreign countries, both because of the possibilities afforded in this field for profitable investments, and because he desired to foster international friendships and business. When he was in France in 1867 he talked with Michel Chevalier and Ferdinand de Lesseps about an isthmian canal across Nicaragua or Panama, and also expressed the wish that with the aid of the governments of France and the United States a transatlantic cable could be laid which would connect with telegraph lines in America not controlled by the monopolistic Great Western Union Telegraph Company.[72] This latter

[70] ‡H. C. Parsons to C. H. McCormick, Jr., Mch. 20, 1881. ‡C. A. Brice to F. O. French, July 27, 1882. In late 1881 a pool was being formed to raise $425,000 and secure control of the Scioto Valley R.R. in Ohio. J. G. Blaine, H. C. Parsons, and C. H. McCormick were prominent in this effort. On ‡Apr. 20, 1882, C. H. McCormick, Jr., wrote to his mother that profits from Richmond & Allegheny might conservatively be estimated at $100,000.

[71] ‡Telegram of H. C. Parsons to C. H. McCormick, Jr., June 25, 1883. ‡Letters of G. MacNeill to C. H. McCormick, Jr., June 26, 28, July 7, Sept. 8, 1883, Jan. 22 and July 1, 1884. G. MacNeill to C. H. McCormick, Jr., Mch. 19, 1887. The McCormicks had bought a goodly block of the stocks and bonds of the Ohio Central R.R. at the time when its junction with the Richmond & Allegheny seemed assured. Its securities were also at low ebb by 1884. Among C. H. McCormick's assets at the time of his death were stocks and bonds of the Ohio Central of a face value of $37,000 and stock of the Richmond & Allegheny R.R. of a face value of $40,000. He then owned also $100,000 worth of Canada Southern R.R. bonds and an equal amount of the bonds of the Pennsylvania R.R.

[72] M. Chevalier to C. H. McCormick, Mch. 12, 1868. Chevalier, economist and engineer, had published several volumes twenty-five years before on life in the U.S., and had written a treatise on the isthmian canal problem. Chevalier was confident that Napoleon III, who was anxious to promote

hope was soon in large measure gratified, and McCormick for several years was a director and member of the Executive Committee of the Atlantic & Pacific Telegraph Company. John Duff was its president, and in other ways also it was quite closely affiliated with the Union Pacific Railroad.[73]

Of a similar nature was McCormick's connection with the Mississippi Valley Society mentioned elsewhere in this narrative. In 1879 he was made a director of the "American Exchange in Europe, Ltd.," formed by Henry F. Gillig and Senator Joseph R. Hawley of Connecticut for the purpose of engaging in an international express, banking, and shipping business, and extending aid to tourists and immigrants.[74]

Franco-American friendship, would at least lend his moral support to a company formed by the capitalists of both countries to build an isthmian canal. C. H. McCormick to M. Chevalier, Sept. 12, 1868, and to C. C. Copeland, Feb. 16, 1869. When in France, McCormick instructed Copeland to see Chevalier and learn his plans for a canal across the Isthmus of Darien. ‡C. Butler to C. H. McCormick, Feb. 26, 1869. De Lesseps visited McCormick in Chicago in March, 1881.

[73] L.P.C.B. No. 119, p. 72, W. J. Hanna to C. H. McCormick, Apr. 7, 1870. ‡C. A. Spring, Jr., to C. H. McCormick, Apr. 25 and May 13, 1870. These letters show that McCormick was entitled to send messages *gratis* over the Atlantic & Pacific Telegraph Company's wires. A pass made out in his name was given to C. A. Spring, Jr., so McCormick could at the same time wire from both Chicago and New York without charge. Up to 1875 he received but one dividend on his stock and he resigned as director in Mch., 1871. In 1882, he invested $25,000 in the stock of the Postal Telegraph Co. ‡Letters to C. H. McCormick of the Atlantic & Pacific Telegraph Co., Mch. 11, 1871, of A. Nelson, July 19, 1872, and of C. H. McCormick, Jr., Aug. 26, 1882. ‡C. H. McCormick to C. H. McCormick, Jr., Aug. 28, 1882.

[74] *Post*, pp. 595 to 600. Senator Hawley had also been the president of the U.S. Centennial Exhibition at Phila. in 1876 and governor of Conn. The Exchange had a "Bureau of Emigration and Travel," which sold tourist guide-books and advertised that it would furnish without charge reliable information about the U.S. It was the sales agent for 5,000,000 acres of improved and unimproved farm lands in the U.S. It issued traveler's checks which were honored by over 1100 banks of the U.S. and Europe. A house and apartment renting-bureau for travelers was another of its services. One of its aims was to overcome in Europe the distrust for American investments aroused by the Panic of 1873. See, Pamphlet, Olive

He who desires to export horses or import cattle [ran its prospectus in 1881], to place his last painting before the eyes of an American millionaire, or to secure a Yankee patent for his latest toy; he who wishes to assure himself whether mining stocks in Arizona are what they are represented, and he who desires to be certain that he is buying a pure article of Bordeaux wine, may apply with confidence to the "American Exchange in Paris." [75]

For several years gratifying dividends were paid to its stock-holders, including Cyrus McCormick, but by 1890 this pioneer enterprise of its kind had succumbed to the competition of more efficiently managed rival concerns which its early success had called into being.[76]

In 1869, Cyrus McCormick and nine others bore the cost of a survey of the mineral resources of Santo Domingo with the hope that President Grant's interest in that negro republic would soon lead to its annexation by the United States. Helped by McCormick's contribution of about $6,400, title to a large tract of land was secured, but Grant was unable to convince the Senate that the acquisition of non-contiguous territory was desirable, and the ten associates lost almost the entire amount of their investment.[77]

Logan, "The American Abroad" (undated and no place of publication stated), and "The American Settler" (London), Apr. 30, 1881, p. 32.

[75] #"Circular No. 1, November 15, 1881. American Exchange in Paris, Ltd." (Paris, 1881), pp. 6-7.

[76] Between 1879 and 1881, McCormick invested $10,000 in this company. Its capitalization by 1884 was $5,000,000 and its central office was in London. #Letters to C. H. McCormick of W. C. Boone, N. Y., July 2, 1881, and of H. F. Gillig, July 29, Dec. 19, 1881, Nov. 2, 1882, and Apr. 5, 1884. C. H. McCormick to #M. Field et al, Mch. 25, 1881, and to the Merchants' Loan and Trust Co., Chicago, June 7, 1883. #Sullivan and Cromwell, N. Y., to C. H. McCormick, Mch. 14, 1884. C. H. McCormick, Jr., MSS., Book "C," p. 31, Nettie F. to C. H. McCormick, Jr., Apr. 24, 1890.

[77] A. C. Rogers for C. H. McCormick, to C. A. Spring, Jr., Feb. 20, 1869. If the result of the survey is an encouraging one, a company with $100,000 capital will be formed "to obtain possession of about ½ the whole mineral wealth of that country." #C. H. McCormick to S. L. M. Barlow, Apr. 9. 1874. #Letters of S. L. M. Barlow to C. H. McCormick, Aug. 8, Dec.

At about this same time McCormick, Anson Bangs, Jesse Hoyt, and several others endeavored to persuade Congress to subsidize with land and federal bonds a company which would undertake the building of a railroad through Mexico to the Pacific Ocean, with a branch to Mexico City. The Union Pacific scandals, however, soon blasted all hope that the United States would aid in financing another transcontinental line.[78]

As the decade of the 1870's neared its close, Edward Learned of Boston, and George S. Coe, the president of the American Exchange National Bank of New York City, secured a favorable concession from Mexico for the Tehuantepec Inter-Ocean Railroad Company to lay a track and telegraph line from the Gulf of Mexico to the Pacific.[79] The company purchased steel rails in England, yellow pine sleepers in Florida, a river-boat called the *Brazil,* and began work on the road-bed before the close of the year. McCormick invested $5,000 in its stock and $50,000 in its bonds.[80] Suits brought against it by those whose earlier concessions for railroad building across the Isthmus of Tehuantepec had been annulled by

20, 1870, and Apr. 13, 1874. That this group kept in touch with the administration is evident from Barlow's word of Dec. 20, 1870: "But Genl. Grant thinks & so does Genl. Butler that annexation in some form will be consummated this winter." In 1874, Barlow was disappointed that the rival Samana Bay Co. refused to merge its interests with theirs. He was still hopeful that some return could be had from their investments.

[78] Letters of C. H. McCormick to A. Bangs, Aug. 10 and Sept. 4, 1868: If you can get a bill through Congress granting your proposed company a subsidy similar to that awarded to the U.P.R.R., I will take a 1/10th interest in the project. ‡Letters of A. Bangs to C. H. McCormick, June 22, July 30, Aug. 4, 6, 23, and Sept. 15, 1868.

[79] ‡Pamphlet, Alex. D. Anderson, "The Tehuantepec Inter-Ocean Railroad" (N. Y., 1880). The Mexican concession was granted to Learned on June 2, 1879, and the company was chartered under the laws of Mass. on Nov. 18, 1879.

[80] ‡E. Learned to C. H. McCormick, Oct. 24, 1879, Mch. 18, May 17, and June 11, 1880. ‡C. H. McCormick to C. C. Copeland, Nov. 28, 1879, and to E. Learned, Feb. 25, 1881. About $150,000 was subscribed for the stock of this company by Chicago men. C. H. McCormick owned a 1/40th interest.

Mexico, were unsuccessful but costly. Labor troubles and much sickness among its employees in Mexico were other items in its long list of misfortunes.[81] By the close of 1881 the company had completed twenty miles of its track and had started work on about as many more, at a cost of approximately $1,500,000. Funds were almost exhausted and the rate of progress had been slower than the terms of its grant from the Mexican government required. After officials from Mexico City inspected the work in the summer of 1882, the government declared the concession void.[82]

The stock of the company was now of little value but the bond-holders, including Cyrus McCormick, at once organized for their own protection and complained to the Mexican Minister at Washington that the action of his government had been an arbitrary one.[83] C. C. Copeland, whom McCormick sent to New York to represent him in the matter, was soon employed by all of the bond-holders at $100 a day to speak for their interests. He knew no Spanish, but he had abundant energy and a ready wit. He approached other American firms with investments south of the Rio Grande urging them to use their influence at Mexico City to secure the reinstatement of the Tehuantepec grant, since if they quietly acquiesced in this unwarranted confiscation, their own properties doubtless would be endangered.[84] The Secretary of State and Minister of

[81] ‡E. Learned to C. H. McCormick, Dec. 16, 1880.
[82] ‡C. H. McCormick, Jr., to C. H. McCormick, June 8, July 31, and Aug. 29, 1882. ‡E. Learned to "Dear Sir," June 21, 1882.
[83] ‡Protest of the 1st Mortgage Bondholders of the T.I-O.R. Co. to His Excellency, C. Romero, Washington, D. C., Aug. 25, 1882.
[84] ‡C. H. McCormick, Jr., to C. H. McCormick, Aug. 4, Oct. 10, 29, 1882. ‡C. C. Copeland to C. H. McCormick, Sept. 26, 30 and Oct. 14, 1882: "I propose to try first all amicable persuasion, then liberal retainers and finally U.S. Governmental interference." On ‡Oct. 25, 1882, he wrote to C. H. McCormick: "It may end in an inside arrangement between a few bond-holders to wreck the whole thing and save themselves by buying it in. I have told them to consider you in on such an arrangement."

International Affairs of Mexico, however, in an unofficial opinion declared that the Tehuantepec bond-holders had no valid claim against his government but must look to the company for redress. He was gracious enough to suggest that Mexico would pay a fair sum for the equipment and machinery along its former right of way.[85] This assurance, of course, by no means satisfied the bond-holders, but Coe believed that all would be well if a reorganized company admitted a few influential Mexicans to its membership. In other words, he interpreted the action of the Mexican government to be inspired solely by the desire of some of its officials to line their pockets.[86] Neither Coe nor Henry Day, another large bondholder, had faith in Copeland's ability to handle the matter delicately at Mexico City.[87] He was replaced by George Tyng, who arranged with Pacheco in December, 1882, that within fifteen months the Mexican government would pay the company for all of its property, $125,000 in Mexican money and $1,500,000 in gold.[88] This sum was considerably less than

[85] ‡Carlos Pacheco, Mexico City, to A. Stickney, N. Y., Sept. 30, 1882: In my opinion, the President of Mexico, "can and will not admit any manifestation that tends to question the legitimacy and equity of his acts." By the terms of the concession, the members of the company agreed that they "*shall be considered Mexicans*" and "shall in no case be entitled to plead the rights of foreigners." ‡E. Learned to C. H. McCormick, Nov. 1, 1882. In this, Learned assured McCormick that Pacheco's letter was "an excellent specimen of diplomatic adroitness . . . but has no other significance."

[86] ‡G. S. Coe to C. C. Copeland, Oct. 6, 1882: "If we can create an interest there [in Mexico] whose self seeking will inure to the general good, we might secure favorable concessions as well as protection to the enterprise afterwards."

[87] C. C. Copeland for services rendered to the Co. between Oct. 28 and Nov. 7, 1882, received over $2800. He went as far on his road to Mexico City as Galveston, but there resigned because he refused to share his mission with another agent of the Co. ‡G. S. Coe to C. H. McCormick, Jr., Nov. 4, 1882. ‡C. C. Copeland to C. H. McCormick, Oct. 14, 1882.

[88] ‡G. S. Coe to C. H. McCormick, Jr., Dec. 2, 1882, Tyng left for Mexico City, on Nov. 23. ‡Memo of a Conversation between G. Tyng and C. Pacheco, Dec. 20, 1882.

enough to cancel the bonds and stock at par, but because it was clear that there was no alternative, the offer was accepted. Each bond-holder and stock-holder was obliged to strike off fifty per cent from the face value of his securities.[89]

Since very little of the $125,000 ever reached the New York office of the company, some of its members hinted that Mexico had paid Tyng that amount to sell out his employers.[90] Tyng's defense left much to the imagination of his reader:

Perhaps I did [get some of the $125,000] but in that case it would not show in the documents. After paying blackmail, expenses and debts of the Co. [in Mexico] there may be a little of that money left, but it is doubtful. . . . I for a while believed that $25,000 was going quietly into the Treasury Dept. That was a mistake, it went elsewhere. . . . I'll send your Treasurer vouchers for a large part of the $125,000. . . . Decorum has compelled me to refuse very fair offers from the Govt. of employment on the Isthmus but in decency I shall have to help them get their work started there. . . . The Govt. knew all about your unwillingness to fight and your anxiety to get out, & took full advantage of it. But you get more this way than though you had gone to court.[91]

By 1884 Mexico was $900,000 in arrears in her payments of the $1,500,000 in gold.[92] Not until the summer of 1888 did

[89] ‡Telegram of A. S. Barnes, G. S. Coe, and E. Learned to C. H. McCormick, Dec. 18, 1882. ‡Telegram of C. H. McCormick to these men, Dec. 20, 1882. ‡C. H. McCormick, Jr., to C. H. McCormick, May 2, 1883. ‡E. Learned to C. H. McCormick, Dec. 23, 1882. Learned believed that the Mexican government had given the company such a short time to accept or reject the proposal with the hope that it would be impossible to obtain the sense of all concerned, before the expiration date. Then Mexico could say that her offer had been spurned. But if this were the intent, it was not successful, since the bond-holders and stock-holders were quickly canvassed by telegram.

[90] ‡G. S. Coe to C. H. McCormick, Jan. 25, 1883. Coe defended Tyng and believed that he had acted with "scrupulous integrity." "We were entirely in the hands of the men in Mexico who commanded the situation for their own benefit."

[91] ‡G. Tyng, Vera Cruz, to E. Learned, Dec. 26, 1882.

[92] ‡Letters of C. Romero to W. A. Booth, Apr. 24, Sept. 19, and Dec. 20, 1883, and to G. S. Coe, Aug. 18, 1883, and Jan. 17, 1884. ‡G. S. Coe

she finally carry out in full the terms of her agreement of six years before.[93]

The craze for mines and mining stocks, so characteristic of the last half of the nineteenth century, in some measure reflected the first gratification of a desire that had been thwarted since the earliest English pioneers came to America. As one after another rich, or allegedly rich, gold-, silver- or copper-bearing region was discovered, many hard-headed business men were lured to exchange their government bonds for the securities of a mining company. To own a gold or silver lode in the Far West lent an air of distinction that could not be gained by trading in railroads and industrials.[94]

Cyrus McCormick's liking for a hazardous game, which led him to make his first purchases of mining stocks, soon changed to a dogged seriousness unaffected by the persistent warning of his friends that he was bound to lose. Being Cyrus McCormick, he could not have acted otherwise, but speculations originally intended to add variety and spice to his many business interests, became vexatious problems to a man already overburdened with them. Stubbornness in continuing to sink money in mines of doubtful value made the final balance-sheet show a heavy loss.

With Jesse Hoyt and others, he was a director of the Schoolcraft Copper Mining Company. Its land adjoined the

to C. H. McCormick, Jr., June 16 and July 12, 1883. ‡W. A. Booth to C. Romero, Sept. 18, 1882, Dec. 19, 1883, and Feb. 18, 1884. ‡G. S. Coe to C. Romero, Oct. 25, 1883, and Jan. 15, 1884. ‡C. H. McCormick, Jr.'s telegram and letter to C. H. McCormick, Apr. 11, and May 2, 1883, respectively.

93 The Tehuantepec Inter-Ocean R. R. Co., N. Y., to the Estate of C. H. McCormick, July 26, 1888.

94 With one unimportant exception, McCormick took no part in the oil stock speculations of his day. In 1866 he invested $3,000 in the stock of the Steam and Vacuum Oil Refining Co., and this netted him a profit of over $20,000 within two years. He declined to invest in Lake Superior iron lands, and probably lost an opportunity for large profits when he refused to purchase the steel-making patents of Henry Bessemer of England. See, ‡Baldwin & Collier to C. H. McCormick, June 25, 1868.

rich Calumet and Hecla properties in Michigan. Year after year he dreamed that his investment of about $38,000 would bring him a large profit.[95] The company spent much money in developing its holdings but was never able to sell its ore for enough to keep clear of debt.

Jesse Hoyt and he were also associated in another abortive and rather costly mining venture. They, with several associates, formed the Montana Mineral Land & Mining Company for the purpose of developing property near Bannock, said to be rich in gold and silver.[96] McCormick risked about $63,000 in this enterprise between 1866 and 1873, and with the exception of a large number of impressive-looking bonds and shares of stock, still preserved to-day, he apparently received nothing in return for his money.[97] After a successful

[95] C. H. McCormick purchased 1250 shares in this Co. in Mch. 1867. Its total capitalization was $500,000, divided into 20,000 shares. It was forced into bankruptcy in 1873 but was later reorganized. C. H. McCormick did not know of this until 1876! ‡J. Hoyt to C. H. McCormick, Mch. 19, 1872. L.P.C.B. No. 132, p. 583, C. H. McCormick to J. Hoyt, Mch. 8, and ‡Apr. 29, 1872. ‡C. H. McCormick to S. L. Smith, May 25, and July 25, 1876. S. L. Smith, Lansing, Mich. to C. H. McCormick, ‡Dec. 15, 1876, and Jan. 29, 1877. Smith believed that since there was a European war in prospect: "our interests are looking up and with it [the war] in active force we shall see tremendous advances in copper & copper shares." He hoped that C. H. McCormick would contribute $10,000 so that a deeper shaft could be sunk at the mine. McCormick probably did not do so, although the records are silent.

[96] L.P.C.B. No. 94, p. 189, C. A. Spring, Jr., to C. H. McCormick, Dec. 11, 1866. ‡C. A. Spring, Jr., to C. H. McCormick, Feb. 4, and July 2, 1867. ‡C. H. McCormick, Journal "A," Nov. 8, 1865 ff. ‡E. Fowler, N. Y., to C. H. McCormick, May 16, 17, 18 and July 28, 1866. H. A. Boardman, Jr., for C. H. McCormick, to C. A. Spring, Jr., Apr. 9, 1867. With McCormick and Hoyt were associated Anson Bangs and S. L. Smith. The property of the Co. was known as the "Black Hawk Vein," the "Wide West," and "Blue Wing" mines. A. Bangs, N. Y., to C. H. McCormick, July 28, 1871. McCormick and Hoyt each had a ⅓ interest. ‡L.P.C.B. No. 3, new ser., p. 49, C. H. McCormick to C. C. Douglass, June 14, 1872: We have too much procrastinated about our Montana mines.

[97] L.P.C.B. No. 132, p. 583, C. H. McCormick to J. Hoyt, Mch. 8, 1872: "Can't something be done now in Montana!" Ibid., No. 132, p. 817, C. H.

lawsuit had insured to the partners a clear title to their property, they were unable to find an honest and competent manager, their holdings were inaccessible, they invested too heavily in machinery, and they failed to pay the taxes levied by the Territory.[98]

The venture of this kind which deserves the most emphasis because of the amount of money and time lavished upon it by McCormick, was the Dorn Mine in western South Carolina near the Georgia border. Now and again gold had been found in paying quantities in the mountain country south of Virginia. A government branch mint at Dahlonega, Georgia, established in President Jackson's day, was evidence of the Treasury's reliance at that time upon this area to supply gold for coinage purposes. Among the landowners who had the good fortune to discover this metal on their property was D. B. Dorn of Abbeville County, South Carolina. By means of surface work-

McCormick to J. Hoyt, Mch. 21, 1872: "Our children may one day be able to go out on the *N. Pacific* & see what should be done there." ‡C. C. Douglass to C. H. McCormick, May 21, 1872: Money can be made in Montana if we are willing to spend between $5,000 and $10,000 for a silver amalgamating mill. ‡J. Hoyt to C. H. McCormick, Jan. 8, 1873: "I have to despair of any good result—notwithstanding there must be great treasure."

[98] ‡S. L. Smith to C. H. McCormick, Jan. 14, 1873: "I have no doubt could we *keep track* of our claims and hold on until the country was reached by rail we should realize handsomely from our investment. The main trouble is to get an honest competent man to take care of it. This want has been the trouble all the way through. . . . Men of supposed honesty and Christian conviction go there, swindle us & leave us as bad as ever. . . . The project is without head or means to take care of itself." Hoyt is withdrawing from the Co. Shall we sell out for $15,000? ‡C. H. McCormick to S. L. Smith, May 25, 1876. D. Ruggles, Fredericksburg, Va., to C. H. McCormick, Apr. 19, 1877. In 1865, McCormick also invested about $3,700 in the stock of the North Clear Creek Gold & Silver Mining Co., which, with John A. Dix as pres., was formed to exploit some property in Gilpin Cy., Colo. McCormick received one dividend of $280, but by 1871, he counted this investment a total loss. ‡T. B. Bunting, N. Y., to C. H. McCormick, May 23, 1865. ‡C. A. Spring, Jr., to C. H. McCormick, Aug. 27, 1866.

ings and shafts sunk at no considerable expense, between $800,000 and $1,000,000 worth of gold was reported to have been removed prior to 1862 when the war compelled a pause.[99] Although this sum was probably an exaggeration, it is pertinent here since it was large enough to invite a further effort to profit from the mine as soon as hostilities had ceased. Dorn, however, was much reduced in fortune when peace came, and leased his property to Captain Thomas S. Morgan, a cotton factor of Augusta, Georgia, and to two other southerners who shortly thereafter formed the Dorn Gold Mining Company.[100]

At this juncture in early 1867, Cyrus McCormick first heard of the mine. Since Morgan and his associates lacked the money to purchase machinery and hire miners, they turned to him for a loan. Without an adequate preliminary investigation, so far as the surviving records show, the inventor advanced Morgan $30,000 for six months at seven per cent interest and took as security a mortgage on one-third of the property, an option to purchase a quarter interest in the venture for $50,000 and a guarantee of his right to sell the mine if the loan were

[99] J. D. Whitney: "The Metallic Wealth of the United States" (Phila., Pa., 1854), p. 133. This account states that Dorn discovered gold on his property in Feb., 1852, and within eighteen months with the aid of a primitive Chilian mill and two mules, had mined $300,000 worth of the metal. According to this author, it was the richest gold mine in the Atlantic seaboard states. While Dorn worked the property, the "New York" and "Pikes Peak" shafts were sunk. They had been driven down to the lower level of the "brown ore," and then stopped, because he did not know how to reduce the pyrites or sulphuret ore beneath. No cross-cutting had been done, and in a word, he had operated the mine in a "loose random sort of way" with an eye to immediate profits rather than to a methodical development of his property.

[100] Morgan was the sole surviving member of the cotton brokerage firm of E. M. Bruce & Co. He held a 7/12th interest in the Dorn Mining Co. His chief associate therein was Colonel S. B. Moe. This Co. was not organized until May 27, 1867, although its members leased Dorn's property on Aug. 25, 1866.

not paid back when due.[101] Even before the date of this loan,
McCormick had invested about $14,000 in gold-mining proper-
ties in North Carolina and Georgia, but this sum was soon
written off as almost a total loss.[102]

When the time came for the Dorn Gold Mining Company
to honor its note, it was unable to do so. McCormick hesitated
either to force it into bankruptcy or to take stock in settlement
of his loan.[103] Although the partners of Morgan had not paid
in all of the money pledged when the company was formed,
he was spending the small funds at his disposal to prepare the
mine for operation. He was most enthusiastic over the prospects of a rich return. He wrote repeatedly in this vein to

[101] C. H. McCormick to C. A. Spring, Jr., Apr. 16, 1867; ‡T. S. Morgan,
Augusta, Ga., to C. H. McCormick, Apr. 8, 1867; A. C. Rogers to C. A.
Spring, Jr., Apr. 27, 1868. The $30,000 loan was made on Mch. 21, 1867,
and about a year later McCormick advanced Morgan $2500 more.

[102] With S. L. M. Barlow of New York, C. H. McCormick invested
$10,000 in Georgia gold lands, location not specified in the records. Accord-
ing to the balance-sheet of Aug. 1, 1871, this sum was a total loss. See,
‡McCormick Journal "A," Nov. 8, 1865 ff. In 1866, McCormick joined
with Theo. Brown and Sam'l. B. Smith of New York to buy 230 acres
from Gen'l. T. L. Clingman, near Charlotte, N. C. This was sometimes
called the "Means' gold property." The associates did not develop it. In
1868, Professor Henry A. Ward was sent to view this property, as well
as the gold lands of Major Hugh Downing. Ward advised that the Downing
property was too poor in metal to repay working. The title to the Clingman
tract was cloudy, and in 1871 McCormick considered the $3,533 paid in,
irretrievably lost. In 1872, S. B. Smith thought the property was worth
$5,000, even though no gold were found on it. See, ‡E. Fowler, Charlotte,
N. C., to C. H. McCormick, Oct. 22, 1866; ‡C. A. Spring, Jr., to H. A.
Boardman, Jr., Apr. 12, 1867; ‡H. A. Ward to C. H. McCormick, June
5, 26, and July 14, 1868; ‡S. B. Smith to C. H. McCormick, July 24,
1872; ‡C. H. McCormick to B. C. Sanders, Dec. 4, 1876, to W. M. Shipp,
Apr. 7, 1877, to W. F. Davidson, June 6, 1877, and to T. L. Clingman,
Oct. 13, 1877. At this time the Means' property was about to be sold for
taxes, and McCormick was eager to dispose of it.

[103] On Mch. 24, 1868, Morgan agreed to extend for six months from that
date, McCormick's option of buying a one-quarter interest in the property.
‡S. L. M. Barlow to H. A. Ward, Aug. 28, 1868.

McCormick, picturing the fortune that beyond all doubt awaited the man who would buy out the interests of the two delinquent members of the company and advance money so that the work could proceed.[104] The inventor was not inattentive to this unceasing flow of eloquence, although his wife, C. A. Spring, Jr., and S. L. M. Barlow, his friend and stockbroker, counseled him that the risk was not worth taking.[105]

To be on the safe side, McCormick now dispatched Henry A. Ward of Rochester, New York, a geologist, mining expert, and paleontologist of sufficient note to be remembered to-day, to the Dorn mines to investigate and report.[106] The professor sent specimens of the ore to the Columbia College School of Mines for assay and the results of the analysis were most disappointing.[107] McCormick thereupon requested Morgan to

[104] T. S. Morgan to C. H. McCormick, May 12, 1868 and to R. M. Funkhauser, July 19 and Aug. 5, 1868.

[105] C. H. McCormick, Jr., MSS. Book "B," Nettie F. to C. H. McCormick, Jr., Mch. 30, 1883: "I wish he [C. H.] would shut it [Dorn Mine] up forever—and I have always, uniformly so advised him . . . since we owned it." ♯S. L. M. Barlow to C. H. McCormick, Oct. 1, 1867, and Sept. 15, 1868. Barlow was of the brokerage firm of Bowdoin, Larocque, Barlow & MacFarland. ♯B. M. Smith to C. H. McCormick, Jan. 14, 1867. Spring spoke with some authority since he had been one of the California gold-seekers of 1849. See his ♯letters to C. H. McCormick of Mch. 17, 1866, Mch. 22 and Apr. 1, 1869: "You doubtless know your own business best, but I do want to say that I have no faith in your South Carolina gold Mine." J. S. Cothran to C. H. McCormick, Dec. 26, 1873.

[106] Ward had made almost a thousand plaster-casts of prehistoric animals, fossils, etc., and on Feb. 26, 1866, asked McCormick to subscribe $5,000 for the erection of a building for their permanent display at any college he might choose. McCormick declined. He probably first met Ward in 1865 in connection with his interest in Montana silver-mines, since the professor had been the manager of the Midas Mining Co. in that Territory. See also, ♯H. A. Ward to C. H. McCormick, Dec. 7, 1868, and June 12, 1869. T. S. Morgan to C. H. McCormick, June 27 and ♯Aug. 8, 1868. Bill to C. H. McCormick, of Assay Dept., Columbia College School of Mines, N. Y., Aug. 28, 1868.

[107] C. H. McCormick to T. S. Morgan, Sept. 4, 1868. The cost of Ward's trip and the assay was $1835, and McCormick expected Morgan to pay it. There are about ten letters of H. A. Ward to C. H. McCormick, dated

repay the $30,000 loan at once.[108] This Morgan could not do, but he endeavored to divert attention from his lack of funds by expressing chagrin that Ward's specimens were so unrepresentative of the general run of the deposits, since "the gold can be seen in almost every piece of ore. It is so rich that we sack it down in the mine." [109] He was convinced that "the thing is big if we only work it big." [110]

Why McCormick early in 1869, contrary to his own first decision and to the advice of friends and experts, consented to purchase an interest in the Dorn Mining Company can only be surmised. Probably the belief that unless he came to its rescue, he would lose the total amount of his loan, was the decisive consideration. Whatever the cause, by February over $50,000 of his money was in the venture.[111] This sum would doubtless increase rapidly since he was committed to an "energetic prosecution" of the work, or in other words, more expensive machinery and a larger laboring force. A new arrangement was made with Dorn at this time, whereby he leased the company for twenty years a tract of about twelve hundred acres in extent.[112] Colonel Moe, the defaulting partner of the original Dorn Mining Company, was disregarded, and hereafter for a time the associates were McCormick, Morgan, Robert M. Funkhauser of New York City,[113] and

between June 3, 1868, and July 30, 1869, in the files of the N. F. McCormick Biog. Asso. Ward found that most of the old shafts had caved in and were full of water. The machinery was in very bad condition.

[108] ‡S. L. M. Barlow to C. H. McCormick, Sept. 24, 1868. C. H. McCormick to T. S. Morgan, Dec. 17, 1868.

[109] T. S. Morgan to R. M. Funkhauser, Oct. 4, 1868.

[110] *Idem* to *idem,* Aug. 27, 1868.

[111] C. H. McCormick to Judge Selden, Feb. 11, 1869.

[112] T. S. Morgan to C. H. McCormick and R. M. Funkhauser, Feb. 16, 26, 1869. Because this land was heavily timbered, fuel was ready at hand. By the terms of the lease, the Co. was given the privilege of purchasing the entire tract for $500,000.

[113] In the N. F. McCormick B. A. files is the letter-press copy-book of McCormick & Funkhauser, covering the period, April 1, 1869, to May 25,

the estate of E. M. Bruce, who until his death had been Morgan's colleague in the cotton-brokerage business. No one of the parties held a majority interest, but McCormick's stake amounted to two-fifths of the whole.[114]

The first misstep of the reorganized company was to appoint Professor Ward the superintendent of the mine at a salary of $600 a month and expenses. He had a deep book-knowledge of minerals and mining, but lacked executive ability and was both physically and temperamentally unfitted for life in the woods among rough men. Friction between him and Morgan, who was also at the scene of operations, began almost at once and continued until Ward's resignation five months later.[115]

1870. In Aug., 1868, Morgan in dire need of funds reduced his own interest in the company by selling Funkhauser a 1/6th interest for $3,000. T. S. Morgan to R. M. Funkhauser, Aug. 17, 1868. ‡R. M. Funkhauser to C. H. McCormick, Mch. 3, 1869.

[114] C. H. McCormick to T. S. Morgan, Mch. 31, 1869. T. S. Morgan's share (including that of the E. M. Bruce estate of which he was trustee) was also 2/5ths and R. M. Funkhauser's, 1/5th. These are the correct proportions if Colonel Moe's 1/6th interest is divided *pro rata* among them. Upon its reorganization, the company petitioned the South Carolina legislature for a charter of incorporation. This was perhaps the most corrupt of all the Reconstruction Assemblies. Morgan wrote McCormick on Feb. 27, 1869, that he did not dare sign his name to the petition since he was suing a member of the legislature, but that his father-in-law, H. R. Casey, a politician of some note in Ga., would go to Columbia to lobby in their behalf. "We may have to expend three or four hundred dollars among the worthy members of the legislature," Morgan added. "Please read and return Hon. F. J. Moses' letter. Don't make it too public as we may find him useful to us now and hereafter." Moses, whom Prof. W. A. Dunning ("Reconstruction, Political and Economic," N. Y., 1907, p. 216) describes as "a notoriously bad character," was soon to be the governor of the state. In 1869 he was Speaker of the House, and Atty. General. The charter was granted Mch. 23, 1869.

[115] Letters of H. A. Ward to C. H. McCormick, June 12, 18, and July 4, 1869. ‡T. S. Morgan to C. H. McCormick and R. M. Funkhauser, July 8, 1869: Ward irritates me at times but he will be serviceable in putting our mine before the public, for in its opinion Ward's approval is a guarantee of a good thing. He has many influential friends and we can not afford to make him our enemy. "I want no scientific ass who can descant

When Ward assumed his duties in March, 1869, McCormick sent another geologist, Professor N. S. Keith, to make a survey of the Dorn property.[116] Keith's report was far more optimistic than Ward's, and must have heartened the inventor as he signed check after check for expensive stamp-mill machinery, engines, pumps, and laborers' wages.[117] Keith believed that the mine would pay large profits if a good mill were erected and the direction of the work were placed in expert hands. He found seams and veins of gold in the strata of quartz and slate. A sample run of this ore through the crusher yielded an average of over $30 worth of gold per ton. In his opinion the gold in the pyrites could be extracted at small expense. There was also a large amount of manganese on the property which would be well worth exploiting if a railroad came to solve the transportation problem.[118]

The spring and summer of 1869 at the mine were spent in repairing and draining old shafts, making bricks, cutting and sawing timber for lumber and fuel, building a mill, and installing the stamp machinery, separators, crushers, and concentrators that McCormick and Funkhauser shipped to the mine

upon chemistry without knowing anything else. I want a business man in the fullest sense."

[116] Ward naturally resented Keith's presence at the mine. C. H. McCormick to C. A. Spring, Jr., Mch. 3, 1869; ‡T. S. Morgan to C. H. McCormick, Mch. 14, 1869.

[117] ‡H. A. Ward to C. H. McCormick, Apr. 29 and May 6, 1869. Telegrams of T. S. Morgan to C. H. McCormick, May 3 and 15, 1869: "Send $5,000 to Dorn or the lease is void." C. H. McCormick to C. H. McCormick & Bros., Mch. 19 and 29, 1869. These letters above all others, reveal his high hopes of large profits. He believed that there would probably be a million tons of ore, worth $40 or $50 per ton, and costing $2.50 per ton, or less, to reduce.

[118] The Dorn Mine was forty miles from Augusta, Ga., and even the nearest town (Abbeville, S. Car.) was twenty-two miles away. All provisions had "to be toted" from Augusta, but Morgan was making a "very nice profit" by selling them to the workmen. ‡T. S. Morgan to C. H. McCormick, Mch. 29, 1869. N. S. Keith to C. H. McCormick, Mch. 17, 1869.

from New York. Discouraging delays, breakages, bickering between the partners, trouble with the workmen, and heavier expenses than had been anticipated, are the subjects most emphasized in the many letters of these months that deal with the venture.[119] During 1869 McCormick drew checks in favor of the company totaling almost $50,000.[120] Although a part of this sum was advanced as a loan and to pay for his share in the enterprise, the distinction between these items and operating costs is unimportant in view of the future history of the mine.

The Dorn Mine and its problems must have strongly reminded McCormick of his unhappy experiences thirty years before when he tried to become an ironmaster in Virginia.[121] By midsummer, 1869, Morgan was writing in confidence to Funkhauser that the inventor was "grasping, overbearing and testy"; had a "selfish, unyielding . . . nature" and "makes the closest hardest trades with me." [122] This explosion came as

[119] As an example of the lack of harmony between the partners at this time, Morgan complained that his Cornish miners were intelligent but lazy. He asked McCormick and Funkhauser to go down to Castle Garden, where the immigrants disembarked, and pick out a new working force. They did so, but to Morgan's disgust, he was sent "a miserable motley crew of Tailors, Barbers, shoe makers etc. Perhaps we can get 4 good men out of the dozen." A miner's day was ten hours "when working dry and eight when working wet." He was paid $2, and an ordinary laborer $1 or $1.25. T. S. Morgan to C. H. McCormick & R. M. Funkhauser, May 15, June 13 and 26, July 8, 1869. ‡R. M. Funkhauser to C. H. McCormick, June 5, 1869. McCormick and Funkhauser sharply differed over the proper type of engine to purchase for the mine. McCormick finally had his way, partly because he was supported by Ward. This made Ward lose favor with Funkhauser. ‡C. H. McCormick to T. S. Morgan, June 24, 1869.

[120] ‡Check stub-books of C. H. McCormick for the period 1868-1870. Between Mch. 30, 1868, and July 2, 1870, the mine cost him over $65,000, and this sum, added to his original loan of $30,000 and unpaid interest due him, made his stake in the company by July, 1870, about $100,000. Apparently up to that time approximately $1,800 in gold had been found.

[121] "Hutchinson," I, Chapter VI.

[122] T. S. Morgan to R. M. Funkhauser, July 9, 1869. ‡R. M. Funkhauser to T. S. Morgan, July 23, 1869.

a result of differences of opinion with McCormick over the purchases of machinery and the accuracy of Morgan's expense-account. Funkhauser handed this letter to McCormick.

Few men ever successfully thwarted McCormick's will for long, and Morgan was not one of them. The inventor at once, without Morgan's knowledge, bought enough of Funkhauser's interest in the company to give him control of its policy.[123] Ward resigned as superintendent, and when McCormick sent Professor Keith in his stead, Morgan refused to accept him and came to New York to make his wishes known to his associates.[124] He stayed only long enough to learn that he had been defeated, since the inventor threatened to dissolve the company and sue for the recovery of his loans unless Morgan carried out the orders sent to him from New York.[125] Having made his position clear, McCormick then characteristically endeavored to please Morgan by agreeing that Keith should be displaced by another superintendent.[126] The company now met

[123] A. C. Rogers to C. A. Spring, Jr., Aug. 4, 1869. This cost McCormick $18,000.

[124] C. H. McCormick believed that Ward had fleeced him by taking commissions from the firms which had supplied the machinery. N. S. Keith was from Colorado and was known as an expert chemist, metallurgist, millwright, and engineer. He had discovered a process for desulphurizing ore. Morgan agreed that Keith was "brainy," but believed that he had no business sense. T. S. Morgan to R. M. Funkhauser, Aug. 17, 1869; #N. S. Keith to McCormick & Funkhauser, Aug. 17, 1869; Funkhauser to C. H. McCormick, Aug. #18, 21, and 25, 1869, and #C. H. McCormick to H. A. Ward, Oct. 22, 1869.

[125] C. H. McCormick to T. S. Morgan, Sept. 23, 1869, and to C. A. Spring, Jr., Sept. 25 and 29, 1869. #W. W. MacFarland to C. H. McCormick, Aug. 31, 1869. C. H. McCormick could dissolve the company by petitioning the proper court in S. C. to appoint a receiver. If the company went into bankruptcy, C. H. McCormick might be able to buy out the entire co-partnership for a nominal sum.

[126] #T. S. Morgan to McCormick & Funkhauser, Sept. 29, 1869; #N. S. Keith to McCormick & Funkhauser, Oct. 24, 1869. Keith was angry because of the unceremonious way in which he had been shelved, but remained at the mine in a subordinate capacity until early in 1870. #C. H. McCormick to N. S. Keith, Dec. 8 and 9, 1869, and Jan. (?), 1870. Keith later sued for salary alleged to be due, and in Mch. 1871, McCormick

at Hamburg, South Carolina, and acting under its state charter acquired earlier in the year, elected McCormick to be the president and treasurer.[127] He was represented at this meeting by his attorney, Perrin & Cothran of Abbeville, a firm which thereafter played an important part in the history of the Dorn Mine. Rev. William S. Plumer of the Columbia Seminary had recommended Colonel Perrin for this assignment, with the persuasive endorsement that he was "an eminent elder in our church."[128]

Thus the year 1869 passed, with much argument, large expenses, and very little gold. Some of the new machinery proved to be unsuited to working slate ore, and the few tons that were run through the crusher yielded a much smaller amount of gold than the samples which had made the inventor so jubilant a few months before.[129] It took courage for McCormick to confess to C. A. Spring, Jr., how completely he had been taken in.

"I desire to remind you also," he wrote, "of the *entire* loss so far as can now be known of all that I have put into the *Dorn* Gold Mine concern. It has been the most *outrageous swindle* that *could be perpetrated*. The *yield* of the vein of gold ore *reported* to me from actual *milling process* was $40 to *$6,000* per ton of ore—from an enormous vein of from 8 to 30 ft. wide; whereas it *now yields* to *better Mill* less than

paid him $750. ♯L.P.C.B. No. 1, 2nd ser., p. 404, C. H. McCormick to ?, Mch. 2, 1871.

[127] Morgan was made vice-president, Funkhauser, sec'y., and Charles W. Allen, gen'l. superintendent, at a salary of $5,000 a year. The company was now styled The Dorn Mining and Manufacturing Company. Its capital stock was $500,000, but it was permitted to begin operations as soon as the paid-in capital amounted to $100,000. Later, its charter was amended so as to allow its capital stock to be reduced to $50,000. In this way the company avoided the payment of so heavy an annual state tax.

[128] ♯W. S. Plumer to C. H. McCormick, Aug. 27, 1869. Perrin, the father-in-law of Cothran, died in Apr., 1878.

[129] ♯C. W. Allen to C. H. McCormick, Apr. 29 and June 20, 1870.

one dollar!" [130] It would have been well for him at this point to have charged his $120,000 loss to experience and closed the Dorn account forever.

Each of the partners was, in fact, ready to unload his shares upon any one of the others "for a reasonable consideration." In McCormick's case, this was fixed at $23,000, or less than twenty per cent of the sum that the venture had already cost him. By November, 1870, as a result of much dickering, McCormick had bought out Funkhauser, and Morgan had disposed of all his rights to Judge Silas M. Stilwell and Richard Remington.[131] They agreed that McCormick should dominate the policy of the company "at all times." [132]

As 1871 opened, after more than six months of inactivity at the mine, three dozen workmen were hired, the machinery was put in good condition, the shafts were drained of water, and operations were ready to begin.[133] The partners resolved to pursue a conservative policy; to move ahead deliberately and economically until the yield in gold had compensated them for

[130] C. H. McCormick to C. A. Spring, Jr., Jan. 20, 1870: The Dorn mine has cost me $119,833.28. ‡C. A. Spring, Jr., to C. H. McCormick, Jan. 24, 1870: "You should be happy because you can deduct the loss on your income tax return." Work was suspended at the mine on May 12, 1870. ‡C. H. McCormick to Perrin & Cothran, May 20, 1870. For much correspondence relating to the mine in the summer of 1870, see ‡L.P.C.B. No. 1, 2nd ser., *passim*.

[131] C. H. McCormick to Perrin & Cothran, July 7, 1870. At this time McCormick bought out Funkhauser for $900, and offered to sell Morgan his entire interest, or buy Morgan's moiety, for $20,000. Morgan owed McCormick about $10,400, but Stilwell and Remington assumed one-half of this debt by the terms of their purchase agreement. ‡W. W. MacFarland to C. H. McCormick, Apr. 20, 28, May 28, 1870. T. S. Morgan to C. H. McCormick, June 15, 1870; ‡C. W. Allen to C. H. McCormick, June 20, 1870; T. S. Morgan to R. M. Funkhauser, Aug. 17, 1870, and Perrin & Cothran to C. H. McCormick, Nov. 30, 1870.

[132] Agreement of November 25, 1870, between the three partners. ‡L.P.C.B. No. 1, 2nd ser., p. 321. Remington was supt. of the mine, and W. P. Jenney, chemist and metallurgist.

[133] R. Remington to C. H. McCormick and S. M. Stilwell, Dec. 10, 21, 1870, and Jan. 6, 17, 1871.

past expenses. But even a cautious course was found to cost about $2,500 a month. Torrential rains fell just as the work was well underway, the shafts refilled with water, the pumps failed, a boiler burst, and the small amounts of ore made ready for shipment averaged only $4 per ton in gold. Since the cost of operation was about as large, there is little wonder that Judge Stilwell wrote in late March that he had "been quite ill for a few days from strong nervous irritability growing out of Dorn business—but am now better." [134] By the summer he and Remington were glad to withdraw and leave McCormick to discover some new way of overcoming the Dorn Mine hoodoo.

Thereupon, McCormick bought the entire property from Dorn for $20,000, although but five years before it had been held for sale at a half-million. One Charles Wright was the inventor's agent in effecting this purchase and he remained at the mine after title was passed. From an old negro squatter on the property, he learned of a vein called "Hidden Treasure," forgotten since the war. It was most aptly named if the first word of its title is given all the emphasis.[135] Wright's

[134] S. M. Stilwell, New York, to C. H. McCormick, Mch. 24, 1871. About six weeks before this time, it had been expected that the operation of the mine would cost only $1500 a month; that for $9 per ton freight about 100 barrels of pyrites could be shipped to N. Y. each month by boat from Savannah, and that each of these barrels would be worth about $100 in gold. Remington did send $500 in gold to the mint in April. See his letters to C. H. McCormick and S. M. Stilwell, Feb. 17, 24, Mch. 4, 17, 28, 29, and Apr. 28, 1871. ‡L.P.C.B. No. 1, 2nd ser., pp. 469, 545, 636.

[135] *Ibid.*, pp. 621-623, C. H. McCormick to C. Wright and to W. W. MacFarland, Aug. 23, 1871. The report of W. Hooper, a mining engineer of Ticonderoga, N. Y., whom McCormick sent to his property in Dec., 1871, urged that more machinery should be installed there. For the next six months McCormick vainly urged Hooper to be the superintendent of the mine. *Ibid.*, No. A, 2nd ser., C. Wright to C. H. McCormick, Dec. 1 and 19, 1871, and Jan. 6, 1872. W. Hooper to C. H. McCormick, Jan. 9, 1872. See also, *ibid.*, No. 3, 2nd ser., pp. 12, 22-23, for McCormick's several letters to Hooper in the spring of 1872. Wright was warned by the Ku Klux Klan not to allow the negroes living on the property to hold evening reli-

assurance that "it would be but a short time before the Dorn Mines would be the most productive . . . on this continent" must have sounded like an old story to the inventor.[136] Thus, on the eve of the great Chicago fire, The Dorn Mining and Manufacturing Company closed its unhappy career, and McCormick was the sole owner of a property that up to that time had been the most costly venture of his life.

The mishaps of Wright need not be detailed here. By the autumn of 1872 McCormick bluntly wrote him that "I have been more heavily fleeced through & by you than any of your predecessors." [137] "Fleeced" was probably too strong a word, but McCormick was angry because Wright was threatening to sue him for salary alleged to be due.[138] Already the inventor had leased the mine to Professor Edward L. Seymour of New York City in return for a guarantee of one-quarter of the net profits.[139] To add to the gloom, reports from samples of manganese sent to England for test indicated that this ore was

gious services since they were too often taught politics rather than the Bible.

[136] C. Wright, Dorn Mines, to C. H. McCormick, Aug. (?), 1871. See also, Wright's nine-page report to McCormick on Nov. 1, 1871, in #L.P.C.B. No. 2, 2nd ser.

[137] C. H. McCormick to C. Wright, Sept. 14, 1872. Wright had found that the stamping machinery was too heavy for the ore, and his expenses, borne mostly by C. H. McCormick, had been very large. See, L.P.C.B. No. 132, p. 844, *Idem* to *idem*, Mch. 23, 1872. Up to June, 1872, Wright's régime had cost McCormick $21,000.

[138] Certified copy of court proceedings in a suit brought in Abbeville Cy. Court by *C. Wright vs. C. H. McCormick,* on Dec. 31, 1872, for $2,350 back salary, alleged to be due. Perrin & Cothran represented McCormick and he won the case. But Wright sued again in the autumn of 1874—this time for a $5,000 claim. McCormick again won. Lord, Day, & Lord to C. H. McCormick, Oct. 20, 1874, and Perrin & Cothran to C. H. McCormick, Jan. 28, 1875.

[139] This arrangement was to begin on Aug. 1, 1872. The contract was made on July 4, 1872. Unknown to McCormick, Seymour entered the story in May when Wright invited him to come to the mine as a consultant. In June, McCormick sent a Chicago friend, Wm. L. Lee, to examine the property. Lee filed a pessimistic report.

worth far less than McCormick had been led to expect. British steel-makers could obtain a considerably higher grade much more conveniently from Spain.[140] The Dorn manganese had commercial value, but until a railroad was built to the mine it cost more to freight it to Savannah than it would sell for in that port.

Seymour, who believed that he had discovered an effective method for reducing refractory ores, spent most of his time in the laboratory of the mine "dreaming over the mysteries of his art." [141] He was the third and last of the line of impractical professors whose total lack of business acumen lends the only touch of humor to the history of McCormick's quest for gold in South Carolina. Under Seymour's very eyes, the small tools used about the mine were carried off by the poor folk of the neighborhood, and the few laborers who could be paid, did about what they pleased to do without regard for the interests of their employer. Seymour's financial backer soon withdrew his support, and the poverty-stricken professor was thrown upon the charity of friends in Abbeville and Augusta, without even enough money to pay his fare back to New York.[142] This doleful situation reached a climax in December, 1873, when his beloved laboratory—his concentrator, crucibles, and test-tubes—and the building which housed much of the mine machinery, burned to the ground.[143]

[140] Peers Naylor, St. Helens, Eng., to C. H. McCormick, June 15, 1872.

[141] Perrin & Cothran to C. H. McCormick, Feb. 7, 1873: "Our judgment of him [Seymour] is that in Metallurgy he is very learned; in business very impracticable and in means (money) utterly impecunious—at the same time artless, enthusiastic and honest." E. L. Seymour to C. H. McCormick, Dec. 26, 1873: "Your ores are worthless by the amalgamation process but . . . I can make them very valuable by my mode of extraction."

[142] Letters to C. H. McCormick of E. L. Seymour, Dec. 26, 1872, W. L. Lee, Apr. 3, 1873, and Perrin & Cothran, Apr. 28, 1873 and Apr. 27, 1874. Seymour had expected monetary aid from Dr. Jas. P. Campbell of Brooklyn, N. Y.

[143] Letters to C. H. McCormick of Perrin & Cothran, Dec. 31, 1873, and Jan. 20, 1874, and of ‡E. L. Seymour, Dec. 30, 1873.

Perrin & Cothran had early taken an interest in Seymour's experiments, and six months before this disaster, induced McCormick to aid him with $5,000. They guaranteed to pay the inventor one half of all the profits that they might make from the mine.[144] In other words, the Seymour contract came to an end and the Abbeville law firm assumed the obligations of the professor and retained him as their expert. McCormick's five thousand dollars were largely used to buy the new machinery that Seymour desired.[145] Then came the fire and additional funds were needed at once. McCormick sent $2,000 more during the next few months.[146] He, as well as all others who knew the mine, believed that it contained gold in paying quantities, but it seemed impossible to find the proper machinery and chemicals to extract it from the ore. Most of the money that was spent on the property at this period was for the purpose of financing experiments to discover this secret. By the autumn of 1874, when Seymour was confident that success was assured if he were provided with a furnace capable of generating a heat of 2300 degrees Fahrenheit,[147] Perrin & Cothran had reached the limit of their small resources, and McCormick, having watched $7,000 disappear without appar-

[144] Letters to C. H. McCormick of W. L. Lee, Mch. 27, 29, and Apr. 3, 1873, and of Perrin & Cothran, June 6, 11, and 16, 1873. ‡Indenture between C. H. McCormick and Perrin & Cothran, July 17, 1873. ‡L.P.C.B. No. 3, 2nd ser., p. 85, C. H. McCormick to Perrin & Cothran, May 30, 1873.

[145] Perrin & Cothran to C. H. McCormick, Sept. 5, Oct. 17, Nov. 11, Dec. 2, and 23, 1873. J. S. Cothran to C. H. McCormick, July 21, 26, Aug. 12, and Dec. 26, 1873.

[146] Perrin & Cothran to C. H. McCormick, Jan. 20, 21, Feb. 28, Mch. 25, and Apr. 27, 1874. By now, since Seymour had decided that the copper pyrites contained too little gold to work profitably, he was directing his attention to the iron pyrites. ‡C. H. McCormick to Perrin & Cothran, Feb. 3 and Mch. 11, 1874.

[147] As early as Apr. 3, 1873, McCormick was informed by W. L. Lee that Ward was able to reduce the virgin ore (copper pyrites) to a sulphurated ore, but that he could not extract the gold from this unless he had hard coal and a furnace which would produce a white heat. See also, J. S. Cothran to C. H. McCormick, Dec. 26, 1873.

ent results, refused to advance any more.[148] Seymour was obliged to quit. In so far as possible the equipment at the mine was put under lock and key, and Perrin & Cothran became its custodian.[149] Thereafter, until the spring of 1876, all was quiet at the Dorn Mine, although apparently the watchman violated his trust by selling tools and machine parts for his own enrichment.[150]

Late in 1874 one Sidney O. Brown of London and San Francisco, first expressed an interest in the property.[151] The agreement with Perrin & Cothran was still in force, however, and over a year went by before McCormick could secure their consent to withdraw temporarily in favor of Brown.[152] He

[148] Perrin & Cothran, to C. H. McCormick, Apr. 27, 1874: "Our debtors at the mine are importunate." See also their letters, stressing the same difficulty, of May 21, June 2, 3, July 13, 25, Aug. 25, Nov. 7, and Dec. 16, 1874. As early as the letter of July 13, Perrin & Cothran hoped that McCormick would help build the furnace. They returned in vain to this subject in their later letters to him. After McCormick both by long silences and by his replies had made abundantly clear that he was weary of writing Dorn Mine checks, Seymour went to Atlanta in Dec., 1874, to seek funds. His quest yielded little and he thereupon returned to New York. ‡C. H. McCormick to Perrin & Cothran, Dec. 25, 1874.

[149] Perrin & Cothran to C. H. McCormick, Jan. 28, Feb. 23, July 29, and Dec. 28, 1875.

[150] An inventory of the equipment at the mine had been made in April, 1873, but due to the petty thieving, it was worthless by the spring of 1875. See, J. Cox to C. H. McCormick, May 1, 1875; ‡S. O. Brown to C. H. McCormick, July 30, 1876: "The loose and dishonest way in which things have been managed here is almost beyond belief. Tools and personal property. . . seem to have been scattered all over the country." Perrin and Cothran were partly to blame because they admitted in a letter to C. H. McCormick on July 29, 1875, that they had not been to the mine "since last fall."

[151] ‡S. O. Brown, Richmond, Va., to C. H. McCormick, Dec. 20, 1874. ‡C. H. McCormick to S. O. Brown, Jan. 5, 1875. ‡D. E. Bradley to S. O. Brown, Dec. 28, 1874.

[152] C. H. McCormick to Perrin & Cothran, May 18, 1876. Letters to C. H. McCormick from H. Day, July 10, 1876, Perrin & Cothran, May 23, 1876, and ‡S. O. Brown, July 3, 1876. Brown & Dunne permitted Perrin & Cothran to go on with its search for free gold.

and his partner, Joseph J. Dunne, agreed to make a thorough survey at the mine, and if the outlook were encouraging, to install a desulphurizing furnace and other machinery at their own expense, paying McCormick one-third of their profits as rent.[153] Brown was at the mine from late May, 1876, until the following autumn. He explored the old shafts, cut several cross-drifts, and found plenty of pyrites but scarcely a trace of gold, "a condition of things anomalous in mining," as he said.[154] So ended the seventh vain attempt to make the property live up to its high reputation of ante-bellum days.

McCormick had now wasted over $195,000 upon a piece of backwood's land that he had never seen. He had been too busy to give it his close attention, and his lack of knowledge about mining obliged him to rely upon others who were often either incompetent or dishonest. Thus Brown discovered during his survey of the mine that Seymour had spent months of time and $7,000 of McCormick's money working with ore that contained only one and three-tenths per cent of copper and $2.75 worth of gold per ton.[155] Perrin and Cothran were men of integrity, but they knew nothing about mining. Because their office in Abbeville was over twenty miles from the mine, they could not watch over it effectively.[156]

Enthusiasm for Dorn Mine gold was at a low ebb by 1877, but the news that a railroad track was to be laid close to the

[153] ‡C. H. McCormick to Perrin & Cothran, Dec. 21, 1875, Jan. 8, Apr. 1, May 29, and June 1, 1876. Telegram of H. Day to C. H. McCormick, Jan. 29, 1876. MS. Agreement of Mch. 25, 1876, between C. H. McCormick and S. O. Brown, and Brown's letter of Mch. 23, 1876, to C. H. McCormick.
[154] ‡S. O. Brown to C. H. McCormick, Oct. 23, 1876. See also, his letters to C. H. McCormick of July 17, Aug. 7, Sept. 14, 18, Oct. ‡26, 1876. Perrin & Cothran to C. H. McCormick, May 17, 1877.
[155] S. O. Brown to C. H. McCormick, Sept. 18, 1876.
[156] J. S. Cothran to C. H. McCormick, May 12, 1877. Cothran was then Atty. Gen'l. of South Carolina. This office required his presence for long periods at Columbia, and hence he was even less able than hitherto to oversee the mine.

property on its way from Greenwood, South Carolina, to
Augusta, Georgia, aroused for the first time a lively hope of
profit from the manganese. McCormick had already been approached on several occasions by men who wished to exploit
these deposits, but their interest had flagged as soon as they
learned of the heavy cost of carriage to the seaboard.[157] The
officers of this railroad, which was being painfully built with
meager funds and convict labor, assured McCormick that if
he would subscribe to its stock and give it a right of way
through his property, they would put a depot there and carry
his manganese to Augusta for $4.00 a ton. They pictured to
him the town that would arise about his station, the several
thousand bales of cotton shipped from it each year, and
the new county that might be formed soon with Dorn Mine
as the county-seat.[158] McCormick was only mildly interested
at first. He tentatively promised to subscribe $1,000 and
shortly thereafter sailed to France for a long visit. J. S.
Cothran and the president of the railroad kept him reminded
of his interests in South Carolina, and finally, in August, 1879,
he purchased $2,000 worth of the stock of the Greenwood &
Augusta line.[159] It was almost three years later before this

[157] E. H. Woodward, Pyrolusite Manganese Co., N. Y., to C. H. McCormick, Feb. 14, 1873. W. J. Leddell, N. Y., to C. H. McCormick, Aug.
27, 1875. ‡S. O. Brown to C. H. McCormick, Oct. 26, 1876.

[158] P. H. Bradley, Greenwood, S. C., to C. H. McCormick, Sept. 5,
Nov. 5, 27, 1877. ‡P. H. Bradley, Millway, S. C., to H. Fay, undated, but
early 1878: "I am afraid I done wrong [to ask C. H. McCormick for $5,000
stock subscription] as Mr. McCormick has not answered any of my letters
since. . . . I have seen the day when there would have been no necessity
for it [asking help] but the war ruined us & we are now poor & strugling
like drowning men to try & improve our section of the country." ‡P. H.
Bradley to Hon. D. W. Aiken, Washington, D. C., Dec. 17, 1878. ‡J. S.
Cothran to C. H. McCormick, Feb. 17, 1879. The project of a railroad to
run near Dorn Mine had been broached at least as early as Dec., 1871.

[159] Letters to C. H. McCormick, May 9, 1878, ‡Feb. 1, 1879, Oct. 27,
1881, from P. H. Bradley; and from D. W. Aiken, ‡Dec. 27, 1878; from
‡J. S. Cothran, Jan. 18, June 5, Aug. 27, 1879, Mch. 16, June 15, Nov. 15,

road was completed. By then, with the help of a small gift from the inventor, Dorn Mine could boast of a station building more appealing to the eye than the unpainted box-like shacks which had been erected here and there along the track.[160] Better still, the Savannah Valley Railroad, coming down toward Augusta from the northwest, was persuaded in 1883 by a $3,000 purchase of its stock, to make McCormick's property its point of intersection with the Greenwood & Augusta line.[161]

Thus, gradually between 1879 and 1883, McCormick came to view his twelve hundred acres of timbered hills not only as a possible source of wealth from manganese and gold, but as a town site where lots could be sold. The mines might be worked in order to build up the community. There were already a dozen families living on his land as squatters, and in the summer of 1878 the caretaker of the mine had asked him to donate an acre or more as a site for a Baptist church.[162] Men without let or hindrance were washing for free gold on his property, and were building cabins, keeping themselves warm, and cook-

1880, and Nov. 14, 21, 22, 1881; from C. C. Copeland, Jan. 4, 1882. McCormick received 100 shares of stock in return for his $2000. In Jan., 1882, they were worth $1500 and Copeland advised C. H. McCormick to sell them. "As a general thing the capitalists who build Rail Roads expect to sell the bonds for enough to reimburse themselves and have the stock and local subscriptions for their profit. This they sell to large trunk lines who want the road for feeders. . . . I have never been a speculator and years ago heard you talk a great deal more about 'Intrinsic values' than you do now. I learned this term from you."

160 #C. C. Copeland to C. H. McCormick, Feb. 7, 1882.

161 Letters to C. H. McCormick from #W. T. Wheless, Augusta and Knoxville R. R. Co., Mch. 8, 1879; #J. S. Cothran, Nov. 22, 1881; J. Cothran, Jr., May 23 and Oct. 16, 1882; #C. H. McCormick, Jr., Aug. 23, 1882, and Dec. 10, 1883. #C. H. McCormick, Jr., to A. A. Stewart, Augusta, Ga., May 4 and June 27, 1883. W. W. Humphreys, Savannah Valley R. R., Anderson, S. C., to C. H. McCormick, Sept. 17 and Oct. 20, 1884. Humphreys believed that the junction at the mine would be completed within a year.

162 #J. B. Holloway to C. H. McCormick, June 3, 1878.

ing their meals with his timber.[163] The Dorn land, due to the neglect of its owner, had become an involuntary philanthropy. Perhaps a way could be found to combine financial profits with social aid.

Early in 1881, R. H. Nesbitt of Red Bud, Georgia, who had been a miner for Dorn before the war, was employed by McCormick and Cothran to operate the mine. For the first time in over four years the old shafts were drained and the machinery set in motion. Soon Nesbitt located a new vein of likely-looking ore and Cothran was confident that at a very modest cost the property would at last begin to make money for its owner.[164] This cheering word, together with the near completion of the railroad, so aroused McCormick's interest that at the close of 1881 he sent his friend and assistant, C. C. Copeland, to the mine on a trip of observation. He found Nesbitt "the worst looking old fellow I ever saw," but an expert miner and one who could be trusted implicitly. "The Parson," as he was known, had with considerable difficulty

[163] Letters to C. H. McCormick, from ♯A. A. Stuart, Augusta, Ga., May (?), 1879; ♯Alexander H. Stephens, Mch. 9, 1879. The late vice-pres. of the Confederacy suggested that the mine should be leased to his close friend, Charles E. Smith of Washington, Ga. Also ♯J. S. Cothran, Nov. 25, 1879, and ♯J. Cothran, Jr., Aug. 3, 1882, to C. H. McCormick. In the summer of 1871, McCormick first suggested that some of the Dorn property might well be leased to farmers. See ♯L.P.C.B. No. 1, 2nd ser., pp. 621-622, C. H. McCormick to C. Wright, Aug. 23, 1871.

[164] ♯C. H. McCormick to J. S. Cothran, Nov. 5, and Dec. 31, 1880; Mch. 23, Apr. 28, and May 24, 1881: "I still believe there is big gold in that mine, while I could wish somebody could point out the way to get at it." ♯J. S. Cothran to C. H. McCormick, Jan. 20, May 2, 23, July 22, Aug. 22, 1881, and from T. P. Cothran, Apr. 7, 1881. Nesbitt's salary depended upon the amount of gold that he found. He was employing about five miners. It is not clear from the correspondence who paid Nesbitt at the outset of his work, but after Jan., 1882, McCormick and Cothran agreed to share the cost or profits at a ratio of about 3 to 1, i.e., in the proportion that Cothran's $2636.70 loss under the Seymour régime bore to McCormick's $7000 loss during the same period. ♯C. H. McCormick to J. S. Cothran, Feb. 2, 1882.

kept an account of his receipts and expenses during his stay at the mine. Apparently the total operating cost had been $3,900, including $1,000 advanced by McCormick, while the receipts from the sale of gold were $2,400. This was not a large deficit, especially if a continuation of the work would lead people to make their homes near the mine.[165]

Copeland believed that Cothran was too sanguine about the speed with which a town would grow about the railroad station. He had surveyed three hundred lots and advertised to auction them on January 10, 1882.[166] The site was a beautiful one, with a fine spring of pure water and a large grove of tall pines near by. At Copeland's suggestion and with the inventor's consent, the embryo village was called McCormick. Its streets were named after members of his family and those, like Copeland, who had been associated with its history.[167] Rain fell steadily on the day of the sale and the railroad was still unfinished for a distance of about three miles out of the town. Only seventeen lots were disposed of, but the president of the road was on hand and promised that if another auction were advertised for early in February, a train would bring prospec-

[165] *Idem* to *idem,* Nov. 17 and Dec. 10, 1881. ‡C. C. Copeland to J. H. Huntington, Dec. 11, 1881, and to ‡C. H. McCormick, Dec. 12, 15, 19 and 23, 1881.

[166] ‡C. C. Copeland to C. H. McCormick, Dec. 12, 1881, and Jan. 2, 1882. ‡J. S. Cothran to C. H. McCormick, Nov. 28 and Dec. 22, 1881. Copeland found little to do and wrote his employer that he was spending much time reading Bacon's "Essays," the work of Goethe, and Thomas à Kempis's, "Imitation of Christ." The tract set aside for the town was about 40 acres in size.

[167] ‡*Idem* to *idem,* Dec. 6, 1881. In this letter Cothran asks if C. H. McCormick has any name to suggest for the town. ‡C. C. Copeland to C. H. McCormick, Dec. 15, 1881. In this, the writer states that Cothran has suggested the name McCormickville but he [Copeland] would like to make the counter-suggestion of McCormick. C. H. McCormick to J. S. Cothran, Dec. 10, 1881. McCormick here writes that he accepts Cothran's suggestion of McCormickville. Copeland's letter of the 15th led him to adopt McCormick. The town was incorporated and officially became McCormick on Apr. 1, 1882.

tive purchasers to McCormick without charge.[168] By ill fortune it rained again at that time, and nine lots were all that Copeland, the auctioneer, could sell.[169] This was discouraging, particularly since the village of Troy about six miles away was also anxious to be the point of intersection with the railroad coming down from Knoxville, which had not yet determined its exact route.[170]

Copeland's optimism, however, was not easily crushed. He soon had four negroes digging out manganese and was negotiating for the erection of a cotton-gin and shingle-mill. Since, in his opinion, profits were in sight from the gold, manganese, and real estate, he advised McCormick that the time had come to ease Cothran and Nesbitt gently out of the picture.[171] In so far as Nesbitt was concerned, Copeland's advice was followed. This was accomplished the more easily, since the old miner's "fissure vein" had not fulfilled his expectations, and his daily harvest of gold flakes had been diminishing for several weeks before orders arrived that his work must cease.[172]

[168] Profit and Loss Statement of J. S. Cothran, Trustee, in account with C. H. McCormick, Feb. 8, 1882. The seventeen lots were sold for a total of $645. ‡C. C. Copeland to C. H. McCormick, Jan. 11, 12, and 23, 1882. Telegram of Copeland to C. H. McCormick, Jan. 20, 1882: The railroad has finally reached the mine.

[169] ‡C. C. Copeland to C. H. McCormick, Feb. 8 and 14, 1882. The nine lots sold for $318.

[170] *Idem* to *idem*, Jan. 21 and 24, 1882.

[171] ‡*Idem* to *idem*, Feb. 21, 25, 27, 28 and Mch. 9, 1882. Cothran had now turned over the active management of the property to his son who lived on a sixty-acre farm near the mine, and paid McCormick rent of $150 a year. Copeland believed he was too young and inexperienced. There were also four other small farms on the Dorn estate, which with the Cothran home, brought C. H. McCormick a total of $550 rent a year. ‡C. H. McCormick to J. S. Cothran, Apr. 18, 1882. J. Cothran, Jr., was running a grist-mill and cotton-gin there, at least by 1883.

[172] ‡Letters from C. C. Copeland to C. H. McCormick, Mch. 12 and 27, 1882; to C. H. McCormick, Jr., Mch. 20, 1882; to R. H. Nesbitt, Mch. 24, 1882, and to J. S. Cothran, Mch. 29, 1882. This suspension of work at the mine made the people of the town restive, and disposed to charge McCormick with breaking faith.

Nevertheless, before he unwillingly left for his home in early May, two new shafts had been sunk in the manganese hill and preparations were going forward to drive down still another one in the hope of finding gold. Nesbitt's work was resumed from the point at which he left it.[173] All of this new expense, however, brought no return excepting to employ the townspeople of McCormick and sell a few more lots. No gold worth mentioning was discovered, and even the best of the manganese was worth only $9.50 a ton at Baltimore.[174]

Mrs. McCormick had always been skeptical concerning the value of the Dorn lands as a mineral property, although she was interested in the town of McCormick as a social investment in the back-country South.[175] She had inspected the diggings in May, 1882, and her belief in the futility of mining there had been strengthened.[176] In the following February, with her husband's consent, she ordered all work suspended.[177]

[173] ‡J. Cothran, Jr., to C. C. Copeland, Apr. 27, 1882, and to C. H. McCormick, May 6, 1882. ‡C. C. Copeland to C. H. McCormick, Jr., Mch. 28, 1882. ‡Ten letters of A. J. Rigby from McCormick, S. C., to C. H. McCormick, between June 28 and Dec. 6, 1882. He was of the firm of Rigby & Murphy, mining and construction engineers of 78 Bdwy., N. Y. C. McCormick paid him $200 a month and board. Rigby, with ten helpers, sunk a new shaft over 100 feet deep, but found very little gold.

[174] ‡Stillwell & Gladding, N. Y., to C. H. McCormick, Mch. 9, 1882, and to ‡C. C. Copeland, Mch. 16, 1882. ‡E. P. White & Co., N. Y., to C. H. McCormick, Mch. 20, 1882.

[175] C. H. McCormick, Jr., wrote for his father to J. S. Cothran on May 4, 1882, that never again would the Dorn Mine be worked unless under the close personal supervision of the McCormicks. In Mch., 1882, Mr. and Mrs. McCormick's daughter, Virginia, with her aunt and cousin, came to the Moore House near Augusta and stayed for about two weeks. Copeland looked after their needs, but they apparently did not visit the mine.

[176] ‡J. S. Cothran to N. F. McCormick, May 22, 1882. ‡J. Cothran, Jr., to C. C. Copeland, May 24, 1882.

[177] ‡J. Cothran, Jr., to C. H. McCormick, Feb. 27, 1883: Mrs. McCormick writes that I should stop all expenses at the mine. ‡J. Cothran, Jr., to C. H. McCormick, Jan. 11, 17, and Mch. 8, 1883. ‡C. C. Copeland to J. Cothran, Jr., Jan. 27, 1883. ‡J. Cothran, Jr., to C. C. Copeland, Jan 29 and Feb. 23, 1883.

Cyrus McCormick, Jr., visited the mine the next month and expressed his mother's own thoughts when he wrote to her:

With sadness I see around me the wrecks of bygone reckless waste of, not thousands alone, but *fortunes*. These decaying mills, tottering buildings, rust eaten machinery, scattered shafts and cog wheels; dilapidated log cabins, time worn & weather beaten dwellings, rotting timbers which once formed the entrances to caves of great and certain depth, but an equally *uncertain* hiding place for the wealth which always eluded and always allured; yawning abysses whose depths are hid from view by the charitable veil of darkness, and whose recesses have been hewn from rock and dug from clay—all in the search after this "ignis fatuus." . . . Through it all runs a dark thread of misrepresentation, deceit, intrigue, imposition and misplaced confidence in sinners who were supposed to be saints. This is the "great gold mine" of today at McCormick, S. C.[178]

Thus the young McCormick wrote the obituary of one of his father's most costly speculations. Thereafter, some hundreds of tons of manganese were sold, but the elusive gold was left in peace.[179] A resolve to help the thriving little community of McCormick supplanted the desire for profits from the Dorn lands. In this work Mrs. McCormick and her eldest son were the leaders. Lots were given for churches, a cemetery, and a newspaper. Stores and a temperance hotel, called "The McCormick," were erected. Street lights were installed and

[178] ‡C. H. McCormick Jr., to N. F. McCormick, Mch. 27, 1883. C. H. McCormick, Jr., MSS. Book "B," N. F. McCormick to C. H. McCormick, Jr., Mch. 22, 1883: "That poor little lump of amalgam left at the jewelers is all we have to show for these enormous expenses. No fortune can stand this long." After receiving her son's letter from which the quotation is given, Mrs. McCormick replied on Mch. 30: "I have your truthful description of that great puzzle which has brought us only *troubles*—and as many of them as Pandora's box held."

[179] ‡F. Blaisdell, Augusta, Ga., to C. H. McCormick, June 14, 1882; "Abbeville Press and Banner," July 22, 1885. C. H. McCormick, Jr., MSS. Book "B," Nettie F. to C. H. McCormick, Jr., Mch. 10, 1886, and to C. H. McCormick, Jr., and Anita McCormick, Mch. 4, 1888.

the town's drainage system was improved.[180] Its population doubled during 1883, and after a fire destroyed two business blocks in the following year, the McCormicks loaned money on easy terms to the merchants so that they could rebuild.[181] In 1885, three thousand bales of cotton were hauled to its freight siding for shipment to market. That year a "genuine, whole-souled South Carolina barbecue" of corn, potatoes, and "eighty-two carcasses of mutton and beef" was held to celebrate the completion of the "Academy" or high school building given by Mrs. McCormick.[182] Not far away at Clinton she provided for the erection and maintenance of the Thornwell Orphanage as a memorial to her husband.[183] McCormick is still a little town, but it is one of the few communities in the United States which owes its origin to the generosity of a mine owner who was foiled in his search for gold on its site.[184]

[180] Letters to C. H. McCormick of ‡J. S. Cothran, Feb. 24, 1883, and of ‡C. H. McCormick, Jr., Apr. 30 and Aug. 17, 1883. Nettie F. McCormick to J. Cothran, Jr., Feb. 10, 1883. J. Cothran, Jr., to C. H. McCormick, Jr., Mch. 17, July 6, Aug. 24, Nov. 19 and 27, 1885.

[181] ‡C. H. McCormick, Jr., to C. H. McCormick, Dec. 10, 1883; C. H. McCormick, Jr., MSS. Book "B," Nettie F. McCormick to C. H. McCormick, Jr., Nov. 17 and 25, 1884.

[182] C. H. McCormick, Jr., MSS., Book "B," Nettie F. McCormick to C. H. McCormick, Jr., Nov. 1, 1884. "Abbeville Press and Banner," July 22, 1885. By this date the town also had a newspaper called "The McCormick Advance."

[183] Pamphlet entitled "The Cyrus Hall McCormick Cottage for Orphan Boys. An Address by Judge J. S. Cothran on the Occasion of the Laying of the Cornerstone, February 14th, 1885" (Clinton, S. C., 1885). C. H. McCormick, Jr., MSS., Book "F," Nettie F. McCormick to C. H. McCormick, Jr., May 11, 1890.

[184] In 1930, McCormick had about fourteen hundred inhabitants. In 1906 several citizens of McCormick formed the McCormick Land and Lumber Company and purchased the Dorn Mine property of Mrs. Nettie F. McCormick for $27,183. In 1916, McCormick County was formed with McCormick as its county-seat. T. H. Williams, Columbia, S. C., to Centennial Comm. of the Inter. Harv. Co., Mch. 11, 1931. Entries from the books of the N. F. McCormick Estate, furnished by I. T. Gladden.

Hardly had the misfortunes of the Dorn venture caused McCormick to lose his first enthusiasm for mining, than it was stimulated anew by reports of rich strikes in Colorado and Arizona. Several years after the Dorn Company was dissolved in 1870, Thomas S. Morgan wrote from Tucson to his former partner about the opportunities for easy wealth in that neighborhood. McCormick also kept in touch with the "rush" to the Tombstone district in the same territory, and by the summer of 1879 was induced to make his first investment in the far Southwest. At that time he and Morgan purchased a controlling interest in four silver-mining claims in the Papago Mountains, and McCormick was also given an option to buy five others near Tombstone.[185]

The very names of some of these claims were alluring: Ruby, Bullion, San Pedro, Burrow, suggesting both romance and riches. These, however, as well as most of the others which McCormick was soon to acquire, were not mines with shafts and machinery but merely claims or prospects. Their surface was thought to be "likely looking" or to hide the extension of a vein that was being exploited with much profit a few hundred yards away. They were staked off on public land and their names and locations were registered at the government land office. Because overlapping and "jumped" claims were common, bickering over titles was a part of the everyday routine of a mining town. The claimant could sell his prospect as soon as it was registered, but title from the United States could not be secured until improvements, known as assessment work and costing at least $500, had been made. The first step in the

---

[185] ‡T. S. Morgan, Tucson, to C. H. McCormick, Sept. 3, 1879; ‡Agreement of Aug. 23, 1879 between C. H. McCormick and A. Lewis *et al.* On C. C. Copeland's advice, McCormick did not take advantage of this option. A letter from ‡Ida Choate, Tucson, Apr. 18, 1878, to McCormick indicates that he then owned a claim near Tucson known as the "Reaper Mine," but this is its only mention in the correspondence.

development of a holding was usually the sinking of a small "prospecting shaft" to the stratum of rock supposed to be rich in gold or silver.[186]

Sitting in Chicago or New York and buying claims by telegraph on the strength of a prospectus, or on the word of a miner far away who was tempted by every circumstance to misrepresent what he had to sell, was sheer speculation.[187] Even those at the scene in Tucson or Tombstone counted themselves fortunate if one out of a dozen of their "mines" yielded a fair return in metal. In their opinion, the hard work at the diggings was not as lucrative as selling claims to "tenderfeet" who were willing to "buy blind." They deserved to be fleeced.[188] If an easterner, before spending his money, sent an agent to have a look, it was often possible, by "salting" a mine

[186] ‡C. C. Copeland to C. H. McCormick, Nov. 19, 1879.

[187] An example of a venture of this kind was the Tiger Mill & Mining Co., formed to work the Tiger Mine near Prescott, Ariz. Terr. Urged by his friends, ex-Gov. R. C. McCormick and Gov. Safford, who were doubtless acting in good faith, C. H. McCormick in 1879 invested $10,000 in its stock and was for a time its president. It *had been* a profitable mine and was still represented so to be, but the rich ore was exhausted and the company was in debt. By 1882, it narrowly missed being sold for taxes; its creditors took over its control, and the stock-holders, including McCormick, received nothing. He ventured $2,000 more in the reorganized company and lost that also. Letters to C. H. McCormick of R. C. McCormick, N. Y., ‡Nov. 17, 1879, ‡L. Bashford, Mch. 3, 1882, ‡C. Churchill, Oct. 22, 1882, A. H. Girard, Jan. 29, 1882. ‡Pamphlet, "Reports on the Property of the Tiger Mill and Mining Company" (N. Y., 1881). ‡C. H. McCormick to C. C. Copeland, Nov. 13 and 28, 1879. R. C. McCormick to C. H. McCormick, Jr., Feb. 15, 1882. ‡C. Churchill to A. H. Girard, Feb. 1, 1882. ‡J. D. Hooker to C. C. Copeland, Feb. 20, Mch. 12, and Apr. 23, 1883.

[188] ‡C. C. Copeland, Tombstone, to C. H. McCormick, Sept. 30, 1879: "If you could see the prospects or claims that have been sold East on representation for 5, 10, 15, 20, 30 & even 60,000$ each you would be astonished. There are many honest miners here but some are swindlers." In late November, 1879, C. H. McCormick wired Copeland to "make further moderate investments in undoubted good things." Copeland, in his letter of ‡Nov. 27, replied: "You can't mean 'undoubted.'"

or a claim with rich ore, to make it appear an Eldorado.[189] Honest business, in the opinion of many on the mining frontier as elsewhere, was whatever could be done with impunity. The Mexican border and trackless mountains were conveniently close in case of need.

In the early autumn of 1879, McCormick dispatched C. C. Copeland to Arizona to report upon the value of his claims and to look for others worth purchasing.[190] Copeland was keenly alive to the fact that "there is more rascality down here than I have ever met before," but with his usual self-confidence he professed his readiness "to encounter heat, robbers, & Comanche Indians." [191] He was soon told by "the Boys" that he was "the sharpest man that ever looked over this camp." [192] Although he was proud of his reputation for shrewdness, most of the claims which he bought were later found to be worthless. This fact, however, is not proof that he was victimized by his flatterers. It was part of the game, and many others who knew far more about mining than did he, gambled with undeveloped mineral lands, and lost.

During his seven months' stay in Arizona, he used about $15,000 of his employer's money to acquire forty claims, parts

[189] ‡J. D. Hooker, Tucson, to C. C. Copeland, Nov. 14, 1882: Sam Hooker, an old miner, says "he thinks the boys salted the mines upon you."

[190] ‡C. C. Copeland to C. H. McCormick, Aug. 31 and Nov. 27, 1879. Copeland was also interested in purchasing on his own account, and he held several claims jointly with McCormick.

[191] ‡*Idem* to *idem,* Sept. 9 and Oct. 22, 1879. On ‡Mch. 3, 1880, he wrote from Tucson: "Capitalists from all the Eastern cities are coming in here and the whole section is rapidly developing. Many sales are being made —rather swindles—being perpetrated. Only a small percentage of the money invested by Eastern people will ever be taken out of the ground." A railroad engine was first seen in Tucson on Mch. 17, when a spur track from the Southern Pacific was finished.

[192] ‡*Idem,* Tombstone, to *idem,* Sept. 30, 1879. In 1880, C. H. McCormick and G. M. Pullman were trustees of the Maxwell Land Grant Co., holding 1,714,765 acres along the route of the Atchison, Topeka, & Santa Fé R. R. G. B. Carpenter to C. H. McCormick, Nov. 23, 1880.

of claims, and mines in the Papago, Patagonia, Comobabi, Santa Rita, and Baboquivari mountains.[193] Morgan's share in certain of these holdings was bought out, and work was begun at the "Empress" and "Burrow" prospects in the Comobabi Mountains, west of Tucson.[194] McCormick's titles to these two claims, as well as to others, were by no means perfect.[195] Within four months after Copeland's return to Chicago in May, 1880, all miners in McCormick's employ were discharged,[196] and for the next two years his Arizona interests were largely neglected. The one hundred dollars' worth of assessment work required by law to be done every year on each claim until the issuance of the patent, was performed in a few instances, but by 1882, forfeiture, abandonment, or the inability to prove a good title, had reduced to twelve the forty holdings of two years before.[197] Although McCormick's law-

[193] ‡Account-book, entitled "Arizona Mines." This shows that of three locations in the Tombstone District, two (a ¼th claim in the "Boss" and "Cedarberg") were still retained in 1882; five were in the Patagonia Mts., and only one (a ¼th claim to the "Rodman") was held in 1882; twenty-eight in the Comobabi Mts. (about fifty miles west of Tucson) and of these, seven ("Pocahontas," "Emperor," "Dutchess," "Cyrus," "Daniels," "Cæsar," and "Francisco") were still owned in 1882; two (the "Montezuma" and Montezuma mill-site) in the Santa Rita Mts., and still held in 1882, and three were in the Baboquivari Mts., but were abandoned by 1882. ‡C. C. Copeland to T. L. Stiles, Tucson, July 17, 1882.

[194] ‡Thirteen letters of C. C. Copeland to C. H. McCormick, dated between Oct. 2 and Dec. 1, 1879. ‡C. H. McCormick to C. C. Copeland, Nov. 13 and 28, 1879. The mines secured from Morgan were all in the Papago district about fifty miles west of Tucson. Copeland preferred this area at the outset because Mexican laborers could be had there for $1.00 a day, while at Tombstone, miners charged $4.00 a day. He took pains to win the friendship of the Catholic priest at Tucson because through him, Mexican and Indian laborers could conveniently be obtained.

[195] ‡C. C. Copeland to C. H. McCormick, Nov. 12, 14, Dec. 8, 1879; Feb. 2, Mch. 3, 17, Apr. 4, 1880. The "Empress," "Emperor," "Dutchess," and "Burrow" were adjacent properties, and largely covered the site of the "Old Cabrisa" claim. For this reason their titles were cloudy.

[196] ‡S. C. Lewis, Tucson, to C. C. Copeland, Sept. 12, 1880.

[197] See, ftn. 193, above. Copeland left Tucson on Apr. 17, and reached Chicago on May 5, 1880. James Buell of Tucson was delegated to care for

yer in Tucson had been instructed to secure deeds for the most promising of these, he had failed to do so, and adverse claimants were issued patents to the "Cyrus" and "Emperor" properties by the United States government.[198]

In 1882, the interest of speculators in the Southwest, at low ebb after the crash of mining stocks in 1880, had revived. McCormick ordered his Tucson representative "to recover lost ground and to prosecute every contest vigorously." [199] Copeland was sent to Washington to handle the Land Office phase of the business, and through friends there secured an official admission from the Department of the Interior that the patent to the "Cyrus" mine had probably been granted to the wrong claimant.[200] Title to this, and to all except one of the other properties that McCormick deemed worth while, were eventually secured.[201] If they were rich in silver, however, his agents in Arizona were unable to find it, and he received no return whatsoever from this new expenditure of effort and money.[202]

C. H. McCormick's interests after Copeland left. ‡Letters to C. H. McCormick of J. Buell, Sept. (?), 1881, and Nov. 1, 1881, and of W. B. Murray, Dec. 8, 1881. ‡C. H. McCormick to J. Buell, May 6 and Nov. 17, 1881, and to W. B. Murray, Tombstone, Nov. 17, 1881.

[198] ‡Twelve letters of J. Buell, Tucson, to C. H. McCormick or C. C. Copeland, between Feb. 4, 1881, and July 17, 1882. The "Cyrus" mine in the Comobabi Mts. was on land formerly located as the "Cokespa." In 1885 the adverse claim was quieted by a payment of $1,000.

[199] ‡C. H. McCormick to J. Buell, July 14, 1882; ‡C. C. Copeland to T. L. Stiles, Tucson, July 17, 1882.

[200] ‡C. C. Copeland, Washington, to C. H. and N. F. McCormick, Aug. 18, 23, 26, 1882. ‡M. L. Joslyn, Actg. Sec'y. of the Interior, to B. H. Brewster, U. S. Atty. Genl., Washington, Aug. 26, 1882. ‡B. H. Brewster to Drummond & Bradford, Washington, Aug. 29, 1882. Here Brewster instructed the U. S. district attorney in Arizona to investigate the method by which the "Cyrus" patent had been obtained in Apr., 1882. If he found evidence of perjury or fraud, he was to permit Copeland to bring suit in the name of the U. S. for the purpose of having the patent voided.

[201] The exception was the "Emperor" mine in the Comobabi Mts. ‡J. Buell to C. C. Copeland, Sept. 27, 1882, Feb. 15, and Nov. 10, 1883.

[202] ‡J. D. Hooker, Tucson, to C. C. Copeland, Nov. 14, Dec. 28, 1882, and Apr. 2, 1883: As you direct, we will have assessment work done on

Nevertheless, Mrs. McCormick and her eldest son continued to believe that they would some day collect in profits from these holdings at least as much as they had cost.[203] With this hope, they engaged the young John Hays Hammond in 1885 to go to Arizona for the purpose of making a survey. His report was not encouraging. Taxes were paid on these claims for the next forty-five years, but except for $3,000 received in 1889 for their quarter interest in the "Boss" Mine, the venture returned nothing to the heirs of the inventor.[204]

This series of losses was broken by one speculation in mines that, by the narrowest of margins, returned to Cyrus McCormick the sum he ventured in it, and a little more. Among the most important of the silver mines at Leadville, Colorado, in the late 1870's were the "Little Chief" and "Little Pittsburg" on Fryer's Hill. Each of these had paid profits to its owners of as much as $100,000 a month, and in 1879 a company of substantial men, including Thomas Ewing and John V. Farwell, was formed to purchase the "Little Chief."[205] Because

six of your claims in the Comobabi Mts., although we do not think there is one promising mine in all of that district. The "Cyrus" appears to be worthless. The "Francisco" is probably the best of your six, but the ore is worth only $5 a ton. Possibly the ore in your "Montezuma" mine in the Santa Rita Mts. is worth $20 a ton. ‡J. D. Hooker to C. H. McCormick, Jr., Nov. 16, 1882; ‡W. B. Murray, Tombstone, to C. H. McCormick, Jr., Jan. 3, 1883: Your Cedarberg claim near here has been jumped.

203 C. H. McCormick, Jr., MSS., Book "B," Nettie F. McCormick to C. H. McCormick, Jr., Oct. 16, and Nov. 1, 1884.

204 Ibid., Nettie F. McCormick to C. H. McCormick, Jr., Dec. 13, 1884, and Feb. 17, 1885. John Hays Hammond, "The Autobiography of John Hays Hammond" (N. Y., 1935), I, pp. 186-187. MS. Diary of C. H. McCormick, Jr., entry of Mch. 20, 1885. Letter of idem to the author, May 25, 1935.

205 The Little Chief Mining Co. owned about eight acres of mineral property at Leadville, and the Little Pittsburg Co., forty acres. The "Little Pittsburg" is uniformly called the "Big Pittsburg" in the correspondence but I have used the name by which it was listed on the stock market. The "Chicago Tribune," Dec. 8, 1879, gives the daily ore output of the thirty mines at Leadville. The "Chrysolite" tops the list with 125 tons and the "Little Chief" and "Little Pittsburg" follow with 100 tons each. The next

they could not carry through the deal without outside aid, they induced Cyrus McCormick to loan them $75,000 with the assurance that a trust fund of their stock had been set aside as a guarantee of his repayment, and that in one year he would be returned double the amount of his advance. This large bonus was in all likelihood promised as a compensation for the boost that Cyrus McCormick's $75,000 gesture of confidence would give to the reputation of the "Little Chief" mine.

McCormick soon learned that a further objective of the company was to pool a majority of its stock with a majority of the shares of the Little Pittsburg Mining Company, to place these securities under the control of a board of trustees, and thereby to create a business organization resembling the Standard Oil "set-up" being erected at this time.[206] He was naturally concerned about the fate of his $150,000 loan and bonus if this plan should be carried out. He was assured that his interests would be even safer than before, but to quiet all of his fears he was made president of the Little Chief Company, and was promised a $50,000 bonus from the Little Pittsburg Company

in line produces only thirty-five tons. *Supreme Court of the State of New York, City and County of New York. Cyrus H. McCormick, Plaintiff, vs. John V. Farwell, Central Trust Company of New York, Jesse Spaulding, Thomas Ewing, Edward H. Potter, Charles P. Shaw and Alexander B. Davis, Defendants. Summons and Complaint.* (New York, 1882). Hereafter cited as *McCormick vs. Farwell et al.* See also, another pamphlet with the same title as this except that "Summons and Complaint" is replaced by the words "Answer of Defendant, Farwell." #W. J. Collins, M. E., to E. H. Potter, Dec. 20, 1879.

[206] #T. Ewing to C. H. McCormick, Dec. 5, 7, and 8, 1879: "They [the managers of the syndicate] could not afford a controversy with you, & will be glad of your cooperation & the influence of your name, as a Chicago man, to counterbalance any suspicion that the Little Chief is not as good as reported." The prestige of your check gave them the standing necessary to bring in all the capital they needed. The "Evening Post" (N. Y.), Dec. 1, 1879: "The mining stocks . . . are attracting more attention, and of these Little Pittsburg Consolidated has today been the most active, having advanced to 34⅛, . . . Dividends of $100,000 per month are declared, they having been begun on June 10 last."

in consideration of his aid in maintaining its solvency.[207] He
declined an opportunity to buy "Little Chief" stock at less than
the market price, but he took advantage of an even more generous offer to purchase seven thousand shares of "Little Pittsburg." [208] In January, 1880, he wrote with much gratification
of the part that he and a few of the best known New York
millionaires were playing in uniting the control of these two
important mines.[209] The trustees, however, were far more
eager to make a killing on Wall Street than to extract silver
from their properties on Fryer's Hill.[210]

The merger was never completed. Mining stocks steadily
dropped and in March, 1880, the crash came. Inefficient management at the mine, an unexpected decline in the quality of
the ore, and labor troubles in Leadville, partly account for the
collapse of the bubble. Two months later McCormick resigned

[207] This aid consisted of opening a $223,000 account in his own name in
a N. Y. bank—the money to be publicized (but not used) as a "bolster"
to the bonds of the company. ‡C. H. McCormick to A. B. Davis, N. Y.,
Dec. 22, 1879; ‡C. H. McCormick's telegram to E. H. Potter, N. Y.,
Dec. 22, 1879, and ‡C. H. McCormick's telegram and letter to C. P. Shaw,
N. Y., Dec. 22, 1879. ‡Telegrams of T. Ewing to C. H. McCormick,
Dec. 13, and 16, 1879. A shaft at the "Little Pittsburg" mine was named
the "McCormick."

[208] On Dec. 19, 1879, "Little Pittsburg" stock was listed @ 61½. On that
day C. H. McCormick accepted the offer of the Co. to buy 7,000 shares
for $31,000. In May, 1880, he loaned the company $2800 and received 400
shares of stock as security for its repayment. ‡C. P. Shaw to C. H. Mc-
Cormick, Dec. 19 and 30, 1879, and Jan. 6 and 12, 1880. In urging C. H.
McCormick to buy "Little Chief" stock, Shaw remarked: "To my mind
the transaction looks very much like buying U. S. Bonds at 40 cents on
the dollar." ‡C. H. McCormick to A. L. Earle, May 10, 1880.

[209] ‡C. H. McCormick to R. W. Hall, Jan. 8, 1880.

[210] ‡C. P. Shaw to C. H. McCormick, Jan. 6 and 12, 1880. "Chicago
Daily Tribune," Mch. 20, 1880: "A long review of the circumstances attending the collapse of the Little Pittsburg is printed editorially in the
'Denver Tribune.' The writer intimates that there was a combination to
'bear' the stock formed, and that some persons interested in the Company
were in the movement. . . . The general opinion among all well-informed
people is that the mine is still rich."

his office of president.[211] He had already received the $50,000 bonus from the Little Pittsburg Company, and in 1881 sold his stock in this concern for about $1.00 a share.[212] The Little Chief Company had paid McCormick about $60,000 of its obligation to him, and now claiming to be bankrupt, offered him $5,000 in full settlement of the $90,000 still due.[213] Naturally he declined to accept it, and inquired concerning the whereabouts of the trust fund which had been set aside for his repayment.[214] When no satisfactory answer was made, he turned to his friend and fellow-church-member, John V. Farwell, for satisfaction. Farwell, who was widely known for his business integrity and generous contributions to many worthy causes, believed that he could not be held to account because

[211] The "R. E. Lee" mine at Leadville now enjoyed the spotlight. *Ibid.*, Mch. 26, 1880: "It seems to be generally admitted that the 'Little Pittsburg' has seen 'its best days' and there is a big row among those who at present advices are badly bitten by the Stock." At that time the stock was quoted at 8. It had been 13 earlier in the month and about 28 in late Jan. ‡C. H. McCormick to Board of Trustees of the Little Chief Mining Co., May (?), 1880. C. H. McCormick was succeeded in the office of president by Adalbert Ames. The stock pool trustees closed up their business in Aug., 1880. ‡J. Spaulding to C. H. McCormick, Mch. 6, 1880. Spaulding was president of the Chicago Mining Board which in the preceding December had opened a mining and stock exchange on Madison Street. ‡C. P. Shaw to C. H. McCormick, Apr. 15 and 29, 1880. ‡A. L. Earle to C. H. McCormick, June 25, 1880.

[212] ‡Letter and telegram of J. Spaulding to C. H. McCormick, Mch. 11 and 24, 1880. ‡C. P. Shaw to J. Spaulding, Dec. 21, 1880. ‡C. H. McCormick to Importers' and Traders' Nat'l. Bank of N. Y., Mch. 19, 1881. McCormick sold the stock for $7800. ‡E. Townsend Co. to C. H. McCormick, Mch. 22, 1881.

[213] ‡J. Spaulding to C. H. McCormick, Aug. 30, 1880. ‡C. P. Shaw to J. Spaulding, Dec. 26, 1880. C. H. McCormick, Jr., to C. H. McCormick, Aug. 28, 1880. ‡Pamphlet entitled "Little Chief Mining Company, Reports of the Superintendent and Management to the Stockholders, Oct. 5, 1880."

[214] ‡C. H. McCormick, Jr., to J. E. Chapman, N. Y., Feb. 3, 1881. ‡C. H. McCormick, Jr., to C. H. McCormick, May 29, 1882. He advises his father to sue those who were members of the Little Chief Co. in 1879. ‡C. C. Copeland to C. H. McCormick, June 6, 1882. Copeland was then in N. Y. preparing the bill of complaint against this group.

Fortune had frowned upon their mutual venture. If "Little Chief" affairs had been mismanaged, McCormick and not he had been its president. Farwell wished to keep the dispute out of the press and suggested that the inventor withdraw his bill of complaint filed in a New York State court, choose "three men of business from our brethren in the Church," and let them "judge between us." [215] Although this method of settling a dispute had biblical sanction, it was not acceptable to the inventor. He was quite in accord with Farwell's desire for privacy, but he also was determined to regain the amount of his loan. Although he might waive his right to the $75,000 bonus, he was at least entitled to the balance due, with interest, on the sum that he had advanced. And so, refusing to drop the suit, he pressed it not only against Farwell but against all the others who had been members of the Little Chief Company in 1879. The outcome of this action is unknown, but most probably it was dropped by the trustees of McCormick's estate after the inventor's death in 1884.[216]

If a detailed statement were prepared showing McCormick's

[215] Farwell appeared to be especially liable to McCormick since it had been his shares of stock that had been deposited at the Central Trust Co. in N. Y. as a fund, the dividends from which were to repay the inventor. ‡C. H. McCormick to C. Bell, N. Y., Feb. 21, and Apr. 19, 1881. ‡J. V. Farwell to C. H. McCormick, Oct. 20 and to C. H. McCormick, Jr., Dec. 25, 1882. Farwell contended that he was not to blame for McCormick's loss, and that his old associates in the Little Chief Co. also owed him (Farwell) much money. On Dec. 7, he met C. H. McCormick and C. H. McCormick, Jr., and by reading from his letter-book of Nov., 1879, endeavored to prove his innocence. The McCormicks were not impressed and on Dec. 25th Farwell again in vain requested that the dispute be "amicably decided by some of our brethren in the church." ‡C. H. McCormick, Jr., to C. H. McCormick, Oct. 25, 1882, May 2, and Nov. 30, 1883. In the last of these letters, the son advised his father to compromise the matter "partly in view of the fact of the recent prospective matrimonial connection between the Farwells and Judge Drummond."

[216] The "Little Chief" mine was written off the books of the McCormick Harv. Mach. Co., as worthless, on July 31, 1888. Letter of Lucile Kellar to the author, May 10, 1935.

loss or profits from each of his many ventures in railroads and mines, the net balance would probably be a small sum on the debit side of the ledger. The large amounts written in red in the Dorn account would be offset by the gains from the Union Pacific and Crédit Mobilier, with enough to spare in all likelihood, to absorb most of his losses from the Southern Railroad Association and the other less costly undertakings.

As a speculator, McCormick was not a success. Bad Luck deserves some of the blame, but he was occasionally victimized by men who used his money and the prestige of his name to pull their chestnuts out of the fire. He hazarded large sums in stocks and bonds without much preliminary training in the ways of Wall Street. This is the more surprising in view of his business shrewdness in all matters relating to his factory and Chicago real estate. These interests, together with the many problems relating to the church and seminary, were more than enough to engage the inventor's entire attention and thought.

His investments in railroads and other methods of communication illustrate one aspect of his dominant nationalism. If there was any thread which bound into a semblance of unity his diverse activities during the last twenty-five years of his life, it was his determination to aid in destroying the intersectional hatreds which had brought so much woe to his country between 1861 and 1865. He believed that his harvesting-machine factory, with its sales in almost every state and territory, was one strand of the economic bond that would help to make a new nation after the war. In his opinion, his aid to railroads stretching the length and breadth of the land was calculated to assist toward the same great end. To unite the South and North again in politics and in religion was his ideal for the Democratic Party and the Presbyterian Church. In the months following Appomattox, while he was deriving so much satisfaction from his share in the work of joining the Far

West with the East by a transcontinental railroad, he was endeavoring with all zeal to banish radicalism from the councils of his denomination so that Presbyterians of the North and South could meet together once more in good fellowship.

CHAPTER VI

RELIGIOUS RADICALISM DEFEATS McCORMICK,
1865-1867

WHEN the Spring Resolutions of 1861 gave the southern members of the Old School Presbyterian Church the option of disloyalty to the Confederacy or withdrawal from the national denomination, they from necessity and by preference, chose the latter alternative. Cyrus McCormick and his fellow-conservatives in the North thereby lost the support of the talent and votes of many presbyteries. The control of the northern General Assembly passed into the hands of the "progressives." The new régime was not unwilling to exercise its power, both by passing the resolutions concerning slavery and secession, already mentioned, and by moving slowly toward a union with the New School Presbyterian Church. This last question was discussed in the Old School General Assembly of 1862, but it was deemed "inexpedient" to take any immediate action.[1] The fusionists in both denominations, however, gained in strength from year to year.[2]

By the close of the war, McCormick and others who were unwilling to make concessions in matters of doctrine and ecclesiastical order, realized that their church faced a new danger

[1] "Minutes of the General Assembly," 1859-1864, *op. cit.*, pp. 211, 222.
[2] "Nevin's Encyclopædia," p. 835. In 1863 the General Assembly (N. S.) received a delegation from the O. S. Church. Dr. Henry Boynton Smith, moderator of that General Assembly, has been called the "Hero of Reunion." "Minutes of the General Assembly," 1859-1864, pp. 387-388, 391. In 1864 an overture for union from the N. S. Gen'l. Assembly was presented to the O. S. Gen'l. Assembly, but that body did nothing but refer it to a committee.

hardly less menacing than the issue which had driven out the southern wing four years before. Those who were working for fusion, however, dared not push their program too rapidly for fear lest three churches would be created instead of one.[3] Presbyteries in the border states, which had been held to the northern church with much difficulty because of its antislavery position, would probably refuse to consent to a modification of the cherished "standards."

In December, 1861, the ten synods of Old School Presbyterians in the Confederacy organized a separate church under their own General Assembly.[4] Some of its most eminent clergymen, and notably Dr. J. H. Thornwell and Dr. B. M. Palmer, had preached secession with the ardor of Old Testament prophets and upheld slavery as a "divine trust."[5] In their General Assembly of 1862, the war was declared to be "for religion, for the Church, for the Gospel, and for existence itself." Two years later their position was further clarified by a resolution affirming that "it is the peculiar mission of the Southern Church to conserve the institution of slavery, and to make it a blessing to the master and the slave."[6] Thus the Old School of the North and the Old School of the South

[3] *Ibid.*, p. 50, i.e., an "United" Presbyterian Church; a church of O. S. members who refused to join, and another of N. S. members who stood out.

[4] "The Presbyterian Church in the Confederate States of America." The New School group of the South, which had seceded in 1857, joined the Old School organization there in 1864.

[5] One of Dr. Palmer's best-known sermons on the eve of the war was entitled, "Slavery a Divine Trust,—Duty of the South to Preserve and Perpetuate It."

[6] Cited in "Minutes of the General Assembly," 1865-1869, *op. cit.*, pp. 66-67. Dr. B. M. Smith, prominent in the southern church, wrote to C. H. McCormick, on Sept. 8, 1865, that northerners should bear in mind the difference between "conserving" slavery (i.e., acknowledging its justification from Scripture) and "preserving" it. In any event, according to Dr. Smith, the resolution of 1864 was never accepted as the "formal, deliberate, and solemn deliverance of the Southern Church," and had been decidedly repudiated since that time by leading ministers and church courts.

traveled rapidly in opposite directions between 1861 and 1865, although it may be more accurate to insist that the southerners still were anchored to their ancient principles at the close of the war while their former friends at the North had moved far away.

In view of these facts, the task of reuniting the northern and southern wings of the Old School Presbyterian Church would be a most difficult one. Presbyterians have always been distinguished for contentiousness and unwillingness to yield on questions of church polity.[7] Their church councils included many of the best-known lawyers of the land, while not a few of their ministers, judging from their conduct during the Reconstruction Period, would have gained eminence in politics and statecraft. The administrative structure of the denomination was very like a state within a state, and if the religious cloak is stripped from the discussions in presbytery meetings and General Assemblies, platforms, parties, terms of peace, and most of the other questions which gave character to the debates in Congress stand revealed. Many of the Presbyterian ministers in 1865 were as eager to punish and humiliate their southern brethren before admitting them to full fellowship as were the radical reconstructionists at Washington. Their letters not infrequently reflect a vindictiveness wholly foreign to the teachings of their Saviour. They spoke for a God of Wrath and reminded the South in 1865 that, "those who have sown the wind must expect to reap the whirlwind."[8] Except

[7] Draft of an article by C. H. McCormick for the "New York Observer," n.d., but probably late 1865. "Their tendency to division has been one of standing reproach to Presbyterians. They are constantly crippling their power and moral influence by splitting among themselves."

[8] "Minutes of the General Assembly," 1865-1869, p. 68. In 1866, this body sent a pastoral letter to its churches, which carries the reader back to the days of John Winthrop. "Any concession touching the offences of such persons [southerners] would have been the height of unkindness. It would have been a connivance at their sin, and would have brought down upon them, and upon us alike, the displeasure of God. . . . We have aimed

for the fact that the northern church had no military force at its disposal to coerce its southern branch, the elements of the situation closely resembled those involved in political reconstruction.

There were, therefore, two chief issues before the Old School Presbyterian Church of the North in 1865. Should the seceders be readmitted to full communion and, if so, on what terms? Should the denomination consolidate with the New School wing, and, if so, how much was it willing to concede in matters of doctrine and church government? Remembering that the Old School Presbyterians in the states of the erstwhile Confederacy were, in the main, ultraconservative, the close interrelationship between these two problems is at once apparent. Those of the North, like Cyrus McCormick who believed "the old Democratic and Presbyterian 'hoops' that were *broken* must be reunited before we can have a *perfectly* restored and reunited country and church," [9] would do their best to prevent a merger of the Old and New Schools. For, if this came about, doubtless some of the "advanced ideas" of the New School would have to be subscribed to, and one more barrier would be erected against the return of those who had been forced out in 1861.[10]

The matter was not so clear-cut as this, but the chief complications will appear as the course of Cyrus McCormick in

---

to reclaim offenders by demanding only what Christ requires of us as rulers in his house." *Ibid.*, pp. 171-172.

[9] From a ⧣"Draft of an address in C. H. McCormick's handwriting, prepared to be delivered before the General Assembly of the (O. S.) Presbyterian Church at St. Louis, 1866." There is no available proof that it was ever delivered, although McCormick attended the Assembly.

[10] C. H. McCormick to E. Erskine, Mch. 10, 1866: "The Church North must first move. Let that be done in the right way and with the right spirit and then look to the South. I believe she will respond nobly. But let the Old and New School Assemblies unite . . . , and I believe the purity of our great Church will have departed." ⧣D. X. Junkin to C. H. McCormick, Mch. 19, 1866.

relation to them is traced. The seminary at Chicago and the position of Dr. Lord were factors of the situation which in his eyes naturally loomed larger than they did in the regard of the church as a whole. If the southern churches returned to the fold, conservatism again would probably be in the ascendency. Dr. Lord could then be eliminated, and the institution could carry out, in so far as the changed national situation permitted, the purposes of its chief founder. On the other hand, if the Old and New Schools came together, Dr. Lord would be more firmly entrenched than ever, and theological students of the North who were resolved not to depart from the beliefs of their fathers, would be obliged to go to southern seminaries for their instruction. Furthermore, with a united northern church, considerations of economy would make advisable the closing of some of the Presbyterian seminaries which had arisen after, and in some measure because of, the schism of 1837.

As before the war, McCormick's program for his church was directed toward promoting harmony and union between the two sections of the country, although as in the earlier period, it was calculated to disturb the peace of the North.[11] He and others appreciated their dependence for success upon the fortunes of President Andrew Johnson, and believed that the relative strength of conservatives and radicals in Congress was a barometer which indicated quite accurately the weather conditions within their church. As a prominent southern Presbyterian wrote early in 1866: "Oh, if the religious people of the Presb. Ch. North had as sound views of Ch. Govt., as that good old sinner of our Govt. [President Johnson], how soon all would be right. . . . All conservatives of the North must rally round him and the country is safe with God's blessing." [12]

[11] ‡C. H. McCormick to Rev. Wm. Brown, Oct. 6, 1865 and to L. J. Halsey, Mch. 12, 1866.
[12] ‡B. M. Smith to C. H. McCormick, Feb. 22, 1866. ‡E. Erskine to C. H. McCormick, Mch. 16, 1866: Johnson's course has helped us wonderfully and will continue to do so.

Owing to the bitterness of politics during the Reconstruction Period, and the conspicuous rôle played by McCormick in the Democratic Party, it was a foregone conclusion that his every move in the religious field would arouse unmeasured abuse from the Republican press.

Hardly had Lee surrendered at Appomattox than Mc-Cormick opened a correspondence with influential northern and southern ministers of his faith to learn their views upon the question of reunion. He became a clearinghouse of conservative opinions from both sides of the Line. It is a matter for wonder how he could find time to write so many lengthy letters on the church situation when he was obliged to give much of his attention to his other important interests.

Dr. Benjamin M. Smith, head of the Union Theological Seminary at Hampden Sidney, Virginia, and at an earlier day a pastor in the Valley near McCormick's old home, was the inventor's chief southern correspondent. If Smith was correctly informed, his views concerning the reunion question were moderate compared to those of the majority of his colleagues.[13] For the next several years McCormick was also more hopeful of success than were most of his northern associates.[14] They reminded him that he was a southern and not a northern conservative in outlook, and that he did not give sufficient weight to the prevailing bitterness felt toward men recently in rebellion.[15] The direction of the wind could be judged from the action of the northern Old School Assembly of 1865, in session

[13] B. M. Smith to C. H. McCormick, Sept. 8, 1865.
[14] ‡Letters to C. H. McCormick of E. Erskine, Nov. 21, 1865, and Mch. 16, 1866, L. J. Halsey, Mch. 5, and 20, 1866, S. Robinson. Mch. 17, 1866, C. H. Read, Richmond, May 6, 1866, and B. M. Smith May 12, 1866. By this date Dr. Smith, who had hitherto been rather optimistic that reunion would come, said he was convinced of its "utter hopelessness" and expected even more radical action by the northern branch of the church. In view of the declaration by its General Assembly before the close of that month he was justified in his prophecy. ‡See D. X. Junkin and B. M. Smith to C. H. McCormick, May 19 and 31, 1866, respectively.
[15] ‡E. Erskine to C. H. McCormick, Mch. 16, 1866.

during the excitement caused by the surrender of Lee and
Johnston, and the assassination of Lincoln. This body reaffirmed that both secession and slaveholding were "great
crimes" against God, and that any southern Presbyterian desiring admission to a northern congregation must "confess and
forsake his sin . . . before he shall be received." [16] In this
manner the church virtually prescribed a test "not recognized
in Presbyterian standards" as a necessary preliminary to renewed fellowship, and also made arrangements to send "missionaries" to the South as to a foreign field.[17]

This was not an auspicious setting for the inauguration of
McCormick's policy of reunion. To him the action of the
Assembly was "without a single redeeming feature of charity
or Christian spirit." By it the church had assumed the pre-
rogative of the government and had condemned and imposed a
punishment without giving the accused the benefit of a
hearing.[18]

Alas, for the poorness of human nature [he wrote], and therefore the consequences of taking a first false step . . . and thus per-
verting a power for infinite good to an instrument of positive
mischief. But for the fatal error committed by the General Assembly in its action taken in 1861 toward its members subject to the
then ill-advised "Confederate Govern't," what an influence and
power might and no doubt would now be exerted by that Church

[16] "Minutes of the General Assembly," 1865-1869, pp. 42, 45. Draft by
C. H. McCormick of an article for the "New York Observer," n.d., but
probably late 1865: "But it is objected that these Southern ministers and
Church-members took an active part in the rebellion and therein committed
a great sin. Grant it. Have not some of the most faithful of God's friends
been led astray under the power of temptation? And has there ever been
a great political conflict in a Christian country, where good men were not
found on both sides? Do false political views necessarily invalidate piety?
. . . Whatever may be said of the recent political course of Southern
Christians no candid mind can deny to them the possession of piety."

[17] The phrase is taken from a letter of B. M. Smith to C. H. McCormick,
Sept. 8, 1865.

[18] C. H. McCormick to B. M. Smith, July 14, 1865.

for good, in reuniting the people North and South, in the bonds of fraternity and Christian fellowship. Whatever differences may have existed hitherto in the church on the abstract question of slavery, practically there could no longer have continued any trouble from that quarter. . . . But now, by the action of the General Assembly, if not reconsidered and changed, the disruption of the Church is to be perpetuated . . . while it is held by *President Johnson* that the status of the *States* remains the same as before the war! [19]

McCormick hoped that the South would return if the northern Old School Presbyterian Church in the 1866 Assembly rescinded its resolutions of the preceding year.[20] In his opinion every member of the denomination should work for their repeal because upon the issue depended the very life of his church. He insisted that the first step must be taken by the North, both because southerners out of regard for their own self-respect could not rejoin as long as the resolutions of 1865 were still spread upon the journal of its supreme legislature, and because it was the northern, and not the southern, branch of the church which had created the schism of 1861.[21] Possibly the Spring Resolutions should also be annulled, if by that additional confession of error the southerners would reunite the more quickly.[22] The matter must be handled in a practical way, and therefore the South must not insist at the outset upon more than the North would ever yield.[23] Christians were expected to be magnanimous, particularly to those of

[19] *Idem* to *idem,* July 14, 1865.

[20] ‡C. H. McCormick to Rev. Wm. Brown, Oct. 6, 1865.

[21] ‡W. Brown, Richmond, Va., to C. H. McCormick, Sept. 8, 1865; C. H. McCormick to S. Robinson, Louisville, Ky., Dec. 7, 1865; to the "Northwestern Presbyterian" (Chicago), n.d., but late 1865 and to the "New York Observer," Apr. 2, 1866.

[22] C. H. McCormick to the "Northwestern Presbyterian." Here he denies that he demands the rescinding of the Spring Resolutions.

[23] C. H. McCormick to S. Robinson, Dec. 7, 1865, and to "The Presbyterian" (Phila.), Dec. 25, 1865.

their own sect, but McCormick apparently forgot that men, whether Christian or otherwise, who are victorious in a civil war, are not often charitable. He took for granted that his northern brethren wished the southern churches to return. Here, too, he misjudged, for many did not desire to strengthen the hands of the conservatives and thus impede the movement toward a union with the New School.[24]

He also found far less sentiment for union in the South than he had hoped. As Dr. Smith explained to him, all in that section were agreed that their Assembly should make no advances and that they should never return unless the northern church repealed some or all of its wartime deliverances. At the outset he believed that to expunge the resolutions of 1861 and 1865 would be sufficient, but others demanded that all declarations bearing upon secession and slavery should be passed into oblivion.[25] Some in the South shrewdly saw a chance to benefit by remaining aloof, for would not the border state presbyteries and a goodly number of the Old School conservatives of the North refuse to join with the New School Church?[26] If so, there might yet be a national Old School Church, but it would arise as a result of northerners seeking affiliation with the southern General Assembly, and not by the ex-Confederates coming "puling and whining about the [northern] church door, like a whipt spaniel, . . . asking for admittance."[27] Many wanted no coöperation with the hated North under any condition, and their number increased as the South

24 ‡E. Erskine to C. H. McCormick, Mch. 16, 1866: "The North is intensely opposed to any reactionary movement."

25 B. M. Smith to C. H. McCormick, Sept. 8, 1865, ‡Oct. 12, 1865, and ‡Feb. 22, 1866. ‡H. A. Boardman to C. H. McCormick, Aug. 1, and Dec. 7, 1866. Dr. Boardman urged against a secession of conservatives from the Old School Church of the North. He admitted, however, that if radicalism maintained its ascendency in this church, the southern denomination would gradually extend its membership north of Mason and Dixon's line.

26 ‡B. M. Smith to C. H. McCormick, Oct. 12, 1865.

27 ‡B. M. Smith to C. H. McCormick, Feb. 22, 1866.

felt the full force of the "thorough" reconstruction policy of Congress.[28] Even the conciliatory position taken by Dr. Hodge and the Princeton group found small favor in the South,[29] and the few northern religious journals which in 1865 tried to present the situation impartially tended to become more critical of the southerners as they found them emphasizing concessions more than compromise.[30]

Little could be expected when southern clergymen wrote in the vein of Dr. Samuel B. Wilson, now eighty-four years of age and for sixty years a preacher of the gospel: "They require us to confess the sin of political error (if it be an error) and all the sin of slavery. We can do neither. Obedience to the powers that be is a Christian duty we believe. But whether obedience be due to the State or the U. S. they have no right to decide. As to slavery—we cannot confess it to be a sin without impeaching the character of God—casting reproach on Moses, the Apostles and our Church from its origin to this day." [31]

In view of these conflicting attitudes, Cyrus McCormick was seeking to achieve the impossible. His southern friends gave him much advice but little help, and even the conserva-

[28] Wm. Brown, Richmond, to C. H. McCormick, Sept. 8, 1865. To paraphrase: There is no reunion sentiment among us worth naming, and its absence is not more due to exasperation, than to a wish to defend a principle. Brown added that the southern position was precisely the stand taken in 1861 by Dr. J. H. Thornwell in his "Address of Our General Assembly to All the Churches of Christ Throughout the Earth."

[29] ‡B. M. Smith to C. H. McCormick, Feb. 22, 1866. To Dr. Hodge's suggestion that the southerners should not require the rescinding of the deliverances of 1862, 1863 and 1864, because they related only to the northern church, Smith answered that they must be expunged because they were unconstitutional. ‡E. Erskine to C. H. McCormick, Mch. 16, 1866.

[30] B. M. Smith to C. H. McCormick, Sept. 8, 1865; C. H. McCormick to L. J. Halsey, n.d., but early 1866; to W. Brown, Jan. 7, 1866, and ‡to E. Erskine, May 5, 1866.

[31] ‡S. B. Wilson, Union Theolog. Sem., Hampden Sidney, Va., to Rev. J. M. Wilson, June 4, 1866.

tives in the North seemed unwilling to make a vigorous fight. Dr. Rice, who might have rendered yeoman service, was broken in health.[32] McCormick paid for the publication of some of his correspondence with leading southern divines.[33] He gave financial aid to the "Central Presbyterian" of Richmond,[34] and the "Free Christian Commonwealth" of Louisville,[35] because he believed that these papers could do much to influence southern church sentiment in the right direction. To his chagrin, however, he found that the northern Presbyterian press, almost without exception, was either hostile or indifferent to the movement.[36] Some editors, professing friendliness toward reunion, urged that to discuss the matter in their columns would merely delay success by still further inflaming opinion on each side.

In late 1865 McCormick conferred with several leaders of the southern church and recommended that their General Assembly at its Macon, Georgia, meeting in December should remain silent on the issue.[37] Since the Confederacy was no more, this Assembly made the necessary change in the name of the denomination, and resolved to continue the separate existence of its church. Although nothing else could well have been

[32] C. H. McCormick to E. Erskine, Jan. 29, 1866.

[33] ‡C. H. McCormick to S. I. Prince, Nov. 4, 1865, and to "The Presbyterian," Dec. 25, 1865, and Jan. 4, 1866. ‡Letters to C. H. McCormick, of B. M. Smith, Sept. 8, 1865, and Apr. 15, 1866, S. I. Prince, Oct. 27, 1865, C. H. Read, May 6, 1866, "The Presbyterian," Jan. 1 and 15, 1866, and of E. Erskine, Nov. 21, 1865. The "New York World," Nov. 13, 1865.

[34] ‡B. M. Smith to C. H. McCormick, July 22, 1865; ‡W. Brown to C. H. McCormick, Sept. 8, 1865.

[35] ‡A. Davidson, Louisville, to C. H. McCormick, Dec. 16, 1865; ‡C. H. McCormick to A. Davidson, Jan. 24, 1866.

[36] Even Dr. Erskine in his "Northwestern Presbyterian" abandoned his position of benevolent neutrality and became mildly anti-southern in tone. ‡M. B. Grier to C. H. McCormick, Sept. 30, 1865; ‡W. Brown to E. Erskine, Nov. 29, 1865; C. H. McCormick to "Northwestern Presbyterian," n.d., but probably late 1865.

[37] ‡M. B. Grier to C. H. McCormick, Sept. 30, 1865; C. H. McCormick to "The Presbyterian," Jan. 4, 1866.

done under the circumstances except to dissolve and beg for admittance to the northern church, "The Presbyterian" of Philadelphia, the most influential of the Old School papers and hitherto friendly to the cause of reunion, now asserted that the southerners had deliberately affronted the North and barred the way to reconciliation. It closed its columns to any further discussion of the subject after expressing the pious hope that the passage of years would serve to change the views of the South.[38]

To widen the breach still further, the General Assembly of the northern church, convening at St. Louis in 1866, reaffirmed in more vigorous terms the resolutions of 1865, and because the Louisville Presbytery had refused to subscribe to those and other wartime deliverances, virtually expelled it from fellowship. "We trust the day is not distant when these dregs of rebellion shall be purged from the Church," ran the pastoral letter adopted by that convention.[39]

[38] "The Presbyterian" continued to print the articles signed "Augustine of Hippo" which were unfriendly to the South. Eds. of "The Presbyterian" to C. H. McCormick, Jan. 1, and 5, 1866; C. H. McCormick to "The Presbyterian," Jan. 4, 1866; ‡B. M. Smith to C. H. McCormick, Feb. 22, 1866.

[39] "Minutes of the Gen'l. Assembly," 1865-69, pp. 160, 166, 169-77. On Sept. 2, 1865, the Presbytery of Louisville adopted a "Declaration and Testimony against the Erroneous and Heretical Doctrines and Practices which have . . . been propagated in the Presbyterian Church . . . during the last five years." These "heretical doctrines" all concerned slavery and rebellion. Forty-one ministers and seventy-eight ruling elders, mostly from the Ky. and Mo. synods, signed this protest, and were often called the "Declaration and Testimony" men. ‡As early as Sept. 30, 1865, M. B. Grier wrote to C. H. McCormick that the "Louisville Movement" was most unfortunate in its effect upon the cause of reunion. It stirred up radical furore, and threatened to reduce still further the conservative strength in the northern church. C. H. McCormick to E. Erskine, Jan. 29, 1866. C. H. McCormick to B. M. Smith, Feb. 4, 1866: "It remains to be seen in what way Christ designs that all these differences shall ultimately promote His Glory, and the good of the Church." ‡A. T. McGill of Princeton to C. H. McCormick, Dec. 20, 1869: The "Declaration and Testimony" men are in dilemma. They can not go South for their connection because Mo. is filling with northerners.

Shortly before this Assembly convened, McCormick expressed the opinion that its action would determine the status of the reunion question for the "next 25 years." [40] At St. Louis he exerted what influence he could in behalf of reconciliation, but he experienced one of the "saddest disappointments" of his life when he found the majority there "a tyrannical mob." Once more it was impressed upon him that the will of the many and not the "Constitution" was the new law of his church. [41] At the close of the convention, he and his friends agreed that reunion in the near future could not be expected. McCormick, however, determined to change his tactics rather than abandon the fight.

His new policy toward the southern question was in part shaped by the action taken by this Assembly on matters relating to the seminary at Chicago. While some of the conservatives in the church liked to believe during 1865 that their numbers were slowly being recruited in the East, they had no doubt that the outlook in the Middle West was most dismal. [42] Perhaps Princeton and Western (Allegheny) seminaries might withstand the radical tide, but Chicago was clearly doomed. The board of directors there began a policy of proscription against all conservatives under its jurisdiction, [43] and Dr. L. J. Halsey, the one friend of McCormick left on the faculty,

If they stay independent they will lose their property. They do not want to join the North again because of the O. S.-N. S. reunion, but by the terms of this reunion all rules adopted by either branch during the period of separation fall to the ground unless reenacted. Hence the Pittsburgh legislation of 1865 so falls, and this is hopeful. In 1868, however, the Ky. presbyteries (and in 1874 the Mo. synod) joined the Southern Presbyterian Church. ‡L.P.C.B. No. 1, 2nd ser., pp. 6-9, C. H. McCormick to B. M. Smith, Apr. 5, 1870.

[40] C. H. McCormick to Editors of "New York Observer," Apr. 2, 1866.

[41] ‡D. X. Junkin to C. H. McCormick, June 11, 1866; C. H. McCormick to J. W. Brockenbrough, June 18, 1866.

[42] ‡M. B. Grier, from Phila., to C. H. McCormick, Sept. 30, 1865; ‡E. Erskine to C. H. McCormick, Jan. 20, 1865.

[43] ‡C. Crosby, Dixon, Ill., to C. H. McCormick, Oct. 28, 1865.

withheld his resignation only because the inventor appealed to his loyalty and sent him small sums of money to supplement his too meager salary.[44] Matters reached a climax in early April, 1866, when the directors by a close vote resolved to request the General Assembly to promote Dr. Lord to the McCormick Chair of Theology.[45] This action signified that the radicals had finally gained control of the administration and with the help of a sympathetic majority in the General Assembly would be able to work their will with the seminary. Furthermore, the Assembly, as a rule, gave much weight to the opinions of the delegates from the Chicago Presbytery about matters relating to the school, and on this occasion its spokesmen would be predominently radical in viewpoint.[46]

These "New Friends," as they were called in the correspondence of the period, were the leaders among the many Presbytrians in the Northwest who had sulked in their tents after the MacMaster forces had been defeated in the Assembly of 1859. Hitherto, most of them had refused to extend financial aid to the school. Although they now talked optimistically about the sums they expected to raise in order to make their period of control a brilliant one, McCormick and his group regarded their poverty as the one ray of hope in a rather desperate situation. He had yet to pay the last $25,000 of his $100,000 pledge, and he had held out the promise of additional sums if all went smoothly. Even his foes might pause before inaugurating a policy which would lead him to withhold these

[44] C. H. McCormick to L. J. Halsey, Mch. 12, 1866: "You are now the salt of the Seminary, and what would it be if you had left? . . . Has his [Dr. Lord's] thirst for blood been slaked? After his failure to get the pastorate of the N. Church, there was some talk of his resigning his professorship. Is there yet no hope of the early realization of that happy event?"

[45] ‡Letters to C. H. McCormick of C. A. Spring, Sr., Apr. 6, 1866, W. W. Harsha, Apr. 9, 1866, J. M. Faris, Apr. 21, 1866, and of E. Erskine, Apr. 27, 1866.

[46] ‡D. C. Marquis to C. H. McCormick, Nov. 24, 1868; ‡E. Erskine to C. H. McCormick, Dec. 24, 1868.

large gifts. Their action, however, in asking for Dr. Lord's
appointment suggested that they had thrown caution to the
winds, although saner views might prevail in the General
Assembly.

When McCormick heard the news from Chicago he determined to go to St. Louis in May and block the move to
elect Dr. Lord. "I rather feel like having a bit of a fight with
the Dr.," he wrote, "and don't feel a bit like being whipped." [47]
He asked the support of eastern clergymen whose word would
be listened to with respect in the convention, and he tried in
vain to prevent news of his projected trip from reaching the
friends of Dr. Lord.[48] That he would not pay the $25,000 in
the event of the election of Dr. Lord, or of another holding
the same views, might well be held in reserve to use as a
devastating surprise in case matters came to a desperate pass.
At the Assembly he would base his opposition to the proposed
appointment on the grounds that considerations of economy
counseled that the fourth Chair should remain vacant for
awhile, and that Dr. Lord, in any event, was not fitted to
teach the theology of the Old School Church.[49]

As has already been mentioned, McCormick was bitterly dis-
appointed at the stand taken by the General Assembly at St.
Louis on the question of reunion with the South. Its provision
for the Chicago Seminary was almost equally unsatisfactory.
It admitted that the opposition to Dr. Lord's appointment was
so "firm and weighty" as to make it inadvisable, but it chose
Dr. E. D. MacMaster, who was hardly more pleasing to Mc-
Cormick.[50] The able old antislavery champion accepted, al-

[47] C. H. McCormick to Rev. J. M. Faris, Apr. 27-30, 1866.
[48] ‡B. M. Smith to C. H. McCormick, May 12, 1866.
[49] ‡D. X. Junkin to C. H. McCormick, May 19, 1866.
[50] "Minutes of the General Assembly," 1865-1869, pp. 133, 152. This body
believed that "both the comfort and usefulness of Dr. Lord will be best
secured by retaining his valuable services in his present department." It
also congratulated him upon the "able and faithful" manner in which he

though with characteristic honesty and forthrightness he refused to draw his salary from funds given by a man who had opposed his views for so long.[51]

Dr. D. X. Junkin believed that the election of MacMaster in defiance of McCormick's wishes would so "shake the confidence of monied men in our Church, as to deter them from any investments of the kind for many years to come. *I never knew a greater outrage."* [52] MacMaster's period of service at the seminary was a very brief one. When he reached Chicago in September, the inventor was informed by his confidential clerk that "the Dr. looks more as though he was fit for a coffin than a Chair of Theology." [53] Exposure to Chicago weather on the way to his classes, so Dr. Halsey wrote, brought Dr. MacMaster's career to a close on December 10.[54] Some years later McCormick, who had always admired his sincerity and courage, helped to pay for the monument erected over his grave at Xenia, Ohio.[55]

Before leaving the General Assembly of 1866 McCormick had for several years taught courses in theology, in addition to his regular duties.

[51] C. H. McCormick to E. Wood, May 25, 1868. "The Presbyter" (Cincinnati), Dec. 2, 1868. This journal, in its issue of Dec. 9, 1869, denied that MacMaster had ever said that he would not accept income from the McCormick endowment.

[52] ‡D. X. Junkin to C. H. McCormick, June 11, 1866. For the same thought see Dr. Erskine's editorial in the "Northwestern Presbyterian," May 8, 1869.

[53] ‡C. A. Spring, Jr., to C. H. McCormick, Sept. 4, 1866: "How shamefully they have treated you in the whole affair. It does seem as though wickedness gets mixed up in the Churches as bad as anywhere else."

[54] ‡L. J. Halsey to C. H. McCormick, Dec. 15, 1866: MacMaster's brief career here was conciliatory. He told me he believed you would be satisfied with him when you came to know him personally.

[55] Memo. by C. H. McCormick, dated Mch. 18, 1867. Here McCormick calls the late Dr. MacMaster "that highminded and noble hearted Christian Professor & gentleman." ‡J. G. Monfort and D. McMillan, Cincinnati, to C. H. McCormick, Feb. 12, 1875. C. H. McCormick sent $20. See, ‡L.P.C.B. of C. H. McCormick, Nov. 1873-June 1876, p. 269, D. E. Bradley, for C. H. McCormick, to J. G. Monfort, Feb. 27, 1875.

talked with Mr. Jesse L. Williams, the close friend of Dr. Lord and able leader of the radical group in control of the board of directors of the seminary. Contrary to Williams's later recollection, McCormick understood from the conversation that he would no longer be expected to pay the $25,000 still due on his original gift. Over two years later when the inventor endeavored to remember what had been said at this parley, he believed that Williams assured him of the "New Friends' " readiness to take their turn at seminary control and of their determination to sustain their administration by funds raised through their own efforts.[56]

Thus the General Assembly adjourned with McCormick defeated on both the seminary and southern church questions, and with the resolution of "fraternal affection and of desire for organic union" with the New School denomination a certain indication that "liberal" theological doctrines were rapidly coming to the fore.[57] Clearly it was time to revise a policy which had brought nothing except defeat. Personal influence, incessant letter-writing, and occasional articles in religious journals had been insufficient to bring a victory. Momentarily, the thought of abandoning his connection with the religious life of Chicago was given consideration. Late in 1866 he purchased a home on Fifth Avenue, New York, and a pew in Dr. Rice's Presbyterian Church not far away.[58] He decided to retain his seat in the North Church of Chicago for a time at least, but for several years he declined to contribute

---

[56] C. H. McCormick to B. M. Smith, June 24, 1866, and to W. Lord, Jan. 16, 1869. Correspondence between C. H. McCormick and J. L. Williams, publish in the "Northwestern Presbyterian," Dec. 19, 1868, and Jan. 9, 1869. Memo. of C. H. McCormick, Mch. 18, 1867.

[57] "Minutes of the General Assembly," 1865-1869, op. cit., p. 138.

[58] ‡C. H. McCormick to B. M. Smith, Dec. 25, 1866. The residence was at 40 5th Ave. (corner of 10th St. and 5th Ave.). C. H. McCormick to D. X. Junkin, Dec. 3, 1866: "Chicago, while a great city, and with a great future before it, has lost much of its interest for me by means of the Radical rule there. What is to become of the Seminary remains to be seen!"

more than the pew rent to its support.[59] He was glad, however, to learn that the aged Dr. D. C. Junkin had retired,[60] and that for the first time since the resignation of Dr. Rice, the Chicago congregation was favored with one of the ablest pastors in the city, the young and eloquent Rev. David C. Marquis.[61]

Although the Chicago Seminary lost its attraction for him now that it was in the control of the radicals, he could not give up his interest in Old School Presbyterianism. If he were unable to help its cause by contributing to the school in the Middle West, there were other places in the country where it needed aid. He had pledged the $25,000 to his denomination, and he believed that it would be unethical to invest this sum for his own profit merely because the original object of his benevolence would no longer heed his counsel.[62] Dr. B. M. Smith had asked him seven years before at Indianapolis to "do something" for the cause of Presbyterian education in Virginia, and McCormick had vaguely promised to lend a hand after the Chicago Seminary was well started.[63] The Civil War destroyed almost one-half of the endowment of Union Theological Seminary in Virginia, and the balance brought only a very uncertain and slender income to the

[59] ‡C. H. McCormick to D. C. Marquis, Jan. 10, 1867; to ‡E. Wood, Jan. 21, 1867; to H. A. Hurlbut, Dec. 3, 1866. ‡H. A. Hurlbut to C. H. McCormick, Jan. 31 and Oct. 11, 1866. ‡E. Wood to C. H. McCormick, Jan. 9, 1867. ‡J. Forsythe to C. H. McCormick, June 27, 1870. ‡L.P.C.B. No. 1, 2nd ser., p. 289, C. H. McCormick to D. C. Marquis, Oct. 30, 1870: I will pay my share of the $12,000 debt of the North Church.

[60] Mary Adams to Nettie F. McCormick, May 7, 1866; Mary Ann to N. F. McCormick, Apr. 16, 1866. Letters to C. H., of L. J. McCormick, Apr. 17, 1866, ‡C. A. Spring, Sr., Apr. 17, 1866, and of ‡C. A. Spring, Jr., Apr. 17, 1866.

[61] Mary Ann to N. F. McCormick, May 8, 1866; Mary Adams to Nettie F. McCormick, May 20, 1866; ‡C. A. Spring, Sr., to C. H. McCormick, May 1, 1866; ‡H. A. Hurlbut to C. H. McCormick, Oct. 11, 1866.

[62] C. H. McCormick to Rev. R. G. Thompson, Nov. 17, 1868.

[63] ‡B. M. Smith to C. H. McCormick, July 7, 1865.

harassed institution.[64] The few buildings were so dilapidated, wrote Dr. Smith, that "we have to keep buckets in our garret when there are heavy rains, to save our ceilings." [65] Here was a needy school which for a long generation before the war had sent out many competent preachers of sound doctrine to pulpits in Virginia and North Carolina. When Dr. Smith reminded McCormick of his promise of 1859, he shrewdly remarked: "We have never had *isms* and fanatical men. The Virginia clergy have always been moderate, conservative men." [66]

This was written in 1865, just after the close of the war, and McCormick sent Smith $1,000 to meet his immediate emergency. The inventor expressed a wish to reserve decision upon the question of a larger gift until the outlook was more hopeful for a reunion of the northern and southern churches.[67] Southern ministers and their congregations were so impoverished that they could not aid the seminary at Hampden Sidney, and without the help of McCormick and other conservative Presbyterians in the North its doors would have closed. Conditions were even worse at the historic seminary at Columbia, South Carolina,[68] and it was doubtful whether it could ever be revived. If it were not, the Union Theological Seminary would have no competitor in the South, east of the Alleghenies. This, to Dr. Smith, was his one reason for good cheer.[69]

[64] "Lynchburg Virginian," June 23, 1866; "Lexington Gazette," June 27, 1866; ‡B. M. Smith to C. H. McCormick, May 31 and June 28, 1866.

[65] ‡*Idem* to *idem*, Dec. 11, 1866.

[66] ‡*Idem* to *idem*, May 12, 1865. It was established in 1824.

[67] Dr. Smith at once came to New York to see McCormick and they went for a drive in Central Park together. C. H. McCormick to B. M. Smith, July 14, 1865; B. M. Smith to C. H. McCormick, ‡July 22, and Sept. 8, 1865.

[68] Dr. Smith believed that the Columbia Seminary should be moved across the mountains, where it would serve as a focus for Presbyterian education in the lower Mississippi area. ‡B. M. Smith to C. H. McCormick, Dec. 11, 1866.

[69] *Idem* to *idem*, May 31, 1866.

Even more significant for the future, so Dr. Smith reasoned, was the swelling tide of radicalism in the North. Soon his seminary, being so close to the border, would be the only haven remaining where "old fashioned sound Presbyterians over the whole land must rally. It must be made such an institution as the crisis and opportunity demand." [70] The course of the General Assembly of 1866 confirmed him in this belief. At its close, taking advantage of the proper psychological moment, he addressed another appeal to Cyrus McCormick. "Aid the Southern Church to resist the assaults of Satan from whatever quarter they may come. You have labored manfully for union, until Radicalism has made that an impossibility. Now you may consistently say, 'Very well then, I'll turn my energies to the Southern Church.' Connect your name with a Professorship here. . . . You will, of course, couple with your gift any conditions by which you may avoid a similar mortification [i.e., as at the Chicago Seminary] hereafter." [71] At the same time, Dr. Samuel B. Wilson, who had taught at Hampden Sidney for twenty-five years, reinforced the plea of the president by reminding McCormick that "the peculiar institutions, character and customs of the South" demanded that her clergymen be trained within her borders. "Northern preachers, from obvious causes," he continued, "are less acceptable than in past time. Their prejudices, their ignorance of the character and feelings of both white and black, utterly unfit them for the ministerial work among us. There may be, I admit, some exceptions to this statement." [72]

These appeals were well timed. Doubtless McCormick would bring down upon his head a new blast of criticism from the radical press for aiding a "rebel" school, but he was happiest

[70] *Idem* to *idem*, Oct. 12 and Dec. 20, 1865, and Apr. 5, 1866. In December, 1865, this seminary had twenty students.
[71] ‡*Idem* to *idem*, May 31, 1866.
[72] ‡S. B. Wilson to C. H. McCormick, June 2, 1866.

when engaged in controversy.[73] Here was the opportunity to
use the money he had set aside for the education of ministers,
in a manner well calculated to promote conservative theology [74]
—not to mention the inward satisfaction of knowing that his
foes would believe the $25,000 was irretrievably lost to the
seminary at Chicago.[75]

In mid-June, 1866, McCormick promised Dr. Smith that he
would endow the professorship of Biblical and Oriental
Literature at Union Theological Seminary with $30,000, and
would begin at once to pay six per cent interest on that sum.
He reserved the right to revoke the grant if the seminary
should ever come under the control of another denomination.
In such an event, the money would be allocated to the aid of
Presbyterian theological education elsewhere in Virginia.[76]
Following the passage by Congress of the Military Reconstruction Acts in the spring of 1867, Dr. Smith feared that
he might be ousted from his position by the negro-carpetbag
government, particularly since the Professor of Theology had
been a captain in the Confederate Army and a considerable
part of the seminary's income depended upon annual appro-

[73] Some of McCormick's church friends in the North erroneously believed
that a gift from him to Union Seminary would help to restore good feeling
between North and South. Letters to C. H. McCormick of ♯M. B. Grier,
Phila., Pa., Sept. 30, 1865, H. A. Boardman, Phila., Pa., July 11, 1866, and
of ♯B. M. Smith, Dec. 11, 1866. C. H. McCormick to B. M. Smith, June 24,
1866. "Chicago Daily Times," July 5, 1866. "Chicago Evening Journal,"
July 19, 1866.

[74] ♯B. M. Smith to C. H. McCormick, Feb. 22, 1866. As early as Mch. 10,
1866, two months before the meeting of the Genl. Assembly, McCormick
wrote Rev. Stuart Robinson of Louisville that he would probably soon "give
something" to the seminary at Hampden Sidney.

[75] C. H. McCormick to B. M. Smith, June 24, 1866, and to S. Robinson,
July 3, 1866.

[76] Memo. of C. H. McCormick, June 18, 1866; ♯B. M. Smith to C. H.
McCormick, June 20, 28, July 5, Aug. 18, Sept. 19, 1866, and May 23, 1867.
The Chair endowed was Dr. Smith's and he soon hung a framed photograph
of C. H. McCormick in his class-room. On July 23, 1866, he sent Dr. Smith
$900 interest in advance of the date when it was due.

priations by the state legislature. He, thereupon, had Mc-
Cormick sign a new instrument making assurance doubly sure
that his gift would not be diverted from the purpose for which
it had been given.[77] By the autumn, however, Dr. Smith could
write that "our lot has been much easier than we had reason
to expect," and four years later the student body had increased
to about sixty.[78]

No one realized better than McCormick that a gift to a
conservative Presbyterian school in the South, while gratifying
as a rebuke to the radicals in Chicago and elsewhere, could
not measurably help toward reuniting the divided church or
promoting sound doctrine in the region where it was most
needed. The battle must be fought in the North, and especially
west of the Alleghenies. Here were the votes which would
determine the course both of the church and the nation. The
conservative Presbyterians of the eastern cities who looked
toward Princeton as their focus could do little in the General
Assembly unless they were supported by some of the ministers
and elders from the prairie belt. The Chicago area had been
predominantly "sound" in the faith in ante-bellum days and
might be made so again, if the Presbyterians there could be
effectively reached.

But what chance did the "old guard" have to influence
opinion in 1865, when political events encouraged radicalism,
and the leading papers of the denomination were bending in
the same direction? There were the radical "Presbyterian Banner" of Pittsburgh, the "noisy 'Presbyter'" of Cincinnati

[77] ‡B. M. Smith to C. H. McCormick, Mch. 4, 12 and Apr. 17, 1867.
[78] B. M. Smith to C. H. McCormick, ‡Oct. 10, 1870, ‡Oct. 20, 1871, and
Dec. 12, 1872. Dr. Smith and some of his seven children occasionally visited
C. H. McCormick in his N. Y. home. By 1880, when McCormick finally
sent his check for the $30,000, he had already paid to the seminary on this
sum interest totaling about $26,000. B. M. Smith to C. H. McCormick,
‡Mch. 9 and ‡June 16, 1869, and Feb. 26, 1876; "Central Presbyterian"
(Richmond), Dec. 8, 1880.

under the editorship of the able but partisan Dr. J. G. Monfort, each with its six thousand or more subscribers; [79] the "Princeton Review," too scholarly to carry a wide appeal; the sleepy "Presbyterian" of Philadelphia, with almost twelve thousand on its mailing list and disinclined to lose them by advocating unpopular issues; [80] and the "Standard" of Philadelphia, as radical as the "Presbyter," and about to publish a Chicago edition.[81] Up to this time the "Presbyterian" had been able to prevent the establishment of a serious rival in New York City.[82] The "Observer" of that metropolis was friendly toward the conservatives but devoted too many of its columns to secular affairs to be a real force. For McCormick to use the "Central Presbyterian" of Richmond, the "Free Christian Commonwealth" of Louisville,[83] or the "Missouri Presbyterian" of St. Louis [84] as his vehicle would be impracticable, for the first two of these had been banned from most northern tables because of their abusive references to the Yankees, while the third was a journal of small circulation and little influence.

As early as the autumn of 1865 Cyrus McCormick learned that Rev. Ebenezer Erskine, lately a pastor at Stirling, Illinois,

[79] ‡E. Erskine to C. H. McCormick, Mch. 16, 1866.

[80] *Idem* to *idem,* Nov. 21, 1865, and Mch. 19, 1866; ‡H. A. Boardman to C. H. McCormick, Apr. 2, 1867; C. H. McCormick to L. J. Halsey, Feb. 28, 1866.

[81] ‡C. Crosby, Dixon, Ill., to C. H. McCormick, Oct. 28, 1865: If the "Standard" is published in Chicago it will *"scatter firebrands, arrows, and death."* ‡E. Erskine to C. H. McCormick, Jan. 20, 1866: The "Standard" was brought here to revolutionize your Seminary, and to drive Copperheadism from the Chicago churches.

[82] ‡D. X. Junkin to C. H. McCormick, Mch. 19, 1866.

[83] ‡A. Davidson to C. H. McCormick, Dec. 16, 1865; E. Erskine to C. H. McCormick, Mch. 1, 1866.

[84] C. H. McCormick to S. Robinson, Mch. 10, 1866; ‡S. Robinson to C. H. McCormick, Mch. 7, 1866; ‡C. A. Spring, Jr., to C. H. McCormick, Nov. 7, 1865. C. H. McCormick subscribed to at least five of these Presbyterian journals in 1866.

planned to establish a conservative Old School paper in Chicago, to be known as the "Northwestern Presbyterian." [85] Its first issue appeared in November, and its editor offered premiums to those who secured subscriptions to the journal. This practice caused some old-time clergymen to frown, but Erskine soon had about four thousand on his mailing list and bought out the Chicago branch of the "Standard." [86] If he were able to continue publication for a year or so, he might make his paper self-supporting. He hoped that McCormick would help him, and the inventor for a time seemed inclined to do so.[87] Only a few years before this time McCormick had learned how expensive a journalistic venture could be, and he was unwilling to embark upon another one unless he were first convinced that the managing editor was a competent business man and thoroughly committed to the views which his financial backer wished to have advanced.[88]

Erskine was unable to persuade McCormick that he was the proper man, although as his policy is viewed from the perspective of seventy years, there is much to be said in its defense.[89] McCormick always believed in a smashing attack with no quarter asked or given before the end of the battle. This was not Erskine's way and he bluntly told the inventor that if those tactics were used the "Northwestern Presbyterian"

---

[85] ‡C. Crosby, Dixon, Ill., to C. H. McCormick, Oct. 28, 1865.

[86] ‡E. Erskine to C. H. McCormick, Jan. 20, Mch. 13, and 16, 1866; ‡A. Davidson to C. H. McCormick, Jan. 24, 1866.

[87] C. H. McCormick to E. Erskine, Jan. 29, and ‡Mch. 10, 1866; to L. J. Halsey, Mch. 12, 1866.

[88] *Idem* to *idem,* Mch. 12, 1866. Writing of the proposed paper, McCormick remarked: "I should deeply regret to be found in a *wrong* position, and the more so when to get there could only be at considerable cost. I am accustomed to acting under decided convictions—may they not in this case be wrong ones?" ‡B. M. Smith to C. H. McCormick, Apr. 5, and Aug. 1, 1866.

[89] C. H. McCormick to L. J. Halsey, Feb. 28, 1866: I can not support Erskine's paper until I learn whether he is made of stern enough stuff to face the ordeal to which he will be subjected. C. H. McCormick to E. Erskine, Jan. 29, 1866; C. H. McCormick to Dr. Magill, Mch. 15, 1866.

would have a very short life.[90] Dr. Halsey and others agreed with Erskine's opinion that the first essential was a large number of subscribers.[91] Care must be taken at the outset not to offend by being too forthright on controversial issues. Far better for him to be impartial in his editorials, and freely to open the rest of his journal to articles from contributors who wished to engage in debate. Gradually the paper could be swung over to champion conservatism and by this subtle change its readers would unwittingly be led to favor the same position.[92] As Dr. D. X. Junkin wrote in a letter, remarkable for its clerical craftiness:

By this process we can *gradually* get them out from under the influence of the *ecclesiastical demagogues* that are now distracting our beloved Zion. If we attempt to drive a wedge *butt foremost, it won't go into* a gnarly log. We must put it *point* foremost and drive it *cautiously* or it will bounce out. . . . Its [the proposed paper's] *ostensible* control must be in the hands of men that we can *trust,* and yet men who are not *specially obnoxious* to the radicals. . . . Our Great Father on high works unseen, yet works mightily. Far be it from me to commend any *deception,* or anything unfair—but I do recommend prudence, and a wise regard to the common sense *possibilities* of the enterprise. . . . Of course this is *confidential* so far as to conceal opinions that would injure me if disclosed.[93]

But McCormick was not prepared to follow this rather sinuous course. If, because of his unpopular political views, it would injure the standing of the paper for his name publicly to be associated with it, he would unwillingly consent to aid it financially and remain in the background. Far better,

[90] ‡E. Erskine to C. H. McCormick, Mch. 13, 1866.

[91] ‡C. Crosby to C. H. McCormick, Oct. 28, 1865; ‡L. J. Halsey to C. H. McCormick, Mch. 5, 1866.

[92] ‡E. Erskine to C. H. McCormick, Dec. 6, 1865, and Mch. 16, 1866: "We mean to be firm and fearless. We have gone just as far as truth and conscience would suffer us to go in order to conciliate the radicals."

[93] ‡Rev. D. X. Junkin to C. H. McCormick, Mch. 19, 1866.

however, in his judgment, to fight in the open, persuade Dr.
Stuart Robinson of Louisville to merge his tottering journal
with the "Northwestern Presbyterian"; immediately and
proudly run up the banner of conservatism at the masthead;
call the new paper the "National Presbyterian," and publish it
both in Chicago and New York.[94] Such a course would fore-
doom the project to failure, countered Erskine, if for no
other reason, because any association with Dr. Robinson would
place an ineradicable stigma on the journal, so far as northern
readers were concerned.[95] By this stage of the deliberations,
McCormick was certain that Erskine was not the man to lead a
desperate charge against heavy odds. By his great zeal to conciliate his foes, he drew too much upon the forbearance of his
friends. He had not boldly championed reunion with the South
in his "Northwestern Presbyterian." In the inventor's estimation his paper was "a miserable thing," and its editor a "poor
stick" and the "weakest brother I know." [96] This judgment was
unfair. He had few truer friends in Chicago during his contest
with Dr. Lord than the Rev. Ebenezer Erskine, but it was
1869, and too late, before McCormick was convinced of the
fact.[97]

Thus, largely because of failure to agree, a year went by
with nothing done toward the establishment of the paper which
all conservative leaders agreed was so much needed. The tem-

[94] ‡Letters to C. H. McCormick of B. M. Smith, May 12 and Aug. 1,
1866, D. X. Junkin, Mch. 19, 1866, and of E. Erskine, Mch. 19, 1866.

[95] ‡Letters to C. H. McCormick of E. Erskine, Jan. 20 and Mch. 16,
1866, D. X. Junkin, Mch. 19, Dec. 6, 1866, and of L. J. Halsey, Mch. 20,
1866.

[96] C. H. McCormick to Rev. J. M. Faris, Apr. 27-30, 1866, to S. Robinson,
July 3, 1866, to H. A. Boardman, July 8, 1866, and to L. J. Halsey, Feb. 28,
1866: "I don't know but that he [Erskine] has sold the control of his paper
to the Radicals! At all events, they now have it, & are using it, as I think,
with a vengeance—& to the greater injury of our cause, as I believe, than
could be affected by the most out & out Radical in the land." ‡D. X. Junkin
to C. H. McCormick, June 11, 1866.

[97] E. Wood to C. H. McCormick, Apr. 17, 1867.

per of the St. Louis General Assembly served to magnify their peril. "We have reached a crisis," wrote Dr. Henry A. Boardman of Philadelphia to McCormick in late June, 1866. "If a stand be not made against radicalism now, our whole Church will soon be enslaved to its unsparing tyranny." [98] If the publication of a paper were desirable before the meeting of this General Assembly, it was now vital as a means of unifying the conservatives and teaching them their strength.[99]

McCormick agreed with his friends in the ministry, but unlike them he felt that the financial cost of such a venture should be taken into consideration.[100] This burden would fall for the most part upon him. The outlook was not a cheering one in the summer of 1866. Now that the Princeton group and the influential Dr. Gurley of Washington were inclining toward a compromise with the radicals,[101] and the conservatives of the Chicago area were reading the "Northwestern Presbyterian," it was doubtful whether a new enterprise centered at New York, could be successfully launched without great expense. Dr. Rice could probably be induced to serve as editor, but the "Presbyterian Expositor" under his management had been a financial failure. No one in the church could debate a question more ably than he, either in writing or from the platform, but his articles were too "solid" and lacking in humor. Even a religious paper must be "sprightly and versatile" in order to live. As Dr. B. M. Smith wrote a few years later: "The religious publick wants excitement—

[98] ‡H. A. Boardman to C. H. McCormick, June 20, 23, July 11, Nov. 6, 1866.

[99] ‡*Idem* to *idem,* Aug. 1, 1866.

[100] C. H. McCormick to H. A. Boardman, July 8, 1866, and ‡Apr. 9, 1867; to D. X. Junkin, Dec. 3, 1866.

[101] C. H. McCormick to B. M. Smith, July 23 & Aug. 11, 1866: "Black Republicanism I am afraid has its influence with Dr. Hodge, while as I have said, . . . [he is] a noble specimen of a Preacher & man." ‡B. M. Smith to C. H. McCormick, Sept. 19, 1866. ‡H. A. Boardman to C. H. McCormick, Aug. 1, 1866. C. H. McCormick to W. S. Plumer, Dec. 3, 1866.

'tickle and entertain us or we die' is the cry—and if that entertainment is provided by flings at our Church so much the better." [102]

In view of the increasing radicalism, potential subscribers to a conservative paper would probably decrease rather than increase as the months went by. It would be foolish to engage in a project which was doomed to fail from the outset. The success of the proposed journal would largely depend, so McCormick reasoned, upon the ability of President Johnson to guide the public away from radicalism. For this reason no definite action should be taken until after the direction of the wind was shown by the autumn elections of 1866.[103] These were as discouraging in result as the course of the St. Louis Assembly six months before. They made clear to the inventor that a conservative religious paper would be a losing venture, and that radicalism in religion and radicalism in politics were closely allied.

Why could not a weekly paper succeed which joined religion and politics and advocated conservatism in both? This should attract both Old School Presbyterians and Democrats, as well as many Republicans who were longing for the return of sanity. Since politics and religion seemed now to be inseparable, it was time to give up trying to keep them apart, and turn to the work of making the union a salutary one for both church and state.[104] By the close of 1866 McCormick was seek-

[102] C. H. McCormick to H. A. Boardman, July 8, 1866. ‡Letters to C. H. McCormick of D. X. Junkin, Dec. 6, 1866, H. A. Boardman, Dec. 10, 1866, and Feb. 27, 1867, and of B. M. Smith, Jan. 22, 1870.

[103] ‡H. A. Boardman to C. H. McCormick, Aug. 1, 1866: "I can appreciate your allusion to Mr. Johnson. If by God's blessing he can make a successful stand ag'st. the Political radicalism of the country, it will react auspiciously upon the churches."

[104] C. H. McCormick to B. M. Smith, Aug. 11, 1866: "About the *paper* I hope much for the success of *Andrew Johnson* in the political church question—if we must have politics with the church." C. H. McCormick to D. X.

ing the proper man to manage the political phase of an enterprise of this kind. He was told by his friend, Reverdy Johnson, that the "ablest editor of the country" was James C.
Welling, formerly a Whig on the staff of the "National Intelligencer" of Washington, but "latterly a Democrat in principle." Welling, however, refused to accept,[105] and McCormick
found that those ministers for whose judgment he had the
highest regard were not agreed upon the wisdom of the plan.
To Dr. Plumer and Dr. D. X. Junkin it was an admirable
suggestion. "It may be, Mr. McCormick," wrote Junkin, "that
God is leading *you* to the rescue of the Church & the country
from the great peril by which both are threatened, by assisting to establish such a journal." On the other hand, Dr. Boardman believed that to join religion and politics was to favor
precisely what all conservatives had heretofore opposed, and
that the "New York Observer," whose "spiritual residuum is
of the homeopathic order," was a melancholy example of an
attempt to present church and state affairs in the same paper.[106]
Dr. Rice, moreover, who was always considered when the
question of a religious editor was discussed, soon resigned his

---

Junkin, Dec. 3, 1866. C. H. McCormick to H. A. Boardman, Dec. 3 and 22,
1866: The secular section wouldn't be Democratic "in politics," but only in
"principles." "Sh'd. not the value of the paper politically help the sale of the
'Presbyterian' paper with *all conservative* men of whatever religious denomination? . . . might not the *course proposed* prove a bold stroke at
popularizing the paper on a great common principle, . . .?"

[105] C. H. McCormick to J. C. Welling, Dec. 12, 1866. J. C. Welling to
C. H. McCormick, Dec. 18, 1866. Dr. J. Leyburn of Baltimore, Dr. H. A.
Boardman of Phila., and Dr. Robt. L. Breckinridge of Kentucky were con-
sidered for the position of religious editor. ‡J. Leyburn to C. H. McCormick,
Dec. 12, 1866. C. H. McCormick to B. M. Smith, Aug. 11, 1866. ‡W. S.
Plumer to C. H. McCormick, Dec. 21, 1866. Plumer advised McCormick to
ask either ex-President Pierce or Buchanan to suggest a secular editor.
R. L. Breckinridge to H. A. Boardman, Feb. 19, 1867, and to ‡C. H.
McCormick, Mch. 26, 1867. H. A. Boardman to C. H. McCormick, Jan. 8,
22; Feb. 25, 27; Mch. 16, 26, 1867.

[106] *Idem* to *idem*, Dec. 7, ‡20, ‡25, 1866, and Jan. 8, Feb. 4, 25, 27, 1867.

Cyrus Hall McCormick

Engraved from a portrait by A. Cabanel, 1867

pastorate of the Fifth Avenue Presbyterian Church because of ill health.[107]

By now it was April, 1867, and although the zeal of Dr. Boardman for a paper was unabated, he felt that it would be best to delay matters for a few weeks until after the meeting of the General Assembly. At this time [108] McCormick was planning an extended trip to Europe and was seeking to interest his friend, S. L. M. Barlow, one of the owners of the "New York World," in his newspaper project.[109] Boardman did not look with favor upon this alliance, and McCormick, tired of arguing the matter and unable to arouse much enthusiasm for it among rich Presbyterians in New York City, decided by mid-May to shelve the whole question until his return from abroad.[110]

As for the seminary at Chicago, Dr. MacMaster's death had once more left vacant the Chair of Theology, and Dr. Lord was as eager as ever to fill it.[111] Since the directors were unable to raise the money needed to endow the Chair and were weary of trying to sustain a financial "white elephant," they wished to reach an accommodation with McCormick.[112] Because he had never formally stated that he would not pay the $25,000 remaining due from his pledge of eight years before, the board outwardly assumed that he would ultimately fulfill what they judged to be his obligation. Un-

[107] Letters to C. H. McCormick of ‡J. Leyburn, Mch. 28, 1867, H. A. Boardman, Mch. 11 and 16, 1867, and of ‡B. M. Smith, Apr. 17, 1867.

[108] ‡H. A. Boardman to C. H. McCormick, Apr. 4, 1867: You must arrange for the financial backing of the paper before you leave for Europe. ‡D. X. Junkin, to C. H. McCormick, July 22, 1867.

[109] ‡C. H. McCormick to H. A. Boardman, Apr. 9, 1867. C. H. McCormick to Manton Marble, Dec. 18, 1866.

[110] ‡H. A. Boardman to C. H. McCormick, Apr. 10; May 7, 13, 14, June 4, 1867. Boardman was "sadly disappointed" at McCormick's decision, but admitted that without a "generous supply" of money, it was unwise to launch the paper.

[111] ‡E. Wood to C. H. McCormick, Jan. 9 and Apr. 29, 1867.

[112] ‡*Idem* to *idem*, Apr. 29, 1867.

willing to widen the breach while in such sore financial straits, it decided at its April meeting not to recommend to the General Assembly of 1867 the appointment of Dr. Lord to the Chair of Theology.[113]

McCormick, however, showed no disposition to compromise. He wrote to a friend in Chicago who was a trustee of the seminary that he would not pay the $25,000 until Dr. Rice, or some one else equally acceptable to him, was appointed to the vacant Chair and his friends who had been forced to resign were reinstated so that the control of the seminary would again be in sympathetic hands. In his opinion, however, it would be wise to let matters hang fire until 1868.[114] He believed that the radicals would compromise with him only long enough to get his money, and once they had it they would again cast him aside.

Learning that nothing was to be hoped for from McCormick unless they agreed to an unconditional surrender, the radicals determined to effect Dr. Lord's appointment. They won their way with the General Assembly. Thus the inventor was defeated on every issue. He soon sailed for France, resolved to banish from his mind the problems of seminary, religious paper, and church reunion while he attended the Universal Exposition at Paris.[115]

[113] E. Wood to C. H. McCormick, Apr. 17, 1867.

[114] C. H. McCormick to E. Wood, Jan. 21 and Apr. 21, 1867, and to N. L. Rice, May 5, 1867.

[115] ‡C. A. Spring, Sr., to C. H. McCormick, May 17 and June 3, 1867. "Minutes of the General Assembly," 1865-1869, pp. 272-273. The Assembly recommended that the friends of the seminary "endeavor to forget all past differences, and coöperate cordially in all practical measures to secure its full endowment."

CHAPTER VII

FROM DEFEAT TO VICTORY ON THE SEMINARY ISSUE,
1867-1884

ILL feeling between the radical and conservative wings of
the Old School Presbyterians in Chicago did not subside
during Cyrus McCormick's eight months' stay in Europe.
Hardly had he returned to New York in March, 1868, than
he reopened the contest by urging his church friends to support Dr. Rice's candidacy for the Chair of Church History at
the seminary.[1] When the General Assembly convened at Albany in May, its Committee on Seminaries and Colleges
unanimously nominated Dr. Rice for the post. Contrary to
custom, however, the Assembly disregarded this recommendation and appointed Dr. William M. Blackburn of Trenton,
New Jersey, who belonged to the Lord wing of the denomination.[2] Thus McCormick lost the initial skirmish of the new
campaign.

The four faculty Chairs were now filled for the first time
since 1861. When the seminary opened that autumn, the directors formally notified McCormick that they would be gratified to receive the $25,000 [3] remaining unpaid from his pledge

[1] C. H. McCormick to E. Wood, Apr. 29 and May 25, 1868. Dr. Rice,
much improved in health, had lived in New Brunswick, N. J., since his
resignation as pastor of the Fifth Avenue (New York) Presbyterian Church.

[2] ‡E. Wood to C. H. McCormick, May 21, 23, 26, 1868; ‡L. J. Halsey to
C. H. McCormick, June 3, 1868. "Minutes of the General Assembly," 1865-
1869, pp. 345, 362, 368, 371.

[3] ‡C. A. Spring, Sr., and R. G. Thompson to C. H. McCormick, Oct. 16,
1868.

of 1859. A month went by before he replied.[4] In this letter, soon published, he reaffirmed his unabated interest in the institution and promised that when its board of control should withdraw from politics, recognize the wishes of its founders, and cease the proscription of his friends, he would pay the $25,000, and add $5,000 more to the endowment of each Chair.[5] Reduced to its simplest terms, this meant that Dr. Lord's tenure of the Chair of Theology, and possibly Dr. Blackburn's occupancy of the Chair of History, were costing the seminary $45,000.

This was the presidential election year and McCormick was active in the campaign. Some of its political heat was carried over into the discussion aroused by the inventor's reply.[6] For the first time since the beginning of the controversy over three years before, McCormick had publicly thrown down the gaunt-

[4] C. H. McCormick to C. A. Spring, Sr., and R. G. Thompson, Nov. 17, 1868. Many of the letters relating to the seminary controversy were published in pamphlet form in 1869 under the title, " 'Important Correspondence' Concerning the Presbyterian Theological Seminary, Between Rev. Willis Lord, D.D., Professor of Theology, . . . and Mr. Cyrus H. McCormick, Founder and Trustee, . . ." (New York, 1869).

[5] C. H. McCormick to Eds., "Northwestern Presbyterian," Nov. 28, 1868. I prefer to remain silent, but matters have "reached the point where, in my judgment, further silence would be improper, and a vindication of myself becomes a duty." ‡D. C. Marquis to C. H. McCormick, Dec. 4, 1868: "Your letter has stirred up the hornet's nest. . . . You have brought the question to a plain square issue which makes it necessary for Dr. Lord's friends either to complete the endowment or retire."

[6] The "Dubuque Herald" (Dubuque, Ia.), Dec. 4, 1868, friendly to McCormick; "New York Observer," Dec. 3, 1868, non-committal; the "Presbyterian Banner" (Pittsburgh), Dec. 2 and 30, 1868, unfriendly to McCormick; "Christian Observer" (Richmond, Va.), Dec. 10, 1868, friendly; the "Presbyter" (Cincinnati), Jan. 6, 1869, unfriendly; the "Evening Bulletin" (Cairo, Ill.), Jan. 7, 1869, friendly; the "World" (New York), Jan. 13, 1869, friendly, and the "Virginia Gazette" (Lexington, Va.), March 3, 1869, friendly. This last paper remarked: "The caustic pen of the celebrated Pascal found a fit theme for its most biting sarcasm in the way in which the ecclesiastics of his day abused the charitable funds entrusted to them. The history of Jesuitism affords no more iniquitous perversion of a sacred trust than we now have been reviewing."

let. The Republican press of Chicago rushed to Dr. Lord's
defense with articles that well illustrate the skill of Reconstruction Period editors in the use of vituperative language.
McCormick was sarcastically hailed as the "Presbyterian
Pope" who sought to make the seminary a mill for the fash-
ioning of Copperhead preachers. His whole war record was
reviewed and even his inventive genius was ridiculed. He was
told that his proper home was not in Chicago but in Virginia.[7]
All except four of the thirty-five students of the seminary
adopted resolutions supporting Dr. Lord.[8] "He" [Mr. Mc-
Cormick], sneered the editor of the "Chicago Evening Post,"
"sees Dr. Lord in his soup, in his wash-bowl, in his wine glass,
in his incomings and outgoings, in his risings and settings,
and in his dreams and visions. Dr. Lord, loyal, fearless, and
devoted, is the bane of his existence, . . . Dr. Lord, like Stanton, sticks." [9] The Democratic "Chicago Times" replied with
equal vigor in his behalf. McCormick's sole purpose, in its
opinion, was to make the seminary a place of "piety instead
of partisanship," and to stop its use as "a manufactory of
political preachers of the Jacobin persuasion." [10]

Dr. Lord and Cyrus McCormick were not willing to stand
aside and let others wage their battles. Soon these two an-
tagonists entered the lists and engaged in a duel of public
letters which lasted from McCormick's first shot of November

[7] "Chicago Daily Tribune," Dec. 2, 1868.

[8] MS. entitled "Facts and Allegations as to Dr. Lord." "Resolutions" of
thirty-one students of Northwestern Theological Seminary, Dec. 5, 1868,
asserting that Dr. Lord had never brought politics into the class-room.

[9] "Chicago Evening Post," Dec. 4, 1868. See also, the issues of Dec. 2,
1868, and Jan. 2, 1869. The reference is to Edwin Stanton, Secretary of
War, who in 1867 and 1868, relying upon the Tenure of Office Act, refused
to resign his office at the behest of President Johnson. "Chicago Daily
Tribune," Dec. 2, 1868: McCormick "will not, if he can prevent it, permit
any man, who contributed by word or deed to the abolition of human
slavery, to educate preachers of the Gospel."

[10] "Chicago Times," Dec. 2, 1868.

28, 1868, to his last on March 20, 1869. The inventor wrote from his home in New York with Dr. Rice at his elbow,[11] and after his letters reached Chicago they were carefully edited for publication in the "Northwestern Presbyterian" by Rev. D. C. Marquis and Rev. E. Erskine.[12] Presbyterian clergymen and elders far and wide hastened to send to McCormick extra rounds of argumentative ammunition for use against his opponent.[13] Those who assisted Dr. Lord to prepare his fulminations are not named in the records, but doubtless Mr. Jesse L. Williams, Drs. Blackburn, R. W. Patterson, and J. G. Monfort, in whose "Presbyter" Lord's replies were published, were valuable allies.[14] Judging from the interest aroused, the Old School Church viewed Lord and McCormick as personifications of the radicalism and conservatism in conflict within their denomination.[15]

Dr. Lord accused McCormick of simony and breach of con-

[11] N. L. Rice to C. H. McCormick, Dec. 26, 1868; C. H. McCormick to N. L. Rice, Dec. 31, 1868; C. H. McCormick to E. Erskine, Dec. 30, 1868 and Jan. 25, 1869. When Dr. Rice came to New York from New Brunswick, N. J., for purposes of consultation, McCormick paid his expenses. Dr. Henry Van Dyke of Brooklyn also read McCormick's second letter before it was published.

[12] ‡E. Erskine to C. H. McCormick, Jan. 9, 13, 14, 26, 27, Feb. 4, Mch. 8, 11, 12, 1869. "Some of your statements are very involved and obscure, (Excuse me but it is so.) . . . It is the most important letter of your life, involving character and a great and important interest." ‡C. H. McCormick to L. J. Halsey, Jan. 6, 1869.

[13] ‡B. M. Smith to C. H. McCormick, Dec. 4, 1868; C. H. McCormick to J. McCosh, Jan. 15, 1869; T. V. Moore to W. Lord, Mch. 5, 1869; ‡C. A. Spring, Jr., to C. H. McCormick, Jan. 15, 1869; ‡D. X. Junkin in the "Presbyterian Banner," Mch. 24, 1869; article signed "Prudence" (J. W. Brockenbrough, Rector of Washington College) in "Virginia Gazette" (Lexington), Mch. 10, 1869.

[14] Letter of J. L. Williams in the "Northwestern Presbyterian," Dec. 19, 1868. C. H. McCormick's reply in *id.*, Jan. 9, 1869. C. H. to E. Erskine, Dec. 30, 1868; C. H. McCormick to J. G. Monfort, Jan. 2, 1869.

[15] MS. entitled "Facts and Allegations as to Dr. Lord"; "Virginia Gazette," Mch. 3, 1869; "Northwestern Presbyterian," May 8, 1869. ‡E. Erskine to C. H. McCormick, Mch. 12, 1869.

tract. With less appropriateness, he tried to divert the argument into a discussion of McCormick's war record and of the
slavery influences attending the birth of the seminary.[16] The
inventor showed that the church, and not he, had "openly and
grossly violated" the *"understood and implied* pledges" of his
1859 agreement, and he stated that his dissatisfaction with
Lord was due to his unorthodoxy and not to his politics or
his position on the slavery issue. Lord was portrayed as the
chief cause of the North Church schism during the war, and
as one who had quickly changed his views when public opinion
in Chicago made it prudent for him to do so.[17] McCormick
argued that the church should show a regard "consistent with
duty" for the wishes of those who contributed to the endowment of the seminary.[18]

"If we do not succeed in the present Seminary controversy,"
wrote McCormick in March, 1869, "I don't know what can
remain worth laboring for. I may *fight* on until I get back the
$75,000 . . . or know why not." [19] As in most debates of
this kind, the winner was apparent only to the friends of each
contestant. Certainly McCormick presented his case with great
force, and to Drs. Rice, Halsey, Junkin, Marquis, and others,
his arguments were "overwhelming." [20] To the "Evening
Post," however, Lord's first letter was "the most triumphant
bit of public letter writing that the year 1868 afforded," while

[16] W. Lord to C. H. McCormick, in the "Presbyter," Dec. 23, 1868, and
Feb. 17, 1869. "Chicago Daily Tribune," Feb. 23, 1869.

[17] C. H. McCormick to W. Lord, in the "Northwestern Presbyterian,"
Feb. 6, 1869. Eight hundred extra copies were struck off to be sent to non-
subscribers. #E. Erskine to C. H. McCormick, Feb. 4, 1869; Letters of C. H.
McCormick to L. J. McCormick, Feb. 4, 1869, and to C. A. Spring, Jr.,
Feb. 6, 1869. C. H. McCormick to W. Lord, in the "Northwestern Presby-
terian," Mch. 20, 1869.

[18] C. H. McCormick to the "Presbyterian," n.d., but probably Feb., 1869.

[19] C. H. McCormick to "My dear Sir," Mch. (?), 1869.

[20] Letters to C. H. McCormick of #L. J. Halsey, Feb. 9, 1869, D. X.
Junkin, Feb. 4, 1869, #E. Wood, Aug. 23, 1869, and L. J. McCormick, Feb. 9,
1869.

his second one, in the view of the "Chicago Tribune," placed "Mr. McCormick in a position from which any man who has a particle of loyalty or patriotism in his composition would be glad to escape." [21]

The test of the success of this debate would be the action taken by the General Assembly of 1869. To give the letters their widest possible influence, McCormick had them published in pamphlet form and distributed to those in the church whose word carried weight.[22] Until the eve of the convention, he hoped that a union of the New and Old School Churches could be prevented, and that the conservative cause could be saved before another year had elapsed, by the readmission of the southern Presbyterians. Pressure was again brought to bear upon him to establish a religious paper to advance the good work, and the "Northwestern Presbyterian" seemed to be the logical foundation upon which to build. Notwithstanding Erskine's services during the controversy with Dr. Lord, McCormick still refused to come to his assistance, and the magazine passed into hostile hands in the early summer of 1869.[23]

Sharp was the battle in Chicago over the election by the presbytery of representatives to the General Assembly of 1869. If the McCormick forces could dominate this delegation, a long step toward victory would be taken. Rev. W. W. Harsha was about to resign the pastorate of the South Church, and efforts were made to induce Dr. Rice to be his successor, with the hope that he could be one of those to speak for the Chicago Presbytery in the Assembly.[24] Although Rice had re-

[21] "Chicago Daily Tribune," Feb. 23, 1869.

[22] C. H. McCormick to E. Erskine, Mch. 15, 1869.

[23] ‡E. Erskine to C. H. McCormick, Mch. 29, Apr. 17, June 5 and 10, 1869.

[24] "Chicago Daily Tribune," Apr. 17, 1869; ‡D. C. Marquis to C. H. McCormick, Nov. 24, 1868; C. H. McCormick to H. A. Boardman, Mch. 15, 1869; ‡C. A. Spring, Jr., to C. H. McCormick, Mch. 12, 19 and Apr. 28, 1869.

cently accepted the presidency of Westminster College at Fulton, Missouri, he viewed the call with favor, until his board of trustees, by extraordinary exertion, succeeded in increasing the endowment of the institution. He then decided that it would be ungrateful of him to resign.[25] The directors of the Chicago Seminary now ousted three members of its board of trustees who were friendly to McCormick, and Dr. Lord tried in vain to rush through the ordination of three students there so that his hand would be strengthened in the presbytery meeting.[26] Although McCormick paid the expenses of ministers and elders friendly to his cause who could not have otherwise attended this gathering, the forces of Dr. Lord controlled the session and the professor was chosen to head the delegation to the Assembly.[27]

Thus McCormick was checkmated, but he wrote that he would not make peace until Dr. Lord resigned as Professor of Theology. "No one thing more, than to do simple justice in this case," he added, "would [so] favor an early restoration of fraternal feeling between the North and South." [28] McCormick worked to have his cause properly presented before the General Assembly by the most eminent ministers of the

25 ‡N. L. Rice to J. Forsythe, June 28, 1869 and to C. H. McCormick, Nov. 9, 1870. In Oct., 1874, Dr. Rice accepted a professorship at Danville Seminary.

26 ‡H. A. Hurlbut to C. H. McCormick, Mch. 26, 1869. ‡E. Erskine to C. H. McCormick, Mch. 29, 1869. In order to strengthen his influence in the presbytery, Dr. Lord secured the election of his friend, Rev. Daniel Lord of Bridgeport, Conn., to the pastorate of the Fullerton Avenue Presbyterian Church of Chicago.

27 ‡H. A. Hurlbut to C. H. McCormick, Apr. 8, 1869; C. H. McCormick to E. Erskine, Apr. 20, 1869; "Chicago Daily Tribune," Apr. 17, 1869. ‡E. Erskine to C. H. McCormick, Apr. 17, 1869: "With a little more expense and more effort in time we'd have had five more votes present." As it was, it was the largest presbytery meeting ever held. "Chicago Times," Apr. 2, 3, 4, 1869.

28 ‡J. G. Monfort to C. H. McCormick, Apr. 14, 1869; C. H. McCormick to J. G. Monfort, Apr. 21, 29, 1869.

East,[29] and although Dr. Rice was not a delegate, he paid his expenses from Missouri so that he could be on hand to use his influence. The inventor's few friends on the board of directors carefully prepared a "Minority Report" vigorously attacking the administration of the seminary and particularly its financial inefficiency.[30] "This is a battle for truth and righteousness," wrote Rev. D. C. Marquis of the North Church.[31]

In so far as the seminary question was concerned, the action of the General Assembly was a victory for neither side. A decision was postponed until a Committee of Investigation could thrash over the whole matter in Chicago, and report its findings to the next meeting. Fortunately for the welfare of the institution, a joint Assembly of the Old and New School Churches was to meet in Pittsburgh in November, and in consequence the seminary issue would not have to await decision for a whole year. The regular Assembly of 1869 with great unanimity endorsed the terms of union between the Old and New School branches, and was gracious enough to "express the desire that the day may not be distant when we [the Presbyterian Churches North and South] may again be united in one great organization." [32] That day has not yet come, but this friendly gesture was cheering to the many who had long hoped that war bitterness would be forgotten in the councils of the denomination.

For nine days at the Tremont House, Chicago, the Committee of Investigation listened to the testimony of C. H. Mc-

[29] ‡E. Erskine to C. H. McCormick, May 7, 10, 22, 1869.

[30] ‡C. A. Spring, Jr., to C. H. McCormick, May 12, 15, 17, 1869. MS. Report of the Minority of the Board of Directors of the Pres. Theo. Sem. of the N.W. to the Committee of Inquiry of the General Assembly, May 15, 1869.

[31] ‡D. C. Marquis to C. H. McCormick, May 15, 1869.

[32] "Minutes of the General Assembly," 1865-1869, pp. 454, 467, 468, 471, 475.

Cormick and all others who had been conspicuous in the seminary controversy during the past five years.[33] McCormick declared that he would not insist upon the election of Dr. Rice to the Chair of Theology. He preferred to recommend no one for that position and was willing to rely upon the fairness of the General Assembly. He did demand, however, "that this settlement should be upon the basis of justice rather than of majorities; that we should inquire what is right rather than what is popular." His services, and those of his friends, to the seminary should be given "a proper recognition." [34]

With the facts before it the committee persuaded the contestants to accept a compromise. All agreed that "bygones shall be bygones." McCormick was released from the payment of the $25,000, and Dr. Lord was retained in the Chair of Theology. The "New Friends" promised to make a "prompt effort" to raise funds to endow his Chair, and new trustees "not unacceptable to either party" were to replace the three who were ousted by the radicals a short time before. The committee also expressed the belief that "times of fearful excitement" had doubtless contributed much to the origin of the dispute, and that "Dr. Lord's character has not been essentially affected by any testimony adduced before it." In matters relating to the seminary, "a courteous consideration" of Mr. McCormick's wishes was declared to be his due. So overjoyed and surprised were the members of the committee to bring the controversy to a close that "in a fervent outburst we sang the Doxology,

[33] A copy of the testimony taken at this meeting from Oct. 25, to Nov. 3, 1869, is in the library of the McCormick Historical Association. ‡D. X. Junkin to C. H. McCormick, Sept. 21, 1869; ‡C. A. Spring, Jr., to C. H. McCormick, Sept. 25, 1869. C. H. McCormick to ?, Oct. 26, 1869. C. H. McCormick to Rev. E. P. Humphrey, Nov. 8, 1869.

[34] Undated Draft of a speech (?) prepared by C. H. McCormick for delivery before the Committee of Investigation. C. H. McCormick to Hon. C. D. Drake, Chairman of this Committee, n.d., but probably the autumn of 1869. C. D. Drake was a U. S. Senator from Missouri.

and lovingly, hopefully concluded our work." The General Assembly at Pittsburgh adopted this report.[35]

Few compromises square with logic and this one was no exception to the rule. If McCormick were released from paying the fourth instalment because the Assembly had broken the spirit of its 1859 agreement with him, as the Committee of Investigation had declared, surely he could rightfully ask for the return of the $75,000 already contributed.[36] The Report of the Committee almost completely vindicated McCormick and it damned Dr. Lord with faint praise. The victory, however, brought small satisfaction to the inventor because the Chair of Theology, bearing his name, was still occupied by his enemy.[37] Furthermore, the seminary was now under the control of a united church, and representation on the faculty and in the directorship would doubtless have to be accorded to the New School element. How could this be done without still more firmly entrenching the radical Old School group in its control of the institution?

By good fortune, a possible way out was soon disclosed. For several years the New School Church had been endeavoring to establish a university in or near Chicago (Lake Forest College), and the movement was at last well under way.[38]

---

[35] "Minutes of the General Assembly," 1865-1869, pp. 505-508. "Chicago Times," Nov. 11 and Dec. 13, 1869.

[36] ‡R. Frame, Morris, Ill., to C. H. McCormick, Nov. 12, 1869. ‡E. Erskine to C. H. McCormick, Nov. 28, 1869.

[37] Undated MS., written by C. H. McCormick, summarizing his opinion of the Report of the Committee of Investigation. He felt that in recommending the retention of Dr. Lord, the committee sacrificed principle for the sake of peace, and did the seminary and himself a "great injustice." "As the Report says that nothing was proved 'essentially' affecting his 'character,' it may be interesting to know just what was proved."

[38] ‡E. S. Skinner to C. H. McCormick, Nov. 25, 1869; ‡D. C. Marquis to C. H. McCormick, Dec. 8, 1869 and Mch. 25, 1870. Marquis saw this effort to interest the Old School conservatives in Lake Forest as a trap set by the Lordites to divert their attention from the seminary and to win New School support for it. ‡Rev. C. P. Jennings, Shelbyville, Ind., to C. H. McCormick, Dec. 2, 1868. In the fall of 1860, the Synod of Illinois resolved

McCormick declined to aid this institution unless its promoters would support him in seminary affairs.[39] For a short while these tactics yielded a return in friendliness from the New School group.[40] McCormick reciprocated by accepting the position of trustee of Lake Forest College and subscribing $5,000 to the stock of a company, headed by New School men, which was formed to rejuvenate the tottering "Northwestern Presbyterian" under the name of "The Interior." He was given to understand that the journal would not be used as a mouthpiece for the Lordites.[41] To help further toward a *rapprochement,* he let it be known that should Dr. Lord leave, and an acceptable appointment were made in his stead, he would complete the payment of his original pledge and add to the endowment of each of the four Chairs.[42] This was the more appealing since the friends of Dr. Lord were having but slight success in raising funds to pay his salary. The day seemed to be won in April, 1870, when Dr. Lord signified his intention of resigning in order to accept the presidency of the University of Wooster in Ohio, and the directors of the seminary reinstated the three trustees friendly to McCormick, who had been ousted two years before.[43]

to campaign for the establishment of a Presbyterian College in its state. "The election of Mr. Lincoln brought such gloom upon the public that we deemed it prudent to lie still." New effort was made in 1864 to found a "Princeton of the Northwest" but to little avail thereafter for several years. *Post,* p. 301, ftn. 102.

[39] C. H. McCormick to E. S. Skinner, Dec. 6, 1869, to R. W. Patterson, June 22, and to D. C. Marquis, Oct. 3, 1870.

[40] #H. G. Miller to C. H. McCormick, Jan. 8, 1870.

[41] The first number of the new magazine appeared about Mch. 1, 1870. #Letters to C. H. McCormick from E. S. Skinner, Mch. 7, 1870; #H. A. Hurlbut, Dec. 24, 1869, #H. Miller, Dec. 26, 1869, and D. C. Marquis, Dec. 27, 1869, Jan. 5, 7, 25, and Feb. 11, 1870.

[42] C. H. McCormick to E. P. Humphrey Nov. 8, 1869; #D. C. Marquis to C. H. McCormick, Nov. 2, 1869. McCormick wished Dr. Humphrey to accept the Chair of Theology.

[43] #L.P.C.B. No. 1, 2nd ser., p. 6, C. H. McCormick to B. M. Smith, Apr. 5, 1870. #E. Erskine to C. H. McCormick, Feb. 24, 1870; #D. C. Marquis to C. H. McCormick, Mch. 9, 17, 20, 25, and Apr. 8, 1870. Dr.

This should have ended the long contest, but almost two years more were to pass before peace descended upon the seminary. Although Dr. Lord left Chicago, his followers were resolved to "carry on," and in fact his departure set the stage for a new campaign. Gloom soon replaced the good cheer of the winter just closed. Who should succeed Dr. Lord at the seminary? The radical Old School group, the New School group, and the conservative Old School group, each had a different answer. The duel had broadened into a three-cornered contest, with each faction of the Old School churchmen playing for the support of the new-comers who held the balance of power. Dr. Robert W. Patterson, pastor of the Second Presbyterian Church of Chicago and leader of the New School forces, was believed to covet a place on the faculty. McCormick was willing for him to occupy a fifth Chair and expound the relationships between science and theology, if his New School admirers would pay his salary and consent to an Old School minister in the Chair of Theology.[44] There was some likelihood that an alliance would be cemented on these terms, until the Patterson forces were told that the inventor had in mind to bring Dr. Rice, Dr. Humphrey, Dr. Boardman, or Dr. Skinner to the Chair which bore his name.[45] These men were too conservative, in the opinion of Dr. Patterson. Even some of

Lord was the first President of the University of Wooster and served until 1873.

[44] ‡*Idem* to *idem,* Feb. 11, 17, Apr. 18, 26, and May 5, 1870. C. H. McCormick to Rev. Mr. McLaren, Feb. 13, 1871, and to ‡H. G. Miller, Feb. 21, 1871. The discontented Dr. Halsey received a call to Danville Seminary in the autumn of 1869, but declined it after a long period of indecision. McCormick privately supplemented his small salary in order to keep one anti-Lordite on the faculty, and to prevent a vacancy which his enemies might fill with a New School man.

[45] ‡L.P.C.B. No. 1, 2nd ser., pp. 1, 26, C. M. McCormick to D. C. Marquis, Apr. 4 and 18, 1870. ‡Letters to C. H. McCormick of E. P. Humphrey, Louisville, Ky., Mch. 25, 1870, Wm. Blackwood, Phila., Mch. 29, 1870, L. J. Halsey, Apr. 7, 9, 22, 1870, and D. C. Marquis, Apr. 3, 8, 18, 22, 26, 1870.

McCormick's friends felt that the seminary should have teachers who were in step with the new age. "Our very foundation questions have to be settled again," he was told by Dr. Blackwood of Philadelphia. "From New England, from Great Britain and from Germany, people and questions are ever and anon coming to the surface that only modern students can ever understand." [46]

To overthrow the Lord faction, McCormick was willing to put aside many of his old prejudices and coöperate with the New School party. Before an agreement could be reached, however, the Chicago Presbytery once again elected a radical delegation to the General Assembly. McCormick went to its sessions at Philadelphia to work for harmony, but witnessed with chagrin the New School men insure for themselves the control of the seminary by electing enough new directors from their own number to hold the balance of power.[47] For several years he had opposed the New School-Old School reunion because he had foreseen that the liberals in theology would dominate the united church. Now his worst fears were realized.

When the Lordian Radicals in the Assembly joined with the New School party to elect the moderately conservative Dr. George L. Prentiss of New York to the Chair of Theology, McCormick was not alone in suspecting that this gesture of conciliation was an act of bad faith.[48] His friends believed that

[46] #Wm. Blackwood to C. H. McCormick, Mch. 29, 1870.

[47] #D. C. Marquis to C. H. McCormick, Apr. 18, 1870; C. H. McCormick to Rev. Dr. Adams, May 30, 1870. #L.P.C.B. No. 1, 2nd ser., p. 83, C. H. McCormick to D. C. Marquis, May 9, 1870: "If we *don't* succeed *properly,* we had better all abandon the cause. *I* am not now under any obligation to give *more* money to that Sem'y., and *if justice* be withheld longer, there will be found the worthy objects for which money may well be applied."

[48] #L.P.C.B. No. 1, 2nd ser., p. 119, C. H. McCormick to D. C. Marquis, June 6, 1870. C. H. McCormick to R. W. Patterson, June 22, 1870. #E. Erskine to C. H. McCormick, June 7, 1870. C. H. McCormick to Rev. Shedd, Feb. 11, 1871. #D. C. Marquis to C. H. McCormick, Apr. 26, 1870. #Report of the Board of Directors of the Chicago Seminary to the General

those who voted for Dr. Prentiss well knew that he would refuse to accept, but before he did so, they hoped that the inventor would pay the $25,000. With that sum in their possession, and with Dr. Prentiss out of the running, the board of directors would then place Dr. R. W. Patterson in the Chair of Theology with the confident expectation that the next General Assembly would make his *ad interim* appointment permanent.[49] So discouraged and disgusted were McCormick's supporters at what they chose to call this "unpardonable outrage" and "premeditated fraud," that they severed whatever official connection they had with the seminary and for a time washed their hands of the whole matter.[50] Rev. D. C. Marquis, who was perhaps the most indignant of all, was unable to withstand the increasing New School membership of the North Church, and yielded his pastorate before the close of the year into the charge of the memorable Dr. David Swing.[51]

When friends gave up the fight in despair, McCormick was at his best.[52] If his enemies had, in fact, prepared a trap

Assembly, May, 1870. McCormick and his friends believed that, in justice, the Old School radicals should now withdraw from the picture, since the agreement of the previous autumn had obliged them to raise funds for the support of the seminary, and they had failed to do so. Dr. Prentiss was a brother of the noted orator and Whig Congressman from Mississippi, Sargent S. Prentiss (died in 1850).

[49] ‡D. C. Marquis to C. H. McCormick, June 8, and July 4, 1870. H. A. Hurlbut to C. H. McCormick, June 11, 1870.

[50] ‡D. C. Marquis to C. H. McCormick, June 16, and July 15, 1870: I am going to try and forget there ever was a seminary. E. Wood to C. H. McCormick, June 20, 1870. "Chicago Times," July 16, 1870.

[51] Letters to C. H. McCormick, from L. J. McCormick, Nov. 14, 1870, R. Hall McCormick, Nov. 25, 1870, and ‡G. Morrison, Dec. 2, 1870. R. Hall McCormick to Nettie F. McCormick, Dec. 5, 1870. In Feb., 1871, the North Church and the Westminster Church united to form the Fourth Presbyterian Church.

[52] C. H. McCormick to D. C. Marquis, Oct. 3, 1870: "With God and right on our side, and in a cause that (if anything) is for the glory of God alone, we can afford to fight so long as he gives us power to stand up to the work." On June 15 (‡L.P.C.B. No. 1, 2nd ser., p. 147) he wrote to

for him, he would see to it that they were caught in their own snare. Perhaps if sufficient inducements were held out to Dr. Prentiss, he would accept and Dr. Patterson would then have to look elsewhere for an opportunity to teach theology. In the meantime, he would correspond occasionally with Dr. Patterson and thus keep open the door for compromise. For over a year McCormick pursued Prentiss, while the group in control of the seminary went deeper and deeper into debt.[53] In August, 1870, Dr. Prentiss definitely declined;[54] by February, 1871, he agreed to reconsider;[55] and by the summer of 1871 he seemed inclined to accept if his teaching would not be censored. By this time McCormick was ready to guarantee him a salary of $6,500 a year, over twice the sum received by any other member of the faculty, and he suspected that Dr. R. W. Patterson was attempting to block the negotiations by covertly reminding Dr. Prentiss that it would be well to learn in advance whether his teaching would be under restraint.[56] On this point, McCormick assured him that he would only be expected to teach "the Theology of the Presbyterian Church according to its 'standards pure and simple.'"[57] This well illustrates his eagerness to end the schism at the seminary,

Dr. Marquis: "Feeling that I have *only commenced* fighting in this case; determined to *see it out,* and finally to *quit* the *Church* and *any Church* in *wh. no justice can be had.* But I *don't despair.*"

[53] C. H. McCormick to R. W. Patterson, June 22, and Aug. 29, 1870. ‡D. C. Marquis to C. H. McCormick, Sept. 6, 1870. The directors, unable to procure donations, were forced to borrow $7,000 in order to pay the faculty. ‡H. G. Miller to C. H. McCormick, Sept. 18, 1870.

[54] ‡L. J. Halsey to C. H. McCormick, Aug. 24, 1870. ‡G. L. Prentiss, D.D. to C. H. McCormick, Aug. 4, and 27, 1870.

[55] ‡C. H. McCormick to G. L. Prentiss, Feb. 14, 1871. ‡C. H. McCormick to H. G. Miller, Feb. 21, 1871.

[56] C. H. McCormick to G. L. Prentiss, Mch. 6 and ‡Apr. 22, 1871, and ‡many others between this date and mid-July. ‡G. L. Prentiss to C. H. McCormick, Feb. 28, 1871.

[57] ‡C. H. McCormick to G. L. Prentiss, July 19 and Aug. 6, 1871. G. L. Prentiss to C. H. McCormick, July 29, 1871.

since but a few weeks before he had written friends in Chicago that he would require Old School theology to be taught there.[58]

Dr. Prentiss, disappointed for the time being in his ambition to join the faculty of Union Theological Seminary in New York City, could no longer afford to refuse McCormick's offer, and in August, 1871, he promised to come. "This seems really like being *'out of the woods,'* " McCormick wrote, "and if there is to be any *'crowing'* in the case, at all, now is about the time for it, I suppose! . . . And let it now be made a point *not to admit of a failure.*"[59] Of the $65,000 endowment needed for Prentiss's Chair, McCormick agreed to give $45,000, and others in Chicago guaranteed to raise the balance by October 1.[60] The New School Presbyterians refused to contribute, but the campaign for funds was yielding encouraging returns when the Great Fire came to render many of the pledges worthless.[61] On that fateful October 9, 1871, when his factory was in flames, McCormick carried out his part of the agreement by signing a check for $45,000 to endow the Chair of Theology.[62] The fire burned to the edge of the seminary grounds, but providentially, so it seemed, Ewing Hall and the residences of the professors, although blistered by the heat, were saved. The securities of the seminary had been kept

[58] C. H. McCormick to G. L. Prentiss, July 10, 1871. #Letters to C. H. McCormick of H. G. Miller, July 11, J. Forsythe, July 18, and S. M. Moore, July 18, 1871.

[59] #C. H. McCormick to H. G. Miller, Aug. 8, 1871; #G. L. Prentiss to C. H. McCormick, Aug. 18, 1871.

[60] S. M. Moore to C. H. McCormick, Aug. 22 and 23, 1871; C. H. McCormick to S. M. Moore, Aug. 27, and to G. L. Prentiss, Sept. 10, 1871.

[61] #C. H. McCormick to G. L. Prentiss, Oct. 15 and 22, 1871.

[62] C. H. McCormick to Trustees of the Presby. Theol. Sem. of the N. W., Oct. 9, 1871. Probably this check never reached its destination, for the receipt from the trustees for $45,000 is dated Mch. 1, 1872. They agreed that this endowment should hold good only as long as "the instruction imparted by said incumbent be in harmony with the Doctrinal Standards of said Church as understood and interpreted by its General Assembly." "Cyrus Hall McCormick, Inventor," in "The Interior" (Chicago), Dec. 14, 1882.

in a safe in the business district of the city, and even these were found to be intact when the strong-box had cooled enough to open it.[63]

When Dr. Prentiss's congregation heard of this disaster, it refused to accept his resignation. The clergyman wrote to McCormick expressing his regret and assuring him that neither the failure to raise the full $65,000 nor the fire was the cause of his inability to fulfil his promise.[64] McCormick could not wholly conceal his anger behind the courteous phrases of his reply.[65] Thus rather ironically ended the long-sustained effort to secure the services of a man whom the New School group had originally supported because they believed he would not accept, and whom McCormick did not highly favor, but was determined to have in order to bring peace to the seminary and block Dr. Patterson's ambition.

The Great Chicago Fire burned out old enmities and reminded some Christians that they should dwell together in love. The group in the saddle at the seminary had heretofore been unable to pay current expenses, and now that they were faced with the task of raising funds from the citizens of a ruined city, they were at last ready to resign the reins into the hands of the only man who had the heart and the means to carry the school through the crisis.

Although McCormick had been waiting for this day for ten

[63] #C. H. McCormick to G. L. Prentiss, Oct. 15 and 22, 1871. #H. G. Miller to C. H. McCormick, Oct. 15, 1871. C. H. McCormick to W. E. McLaren, Detroit, Nov. 3, 1871.

[64] #G. L. Prentiss to C. H. McCormick, Oct. 30, 1871. C. Butler to C. H. McCormick, Nov. 4, 1871. Butler, a leading member of Dr. Prentiss's church, stated that the members of the congregation believed that in view of the now depleted resources of the seminary it was doing the institution a service by not releasing their pastor. #Rev. G. Morrison to C. H. McCormick, Nov. 17, 1871.

[65] #C. H. McCormick to G. L. Prentiss, Nov. 19, 1871. C. H. McCormick to C. Butler, Nov. 19, 1871. In 1873, Dr. Prentiss became a member of the faculty of Union Theological Seminary in New York City.

years, he realized that if the institution were to prosper it must be so conducted as to secure the coöperation of the whole church. "We are looking for a New School man of Old School theology," he wrote to Dr. W. E. McLaren of Detroit, at the close of November.[66] Dr. A. A. Hodge of Western Seminary was his first choice, but he declined. He suggested that McCormick approach the young and brilliant friend of Dr. Henry J. Van Dyke, Francis L. Patton,[67] who was "decidedly orthodox" and had entered the ministry too recently to be distinctly identified with either the New or the Old School. A committee was at once dispatched to Brooklyn to listen to Mr. Patton's preaching, and to talk with his father-in-law, Dr. J. M. Stevenson. The report which came back to Chicago was most enthusiastic [68] and soon Mr. Patton visited McCormick in his Chicago home in order to come to a decision more quickly. On February 7, 1872, he signified his acceptance, and with his arrival in Chicago about March 1 a new day dawned for the Presbyterian Theological Seminary of the Northwest.

As an offset to Dr. Patton, Dr. Robert W. Patterson, the "Nestor of the New School" in Chicago, accepted the invitation of the board of directors to teach Apologetics without pay.[69] The four Chairs at the seminary were once more filled,

[66] ‡C. H. McCormick to W. E. McLaren, Nov. 3, and 12, 1871.

[67] ‡W. E. McLaren to C. H. McCormick, Nov. 29, 1871: *"I deliberately and earnestly hold that he is the very best man in the whole church for the place, who is in any probability available."* ‡W. H. Hornblower to A. A. Hodge, from Allegheny City, Nov. 27, 1871.

[68] S. M. Moore to C. H. McCormick, Dec. 9 and 11, 1871. W. W. Harsha to C. H. McCormick, Dec. 12, 1871: His sermon brought out the "great doctrines of *imputation and vicarious atonement* in a manner which indicated his soundness in the faith and his love for those truths so fundamental to our system. He is a mental master of those much older than he."

[69] ‡F. L. Patton to C. H. McCormick, Jan. 29, and Feb. 7, 1872. ‡C. H. McCormick to F. L. Patton, Feb. 10, 1872. "Annual Announcement of the Presbyterian Theological Seminary of the Northwest," June 1, 1872. "Chicago Times," June 2, 1874. Although Dr. Patterson received no salary from the seminary, his congregation established a small endowment which yielded

and for the first time in over ten years, Cyrus McCormick was satisfied. As he wrote to his old friend, Charles A. Spring, Sr.: "We may yet feel compensated for the great delay and trouble we have been subjected to in accomplishing the great result we have achieved—and this is saying a good deal—but God reigns." [70] For the sake of peace, McCormick would no longer endeavor to foist Old School principles upon an unwilling church, but for his own spiritual satisfaction, he would cling to them until the end.

Shortly before January, 1870, when McCormick invested $5,000 in the stock of the Western Presbyterian Publishing Company to promote the publication of "The Interior," [71] he dreamed of issuing without charge a very large number of copies of "a missionary paper" to furnish religious reading to people not reached by Presbyterian ministers or missionaries, to promote the reunion of the northern and southern churches, and "to look after the purity & democracy of the world." [72] This ambitious program was never inaugurated, and his friends urged him to adopt the more practicable course of buying out the "moribund *Presbyterian*" of Philadelphia.[73] McCormick showed an interest in this suggestion for a time, but he turned his attention elsewhere after learning of the very high price that its editor demanded.[74] It was then that he de-

him a "very meagre income" as a compensation for his teaching. He continued to teach at the seminary until 1881. Between 1876 and 1878 he was president of Lake Forest College. ‡L.P.C.B. of C. H. McCormick, Nov. 1880-May 1881, p. 289, C. H. McCormick to Dr. McCosh, Mch. 14, 1881.

[70] C. H. McCormick to C. A. Spring, Sr., Mch. 7, 1872. ‡C. A. Spring, Sr., to C. H. McCormick, Mch. 1, 1872.

[71] *Supra*, p. 243.

[72] C. H. McCormick to D. C. Marquis, Dec. 3, 1869. ‡L.P.C.B. No. 1, 2nd ser., pp. 6-9, C. H. McCormick to B. M. Smith, Apr. 5, 1870.

[73] ‡A. T. McGill, Princeton, N. J., to C. H. McCormick, Dec. 20, 1869. ‡D. C. Marquis to C. H. McCormick, Dec. 15, 1869.

[74] ‡J. M. Backus, Baltimore, Md., to C. H. McCormick, Jan. 5, 1870. ‡B. M. Smith to C. H. McCormick, Jan. 22, May 7, 10, and June 3, 1870.

cided to support the Chicago project, mentioned above. He had been assured that Dr. Arthur Swazey, the senior editor of "The Interior," would be fair to both the Old and New Schools, but within three months after its first number appeared McCormick found that the journal had become wholly New School in its position and was supporting radicalism in its editorials.[75] The paper was inefficiently managed, and although it had nearly twelve thousand subscribers when its plant was destroyed by the Great Fire, it was heavily in debt.

After the fire, the magazine was quickly revived, but its unpaid obligations grew from month to month.[76] McCormick's friends urged him to acquire a majority interest in the venture in order to promote the welfare of the seminary and the cause of reunion with the southern Presbyterian church.[77] When Professor Patton reached Chicago in March, 1872, he expressed his willingness to be an associate editor, but Dr. Swazey refused to admit him to his staff.[78] Before the close of that summer the control of the paper fell into new hands and Dr.

[75] ‡L.P.C.B. No. 2, 2nd ser., p. 444, C. H. McCormick to ?, Apr. 20, 1872. ‡Letters to C. H. McCormick from D. C. Marquis, June 8, 1870, E. Erskine, June 7, 1870, H. G. Miller, Apr. 19, 1871, and ‡C. A. Spring, Jr., July 10, 1871. Spring had been told that "The Interior" would "run behind" about $30,000 that year.

[76] ‡W. C. Gray to C. H. McCormick, Sept. 13, 1873. At the time of the fire the paper was $10,000 in debt.

[77] The Northern Presbyterian General Assembly of 1869 sent a delegation to the Southern Presb. Gen'l. Assembly with the proposal that reunion should be accomplished by each branch agreeing to treat as of no effect the resolutions enacted by the other since 1860, with the exception of those accepted by both. This reasonable offer was rejected by the southerners who demanded that the northern church specifically repeal its offensive measures. Dr. Smith had warned C. H. McCormick that the times were not yet ripe for such an overture and he regretted the "lamentably unfortunate" result. McCormick was both disappointed and angry at the outcome. "Alas that men of talent and genius are so often deficient in practical common sense." ‡B. M. Smith to C. H. McCormick, May 7, 1870. C. H. McCormick to B. M. Smith, July 20, 1870, in ‡L.P.C.B. No, 1, 2nd ser., p. 137.

[78] C. H. McCormick in "The Interior," Feb. 1, 1873.

Swazey was obliged to resign.[79] The two clergymen who now tried to earn a livelihood by its publication found their subscribers falling away, and their debts alarmingly increasing.[80]

In mid-January, 1873, Cyrus McCormick reluctantly yielded to the pressure of his friends, paid $15,000, and became sole owner of the enterprise.[81] The first issue of "The Interior" under the new régime showed at the head of its editorial page that he was its publisher, Francis L. Patton, editor, and William C. Gray, managing editor.[82] Gray had entered the service of the Western Presbyterian Publishing Company in October, 1871.[83] He and McCormick became warm friends, and largely owing to Gray's business ability and devotion to his task, "The Interior" within a decade was one of the most widely read religious journals in the land.

The four-fold purpose of this magazine, announced by Cyrus McCormick in its first issue after he had gained control, was thenceforward followed in the main during the rest of his life—no party politics, impartiality between the Old and

[79] ‡H. G. Miller to C. H. McCormick, July 22, 25, 31, 1872. ‡R. B. Mason to C. H. McCormick, Aug. 14, 1872.

[80] These two men were Rev. Benjamin W. Dwight and Rev. James H. Trowbridge. See ‡W. C. Gray to C. H. McCormick, Jan. 18, 1873. The financial accounts of "The Interior" had become so confused that an accurate balance could not be drawn. ‡W. J. Hanna to C. H. McCormick, Sept. 10, 1873. L.P.C.B. No. 145, p. 254, D. W. Cobb to C. H. McCormick, Sept. 10, 1873. "Chicago Times," May 26, 1874.

[81] At No. 400, 606 South Michigan Ave., is the agreement of C. H. McCormick and B. W. Dwight, Jan. 20, 1873. C. H. McCormick to the Faculty of the Seminary, n.d., but probably Jan. 1874: "I accepted the responsibility solely for the benefit of the Seminary and the cause of Presbyterianism generally." "The Interior," Dec. 14, 1882, p. 4. "Chicago Times," Jan. 26 and Feb. 2, 1873.

[82] "The Interior," Feb. 1, 1873. This was McCormick's first issue. ‡L.P.C.B. No. 3, 2nd ser., p. 77, C. H. McCormick to L. J. Halsey, n.d. but about May 1, 1873: I am told you and others are in doubt whether you will be paid for articles written for "The Interior." I hope you will contribute *gratis* this year.

[83] ‡W. C. Gray to C. H. McCormick, Sept. 13, 1873.

New Schools, promotion of the interests of the seminary, and the advancement of the cause of reunion between the northern and southern branches of the Presbyterian Church.[84]

By 1879, "The Interior" had about thirteen thousand subscribers.[85] Hitherto, it had been operated at a net loss of over $11,000,[86] but Gray reminded McCormick that he should judge of its success in terms of the good that it had accomplished for the church.[87] After 1879, it was self-sustaining and its managing-editor welcomed the opportunity in March, 1884, to purchase a one-half interest in it from the inventor.[88]

Although its competitors had long since ceased strongly to urge reunion between the northern and southern branches of the church, "The Interior" never wearied of championing this cause. For this reason, it was the one Presbyterian publication in the North which had a growing circulation below Mason and Dixon's Line, and Gray spoke with truth when he called it the only national paper of his church. Each year after 1872, McCormick and Gray prepared a reunion article for its columns and distributed reprints of it to the delegates at the

[84] The resolve of McCormick to hold an even balance in "The Interior" between the Old and the New Schools, caused some heart-burning among the arch-conservatives. ♯G. Morrison to C. H. McCormick, Apr. 12, 1873; ♯D. X. Junkin to C. H. McCormick, Apr. 9, 1875.

[85] ♯C. A. Spring, Jr., to C. H. McCormick, Feb. 12 and Nov. 7, 1879. W. C. Gray to C. H. McCormick, Aug. 23, 1875, ♯Sept. 1, 1876, Aug. 6, 1877, and Nov. 29, 1878. L. J. Halsey to C. H. McCormick, Nov. 31, 1878. Its subscription price was $2.50 a year.

[86] ♯C. A. Spring, Jr., to C. H. McCormick, Feb. 12, 1879. ♯Statement of Assets and Liabilities of C. H. McCormick, Aug. 1, 1881. "The Interior" is here listed as a net asset of $45,000.

[87] ♯W. C. Gray to C. H. McCormick, Sept. 16, 1879. ♯L. J. Halsey to C. H. McCormick, Sept. 24, 1879.

[88] ♯Agreement between W. C. Gray and C. H. McCormick, Mch. 18, 1884. McCormick stipulated that he should control the policy of the paper as long as he lived and that it should bear his name forever. In recognition of Gray's faithful and able service as editor and business manager, McCormick paid his expenses to Europe for a vacation in the summer of 1881. ♯W. C. Gray to C. H. McCormick, May 2, 1881; Feb. 28, 1883. C. H. McCormick to Dr. H. Calderwood, Edinburgh, Scotland, July 11, 1881.

northern General Assembly.[89] It was a discouraging task since
southern leaders were still insisting upon larger concessions on
questions of property, church discipline, and wartime deliverances than most northern Presbyterians were prepared to
yield. The members of the southern branch were apparently
quite happy to go their own way unless the North would make
an unconditional surrender.[90] Finally, in 1882, the two wings
established fraternal relations by exchanging delegates, and
McCormick and Gray felt that they and "The Interior" deserved some credit for the victory. The "half-way house" to
organic union, so they believed, had at last been reached, and
fusion was without doubt "among the blessings foreordained
from all eternity!" [91]

Many believed that the compromise effected by the appointment of Professors Patton and R. W. Patterson to the faculty
of the seminary in Chicago in 1872, would lead the churches of
the Northwest to rally to its support.[92] In this hope McCormick and others who were anxious to promote the welfare of
the institution were disappointed. The New School congregations still viewed the seminary with distrust.[93] The forceful

[89] ‡L.P.C.B. of C. H. McCormick, Nov. 1873-June 1876, p. 406, C. H.
McCormick to B. M. Smith, Apr. 5, 1876. ‡W. C. Gray to C. H. Mc-
Cormick, June 2 and Nov. 15, 1882. In the N. F. McCormick Biog. Asso.
Files is a folder containing fifteen letters from W. C. Gray to C. H. Mc-
Cormick between 1879 and 1884.

[90] B. M. Smith, Hampden Sidney, Va., to C. H. McCormick, July 23,
1873, March 2, 1875, Apr. 13 and May 9, 1877.

[91] "The Interior," June 1, 1882; ‡W. C. Gray to C. H. McCormick, June
2, 1882. C. H. McCormick to W. C. Gray, June 8, 1882: "And now for
Part 2—Reunion. This is even more important and should be looked to as
the final consummation of what has been so happily begun by the two
assemblies. I hope to see more about that in 'The Interior.' " H. Johnson to
C. H. McCormick, June 6, 1882: The northern Church has withdrawn its
wartime changes of schism, heresy and blasphemy.

[92] W. W. Harsha, Jacksonville, Ill., to C. H. McCormick, Mch. 18, 1881,
and ‡R. W. Patterson to W. S. Curtis, Rockford, Ill., Feb. 4, 1881.

[93] D. Marquis to C. H. McCormick, Apr. 19, 1876. H. A. Hurlbut to
C. H. McCormick, Sept. 19, 1876. He wrote of the lack of support of the
seminary by the Fourth Presbyterian Church and hoped that if Dr. French

figure of Dr. Patton dominated the life of the campus, and his courses in theology, in the view of some of his colleagues, held too prominent a place in the curriculum.[94] His post as editor of "The Interior" also brought him the attention of the religious public, and he there advocated more conservative doctrines than many of his fellow-clergymen could endorse.

The aversion of the Presbyterian liberals for Patton changed to open hostility in April, 1874, when he laid before the Chicago Presbytery two charges of heresy against the Rev. David Swing. Among the twenty-eight specifications comprising this indictment were a tendency toward Unitarianism and mysticism, laudation of John Stuart Mill, sympathy for "the doctrine commonly known as 'Evolution,'" denial of the infallibility of the Bible, "flippant" references to infant baptism, and the use of "language in respect of Penelope and Socrates which is . . . contrary to . . . the Confession of Faith."[95] Swing had come to Chicago in 1866 from a professor's chair at Miami University in Ohio, to accept the pastorate of the Westminster Church. Five years later his congregation united with the members of the North Church to form the Fourth

were called to its pulpit, he would work a change of feeling. C. H. McCormick to Rev. Dr. Niccolls, St. Louis, Sept. 24, 1876. Niccolls was being considered for the place also and C. H. McCormick, although not favoring him because of his "unsound" theological views, was glad to find that he was a friend of the seminary and "The Interior." In McCormick's opinion, these two agencies, with the church, constituted "the foundation of our Presbyterian system." W. C. Gray to C. H. McCormick, Oct. 26, 1877. In this letter Gray expressed the belief that the prejudice against Patton among Chicago preachers was dying out.

[94] J. M. Faris to C. H. McCormick, June 11, 1879; #C. Elliott to C. H. McCormick, May 29, 1880.

[95] The twenty-eight specifications will be found in A. T. Andreas, "History of Chicago from the Earliest Period to the Present Time" (3 vols., Chicago, 1885), II, pp. 802-803. See also, "Chicago Times," Feb. 24, 25, and Mch. 1, 1874; "Chicago Daily Tribune," Apr. 14, 15, 1874. Dr. Swing had also offended by saying that Catherine II of Russia was less likely than the pagan Socrates to go to Heaven.

Presbyterian Church.[96] When McCormick reëstablished his home in Chicago in October, 1871, he refused to abide Swing's preaching, and joined the Third Presbyterian congregation, of which Dr. Abbott E. Kittredge was the pastor. Swing's sermons, however, drew larger and larger audiences, and editors found that the circulation of their newspapers increased when they printed his discourses and essays. He was soon acknowledged to be the most dangerous foe of conservative Presbyterianism in the Chicago area. To the editor of the "Chicago Tribune," on the other hand, Professor Patton was a "16th Century bigot brought to the city by C. H. McCormick to extirpate heresy." [97]

The attitude of the conservative Presbyterians toward Dr. Swing is well summarized in a letter received by McCormick early in 1874. "If Prof. S[wing's] positions are sustained, no one can tell what is the Bible, & what is not. . . . If our Church can tolerate views, which Unitarians & other sceptics endorse, and which all evangelical Christians ignore, the time has arrived, when another Division of the Church will take place. It has become fashionable to reduce the word of God to the level of . . . 'the inspired platform of Plato.' " [98]

The memorable Swing heresy trial of May, 1874, is unmentioned in the letters of Cyrus McCormick, but messages received by him from sympathetic clergymen, and articles in

---

[96] The Fourth Presbyterian Church was burned in the fire of 1871. Thereafter for over two years, Dr. Swing gathered about him the members of his congregation and many other people in Standard Hall or McVicker's Theatre. Finally, on Jan. 4, 1874, a new Fourth Presbyterian Church edifice, at the corner of Rush and Superior streets, was ready for services.

[97] "Chicago Daily Tribune," March 1, 1874.

[98] ‡Rev. W. H. Van Doren, Clifton Springs, N. Y. to C. H. McCormick, Feb. 28, 1874. Van Doren in 1884 gave 1,300 volumes to the Chicago Seminary. See, A Committee of the Presbytery, editor, "The Trial of the Rev. David Swing before the Presbytery of Chicago" (Chicago, 1874), and "The World's Edition of the Great Presbyterian Conflict: Patton vs. Swing" (Chicago, 1874).

the daily press, leave no doubt that he supported the prosecution.[99] The pastor of his church, Dr. Abbott Kittredge, defended the accused and was with difficulty restrained from resigning his charge before the summer was over.[100] Even prior to the opening of the trial, Swing announced that he would sever his connection with a denomination that emphasized "dogma rather than love." He was vindicated by a three to one vote of the Chicago Presbytery, but the Synod of Northern Illinois, composed largely of preachers from rural churches, resolved by an overwhelming majority to eject him from its fellowship. Dr. Swing, of his own volition, had withdrawn from the denomination five months before.[101] About one-third of the congregation of the Fourth Church gave up their membership rather than abandon their pastor. His reputation increased, and by 1878 he was obliged to preach in Central Music Hall in order to provide seats for all who wished to listen to him.

[99] ‡L.P.C.B. of C. H. McCormick, Nov. 1873-June 1876, p. 162, D. E. Bradley (secretary of C. H. McCormick) to Nettie F. McCormick, Sept. 28, 1874: "Dr. Patton will require my services no doubt and I hold myself at his call, which he understands. Some 30 copies of the 'Trial' were sent in and have been mailed to the Synod." In the previous May, during the trial, several meetings of the Chicago Presbytery were held in the "Presbyterian Room" of the McCormick Block. ‡B. M. Smith to C. H. McCormick, Oct. 2, 1874; T. H. Skinner to C. H. McCormick, Sept. 12, 1874. H. G. Miller, L. J. Halsey, and W. C. Goudy, friends of C. H. McCormick, testified against Mr. Swing. The trial was conducted with dignity. Swing pleaded "Not Guilty," and contended that Patton's charges for the most part consisted of sentences torn from the context of his sermons. See also, "Chicago Daily Tribune," March 5, 6, 8, and June 6, 1874. According to "Chicago Times" of Jan. 17, 1875, the outspoken attacks upon Swing by "The Interior" led many to cancel their subscriptions by the close of 1874.

[100] ‡A. E. Kittredge to C. H. McCormick, Feb. 10, and July 14, 1874; "Chicago Daily Tribune," June 6, 1874; "Chicago Times," June 6 and 9, 1874.

[101] "Chicago Daily Tribune," Apr. 29, May 21, 26, and Oct. 24, 1874. "Chicago Times," May 22, and Oct. 17, 24, and Nov. 1, 1874. To recover lost ground and to make "The Interior" the voice of an united Presbyterian Church, Rev. C. L. Thompson, the new school pastor of the 5th Presbyterian Church of Chicago, was made co-editor with Dr. Patton in Jan., 1875.

This episode widened the breach between the two wings of Presbyterians in the Middle West, and made assurance doubly sure that the liberals would not support the seminary as long as Professor Patton occupied its senior Chair. Nevertheless, Jesse L. Williams, no longer a political radical, joined with Cyrus McCormick and C. B. Nelson of Chicago in 1874, to make possible the erection of a new building on the seminary campus—a chapel, library, and recitation hall combined. This was dedicated in the spring of 1876.[102] Conservatives comforted themselves with the belief that the church was moving slowly back to orthodoxy, and they viewed Dr. Patton's election as moderator of the General Assembly of 1878 as a cheering indication of this tendency.[103]

Early that year the agent of the seminary, John M. Faris, summarized in a circular letter the critical financial condition of the school. By a strange chance, one of its greatest future assets was at this time a heavy liability. Those who gave the institution twenty-five acres of land on the North Side in 1863 had stipulated that this property could not be sold or mortgaged before 1888. Following the Great Fire, the city grew rapidly in the neighborhood of the seminary, and it was harassed by heavy taxes and special assessments. The value of the real estate increased from year to year but it returned no income. Five of the twenty-five acres were to be reserved for the campus, and the balance by sale or lease would some day add substantially to the endowment. The chief financial prob-

102 "Chicago Times," Apr. 3, 1874, and Apr. 7, 1876. Each of these men gave $5,000, and $15,000 more was raised in New York. J. M. Faris to C. H. McCormick, Aug. 16, 1875; J. L. Williams, Fort Wayne, to C. H. McCormick, May 29, 1878. Pamphlet, "Services at the Laying of the Corner Stone, and Addresses at the Dedication of the Chapel and Library of the Presbyterian Theological Seminary of the Northwest" (Chicago, 1876), p. 6.

103 C. H. McCormick, Jr., MSS. Book "B," N. F. to C. H. McCormick, Jr., June 3, 1878: "What a triumph and what a just recognition by the church of one who has defended truths so dear to her, and away from which there has been such a tendency to drift."

Jem of the fifteen years after the fire was to keep the institution out of debt until that happy day arrived. By then it was expected that the twenty acres would have a value of $400,000, or double their estimated worth in 1878.[104]

The crisis at the seminary at this time was the more serious because the money given by Cyrus McCormick to endow the Chair of Theology had for the most part been loaned to John Forsythe of Chicago, who had invested it in suburban lands. These properties were now unproductive and Forsythe was unable to pay to the seminary each year the interest guaranteed when the loan was made. By March 1, 1879, Patton's salary was $10,000 in arrears, and as early as 1875 he had been obliged to accept the pastorate of the Jefferson Park Presbyterian Church in order to support his increasing family.[105] The endowment of the other Chairs also failed to return an income adequate to pay the living expenses of their incumbents. Dr. L. J. Halsey, in poor health and often on the point of leaving, managed to keep out of debt by serving as senior editor of "The Interior" after Patton resigned in 1876.[106] McCormick expected that the members of the faculty would contribute articles to this weekly without charge, but the pressure of their seminary duties and the need of devoting their spare time to tasks which would supplement their salaries, rendered this impossible.[107]

[104] Circular letter of J. M. Faris, Jan. 10, 1878. J. M. Faris to C. H. McCormick, June 11, 1879. C. H. McCormick to T. H. Skinner, June 20, 1881.

[105] J. M. Faris to C. H. McCormick, May 15, 1879; W. C. Gray to C. H. McCormick, Jr., May 3, 1879; H. G. Miller to C. H. McCormick, June 9, 1879. "Chicago Times," Sept. 1, 1879.

[106] "Chicago Times," Jan. 30, 1876. Letters to C. H. McCormick of ‡F. L. Patton, Jan. 22, 1876, D. C. Marquis, Apr. 19, 1876; ‡L. J. Halsey, Jan. 7, 1874, ‡March 18, 1876, and ‡Sept. 24, 1879, C. L. Thompson, Oct. 22, 1877, and from W. C. Gray, Oct. 26, 1877. ‡Circular letter of J. M. Faris, Jan. 10, 1878. ‡L.P.C.B. No. 4, 2nd ser., p. 48, C. H. McCormick to W. Gray, Oct. 21, 1877.

[107] L. J. Halsey to C. H. McCormick, May 9, 1873, and ‡Jan. 7, 1874. He thought that his ideas were too old-fashioned, and his style "too grave and

When the seminary was founded, the inventor hoped that each professor would also be a pastor in the city. From financial necessity, and not by choice, this had come to be the rule,[108] but during the past twenty years those in charge of the leading seminaries in the land had decided that these two functions should not be combined. "I know the tastes of students well," wrote Dr. James McCosh of Princeton to McCormick in 1881, "and of all things they hate the sermonizing hortatory style. They simply will not tolerate it; if forced upon them, it will disgust them. This is the case in all countries & in all Theological seminaries. They must have Theological subjects treated scientifically. We have it now in all our Eastern Theological Seminaries. Students will not go now either to Colleges or Seminaries where the Professors are dividing their time between preaching & lecturing." [109] If the seminary at Chicago followed this trend, the endowment of each chair would have to be increased.

Dr. McCosh's letter also suggested another problem at Chicago. The homes of the members of the faculty were widely separated because they were obliged to be near their churches, or to live where rents were low. As a result, there were lacking that professional *esprit de corps* and feeling of oneness between the teaching staff and the students which were

serious" to suit the prevailing mode, or to interest the younger generation. C. H. McCormick to Faculty of Presbyterian Theological Seminary of N. W., n.d. but probably early Jan., 1874. Up to this time, he writes, he has been publishing "The Interior" at a loss, and suggests that he cannot afford to continue the paper unless its expense can be reduced. W. M. Blackburn to C. H. McCormick, Jan. 27, 1874. He was too busy cataloging the 4,000 volumes in the seminary's library to write for "The Interior." Although Dr. Halsey was the titular senior editor for a short time after Dr. Patton's resignation, W. C. Gray was the active directing head, under C. H. McCormick. See, #L.P.C.B. of C. H. McCormick, Nov., 1873-June, 1876, pp. 369-370, C. H. McCormick to L. J. Halsey, Feb. 11, 1876.

108 W. C. Gray to C. H. McCormick, Oct. 26, 1877.

109 #J. McCosh to C. H. McCormick, March 28 and 29, 1881.

so desirable at a theological seminary.[110] To secure these advantages, houses for the faculty should be erected on the campus. If this were done, the portion of a salary which could be equated as rent would be a sum larger than the annual income to be expected from a safe investment of the money in another way.[111] In short, quite apart from considerations of morale, the erection of four or five dwellings would be a shrewd financial stroke.

Furthermore, by 1879, with the exception of Professor Patton, the members of the faculty were either too old or were not in accord with the theological views of the few "giving members," as they were called, of the Presbyterian Church in or near Chicago. Patton was the only professor of national reputation on the staff, although it had been McCormick's early dream to make this seminary the equal of the best in the land.[112] To do this he had expected the coöperation of the whole church, but it had not been given, probably in some measure because he had said more than once after 1872 that he would not let the institution fail. With this assurance, even the friends of the seminary felt satisfied to sit back and permit him to carry most of the burden.[113] The Fire of 1871 and the

[110] H. Johnson, Chicago, to C. H. McCormick, Sept. 9, 1881.

[111] ‡J. M. Faris to C. H. McCormick, Jan. 20, 1881. He believed that each house, erected at a cost of about $8,000, would permit the salary of each professor to be reduced by as much as $900 or $1,000 a year. Thus the investment would yield the seminary about 12% income.

[112] ‡J. Milligan, Princeton, Ill., to C. H. McCormick, Oct. 28, 1880. C. H. McCormick to B. B. Warfield, Allegheny, Pa., May 15, 1881.

[113] S. M. Moore to F. L. Patton, July 16, 1880: What is the use of maintaining a board of directors and trustees if McCormick is obliged to pay all the costs of the seminary? S. M. Moore to C. H. McCormick, Aug. 9, 1880. W. C. Gray to C. H. McCormick, Aug. 11, 1880: "I confess I get mad when I notice one of the brethren sit down, stick his heels high, light a cigar, and say: 'Mr. McCormick must do so and so.'" ‡L.P.C.B. of C. H. McCormick, Nov., 1880-May, 1881, pp. 4-6, C. H. McCormick to H. Johnson, Nov. 13, 1880: I am ready to help in the seminary crisis but I don't think all the burden should fall on me. The seminary is central in the present church emergency and should be aided by all Presbyterian congrega-

years of depression between 1873 and 1879 doubtless increased the difficulty of raising money. No wonder that Rev. J. M. Faris in the summer of 1879 suggested that the "McCormick" Theological Seminary would be a more appropriate name for the institution.[114]

In the spring of that year, when Dr. Patton received a tempting offer from the Presbyterian Theological Seminary of London, McCormick induced him to decline by paying him one-half of his back salary, and guaranteeing that he would receive $4,500 a year until 1882. The fear that a New School man would be appointed to the Chair of Theology if Patton should leave, was one consideration influencing McCormick to make this pledge.[115] Hardly had this danger been avoided than the professor was approached by representatives of the Princeton Theological Seminary who wished him to return and serve his Alma Mater. These negotiations were soon common knowledge. They brought the troubles of a decade to a focus, and precipitated one of the most serious crises in the life of the Chicago institution.

Following McCormick's arrangement with Patton in the summer of 1879, his colleagues, and particularly Dr. Elliott,

tions. *Ibid.*, p. 324, C. H. McCormick to W. W. Harsha, Jacksonville, Ill., March 22, 1881. C. H. McCormick to D. L. Moody, Feb. 23, 1881. #C. H. McCormick, Jr., to T. H. Skinner, Oct. 4, 1883.

[114] #J. M. Faris to C. H. McCormick, June 3, 1879. This is the first time that this suggestion was made, so far as I have found.

[115] W. C. Gray to C. H. McCormick, Jr., May 3, 1879; J. M. Faris to C. H. McCormick, May 15, and #Oct. 24, 1879; H. G. Miller to C. H. McCormick, June 9, 1879; #C. H. McCormick to F. L. Patton, June 26, 1879. C. H. McCormick was to receive the coupon notes of the Forsythe loan and endeavor to gain reimbursement in that way. By Nov. 1879, Forsythe owed the seminary about $60,000, but at that time one of his friends assumed the obligation. See, #R. B. Mason to C. H. McCormick, Nov. 3, 1879. #F. L. Patton to C. H. McCormick, July 1, 1879. Patton here states that he declined the London call largely because McCormick told him that his resignation would be disastrous to the seminary. "Chicago Times," July 2, 1879.

took no pains to hide their displeasure at the preferred treatment which he had been accorded.[116] To allay this discontent, McCormick promised to pay the arrears of salary due to each member of the faculty,[117] but he approved and most probably inspired the action of the board of directors in the spring of 1880, inviting all of the teaching staff with the exception of Patton to hand in their resignations by the close of the next academic year. Dr. Halsey, in recognition of his long and faithful service, would retire with the rank of Professor Emeritus.[118] Every possible expedient was employed to influence Dr. Patton to remain. McCormick told him that his departure would bring "almost temporary ruin" to Presbyterian interests in the entire Northwest, and that he would gladly loan him $10,000 without interest so that he could build a home near the seminary. He would also assure him of a salary of $4,500 until 1888.[119] Mr. R. L. Stuart of New York, who

[116] ‡C. Elliott to C. H. McCormick, May 29, 1880; S. M. Moore to C. H. McCormick, Nov. 10, 1880.

[117] C. C. Brown, Springfield, Ill., to C. H. McCormick, Apr. 2, 1880. "Chicago Times," Apr. 2, 4, 6, 1880.

[118] ‡C. M. Howe to C. H. McCormick, Apr. 19, 1880; ‡C. Elliott to C. H. McCormick, May 29, 1880: "If you search the annals of the Presbyterian Church, you will not find an action, by men professing to be ministers and servants of Christ, so mean and so disgraceful. We were given no chance to speak in our own defense, and we are asked to resign on the alleged ground that the Seminary is financially embarrassed." In a letter to ‡R. L. Stuart, New York City, Aug. 2, 1880, C. H. McCormick stated that the faculty were ousted in order to rid the seminary of the "unsoundness" which prevented the churches of the Northwest from supporting it. Viewed from one angle, this housecleaning was the last gun in the Lord-McCormick controversy, for Professor Blackburn had been appointed by a radical General Assembly, and was one of Dr. Lord's close friends. He was also a stanch supporter of Dr. Swing. ‡R. W. Patterson to W. S. Curtis, Feb. 4, 1881; S. M. Moore to C. H. McCormick, Nov. 4, 1880; C. H. McCormick to B. B. Warfield, May 15, 1881. In April, 1880, C. H. McCormick was elected president of the board of trustees of the seminary.

[119] C. H. McCormick to F. L. Patton, Dec. 5, 1880. There is a notation on this letter that it was never sent, since C. H. McCormick, Jr., went to Dr. Patton's house that day and made the offer verbally.

had endowed the new Chair at Princeton with Patton in mind, was made aware of the serious injury he was doing to one seminary by his gift to the other.[120] But Patton, now thirty-seven years of age, felt that his advancement at Chicago had not been sufficiently rapid. He desired an opportunity to specialize, and he was tired of the gloomy outlook with its "suspicions, conflicts, delays, and cliques."[121] Before he fully realized how much McCormick would do to tide the seminary over the lean years until its land endowment could be sold, he promised his admirers at Princeton that if he received a formal call to come there, he would accept.[122]

This came in due season, but not before McCormick had let it be known that he would give $100,000 to the seminary if a like sum could be raised from other sources.[123] He also induced Dr. Herrick Johnson, the able pastor of the Fourth Presbyterian Church of Chicago, whither the inventor had transferred his membership in 1877, to lecture at the seminary during the session of 1880-1881.[124] Thus both the qual-

[120] ‡C. H. McCormick to R. L. Stuart, Aug. 2, 1880. Stuart was a wealthy sugar-refiner. W. M. Paxton, Princeton, to C. H. McCormick, Sept. 16, 1880.

[121] F. L. Patton to C. H. McCormick, Sept. 6 and Dec. 17, 1880; to W. S. Plumer, Sept. 6, 1880; H. Johnson to C. H. McCormick, Nov. 9, 1880.

[122] S. M. Moore to C. H. McCormick, July 23, Aug. 23, Sept. 13, and Oct. 1, 1880; F. L. Patton to C. H. McCormick, Sept. 6, 1880, and to the board of directors, Nov. 24, 1880. The first advances of Princeton to Dr. Patton were made during the absence, and without the knowledge of Dr. McCosh. See his letter to C. H. McCormick, Apr. 29, 1880.

[123] S. M. Moore to F. L. Patton, July 16, 1880. This letter indicates that McCormick's original proposal was to give $50,000 if a like sum were raised by the churches. Moore urged Patton to stay, on the ground that if he left, McCormick would not give so much to the seminary. Letters to C. H. McCormick of S. M. Moore, Aug. 9, 23, 1880; W. C. Gray, Aug. 11, 1880, and of H. Johnson, Aug. 16, 1880.

[124] S. M. Moore to C. H. McCormick, July 6, 1880. C. H. McCormick was to pay the bill—$2,000 a year. As pastor of the Fourth Church, Dr. Johnson received $8,000 a year. The Fourth Church steadily grew in membership and influence. In a memorable two weeks' "drive" in 1878, with C. H. McCormick as the "pivot man," its burdensome debt of $35,000 had all been

ity of its faculty and the state of its finances seemed to augur a brighter future in the late summer of 1880, and McCormick hoped that these advantages would resolve any doubts which Patton might have as to his proper course. Patton did hesitate, so much so in fact that his health was temporarily impaired, and the liberals among the Presbyterians of the city began to fear that he might choose to remain. As the weeks went by, his inability to reach a decision embarrassed the directors of both seminaries.[125] Finally, in December, he declared, "The verdict of my judgment is preponderating in the direction of Princeton as the field of my life work." [126] By so narrow a margin did Princeton secure a man who within eight years would be her president.[127]

A few men, and notably Dr. Herrick Johnson, felt that the seminary had been placed in a humiliating position by the too insistent efforts of its officials to retain Patton.[128] Nor could

paid—the inventor contributing $5,000. Following Dr. Swing's resignation in 1874, the church had no regular pastor until the well-beloved Rev. John A. French of Morristown, New Jersey, was installed in the spring of 1877. Ill health obliged him to resign on Jan. 1, 1880. Dr. Johnson became pastor in April of that year and served until July 1, 1883. Johnson was puritanical in his attitude toward amusements. He was known as "the scourge of the Chicago theatre." He had formerly been a professor in the Auburn (N. Y.) Seminary. C. H. McCormick, Jr., MSS. Book "B," Nettie F. McCormick to C. H. McCormick, Jr., Jan. 30, 1878; H. W. King to C. H. McCormick, March 19, 1877.

[125] H. Johnson to C. H. McCormick, Oct. 21, 1880: Patton should make up his mind at once. He too often puts himself in a posture to be urged and pleaded with.

[126] ‡F. L. Patton to S. M. Moore, Dec. 10, 1880. Patton's decision seems to have been forced by the determination to send a committee to Princeton to endeavor to secure a release for him from his pledge.

[127] C. H. McCormick, Jr., MSS. Book "B," Nettie F. McCormick to C. H. McCormick, Jr., March 24, 1888. She expressed her gratification at the news that Dr. Patton had been elected President of Princeton College. C. H. McCormick in 1881, however, believed that Patton had made "the mistake of his life" in going to Princeton. See, C. H. McCormick to H. Johnson, Aug. 6, and ‡10, 1881.

[128] H. Johnson to C. H. McCormick, Aug. 16 and Oct. 21, 1880: "Institutions are stronger than men." "Chicago Times," Dec. 5, 1880.

W. C. Gray, the editor of "The Interior," account for the general air of despondency occasioned by the news of Patton's resignation. "We must galvanize new life into the Directory," he wrote McCormick. "We need hopeful, vigorous, aggressive leadership. . . . If the Chair of Theology is occupied by a man who is satisfactory to yourself, and to the more conservative element of the Church, the Ship is secure. Put young, enthusiastic men in the other chairs." [129] This was one aspect of the task which faced the friends of the seminary in the autumn of 1880. The other was well summarized by Dr. Johnson: "We want a contingent fund," he wrote, "that will make it unnecessary for the Seminary to go every year and lie like a pauper at the gates of opulent churches begging for a few pittances with which to get its daily bread." [130] Men and money would bring the renaissance.

While the seminary officials, without much hope of success, were considering ways and means of raising $100,000 in order to meet McCormick's offer of a like amount,[131] the inventor

[129] W. C. Gray to C. H. McCormick, Aug. 11, and Sept. 30, 1880. ‡L.P.C.B. of C. H. McCormick, Nov. 1880-May, 1881, pp. 66-69. C. H. McCormick to Dr. Hall, New York, Dec. 19, 1880: "The great agony now over, Professor Patton goes to Princeton next spring. I need not now trouble you with the long, tedious, and inconsistent course of Professor Patton in coming to a decision. . . . I do not know a single person who would now, under all the circumstances, have it otherwise. The universal feeling already seems to be in accord with the expression once made by yourself, that such an institution could not depend upon the action or agency of any one man." Apparently this was never mailed to Dr. Hall, but it doubtless expressed C. H. McCormick's true feeling. ‡C. H. McCormick to D. Marquis, June 28, 1881: The seminary should be "extended and liberalized" and lifted out of "old ruts." My name has been to some extent connected with this "old rut charge." The narrow and contracted course has kept prominent men from helping the school.

[130] H. Johnson to C. H. McCormick, Aug. 16, 1880.

[131] Letters to C. H. McCormick of S. M. Moore, Aug. 9, 1880, F. L. Patton, Sept. 6, 1880, and H. Johnson, Sept. 10, 1880. In view of the poor success attending the drive for funds from the churches, McCormick by this date had apparently revised his proposal a third time, and now promised $50,000 unconditionally and $50,000 more if a like sum were raised from other sources.

was wondering who could be found to succeed Dr. Patton in the Chair of Theology. His first choice for the position was Professor Henry Calderwood of the University of Edinburgh, but his name failed to arouse much enthusiasm from McCormick's associates.[132] Dr. Faris believed that his appointment would "exert a depressing influence on home scholarship," and that he would most likely be "tainted with the prevalent and growing rationalism." If he should come he "would bring a degree of British lordliness that would be odious in Republican America, and especially in our 'free and easy' Chicago and the North West. Students cannot brook haughtiness in a Professor." [133]

In view of these "perils," it was perhaps fortunate that Calderwood declined, and McCormick turned for advice to Dr. McCosh, who had lived over fifty years under the British flag. This oracle of sound Presbyterianism, now that Dr. Charles Hodge had gone to his reward, warned McCormick that the heresy he was "most likely to meet with in the present age does not relate to soundness of doctrine but to the authenticity of the books of Scripture. This error comes from Germany and . . . is far deeper and more dangerous than the other. You must watch specially over the Chair of Biblical Criticism." [134] "The danger," he resumed in a later letter, ". . . comes from those who . . . tell you that Moses did not write

[132] ‡L.P.C.B. of C. H. McCormick, Nov., 1880-May, 1881, pp. 72, 95-96, 121, 145, C. H. McCormick to Dr. McCosh, Dec. 21, 1880, Jan. 3, 13 and 23, 1881. C. H. McCormick thought Calderwood's appointment would be worth $50,000 to the seminary and was willing to build him a house. See, "Dictionary of National Biography" (N. Y., 1909), XXII, p. 373. J. M. McCue, Afton, Va., to J. D. Davidson, Apr. 8, 1881.

[133] Letters to C. H. McCormick of ‡J. M. Faris, Dec. 22, 1880, and of H. Calderwood, Edinburgh, Mch. 22, 1881.

[134] J. McCosh to C. H. McCormick, Jan. 18, 1881. ‡L.P.C.B. of C. H. McCormick, Nov., 1880-May, 1881, p. 308. C. H. McCormick to J. McCosh, Mch. 19, 1881: I'd like to find an "old light" man for Theology and a "new light" one for Exegesis.

the Pentateuch, that the commandments were not delivered from Mt. Sinai [and], that the Gospel usually ascribed to John was not written by him." [135]

Finally, after scores of letters had been exchanged and the first half of 1881 had brought little return except discouragement and conflicting counsel,[136] a tentative slate of professors was agreed upon. Dr. Thomas H. Skinner, pastor of Lyman Beecher's old church in Cincinnati, was the choice for Theology. After much hesitation, in some degree due to his absence in Europe, he accepted and reached the campus by late October.[137] He entered upon his new work with enthusiasm, and was soon spending more of his modest fortune in behalf of the seminary than he was receiving in salary.[138] Dr. Herrick Johnson was Professor of Homiletics, and in 1883 resigned his pastorate in order to devote all of his time to teaching.[139] Dr. David C. Marquis, an alumnus of the seminary and now a successful preacher in St. Louis, promised to occupy the Chair of Exegesis as soon as his unwilling congregation would release him. He was unable to assume his duties before the

[135] J. McCosh to C. H. McCormick, Mch. 11, 1881.

[136] ‡S. J. Niccolls, St. Louis, to C. H. McCormick, June 11, 1881; ‡W. W. Harsha, Jacksonville, Ill., to C. H. McCormick, Apr. 20, May 12, and 28, 1881; C. H. McCormick to B. B. Warfield, Allegheny, Pa., Apr. ‡8, ‡15, ‡27, May 15, 1881. Dr. Warfield, a grandson of Dr. R. J. Breckinridge, was offered the Chicago Chair of Theology at this time, but he declined. So, also, did Dr. A. T. Pierson of Detroit.

[137] C. H. McCormick to T. H. Skinner, June 20, 1881; ‡T. H. Skinner, Constance, Switzerland, to C. H. McCormick, July 8, 1881; Dr. Herrick Johnson did not favor Skinner for the Chair. He wrote to C. H. McCormick in a tone of irritation about seminary matters on ‡Aug. 4, 1881, complaining that his advice was not followed. C. H. McCormick to C. H. McCormick, Jr., July 20, 1881; ‡W. W. Harsha to C. H. McCormick, Nov. 2, 1881. "Chicago Times," Sept. 7, 1881.

[138] ‡L.P.C.B. of C. H. McCormick, May, 1881-Jan., 1882, p. 204, C. H. McCormick to D. C. Marquis, Dec. 29, 1881. ‡T. H. Skinner to C. H. McCormick, Sept. 1, 1882; Apr. 14, 1883.

[139] ‡Idem to idem, Apr. 6, 1883; C. H. McCormick to C. H. McCormick, Jr., July 17, 1883.

spring of 1883, and Dr. Halsey substituted for him until that time.[140] Dr. Willis G. Craig of Keokuk, Iowa, who had been chosen for the Chair of Biblical History, finally secured the consent of his presbytery to the appointment in April, 1882.[141]

The forced resignation of the old faculty, and the uncertainty whether there would be either professors or money on hand in the autumn of 1881 to begin the new academic year, reduced the student enrolment from its normal number of over thirty, to ten.[142] Because the New School Presbyterians viewed the appointments with distrust, little financial aid could be expected from them.[143] Furthermore, it was well known that the delay of Marquis and Craig in coming to Chicago was in large measure due to the fact that there were no homes provided for the use of the faculty.[144] Letter after letter came to McCormick in 1881 urging him to bear the expense of erecting three or four houses on the seminary campus.[145] He, thereupon, withdrew his earlier proposals and eventually agreed to give $100,000 unconditionally to the endowment fund. In addition, he promised to have three residences built at a cost of about $9,000 each.[146] He hoped that if Dr. Her-

[140] Letters to C. H. McCormick of ‡J. Milligan, Apr. 4, 1882, C. H. McCormick, Jr., May 18, 1882, D. C. Marquis, June 5 and 15, 1882, and ‡S. J. Niccolls, June 19, 1882. Letters of C. H. McCormick to D. C. Marquis, May 9 and June 15, 1882, to C. H. McCormick, Jr., May 13, 1882, and to Nettie F. McCormick, June 7, 1882. "Chicago Times," Apr. 10, 1883.

[141] ‡W. G. Craig to C. H. McCormick, Jan. 3 and March 19, 1881; Jan. 3, and Apr. 22, 1882.

[142] ‡Letters to C. H. McCormick, of J. Milligan, Aug. 29, and Sept. 24, 1881, of H. Johnson, Aug. 12, 1881, and of S. M. Moore, Sept. 2, 1881.

[143] W. W. Harsha, Jacksonville, Ill., to C. H. McCormick, March 18, ‡June 16, and ‡Nov. 2, 1881.

[144] ‡S. J. Niccolls, St. Louis, to C. C. Brown, Apr. 13, 1881. ‡J. Milligan to C. H. McCormick, Aug. 11, 1881.

[145] ‡Letters to C. H. McCormick of W. W. Harsha, May 24, 1881, S. M. Moore, Aug. 29, 31, Sept. 2, and 27, 1881, J. Milligan, Sept. 13, 1881, and of H. Johnson, Sept. 9, 1881. C. H. McCormick, Jr., to C. H. McCormick, Sept. 5, 1881.

[146] C. H. McCormick to D. L. Moody, Feb. 23, 1881. In this, C. H. McCormick states that he has agreed to give $75,000 unconditionally. C. H.

Professor's House.   Professor's House.   M'Cormick Hall.   Central Hall.   Chapel.   Foster Hall.   Professor's House.

The McCormick Theological Seminary, 1888

rick Johnson resigned his pastorate, those members of his congregation who disliked his liberal theological views would offer to provide a house for him in order to speed his departure.[147] It was too patent, however, that McCormick would do it, if they did not, and thus it turned out.[148] By the close of 1881, each professor or prospective professor, was assured of a salary of $3,000 a year and a dwelling.[149]

Word of the new day at the seminary brought a quick return in increased enrolment and reputation. By the autumn of 1883 the student body numbered over fifty. The dormitory was now too small.[150] Professors went from door to door in the neighborhood seeking lodgings for their flock, and some students were obliged to room so far from the campus that they asked to be excused from attending early-morning prayers.[151] McCormick's generosity had been most largely respon-

McCormick, Jr., to C. H. McCormick, Sept. 5, 1881. McCormick is now urged to increase the $75,000 promise by $25,000. "Further he [Judge S. M. Moore] does not advise your requiring the right to nominate all the Profs. for that you will have *anyway* as the Committees have *always* deferred to you and always will!" Shortly thereafter, McCormick agreed to give $100,000. W. C. Goudy, H. Johnson, and others at this time hoped that he would donate $500,000. ⧣W. C. Goudy to C. H. McCormick, July (?), 1881; ⧣H. Johnson to C. H. McCormick, Sept. 9, 1881. In Dec., 1881, McCormick gave $50,000; half of this sum was for the Chair of Theology and half for the Chair of History. In 1882, he paid another $25,000 and a like amount was given shortly after his death. Virginia McCormick to C. H. McCormick, Jr., Dec. 12, 1881; C. H. McCormick to C. H. McCormick, Jr., Dec. 13, 1881, and June 5, 1882. The three residences were started in the autumn of 1882, and by the first of the next year McCormick had paid $27,000 for them. "Chicago Times," Oct. 2, 1881.

147 ⧣W. C. Gray to C. H. McCormick, Apr. 6, 1882 and May 17, 1883; C. H. McCormick to W. C. Gray, May 17, 1883.

148 T. H. Skinner to C. H. McCormick, Oct. 8, 1883.

149 C. H. McCormick to H. Johnson, Aug. 6 and ⧣10, 1881. C. H. McCormick, Jr., to C. H. McCormick, Sept. 13, 1881.

150 T. H. Skinner to C. H. McCormick, Aug. 24 and Sept. 17, 1883: "Your large generosity to the Institution is now being recompensed and your wise foresight vindicated. I rejoice that you have lived to see this day. . . . Your name will be cherished in the Church as the Benefactor of Education."

151 *Idem* to *idem*, Sept. 24, and Oct. 8, 1883.

sible for this growth. Because of it, new demands were now made upon his benevolence. Urged for four years to allow the seminary to bear his name,[152] he now authorized his eldest son to write that, under the circumstances, the proposal "seems not unreasonable or out of place," and that plans for a new dormitory should be prepared without delay.[153] In early February, 1884, the faculty and fifty-nine students met at his home to give thanks for a seminary which at last, after twenty-five years of trial, exemplified "the fruition of his hopes and ambitions." Dr. Skinner told of the transformation of the campus from its dreary aspect of 1881 when the "weeds were almost waist high," and he emphasized the even more significant improvement in morale. To Dr. Craig, and probably also to McCormick, this institution, with its dozen graduates a year, was as satisfying a monument to his persistence and devotion to a cause as his factory with its annual output of fifty thousand machines.[154]

The inventor did not live to witness the dedication of "McCormick Hall," as the new dormitory was called. In the spring of 1884 the members of the board of directors expressed their:

sense of profound gratitude to Almighty God that He raised up and qualified one for a work so great, at a period in the world's history so full of peril to the cause of evangelical religion. With rationalism spreading itself abroad so widely, especially in the

[152] C. H. McCormick to S. M. Moore, Sept. 2, 1881: The idea that the seminary should bear my name did not originate with me, and has never been "a cherished thought of mine." J. M. Faris to C. H. McCormick, June 3, 1879; ‡H. Johnson to C. H. McCormick, Sept. 9, 1881; C. H. McCormick, Jr., to C. H. McCormick, Sept. 5 and 13, 1881. The institution took its new name in 1886, but in 1928 it was rechanged to the Presbyterian Theological Seminary of Chicago.

[153] ‡C. H. McCormick, Jr., to T. H. Skinner, Oct. 4, 1883; T. H. Skinner to C. H. McCormick, Oct. 8, 1883. The "Chicago Daily Tribune," Jan. 30, 1884, p. 8. At this time the cornerstone was laid.

[154] ‡Typewritten "Report of Meeting of Professors and Students of the Seminary at the Residence of Mr. C. H. McCormick, February 8, 1884." "Chicago Times," Apr. 15, 1884.

Great Northwest . . . with materialism massing its forces on every hand for the overthrow of spiritual Christianity . . . with Romanism girding itself for a conflict that is to determine the religious control of the new world . . . we can but regard it as a special mark of the Divine favor that the King and Head of the Church raised up, at such a crisis, one who, by his beneficence in the past, and by a wise and prudent provision for the future, has reared at this great center of influence a bulwark against these varied powers of evil.[155]

[155] The four professors' residences and the gift of the dormitory were formally presented to the seminary in April, 1884. "Chicago Daily Tribune," Apr. 14, 1884, p. 6. On October 14, 1884, when McCormick Hall was dedicated, C. H. McCormick, Jr., spoke in behalf of the donor. The building with its 52 rooms cost about $80,000. (*Ibid.*, Oct. 14, 1884, p. 8.) The total of McCormick's gifts to the seminary during his lifetime was about $325,000. In 1885, $104,361.09 more was given mainly in payment of pledges made by McCormick before his death. Year by year thereafter, the trustees of his estate extended additional help to the institution, $92,936.37 in 1886; $10,400 in 1887; $35,783.58 in 1888; $157,194.19 in 1889. "The Interior" of Aug. 7, 1884, gives the sum donated by McCormick as $400,000. This would appear to be an exaggeration.

CHAPTER VIII

CYRUS McCORMICK, PHILANTHROPIST

M ANY Virginians turned to Cyrus McCormick for aid in 1865. He was one of the few men of wealth and influence in the North who did not assume that they richly merited their humiliation. His native Valley of Virginia had been repeatedly ravaged by northern armies, while in the low country were broad areas where little remained except the land.[1] With their buildings burned, slaves freed, and Confederate currency and bonds worthless, planters were reminded of the man who had dared to champion peace when enthusiasm for the war was the test of loyalty.[2] Money was very scarce in the Old Dominion, interest rates were exorbitant, and creditors could not collect because of the stay laws.[3] Land was a drug upon the market, and those who trusted that better times would come in the near future hesitated to sell their one asset when prices were ruinously low. Cash was immediately needed, however, to buy food and clothing for their large families, to satisfy the tax collectors of the national government, and to pay for the labor and seed required to "put in

[1] ‡R. Ridgeway, Congressman-elect, Amherst Co., Va., to C. H. McCormick, June 18, 1866, describes the devastation between Petersburg and Appomattox C. H. "Two or three thousand people in this district, mostly women and children, need food until the corn can be harvested in November. But I do not want to put my people before the public in the attitude of beggars."

[2] ‡T. J. Michie, Staunton, Va., Jan. 12, 1866, to C. H. McCormick. He had lost four of his five sons in the war, and wished to borrow $3,000 or $5,000 for about two years.

[3] ‡D. E. Moore, Lexington, Va., to C. H. McCormick, Nov. 21, 1865.

a crop."[4] Under these circumstances, a few planters decided to sell out at a sacrifice and move to Mexico or Brazil. Financial embarrassment was not the only cause for this decision. Refusal to live under the United States flag, to submit to the indignity of caring for negroes who had once been their property, or perhaps even to be ruled by them, were other considerations of much weight.[5]

Members of this social class sought loans or gifts from Cyrus McCormick to enable them to start life anew. In every instance, he refused to assist men to desert the "dear old state." Due to the failure of the wheat-harvest in Virginia in 1866, the partial failure of 1867, and the inauguration of a negro-carpetbag government that spring, calls of this kind became more numerous and insistent. The plea of J. Marshall McCue, a large landholder in the Valley of Virginia, is typical:

The impending ills of which the present is only a foreshadowing, . . . cause thousands of our down-trodden people, sad as it may be, to expatriate themselves and to leave the graves of their fathers & Virginia, proud, glorious, noble, Old Virginia, and find a home down there [Brazil], . . . We are now under a military satrap whose *ipse dixit* overrides our code. I have given my last vote. My boy Sander (ex-slave) yet in my employ, in the estimation of our masters at Washington, is a better man than your unworthy correspondent. My spirit is too unbending to brook this, . . . *I will not do it.* . . . Have you not made money enough in the icy north, my dear sir, to determine now when like ours your raven locks are mixing with gray, to find a sunnier and more congenial clime south of the equator, . . . The change . . . would seem like stepping out of Purgatory into Paradise.[6]

[4] Sallie M. Paxton, Pleasant View, Va., to C. H. McCormick, Feb. 19, 1866. Miss S. A. Roane, Fredericksburg, Va., to C. H. McCormick, Aug. 9, 1866.

[5] ‡W. I. Massie, to C. H. McCormick, May 29, 1868.

[6] J. M. McCue, Mt. Solon, Va., to C. H. McCormick, Apr. 11, 1867. McCue remained in Va.

Here are illustrated the discontent, the personal pride, the love of state, and withal, the eloquence, characteristic of many of these requests for help. "When I form the acquaintance of a perfect lady or Gentleman I take it for granted that they are Virginians," admitted an exile who was languishing in Tennessee; "*I* am a Virginian and my devotion to the old precious state will cease only with my life." [7]

Closely akin in spirit to those who would leave the state or the country rather than accommodate their lives to the new day, were the pleas for aid received by Cyrus McCormick from the Virginia Historical Society, and other organizations designed to preserve a civilization that already lay in ruins. In no way better than by a study and contemplation of the past, ran its appeal, "can our people be prevented from leaving those good and ancient paths which have been trodden by their fathers." A knowledge of Virginia's history will act as an antidote for "these days of materialism, when so much is thought about laying up treasure." [8] Cyrus McCormick was a conservative on most questions, but he knew that this was not the thread to lead Virginia out of her maze of difficulties. He was grateful for a sprig of evergreen from Stonewall Jackson's grave,[9] and he helped those who had associated to care for the cemeteries of the Confederate dead, but although the southern cause was a most honorable one to have died for, it was now a "lost cause" for all that.[10]

[7] ‡Mrs. L. F. Johnson, Bristol, Tenn., to C. H. McCormick, July 2, 1866. T. H. Ellis, Chicago, to C. H. McCormick, Sept. 10, 1881.

[8] ‡Virginia Historical Society, Richmond, Va., to C. H. McCormick, Apr. 19, 1869. ‡B. M. Smith, to C. H. McCormick, Jan. 14, 1867: "Our folks are generally quiet to publick matters—Corn & Tobacco—Cabbages & Potatoes *are* more interesting topicks than Federal Relations. It seems Virginia is now to live in *a present* for a long time; heretofore, our people have lived on the fame of the past—they are now as comfortably congratulating themselves on the fame that is to be."

[9] ‡Rev. S. D. Stuart to C. H. McCormick, from Staunton, Va., Apr. 14, 1866.

[10] Mrs. Wm. Brown, Richmond, Va., to C. H. McCormick, June 22, 1866. ‡W. R. Denny, Winchester, Va., to C. H. McCormick, Oct. 10, 1879. He

Most Virginians of gentle breeding, however, were willing to remain in the state if by any means they could ward off starvation. They freely admitted that the war had worked a revolution, and that former ways of life were no longer adequate. They wrote to McCormick asking him to advance money at reasonable rates of interest for two or three years so that they could begin anew at their old homes. They would secure his loans by giving him mortgages on their land.[11] The feeling was widespread that tobacco could no longer be profitably raised by free labor, and that plantations must be divided into smaller units with more attention given to intensive farming, fertilizers, and crop rotation.[12] Capital was required in order to make the shift from tobacco to small grains and to purchase the machinery necessary for its cultivation. Some expected the negroes to move to the North or West, and that immigrants from Europe would soon be the "hired hands" of the South.[13]

The apex of the social pyramid of Virginia was represented among the many persons who sought to borrow or to receive a gift from Cyrus McCormick. The Tuckers, Lees, Garnetts,[14]

wished McCormick to contribute to a $10,000 monument to the "Unknown and Unrecorded Dead,"—the only one of its kind in the world.

[11] ♯C. H. McCormick to T. J. Massie, Aug. 6, 1866; Letters to C. H. McCormick from ♯T. T. Tredway, Prince Edward Co., Va., July 5, 1866; J. M. McCue, Mt. Solon, Va., May 8, 1868; ♯M. C. Massie, Tharsalia, Va., June 5, 1869; ♯J. Horace Lacy, Chatham, Va., Oct. 27, 1870. ♯Ex-Senator C. C. Clay, U.S.A., C.S.A., Huntsville, Ala., to C. H. McCormick, Mch. 29, 1869, and May 13, 1870. McCormick loaned Clay $1,000 @ 7%. Check Stubs, Importers' and Traders' National Bank, New York City, July 1, 1870.

[12] ♯T. J. Massie, Nelson Cy., Va., to C. H. McCormick, July 2, 1866. No one in Virginia has money "except a few dogs that speculated in cotton & tobacco during the war." As soon as the northern soldiers leave, the negroes "will as a people, die before they will work. The 'Bureau' sometimes handles them very roughly, a great deal more so than we ever did & it drives them into work." ♯S. C. Robinson, Richmond, Va., to C. H. McCormick, Feb. 16, 1868.

[13] ♯A. M. Paxton, Vicksburg, Miss., to C. H. McCormick, May 12, 1868.
[14] ♯H. T. Garnett, Baltimore, to C. H. McCormick, Mch. 22, 1866.

Hills, Blands,[15] Stuarts,[16] Braxtons,[17] Gilmers,[18] and Cockes [19] are a few of the better-known families represented in this extensive correspondence. R. H. Glass, editor of the "Lynchburg Republican," [20] and C. C. Baldwin,[21] former publisher of the "Lexington Gazette," asked for loans in order to start in business once more. Most wrote with evident hesitation, and some asked that their names should not be divulged. Not a few of these manuscripts run for page after page of closely written script, but McCormick's replies usually show that he had read them to their close. N. Beverley Tucker, who had gone to Canada in the service of the Confederacy, wrote that he was "terribly and most unjustly persecuted" and in dire need of money.[22] S. Adams Lee, a war invalid and cousin of Robert E. Lee, wished McCormick to aid him by purchasing his complete set of autographs of the signers of the Declaration of Independence.[23] Thomas T. Hill, brother of the late General A. P. Hill, remarked that he became "sick whenever I let my pen run into politicks" and wondered whether the "atmosphere of Chicago" would be prejudicial to the success of a good Virginia lawyer who had lost his all in

[15] Mrs. J. R. Bland, Prince Edward Cy., Va., to C. H. McCormick, July 16, 1866.

[16] A. A. Stuart, Waynesborough, Va., to C. H. McCormick, Mch. 2, 1868. "The morals of our once happy and law abiding people have become very much corrupted, & horse stealing and burglary are common." For the same thought, see A. M. Hamilton, Keswick, Va., to C. H. McCormick, Aug. 15, 1872.

[17] ‡Henrietta Braxton, Hybla, Va., to C. H. McCormick, Mch. 5, Apr. 24, 1866; July 25, 1868; Mch. 26, 1871.

[18] ‡W. W. Gilmer, Ivy Creek, Va., to C. H. McCormick, Sept. 21, 1868.

[19] ‡C. C. Cocke, Fluvanna Cy., Va., to C. H. McCormick, Feb. 16, 1870.

[20] ‡R. H. Glass, Lynchburg, Va., to C. H. McCormick, July 4, 1866.

[21] ‡C. C. Baldwin, Balcony Falls, Va., to C. H. McCormick, July 7, 1866. C. H. McCormick to C. C. Baldwin, Aug. 14, 1866.

[22] ‡B. Tucker, St. Catharines, Canada, to C. H. McCormick, Sept. 8, 1868. ‡Check stub of C. H. McCormick, Sept. 15, 1868.

[23] ‡S. A. Lee, Winchester, Va., to C. H. McCormick, July 13, 1869. McCormick declined to buy, and thus missed a real opportunity.

the war.[24] Judge John W. Brockenbrough, Rector of Washington College, was hounded by the tax-collector, and requested McCormick to buy a portrait, said to be by Gainsborough or Lawrence, for one hundred dollars. The painting was forwarded to New York and the inventor returned a check for the amount asked.[25]

Among the letters none is more characteristic of the mood, or better reflects the dignity of a Virginian leader in defeat, than the following from ex-Governor ("Honest") John Letcher:

Since released from prison on parole, I have been quietly at home engaged in the practice of law, and expect to devote my remaining days to my profession, in hope of laying up something for the evening of life. The war has swept from me all my property, and I am now commencing life anew. I have health, energy and industry, and I feel confident of success. . . .

I have not cast a vote since May, 1861, nor do I expect either as a voter or otherwise, to meddle in politics. I have no desire to do so, and even if I had, it would in my present condition, be little short of absolute madness. I served the country faithfully in the better days of the Republic; I have no desire to serve in these days of its decline.[26]

Those, like Alexander Rives, who did not know McCormick well, wrongly imagined that they could win his sympathy by

[24] ‡T. T. Hill, Culpeper C. H., Va., to C. H. McCormick, July 11, 1866; ‡F. H. Hill, Madison C. H., Va., to C. H. McCormick, July 29, 1867.

[25] ‡J. W. Brockenbrough to C. H. McCormick, Apr. 28 and May 3, 1868. ‡Check stub of C. H. McCormick, Feb. 22, 1869. The portrait was found later to have been painted by an inferior artist.

[26] J. Letcher, Lexington, Va., to C. H. McCormick, Apr. 23, 1866. ‡T. J. Massie, Nelson Cy., Va., to C. H. McCormick, Sept. 22, 1866: "I sometimes feel ready to exclaim 'N'importe'—from the conviction that we have, North & South, verified the lesson of all past history that man is incapable of self-government, and the sooner we run the race of mobocracy the better for the whole country—tho' I had hoped the thing would last a little longer untill [sic] my hour was over."

condemning the course taken by "that vile party" which had led the South out of the Union.[27] The inventor would aid northern ministers who had been driven from their pulpits because they would not preach political sermons,[28] but although he had opposed secession, he would not lend a hand to a southerner who had been untrue to his state. Some in Virginia and elsewhere in the South enticed him to join with them in buying up the debts of the planters, in order promptly to foreclose upon their rich bottom-lands as soon as the stay laws were lifted. Others urged the purchase of deserted factories or a speculation in city lots.[29] These letters went unanswered, for McCormick was determined not to profit from the distress of the South.

By far the largest number of requests for private aid came from those who were not of the South's first families. These spin out their pitiable stories of privation at greater length, if possible, than those already mentioned, and unrestrained emotion is their chief characteristic.[30] Some were alleged relatives

[27] A. Rives, Carlton, Va., to C. H. McCormick, June 27, 1865. ‡D. E. Moore, Lexington, Va., to C. H. McCormick, Nov. 21, 1865. Moore's letter must have been particularly offensive to McCormick since it bitterly arraigned his close friend, General Roger Pryor, for leading the "infamous deputation" to South Carolina in order to precipitate war by firing on Fort Sumter.

[28] ‡Letters to C. H. McCormick from the Revs. J. N. Schultz, Michigan City, Ind., Dec. 4, 1864, W. M. Ferguson, Washington, O., July 13, 1866, C. Axtell, Bellevue, Ia., Mch. 18, 1869, G. Morrison, Brighton, Ill., Dec. 2, 1870, and J. Ustick, Earlville, Ill., June 9, 1875.

[29] ‡S. C. Robinson, Richmond, Va., to C. H. McCormick, Feb. 16, 1868. He argued that if McCormick took over three iron- and wood-working factories in the city, his example would draw more capital to Virginia for investment. ‡A. M. Paxton, Vicksburg, Miss., to C. H. McCormick, May 12, 1868. ‡B. M. Smith, D.D., to C. H. McCormick, Jan. 14, 1867.

[30] A most noteworthy series of letters was written by Mrs. C. M. Legaré, who had evidently known better days, but was then living in extreme poverty in the piney woods country of South Carolina. Her long, almost hysterical, descriptions of life there are remarkably realistic. McCormick sent money and clothing to her several times. See, ‡Mrs. C. M. (James) Legaré, Adams Run, S. Car., to C. H. McCormick, Sept. 15, 1867. ‡*Idem,*

and old friends of Cyrus McCormick; many believed that residence in Rockbridge or Augusta counties, Virginia, gave them a special claim to his favor, while others professed to have been of material assistance in launching the reaper upon its successful career.[31] A few assumed that they could rightfully demand his help, but most believed that flattery, couched in some variation of the phrase "your proverbial kindness and generosity," was the surest road to his heart.[32] Prior to 1865, Cyrus McCormick had received few letters of this kind and for a short while following the war he attempted to reply briefly and courteously to each. The publicity given to his gifts to seminaries and colleges, and the announcement each year in the press of the amount of his taxable income, encouraged a flood of solicitations. To answer all of them was impossible. A favorable response led to less modest requests and brought similar petitions from the neighbors of the one who had been fortunate. Worthy persons whom he knew were given assistance,[33] and his several former slaves in Virginia never asked

to D. L. Moody, Apr. 23, 1868: "We are in a Pine Land Village—and you can't think how barren and desolate everwhere (sic) looks—the very night birds have a sadder cry than anywhere I ever heard them—the place looks like a vast Cemetery—just the white pillars showing through the weeds as you pass along—and famine seems to be our fate. . . . Can you think what it is to have the grim Wolf hunger hanging around your door all the while?" ‡J. Craig, Yorkville, S. Car., to C. H. McCormick, June 30, 1867: "Many farmers running from one to three ploughs will mortgage their whole crops for a loan of from 10 to 50 $ to buy them corn enough to put them over to oats & wheat which will be coming in now in a very few weeks."

[31] Letters to C. H. McCormick of J. M. Hite, Guilford, Va., Oct. 10, 1865, ‡Mch. 19 and May 3, 1866, A. McCormick, Warrenton, Va., Feb. 20, 1866, ‡G. Holbrook, Wytheville, Va., Dec. 18, 1868, ‡L. P. Holbrook, Port Republic, Va., Nov. 11, 1880, ‡"Old Fellows Citizens" of South River, Va., June 8, 1869.

[32] ‡K. G. Hering, Bridgewater, Va., to C. H. McCormick, Oct. 13, 1879.

[33] ‡C. H. McCormick to D. S. Evans, M.D., Concord Depot, Va., Sept. 20, 1880: "It is not often that I feel warranted in responding to the calls that come to me in considerable numbers for assistance; and indeed I could nót. . . . If the small sum of one hundred dollars would be of any assistance

in vain. He bought a cabin and a lot "lying well to the sun" for his old body servant, "Jo" Anderson.[34] Dr. B. M. Smith was his almoner for the neighborhood about Hampden Sidney, Virginia, and relief associations in southern cities rarely met a refusal if they presented their cases briefly.[35] He and his brother, L. J. McCormick, occasionally instructed the factory office to forward small sums of money or a machine to help the needy in the South.[36]

Although the total of McCormick's gifts and loans for the relief of individuals in the South was a large one, his more notable service there was in behalf of religious and secular

toward the education of one of your boys I cheerfully give it to you, with the single request that he employ his education with a view to the *benefit of his fellow men*. I prefer that you would not mention the matter to anyone." H. A. Kellar, in a letter to Cyrus Bentley on Aug. 24, 1925, stated that between 1865 and 1878, C. H. McCormick received 199 calls for aid from institutions in Virginia or residents of that state. Of these he granted thirty-nine in whole or in part, refused twenty-five, and ignored 135. The total sought approximated $250,000. He sent or pledged $63,000, refused requests for a total of $113,000, and ignored others asking for a total of $74,000.

[34] Check stubs, Importers' and Traders' Bank, New York City, checks of May 22, 1868. ‡"Jo" Anderson to "Dear Master" from Greenville, Va., June 12, July 12, Nov. 23, 1869: Some one has stolen all my salted meat, and "I'm sorry to say I think one of my own colour got it." In his letter to "Jo" Anderson on Jan. 19, 1870, McCormick expressed regret that "Jo" had not followed his advice and gone West before the war. McCormick gave him $800 to purchase the property he desired. ‡Emily Harris to C. H. McCormick, June 1, 1870, from Greenville. She had named one of her sons for her former master. "I'm very hard run at this time."

[35] ‡J. E. Edwards, Richmond, Va., to C. H. McCormick, Feb. 16, 1866. ‡Check stubs, Importers' and Traders' Bank, New York City, Checks of Feb. 14, 1866, Apr. 23, 1868, Aug., 1869, *passim*. ‡B. M. Smith, D.D., to C. H. McCormick, Jan. 14 and 30, 1867. ‡M. D. Hoge, Richmond, to C. H. McCormick, Apr. 9, 1870.

[36] L.P.C.B. No. 80, p. 559, C. A. Spring, Jr., to J. S. Campbell, Confederate Prisoner at Fort Delaware, Del., June 6, 1865. L. J. to C. H. McCormick, Mch. 12, 1866. No. 93, p. 525, C. A. Spring, Jr., to I. W. Martin, Ky. Relief Society, Spring Station, Ky., Nov. 9, 1866. No. 97, p. 865, W. J. Hanna to Rev. S. Robinson, Louisville, Ky., Mch. 23, 1867. No. 105, p. 315, L. J. McCormick to Mrs. Chas. Gennet, Richmond, Va., June 9, 1868.

education. The endowment of a Chair in the Union Theological Seminary has been mentioned in an earlier chapter.[37] As soon as the war was over, he was impressed by the challenge offered to his denomination by conditions within the prostrate Confederacy. If Presbyterianism were to be kept to the fore, aid from the North was essential.[38] Over twelve hundred churches had been destroyed; congregations were unable to support their ministers or contribute to the rebuilding of their houses of worship, parsonages, and seminaries.[39] Devout southerners turned to their Bibles for consolation. "Our religious liberty and our Church privileges are all that we have left now to cheer and comfort us in our oppressed and sad condition. There is no music now so sweet to us as the sound of the church bell summoning us to the sanctuary on the Sabbath morn." So wrote a Virginian from Culpeper Court House in 1869.[40] Ex-Governor Patton of Alabama believed that "nothing except bread could be more acceptable than books to replace the burnt libraries." [41]

Several million negroes, ignorant, impressionable, and fit subjects for the propaganda of the Freedmen's Bureau, northern missionaries, ministers, and religio-political tracts published in northern cities, should be gathered into Sunday-schools and taught the fundamentals of peaceful and

[37] *Supra,* pp. 220 ff.
[38] Rough draft of an article by C. H. McCormick, for the "New York Observer," n.d., but probably early 1866. ‡Mrs. T. M. Joseph, Galveston, Texas, to C. H. McCormick, Apr. 24, 1876. She complained of the inroads of the Episcopalians because of the poverty of the Presbyterian Church.
[39] ‡Rev. W. W. Morrison, Houston, Fla., June 11, 1866. He and many other ministers had been obliged to enter business, in order to support their families. ‡R. J. Taylor, Rockbridge Baths, Va., to C. H. McCormick, Dec. 19, 1868: Due to emancipation and the necessary changes in our household arrangements, we are no longer able to board our ministers and their families. There are no houses for rent, so we have to build parsonages.
[40] ‡G. D. Gray to C. H. McCormick, Feb. 5, 1869.
[41] ‡L. J. Halsey to C. H. McCormick, Dec. 15, 1866.

purposeful living by southerners who understood them best.[42] "There are among the colered [sic] people," confided Robert Logan of LaGrange, Georgia, in the autumn of 1865, "a great many who have been restrained only by the severity of the lash from being outlaws. Now that fear is removed and they are developing their true character. We have no civil law, and the military are on the side of the negro so that crime goes unpunished."[43] Christianity, taught from the southern viewpoint, was the proper corrective. McCormick's interest in the welfare of the Negro was shown by his continued support of the American Colonization Society, and by donations to southern secular schools established for their education.[44]

Southern ministers urged that the frontier line from Baltimore to St. Louis should be held for Old School Presbyterianism against the incursions of the northern liberals and radicals of the church.[45] Hundreds of young Virginians moved to Baltimore after the war and the church buildings of that city were soon overtaxed. A new edifice was needed, manned by a Presbyterian minister from Virginia, who should "preach and pray without saying anything to jar on their feelings or wound their sensibilities."[46] By 1869, Baltimore was more southern in tone than in 1861. Dixie was moving north.

[42] S. B. S. Bissell, New York, to C. H. McCormick, Dec. 10, 1866; G. Owen, Secretary of Md. S.S. Union, Baltimore, to C. H. McCormick, Dec. 25, 1866: "Jay Cooke declines to aid us until 'a better spirit pervades the people' of the South. Jas. Lenox of New York gave us $400." J. McCullagh, Henderson, Ky., to C. H. McCormick, Mch. 25, 1868.

[43] ‡R. Logan, LaGrange, Ga., to C. H. McCormick, Nov. 10, 1865.

[44] C. H. McCormick contributed $100 annually for several years to the American Colonization Society. ‡Check stubs of May 21, 1868, Mch. 31, 1869, and Feb. 15, 1870. These show that on July 16, 1868, he made a donation to the Biddle Memorial Institute of Charlotte, N. C., and on Mch. 23, 1869, to the Southern Pioneer Aid Society Boys' School, of Charleston, S. C.

[45] ‡Rev. R. Carson, Louisville, Ky., to C. H. McCormick, Sept. 10, 1866.

[46] ‡B. M. Smith, et al., Hampden Sidney, Va., to C. H. McCormick, Apr. (?), 1869. $100,000 was soon given for this purpose by the widow of George Brown, late of Brown, Shipley & Company, international bankers.

To meet this religious crisis in his church, McCormick gave financial aid to many ministers and individual congregations.[47] Rev. John Leyburn of Virginia was employed as his secretary until he was able to start on his long and notable career as a pastor in Baltimore.[48] He assisted his old friend, Dr. W. S. Plumer, to move his family to Columbia Seminary in South Carolina, where he succeeded the distinguished Dr. J. H. Thornwell as Professor of Theology.[49] He sent money to Plumer to glaze the windows of his war-ruined home and to pay taxes which equaled over ten per cent of his meager salary. As this indefatigable clergyman completed one after another of his thirty volumes of religious writings, and over one hundred and fifty tracts, the inventor often supplied him with the funds to finance their publication, and occasionally purchased copies enough for each student in the seminary at Chicago.[50] As a director and member of the Executive Com-

[47] ‡Mrs. E. H. Brown, Richmond, Va., to C. H. McCormick, Mch. 10, 26, 1870, and ‡M. D. Hoge, D.D., Richmond, to C. H. McCormick, Apr. 9, 1870. ‡Check stubs of May 19, 1868, and Mch. 22, 1870, in favor, respectively, of Rev. Philo Calhoun and "the needy ministers of East Hanover Presbytery, Va."

[48] Leyburn was Secretary of the Presbyterian Board of Missions in 1861, but resigned at that time to accept a similar position in the southern church. C. H. McCormick to A. Leyburn, Oct. 9, 1865; ‡C. H. McCormick to B. M. Smith, Feb. 22 and Aug. 12, 1866; ‡J. Leyburn to C. H. McCormick, Dec. 12, 1866.

[49] ‡W. S. Plumer, D.D., to C. H. McCormick, Dec. 21, 1866. ‡Check stubs, Importers' and Traders' Bank, New York City, check of Jan. 10, 1867. Letter of J. Plumer to C. H. McCormick, June 1, 1880. Plumer was compelled by the Columbia Seminary to retire in 1880. In that year, when seventy-eight years of age, he traveled 12,500 miles, preached ninety-seven times, and raised more than the amount of his salary for the seminary. He died before the close of the year. He had given away all that he made during his lifetime and a Plumer Memorial Fund was started to support his two daughters. See, the Committee to C. H. McCormick, from Baltimore, Nov. 1, 1880. C. H. McCormick donated $600, and four years later C. H. McCormick, Jr., sent another $100. C. H. McCormick was also interested in a project to publish the works of Dr. N. L. Rice, who died in 1877. See, J. W. Dulles, Phila., to C. H. McCormick, Dec. 10 and 19, 1877.

[50] C. H. McCormick to W. S. Plumer, D.D., Jan. 2, and Dec. 3, 1866; ‡W. S. Plumer to C. H. McCormick, Dec. 5, 7, 1866; Jan. 18, 22, 1867;

mittee of the Southern Aid Society for the assistance of struggling churches, he contributed generously to its work.[51] The daughter of at least one impoverished minister in the Valley of Virginia owed her training in a "female seminary" to him,[52] and his money helped rebuild several churches in the South.[53] In 1869, and for several years thereafter, he paid the salary of Rev. J. S. K. Legaré, a Yale graduate from South Carolina, who was the first, and a very successful, organizer of Sabbath schools for negroes and poor whites in the Virginia Piedmont.[54]

During the early Reconstruction Period many southern colleges, institutes, and academies asked assistance of Cyrus McCormick. The reasons given for their needs followed a definite pattern—buildings burned by northern or southern troops, libraries scattered or destroyed, investments in Con-

May 9, Aug. 25, Oct. 10, 1870; Apr. 10, May 27, 1871; Sept. 1, 1873; Mch. 4, Aug. 22, 1874; July 14, 1879. Check stubs, Importers' and Traders' Bank, New York City, checks of July 2 and Aug. 2, 1868. ‡J. B. Andrews, Chicago, to C. H. McCormick, Apr. 7, 1874.

[51] ‡Check stubs, Importers' and Traders' Bank, New York City, checks of mid-Jan., 1866, and Jan. 29, 1867. ‡J. B. Waterbury, New York, to C. H. McCormick, Nov. 29, and Dec. 8, 1865.

[52] ‡J. M. M. Caldwell, President of Edgeworth Female Seminary, Greensboro, N. C., to C. H. McCormick, Mch. 17, and Aug. 6, 1870; ‡Lucy C. Martin, Lynchburg, Va., to C. H. McCormick, Mch. 23, 1870.

[53] Check stubs, Importers' and Traders' Bank, New York City, checks of Feb. 12, Apr. 7, May 2, Nov. 20, 1866, in favor of the churches at Brandy Station, Woodstock, and Warrenton, Va., and of Holly Springs, Miss. Others of Sept. 29, and Oct. 3, 1869, for aid to churches in Miss. and N. C. ‡R. J. Taylor, Rockbridge Baths, Va., to C. H. McCormick, Jan. 23, 1871, thanking him for sending $100 to the Timber Ridge Church.

[54] J. S. K. Legaré, Lynchburg, Va., to C. H. McCormick, ‡Mch. 19, ‡July 20, ‡Dec. 20, 1869; Oct. 23, Nov. 20, Dec. 20, 1871. During a five-weeks period in the summer of 1869, he established seven negro and one white Sunday-schools, with a total of 551 pupils. Reading, as well as religion was taught, and he tried to provide stoves so that these schools could remain open in winter. He mentioned with pride in one letter that a negro girl "last Sunday recited 110 verses from Luke." His salary was $1,000 a year. ‡J. McCullaugh, Phila., Pa., to C. H. McCormick, Sept. 26, 1870, and from New York City, Mch. 17, 1872.

federate bonds or state stock either worthless or unremunerative, and the high cost of living and the poverty of southern families making increased salaries and the endowment of scholarships imperative. Because college professors customarily received as a part of their stipend a percentage of the fees paid by the students, a smaller sum was required to endow a Chair in a college than in a theological seminary where no tuition was charged.[55] An amount which would yield about $1,200 in interest a year would be sufficient to sustain a professor if his share of the tuition receipts were as much as $1,000.

Perhaps the most striking characteristic of the letters written to McCormick by college authorities, and particularly by those in Virginia, is the determination expressed by so many of them to introduce the study of scientific subjects, engineering, chemistry, and agriculture. The feeling was prevalent that the emphasis in southern higher education should be changed. Less stress should be given to the classics, law, and oratory, because, as some said, the bane of Virginia had been her politicians. The youth of that state who no longer could look forward to careers in Congress, the Army, or as planters growing tobacco with slave labor, must now for the good of their commonwealth learn how to develop its mineral and timber resources, build its canals and railroads, and till its soil intensively. This was the note struck by General Francis H. Smith, the Commandant of the Virginia Military Institute at Lexington, when he called upon McCormick to help him restore the results of twenty-six years of work, which had been destroyed in a few hours time in 1864 by the "Vandal Hunter." [56] The same objectives were stressed by Professor

[55] ♯B. M. Smith to C. H. McCormick, May 12, 1866. He estimated that double the amount was needed for the endowment of a Chair in a theological seminary.

[56] General David Hunter, U.S.A., had gained this sobriquet among the folk of the Shenandoah Valley, by his campaign there in May and June,

Charles S. Venable, and A. Johnson Barber, the rector, in their letters asking aid for the University of Virginia.[57]

On the other hand, General Benjamin S. Ewell, President of William and Mary College, and for long a vigorous advocate of renewed harmony between the North and the South, requested funds to erect new buildings over the "mass of ruins" in his charge, for the sake of removing a "painful reminiscence of civil strife."[58] Davidson College in North Carolina,[59] soon to welcome young Woodrow Wilson as an undergraduate, Cumberland University at Lebanon, Tennessee, with its new motto, *"E cineribus resurgo,"*[60] and the Presbyterian Seminary at Columbia, South Carolina,[61] which re-

1864. ‡F. H. Smith to C. H. McCormick, Aug. 25, and Nov. 23, 1865; Nov. 19, 1866; June 2 and 25, 1868. ‡Col. J. T. L. Preston, Lexington, Va., to C. H. McCormick, May 20, 1868. By this time V.M.I. again had 250 cadets. McCormick declined to contribute to the $150,000 endowment drive, but he gave $500 for the purchase of books.

[57] ‡C. S. Venable, Charlottesville, Va., to C. H. McCormick, July 31, 1866. The University then had 260 students. ‡A. J. Barber, Gordonsville, Va., to C. H. McCormick, Dec. 10, 1868. We wish to teach the young men of the South the "dignity of Labor." We must accommodate our teaching to the new order of things, and make our courses more practical.

[58] ‡B. S. Ewell's circular letter of Jan. 6, 1869; ‡J. Tyler, Richmond, Va., to C. H. McCormick, July 26, 1866; ‡C. B. T. Coleman, Williamsburg, Va., to C. H. McCormick, Dec. 29, 1866.

[59] ‡E. N. Hutchison, Davidson College, N. C., to C. H. McCormick, Sept. 1, 1866; ‡Mrs. J. M. Anderson, Davidson College, to C. H. McCormick, Jan. 13, 1871.

[60] This institution had been burned by Confederate troops. ‡President B. W. McDonald, Lebanon, Tenn., to C. H. McCormick, Mch. 13, 1870. By this date it was said to have 400 students, as well as 350 more in its preparatory school. "I've pledged my life to develop this stronghold of evangelism and conservative politics."

[61] ‡W. S. Plumer to C. H. McCormick, Dec. 7, 1866. It was probably with a view to aiding southern schools that McCormick in 1867 invested in the stock of the University Publishing Company of New York. Its president was General J. B. Gordon, and secretary, Henry Heath. This firm specialized in the publication of textbooks for southern schools, "written without sectionalism and by southern writers." ‡J. Leyburn to C. H. McCormick, Jan. 26, 1870.

garded General Sherman as a modern Alaric, were three other institutions whose appeals were regretfully declined by the inventor.[62] Shortly after his death in 1884, $7,000 from his estate was used to help construct a hall at Tusculum University, Greenville, Tennessee; $4,000 to purchase land for Park College in Missouri; and additional sums to erect Thornwell Orphanage at Clinton, South Carolina, a school-building at McCormick in the same state, and to assist Maryville College, in Tennessee.[63]

Perhaps the chief reason why McCormick felt obliged to refuse most of the requests for aid from southern centers of learning, was his decision to help Washington College at Lexington, Virginia, in the county of his birth. He was interested in its welfare as early as the summer of 1865 when he learned that its board of trustees, by a happy inspiration, had asked Judge Brockenbrough to make a pilgrimage to that "noble patriot," General Robert E. Lee, and offer him the presidency of the institution. Lexington was not served by a railroad, and it held out to the General the seclusion which his modesty and sensitiveness so much welcomed. Since he

[62] Still others were Hampden Sidney College, Va. (Letters to C. H. McCormick of ‡T. T. Tredway, Prince Edward Co., Va., July 5, 1866, and of ‡R. McIlwaine, Farmville, Va., Jan. 17, 1868) ; Ann Smith Academy, Lexington, Va. (‡J. A. Scott, Lexington, to C. H. McCormick, Dec. 7, 1866) ; Presbyterian Female School, Yorkville, S. C. (‡J. Craig, Yorkville, S. C., to C. H. McCormick, June 30, 1867) ; East Alabama Methodist College (‡E. J. Hamill, Auburn, Ala., to C. H. McCormick, Feb. 3, 1868) ; King's College, Bristol, Tenn. (‡Check sent for $100, June 13, 1868, to Rev. C. A. Caldwell) ; and Westminster College, Fulton, Mo. (‡N. L. Rice, Fulton, Mo., to C. H. McCormick, Nov. 9, 1870, Check for $1,000 sent, Dec. 7, 1870).

[63] P. M. Bartlett, Maryville, Tenn., to Nettie F. McCormick, Apr. 27, Aug. 30, and Nov. 20, 1885; C. H. McCormick, Jr., MSS. Book "B," Nettie F. McCormick, to C. H. McCormick, Jr., Oct. 23, Nov. 1, and 17, Dec. 9, 1884, and Feb. 12, 1885. "Second Annual Report of the Board of Aid for Colleges and Academies of the Presbyterian Church in the United States of America" (Chicago, 1885), pp. 10-12. The "Press and Banner," Abbeville, S. C., July 22, 1885.

was in great financial need, and refused the many gratuities offered to him, the salary of $2,500 a year and a house added to the attractiveness of the proposal.[64] So he mounted his famous gray charger, "Traveller," and rode to the campus in the Valley of Virginia.

Although his experience as Commandant of West Point, about fifteen years before, was not the best preparation for his new work, his renown immediately became the chief asset of the college. Those who were most closely connected with its life, were soon convinced that the institution could hardly survive without the influence and inspiration of his presence.[65] Many of the ninety-seven students who matriculated there in the autumn of 1865 had recently put aside their gray uniforms, and they probably accepted Lee's strict discipline as a matter of course. Judge Brockenbrough reflected the campus atmosphere in a letter to McCormick in January, 1866:

The distinguished President of the College has not as yet taken charge of any special class, but exercises a wise and unremitting supervision over all. He requires the Professors to make a detailed report à la West Point . . . of the standing of each student in scholarship and conduct, at the end of each week, and when he finds that any youth is falling behind in his studies he is invited to a private interview with the late "Commander in Chief of the

[64] J. W. Brockenbrough, to C. H. McCormick, Nov. 28, 1865. Lee's actual salary was $1,500, but his share of tuition fees was expected to add another $1,000. The expression "noble patriot" is taken from C. H. McCormick's letter to A. Leyburn, Oct. 9, 1865.

[65] ‡Letters to C. H. McCormick of J. M. McCue and B. Christian of Staunton, Va., Apr. 21, and Apr. 6, 1870, respectively. Washington College had been under Presbyterian influence and at least one trustee feared that Lee, supported by most of the faculty of V.M.I., would swing the college toward Episcopalianism. He hoped McCormick would buy an organ for the Presbyterian meeting-house at Lexington to help counteract this adverse influence. ‡A. Leyburn to C. H. McCormick, Jan. 3, 1867. Whether the college was, or was not, denominational, disturbed the trustees as late as 1873, when they decided by a vote of 11 to 2 in the negative. ‡B. Christian to C. H. McCormick, Feb. 4, 1874.

Armies of the Confed. States of America." The unhappy delinquent is tremblingly ushered into the august presence, and is in no danger of soon forgetting the admonition, stern but paternal, then and there administered! He retires profoundly impressed with the simple grandeur of the character of his illustrious preceptor, and the next week's report attests the influence of this private audience. . . . In short, my dear sir, I think we may justly claim that our College is, today, the best governed school on the Continent.[66]

General Hunter and his troops in 1864 had slaked their thirst for destruction chiefly upon the property of the Virginia Military Institute, but they had plundered the library of Washington College and broken its windows and "extensive Chemical and Philosophical Apparatus." Its endowment had been much reduced by investments in Confederate securities. The board of trustees in July, 1865, however, agreed upon an ambitious program of expansion, later endorsed by Lee. If money could be secured for the endowment of five new Chairs, the college would give more emphasis to training in scientific subjects. Of the $150,000 needed, not over $50,000 could probably be raised in the South, and Cyrus McCormick, among others in the North, was asked for "a good round sum." [67]

Dr. Adam Leyburn, a close friend of McCormick, was the first to approach him in behalf of the college,[68] but his letter was quickly followed by others from Judge Brockenbrough and General Lee. "To you who are so conversant with the necessities of the Country, & its vast undeveloped resources," wrote Lee in November, 1865, "the benefit of applying scientific knowledge & research, to agriculture, mining, manufac-

<hr>

[66] J. W. Brockenbrough to C. H. McCormick, Jan. 16, 1866.

[67] *Idem* to *Idem*, Nov. 28, 1865: "Nor is there another capitalist living to whom I would have addressed" a similar appeal. The endowment of the college was then about $100,000.

[68] A. Leyburn to C. H. McCormick, Sept. 21, 1865. C. H. McCormick to A. Leyburn, Oct. 9, 1865, and Jan. 2, 1866.

turing, architecture, & to the construction of ordinary roads, R. Roads, Canals, bridges etc., will be at once apparent, & it is hoped will elicit your approval." [69] McCormick replied to Brockenbrough that his finances were not in the happy state "so elegantly portrayed by you." He believed that the college was attempting to do too much but he would give $10,000, "reserving the *privilege* of adding to it thereafter, when it shall become clear that the full complement of Professorships embraced in your plans will be met by corresponding contributions." [70] Within six months he added $5,000 to his gift and a like sum three years later.[71] The interest from $20,000 was enough to pay the salary of a professor, if it were supplemented by a share of the tuition fees, but no money remained with which to obtain the apparatus customarily provided when a Chair was endowed.[72]

This gift was used to create the "McCormick Professorship of Experimental Philosophy and Practical Mechanics." Richard S. McCulloch, who had taught at Columbia College in New York City until the war made him a colonel in charge of the Bureau of Nitre and Mines at Richmond, was the first occupant of the Chair.[73] McCormick's donation, together with his contribution to the Union Theological Seminary at the same time, brought him widespread criticism from the north-

[69] R. E. Lee to C. H. McCormick, Nov. 28, 1865.

[70] C. H. McCormick to J. W. Brockenbrough, Jan. 1, 1866, and to R. E. Lee, Dec. 30, 1865. J. W. Brockenbrough to C. H. McCormick, Jan. 16, 1866. "Lexington Gazette," Jan. 10, 1866. McCormick paid the $10,000 on March 5, 1866.

[71] *Ibid.*, June 27, 1866. C. H. McCormick to J. W. Brockenbrough, June 18, 1866. He paid 6% interest on the $5,000 pledged in the summer of 1866, until he sent a check for the principal in Apr., 1868. He sent the last $5,000 on June 17, 1870, with six months' interest.

[72] ‡A. Leyburn to C. H. McCormick, Nov. 10, 1866; C. H. McCormick to A. Leyburn, Dec. 4, 1866.

[73] ‡A. Leyburn to C. H. McCormick, May 3, 1866; ‡J. W. Brockenbrough to C. H. McCormick, May 14, 1866. McCulloch was to receive $1,000 a year. His ninth of the tuition fees would probably add $1,000 or more to this sum.

ern press for aiding the "nest of rebels" headed by the "traitor" Lee.[74]

Under Lee's auspices, the student body increased to about four hundred by the autumn of 1867. The endowment fund grew more slowly, but a house for the president and a chapel-library building were erected in 1869. Here portraits of Lee and Cyrus McCormick were hung side by side, and Judge Brockenbrough, with some exaggeration, informed the inventor that his gift to the institution was larger than any since Washington's.[75] When, in the spring of that year, McCormick was elected to the board of trustees, he hesitated long before accepting the appointment. Although he wished to serve the college which was "dearer to me [him] than any other of its kind in the country," he realized that his business cares in the North would oblige him to be absent from most of the meetings.[76] Not until the autumn of 1875 was he able to visit the campus.[77]

[74] C. H. McCormick to W. Lord, Jan. 6, 1869. McCormick reminded Dr. Lord of the gift of Henry Ward Beecher to Washington College, and of the southern philanthropies of George Peabody.

[75] ‡J. W. Brockenbrough to C. H. McCormick, Feb. 11, 1869. Washington had given $50,000. McCormick's gift at this time totaled $15,000. The Cincinnati Society of Virginia in 1807 made a donation which eventually brought $25,000 to the college, and in 1826 John Robinson of Rockbridge County bequeathed it an estate valued at $46,500. For a summary of the sources of the endowment of Washington and Lee University in 1885, see "Richmond Dispatch," Aug. 14, 1885. J. D. Davidson, Lexington, Va., June 20, 1868, to C. H. McCormick. This indicates that McCormick's portrait was in reality a photograph.

[76] C. H. McCormick to J. W. Brockenbrough, Apr. 26, June 17, 1869; R. E. Lee to C. H. McCormick, Apr. 26, 1869. McCormick was elected to fill the vacancy left by the resignation of the venerable S. McDowell Reid who had been a trustee for fifty years. Judge Brockenbrough hoped that McCormick's election would not occasion a "fresh radical attack" upon him. ‡J. D. Davidson to C. H. McCormick, Apr. 19, and Apr. 30, 1869. C. H. McCormick to J. D. Davidson, Apr. 27, 1869. On the plea that he could not find time to attend the meetings, C. H. McCormick sent in his resignation in 1874, but the board refused to accept it. ‡J. Fuller, Lexington, Va., to C. H. McCormick, June 26, 1874.

[77] C. H. McCormick, Jr., MSS. Book "B," Nettie F. McCormick, to C. H. McCormick, Jr., Oct. 4, 1875, from Lexington, Va.

By that time the old college had undergone and partially recovered from a severe crisis. Early in 1870 McCormick was told that Lee, because of ill health, would be unable to join him at Boston, as a member of the committee sent to represent the college at the funeral of George Peabody.[78] While the General was absent that spring on a visit to Georgia, his friends took counsel together for the purpose of finding a way of gaining his consent to a trip abroad for the sake of his health. Lee hesitated to make the voyage at the expense of the college, and he shrunk from any course which might tax the generosity of his friends or appear to be a bid for honors or notoriety. He did not wish to be an "incubus" to the college, and was with difficulty persuaded not to resign by associates who believed that the welfare of the institution and his continuance in the presidency were synonymous.[79] He was also distressed by his inability to provide adequately for his invalid wife in the event of his death. In April, 1870, during his absence, the trustees agreed to arrange for Mrs. Lee's future in a manner calculated to relieve her husband's anxiety. Several of them wrote to McCormick, urging him to invite the General to go with him to the Continent.[80] "Could you, do you think," asked J. Marshall McCue, "induce Lee to visit Europe *in company with you,* say with the pretext of viewing

[78] ‡B. Christian, Staunton, Va., to C. H. McCormick, Jan. 24, 1870: "There is some unhealthy adhesion or growing fast of some of the viscera that prevents him [Lee] taking his favorite mode of exercise entirely, i.e., horseback riding & affects his walking very seriously." ‡J. W. Brockenbrough, Lexington, Va., to C. H. McCormick, Jan. 10, and 25, 1870. In 1869, Peabody transferred to the college his claim against the state of Virginia for bonds lost in the SS. *Arctic* disaster in 1854. For long, it was believed that it could not be realized upon, but eventually it brought the institution over $150,000. ‡L.P.C.B. of McCormick & Funkhauser, p. 83, C. H. McCormick to C. W. Allen, Feb. 10, 1870.

[79] ‡B. Christian, Staunton, Va., to C. H. McCormick, Apr. 6, 1870; ‡J. Echols, Staunton, to C. H. McCormick, Apr. 13, 1870.

[80] ‡J. M. McCue, Staunton, to C. H. McCormick, Apr. 21, 1870.

the great universities of Europe and examining their improvements in the astronomical, chemical, and other instruments, or their libraries, or their most noted agricultural schools, etc?" Mr. and Mrs. McCormick expected to go overseas in early July, and "it wd. give us the greatest pleasure . . . to be able to join the Gen'l. in crossing—shd. *that time* suit him." [81] The General was back in Lexington by early June and was half-way persuaded to accept his friends' suggestion, especially since two railroad companies and a southern insurance concern were competing for the privilege of paying him a salary and all expenses if he would make the journey "even incidentally in their interest." [82] The trip was never made. Lee died on October 12, 1870, and his son, General G. W. Custis Lee, then teaching at the Virginia Military Institute, was chosen to be his successor.[83]

A Lee Memorial Association was at once formed in Lexington to raise money for a tomb, and McCormick accepted

[81] ‡L.P.C.B. No. 1, 2nd ser., pp. 12-15, 35, 131, C. H. McCormick to B. Christian, Apr. 9 and June 17, 1870, and to R. E. Lee, Apr. 19, 1870. McCormick wished Lee to come to his home in New York for a visit.

[82] ‡B. Christian to C. H. McCormick, June 6 and Oct. 31, 1870. Lee accepted the presidency of the Shenandoah Valley Railroad because he believed that his influence might hasten the completion of a project that would mean much to Lexington and to the college.

[83] ‡*Idem* to *idem*, Oct. 31, 1870. "The Southern Collegian" (Lexington, Va.), Oct. 15, 1870. Lee's death came as a surprise. This student paper comments that he characteristically, in his last illness, said "nothing for the sensational press to seize upon." During the closing months of his life, Lee was especially eager to secure funds for an astronomical observatory. The University of Virginia also wished one. L. J. McCormick purchased an exceptionally powerful telescope, and, after considerable hesitation occasioned by the inability of either institution to raise the funds necessary to build and maintain an observatory, gave it to the University of Virginia. The competition of the two colleges for this instrument was embarrassing to its owner, and he wrote to Professor C. S. Venable of Charlottesville on Apr. 17, 1878: "I can assure you that I was never more perplexed by any question in my life." For this letter, see L.P.C.B. No. 179, pp. 262-265. See also, No. 177, pp. 570-572, 756-757, and No. 132, p. 612.

the presidency of the New York City branch.[84] After Mrs. Lee had made clear to citizens of Richmond that Lexington and not the capital city would be her husband's last resting place, the campaign for funds was pressed with vigor. The sarcophagus, with its recumbent statue of the General by the Virginia-born sculptor, Edward V. Valentine, cost about $25,000 and was unveiled in 1883.[85]

The financial needs of Washington and Lee College, as it was now called, caused real concern to its trustees during the 1870's.[86] A meeting was held in Independence Hall at the time of the Centennial Exposition to launch a drive for an endowment fund of a million dollars. McCormick, W. W. Corcoran, Morrison R. Waite, Robert C. Winthrop, William M. Evarts, Charles F. Adams, and other men of like prominence, sponsored the movement.[87] The campaign was heralded as an excellent method of bringing the North and South into closer harmony. Although the inventor was asked to "do something handsome" for the college, he declined to add to his previous gifts.[88] Shortly after his death, the trustees of his estate con-

[84] ‡E. C. Cabell to C. H. McCormick, Dec. 11, 1870, and ‡J. B. Dorman, of Lexington, to C. H. McCormick, Jan. 13, and Feb. 1, 1871.

[85] ‡*Idem* to *idem*, June 24, 1871.

[86] ‡A. Leyburn to C. H. McCormick, June 2, 1874. Leyburn, who was then the Rector of the College, urged McCormick to complete the endowment of the Chair that bore his name.

[87] Between 1880 and 1886 the income of Washington and Lee doubled. Pamphlet, "Centennial Organization for the Better Endowment of Washington and Lee University. Report of the Meetings Held in Independence Hall, Philadelphia, Oct. 10, 1876, and June 8, 1881" (New York, 1882). ‡R. D. Lilley, Phila., Pa., to C. H. McCormick, Sept. 2, 1876.

[88] ‡R. D. Lilley, Lexington, to C. H. McCormick, Nov. 7, 1882: "Your example with a small gift now would be worth to us ten times the face value of the donation." It is perhaps significant that McCormick's aid to Washington and Lee ceased after its board of trustees had resolved that it was non-denominational, although there is nothing in his correspondence referring to this resolution. On the other hand, in his letter (‡L.P.C.B. of C. H. McCormick, Nov., 1873-June, 1876, pp. 267-268) to A. H. Pomeroy (?) on Feb. 7, 1875, he said: "I shall be most glad to add still more to it

tributed $20,000 to the endowment of the McCormick Chair, and by 1931 his children had given $200,000 more. In the autumn of that year a statue of Cyrus McCormick was unveiled on the Washington and Lee campus, in recognition of the services of a son of Rockbridge County to the university, and to agriculture wherever grain is grown.[89]

McCormick's gifts during the period of Reconstruction were not confined to men and institutions in the South or to southerners who were stranded north of the Ohio.[90] Presbyterian missions, both foreign and domestic, received his continued aid, and for many years he furnished a room without charge in the McCormick Block in Chicago to the Women's Presbyterian Board of Missions of the Northwest.[91] He was a spon-

[his gift to W. & L.] whenever I can see my way clear to do so, feeling myself, that there is hardly any more worthy object of beneficence to be found than W. & Lee. University."

[89] "Lynchburg Virginian," July 11, 1884; "Rockbridge County News" (Lexington, Va.), Jan. 27, 1888; "The Interior" (Chicago), Aug. 7, 1884; Pamphlet entitled "McCormick Celebration, Washington and Lee University, September 25, 1931."

[90] The most noteworthy of these, besides Beverley Tucker already mentioned, was Col. W. H. H. Taylor, who had probably been McCormick's agent in southern Ohio over twenty years before. In 1868 he was seeking to support his ten children by truck-gardening near Minneapolis. Owning land in Virginia and Ohio, at the outset of the war, he had, to his regret, fought for the North. "I was unfortunately a Democrat, and went into the Army like a fool, to help them steal my own negroes, abuse my own people, destroy my own government, and then be denounced as a traitor and Copperhead." ‡W. H. H. Taylor, to C. H. McCormick, Apr. 15, and June 1, 1868. He asked for a loan of $2,000, and McCormick, on May 16, sent him a gift of $100.

[91] C. H. McCormick, Jr., MSS. Book "D," MS. sketch of Nettie F. McCormick by Dr. J. G. K. McClure. On Aug. 29, 1873 this board began to hold its regular Friday morning meetings at No. 48 McCormick Block. Mrs. McCormick participated actively in its work and served it in several official capacities. On p. 8 of its 7th Annual Report (1878) it is stated that "This donation of rent [for 5 years in the past] is a larger gift than has been received from any other individual." C. H. McCormick, Sr., to Mrs. G. H. Laflin, Feb. 7, 1883, Room 48, McCormick Block, can be the home of the board, "as long as it cares to stay there." C. H. McCormick, Jr., MSS.,

sor of the Christian School of Philosophy, a Presbyterian enterprise which met each summer at Richfield Springs, where he spent some weeks almost annually.[92] For several years, a Bible-worker in Chicago and a missionary in Iowa were largely supported at his charge.[93] He declined to heed the repeated requests of C. A. Spring, Sr., that he carry out one of the last wishes of William S. McCormick and found a home where girls from five to ten years of age would be taken "from destructive Parental & other influence" and be clothed, fed, and educated in a religious and moral environment so that they "may safely be trusted to be good domestics, nurses, milliners, Box makers, etc." [94] The American Sunday School Union, city missions, the Chicago "Home for the Friendless," the Presbyterian Hospital in that city, the American Tract

Book "C," N. F. McCormick to C. H. McCormick, Jr., Feb. 26, 1891. C. H. McCormick to C. H. McCormick, Jr., Nov. 4, 1882. He gave $1,000 to home missions and $500 to foreign missions almost every year.

[92] C. H. McCormick to C. H. McCormick, Jr., Aug. 28, 1883; #C. H. McCormick, Jr., to C. H. McCormick, Aug. 2, 1883. No attempt has been made in this paragraph to differentiate the sums donated by Cyrus McCormick from those given by his wife. To do so would be without significance, because their ideas of worthy benevolences harmonized.

[93] Helen B. Syme was the Chicago Bible-worker who in the late 1870's was sending Mrs. McCormick monthly reports of cottage prayer-meetings, "scripture readings & conversations held," Bibles given, "backsliders reclaimed," "hopeful conversions," etc. #Check stubs of Dec., 1881.

[94] C. A. Spring, Sr., to C. H. McCormick, Oct. 1, Nov. 15, 1865, Feb. 17 and Sept. 28, 1866. Spring's influence had finally induced the city council of Chicago to vote funds for the establishment of a Chicago Juvenile Reform School for Boys, and he was now eager that a similar provision should be made for girls. He believed that too much emphasis was placed upon punishment, and not enough upon the prevention of crime. #C. A. Spring to C. H. McCormick, Mch. 2, May 12, 1866. C. A. Spring, Jr., to C. H. McCormick, July 25, 1866. Spring, Sr., lived to be a very old man. He was troubled by weak eyesight after (cir.) 1868 and spent most of each year at Manteno, Ill., where, as he said, he "raised strawberries and grandchildren" (#His letter of May 1, 1865 to C. H. McCormick). He was an indefatigable worker for Presbyterianism and was especially interested in religious training for children. McCormick aided his church at Manteno. He moved to LeMars, Ia., in 1878, and outlived McCormick.

Society, orphan asylums, the Illinois Industrial School for Girls, the Citizens' League for the Suppression of the Sale of Liquor to Minors, and the Society for Promoting the Gospel Among Seamen in the Port of New York, were some of the institutions or causes to which he annually rendered assistance.[95] His espousal of the Port Society, as the organization last named was usually known, probably induced Captain W. J. Murphy of New York to name his sea-going wrecking vessel "Cyrus Hall McCormick." McCormick, in accordance with the custom, furnished it with its first suit of flags.[96]

Unless the circumstances were exceptional, he refused to rent his Chicago store properties to saloon-keepers.[97] While Mrs. Rutherford B. Hayes, the wife of the President, was attracting international comment by her stand against liquor, McCormick wrote to congratulate her upon her courage. "You have set an example which will prove to be of very high value to the moral and material interests of the country at large,

[95] *Victims of the Boston Fire of Nov. 1872;* McCormick contributed $1,000. See, "Chicago Times," Nov. 12, 1872. *Sabbath School Work;* L.P.C.B. No. 145, p. 269, W. J. Hanna to Mrs. C. H. McCormick, Avon Springs, N. Y., Sept. 10, 1873: You have subscribed $1,500 to this in 1872-73. *City Missions:* ‡Rev. D. C. Marquis, Chicago, to C. H. McCormick, Mch. 25, 1868. *Presbyterian Hospital;* the "Chicago Daily Tribune," July 22, 1883. *Home for the Friendless;* ‡E. C. Boring, Chicago, to C. H. McCormick, May 7, 1868. *Orphan Asylums;* ‡Check stubs, Importers' and Traders' Bank, checks of Apr. 28, 1868, Mch. 22, and Apr. 7, 1870, Dec., 1881. *American Tract Society;* In 1871, C. H. McCormick pledged $1,000 to this Society but either due to his losses in the Great Fire, or because he did not like the political tenor of some of the tracts sent to the South, he never paid it. Nevertheless, he contributed smaller sums to its work. ‡J. L. Shearer, New York, to C. H. McCormick, Dec. 4, 1872; Sept. 27, 1873. J. M. Stevenson to C. H. McCormick, Apr. 25, 1874. *Port Society;* ‡Check stubs, Importers' and Traders' bank, New York City, checks of Apr. 16, 1868, May 25, 1869, June 8, 1870.

[96] ‡W. J. Murphy, to C. H. McCormick, July 25, Aug. 27, 29, 1872; Jan. 12, 1876.

[97] ‡M. Evans to C. H. McCormick, Mch. 6, 1871. Evans, who was a saloon-keeper, furnished an endorsement from Lambert Tree, and W. C. Goudy added that he was a "stirling and unflinching democrat."

and especially to the working men upon whose industry, so-
briety and integrity, the great manufacturing interests of our
country depend. . . . 'Many daughters have done virtuou'sly,
but thou excellest them all.' " [98] This is the more surprising,
since McCormick was not a total abstainer and occasionally
imported wines and liqueurs from France for his own table.[99]
He believed in temperance, however, and thought that only
those should drink who could afford to do so.

Of the northern institutions of learning which asked him
to help, he refused aid to the Princeton Theological Seminary
on the grounds that others were in more need of assistance,[100]

[98] C. H. McCormick to Mrs. R. B. Hayes, Jan. 31, 1881. In that year,
McCormick was a vice-president of the Citizens' League for the Suppression
of the Sale of Liquor to Minors. #A. M. Luynes, S.J., N.Y., July 4, 1869,
to C. H. McCormick. Before McCormick would continue Thomas Meighan
as his coachman, he obliged him to sign a temperance pledge in the presence
of this priest. N. F. McCormick contributed about $100 annually to the
work of the W.C.T.U. L.P.C.B., No. 225, p. 447, C. H. McCormick, Jr.,
to A. Kimball, Iowa State Temperance Association, Des Moines, Ia., July 3,
1882. In 1882, C. H. McCormick, Jr., was one of a committee formed in
Chicago to sponsor a nation-wide series of meetings against "polygamous
Mormonism." "Let the moral sentiment of the Country be felt in Washington." The Edmunds Anti-Polygamy Act became a law that year. By 1884
he was an active member of the Civil Service Reform League.

[99] Cyrus Adams to J. B. McCormick, Oct. 14, 1868: "Uncle Cyrus has
bought twenty gallons of very superior Kentucky Whiskey @ $8.00." C. A.
Spring, Jr., to D. R. Riddle, July 11, 1879; C. H. McCormick to J. B. Mc-
Cormick, June 9, 1868: "I am now using the best *whiskey,* I think that I
have found—Ky. made—at $10 a single gallon here. . . . You may send
me some of the best for purity & health." In September, 1873, a group in
Chicago approached him to learn whether he was in sufficient agreement
with its program to be its candidate for mayor. One of its planks read,
"Intemperance in all things whatever ought to be combated with all suitable
means." On this, McCormick commented as follows: "I should hardly say
that these objects can only be accomplished by elevating the moral standard
of the people through enlightened education; but should think that some
other suitable means. . . ." He did not elaborate, but his words suggest
action by the government. According to the "Chicago Times" of Oct. 20,
1882, C. H. McCormick, Jr., believed "the prohibition movement would be
simply local and never would become a prominent national issue."

[100] He occasionally sent small sums to assist deserving students at Princeton. #A. T. McGill, Princeton, N. J., to C. H. McCormick, Dec. 15, 1865;

declined to sponsor the establishment of a Presbyterian Female Academy at Terre Haute, Indiana,[101] and although he
was a trustee of Lake Forest (Illinois) College, he contributed during his lifetime, so far as the records show, but $1,000
to its support.[102] Through the columns of "The Interior," he
endeavored to have Danville (Kentucky) Seminary transferred to the control of the southern branch of the Presby-
terial Church,—his editor, W. C. Gray, reminding him in
confidence that if this were done, more northern students
would be drawn to the seminary at Chicago.[103] The laying of
the corner-stone at McCormick Hall at Hastings College in
Nebraska, in 1883, was made possible by his benevolence, and
an additional sum was later given to this institution by the
trustees of his estate.[104] They also, in 1884 and 1885, ren-

Dec. 17, 20, 1869; C. H. McCormick to A. T. McGill, n.d. but early Jan.,
1866.
[101] #Many letters between C. H. McCormick and Rev. Geo. Morrison in
1868.
[102] #J. V. Farwell, Chicago, to C. H. McCormick, Feb. 3, 16, 1874;
"Chicago Times," Apr. 2, 1878; C. A. Spring, Jr., to C. H. McCormick,
Dec. 10, 1878, and Jan. 18, 1879. These last two letters show that the $1,000
was paid at this time. Rev. D. S. Gregory, Lake Forest, Ill., to C. H. Mc-
Cormick, Apr. 18, 1881, #Feb. 8, 1882, and Apr. 24, 1884. The trustees of
his estate gave $500 more to this college. C. B. Farwell to C. H. Mc-
Cormick, Jr., July 9, 1885. Perhaps McCormick's unwillingness to extend
substantial aid to Lake Forest was in part due to the fact that it was under
"New School" control. However, President Gregory in a letter to C. H.
McCormick, Jr., on May 18, 1885, wrote: "It was the earnest endorsement
which your father gave to the enterprise here at Lake Forest that more
than anything else, induced me to undertake the difficult task of carrying
it forward in the interests of Presbyterianism." "Chicago Times," May 15,
1884, p. 8.
[103] #Converse & Co., Louisville, Ky., to W. C. Gray, Apr. 25, 1883. In
1883 the seminary was closed by order of the General Assembly of the
northern Presbyterian Church. #W. C. Gray to C. H. McCormick, May 3,
1883.
[104] #H. Johnson to C. H. McCormick, Apr. 30, 1883; C. H. McCormick,
Jr., MSS. Nettie F. McCormick to C. H. McCormick, Jr., May 14, 1883.
"The Observer" (Omaha, Neb.), July 27, 1883. C. H. McCormick to C. H.
McCormick, Jr., July 28, 1883. The total gift to Hastings College between
1883 and 1885 was $8,000. To Pierre University, an institution under the

dered financial assistance to a number of other academies and colleges in the upper Mississippi Valley.[105] In almost every instance, the educational organization which benefited by his help was under Presbyterian control, and often it was so located that it could aid this denomination keep step with the moving frontier. With increasing frequency in his later life, he asked his pastor or the Board of Aid of his church to investigate pleas for contributions from individuals or institutions before he made his decision.[106]

With the exception of the seminary and his church, the Young Men's Christian Association in Chicago appealed most strongly to Cyrus McCormick.[107] Due to the effectiveness of his work among the poor, and the success of his large Sunday-school, the young Dwight L. Moody won the support of several of the city's leading citizens even before the Civil War. His enthusiasm and eloquence, and the "drive" with which he accomplished the seemingly impossible, aroused McCormick's interest upon his return from Europe in 1864. By that time,

aegis of the Presbytery of Southern Dakota, the trustees of his estate contributed $7,500 for a McCormick Hall in 1885. The "Chicago Daily Tribune," Sept. 15, 1884. Gov. Gilbert A. Pierce, Bismarck, Territory of Dakota, to C. H. McCormick, Jr., Oct. 21, 1885.

[105] "Second Annual Report of the Board of Aid," op. cit., pp. 10-12, $500 to Galesville University in Wisconsin; $500 to Union Academy, Anna, Ill.; $250 to Corning Academy at Corning, Ia. C. M. Charnley, Chicago, to C. H. McCormick, Jr., June 27, 1885. S. M. Johnson to C. H. McCormick, Jr., Oct. 26, 1885.

[106] C. H. McCormick, Jr., MSS. Book "B," Nettie F. to C. H. McCormick, Jr., Nov. 20, 1884: "Mrs. Vanderbilt was here today and says she don't even pretend to reply to all her begging letters. Dr. Hall tells me he has sifted cases from south and has found them unworthy." C. H. McCormick's interest in Protestantism in Europe is illustrated by his gifts to the Scotch Church in Rome and the Protestant Evangelical Church in Seville.

[107] "Chicago Daily Press," June 21, 25, 1858. The Y.M.C.A., which then had 150 members, held its first regular meeting on June 21, and Cyrus Bentley, its president, presided. The Y.M.C.A. boycotted the "Chicago Times" in 1863. See, A. C. Cole, "The Era of the Civil War, 1848-1870" (Springfield, Ill., 1919), p. 303.

Moody had enlisted in the cause of the Y. M. C. A., and in the following year began to campaign for $125,000 with which to purchase land and erect an Association building, "bigger than the Crosby Opera House."

The evangelist asked McCormick to subscribe to this venture, and with J. V. Farwell, T. W. Avery, George Armour, and others, to be one of the original trustees. This was not a bid for charity. Each investor was to receive stock, and eventually, so it was hoped, the sums advanced would be returned from the rent paid by the occupants of the offices in the proposed building. Thereafter, the profits would be used for city benevolences. *"More depends on your decision than on that of any other man,"* wrote Moody in April, 1866. "Your name will help us through. The public will think if you take hold of it, it must succeed." [108] Few were able to resist Moody's appeals. McCormick promised $10,000 to the "commendable and plausible enterprise," and consented to be a trustee. By May, 1866, the full sum had been pledged, and work on the building was commenced.[109] Hardly was the structure finished than it burned to the ground, with a loss of $75,000. Before the close of 1867, Moody was pushing forward a rebuilding program involving an expenditure of $135,000.[110] McCormick again purchased $10,000 worth of stock. By January, 1869, the large new hall was ready for use, but the fire

[108] Letters to C. H. McCormick from D. L. Moody, Apr. 5, 17, 1866; J. V. Farwell, Apr. 3, 1866, #C. A. Spring, Sr., Mch. 29, 1866, and C. A. Spring, Jr., Feb. 22, 1866.

[109] McCormick paid the $10,000 for the stock in Jan., 1867. L.P.C.B. No. 94, p. 510, C. A. Spring, Jr., to D. L. Moody, Jan. 2, 1867. D. L. Moody to C. H. McCormick, Apr. 25, May 5, 1866. C. H. McCormick to D. L. Moody, Apr. 24, 1866.

[110] D. L. Moody to C. H. McCormick, Apr. 15, 1868: We won't start the new building until the money is raised. "The harvest is already perishing for want of the reapers." The completed structure, with the "finest public hall in the country," was dedicated on Jan. 19, 1869. See, *idem* to C. H. McCormick, Jan. 1, 1869.

of 1871 completely destroyed it. Three years later the Chicago Y. M. C. A. was ready to open its third home.

Although Moody preached thrice each Sabbath and made two addresses each week-day, he now found time to solicit funds for a library building to be erected on land adjoining the Y. M. C. A. Chicago had no public library or reading-rooms, and the book collection of the Young Men's Association, so Moody complained, was too much dominated by a Unitarian minister. "We want the leading library of the Northwest under the control of the friends of Christ," he added.[111] John V. Farwell was the layman who gave most generously of his wealth and time to the cause of the Y. M. C. A. in Chicago, but McCormick and others who had subscribed to its building now converted their investments into gifts, in order to help erect the library.[112] By the close of 1870 it was completed.[113]

Thereafter, the inventor contributed almost yearly to the support of the Association in Chicago,[114] and in 1881, at Moody's request, donated $1,000 toward a Y.M.C.A. building for San Francisco.[115] In February of that year he ten-

[111] *Idem* to *idem*, Jan. 1, 1869.

[112] *Idem* to *idem*, Aug. 6 and 27, 1869. "Report to the Stockholders of the Y.M.C.A., Chicago," Aug. 16, 1869.

[113] D. L. Moody to C. H. McCormick, Dec. 1, 1870. In 1874 the Y.M.C.A. established an employment bureau in Chicago to assist young men who were strangers in the city to find work. "We thought this was the best help we could give young men in temporal matters and through this help obtaining an influence over them that would lead to *spiritual good.*"

[114] W. W. VanArsdale to C. H. McCormick, Sept. (?), 1875; J. V. Farwell to C. H. McCormick, June 5, 1876. C. H. McCormick to J. A. Weeks, Nov. 18, 1876, *in re* his $1,000 subscription to Moody and Farwell Hall. N. F. McCormick to McCormick Co., Oct. 10, 1877: "Pay $1,000 to Mr. Henry Field for my pledge to Moody and Farwell Hall." This may be the same subscription that is mentioned in the letter above. C. H. McCormick, Jr., MSS. Book "B," Memo. of N. F. McCormick, Dec. 13, 1881,—$1,000 to D. L. Moody. Purpose not specified.

[115] ‡L.P.C.B. of C. H. McCormick, Nov. 1880-May, 1881, pp. 233-236, C. H. McCormick to D. L. Moody, Feb. 23, 1881. In this letter, the inventor refused, but he reconsidered by early summer. D. L. Moody to C. H. Mc-

dered a reception in his home to the members of the International Committee of the Association, and invited to meet them, wealthy citizens of the city who might be persuaded to help the cause.[116]

In the same year, a Virginian who had on several occasions tried without success to borrow money from McCormick, wrote that he threw appeals from the poor into the waste-basket and limited his donations to conspicuous enterprises which would give him extended notice in the press. The earlier pages of this chapter have shown the injustice of this charge, although it is true that he was primarily interested in large causes and disliked to loan money to any one.[117] Contributions to reputable institutions or to societies which extended intelligent aid to the unfortunate, were less likely to be squandered than those sent in response to pleas by mail from unknown persons who might well be impostors. In the household account books, carefully kept by Mr. and Mrs. McCormick during at least some of their twenty-six years of life together, are many notations of "gifts" ranging in amount from ten

Cormick, Feb. 9, ♯Mch. 4, and July 14, 1881; T. K. Cree, San Francisco, Cal., to C. H. McCormick, June 14, 1881.

[116] "Chicago Daily Tribune," Feb. 25, 1881; "Daily Inter Ocean," Feb. 25, 1881. On this occasion, C. H. McCormick, Jr., talked to the gathering on the importance and needs of the Y.M.C.A. in the colleges of the land. The Chickering Quartet played and Miss Fanny Kellogg, of Boston, sang. ♯L.P.C.B. of C. H. McCormick, Nov. 1880-May, 1881, p. 284. C. H. McCormick to E. G. Keith, Chicago, Mch. 9, 1881: "The Young Men's Christian Association . . . is as much an object of interest to me as ever it was. . . . I shall be at all times ready to cooperate with you in the noble work of the Association." See also, C. H. McCormick, Jr., MSS. Book "B," N. F. McCormick to C. H. McCormick, Jr., Feb. 12, 1878. She was then entertaining Major Hardee of Selma, Ala., one of the national commanders of the Y.M.C.A. C. H. McCormick, Jr., held several official positions in the Y.M.C.A. after 1880. The friendship between Moody and McCormick is reviewed by Mrs. N. F. McCormick in "The Interior," Jan. 4, 1900, p. 3.

[117] J. M. McCue, Afton, Va., to J. D. Davidson, Apr. 8, 1881. C. H. McCormick to H. Chrisman, St. Augustine, Ill., Apr. 27, 1877: "I have had to adopt as a rule of business for *my protection* to loan no money."

cents to one dollar. Probably these were tips, or gratuities to beggars who came to their door or approached them on the street.

In point of time, McCormick was most generous between 1858 and 1861, 1866 and 1871, and from 1880 until his death four years later. The outbreak of the Civil War and the severe setback occasioned by the Great Fire restrained him from making new commitments until he could see light ahead, recoup his losses, and carry out pledges already given. In each of these periods the seminary at Chicago was the most favored of his interests. The Presbyterian Church, its seminaries and secular schools, received by far the largest portion of the total sum donated by him during his lifetime.

This total can not be precisely determined, but $550,000 is approximately the correct figure. Of this amount about $445,-000 was devoted to enterprises directly or indirectly connected with his church; $45,000 to the Democratic Party, $25,000 to his sisters and several nieces and nephews, $25,000 to the Y.M.C.A., and about $10,000 to such miscellaneous purposes as literary, art, and music societies, commemorative statues, sanitary fairs, Confederate prisoners, war orphans and widows, newsboys, and firemen.[118] Compared with the philanthropies of George Peabody, James Lenox, and several other very wealthy men of his own day, McCormick's contributions

[118] Included in the $445,000 is his $20,000 gift to Washington (and Lee) College, although its Presbyterian "flavor" was probably not the factor chiefly responsible for his interest in this institution. The files of the N. F. McCormick Biographical Association contain a statement itemizing gifts made by him totaling $124,462.41 between June 1, 1880, and May 9, 1883. Of this sum, about $85,000 was donated to the church and seminary, $13,000 to the Democratic Party, $8,000 to a sister, a niece, and a nephew, $1,000 to the Y.M.C.A., etc. See, Chapters One, Six and Seven for his contributions to the Presbyterian Church, and Chapters Two and Nine for his gifts to the Democratic Party. His subscriptions totaling $45,000 or more to the campaign funds of his party do not include his probable losses of $20,000 from the "Chicago Times" or of $6,500 from the "Chicago News."

were not impressive in amount. His fortune, however, was much smaller than theirs. About one dollar of every twenty that he made, was given away. With unimportant exceptions, his largess was never impersonally bestowed as in performance of a duty required by his ample wealth. His heart was in the causes he supported and he usually insisted that his gift should be used to help toward the attainment of a definite objective that he considered to be desirable.

Within five years after his death nearly $475,000 was given from his estate to the Presbyterian Church, seminary, and a dozen institutions of collegiate rank. These benefactions, and many others taken from the same fund, were dispensed in fulfilment of a provision of his will. This clause, wisely allowing the trustees of his property almost complete discretion, stated that they were empowered "to make such reasonable donations therefrom to charitable or benevolent purposes as in their judgment I would have made if living." [119]

[119] "Chicago Daily Tribune," May 20 and July 25, 1884.

CHAPTER IX

CYRUS MCCORMICK, DEMOCRAT, 1865-1884

FOR seven years following his return from Europe in 1864, Cyrus McCormick spent most of his time in New York City. By 1866, he was a member of the Manhattan Club, the Democratic counterpart of the Union League.[1] In its rooms on lower Fifth Avenue, a short walk from his residence and his church, he shared the friendship and political counsels of Samuel J. Tilden, Manton Marble, S. L. M. Barlow, John Van Buren, August Belmont, George Ticknor Curtis, and other leaders who were seeking to rebuild the fallen fortunes of their party. Reverdy Johnson was his chief political correspondent at Washington, and borrowed money from him on easy terms.[2] William Marcy Tweed counted him among the many advocates of honest city government whom he had deceived. In the summer of 1871, when the notorious boss was already under heavy fire, McCormick wrote to him, endorsing his administration. "They [the reformers] are honest men, and conscientious, but they forgot the fable! Better prove all things, and hold fast that which is good—not adopt the insane policy of burning down the barn to insure the extermination of unseen rats!"[3] Before the end of the year,

[1] ‡M. Marble to C. H. McCormick, Jan. (?), 1866. The initiation fee of the Manhattan Club was $150, and the annual dues $50.

[2] C. A. Spring, Jr., to C. H. McCormick, ‡Aug. 6, 11, and ‡Dec. 12, 1866; Jan. ‡3, 10, Feb. 21, Mch. 30, and Apr. 1, 1867. C. H. McCormick to R. Johnson, Jan. 6, 1886, Jan. 7, and ‡17, 1867. ‡G. T. Curtis to C. H. McCormick, Oct. 7, 1869. Curtis sought a loan of $1,200.

[3] ‡C. H. McCormick to W. M. Tweed, 1871, either late June or early July. A bi-partisan movement was on foot to end Democratic control at

Charles O'Conor and other associates of McCormick in the Manhattan Club had proved much, and the inventor doubtless wished that he had left unanswered Tweed's invitation to Tammany's Fourth of July celebration.

While living in New York City, McCormick retained his citizenship in Illinois,[4] and Democratic leaders there expected and received his financial aid in their campaigns for office.[5] The New York group also made demands upon his purse, and Virginia Democrats, too poor to pay their own expenses to national conventions, were grateful for his checks.[6] Politicians both from Virginia and Illinois were welcomed in his home, and although some friends cautioned him that his hospitality and generosity were abused by those who sought his money, he felt that he was, thereby, aiding a most deserving cause.[7]

The cause was, of course, the overthrow of radical rule at Washington and in the South. The Republican "redestruction" policy, as he called it, must be ended, since the Union and national prosperity could not be completely restored until

Albany in order to oust Tweed in New York City. McCormick opposed this move. "Third parties in politics have never yet accomplished anything important."

[4] C. H. McCormick to I. R. Diller, Dec. 3, 1866, and to T. H. Hoyne, June 17, 1869.

[5] I. R. Diller to C. H. McCormick, July 23 and Nov. 4, 1866, and Apr. 22, 1867.

[6] ‡Check stub, July 6, 1868, for $250, "to enable the gentlemen of Richmond to come to Democratic Convention."

[7] C. H. McCormick to C. A. Spring, Jr., June 6, 1868. He wished the Chicago delegation to stay at his New York home during the national nominating convention, but all except Isaac Diller, the Chairman, "with one accord began to make excuses." See ‡C. A. Spring, Jr., to C. H. McCormick, June 11 and 12, 1868; I. R. Diller to C. H. McCormick, June 25, 1868; W. C. Goudy to C. H. McCormick, June 19, 1868. Goudy promised to call on McCormick and learn his views as to the proper course for the Chicago delegation to follow in the convention. Young Men's Democratic Association of Chicago to C. H. McCormick, June 12, 1868: We are coming between five hundred and a thousand strong to the Convention. Will you please arrange accommodations for us?

the Democratic Party was again in control.[8] President Johnson deserved the support of all conservative men who desired peace and reconciliation. Although McCormick agreed with the President's objectives, he did not always approve of his method of attaining them.[9] The inventor's optimism during these trying days is the only unusual characteristic of his political outlook. He underestimated the strength of the Radicals, and expected an early end to their rule. Once the soldiers were withdrawn from the late Confederate states, the whites there, in his opinion, would readily dominate the negroes, and the traditional alliance in politics of the South and West could then be reëstablished. Until that time arrived, the southerners would be well advised to submit peacefully to the measures of Congress, since resistance strengthened the hands of the Vindictives and prolonged their control.[10] The United States was destined to be the greatest country in the world, the southerners should remain under the flag, and turn their faces toward the glorious future.[11]

McCormick was as ready to offer his services as his wealth, to hasten the happy day when this dream would come true. He did not care to enter the arena, however, unless his chances of victory were fair. Reports from the West were far from encouraging when he sailed for Europe in 1867. While abroad, he confided to Reverdy Johnson his willingness to be United States Ambassador to Austria-Hungary, if President Johnson

[8] C. H. McCormick to J. D. Davidson, Lexington, Va., Mch. #9 and 18, 1867; C. H. McCormick to R. Johnson, #Mch. 9, 1867.

[9] C. H. McCormick to L. J. Halsey, Mch. 12, 1866; to R. Johnson, Jan. 6, 1866: "I have been pleased with the President's message [to Congress] under the circumstances. He has had a hard trial, but I trust his courage will be found equal to it. He is favored with the opportunity to display greatness, while I have slight misgivings as to his improving it to that extent." C. H. McCormick to J. D. Davidson, Mch. 18, 1867: "Andy Johnson is still the best trump in the pack. . . . The future is dark, but still the Lord reigns!"

[10] Letters of C. H. McCormick to J. W. Brockenbrough, Lexington, Va., Apr. 9, 1867, and to J. M. McCue, Mt. Solon, Va., Apr. 24, 1867.

[11] C. H. McCormick to B. Tucker, Sept. 15, 1868.

were unable to secure a hostile Senate's consent to the appointment to that post of a "professional politician." "I need not say to you, my dear sir," McCormick continued, "that my ambition is quite satisfied in having reached the highest point of success in the pursuit of my own business, . . . But if . . . the popularity of my name in Europe . . . might . . . make my services useful at Vienna . . . I might be able to meet such a call to the best of my ability. This is all I could or need say. I leave all else with you." [12] Almost before Reverdy Johnson received this letter, the House of Representatives resolved to impeach the President for high crimes and misdemeanors. The post at Vienna remained vacant.[13]

Upon his return to America in the spring of 1868, McCormick tried to gain an appointment as a delegate of his party in Illinois to the national nominating convention.[14] Again he failed, but he attended its sessions in New York City in July, and was named one of a special committee of nine men to assist the national committee in organizing the campaign.[15] During the convention, he sought to persuade its southern members to vote for Salmon P. Chase for the presidential nomination, since he believed the only hope of success lay in the choice of a candidate who could draw some Republican support.[16] In this he was unsuccessful, and when the chair-

[12] C. H. McCormick, Paris, to R. Johnson, Feb. 4, 1868.
[13] C. H. McCormick to B. M. Smith, Apr. 24, 1868: "Nor do I now think the Prest. will be *convicted*."
[14] ‡C. A. Spring, Jr., to C. H. McCormick, Mch. 31, Apr. 16 and 17, 1868.
[15] C. H. Adams to M. Andrews, June 27, 1868; C. H. McCormick to C. B. Norton, July 29, 1868; S. G. Selden to C. H. McCormick, Sept. 19, 1868; J. C. Spencer to C. H. McCormick, July 29, Aug. 1 and 6, 1868. Spencer, of the law firm of Rapallo and Spencer of New York, was the most active member of the Committee of Nine. He stayed at McCormick's home in New York, while the inventor was at Avon Springs. The work of this committee was chiefly to arouse enthusiasm by organizing an "Order of the Union Democracy," and Spencer felt very much encouraged by the response received. Its motto was "Our Federal Union: It Must Be Preserved."
[16] C. H. McCormick to B. Tucker, Sept. 15, 1868.

man of the convention, Horatio Seymour, became the unwilling nominee and repudiated the "easy" money plank of the platform in his acceptance speech, McCormick was the more convinced that a fatal mistake had been made. He was a "gold" Democrat, but he was ready to support a stand for the taxing of United States bonds, and the issuance of several millions more of greenbacks, if thereby the discordant wings of his party could be held together long enough to win the national election. To wrangle over money or tariff questions when radical rule at Washington threatened the very existence of the Union, seemed to him to be a fatuous course leading surely to ruin. As always, he saw only the main goal, and was impatient when his fellow-workers allowed their energy and attention to be diverted to issues which, in his estimation, were relatively unimportant.

From the outset of the campaign, McCormick felt that his friend Seymour was not the man to win. The Republicans, as in 1864, helped their own cause by misrepresenting the platform of their opponents. Bond-holders were assured that a vote for Seymour was a ballot cast in favor of the repudiation of the war debt, and the negroes were warned that the Democrats would return them to slavery. Seymour made no ringing declaration of purpose to counteract the effect of these falsehoods. He had accepted the nomination against his better judgment, and although he congratulated himself that he was "free from all pledges, alliances or other entanglements," he was unwilling to wage a vigorous campaign. "My theory is," he assured McCormick, "that this election is in the hands of business men. It will go as their judgments shall dictate. I am very anxious to lay my theories before you and to get your opinions. If you can come [to my home at Utica] let me know when." [17]

[17] H. Seymour to C. H. McCormick, Sept. 15, 1868: "My nomination was made under circumstances in many respects embarrassing. In other ways I

The inventor contributed about $12,000 to the Democratic war chest,[18] and conferred with Seymour on several occasions. "I venture to suggest," he wrote to the candidate in late September, "whether . . . it may not be in your power to checkmate the course of fanciful misrepresentations upon which, manifestly, the Radicals depend for success, by a simple and concise statement of . . . the course your administration (if elected) will pursue on the great issues . . . before the country." [19] But this was not forthcoming, and in early October, Tilden, McCormick, S. L. M. Barlow and others considered the advisability of asking both Seymour and Francis P. Blair, Jr., the vice-presidential candidate, to resign in order to place Chase (with possibly Tilden) at the head of the ticket. When news arrived that the October elections in Pennsylvania, Ohio, and Iowa had brought Republican victories, McCormick felt that it was time to act "to save the Constitution and the Country." On October 15, without Tilden's approval, he wrote Seymour, frankly stating that his New York friends believed the outlook, as matters then stood, was "hopeless," and asked whether he would resign his candidacy to Chase, provided the Chief Justice would accept.[20]

have some great advantages. . . . As I did not seek a place upon the ticket, . . . I can take such positions as I may deem wise as to men and in some degree as to measures. I do not know how the election may turn but I must now contemplate success so that I may avoid false positions and not drift into any difficulties."

[18] ‡Check stubs, Importers' & Traders' Bank of New York; checks of July 21, Sept. 30, Oct. 2, 8, 1868. C. H. McCormick's telegram to H. Seymour, from Sheldon, Vt., Sept. 21, 1868.

[19] ‡C. H. McCormick to H. Seymour from Missisquoi Springs, Vt., Sept. 24, 1868: "believing as I do that upon the result of this election to a great extent depends the stupendous fact whether this Republic is to last, or be destroyed by the party now in possession of it."

[20] ‡*Idem* to *idem*, Oct. 15, 1868, from New York City: "Your closest friends here consider success in Novr. hopeless as we stand. . . . Chase's friends say, and it [is] *generally* conceded that large numbers of conservative Republicans, and wavering or fence Democrats would be secured by

It was a most difficult letter to write, and that their friendship remained unbroken, is a tribute to the character of Seymour and to the ability of McCormick to express a blunt thought tactfully. "I have been very much perplexed," answered Seymour on the twentieth. "The events of the past six days have been so pregnant with consequences that I have needed the counsel of my friends. . . . You knew I had no wish to go upon the ticket nor have I a wish to remain on it. I should be glad to have another name in place of my own, but I do not wish to shrink from defeat, or to shove it off upon another. . . . I must be governed by the [National] Committee. If they can see that I can with honor decline, can any candidate be found who will give us strength? I do not believe Mr. Chase would take a nomination." [21] There the matter rested, although Seymour consented to make an address at Buffalo to clarify his position upon the issues of the campaign. The Republicans won by a large margin of electoral votes, and McCormick took comfort in the thought that he had decided against returning to Chicago for the purpose of running for Congress that autumn.[22]

his acceptance of the candidacy, that would otherwise be lost. It would surely be a grand and glorious achievement by a bold manoeuvre of this sort to save the Constitution and the Country, while its novelty and greatness would stamp your name more indelibly in connection with it than if you had been elected President of the U. States." This was not mailed until Oct. 16 and then he added a P.S. "Mr. Tilden appears more decidedly opposed to the course suggested above this A.M. than yesterday."

[21] After C. H. McCormick wrote the letter of Oct. 15-16 in New York he went to Utica, but Seymour was on his farm, and the inventor did not see him. H. Seymour to C. H. McCormick, Oct. 20, 1868: "I am now urged from every quarter to make some speeches. I wanted your advice upon that point. It is very disagreeable to do so. In addition to other things which make it unpleasant is the fact that the labors of the Canvass have worn me down."

[22] ‡C. A. Spring, Jr., to C. H. McCormick, Aug. 24, 1868. Spring warned McCormick that the party only wished to run him for Congress in order "to bleed him." C. C. Copeland to C. H. McCormick, Aug. 28, 1868: "You couldn't succeed to the nomination and election without spending your entire

Following the Democratic fiasco of 1868, over three years passed with hardly a mention of politics in the correspondence of McCormick. He rejoiced in 1869 when the carpet-bag rule in Virginia was overthrown,[23] and his good Presbyterian and political friend, Roswell B. Mason, was elected the reform mayor of Chicago.[24] During these years his controversy with Dr. Lord and the New School group within his church reached a climax, and occupied much of the time that he could spare from his rapidly growing business interests.[25] The Great Fire in 1871 led him to reëstablish his home in Chicago and, thereafter, for several years the task of rebuilding his factory and other city [26] properties absorbed most of his attention. Nevertheless, the future of his party, the South, and the nation at large seemed to hang upon the issue of the campaign of 1872, and he felt that he could not stand aloof.[27]

In 1868 the Democrats had unwisely, in his opinion, nominated a candidate who could not draw the vote of Republicans weary of radical rule. Now on May 1, 1872, members of this discontented group met at Cincinnati and selected Horace

time & money without limit. . . . No true Democrat can be elected. I don't think it wise for you to run. You are too busy." C. H. McCormick did not vote in this election. He came to Chicago to do so, but was told that since he lived in New York, his right to cast his ballot would probably be challenged. *C. H. McCormick vs. the Pennsylvania Central RR., Case on Appeal, 1879,* testimony of C. H. McCormick, p. 39.

[23] ‡J. D. Davidson to C. H. McCormick from Lexington, Va., July 11, 1869: "The 'Vinegar aspect' so prevalent amongst us some time ago, has disappeared from the faces of our people, & we are already singing, 'O Carry Me Back to Old Virginny.'"

[24] D. Cameron to C. H. McCormick, Oct. 7, 1869; I. R. Diller to C. H. McCormick, Oct. 5, 1869.

[25] *Supra,* Chaps. VI and VII.

[26] ‡C. H. McCormick to Hons. Messrs. Stevenson, Thurman, and Lewis of U. S. Senate; Brooks of New York; and Harris of Virginia, House of Representatives, Feb. 22, 1872. In this, McCormick urged all Democrats to support the bill then before Congress to extend relief to Chicago.

[27] S. J. Tilden to C. H. McCormick, Sept. 27, 1871: "These are times which call on such men as you to come to the front."

Greeley as their standard-bearer. They obviously hoped that the Democrats would also make him their choice for the presidency. Although differing in their position on most issues, Horace Greeley and Cyrus McCormick had been friends for over twenty years. Their mutual interest in agricultural reform had first drawn them together, and Greeley had graciously given publicity in the "New York Tribune" to the inventor's triumphs abroad. Now and again, during the Civil War, they had corresponded on the subject of peace, and in 1867 Greeley had been one of the sureties of Jefferson Davis when he was released from prison on bail. This last should work to Greeley's advantage in the South, although his former arch-Republicanism, his lead in the abolition movement, and his support of high tariffs would certainly make the Democrats most reluctant to accept him as their candidate.[28] If McCormick were correct, a Democratic-Liberal Republican fusion was the only formula of victory, and whatever had been the "Tribune" editor's stand on slavery mattered little now, since that issue was (or should be) dead. These practical considerations, as well as a desire to aid a friend, were additional reasons which impelled the inventor to come to the front in the campaign of 1872.[29]

As soon as he heard of Greeley's nomination by the Liberal Republicans, he urged the two Democratic newspapers of Chi-

[28] C. H. McCormick to H. Greeley, from Chicago, May 10, 1872: "Although silent so long since your nomination at Cincinnati, I have not I assure you been idle or indifferent about the matter. Please command me if I can in any way do anything for you. . . . Please have the Tribune sent to me." H. Greeley to C. H. McCormick, May 13 and June 8, 1872: "I cannot foresee the issue of this contest, but I know that the Cincinnati movement affords a basis for a genuine and hearty reunion of our whole people. How long I have labored and what sacrifices I have made for that end you partly (?) know. If it fails now, I hope not to be blamed."

[29] Letter of C. H. McCormick in "Chicago Daily News," May 17, 1872. McCormick here tells the Democrats that Greeley is "fairly pledged to non interference . . . with the tariff question."

cago—the "Times" and the "News"—to come out in his support. Wilbur F. Storey of the "Times" refused to do so and during the rest of the campaign occupied a hostile or "Bourbon" position.[30] McCormick was a stock-holder of the recently established "News," and its editor, Daniel Cameron, had been active on the "Times" ten years before.[31] From conviction, and perhaps also because he much needed financial aid, he at once ran up the Greeley flag. Within a few weeks, he became McCormick's recognized political agent and spokesman in Illinois. Before the close of June, McCormick reported to Greeley that of sixty-one Democratic papers in the state, all except four supported his candidacy.[32] Even the powerful "Chicago Tribune," now under the editorship of Horace White, threw its influence on the same side.[33] Certainly a new era had arrived when McCormick and the "Tribune" were in agreement upon a public issue.

The first damper to the enthusiasm of McCormick over the political outlook came in late June when the Democratic leaders of Illinois met at Springfield to choose delegates to the national nominating convention at Baltimore. These were in-

[30] *Ibid.,* Greeley's plea for "a genuine and hearty reunion of our whole people" must be the "*keynote* of the *democracy* in this presidential contest. This and the platform adopted at Cincinnati, furnish the best compromise for uniting with Liberal Republicans. . . . It is *now certain* that the endorsement of Greeley by the Baltimore [Democratic] Convention will elect him. . . . Let us not, then, . . . risk another suicide." C. H. McCormick to H. Greeley, June 4, 1872. D. Cameron to C. H. McCormick, July 18, 1872. H. Greeley to C. H. McCormick, Sept. 15, 1872, "I do not approve of meetings anywhere to denounce the Bourbons. They are simply Grant men in disguise. Holding meetings to denounce them would only give them undue importance." The "Bourbons" met in convention at Louisville in September and nominated Charles O'Conor for President. See, J. F. Blackburn, Fairburg, Ill., to O. M. Hatch, Sept. 13, 1872.
[31] D. Cameron to C. H. McCormick, Mch. 19, 21, 1872.
[32] C. H. McCormick to H. Greeley, June 22, 1872.
[33] H. White to C. H. McCormick, May 31 and Aug. 1, 1872; H. White to E. L. Gross, Springfield, Ill., July 14, 1872.

structed to support Greeley's candidacy, and McCormick was named chairman of the state central committee.[34] This was gratifying, but due to the machinations of W. F. Coolbaugh, president of the Union National Bank of Chicago, and his son-in-law, the future Chief Justice of the United States Supreme Court, Melville W. Fuller, the Springfield meeting failed to name McCormick as a delegate-at-large to the Baltimore convention.[35] This was perhaps a petty matter at best, but most of the Cook County spokesmen at Springfield had wished him to be a delegate, and it was humiliating for the chosen head of the party in the state to be overlooked when its official representatives in the national get-together were selected. For the next two months the rift in Illinois Democratic councils caused by this episode threatened seriously to affect the conduct of the campaign in that state.[36] McCormick temporarily refused to accept the chairmanship of the state central committee, and those who knew him best were convinced that he would not rest until young Fuller had been properly disciplined.[37]

[34] L.P.C.B. No. 135, p. 282, C. A. Spring, Jr., to J. B. McCormick, June 25, 1872: C. H. McCormick goes as a delegate to the Democratic Convention at Springfield tonight. "Chicago Times," June 23, 1872.

[35] "Daily Illinois State Register" (Springfield), June 27, 1872. Carter H. Harrison supported C. H. McCormick, urging that Coolbaugh was an anti-Greeley man. Fuller replied that he was certain Coolbaugh would be for Greeley. C. H. McCormick was elected *alternate* delegate at large but refused to accept. C. H. McCormick to H. Greeley, July 2, 1872. Fuller was president of the Democratic Invincible Club of Chicago in 1863, then an anti-abolitionist organization, but formed five years before to aid Stephen Douglas. "Chicago Times," Sept. 23, 1863.

[36] H. White to C. H. McCormick, Aug. 1, 1872. White diplomatically assumed in this letter that Cameron was to blame for the "pitiful and small" quarrel, and that McCormick had of course not "entertain[ed] it for a moment." L. Trumbull on July 22 wrote to McCormick in the same vein: "If you would come to Chicago, I think you could settle their bickerings in an hour."

[37] "Chicago Daily News," July 18, 1872; D. Cameron's telegram to C. H. McCormick, July 17, 1872.

Although not a delegate, McCormick engaged a suite of rooms in the Eutaw Hotel at Baltimore and with Cameron and other friends was on hand when the national convention opened on July 9. Greeley was nominated on the first ballot and McCormick was a member of the Committee of Notification.[38] The platform of the Liberal Republicans was accepted in its entirety. The inventor took the place of the recalcitrant Wilbur F. Storey on the national committee of the party and barely failed of selection as its chairman.[39] This recognition strengthened his hand in Illinois, and boded ill for those who were opposing him there.

McCormick often found suspense a most effective weapon to use against his foes. At the close of the convention he went to New York City to attend the first meeting of the national committee and promised to contribute $10,000 to the campaign fund.[40] He stipulated, however, that this should be used for the cause in Illinois, a doubtful state, whose twenty-one elec-

[38] H. Greeley to C. H. McCormick, June 24, 1872: "It looks as though we were bound to win." C. H. McCormick to H. Greeley, July 2, 1872: I must go to Baltimore "because I think I can be of some service to your cause there. . . . My friends say they will move in Baltimore Convention to put me in Storey's place on the National Committee."

[39] "Richmond Daily Whig," July 10, 1872. C. H. McCormick was also named one of the ten men on the executive committee of the national committee. C. H. McCormick to D. Cameron, July 16, 1872: "I would have been elected [chairman of national committee] but for the usual intrigue and fraud as practiced by *Chicago* anti-Greeley men, who want the offices without Greeley, but in any event *want the offices!*" I desired the position, and the southern delegates supported me. "I have subscribed as much as any other member of the Committee." In his MS. Reminiscences, Judge M. F. Tuley says that McCormick was to be an ambassador if Greeley won. "C. H. was no diplomat, and he was too much of a democrat to wear knee breeches." No mention of this ambition is made in McCormick's letters of 1871-1872. H. Chrisman, St. Augustine, Ill., to ? (probably D. Cameron), Dec. 16, 1876: "I had him (C. H.) elected once, within $1,000, Chairman of Natl. Democratic Central Committee, and he declined the honor. . . . I inferred he didn't approve of the principle of purchase." "Chicago Times," July 10, 1872.

[40] C. H. McCormick to D. Cameron, July 15, 1872.

toral votes were well worth fighting for.[41] Democratic and
Liberal Republican leaders there were hard pressed for money
and were, of course, aware of McCormick's pledge, but it was
some weeks before they realized that he had characteristically
attached some implied qualifications to his gift.[42] It finally
occurred to them that the money would be paid over when
their campaign organization and leadership were changed to
meet his approval. To give them time to puzzle this out for
themselves, ill health furnished McCormick a valid excuse to
withdraw for the two months following the convention to
Richfield Springs, New York. He asked Daniel Cameron to
act for him in Illinois.[43]

In mid-July, without McCormick's knowledge or approval,
the Liberal Republican state committee, led by Governor John
M. Palmer, and three-fourths of the members of the Democratic state committee, met at Springfield and named a bi-
partisan executive committee to manage the state campaign.[44]
McCormick was not a member. Palmer was its chairman and
the headquarters were to be at the state capitol. Melville Fuller
was on this board, although he had no place on the Democratic
state central committee. Learning of this action from the

[41] C. H. McCormick to F. O. Prince, July 24, 1872.

[42] Letters of C. H. McCormick to D. Cameron, July 16, 1872, and to
A. Schell, July 19, Aug. 16 and 18, 1872. D. Cameron to C. H. McCormick,
Aug. 1, 1872.

[43] Telegram and two letters of C. H. McCormick to D. Cameron, July 17,
23, and 25, 1872. For a good summary of McCormick's position in this
controversy, see the draft of his speech to the Democratic state central committee, Aug. 27, 1872.

[44] Horace White had advised against this fusion, before the meeting on
July 16. See, his letter to E. L. Gross, Springfield, Ill., July 14, 1872. The
letter-press copy-book of this committee is in the files of the Nettie F.
McCormick Biographical Association. The first letters are dated July 19,
1872, and thereafter until Sept. 7, 1872, they are mailed from Springfield.
Then follows a week when no letters were sent and beginning in mid-
September, they were written in Chicago. The last letter in the book is
dated Nov. 6, 1872. D. Cameron to C. H. McCormick, July 17 and 23, 1872;
G. Kimberly, Chicago, to C. H. McCormick, July 19, 1872.

faithful Cameron, McCormick determined that he, and not
Palmer, was entitled to the chairmanship, and that Fuller must
be ousted.[45] Until these changes were made, the rebels might
rely upon whatever paltry funds they could raise in a Chicago
impoverished by the fire.[46] Apparently his enemies within his
own party planned to leave him with the empty honor of chairman of the state central committee; give the *de facto* control
of the canvass to the so-called executive committee, and expect
him to pay the bills.

The Palmer-Fuller group was not without its defense.
Coöperation between the Liberal Republicans and Democrats
was necessary if victory were to be won, and all personal
grievances should be shelved for the good of the common
cause. Probably the chief tasks of the campaign would be to
persuade Democrats to vote for Greeley and to induce Republicans to associate with men who had been in many instances
unenthusiastic, or even disloyal, during the Civil War.[47] It

[45] D. Cameron to C. H. McCormick, July 18, 1872; C. H. McCormick
to D. Cameron, July 24 and 31, 1872; M. W. Fuller to ? (probably J. M.
Palmer), Aug. 15, 1872. After speaking of McCormick's "silliness," he
adds: "If my presence on the Comm. interferes with McCormick's liberality,
it is little to sacrifice me and let him shell vigorously. . . . When a man
of his wealth seeks political notoriety or preferment, he should be willing
to pay liberally, and such is my hope in regard to him. . . . Consider my
head in the basket so soon as the proper number of ducats can be coined
out of the political life stream expected thereupon to leave my veins—'the
blood of the martyrs is the seed of the Church.' "

[46] W. Trumbull to C. H. McCormick, July 22, 1872; Greeley and Brown
Campaign Committee to O. M. Hatch, Sept. 20, 1872.

[47] #L.P.C.B. of Lib. Exec. Comm., pp. 55-64, the Comm. to A. Schell,
New York, Aug. 16, 1872: C. H. McCormick claims "the authority to
relocate Head Quarters and substantially demands that the whole control
of the campaign shall be placed in his hands. Something more than money
is needed; every overture for conciliation that the vital necessities of the
campaign or the common proprieties of life could justify has been unsuccessfully made." C. H. McCormick to H. Greeley, June 22, 1872: "I have for
some time thought that the most important if not the *only* point in the
canvass that required attention was to checkmate the effort by the Grant
party to make it appear to Republicans that your election would be a

was foreseen early in the canvass that there would be far more Republicans in Illinois who would hesitate to vote for Greeley, than Democrats who would actively work against him. The Bourbon element could, therefore, be disregarded, and, in fact, they numbered only three thousand in the election returns. For this reason, sound campaign strategy dictated that everything possible should be done to entice Republicans away from the Grant banner. This was the justification, in the opinion of Palmer, Lyman Trumbull and others, for the strong Republican representation upon the joint executive committee which McCormick so much disliked. He argued that the Democrats would furnish most of the votes, and in fact most of the money, and should therefore have a majority voice in the directing of the campaign.[48] The obvious answer to this contention was that in any election, primary attention must be given to the "floating vote," and since this mainly consisted of undecided Republicans, they should be assured of an equal share in party honors and offices both before and after the election.

The unusually large number of Illinoians who were "on the fence" in the summer of 1872, made it imperative that the campaign should start early and vigorously. The party which first reached these doubtful ones with their propaganda and their promises would likely capture their support on election day.[49] Since the Grant forces controlled all the postoffices and

Democratic triumph. . . . It now seems that your election is assured by an overwhelming majority." In truth, the chief difficulty came to be to arouse enough Greeley enthusiasm among Democrats to make them take the trouble to vote. See, L. Trumbull to C. H. McCormick, Sept. 16 and Oct. 17, 1872; G. A. Bixby, Plum River, Ill., to O. M. Hatch, Aug. 13, 1872; C. H. Moore, Clinton, Ill., to C. H. McCormick, Sept. 23, 1872.

[48] C. H. McCormick's telegram to D. Cameron, July 30, 1872. C. H. McCormick to D. Cameron, July 31, 1872.

[49] J. R. Blackford, Clinton, Ill., to H. White, July 29, 1872. G. W. Brockhaus, Mascoutah, Ill., Sept. 16, 1872: "We have nearly all the leading Republicans on our side excepting the Methodists and they are not very strong here in numbers." T. J. Johnson, Dwight, Ill., to O. M. Hatch,

most of the national banks, they had every advantage.[50] There was not time to wait until Cyrus McCormick felt that his health was sufficiently restored to return to Chicago. Because he had never directed a state-wide campaign, veteran "wheelhorses" in Illinois wrongly believed that he would be satisfied to acquiesce in whatever tactics they advised. But, if for no other reason, McCormick always demanded a controlling voice in the spending of his own money, and although he was quite willing to let Cameron handle all the details, he wished to be more than a nominal head.[51] The national committee refused to extend aid to the Illinois Democracy until it had made its peace with the inventor.[52] As a gesture of conciliation, Governor Palmer offered to resign in McCormick's favor as chairman of the executive committee, and to recommend that its office should be moved to Chicago.[53] The Democratic members of the committee would not agree to this, and the deadlock was still unbroken when McCormick returned to Chicago about August 8.

Although a gathering of "prominent gentlemen" from all parts of the state [54] had been summoned by Palmer to meet

Aug. 26, 1872: "It now looks to me to be a *nip* & *tuck* race with the Phylosopher about 4½ ft. ahead and he seems to be gaining all the time . . . quite a goodly number are in the Suspension State (in a State of betwixity)."

[50] O. C. Royce, Ashton, Ill., Aug. 4, 1872, to C. H. McCormick. R. A. Mills, Galena, Ill., Sept. 14, 1872, to C. H. McCormick. It was charged that government funds were loaned by the national banks to Republicans for electioneering purposes.

[51] C. H. McCormick to D. Cameron, July 25, 1872: "There is now for us the job of getting subscription list, competent secretary, accountant, offices, speakers, documents distributed. I can never do *this work!* I can only advise and keep an oversight. You do it."

[52] A. Schell to C. H. McCormick, Aug. 7, 1872.

[53] J. M. Palmer to C. H. McCormick, July 19, 1872; W. Trumbull to C. H. McCormick, July 22, 1872.

[54] J. M. Palmer to D. Cameron, Aug. 7, 1872, and to C. H. McCormick, Aug. 9, 1872; J. A. McClernand to C. H. McCormick, Aug. 12, 1872; J. C. Robinson, G. W. Shutt, and J. W. Patten's telegram to C. H. McCormick, from Springfield, Aug. 13, 1872.

at Springfield, the inventor declined his pressing invitation to attend. At this assembly a definite plan of campaign was decided upon, but the executive committee refused to yield to McCormick's wishes.[55] Thereupon he summoned the Democratic central committee together in Chicago on August 27, and to this body he presented his grievances and laid down his terms.[56] Up to this time he had paid only $1,000 of his $10,000 pledge, and the early optimism of the Greeley forces had been cooled by the reports of the large amounts of money which the regular Republicans were spending in their canvass.[57] McCormick's golden argument was unanswerable, and within ten days Governor Palmer and Melville Fuller had resigned from the executive committee, and its office had been transferred from Springfield to Chicago.[58] Whether the unconditional surrender demanded by McCormick was conducive to party and interparty harmony may well be doubted, and perhaps the "illness" which kept several of the most popular Liberal Republican orators from meeting their appointments in early September may be laid at the inventor's door.[59]

In the meantime, steps were going forward to press a close

[55] J. M. Palmer to C. H. McCormick, Aug. 13, 1872; telegram of J. W. Patten to C. H. McCormick, Aug. 16, 1872.

[56] H. White to O. M. Hatch, Aug. 8, 1872: "He [C. H. McCormick] does not talk unreasonably at all, except on the point of Fuller's election. Whether he is *unreasonable* as to that or not I am not able to say." Draft of a speech of C. H. McCormick to State Democratic Central Committee at Chicago, Aug. 27, 1872. C. H. McCormick to O. M. Hatch, Aug. 29, 1872.

[57] MS. undated Reminiscences of Judge M. F. Tuley. He recalled that McCormick assigned him the task of supervising the campaign finances. "He demanded a rigid accounting—even of the smallest items."

[58] "Daily Illinois State Journal" (Springfield), Sept. 9, 1872. The move of the committee to Chicago was "to get it out of the control of Springfield Liberals and nearer to the dollars and dimes of McCormick."

[59] J. A. McClernand to C. H. McCormick, Sept. 16, 1872; G. W. Koerner to O. M. Hatch, Sept. 11, 1872; C. H. McCormick to A. Schell, Sept. 9, and to H. Greeley, Sept. 11, 1872. Koerner, Palmer, and Black, the candidate for Lieut. Gov., were either ill or had illnesses in their family.

canvass in every part of the state.[60] Contrary to plan, some county organizations refused to endorse a fusion ticket for their local offices.[61] Hundreds of Greeley and Brown clubs were formed, with "White Hat, White Coat, White House" as their slogan, and with their members appropriately uniformed whenever their treasury could stand the strain.[62] One Liberal and one Democrat in each county, or a board of four or five men, were appointed by the state executive committee to direct the local campaigns, and to receive and distribute printed matter from the national and state headquarters.[63] The county board had the duty of naming a correspondent in each township and precinct, who kept them and the executive committee informed of the state of opinion in his neighborhood. He should prepare a list of all voters in his district, visit every one of them, and note down their political preferences. These lists, or "window books," as they were occasionally called, revealed the weak spots in the state and could also be used effectively on election day both to round up tardy voters and to influence balloting at the polls.[64]

[60] Circular letter of O. M. Hatch, Secy. of Exec. Comm., July 21, 1872.

[61] A. M. Herrington, Geneva, Ill., to J. M. Palmer, Aug. 7, 1872; J. B. Jones, Sparta, Ill., to Lib. Repub. Exec. Comm., Aug. 31, 1872. Nominations for county offices were made at mass conventions of the party, often enlivened by a barbecue.

[62] Hand and Metzke, Chicago, to C. H. McCormick, Aug. 17, 1872. The cost of a complete Greeley-Brown uniform was $1.50, including cap, cape, torch and flag. J. N. Cornett, Chicago, to O. M. Hatch, Aug. 13, 1872.

[63] The state central committee was made up of one man from each county. The Cook County committee, which managed the Chicago campaign, coöperated with, but did not consider itself to be subject to, the direction of the state organization. Chicago Democrats, unlike those of rural Illinois, were permanently grouped into ward clubs, etc., and the state executive committee had no reason to interfere with their work. For this reason, Governor Palmer was probably correct in his opinion that the executive committee for the state should have its headquarters in central Illinois, at Springfield, and not at Chicago.

[64] C. H. Munger, Marion, Ill., to Lib. Exec. Comm., Aug. 11, 1872. J. S. Moore, Lebanon, Ill., Sept. 18, 1872.

Whitelaw Reid of the "New York Tribune" office prepared "boiler plate" material for the rural press, and Theodore Tilton who edited the "Golden Age" in the Tribune building, offered to send to every new subscriber a large and handsome lithograph of Horace Greeley.[65] A total of twenty different campaign pamphlets was distributed in Illinois. Some appeared in English, German and Scandinavian editions. The many Germans who for ten years and more had been a source of strength to the Republican side, now hesitated to vote for a party whose administration had allowed arms to be sold to France in the Franco-Prussian war,[66] and which had as its vice-presidential candidate the old "Know-Nothing," Henry L. Wilson.[67] They believed in honest government, and the Democrats in their appeal to them, made much of the scandals that had disgraced Grant's term of office. Furthermore, Gustave Koerner, of their own race, was the Liberal Republican-Democratic candidate for Governor, and he, Carl Schurz, and the Chicago boss, Caspar Butz, were relied upon to wield large influence over German audiences.[68]

To offset these men the Grantites sent to the state Franz Sigel, a German hero made by the Civil War. He and other speakers pictured Greeley as a rabid temperance agitator, and as one who would, if elected, return to the South all the fruits

[65] T. Tilton to Democratic and Liberal Republican State Committee of Ill., Oct. 14, 1872. ‡L.P.C.B. of Lib. Exec. Comm., O. M. Hatch, Secretary, to W. Reid, Aug. 7, 1872. Whitelaw Reid was a close friend of C. H. McCormick.

[66] G. W. Brown, Butler, Ill., to J. M. Palmer, July 26, 1872. G. W. Koerner to O. M. Hatch, Sept. 11, 1872.

[67] L. North, Kewanee, Ill., to E. L. & W. L. Gross, June 19, 1872. H. L. Wilson was "the Grand High Cockalorum of the Know-Nothings—who organized every lodge in Mass. and was one of the authors of the reading and writing test in Mass."

[68] G. W. Brockhaus, Mascoutah, Ill., to C. H. McCormick, Sept. 16, 1872. F. M. Annis, Aurora, Ill., to O. M. Hatch, Sept. 2, 1872. G. W. Koerner to O. M. Hatch, July 31, 1872, and to D. S. Phillips, Sept. 22, 1872.

of the war.[69] The early hope of carrying the German votes to Greeley proved delusive. The powerful "Staats-Zeitung" of Chicago stood for Grant, and it was difficult at any time to make Germans believe that a ticket backed by the Irish deserved their support. The Swedes and Norwegians of Illinois had been almost solidly for Grant in the 1868 election. They were harder to convert than the Germans, since for the most part they did not speak English, and their political opinions were derived from their clergymen who were Republicans almost without exception.[70] The large Irish vote of northern Illinois was expected, as always, to be predominantly Democratic.[71]

Naturally there was much bickering between the Liberal Republicans and the Democrats, but the many campaign letters sent to the executive committee by workers in all parts of the state also reveal an astonishing lack of coördination between the local organizations and the central body. Until harvest was over in mid-August, the Greeley partisans in the rural districts were satisfied to assemble occasionally in the school-houses and listen to local leaders discuss the issues.[72] Once the grain was in the shock, however, they demanded an opportunity to gather of a Saturday at the county seat and applaud prominent orators whose eloquence would be fortified by a barbecue, band, and parade. One Liberal Republican and one Democratic speaker were usually the core of these pro-

[69] R. R. Finley, Galesburg, Ill., to J. K. DuBois, Aug. 29, 1872. R. A. Mills, Galena, Ill., to C. H. McCormick, Sept. 14, 1872: "A little money expended judiciously amongst the Brewers and with the 'Volksfreund' (of this city) will prevent the Radicals from making any further accessions from the Germans."

[70] S. Peterson, Knoxville, Ill., to State Central Committee, Aug. 27 and Sept. 30, 1872. Bill of J. C. Hansen, Printer, Oct. 24, 1872. J. C. Bundy, St. Charles, Ill., to O. M. Hatch, Aug. 4, 1872.

[71] J. N. Cornett, Chicago, to O. M. Hatch, Aug. 13, 1872. R. A. Mills, Galena, Ill., to O. M. Hatch, Sept. 14, 1872.

[72] R. C. Burchell, Oregon, Ill., Aug. 12, 1872, to Lib. Exec. Comm.

grams, but if choice had to be made, a Liberal Republican was always preferred.[73] Koerner, Trumbull, Palmer, Schurz and Cassius M. Clay were the most popular of all. General John A. McClernand and other soldiers of Democratic persuasion were welcome on any platform, since their very presence disproved the threadbare Republican charge that the Democrats had been disloyal during the recent struggle.[74] The votes of the veterans were worth having, for, as Sergeant Bates of Saybrook, Illinois, remarked, "100 soldiers of the late war have more influence politically in any community than 200 citizens who never robbed *henroosts* or masticated Hard-Tack in range of Rebel guns." [75]

Local committees were expected to request the Chicago headquarters for speakers, and they invariably asked for the most prominent men. They sometimes, however, negotiated directly with the orator, and he would learn from the executive committee, too late to make any change of plan agreeable to all concerned, that he was scheduled to address two audiences at widely separated points at the same time.[76] At the central office was kept a record of the engagements and open dates of each spell-binder. The local organization would be informed that Cassius Clay, for example, would be on hand at Bloomington at 8:30 P.M. on November 1. Hand-bills and posters would be printed and elaborate preparations would be made for a torch-light procession to escort him from the depot to the "Opera House." Farmers would come to town on the appointed evening, sometimes from a considerable distance, and would learn to their disappointment and anger that illness, bad

---

[73] C. Bennett, Mattoon, Ill., to O. M. Hatch, Sept. 26, 1872. G. Berry, Greenville, Ill., to J. M. Palmer, Aug. 5, 1872. J. F. Blackburn, Fairburg, Ill., to O. M. Hatch, Sept. 19, 1972.

[74] F. P. Griffith, Lagrange, Ind., Aug. 2, 1872. J. A. McClernand to C. H. McCormick, Aug. 26, 1872.

[75] G. H. Bates to G. W. Shutt, Springfield, Ill., Aug. 12, 1872.

[76] G. Koerner to O. M. Hatch, July 31, 1872.

roads, faulty train connections, or an emergency call from some center that could poll more votes, had made it necessary for a substitute orator to take the place of the promised lion. Occurrences of this kind, all too frequent, dampened enthusiasm and lost votes.[77]

McCormick and his committee were warned by the national headquarters to be on their guard against the plan of the Republicans to "colonize" negro voters from Dixie in the "Egypt" section of Illinois just before election day.[78] They also must keep a sharp watch over the Chicago area, for the elections in Indiana took place in October, and it was to be expected that their rivals would rush "floaters" from Illinois across the border to swamp the polls in the northern counties of the Hoosier state.[79] General John A. Logan, one of the most popular of the Republican orators, was, with a degree of truth at least, charged with raising a company in southern Illinois in 1861 to fight for the Confederacy.[80] A Democrat of Chicago, who was a friend of the routemaster of Forepaugh's circus, secured from him the confidential schedule of the dates when the show would be at different towns in Illinois during the summer and early autumn. Democratic rallies were arranged for those dates and large crowds assured.[81] Sometimes local celebrities had to be outfitted with

[77] W. H. Neeces, Macomb, Ill., to C. H. McCormick, Sept. 28, 1872. J. C. Crooker, Mendota, Ill., to C. H. McCormick, Sept. 17, 1872. File of letters dated from Aug. to Oct., 1872 from Stewart Crawford of Galena to State Central Committee.

[78] A. Schell, Chairman of National Committee, to C. H. McCormick, July 25, 1872. This was possible since there was no preliminary registration of voters.

[79] E. S. Alvord, Indianapolis, to Illinois State Central Committee, Sept. 21, 1872.

[80] G. Abbott to O. M. Hatch, from Duquoin, Ill., Aug. 20, 1872: "Send me anything to make his [Logan's] record obnoxious in print as a Republican. I can get up some affidavits here that he raised a rebel company in '61 in Marion & Williamson counties."

[81] J. Garrick, Chicago, to O. M. Hatch, Aug. 9, 1872.

clothes so that they could make a presentable appearance before their audiences.[82]

Thus the campaign ran its course, with McCormick irked by the details which required his attention and disappointed because his party seemed determined to saddle him with the whole cost of the canvass. The "Chicago News" was the only Democratic Greeley paper of importance in the city. In July, 1872, it had a circulation of 3,500 and its subscribers were increasing at the rate of about one hundred a day. McCormick owned $2,500 worth of its stock and he was one of the few holders who had paid in full for his shares. The journal could not be allowed to fail during the campaign, but it was running behind about $1,000 a month.[83] To no avail McCormick stormed at the delinquent stock-holders, and finally in September, after making several small gifts of money to its editor, loaned the paper $4,000 at ten per cent interest, taking a chattel mortgage on the plant (estimated to be worth $6,000) as his security.[84] On the day before election a petition was filed to place the "News" in the hands of a receiver. Republican papers here and there in Illinois, which had turned to the support of Greeley, were boycotted by many former subscribers and advertisers, and begged for aid from McCormick and his committee.[85]

[82] D. G. Hay, Burnt Prairie, Ill., to "Dear Brown," July 26, 1872.

[83] C. H. McCormick to D. Cameron, July 15, 23, 25, 1872: "How then *can* I get along *carrying the News,* and how *could* I get on without it! . . . Why do they [the other stock-holders] throw the load on me whose boat, as you know, is already so heavily loaded down as to be in danger of swamping!" D. Cameron, to C. H. McCormick, July 18, 23, 24, 26, 1872.

[84] Inventory of "Daily News" Property, Nov. 12, 1872. Account-sheet of C. H. McCormick with the "Chicago Daily News" Company, 1872. "Chicago Times," Nov. 4, 1872.

[85] H. M. Hale, Galesburg, Ill., to C. H. McCormick, Sept. 9, 1872: the "Galesburg Free Press" shifted to Liberal Republicanism and is "now being starved out." D. Randall, Aurora, Ill., to C. H. McCormick, Aug. 30 and Oct. 1, 1872; J. L. Stickney, ed. of "Fox River Press," Aurora, to State Exec. Comm., Sept. 21, 1872.

The national committee called upon Illinois for money and speakers to help in the eastern campaign, and McCormick countered by requesting funds from the New York headquarters for use in his own state.[86] Although Greeley maintained a brave front, he had lost most of his initial optimism by mid-September. At that time McCormick managed to decipher enough of a letter from the editor to read: "We have many discouragements. Our Committees lack both experience and money. But criticism is vain. We must do our best and trust Providence." [87] The critical illness of Greeley's wife added to his despondency, and on her account he refused to venture west of Cincinnati during the last weeks of the campaign, fearing that she might die before he could reach her bedside.[88]

When the news of Republican victories in the October elections in a number of northern states reached McCormick, he must have realized that defeat was certain the next month. The campaign in Illinois had been almost at a stand early in October in order to aid the cause of Democracy in the hard-fought state of Indiana,[89] and the inventor immediately there-

[86] A. Schell to C. H. McCormick, Aug. 7, 20, 24, 1872; to J. M. Palmer, Aug. 13, 1872. C. H. McCormick to H. Greeley, Sept. 11, 1872. ‡L.P.C.B. of Lib. Exec. Comm., p. 189, C. H. McCormick to A. Schell, New York, Oct. 2, 1872: "The fact is that we have to this time been able to collect next to nothing."

[87] H. Greeley to C. H. McCormick, Sept. 15, 1872; C. H. McCormick to J. D. Davidson, March 30, 1881.

[88] H. Greeley to C. H. McCormick, Sept. 17, Oct. 6, 8, 21, 1872; Telegram of "New York Tribune" office to C. H. McCormick, Sept. 18, 1872. ‡L.P.C.B. of Lib. Exec. Comm., pp. 148, 192-194, C. H. McCormick to H. Greeley, Sept. 17 (?) and Oct. 4, 1872. In these, McCormick expresses his great disappointment because Greeley will not come to Chicago. McCormick hopes that Greeley will at least attend the big political rally in the city on Oct. 11.

[89] J. S. Williams, Indianapolis, to J. C. Robinson, Aug. 13, 1872: "We are in trouble and need assistance. If we lose Indiana you are gone up in Illinois, and what you do for us, you do for yourselves. Morton is working as he never worked before and spending money like water." E. S. Alvord, Indianapolis, to C. H. McCormick, Oct. 3, 1872: I will draw on you for

after hurried to New York to attend a meeting of the national committee.[90] Upon his return he, George Pendleton, and Thomas A. Hendricks addressed a large Democratic mass-meeting in Chicago on October 22. McCormick presented a most rosy view of the political situation and prophesied victory. He closed his address by denouncing Wilbur F. Storey of the "Chicago Times" for his desertion of the cause.[91] As late as November 1, the chairman of the national committee telegraphed him that Greeley would carry New York state by a big majority.[92] Doubtless these extravagant predictions, in the face of many signs pointing in quite the opposite direction, were designed to exalt the spirits of the rank and file on election-day. The returns gave Grant the victory by a very large margin of electoral votes. The Republican majority in Illinois was bigger than ever before in her history, and Grant also carried every other state north of Mason and Dixon's Line.

$5,000 "as it will aid much in protecting us from the frauds being practiced by the Rads. who are desperate. The Legal Vote of the State will Elect Hendricks handsomely." Alvord was Chairman of the Ind. Democ. State Central Committee. There are many other letters from him in the McCormick Histor. Asso. Library.

[90] L.P.C.B. No. 138, telegram of C. H. McCormick to H. Baldwin, Philadelphia, Oct. 12, 1872. S. M. Moore and B. G. Caulfield, Chicago, to C. H. McCormick, Oct. 12, 1872. They urged McCormick to persuade Greeley to resign in favor of a Hendricks-Hancock ticket, or ex-Governor Curtin of Pennsylvania. "Any change is better than the condition we are in now, provided it would save our party organization."

[91] C. H. McCormick had hoped to have Seymour at this meeting, but the latter wrote: "it annoys and mortifies me to be unable to meet any request you may make." H. Seymour to C. H. McCormick, Oct. 19, 1872; MS. draft of speech of C. H. McCormick to Democratic mass-meeting, Oct. 22, 1872. "Chicago Times," Oct. 23, 24, 26, 28, 1872. This paper uniformly refers to the inventor as "Boss" McCormick.

[92] A. Schell's telegram to C. H. McCormick, Nov. 1, 1872; A. Schell to C. H. McCormick, Oct. 18, 1872: "So far in this campaign our disasters have come from a concentration of the whole power of the administration on separate states. Now we have an opportunity to diffuse this pressure. Hence the importance of a general fight all along the line."

Many Democrats stayed away from the polls rather than support Horace Greeley, and the Illinois vote by no means accurately indicated the strength of their party. McCormick turned back to his business, noting with regret that his political account was overdrawn by almost $3,000.[93]

For six years following 1872, party lines in Illinois were not clearly drawn. A goodly number of Liberal Republicans resumed their old allegiance, but many too, like John M. Palmer and Gustave Koerner, held aloof, and played for the support of the discontented farmer groups. The smoke of the 1872 battle still hovered over the political field when the Granger forces arrived in strength to take the place of the scattered Liberal Republicans and keep the contest a three-sided one. Times were hard and Illinois farmers were more interested in economic than in political ills. In their estimation, the Liberal Republican-Democratic alliance of 1872 had placed too much emphasis upon dishonest government at Washington and in the South, and too little upon ways of raising the price of corn and lowering transportation costs to the eastern seaboard. Although the grain growers were not ready as yet to make common cause with the erstwhile "rebels" of the South for lower tariffs, they strongly felt that import duties were too high and lessened the foreign market for their crops. Above all, so far as the central government was concerned, they wished "soft" money in abundance, so that prices would rise and old debts could be paid off for less, or at least not more, value than they had received at the time the obligation was incurred. Although railroads could be regulated by the state legislature, only Washington could adjust the money

[93] Free Press Printing Company to C. H. McCormick, Oct. 21, 1872. The company threatened to sue for a bill of $652. L.P.C.B. No. 138, pp. 452, 472, C. A. Spring, Jr., to C. Henrotin, Nov. 6, 1872, and to C. H. McCormick, Nov. 7, 1872. Voters who failed to come to the polls by noon on election-day were furnished free transportation by their respective party organizations.

situation, and for this reason farmers must make their strength felt at the national capital.

To the Democratic Party of Illinois, following the election of 1872, the question of whether the alliance with the Liberal Republicans should be maintained was relatively unimportant when compared with the need and difficulty of determining its official attitude toward the Grangers. Their success in the state elections of 1873 was a most convincing evidence of their power. They had mostly been Republicans, and their votes were urgently needed by the Democrats. To gain them, however, would require an adoption of their principles, and this would most likely repel the few rich men of Chicago who supplied the necessary funds for the campaigns. Of these, Cyrus McCormick was the chief. He was still the chairman of the Democratic state central committee.

The issue touched him very closely because his business depended upon the good-will of the farmers, and the high price of agricultural machinery was one of their many grievances. Although his factory conceded less to them in the matter of prices than did many other reaper manufacturers,[94] he as a politician was willing to make a stronger bid for their votes than were most Republicans. While in 1873 he believed that "masterly inactivity" was the best policy in order to allow the full extent and nature of the Granger movement to become clear,[95] by the next year he was ready to announce how far his party should go so as to profit by it. He would support the farmers in their desire for adequate railroad regulation and lower tariffs, and he would follow them far enough along the road of inflation to convince them of his sympathy. "No immediate resumption of specie payments, and no sudden, reckless inflation," summarizes his position on the money question. "The agricultural community has unquestioned and grievous

[94] *Post,* pp. 582 ff.
[95] C. H. McCormick to J. B. Danforth, Aug. 16, 1873.

wrongs to complain of," he told the central committee in the summer of 1874, "and the Democracy should stand pledged to their redress, without however violating a single vested right or resorting to the extreme legislation which has proved so embarrassing to other States." [96] He was accustomed to say "This is a big country, and government must go by compromise." [97]

When this advice was given, probably a majority of the Democratic leaders in the state, as well as Liberal Republicans like John M. Palmer, favored an immediate resumption of specie payments. The Democrats and their Liberal friends assembled in convention at Springfield in the late summer of 1874.[98] In spite of Cameron's urgent request, McCormick did

[96] ‡Speech of C. H. McCormick to Illinois Democratic State Central Committee, July 29, 1874. "Chicago Daily Tribune," July 30, 1874. D. Cameron to C. H. McCormick, Aug. 25, 1874: "The East looks today to Illinois on the *finance* question, and you are regarded as the one who is producing a healthful influence on that great subject." In the 1868 letter file of C. H. McCormick there is an undated memo. which expresses his views of the money question at that time: "Pay $25,000,000 of debt annually. Fund all 5-20's [U. S. Bonds] for 40 years and pay in gold bonds @ 5% if desired. Tax the govt. bonds and issue several millions more of greenbacks to add to the volume of currency for prompt relief, reducing taxation, etc. This should satisfy both East and West." In this connection it should be remembered that he had purchased very few U. S. Bonds during the war. G. T. Lanigan, Chicago, to C. H. McCormick, May 23, 1874; A. Schell to C. H. McCormick, June 5, 1874; B. D. Buford, Rock Island, Ill., to C. H. McCormick, July 23, 1874. ‡L.P.C.B., Nov., 1873-June, 1876, pp. 77, 97, 105, 110, letters of C. H. McCormick to A. Schell, New York, May 22; to E. S. Merritt, Springfield, Ill., July 13; to J. M. Palmer, July (?), and to W. T. Dowdall, Peoria, Ill., July 31, 1874.

[97] MS. speech of C. H. McCormick to Dem. State Cent. Comm., n.d. but summer of 1876. "Chicago Daily Tribune," Jan. 9, 1876.

[98] Letters to C. H. McCormick of ‡E. L. Merritt, Springfield, July 8, 14, and 18, 1874; J. M. Palmer, July 27, 1874; J. A. McClernand, July ‡16 and 28, 1874; W. L. Hamilton, Carthage, Ill., July 27, 1874; S. Heagy, Hampton, Ill., July 14, 1874, and E. Barrett, Niota, Ill., July 27, 1874. Letters of C. H. McCormick to D. Cameron, July 9, 1874; W. A. J. Sparks, July 16, 1874, and to E. L. Merritt, ‡July 15 and 21, 1874. In general, Democratic leaders in southern Illinois wanted their party divorced from the Liberal Republicans and a return to "Democracy pure and simple."

not attend.[99] Here a sharp contest over the money issue occurred, but finally a plank very similar to the McCormick "straddle" mentioned above, was agreed to. The elections that autumn, both in Illinois and throughout the North, greatly encouraged the Democrats and pointed the way toward victory in 1876. After 1874 the Grangers, as an organized political group in Illinois, were no longer important, but their principles remained to the fore, and because many of them transferred their support to the Independent National (Greenback) Party, the Republicans and Democrats still had to reckon with a third party of uncertain strength.

McCormick's share in forming a Jefferson Club in Chicago as a preparation for the 1876 election, won him the congratulations of both Seymour and Tilden.[100] In the interest of party harmony, he urged that "Reform," and not the controversial money question, should be the chief rallying cry of 1876. Not that inflation was the demand solely of the rural folk of Illinois. The currency question caused no clear-cut division between city and country-side. Men in Chicago told McCormick that if resumption of specie payments should come in the midst of the hard times, many of the most substantial men of the city would be ruined.[101] Chicago was not suffering as

On the other hand, McCormick, McClernand and other leaders of central and northern Illinois wished if possible, to preserve the *entente*.

[99] C. H. McCormick, in poor health, was spending a few days at Waukesha, Wisconsin. Cameron, jealous of McClernand's influence over McCormick, thought that he should be at Springfield to promote his (C. H. McCormick's) senatorial hopes.

[100] "Chicago Times," May 26, 1875, p. 4. C. H. McCormick to Jefferson Club, Chicago, June 22, 1875; S. J. Tilden and H. Seymour to C. H. McCormick, July 26 and 29, 1875, respectively. ‡L.P.C.B., Nov. 1873-June, 1876, pp. 267-268, C. H. McCormick to A. H. Pomeroy, Feb. 7, 1875: "Agreeing with you that scarcely anything short of madness in the management of our political leaders stands in the way of the election of a Democratic President in 1876, which however would not be new to us." In 1876, C. H. McCormick was also a member of the Municipal Reform Club of Chicago. "Chicago Times," Dec. 3, 1875.

[101] E. W. Cummings, Chicago, to C. H. McCormick, July 28, 1876.

much as New York from the depression, since the Great Fire
had kept most of its citizens from participating in the reckless
speculation preceding the crash in 1873. The hard times were,
in fact, a chief asset of the Democratic Party, if it refrained
from too much forthrightness in advocating definite ways and
means to restore prosperity.[102]

Between 1874 and 1876, McCormick was mentioned time
and again as a likely candidate for governor,[103] vice-president,[104] or United States Senator. So far as the evidence
shows,[105] he wrote little either to encourage, or to discourage,

[102] O. B. Ficklin, Charleston, Ill., to C. H. McCormick, Sept. 21, 1876.
[103] "Chicago Times," Apr. 8, 20, and May 21, 1876. "Daily Illinois State
Register," July 15, 1876. D. Cameron to C. H. McCormick, Mch. 24 and
June 4, 1876. By late March, C. H. McCormick had evidently authorized
him to "sound out" the possibility of his nomination for governor. W. T.
Dowdall, Ed. of "National Democrat" (Peoria), to C. H. McCormick, July
27, 1875. Dowdall urged him to announce his candidacy for governor. It is
perhaps of significance that Dowdall owed McCormick money, which Mc-
Cormick for long was unable to collect. D. Cameron thought Dowdall
had too many enemies to be a helpful sponsor.

[104] Column in "Chicago Times," June 2, 1876, headed, "Cyrus the Great.
At Least He is Willing to Take the Second Place on a Presidential Ticket.
. . . If McCormick Can't Get the Vice Presidency, He's Willing to be
Governor of Illinois. 'Barcus is Willin'.' " J. V. Farwell to C. H. McCormick, June 5, 1876. Farwell believed that if C. H. McCormick gave $5,000
to Dwight L. Moody's cause in Chicago, the gift would be widely advertised
through the Associated Press and help C. H. McCormick more toward the
vice-presidency "than all the money you could put into the hands of political wire pullers." "Daily Inter Ocean," May 14, 1884. This account states
that in 1876 C. H. McCormick was urged for the vice-presidential nomination at St. Louis but withdrew when Hendricks appeared to be the
choice of the close states. McCormick was mentioned at the convention for
this office but Hendricks was nominated by a unanimous vote on the first
ballot. "Daily Illinois State Journal," June 9, 1876. The editor thought
that the move to get the vice-presidential nomination for McCormick was
merely to divert him from seeking to be the candidate for governor. Mc-
Cormick attended the convention at St. Louis. "Chicago Times," June 28,
1876.

[105] D. E. Bradley to C. H. McCormick, Aug. 26, 1874. ‡L.P.C.B., Nov.,
1873-June, 1876, p. 413, C. H. McCormick to J. Reilley, Apr. 25, 1876.
McCormick here thanked Reilley for nominating him for President. This

these proposals. Doubtless he was receptive, but he did not wish to start a premature boom in his behalf, and he seemed unable to decide which of the three offices held the most attraction for him.[106] He knew that he was not fitted for a rough and tumble campaign, and he did not wish to spend much money unless the prospects were favorable for success. His business advisers cautioned him that his interests would suffer, as well as his health, if he added to the burdens on his already overloaded shoulders. He was ever reminded that he had reached the top of the manufacturing world, and to venture at his age upon a new career in politics, with success at least problematical, would be an anticlimax. His wife, so far as is known, did not permit her views in this matter to influence his course, and, taking him at his word, the only reasons why he might decide to throw his hat in the ring would be to help advance the principles for which he stood, and to aid in overthrowing the radical rule in Washington.

McCormick tried in vain to persuade the Democrats to hold their 1876 national convention in Chicago, and hoped that either Samuel J. Tilden or Thomas A. Hendricks of Indiana would be the candidate for the presidency.[107] Many of his party in Illinois, including the formerly hostile Coolbaugh-Fuller faction in Chicago, and Storey of the "Times," agreed with him.[108] Not a few rural Democrats, however, favored

probably referred to a magazine article, which the writer has been unable to locate.

[106] W. T. Dowdall to C. H. McCormick, Feb. 11, 1876: Cameron now tells me you want to be senator. "I advise you as a friend to make up your mind what you want and I think, indeed I feel sure, we can with your power secure it for you."

[107] #L.P.C.B., Nov., 1873-June, 1876, pp. 344, 364, C. H. McCormick to A. Schell, New York, Dec. 23, 1875, and to H. Seymour, Utica, New York, Jan. 26, 1876. C. H. McCormick to S. J. Tilden, May (?), 1876: "Men must be nothing—principles everything. But principles must be coupled with *availability*. *The soundest principles* can avail nothing if a candidate can't be elected, for whatever cause."

[108] D. Cameron to C. H. McCormick, June 4, 1876.

David Davis, an associate justice of the United States Supreme Court who because of his stand in the Legal Tender Cases was believed to be a friend of the greenbacks.[109] For this very reason McCormick opposed him and urged an assemblage of Illinois Democrats in January, 1876, to remain true to the innocuous money plank of 1874.[110] In February, the "greenbackers" met in Decatur, Illinois, and nominated Lewis Steward of Kendall County for governor.[111] They were more interested in warding off a resumption of specie payments, than in expanding the amount of money then in circulation. During the next five months the Democrats of the state debated whether they should endorse Steward or nominate one of their own regulars. Finally in July, in the face of vigorous dissent from many of their leaders, they accepted him, but continued to stand upon the ambiguous currency platform adopted the preceding month by the national convention at St. Louis.[112]

[109] ‡H. Chrisman, St. Augustine, Ill., to C. H. McCormick, Feb. 7, 1876. C. H. McCormick to H. H. Metcalf, Dover, N. H., Apr. 13, 1876. McCormick would not favor the nomination of David Davis since he would probably split his party on the money question.

[110] MS. draft of speech of C. H. McCormick to meeting of Democrats, n.d., but January 8, 1876 (Jackson Day speech). H. Seymour, Utica, to C. H. McCormick, Jan. 10, 1876. Seymour desired a conference. "Chicago Times," Jan. 9, 1876. This hostile paper often refers to C. H. McCormick as "a moss-back Democrat," "a centenarian politician," an "old Democratic warhorse," and as "a general by commission of Jeff Davis."

[111] H. Chrisman of St. Augustine, Ill., was present at this meeting as a scout for the Democrats. He reported to C. H. McCormick on ‡Feb. 7, 1876, that the Grangers did not demand more inflation but would only vote with the Democrats if they stood against immediate resumption. H. Chrisman to C. H. McCormick, Dec. 8, 1876: "You could have been elected Govr. if I had had the presence of mind to buy the Decatur Convention—Stewart [sic] only paid $2,000 for it. . . . I fear you are a trifle too modest for the best interests of the Country."

[112] MS. address of C. H. McCormick to state Democratic central committee, n.d., but July, 1876. D. Cameron to C. H. McCormick, Aug. 11, 16, 1876. ‡L.P.C.B., Nov., 1873-June, 1876, p. 389, C. H. McCormick to M. Marble, March 23, 1876, enclosing a printed copy of an address which

Thus, whatever hope McCormick may have had of being the party's candidate for governor, was ended by the choice of a man who was prominently associated with the manufacture of the Marsh Harvester. For the second time, however, the inventor was drafted to manage the state campaign in a presidential election year, and he was still a member of the Democratic national committee.[113] Repeating his tactics of 1872, and disregarding the criticism directed against him for his inactivity, he turned over the active management of the canvass to Daniel Cameron, and stayed at Richfield Springs from late August until early October.[114]

During these months a better county, township, and ward organization was perfected by the Democrats than ever before, and their enthusiasm reached a pitch unequaled since the days of Douglas, fifteen years earlier.[115] The demand for campaign documents was unprecedented. As always, the Democratic treasury was not as ample as the Republican, but it was full compared with its condition when Greeley was the candidate.[116] More help was given by the national headquarters to Illinois than in 1872. No longer was it necessary for the local

McCormick had made on "the issues of the day." McCormick hoped that his compromise stand on the money issue, known to many in Illinois as the "McCormick Platform," would be accepted by the Democratic Party at its national convention.

[113] "Chicago Times," Aug. 9, 10, 13, 1876; "Daily Illinois State Register," Aug. 10, 1876. *Post,* p. 527.

[114] C. H. McCormick's telegram to T. Shirley, Secy. of the State Dem. Comm., Sept. 26, 1876. D. Cameron to C. H. McCormick, Sept. 6, 1876. On Oct. 2, he telegraphed: "Great dissatisfaction about your absence and silence. Earnestly ask your return or campaign will be ruined." At the close of the campaign, Cameron was extremely angry because C. H. McCormick only allowed him the "contemptible pittance" of $2.00 a day for his expenses during the canvass. D. Cameron to C. H. McCormick, Nov. 4, 1876.

[115] D. Cameron to C. H. McCormick, Aug. 26, and Sept. 11, 1876. J. Jackson, Amboy, Ill., to T. Shirley, Sept. 12, 1876.

[116] J. Jackson to Dem. Exec. Comm., Oct. 20, 1876. W. S. Andrews, New York, to W. Brown, Sept. 11, 14, 1876. D. Cameron to C. H. McCormick, Aug. 31, 1876.

committees to furnish their own canvassing books and blanks
for the organization of clubs.[117] They were now standardized
and sent on request by the national committee. This board also
despatched skilled workers to assist in regimenting the voters
in doubtful states.[118] It even forwarded to the state central
committee stamped envelops, addressed to each county in Illinois, containing campaign propaganda. All that the Chicago
bureau had to do was to write the name of the appropriate
county chairman on each envelop and drop it in the mail.[119]
Before the close of August, the work of organizing three-
quarters of the counties of Illinois was completed, and the task
in the balance of them was well advanced.[120] During the first
two weeks of the next month, the Democratic leaders of
Illinois spent most of their time assisting their brethren in
Indiana. Torches and calcium lights were sent across the
border to help manufacture enthusiasm. The belief was widespread in 1876, as in 1872, that Indiana was the key to the
vote of the Old Northwest, and the apparently inexhaustible
financial resources of Senator O. P. Morton needed to be
offset by oratory, bands, and parades. It would be a fatal
blow if Hendricks, the vice-presidential candidate, could not
carry his own state in the elections of mid-October.[121]

The political "set-up" varied widely from county to county.

[117] G. Q. Leake, New York, to C. H. McCormick, Sept. 16, 1876.

[118] H. H. Finley, Milwaukee, Wis., to C. H. McCormick, Oct. 30, 1876.

[119] W. S. Andrews to W. Brown, July 26, 1876; W. A. Anderson, Madison, Wis., to T. Shirley, Sept. 8, 1876. The temper of the local workers
is illustrated by the following word from J. M. Campbell, Macomb, Ill.,
to the Dem. Cent. Comm., Sept. 18, 1876: "James C. Allen or Judge
Doolittle etc., will make Grant and his co-workers tremble with consuous
[sic] gilt [sic]. Their doom is fixed and the Glory of our Country made
manifest. . . . We do not want any one who cannot denounce the crime of
'Sallery [sic] Grabing [sic].'"

[120] D. Cameron to C. H. McCormick, Aug. 23, 1876.

[121] Letters to R. E. Goodell of E. J. Church, La Porte, Ind., Oct. 24,
1876; J. W. Clampett, Indianapolis, Oct. 2, 1876; J. G. Thompson, Columbus, O., Sept. 19, 1876, and of W. W. Boyd, Vienna, Ill., Oct. 14, 1876.
C. M. Babcock, Galesburg, Ill., to B. F. Bergen, Oct. 10, 1876.

In some the Greenbackers and the Democrats worked arm in arm and ran but one ticket for the local offices. In others there was a distinct committee of each party and each had its own slate of candidates.[122] In still others, harmony or jealousy at the outset of the campaign changed to the opposite feeling after a few weeks, and necessitated changes in the names and the number of the office-seekers.[123] The Democratic chairman of each county central committee was asked to state from which major party the Greenbackers were gaining the more recruits for the national ticket. The many answers received to this question indicate that the Republicans were believed to be suffering the most casualties, but, in the light of the final returns, these preliminary estimates greatly exaggerated the number of defections, since only seventeen thousand out of over 535,000 voters on election day gave their preference to Peter Cooper, the Greenback presidential candidate.[124] A Republican or a Democratic leader occasionally encouraged the Greenback movement as one way of weakening the strength of his chief rival.[125]

The many letters from party-workers throughout the state sent to the Chicago headquarters during the canvass leave no

[122] Letters to Dem. Cent. Comm. of G. Thode, Metamora, Ill., Aug. (?), 1876; Power & Harl, Metamora, Ill., Sept. 23, Oct. 31, 1876, and G. W. Andrews, Murphysboro, Ill., Sept. 13, 1876. J. A. McClernand to C. H. McCormick, Oct. 27, 1876. He opposed the tendency to fuse the tickets.

[123] W. A. Sparks, Carlyle, Ill., to "Dear Gen'l.", July 31, 1876. T. W. S. Kidd, Springfield, Ill., to R. E. Goodell, Oct. 27, 1876. W. C. Green, Fulton, Ill., to C. D. Hoiles, Aug. 28, 1876.

[124] J. F. Snyder, Virginia, Ill., to Dem. Exec. Comm., Oct. 16, 1876. J. T. Hoblit, Lincoln, Ill., to C. D. Hoiles, Aug. 28, 1876. F. H. Marsh, Oregon, Ill., to B. F. Bergen, Aug. 28, 1876. D. Cameron to C. H. McCormick, Sept. 11, 1876. In this, Cameron quite accurately predicted that the Cooper strength might possibly total 20,000, of which three-fourths would be Republicans and one-fourth Democrats.

[125] J. W. Chapman, Oswego, Ill., to State Cent. Comm., Oct. 16, 1876. C. H. Lanphier, Springfield, Ill., to B. F. Bergen, Sept. 3, 1876. G. M. Andrews, Murphysboro, Ill., to T. Shirley, Sept. 28, 1876. R. Babcock, Pontiac, Ill., to T. Shirley, Oct. 27, 1876.

doubt that the winning of the Germans was scarcely secondary in interest to the unnecessary concern about the Greenback movement. Of the hundreds of Republicans who appeared to be "on the fence," the Germans comprised a principal part, and the Tilden leaders made special efforts to gain their favor.[126] Both parties rounded up foreigners and rushed through their naturalization papers so that they could vote.[127] Carl Schurz was no longer available to aid in the good work, for he, together with many other Liberal Republicans, supported Hayes with a clear conscience. But Joseph Pulitzer, the rising young Democratic editor of St. Louis, was listened to with respect by many Germans in southern Illinois, and the "National Demokrat" of Chicago was laboring in the same cause.[128] Even before the end of August, Daniel Cameron believed that the Germans, "almost to a man," would be for Tilden and Hendricks.[129] His viewpoint was not an impartial one, but probably was to a degree justified since Chicago and certain southern counties, although Republican in 1872, shifted to the Democratic column in 1876.

For the first time, the Democrats made an extra effort to win the coal-miners of Illinois to their standard. Much stress was laid in the pamphlets and posters, prepared for their

[126] E. B. Shumway, Peotone, Ill., to C. H. McCormick, Oct. 24, 1876. H. M. Gallagher, Peru, Ill., to State Dem. Comm., Oct. 13, 1876. S. D. Stevenson, Tuscola, Ill., Sept. 19, 1876. J. W. Alexander, Sterling, Ill., to R. E. Goodell, Oct. 23, 1876.

[127] W. E. Cook, Lacon, Ill., to R. E. Goodell, Oct. 31, 1876. Judge D. Kyes, Pekin, Ill., to T. Shirley, Oct. 23, 1876: "Parties are coming in at all hours of each day for the purpose of being Naturalized." J. Braun, Joliet, Ill., telegram to R. E. Goodell, Nov. 3, 1876.

[128] W. J. Onahan, Chicago, to C. C. Copeland, Nov. 28, 1876. E. Rummel, Chicago, to L. Steward, Aug. 18, 1876. F. Schell, ed. of "Stern des Westens," Belleville, Ill., to E. Rummel, Oct. 9, 1876.

[129] D. Cameron to C. H. McCormick, Aug. 23, 1876. H. C. Conde, St. Louis, to J. M. Corse, Sept. 29, 1876. E. Hoechster, Peru, Ill., to R. E. Goodell, Oct. 27, 1876. J. H. Mann, Danville, Ill., to B. F. Bergen, Sept. 1, 1876.

benefit, upon Governor Hayes' support of the operators in mine-labor disputes in Ohio.[130] A Soldiers' and Sailors' National Reform Association was organized to appeal to the members of the G. A. R. and Cyrus McCormick paid for the transportation of a car-full of veterans to an enthusiastic rally in Indianapolis early in October.[131] Both political parties made arrangements with railroad and steamboat lines to carry voters to political meetings at half-fare rates,[132] and every student at Rush Medical College, who was old enough to cast a ballot, was given a round-trip ticket to his home on election-day.[133] The usual effort was made by the Democrats to prevent the migration of negroes to southern Illinois during the last weeks of the campaign, and several colored orators attempted with poor success to persuade men of their own race to vote for Tilden.[134]

In fact, nothing was left undone to insure victory.[135] Over one hundred thousand more Illinoians than in 1872 came to the polls and the number of Democratic voters increased by 70,000. Although the Republicans carried the state by a nar-

[130] J. G. Armstrong, Ottawa, Ill., to W. F. Storey, Oct. 30, 1876. G. M. Andrews, Murphysboro, Ill., to T. Shirley, Sept. 28, 1876.

[131] Letters to C. H. McCormick of D. Cameron, Oct. 3, and Nov. 2, 1876; R. Magee, Indianapolis, Ind., Sept. 20, 1876, and of D. Downing, National Soldiers' Home, Dayton, O., Aug. 17, 1876. Many of the 400 Illinois soldiers here are Democrats but the Govt. only supplies us with the "Chicago Tribune." Send us a Democratic paper. Many of the 2,500 here "are getting tired of Grantism."

[132] W. F. Pitney, Quincy, Ill., to C. H. McCormick, Oct. 9, 1876.

[133] W. H. Boak and J. S. Barry, Chicago, to Dem. State Cent. Comm., Nov. 6, 1876.

[134] O. Edson, Villa Ridge, Ill., to Dem. Cent. Comm., Oct. 28, 1876. J. W. Clampett, Fort Wayne, Ind., to R. E. Goodell, Sept. 27, 1876. For the effort to prevent "floaters" entering Indiana from the Chicago area on election-day, see T. J. Wood, Crown Point, Ind., to C. H. McCormick, Sept. 21, 1876. T. W. Halliday, Cairo, Ill., to R. E. Goodell, Oct. 6, 1876: "Negroes are passing through here in small squads bound Eastward—bound for Indiana, we suppose, to help the Rads. out of their scrape." See also, his letters of Oct. 19, 27, 1876.

[135] W. T. Pelton to C. H. McCormick, Nov. 3, 1876.

row margin, the Democratic national committee warmly
thanked McCormick for the energy with which he and his co-
workers had prosecuted the campaign, and unofficially informed him that it would be most gratified if he were chosen
to succeed John A. Logan in the United States Senate. In any
event, he deserved well of his party, and if Tilden were inaugurated President, he would not be forgotten.[136]

That this hoped-for event would ever take place, was by
no means certain in mid-November. The issue of the national
election hung upon the disputed returns from Florida,[137]
South Carolina [138] and Louisiana.[139] Although the Democrats
were convinced that the majority of the voters in those states
had expressed their preference for Tilden and Hendricks, they
saw with anger and dismay that their opponents were resolved,
through their control of the "carpet bag" canvassing boards,
so to juggle the ballots that each of these commonwealths
would officially report its electoral vote for Hayes and
Wheeler. The details of this dramatic story have been too
often told to bear repetition here. Excitement in Illinois was
intense, and in some towns business for several days was
almost at a standstill.[140] The Democratic state central com-

---

[136] H. H. Finley, Milwaukee, Wis., to C. H. McCormick, Nov. 6, 7, 28,
29, and Dec. 13, 1876. W. T. Pelton, New York City, to C. H. McCormick, Dec. 13, 1876. H. H. Finley's telegram to C. H. McCormick, Dec.
15, 1876. "Chicago Times," Oct. 19, 1876, mentions C. H. McCormick's
senatorial hopes.

[137] Two telegrams from Lake City, Fla., to Dem. Cent. Comm., Chicago,
Nov. 9, 1876.

[138] A. C. Haskell's telegram from Columbia, S. Car., to D. Cameron,
Nov. 10, 1876. Wade Hampton's telegram from Columbia, S. Car., to D.
Cameron, Nov. 7, 1876: "All reports in South Carolina quite favorable."

[139] J. W. Patton's telegram to C. H. McCormick, Nov. 7, 1876: "We
carry city and State beyond doubt and despite of fraud." Telegraphic bulletin from New Orleans, Nov. 10, 1876, stating that the Democrats probably
had won Louisiana. P. H. Smith's telegram from New Orleans to J. M.
Corse, Nov. 15, 1876.

[140] A mass-meeting in Chicago was addressed by C. H. McCormick, who
opposed forcible resistance, "relying upon the supremacy of the law."

mittee was showered with telegrams from anxious party-workers asking the latest news, the current betting odds on the outcome, and in not a few instances, urging the use of force to place Tilden and Hendricks in office.[141]

There were moments when revolution seemed to threaten. Differences of opinion upon the proper course for the Illinois Democrats to pursue in the crisis made McCormick's life exciting for several weeks. As might be expected, he stood for peace, believing that right would eventually triumph because there were many honest Republicans both in Congress and out, who would join with the Democrats to prevent the defeat by fraud of the people's will.[142] Members of his committee, Daniel Cameron, E. L. Merritt of the influential "Illinois State Register," and others, chafed at his inactivity and his apparent intention to "sit on the lid until it bursts with emotion." [143] Most of those who demanded action were young men or those whose hopes of federal jobs would be blasted if Hayes were inaugurated. The national Democratic committee supported the inventor in his refusal to sponsor mass-meetings or any other demonstration by his party which would

[141] J. G. Sherman, Geneva Lake, Wis., to R. Goodell, Nov. 11, 1876; J. M. Hall, Paxton, Ill., telegraphed R. E. Goodell, Nov. 10, 1876: "Is it safe to bet on Tilden?" H. M. Brown, Columbus, Wis., telegraphed to T. Shirley, Nov. 10, 1876: "For God's sake give me your latest from Doubtful States." Telegrams to R. E. Goodell on Nov. 10, of J. S. Eckels, Princeton, Ill., and Ed. Keogh, Elgin, Ill., and on Nov. 11, of J. C. Campbell, Streator, Ill. Telegrams of J. W. Duncan, La Salle, Ill., to T. Shirley, Nov. 10, of J. M. Brown, Atkinson, Ill., to J. J. Crowley, Nov. 11, and of E. S. Bragg, Fond du Lac, Wis., to P. H. Smith, Nov. 11, 1876.

[142] Telegram of C. D. Hoiles from Greenville, Ill., to C. H. McCormick, Dec. 15, 1876. Telegram of C. H. McCormick to A. S. Hewitt, Nov. 17, 1876: "My advice here as there [Louisiana]. All peaceful measures first exhausted for right."

[143] D. Cameron to C. H. McCormick, Nov. 25, 1876; R. M. Andrews, Pittsfield, Ill., to C. H. McCormick, Nov. 27, 1876. "Chicago Daily Tribune," Dec. 17, 1876.

still further inflame those who were well nigh already beyond control.[144]

This tense situation caused a schism within party ranks and led discontented Democrats to criticize McCormick publicly in terms so abusive that he must have been reminded of Civil War days and his controversy with Dr. Lord.[145] Worse still, he was unable to hold in check all the members of the Democratic state central committee. A few of them telegraphed to the New York headquarters that "We have 100,000 ex-soldiers in the North as a nucleus to prevent anything like violence in case of necessity. Tell the Governor [Tilden] he shall not be defrauded of his seat." [146] Against his wish, a call was issued for a meeting of the central committee at Springfield in late December,[147] and the "Illinois State Register" let it be known that the chief business of the meeting would be to oust "the imbecile" chairman.[148] Nevertheless, when the obstreperous few gathered together on the appointed day they

[144] A. S. Hewitt to C. H. McCormick, Nov. 13, 1876. "Daily Illinois State Journal," Dec. 13, 1876. W. Kirkwood, Sullivan, Ill., to C. H. McCormick, Nov. 27, 1876: "I do not believe in resorting to the bayonet to settle every little question. We have had too much of it already to be tolerated in a free government." ‡F. F. Marsh, to C. H. McCormick, Dec. 15, 1876: "*I think that if finances was required, some of the so-called leaders would be willing to listen to your advice.*"

[145] "Daily Illinois State Register," Dec. 2, and 20, 1876. "Daily Illinois State Journal," Dec. 14, 1876. This Republican paper defended C. H. McCormick and remarked that he had "long carried the Democratic party of Illinois . . . Atlas like . . . on his shoulders." ‡B. F. Bergen to C. H. McCormick, Dec. 25, 1876.

[146] Telegram of Dem. State Cent. Comm., Chicago, to W. T. Pelton, Nov. 8, 1876; B. F. Bergen's telegram and letter to C. H. McCormick, Nov. 20 and 21, 1876.

[147] Letters to C. H. McCormick of G. Edmunds, Jr., Carthage, Ill., Dec. 18, and L. B. Parsons, Flora, Ill., Dec. 19, 1876. "Chicago Daily Tribune," Dec. 17, 1876. This paper also supported C. H. McCormick in the crisis.

[148] "Daily Illinois State Journal," Dec. 19, 1876; "Daily Illinois State Register," Dec. 12, 1876. "Chicago Daily Tribune," Dec. 23, 1876.

were surprised to find McCormick there. His better counsel prevailed. In view of the approaching election of an United States Senator by the legislature, it seemed unwise to advertise and sharpen the dissension within the ranks of the party. There was no denying that without McCormick's money in 1872 and 1876 the state campaign could hardly have been carried on at all, and to dispense with him before victory was gained, would be sheer madness.[149] This conference adjourned after McCormick agreed to call a Democratic convention to assemble at Springfield on January 8, 1877, in time, so it was hoped, to influence the senatorial election there and the counting of the national electoral vote at Washington.[150]

Cheered by the favorable attitude of the national Democratic committee, and very anxious that a Democrat should replace John A. Logan in the United States Senate, McCormick was not unwilling to be the choice of the legislature for this office. Political lines in that body were narrowly drawn and the Greenback group held the balance of power. His known middle-of-the-way position upon the currency question was hardly a disqualification, since he and the soft-money men of Illinois agreed that the resumption of specie payments should be postponed. His office superintendent at the factory

[149] "Daily Illinois State Register," Dec. 26, 1876; "Daily Illinois State Journal," Dec. 22, 1876; J. A. McClernand and C. A. Keys's telegram to C. H. McCormick from Springfield, Dec. 20, 1876; W. T. Steele, Springfield, to C. H. McCormick, Dec. 22, 1876. #L.P.C.B., June 1876-Apr. 1878, p. 497, C. H. McCormick to H. H. Finley, Dec. 22, 1876: "I thought it best to meet the Committee at Springfield yesterday. . . . I had in the meantime ascertained that the thing was a complete flash in the pan. . . . I went down as requested by many members to make the meeting regular, and thought something useful might grow out of it. . . . I have never attended a meeting of the kind with more real satisfaction. . . . I had fully informed the members (all) of the game, and there were special pains taken by them to show their sympathy and *appreciation*."

[150] "Daily Illinois State Register," Dec. 28, 1876. G. A. Fitch, Chicago, to C. H. McCormick, Dec. 30, 1876; telegram of J. S. Drake, Rock Island, to C. H. McCormick, Dec. 19, 1876.

corresponded with leading agents in Illinois, asking them to say a good word for the inventor to their friends.[151]

H. H. Finley, a New York lawyer and member of the Democratic national committee, who was at Washington working in Tilden's behalf, suggested that $2,000 could persuade the party press of the capital city and throughout the northwest, as of its own initiative, to sponsor McCormick's candidacy for the Senate. Such weighty support, so it was believed, would exercise a salutary influence upon the Illinois legislature.[152] A friend in Illinois wrote McCormick with disarming frankness that a not unusual way to reach the United States Senate was to buy enough votes in a state legislature to insure a majority, and he was confident that the outcome of the election in this instance would be determined by the "arbitrament of cash." [153] Rejecting the advice of both of these well-wishers,

[151] F. H. Matthews to G. A. Willey, Belleville, Ill., Nov. 25, 1876. Matthews of the factory office asks this agent whether "you could bring any influence to bear either through yourself or others to induce them [state senators and representatives] to vote and work for the right kind of man for Senator. . . . I would suggest that Mr. C. H. McCormick is just the man needed in this emergency. . . . Please consider what I have said as confidential." ‡L.P.C.B., June 1876-Apr. 1878, p. 27, C. H. McCormick to H. Chrisman, St. Augustine, Ill., Dec. 6, 1876. Here McCormick asked Chrisman to help him become U. S. Senator. McCormick believed that some of the Republicans in the state legislature would not vote for Logan. H. O. Goodrich (agent), Jerseyville, Ill., to C. H. McCormick, Dec. 9, 1876: "I think I can influence some of the members from this part of the state." D. W. Cobb from Belleville, Ill., to Co., Sept. 17, 1877.

[152] H. H. Finley, Washington, D. C., to C. H. McCormick or to C. C. Copeland, Dec. 2, 3, 6, 7, 1876. On the 3rd he wrote: "Tonight I have positive information from Mr. Grant that he will not interfere and that Mr. Tilden will be declared elected unless some new complications arise." C. C. Copeland to H. H. Finley, Dec. 9, 1876.

[153] H. Chrisman, St. Augustine, Ill., to C. H. McCormick, D. Cameron, or C. C. Copeland, Dec. 8, 15, 16, 22, 1876. On the 16th he wrote either to Cameron or Copeland: "C. H. is the only man among us all that has money enough to gain us one vote in the Senate. One more vote in that body may prove vital. We know he has the public spirit to spend the money. But will he think it proper to do it; that is the question. . . . Believing that it

he encouraged his close friend, C. C. Copeland, and several others, to engage in a "still hunt" among the Democratic assemblymen in an effort to pledge them to vote for him.[154] Reports from these scouts in early December were optimistic in tone, but if any member of the legislature bound himself to support the inventor's candidacy, he flagrantly violated his promise as soon as the balloting began.[155] The official journals of that body make no mention of McCormick.

He presided at the opening session of the Democratic convention at Springfield on January 8. He was disappointed in the hope that many Republicans would join with his party

can only be done with money it becomes important to know his views. . . . I could render him very valuable aid . . . with a very moderate sum, yet I should never venture to suggest it to him unless you advise me." On the 22nd he wrote C. H. McCormick: "I feel well satisfied that your judgment is correct not to *invest* in the Senatorial nomination but to remain a careful observer and withhold decision until it becomes reasonably apparent that the means will secure the end."

[154] J. H. Oberly, editor of "Cairo Bulletin," to C. H. McCormick, Dec. 24, 1876. He hoped C. H. McCormick would win, but he feared the opposition was too strong. W. J. Onahan, Chicago, to C. C. Copeland, Nov. 28, 1876. M. W. Robinson's telegram to C. H. McCormick from Springfield, Ill., Jan. 3, 1877: "I find matters looking very favorable. Why are you not down here?" ‡L.P.C.B., June, 1876-Apr. 1878, pp. 34, 37, C. H. McCormick to H. Chrisman and to H. H. Finley, Jan. 2, 1877. In these letters, McCormick admits that his senatorial chances "look so blue" that he doubts whether he will come out openly as a candidate. But the next day (*id.*, p. 492) in a letter to M. W. Robinson, Springfield, he wrote: "There have seemed to be so many aspirants to this high honor among the best men of our State that I have at least felt it became me to wait for some indication that my services in the capacity referred [to] might be called for. Your telegram to me is one that I can not ignore, and for which accept my thanks. . . . While it may hardly be essential that I go immediately [to Springfield]. . . . I have expected to attend the Convention . . . and may get down a day or two earlier than the 8th."

[155] C. C. Copeland to H. H. Finley, Dec. 9, 1876. Momentarily in mid-December C. H. McCormick decided to withdraw his candidacy, but he received a letter from New York Democratic headquarters urging him to go on. C. H. McCormick to H. H. Finley, Dec. 15, 1876. W. T. Pelton, New York, to C. H. McCormick, Dec. 13, 1876. H. H. Finley to C. H. McCormick, from Washington, D. C., Dec. 16, 1876.

and endorse the resolutions drafted by this meeting, condemning the "conspiracy" to defraud Tilden, and demanding that the electoral vote be counted, not by the Republican presiding officer of the United States Senate, but by the members of both Houses in joint session. Since the House of Representatives had a Democratic majority, and was, of course, much larger in membership than the Senate, this manner of determining the valid returns from the three southern states would result in making Tilden the victor. This peaceful expression of protest, in accord as it was with instructions from the national committee, had McCormick's hearty approval, and signified that the conservative wing of the party was in control.[156]

Interest then shifted from the situation at Washington to the Illinois Assembly which for the first time convened in the new state capitol, "a structure so magnificent that he who walks its pillared halls, and gazes on its granite and marble stairways, must feel himself lifted into a broader appreciation of our loved Prairie State, and the great resources garnered from its rich, virgin soil." [157] Having been warmed by this eloquence of James Shaw, the Speaker, the two houses soon deadlocked over the choice of an United States Senator. The lower chamber of the 45th Congress would have a Democratic majority, but the division in the Senate was so close that Illinois's decision might determine which party would control that body. For that reason, the election was of more than ordinary national interest, and McCormick keenly felt his responsibility.[158]

[156] W. T. Pelton, Natl. Dem. Comm., to C. H. McCormick, Jan. 5, 1877. The resolutions adopted at Springfield were almost identical with the suggestions of this letter. "Illinois State Register," Jan. 8, 1877. "Chicago Times," Jan. 8, 1877.

[157] "Journal of the House of Representatives of the Thirtieth General Assembly of the State of Illinois" (Springfield, 1877), p. 11.

[158] See, ftn. No. 153, supra.

On January 16, 1877, the balloting at Springfield began. As had been expected, the Greenbackers controlled enough votes to prevent the election of either John A. Logan or John M. Palmer, the two candidates who had marshalled the most support.[159] Evidently the aspirant that could gain the favor of those who held the balance of power, would win. McCormick believed that the Republicans might use money as a last resort to effect their purpose, and on January 18 wrote to Chicago for $5,000 as an emergency fund. "Prospects strong for us here," he added, "and no expectation that anything but incidental expenses wanted." [160] However, the matter seemed vital, and he was prepared to fight fire with fire, if need should arise. Finally, on January 25, 1877, on the fortieth ballot, a union between the Democrats and members of the Greenback party, gave the victory (with no votes to spare) to David Davis.[161]

[159] "House Journal," *op. cit.*, pp. 85-150, *passim*. D. Cameron to C. H. McCormick, Jan. 15, 1877. "Daily Illinois State Journal," Jan. 15, 1877, p. 4.

[160] C. H. McCormick to Nettie F. McCormick, via Amanda Adams, from Springfield, Jan. 18, 1877. #L.P.C.B., June 1876-Apr. 1878, p. 497. C. H. McCormick to H. H. Finley, Dec. 22, 1876. At Springfield it is said that no one except myself can beat Logan's money. "I am terribly disgusted with much that I see in connection with these matters, but if I could be instrumental in defeating &c. I should submit to a great deal to accomplish it. . . . If thought desirable by Govr. T. (whose election I *consider* still certain) I should still do all I could in some way, etc. etc. Please write me."

[161] "Chicago Times," Jan. 10 to 27, 1877. An editorial on Jan. 19 states that few at Springfield take McCormick's candidacy seriously, but many encourage him to stay in the race so as "to keep up the market price of members" of the Assembly. C. H. McCormick to C. H. McCormick, Jr., June 19, 1882. In this, C. H. McCormick recalls that his friend, C. C. Copeland, controlled some Chicago votes which were to be cast for Davis on the first ballot, and then to be shifted to him. But on that ballot, writes C. H. McCormick, enough votes were cast for Davis to give him the election. The "House Journal" of Illinois for 1877 does not bear out this statement, although it is quite possible that some of the Chicago representatives may have expected to shift to C. H. McCormick after giving Davis a com-

McCormick was dissatisfied because he believed that Davis, who was known for the impartiality of his political views, had promised to accept a place on the Electoral Commission. In fact, the Democrats had been induced to accept this method of reaching a decision upon the disputed electoral returns, only with the understanding that Davis would hold the balance between the other fourteen members who were equally divided in their party affiliations. McCormick's state of mind was probably quite accurately reflected by H. H. Finley, who wrote on February 11 that

the duplicity of Judge Davis now well known and understood has placed him lower in the estimation of our people than Bradley's perfidy or Miller's bigotry. Davis could have saved us. He promised to do so and . . . then connived to have himself rejected. Judge Clifford refuses ever to speak to Davis again and he has left here in disgrace. I mention these facts because I think that you should know the standing of Senator Davis with Mr. Tilden and his friends. No blame attaches to us for his election as Senator. He would have been false to us, if he had not been elected.[162]

This was probably an unfair judgment of Davis's course, but it was the characteristic reaction of an ardent Democrat who was just then witnessing the Electoral Commission, by eight to seven divisions, give the presidency to Rutherford B. Hayes.

plimentary vote. On this, see D. Cameron to C. H. McCormick, n.d., but either late Dec. 1876, or early Jan., 1877. H. Chrisman, Galesburg, to C. H. McCormick, Jan. 26, 29, 1877. Chrisman had heard that with C. H. McCormick in the race, Logan would have been elected, and that to prevent this, C. H. McCormick gave up his chances and released his supporters to Davis. Chrisman, however, wanted a loan, was a sycophant, and too much trust cannot be placed in his word. See, "Mississippi Valley Historical Review," XX, No. 2, Sept. 1933, p. 235.

    162 H. H. Finley to C. H. McCormick from Washington, Feb. 11, 1877. He is confident that Tilden will win. On Feb. 9, 1877, C. H. McCormick wrote to H. B. Tomlin of Virginia: "I have still myself however strong confidence that Tilden will be the next Pres.! with a strong probability that *Wheeler* will be the Vice! While to satisfy Mr. Tilden & friends, I consented to take the *chance* of a hand at Politics for a time, though at the expense of great discomfort to my family & self."

To the end of his life, McCormick believed that Tilden rightfully should have been inaugurated in March, 1877. Hayes won his praise by his benevolent southern policy and sympathy for civil service reform,[163] but he was glad that the new Chief Executive was determined to serve only one term, since in his opinion the people must as an act of simple justice repudiate in 1880 a party which had been guilty of the bare-faced frauds of 1876.

In April, 1878, because of illness, he was obliged to have a friend read his speech on the issues of the day to a Democratic convention at Springfield. This was destined to be his political valedictory.

Ours will be the responsibility and trust of governing soon [he predicted]. It has not been and must not be a question of honors and offices. We must govern to bring honor, respect, prosperity, peace and happiness.

Although he favored the Bland-Allison bill then before Congress, he warned his hearers not to expect it to bring prosperity.

My preference [to the Bland-Allison bill] would be the adoption of the trade dollar of 120 grains with free coinage privileges, and the call of an International Congress in twelve months for the final settlement of the . . . question. . . . With these provisions, I do not think it necessary to require the resumption of specie payment . . . on the 1st of January, 1879. The present financial crisis . . . is due to improvidence, extravagance, overtrading,

163 "While in New York last November [1877] I talked with Hayes and was satisfied with his original and honest intention to bring about, so far as his influence would go, . . . a fraternal state of feeling . . . and to do what he could in the way of the reform of the government service." From a MS. speech of C. H. McCormick written for delivery to Dem. Cent. Comm. in late winter of 1877-1878. C. H. McCormick to Dem. Members of the H. of R., 45th Congress, Apr. 18, 1877. He recommended J. W. Clampett for postmaster of the House of Representatives for his efficient services in the campaign of 1876. "Chicago Times," Apr. 18, 1878.

and excesses, and recovery can only come from economy, industry and frugality. . . . With old fashioned Democracy . . . the financial question will take care of itself, because these political virtues bring national wealth.

While abroad he followed the course of European events with more interest than those at home. Disraeli and his foreign policy won his unqualified praise, and the views expressed by the "London Times" so pleased him that he resolved thereafter to have it always in his home.[164] He returned from Europe broken in health and he was no longer a member of the Democratic national and state committees. Because the Presbyterian Theological Seminary required so much of his time and thought during the last five years of his life, and business problems crowded upon him daily, he was obliged to make some concessions to his advancing age and ill health. He therefore gave up politics—the interest which was the least near to his heart—although he attended the national nominating convention of his party at Cincinnati in 1880 with some hope that he would be the vice-presidential nominee. To the relief of his eldest son, his claims were overlooked.[165] In the same

[164] ‡C. H. McCormick to "Dear Sir" (prob. W. C. Gray) from Paris, March 30, 1879.

[165] "Chicago Times," Apr. 5, 1878: "Cyrus H. McCormick is understood to be a candidate for re-election [to the State Central Committee] but there seems to be a general opinion that he has outlived his usefulness as a party manager, and he will no doubt be placed on the retired list." As early as Dec. 10, 1879, the "Chicago Times" mentioned C. H. McCormick's vice-presidential hopes. ‡C. H. McCormick, Jr., to Nettie F. McCormick, June 19, 1880: "Father leaves tonight for Cincinnati. There has been some talk lately of his being put up for Vice President! He seems not averse to the idea. Mr. Copeland however goes with him and will keep off the sharks. . . . The idea seems to be that Illinois must be carried, hence a Vice President from Chicago! I hope the plan will not go through." ‡C. H. McCormick, Jr., to Nettie F. McCormick, June 28, 1880: Father had a first rate time at Cincinnati and saw many friends. He "spent no money in subscribing to campaign &c . . . is well pleased with Hancock & English &c." Before going to Cincinnati, McCormick had attended the Republican national convention in Chicago and seen Garfield nominated.

year he declined an invitation to serve as the chairman of the executive council of the state central committee.[166]

His interest in politics never flagged.[167] He was much pleased in 1879 when his close friend C. C. Copeland served as manager for Carter Harrison and helped elect the first Democratic mayor that Chicago had had in many years.[168] It was gratifying in the campaign of 1880 to have party giants like Seymour and Tilden come to him for consultation, and to receive letters from Melville Fuller and other new leaders of the party in his state, asking for advice.[169] He attended several of the party's councils of war during this canvass,[170] and Hancock, after his defeat, took pains to send him his impressions of the election. "There is no doubt we would have gotten through safely," wrote the distinguished general, "but for the peculiar results in the cities of New York and Brook-

[166] R. B. Mason, Chicago, to C. H. McCormick, June 30, 1880.

[167] C. H. McCormick to J. G. Priest, St. Louis, Oct. 7, 1879. He thinks that Tilden could not be elected in 1880, and should not be the nominee. "His managers blunder." According to "Chicago Times" of Dec. 9, 1879, McCormick had just been informed by Tilden that he was ready to be the presidential nominee of the Democratic Party in 1880, "if the people wanted him." By June, 1880, McCormick declared that he favored Tilden, if his views were accurately set forth in the "Daily Inter Ocean," of June 12, 1880.

[168] C. C. Copeland to C. H. McCormick, March 28, Apr. 5, 1879: The campaign cost us only about $3,000. "The main object [of Harrison] will be to strengthen the party and retain the control of the city." An ominous feature of this election was that the Socialists polled 12,000 votes, but in the November election their strength fell to 4,000.

[169] M. W. Fuller, Chicago, to C. H. McCormick, Sept. 7, Oct. 20, 30, 1880. S. M. Moore, Chicago, to C. H. McCormick, Oct. 9, Nov. 4, 1880. C. H. McCormick to S. J. Tilden, June 12, 1880. W. H. Barnum, Chairman of Nat. Dem. Comm., to C. H. McCormick, Sept. 3, 30, 1880. C. H. McCormick's $10,000 contribution in this campaign was used to help the Democrats in Indiana and Ohio. "We only wish we had more like you in our party and success would be assured." W. S. Scott to C. H. McCormick, Oct. 5, 1880. "Chicago Times," Oct. 10 and 17, 1880.

[170] R. A. Pryor, to C. H. McCormick, Oct. 2, 1880. C. H. McCormick was a member of the "Campaign Finance Committee" appointed by the Democratic national committee.

lyn. . . . I never felt in better spirits than I have since the election. Although I hoped for success; yet when unsuccessful, I felt as if a great load of responsibility and care had been lifted from my shoulders." [171] C. H. McCormick, Jr., who had reached his majority in May of that year, received a telegram from his father on the eve of election, cautioning him not to forget to vote.[172] Shortly, thereafter, Poultney Bigelow persuaded both father and son to join the Free Trade Club of New York.[173]

Occasional mention of long conversations with Roger Pryor on political subjects and the record of contributions sent to help the Democratic cause in Virginia are the only glimpses afforded of McCormick's interest in politics between 1881 and 1883.[174] Although he was an unswerving Democrat at all times, he gave $100 to help erect a building at Richfield Springs for a Republican state convention,[175] and employed

[171] W. S. Hancock from New York to C. H. McCormick, Nov. 28, 1880. ‡L.P.C.B., Nov. 5, 1880-May 9, 1881, pp. 20-21, C. H. McCormick to W. S. Hancock, Nov. 19, 1880: Once more we have been "cheated out of our election." You would have been President "could the fair vote of the people of New York . . . have been obtained."

[172] C. H. McCormick's telegram to C. H. McCormick, Jr., from New York, Nov. 1, 1880. ‡C. H. McCormick, Jr., to Nettie F. McCormick, Nov. 1, 1880: "I smiled audibly at Father's telegram 'be sure & vote'! . . . We shall try & carry this county by at least *one* vote! . . . I felt as big as a Thanksgiving turkey when I went to register!"

[173] P. Bigelow to C. H. McCormick, Jan. 16, 1882, and to C. H. McCormick, Jr., ‡March 2, 1882.

[174] C. H. McCormick draped his house at Richfield Springs in black on the death of President Garfield, and Mrs. C. H. McCormick advised her son to do the same to their Chicago home. Cyrus, Jr., MSS. Book "B," Nettie F. to C. H. McCormick, Jr., Sept. 21, 1881: "Oh, why should a life so grand be cut off in darkness by a life so mean and low as that of the assassin?" R. A. Pryor to C. H. McCormick, Oct. 19, 1880. ‡C. H. McCormick to R. Pryor, Nov. 11, 1881. C. H. McCormick to H. Shepperd, Alexandria, Va., Oct. 27, 1883. C. H. McCormick sends $500 for campaign expenses. ‡H. Shepperd, Alexandria, Va., to C. H. McCormick, Oct. 15, 1883.

[175] ‡Check stubs, Importers' & Traders' Bank, check of Sept. 17, 1883.

Roscoe Conkling as one of his counsel.[176] In the early spring of 1884, he wrote twice to Tilden urging him for the sake of his country and his party to stand for the presidential nomination in the approaching campaign.[177] He believed that Senator Joseph E. McDonald of Indiana should be the vice-presidential candidate. In the interest of this idea, he entertained in his home on the evening of April 4, 1884, McDonald and eight leaders of the Democratic Party in Chicago. All of his guests favored his proposal except the senator. He was not unwilling, but did not wish to come out for the nomination in advance of the convention, for fear of alienating Hendricks of his own state. Following this dinner, McCormick wrote to Tilden, telling him that "all felt that no other name could draw so many Democratic votes as yours," and requesting him to permit the launching of a boom for a Tilden-McDonald ticket.[178] The New York statesman had already informed McCormick that he did not wish "to deprive" himself of his "home comforts," although he had not positively stated that he would not accept the nomination if offered. His reply to McCormick's second letter is lost, but most probably it was unfavorable since no further step was taken by the inventor in the matter except to urge his eldest son to call on Tilden when he was in New York in late April.[179]

It was quite fitting that McCormick, when seventy-five years of age, should close his political activities by advising a man who had just reached seventy that his candidacy was necessary for the country's good. Grover Cleveland, who would be President before another April had come, never appeared above McCormick's horizon. The inventor was a conservative

[176] *Post,* p. 758.
[177] C. H. McCormick to S. J. Tilden, March 27, 1884.
[178] *Idem* to *idem,* Apr. 5, 1884.
[179] Telegram of C. H. McCormick to C. H. McCormick, Jr., Apr. 30, 1884. Entry of May 1, 1884, in MSS. diary of C. H. McCormick, Jr., "Saw S. J. Tilden—said would not run for Pres.—seems very feeble."

to the last, clinging to the belief that the elder statesmen alone could save the nation. The inward satisfaction of espousing certain principles that were dear to him, and the friendship of men whose names, like his own, were household words, were his only rewards for twenty-five years of service to the Democratic Party.[180]

[180] In each presidential year from 1868 to the end of his life he gave $10,000 to advance the cause, as well as other smaller sums to the Democrats of his own state and Virginia.

CHAPTER X

MOWER AND SELF-RAKE RIVALRIES, 1856-1879

CYRUS McCORMICK'S fame as an inventor rests upon his patents of 1834, 1845, and 1847. Wherever he traveled during the last thirty years of his life, people came to congratulate him for lessening the toil of the annual harvest season. At the Centennial Exposition of 1876, visitors were more eager to see him than to examine the machines displayed there by his company. His title of "inventor" was richly merited, but those who thought of him in terms of self-rake reapers, harvesters and automatic binders, forgot that although many of these machines bore his name, they were not the product of his inventive skill. Their success, to be sure, depended upon the utilization of the basic mechanical elements first successfully combined in one machine by him, but the distinctive devices which set them apart as an advance over the hand-rake reaper of 1850 were first fashioned by other men. Occasional trips to the field after 1855 to watch an experimental machine in operation, and a letter now and again to his brothers suggesting methods whereby mechanical difficulties might be overcome, are evidences of his continued interest in this aspect of his business, but his days as an inventor closed with his patent of 1847.

To explain this change of emphasis in the life of Cyrus McCormick by writing that his talent for invention disappeared with his youth, is hardly convincing. In the late 1850's, and thereafter, the general oversight of his rapidly expanding plant, the need to be ever on the alert to meet the sharp challenges of more and more competitors, and the responsibilities arising from the management of an increasing fortune, absorbed most of his attention and gradually widened the gap which separated him from the harvest field and the machine shops of his factory. Chicago grew apace, and the line between city and country-side became more and more distinct. Of necessity, McCormick had to make his choice, and every circumstance constrained him to turn the last thirty years of his life about an urban focus. Doubtless, he did not sense the alternative thus presented to him, but after 1855 he most frequently saw the farmer from the window of a railroad car, or from his carriage on an afternoon's drive from his summer-home. News from the grain fields now reached him indirectly through the office of his factory, whence clerks forwarded generalizations made after a study of the minutiæ contained in the monthly or weekly reports of the many agents. His subordinates endeavored to spare him the annoyance of petty problems, and the worthwhile suggestions from farmers or salesmen for the improvement of the reaper were shunted, as a rule, to the superintendent of construction at the factory, and rarely came to the immediate attention of the master who had founded the business.

Although real loss resulted from thus breaking his direct contact with the daily routine of farm and factory, a proper perspective for the wise conduct of a large enterprise could be gained only from a position of considerable isolation. That McCormick, manufacturer and capitalist, tended to crowd out McCormick the inventor, accorded well with the trend of the times. Although the momentum of a society becoming increasingly industrialized depended in large degree upon the progress of invention, the post-war generation of inventors, with a few conspicuous exceptions, were eclipsed by the business giants who exploited the new devices chiefly for their own profit. The remarkable increase in the annual number of patents granted by the United States government between 1855 and 1885 was both a cause and an effect of the Industrial Revolution, but it also suggests that both inventions and inventors paid the penalty of the commonplace.

The laboratory of the inventor of harvesting implements moved from the workshop of the farm to the machine-shop of the factory. Invention became the tool, and the inventor the employee of the manufacturer. Doubtless mechanical skill was still assisted by inspiration, but to cage a genius within the brick walls of a factory stripped invention of much of its romance. Invention was now a business, and ingenious mechanics were as customary a segment of a big manufacturer's laboring force, as were his moulders and salesmen.

The pressure of competition, translated into a crisp order from the office of the superintendent to the expert at the works, was the chief stimulus to invention. After the battle-smoke of each hectic harvest season had blown away, there often stood revealed some machine which had found favor with the farmer in spite of the ridicule and high-pressure salesmanship of its rivals. Common prudence at once dictated that invention should go forward at the factory under forced draft so that an improved implement for next year would compel last summer's "favorite" to retire from the field in shame.

To help toward this end as speedily as possible, McCormick's agent, acting incognito, would purchase and ship to Chicago one of the machines which had been so successful in the harvest just closed.[1] The inventors at the factory then

---

[1] L.P.C.B. No. 145, p. 124. W. J. Hanna to E. C. Beardsley, Aurora, Ill., Sept. 1, 1873: "You might ship it [a Marsh Harvester] to your own name here, and then come to Chicago to get it at RRd depot. We don't at present want our name known in it." *Minneapolis Harvester Works vs. McCormick Harvesting Machine Company, Defendant's Record, United States Circuit Court, District of Minnesota* (1890), pp. 120, 127, testimony of Dr. Edwin D. Bishop: "All machine manufacturers have a code of

Men of Progress—American Inventors

From an engraving by John Sartain of a painting by Christian Schussele, 1861

Left to right: Dr. Morton, anaesthetics; Bogardus, iron architecture; Colt, revolvers; McCormick, reapers; Saxton, mint and coin machines; Goodyear, vulcanizing gum elastic; Cooper, gelatine; Mott, works on iron, fuel, etc.; Prof. Henry, electric motor; Dr. Nott, management of heat; Ericsson, caloric engine; Sickles, steam cut-off; Morse, telegraph; Burden, horse-shoe machine; Hoe, rotary press; Bigelow, carpet loom; Jennings, friction matches; Blanchard, eccentric lathe; Howe, sewing machine. (Reproduced by courtesy of the *Scientific American*, New York.)

studied it carefully for the purpose of discovering a way whereby the implements in their charge might attain a similar perfection of operation, without making their employer liable to a suit for an infringement of patent-rights. If this could be done, the law still required that the patent should be granted to the expert who had made the invention—but he immediately thereafter assigned all of his interest in the monopoly to his employer. Thereupon, the latter gave him a new problem to master, and the process was repeated. In this fashion the inventor of machinery was himself mechanized. The patrons of this Renaissance overshadowed the artists.

Invention of harvesting implements was not confined altogether to the machine-shop of the industrialist between 1855 and 1885. In fact, the half-dozen most significant of the hundreds of patents for improvements in self-raking reapers, harvesters, and binders during these years were granted to farmers or to small-town mechanics. Nevertheless, the control of these inventions tended quickly to gravitate to the big manufacturers. They, alone, had the capital to exploit a new mechanism. Their scouts, or "patent experts," searched the country-side for valuable devices. These might often be secured for a very small sum.

This increasing tempo of invention in some degree reflected the insistent demand of the farmer for machinery whereby he might harvest larger crops at less cost, but it more truly

morals of their own. Anything is public property that they can see anywhere, and one manufacturer does not differ from another in that respect, so far as my experience goes. . . . If they can discover an invention, that another one is bringing out, they take pains to examine it, and look it over." A patent was sometimes purchased through an obscure person, who then assigned it to the company. In this way a lower price was paid, and unknown to its rivals, a company had valuable monopolies "up its sleeve" to use effectively at the proper moment. L.P.C.B. No. 171, p. 150, the Co. to Baldwin, Hopkins, & Peyton, March 23, 1877. If a company wished the services of an inventor working for another firm, the letter to him was mailed in a plain envelop, not bearing the sender's name.

represented a widening of the industrial battle line. Without question, the number of patents bore a direct relationship to the perfection of the implement, but they were sought the more eagerly because they were effective weapons to embarrass a competitor by assessing him with heavy damages for infringement. The manufacturer who controlled an essential device could oblige a rival to pay large royalties, could nip small producers in the bud, and could withhold an improvement from the market until he had sold out his old stock of implements or was prepared to make the costly alterations in factory equipment which were, oftentimes, a necessary preliminary to the building of new-style machines.

A lawsuit was also an excellent method of advertising. Newspapers gave it free publicity, and its course and probable results were "played up to the limit" in the pamphlets, posters, and handbills of the parties to the action. The peak of the selling season was the usual time to seek a court injunction against a rival, for the complainant company could then warn farmers that if they used the offending machine, they would also be liable for damages.[2] The advertisements, the rodomontade of agents, and the field contests at county and state fairs, leave the impression that the makers of reapers and mowers were ever at one another's throats. Without doubt they usually were, but the most bitter phase of the conflict— the struggle for a strategic patent position—was almost entirely fought behind a curtain which the public could rarely penetrate. In fact, two firms, engaged in war without stint in a sales territory, might be working in close agreement in patent purchasing or in opposition to a third manufacturer who menaced the safety of both.

Under these circumstances, invention could well be left to subordinates, but the acquisition and wise use of patents were

---

[2] L.P.C.B. No. 224, p. 328, telegram of the Co. to C. Colahan, St. Paul, Minn., June 1, 1882.

vital to the success of the firm. For this reason also, Cyrus McCormick devoted more and more of his attention during the last thirty years of his life to this most intricate aspect of his business. The profits or losses to be anticipated from lawsuits, royalties, and shop rights, were reckoned by the hundreds of thousands of dollars, and in some years equaled in amount the proceeds derived from the sale of machines.

The exceptionally liberal patent laws of the United States permitting an inventor to secure a monopoly for fourteen years (and perhaps a renewal for an additional seven years) on a device differing in no fundamental respect from another already patented, stimulated invention, but they also led to a veritable labyrinth of patents on harvesting machinery, wherein even the best of lawyers frequently lost their way. The resulting crop of "interferences" and lawsuits was naturally very large. The retainers and counsel fees charged by the dozen or so outstanding patent attorneys of the country were in proportion to the unremitting efforts made by as many major manufacturers of harvesting machinery to secure their services. It was a quiet year when the McCormicks, the Deerings, or Walter A. Wood were not parties to three or four lawsuits of the first importance.

Even though good fortune secured the aid of redoubtable Peter H. Watson,[3] George Harding, Edward N. Dickerson, or Moses Keller, the factor of chance in litigation was still a very considerable one.[4] Politics, the patent-maze, the peculiar

[3] Peter H. Watson's clerk in 1860 was Henry Baldwin, Jr., who with his brother, William D., soon became McCormick's chief attorneys.

[4] C. H. McCormick to H. Day, Dec. 31, 1874. C. H. McCormick to C. A. Spring, Jr., Nov. 30, 1868: "*Now* is the time to do all at Washington, The present Commr. of Patents is I think *honest*—used to be friendly with me, and I may have to go to Washington. *Judge Foot[e]*. Well that these *extensions* are before him. He will be removed after Mch. next, I look for! So *hurry up!*" ‡C. H. McCormick to Hon. Mr. Goode, March 24, 1876: "Since I have never had a patent extended, I do not think it is just that a competitor should be granted an extension of a patent covering an im-

temper of a judge, and the meager knowledge possessed by Patent Office officials who too often owed their positions to party preference, made this branch of the business even more speculative than the sale of machines, so dependent upon "Acts of God" as manifested in the weather and the ravages of insects.

One who seeks to trace the rise of the harvesting-machinery industry in the United States must discuss at some length the never-ending patent war of the years following 1855. The complexity of the subject warns the student to avoid it or to dismiss it with a few words, but by doing so, one of the prime reasons why a few manufacturers dominated the field before the close of the century would be unduly subordinated. From the standpoints of money involved, energy and time expended, interests at stake, and results for the future, this phase of the history of the business is second in importance to none. Although to simplify the story is to distort it, to follow all of its ramifications renders it unintelligible.

By 1858, the three basic patents of Cyrus McCormick either had expired or were about to do so. He was then engaged in a long and fruitless endeavor to secure their extensions from the Patent Office or from Congress. Suits brought by him at this time against his several chief rivals for infringement were, in the main, unsuccessful. As late as 1865, he was still trying to collect royalties for infringement of his reissued patent of 1847, which had lapsed four years before. His stand on the war issues, his active share in the councils of the discredited Democratic Party, and his absence in Europe between 1862 and 1864, made it unlikely that he could gain either favorable judgments in actions before the courts, or a revival of his

provement of my own invention." Occasionally, a firm paid an able lawyer "a shelving retainer." Although it might not wish to use his services, it could by this means prevent his employment in any case in which it was the defendant. Coburn & Thatcher, Chicago, to the Co., Jan. 5, 1878.

patents by acts of Congress.[5] For these reasons, among others, the first chapter in the history of harvesting-machinery patents properly closes with the opening of the Civil War. The expiration of McCormick's monopolies, the emergence of the country from a period of economic hard times, and the stimulus given to sales by the war, brought many new firms into the field, and shifted the patent battle-front from the hand-rake reaper to the self-rake machine.

During the next twenty-five years, rivalry in the harvest field, patent office, and court-room chiefly revolved about four implements: the mower, the self-rake reaper, and its two successors, the harvester and harvester-binder. Certain patents covered devices common to all of these machines, but for the sake of clarity, the main lines of the controversy involving each, will be separately treated.

For thirty years prior to 1860, inventors and manufacturers endeavored to develop a machine which would cut both grain and grass with equal ease. In spite of the extravagant claims made in the advertisements of the time, it had been impossible to fashion a blade which would perform this dual task to perfection. One knife-bar for mowing and another for reaping became the rule, although it was inconvenient to make the substitution during the rush of harvest. The sickle needed to vibrate more rapidly in cutting grass than in reaping grain, but this acceleration could not be obtained when a single machine was used for both services. During the 1850's the demand for a separate grass-cutter became more and more insistent, particularly in the many districts which were turning from

[5] ‡H. Baldwin, Jr., to C. H. McCormick, Aug. 7, Oct. 14 and Dec. 23, 1865. L.P.C.B. No. 48, p. 304, C. H. McCormick to H. Baldwin, May 2, 1862. His patent of 1847 was reissued as ten separate patents in 1859. The "Press and Tribune," Sept. 23, 1859. For the close relationship between politics and C. H. McCormick's unsuccessful efforts to have his patents of 1845 and 1847 extended, see, "Chicago Daily Tribune," Feb. 4, 7, 11, 12, 14, 1861.

grain to hay. and stock-raising. A fortune awaited the manufacturer who could develop an inexpensive, light, and efficient
mower.[6]

It is not without significance that the first single mowers
to satisfy a large demand were the inventions of men of New
York State, where so much emphasis was placed upon the
hay crop. Here, in the 1850's, the machines made under the
patents of Rufus Dutton,[7] Eliakim B. Forbush,[8] S. S. and
R. L. Allen,[9] W. A. Kirby,[10] William F. Ketchum,[11] or Moses

[6] L.P.C.B. No. 84, p. 137, McCormick Co. to S. Durpee, Malta, Ill., Sept.
11, 1865. By the 1870's, however, through the use of "interchangeable pinions," the knife could be vibrated with either a fast or a slow motion. See,
"Catalog" of the McCormick Harvesting Manufacturing Co. for 1880.

[7] Dutton manufactured his Clipper Mower at Yonkers from 1854 to at
least 1874. Two of his licensees were Horton & Mabie of Peekskill, N. Y.,
and R. L. Allen of Brooklyn. Dutton was sued by the Hinged-Bar Pool
and forced to take a license from it in 1872. See, *Before the Commissioner
of Patents, In the matter of the Application for an Extension of Robert T.
Osgood's Patents, dated February 17, 1852, as reissued December 24,
1861, Opponents' Brief and Points* (Philadelphia, 1866), pp. 4 ff. *Cyrenus
Wheeler, Jr. vs. The Clipper Mower and Reaper Company, Circ. Ct. of
U. S. in and for the Southern District of New York. In Equity,* (N. Y.,
1869), *passim.*

[8] After receiving his patent of July 20, 1852 (reissued in 1859), Forbush
formed E. B. Forbush & Co. at Buffalo. Several misadventures, including a
costly infringement suit won by R. L. Howard & Co., maker of Ketchum's
mower in Buffalo, forced the Forbush firm to reorganize as the American
Mowing and Reaping Machine Co. of Buffalo in early 1854. It failed after
two harvests. Eventually the Forbush patents came into the possession of
J. P. Adriance and C. Wheeler, Jr., and were placed in the Hinged-Bar
Pool. Love of Beloit made 50 Forbush machines in 1854 and J. P. Adriance
also manufactured a few between 1855 and 1857.

[9] Allen's patent mower was chiefly made in New York City.

[10] The chief manufacturers of the Kirby mower were the Buffalo Agricultural Machine Works (G. L. Squier), and D. M. Osborne & Co. of
Auburn, N. Y. Kirby's patent was dated 1856, and Squier made 2,000 of
his mowers between 1857 and 1860 (inc.). Apparently Osborne was manufacturing Kirby mowers as late as 1872 for in that year he settled with
the Hinged-Bar Pool for infringing certain of its patents in making these
machines.

[11] Ketchum, due to financial troubles, was forced to sell his patent to
R. L. Howard & Co. in 1849. This firm for a time was the chief manu-

G. Hubbard enjoyed a large sale until the inventions of Cyrenus Wheeler, Jr., of Poplar Ridge, New York, and Lewis F. Miller of Canton, Ohio, swept all before them. These two-wheeled implements, brought forward by men who for long were to speak with authority in the world of harvesting machinery, not only worked well, but offered the great additional advantage of a hinged, "floating," and "rocking" cutter-bar. This jointed beam, when combined with a mechanism whereby the points of the fingers could be raised or lowered by the operator, was one of the most significant developments in the evolution of the modern mowing machine. With it, the driver could ungear the knife at will, and either raise the mowing arm by a lever to a position perpendicular to the ground, or "fold it up" entirely in front of the wheels. Much less space was needed to store it under cover, and stones on the highway could not break off its knife sections as it was drawn to or from the field. If the horses became frightened, the operator had little fear of being thrown in the path of the moving knife.[12] This danger was also greatly reduced by the development of a front-cut machine with its mowing-bar extending

facturer of his machine, and was said to have made 20,000 through 1861. The Patent Office refused to extend his patent in 1861, C. H. McCormick being one of those who opposed its extension. Besides Howard & Co., other important manufacturers of Ketchum mowers in the 1850's were Ruggles, Nourse & Mason of Boston, Seymour & Morgan of Brockport, N. Y., Warder & Brokaw of Springfield, O., J. M. Champlin of Cleveland, and Hall of Poughkeepsie. Letters of McCormick agents to their employer are filled with references to Ketchum's competition. Ebenezer Danford's mower, made by the inventor at Geneva, Ill., Beard & Sinex at Richmond, Ind., F. S. Boas, Reading, Pa., and in the Genesee Valley, N. Y., also enjoyed a considerable sale until the failure of the home company in 1857.

12 J. M. Thacher to Elisha Foote, Commr. of Patents, Nov. 28, 1868. *In Circuit Court of the United States, in and for the Northern District of Illinois, Cyrenus Wheeler, Jr., vs. Cyrus H. McCormick and Leander J. McCormick. In Equity* (No date or place of publication shown), pp. 783-786, evidence was offered to prove that Wheeler had made his first hinged-bar machine in 1853. L. F. Miller, the father-in-law of T. A. Edison, was one of the originators of the Chautauqua movement.

to the side on a line ahead of the position of the wheel and the driver's seat. But "front-cut," when compared with "rear-cut" mowers, had certain disadvantages which prevented their extensive use for some years.[13]

During his early business career Cyrenus Wheeler, an astute Yankee who in his youth had moved to Poplar Ridge, was an inventor and a promoter rather than a manufacturer. In 1854 'he was granted the first of seventeen patents for devices of his own invention, and when to these are added the sixty-seven others which he purchased during the next dozen years, it is small wonder that he was soon known as the "patent king." [14] In late 1859 he formed the Wheeler Association, comprising himself, one Henry Morgan, a firm of machinists, and two mower concerns—Ross, Dodge & Pomeroy and Sheldon & Company of Auburn, New York. To these he allotted a four-fifths interest in his several monopolies. Through this organization he proposed to prosecute infringers and to make and sell "Cayuga Chief" machines.[15]

[13] Of the 21 mowers exhibited at the 1876 Centennial, 15 were front-cut and six were rear-cut. *U. S. Circ. Ct. N. Dist. of N. Y. In Equity, W. Sprague & J. R. Parsons vs. J. P. Adriance & S. R. and I. S. Platt, Defendants' Record* (N. Y., 1874), pp. 605-614. One alleged advantage of a rear-cut machine was that it required less power, since the point of cutting and the point of delivery were brought closer together.

[14] On Wheeler's patents see, *United States Patent Office. In the Matter of the Application of Cyrenus Wheeler, Jr. For the Extension of the Reissues of his Harvester Patents of December 5, 1854, and February 6, 1855. Opponents' Brief and Points* (Washington, 1868), pp. 15-16; "Farm Implement News" (Chicago), May, 1888, pp. 16 ff. and July, 1888, pt. 2, p. 15.

[15] The firm of Sheldon & Co. (or Barber, Sheldon & Co.) was known as Burtis & Beardsley between 1864 and 1866 and thereafter as the Cayuga Chief Manufacturing Co., with Wheeler as its president. In 1874 it consolidated with D. M. Osborne & Co., also of Auburn. Eight years later, Wheeler sold out his interest and retired. On July 8, 1868, he had resecured complete control of his patents from the defunct Association. *Opponents' Brief, Wheeler Extension Case,* pp. 21, 36, ff. *Sprague & Parsons vs. Adriance & Platt,* pp. 371, 600. For a time, Ross, Dodge &

The identification of Canton, Ohio, with the manufacture of agricultural machinery, dates from 1849. At that time Cornelius Aultman, only twenty-two years of age, began to build threshers and Hussey reapers there.[16] His annual output was at first very small, but it was the beginning of a notable enterprise. Ephraim Ball, a reaper-maker of Greentown, Ohio, his helper, Lewis F. Miller, James A. Saxton and others, joined Aultman in 1852 to form Ball, Aultman & Co. In 1854 Ball perfected an excellent rear-cut mower, and the firm marketed this machine with success during the next two harvests.[17] Undiscouraged by a costly fire in 1855 and a judgment by a court against it in favor of Jonathan Haines, who for long manufactured headers at Pekin, Illinois, the company rebuilt its factory and bought a shop right from Haines in the patent which it had infringed.[18] In 1856, Miller made the first of the famous two-wheeled, front-cut, "Buckeye" mowers, and the firm decided to concentrate upon their production.[19] Shortly thereafter, Ephraim Ball, who together with Saxton and several others controlled a number of valuable mower patents, withdrew from the enterprise, and until his death about fifteen

Pomeroy made Ball's Mower. See, "The Cultivator" (Albany, N. Y.), Sept., 1861. Although Obed Hussey is scarcely mentioned in this discussion, it should be remembered that his work was basic. As long as his patents on the knife and finger-guard were in force, virtually every manufacturer of reapers and mowers was obliged to pay a royalty to his heirs. "Hutchinson," I, pp. 163-164, 449-542.

[16] *Record in Hussey vs. Whiteley, et als., U. S. Circuit Court, Southern District of Ohio,* (1860-1861).

[17] "Ohio Cultivator" (Columbus, O.), Apr. 15, 1856, p. 128; July 15, 1856, p. 216; Aug. 1, 1856, p. 232, Oct. 15, 1856, p. 307; Nov. 15, 1856, p. 344. E. Laizure, Cadiz, O., to C. H. McCormick, Aug. 25, 1856; G. Young, Hamilton, O., to C. H. McCormick, July 8, 1857.

[18] *Sprague & Parsons vs. Adriance & Platt,* pp. 380-391, 421 ff, testimony of C. Aultman. Haines, either alone or in partnership with I. A. Hawley, manufactured at Pekin until his death in 1868.

[19] "The Cultivator," May, 1859, p. 164; "American Farmer" (Baltimore), Feb., 1858, p. 269; J. T. Griffin from Massillon and Orrville, O., to C. H. McCormick, July 21 and Aug. 6, 1858.

years later manufactured his own "Ohio Mower" and "New American Harvester" in a separate plant at Canton.[20]

Aultman and Miller enjoyed instant success with their "Buckeye" mower. They shrewdly began to buy up patents and to license or sell shop rights to other manufacturers who anticipated large profits from making this machine.[21] One of their earliest and most important licensees was John P. Adriance (Adriance, Platt & Co.) of Poughkeepsie, New York, who heretofore had been building J. H. Manny reaper-mowers and Forbush mowers for the New England trade at his Worcester factory. For almost fifty years Adriance was a prominent figure in harvesting-machinery circles. Fortunately for his future, he purchased several valuable mower patents in the late 1850's, and was thus enabled to bargain with those who insisted that he was infringing their monopolies.[22]

Thus, by 1860, Wheeler and Adriance in New York, and Ball, Aultman, Miller and their associates in Ohio, controlled

[20] "Michigan Farmer" (Detroit), June 23, 1860, p. 193; L.P.C.B. No. 31, p. 211, the Co. to W. C. Leyburn, Galesburg, Ill., Apr. (?), 1860; "The Cultivator," Dec., 1862, p. 377. ‡Aultman Steel Co. to C. H. McCormick & Co., from Canton, O., Oct. 20, 1871.

[21] U. S. Senate, 45th Congress, 2nd Sess., *Misc. Doc. No. 50* (Washington, 1878). Between 1857 and 1865 (both inclusive) the "Buckeye" works, or its licensees, built 24,000 machines. By 1861, C. Aultman & Co. owned 34 patents, embracing over 50 claims. Perhaps the most important of these, besides those covering their own inventions, was the hinged-bar patent of Sylla and Adams, 1853, purchased in Apr. 1858. This was extended in 1867.

[22] Adriance took a "Buckeye" license in Oct. 1857. He began to manufacture at Worcester, Mass., in 1855. *Sprague & Parsons vs. Adriance & Platt,* pp. 350-351, 660-667; "Ohio Cultivator," July 1, 1855, p. 198; "Genesee Farmer" (Rochester, N. Y.), June, 1860, p. 194; Adriance, Platt & Co. "Catalogs" for 1896 and 1900. At the close of the century this company bought out D. S. Morgan & Co. of Brockport, N. Y. It is interesting to note that for over forty years, Adriance's factory superintendent was Thomas S. Brown, whose father, Thomas, a smith and founder of Alnwick, England, invented with Henry Ogle, a reaper of significant construction about 1820. See, an unsigned pamphlet, "Light from the Past" (Poughkeepsie, 1901); T. S. Brown to McCormick Harvesting Machine Co., Oct. 3, 1905; "Hutchinson," I, pp. 63-64.

a score or more of mower patents. In short, the "Buckeye" and "Cayuga Chief" interests dominated the mower trade of the country, but because their patent claims overlapped, the stage was set for a series of expensive suits for infringement which in all probability would dwarf any heretofore known in the history of the industry. Under these circumstances, on January 27, 1860, many of the Aultman-Miller, Wheeler and Adriance patents were pooled, and a definite sales territory for each firm was designated. More patents were to be purchased and the types of machines to be manufactured by each associate were standardized. Ball and his colleague, J. A. Saxton, forced their way into the "Ring" two years later.

This combination assumed that their patents covered all essential features of every two-wheeled, flexible-bar mower made in the United States, as well as many devices commonly employed in one-wheel machines. Therefore, any manufacturer who had the temerity to make these implements would be compelled by suit, or by a threat of suit, to pay tribute to the pool, varying from $7.50 to $10 a machine.[23] Although the licensees of Wheeler were then producing only one-eighth as many machines annually as were the "Buckeye" manufacturers, his patents were so numerous and so important that his association was allotted one-third of the profits of the pool. Up to 1868, the members of the pool built over 120,000 machines and received more than $530,000 in license fees from twenty-five or more manufacturers.[24] William Allen, the at-

[23] *Osgood Extension Case.* Here will be found listed the various patents merged in the pool. *Opponents' Brief, Wheeler Extension Case,* pp. 6, 27 ff., 44, 56-57; *Wheeler vs. McCormicks,* pp. 832-838. For the pool agreement itself, see, *Aultman vs. Holley and Fittz,* op. cit., pp. 83-90, 94-96.

[24] *United States Patent Office. Sylla and Adams Extensions. Patent Dated September 20, 1853. Part II, Opponents' Proof* (Philadelphia, 1867), p. 80. Some of the licensees of the Hinged-Bar Pool were F. W. Parmenter, Troy; M. Hallenbeck, Albany; R. Dutton, Yonkers, F. Nishwitz, Brooklyn, Kniffen Mowing Machine Co. (made about 4,000 mowers 1861-65), Worcester, Mass., Chapman, Donnelly & Co., Lima, O., Reynolds & Co., Aurora,

torney for the pool, was ever on the alert to sue unsubmissive firms.[25] The "Ring," however, insisted that it worked to the benefit of both the manufacturer and the farmer, since the one was guaranteed against prosecution if he took a license, and the other was told that by this interlocking of patents, better mowers than ever before were being made for his use.[26] Probably a more realistic view would emphasize that protection for themselves and the plunder of all others were the chief objectives.

Although the combination was profitable, its ten years of life were filled with discord. All of the patents owned by the several members of the pool had not been merged, and for this reason each associate continue to grant licenses under his reserved monopolies. Since some of these apparently covered features which were also embraced by the pool patents, there was a deal of bickering among the confederates and uncertainty on the part of the licensees. To add to the confusion, there were many "outsiders" who believed that Miller and Wheeler were not the first to invent a hinged-bar machine. As early as the late 1830's, in their opinion, Abram Randall of Oneida, New York, and Hazard Knowles of Washington, D. C., had employed this device in their unsuccessful reapers. Although Knowles had been prevented from securing a patent because he was an employee of the Patent Office, his implement in altered form, and Randall's also, were still in exist-

N. Y., Nixon & Co., Alliance, O., Woodman & Burnham, Biddeford, Me., C. J. Shuttleworth, Springville, N. Y., Walter A. Wood & Co., and Barber, Sheldon & Co., of Auburn, N. Y. See, *Osgood Extension Case,* pp. 4 ff., and C. Wheeler, Jr., to C. H. McCormick, Oct. 31, Dec. 2 and 12, 1864. For the sums collected annually by this pool between 1862 and 1868 (both inc.) see *Opponents' Brief, Wheeler Extension Case,* pp. 36 ff. These range from $6,463 in 1862 to $138,517.02 in 1865.

[25] *Aultman vs. Holley and Fitts,* pp. 614-615, 835 ff. lists some of the suits launched by the pool against infringers.

[26] Printed Circular of the Hinged-Bar Pool, 1866.

ence.[27] The Randall patent came into the possession of Walter A. Wood of Hoosick Falls, New York, and thanks largely to it, he was able to make a mutual licensing agreement with the pool in 1862.[28]

Perhaps Moses G. Hubbard of Syracuse, New York, was the most untiring in his efforts to break the strangle hold of the pool. With a dozen sub-manufacturers in 1862 paying him royalties under his several valuable mower patents, he seemed destined eventually to wield as much power in harvesting-machine circles as Wheeler. He bought what purported to be the old Knowles machine and borrowed the use of the Randall reaper, and they were seen in many court rooms during the early years of the Civil War.[29] Hubbard, with too

[27] *Sylla and Adams Extension Case, Opponents' Proofs*, Part II, pp. 4, 13. *United States Patent Office. In the Matter of the Application for the Extension of the Reissues of the Patents of J. E. Brown and S. S. Bartlett, for Grain and Grass Harvesters of January 2, 1855. Testimony* (Washington, 1868), pp. 86-87, 107. Among the early inventors challenging the pool's right to claim the hinged-bar, was S. S. Bartlett (d. 1868) of Woonsocket, Rhode Island, who was financed by J. E. Brown (d. 1865), a tailor. They began experimenting with hinged-bar machines in 1849. Their patents, however, were eventually sold to the Saxton-Ball interest, and merged in the Hinged-Bar Pool. See, M. S. Stetson, Salem, Ohio, to C. H. & L. J. McCormick, Dec. 15, 1864. Note also, the Sylla and Adams hinged-bar patent of 1853, already mentioned (*supra*, ftn. 21). At a later date, W. Gage of Buffalo claimed that he invented in 1850 the first "Buckeye" for J. P. Adriance. ‡C. Colahan to C. H. McCormick, July 2 and Nov. 27, 1874; Mch. 10, 1875.

[28] *Sylla and Adams Extension, Opponents' Proofs*, Part II, pp. 44, 46, 53, 60, 91-97.

[29] *Aultman vs. Holley and Fittz*, pp. 513 ff., 769. *Sylla and Adams Extension Case, Opponents' Proofs*, Part II, pp. 4, 13, 40-41, 74-75. *Wheeler vs. McCormicks*, pp. 401-402; 683-86, 700-01, 716. Hubbard was interested in mowers as early as 1853. Some of his sub-manufacturers were Silliman Bros. & Co. of Brockport, N. Y., Hallenbeck & Cunningham, Albany, N. Y., and Bradley & Bradley of Syracuse, N. Y. On the early history of the Randall and Knowles machines, see, "Hutchinson," I, pp. 155, 157. Although Hubbard had bought the Knowles machine, Knowles in 1867 assigned all of his rights in his unpatented invention to Frederick Nishwitz

much self-confidence, failed to follow the prudent example of the pool, of paying royalty to the Hussey heirs for the use of their open-back guard-finger. Consequently they brought him to heel in 1863. Early in the same year, however, he made a very favorable arrangement with the Hinged-Bar Pool, whereby he was permitted to sub-license others under its patents.[30] Thereupon, the Knowles and Randall reapers, which might well prove embarrassing to the "Ring," were opportunely "lost." [31]

When Cyrus McCormick returned from Europe in 1864, he at once learned that the mower question was among the chief business problems demanding his immediate attention. For six years his agents had complained of their inability to make headway against the "Buckeye" competition in the Middle West, and obviously the time was ripe for the Chicago partners to build a two-wheeled, hinged-bar mower of their own. The old style, one-wheeled, rigid, wooden-beam machine was outmoded, and unless they were willing to abandon the mower trade to their rivals, some change was imperative. By 1864, however, patents on mowers embraced such a wide

who manufactured the Monitor mower in Brooklyn, 1862 ff. Nishwitz had made several valuable improvements on single mowers, but had been obliged to take license from the Hinged-Bar Pool in 1864. By 1871, aided by the Sprague Mowing Machine Co., of Providence, R. I., he was using his lifting-lever patent of 1858 to bring J. P. Adriance to book. *Sprague & Parsons vs. Adriance & Platt*, p. 667; ‡J. Pine, Troy, N. Y., to C. H. McCormick, Nov. 21, 1872.

[30] C. Wheeler, Jr., to C. H. McCormick, Oct. 31, 1864. The pool members paid the Hussey heirs $2.50 per machine. *Record in Hussey vs. Bradley et als. U. S. Circuit Court, Northern District of New York* (1861-1863). Hubbard was also sued for infringing the Sylla and Adams patent owned by Aultman. *Sylla and Adams Extension Case, Opponents' Proofs*, Part II, pp. 63-71.

[31] *Aultman vs. Holley & Fitts*, pp. 515-518; *Wheeler vs. McCormicks*, pp. 213, 721 ff. In the early 1870's, Hubbard's rear-cut "Meadow Lark" mower was widely sold. It was manufactured by James Brayley, proprietor of Rochester Agricultural Works of Rochester, N. Y. See, "Brenton, Terry & Belden's Monthly" (Chicago), Mch. 1, 1873.

range of devices that it was hardly possible for them to modernize their machines without infringing the monopolies of their rivals. Little mercy could be expected from the pool, because several years before Cyrus McCormick had compelled the Aultman-Miller Company to pay him royalties under his reissued patent of 1847.[32]

In the early autumn of 1864, the McCormicks made a careful examination of the several types of two-wheeled, hinged-bar mowers then on the market,[33] and by December resolved to choose either the Hubbard or the "Cayuga Chief" machines of Wheeler. Month after month into 1865 the negotiations continued with Wheeler and the Hinged-Bar Pool. In the meantime, an agreement was closed with Hubbard to make one thousand of his mowers for the harvest of that year, paying him $5.00 royalty per machine. Although the McCormicks expected to clear $100,000 on this contract, it was not wholly satisfactory, since the field of sale was limited to Iowa, Kansas, Nebraska Territory, and Missouri.[34] Long before harvest came, it was well understood at the factory that the arrange-

[32] L.P.C.B. No. 47, p. 159, C. H. McCormick to G. Harding, Mch. 20, 1862; No. 48, p. 390, to T. H. Dodge, May 5, 1862; No. 52, p. 2, C. A. Spring, Jr., to E. P. Grant, Canton, O., Sept. 1, 1862. ‡C. H. McCormick to C. Aultman & Co., Canton, O., July 14, 1862. This Co. paid McCormick about $8,800, or $7.50 per machine. ‡C. Copeland to C. H. McCormick, Apr. 8, 1864.

[33] Letters of W. S. McCormick in L.P.C.B. No. 74, pp. 846, to W. H. B. Warren, Indianapolis, Sept. 26, 1864; No. 76, p. 309, to Kniffen & Harrington, Worcester, Mass., Nov. 24, 1864; No. 75, p. 192, to E. Ball, Canton, O., Oct. 5, 1864. No. 76, p. 613, W. J. Hanna to (?) Woodhull, Dayton, O., Dec. 12, 1864.

[34] *Ibid.*, No. 75 and No. 76 (Oct.-Dec., 1864), *passim.*, letters too numerous to list from C. H. McCormick & Bros. to Burtis & Beardsley and C. Wheeler, Jr. W. S. McCormick to C. H. McCormick, Dec. 31, 1864, Feb. 22 and Mch. 9, 1865. Letters of C. Wheeler, Jr., to C. H. and L. J. McCormick, Oct. 31, Nov. 21, Dec. 2, 3, 12, 13, 15 and 23, 1864 and Jan. 10, 1865. *Wheeler vs. McCormicks,* pp. 637-643, 649. MS. agreement of C. H. McCormick & Bros. with Ebenezer E. Lewis (for M. G. Hubbard) on Oct. 4, 1865.

ment would not be renewed for another year, although advantage might be taken of their option to buy an exclusive and permanent shop right of Hubbard for $9,000, in order to be free forever from the competition of his mowers in the region mentioned above. This was done in the following autumn.[35]

Late in 1864 Leander McCormick, in charge of machine building, and Lambert Erpelding, his chief assistant, turned their attention to the construction of a mower incorporating, in so far as possible, all of the best features of the Hinged-Bar Pool machines, without infringing its patents. A study of these patents had convinced them that the idea was a practicable one.[36] Fortified with a machine of their own, and exerting all pressure possible at Washington to prevent the extension of several key patents of the pool which were about to expire,[37] the McCormicks believed that they might compel it, in exchange for a withdrawal of their opposition, to give them a free license to make whatever type of mower they desired.[38] To help toward this end, as well as to have a de-

[35] W. S. to C. H. McCormick, Feb. 16, 1865. ‡C. H. McCormick & Bros. to C. Wheeler, Jr., Mch. 15, 1865. ‡C. A. Spring, Jr., to C. H. McCormick, Aug. 22 and Oct. 16, 1865. L.P.C.B. No. 77, pp. 97, 330, W. S. McCormick to C. Wheeler, Jr., Feb. 3 and 16, 1865; No. 83, pp. 588, 824, C. A. Spring, Jr., to C. H. McCormick, Aug. 23, and 30, 1865.

[36] *Ibid.*, No. 75, pp. 574, 642, C. A. Spring, Jr., to Burtis & Beardsley, Auburn, N. Y., and to C. Wheeler, Jr., Poplar Ridge, N. Y., Oct. 21, 1864. W. S. to C. H. McCormick, March 28 and Apr. 6, 1865. Nevertheless, Andrew Whiteley, of Springfield, O., believed that the McCormick hinged-bar mower infringed several of his patents, and threatened to sue. Threats, but no suit, seemed to be an almost yearly custom of the Whiteleys.

[37] *Opponents' Brief, Wheeler Extension Case,* p. 59.

[38] W. S. to C. H. McCormick, March 14, 1865: Nearly all that is valuable in the two-wheeled mower should belong to the public. "It *may* be for *our* interest however that the public should not have all. The *joint* & some other patents run out this year & I have seen Aultman & Wheeler . . . & they admit I think that when they apply for an *extension* it will be their interest to *arrange* with us. I talked the point up to them." ‡H. Baldwin, Jr., to C. H. McCormick, May 17, 1866.

fense in case of failure, an exhaustive and measurably successful search was made to discover patents of an early date which
appeared to anticipate the devices claimed by the combination.
These were purchased.[39] If, by these tactics, the McCormicks
could force their way into the pool, they would be more than
willing that any or all of its patents should be renewed for
another seven years.[40]

This plan could not be carried out. The L. J. McCormick-
Erpelding mower ran well in the factory, but was not immediately successful in the field. For this reason it seemed best
to make an agreement with the pool. William Allen was invited to come to Chicago, and in late April, 1865, a contract
was drawn whereby the partners were licensed to build mowers to sell in all of the Middle West except Ohio. They were
to pay $5.00 royalty on each machine, and to abandon all
opposition to the extension of the Wheeler patents.[41] Since the
usual fee charged by the combination was between $7.50 and
$10 a mower, the McCormicks gained a marked advantage
over some of their competitors. Nevertheless, they had no
intention of abiding by the terms of this treaty unless a further
search in the Patent Office made clear that they could not
defend themselves successfully if an action for infringement
were brought against them by the pool.[42]

[39] E.g., the patent of Feb. 23, 1858, of Hamilton A. Parkhurst of Fairfield, N. Y. ♯H. Baldwin to the Co., Aug. 24, 1867. H. Baldwin, Jr., to
the Co., Nov. 29, 1857. "Farm Implement News," May, 1888, pp. 16 ff.
This patent expired in Feb., 1872, and was not renewed. H. Baldwin, Jr.,
to C. H. McCormick, June 11, 1872.

[40] W. S. to C. H. McCormick, March 14 and 29, 1865.

[41] *Idem* to *idem,* Apr. 6, 8 and 10, 1865. Letters of W. S. McCormick to
W. Allen, Auburn, N. Y., in L.P.C.B. No. 79, p. 765, on Apr. 10, 1865,
and in ♯78, p. 216, on Apr. 22, 1865. No. 78, p. 443, W. J. Hanna to G. W.
Russell, Woodstock, Ill., May 3, 1865. The contract was signed Apr. 26,
1865. *Osgood Extension Case,* p. 30; L.P.C.B. No. 82, p. 200, C. A. Spring,
Jr., to Baldwin & Son, Washington, D. C., July 8, 1865; W. S. to C. H.
McCormick, Apr. 28, 1865.

[42] W. S. to C. H. McCormick, Apr. 6, 1865.

Almost no royalties were paid, and in the autumn of 1865, when the "Ring" threatened suit, Henry Baldwin, a leading patent attorney of Washington, assured Cyrus McCormick that any action it might bring against him was certain to result in his favor, although most probably his mower infringed certain "un-merged" patents owned by individual members of the combination.[43] Unfortunately, at this time William S. McCormick was critically ill, and Cyrus and Leander J., were in disagreement. The latter, fearing the outcome of a suit, believed that the contract with the pool should be carried out, and possibly in violation of the articles of partnership with his brother, he refused to assign to the firm the patents issued in his name as the inventor of certain devices included in the new McCormick mower.[44] Soon Cyrus and Leander suspected that their attorneys, Henry and William D. Baldwin, were "running with the hounds and playing with the hares." The Baldwins on their part, were irritated by this distrust, by the slowness with which the McCormicks met their requests for funds, and by Cyrus's insistence upon a rigid accounting of all sums advanced. These lawyers, however, were too much "on the inside" to be dropped, since in that case they might accept a retainer from the opposition.[45]

[43] In L.P.C.B. No. 96, p. 42 is a memo. headed "Fees Paid Sundry Parties for Use of Patents," which shows that on Sept. 11, 1865, W. Allen was paid $1,175 on 235 of "L. J. McCormick's mowers." ‡C. A. Spring, Jr., to C. H. McCormick, Mch. 5 and 8, 1866. ‡H. Baldwin, Jr., to C. H. McCormick, Feb. 28, Mch. 5, 14 and 24, June 25, Sept. 18 and 25, 1866.

[44] L.P.C.B. No. 81, pp. 792-3, L. J. McCormick to Baldwin & Son, Washington, D. C., July 1, 1865; No. 83, p. 374, C. A. Spring, Jr., to L. J. McCormick, Aug. 8, 1865; No. 113, p. 186, C. A. Spring, Jr., to H. Baldwin, Jr., May 24, 1869; No. 105, p. 186, the Co. to W. D. Baldwin & Son, June 4, 1868. C. A. Spring, Jr., to C. H. McCormick, ‡Jan. 9, Feb. 16 and ‡17, ‡June 18, 29 and ‡July 6, 1866. L. J. to C. H. McCormick, Feb. 24 and Apr. 17, 1866.

[45] C. H. to L. J. McCormick, Dec. 9, 1868. L. J. to C. H. McCormick, Nov. 11, 1870, and June 30, 1871. H. Baldwin, Jr., to C. H. McCormick, Jan. 18, 21 and 27, 1871. L.P.C.B. No. 147, pp. 680-82, C. H. McCormick

With harmony lacking, no certain course could be pursued, although the Baldwins worked diligently to undermine the validity of the pool patents and to defeat every attempt made to secure an extension or reissue of any of them.[46]

The pool manifested a strange hesitation to hale the McCormick Company before a court, probably preferring if possible to get its mower under license, and thus escape its competition.[47] Finally, it was Wheeler alone, and not the "Ring," who sought redress at law for alleged infringements by the partners. His bill of complaint was filed in the federal court of the Chicago district in May, 1869, and shortly thereafter he launched a second attack against them in New York, where the inventor was then a resident. Although the Chicago suit was for infringement by the mower of the McCormicks, while the other focused upon their combined machine (reaper-mower), the same points were at issue in both.[48] Wheeler was in fine fettle because of his recent successes in securing extensions of some of his chief patents, as well as the reissue of others in more inclusive terms than had been used in the

to H. Baldwin, Jr., Jan. 16, 1874. ‡H. Baldwin's telegram to C. H. McCormick, Dec. 13, 1870. ‡Memo. of C. H. McCormick, Feb. 21, 1874. ‡H. Baldwin, Jr., to C. H. McCormick, Feb. 21, 1871. In this letter Baldwin returned C. H.'s frankness in full measure: "You are all wrong and you behave so that no man with proper self respect can deal with you. . . . You are making your case difficult in every way. I cannot do more than I have done and will not again do so much. . . . Stop this wretched system of business. Be a man and a man of business."

[46] Most of these efforts were unsuccessful. ‡*Idem* to *idem*, Apr. 18, May 17 and Sept. 18, 1866. ‡W. D. Baldwin to C. H. McCormick, Dec. 7 and 12, 1868; Oct. 1, 19, 23 and 26, 1868; Feb. 18 and 20, 1869. F. Nishwitz promised to help C. H. McCormick defeat the efforts of the pool to extend some of its patents. ‡C. A. Spring, Jr., to C. H. McCormick, Oct. 1, 1868. ‡The Co. to W. D. Baldwin, Oct. 19, 1868.

[47] ‡C. A. Spring, Jr., to C. H. McCormick, Mch. 6, 12 and 19, 1869.

[48] ‡*Idem* to *idem*, May 11, 1869; ‡W. D. Baldwin to C. H. McCormick, May 12, 1869; L.P.C.B. No. 113, p. 17, C. A. Spring, Jr., to Goodwin & Larned, Chicago, May 15, 1869; ‡H. Baldwin, Jr., to C. H. McCormick, Sept. 1, 1870.

original grants. Doubtless this last was not in accord with either the letter or the spirit of the law, but it was commonly done, and the McCormicks but a few months before had been congratulated by their attorneys upon a similar stroke of good luck.[49]

The case moved ahead very slowly. For some months in 1870, Cyrus McCormick annoyed by the expense involved and possibly influenced by his brother with whom he had a temporary reconciliation,[50] wished to seek a compromise with Wheeler.[51] Quite apart from the merits of Wheeler's claims, there was no doubt that his attorney, George Harding, was almost invincible in hearings before the Patent Office officials and even in actions before the courts in the latter years of the Johnson, and during the entire Grant, administration.[52] The Baldwins, however, were confident of victory, although their judgment may have been colored by their vision of the fat fees in prospect.[53]

In the autumn of 1870, the Sprague Mowing Machine Company of Providence, Rhode Island, which was the defendant in a suit brought against it by members of the pool, arranged with the McCormicks for a mutual interchange of testimony favorable to the cause of each.[54] A few weeks earlier William

[49] ♯W. D. Baldwin to C. H. McCormick, Feb. 18, 20, Mch. 8 and May 3, 1869. This was the Parkhurst patent.

[50] L. J. to C. H. McCormick, May 27, 1869. ♯H. Baldwin, Jr., to C. H. McCormick, July 8, 1870.

[51] ♯H. Baldwin, Jr., to C. H. McCormick, Aug. 5, 24, Sept. 1, 1870. ♯L.P.C.B. No. 1, 2nd ser., p. 284, C. H. McCormick to H. and W. D. Baldwin, Sept. 6, 1870.

[52] ♯W. D. Baldwin to C. H. McCormick, Dec. 7, and 12, 1868; ♯C. Colahan to C. H. McCormick, June 10 and 13, 1874; ♯H. Baldwin, Jr., to the Co., Sept. 24, 1867. He said the "Patent Office Ring" included Harding, I. I. Combs, and Addison M. Smith.

[53] ♯H. Baldwin, Jr., to the Co., Sept. 24, 1867, to ♯C. H. McCormick, Mch. 6, 1871, and to the Co., June 10, 1871.

[54] The principal in this company was Senator William Sprague, who had married the daughter of Salmon P. Chase. The company made many

Wallace, who held a large interest in the Hubbard patents and was a stock-holder in Hubbard's Syracuse Mower & Reaper Improvement Company, offered for a price to tell why the Hinged-Bar Pool had been glad to *give* Hubbard a license seven years before. Wallace had in mind the "lost" reapers of Randall and Knowles. McCormick agreed to pay Wallace $2,500 if these machines could be found. With the aid of Pinkerton detectives, Wallace early in December ran these "relics" to earth in Chicago, whither they had been shipped for some undetermined reason four years before.[55] But the outcome was disappointing to the McCormicks. Wheeler's counsel was able to show that the Knowles machine had been significantly altered in construction since its invention almost thirty-five years before,[56] while the Randall reaper, although more useful in casting doubt upon the originality of Wheeler's hinged-bar claim, was destroyed in the Chicago fire of Octo-

mowers in the early 1870's for resale by Gammon & Deering of Plano, Ill. By 1878, after it had manufactured in all about 10,000 machines, it was bankrupt. Nevertheless it continued to do business under its old name at least as late as 1883. See, *Supreme Court of the United States. October Term, 1887, No. 379. Cyrus H. McCormick and Nettie Fowler McCormick, Executor and Executrix of Cyrus H. McCormick, Deceased, Leander J. Mc-Cormick, and Robert H. McCormick, Appellants, vs. Peter Whitmer, Administrator of Hugh Graham, Deceased, Appeal from the Circuit Court of the United States for the Northern District of Illinois* (Washington, 1888), pp. 517-520, 532. ‡H. Baldwin, Jr., to C. H. McCormick, Nov. 15, 1870 and July 18, 1871.

[55] ‡L.P.C.B. No. 1, 2nd ser., p. 330, C. H. McCormick to H. Baldwin, Dec. 23, 1870 and Jan. 12, 1871. *Aultman vs. Holley and Fittz*, pp. 524-535, testimony of W. Wallace. See also, pp. 888-890. These machines were found in an old shed at 595 State Street. *Wheeler vs. McCormicks*, pp. 683-686, 704. ‡W. Wallace to C. H. McCormick, Sept. 3, Oct. 21, and Dec. 6, 1870, and his telegram of Dec. 8, 1870.

[56] *Aultman vs. Holley and Fittz*, pp. 972-973. Here M. G. Hubbard admitted that after he had bought the Knowles machine he had altered its cutter-bar so as to make it a "floating" one. *Wheeler vs. McCormicks*, pp. 700-01, 716, 721. ‡H. Baldwin, Jr., to C. H. McCormick, Jan. 9, 1867 and Feb. 21, 1871. L. J. to C. H. McCormick, Feb. 18, 1871.

ber, 1871, before it could serve its full purpose in the suit.[57] As a matter of fact, the subsequent decision made clear that its construction had failed to impress the bench.

From the outset of the lawsuit, Harding had been anxious to complete the testimony in the New York case and gain a decree from his friend, Judge Woodruff, before a decision could be reached in the Chicago court, where Judge Drummond was believed to be partial to the McCormicks.[58] Henry Baldwin was stricken with pneumonia in the winter of 1871-1872, and before the hearing of the McCormick cases could be resumed, Wheeler was successful before Woodruff's court in his suit against the Clipper Mower & Reaper Company of Yonkers, New York, for infringement. Since this action had involved a number of points also at issue in the McCormick case, the decision naturally worked to the disadvantage of the partners. Cheered by this good augury, but fearing an unfavorable outcome in the West, Wheeler in early October,[59] 1872, had his suit dismissed there and concentrated his efforts upon the New York case.[60]

Cyrus McCormick, who was not sanguine of the outcome, disregarded his attorneys' advice and entered into fruitless negotiations with Hubbard to secure a withdrawal of the suit in the East. The rough draft of a letter from the inventor to him, dated November 21, 1872, and marked "Sacredly Confi-

[57] *Aultman vs. Holley and Fittz*, pp. 895, 906, 977. ‡S. A. Goodwin to C. H. McCormick, Nov. 3, 1871. The taking of testimony in the Wheeler suit was completed in Apr. 1871, and the case was argued in October. ‡L.P.C.B. No. 1, p. 466, C. H. McCormick to W. Whitney, Apr. 5, 1871.

[58] ‡H. Baldwin, Jr., to C. H. McCormick, May 8, 13 and July 18, 1871; Jan. 27, 1872.

[59] ‡J. S. Bell to C. H. McCormick, Feb. 23, 1872. L.P.C.B. No. 132, p. 580, C. H. McCormick to S. A. Goodwin, Mch. 8, 1872, and p. 705 to W. Whitney, Mch. 16, 1872. H. Baldwin, Jr., to S. A. Goodwin, Oct. 3, 1872. *Wheeler vs. Clipper Mower & Reaper Co.*

[60] Wheeler had contemplated doing this as early as Oct., 1870. ‡Telegram of H. Baldwin, Jr., to C. H. McCormick, Oct. 31, 1870.

dential," affords a fleeting glimpse of the heart of the matter, and suggests how unsatisfying must be the court records and lawyers' briefs to one who wishes to penetrate beneath the surface.

In the Wheeler suit brot. by Harding *vs.* us, we believe we are *right* & shall therefore defend it to fullest extent. Our immed. success would of course ruin the Patent [i.e. Wheeler's Patent] & the time required to obtain a final *decree* would in any event be nearly as injurious. It is our interest that the Patent should be sustained *vs.* those legally infringing it. We would favor that result by a fair cooperation & we also understand that you favor sustaining the Patent by some judicious arrangement. So we propose —that if you will obtain the withdrawal of said suit, or some equiv. arrangement, & obtain for us Harding's written agreement that he will not hereafter act for any Party in commencing or conducting Suits against us, we will upon receipt of such agreement, pay you the sum of fifty thousand dollars in our negotiable notes on interest, or ten thousand per year for five years.[61]

It is perhaps significant that on this same day the McCormicks agreed to pay Hubbard $1.00 per machine for the use of his changeable speed gearing. Hints in later correspondence indicate that he attempted to carry out McCormick's wishes, but accomplished nothing. In October, 1873, Judge Woodruff in his decision, declared in favor of the Wheeler claim and held that the McCormicks were liable to the plaintiff for the profits (to be fixed by a Master) they had made from the sale of their flexible-bar machines between July 8, 1868, when

[61] There were two ways in which McCormick might win the suit: (a) by demonstrating that he did not infringe the patent in question, or (b) by showing that this patent was invalid because its claims had been anticipated by earlier inventors. McCormick hoped that (a) and not (b) could be shown, for if he could establish his immunity against a most important valid patent, he would have a decided advantage in the selling field over others who were not so fortunate. See also, M. G. Hubbard to C. H. McCormick, Feb. 25, 1873. This shows that Baldwin had strongly advised C. H. McCormick not to have anything to do with Hubbard, for he believed that Hubbard was probably trying to "double cross" him.

Wheeler recovered control of his patents from the Wheeler Association, and July 3, 1872, when he sold all of them, together with his interest in lawsuits then in progress, to Aultman.[62] Of course, the latter now demanded the profits for the period after July 3, 1872. The McCormicks threatened to appeal the decision in the Wheeler case to the United States Supreme Court.[63]

For some time before the Hinged-Bar Pool dissolved in 1871, Wheeler, because of the value of his patents, had been pushing his associates into the background, while Harding usurped the influential rôle hitherto played by William Allen.[64] When Wheeler, however, sold his patents to Aultman, the center of interest once more shifted from Auburn, New York, to Canton, Ohio. By 1872, evidences of Aultman's increasing prosperity were on every hand. For nine years at Akron he had been treasurer, and Lewis F. Miller, president, of Aultman, Miller & Company, which manufactured several thousand "Buckeye" mowers and reapers each season. At Canton were the Aultman Steel Company and C. Aultman & Company, while at Mansfield, Ohio, the Aultman & Taylor Manu-

---

[62] This would affect about 25,000 machines made by the McCormicks. *In the Circuit Court of the United States, Southern District of New York. In Equity, Cyrenus Wheeler, Jr. vs. Cyrus H. McCormick. Opinion of the Court* (Philadelphia, 1873). See also, L.P.C.B. No. 150, p. 455, Hanna to H. Baldwin, Jr., May 26, 1874. The Judge did not file the decree until mid-Feb., 1874. S. A. Goodwin to C. H. McCormick, Sept. 19 and Nov. 14, 1872.

[63] The patent in question would not expire until Dec. 5, 1875. Eventually, Aultman was the plaintiff in three suits against the McCormicks—the one inaugurated in New York by Wheeler and two others in Illinois of his own initiation.

[64] ♯H. Baldwin, Jr., to the Co., Mch. 8, 1869: "Wheeler has gradually absorbed the blood and muscle of the combination and only waits the expiration of his contract to claim against them [i.e. the other members of the pool]. He will then put his fee down so low that we can afford to pay it. They will not pull together in the meantime and so—when rogues fall out, honest men may come by their own."

facturing Company gratified its senior partner's ambition to supply farmers with threshing machines.[65]

In the autumn of 1872, Aultman and Saxton were deep in a pamphlet war over the question of title to certain patents, including those originally issued to Ephraim Ball.[66] Some months later, Aultman agreed to pay Saxton $170,000 for almost all of his monopolies, as well as for his prospective share of damages from a number of "Pool" infringement suits still before the courts. The terms of this contract were by no means clear, but Saxton chose to believe that his retained patents were sufficiently broad in their scope to permit him by license to protect mower manufacturers from most of Aultman's claims. Following the adverse decision in the Wheeler case, Saxton approached Cyrus McCormick and induced him to pay a royalty of $2.50 a machine for the privileges of making the Ohio or Ball single-frame mower for the harvest of 1874. This was continued from year to year until 1878, when Saxton's chief patent expired. By then he had received royalties from the McCormicks totaling more than $57,000.[67] Henry Baldwin had opposed McCormick's determination to enter this contract because he believed that a Saxton license gave no immunity from Aultman's [68] patents, unless his client intended to build simply the obsolete Ball

[65] Circular Letter of C. Aultman & Co., Canton, O., June 10, 1870. The "Scientific American," June 10, 1882, pp. 359 ff.

[66] The E. Ball & Company, Reaper, Mower & Threshing Machine Works, went out of existence in the spring of 1871. Circular Letter of J. A. Saxton, Canton, O., Nov., 1872. Pamphlet of J. A. Saxton, Nov., 1872, addressed to "Manufacturers of Reapers and Mowers."

[67] L.P.C.B. No. 188, pp. 50, 142, the Co. to J. A. Saxton, Canton, O., Feb. 11 and 14, 1879.

[68] J. A. Saxton's telegram to C. H. McCormick, Dec. 31, 1873; #H. Baldwin, Jr., to H. Day, Feb. 13, 1874; C. H. McCormick to H. Baldwin, Jr., Feb. 12, 1874 and #Feb. 21, 1874; H. Baldwin, Jr., to C. H. McCormick, Feb. 25, 1874; #H. Day to R. H. McCormick, Mch. 6, 1874 and to C. H. & L. J. McCormick, Mch. 7, 1874; J. A. Saxton to McCormick Co., Jan. 24, and May 24, 1878.

mower which had been popular twenty years before. Almost immediately, as Baldwin had foretold, Aultman threatened to start a new suit if the McCormicks presumed to rely upon Saxton for protection.[69]

At this critical juncture in McCormick's affairs in the spring of 1874,[70] the inventor accepted the services of a man who for the next ten years was to figure prominently in the patent history of the harvesting-machine industry. Charles Colahan of Cleveland, Ohio, describing himself as one of the new profession of "patent specialists," laid his claim to attention before McCormick in the following words: "If you are of opinion I can aid you, it would be desirable to say as little as possible in regard to my work, as it is really a sort of detective prying out service—& it may at times be necessary to invade the enemy's camp & find information. . . . I believe you are a victim of a conspiracy & humbug, & one of the enormous kind altho the courts sustain the delusion. Do you want my help?" [71]

[69] *Idem* to *ibid.,* Mch. 26, 1874; L.P.C.B. No. 149, p. 70, W. J. Hanna to J. A. Saxton, Canton, Mch. 30, 1874. C. H. McCormick to J. A. Saxton, #Mch. 11, Apr. 9, #24, 1874.

[70] At about this time, also, another of the McCormicks' chief rivals, Whiteley, Fassler & Kelly of Springfield, Ohio, made an advantageous agreement with Wheeler. #C. Colahan to C. H. McCormick, Nov. 27, 1874. To paraphrase: There is much mystery about the Wheeler-Whiteley settlement but I believe it was a "straw compromise" and that Whiteley paid Wheeler no money for the use of his patents. Soon Whiteley, who was virtually an ally of the Wheeler-Aultman group, entered an "interference" at the Patent Office to prevent an issue to the McCormicks of a patent upon certain improvements of the drag-bar and lifting-lever of their mower. Eventually, after appeal, priority was awarded to the McCormicks.

[71] C. Colahan to C. H. McCormick, Apr. 7, 11, #20 and #25, 1874. By McCormick's one-year contract with Colahan, made on May 6, 1874, Colahan was to receive $1,000 a year and traveling expenses. If, however, he discovered evidence in connection with the Wheeler suit, worth $10,000 in Baldwin's opinion, he would be paid $3,000 for the year's work. See also, C. Colahan to C. H. McCormick, #May 9 and 19, 1874. It is very probable that C. H. McCormick was the more willing to employ Colahan because he might serve at Chicago as a check to Leander's son, Robert Hall, who

McCormick was most dissatisfied with his attorneys, and now found himself becoming enmeshed ever more tightly in a patent snarl involving self-rakes, harvesters, wire-binders, and mowers. He decided that perhaps this secretive and self-confident man from Cleveland, who had been "schooled in the best merchantile [sic] houses in New York," could render assistance by ascertaining the intention of his opponents and by locating patents which might anticipate those that were being used against him. The value of his work for the McCormicks was variously appraised by those who knew him. In Colahan's opinion, frankly expressed as always to his employer, Henry Baldwin was not a "good business man" and only an "ordinary lawyer." [72] Baldwin returned Colahan's dislike in full measure and warned McCormick, to no avail, that his agent was "simply fooling away your [his] money." [73] Leander McCormick, and his son Robert Hall, agreed with Baldwin's estimate, and when Cyrus McCormick, Jr., entered the office of the company in 1879, he found it difficult either to endure Colahan's officious manner or to dispense with his aid. Apparently all who had to work at close quarters with him were repelled by his proneness to criticise, his assumption of infallibility, and his willingness to let the end justify the means. Cyrus McCormick, Sr., whose contacts with his scout were chiefly by letter, judged him solely from the standpoint of services rendered, and there is little reason to doubt that he amply earned his pay.[74]

was, in C. H. McCormick's opinion, taking too much interest in patent matters. L.P.C.B. No. 149, p. 232, the Co. to W. D. Baldwin, Apr. 8, 1874.

[72] ‡C. Colahan to C. H. McCormick, May 16, July 30, Sept. 15, 17, Oct. 23, and Nov. 3, 1874.

[73] ‡H. Baldwin, Jr., to C. H. & L. J. McCormick, Sept. 28, 1874; ‡C. Colahan to C. H. McCormick, Feb. (?), 1875; ‡H. Baldwin to C. H. McCormick, July 28, 1874; W. D. Baldwin to the Co., Apr. 19, 1879.

[74] C. H. McCormick to C. Colahan, June 13, 1874. At this time C. H. McCormick customarily signed his letters to Colahan merely with an "X"

Between 1874 and 1878 there were many conferences between the McCormicks and Aultman on the subject of the amount that the Chicago partners should pay. When Aultman blustered that he would not be satisfied with less than $500,000, or some other almost equally extravagant sum, the McCormicks countered with a threat to appeal the case to the United States Supreme Court.[75] Neither Aultman nor McCormick wished to be saddled with the heavy expenses which this further action would entail. Little by little Aultman moderated his demands, and finally in 1881 agreed to have his suit dismissed upon the payment by the McCormicks of $25,000.[76]

But the court history of the McCormick mower was not yet ended. Hugh Graham of Bloomington, Illinois, encouraged by his success in an action against Gammon & Deering of

and cautioned him that they "should be carefully dealt with." In his correspondence with the Baldwins, Colahan was disguised under the title "the man from Cleveland." By the autumn of 1874, however, Colahan's rôle was no longer unknown to Aultman. ‡C. Colahan to C. H. McCormick, June 10, 27, July 2, Aug. 18, 20, Sept. 15, 17, 26, Oct. 6, 31 and Nov. 27, 1874; Jan. 16, Feb. 22 and Mch. 10, 1875.

[75] ‡C. H. McCormick to H. Baldwin, Apr. 29, 1874, and Jan. 9, 1875. Baldwin believed the McCormicks could gain a reversal of the decision in the Supreme Court. Even L. J. McCormick, hitherto so pessimistic of the outcome, now was encouraged by the "errors" of the opinion to hope for victory on appeal. L.P.C.B. No. 147, pp. 439-445, L. J. McCormick to H. Baldwin, Jan. 5, 1874; No. 146, p. 639, C. H. & L. J. McCormick to C. Aultman, Dec. 2, 1873. C. Aultman to C. H. & L. J. McCormick, Nov. 28, Dec. 10 and ‡31, 1873. C. H. McCormick to C. Aultman, Jan. 2, 1874; G. Harding to H. Baldwin, Jan. 19, 1875. E. N. Dickerson to Co., Apr. 6, 1877. C. H. McCormick to E. N. Dickerson, Mch. 31, 1877, and to H. Baldwin, Jr., Apr. 29 and July 4, 1874. H. Baldwin, Jr., to C. H. McCormick, Apr. 16, 1875. ‡Dickerson & Beaman, N. Y., to C. H. & L. J. McCormick, July 16, 1875.

[76] MS. Diary of C. H. McCormick, Jr., entry of Feb. 5, 1881. ‡C. H. & L. J. McCormick to Aultman, Miller & Co., Apr. 5, 1876; ‡C. H. McCormick to E. N. Dickerson, Dec. 14, 1876; Mch. 31, 1877, Nov. 19, 27, 1880, and Jan. 8, 1881; ‡C. H. McCormick to E. C. Larned, Feb. 7, 1881. L.P.C.B. No. 195, pp. 728-29, the Co. to C. H. McCormick, Nov. 13, 1879. ‡C. Colahan to C. H. McCormick, Nov. 23, and Dec. 30, 1879. ‡C. A. Spring, Jr., to C. H. McCormick, Nov. 13, 1879.

Plano for infringing his 1868 patent covering certain features of the finger-beam of single-frame mowers, brought the McCormicks before a federal tribunal in 1877 to defend themselves against a similar charge.[77] The partners believed that their license from Saxton covered the feature at issue, but to make doubly certain that they were protected, they bought a shop right from Cyrus A. and William B. Werden of Berkshire County, Massachusetts, in 1878, who were supposed to own an interest in the Graham patent. To the partners' chagrin, it was adjudged that the Saxton license afforded no security and that the Werdens were unable to grant a valid shop right. In 1880 the United States Circuit Court in Chicago issued a decree in Graham's favor and a second hearing of the case led only to a reaffirmance two years later.[78] In the summer of 1884 a Master appointed by the court recommended a decree requiring the McCormicks to pay the plaintiff nearly $103,000 on over twenty-seven thousand infringing mowers sold between 1874 and 1879, when a change in the construction of these machines avoided the device in question.[79] When the McCormick Company objected to the Master's findings, they were reviewed by the chancellor, Judge Walter Q. Gresham, and the damages were scaled down to approximately $85,550 and costs.[80] This satisfied neither party to the case, and McCormick appealed to the Supreme Court.

[77] *McCormicks vs. Graham, op. cit.,* pp. 1, 11-12, 50-51, 200, 208 and 519-520. L.P.C.B. No. 172, p. 636, the Co. to W. D. Baldwin, June 11, 1877. ‡C. H. & L. J. McCormick to E. N. Dickerson, Mch. 26, 1878. ‡C. A. Spring, Jr., to C. H. McCormick, Sept. 10, 1879. "Chicago Daily Tribune," Sept. 9, 1879. F. H. Matthews to C. H. McCormick, Apr. 23, 1879. Baldwin, Hopkins & Peyton to the Co., Dec. 31, 1879. The rocking finger-beam controlled by a lever was chiefly at issue.

[78] *McCormicks vs. Graham,* pp. 25, 48-56, 164. M. D. Leggett, Cleveland, to the Co., Mch. 18 and 19, 1880. C. H. McCormick, Jr.'s, telegram to C. H. McCormick, Mch. 29, 1880. "Chicago Times," Jan. 15 and Mch. 15, 1880.

[79] *McCormicks vs. Graham,* pp. 56-65. J. R. Bennett to C. H. McCormick, Jr., Oct. 19, 1883.

[80] *McCormicks vs. Graham,* pp. 65-69.

Here, in 1889, he won a complete victory, since the cause was remanded with a direction to dismiss the bill of complaint with costs.[81]

During most of the thirty-year period just surveyed, when every leading manufacturer of harvesting machinery was endeavoring to out-maneuver his rivals in the mower war, a similar conflict was in progress for control of the key patents covering the self-rake reaper. This struggle ended by the mid-1870's, not because a decisive victory had been gained by any contestant, but because by that time the growing popularity of the harvester and binder minimized the importance of the self-rakes.

If the abortive efforts of several English inventors early in the nineteenth century to discharge the cut grain automatically either by means of a tilt-platform or by a revolving or reciprocating rake, are omitted, the history of the self-rake reaper should probably begin with a brief mention of Andrew J. Cook of Richmond, Indiana. Under his patent of 1846, Love & Otis of Beloit, Wisconsin, and Hatch & Whiteley of Springfield, Ohio, in 1851 and 1852 made a few machines with a rake revolving about a vertical axis.[82] They did not work well, but Cook, and perhaps Homer Adkins [83] of Round Prairie, Illinois, with his reciprocating rake invention of 1850, deserve credit for being the first of the many inventors who demonstrated that automatic delivery was practicable. Ob-

[81] U. S. Supreme Court Records, CXXIX (Oct. Term, 1888), pp. 1, 19.
[82] "Hutchinson," I, pp. 58-59; "Southern Planter" (Richmond), Jan., 1847, p. 32; "Prairie Farmer," Oct., 1848; Dorsey Extension, Henry Baldwin, Jr., Attorney for William D. Baldwin, a Contestant (Philadelphia, 1870), p. 271, testimony of J. Fassler. Henry F. Mann vs. the Slifer, Walls and Shriner Manufacturing Company. The Circuit Court of the United States. In and for the Western District of Pennsylvania, #29 of the November Term, 1871 (Pittsburgh, 1873), p. 215.
[83] "Prairie Farmer," Jan. 1850, pp. 30-38. "Scientific American," June 5, 1915. Here Adkins is given credit for beginning the era of the self-rake reapers.

viously it was desirable to discharge the grain at the side rather than at the rear of the machine, but should this be done by attaching a rake to the revolving reel, or by giving the rake its own separate gears and independent motion? If the latter, should the rake teeth push up through a slotted platform and move across it at regular intervals,[84] or would more efficient operation be secured if the rake were suspended on a vertical or horizontal axis and reciprocated across a solid platform from above? These were the chief questions which inventors were trying to answer during the decade of experiment ending in 1860. By then, the slotted platform principle had been abandoned as impracticable, but whether the rake should be separate from the reel, or revolve with it, was still a matter of doubt.[85] The old hand-rake reapers were preferred by most farmers as late as 1860, although by that date probably twenty thousand machines with automatic delivery were already in use.

By the close of that harvest the McCormick Company realized that its attempt during the preceding four or five years to drive these "new-fangled" inventions from the field by ridicule, had been unavailing. It was now time to secure the right to build the best of the self-rakes and keep step with progress. Which of the several types already on the market was the most efficient, was by no means clear. Certainly, the ingenious

[84] The best-known self-rake on this principle was D. C. Henderson's Grain and Grass Harvester of Sandusky, O. Henderson had purchased the mower patent of John E. Heath, of Warren, O., and with this mower he combined the self-rake device of A. H. Caryl of Sandusky. It was frequently mentioned with respect in the letters of McCormick's agents in 1856 and 1857. It aroused considerable attention in 1856 when it was said that 2,000 were made, but it did not work well and was soon forgotten. See, "Ohio Cultivator," Mch. 1, 1856, p. 67, Apr. 1, 1856, p. 111, Apr. 15, 1856, p. 117. "Michigan Farmer," Sept., 1856, p. 267.

[85] *Dorsey Extension Case*, p. 195. The Wright-Atkins "Automaton," the self-rake of Byron Densmore, made by B. Warder at Springfield, O., and the Palmer and Williams self-rake, were the chief ones on the market prior to 1860.

Atkins "Automaton" need not be considered, although it had been one of the wonders of the farmers' world in the mid-1850's. The mechanism of the several thousand sold by its two principal manufacturers, John S. Wright of Chicago and W. C. Dutton [86] of Dayton, Ohio, was too delicate and complicated to resist hard usage in the harvest field. Its day was over by 1860 and its influence upon reaper history was not an enduring one. Much less sensational, but far more important for the future, was the Palmer and Williams Self-Rake, manufactured after 1853 by Ganson, Huntley & Company and Seymour & Morgan of Brockport, New York, and still later in the decade by several firms in the Middle West. [87] This rake swept over a quadrant-shaped platform invented by William H. Seymour, and his patent of 1851 covering this platform became one of the most valuable monopolies associated with self-rake history during the next twenty years. The McCormicks alone paid Seymour & Morgan over $60,000 between 1862 and 1872 for the privilege of using it in their machines. [88]

[86] Wright brought out the first Atkins in 1852, but was forced to suspend manufacture in 1858. Dutton made his first "Automaton" in 1854 and was still producing a few in 1860.

[87] Warder, Mitchell & Co., and Whiteley, Fassler & Kelly of Springfield, O., Long, Black & Allstatter of Hamilton, O., Newton & Co. of Batavia, Ill., and Adriance, Platt & Co., also made the Seymour & Morgan rake in 1860. *Dorsey Extension Case,* pp. 168, 181. "Michigan Farmer," Jan., 1855, p. 23; Apr., 1855, p. 123; June, 1855, pp. 166-167. "Genesee Farmer," July, 1860, p. 228. In 1861 Williams, in bad health, and Palmer, in dire need of money, sold their patent rights to Seymour & Morgan. By 1860, Morgan had moved his residence to Springfield, O.

[88] The five patents controlled by Seymour & Morgan covered a quadrant-shaped platform in combination with an overhanging reel (i.e. beyond the cutter and over the grain), and an automatic sweep-rake. By the license of June 4, 1862, from Seymour & Morgan (Seymour, Morgan, & Allen), Cyrus McCormick agreed to pay $10.00 per machine "less a certain discount" until $30,000 had been paid. He would not oppose any effort Seymour & Morgan might make to extend their self-rake patents, and if extension were gained, he would pay an additional $32,000 at the rate of $2.50 per machine.

But when the Chicago partners placed their first self-rake reapers upon the market in the harvest of 1862, they were chiefly protected by the patents of four inventors living in Maryland. By a strange chance, several men of that state, working independently, had turned their attention to the problem of the self-rake in the late 1850's. The earliest of these in point of time was Owen Dorsey of Triadelphia, who with the financial aid of Hussey's good friend, Edward Stabler, constructed the first reel-rake in history in 1853. Having secured his patent three years later, Dorsey sold manufacturing rights to a number of small firms in Maryland, New Jersey, Pennsylvania, and Ohio. Not over a few hundred of these reel-rakes had been sold by 1862, when Dorsey because of his stanch Unionism, deemed it unwise to remain longer in his Maryland home. He moved to Newark, Ohio, and shortly thereafter three new licensees, Pritz & Kuhn of Dayton, James S. Marsh & Co., of Lewisburg, Pennsylvania, and Reese, Staats & Mellick of Phillipsburg, New Jersey, began to make and sell a considerable number of his rakes.[89]

By 1866 he had sent Morgan over $36,000 under this contract; $10,000 more was paid in 1867; $8,805 in 1868, etc. *U. S. Supreme Court, December Term, 1870, No. 65, William H. Seymour and Dayton S. Morgan, Appellants, vs. David M. Osborne and John H. Osborne. Decision of the Supreme Court of the United States in favor of the Five Harvester Patents of Seymour & Morgan* (New York, 1871), *passim. Before the Honorable Commission of Patents. In the Matter of the Application of Aaron Palmer and Stephen G. Williams for an Extension of their Re-issued Letters Patent for Inventions on Reaping Machines, dated the 1st day of January, 1861 . . . the Original of which Patent was issued to them, dated July 1, 1851 . . . and the patent . . . dated 31st day of May, 1864 . . . the original of which . . . was . . . dated July 1st, 1851, passim.* H. Baldwin, Jr., to C. H. McCormick, Apr. 3, 1865.

[89] *Dorsey Extension Case,* pp. 148 ff., 196, 200, 271. One of the distinctive features of the Dorsey rake was the overhanging reel which permitted the rake to operate without interfering with the driver. Slifer, Walls & Shriner Mfg. Co., of Lewisburg, Pa., made a few Dorsey rakes, 1867 ff. In 1870, Dorsey believed that about 20,000 of his rakes had been sold. Marsh of Lewisburg was the first to devise a method of placing a revolving reel-rake

Probably the McCormicks should have purchased a shop right under this important patent, but they chose to deal with Benjamin G. Fitzhugh and McClintock Young, Jr., of Frederick, Maryland. The three patents on reel-rakes granted to these men between 1858 and 1860 were sold for $10,000 to Cyrus McCormick on July 12, 1861. One year later he purchased for about $9,500 the 1859 patent on reel-rakes of Isaac S. and Henry R. Russell of New Market, Maryland.[90] Thus, by the harvest in which McCormick sold his first automatic delivery reapers, he was safe-guarded by a license from Seymour & Morgan, and by the ownership of the Fitzhugh, Young, and Russells' patents.

The Civil War accentuated the shortage of harvest labor both by drawing men to the armies of the North and by stimulating small-grain production. With good reason, therefore, the self-rake reaper came into its own during the four years of conflict. Hundreds of patents covering details of machines of this type were granted,[91] and the Hinged-Bar Pool soon had its counterpart in the domain of the self-rake.

with a vertical axis on a rear-cut machine. *Decisions of the Commissioner of Patents for the Year 1871* (Washington, 1872), pp. 253-55. The reel-rake, proper, was uncontrollable since it operated as long as the reel was in motion. It revolved on either a horizontal or vertical axis. Those, like the Dorsey, which were on a vertical axis, were often called "pigeon wing" rakes. The Young reel-rake revolved on the horizontal shaft of the reel. On the other hand, the reciprocating rake of the Palmer and Williams type revolved about two axes—one vertical and the other horizontal. See, "The Iron Age" (N. Y.), Sept. 27, 1877.

[90] The agreement with the Russells was on July 5, 1862. Two years before this time they had exhibited their machine in Chicago. The McCormicks were sufficiently impressed to use several in the 1861 harvest, after the gearing had been improved by Lambert Erpelding. They, however, did not work well, and the partners were better pleased with a Young self-rake which they had tried out near Lodi, Wisconsin. Further experiments with this machine, led them to make 200 for the 1862 harvest and to purchase the three patents.

[91] By 1877, over six hundred patents had been granted for improvements of the reel-rake, alone. *Ibid.*, Sept. 27, 1877.

Thus, in late 1865 Hubbard purchased the Dorsey monopoly for $15,000, and with several other owners of patents formed a Harvester Rake Pool on March 17, 1866. Hubbard was guaranteed one-third of the profits expected from the sale of licenses and from damages to be won by suits for infringements.[92] Immediately it was rumored that the McCormick Company would be one of the first to be humbled, but for the moment the pool organization was unstable. Not until the close of 1867, when Hubbard yielded control to Harding and to Samuel Johnston of Syracuse, was the league ready to take the offensive.[93]

For almost fifteen years, Johnston had been slowly climbing toward a place of eminence in the world of harvesting machinery.[94] His dominance of the rake pool made clear that he had finally arrived. As an inventor, he was early interested in discovering a method whereby the self-rake could be "controlled." The Dorsey rake swept a gavel from the platform with each revolution of the reel. Johnston's improvement consisted of

[92] *Dorsey Extension Case,* pp. 68-70, 252. Robert W. Brown of Newark, Ohio, son-in-law of Dorsey, took out three patents on reel-rakes between 1861 and 1866. These were placed in the pool. Others therein were those of Jearum Atkins of Chicago and of Reuben Hoffheins of York, Pa. The latter had been granted three patents between 1862 and 1865, covering particularly a method of mounting the reel-post on the finger-beam of the machines employing the pigeon-wing rake. The owners of Atkins's patent were guaranteed 1/6 of the profits; the Brown patents-holders 1/6, and all the rest save Hubbard, 1/3.

[93] ‡H. Baldwin, Jr., to C. H. McCormick, Mch. 31, Apr. 6, 13 and 19, 1866; Jan. 9, 1867. *Dorsey Extension Case,* pp. 75, 88, 94, 293. Johnston and Aultman entered the Hubbard Pool on Sept. 20, 1866. The pool bought the Dorsey patent of Hubbard for $37,386, and other rake patents for over $75,000.

[94] Johnston had been experimenting with, and manufacturing, self-rakes since the early 1850's at Buffalo and Syracuse. On Feb. 7, 1865, he patented an excellent automatic delivery of the revolving type. Johnston, Huntley & Co. was established at Syracuse in 1868 but was superseded by the Johnston Harvester Co. of Brockport, in 1871. Johnston retired in 1879 and died in 1911. *McCormicks vs. Graham,* p. 501.

a mechanism operated by the foot of the driver, whereby the speed of the rake could be proportioned to the heaviness of the crop. Thus the driver of the machine could size the gavels to suit himself. Since each of the four fans of the reel was also a rake, he was able to make all of them in turn, or only one or two of them, discharge a bundle of grain at each revolution. Johnston's success in this field of invention spelled the doom of vibrating rakes of the Palmer and Williams style, and by 1867, firms such as Adriance, Platt & Co., Warder, Mitchell & Co., and Whiteley, Fassler & Kelly abandoned this type and began to manufacture the "Johnston Rake." [95]

With the formation of the pool, it was for the first time possible to differentiate clearly between friend and foe in the contest for preëminence in self-rake manufacturing. The pool was a checkmate to the McCormicks, who after 1864 were discussing the possibility of gaining a whip hand in this field by buying a share in the Dorsey patent, securing control of early patents on quadrant-shaped platforms so as to be freed from their irksome annual tribute to Seymour & Morgan, and by having their Young monopolies reissued in order to broaden the field of their incidence. [96] The Whiteleys (Abner, Amos, Andrew, William and William N.) of Springfield, Ohio, who until 1886 were in the forefront of reaper and mower manufacturing, were also injured by the pool, because they had for long been making self-rakes and owned some patents which

[95] Benjamin Warder of Springfield, Ohio (Warder, Brokaw & Child), began to manufacture reapers and mowers in 1850. He at first made Ketchum mowers and Seymour & Morgan reapers, but his Co. is usually remembered as one of the "Champion system" of firms. In fact Seymour & Morgan was soon paying a license fee to Johnston, while the "Buckeye" folk (at least Aultman) became members of the rake pool. *Dorsey Extension Case,* p. 101.

[96] It is rather significant that at this time Tench Tilghman, of Oxford, Maryland—early patron of Obed Hussey and now a railroad president—offered for $10,000 to prove to C. H. McCormick that a quadrant-shaped platform had been used long before the Seymour patent of 1851. ‡T. Tilghman to C. H. McCormick, Apr. 24, 1865.

they believed both McCormick and the Dorsey-Johnston folk infringed. But, as we have seen, they took a license from Johnston in 1867, and were soon the largest manufacturers of his style of self-rake.[97] In the harvest of that year, for the first time, McCormick's agents had much to say about the stiff competition furnished by this machine.[98]

As its first important move on the offensive, the rake pool secured an extension and reissue of the Dorsey patent of 1856, despite all that the McCormicks could do to prevent.[99] Harding, who had handled the matter before the Patent Office, hoped that the broad claims of the reissue would subordinate every rotating rake made in the United States. If this could be done, the $27,500 which the "Ring" paid to Dorsey for his aid and consent in applying for an extension would be a most profitable investment.

To strengthen his defense against the threatened onslaught, Cyrus McCormick endeavored to secure extensions and reissues of the Young and Fitzhugh patents. To his surprise

[97] The Whiteleys came to Springfield in the early 1850's. The firm of Hatch & (William) Whiteley was succeeded about 1857 by Whiteley (William N., nephew of William), Fassler & Kelly. The company was aggressive from the outset. In 1860 it endeavored to unite manufacturers to resist paying license fees to the heirs of Obed Hussey. In this it was unsuccessful. Warder, Mitchell & Co., the Champion Machine Co., and Whiteley, Fassler & Kelly, all at Springfield, made nearly 40,000 machines in 1867. By 1880, Whiteley, Fassler & Kelly had one of the largest agricultural machinery factories in the world. It, with its licensees, made "Champion" Reapers and Mowers. "Circular" of Whiteley, Fassler & Kelly, May, 1858; S. S. Fisher, "Patent Cases" (Cincinnati, 1868), II, 120, 362; Patent Office Records, *Hussey Extension Case, Patent of 1847* (Washington, 1861), p. 7. *Hussey vs. Whiteley*, pp. 29, 31, 33, 48. "Frank Leslie's Illustrated Newspaper" (N. Y.), July 22, 1876.

[98] H. G. Grattan, Cresco, Iowa, to the Co., Aug. 6, 1867; E. W. Brooks, Red Wing, Minn., Oct. 3, and Dec. 25, 1867.

[99] C. H. to L. J. McCormick, Dec. 24, 1869. McCormick hoped that by putting up a stiff fight against the Dorsey extension, the rake pool might grant him a free license under the patent, in order to induce him to drop his opposition. This was a usual ruse.

and alarm, he learned for the first time that these inventors
had so construed their contract with him as to justify the sale
of their self-rake improvements to Aultman (of the rake pool)
and Walter A. Wood.[100] In McCormick's opinion—and he
finally convinced his attorney, Henry Baldwin, that he was
correct—they had obligated themselves to give him the exclusive benefit of all their inventions relating to self-rakes.[101]
McCormick, however, was unable to make good his position
with Young, and his effort to do so left the latter in ill humor.
Knowing that his patents could not be extended or reissued
without his consent, and that they were essential to Cyrus
McCormick in his fight against the pool, he compelled the
inventor to pay him liberally and to loan him funds to relieve
his chronic need.[102] At the same time, McCormick had to buy
the continued support of the Russells, since his contract with
them did not give him an exclusive control of their patent,
and they were hobnobbing with the Whiteleys and the rake
pool.[103]

By these measures the McCormicks mustered their forces

---

[100] ‡H. Baldwin, Jr., to C. H. McCormick, Apr. 18, 19 and May 8, 1866;
C. H. McCormick to Baldwin & Collier, Oct. 2, 1868; C. H. McCormick to
W. D. Baldwin, Feb. 3 and Mch. 25, 1869; ‡W. D. Baldwin to C. H. Mc-
Cormick, Mch. 28, 1870; A. C. Rogers to C. A. Spring, Jr., Mch. 30, 1870.

[101] MS. Opinion of W. D. Baldwin, Feb. 16, 1869; B. R. Curtis to C. H.
McCormick, May 29, 1869.

[102] ‡M. Young, Frederick, Md., to C. H. McCormick, May 5, 1870, and
Jan. 16, 1874. C. H. McCormick to M. Young, Apr. 7, 1870. H. Baldwin,
Jr., to C. H. McCormick, May 7, 1870, Dec. 17 and 27, 1872, Apr. 18 and
22, 1874. C. H. McCormick to H. Baldwin, Jr., Aug. 2, 1872: "If necessary,
pay Young $20,000 to have his patent of 1858 extended." However, finally he
paid $15,000 for the extended patent of 1858 and $5,000 for 1859. ‡H.
Baldwin, Jr., to C. H. & L. J. McCormick, Apr. 21 and Sept. 28, 1874:
You are to pay $10,000 for the extended patent of 1860.

[103] H. Baldwin, Jr., to C. H. McCormick, May 7 and ‡8, 1870, ‡Dec. 27,
1872, ‡Mch. 18, 1873, and to the Co., ‡Mch. 31, 1873. MS. Agreement of
Dec. 27, 1872, between Henry R. and Isaac S. Russell and C. H. Mc-
Cormick: C. H. McCormick will pay $5,000 to the Russells if their patent
is extended.

for war. The court contest began in 1870, when the pool brought suit against them for infringement of the Dorsey patent.[104] The ardor of Harding was considerably cooled when he discovered that his witnesses were unable to prove some of Dorsey's mechanical devices back to a time antedating their first use by Young or the Russells.[105] As early as March, 1871, Harding was ready to talk about compromise, and although several conferences failed to bring an agreement, the case was not pressed.[106] Between 1872 and 1874 McCormick gained extensions of the four Young and Russell patents,[107] as well as a reissue of several of them.

For a number of months in the latter year he listened with favor to a proposal of alliance with Walter A. Wood & Co., whereby it would coöperate with him in suing rivals for infringement and securing the Young reissues in a more effective form. The patents were the McCormicks', the costs of prosecuting infringers would be Wood's, and the profits, if any,

[104] As early as May, 1867, the McCormicks were told that Johnston, through Harding, would begin suit. #Goodwin & Larned to C. H. and L. J. McCormick, May 8, 1867. W. D. Baldwin to C. H. McCormick and Co., Apr. 2, 1870. H. Baldwin, Jr., to C. H. McCormick, Apr. 20, and #Apr. 30, 1870. L. J. to C. H. McCormick, Jan. 7 and 24, 1870. L. J. McCormick feared a suit by the rake pool, because he believed that the Dorsey patent anticipated Young's.

[105] Since the extension of the Dorsey patent had been granted by a subordinate in the Patent Office and not by the Commissioner, doubt was raised concerning its validity. This fact also apparently operated to McCormick's advantage in the suit. #H. Baldwin, Jr., to C. H. McCormick, Mch. 8, 1871.

[106] C. H. McCormick to H. Day, Dec. 21, 1874.

[107] A paraphrase of the #memo. written by C. H. McCormick on Feb. 21, 1874, will show the basis of his hopes: The Young patents were reissued to secure to us the exclusive right to every rake device which entered the grain *in front* of the cutting apparatus, and after pushing the grain back upon the platform, swept it off, and then rose to a perpendicular position and passed over the reel. The rake was made so to enter the grain as not to interfere with the driver seated on the machine. The original Dorsey rake could not be used if the driver remained upon the machine—he had to ride on the back of one of the horses. For this reason we have a whip hand over the Dorsey.

would be divided equally between them. This plan to unite two of the biggest firms in the country for the purpose of fighting Whiteley and the rake pool with their own weapons was never carried out. Cyrus McCormick conferred many times on this subject with J. Russell Parsons, the son-in-law of Walter A. Wood and the vice-president of his company.[108] Parson's health failed in the autumn of 1874 and he felt obliged to go to California to recuperate.[109] During his absence, McCormick lost his first enthusiasm for the *entente,* and although Parsons was eager for the fray when he returned at the beginning of the new year, the moment for action had passed. McCormick had discovered that to reissue one of the Young patents in such a form as to make it effective against his competitors it must include claims to certain combinations of mechanical elements which he had held to be unpatentable in his Dorsey suit defense. Surely, if this were done, the rake pool would revive their case and stand an excellent chance of gaining a favorable verdict. Far better to let sleeping dogs lie, even at the cost of sacrificing the Wood alliance. The extended Dorsey patent would lapse for good and all in 1877, and until then it was wise to go slowly.[110]

[108] J. R. Parsons had been associated with D. C. Ball in making Manny machines at Hoosick Falls, at least as early as 1852 or 1853. See, "Pennsylvania Farm Journal" (West Chester, Pa.), July, 1855, p. 208. Letters to C. H. McCormick from A. D. Hager, Proctorsville, Vt., June 1, 1857, ‡H. Day, Mch. 3, 1874, ‡H. Baldwin, Jr., May 16, July 28 and Aug. 4, 1874, and ‡J. R. Parsons, ‡June 23, and July 25, 1874. ‡H. Day to C. H. & L. J. McCormick, Mch. 7, 1874; J. R. Parsons to C. H. & L. J. McCormick, Sept. 19, 1874. ‡C. H. McCormick to H. Baldwin, Jr., Feb. 21, Sept. 8 and 28, 1874.

[109] ‡H. Baldwin, Jr.'s telegram to C. H. McCormick, Oct. 28, 1874; C. H. McCormick to H. Day, Dec. 21, 1874.

[110] H. Baldwin, Jr., to C. H. McCormick, Feb. 25, 1874 and Dec. ‡21 and ‡31, 1874; C. H. McCormick to H. Day, Dec. 21, 1874; H. Baldwin, Jr., to C. H. & L. J. McCormick, June 21, 1875; H. Day to C. H. & L. J. McCormick, Jan. 20, 1875. Day was anxious for C. H. McCormick to close with Wood. Baldwin advised against it.

Although the McCormicks had so well fortified their machine with patents that the members of the pool concluded that it would be unprofitable to push their suit against them for infringement, there was no doubt that the Johnston-Dorsey type of rake gave excellent service. The McCormick self-rake was non-controllable, and its center of gravity was so high that it could not be used on hillsides. This handicap barred it from sale in many parts of the country.[111] Wishing to sound out Johnston on the subject of a license, but unwilling to furnish him with good advertising copy unless an agreement could be reached, the McCormicks commissioned Saxton late in 1877 to broach the matter to him without mentioning their name.[112] Thus began the dickering which led to the contract of the summer of 1879 whereby the McCormicks were licensed by Johnston to build his self-rake for a royalty fee of about $3.25 per machine.[113] In the same year the Harvester Rake Pool dissolved when Johnston's key patent of 1865 expired.[114]

[111] McCormick Co. to C. H. McCormick, Oct. 8, 1877. L.P.C.B. No. 174, pp. 720, 808, F. H. Matthews to C. H. McCormick, Oct. 1 and 8, 1877. The Johnston reel-rake had a worthy competitor after 1870 in the "table-rake," invented by Jacob and Lewis Miller, and soon manufactured in large numbers by all the "Buckeye" firms, and by W. A. Wood. It was pivoted close to the platform and was entirely distinct from the reel. Compared with the reel-rake, it was said to be more durable, more easily controlled, less complicated, and to deliver more compact gavels. The reel-rake, however, rendered better service in tangled grain. As early as 1863 there was demand for a controllable rake but the McCormicks thought it would be too complicated. *Ibid.*, No. 64, p. 465, the Co. to L. Wisler, Townsend, O., Sept. 21, 1863.

[112] *Ibid.*, No. 175, p. 358, the Co. to J. A. Saxton, Canton, Nov. 6, 1877, and p. 735, to W. D. Baldwin, Nov. 26, 1877.

[113] ‡C. Colahan to C. H. McCormick, July 8 and Nov. 10, 1879, and Oct. 16, 1882; ‡C. Colahan's telegram to C. H. & L. J. McCormick, July 14, 1879. "The Farmers' Advance" (Chicago), May 1, 1880, p. 4. C. H. McCormick, Jr., to S. Johnston, Brockport, N. Y., Mch. 24, 1881. This shows that the McCormicks sold 1456 Johnston rakes in 1880. S. Johnston to C. Colahan, Feb. 27 and Apr. 7, 1882.

[114] S. Johnston, Brockport, N. Y., to McCormick Harvesting Machine Co., Jan. 26, 1884. Here Johnston states that the rake pool "died" when his

Thereupon, the McCormicks purchased at least one of the important self-rake patents which had heretofore been locked in the combine.[115] As we have seen earlier in this chapter, 1879 also marked the close of the long contest with the "Buckeye" folk over mower patents. Probably there was more than chance in this coincidence of dates. The big manufacturers were anxious to clear their desks of old issues in order to devote their entire attention and resources to the harvester-binder war already in progress.

1865 patent expired, but in a telegram of G. Harding to C. H. McCormick, Apr. 12, 1882, he speaks of the "Self-Rake Association" being in session in Philadelphia. In like manner, C. Colahan in a letter to C. H. McCormick, Oct. 2, 1882, refers to the "Johnston-Harding Rake Pool" as still in existence. Up to Jan. 1, 1870, the pool had collected about $120,000 in license fees. See, *Dorsey Extension Case*, p. 293.

115 This was the reel-rake patent, dated Mch. 10, 1868, of Thomas Harding of Springfield, O., which was assigned to the McCormick Harv. Mach. Co. on Jan. 10, 1880. T. Harding to C. H. McCormick, Jr., Dec. 7, 1883. Hardly had the McCormicks started to manufacture the Johnston self-rake than W. N. Whiteley charged that its mechanism invaded some of his patent-rights. The McCormicks at once sought from Johnston a guarantee of protection against suit by the Whiteleys. Johnston finally gave it in late 1882 after the McCormicks had withheld the royalties due him on the rakes they had manufactured. Doubtless Whiteley tried by his threat to gain from the McCormicks the use of some of their patents on binders. L.P.C.B. No. 201, p. 384, the Co. to W. R. B. Smyth, Freeport, Ill., May 7, 1880. C. Colahan to C. H. McCormick, #Nov. 9, 1880 and Oct. 28, 1882. S. Johnston, Brockport, to C. Colahan, Feb. 27 and Apr. 4, 1882. S. Johnston's telegram to the Co., Apr. 8, 1882.

CHAPTER XI

THE RISE AND FALL OF THE TRANSATLANTIC
MARKET, 1856-1876

WITH the close of the Crimean War in 1856, and the opening of a period of agricultural depression in the United States lasting until 1862, the principal American manufacturers of harvesting machinery sought to offset hard times at home by extending their markets overseas. Cyrus McCormick and Obed Hussey had first opened the way for foreign sales by the display of their reapers at the Exhibition of the Industry of All Nations in the Crystal Palace at London in 1851. There and at the Paris World's Fair four years later, McCormick won the highest awards, but his rival also attained a gratifying measure of success and the machine of each inventor was championed by an increasing number of English grain-growers.

By 1860, however, they were not the only American reaper manufacturers in the foreign field. John H. Manny and John S. Wright of Illinois, Eliakim Forbush and Seymour & Morgan of New York early entered the lists.[1] From the Empire State soon came Walter A. Wood, who was destined for long to be one of the chief American competitors of McCormick for the favor of English and European farmers. To these should be added Patrick Bell and his Scottish reaper which was at work again after a long sleep of twenty years. When,

[1] John Palmer of Stockton-on-Tees manufactured the Forbush Reaper, while the Manny, Wright, and Seymour & Morgan machines were supplied from the United States.

in 1854, its principal manufacturer, William & Alfred Cross-kill of Beverley in Yorkshire, adopted the knife of McCormick without his authorization and further improved the machine in detail, it won the patronage of those who believed that home talent should be encouraged.[2] Lord Kinnaird, one of the first advocates of mechanical reaping in Scotland, associated with John Burry, a skilled mechanic, and for about seven years sold a few machines which were said to combine the best features of the inventions of McCormick and Bell.[3]

At the outset, the leading reaper-makers of the United States assumed that they could not profitably supply the over-seas market from their home factories. Freight rates were too high, and a farmer for patriotic reasons was supposed to pre-fer a machine that bore the stamp of a firm in his own country. Harvest conditions in America were unlike those abroad, and reapers had to be adapted to the new environment. This could best be done by craftsmen of the land in which the machines were to be sold. Using England as an example, fields there averaged smaller in size than those in the United States; they were often ridged, and as a rule the grain was tall, tangled, and tough of stalk. In southern Russia and the lower Danube Valley alone, field and crop conditions were quite similar to those of the prairie belt. For these reasons American inventors applied for foreign patents and engaged manufacturers in England and on the Continent who would pay them £4 and £5 royalty for each of their reapers, made and sold.

The United States encouraged the ingenuity of its citizens by the enactment of patent laws which at a small cost insured

[2] The efforts to compel the Crosskills and other English firms to pay C. H. McCormick a royalty can be traced in ‡C. H. Collette to C. H. Mc-Cormick, Jan. 8, 1856, and in the ‡correspondence between Prichard & Collette and Robinson & Atkinson, both of London, Aug. 26, 1857, to Apr. 29, 1858. "Gardeners' Chronicle and Agricultural Gazette" (London), July 29, 1856, p. 508. Hereafter cited as "Gardeners' Chronicle."

[3] "Farmer's Magazine" (London), Oct., 1855, p. 314.

a maximum of protection for a long term of years to an inventor.[4] European countries in 1860 required an inventor to pay heavy fees for a patent.[5] These were not usually collected in a lump sum at the time the patent was granted, but came due year after year during the life of the monopoly. If they were not paid, the patent lapsed and the protection was lost. For this reason an American manufacturer was wise to retain a solicitor in each foreign country in which he sold reapers, to keep him reminded of his recurring obligations. Unlike the United States, European countries permitted only important discoveries or basic changes in the construction of a machine to be patented. An extension of patent beyond its original term was rarely granted. Many improvements deemed valuable by an American were, therefore, freely open to use by a foreign firm. For these reasons litigation over patents was less commonly resorted to than in the United States. In any event, an American hesitated to carry a complaint of infringement before a foreign court unless he were confident that he had a strong case. Before the unification of 1871, the cost of securing patents in all of the German states was almost prohibitive, while in Italy and Spain too few reaper sales could be expected to warrant the expense. According to McCormick's English

[4] "Engineering" (London), XVI (1873), pp. 88-89, American implements reveal "a tendency to excess of ingenuity, which often appears to be exercised rather for the purpose of evading an existing patent than for the sake of efficiency." In so far as harvesting machinery was concerned, this was doubtless true. The intricacy of patent claims in the United States was always a source of amazement to English lawyers. Robertson, Brooman & Co., London, to C. H. McCormick, Oct. 25, 1877: "Fancy sixty-two claims in four patents on Binder mechanism, from two men! It's like registration of shapes and configurations."

[5] C. H. McCormick to Baldwin & Son, June 30, 1860. European countries represented at the Centennial Exhibition at Philadelphia in 1876, were forcibly reminded that their patent laws discouraged invention. See, U. S. Senate, 45th Cong., 2nd Sess., *Misc. Doc. No. 50*, pp. 97, 271, 446-448. England charged an inventor £175 in stamp duties for a patent, while in the U. S. the fee was $35.

solicitors, German manufacturers were the most notorious "pirates" of inventions in Europe, although probably they were most often merely appropriating as their own, discoveries which had not been patented in their homeland.[6]

Charges for patents were but one of the many items which made the introduction of reapers abroad a most expensive business. Much more important was the conservatism of the European landowners and in some areas the hostility of farm laborers to the use of machines.[7] An American manufacturer who, like McCormick, blazed the way, faced a loss year after year. With the aid of agricultural journals and societies, he slowly taught English, German, and Russian landowners that on a farm of moderate size a reaper would almost pay for itself in a single harvest by its saving of grain, time, and labor cost. But to do this, hedge-rows must be sacrificed for the sake of larger fields, deep furrows erased, and the operator of the implement must acquire enough mechanical sense to oil its moving parts, and to repair it in case of a minor mishap. The agricultural press of Great Britain in the late 1850's emphasized that harvesting machinery demanded intelligent farm labor, and that the day of the stupid husbandman had closed. At this time improvements were added to the reaper in almost every harvest and the European grain-grower, accustomed

---

[6] ‡Robertson, Brooman & Co., London, to C. H. McCormick, Mch. 28, 1872. ‡J. T. Griffin, Berlin, to C. H. McCormick, Feb. 28 and May 30, 1863. The life of a Prussian patent was only five years (compared with fourteen years in the U. S.), and could be renewed only with great difficulty. The sole benefit derived from a patent granted by any one of the many German states was to prevent manufacture there by an interloper. Since there were no custom's barriers between the German states, a manufacturer in a state where McCormick had no patent, could freely make his reapers without royalty and ship them at little cost to states where McCormick was protected. A Russian patent was good for ten years but cost £110.

[7] The "Scientific American," Apr. 12, 1856, p. 242. "Gardeners' Chronicle," May 24, 1856, p. 364; Nov. 1, 1856, p. 730; Nov. 8, 1856, p. 745. "Chicago Daily Press," Aug. 31, 1858.

to low-priced tools which would last a lifetime or more, hesitated to invest £30 or £40 in a machine that would be worn out and obsolete within eight or ten years.

There were, however, several favoring factors tending to counterbalance these handicaps. When the reaper crossed the sea, it was already a success in America, and European farmers unlike those in the United States, were not obliged to suffer with it through a long period of experiment. Thanks to the great fairs at London and Paris, it had been introduced with much *éclat,* and foreign visitors interested in agricultural reform carried the good news to their homes. In each country of Europe there were a few influential men who immediately made its cause their own, bought machines for their farms, arranged for trials in their harvests, and urged their friends to buy them. Notable among these were Squire J. Mechi of England, Lord Kinnaird of Scotland, Michel Chevalier of France, Baron Bettino Ricasoli of Sardinia, and C. S. Schneitler, the editor of an important farm journal of Berlin. Agricultural periodicals without exception were on the side of the reaper,[8] and members of the ruling houses of Europe extended it their patronage in order to set a good example for their subjects to follow.[9]

In the decade before the Civil War, the British Isles, of all the territory of Europe, appeared to promise the largest imme-

[8] "Gardeners' Chronicle," Aug. 23, 1856, p. 569; Sept. 19, 1857, pp. 651-652. "Landwirtschaftliche Zeitung für Nord und Mittel Deutschland" (Berlin), Mch. 28, 1856, pp. 100, 102; Aug. 15, 1856, pp. 257 ff.; Aug. 28, 1856, pp. 275-276; Sept. 12, 1856, pp. 292-293; Oct. 31, 1856, pp. 349-351; May 22, 1857, p. 168; July 10, 1857, p. 224; Aug. 1, 1857, p. 254. "Mechanics' Magazine, Museum, Register, Journal, and Gazette," of London (hereafter cited as "Mechanics' Magazine"), May 22, 1858, pp. 482-485. Ricasoli bought two reapers of Burgess & Key in 1857. R. A. Brooman, London, to C. H. McCormick, Aug. 26, 1859.

[9] "Gardeners' Chronicle," June 7, 1856, p. 395. Napoleon III took great interest in the Agricultural Exposition at Paris in 1856. When the Empress Eugenie visited it, she "was wheeled about in a perambulator."

diate profits to American reaper manufacturers. Although McCormick's agents there often complained about the seeming inability of an English farmer to observe the simplest rules for the care of a machine, and marveled at the force of the inertia which led him to defend the slowest methods of harvesting, at least they could argue with him in his own language. Many forward-looking men were trying to promote the culture of grain in England in order to lessen her dependence for that staple upon imports. There were more societies and journals in Great Britain devoted to agricultural progress than in the other countries in Europe. Several American bankers and exporting firms of great respectability— George Peabody & Co.,[10] Brown, Shipley & Co., and Naylor & Benson [11]—were ready in Liverpool and London to place their services at the disposal of United States manufacturers. No people in the world were more skilled in the use of iron and steel than the English, and although they lacked an adequate supply of wood, their factories could build reapers as efficiently as those in America. In fact, England led the United States by at least twenty years in the use of reapers made largely of steel.[12] Harvest in the British Isles began at about the time the prairie belt was cutting its last grain, and for this reason an American manufacturer could be on hand to supervise during the busiest season in both countries. The small and compact grain area of Great Britain, when compared with Germany, Austria Hungary, or Russia, was also attractive to reaper-makers who wished to try out their wings

[10] ‡George Peabody & Co. to C. H. McCormick, Oct. 1, 1864. Herein, McCormick was informed that the firm had "expired by the effluxion of time" on Sept. 30, and was succeeded by Junius S. Morgan & Co.

[11] ‡Nettie F. McCormick, London, to E. L. Benson, July 29, 1864.

[12] Bamlett's steel reaper, made by Samuelson of Banbury, was in the field at least as early as the 1860 harvest. See, "Gardeners' Chronicle," Sept. 22, 1860, p. 859; June 22, 1861, p. 582. This was probably the invention of Adam Carlisle Bamlett of Thirsk, Yorkshire.

cautiously in a foreign field, although they could not have selected a region in Europe where the harvest season was more likely to be rainy, or where the grain would put their machines to a severer test. Nor were the hills of Scotland and northern England a welcome sight to a reaper which had won its laurels on the level fields of Iowa and Illinois.

When Cyrus McCormick first explored the possibilities of a European market in the years 1851 to 1853, he hoped to find several manufacturers in each of the principal grain-growing countries who would extend their sales under the spur of healthy competition. Obed Hussey had the same idea in so far as the British Isles were concerned, and before 1860 three or four factories were making a modified form of his machine. Several English firms were selected by McCormick to build his reaper, but by 1857, as a result of disagreements over royalties, Burgess & Key of Brentwood, Essex, was its only manufacturer in England.[13]

Sir Kingsmill Grove Key, Baronet, handled the financial affairs of this partnership, while William Burgess, and within a few years his son Charles, furnished the mechanical skill. Because English wheat and rye were often too heavy to rake hour after hour by hand from the platform of a reaper, Burgess as early as 1854 invented and patented an ingenious

[13] This does not include Kinnaird & Burry of Scotland, who added an endless web delivery to the McCormick reaper, but sold too few to deserve much emphasis. See, "Gardeners' Chronicle," June 29, 1861, p. 611 and ‡the contracts of 1853 between McCormick and Ransome & Sims of Ipswich, and Richard Garrett & Son of Saxmundham. These were probably never carried into effect, although "Gardeners' Chronicle," Sept. 1, 1855, p. 589, announced that these two firms "will make" Burgess & Key's McCormick machines. This was probably the outcome of the letter from ‡C. H. McCormick to Burgess & Key, Mch. 26, 1855, in which he asked the partners if they could draw Garrett and Ransome into a "mutual arrangement." "The object . . . of course is to consolidate and monopolize the trade by such a combination of machinery, means, men & influence, as will accomplish the object to the fullest extent." ‡R. A. Brooman to C. H. McCormick, Apr. 1, 1858; ‡C. H. Collette to C. H. McCormick, Dec. 23, 1858.

Archimedian screw device which automatically laid the cut grain in swath on the stubble at the side of the moving machine.[14] Prairie farmers much preferred delivery in gavels ready for the bandster, even though the grain had to be cleared from the platform by manual labor. For this reason, McCormick was unwilling to place the screw on his Chicago-made reapers, although Burgess urged its adoption, hoping thereby to be released from paying so heavy a royalty to McCormick for the use of his English patents.[15] This difference of opinion was the first of many which arose to trouble his relations with Burgess & Key during the next fifteen years.

The Burgesses were forever tinkering with the machine and McCormick was displeased by their apparent effort to change the construction of each patented element sufficiently to avoid paying him a royalty. If this were their objective, they were unsuccessful prior to 1859, for in that year they agreed to give him £4,000 in lieu of any further fees under his three English patents. By this time Burgess & Key led the field in England and had made and sold about two thousand machines.[16] The several British factories manufacturing Hussey and Bell reapers were disposed to use the knife and divider

[14] "Mechanics' Magazine," Mch. 17, 1855, pp. 241-242. As late as 1867, Burgess & Key reapers still used this type of self-delivery. See, ‡J. T. Griffin, London, to C. H. McCormick, Aug. 11 and Oct. 6, 1866; Aug. 17, 1867.

[15] ‡C. H. McCormick to Burgess & Key, Mch. 26, 1855: "I have no disposition too heavily to burthen the *general introduction* of the Reaper into use by heavy Royalties." ‡Burgess & Key to C. H. McCormick, May 5, 1857.

[16] McCormick was not pleased with Burgess & Key's work. He wrote to W. S. McCormick, on Apr. 20, 1857: "If I could have had a good and efficient man in England, I am satisfied that by this time a *large business* might have been doing there." ‡R. A. Brooman to C. H. McCormick, Apr. 1 and 15, 1858; Aug. 26, 1859; C. H. Collette to C. H. McCormick, Dec. 23, 1858. C. H. to W. S. McCormick, Apr. 15 and May 3, 1858. ‡MS. Undated Agreement between C. H. McCormick and Sir Kingsmill Grove Key, but apparently signed by McCormick on June 16, 1859.

of McCormick without his permission. Time and again, through his solicitors, Prichard & Collette of London, he threatened to sue for infringement. In so far as the available records show, however, his grievances were never brought before the courts.[17]

Although more Burgess & Key McCormick reapers were sold in the British Isles during the years 1851-1861 than those of any other manufacturer, expert opinion was by no means unanimous in their support. Hussey, Bell, and Wood had their ardent champions, and the first two of these and McCormick each won the highest prize three times during this decade in the annual field trials of the Royal Agricultural Society of England. This association included within its membership the leading agriculturalists of the kingdom, and its inconclusive verdict merely reflected the divided opinion of the many other organizations of farmers which furnished reaper-makers a yearly opportunity to compete for premiums. The victors in these contests widely advertised their prowess both at home and abroad, but as in the United States, the amount and superior quality of the roast beef and champagne furnished to the jury of award by an aspirant for the first prize, often went far toward determining the result.[18]

With the exception of the Bell reapers as made by William & Alfred Crosskill (Crosskill's Trustees), the McCormick commanded the highest price on the English market. By 1860,

[17] #Correspondence between Prichard & Collette and Robinson & Atkinson of London, Aug. 26, 1857 to Apr. 29, 1858. #Account of C. H. McCormick with Prichard & Collette, Easter Term, 1855. #C. H. Collette to C. H. McCormick, Jan. 8, 1856; #C. H. McCormick to R. A. Brooman, Mch. 20, 1859; #R. A. Brooman to C. H. McCormick, Apr. 7, 1859. "Mechanics' Magazine," Dec. 21, 1860, p. 433.

[18] S. Sidney in a paper read before the Society of Arts, blamed the slow progress of the reaper in England upon the "contradictory decisions of the Royal Agricultural Society." "Gardeners' Chronicle," Dec. 12, 1857, p. 844. For a summary list of the prizes granted by the Royal Agricultural Society during the decade beginning in 1851, see, ibid., Aug. 31, 1861, p. 795.

most landlords who could afford to give £42 had made their purchases, and there was an insistent demand for a lighter and less expensive machine. Because of this pressure, the Hussey reaper priced at about £30 by its British makers, William Dray & Co., Spencer, Wray & Son, Robert Cuthbert & Co., Gardner & Lindsay, and others, gained increasing favor, especially in Scotland where self-rakes carried little appeal.[19] Walter A. Wood was rapidly winning fame and fortune in America by demonstrating that it was possible to unite cheapness, light draught, and fair durability in a single implement, and his English manufacturer, W. H. Cranston of London, sold over two thousand reapers in four years (1858-1862).[20] As a reaper, the Wood combined-machine was inferior to the McCormick, but in grass it was surpassed by none. To meet this competition, Burgess & Key about 1858 arranged to build the excellent mower of A. B. Allen of New York.[21] At this time, also, Bernard Samuelson of Banbury contracted to make the Owen Dorsey reel-rakes (a self-rake reaper-mower [22]) and Ball mowers. Within a few years, Wood

[19] "Farmer's Magazine," Sept. 1859, p. 211; Dec. 1859, p. 503. "Transaction of the Highland and Agricultural Society of Scotland," Vol. XI (3rd ser.), pp. 123-147. The trend toward the use of cheaper and lighter machines than the McCormick is noticeable as early as 1860. See, "Gardeners' Chronicle," Sept. 15, 1860, p. 837; Sept. 29, 1860, p. 880; Oct. 27, 1860, p. 959; Nov. 10, 1860, p. 1008, ‡E. Alexander, Stirling, Scotland, to C. H. McCormick, Sept. 20, 1865. This writer claimed that Scottish farmers still preferred manual delivery because of the wet harvests. In other words, grain had to be spread on the stubble to dry, before it could be safely tied into sheaves. Letter to C. H. McCormick in "North British Agriculturist" (Edinburgh), Sept. 30, 1863.

[20] Peltier in France was also manufacturing the Wood machine. *Dorsey Extension Case*, p. 289. Here Wm. N. Cranston testified that he went to England in 1858, and from 1863 to May, 1869, remained there as a partner of Walter A. Wood. He probably began to manufacture Wood machines in 1858.

[21] "Scientific American," Oct. 1, 1859, p. 219.

[22] "Gardeners' Chronicle," Sept. 25, 1858, p. 722. "Mechanics' Magazine," Jan. 17, 1862, p. 32.

alone was able to hold his own against the popularity of these light machines both in England and on the continent.

Shortly after McCormick made his initial arrangement with Burgess & Key, these partners sub-leased manufacturing rights to several firms in Europe. France was always an excellent place in which to win prizes, but few countries offered less encouragement as a market. D. L. Laurent of Paris and Francois Bella of Grignon made a few McCormick machines for sale in France and Algeria, but during the entire period covered in this chapter, by far the most of the thrifty French peasants on their small holdings continued complacently to swing their hooks and sickles. Neither McCormick nor any other reaper manufacturer could make headway against Gallic conservatism.[23]

Even less encouragement was found in the Low Countries, although Burgess & Key received the first premium for two successive years in trials held under the auspices of the Royal Agricultural Society of The Netherlands, and other awards were gained in Belgium from an association formed there to promote the introduction of farm machinery.[24] There is no record of sales in Portugal or Spain prior to 1864. At least

[23] "Journal de l'Agriculture Pratique et du Jardinage" (Paris), VI, 4th ser. (1856), pp. 125, 228; VII (1857), p. 110; II, 5th ser. (1859), pp. 52, 156-159, 196; II, 6th ser. (1864), pp. 195, 255. ‡D. C. McKenzie from London to C. H. McCormick, Apr. 10, 1857. "Prairie Farmer," Sept. 1, 1859, p. 137. "Frank Leslie's Illustrated Newspaper," Sept. 10, 1859, p. 234; "Farmer's Magazine," Feb. 1860, pp. 132-135; Sept. 1860, p. 193. "The Cultivator," Sept. 1860, p. 293. "Scientific American," Oct. 20, 1860, p. 265. The Prince Imperial visited the McCormick factory in Chicago in Sept., 1861. L.P.C.B. No. 45, pp. 327, 334, W. S. McCormick to H. O. Goodrich, Jerseyville, Ill., Sept. 3, 1861. ‡Albaret et Cie. to J. T. Griffin, July 20, 1865.

[24] H. Van Houten, Pella, Ia., to C. H. McCormick, Mch. 30, 1857. "Journal de l'Agriculture Pratique," Vol. II (1859), pp. 181-182, 259-260; "Scientific American," Sept. 17, 1859. ‡Programme du Concours International de Machines à Moissonner, Ouvert Par La Société Centrale d'Agriculture de Belgique, Bruxelles, le 15 Janvier, 1859. "The Cultivator," Sept. 1861, p. 292. "Gardeners' Chronicle," Sept. 1, 1860, p. 798.

eight reapers had been sent by Burgess & Key to prominent landowners of north Italy before the American Civil War, and a first prize was won at Grosseto in Tuscany in 1857.[25]

Whether Anton Burg of Vienna, Schneitler & Andrée of Berlin, Dr. Hamm of Leipsig, Talbot & Herbrand of Aachen, and Evans & Lilpop of Warsaw paid either Burgess & Key or Cyrus McCormick any fees for the machines which they made may well be doubted. Taking them at their word, they manufactured and sold several hundred McCormick reapers in Austria-Hungary, the German states, and Russia before 1861.[26] To these must be added a few marketed there by Burgess & Key, and several more sent direct from Chicago. Of these three regions, Austria-Hungary appeared to be the most promising because of the scarcity of harvest labor in the Danube Valley. In 1857, in a field trial in heavy rye near Budapest, a Burgess & Key McCormick defeated a Hussey reaper made by Baron Ward of Vienna. Archduke Albrecht and several high state officials who had witnessed the contest, expressed the hope that the English firm would endeavor to

[25] "Farmer's Magazine," July, 1860, p. 1. #Royalty Account of Burgess & Key with C. H. McCormick for 1864 shows that eight of its reapers were shipped to Spain, and five more were sent there from Chicago. W. A. Wood already had an office in Madrid. In 1865, Burgess & Key sent twenty McCormick reapers to Spain but very few were sold. #J. T. Griffin, London, to C. H. McCormick, Mch. 17, 1866: "Italy is a dead field and Spain, due to political troubles and lack of money, not much better. Wood sells for £36 in Spain, but we have to charge £40." Another first prize was won at Grosseto by C. H. McCormick in 1883, but the sales in Italy were always very few. A Cosimini e Figli, Grosseto, to C. H. McCormick, July 1, 1883. "Chicago Times," Sept. 1, 1883.

[26] "Landwirtschaftliche Zeitung," May 22, 1857, p. 168; July 10, 1857, p. 224; Aug. 7, 1857, pp. 254-255; Sept. 1, 1859, pp. 278-9, Sept. 8, 1859, pp. 282-5, Sept. 15, 1859, pp. 293-96; and Dec. 29, 1859, pp. 411-412. "Agronomische Zeitung" (Leipzig), Mch. 19, 1857, p. 184, and July 30, 1857, pp. 488-89. "Landwirtschaftlicher Anzeiger für Kurhessen" (Cassel), Oct. 19, 1859, pp. 149-152. Butenose Bros., Moscow, to C. H. McCormick, May 16, 1859. L.P.C.B. No. 35, p. 461, C. H. McCormick & Bros. to Butenose Bros., Sept. 29, 1860.

increase its sales in their country.[27] Agricultural editors in Germany urged their subscribers to cease complaining of high labor costs and to buy reapers; not those imported from England, but the even more efficient ones made in their own country. By 1860 Wood claimed to have sold fifty machines in Russia, and he anticipated a profitable trade in the Volga Valley and Siberia. In the same year the office of the McCormick factory informed the Consul General of Russia at New York of its interest in extending the use of its machines in his country. In his reply he requested that the new Imperial Agricultural Museum at St. Petersburg should be favored with a model of the machine.[28] Erzerum, in Turkey, was soon the farthest outpost of the McCormick reaper.[29]

By 1862 Cyrus McCormick was ready to introduce his new self-rake reaper to the grain-growers of the world. Thanks to his brothers, he could leave the country for an indefinite stay with the knowledge that his interests were in competent hands. The lawsuits and patent-extension cases which had prevented

[27] "Agronomische Zeitung," July 23, 1857, pp. 473-474. "Farmer's Magazine," Aug. 1857, pp. 130-131. The "Scientific American," Aug. 1, 1857, p. 374.
[28] L.P.C.B. No. 37, p. 311, McCormick Co. to J. de Nottbeck, N. Y. City, Dec. 7, 1860. ‡J. de Nottbeck to McCormick Co., Dec. 11, 1860. ‡J. T. Griffin, London, to C. H. McCormick, Dec. 10, 1864: Wood claims to have sold as many as two hundred in one season in Moscow, and to have sent fifty machines to Russia as early as 1860. See, L.P.C.B. No. 35, p. 461, the Co. to Butenose Bros., Moscow, Sept. 29, 1860.
[29] ‡T. C. Trowbridge, Constantinople, to C. H. McCormick, Mch. 5, 1864. Letters from the Co. in L.P.C.B. No. 88, p. 395, to L. S. Durfee, Phila., Mch. 14, 1866; No. 220, p. 604, to E. Benedict, N. Y. City, Feb. 1, 1882, *in re* shipping a machine to Mersine, Turkey; No. 249, pp. 215, 232, to D. Offley, Smyrna, Jan. 13, 1882, and to Rev. T. D. Christie, Adana, Turkey, Jan. 30, 1882; No. 240, p. 148, to Mrs. J. O. Keller, Ft. Wayne, Ind., Feb. 5, 1884. In 1881, C. H. McCormick declined to send two harvester-binders to Thessaly on the grounds that field conditions there were too primitive to permit their success. See, ‡L.P.C.B. of C. H. McCormick, Nov. 1880-May, 1881, p. 364. C. H. McCormick to R. C. Ransome, Ipswich, Eng., Mch. 29, 1881.

an extended wedding trip four years before, were settled. Europe was the more attractive to him because his emphatic stand for peace after Lincoln's election brought him its social penalty as soon as hostilities began. Perhaps Napoleon III could be persuaded to offer to mediate between the warring sections.[30]

Although these general considerations influenced McCormick to journey overseas in 1862, his immediate objective was the London International Exposition. To prepare for this, men at his factory in late 1861 built a self-rake reaper with special care. Its platform was covered with "planished copper . . . sometimes used in making bath tubs" and its iron pieces were highly polished.[31] John Skirving, who had been associated with Christian Schussele in the painting of a canvas entitled "American Men of Progress," showing McCormick conspicuously in the foreground, was employed to varnish and gold stripe in his best style the beautifully grained ash used for its woodwork. The inventor was obliged to restrain him, however, when he proposed to emblazon "Our Whole Country, or *None*" on the platform of the machine.[32] Skirving, with the implement in his charge, sailed for the Crystal Palace early in April, 1862.[33] Once in London, he joined the other "dis-

[30] H. Greeley to W. L. Dayton, Paris, July 14, 1862.

[31] L.P.C.B. No. 54, p. 140, C. H. McCormick & Bros. to T. B. Bunting & Co., N. Y. City, Dec. 25, 1861; No. 47, pp. 86, 166, to U. S. Express Co., Chicago, Mch. 18, 1862, and to H. S. Champlin & Co., Courtland, Ill., Mch. 20, 1862. "Chicago Times," Mch. 21, 1862. "Prairie Farmer," Mch. 29, 1862, p. 200. "Chicago Daily Tribune," Mch. 22, 1862.

[32] Schussele was a professor of Fine Arts at the Pennsylvania Academy of Fine Arts. L.P.C.B. No. 47, pp. 154-155, 351, C. H. McCormick to J. Skirving, Mch. 20 and 31, 1862. McCormick was a little fearful of Skirving's habits. "I *proposed* to you at dinner to have Scotch ale (which I like sometimes) which you declined, adding that you sometimes drank *wine,* whereupon I ordered a bottle. *After this* you seemed to have been drinking which I observed in my room before you left."

[33] *Ibid.,* No. 47, p. 366, C. H. McCormick & Bros. to T. B. Bunting & Co., Apr. 1, 1862. ‡J. Skirving to C. H. McCormick, Mch. 19, 1862; ‡R. A. Brooman to C. H. McCormick, Mch. 27, 1862.

gusted" representatives of the sixty American exhibitors who were at work on the five thousand square feet of floor space assigned to them in an out-of-the-way corner of the leaky building.[34]

The Virginia Reaper was soon in its place on a low platform backed by a curtain of the "dark maroon stuff . . . authorized by the Commissioners." By then the Exposition had opened, and the inexperienced Skirving was reinforced by the arrival of Leander McCormick and James T. Griffin of the factory office.[35] While the display machine was receiving the flattering attention of the crowds, twelve other self-rake reapers were made ready for field use in the harvests of England and the Continent.[36] Thus was the way prepared for the coming of Cyrus McCormick.

When he, with his wife and two children, occupied the "choice accommodations . . . not against the wheels or smoke chimney" of the SS. Scotia bound for Liverpool in July, 1862,[37] he little dreamed that two years would pass before his

[34] "Gardeners' Chronicle," May 10, 1862, p. 434.

[35] L.P.C.B. No. 47, p. 595, telegram of C. H. McCormick & Bros. to Naylor & Co., Boston, Mass., Apr. 12, 1862; ibid., pp. 648, 691, 761, C. H. McCormick to Naylor & Co., Apr. 15, 1862. This shows that Griffin carried letters from C. H. McCormick to Prince Napoleon, Charles Francis Adams, George Peabody, Joshua Bates, etc. L.P.C.B. No. 48, pp. 16, 128, 279, 289, 389, 487, C. H. McCormick to J. T. Griffin, May 1, 1862. Leander was accompanied by his wife, three children, and a nurse. ‡Letters to C. H. McCormick from J. Skirving, Apr. 28, 1862; ‡J. T. Griffin, May 9, 1862, and L. J. McCormick, May 14, and 24, 1862.

[36] L.P.C.B. No. 48, p. 511, C. H. McCormick & Bros. to J. T. Griffin, May 9, 1862. The comment of Eugene Tisserand, called forth by the Vienna Exposition of 1873, was equally in point at London. "The inventors love their machines, and their wits are continually at work to improve them; hence the unequalled finish, elegance, and exquisite work employed in their construction. The machines exhibited in their hall, especially their models, are perfect gems, wrought and polished with true artistic taste." R. H. Thurston, ed., "Reports of the Commissioners of the U. S. to the International Exhibition Held at Vienna, 1873" (Washington, 1876), I, p. 304. Hereafter cited as "R. H. Thurston."

[37] L.P.C.B. No. 48, pp. 434-435. C. H. McCormick to Naylor & Co., Boston, May 6, 1862, and No. 50, pp. 156, 725, C. H. McCormick & Bros.

return to the United States. Nor could his brothers understand why he stayed away so long.[38] Leander, very seasick on his Atlantic crossing and homesick almost as soon as he reached London, was outraged by the prices asked of Americans in European hotels and shops. At the close of the year he was more than glad to return to his native land and take his chance with the draft.[39] In his judgment, his trip was one of the blunders of his life and he desired no further connection with the foreign trade of the firm.[40] William S. McCormick, holding the Chicago fort alone for five months and daily confronted with perplexing problems, wondered why Cyrus wished "to be involved in business in Europe, unless to flee away from this land of blood & death, where we are downtrodden by abolitionism in the *North—without* liberty of speech—& with utter ruin in the South, as I suppose." [41]

For Cyrus McCormick and his wife, however, the days abroad were all too short. Comfortably settled at Edward's Hotel in Hanover Square in their "front grand drawing room with its two fireplaces opposite to each other," they followed the course of the struggle at home in the "London Times," and enjoyed the society of Baron James Rothschild, Junius

to Naylor & Co., June 28, 1862: "C. H. McCormick wishes to sail July 16th from Boston. He is to be accompanied by his wife, two children, niece, and servant." The niece was Miss Mary Adams.

[38] C. H. to W. S. McCormick, n.d., but probably the autumn of 1862: "Can say not returning this year (though I may still see about it). . . . Don't see that it can be important for me to be with you, but *may* be able to go over if still thought so."

[39] W. S. McCormick to "Dear Brother," Sept. 24, 1862: "I think the draft should not delay you as substitutes can be hired & at no very great price no doubt," L. J. to C. H. McCormick, May 24 and 29, 1862, and to Nettie F. McCormick, Dec. 4, 1862. Henrietta to Nettie F. McCormick, Dec. ?, 1862.

[40] L. J. to C. H. McCormick, Apr. 7, 1863, and Jan. 5, 1870; C. H. to L. J. McCormick, Dec. 31, 1869.

[41] W. S. to C. H. McCormick, Sept. 27, 1862.

Morgan, and George Peabody.[42] Frequent letters from William S. told of large cash balances and profitable investments in gold and real estate. Nearer at hand the self-rake reapers were winning Cyrus McCormick "trophies like the row of scalps worn by a successful Choctaw warrior." [43] During his long absences from London in the interests of his machine, his wife took their children to Brighton, Tunbridge Wells, or to one of the fashionable spas on the Continent.[44]

The reception accorded the McCormick reaper left little to be desired. Medals from the London Exposition and the Imperial Society of Agriculture in France were only the two most notable awards of the 1862 season. Exhibitions and field trials in England, Scotland, France, Belgium, Italy, Austria-Hungary, the German States, and Russia, brought Cyrus McCormick a most gratifying harvest of prizes and com-

[42] C. H. to W. S. McCormick, Dec. 2, 1862; J. T. Griffin to C. H. McCormick, Jan. 13, 1865. C. H. McCormick, Jr. MSS., Nettie F. to C. H. McCormick, Jr., July 29, 1907.
[43] 1864 Pamphlet of C. H. McCormick & Bros., p. 7.
[44] In Mch., 1864, C. H. McCormick was living at 7 Montague Place, London. When he returned to the U. S. three months later, he probably planned to go back to England after a short visit. This is indicated by his letter of Mch. 23, 1864, to his London pastor, Rev. L. Cumming, D.D. In this he writes that Mrs. McCormick would not go to America with him and that she "would be pleased to become acquainted with some English society, while our niece, who has been at school at Geneva about a year, may return and accompany her." Mrs. McCormick came back to the U. S. in Nov. 1864. Receipted hotel bills in the files of the N. F. McCormick Biog. Asso. reveal the itinerary of the McCormicks while they were in Europe. In August, 1862, for example, they were registered at Fenton's Hotel in London. In both the autumn of 1862 and 1863, C. H. McCormick was with his reaper in the harvest fields of northern England and Scotland. Their address in the winter of 1862-1863, was Edward's Hotel, London, and Brighton in the following spring. Part of the late summer and autumn of 1863 was spent at the Palace Hotel, London, and at Tunbridge Wells, but in November they opened a residence in Upper Norwood. Apparently they stayed there until C. H. McCormick sailed for home in June, 1864. From that time until Mrs. McCormick left England five months later, she lived at 17 Marlborough Rd., St. John's Wood.

mendatory press notices.[45] The "St. Petersburg Agricultural Gazette" pronounced his reaper "the best thing of the kind known as yet," and the "Hungarian News" of Budapest commented that "never before has a machine met with such general approval from our people."[46] The Duke of Athol of Scotland, Prince Alexander Baschmakoff of Russia, and the Marquis de Sambuy of Italy, were among the high-born who bought McCormick reapers for use on their estates.[47] Little wonder that the inventor was content to linger in Europe!

The climax of this round of victories came in July, 1863, when the Hamburg International Agricultural Exhibition awarded McCormick its highest prize "for the practical introduction and improvement of the Reaping Machine."[48] Ex-

[45] Pamphlet of 1863 entitled "McCormick's Reaping and Mowing Machine." "Gardeners' Chronicle," Aug. 16, 1862, p. 769; Aug. 30, 1862, p. 823; Oct. 18, 1862, p. 990. "Farmer's Magazine," Oct. 1862, pp. 308, 321, 330. "Genesee Farmer," Sept., 1862, p. 306. L.P.C.B. No. 50, p. 258, C. H. McCormick & Bros. to J. T. Griffin, London, June 18, 1862; No. 49, p. 858, C. A. Spring, Jr., to W. S. McCormick, Aug. 12, 1862. ‡J. T. Griffin to C. H. McCormick, June 19, 1862. One A. Vattemare "was the lever that we used to move the 'body of state' (Imperial Society of Agriculture in France) and to him we owe much." "Journal de l'Agriculture Pratique," Vol. II (5th ser.), pp. 110, 169, 540. "Mark Lane Express" (London), Aug. 11, 1862. "Le Siècle" (Paris), July 28, 1862. "Bell's Weekly Messenger" (London), Aug. 18 and Sept. 8, 1862. "London Times," Aug. 15 and Sept. 13, 1862. "The Daily Review" (Edinburgh), Sept. 15, 1862. "The Scotsman" (Edinburgh), Oct. 10, 1862. "North British Agriculturist," Oct. 1, 1862. "Allegemeine Land- und Forstwirtschaftliche Zeitung" (Vienna), XII, July 28, 1862, pp. 662-664.

[46] "Hungarian News" (Pesth), July 11, 1862; "St. Petersburg Agricultural Gazette," Sept. 27, 1862; ‡J. T. Griffin, St. Petersburg, Aug. 18, 1862 to C. H. McCormick, and from Moscow to C. H. McCormick, Aug. 22, 1862.

[47] A. Baschmakoff to C. H. McCormick, Aug. 10 and Oct. 22, 1862; C. H. McCormick to A. Baschmakoff, Dec. 17, 1862. The Marquis de Sambuy was President of the Italian Agricultural Association. ‡J. T. Griffin, Berlin, to C. H. McCormick, May 29 and 30, 1863, and from London, Apr. 21, 1866.

[48] "Gardeners' Chronicle," July 25, 1863, p. 706. "Prairie Farmer," Aug. 8 and 22, 1863, pp. 88, 114: "McCormick thrashed all the nations and

hibitors from thirty-four nations were there and over three thousand implements were on display. The Commissioner of the United States reported to President Lincoln that McCormick's reaper "surpassed in elegance of workmanship any agricultural machine on the ground, while his working machine at the trial only more fully demonstrated . . . the superiority which he had so long maintained in Europe and in America." Leading German merchants and bankers of New York donated a large assortment of American-made machines for permanent display in an agricultural museum to be opened at Hamburg.[49] McCormick added his prize reaper to this collection, and the United States Commissioner was of the opinion that these evidences of international good-will had helped to gain favor for the northern cause in Germany.[50]

McCormick attended this Exposition and enjoyed his triumph. He spent several weeks that summer in Germany overseeing the work of his machine in the harvest, and arranging with James R. McDonald, the acting United States consul at Hamburg, to be his agent. Gustave Koerner met the inventor in Berlin and later referred to him in his "Memoirs" as an excellent example of the American with a "business mania" who could talk only about his work or local politics and had no time to visit the cathedrals and picture-galleries of the Old

walks off with the golden medal. . . . May our glorious army be as successful in thrashing the rebels as Campbell [exhibitor of sheep from Vermont], McCormick and other Americans are, in competition, with the nations here assembled." Wiegandt und Hempel, "Annalen der Landwirtschaft in den Preussischen Staaten" (Berlin, 1869), pp. 351-352. "North British Agriculturist," Sept. 16, 1863.

[49] The Executive Committee of the Hamburg International Agricultural Exhibition of 1863 to C. H. McCormick, July 31, 1863. ‡J. R. McDonald, Hamburg, to C. H. McCormick, Aug. 19, 1865.

[50] "Daily Morning Chronicle" (Wash., D. C.), Jan. 21, 1864, Rept. of the Hon. Jos. A. Wright, Commr. of U. S., on the Internat'l. Agr'l. Exhib. at Hamburg. Twenty-three U. S. exhibitors received awards. Five steam ploughs from Great Britain attracted particular attention.

World.[51] McCormick would probably have replied that his wife was his very willing and appreciative envoy to the art museums, while his absorption in his task was amply justified by the value of his machine to the farmers of Europe.

But the grain-growers of the Continent were slow to take advantage of the opportunity afforded them. For reasons suggested earlier in this chapter, medals and newspaper "puffs" in Europe did not sell many reapers there, nor did the rather imposing number of agents whom Griffin appointed in 1862 and 1863 in a score of cities between Madrid and Moscow. Labor was said to be too cheap in Prussia, farms too small in France, ridges too high in the fields of Italy, and money too scarce in Russia where the big landowners were going through a difficult transition from serf to free labor.[52] Albaret et Cie. of Liancourt-Rantigny (Oise), licensed after 1862 to manufacture McCormick reapers for France, were able to sell less than five a year.

[51] Thomas J. McCormack, ed., "Memoirs of Gustave Koerner" (2 vols., Cedar Rapids, Ia., 1909), II, pp. 352-353. ‡J. R. McDonald & Co., Hamburg, to C. H. McCormick, Oct. 26, 1864. In the 1864 harvest this firm sold four reapers, but having distributed 13,000 circulars, the expenses were £50 more than it received from the sales.

[52] C. H. McCormick to L. Wyrzakowski (no address given), Dec. 18, 1862. ‡J. T. Griffin, Turin, to C. H. McCormick, June 17, 1863, Nov. 26 and Dec. 10, 1864. In 1864 the McCormick "trade in Russia was zero," but a ‡J. T. Griffin-McCormick account-sheet for that year shows that sixteen reapers were sent to Bellino Tendinck, of Odessa; ‡J. T. Griffin, Budapest, to C. H. McCormick, May 30, 1865: "The situation in Russia looks even more hopeless than last season." ‡Idem to C. H. McCormick, from Dresden, June 29, 1865, and from London, June 23, 1866. "The Cultivator," July 1863, pp. 201-202. Judging from the report of J. C. Morton, Chairman of the Jury on Agr'l. Machs. at the Internatl. Exhib. in London, 1862, England was using many reapers and mowers. "There is now no large arable district in the country where the reaping machine is not employed, nor any extensive district of pasture land where the mower is not at work. In some counties most of the reaping is now done by machinery." This was particularly true in the north of England. "Mechanics' Magazine," Jan. 8, 1864, p. 17: Since 1851, 10,000 reapers have been made in England.

McCormick's entire stay in Europe up to March, 1864, was punctuated by controversy with Burgess & Key over royalties past and future, and the amount of emphasis they should give to his name and his machine at their factory and in their advertisements.[53] Because of this dispute, he was obliged between 1862 and 1865 to bring most of the machines needed for the Continental market (except France) from Chicago.[54] The costly transportation charges made their price too high to compete advantageously with the reapers of Cranston-Wood or Samuelson. The McCormick machines were heavy of draft, unattractive in appearance, and often damaged as a result of their several transshipments between Chicago and their European destinations.[55] Except in the Low Countries and Central

[53] ‡J. T. Griffin to C. H. McCormick, May 9 and June 19, 1862. L. J. to C. H. McCormick, May 29, 1862. ‡Account of C. H. McCormick with Prichard & Collette, Nov. 21, 1861, to May 6, 1863. "Bell's Weekly Messenger," Aug. 18, 1862. Here Burgess & Key states that it has made arrangement to build McCormick's self-rake machine. This was a contract made for two years on Aug. 4, 1862, but it was ambiguous and question at once arose as to what royalty B. & K. should pay. A fee of £2 per machine was finally agreed upon, to be increased to £4 after 1864. ‡E. Alexander, Sterling, Scotland, to C. H. McCormick, May 30, 1863. ‡R. A. Brooman to C. H. McCormick, Mch. 4, 1864. To paraphrase: I view the amicable settlement of all matters between you and Burgess & Key as a great occasion. So will you celebrate with these partners as my guest at my club at 15 George St., Hanover Square, next Monday evening? Fearing that the lawyers might quarrel, I haven't invited them. See also, the elaborate parchment license granted to Burgess & Key on Mch. 4, 1864.

[54] C. H. McCormick to A. Baschmakoff, Dec. 17, 1862, and to W. S. McCormick, Dec. 19, 1862. C. H. McCormick feared that captures by Confederate cruisers might raise freight rates on reapers from New York. ‡C. H. McCormick to J. T. Griffin, Nov. 22, 1864: "If the business is *well worked,* I am not anxious to manufacture here [in Chicago] for Europe."

[55] ‡J. T. Griffin, Berlin, Budapest, Dresden and Frankfort-am-Main, to C. H. McCormick, Feb. 28, May 28, 30, June 4, 5, 7, 9, 12 and 13, 1863. R. Nestle, Frankfort-am-Main to E. Baxter, Mch. 10, 1863. In 1862 the freight on a reaper via Lakes and rail from Chicago to New York was about $9.50; from N. Y. to Liverpool about $40, and from Liverpool to Berlin about $35. Directions written in German for setting up and operating the machines sent to Central Europe were prepared at the Chicago factory.

Europe, work horses were smaller in size than in the United States, and farmers complained that the McCormick reapers were too heavy for their use.[56] Not infrequently they arrived late for the harvest, to the disgust of the agents who had managed with difficulty to persuade a few farmers to place orders. Their tardy coming could sometimes be justly blamed upon the Chicago factory which viewed with disfavor the interruption of its routine by the necessity of making a hundred or so reapers of a special pattern, boxing them for shipment, and dickering with the overcrowded wartime railroad and steamship companies for their carriage overseas.[57] If there had been immediate profits in the venture, the trouble would have seemed worth while, but to Leander McCormick, who was hard pressed to finish enough machines for the domestic supply, this European diversion was merely an expensive whim of a brother chiefly interested in adding to his personal prestige.[58]

Under these circumstances the yearly market for McCor-

[56] ‡J. T. Griffin, London, to C. H. McCormick, Nov. 26, Dec. 6, 1864, and July 8, 1865. ‡M. Helferich, Charkoff, Russia, to J. T. Griffin, Nov. 16, 1865.

[57] L. J. to C. H. McCormick, Jan. 26, 1864. L.P.C.B. No. 58, pp. 335, 344, 376, 379, 467, 492, 505, 507, 790, letters of C. H. McCormick & Bros. to H. H. Taylor & Co. and T. B. Bunting & Co., of N. Y., during the spring of 1863. L.P.C.B. No. 57, p. 507, C. H. McCormick & Bros. to W. H. B. Warren, Cincinnati, O., Mch. 5, 1863. See also, L.P.C.B. No. 59, pp. 18, 24, 149, 667, 669; No. 65, p. 284; No. 71, p. 568 and No. 66, pp. 127-128.

[58] As examples of the publicity value in the U. S. of reaper victories abroad, see, "Prairie Farmer," Sept. 6 and 13, 1862, pp. 152, 162; "Farmer and Gardener" (Phila.), Nov. 1862, p. 140; "The Cultivator," Sept. 1863, p. 273; F. G. Smyth, Madison, Wis., to McCormick Co., June 29, 1867: "I got him [Wood's agent] fairly rearing mad, so much so that when my back was turned, he commenced bluffing some Farmers offering to bet them that Woods had taken the Gold Medal. I . . . hurried up and pulled out a Hundred dollar Bill, put it right up to His Nose & told him *that that said Wood's Mower had taken no medal* yet . . . & that He had a plagued poor show with us. He soon drew in His Horns . . . and turned a heavy Hurrah for McCormick & laugh against Him."

mick reapers in England and Europe was very small. Griffin, who was McCormick's traveling agent there, hoped by 1867 to sell as many as three hundred a year on the Continent. This was surely not an ambitious figure when compared with the several thousand already disposed of there by Wood and the Johnston Harvester Company.[59] But the demand for Virginia Reapers declined rather than increased. In 1863 crops were light in the Danube Valley, and two years later that region, together with all Central Europe and Russia, had poor harvests.[60] In 1864 there were too few McCormick reapers in Saxony and Prussia to meet the demand, but during the spring selling season of 1866 the encouraging outlook in the German

[59] As early as 1862, Wood was reported to have sold about 2500 machines in England, and to have enjoyed a profitable market in Russia for three years. By the close of the 1864 harvest he was said to have sold over 4000 mowers in foreign countries, and in 1867 nearly 1000 of these machines were reported to be at work in France. In 1867 he advertised that he had disposed of 10,000 machines (one-fifth of his entire output) abroad in five years. C. H. McCormick was told that his rival found sales for over 400 in Ireland that season. By 1870, Wood claimed to have reached his 18,000th sale in England. See, "Genesee Farmer," Aug. 1862, p. 258. Letters of J. T. Griffin to C. H. McCormick, ‡Aug. 18, 1862, ‡Dec. 10, 1864, Jan. 13, 1865 and ‡Aug. 23, 1867. Pamphlet, "Machines à Faucher et à Moissonner de Wood: 1867." Catalog of Wood's Mowing & Reaping Machines, 1870, No. 94. ‡J. R. McDonald & Co. to C. H. McCormick, Mch. 5, 1872. ‡W. Anson Wood to C. H. McCormick, Feb. 9 and July 15, 1872. In the latter of these Wood reported that the Johnston Harvester Co. had sold over five hundred machines in Russia in 1872; seventy in England, and many in Germany. The Osborne-Kirby output was also favored abroad.

[60] ‡J. T. Griffin, Budapest and Dresden, to C. H. McCormick, June 3, and 7, 1863, May 30, Aug. 9 and Sept. 9, 1865. With failing crops, wrote Griffin, peasants in Austria-Hungary will work for a pittance, and thus it is more difficult to sell reapers. Helmsing & Grimm, Riga, to J. T. Griffin, Sept. 9, 1865: "people are so awfully slow here." Wood's is the only successful reaper in the Riga neighborhood but no manufacturer has sold many in Russia in the last few years. ‡J. T. Griffin to C. H. McCormick, Dec. 2, 1865. ‡M. Helferich, Charkoff, to J. T. Griffin, Nov. 16, 1865: We had no harvest in Russia. Drought, hot winds, and "land rats or those little earth hares" arrived by millions from south Russia, and devastated. We couldn't sell even at the Charkoff Wool Fair.

States and Austria-Hungary disappeared with the outbreak of war.[61] Griffin, dissatisfied with his low salary and the few sales rewarding his hard work, was ready to resign.[62]

To some extent, McCormick's inability to widen his foreign market was a result of his continued reliance upon Burgess & Key. In the United States he would have refused an agency, or a license to manufacture, to a firm making its own style of machines. The outcome was almost a foregone conclusion. Burgess & Key built a few McCormick self-rakes but tried far harder to sell the screw-delivery machine of their own invention. In 1864 they developed a new mower and its popularity still further cooled their interest in a heavy reaper, hard to sell, which cost them a £4 royalty.[63] McCormick might well write in the late winter of 1863-1864, "I've been *working hard* & hope to accomplish something but time is required to effect the general & extensive introduction of a new implement in Europe." [64]

Early in 1865, he tried to rouse the English partners to more vigorous effort in his behalf, by promising them for the harvest of the following year and thereafter, the exclusive privilege of making his reapers for the British Isles and all of Europe. If they sold less than one hundred and fifty in any one season on the Continent, he reserved the right to declare the agreement void. Shipments from Chicago were stopped (excepting to France), and although Griffin continued to represent McCormick on the Continent, Burgess & Key

61 ‡J. T. Griffin, Mannheim, Brussels and London, to C. H. McCormick, July 14, Aug. 4, Oct. 22, Nov. 12, 26, and Dec. 6, 1864; Apr. 7, May 19, June 23, and July 7, 1866. ‡J. P. Lanz & Co., Mannheim, to J. T. Griffin, July 2, 1866.

62 ‡J. T. Griffin to C. H. McCormick, Aug. 9, 1865, Mch. 1, Apr. 5, 1866, and Mch. 1, 1867.

63 *Idem* to *idem,* Dec. 17, 1864; Jan. 21, 27, Feb. 25, Mch. 4, July 8, 21, and Dec. 9, 1865.

64 ‡C. H. McCormick to B. P. Johnson, Feb. 27, 1864.

filled his orders and paid a portion of his annual salary.[65] Then came the Austro-German War of 1866 to blast the new hope awakened by this contract. At the close of the harvest Griffin was astonished to learn that "too heavy outlays" in cotton-gins for the Egyptian market, and questionable financial manipulations by Sir Kingsmill Key, had bankrupted the firm. Several of its chief creditors advanced enough money to keep the factory humming, but McCormick's refusal to come to its aid made Burgess almost completely indifferent to the success of the Virginia reaper. Thereafter he concentrated upon his own mower, and the McCormick self-rake became a very subordinate part of his output.[66]

In 1867 Emperor Napoleon III sought to revive his waning popularity and perhaps to divert attention from the continued rumor of approaching war, by staging in Paris an international exposition far larger and more magnificent than the Crystal Palace show of five years before. Cyrus McCormick hesitated to attend. He did not wish to exhibit unless he could win the highest award, and because of the hostility of the Johnson administration toward Maximilian in Mexico, Americans were not regarded with favor in Paris. McCormick's reaper had found few purchasers in Europe and had not been markedly improved since its success at the London Exhibition of 1862. It was, therefore, very doubtful whether his entrance into the arena at Paris would do more than afford Walter A. Wood a splendid opportunity to gain valuable publicity at his expense. But, as McCormick later wrote, "I had taken the highest prizes at all former Universal Expositions and could not stop short of the last & greatest of them all." [67]

In view of these apparent handicaps, he knew that he must play his few strong cards to the best advantage. He was a

[65] ‡J. T. Griffin to C. H. McCormick, Feb. 4, 11, 25, Mch. 4, and 11, 1865.
[66] ‡J. T. Griffin to C. H. McCormick, Jan. 20, Mch. 1, June 23, July 7, Aug. 11, Oct. 6, 24, 27, Nov. 3, 17 and 24, 1866.
[67] C. H. McCormick to B. M. Smith, Apr. 24, 1868.

realist, and had participated in too many field contests and fairs to be unaware that adroit management was almost as necessary for prize-winning as an excellent machine. At first thought it seemed well to arrange with Albaret to exhibit his machine in the French Department of the Exposition, and thus perhaps counteract, so far as McCormick was concerned, the anti-Yankee sentiment in Paris.[68] He soon concluded, however, that this expedient would cost far more than it was worth, since the Civil War was not long over and his competitors at home would once again charge him with a lack of patriotism. Eventually he paid Burgess to build him a display machine and to mark it simply:

McCORMICK'S AUTOMATIC SIDE SHEAF DELIVERY REAPER
78,351 REAPERS MADE AND SOLD BY
CYRUS HALL McCORMICK,
PATENTED IN ALL EUROPE.

The manufacturer's name did not appear on the implement, and in truth it was of McCormick's own design.[69] Under the direction of Leander J. McCormick an excellent light mower had been developed at the Chicago factory. Although he refused to share in the cost of exhibiting at Paris, or to permit the mower to be patented in Europe, he did not object to the purchase by his older brother of several of these new machines for use in connection with the Fair.[70] The display mower was marked:

[68] J. T. Griffin to C. H. McCormick, Jan. 20, 1866. C. H. McCormick to J. T. Griffin, Sept. 24, 1866.
[69] ‡J. T. Griffin to C. H. McCormick, Nov. 9, 1866; Jan. 5, Feb. 23, and Apr. 19, 1867.
[70] Letters from C. H. McCormick to Baldwin & Sons, June 21, 1866, and to J. T. Griffin, Feb. 12, 1867; to C. A. Spring, Jr., Feb. 25, 1867; to L. J. McCormick, Oct. 10, 1866, and another to L. J. McCormick begun Nov. 3, 1866, and completed Jan. 15, 1867. J. C. Derby to C. H. McCormick, Sept. 8, and Nov. 26, 1866. ‡C. A. Spring, Jr., to C. H. McCormick, Jan. 15, 1867. L.P.C.B. No. 95, p. 581, C. A. Spring, Jr., to A. Baldwin, Feb. 16, 1867.

McCORMICK'S MOWER, CHICAGO, ILL., U. S. A.
10,137 MADE AND SOLD IN TWO YEARS.

Cyrus believed that his invention of the first practical reaper, his leadership in its production for sale, and his unique record of unremunerative pioneer work for fifteen years in behalf of machine harvesting in Europe, should weigh heavily with the Jury of Award and perhaps gain him admittance to the Legion of Honor.[71] Four years before, following the Hamburg Agricultural Fair, he engaged in a long press-battle with Patrick Bell, and had convincingly defended his right to the title "Inventor of the Reaper." [72] Now he directed his counsel, Henry Baldwin, Jr., to prepare a pamphlet on the same subject for distribution where it would do the most good.[73]

Thus, as early as November 21, 1866, McCormick wrote in his characteristic telegraphic style to J. T. Griffin:

With nothing *strikingly new now* (in machine design) I might (with my pamphlet discussion & no competition on the *invention* strong) get the "cross of Honor" for the Invention & improvement of the Reaping Machine. Could have had that in '55 *if applied for* and *Albaret* would perhaps be good help in that. . . . Gen'l (J. A.) Dix *now* going out as (U. S.) *Minister* (to France)

[71] C. H. McCormick to J. T. Griffin, Mch. 12, 1867.
[72] Letters of C. H. McCormick in the "North British Agriculturist," Sept. 30, Oct. 7 and 14, 1863. "Mark Lane Express," Oct. 26, 1863; "Farmer's Magazine," Nov. 1863, p. 452. In 1866 and 1867 the Bell-McCormick controversy was still a matter of considerable discussion. See, "Gardeners' Chronicle," Aug. 25, 1866, p. 817; Oct. 13, 1866, p. 978; Jan. 5, 1867, pp. 11, 14; Jan. 19, 1867, p. 58; Jan. 26, 1867, pp. 89-90. ‡J. T. Griffin to C. H. McCormick, Dec. 15, 1866: "Stephenson of the 'North British Agriculturist' asked me dryly if you wished to contribute to the Bell testimonial in honor of his invention of the reaper." ‡J. T. Griffin, Sterling, Scotland, to C. H. McCormick, Oct. 2, 1867. "Landwirtschaftliches Centralblatt für Deutschland," XVI (1868), p. 81. Bell died on Apr. 22, 1869.
[73] ‡C. H. McCormick to H. Baldwin, Jr., Mch. 7, 1867, and to M. Chevalier, Jan. 19 (?), 1868. L.P.C.B. No. 96, p. 565, C. A. Spring, Jr., to C. H. McCormick, Mch. 20, 1867.

is good friend &c. Some friends in the U. S. Commission (to the Exposition) &c. But whether to trouble myself at all is the first *question*.

Griffin replied that the coveted honor might be secured "with proper management," and for the next few months McCormick in the United States, and his agent abroad, made ready for the day when the great Exposition would open.[74] Samuel B. Ruggles of the American Commission was particularly helpful, and McCormick contributed $1150 for the building of a western farmer's home as a part of the national display.[75] The United States Ambassador at Paris, John A. Dix, had been closely associated with McCormick on the board of directors of the Union Pacific Railroad.[76] Michel Chevalier, an official of the Exposition and with some influence at Napoleon's Court, had been McCormick's good friend since the Paris Exposition of 1855. Albaret for obvious reasons was also working to turn French opinion in McCormick's favor. Griffin blundered by influencing the appointment of Joseph S. Reynolds of Illinois to the Jury named to choose the victors in the grueling field contests arranged for reapers and mowers. He, together with James H. Bowen, his associate

[74] ‡J. T. Griffin to C. H. McCormick, Dec. 8, 1866: "Some of those on the Commission I know well, and think I could influence." ‡*Idem* to *idem*, Apr. 13 and 26, 1867: "There are so many influences at work that it is not safe to rely upon anything or anybody. I will try to keep *facts* before the Jury & see as many as possible."

[75] ‡C. H. McCormick to J. H. Bowen, Feb. 8, 1867: ‡J. T. Griffin to C. H. McCormick, from Paris, Apr. 5, 1867: "I don't fear *fair* competition but France & England are both opposed to America. This is patent to all. A more down & disappointed set than the American Exhibitors, I never saw. . . . They feel *sold,* and one half would retire, could they do so. Indeed a few will not exhibit. . . . As we have Albaret & Co. to help us, therefore will have French influence." C. H. McCormick to C. A. Spring, Jr., Feb. 25, 1867. ‡S. B. Ruggles, London, to C. H. McCormick, July 15, 1867, and J. H. Bowen to him on Apr. 17, 1867.

[76] ‡J. A. Dix, Paris, to C. H. McCormick, July 17, 1867: "I will try to meet your wishes in regard to the reaper."

on the commission, proved to be friendly to Walter A. Wood.[77] This emphasis upon McCormick's strategy should not obscure the fact that his rivals were playing a similar game. Excepting for its scope on this occasion, there was nothing unusual about it. It was as customary an aspect of competition for prizes at a Fair as was the exhibition of the machines themselves.

On May 23 the mower contest opened on the Emperor's farm at Fouilleuse. Six English, one Canadian, six French and five machines from the United States took the field. They were grouped in two divisions and each driver drew by lot to determine which two-acre strip he should cut. In view of the threatening weather, Wood's operator, with his machine of carved walnut and polished iron, had the good fortune to be assigned to the first brigade and finished his stint before the wind and rain commenced. Thereupon, the McCormick mower moved off with the rest of the second division, and was the only one able to complete its task. The test was inconclusive and the trial was continued about two months later on the same estate.[78] By then Cyrus McCormick and his wife had arrived in Paris and were staying at the Grand Hotel.[79] The trial jury awarded Wood's mower the first prize, Perry's of Worcester, Massachusetts (or Kingston, Rhode Island), second, and McCormick's third. Perhaps McCormick's first impulse had been a correct one, and he should not have exhibited at Paris!

[77] ‡J. T. Griffin to C. H. McCormick, May 3 and 18, 1867. C. H. McCormick to J. H. Bowen, May 19, 1868, and to M. Chevalier, Sept. 12, 1868.
[78] "Prairie Farmer," June 22 and Aug. 24, 1867, pp. 113, 409. ‡J. T. Griffin to C. H. McCormick, Apr. 13 and May 29, 1867: Your reaper is plain in appearance. "I feared to put too much cost in it, while Wood is said to have spent over $4,000 on his machine." J. T. Griffin to C. A. Spring, Jr., June 1, 1867. "Farmer's Magazine," Sept. 1867, p. 257.
[79] C. H. McCormick sailed from N. Y. on June 15, 1867. See, ‡C. A. Spring, Jr., to C. H. McCormick, June 12, 1867; L.P.C.B. No. 99, p. 656, C. A. Spring, Jr., to S. L. M. Barlow, N. Y., June 18, 1867.

On July 27, the day following the final mower contest, the reapers were given an opportunity to demonstrate their quality in a field of badly tangled wheat at Fouilleuse. Only four machines could complete their assignment, and of these McCormick's required twenty-seven minutes and Wood's over twice as long. When the contest was resumed in oats at Vincennes three days later, the excellent performance of the McCormick only confirmed the verdict of Fouilleuse.[80] The Virginia Reaper was supreme in grain. Thus the tide turned in McCormick's favor.

About two weeks later the inventor was invited by the Emperor to come to his estate at Chalons and operate the reaper in his presence. Following his arrival and an annoying delay in a "dirty hotel," McCormick was privileged to talk for nearly an hour with Napoleon while his machine was at work. The Emperor was highly pleased, and Eugene Tisserand, the "Director of the Emperor's Domains," restrained his sovereign with difficulty from making the American a Chevalier of the Legion of Honor on the field.[81] Nevertheless, this was probably the proudest moment of McCormick's life up to that time. He returned to Paris, assured of the favor of the court, and with the promise of the Emperor to purchase three machines for use on his estates. Thereupon, McCormick commissioned Griffin to look up the Irish coat-of-arms of his family [82] and secured permission from the General Agent of the New York Associated Press to cable a report of his triumphs. Usually so terse in his telegrams, now in this his first cable, he wrote one hundred and thirty-one words. The London of-

[80] "New York Times," Aug. 14, 1867. "Journal de l'Agriculture Pratique," 5th Ser., I (1868), p. 467. "Gardeners' Chronicle," Aug. 10, 1867, p. 837.

[81] M. Chevalier to C. H. McCormick, Aug. 11, 1867. "Le Moniteur Universel" (Paris), Aug. 20, 1867. J. Parton, "Sketches of Men of Progress" (N. Y., 1870), p. 31. Letters of C. H. McCormick to ‡Mr. Ryan, "N. Y. Times," Jan. 10 (no year given), M. Chevalier, Sept. 12, 1868, and to C. C. Copeland, Dec. 15, 1868. "The News of the Week" (Paris), Aug. 26, 1867, p. 2.

[82] ‡J. T. Griffin to C. H. McCormick, Oct. 18 and 19, 1867.

fice of the Associated Press felt obliged to reduce its length by almost one-half before relaying it to New York.[83] It cost McCormick about $175, but when the newspapers of the United States copied and elaborated upon the dispatch, he was informed by C. A. Spring, Jr., of the factory office, that "Half a million dollars would not give you the advertising that you are getting gratis." [84] Again it was apparent that European medals did not induce European sales, but were more than worth their cost and trouble because of the impression they made upon the buying public at home. In view of this fact, McCormick could not sympathize with his brother's insistence that the firm should not be burdened with the expense of exhibiting abroad.[85]

The work of Cyrus McCormick at the Exposition was now finished and little remained to be done but to wait in Paris for the conferral of the honors. This was done by the Emperor at a colorful ceremony in the Tuileries on January 5, 1868.[86] He was the only American exhibitor of harvesting machinery to receive the Grand Prize of 10,000 francs. This was bestowed upon him both as a "benefactor of mankind" and as a "skillful mechanician." [87] By an imperial decree of the day before, he was admitted to the rank of Chevalier in the Order of the Legion of Honor, as "the inventor of the reaper machine." [88]

[83] ‡A. C. Wilson, Office of the Associated Press, London, to C. H. McCormick, Aug. 19, 1867: I give no warrant that it will be published as transmitted. If the Gen'l. Agt. had not so authorized, I would have declined to forward news so largely affecting a private interest.

[84] ‡C. A. Spring, Jr., to C. H. McCormick, Aug. 30, 1867. "Chicago Times," July 15 and 28, 1867.

[85] C. H. to L. J. McCormick, Oct. 10, 1866, and Feb. 13, 1867.

[86] "Le Moniteur Universel," Jan. 6, 1868. N. M. Beckwith to C. H. McCormick, Jan. 4, 1868.

[87] M. Chevalier (ed.), "Universal Exposition of 1867 at Paris. Reports of the International Jury" (Paris, 1867), Vol. XII, Group 8, Chap. 5, Sect. 5, p. 45.

[88] N. M. Beckwith to C. H. McCormick, Jan. 5, 1868. W. Hoffman, U. S. Legation, Paris, to C. H. McCormick, Jan. 6, 1868.

Walter A. Wood was similarly rewarded for his prominence "as constructor of agricultural machines." No other honor received by McCormick during his career was more highly prized by him, and thereafter he wore the red rosette on the lapel of his coat with great pride. To be acclaimed officially by France as "the inventor of the reaper" and a "benefactor of mankind" was exceedingly gratifying, and he took much pains to have the reports of the Group Jury of the Exposition and of the United States Commissioners corrected so that they included these phrases in their references to his success.[89] He was, thereby, distinguished from Walter A. Wood. Patrick Bell was doubtless also in his thoughts and so too was his lifelong desire to be known as one whose genius had served his fellow men. Before he left Paris in February, McCormick presented Napoleon III, through the United States Ambassador, with a mowing machine and an engraving of Schussele's painting, "American Men of Progress."[90]

McCormick had won all of his objectives at the Exposition, but he found little time to enjoy his victories. In their train came controversies with Griffin and Burgess which occupied much of his attention during the last four months of his stay in Europe. Without his authorization, Griffin made an agreement with Burgess early in 1867 concerning the old stock of

[89] "Official Report of Hon. N. M. Beckwith, Comm'r. General and President of the United States Commission at the Universal Exhibition, Paris, 1867," pp. 11-12. #C. H. McCormick, Paris, to M. Chevalier, Jan. 19 (?), 1868: Unless I were called the inventor, to wear the red ribbon "would have no charms for me." When I won the highest prizes of the Expositions of 1851, 1855, and 1863, they were given to me as "inventor." Letters of C. H. McCormick to Speaker of the House of Representatives, May 12, 1868; to J. P. Haswell, May 23, 1868, and to N. P. Banks, May 25, 1868. L.P.C.B. No. 105, C. H. McCormick & Bro. to A. M. Hamilton, Keswick Depot, Va., June 4, 1868.

[90] Marshall Vaillant, Paris, to C. H. McCormick, Feb. 19, 1868. C. H. McCormick to Marshall Vaillant, Feb. 14, 1868. #A. Albaret & Cie. to C. H. McCormick, Mch. 20 and Aug. 18, 1868. C. H. McCormick to J. A. Dix, Apr. 3, 1868. #J. A. Dix to C. H. McCormick, Apr. 17, 1868.

machines on hand.[91] McCormick repudiated its terms after his arrival in France and demanded from Griffin a detailed statement of his sales and collections in Europe during the past four years. Although Griffin was honest he was unable to furnish a satisfactory balance-sheet.[92] He countered with a few grievances of his own. His small fixed salary was supplemented by commissions for each McCormick reaper sold by him in Europe. Because of his duties at the Fair, he had been unable to make a thorough canvass in 1867 and had sold only sixty machines. He believed that his employer should lessen his probable loss, and indiscreetly reminded him that the triumph at the Fair was due largely to his efforts.[93] At the same time he asked for a one-sixth interest in any partnership arrangement made between McCormick and Burgess for 1868. McCormick stood on one-eighth, and when Burgess supported Griffin, the negotiations were deadlocked. The angry inventor, seeing the next year's selling campaign jeopardized by the impertinence of an employee, dismissed Griffin from his service.[94]

Since Griffin was penniless and had a wife and children to support, he made partial amends and repented his hasty words.

[91] ‡J. T. Griffin to C. H. McCormick, Feb. 9, 1867.

[92] *Idem* to *idem*, Oct. 21, 23 and 26, 1867.

[93] ‡J. T. Griffin, Frankfort-am-Main, to C. H. McCormick, Aug. 5, 1867. ‡C. H. McCormick to J. T. Griffin, Dec. 13 and 14, 1867: As to your influence at Paris, "if I had not myself been *present* to guard my interests in the private trials of the machine and [made] improvement in the separation of tangled grain, *the award would not have been as now*. . . . I have not counted the cost to me at all in what I have done [to you]. I have acted only on *principle*." Memo. by C. H. McCormick, undated, but probably late 1867: "I had *no other person* [than Griffin] knowing anything about the business, and was dependent on him, and he happened to know that."

[94] C. H. McCormick to "the Referees," n.d., but probably early Dec. 1867. ‡C. H. McCormick to J. T. Griffin, Dec. 2, 7, 10 and 17, 1867. ‡J. T. Griffin to C. H. McCormick, Sept. 23, Oct. 2, 18, Dec. 1, 12 and 16, 1867. ‡C. B. Norton to J. T. Griffin, Dec. 26, 1867. ‡Mrs. E. D. Griffin to Nettie F. McCormick, Dec. 9, 1867.

McCormick also took second thought and realized that Griffin alone knew the details of the old business and the location of the unsold machines. The cordial relations between the two men were never restored, but mutual need drew them together for a few more months. Griffin consented to visit the European agencies, put the accounts in order, and place all unsold reapers in the charge of J. R. McDonald & Co., of Hamburg.[95] When this work was finished, he had the good fortune to be appointed agent for Great Britain by Walter A. Wood. He remained a bitter enemy of the Chicago firm, although as late as 1870 Cyrus McCormick was paying him a ten per cent commission on all monies collected from sales of the period 1862-1867.[96]

The Griffin affair so complicated the McCormick-Burgess negotiations that the inventor was obliged to sail for home in late February before any satisfactory arrangement had been made.[97] This was the more unfortunate since his success at Paris augured well for larger sales in Europe.[98] McCormick

[95] ‡C. H. McCormick to J. T. Griffin, Dec. 19, 20, 24, 1867; Jan. 16 and 17, 1868. ‡J. T. Griffin to C. H. McCormick, Jan. 15, 17, 21, 25, 30 and Feb. 1, 1868. J. R. McDonald & Co. to C. C. Copeland, Jan. 13, 1869.

[96] Griffin returned to the U. S. in Mch., 1868, and sought to borrow $1500 of C. H. McCormick. McCormick was inclined to make the loan in order "to keep him quiet," but whether he did so, does not appear in the records. ‡C. A. Spring, Jr., to C. H. McCormick, Apr. 13 and 24, 1868; C. H. McCormick to C. H. McCormick & Bros., Apr. 9, 1868; to J. R. McDonald & Co., May 8, 1868; to J. T. Griffin, Apr. 9 and Oct. 9, 1868. ‡J. T. Griffin to C. H. McCormick, Apr. 7, 11, May 1, June 23, Aug. 15 and Sept. 11, 1868, and Mch. 19, 1870. J. T. Griffin to C. A. Spring, Jr., Apr. 6, 1868.

[97] ‡J. T. Griffin to C. H. McCormick, Jan. 11, 1868; ‡C. H. McCormick to J. T. Griffin, Jan. 14, 1868: I am "still hesitating as to the expediency of taking the trouble myself of continuing the sale of the Reapers here at all." C. H. McCormick reached the United States on March 5.

[98] C. H. McCormick to M. Lafont, Dec. 11, 1867: The "great object of us all now being to get the most extensive introduction of it [the reaper] into France under the strong patronage of the Emperor, that the greatest advantages from its use may be realized to the country, as have been realized in my own country." J. A. Dix, Paris, to C. M. Clay, Sept. 27, 1867. L.P.C.B. No. 100, p. 366, C. A. Spring, Jr., to J. T. Griffin, Aug. 17, 1867.

was greatly annoyed when Burgess advertised that a Brentwood-built reaper had won the Grand Prize at the Exposition. Both men were hard bargainers and any negotiations between them were bound to spin out almost interminably. The creditors of Burgess controlled his policy and insisted that he should devote his chief attention to the building of his mowers for the home market.[99] But Burgess knew the advertising value of the McCormick name, and in order to gain it was willing to make a few of the American machines for sale both in England and on the Continent. His resources were too limited to manufacture many of them and McCormick refused to loan him money.[100] The inventor insisted that his name should be kept prominently to the fore. The long association of Burgess with Virginia reapers was a strong point in his favor, although if McCormick had not been in a hurry to return to the United States, he would probably have looked for a builder who would coöperate more enthusiastically. Burgess finally consented to paint "McCormick" conspicuously and pay £2 royalty on each reaper he should make for the British market. For £20 each (f.o.b. London) he would supply McDonald & Co. with as many reapers as it should order for sale in central Europe. These machines were to bear McCormick's name only, and on each of them McDonald & Co. would pay the inventor a fee of £3.[101]

‡J. T. Griffin to C. H. McCormick, Aug. 30, 1867. The McCormick reaper exhibited at Paris was purchased by the Prussian Commrs. at the Fair for the Agrl. Museum of Berlin. ‡C. H. McCormick to Hon. Mr. Santos, Spanish Commr., Sept. 3, 1867.

[99] ‡W. Burgess to C. H. McCormick, Dec. 8, 15 and 24, 1867; ‡C. H. McCormick to W. Burgess, ‡Dec. 13, 25, 1867, to J. T. Griffin, Dec. 26, 1867, to E. Tisserand, Nov. 27, 1868, and to C. C. Copeland, Dec. (?), 1868. ‡J. T. Griffin to C. H. McCormick, Dec. 23, 1867.

[100] Letters to C. H. McCormick from ‡J. T. Griffin, Aug. 24, 1867, ‡C. C. Copeland, Aug. 5, 1870, and ‡A. M. Hamilton, July 29, 1871. ‡C. H. McCormick to W. Burgess, Dec. 30, 1867, and Jan. 24, 1868.

[101] Letters to C. H. McCormick, from ‡J. T. Griffin, Sept. 11, 1868, ‡W. Burgess, Jan. 28, Sept. 24, and Dec. 15, 1868, ‡J. R. McDonald & Co.,

From 1868 to 1876 the sales of McCormick machines in Great Britain and Europe were too few to be of any significance in the agricultural life of that area. While Wood, Osborne, Johnston and other American firms were enjoying a large and growing foreign business and were driving English-made harvesting machinery from the Continental market,[102] the number of purchasers of McCormick reapers never exceeded two hundred a year.

Year	McCormick Machines bought from Burgess & Key by McDonald & Co.	McCormick Machines sold in Germany and Austria by McDonald & Co.	McCormick Machines sold by Burgess & Key in Great Britain	Albaret's Sales of McCormick's Machines
1868	100	63	36	6
1869	200	160	25	?
1870	112	110	?	?
1871	13	31	?	?
1872	24	47	?	?
1873	100	30	?	?
1874	0	14	?	?
1875	0	6	?	?
1876	0	0	?	?
1877	0	61 at auction	0	0
TOTALS	549	522	61	6

McDonald & Company was discouraged long before 1875. It admitted that McCormick's reaper gave better service than Wood's or Samuelson's, but because it was so heavy and costly very few farmers would buy it. After 1871 the firm

Aug. 21 and Oct. 2, 1868. Letters from C. H. McCormick to #W. Burgess, Jan. 24, 1868, Burgess & Key, July 29, 1868, J. R. McDonald & Co., July 31 and Oct. 10, 1868, M. Chevalier, Sept. 12, 1868, and to M. Aureliano, Bucharest, Oct. 23, 1868.

102 The preference for American rather than English-built reapers was noticed by J. T. Griffin as early as 1865. See, his letter of #Sept. 16, 1865, to C. H. McCormick. Also #J. R. McDonald & Co. to C. H. McCormick, Apr. 28, 1868. "Engineering," XVI (1873), pp. 68-69, 88-89.

reproached McCormick for neglecting the business opportunity presented by a unified Germany, ready to liberalize its patent and tariff laws and eager to buy harvesting machinery to offset the rising labor costs occasioned in part by the large immigration to the United States. He was urged to establish a factory in Germany where wages were low and iron and coal cheap, compared with their price in his own country.[103]

The inventor was unwilling to relinquish his foothold in Europe where some of his greatest triumphs had been won. To maintain it properly, however, demanded more of his attention that he was able to give. His home, rather than the factory office, had always been the control center of his reaper overseas. Upon his return from Europe in 1868, important questions connected with his many other interests pressed upon him almost daily for solution. His correspondence was very large, and he disliked to employ a private secretary. News from Burgess, McDonald and his patent lawyers in London came but seldom. Since there were too few hours in his day to accomplish all that he had to do, he naturally neglected the least insistent, and most distant of his problems.[104] Further-

[103] ‡J. R. McDonald & Co., to C. H. McCormick, May 19, June 12, and Aug. 21, 1868; Apr. 4, 1871; Mch. 5, May 11, 1872; June 4 and Aug. 2, 1873; Feb. 3, 1874. By 1873, this firm was also acting as forwarding agent for Wood. Samuelson & Co. was one of the largest manufacturers of reapers in England by 1865. In 1868 it made 1200 self-rakes, and from 1600-2000 for 1869. See, testimony of W. N. Cranston on pp. 289-290 of *Dorsey Extension Case,* and ‡J. T. Griffin to C. H. McCormick, Feb. 19, 1866. By 1871, however, Samuelson was turning more and more to the building of traction engines. ‡Robertson, Brooman & Co. wrote to C. H. McCormick on Feb. 4, 1871, that Burgess & Key and W. A. Wood would soon be the only prominent reaper- and mower-makers in England. For a time in 1870, McCormick hoped that Wood might agree to make "The Advance" in his English factory for Europe. ‡L.P.C.B. No. 1, 2nd ser., pp. 3, 122, 139, C. H. to L. J. McCormick, Apr. 5, 1870, and to Robertson & Co., London, June 7 and 20, 1870.

[104] ‡J. R. McDonald & Co. to C. H. McCormick, Jan. 29, 1869. C. H. McCormick to J. R. McDonald & Co., Jan. 29, and Feb. 16, 1869.

more, the Chicago factory reported that it could not supply the domestic demand and it was inadvisable to enlarge the plant unless it were moved to a new site.

With the approach of harvest-time in the United States, McCormick was often reminded of the ripening grain across the ocean. In both the summer of 1870 and 1871 he was on the point of sailing for Europe, when home affairs obliged him to change his plans.[105] In his stead, in 1870 he sent his friend C. C. Copeland with one of his new reaper-mowers known as "The Advance." He was unable to interest Burgess or any other English manufacturer in the machine. Copeland had it patented in Great Britain but the grant soon lapsed through failure to make the necessary payments.[106] A. M. Hamilton, an agent and kinsman from the Valley of Virginia, took several of "The Advance" machines to England for exhibition in the harvest of 1871. They drew some little attention, but the trip had no practical result since Hamilton was kept too busy in the field to spare time to negotiate with manufacturers. His reports make frequent reference to the "old fogyism" of English landowners and to farm laborers "as

[105] McCormick believed, and his friends overseas emphasized, that he must come to England and Europe for a time, if he wished his business there to be a success. ‡Robertson, Brooman & Co. to C. H. McCormick, Feb. 4, 1871: "Your name will die out here unless you come over & see to it yourself." ‡C. A. Spring, Jr., to C. H. McCormick, July 3, 1871. ‡C. H. McCormick to Burgess & Key, June 7, 1871.

[106] "The Advance" was a combined reaper-mower, and as early as 1861 the "Gardeners' Chronicle" (Aug. 31, 1861, p. 797) had noted that combined machines were not suited to English needs. ‡J. R. McDonald & Co. to A. M. Hamilton, Aug. 5, 1871, and A. M. Hamilton to C. H. McCormick, Sept. 7, 1871. C. C. Copeland was also in Europe in 1869 and made inquiries about McCormick's business. C. H. McCormick to J. R. McDonald & Co., Mch. 26, 1869 and to C. C. Copeland, Feb. 16, 1869. Letters to C. H. McCormick from ‡J. R. McDonald & Co., Apr. 13, 1869, and Mch. 29, 1870; from ‡C. C. Copeland, Mch. 26, 30, Apr. 1, July 23, Aug. 5, 10 and 11, 1870; from ‡W. Burgess, Mch. 24, 1870, and from ‡Robertson, Brooman & Co., May 7, June 24, July 16, Aug. 6, 1870, and May 17, 1873, ‡J. R. McDonald & Co., to C. C. Copeland, Mch. 23 and Aug. 23, 1870.

clumsy as Elephants and dumb as the Ox." [107] Upon his return to the United States he found Cyrus McCormick completely absorbed in the work of reconstruction following the Great Fire in Chicago. By March, 1872, the inventor was so much out of touch with his overseas interests that he did not know whether Burgess was still manufacturing for him, or whether McDonald & Company was selling his reapers in Central Europe.[108] Over six million dollars' worth of agricultural machinery left the United States for Europe in 1871, but scarcely a packing case was marked with the McCormick stencil.[109]

For the next five or six years McCormick fortunes in the foreign field were at their lowest ebb.[110] The disastrous fire of October, 1871, was partly to blame, but it led to the erection of a new factory, so large that the building of reapers for

[107] Letters to C. H. McCormick from A. M. Hamilton, July 26, #29, Aug. #6, #13, #16, 24, Sept. 7, 16, Oct. 25, 1871; #Robertson, Brooman & Co., Feb. 4, Apr. 10 and May 27, 1871, and Ransome, Sims & Head, Ipswich, Feb. 8, 1871. #L.P.C.B. No. 1, 2nd ser., pp. 553-556, C. H. McCormick to A. M. Hamilton, July 12, 1871: "Mr. Peabody *lived in a single bedroom,* no separate sitting room! This was *surprising* for *him,* but I mention it to show that respectability don't require much *show* in Engd. of this sort. *Americans* are often foolish in these matters."

[108] L.P.C.B. No. 132, p. 581, C. H. McCormick to Robertson, Brooman & Co., Mch. 8, 1872: "I met the Grand Duke [Alexis] & Russian party *here* pleasantly some two months since—exchanged Photographs with the G.D. & some others of the party, wh. *might help* out some at St. Petersburgh [*sic*] possibly!" "Chicago Times," Jan. 3, 5, 1872. #Robertson, Brooman & Co. to C. H. McCormick, May 17, 1873: We could not even learn whether you were still in business.

[109] R. H. Thurston, I, pp. 315 ff. There was a growing tendency after 1865 for American builders of harvesting machinery not to seek sub-manufacturers on the Continent but to ship there direct from the U.S. #J. R. McDonald & Co. to C. H. McCormick, June 12, 1868. #Robertson, Brooman & Co., to C. H. McCormick, Feb. 4, 1871.

[110] Nevertheless, at a three-day field trial at Altenburg, Hungary, in July, 1869, against thirty-seven different machines, the Burgess & Key McCormick won first prize. #J. R. McDonald & Co. to C. H. McCormick, March 2, 1870.

export waited only upon the word of its owners. No longer would it be necessary to tolerate the whims of William Burgess.[111] But the signal for the drive to begin was slow in appearing. In 1873, almost on the spur of the moment, Cyrus McCormick sent John F. Fullen, a skilled mechanic, to the Vienna Exposition with a reaper and reaper-mower. The machines were not completely finished when they were boxed for shipment, and in striking contrast to his careful preparation for the Paris and London Fairs, McCormick failed to notify McDonald & Company of his plans until it was too late for that influential firm to be of much service at Vienna.[112] Walter A. Wood attended in person, bringing with him a staff of experts and enough money to entertain freely. The most interesting feature of his display was a Locke binder, the first ever seen in Europe. It was not ready for work in the field but it amused the crowd by tying "bundles of newspapers" in the Exposition Building.[113] After a field trial at Leopolds-

[111] L.P.C.B. No. 146, pp. 83-85, C. H. & L. J. McCormick to H. Weil, N. Y. City, Oct. 27, 1873: We will sell for foreign shipment in lots of five or more, packed in iron-strapped cases, at a discount of 20% from cash prices, f.o.b. Chicago. The Chicago office wrote that it had no wish to establish European agencies, since "we have satisfied ourselves that they would not pay." L.P.C.B. No. 143, p. 475, the Co. to P. Mohan, St. Louis, Mo., July 9, 1873. ‡Burgess & Key to J. R. McDonald, Apr. 25, 1872: We no longer wish to make McCormick machines for you unless you will give us a large order. There is no more call for them in England. C. F. Burgess to C. H. McCormick, Apr. 28, 1877.

[112] "Chicago Times," Mch. 13, 1873. ‡D. Lord, Jr., to C. H. McCormick, Mch. 19, 1873. H. White, ed. of the "Chicago Tribune," to J. Kune, Apr. 17, 1873: "I give this note to Mr. McCormick at his request with the suggestion that you shall do justice in your correspondence to his machines in the Vienna Exposition." ‡L.P.C.B. No. 3, 2nd ser., C. H. McCormick to J. R. McDonald & Co., Apr. 28, 1873. ‡J. F. Fullen to C. H. McCormick, Feb. 8, 1874. ‡J. R. McDonald & Co. to C. H. McCormick, Dec. 2, 1873. If McDonald had known in time he "would have taken advantage of his acquaintance with Prof. Dr. Arenstain and others, to push your interests."

[113] Published letter of W. A. Wood to J. E. Haynes & Co., St. Louis, Mo., Aug. 8, 1873. The Marsh Harvester had been taken to Europe at least as early as 1870. See Marsh Extension Case, p. 8. In 1873, J. F. Steward began

dorf in upstanding grain, each of the McCormick machines received a medal for merit. Wood's mower, however, was awarded one of the Grand Prizes of the Exposition, and Eugene Tisserand mentioned the Chicago inventor but briefly in his long report on the agricultural implements displayed there.[114] The contrast between McCormick at Paris in 1867 and McCormick at Vienna in 1873 was painfully apparent, and there was a widespread feeling that the old master was now "out of date." [115]

This half-hearted effort had not helped at all. McDonald decided that McCormick intended to abandon the European field and his silence during the next three years gave ample warrant for this belief.[116] The Centennial Exposition at Philadelphia in 1876 came opportunely to turn the tide. Here the many sight-seers from foreign lands examined his new wirebinder and the other machines in his large exhibit. The myth

his two-year service of introducing Marsh harvesters abroad, *McCormick vs. Aultman et al. Defendant's Record*, p. 508. The harvester was described as a "curiosity" in "Iron" (London), II (1873), p. 310. "Chicago Times," July 31 and Aug. 22, 1873.

[114] ‡J. F. Fullen to C. H. McCormick, Aug. 21 and Oct. 17, 1873. Nettie F. McCormick to W. J. Hanna, Sept. 3, 1873. ‡Walter A. Wood & Co. to "Our Agents and Patrons," Aug. 22, 1873. "Engineering," Vol. XVI (1873), pp. 52-53. "Report on Vienna Universal Exhibition of 1873" (London, 1874), Pt. II, pp. 195-197. "Auftrage der Kaiserl. Königl. Ackerbau Ministeriums" (Vienna, 1874), pp. 416 ff.

[115] Wood & Co. sold about one thousand reapers and mowers in central Europe in 1873. It intended, so it was said, to send about five thousand there for 1874. McCormick sold less than twenty-five abroad that year. ‡J. R. McDonald & Co. to C. H. McCormick, June 4, Aug. 2, Dec. 2, 1873, and Feb. 3, 1874. R. H. Thurston, p. 306: Wood has sold about 30,000 machines, or 16% of his entire output since 1853, in Europe.

[116] ‡J. R. McDonald & Co. to C. H. McCormick, June 6, 1871. This company was unable to sell any Burgess & Key McCormicks in 1876, and soon auctioned off the sixty-one on hand at an average price of £5 each: "an excellent acquisition surely for the farmers who purchased but leaving us badly in the cold." Letters of J. R. McDonald & Co. to the McCormick Co. or to C. H. McCormick, Feb. 6, June 19, July 7, 1877, Jan. 16, and Mch. 12, 1878.

that McCormick was behind the times suddenly exploded. His name was still a magical one in the world of harvesting machinery and the inventor was on hand at Philadelphia to flatter distinguished visitors and delegates from overseas with his attention.[117] The suave Charles Colahan, in immediate charge of the McCormick exhibit, distributed attractive pamphlets to those who came to watch the binder tying sheaves of straw. From the Exposition went word to the grain-fields of the world that McCormick had kept step with progress and was preparing to sell his machines wherever wheat was harvested.

Cyrus McCormick's importance in the history of grain culture in Great Britain and Europe prior to 1876, does not chiefly depend upon the number of his machines at work in those areas. Probably not more than four thousand reapers, made at Brentwood, Chicago, or Liancourt, were sold there during this period.[118] He made little money, if any, from his

[117] C. H. McCormick was a member of the Illinois Centennial Committee and attended the opening of the Fair. C. Henrotin, Chicago, to the Co., Oct. 12, 1876: C. Colahan to C. H. McCormick, July 28, 1876; W. Hall, Phila., to the Co., Oct. 16, 1876; P. Mohan to the Co., from San Francisco, May 6, 1876: "I have sold two reapers to the Japanese Consul." These were the first (and probably the only) McCormick machines sent to Japan prior to 1885. Possibly the earliest sales in Hawaii were in 1879. See, "Chicago Times," June 15, 1875 and L.P.C.B. No. 190, p. 427. Co. to A. A. Cox, San Francisco, Cal., May 13, 1879. The first mention of a potential market in China is in a letter in L.P.C.B. No. 234, p. 529, June 25, 1883, to Ling Fong & Co. of N. Y. For the effect of the Centennial upon the foreign market, see U. S. Senate, 45th Cong. 2nd Sess., *Misc. Doc. No. 50,* pp. 443-449. According to E. Bally, one of the Commissioners from Switzerland: "The Universal Exhibition of Philadelphia has been, so to speak, the key by which American industry will unlock for itself the road to Europe and to its colonies." The Bavarian Government paid Dr. Geo. Seelhorst, of the Nuremberg Industrial Museum, to make a lecture tour of his country, explaining what he had seen at Philadelphia.

[118] MS. entitled "Reaper Statement—McCormick's Reapers." n.d., but probably early 1867. Burgess & Key seem to have sold about 400 McCormick Reapers in the British Isles between 1862 and 1872; McDonald & Co. disposed of about 465 B. & K. McCormick's between 1868 and 1876; Albaret & Co. most likely did not market over 75 of their own manufac-

transatlantic business, and several other American manufacturers could boast a far more imposing record of annual sales. Their profits, however, were due in considerable degree to McCormick's path-breaking during the fifteen years following the London Exhibition of 1851. When his pioneer work was about completed in his own country, he sought new frontiers overseas. As long as it was an outpost of the reaper it held his interest, but by 1868 most farmers of Europe at least were aware that grain could be cut effectively by machinery, and McCormick characteristically turned his attention to new problems at home.

Because his interest in the foreign phase of his business was at its height whenever a World's Fair was held abroad, it may be said that medals and personal renown were his chief objectives. Without question, these rewards were always in his thoughts.[119] Fame did not steal upon him unawares. He consciously sought it, and gloried in the full measure of it that he won. But the desire to sell his reaper, to fight where the odds were heavily against him, and to earn the right to be known as one who had done much good in the world, were as influential as the lure of ribbons and prizes. By 1876 the success of his competitors abroad was a challenge that could no longer be ignored.

ture; McCormick found European purchasers for approximately 300 built in Chicago between 1855 and 1875; Laurent of Paris was said to have made and sold 150 B. & K. McCormick's by 1861. These total 1390 machines. The biggest item, as well as the most problematical, is the number of McCormick reapers made and sold by Burgess & Key between 1852 and 1862. In "Gardeners' Chronicle," July 27, 1861, p. 703, this firm was said to have sold a total of 2800, but this number probably includes several hundred Allen mowers, not under McCormick's patents.

[119] Letters from C. H. McCormick to B. M. Smith, Apr. 24, 1868, to J. H. Bowen, May 19, 1868, and to N. P. Banks, May 25, 1868.

CHAPTER XII

OUT OF THE WAR AND THROUGH THE FIRE,
1865-1873

WHILE Cyrus McCormick, with his money and counsel was aiding Presbyterianism, the Democratic Party, and the South to recover from the effects of the civil conflict, his factory passed through the transition from war to peace with considerable ease. Because reapers and mowers helped to increase and feed the northern forces, and to bring them victory, the manufacturing of harvesting machinery may be called a war industry. Unlike many owners of textile, iron and steel mills, however, implement-makers had not needed to alter the nature of their output in order to meet the peculiar demands of a nation in arms. Compared with the critical problems faced by those who hitherto had been relying for business upon government contracts, the McCormick partners were not obliged to undergo a severe period of reconstruction following the war.

Although a half-million men or more returned to northern farms after they were mustered out of the service, the demand for harvesting machinery remained unchecked. Many veterans, in fact, who had spent their youth in the cities, took up homesteads at the close of the struggle and were soon ready to buy reapers and mowers. Uniting their influence, implement manufacturers quickly persuaded a well-disposed Congress to remove the heavy tax upon their gross sales.[1] By 1867, nothing

[1] See, *post,* p. 476, footnote 90. L.P.C.B. No. 87, p. 361, the Co. to N. B. Smith, Syracuse, N. Y., Feb. 2, 1866: "We ask no favors from Congress in the shape of protection, for agricultural implement makers *can defy the*

remained of the federal war levies upon industry except the income tax and a light impost upon several of the materials needed in the building of harvesting machines. Reconstruction, therefore, to the McCormick firm meant little except the reëstablishment and extension of its small ante-bellum market in the South, and the collection there of its old debts.

Many southerners, believing that the freed negroes would not work, wrote to the Chicago firm of their need for labor-saving machinery.[2] They talked of turning from the culture of cotton or tobacco to the raising of grain. One Louisiana planter hoped that midwestern farmers would come South each year during their slack season to help harvest the crops of the lower Mississippi Valley.[3] In Virginia an Immigration

world. . . . All we ask is to be left untrammeled by onerous or special taxation in furnishing implements, tending directly to the development and expansion of the agricultural resources of the country, and which largely promote the ability of the nation to pay its taxes. . . . We feel that the production of the food of a nation and all that directly tends thereto should not be burdened by any taxation beyond the income tax which all pay, and which by the adoption of our proposition would be very largely increased." "Chicago Times," Nov. 20, 1867.

[2] L.P.C.B. No. 66, pp. 585, 662, the Co. to W. Burke, La Prairie, Ill., Feb. 6, 1864. Letters to the Co. of W. P. Grayson, Henderson, Ky., Aug. 8, 1867, W. Cartmell, Lebanon, Tenn., Aug. 15, 1867, ‡J. Naylor, Tyro, Miss., Nov. 30, 1867, C. W. Greene & Co., Columbus, Ky., Dec. 25, 1867, Hamilton & Cunningham, Nashville, Tenn., May 12, 1868, D. Spring, Winchester, Tenn., May 30, 1868, J. F. McLeod, Macon, Miss., Apr. 16, 1869, M. Fry, Lynnville, Tenn., Jan. 7, 1870, and ‡J. V. Jones, Herndon, Ga., Mch. 8, 1870. This correspondence reveals an expectation of a larger market in the South for reapers and mowers because of the greater breadth of grain sown there; the money scarcity which would compel the planters to raise their own food; the favorable market price of grain as compared with tobacco or cotton; the exodus of negroes, the unwillingness to hire former slaves, the high price of labor, and because the white laborer, unlike the careless slave, could be trusted to operate delicate machinery.

[3] ‡W. H. Compton, Bastrop, La., to C. H. McCormick, Feb. 8, 1866. This writer also hoped that McCormick would invent machines to plant, cultivate and harvest cotton. A practical cotton-picking machine has only very recently been constructed. See "Time" (New York), XXV, No. 16 (Apr. 22, 1935), p. 36.

Society was formed to encourage the introduction of "labour, capital and the useful arts . . . from those countries where they are in excess." [4]

Cyrus McCormick was ready to expand his trade in the ex-Confederate States both for business reasons and because he was confident that reapers and mowers would help the South to recover more quickly from the effects of the war.[5] He was willing to grant easy terms of payment to the impoverished planters, but the clerks in his office, who were expected to send him a balance-sheet each August showing a goodly margin of profits from the year's business, were not so strongly influenced by altruistic motives. Their employer's sympathy for the "rebel" South sometimes embarrassed their efforts to defeat competitors in the Middle West.[6] Pre-war accounts should be settled if possible, but poverty, stay laws, and unsympathetic neighborhood juries were hurdles most difficult to surmount.[7] Southern agents sadly commented upon the decline of business morality in their districts, and advised the firm to sell only for cash. The men in the factory office, on the other hand, were of the opinion that these canvassers, as well as

[4] ‡W. B. Robinson, Secy. and Treas. of the Va. Immigration Society, Lynchburg, Va., to C. H. McCormick, May 31, 1866. Little capital was available in Virginia for the use of this society, but it sought to borrow money in the North, on land as security.

[5] C. H. McCormick, from Sheldon, Vt., to C. C. Baldwin, Aug. 14, 1866.

[6] D. N. Barnhill, La Grange, Ill., to the Co., July 17, 1866.

[7] Letters of the Co. in L.P.C.B. No. 84, p. 80, to H. M. Smith, Richmond, Va., Sept. 7, 1865; No. 88, p. 633, to M. G. Bush, Farmington, Texas, Mch. 24, 1866; No. 92, p. 414 and No. 93, pp. 497, 688-690, to T. Berry, Staunton, Va., Sept. 10, and Nov. 7, 1866; No. 105, p. 728, to D. N. Barnhill, Sherman, Texas, June 19, 1868; No. 116, p. 853, to Broughton & Porter, Sherman, Texas, Aug. 24, 1869. ‡C. A. Spring, Jr., to C. H. McCormick, Mch. 20, 1866. ‡A. M. Hamilton, Alexandria, Va., to C. H. McCormick, Feb. 9, 1866. H. M. Smith & Co., Richmond, Va., to the Co., Apr. 1, 1868. M. G. Bush, Farmington, Texas, to the Co., Sept. 30, 1868. The attitude of southerners toward their northern pre-war creditors, and the embarrassment of the latter because of the practical situation making recovery so difficult, strongly remind the student of the planters and their debts owed to Englishmen at the close of the American Revolution.

purchasers of machines, would bear watching more closely than ever before.[8]

Planters who had written enthusiastically of raising wheat found that the country bankers or cross-road merchants from whom they borrowed money, demanded that the land, as always, should be devoted to cotton or tobacco. Negroes continued to be the only available labor force, and they usually gave their best service when tending the normal staple crops.[9] The climate of some sections of the lower South, where crop diversification had been urged, was found to be unsuited to the growth of wheat. In view of the large and rapidly expanding market for harvesting machinery in the central and northern belt, the McCormicks could not be expected for long to push vigorously into an area where sales were few and collections difficult.[10] By 1872, their enthusiasm for the southern trade had disappeared.

During the seven years before that time, Virginia, Tennessee, and particularly Texas had received more attention than the other southern states.[11] To Cyrus McCormick's displeas-

[8] Dishonesty on the part of a reaper agent was very rare, although occasionally one was taken to task for faulty bookkeeping. W. J. Hanna, in May, 1870 (L.P.C.B. No. 119, p. 629), wrote that since 1849 he could remember but one instance when the firm was obliged to sue an agent. The present writer believes this to be an understatement, but the cases were exceptionally few. L.P.C.B. No. 89, p. 143, the Co. to H. A. Pitts & Co., Chicago, Apr. 9, 1866; W. Lyon, Nashville, Tenn., to Co., Feb. 15, 1867. M. Fry, Lynnville, Tenn., (?), 1869, to the Co.: "Old Tennessee is the garden spot but awfully cussed with a bad Government but we still live in hope of better times somewhere. Oh, I had better quit for I don't know your politics. I may be too hard on your toes. Please excuse such nonsense." A. M. Hamilton, Keswick, Va., to the Co., Aug. 15, 1872.

[9] A. J. Hamilton, Richmond, Va., to Co., July 15, 1869.

[10] Letters of the Co. in L.P.C.B. No. 110, p. 715, to C. McCorkle, Wytheville, Va., Feb. 18, 1869; No. 113, p. 379, to R. A. Hardaway, Union Springs, Ala., May 31, 1869. J. H. Robinson, Austin, Texas, to Co., Oct. 16, 1869.

[11] Because of the sand hills back from the coast, the broad, deep drains on the tide-water plantations, and the little grain that was grown, the Co. decided not to try to sell reapers in North Carolina. L.P.C.B., No. 88, p. 540, Co. to S. A. Stanfield, Milton, N. Car., Mch. 21, 1866. See also, *ibid.*,

ure, the Lexington and Lynchburg company of Leander's brother-in-law was appointed chief agent for all of the Old Dominion except the tide-water counties.[12] Reapers and mowers were shipped there for sale through a forwarding house at Baltimore, and the Chicago firm gave assurance that it would bear the heavy freight charges and allow the planters time to raise a crop before pressing them to settle for their implements. Because of their bountiful harvest in 1867, Virginians bought over two hundred machines, but this good augury for the future was unfulfilled on account of droughts in 1869, 1871, and 1872. The farmers of the Shenandoah Valley continued to provide a small market each year, although exorbitant freight rates on the Baltimore and Ohio Railroad often threatened to end the trade altogether.[13] Long before this time New York State had been virtually abandoned as a sales territory; New England had never been entered; purchasers from New Jersey were very few, and Maryland, Delaware and Pennsylvania markets were always unimportant.[14] In Ohio, where thousands of "Buckeye" and "Champion" machines were made each year, the McCormicks were unable to secure a firm foothold until 1880.[15] On the middle seaboard, farmers

No. 110, p. 118; No. 111, p. 644, Co. to J. Chesnut, Camden, S. Car., Mch. 5 and Apr. 3, 1869.

[12] Adv. of Hamilton, Waesche & Co. in "Lexington (Va.) Gazette," Jan. 3, 1866. #C. A. Spring, Jr., to C. H. McCormick, Feb. 17, 1866. L.P.C.B. No. 95, pp. 245-246, Co. to A. M. Hamilton, Lexington, Feb. 1, 1867.

[13] Ibid., No. 104, p. 386, Co. to A. M. Hamilton, Apr. 10, 1868. The carload freight rate from Chicago to Charlestown, W. Va., advanced from $155 in 1867 to $273 in 1868. In 1869 the rate to Indianapolis was $50; Cincinnati, $60; Louisville, $72; and Baltimore, $176.

[14] Ibid., No. 90, p. 55, Co. to H. N. McAllister, Bellefonte, Pa., May 12, 1866: "Our business in Pa. has been so expensive that hereafter we will confine it to the 'Cumberland Valley & thereabouts.'" J. McElwain, Buffalo, to Co., Aug. 5, 1869.

[15] L.P.C.B. No. 86, pp. 364, 466, Co. to W. D. Cobb, Bellefontaine, O., Dec. 16, 1865: "Our Ohio business pays us less and less each year, and next season we will have only ten agents there." Ohio wheat in 1866 and

wished to buy combined machines which were primarily mowers. The McCormick reaper-mower, however, was above all a reaper.[16] Failure to extend the eastern and Virginia market was not a matter of large importance. "Our trade is now essentially western," wrote William J. Hanna of the factory office in 1870, "and the demand west takes all the machines we can make—hence we attach *little* importance to a Baltimore agency."[17]

Heedless of their costly experience in Texas on the eve of the Civil War, the McCormicks after the conflict was over prepared to reënter the state in force.[18] Northern and southern Texas agencies, with the Brazos River as the dividing line, were organized, and machines were shipped there both by way of New Orleans and New York.[19] An Illinoian who was sent to manage the business in the Sabine and Red River valleys had a brief and colorful experience. Many Confederate

1867 was very light. J. Ackerman, Columbus, O., to Co., Feb. 20, 1867; T. H. Ritter, Columbus, to Co., June 9, 1872; L.P.C.B., No. 118, p. 336, Co. to T. H. Ritter, Urbana, O., June 6, 1871.

[16] W. C. Koons, Newville, Pa., to Co., July 26, 1867.

[17] L.P.C.B. No. 122, p. 59, Co. to W. B. Tilghman, Baltimore, Oct. 20, 1870. See also, *ibid.*, No. 118, p. 46, Co. to W. B. Harman & Co., Westminster, Md., Mch. 1, 1870; No. 101, p. 591, Co. to H. B. Blair, Clear Spring, Md., Oct. 20, 1867: "Our aim at the present time is to rather centralize our Eastern business than to increase the number of agents." In the spring of 1874, the Co. again appointed a general agent for eastern Tennessee. On Jan. 10, 1881 (L.P.C.B. No. 209, p. 244), the Co. wrote W. N. Baker of Baltimore that "The Messrs. McCormick have great pride in their native state but have decided that they have done business on the give-away plan there long enough." Late in 1882 the Richmond agency was closed (No. 228, p. 434).

[18] In 1861, the McCormick Co. had one general agent, five agents, seventeen sub-agents, and over one hundred unsold machines in Texas. These machines, together with about $20,000 in reaper notes held by the general agent, were almost a total loss as a result of the war and the dishonesty of this salesman. Most of the debts were outlawed in 1874 under the statute of limitations.

[19] The focus of the southern district was at Austin, and of the northern at Jefferson, and later at Sherman. Other consignees were at Waco, Dallas, and Fort Worth. See, L.P.C.B. No. 94 (Dec., 1866), *passim*.

veterans migrated to the region about Sherman and Jefferson in the northeastern part of the state, carrying with them their dislike for all Yankees. Here, in a virgin country well watered by many broad and deep streams, these new-comers herded cattle and tried to grow wheat and cotton. Money was scarce, grasshoppers abundant, and men from the North found it wise to forget which section had won the war.[20] D. N. Barnhill, the agent, was coached by his home office in the tactics he should follow. "C. H. McCormick & Bros.," he was reminded, "are Southern men and Known as such, and it is perfectly right and proper to make use of all such facts in the business, *without* entering into the dirty muddle of politics on any account. The accident of a man's birthplace often gives him advantages and he should not fail to make use of them." [21] So Barnhill, whose predecessor in Texas had lasted less than a month,[22] tucked his trousers into his boots, bought a broad-brimmed hat and six-shooter, and professed to be a "Rebel." [23] His frequent letters to the company portrayed a state of society in his district which might well have furnished material for authors of "penny dreadfuls" about the Wild West. "I am trying to get all strait so as to avoid trouble in case I should get killed or die," he mournfully assured his employer in the spring of 1868. "The morrals of the country is verry bad at this time. There has been over thirty men killed in the vicinity of the country I have been in within the last 30 days." [24]

[20] D. N. Barnhill, Jefferson, Texas, to Co., Apr. 15 and Dec. 12, 1867.
[21] L.P.C.B. No. 94, pp. 237-238, Co. to D. N. Barnhill, Dec. 14, 1866.
[22] *Ibid.*, No. 85, p. 595, No. 86, pp. 412, 587, letters of the Co. to W. C. Stacy, Indianapolis and New Orleans, Nov. 15 and Dec. 20, 1865, and to Horton, Newton & Co., Houston, Texas, Dec. 30, 1865.
[23] D. N. Barnhill to the Co., Apr. 8, 1867.
[24] *Idem* to *idem*, May 19, 1868. See also, his many letters in 1867 and up to August, 1868. L.P.C.B. No. 96, pp. 130-131, Co. to D. N. Barnhill, Mch. 4, 1867: "Remember that 'California soon tamed down' in the early 1850's."

Although his life was threatened because he was a "damned Yankee," and he finally abandoned his post at Jefferson, the "emporium of trade," under cover of darkness in order to avoid being robbed of his employer's funds,[25] poor transportation facilities, poverty, grasshoppers, and crop failures, rather than prejudice against northern wares, were the chief causes of his ultimate defeat.[26] Farmers, with four or five yoke of oxen drawing their wagons, were accustomed to start out in the spring on a journey of a hundred miles or more to Jefferson to buy reapers and other supplies. Many swollen streams swept across the long, muddy trail. In 1867, one eager purchaser spent four weeks in coming for a machine and feared he could not get back to his few acres of wheat in time for the harvest.[27] In that same season, Barnhill had over sixty orders, but finally delivered only nineteen machines because most of the buyers were unable to ford the rivers on the road to Jefferson.[28]

After this unencouraging experience, the McCormicks declined for several years to send any further shipments to Texas, and were chiefly concerned to dispose of the one hundred and thirty-six old reapers and mowers there which even at greatly reduced prices went begging for buyers. "We are sick and tired of Texas," wrote C. A. Spring, Jr., in 1871, ". . . The fact is the Country has no money, and of late years the wheat crop has failed year after year. We have tried to trade our machines for land or Bitch Pups but no Sale—Don't

[25] D. N. Barnhill to the Co., Aug. 3, 1868.
[26] A. N. Wright & Co., Jefferson, Texas, to Co., Dec. 27, 1867. Grasshoppers and rust destroyed virtually all the grain in Texas in 1868, and left the farmers too poor to send North for seed wheat. J. H. Robinson, Austin, Texas, to the Co., Jan. 29, Feb. 24, and Aug. 24, 1868.
[27] D. N. Barnhill to the Co., May 30, 1867.
[28] Idem to idem, July 1, 1867. The agency moved its headquarters to Sherman after the 1868 season, in order to have a distributing place with better transportation facilities, more centrally located in the wheat area of north Texas, and in a town which was less completely surrounded by deep streams.

think we will try it again."[29] By then the company had no
regular agent in the state and any Texan who wished to purchase a new McCormick machine was obliged to pay cash
with his order.[30] In the opinion of the Chicago firm, the early
harvest of Texas was worthy of note merely because it was
a convenient place in which to try out improvements before
the grain ripened in the central belt.

While the McCormicks attempted with small success to increase their sales in the southern states, they also sent car-
loads of reapers and mowers to New York for transfer to
ships bound for San Francisco and Portland. The expansion
of the wheat fields of California and Oregon during the early
sixties invited a more determined effort to market machines
there than ever before. The Portland agent boasted that Oregon grain and flour was of such superior quality that it outsold the export of California in the New York market. With
evident pride, he sent the McCormicks some seed wheat for
trial in prairie soil.[31]

The cost of the iron-bound cases in which machines were
shipped to the Pacific Coast, together with the heavy freight
charges both by land and by sea, added about $80.00 to the
Chicago price of a reaper. The completion of the transconti-

[29] L.P.C.B. No. 127, p. 464, C. A. Spring, Jr., to J. F. Fullen, St. Louis,
Mo., June 27, 1871; No. 128, p. 756, the Co. to P. Mohan, St. Louis, Mo.,
July 25, 1871: "Inasmuch as cattle can be wintered outdoors [in Texas] we
cannot see how mowing machines would be in demand to any extent." See
also, its letters to P. Mohan in No. 129, pp. 275, 446, No. 138, pp. 727, 793,
Aug. 10 and 22, 1871, Nov. 27 and Dec. 3, 1872. *Ibid.,* No. 133, pp. 406, 460,
Co. to Broughton & Porter, Sherman, Texas, Apr. 18, 1872; No. 133, p. 609,
to Harwood & Co., Dallas, Texas, May 2, 1872. As late as Nov., 1872, 129
of these 136 machines were still unsold. *Ibid.,* No. 139, p. 802, Co. to J. H.
Robinson, Austin, Texas, Feb. 17, 1873.

[30] *Post,* Chap. XIV, ftn. 111. *Ibid.,* No. 126, p. 311, the Co. to G. O. Evans,
Paris, Texas, June 5, 1871.

[31] *Ibid.,* No. 90, p. 768, the Co. to Knapp, Burrell & Co., Portland, Ore.,
June 12, 1866. Knapp, Burrell & Co., to the Co., Apr. 10, 1867.

nental railroad in 1869 brought no relief, since the Union
Pacific presumed upon its monopoly to charge such prohibitive
rates on harvesting machinery consigned to the far-western
market that the ocean route was still preferred.[32] Thus, because of the cost of transportation by rail from Chicago to
New York, midwestern manufacturers could be undersold in
California and Oregon by Atlantic seaboard firms who were
almost a thousand miles farther away from these grain
areas.[33]

Nevertheless, no maker of reapers and mowers whose factory was east of the Rocky Mountains long enjoyed a profitable business on the Pacific Coast. The McCormicks shipped
less than two hundred machines there during the five years
following the war and by 1870 they were happy to dispose of
the fifty still unsold at a big reduction in price.[34] West-coast
farmers, chafing under the high cost of eastern implements,
were soon supplied with headers and mowers made in their
own neighborhood.

In the meantime, the McCormicks directed their agents to
follow the Union Pacific Railroad as it was pushed farther
and farther toward the mountains. Omaha was the center for
this trade and their representative was aboard the first regular
train which started west from that town over the newly laid

[32] L.P.C.B. No. 133, p. 395, the Co. to H. G. Grattan, Waukon, Ia.,
Apr. 17, 1872.
[33] Knapp, Burrell & Co., Portland, Ore., to the Co., July 15, 1867. Short
crops in Oregon in 1867 also hurt the sale of machines there. In 1869
McCormick could ship a self-rake reaper by lake and rail from Chicago to
New York for $10.08, or by lake and canal for $8.28. See, L.P.C.B., No. 116,
p. 451, the Co. to Baker & Hamilton, N. Y., Aug. 5, 1869, and *supra*,
Chap. XI, ftn. 55.
[34] *Post*, Chap. XIV, ftn. 128. Letters of the Co. to Knapp, Burrell & Co.,
in *ibid.*, No. 118, p. 133; No. 122, p. 320; No. 123, p. 159; No. 129, p. 712,
Jan. 11, Mch. 4, Nov. 14, 1870, and Sept. 8, 1871. *Ibid.*, No. 127, p. 661, the
Co. to O. Haupt, St. Peter, Minn., June 30, 1871; *ibid.*, No. 139, p. 752, Co.
to K. W. Waterman, Wilmington, Ill., Feb. 12, 1873: "We have no agent
on the Pacific Coast."

tracks.[35] Even before the railroad opened up a market in Colorado and Utah Territories, the factory office had been ready
to wagon reapers and mowers there from Nebraska City or
Council Bluffs.[36] The heavy cost of carriage rendered this impracticable, but in the spring of 1869 consignees were appointed in Denver and Salt Lake City. When McCormick's
scout reached the Mormon capital he was obliged to work
through the "Zion's Cooperative Mercantile Institution," managed by a son-in-law of Brigham Young, since "all business
in the country must be done through that channel." [37] The
clerks in the factory office shared the prejudice of the agent
against these "poor deluded" people, but consoled him with
the word that "so long as they will buy machines and pay for
them, we can afford to leave them and their institutions to the
[civilizing] influence of the Pacific RRd." [38] The machines

[35] H. C. Addis, Omaha, Neb., to the Co., Mch. 26, and Apr. 23, 1867.
L.P.C.B. No. 97, p. 37, the Co. to H. C. Addis, Apr. 1, 1867; No. 109,
p. 563, the Co. to H. A. Honeywell, Centreville, Mich., Dec. 22, 1868.

[36] Letters of the Co. in *ibid.*, No. 86, p. 639, to Hardy & White, Nebraska
City, Neb. Terr., Jan. 3, 1866, and p. 644, to Partridge & Morrison, Denver,
Colo. Terr., Jan. 3, 1866; No. 88, p. 143, to L. O. D. Clom, Payson, Utah
Terr., Mch. 5, 1866; No. 98, p. 815, to A. K. Younst, Big Thompson, Colo.
Terr., May 27, 1867. The heavy expense of freighting agricultural machinery long distances by rail or wagon, led farmers to demand that reapers
and mowers should be made lighter. Thus another factor was added to those
already mentioned impelling manufacturers to reduce the weight of their
implements.

[37] H. C. Addis, Salt Lake City, to the Co., Apr. 8 and 22, 1869. He believed that 250 reapers and mowers would be sold in Utah for the 1869
harvest, and he hoped that at least one hundred of them would be Mc-
Cormicks'. Before the Union Pacific reached Salt Lake the small number
of harvesting implements on sale in Utah had commanded prices ranging
from $450 to $1,000 a machine. Cash was almost always paid.

[38] L.P.C.B. No. 111, p. 831, and No. 112, pp. 247, 342, the Co. to H. C.
Addis, Apr. 5, 19, and 22, 1869. In the letter of Apr. 5, the Co. wrote:
"This is the first letter we have had the pleasure of writing to the 'City
of Saints' and hope it will mark an epoch in our business. A view back
twenty years makes the whole western progress seem like the stories of
the 'Arabian Nights' or 'Gulliver's Travels.'" *Ibid.*, No. 113, p. 917, the Co.

sent to Salt Lake for the 1869 harvest did not work well, and when only four were sold during the next year, the McCormick Company was glad to close out the surplus to the Mormon Association at bargain prices.[39] A few purchasers were found each season in the neighborhood of Denver, but a year or two often elapsed between shipments there, since the company wished the old stock to be sold before machines of the latest model were sent.[40]

More important from the business standpoint than these excursions so far afield, although probably less gratifying to pride, was the slowly mounting volume of orders reaching the office from the southeastern Dakotas, eastern Nebraska, and central Kansas. This new grain region, depending so largely for its existence upon railroads, homesteaders, and agricultural machinery, was destined to have much greater significance for the McCormick Company than the wheat lands of the eastern, southern and far-western states. At the outset of the race for the trade of this vast country, the firm had a decided strategic advantage because it was located farther west than any other large manufacturer of harvesting implements. Even before the close of the Civil War, St. Joseph, Missouri, was an important distributing point for reapers and mowers shipped there from Chicago by way of St. Louis.[41]

to Walker Bros., Salt Lake City, June 15, 1869: "We sell in Utah at Chicago prices, plus freight."

[39] Letters from the Co. in *ibid.*, No. 116, p. 432, No. 121, p. 496, to H. C. Addis, Aug. 4, 1869, and Sept. 10, 1870; No. 119, p. 596, to A. W. Farnesworth, Beaver City, Utah Terr., May 3, 1870. No. 122, p. 438, to D. W. Cobb, Omaha, Neb., Nov. 28, 1870.

[40] Letters of the Co. in *ibid.*, No. 118, p. 243, to H. C. Addis, Mch. 10, 1870; No. 134, p. 264 to J. F. Brooke, Huerfano Canon, Colo. Terr., May 23, 1872. *Post,* Chap. XIV, ftn. 112.

[41] *Ibid.*, No. 66, p. 681, Co. to D. A. Constable, St. Joseph, Mo., Feb. 8, 1864; No. 86, p. 820, to the Genl. Frght. Agt., Chicago and Alton RRd., Jan. 9, 1866. The firm wished to make St. Louis a transhipment place for the Kansas and Nebraska trade, if railroad rates were made low enough from Chicago to St. Louis. *Ibid.,* No. 89, pp. 220, 384, Co. to Hawley &

Nebraska City, Brownville, Plattsmouth, Council Bluffs, and Omaha began to figure prominently in the correspondence by 1866, and within the next five years Sioux City and the Yankton district of southern Dakota territory became familiar names to the clerks in the office.[42]

Around these towns and in Kansas the story made familiar by experiences on earlier frontiers was repeated with certain variations for which grasshoppers and a perverse climate were largely to blame. The rush of settlers, the early optimism both of agents and buyers, the pride in the quality of the grain grown on virgin soil, the competition between neighboring settlements for a station and water-tower on the proposed railroad line, the speculative boom both in and near these little communities, and harvesting-machinery salesmen vying one with another to "get in solid from the word 'go,'" sum up the hopeful years from 1865 to 1868.[43] Before the end of

White, Nebraska City, Neb. Terr., Apr. 12, 1866. Freight charges on machines to Nebraska City by rail and water through St. Louis were as low as the rail rate direct from Chicago. To ship a reaper and a mower from Chicago to Nebraska City cost $19 and $9, respectively.

[42] Letters to the Co. of E. H. Wilcox, Brownville, Neb., Feb. 3 and July 2, 1867, Apr. 23, 1868, and Oct. 28, 1869; of Clark & Plummer, Plattsmouth, Neb., June 2, 1868, and of G. W. Edgar, Lincoln, Neb., July 7, 1869. H. C. Addis, the agent at Omaha, wrote on Dec. 16, 1867, that Sioux City was second only to Omaha as a sales center. John Edgar of Missouri Valley, Ia., urged the Co. in Dec., 1872, to push into the Yankton district because it was being settled very fast and doubtless had a great future. In 1872, the Co. sold two hundred machines in Neb., 110 in Kan., 405 in Mo., and 1,999 in Ia. W. N. Spring, Sioux City, to Co., June 25, 1873: "There is no time of day when one can not see white covered wagons in our streets. Dakota is fast filling up."

[43] J. Hammond, Council Grove, Kan., to the Co., Nov. 9, 1867: Government land sells at $1.25 an acre, improved land from $5 to $10 an acre, and lots in this town for $25 to $300. Labor is in demand and the railroad will soon come. H. C. Addis, Omaha, to the Co., Mch. 26, Apr. 4, Dec. 6, 7, 16 and 22, 1867, and Jan. 11, 1868: If we buy a corner lot (66 ft. front and 120 ft. deep) in Omaha for $10,000, we can sell a part of it next spring for as much as we now pay for it all. If the railroad bridge does not cross the river at this point, however, Omaha, will be dead. Excitement on this sub-

this brief period, and with increasing emphasis as the new decade began, came word of grasshoppers innumerable, grain drowned out in Kansas, cattle starving during the winter months, wheat scorched by the summer's heat, "iniquitous" stay laws, heavy taxes and freight rates, a poor quality of immigrants, a surfeit of machines, declining prices of grain, no money among farmers, and general discontent.[44]

"Kansas is made up of a class of people who have suffered reverses of fortune," the McCormicks were informed in the

ject is intense. E. H. Wilcox, Brownville, Neb., to the Co., Feb. 3, 1867: Nebraska wheat commands from 10¢ to 15¢ a bus. more than any other in the St. Louis market. I. N. Van Hoesen, Fort Scott, Kan., to the Co., Apr. 9, 1867: There is immense immigration to Neosho and Cherokee Counties. I sell mowers to homesteaders as they go by my store. W. F. Carr, Lawrence, Kan., to the Co., May 2, 1868: "I can not sell much this year in Neosho, Labette, Crawford, and Cherokee Cys. since the settlers are saving all their money, or borrowing @ 50 per cent a year, to buy the land which the government will soon put on the market." After the bountiful harvest of 1868, H. C. Addis wrote to the Co. on July 27, that "Nebraska is bound to beat the world on small grains." L. A. Smith, St. Joseph, Mo., to the Co., May 3, 1873.

[44] I. N. Van Hoesen, Fort Scott, Kan., to the Co., Apr. 9, and July 7, 1867. L.P.C.B. No. 96, p. 388, No. 97, p. 234, the Co. to W. F. Carr, Leavenworth, Kan., Mch. 14, 1867. H. C. Addis, Omaha, to the Co., Sept. 7 and Oct. 5, 1867, Mch. 23, May 17 and 20, 1868. The Kansas and Nebraska harvest seasons of 1867, 1869 and 1872, were too wet, but the crop of 1868 was excellent and Van Hoesen expected his state to "beat Iowa" by 1869 as a sales territory. He was disappointed in this hope but in spite of the wet weather, he found more purchasers than ever before. In 1870, due to the dry winter and spring, and the excess buying of 1869, Van Hoesen sold ⅓ less machines, than in that year. E. W. Wilcox of Brownville, Neb., informed the Co. on Oct. 28, 1869, that farmers would not sell their grain as long as the price was 40 to 60¢ a bushel. In July, 1870, #1 Fall Wheat was selling in Kansas for 75¢ a bushel but farmers held it back from market hoping that European war rumors would drive up the price still further. In that month, according to I. N. Van Hoesen, "Every city and town is full of machines laying around in the mud." The expected rise in price did not come, however, and by Feb., 1871, the same agent lamented to the home office: "As soon as the large immigration stops or slacks, money will be *non est.* A reaction is bound to take place in any country where things have gone as they have here, and I think it's come now."

spring of 1867, "and have come to retrieve it. They are, or think they are, very sharp at a bargain, and from the fact that they are themselves rascally (having in most cases debts for McCormick Reapers &c still hanging over their heads) are suspicious of everyone else. . . . They won't sign an order blank but will promise on their honor to pay if the mach. on arrival is as represented." [45]

Every season an increasing number of hard-luck stories came to the McCormicks from this area, but they continued to press for sales there, hoping, with the farmers, that "next year a big crop will bring matters out all right." But a "next year" of this kind was very slow in coming and debts and unpaid taxes accumulated to disheartening amounts. In sections where wheat was of secondary importance, a good crop of corn or a high price for pork sometimes allowed a farmer to pay for his reaper on time.[46] Then, too, many landowners in central Kansas were fattening Texas cattle, and needed mowers to put by hay for the winter months.[47] In short, the situation was never one of unrelieved gloom, but the general outlook by the close of 1872 warranted pessimism.

Collections are *impossible* [reported an agent at Lawrence in December of that year]. Kansas is in a deplorable condition, in

[45] As a matter of fact, by 1871, the bulk of McCormicks' sales were made without the formality of the purchaser signing an order-blank. See, L.P.C.B. No. 125, p. 873, the Co. to C. H. Smith, Warrensburgh, Mo., Apr. 13, 1871. I. N. Van Hoesen, Manhattan, Kan., to the Co., Apr. 16, 1867. In a letter of Mch. 24, 1867, he wrote, in summary: I can't extend credit because of the stay laws, which provide that a note is not collectable longer than three years after its maturity, and exempts 160 acres, and stock and implements in proportion, from seizure for a debt. I won't try to sell west of Salina. Most farmers around Manhattan are homesteaders who have bought a pair of condemned army horses, and are now scraping around to get money to buy fencing material.

[46] *Idem,* Macomb, Kan., to *idem,* June 3, 1867. H. Tucker, Holton, Kan., to the Co., May 8, 1871.

[47] D. R. B. Greenlee, Junction City, Kan., to J. G. Hamilton, June 29, 1869.

fact bankrupt. . . . Prices of such stuff as the farmers have for sale is very low. Oats the principal grain . . . is a Drug at 16⅔¢. Taxes are coming due, and every cent is being hoarded to pay them. Banks are holding their funds at an advanced price—and farmers can't touch money at the rate of interest asked. . . . Rich firm of C. H. McCormick & Bros., who "don't want money, only the interest on the note," every man in Kansas seems sometime or other to have heard this, although I've been since 1866 trying to convince them otherwise.[48]

The six states flanking the Mississippi River from Kentucky and Missouri northward to the Canadian border, continued to be the chief sales territory for McCormick machines.[49] Aided by agricultural implements, the tide of Scandinavian and German immigration, and by the rapid construction of railroad lines, the production of spring wheat during this period greatly increased in northern Iowa, Wisconsin and Minnesota. The opening of the Red River Valley of the North, however, was still a few years in the future.[50]

[48] I. N. Van Hoesen, Lawrence, Kan., to the Co., Dec. 23, 1872. In a similar vein, Nye, Colson & Co. of Fremont in eastern Neb. wrote to the firm on Jan. 2, 1872: "It is *very*, VERY hard collecting. Our farmers are, in consequence of hurricanes, hailstorms, Drouths, and low prices for the little they have, certainly in a deplorable condition." See, letters to the Co. from J. Edgar, Rochester, Minn., Oct. 14, 1868; H. G. Grattan, Ludlow, Ia., Oct. 19, 1868, and W. C. Orr, Plum Valley, Neb., Dec. 10, 1872.

[49] The McCormick reaper trade in Missouri had not been satisfactorily managed by the aged J. B. McCormick during the Civil War. He was shelved in 1865, and Kentucky was no longer controlled from the St. Louis office. Not until 1867, however, when Patrick Mohan took over the general agency for Missouri, did business in that state again become remunerative.

[50] J. Rhodes, Hastings, Minn., to the Co., Mch. 2, 1867, and Mch. 17, 1869. To paraphrase the letter of Mch., 1867: The people of Scott Cy., Minn., are nine-tenth German and Irish, and the rest of them are "smart-dealing" Yankee merchants and large farmers who govern and lead the foreigners. On June 24, 1867, he wrote of the competition among agents for the patronage of Oliver Dalrymple, who with nearly two thousand acres of grain, was in his first year as a "bonanza" farmer. Dalrymple, a lawyer of St. Paul, had three large farms about fifteen miles south of the town. One was named "Grant," another "Sherman," and the third, "Sheridan."

In view of this development, it mattered little to the McCormicks that many farmers in Illinois and Indiana were shifting their emphasis from winter wheat to corn and live stock. They could at least be persuaded to purchase the excellent mowers made by the firm during these years.

In 1866, the wheat crop failed in Kentucky, Indiana, Minnesota and northern Iowa, but elsewhere in the Middle West it was splendid.[51] Following an unusually cold winter and rainy spring, when much live stock starved or froze to death, the grain harvest of the next season was of about average size.[52] Farmers in Iowa and Illinois, however, complained of the poor yield of corn and the ravages of hog cholera.[53] Except for depredations by grasshoppers in some localities, 1868 was a boom year in Iowa and Minnesota, but the stand of wheat in Illinois, Indiana and Kentucky was lighter than

Rhodes secured as sub-agents men who were also engaged in promoting immigration from northern Europe. Edgar & Aiken, Rochester, Minn., to the Co., Apr. 4, 1867, and Oct. 3, 1868: The railroad has opened up Waseca Cy. so we should sell fifty more machines this year than last. As soon as the farmers pull the stumps out of their fields we can sell more machines. Building a railroad furnishes farmers along the line an excellent market for their produce, but it occasionally entices them to use all their cash to buy its stock.

[51] C. A. Spring, Jr., to C. H. McCormick, May 25, 1866. H. G. Grattan, Waukon, Ia., to the Co., Dec. 31, 1866. Harvest almost everywhere in the Middle West in 1866 was about a month later than usual due to the dry spring. See, L.P.C.B., No. 90, p. 496, the Co. of J. J. Barnhill, Vincennes, Ind., May 31, 1866.

[52] Letters to the Co. from W. H. Sibley, Des Moines, Ia., Jan. 14, Feb. 4, Apr. 22, June 4, 22, and July 14, 1867; from H. G. Grattan, Waukon, Ia., July 15, 1867; from J. Rhodes, Hastings, Minn., Sept. 7, 1867, and from T. L. French, Cedar Falls, Ia., June 3, 1867.

[53] Letters to the Co. from O. H. Loomis, Kewanee, Ill., between Jan. 29 and Aug. 8, 1867; from H. O. Goodrich, Jerseyville, Ill., on Mch. 24, June 10, July 11, Aug. 16 and Sept. 13, 1867; from J. S. Andrews, Wapello, Ia., Oct. 2, 1867 and from G. Monser, Wenona, Ill., July 19, 1867. On Jan. 19, 1867, T. Flick, of Clinton, Ia., wrote that the cattle-feeders had bought much corn but since the banks would not loan to them, they were unable to pay for it.

usual.[54] Prices sharply declined that autumn, and farmers held back their grain with the hope that the market would be more favorable after the presidential election in November, or after "combinations among speculators" stopped "rioting upon the ruins of honest industry." [55] But there was no upward trend, and they were eventually obliged to sell at a figure insufficient in many cases to pay their debts and buy seed for the spring planting.

After the cold, wet, spring and early summer in 1869 ruined the corn and rusted the small grain in some sections, wheat commanded only from fifty to seventy cents a bushel, and farmers were desperate.[56] Many fields at harvest time had

[54] Letters to the Co. from D. H. Smith, Lafayette, Ind., May 6 and 25, 1867; D. W. Cobb, Lexington, Ky., June 1, 1867; C. B. Pinkham, Marshalltown, Ia., May 9 and June 4, 1868; J. V. Hinchman, Glenwood, Ia., June 6, 1868; E. A. McNair, Davenport, Ia., July 3, 1868, and A. Burlingame, Cedar Falls, Ia., July 26, 1868. C. Morgan, Galveston, Ind., June 20, 1868: "Crops have failed around here for three or four years and farmers are discouraged." L.P.C.B. No. 105, p. 784, the Co. to J. Rhodes, Hastings, Minn., June 20, 1868. The Co. had already shipped 363 machines for sale in the Minnesota harvest, and this agent begged in vain for four more car-loads.

[55] D. H. Smith, Sparta, Wis., to the Co., Nov. 4, 1868. Where the corn crop was large but low in price compared with that of pork, farmers tended to postpone hog-killing until later than usual in the autumn. Letters to the Co. from H. G. Grattan, Ludlow, Ia., Oct. 19, 1868; O. H. Loomis, Kewanee, Ill., Oct. 31, 1868; J. H. Osborne, Mattoon, Ill., Nov. 2, 1868; and W. J. Hays, Bloomington, Ill., Nov. 23, 1868. Wheat that was selling as high as $1.75 a bus. in the summer was down to a dollar by November. Shelled corn brought 60¢ a bus. in May and 30¢ in November. Pork and beef were also "a drug on the market" that autumn. Farmers were said to have bought equipment, fencing, etc., with the expectation that their wheat would sell @ $1.50 a bushel.

[56] Letters to the Co. from E. C. Beardsley, Sycamore, Ill., Apr. 21 and July 16, 1869: "The oldest inhabitants do not remember a more rainy season than this;" C. F. Johnson, Galesburg, Ill., June 28, 1869; A. Dickey, Farmington, Ia., July 15, 1869, H. H. Johnson, Palmyra, Mo., July 20, 1869, and L. H. Shepard, Burnett, Wis., Nov. 15, 1869: "Cattle are drowning and the Mississippi River is higher than since 1851." The region about Cedar Falls and Waverly, Ia., enjoyed fine crops but was an exception to the rule. L.P.C.B. No. 116, p. 330, the Co. to A. T. French, Cedar Rapids, Ia.,

been so muddy that reapers and mowers could not work in them, grain sprouted in the shock, and country roads hub-deep in mud made it impossible either for the farmer to move his crop to market, or for the reaper agent to go about the country-side on his futile mission of collecting.[57] Farmers generally estimated that wheat cost seventy-five cents a bushel to raise. With its sale price considerably below that figure, and with insistent tax collectors and agents adding to the cheerlessness of the soggy weather, it is little wonder that many grain-growers saw only ruin ahead.[58] Farmers in southern Minnesota were especially hard hit. There was no money to borrow except at twenty-four per cent to thirty-six per cent interest a year, and they were clamoring for their legislature to enact a stay law. From Illinois, as well, came the word in August: "I never saw anything like the present money stringency, & it has come like a clap of thunder. The Bank is dry & the money dead. Is the govt. still diminishing the supply of money? If so, we'll have the biggest smash up you ever saw. If Uncle Sam's debt is paid, it will be through the *prosperity* of the people. Or is this stringency due to some speculative movement & will it soon be over?" [59] A widespread demand for inflation was a natural outcome of this situation.

The next three years brought little relief to the farmers in the diversified farming belt from Indiana to Iowa, although apparently those who relied for most of their income upon

July 31, 1869, "We cannot take back Reliables because the season is wet. Such a season may never occur during our lifetime again."

[57] Letters to the Co. from J. H. Shaffer, Kankakee, Ill., between Apr. 26 and Nov. 29, 1869, McNair & Co., Washington, Ia., July 18, 1869, E. W. Brooks, Red Wing, Minn., Sept. 11, 1869, and W. Burke, La Prairie, Ill., July 8, 1869.

[58] J. Edgar, Ackley, Ia., to the Co., Nov. 16, 1869: "*Collections are coming very hard & must be short.* With wheat at 40 to 60 cts. which cost the Farmer 75 cents, the whole matter is plain—*he cannot pay his debts.*"

[59] Letters to the Co., from O. H. Loomis, Kewanee, Ill., Aug. 5, 1869, J. Edgar, Rochester, Minn., Dec. 17, 1869, and H. H. Johnson, Pana, Ill., Oct. 8, 1870.

corn and live stock were somewhat less unfortunate than growers of the small grains.[60] These last suffered from drought in 1870 and from drought and chinch-bugs in 1871.[61] Prices of farm products remained low and dairymen and cattle-fatteners alone had any money.[62] The exceptionally cold winter of 1871-1872 killed much winter wheat, and with the return of warm weather Hessian fly and chinch-bug once again took a heavy toll in some localities.[63] Crops, however, were excellent in the spring wheat section of northern Iowa and Minnesota, and agents there wrote less about "constables and sheriffs . . . busy on all sides." [64] The McCormick agent at Rochester, Minnesota, who had been the gloomiest member of the force for several years, sold almost seven hundred machines, and grumbled because the company could not send three hundred more.[65] Nevertheless, the very low price of

[60] Letters to the Co. from C. F. Johnson, Galesburg, Ill., Apr. 11, 1870, O. H. Loomis, Kewanee, Ill., July 8, Oct. 13 and Nov. 5, 1870: "Ruined farmers also bankrupt everybody in these small towns;" A. D. Rogers, Elmwood, Ill., Sept. 14, 1870, and A. Perry & Co., Farmington, Ia., Oct. 17, 1870.

[61] Letters to the Co. of H. H. Johnson, Palmyra, Mo., Apr. 26, 1870, L. H. Shepard, Burnett, Wis., June 7, 1870, W. A. Boyd, La Porte, Ind., May 16, 1870, F. W. Haxford, Cherokee, Ia., July 5, 1870, G. Monser, Wenona, Ill., July 25, 1870, and J. Edgar, Rochester, Minn., Aug. 22, 1870. Crops were of average size in Minnesota, although some sections were injured by hail.

[62] This was particularly true of Illinois and Wisconsin in 1871. See letters to the Co. of J. H. Shaffer, Kankakee, Ill., May 27, June 15, and July 19, 1871, F. G. Smyth, Madison, Wis., July 17, 1871, and of W. H. Hays, Bloomington, Ill., May 15, 1871. Wheat was selling @ fifty cents a bus. in May, 1870. See, W. Case, Ottawa, Ill., to the Co., May 1, 1870.

[63] L.P.C.B. No. 133, p. 647, Co. to L. H. Smith, St. Joseph, Mo., May 6, 1872. I. A. Seaver, Quincy, Ill., to the Co., May 25, 1872.

[64] Letters to the Co. of A. Perry & Co., Farmington, Ia., between Jan. 2, and Oct. 1, 1872, F. G. Smith, Madison, Wis., June 28, 1872, C. E. Hedges, Sioux City, Ia., July 23, 1872, and of J. Edgar, Rochester, Minn., Aug. 20, 1872. C. A. Spring, Jr., to C. H. McCormick, July 24, 1872.

[65] In 1866, this agency sold only 163 machines. The increase during the next six years is typical of the growth of the market in Minnesota during that period. J. Edgar to the Co., Nov. 17, 1870.

grain made it most difficult for farmers to pay for their implements.[66] The salesman at Farmington, Iowa, described a situation common to many districts in the Middle West, when he wrote in the autumn of 1872: "Every dollar farmers can get they are investing in hogs & cattle to eat the product [grain and hay] rather than sell [it] at these prices. There will be a big hog crop to market if nothing gets among them to destroy them. . . . Last Spring ['s] Calves are selling at from 12 to 15 dollars apiece in many places which is too high but buyers say they must have them to eat the product of farm as they can't sell it." [67]

The conditions, just described, in part account for the vigor of the Granger movement in the early 'seventies. Many farmers who were debt-free at the close of the war were heavily burdened once again by 1872. Because of the hard times, grain-growers might be expected to buy very few implements. Quite the contrary was true. "Easy to sell and hard to collect," summarizes these seven years from the standpoint of the builders of machines. The McCormick Company was embarrassed in almost every season by its inability to fill all of the orders sent in by its agents.[68] The popularity of its output increased in spite of the fact that the generally dry summers of this period favored the success of the Marsh Harvester.[69]

[66] G. Monser, Wenona, Ill., to the Co., Oct. 16, 1872. Oats sell here for 15¢ a bushel, old corn @ 22¢, and rye @ 40¢.

[67] A. Perry & Co., Farmington, Ia., to the Co., Oct. 28, 1872. N. J. Hays, Champaign, Ill., to the Co., Oct. 21, 1872: "There never has been such a corn crop as now and never I think so many hogs. . . . From the amount of hogs of all ages [I] think collections will keep up during the winter." But pork brought the "ruinously low" price of 3½ to 5¢ a lb., by the new year.

[68] L.P.C.B. No. 90, p. 617, the Co. to Crosby Bros., Grasshopper Falls, Kan., June 5, 1866: "We will sell about 7,500 machines this year. It seems that the more we sell the more we can sell. No spot is ever oversupplied for long."

[69] G. A. Willey, Belleville, Ill., to the Co., Mch. 28, 1872. J. Edgar, Mason City, Ia., to the Co., Aug. 1, 1872.

There was but small inducement to lower the price of reapers and mowers while the demand for them could not be supplied. The cost of the raw materials used in machine construction was between a quarter and a third greater in 1865 than in 1870.[70] In the latter year, for the first time in its history, the McCormick firm put down the selling price of its implements, but the competition of rival manufacturers, rather than a buyers' strike, was the main cause for the reduction.[71]

In view of the critical agricultural situation, the agents of the McCormick Company necessarily devoted more time to collecting and securing debts than to selling machines. Under ordinary conditions they were busiest from April to August of each year, but special vigilance was now demanded in the autumn and early winter when a farmer, having completed his threshing or slaughtered his hogs, was moving his crop to market. Because he lacked money enough to pay all of his obligations, he was prone to satisfy his most insistent creditors. Therefore, it was the duty of the McCormick salesmen to be as conspicuous as the tax collector or the village storekeeper. Their own interest also prompted them to be on hand when a farmer sold his pork and grain, because as a rule ont-

[70] In the autumn of 1865, the McCormicks paid $46 per ton for No. 1 Lake Superior iron, $26 per M. for 3 inch white-ash plank, 15¢ (gold) per lb. for steel, and about $8 per ton for blacksmith's coal. In 1871, Lake Superior iron cost $35 a ton, ash plank $20 per M., steel about 16¢ (gold) per lb., and blacksmith's coal, $6.80 a ton. These figures, to which the prices of many other materials in use at the factory might be added, have been gleaned from the letter-books covering the period in question. The terms of purchase were c.o.d., and included delivery upon the factory-dock. Lumber was usually secured from Michigan and Indiana dealers, steel from Pittsburgh and New York, coal from Chicago firms, and iron from a half-dozen or more dealers in the eastern United States and Canada.

[71] Letters to the Co. of H. H. Johnson, Palmyra, Mo., Apr. 26, 1870, and of E. Healy, Earlville, Ia., May 8, 1870. L.P.C.B. No. 119, p. 729, Co. to J. Edgar, Rochester, Minn., May 9, 1870. In this letter, the price reduction is explained on the ground that greenbacks are rising to a parity with gold. This is also the reason stated in the McCormick Co. Catalog, for 1871, p. 6.

half of their ten or twelve per cent commission was paid only after the purchaser had settled for his implement.[72] Since many debtors were unable to honor their reaper notes when due, the agents were engaged in the tedious and unpleasant work of taking mortgages on farms in order to secure the debts, or of suing an impecunious friend at the behest of their employers. In short, the salesmen's duties became more onerous and distasteful in the very seasons when they were receiving the least money from commissions.

As a result, McCormick's representatives in the stricken districts were dissatisfied by 1870, particularly since the canvassers for other makers of harvesting machinery were paid considerably larger commissions.[73] They wished either to be given a salary or an increased percentage upon their sales. One of the many grievances of the Grangers was the allegedly high commissions garnered by the reaper and mower agents. These salesmen, however, complained that they were underpaid, and laid their troubles at the door of the farmers, who were unable to settle for their machines. Thus another economic circle revolved. The manufacturer said he was unable to increase the remuneration of his agents because he could not collect from the farmers; the farmers believed that commissions came from

[72] Edgar & Aiken, Rochester, Minn., to the Co., Oct. 14, 1867.

[73] Agents were as prone to grumble when the demand exceeded the supply of machines as in years when the reverse was true. For example, in the summer of 1868 when the McCormicks could not fill all of the orders sent in, there was considerable discontent. See, L.P.C.B., No. 107 (July and Aug., 1868), passim. Ibid., No. 126, p. 139, Co. to J. P. Mohan, St. Louis, Mo., May 30, 1871: "We are well aware that several concerns are underselling us, and offering higher commissions than we—but we are just as well aware that they cannot stand up to it. We are certain that they or we must abandon this Reaper business for when it comes to the point of making and selling machines at a positive loss . . . we must be counted out of the game!" Letters to the Co. of J. Edgar, Rochester, Minn., June 8, 1868, June 1, and Dec. 17, 1869: The Manny firm pays its agents about 15 per cent. Marsh agents receive $40 for each harvester they sell. I pay my sub-agents $12 for selling a reaper and $9 for a mower.

their own pockets and should be abolished; the agents clamored for increased compensation because agricultural distress compelled them to work harder and receive less than ever before.

As early as August, 1866, C. A. Spring, Jr., of the factory office, complained to his chief that "Farmers seem to be getting into the old track they were in before the war"—no money until they have sold their grain.[74] Collections were so light during the next two winters that the company had to borrow heavily in order to pay its current expenses. No longer was it possible, as during the Civil War, to loan money to farmers.[75] The resolution of the firm never again to trade a machine for wheat or cattle was soon broken in "hard cases" where a refusal to take these commodities meant that the sale would be a total loss.[76] Of necessity, agents asked McCormick to advance the money required to pay the freight on the machines consigned to them, since they were unable to collect enough from the purchasers to meet even this comparatively small bill.[77]

[74] C. A. Spring, Jr., to C. H. McCormick, Aug. 9, 1866. See also, his letter to C. H. McCormick, July 24, 1866.

[75] L.P.C.B. No. 96, p. 586, C. A. Spring, Jr., to Chadbourn & Whitney, Rochester, Minn., Mch. 21, 1867. #C. A. Spring, Jr., to C. H. McCormick, May 18, 1867, and June 1, 1868.

[76] L.P.C.B. No. 89, p. 150, Co. to G. W. Russell, Woodstock, Ill., Apr. 10, 1866; No. 122, pp. 504, 759, to H. J. Prier, Indianapolis, Ind., Dec. 3 and 20, 1870; No. 138, p. 255, to A. L. Horton, Rochester, Minn., Oct. 25, 1872. A sub-agent of H. J. Prier took a piano in settlement for a reaper note and, it would appear, he soon traded it for eighty acres of land in White Cy., Ind.

[77] During these years each agent, and not the company office, was expected to arrange about freights with the railroads and with the farmers in his district. The company merely insisted that the purchaser should pay the cost of transportation, and it advised the agents to "equalize the fee" as much as possible. This was done by collecting a little more than the actual freight charge from each customer, in order to lighten the fee for buyers whose machines had had to be transhipped one or more times from other agencies. Machines were despatched from Chicago in car-load lots so as to keep the freight charge to each buyer as low as possible. Farmers,

Up to the early summer of 1869, however, there are few signs of real alarm in the letters written by the clerks of the office. At that time Cyrus McCormick was informed that farmers had paid fifty-one and one-half per cent of their notes when due during the fiscal year 1868-1869, fifty-seven and one-half per cent in 1867-1868, and that if it were borne in mind that sixty-six per cent had been the average of the war period, collections had been about as good as could be expected, in view of the low price of grain.[78] Without doubt, the staff in the office usually minimized its troubles to Cyrus McCormick, and exaggerated its concern when writing to agents who were dilatory in sending money.[79]

The sharp break in the price of grain in the winter of 1868-1869, combined with the rainy harvest of the next summer, marked the beginning of a severe and long-extended crisis. In July, agents were complaining that "everybody is buying cradles and wading in mud and water over their shoe tops to save what [grain] they can."[80] By November, Leander Mc-

however, occasionally complained that agents asked more than the actual rate, and pocketed the difference. The correspondence furnishes no evidence in support of this accusation. In 1867 a standard-sized freight car held 14 self-rake reapers or 30 mowers. Where two or more railroads served the same agency town, the salesman was advised to divide shipments equally between them so as to keep on good terms with all. See, "Private Circular of C. H. McCormick & Bros., to Agents," Mch., 1867.

[78] ‡C. A. Spring, Jr., to C. H. McCormick, June 8, 1869. See also, L.P.C.B. No. 94, p. 707, C. A. Spring, Jr., to N. M. Lester, Eddyville, Ia., Jan. 12, 1867.

[79] *Ibid.*, No. 90, p. 126, the Co. to W. S. Crouch, St. Louis, May 17, 1866: "We need hardly say to you that we don't want you to mention to Mr. C. H. the little difficulty about the mower. He being in N. Y. don't know of it and as it is all over now he need not be *worried about it.*" In fact, ‡C. A. Spring, Jr., wrote to C. H. McCormick on July 13, 1867, that since 1855 he had never seen a time when everything promised so well. Sales were beyond his most sanguine hopes. See also, L.P.C.B. No. 107, p. 10, C. A. Spring, Jr., to H. H. Johnson, Sparta, Wis., July 29, 1868: "We never stood so high on the ladder, and it will help sales next year."

[80] ‡C. A. Spring, Jr., to C. H. McCormick, July 17, 1869. Due to the muddy grain-fields, some farmers wished to give up their reapers and to have their down payment refunded. They were asked whether, if they

Cormick urged his brother to write a "driving letter" to the men in the factory office, ordering them to press the agents harder for money.[81] Whether Cyrus followed this suggestion is not known, but thereafter for several years the letter-books of the firm emphasized above all other subjects the desperate need of bringing the farmers to book. "We feel that all our customers want us to carry them on our Shoulders," a Minnesota agent was told in early 1870, "and it is more than we can manage! At least one half of them have got to *come down* —for the load is greater than we can bear." [82] Salesmen were warned, however, not to indulge in a policy of "general suing," but to protect all doubtful notes by requiring either that they be endorsed by responsible farmers or that real estate and chattel mortgages be taken as security.[83]

The general policy of the company in regard to granting additional time for the payment of over-due reaper notes, is well summarized in these words. "We *must have* money, and we can't make any extensions, without it is absolutely impossible for a man to pay without taking everything he has on earth." [84] In other words, a realization that it would be

bought a wagon, they would think of returning it because of wet roads. L.P.C.B. No. 115, p. 168, the Co. to J. A. McElwaine, Buffalo, N. Y., July 8, 1869.

[81] L. J. to C. H. McCormick, Nov. 22, 1869: "You come & go and say but little on that subject and it is pleasant for the office men to think that all is well and satisfied."

[82] L.P.C.B., No. 123, p. 603, the Co. to John Rhodes & Son, Hastings, Minn., Feb. 8, 1870.

[83] *Ibid.,* No. 119, p. 495, Co. to W. H. Ditmar, St. Joseph, Mo., Apr. 28, 1870: We recommend that you sue only when a debt would otherwise be surely lost, or when a man can pay and absolutely refuses to do so. No. 121, p. 352, Co. to J. Edgar, Rochester, Minn., Aug. 31, 1870: Never buy a mortgage to secure a debt unless you submit the case to us and have our approval. No. 123, p. 218, to G. R. Hersey, River Falls, Wis., Jan. 15, 1870; No. 124, p. 560, to G. A. Willey, Belleville, Ill., Jan. 30, 1871.

[84] *Ibid.,* No. 122, p. 509, Co. to W. N. Spring, Manteno, Ill., Dec. 3, 1870; No. 109, p. 237, to M. T. Grattan, Preston, Minn., Nov. 28, 1868; No. 127, p. 483, to D. O. Breuer, Kasson, Minn., June 27, 1871: "We believe every word you say, but then the fact that men are feeling their poverty is the

stupid business to ruin farmers who otherwise would probably soon need to buy more machinery, was in most instances a factor restraining both agent and manufacturer from being as harsh in practice as their words often suggest.[85] Another consideration working in the debtor's favor, was the unwillingness of a reaper-maker, when competition was so keen, to antagonize a whole neighborhood by a policy of ruthlessness which would net him little except unsaleable property heavily encumbered by unpaid taxes and mortgages.[86] Many debtors spoke the truth when they claimed that they had absolutely nothing to offer in satisfaction of their obligations except a determination to work hard and pay as soon as Providence should send good weather and a remunerative market.[87] Very

very reason [why] we should run no great risks by giving long time. We are willing to give the long-winded customers to the opposition—for nothing in the world will so soon sink their capital & make them bankrupt." No. 127, p. 51, to N. Phelps, Charles City, Ia., June 19, 1871: "We have been fighting this 'long time' question stubbornly & have lost some sales by it but it will *pay* us in the long run to keep a firm front." No. 128, p. 206, to W. Carr, Ottawa, Ill., July 12, 1871: "When men have lost their crops by Storm or anything else, you had better give them one year's extra time [to pay] without interest for the year."

[85] L.P.C.B. No. 117, for Oct. 1869, furnishes many examples of uncompromising letters on the subject of collections. They are, as always, written to the agents, and not to the farmers. L.P.C.B. No. 122, p. 328, the Co. to P. Neuman, Independence, Ia., Nov. 14, 1870: "Our experience has been that it is unsafe to retire notes [as worthless] as long as the maker thereof is living, because the chances in this western country are that an industrious man will at some time, 'dig out.'" L.P.C.B. No. 123, p. 782, the Co. to W. J. Hays, Bloomington, Ill., Feb. 18, 1870: "We know farmers will feel *poor*—but then we know they won't stop planting their farms & run into a state of barbarism—they cannot afford *that!* & so although we expect a rough rugged Season, that will tax our patience, yet we believe we shall sell a fair portion of machines."

[86] Letters to the Co. of H. G. Grattan, Ludlow, Ia., Oct. 19, 1868, and of A. Perry & Co., Farmington, Ia., Oct. 28, 1872.

[87] Not infrequently, agents wrote to the home office that farmers had produce to sell, but no buyers could be found. As a result, there was no money in the district. Those who wished to settle for their machines were thus in a dilemma, since there was no money to borrow and no market for

few farmers were scalawags, and it was simply sound business for the manufacturer to wait until the future brought a plentiful crop and fair prices.

If the very large total of unpaid reaper notes is listed as an asset, the years from 1865 to 1872 were most profitable ones for the McCormick firm. Because of the conflicting evidence, the average net profit made on the sale of a reaper or mower cannot be stated with assurance, but about $55 would seem to be the correct figure. This was by no means as large as the aggrieved farmers liked to believe. Since the average price of a self-rake reaper was about $200, and of a mower about $130, a net profit of approximately thirty-five per cent was derived from each sale.[88] Grangers, basing their estimate upon the testimony given in the many patent lawsuits of the time, or upon nothing more substantial than their own emo-

their crops. The farmers, in other instances, overlooked the reaper agents because they were using every spare dollar to build fences and break new soil. They preferred to continue paying the McCormicks 10% interest, since if they discharged their debt to him, they would be obliged to borrow at a higher rate in order to extend and improve their holdings. This optimism, encouraged by the high prices of farm produce between 1865 and 1868, led to reckless expenditures for land and machinery, and the inevitable collapse when prices crashed in the winter of 1868-1869. See, the letters to the Co. of W. H. Sibley, Des Moines, Ia., Apr. 18, 1868, of O. H. Loomis, Kewanee, Ill., Dec. 31, 1868, of C. B. Pinkham, Marshalltown, Ia., Jan. 1, 1869, of J. Edgar, Rochester, Minn., June 1, 1869, and of G. R. Hersey, Hudson, Wis., Oct. 11, 1869.

[88] This estimate is based upon a study of the annual balance-sheets prepared by the factory office in August of each year. As a rule, these give the average manufacturer's cost per machine, but clearly do not include extra-factory items of expense. These figures have been compared with relevant material in the correspondence of the firm. Samples of these letters are, C. A. Spring, Jr., to C. H. McCormick, Sept. 19, 1867, Sept. 1, 1869, and ‡Aug. 31, 1870. L.P.C.B. No. 158, pp. 130-132, F. H. Matthews to H. Baldwin, Jr., Philadelphia, Pa., May 20, 1875. The office clerks assured agents between 1865 and 1870 that there was no profit in selling machines at current prices, but the untruth of these statements can be demonstrated by citing other letters written by these same scribes. *Ibid.*, No. 90, p. 675, Co. to W. C. Stacy, Princeton, Ill., June 7, 1866; No. 87, p. 482, Co. to T. Flick, Feb. 9, 1866.

tion, charged that the manufacturers were selling their output for an advance of three hundred per cent or more over cost of production. They apparently forgot that agents' commissions, and the cost of the labor and raw materials needed to build a reaper, did not include interest on the capital invested, taxes collected by local, state and federal governments, patent fees, losses arising from "bad" sales, storage charges on unsold reapers and mowers, and the expense necessary to replace worn-out factory machinery.[89] Because McCormick's sales price for a machine usually averaged about $20 more than that charged by most of his competitors, while his large capital and plant permitted him to build machines with a maximum of efficiency, his net profit on each sale was probably larger than theirs. The abolition by Congress in 1866 of the wartime six per cent tax on gross sales, and the drop in the cost of raw materials for several years prior to the harvest of 1870 when the McCormicks lowered their prices, made their profit per machine larger in 1869 than it had been in 1865.[90]

Pressure from the farmers was second only in importance

[89] Winter storage charges on unsold machines in the possession of the agents averaged between $2 and $3 apiece. The office found it difficult to prevent agents selling pieces of these for "spare parts." The McCormicks were obliged to pay state taxes on surplus machines and parts in the charge of their agents, and occasionally, over their protest, they were assessed upon the cash and reaper notes held by these salesmen. *Ibid.*, No. 124, pp. 618, 670, Co. to E. Healy, Earlville, Ia., Feb. 1, 1871, and to J. N. Van Hoesen, Leavenworth, Kan., Feb. 2, 1871; No. 125, p. 80, to J. N. Hall, Mankato, Minn., Feb. 27, 1871; No. 127, p. 407, to C. H. Russell, Mineral Point, Wis., June 26, 1871: "Over and over again it has been decided that we cannot be taxed on unpaid reaper notes, and no assessor short of an idiot would pretend to anything else. . . . All we can legally be taxed on is the old machines . . . and the old castings also—and they estimated at what they would bring in cash under the hammer."

[90] The repeal of the sales tax, effective on Aug. 1, 1866, increased the Co.'s annual profit by between $60,000 and $75,000 a year. They continued to pay a tax of about $7,000 annually on the bolts, castings, and sickles used in their machines. See, C. A. Spring, Jr., to C. H. McCormick, Feb. 2, July 20, and ♯Aug. 10, 1866.

to competition between manufacturers and the ingenuity of inventors in promoting the change and improvement of harvesting implements. There were mutations of style in reapers and mowers as in dress. Certain types of machines were "fads" in certain sections of the country. If one manufacturer were permitted by his rivals to entrench himself in the favor of a locality, it was difficult to dislodge him at some later time. Partially because of this "inertia" among buyers, the McCormicks, as well as other firms, annually continued to send at a loss a few reapers and mowers to districts where they wished to be remembered until they were prepared to enter them in force. Then, as now, manufacturers realized that prospective purchasers anywhere were attracted to a product which they knew to be in use far and wide throughout the land.

Farmers had long complained of the weight of McCormick's machines, while praising them for their durability and efficiency of operation. The agents of other manufacturers encouraged grain-growers to grumble about the weight and side draft of the Chicago "Horse Killer." [91] Although some concessions had been made at the factory by 1865 as a result of this criticism, it could not be denied that there were reapers on the market at that time which gave good service and were less taxing upon the horses. Their greater facility of operation had been effected in part by substituting two wheels for the one hitherto customarily used. As a result of this change, the machine was also less likely to tip over when employed on sideling land. [92]

Farmers who disliked the heavy draft of the McCormick reaper-mower sometimes lengthened their letters of criticism

[91] Letters to the Co., from J. Edgar, Rochester, Minn., June 8, 1868, and F. G. Smyth, Madison, Wis., June 15, and 29, 1868. Men tell me they would rather buy reapers than horses. H. O. Goodrich, Alton, Ill., to Co., June 26, 1869.

[92] D. W. Fairbanks, Concord, Ill., to the Co., June 9, 1868. H. G. Grattan, Ludlow, Ia., to the Co., June 22, 1868.

by suggesting that the factory had slighted the grass-cutting problem in its effort to produce a perfect machine to harvest grain. This complaint was in a measure justifiable. Cyrus Mc-Cormick's first invention had been a reaper, and when he established his factory in Chicago he found that prairie farmers were interested, above all, in an implement to cut wheat and rye effectively. Compared with several other manufacturers whose factories had been in operation before the Civil War, he had been late in developing a good single mower. His combined machine, known as the "Reliable," was primarily a reaper, although after a rather tedious shift of some of its elements, it could be transmuted into a mower of average quality.

During McCormick's twenty years in the Middle West, some districts had turned largely from a cultivation of the small grains to live-stock farming.[93] Not only was this true in sections long settled which could no longer compete in wheat culture with the virgin lands of Iowa and Minnesota, but the fattening of steers driven north from Texas was attracting more and more landowners in the states west of the Mississippi River. Due, also, to a succession of poor grain harvests in the winter wheat section of the border states and Middle West, many farmers there were devoting a larger acreage than ever before to pasturage. To the manufacturer of harvesting machinery, this tendency meant an increased demand for mowers.

Judging from the correspondence of the McCormick factory, Indiana and Missouri farmers above all others clamored for a combined machine which should be an excellent mower, and as good a reaper as possible. They were too poor, so they wrote, to buy one implement for grain and another for grass, but they much needed a mower-reaper light enough to be

[93] L.P.C.B., No. 88, p. 395, the Co. to L. S. Durfee, Philadelphia, Pa., Mch. 14, 1866. W. W. DeMerritt, Decatur, Ill., to the Co., May 18, 1867.

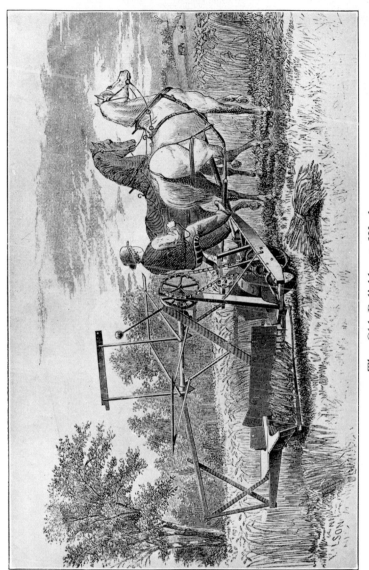

The Old Reliable at Work

drawn readily over quite rough land by one or two horses, and suited in price to their thin purses.[94]

The McCormicks made their first response to these suggestions in 1868, when they placed about five hundred "droppers" upon the market. The dropper was a mower to which a self-rake, platform, and tilt-board could be added. At each revolution of the rake one gavel of grain was swept from the platform to the tilt-board, whence it was dropped to the stubble behind the machine.[95] Since delivery was at the rear rather than at the side of the implement, the sheaves had to be bound and removed quickly so that they would not be trampled by the horses when the next course was run. Leander McCormick, and expert mechanics working under his supervision in the factory, devised this machine and it worked well when tried out in Alabama in early June.[96] It failed, however, in almost every instance, in the tall, rank grain of the prairie belt, and by the first of July the office declined to fill any further orders for it. The field experience of that harvest suggested the improvements needed to remedy most of its faults, but more significant, perhaps, is the fact that this implement was never again manufactured for sale. Soon thereafter, how-

[94] Letters of P. Mohan to the Co. from Warrensburgh, Mo., Apr. 30, 1867, and from St. Louis, Feb. 19, 1868; H. J. Prier, Indianapolis, Ind., July 12, 1867; F. Craycroft, Syracuse, Mo., Mch. 17, 1869; G. Bacon & Sons, Hannibal, Mo., Mch. 19, 1869; and A. E. Shepherd, Wellsville, Mo., Aug. 12, 1869. C. A. Spring, Jr., to C. H. McCormick, Aug. 2, 1866: We need very badly a machine that will mow well, and reap a few acres each year indifferently well. ‡C. A. Spring, Jr., to C. H. McCormick, July 2 and Sept. 21, 1867: You should come here and stay until you persuade L. J. McCormick to add a reaping attachment to our mower. We could thus double our sales and profits.

[95] L.P.C.B., No. 103, p. 210, the Co. to A. M. Lester, Eddyville, Ia., Feb. 26, 1868; No. 106, p. 2, the Co. to D. M. Stump, Avon, Ill., June 24, 1868.

[96] L. J. McCormick, W. R. Baker, and L. Erpelding constructed the dropper. See, ibid., No. 105, p. 136.

ever, the company began to build droppers under license from
J. F. Seiberling of Akron, Ohio.[97]

During the summer of 1868 the craftsmen of the factory
divided their attention between the unsuccessful dropper and
an experimental, light, two-wheeled, combined machine designed to mow as well as reap, and to deliver automatically
at the side of the machine gavels of grain which could be
sized at the will of the driver.[98] Such an implement had been
the dream of manufacturers for many years. Six machines
constructed with the hope of realizing this ideal were given
field trials late in the harvest of 1868.[99] According to the office
superintendent, Charles A. Spring, Jr., they were "as much
ahead of our old Self-Rake as light is ahead of darkness."
Premature enthusiasm aroused by inadequate tests in upstanding grain and grass had been very costly on several occasions
in the past, and the McCormicks determined in this instance

[97] Letters to the Co. of D. W. Fairbank, Concord, Ill., July 13, 1868,
N. L. Fish, Mexico, Ill., July 6, 1868, H. J. Prier, Indianapolis, Ind., July 3,
1868; W. H. Rhodes, Rensselaer, Ind., July 12, 1868, G. W. Russell, Water-
ford, Wis., July 24, 1868, G. Monser, Wenona, Ill., June 26, 1868, and
H. G. Grattan, Ludlow, Ia., July 27, 1868. Judging from these letters, the
reel and rake of the dropper ran too fast, made too small sheaves, and
scattered the grain. It was too difficult to change the machine from a
mower to a reaper, and it had too much side draft. Before the close of the
harvest, the 534 droppers shipped to the agents had been repaired and almost
all of them were sold. L.P.C.B., No. 106, pp. 347, 502, 889, the Co. to D. W.
Fairbank, Jacksonville, Ill., July 1, 1868, Holland & Hays, Champaign, Ill.,
July 3, 1868, and to G. W. Russell, Woodstock, Ill., July 9, 1868; No. 108,
p. 405, the Co. to C. B. Pinkham, Marshalltown, Ia., Oct. 6, 1868. Rice,
McConnell & Co., Jackson, Mich., to the Co., July 4, 1868. C. H. McCormick
& Bros., Balance sheet, Aug. 1, 1868. *Post,* Chap. XIV, ftn. 98.

[98] *Ibid.,* No. 105, p. 226, the Co. to W. D. Baldwin & Son, Washington,
D. C., June 5, 1868. The driver could not regulate the sheaf in the sense
that he could vary the size of each successive one swept off by the rake,
but he could set the latter so that it would discharge a gavel at every revolution, or at each 1¼, 1¾, etc., revolutions.

[99] *Ibid.,* No. 107, pp. 130, 186, C. A. Spring, Jr., to W. F. Carr, Lawrence, Kan., Aug. 6 and 10, 1868; No. 107, p. 74 to H. B. Prier, Indianapolis, Ind., Aug. 3, 1868. McCormick Co. Catalog for 1871, p. 7.

to subject their new reaper-mower to a full season of testing before offering it widely for sale.[100] If it should prove its worth under all harvest conditions, it would doubtless supplant the heavy, one-wheeled "Reliable," and in all likelihood become the most popular machine that had ever borne the McCormick stamp. Late in 1868, it was decided to name the new model "The Advance."[101] The nucleus or base of this implement was the McCormick single-mower. This, too, had been much improved during the preceding two years, and the work still went on.[102]

Experiments with "The Advance" continued at the factory until mid-March, 1869, and not until then was it possible to finish the patterns for the manufacture of the machines. Some of these eleventh-hour changes, introduced without any test in the field, were unwisely made.[103] About three thousand

---

[100] L.P.C.B. No. 107, p. 197, the Co. to W. N. Spring, Manteno, Ill., Aug. 11, 1868: "No matter how well these machines work in dead ripe Spring wheat, we must *go slow* in adopting improvements, for Rye, Barley & full bearded winter wheat present difficulties not found at this season." No. 111, p. 693, the Co. to A. M. Hamilton, Keswick, Va., Mch. 31, 1869. ‡C. A. Spring, Jr., to C. H. McCormick, Aug. 20, 1868.

[101] *Ibid.*, No. 109, p. 270, the Co. to T. Thompson, Elkader, Ia., Dec. 1, 1868.

[102] *Supra*, p. 376, ‡C. A. Spring, Jr., to C. H. McCormick, June 27, 1867. L.P.C.B., No. 98, p. 538, the Co. to N. M. Lester, Eddyville, Ia., May 16, 1867. E. W. Brooks, Red Wing, Minn., to the Co., Dec. 25, 1867. H. J. Prier, Indianapolis, Ind., to the Co., Aug. 8, 1868. *Ibid.*, No. 108, p. 2, the Co. to H. J. Prier, Sept. 16, 1868: The most important improvement in the mower for next year will be a spring under the tongue attached to the lower frame. This will throw the whole weight of the machine upon its two wheels, and will lessen its draft about forty pounds. L. J. to C. H. McCormick, Jan. 23 and 25, 1869. In these post-war years, the McCormicks stressed the building and sale of mowers more than ever before. C. A. Spring deemed that hay was a more certain crop than wheat. ‡C. A. Spring, Jr., to C. H. McCormick, June 27, July 26, and Aug. 17, 1867.

[103] ‡*Idem* to *idem*, Mch. 12, 19, Aug. 5, 13, 16 and 19, 1869. Spring and Hanna of the office force complained of L. J. McCormick's tendency to make alterations in machine patterns during the winter months when they

were completed by harvest time, and the exceptionally rainy summer provided the most grueling of tests. Leander McCormick, who had cause to be proud of the ingenious construction of "The Advance," believed that "the wet & mud of this Harvest has completely drowned 'The Reliable.' *It has gone under.*" [104] In his opinion the new model should be made the principal machine of the company in the next harvest. Others at the factory were not so certain. In the rush of making the first deliveries of "The Advance," several parts had been forgotten,[105] while those complete in every respect were soon found to need simplification before the ordinary farmer could be entrusted with them. The general verdict of the harvest was that "The Advance" was "a great success"—if the operator understood it.[106] Even Leander McCormick admitted that the firm had lost money by building so many of them in 1869, but he argued that grain-growers were heartily tired of clumsy old style "Reliables," and that "something new" were now the "popular words" of the country-side. The Marsh Harvester and Johnston's light, controllable, self-rake reapers were

could not be given practical tests in the field. To paraphrase the letter of Aug. 5: He (L. J.) leaves us in the office to take care of the complaints that arise, and he won't read farmers' letters. He is the one who determines what kind of a machine shall be built and in this he has always pleased himself without consulting you or anybody else. You must veto making machines until they have been thoroughly tested from *far* South to *far* North. We don't do enough of this and have trouble every year.

[104] L. J. McCormick to C. A. Spring, Jr., Aug. 9, 18 and Oct. 12, 1869. L. J. believed that "The Advance" machines, in spite of their breakages, were "the salvation" of the 1869 season. He reminded Spring that for the last twenty years decisions of mechanical questions at the factory had been mainly left to him (L. J.), although on important issues C. H. McCormick had insisted, as was his right, in having a ⅔ vote.

[105] L.P.C.B., No. 111 (Apr. 1869), pp. 787 ff.

[106] *Ibid.*, No. 113, p. 543, the Co. to J. Edgar, Rochester, Minn., June 5, 1869: "All depends on the agent's skill in setting them up & working them." *Ibid.*, No. 114, p. 539, telegram of the Co. to C. H. McCormick, June 28, 1869.

making surprising headway. The McCormick Company could not afford to lag behind.[107]

Fortunately Leander's advice was in the main followed, and "The Advance," considerably altered as a result of the 1869 experience, became for several years McCormick's leading implement.[108] The "Old Reliable," hitherto the mainstay, was manufactured for the last time for the season of 1870. Both machines were priced at $190 cash, and the preference of farmers was then given so emphatically to "The Advance" that the supply of six thousand fell considerably short of the demand.[109] So enthusiastic was its reception that William J. Hanna of the office staff could not hide his excitement in a letter to Leander early in July: "Twelve thousand Advances won't supply the market [for 1871] and to build them not an hour should now be lost, and not an item changed about the machine. . . . If we halt now to hear from experimental machines & then change or make new patterns, we shall lose

---

[107] Letters of L. J. to C. H. McCormick, Aug. 8, 1869, and to C. A. Spring, Jr., Aug. 18, 1869. E. W. Brooks, Red Wing, Minn., to the Co., Dec. 25, 1867. *Post*, Chap. XIII, ftn. 22.

[108] Complaints against "The Advance" in the 1869 harvest included weak castings, too small gavels in light grain, too short sickle in the sickle-bar, fragile reel-post, non-controllable rake, heavy side draft, and wobbly reel. See, letters to the Co. of J. H. Shaffer, Kankakee, Ill., Aug. 26, 1869, C. F. Johnson, Galesburg, Ill., Aug. 24, 1869, and of E. C. Beardsley, Sycamore, Ill., Oct. 4, 1869. L.P.C.B., No. 116, p. 196, Co. to O. H. Loomis, Kewanee, Ill., July 28, 1869, and No. 117, p. 234, to P. Mohan, St. Louis, Sept. 10, 1869.

[109] *Ibid.*, No. 120, p. 54, Co. to H. C. Addis, Omaha, July 7, 1870. A few improved "Reliables" were also worked in the harvest of 1870, and L. J. McCormick thought that they performed better than "The Advance." Practically all "Reliables" sold during the season, however, were of the old type. *Ibid.*, No. 118, p. 730, Co. to A. M. Hamilton, Keswick, Va., Mch. 29, 1870, No. 120, p. 72, to L. J. McCormick, July 7, 1870, No. 120, p. 518, to A. J. Merton, Butler, Mo., July 15, 1870. L. J. to C. H. McCormick, June 22, July 1 and 29, 1870.

two months time." [110] As for "The Reliable," it was, in his opinion, already relegated to the class of machines that might be wanted in the future by "old fogies" or by the few whose grain was too heavy for "The Advance" to cut.[111] This well illustrates the speed with which office clerks, for the sake of business, learned to make mental somersaults in their estimate of the output of their employer. In Hanna's opinion, "The Advance" had "revolutionized the business," and it would be necessary to enlarge the factory because it outsold "all other machines on the market." [112] This "perfect" implement of 1870 gave complete satisfaction in the next harvest, but the company continued to "perfect" it still more by alterations designed to lessen its draft by almost one-third.[113]

[110] *Ibid.,* No. 120, p. 203, W. J. Hanna to L. J. McCormick, July 9, 1870. Hanna's covert purpose was to forestall L. J. McCormick's inclination to keep on experimenting until it was too late to manufacture all the machines needed. In fact, the letter closes with these words, "Feeling sure you will endorse these views, we are now at work on 1871 machines, and shall press the work in all the departments without change."

[111] *Ibid.,* No. 120, p. 360, Hanna to J. Edgar, Rochester, Minn., July 12, 1870. No. "Reliables" were constructed for 1871, but there was a considerable surplus unsold from the previous year. Their price was $170 cash in 1871 and $100 in 1872. See, *post,* pp. 585, 602.

[112] *Ibid.,* No. 120, p. 453, Hanna to L. J. McCormick, July 14, 1870. *Id.,* No. 113, p. 789, the Co. to A. J. Hamilton, Richmond, Va., June 11, 1869.

[113] For the harvest of 1871, "The Advance" was improved by the addition of a mechanism which permitted the operator to throw the rake out of gear when it was not being used. A few of these machines that season also had a lever whereby the driver, without rising from his seat, could elevate or lower the cutting edge of the knife as much as four or five inches. This machine made a sheaf about every sixteen feet, the size depending, of course, upon the heaviness of the grain. *Ibid.,* No. 128, p. 712, the Co. to G. W. Russell, Woodstock, Ill., July 25, 1871. During the harvest of 1870 L. J. McCormick was for a time enthusiastic about a one-wheeled, inexpensive "velocipede" mower of his own invention, but it failed. See, the letters of L. J. to C. H. McCormick on June 3, 10 and 22, 1870; *ibid.,* No. 120, pp. 363, 405, Hanna to C. A. Spring, Jr., July 12, and 13, 1870: "Leander's Velocipede Mower—failed—choked—finally broke Cutter bar— Shoo fly!"

The McCormick partners often referred with pride to the loyalty of their employees in office, shop and field.[114] Except during the Civil War period, very few strikes interrupted the routine of the factory, and of all the subjects relating to manufacturing which the student would expect to find discussed frequently in the letter files of the company, that of the labor force in the plant is the most seldom mentioned.[115] True, the "eight hour day" movement led the partners on May Day in 1867, to close their shop for a few hours so that their men could march in a parade.[116] In spite of these little flurries of excitement, there were no walk-outs, and the men continued to work in the plant ten or twelve hours out of the twenty-four. The growing strength of unions at that time caused Leander to suggest to his brother, to no avail, that German immigrants should be engaged on two-year contracts.[117]

[114] *Ibid.*, No. 137, p. 462, the Co. to Rodgers & Son, Elmwood, Ill., Sept. 5, 1872: "We pay our men their wages in cash once a week & let them buy their groceries where they please. We are sure if they would cooperate in their purchases, they could save money, but that is their business and not ours."

[115] "Lexington (Va.) Gazette," Apr. 28, 1859. After referring to the long service of seven employees of Cyrus McCormick holding positions of responsibility in his factory, this account adds: "Can many manufacturers or their employees show a better record of mutual cooperation for mutual interest?"

[116] ‡C. A. Spring, Jr., to C. H. McCormick, May 1, 1867. In a ‡letter on May 4 to C. H. McCormick, Spring said that nearly all the workmen in the city were on a strike for an eight-hour day, but that those in the McCormick factory were still at their tasks. On May 1, 1867, the McCormicks advanced the wages of their employees 10%. "Chicago Times," May 1, 4, 7, 22, 31, 1867.

[117] L. J. to C. H. McCormick, May 25, 1867: "The Union is controlling our Shop complete . . . and we ought at whatever cost to hire men outside of it." On June 19, 1872, the J. W. Orr Engraving Co. of New York explained its slowness in sending cuts for use in McCormick's advertisements on the grounds that "communist feeling has been rapidly extending in this city, & has, for some time, unsettled the minds of all skilled workmen. Engravers, who were glad to get $20 a week a few years since, now demand & receive $60 per week of 54 hours. . . . Finally, when we do get good men,

The factory force numbered about four hundred skilled mechanics and laborers during the busy season, but most of these were laid off for several weeks in late summer of each year while the annual inventory was taken and broken factory machinery repaired.[118] Although farmers were obliged to pay from $3 to $4.25 a day for field help at harvest-time,[119] unskilled labor was always abundant in Chicago during the years following the Civil War.[120] The foreman of the several departments of the factory customarily went to the gate in the early morning and selected from the many job-seekers there the few extra hands they needed for the day's work. The insecurity of persons and property in the city was blamed upon the great number of unemployed. An agent who was timidly trying to sell reapers in a section of Texas where men carried the law in their holsters, was consoled by an office clerk with the words, "We think if a premium were offered

it is almost impossible to keep them steadily at work." Not until 1877, and occasionally thereafter, were the McCormicks to experience a similar situation.

[118] L.P.C.B., No. 91, p. 672, the Co. to R. M. Wiley, Sinking Creek, Va., Aug. 7, 1866: We pay agents $50 to $75 a month and expenses. General agents, however, receive about $1,500 a year. Ibid., No. 95, pp. 245-246, the Co. to A. M. Hamilton, Lexington, Va., Feb. 1, 1867; No. 107, p. 122, C. A. Spring, Jr., to R. Smithers, Aurora, Ill., Aug. 6, 1868; No. 128, p. 660, the Co. to Plumb & Burdett, Buffalo, July 24, 1871. On the 28th of this month we close the factory three weeks for stock-taking. The Co. also discharged many of its agents in Aug. of each year when the selling season was over. For a description of the McCormick factory in 1868, see "Chicago Times," Nov. 18, 1868.

[119] Letters to the Co. of G. H. Spring, Manteno, Ill., July 24, 1868, J. Edgar, Rochester, Minn., July 24, 1868, A. Burlingame, Cedar Falls, Ia., July 26, 1868, and A. D. Wright, Cresco, Ia., June 7, 1869.

[120] L.P.C.B., No. 94, p. 674, C. A. Spring, Jr., to E. W. Brooks, Red Wing, Minn., Jan. 11, 1867: Chicago is overrun with young job seekers who have fled dull times in the East expecting to find conditions better here. Ibid., No. 99, p. 160, the Co. to T. L. French, Cedar Falls, Ia., June 4, 1867: "More men must quit loafing around towns and go to work tilling the soil. The present condition of things is a disgrace to the country." Ibid., No. 121, p. 599, the Co. to A. C. Rogers, Middletown, Vt., Sept. 19, 1870.

for crime that Chicago could carry off the prize." [121] The many farmer boys who wrote to the company seeking an opportunity to move to Chicago were usually advised to remain where they were.[122] In its advertising material for 1867, it pointed with satisfaction to the fact that it was the biggest establishment in the Middle West and that it gave work in winter to men in Chicago who would otherwise be jobless.

Cyrus McCormick was occasionally advised by his friends that he was paying too high salaries to the principal men in the factory office. Several of them, however, had been with him for many years, and because of his infrequent visits to Chicago between 1862 and 1871, he was obliged to place implicit confidence in their efficiency and loyalty. Among the faithful, Charles A. Spring, Jr., was the chief. His term of service had begun in 1855. Following the death of William S. McCormick, he was the general superintendent of the concern as well as the inventor's confidential clerk and the manager of his extensive real estate holdings in Chicago and elsewhere. Although his seven-thousand-dollar salary of 1866 was more than doubled by 1872, he was obliged to retire in the following year because the heavy responsibilities of his position had undermined his health.[123] William J. Hanna, who

[121] *Ibid.*, No. 98, p. 756, the Co. to O. N. Barnhill, Jefferson, Texas, May 24, 1867.

[122] *Ibid.*, No. 141, p. 71, the Co. to J. D. Patterson, Greensboro, N. Car., Apr. 21, 1873.

[123] ‡C. A. Spring, Jr., to C. H. McCormick & Bros., June 15, 1866. Of his $12,000 salary in 1871, C. H. McCormick personally paid 1/6th and the firm the balance. By this date he was permitted to take as much recreation as his health demanded, but he explained his resignation of Aug. 1, 1873, on the score of lack of time to rest. For his last year of service he was apparently paid $15,000. C. A. Spring, Jr., to C. H. McCormick., Oct. 4, 1871. C. H. McCormick to C. A. Spring, Jr., July 31, 1873: "As this day closes a business connection between us of eighteen years' standing, I cannot let the occasion pass without some testimonial of my appreciation of one who, tried through so long a period, and with responsibilities so varied as well as great, has born himself throughout with the highest honor and credit."

supervised the agencies, received $4,000 annually by 1870, while W. R. Selleck, the cashier, was paid $3,000.[124] Compared with positions of like importance to-day, these salaries were small, but they were well abreast of the standard of sixty years ago. No regular vacations were granted, but the members of the office force took off a few days now and then, principally, it would seem, to shoot wild pigeons in Wisconsin or ducks along the Fox River in Illinois.

As more and more reaper-makers entered the field, and as new types of agricultural machinery appeared in each harvest season, competition for the favor of the farmers and for the services of the most persuasive agents became ever more keen.[125] "High powered" advertising methods were employed, and probably many were induced to buy who either could not afford a machine or had too few acres of grain or grass to use one with profit. McCormick's agents complained that they

As a matter of fact, Spring continued to work for the McCormicks until about Oct. 1 of that year, and returned to their service in 1879. As early as 1875, he was once again managing C. H. McCormick's Chicago real estate.

[124] ‡C. A. Spring, Jr., to C. H. McCormick, Mch. 7, 1870, and Feb. 6, 1873. In Sept., 1866, a three-year contract @ $2,000 was made with W. R. Baker, who had hitherto been the partner of J. B. McCormick in St. Louis. Baker, an expert mechanic, was at his best in the field experimenting with new devices. In addition to his wages, he was allowed to build a small home on company land without charge. C. A. Spring, Jr., to C. H. McCormick, Sept. 24, 1866. On Dec. 9, 1872, a three-year contract was made with F. H. Matthews to be chief bookkeeper. He agreed to work ten hours a day for $3,000 a yr., with extra pay prorated for overtime. Hanna, who entered the factory office in 1849, resigned in 1874 to be a partner in a Chicago commission house. He returned to the McCormick Co. in 1878 and remained until his death in 1887. Copyists for the office could be hired for $7 a week.

[125] L.P.C.B. No. 101, p. 731, the Co. to R. L. Scott, St. Cloud, Minn., Oct. 28, 1867. In the spring of 1871, there were twelve McCormick agents in Ohio, each of whom received 8% for selling, and 7% for collecting. Ibid., No. 124, p. 701, the Co. to P. Mohan, Warrensburgh, Mo., Feb. 6, 1871, and p. 720, to F. G. Smyth, Madison, Wis., Feb. 7, 1871: "We won't pay over 12% commissions and don't like to do that." As a matter of fact, the firm occasionally did pay as much as 15%, but more usually 10%.

had to fight the combined opposition of rival salesmen, and while they probably exaggerated their troubles, there is no doubt that the smaller firms united against the big producer who had for so long led the pack. If for no other reason, self-preservation alone inclined them to this course.[126] When Mc-Cormick had no other choice, he built reapers and mowers under license from his rivals, but he rarely granted shop rights under his own patents, and never employed sub-manufacturers to make his machines.

Two customary methods of competition were seldom employed by the McCormick firm at this time. Because it took pride in its motto of "One Price to All, and Satisfaction Guaranteed," [127] it stood aloof from the price-slashing campaigns employed by other makers during the month or so preceding the harvest. After the summer season was well advanced, however, and it was clear that many machines would remain unsold in the district of an agent, he was often authorized by the home office to reduce prices or to offer hesitating farmers a longer time in which to pay.[128] Nor would the McCor-

[126] W. J. Hays, Bloomington, Ill., to C. H. McCormick, Apr. 22, 1869. L.P.C.B., No. 91, p. 281, the Co. to A. M. Jones, Warren, Ill., July 21, 1866: "We have more to contend with in the shape of opposition agents poisoning & prejudicing farmers' minds and magnifying defects of small things into great matters than we have from any other source." *Ibid.*, No. 133, p. 115, the Co. to G. A. Willey, Belleville, Ill., Apr. 1, 1872.

[127] McCormick Co. Catalog for 1871. As early as 1866 (L.P.C.B., No. 91, p. 180, a letter of July 19), an agent was assured that every mower was tried out in the factory before it was shipped. In spite of this care, field use occasionally revealed defects in a large portion of a season's output of one type of machine. In case of a misfortune of this kind, experts or new pieces were rushed to the purchasers. If these could not remedy the trouble, improved parts were sent to them without charge before the next harvest. *Ibid.*, No. 89 (Apr. 1866), *passim.*

[128] This was true in 1865 and 1871 when sales were dull. *Ibid.*, No. 82 (July and Aug. 1865), and No. 129 (Aug. and Sept. 1871), *passim. Ibid.*, No. 126, p. 139, the Co. to P. Mohan, St. Louis, Mo., May 30, 1871: "There is nothing so demoralizing as changing prices after the Season has commenced for it *educates* the people to expect a reduction as a matter of course

micks sanction large advertisements by their salesmen in local newspapers,[129] nor often permit them to compete for premiums at a county fair [130] or in an impromptu field trial against the machine of a little-known manufacturer who was seeking to gain a reputation by winning chance victories over those of long-established reputation. McCormick reapers and mowers were displayed at expositions where no prizes were awarded, and of these the agricultural fair at St. Louis was soon "recognized as the best . . . of the kind in the U.S." [131]

During these post-war years, the McCormicks succeeded in making both their machines and their advertisements more attractive. The clerks in the office found that the dusty-brown every season. We are aware most farmers believe there is an immense profit in the reaper trade and frequent reductions near harvest time confirm them in this view." *Ibid.*, No. 127, p. 457, the Co. to F. Craycroft, Chillicothe, Mo., June 27, 1871: "The public must be taught that we make no cheap machs. & have but *one price."*

[129] *Ibid.*, No. 118, p. 617, the Co. to A. M. Lester, Eddyville, Ia., Mch. 24, 1870: " 'Small racey notices' in local newspapers pay better than the best displayed advertisements." *Ibid.*, No. 95, p. 385, the Co. to N. L. Fish, Concord, Mo., Feb. 8, 1867: Don't spend over $25 or $30 on advertisements in the press. House to house canvassing is worth much more. "We would place more value in a *Little Puff* written by the Editor and paid for, than a regular advertisement."

[130] *Ibid.*, No. 91, p. 31, the Co. to J. H. Hall, Henry, Ill., July 13, 1866, and No. 100, p. 853, the Co. to P. Mohan, St. Louis, Sept. 13, 1867, We will exhibit a mower at the St. Louis Fair because they offer no premium. F. G. Smyth, Madison, Wis., to the Co., July 5, 1867.

[131] L.P.C.B., No. 91, p. 31, Co. to J. H. Hall, Henry, Ill., July 13, 1866; No. 129, p. 475, Co. to P. Mohan, St. Louis, Mo., Sept. 10, 1869, and Aug. 23, 1871; No. 128, p. 905, to G. A. Willey, Belleville, Ill., July 28, 1871; No. 128, p. 462, to G. W. Russell, Woodstock, Ill., July 19, 1871: "We wonder our Agents place so much value on these trials, for they amt. to nothing and prove nothing! Is it not strange that these 'Committees' all over the country for the sake of a free lunch are busily engaged every year in finding out which machine is best and never succeed! It is really becoming a mockery! We are under no obligations to submit our machine to the judgment of Tom Dick & Harry who don't want to buy machines, but set themselves up as judges of what farmers should buy! We are opposed to all public trials before judges & intend next year to make it a rule that none shall be entered into."

color of the reapers and mowers of 1865 did not sell them as easily as the vermilion paint of the next year.[132] Even the posters were brightened by the use of five or six different tints.[133] As a result of the insistence of their Minnesota and Wisconsin agents, their pamphlets included supplementary pages in German and Norwegian.[134] In 1868 it was learned that the "Champion" firms of Ohio were publishing a trade newspaper in Springfield,[135] and three seasons later the Mc-Cormicks issued the first number of "The Farmers' Advance," which thereafter appeared two or three times a year.[136] This journal, distributed gratis to the number of one hundred thousand or more by the agents, was soon said to have the largest rural circulation of any paper in the land. It quickly supplanted the pamphlet as the most important method used by the Chicago firm to publicize its machines, although its

[132] *Ibid.*, No. 90, p. 475, Co. to J. V. Hinchman, Glenwood, Ia., May 30, 1866.

[133] These multi-colored posters were first used in 1867, and a blank space was left at the bottom of each for the agent's name to be printed in red. Eighteen thousand were prepared in 1871, and the supply was exhausted by the end of May. *Ibid.*, No. 126, p. 89, Co. to J. Edgar, Ackley, Ia., May 30, 1871.

[134] Two editions of these pamphlets appeared each year. One was known as the "Northwest Edition" and the other as the "General Edition," for use in the South and East. The total number printed for each season's use was about 100,000. Engravers in New York City had to be employed because "we find it impossible to get any artist here [Chicago] to make even a passable engraving of a horse at work." *Ibid.*, No. 103, p. 46, Co. to E. A. McNair, Davenport, Ia., Feb. 18, 1868; No. 101, p. 471, to Bunting Bros., N. Y. City, Oct. 14, 1867. J. W. Orr Engraving Co., N. Y. City to Co., June 19, 1872; C. Tesseberg, ed., "Emigranten," Madison, Wis., to Co., Apr. 2, 1867.

[135] Letters to the Co. of J. H. Whitaker, Monterey, O., Apr. 8, 1868, and of T. H. Ritter, Columbus, O., Mch. 26, 1872.

[136] L.P.C.B., No. 122, p. 186, Co. to E. C. Beardsley, De Kalb, Ill., Nov. 2, 1870; No. 124, p. 863, to J. H. Osborn, Mattoon, Ill., Feb. 17, 1871; No. 125, p. 112, to H. Gilbert & Co., Lincoln, Neb., Mch. 1, 1871. The original intention apparently was to discontinue the use of pamphlets altogether, after "The Farmers' Advance" made its appearance.

columns were scarcely more devoted to news about McCormicks' reapers and mowers than to articles designed to amuse and instruct its readers. The moral tone of its pages was always high; copy from other advertisers was carefully scanned before acceptance, and if the homilies upon ethics and the general business of living seem somewhat banal and hypersentimental to-day, they were quite in accord with the taste of country folk sixty years ago.[137] Many of McCormicks' subagents were the salesmen of other products desired by farmers. Whenever they refused to distribute "The Farmers' Advance" because it advertised goods which competed with their own wares, they were given the choice of resigning or complying with the orders of the Chicago office.[138]

Although some machines were left unsold at the end of each harvest season, the surplus in all except two of the first seven years following the Civil War was due to the inability of the McCormicks to forecast the exact demand of each of the many sales points to which they sent their output during the spring. In every harvest of this period, except 1865 and 1871 when purchasers were few, they could have increased their total of sales if more reapers and mowers had been available to fill the orders of certain districts where the call for them

[137] As a sample, see "The Farmers' Advance," January, 1883, p. 6: "The girly girl is the truest girl. She is what she seems, and is not a sham and a pretense. The slangy girl has a hard job of it not to forget her character. The boy girl and the rapid girl are likewise wearers of masks. The girly girl never bothers about woman's rights and woman's wrongs. She is a girl, and is glad of it. She would not be a boy and grow up into a man and vote, and go to war and puzzle her brain about stocks for a kingdom. She knows nothing about business, and does not want to know anything about it. Her aim is to marry some good fellow and make him a good wife, and she generally succeeds in doing both."

[138] Letters to the Co. of J. Edgar, Rochester, Minn., Mch. 28, 1873, and of O. M. Carter, Ashland, Neb., Sept. 1, 1873. L.P.C.B., No. 140, p. 676, Co. to J. Edgar, Apr. 8, 1873. By 1883, however, the company had yielded to the wish of its agents, and declined to accept advertisements of plows, threshers, etc.

was unexpectedly heavy. Because the harvest-time in any locality was so short, and because grain-growers usually delayed placing their orders until they were certain that their crop would be worth cutting, lack of time made it impossible to reallocate many machines after the original distribution had been completed. In any event, farmers were unwilling to bear the heavy freight charges resulting from shipping and reshipping a machine about the country in search of a buyer.

Between 1868 and 1870 the average annual sales were almost double those of the war period.[139] Because of the growth of the West, an expanding market was assured for many years to come, but the McCormick factory near the mouth of the Chicago River was already embarrassed to complete seven or eight thousand reapers and mowers in time for harvest each year. The site was already utilized to the fullest extent; adjoining land was not available for purchase at a reasonable price, and the partners knew that if they were to regain from Walter A. Wood, the "Champion," and the "Buckeye" firms the title of "biggest building of harvesting machinery in the world," they would be obliged to erect larger works at a new location.[140] Partly because of their cramped quarters, they were unable to develop their eastern, southern, and foreign markets as much as they desired to do.

Nor was lack of room the only consideration which counseled a move. Business prosperity and leisure brought to leading Chicagoans a feeling of civic pride. Factories and railroad tracks along the otherwise beautiful lake-shore were frowned upon, and parks were laid out within the city and on its out-

[139] Sales rose from about 6,125 in 1866, to about 9,975 in both the harvests of 1868 and 1869. By 1871, however, the number had fallen to 8,356, and in the following year, due to the shortage of machines caused by the Chicago fire—to 6,874.

[140] *Ibid.*, No. 121, p. 414, the Co. to W. O. Tillottson, Wooster, O., Sept. 5, 1870; No. 123, pp. 290, 292, to P. Mohan, St. Louis, and to M. Fry, Lynnville, Tenn., Jan. 20, 1870.

skirts.[141] Recurring cholera epidemics, as late as 1866, led to provision for a new water supply, and meat-packers and others were no longer permitted to make the river a nauseating reproach to the community. Some factory owners who counted their high social position as the chief dividend gained from their large wealth, may have wished to make their connection with "trade" less conspicuous by moving their plants away from Chicago's avenue of fashion, but this motive influenced McCormick not at all. He was proud of his industry, and to have his name synonymous with harvesting machinery the world over was the chief ambition of his life. Land values in the business section near which the McCormick plant was located were now too high to encourage the erection or enlargement of factories there, particularly since adequate water and superior railroad facilities were available on the near-by prairie to the west. In this area, in the late 1860's, a land boom was under way, and early purchasers of lots might expect to

[141] At this time, the Illinois Assembly enacted the so-called "Lake Shore Bill," permitting the Illinois Central Railroad to take the land on the east side of Michigan Ave. up to their tracks running from Randolph St. south to Monroe St. Property owners on Michigan Ave., including Cyrus McCormick, were indignant at this "ruthless act of spoliation & plunder." Thos. Hoyne, of the firm of Hoyne & Horton, urged McCormick as a citizen of New York, to seek an injunction in a federal court to restrain the railroad from appropriating this land, relying upon earlier official assurances that the lake shore fronting Michigan Ave. should be kept open. Citizens of Illinois could only bring an action of this kind in a state court, but a federal tribunal was preferred since there "no corrupt or insolent power or corporation can have the merest chance of influencing Justice or continuing Injustice!" For the moment, McCormick gave his consent, and a bill was prepared to commence suit in the federal court. He soon regretted however that he had allowed himself to be designated a citizen of N. Y. and for both political and business reasons, he resolved to remain a citizen of Chicago. Thereupon, the venue of the case was changed to the Circuit Court of Illinois. This action was merely one skirmish of the battle which was revived time and again between 1852 and 1919. Until the latter year, the victory rested in the main with the railroad. ‡Letters of T. Hoyne to C. H. McCormick, May 4, 20, June 15 and 23, 1869. ‡Letters of C. A. Spring Jr., to C. H. McCormick, June 15 and Dec. 20, 1869. "Chicago Daily Tribune," June 24, 1869. "Chicago Times," June 26 and Aug. 14, 1869.

realize handsomely from their investments within a few years.[142]

Among the promoters who were seeking to develop the property along the several branches of the Chicago River to the west of the city, Samuel J. Walker of Covington, Kentucky, was doubtless the chief. His readiness to promise sometimes exceeded his ability to carry out what he engaged to do; all of the titles to the many acres in his name were not of the best, but he controlled most of the desirable factory sites on the prairie, and manufacturers who desired to locate there had no choice but to deal with him.[143] Even though he could furnish a guaranteed title to a purchaser, there were squatters on the flat and often marshy waste who had no intention of peaceably abandoning their ramshackle cabins, pig-sties, and little garden patches.

As early as 1864 and 1865, the McCormicks were dickering with Walker because of the "miserable cramped arrangement of things" in their busy factory.[144] No agreement was reached,

[142] ‡C. C. Copeland to C. H. McCormick, Aug. 22, 1868: "The outside real estate mania is far ahead of 1856-57." ‡C. A. Spring, Jr., to C. H. McCormick, July 7, 1868, and Feb. 2, 1869. The most sought-for residential property at this time was located a mile or two south and southwest of the business district. For the "style and show" on Wabash Ave. "upon a summer's evening," see "Chicago Times," Aug. 3, 1867, "C. H. McCormick has a splendid clarence, drawn by a coal-black team."

[143] ‡C. A. Spring, Jr., to C. H. McCormick, Nov. 27 and Dec. 1, 1868: (Enos) "Ayres tells me that Walker is such a man as Honoré, only more so—you can't tell whether he is worth anything or not. Rich today, poor tomorrow, if his debts were paid he might be worth nothing. Long John Wentworth also speaks disparagingly of Walker & his visionary ideas." Enos Ayres was an important realtor of Chicago who in that year had been named one of a board to apportion the properties of the McCormick firm among the two brothers and the heirs of William S. McCormick. Walker had been dealing in Chicago real estate since 1853. He moved to the city in 1872 and by the next year, when he was caught in the Panic, he was said to own 1,500 acres there.

[144] L. J. to C. H. McCormick, Nov. 29, 1865. In this letter L. J. McCormick urged C. H. to erect a new six-story building 50 by 55 feet in size. In letters of Mch. 22 and Nov. 22, 1863, W. S. McCormick complained that the office of the factory was "utterly unfit," and that the plant was too small,

and for the time being Leander's preference for an enlargement of their present works and river dock was accepted as
the program of the company. The death of William S. Mc-
Cormick in September, 1865, making necessary the difficult
task of unscrambling the merged assets of the partners, postponed the consideration of any plan calculated to complicate
still further the relations between Cyrus and Leander. By
1868 this property tangle had been largely unsnarled, and
Walker's name again appears in the correspondence of the
firm.[145] Now, however, he had a competitor in the person of
one William F. Dominick, who induced Cyrus McCormick to
pay $70,000 for twenty-two acres of land on the north branch
of the Chicago River.[146] The inventor apparently had a promising investment in mind, as much as a future site for his
factory, when he bought this tract.[147] Undiscouraged, Walker
continued to press the advantages of his property upon the
attention of the partners. Although the water-front of Walker's land on the south arm of the river was shallow, it was
closer than the new purchase to a street leading to the city
and to good rail connections. Early in the new year, the Mc-
Cormicks sufficiently overcame their lack of faith in Walker
to agree to pay him $3,800 per acre for about twenty-two

even with the addition of the lot recently purchased. C. H. McCormick to
C. H. McCormick & Bros., Dec. 1, 1864. The dock was improved in the
summer of 1869.

[145] ‡C. A. Spring, Jr., to C. H. McCormick, Nov. 21, 1868. Walker
wished to sell McCormick about 30 acres on the south branch of the south
branch of the Chicago River.

[146] E. Ayres to C. H. McCormick, Nov. 24, 1868. He advised C. H. Mc-
Cormick that $70,000 was a "very cheap" price. ‡C. A. Spring, Jr., to C. H.
McCormick, Nov. 26, Dec. 9, 1868, and Feb. 24, 1869. On the latter date,
he wrote that Dominick regretted the sale, since real estate values on the
outskirts of Chicago were mounting very rapidly.

[147] ‡C. A. Spring, Jr., to C. H. McCormick, Dec. 2 and 5, 1868. Spring
advised C. H. McCormick to purchase also from Walker: "As an investment, quite apart from putting factory there, it's a good buy."

acres on the south branch, with the understanding that he would show an air-tight title to this land, dredge the stream to a depth of twelve feet, and lay down a track to connect it with the main line of railroad.[148]

Although there is no question that this land was intended to be used as a site for a new factory, Cyrus and especially Leander, hesitated to take the next step.[149] At times, as in January, 1870, when the office clerks wrote to agents that "we shall very likely move our works another year," [150] the matter seemed to be settled, but by autumn it was once again doubtful whether the big plant would ever be erected. And yet, hardly had the new year opened when Cyrus McCormick bought of Walker about 130 acres (in two parcels of 120 and about ten acres each) near the first purchase for over

[148] This purchase was made from both Henry H. and his brother, S. J. Walker. Apparently 10 acres of it was bought by C. H. McCormick and the balance by L. J. McCormick. The land was described as Block 8 (10 acres) in Moore's Subdivision, and the 11 or 12 acres south of that block along the south branch of the Chicago River. ‡C. A. Spring, Jr., to C. H. McCormick, Dec. 19, 1868, Jan. 8, 9, 15, Mch. 19 and Apr. 15, 1869. Walker's opening offer was $4,000 an acre. The improved street was Blue Island Ave. C. H. McCormick to C. A. Spring, Jr., Dec. 26, 1868. C. H. hesitated to buy of Walker for fear lest the Supreme Court would hold greenbacks to be unconstitutional. In such case, property values would probably fall materially. On Jan. 2, 1869, he authorized Spring to close the deal. The decision of the Supreme Court to this effect was not announced until Feb., 1870, and was reversed fifteen months later. C. H. McCormick gave Walker notes for $38,000 @ 7% interest. Walker placed them on the market, and Spring managed to buy back one for $14,000 at par. Then he loaned it out at 6%, thus saving his employer 13% interest on $14,000. Up to mid-June, 1869, Walker had not been able to show a clear title to this property as he had pledged to do. L.P.C.B., No. 113, p. 785, C. A. Spring, Jr., to S. J. Walker, June 12, 1869.

[149] C. H. McCormick to C. A. Spring, Dec. 26, 1868: Suggest to Leander that it may be well to remove the factory to a new site, especially if conditions warrant a continuance of our business when my three year partnership with him expires [Nov., 1871].

[150] L.P.C.B. No. 123, p. 315, C. A. Spring, Jr., to G. F. Simonds, Fitchburg, Mass., Jan. 21, 1870. No. 119, p. 639, the Co. to T. W. Kern, West Alexandria, O., May 5, 1870.

$300,000.[151] In March, however, Leander was decidedly of the opinion that no change should be made, or at least that a new plant should not be built so far out on the prairie.[152] After a spring and summer of indecision,[153] Walker and McCormick were on the point of signing a third and most complicated agreement relating to the proposed works and the land in its vicinity, when the fire in O'Leary's cow-barn brought a sudden pause to the negotiations.[154]

Much of the brothers' vacillation may be explained by referring again to the lack of harmony between them. Differences of opinion over the settlement of their brother's estate, the overseas business of the firm, and the ownership and use of patents, have already been mentioned. Leander was more cautious than his brother in his estimate of the number of reapers and mowers to build for each season's trade, but was too prone, in Cyrus's opinion, to make last-minute and untested changes in details of machine construction.[155] Leander

[151] ‡C. A. Spring, Jr., to C. H. McCormick, Nov. 12, 1870, Jan. 9, 23, and Feb. 28, 1871. In the letter of Jan. 9, Spring advised its purchase on the grounds that if the factory were built near there, "a very large sum of money could be made out of . . . that tract by laying it out & selling it to employees, etc." Of this purchase, 120 acres were flanked by Western Ave. and 22nd St. on the east and north respectively. The other nine or ten acres were north of the river. The contracts of sale were dated Jan. 25, 1871.

[152] L. J. to C. H. McCormick, Mch. (?), 1871. Leander suggested that they should buy "the old Sugar Refinery" in the city for factory use. ‡L.P.C.B. No. 1, 2nd ser., pp. 433-434, C. H. to L. J. McCormick, Mch. 13, 1871: "I understood that we bought the land from Walker in order to locate our new factory there. If your son intends to enter the business, he should delay building his house until we decide where the plant is to be erected. With greatly enlarged facilities, we might make other types of implements."

[153] ‡C. A. Spring, Jr., to C. H. McCormick, July 5 and 7, 1871. He urged C. H. either to quit manufacturing and invest in something else, or build machines on a grand scale, and by means of a two-year price war, drive all eastern manufacturers out of the midwestern market.

[154] This contract was dated Oct. 6, 1871, but it was never carried out.

[155] ‡C. A. Spring, Jr., to C. H. McCormick, Sept. 21, 1867, and Aug. 7, 1871.

was usually content to leave well enough alone, but Cyrus had no interest in continuing the business unless it were one of the largest harvesting machinery firms in the world.[156] Leander was annoyed by the demands made by his brother's private affairs upon the time of C. A. Spring, Jr., the superintendent. He wished his son, Robert Hall McCormick, admitted to the partnership, and believed that Cyrus received too high a salary and charged too much rent for the factory and its site. Cyrus's eldest son was still a boy, and although the inventor pleased his brother by helping Hall at the time of his courtship and marriage in 1870 and 1871, he was loath to admit him to the firm until his own son, Cyrus, Jr., was old enough to enter the business.

The contract of 1866 between the partners was to expire in November, 1871, and the matters mentioned in the preceding paragraph, as well as the problem of a new factory, made it very difficult to come to a new agreement. Leander's outlook upon the future swung back and forth between enthusiasm and gloom within a very short period of time. When matters moved smoothly in factory and field he was keenly interested in the business, as in early July, 1871, when he informed Cyrus of his readiness to be bound by a revised partnership agreement for "1, 5, or 10 years." [157] As soon as the next few weeks, however, had made clear that a large number of machines would remain unsold, he warned his brother that "before I go in a new contract I want to be sure of a more conservative policy in the future." [158] The inventor, on his part, was daily distracted by the many problems relating to his religious, political, and business interests. He could not spare

156 L. J. to C. H. McCormick, Aug. 22, 1871.

157 ‡L.P.C.B. No. 1, 2nd ser., pp. 572, 600, C.H. to L. J. McCormick, July 26 and Aug. 15, 1871. L. J. to C. H. McCormick, July 4 and 12, 1871. ‡C. A. Spring, Jr., to C. H. McCormick, Aug. 1, 1868: L. J. does not carry "a straw's weight of the responsibility of this business."

158 L. J. to C. H. McCormick, Aug. 10, 22 and Sept. 1, 1871.

enough unbroken time to reach a considered conclusion about the partnership question, and even the loyal Charles Spring, Jr., was annoyed by his hesitation in coming to a definite decision.[159] Finally, in September, 1871, the brothers found common ground in their negotiations, but the Chicago fire early in the next month quickly made an anachronism of the treaty concluded after so much toil.[160]

The fear that the factory would some day burn down had been kept alive by several small fires there since its erection twenty-five years before. Much wood, paint, and oil used in the construction of machines, and sparks from the factory chimneys or from steamboats on the river, were always a menace. Care was taken to keep combustibles stored away from the boilers and to sweep up wood shavings as fast as they accumulated.[161] Fireproof doors separated the different departments, a wall was built between the McCormick plant and the adjoining soap factory, and all new buildings erected were of brick.[162] Day and night watchmen were em-

[159] ‡C. A. Spring, Jr., to C. H. McCormick, July 3, 1871. L. J. to C. H. McCormick, Aug. 22, 1871. L.P.C.B., No. 129, p. 284, the Co. to H. G. Grattan, Ludlow, Ia., Aug. 10, 1871. Spring threatened to resign, and C. H. McCormick wrote to his brother on ‡July 26, 1871: "Can we do business without Spring!"

[160] ‡L.P.C.B. No. 2, new ser., C. H. to L. J. McCormick, Sept. 16 (?), 1871. By this partnership agreement, the name of the firm was to be C. H. McCormick & Bro. The senior partner had a ⅔, and the junior a ⅓, interest. Each was to receive a salary of $5,000 a year, and Cyrus was also assured $20,000 annual rental as long as the old plant was used. If a new factory were erected, the machinery owned by Cyrus was to be bought by the firm. If the new factory should be built on Cyrus' land, Leander could buy a ⅓ interest in it.

[161] "Lexington (Va.) Gazette," Apr. 28, 1859. The chips and shavings were used to feed the fire in the boiler.

[162] Ibid., Apr. 28, 1859: The McCormick factory comprises five buildings, of from two to five stories high, providing 110,000 square feet of floor space. There is a dock about three hundred feet long. The labor force consists of 120 carpenters, 115 iron finishers, 40 blacksmiths and 25 unskilled laborers. L.P.C.B. No. 121, p. 774, C. A. Spring, Jr., to J. S. Kirk, Oct. 5, 1870.

ployed, and as early as 1856, a punch-clock on each floor of the plant told every morning whether the man on night duty had faithfully made his hourly rounds.[163]

As the business grew and conditions at the works became more and more crowded, the danger of fire increased. Finished machines were shipped earlier each spring, not only because the space that they occupied was needed for other purposes and enough freight cars might not be available during the rush of harvest, but also to lessen the likelihood of fire and the amount of damage it would do in case it should occur.[164] Not until 1866, however, was insurance carried upon the raw materials and the stock of machines at the plant, and as late as 1870 the factory buildings themselves were covered by only a very small sum.[165] Even machines in transit were rarely insured against damage. The plant of Walter A. Wood at Hoosick Falls, New York, was leveled by fire early in 1870, and although those in the office of the McCormick Works regarded this disaster as a warning, little more could be done

---

[163] MS. "Diary of Greenlee Davidson of Lexington, Va.," Entry of Sept. 19, 1856, describing a visit to the McCormick Works. "I saw on each floor what is called a watchman's clock. . . . On the dial is a brass circle with a number of pins at regular intervals. . . . Every time he [the watchman] makes his round he pushes a screw & if it is within five minutes since the clock struck, one of the pins in the brass circle will fall back; if it is not, it is impossible to force one of them in. In the morning the overseer counts the number of pins out of place and thus tells whether the watchman had done his duty."

[164] L.P.C.B. No. 111, p. 875, the Co. to A. J. Hamilton, Richmond, Va., Apr. 8, 1869: "Just now the warehouse is over flowing and we *must* Ship from 3 to 5 carloads a day. To do so we must ship on the roads that can furnish cars promptly. If we should make up our minds to ship only certain cars first and no others we could not get half the shipping done."

[165] ‡C. A. Spring, Jr., to C. H. McCormick, Mch. 28 and Apr. 17, 1866: I have insured for $20,000 the stock in the factory @ 2½%, and for $50,000 the stock in the warehouses @ ¾%. This is for a three months' period only. ‡C. A. Spring, Jr., to C. H. McCormick, Nov. 28, 1870: With the exception of $10,000 on the west warehouse, there is no insurance on the factory buildings.

to avert the danger as long as the factory remained upon its original site.

The Great Fire of October 8 and 9, 1871, which made Chicago "a howling wilderness from Harrison St. on the South to beyond the City limits on the North," included in its broad path of destruction the McCormick Works, all the stores, and nearly all the residences owned by the brothers individually or in partnership.[166] Although Cyrus was in the city, his course of action while the flames were destroying so much of his property is not known. Sometime during that fearful night and day, and most probably early on October 9 when it was clear that the factory could not be saved, he telegraphed to his wife at Richfield Springs, urging her to join him in Chicago. She left the children in charge of the servants and came posthaste. In all likelihood she reached the city on the afternoon of the eleventh. When a temporary factory office was opened next morning opposite the old Bull's Head Tavern on Ashland Avenue, the clerks did not know what their employers planned to do.[167] Before the day was over, however,

---

[166] L.P.C.B. No. 130, p. 41, Co. to A. T. Averill, Cedar Rapids, Ia., Oct. 14, 1871. As a matter of fact, about six hundred houses in the North Division escaped destruction. The McCormick factory burned early on October 9, when the flames leaped the river. Because of the fire, it was McCormick's good fortune that he had not yielded to his impulse of the summer of 1868 to erect, either alone or with Wm. Armour, "the great hotel Chicago needs," on Michigan Ave. between Madison and Monroe streets. McCormick planned to keep his intention a secret until he had purchased the property on each side of the proposed hotel site. Armour declined to join in this enterprise, and McCormick soon concluded that his dream might prove to be "an elephant" in reality. ‡C. A. Spring, Jr., to C. H. McCormick, July 21, Aug. 1, and Sept. 21, 1868; C. H. McCormick to C. A. Spring, Jr., July 17 and 28, 1868; J. H. Rees & Co. to C. H. McCormick, Dec. 13, 1871.

[167] L.P.C.B. No. 130, p. 2, Co. to Graff, Bennett & Co., Pittsburgh, Pa., Oct. 12, 1871. This despatch, and others mailed that morning, suspended orders previously given for lumber, iron, steel, and cutter-bars. Within two weeks, however, orders were placed for reduced amounts of these materials. Early in Feb., 1872, the factory office was moved back from 71 Ash-

a circular prepared for mailing to all farmers who were in debt to the company, announced: "We intend to put everything in operation again as fast as Men and Money can do it." [168] From this, it would appear that the decision to rebuild was reached on the evening of the eleventh or early on the twelfth. If so, the McCormick family tradition that Cyrus allowed his wife to decide whether he should retire or continue to manufacture harvesting machinery may have some basis in fact.[169] He was accustomed to seek her advice on business matters, although in view of his character and ambition, the question whether he should rebuild hardly admitted of more than one answer.

Merely to resolve to make a fresh start, left the site for the new works undetermined. Because this problem required most careful consideration, and a large plant could not in any event be completed in time for the harvest of 1872, the immediate task at hand was to erect temporary buildings at the old location.[170] Thousands of other property-owners in Chi-

land Ave. to the old site. *Ibid.*, No. 132, p. 219, C. A. Spring, Jr., to C. E. Vail, Blairstown, N. J., Feb. 20, 1872. In a conversation with Mrs. Emmons Blaine and Mr. Cyrus Bentley on Apr. 24, 1913, Mrs. McCormick said that her husband left his hotel during the fire and by a timely warning enabled his brother to remove some of his goods before his home was destroyed.

[168] Notice of C. H. McCormick & Bro., Oct. 12, 1871, to all Debtors.

[169] McCormick wrote in a MS. draft of an address, probably delivered in 1873, that he telegraphed during the fire to his wife and that she was with him two days later, "when I at once determined to proceed with . . . rebuilding."

[170] Several agricultural machinery manufacturers offered to make McCormick implements for 1872, but their proposals were declined. The Aultman Steel Co. of Canton, O., wished the McCormicks to take over as their permanent plant the vacant factory of E. Ball & Co. in that town. A letter of C. H. McCormick to J. I. Case & Co. Threshing Machine Works of Racine, Wis., indicates that the offer of that company to make his machines was given more than perfunctory notice. #Aultman Steel Co. to C. H. McCormick & Bro., Oct. 20, 1871; #J. I. Case & Co. to C. H. McCormick & Bro., Oct. 28, 1871; L.P.C.B. No. 130, p. 329, C. H. McCormick to J. I. Case & Co., Nov. 2, 1871, and No. 131, p. 366, Co. to

cago were engaged in similar work, and labor and materials were scarce and high priced. Winter was coming on, and all outside plastering needed to be finished before the first hard freeze.[171] Even with a well-equipped factory in operation throughout the year, the firm had been hard pressed to make enough implements to meet the demand. How extravagant was the hope of holding its own with a makeshift plant which would not be ready for use before the winter was far advanced! That a large number of machines had been left unsold at the close of the 1871 season was now viewed as a blessing rather than a misfortune. Almost two thousand of them had been destroyed in the fire, but the remaining four thousand in agents' hands were a most welcome foundation to build upon for the business of the next summer.[172]

While millions of bricks and hundreds of thousands of feet of lumber were on their way to the McCormicks from dealers as far away as Canada,[173] workmen cleared away the debris, salvaged the factory vault with its record books all intact, and repaired such odds and ends of machinery as could again be made serviceable.[174] In general, however, the old factory

P. E. Merrihew, Racine, Jan. 1, 1872. In the last of these letters, the Co., contrary to the tenor of McCormick's note to the Case Co., wrote, "We . . . have never contemplated leaving Chicago."

[171] Chicago contractors discovered, however, that if bricks were bedded well down in the mortar, they could be laid except in extremely cold weather. *Ibid.*, No. 138, p. 677, Co. to Lye & Walsh, Delphos, O., Nov. 13, 1872.

[172] The fire destroyed 698 "Reliables," 1,053 "Advances," and 218 mowers.

[173] MS. agreement of A. J. Kinseley with C. H. McCormick, Nov. 23, 1871, to furnish 6,000,000 brick during 1872 at prices ranging between $8 and $9 per thousand. See, letters of Oct. 21, 1871, ff. in L.P.C.B. No. 130, pp. 150, 154, 177, 188, 296.

[174] *Ibid.*, No. 130, p. 20, Co. to J. B. McCormick, Dayton, O., Oct. 13, 1871: "We have commenced to clear away the rubbish." No. 130, pp. 288, 289, 694, Co. to L. W. Pond, Worcester, Mass., to New York Tool Co., N. Y., Oct. 31, 1871, and to Corliss Steam Engine Co., Providence, R. I., Nov. 14, 1871. These letters deal with the purchase of new factory machinery. No. 130, p. 275, Co. to J. G. Beckerley, Chicago, Oct. 30, 1871.

and all that it contained had become history. Even new machine patterns had to be fashioned, and the stock of pig-iron was "in such a molten condition [it] can hardly be extricated for scrap." [175]

Faced by the necessity of doing so much in so short a time against the handicap of bad weather and the lively competition for the small available supply of labor and materials, the spirit brought to the task of reconstruction by the McCormicks and their employees is more remarkable than the extent and completeness of the destruction.[176] Doubtless there was much of pose and bravado and a determination to mask their true feelings behind a bold front. But these are unimportant considerations when compared with the fact that they carried the work through with success. The instant sympathy and aid extended to Chicagoans by people all over the world might well have led them to be self-piteous, but amid the smoking ruins they asserted that they were "masters of the situation" and would speedily rebuild "in better style than ever before." [177] History furnishes no better example of the spirit

[175] *Ibid.,* No. 130, pp. 190, 255, 347, letters of Co. to H. S. Butler, Des Moines, Ia., Oct. 24, 1871, to A. M. Hamilton, Keswick, Va., Oct. 29, 1871, and to A. D. Forbes & Co., Roslyn, Ill., Nov. 4, 1871. Even an "Advance" sent to the Elgin Fair, had to be brought back because it was needed for pattern-making. *Ibid.,* No. 130, p. 129, Co. to E. C. Beardsley, Aurora, Ill., Oct. 19, 1871.

[176] All of the office force, except F. H. Matthews, lost their homes, and in most instances, their furniture and clothing. *Ibid.,* No. 130, p. 56, Co. to H. O. Goodrich, Jerseyville, Ill., Oct. 16, 1871. C. A. Spring, Jr., with his family and many others, took refuge during the fire on the lake shore, and when that grew too hot he went to the lighthouse and stayed for two nights. By Oct. 13, "all our men are now provided with homes so far as we know." No. 130, pp. 12, 615, Co. to H. J. Prier, Indianapolis, Oct. 13, and to A. Burlingame, Ackley, Ia., Nov. 9, 1871.

[177] Letters from the Co. in *Ibid.,* No. 130, p. 3, to Naylor & Co., New York City, Oct. 12, 1871: "Though in ruins the Spirit of our people is unbroken & Chicago shall before long be herself again"; p. 5, to Jones & Laughlin, Pittsburgh, Oct. 12, 1871: "Loss is great but we can stand it and more too"; p. 71, to H. O. Goodrich, Jerseyville, Ill., Oct. 17, 1871: "Our

and optimism of the Middle West. Nor could even this calamity cause them to forget to boast. With unconscious humor, a clerk in the McCormick office hastened to remind a correspondent at Sheffield, England, that "It has been the greatest fire of the Age!—far exceeding the Great Fire of London in 1666!" [178] There was comfort in the realization, and in having others agree, that the ruin was widespread enough to be memorable.

Business considerations, as well as a lack of certain knowledge, led those in the McCormick office who were in charge of collections, to exaggerate the extent of their employers' losses. While Cyrus was assuring needy kinsfolk and those from whom he desired to borrow money, that he was still worth "five or six millions," and that his land in Chicago commanded almost as high a price as before the fire,[179] clerks informed the agents and farmers that the conflagration had cost the senior partner about two millions of dollars; that the list of debtors had not been destroyed, and that reaper obligations must now be met without fail.[180] The firm had in-

people don't cry at the desolation around us, but tears do come unbidden from reading such letters as yours"; p. 78: "The prompt rescue measures of eastern cities & universal sympathy alone unmans us"; p. 310, to E. K. Butler, Davenport, Ia., Nov. 1, 1871: "Chicago was never so full of life, business, nerve and work as it is today. There seems to be no time for despondency."

[178] *Ibid.*, No. 130, p. 24, the Co. to T. Jowitt & Co., Scotia Works, Sheffield, England, Oct. 13, 1871. This firm on Oct. 17, wrote to McCormick that the Chamber of Commerce of Sheffield had raised about £5,000 for the sufferers in Chicago, and it was hoped that the sum would be more than doubled by contributions from the workmen.

[179] Letters from C. H. McCormick in L.P.C.B. No. 130, p. 328, to J. B. Dorman, Nov. 2, 1871: "All in as good spirits as can be expected. . . . Thanking God that it is no worse with us. . . ." pp. 731-732, to M. Skinner, Hartford, Conn., Nov. 16, 1871. According to the balance-sheet of Aug. 1, 1871, McCormick's net fortune was then $6,500,000. On Feb. 24, 1872, it was estimated to be $5,882,878. ‡C. H. McCormick to W. E. McLaren, Detroit, Nov. 3, and 12, 1871.

[180] Letters to agents between Oct. 12 and 20, 1871, in L.P.C.B. No. 130, pp. 1, 8, 14, 25, 45, 67, 72, 143. Banks resumed business on Oct. 17 and thenceforward drafts on Chicago could be cashed.

dulged the farmers when they had failed to make a crop, and they should now help in its day of need. When the situation could be seen in better perspective and agreements had been reached with the insurance companies concerned, it was found that Cyrus McCormick's net loss was about $600,000.[181] Nevertheless, it was good policy to make use of the feeling of sympathy for suffering Chicago, to reduce the very large total of debt owed the company by the farmers of the Middle West. That the fervor which characterized the pleas for money was in some measure simulated, is made evident by the following sentence from the letter of a clerk to an agent: "We want you to make believe that we shall force collections." [182] Farmers who could pay were obliged to do so, but there were many who had neither money nor resources to convert into cash, and the result of this drive for funds was disappointing.[183]

---

[181] All save one (142-144 South Water St.) of McCormick's store properties were a total loss, and several of the insurance companies were so hard hit by the Chicago Fire that he could collect only 35 to 50 cents on the dollar from them. He placed the work of coming to terms with these firms in the hands of Lord, Day & Lord of New York City. According to the balance-sheet of Aug. 1, 1871, the factory buildings had cost McCormick $67,400 and were then worth $200,000. In 1867 the McCormick Block, worth at least $200,000, was insured for only $40,000; the State Street stores, worth $65,000, were insured for $15,000, and the stores on South Water St., valued at $60,000, were insured for $20,000. The Larmon Block on S. Clark St. was said to be worth $400,000 in 1868. At that time there was a mortgage on it of $76,000 which McCormick paid off early in the next year. His net loss from his stores and dwellings, over the insurance expected to be paid, was $300,595, and his loss from the burning of the factory, $272,160. Adding to these sums about $360,000 depreciation in real estate values and his total loss was over $900,000. This decline in real estate values was only temporary, and thus McCormick's ultimate loss was about $600,000. By Aug. 1, 1874, his net assets were estimated to be about $6,500,000 or as large as they had been just prior to the fire.

[182] L.P.C.B. No. 130, p. 294, the Co. to F. Craycroft, Chillicothe, Mo., Oct. 30, 1871.

[183] From Feb. 1, to June 1, 1872, the Co. collected $286,000 from farmers. During the same period in 1873 the total was $313,000.

Cyrus McCormick was never busier in his life than in 1872. Quite apart from problems arising from the factory, the crisis at the seminary, and the presidential campaign, he was absorbed in the work of rebuilding the business blocks and homes which before the fire had brought him rents of about $175,000 a year.[184] His residence in New York City was almost forgotten, his church pew there was subleased to friends, and from this time forward until his death his home was in Chicago. From their apartment in the St. Caroline's Court Hotel,[185] Mrs. McCormick and he supervised the erection of the large Larmon, McCormick, Hilliard, and Reaper buildings, and of a dozen stores and dwelling-houses besides. When he unwillingly was obliged to go to New York or Washington on business, she remained to direct the work of reconstruction. Architects, contractors, and labor foremen soon recognized that she had his implicit confidence, and they ungrudgingly paid tribute to the soundness of her business judgment, and to her ability as an executive. By 1874, McCormick had spent about three-quarters of a million dollars upon these proper-

184 From 1865 to 1870, rents in the Chicago business district were rising, but the movement was downward during the year preceding the fire. Thus McCormick received $177,243 in 1869 and $166,610 in 1870. The balance-sheet of Aug. 1, 1871, estimated that real estate which had cost him $1,-108,438 was then worth $2,364,795. At the time of the fire, C. H. McCormick owned in the North Division of the city, 1 entire block, 3 half blocks, and the 7 lots on which the factory was located. In the South Division, his property included the Larmon Block, the McCormick Building, at the corner of Dearborn and Randolph Sts., seven numbers on Lake St., four on S. Water St., three on Michigan Ave., two on Wabash Ave., and two on State St. See, L.P.C.B. No. 130 (Oct., 1871), pp. 662-664.

185 This hotel was on Elizabeth St. In 1872, the McCormicks moved to 62 N. Sheldon St. *Ibid.,* No. 130, p. 645, C. H. McCormick to H. A. Hurlbut, Nov. 10, 1871; No. 131, p. 189, the Co. to L. P. Hilliard, Chicago, Dec. 14, 1871: "He [C. H. McCormick] can always be found at his Rooms in above Hotel up to 10 o'clock A.M. each day." On Apr. 16, 1874, C. H. McCormick wrote to Robertson, Brooman & Co. of London, Eng., that he had not been at his residence at 40 5th Ave., N. Y., since the Great Fire.

ties,[186] and he was among the foremost of those who were restoring the city by "uniting the useful and beautiful in his fine buildings." The fire burned away old enmities born of the Civil War, and Joseph Medill, who as editor of the "Chicago Tribune" bitterly criticized the course of the inventor during the conflict, now as mayor of the city named him one of a committee to welcome the Russian Grand Duke Alexis upon his visit in late December, 1871.[187]

About a year later, after complimenting the McCormicks upon the magnitude of their building operations, "The Land Owner" of Chicago added with characteristic extravagance:

There has been but one parallel to the mighty creation recorded in Genesis, and that parallel is the rebuilding of Chicago in twelve months. That God made the world in six days, by the exercise of divine power, is no greater a marvel than that men have erected three thousand brick and stone structures—a majority of them as costly and massive buildings as the world can boast—in three hundred working days. . . . Twelve months have seen accomplished the work of centuries. . . . Four Hundred Thousand People now will bring a million in eight years, at the rate of increase the past year has shown. Laugh at this St. Louis; weep at it New York and *effete* Cincinnati; but the result will come, nevertheless. This city has never retrograded. The total loss of Three Hundred Millions of Property in forty-eight hours could

[186] C. H. McCormick financed this rebuilding in part by loans from the Equitable Insurance Co. and the Connecticut Mutual Life Ins. Co. *Ibid.*, No. 134, p. 418, the Co. to J. H. Shaffer, Kankakee, Ill., May 27, 1872; No. 135, pp. 207, 604, C. A. Spring, Jr., to J. B. McCormick, Dayton, O., June 22 and July 3, 1872. Letters of C. A. Spring, Jr., to C. H. McCormick, July 10, 11, 17, 24 and Aug. 2, 1872: "Mrs. McCormick keeps you posted as to the Buildings and knows far more about them than I do." "The Daily Inter Ocean," Oct. 8, 1872: C. H. McCormick is building fourteen structures at a cost of over $900,000.

[187] J. Medill to C. H. McCormick, Dec. 28, 1871. "Lexington (Va.) Gazette," Jan. 19, 1872. Mayor Medill, C. H. McCormick, and John Y. Scammon comprised Chicago's committee of welcome. They escorted the Duke on a carriage-ride about the ruined city, and both the inventor and his wife attended the banquet and ball given in honor of the occasion.

not stop its onward stride. What, then, will your sneers and back-biting be able to accomplish? [188]

While workmen were busy with McCormick's office buildings and "marble-front" stores during the winter of 1871-1872, a two-story, shed-like structure arose on the old factory site. By the new year enough new machinery had been assembled there to begin work on three thousand "Advance" reaper-mowers for the next harvest. News soon came from the agents that the makers of "Champion" machines were selling their product at sacrifice prices. Since the McCormicks had a large surplus of 1871 implements on hand, they resolved to shelve their resolutions of former years, and beat their rivals at their own game. "Do not let any opposition machine undersell you," ran the word to the salesmen by mid-June: "We authorize you to sell a little lower than any machine in market! We intend to make the opposition *sick* enough of the *cheap machine* business." [189] "The Reliables" and mowers were advertised for as little as $75 apiece, and "The Advance" for $150. Never had McCormick machines been sold for such low prices, and the resulting demand was unprecedented. Farmers badgered the agents for implements, and they in turn passed on their troubles to the shipping clerks at Chicago. The latter, cramped in a tiny office, sought to speed up production in the factory, which for the first time in the history of the firm, was operating both day and night. Exceptionally fine crops in the wheat belt intensified the pressure by mid-summer, and angry farmers whose orders went unfilled left the McCormicks in no doubt that they had oversold their supply by many hun-

[188] "The Land Owner" (Chicago), Vol. X, No. 10 (Oct. 1872). This article is accompanied by a large picture showing the buildings constructed by Cyrus, Leander and the heirs of W. S. McCormick since the fire. See also, "Chicago Times," Jan. 14, 1872, and Apr. 22, 1876.

[189] L.P.C.B. No. 135, p. 51, the Co. to W. H. Boyd, La Porte, Ind., June 17, 1872.

dreds of machines.[190] "We are now completely out of all kinds, sizes and ages of machines," the salesman at Red Wing, Minnesota, was told late in July, "and consider the Shipping season closed. Hurrah for our side! All our time, money, and attention now goes into the building of a monster Reaper Factory for the coming season." [191] When that is finished, "we can build 20,000 machs. at a lick. If the opposition think we are dead, they will find themselves woefully mistaken." [192] "The building will be near the City Bridewell or House of Correction which it is hoped will be a standing warning to clerks and agents to walk uprightly." [193]

In truth, the brothers had at last decided to unite in erecting a huge plant, although the drafting of a new partnership contract was necessarily postponed because they could not agree upon its terms.[194] When Walker sold Cyrus McCormick 120 acres in January, 1871, he had promised to make the place accessible to boats, teams, and freight cars by deepening the adjacent stream, building a road, and running a spur line to the near-by railway. These he had failed to do, and a new arrangement was concluded with him in February, 1872.[195]

[190] These low prices applied only to the old stock. *Ibid.*, No. 133, p. 470, Co. to C. H. Russell, Mineral Point, Wis., Apr. 22, 1872; No. 134 (May and June, 1872), *passim,* and particularly, pp. 138, 424, 431, 481; No. 135 (June and July, 1872) *passim,* and particularly pp. 255, 259, 307, 607; No. 136 (July and Aug., 1872) *passim,* and particularly pp. 405, 727, 812. J. Edgar, Rochester, Minn., to the Co., Aug. 12, 1872: "The demand is unprecedented in this neighborhood."

[191] L.P.C.B. No. 136, p. 702, the Co. to E. W. Brooks, Red Wing, Minn., July 25, 1872. C. A. Spring, Jr., to C. H. McCormick, July 10, 1872.

[192] *Ibid.*, No. 132, p. 444, the Co. to Kuhnen & Roth, Highland, Ill., Feb. 29, 1872.

[193] *Ibid.*, No. 136, p. 136, the Co. to J. Edgar, Rochester, Minn., July 11, 1872.

[194] ♯H. Day, New York City, to C. H. McCormick, Nov. 15, 1871. Judging from the tone of the factory correspondence, the brothers in Jan., 1872, agreed in general where the new works should be located.

[195] L.P.C.B. No. 131, p. 734, C. A. Spring, Jr., to C. H. McCormick, Jan. 25, 1872. MS. Agreement of S. J. Walker with C. H. and L. J.

Therein, he pledged to complete these improvements, and also agreed to pay the partners $100,000 for a return to him of forty acres of this tract. On their part, they bought the remaining eighty acres for $200,000, as well as another plot of about forty more. Walker's financial fortunes ebbed and flowed like an erratic tide and he was unable to carry out all that he had promised. But the brothers had made their decision and pressed forward with the work, even while they used every means in their power to compel the promoter to live up to the contract.[196] By summer, a definite site for the plant had been agreed upon, and a lawyer from New York City was summoned to assist Walker in clearing it of squatters.[197]

The two brothers broke ground at Canalport for the new factory in mid-August. Thereafter, Cyrus was often seen

McCormick, Feb. 17, 1872. The $100,000 represented not only the worth of the forty acres returned, but also a partial money equivalent for the increased value accruing to Walker's property as a result of the erection near it of the new works. Walker's dream was to create a manufacturing district on the land owned by him southwest of the city.

[196] C. H. McCormick to S. J. Walker, May 10, 1872. ♯MS. Agreement of July 5, 1872, between Walker and C. H. and L. J. McCormick. By this, Walker bound himself for $200,000 with Henry J. Walker as surety, to pay his debt to the partners. L.P.C.B. No. 133, p. 541, Memo. of C. A. Spring, Jr., Apr. 27, 1872; No. 138, p. 515, C. A. Spring, Jr., to C. H. McCormick, Nov. 12, 1872. W. J. Hanna to C. H. McCormick, Sept. 13, 1873. Walker still owed the McCormicks over $81,000. L. J. to C. H. McCormick, Dec. 5, 1873.

[197] The new works were on Blue Island Ave., near Western Ave., in the subdivision known as Canalport. As late as 1885, the court battle still went on to eject Patrick Flaherty, a drayman, who as a squatter claimed title to fourteen acres that the McCormicks had purchased of Walker. "Chicago Daily News," Sept. 26, 1885. L.P.C.B. No. 136, p. 554, the Co. to D. W. Cobb, Sparta, Wis., July 20, 1872: "Neither Mr. [L. J.] McCormick nor Baker can leave Chicago for an hour now. All their attention and time is centered on the new factory business—perfecting plans, location, Dock lines, Dredging and a thousand other matters connected therewith." L. J. to C. H. McCormick, July 25, 1872: "I am doing all I can to get plans ready when we will at once & as quickly as possible let the work to the lowest bidder." H. Day to C. H. McCormick, Aug. 2, 1872.

astride his favorite saddle horse watching the workmen lay the courses of brick or set the bed-plate for the big engine. Supervision over construction, however, was chiefly exercised by Leander, and the press reported that he could be found almost every day at the factory site with a roll of blue-prints under his arm.[198] Although Canalport was only about six miles southwest of the business section of the city, it was difficult to reach. After a slow and uncomfortable ride on the Brickmaker's Bus Line to the end of the road, a muddy or dusty mile of prairie still faced the pedestrian who wished to see Chicago's new manufacturing district.[199] Under these conditions, laborers could not be expected to reach the factory gate by seven o'clock in the morning, and the McCormicks, who were not unaware of the profits in prospect, erected near their plant a boarding-house of thirty rooms, and about forty cottages of one or two stories each.[200]

When the contracts were let for the erection of the big central building of the works, the masons and carpenters guaranteed that they would complete their tasks before the close of

[198] "Chicago Times," July 21, 26, and Aug. 18, 1872. "The Land Owner," Oct., 1872, p. 167. L.P.C.B. No. 138, pp. 448-449, W. J. Hanna to A. M. Hamilton, Keswick Depot, Va., Nov. 5, 1872: L. J. McCormick is doing "more than three men could well do."

[199] *Ibid.*, No. 139, p. 681, the Co. to A. D. Forbes & Co., Feb. 6, 1873: "After a few days our office will be down a few miles this side Cairo. Pray for us, when the mud comes!!" No. 140, p. 441, W. J. Hanna to H. O. Goodrich, Jerseyville, Ill., Mch. 21, 1873: "Our office is fine and pleasant enough, but oh the getting here & getting home is terrible. The writer walks 6 to 9 miles daily & hopes soon to be able to beat Weston." This bus-line started at the corner of Madison and Halsted streets.

[200] L. J. to C. H. McCormick, July 25, 1872. ‡W. J. Hanna to C. H. McCormick, Dec. 8, 1873. "The Land Owner," Oct., 1872, p. 167. This account mentions the three-story boarding-house, two-story cottages for mechanics, and one-story homes for workmen, "with other tenements upward of fifty in number." L.P.C.B. No. 139, pp. 168-170. Here, L. J. McCormick in a letter of Dec. 28, 1872, to Miller, Kaumacher, Denig & Co., refers to the "38 houses for workmen" being erected. "Chicago Times," Oct. 9, 1872.

November. The McCormicks soon decided to add an extra floor to the four-story main structure originally planned,[201] and further delays occurred when New England and Cleveland firms failed to send the factory machinery at the time agreed upon.[202] Furthermore, in the late autumn, most of the horses and mules throughout the entire country were stricken by a disease, generally known as the epizoötic or influenza. The dependence of that generation upon the horse was at once made clear. Every day became as Sunday in the small towns, livery-stables closed, and farmers on foot were met everywhere along the country roads, going for medicine to the nearest veterinary or drug-store.[203] The scourge was at its height in Chicago during the first two weeks in November. Business and building operations, requiring the use of teams, were almost at a stand just when every hour of good weather was at a premium because of the near approach of winter.[204] The McCormicks telegraphed their agents and Michigan logging camps to rush oxen to Chicago. Soon they had a dozen

[201] F. & E. Baumann were the architects of the new factory, and Miller, Kaumacher, Denig & Co., the contractors. *Ibid.*, No. 139, pp. 168-170, L. J. McCormick to Miller, Kaumacher, Denig & Co., Dec. 28, 1872.

[202] For letters regarding the purchase of machinery and an engine for the new factory, see *ibid.*, No. 137 (Aug. and Sept., 1872), pp. 150, 584, 616, 673. L. J. McCormick made a two-weeks' trip to the East in Sept., chiefly for the purpose of buying machinery. No. 138, p. 586, the Co. to Cuyahoga Steam Furnace Co., Cleveland, O., Nov. 15, 1872.

[203] Letters to the Co. of J. H. Shaffer, Kankakee, Ill., Nov. 11, 13 and 27, 1872; J. S. Buck, Princeton, Ill., Nov. 5, 16 and 22, 1872; J. A. McElwaine, Cedar Falls, Ia., Nov. 29, 1872; D. H. Smith, Sparta, Wis., Dec. 3, 1872; W. F. Cowhan, Jackson, Mich., Nov. 30, 1872; C. W. Brooks, Red Wing, Minn., Dec. 16, 1872.

[204] L.P.C.B. No. 138, p. 470, the Co. to A. T. Averill, Cedar Rapids, Ia., Nov. 6, 1872: "You have no idea of the mess we are in here in Chicago— all horses sick and deadlock on everything, and of course our New Works at a dead stand." No. 138, p. 494, the Co. to G. W. Russell, Mineral Point, Wis., Nov. 8, 1872: "All that can be done for horses now is not to work them at all. Disinfect stable with carbolic acid. Keep the horses clean, quiet and warm. To work them is death." Chicago's first snow that autumn was on Nov. 15.

yoke drawing their wagons—probably the last time that these patient beasts were seen at work in the streets of the city.[205]

In the meantime, iron and lumber, reapers and mowers, and factory machinery were being moved by scow and wagon from the old site to the new. In early January, 1873, steam was raised for the first time at the new works, but it was the following month before the wheels stopped turning at the down-town plant and its tiny twelve-foot square office finally closed.[206] At a dinner given to celebrate the occasion, Cyrus McCormick told about the progress of his industry since he had invented the first practical reaper in the little blacksmith shop at "Walnut Grove" over forty years before.[207] For the second and last time, his machine had a new home, and the contrasts between his circumstances in 1831, 1847, and 1873, were too apparent to require extended comment.

[205] *Ibid.,* No. 138, pp. 421-424, 479, Co. to L. J. McCormick, Nov. 8, 1872; No. 138, p. 530, to J. Edgar, Rochester, Minn., Nov. 12, 1872: ". . . indeed oxen are more common in Chicago than horses now. Horses are improving and we expect in a few days to see oxen at a big discount here." No. 139, p. 407, Agreement of the Co. with H. F. Seffer, Sycamore, Ill., Jan. 4, 1873, whereby the farmer was to take the oxen and fatten them for sale as beef.

[206] The McCormick tug, the *Eustaphieve,* assisted in the moving. *Ibid.,* No. 139, p. 189, Co. to F. Douglass & Co., Dec. 31, 1872: "We will start the big engine next Monday." No. 139, p. 22, Co. to J. Edgar, Feb. 26, 1873: "We have just got into our new office." ‡C. A. Spring, Jr., to C. H. McCormick, Feb. 8, 1873: "The Engine at the Old Works stopped to-night." The old dock was soon rented to J. S. Kirk & Co., but the temporary factory, erected after the fire, and its 100 H.P. Engine, remained unused at least as late as Oct., 1874. Naylor & Co., a Boston forwarding house often employed by the McCormick Co., gave the new works a 42-inch bell with a "G" sharp note. The factory bell destroyed in the fire had been given by this concern in 1859. By 1879, the factory office was under the impression that the bell had been purchased of Naylor & Co. ‡Naylor & Co. to C. H. McCormick & Bro., Oct. 31, 1872; L.P.C.B. No. 138, p. 669, No. 190, p. 618, Co. to Naylor & Co., Nov. 22, 1872, and May 19, 1879; No. 206, p. 570, to J. S. Kirk & Co., Oct. 7, 1880.

[207] This dinner was given without L. J. McCormick's consent, and he refused to share its cost of $600. *Ibid.,* No. 144, p. 826, W. J. Hanna to C. H. McCormick, Aug. 19, 1873.

Credulous farmers who had taken the word of rival agents that the Great Fire was the grave of the Chicago firm, could now learn how they had been hoodwinked.[208] The new works comprised a group of four large buildings, equipped with the best of factory machinery, heated by steam, lighted by gas, protected against fire by all the devices then known, and soon to have its own full-time fire-fighting force.[209] Compared with the old plant, there was now abundant room for growth, and the factory from the outset was able to turn out ten or fifteen thousand implements each season. Because of the opening of the harvester-binder war and the Red River Valley of the North within the next few years, the McCormicks were soon aware that they had enlarged their production facilities at just the right time. The Chicago Fire had been a blessing in disguise.

If, however, they had been asked for a confidential opinion in the spring of 1873, they would not have painted so rosy a picture. Quite apart from the growing threat of the Granger societies and the impossibility of collecting from purchasers more than a small percentage of the amounts that they

[208] *Ibid.*, No. 138, p. 537, Co. to Hatch Lithographic Co., New York, Nov. 13, 1872. The plan to show the new plant on their 1873 poster, failed because of poor work by the engravers.

[209] The new works, its site, its dock, its machinery, and the cottages and boarding-house for its workmen, cost about $619,000, according to an account-sheet dated June 27, 1879. The main factory building was 209' x 360' in size, the warehouse 400' x 100', the foundry 90' x 300', the blacksmith shop, 160' x 160', and there was also a power-house. The river frontage of the works was 1,320 feet long. Besides the brick and stone construction, interior division walls, and double iron fire-doors, there were hoses and hydrants on every floor. Each room could be smothered with steam. A pipe-line was laid to the river, and this together with the fire-pump in the engine-room, assured an abundant water supply. In 1875, as a further protection against fire, thermostats were installed twenty feet apart throughout the works. The "Scientific American," May 3, 1873, p. 279; Western Electric Mfg. Co. to McCormick Co., June 25, 1875. See, *post*, p. 689.

The McCormick Reaper Factory

From the catalog of the McCormick Harvesting Machine Company, 1881

owed,[210] the general business outlook of the country was dark, and conditions at the factory were well calculated to try the patience of a saint. "All is mud—mud—mud. . . . It is awful," lamented Leander to his brother at that time. Plank roads had to be laid so that the out-of-door supplies of coal, iron, lumber, and sand could be reached; the spongy prairie sucked in gravel by the car-load with little result, and lacking a firm bed the spur track to the factory yard from the main line of railroad could not be used. "The Locomotive sinks in it [the mud] and is *continually* off the track. They are having *great* trouble." [211] Because Walker failed to dredge the stream, the McCormicks had to do it themselves.[212] The big engine

[210] L.P.C.B. No. 138, p. 542, Co. to W. C. Chamberlain, Dubuque, Ia., Nov. 13, 1872: "The Banks have now refused further accommodation and we are left wholly dependent upon the efforts of our agents to collect from our Notes in their hands." This was probably an exaggeration, although the partners had borrowed heavily and needed funds. See, No. 138, pp. 554, 672, C. A. Spring, Jr., to Importers' and Traders' Natl. Bank, N. Y. City, Nov. 14, 1872, and to C. H. McCormick, Feb. 5, 1873. The first of these letters sought to arrange for C. H. McCormick a loan of $50,000, and in the second, Spring informed his employer that the firm would probably need to borrow $370,000 before June 1. The partners were accommodated with approximately this sum by the Equitable Life Insurance Co. and the Connecticut Mutual Life Insurance Co., but to raise still more money, C. H. McCormick mortgaged his New York home and sold most of his Union Pacific R.R. securities.

[211] This quotation and the one preceding it in this paragraph, are taken from two undated letters from L. J. to C. H. McCormick, which were undoubtedly written in the spring of 1873. High water had submerged both ends of the spur line. The P. C. & St. L. R.R., Danville R.R., and Northwestern R.R., ran quite close to the factory, but a half-mile track had to be laid to make connection with the Pittsburgh & Ft. Wayne R.R. These companies wished to charge $10 per car for switching, and this was another problem which early arose in connection with the new factory.

[212] L. J. to C. H. McCormick, Dec. 5, 1873. Walker was almost, if not quite, bankrupt. The McCormicks, however, owed him over $500,000 and portions of this sum fell due at stated times during the next five years. L.P.C.B. No. 153, p. 379, Co. to Rogers & Co., Aug. 6, 1874. The last of the notes held by Walker was paid in Oct., 1878. See, F. H. Matthews to Nettie F. McCormick, Oct. 9, 1878.

of three hundred horse-power did not operate properly at first, and at least on one occasion when the gas lights went out, the night-shift had to be sent home.[213] The clerks in the office were handicapped by the inaccessibility of the city, and the McCormicks were obliged to buy an omnibus so that they could get to their desks by seven o'clock every morning.[214] In 1879 the office was moved back to the business district, and thereafter contact was maintained with the factory by a private telegraph wire, and soon by telephone.[215]

Most important of all, however, now that the factory was completed, was the inability of the partners to agree upon the terms under which it should be operated. At least as early as the summer of 1872, Cyrus McCormick had become reconciled to his brother's proposal to admit Robert Hall McCormick to a small share in the business, but there were many other questions to be settled.[216] C. A. Spring, Jr., together with Henry Day of New York City, a mutual friend of the McCormicks and the father of Hall's bride, acted as intermediaries whenever the situation became too tense to permit correspondence between the brothers. In February, 1873, Leander sold one-fourth of his interest in the company to

[213] L.P.C.B. No. 139, p. 498, No. 140, p. 539, Co. to Cuyahoga Steam Furnace Co., Jan. 22, 1873, and to The Peoples Gas & Coke Co., Chicago, Apr. 1, 1873.

[214] *Ibid.*, No. 140, p. 410, Co. to E. C. Beardsley, Aurora, Ill., Mch. 20, 1873.

[215] While the Co. office was at the works, it was necessary to appoint an agent in Chicago. W. H. Banks & Co. served in this capacity from the spring of 1874 until its failure at the close of the next year. Telegraphic connection with the factory had been established even before the office was moved there. *Ibid.*, No. 138, p. 678, the Co. to W. Hopkins, Nov. 25, 1872. No. 132, pp. 687-8, the Co. to P. Mohan, St. Louis, Mch. 15, 1872.

[216] MS. draft of a partnership agreement in C. H. McCormick's handwriting, summer of 1872. R. H. McCormick had been employed by the McCormick Co. since shortly after his marriage to Miss Sarah (Daisy) Day in 1871. He was then twenty-four years old.

Cyrus,[217] but by May they were further apart than ever before. "I cannot continue longer in business with you on such terms as you are disposed to exact," Leander informed Cyrus at that time. "It is apparently useless and unprofitable for us to discuss the question further. . . . I am willing to sell you my interest in the Factory or to allow you to occupy and use it at a fair rental." [218]

This was neither the first nor the last occasion when the partnership seemed about to dissolve. It is probable that Leander had no serious intention of abandoning a most profitable enterprise, but merely wished by his ultimatum to bring matters to a conclusion. If this were his purpose, he was disappointed, since it was September, 1874, before a new five-year contract was finally signed.[219] By its terms, Cyrus, Leander,

[217] ‡C. A. Spring, Jr., to C. H. McCormick, Feb. 6, 1873. L.P.C.B. No. 139, p. 682, telegram of L. J. to C. H. McCormick, Feb. 7, 1873. ‡L. J. to C. H. McCormick, Feb. 7, 1872 (should probably be 1873). ‡L.P.C.B. No. 3, 2nd ser., p. 54, C. H. to L. J. McCormick, Dec. 9, 1872. From this letter it is clear that the partners were also at odds over the terms of the real estate purchase from Walker in Feb. 1872. Each brother charged the other with a determination "to rule or ruin." Perhaps for the first time, C. H. McCormick suggested a joint stock arrangement as a possible means of compromise.

[218] L. J. to C. H. McCormick, May 17, 1873. L.P.C.B. No. 141, p. 523, C. A. Spring, Jr., to C. H. McCormick, May 13, 1873: "I gave your message to Leander but got no definite reply from him. I spoke of the importance of having a Contract made at once but he seemed to care very little about it." ‡L.P.C.B. No. 3, 2nd ser., pp. 95, 493, C. H. to L. J. McCormick, May 19 and July 28, 1873. ‡L.P.C.B. of C. H. McCormick, Nov., 1873-June, 1876, p. 118, C. H. McCormick to H. Day, Aug. 12, 1874. Much of this letter is illegible but enough of it can be read to learn that C. H. McCormick wished the new business agreement, whatever it should be, to be made for only one year, so that in case trouble arose, it would end soon. His brother desired a contract to be concluded for a term of from three to five years.

[219] The firm of C. H. & L. J. McCormick dated from Aug. 1, 1873, but the question of what R. H. McCormick's interest should be, prevented a full settlement for another year. H. Day to C. H. McCormick, ‡July 28, Aug. 18, and Sept. 19, 1874: "I can say with confidence that I think Mr. L. J. is determined to work with all his might, & I know he will work with a

and Robert Hall McCormick united in a partnership under the name of C. H. & L. J. McCormick. Cyrus's interest was three-fourths, Leander's three-sixteenths, and Robert Hall's one-sixteenth.[220] In case a disagreement over a question of factory policy arose, Hall's vote should not be used to offset the wish of his uncle. The question concerning the ownership and use of patents, which had so sharply divided the brothers for eight years, was answered by these words: "All improvements or patents for improvements on machines manufactured by the said firm, made or procured by either of the said partners, as well as those purchased for use in said business, shall be for the benefit of the firm." [221] This provision seemed to be clear enough, but it did not prevent trouble over the matter in the future.

heart in this if it now goes on. I have never seen him so much interested in this business as he now seems. . . . I know you are both positive men & have decided opinions of your own, but that is no reason why you should not compromise upon fair terms, & each be allowed to express his own peculiar views."

[220] C. H. and L. J. McCormick were each to receive an annual salary of $7,500, and Hall, $2,000. A paragraph of the document was devoted to the manner in which L. J. McCormick should repay, by 1877, loans of $200,000 from C. H. McCormick. These loans, with the interest charged, and the time of repayments, were one matter of importance which served to embitter the brothers between 1870 and 1874. Too much space would be required to make their complicated history understandable, and for that reason they have probably been given too little emphasis in the text of this narrative. One point in connection with them, unsettled in the contract of 1874 and still rankling L. J. as late as 1898, was that when he borrowed the first $100,000 in May, 1870, C. H. took out insurance on the property which L. J. offered as security. C. H. paid the premium for a little over a year, the Great Fire destroyed the property, and C. H. collected the insurance. So, Leander's building was burned down, his brother had the insurance, while he (L. J.) still owed the $100,000. For a summary statement, see L.P.C.B. No. 153, pp. 225, 370-371, F. H. Matthews to C. H. McCormick, July 29 and Aug. 6, 1874.

[221] It was also provided that if the firm should disband, these patents were to be the common property of the two brothers, and each could use them freely in his own factory. The returns from all licenses granted under them, however, were to go ¾ths to C. H. and ¼th to L. J. McCormick.

All in all, the new arrangement was satisfactory to no one of the parties in interest. It was little better than a truce. No father was ever more jealous of the future of his eldest son than Cyrus McCormick, and in four or five years, when Cyrus, Jr., would be old enough to enter the business, a new crisis was bound to arise. In the meantime, Grangers, grasshoppers, financial depression, the transition to the harvester and self-binder and the resignation of the experienced and conciliatory C. A. Spring, Jr., and W. J. Hanna, made the years between 1873 and 1879 among the most precarious in the history of the firm. The outside world knew only of its amazing growth and its many hard-fought battles with rivals in court-rooms and harvest fields. The brothers were justly proud of this record of achievement, but their inability to work together in harmony always denied them a full measure of satisfaction from their success.

CHAPTER XIII

HARVESTER AND BINDER RIVALRIES, 1868-1885

THE development of the harvester and automatic binder during the twenty years following the Civil War was attended by a patent maze so intricate and perplexing that the mower and self-rake controversies, already summarized, seem simple by comparison. In no other phase of the history of harvesting machinery is the student more baffled in his effort to find a clear path. With each of several hundred inventors patenting one or more devices designed to speed the work of the reaper, and to render it more efficient, the task of sifting out the few who made contributions of lasting value is no easy one. In the judgment of their contemporaries, about a dozen men, all living within a short distance of Chicago, stood head and shoulders above the rest.[1] Back of them, however, were their many co-workers in machine-shop and harvest field who often added the "here a little, and there a little," which transformed imperfect mechanisms into inventions of significance. By 1865, few inventors were experimenting in isolation as Cyrus McCormick had done when he constructed his first reaper in the Valley of Virginia about thirty-five years before.

The evolutionary or coöperative character of invention in the "machine age" is aptly illustrated by the story of the har-

[1] It is interesting to note that although inventors living in New York and Maryland chiefly developed the mower and self-rake reaper, men of the prairie belt were foremost in the invention of harvesters and binders.

vester. Carried upon this implement were two men who made and tied the sheaves on a binding table to which the grain was elevated from the platform by a revolving apron of canvas or wooden slats. Their place of work was a fairly comfortable one and they could bind almost as much in a day as the four laborers who customarily followed the self-rake reaper and bent to their task under the hot sun.

The brothers, Charles W. and William W. Marsh of Shabbona Grove, Illinois, are alone remembered now as the inventors of the harvester. The Commissioner of Patents declared in 1872: "The Marsh Harvester was the first really successful machine put into the field on which the grain was bound on the machine, . . . the difference . . . between the Marsh machine and its predecessors is the difference between *failure* and *success*." [2] This statement is true as far as it goes, but that it needs some qualification will be made clear if the circumstances preceding and attending the invention are noted.

Reducing the problem to its simplest terms, the transformation of a reaper into a harvester depended first of all upon the discovery of a way to lift the cut grain over the main wheel of the machine. As early as 1827 Patrick Bell in Scotland had used an endless apron to discharge the grain in swath at the stubble side of his implement.[3] This belt was not designed to raise the straw, but it did demonstrate a method whereby grain could be easily moved. About twenty-three years later George Esterly of White Water, Wisconsin, employed a revolving cloth apron to elevate grain over the wheel to the threshing mechanism of his big header-thresher.[4] Shortly thereafter, the Haines Header, as made at Union Grove, Illinois, featured a moving canvas on which the grain heads were con-

2 MS. Decision of Commissioner of Patents, Aug. 9, 1872, on the application of the Marsh brothers for an extension of their patent.
3 "Hutchinson," I, chart facing p. 58.
4 *Ibid.*, I, pp. 346-349. "Prairie Farmer," Oct. 1846, p. 305.

veyed to a receptacle for transferral into an attendant wagon.[5]
At this time in Clinton, Indiana, Jacob J. Mann and his son,
Henry F., also similarly lifted the straw to a wooden box above
the driving-wheel of their harvester. A boy stood upon the
machine and operated a revolving rake to sweep the unbound
gavels from this container to the ground. Jacob Mann and his
licensees continued to build and sell a few of these harvesters
annually for the next fifteen years. Bell, Esterly, Haines, and
Mann were only a few of the early inventors to whom the
endless apron was well known.[6]

Turning to the other main aspect of the harvester problem
—the placing of men upon the implement to do the binding—
Seth Lamb of New York City led the way in 1840, although
his experiments were not sufficiently successful to attract much
notice.[7] Ten years later, Augustus Adams and James T.
Gifford of Elgin, Illinois, removed the rake and box from a
Mann machine and placed thereon a binding table, stand, and

[5] *Ibid.,* Dec. 1849, p. 382, Jan. 1850, p. 19. "Gem of the Prairie" (Chicago), May 11, 1850. The Jonathan Haines patent was dated Mch. 27, 1849. *Sprague and Parsons vs. Adriance and Platts,* pp. 391, 421.

[6] In "Easter's Implement World" (Chicago), June, 1893, p. 7, H. F. Mann states that between 2500 and 3000 of his harvesters were made and sold. Earlier evidence indicates that these figures are over twice too large. See, "Gem of the Prairie," May 11, 1850; "Prairie Farmer," July 14, 1859, p. 24; *Mann vs. Slifer, Walls & Shriner Mfg. Co.* (1873), pp. 54, 61, 87, 95, 137, 157, 208, ff. When Mann attempted to compel E. Bayliss, the manufacturer of the Massillon (O.) Harvester, to pay him a royalty in 1876, the court held that the leading features of the Mann invention had been anticipated, with the probable exception of his use of a revolving rake to discharge the gavels from the grain-receiver. *Henry F. Mann vs. Edwin Bayliss, In Equity, Circuit Court of the U. S., in and for the Northern District of O., No. 2623.* MS. H. F. Mann, "A Brief History of the Invention and Development of the Mann Harvester" (1893). Other inventors who had early used a revolving apron for lifting or discharging cut grain were Moore and Hascall of Mich. in 1836 ff; Ira Wheeler of N. H., 1838 ff; D. A. Church of N. Y., 1841 ff; and A. J. Cook of O., 1846 ff.

[7] Edward H. Knight, "American Mechanical Dictionary" (N. Y., 1877), III., p. 1891.

riding bandsters. Because the endless apron was also dispensed with, the cut grain had to be lifted to the table by a man walking beside the machine. After Gifford, who was more ingenious than his colleague, died in 1850, Adams and his new associate, Philo Sylla, were unable to perfect their harvester.[8]

Among the several manufacturers of the Mann Harvester was Haskell, Barker & Aldridge of Michigan City, Indiana. Charles W. Marsh, a young farmer of mechanical bent who hoped to be a lawyer, was the agent for this firm in the district about his home. According to his story, he was seated upon a Mann machine in the early summer of 1857, thinking of the back-breaking toil of making sheaves in the harvest field, when it occurred to him that if a grain receptacle, stand, and a table were placed upon the reaper, the binders might ride while doing their work.[9] This idea, as we have seen, was not new, but hitherto no attempt to carry it into practice had been wholly successful. Most probably Marsh and his brother, living only forty-five miles by road from Elgin, had heard of

[8] Nevertheless, Easter, Gammon & Co., of Chicago, makers of Marsh harvesters, found it worth while to protect their output in 1872 by purchasing the harvester patent of Sylla and Adams for $25,000. The Slifer, Walls & Shriner Mfg. Co. of Lewisburg, Pa., was also licensed under this patent, and the McCormicks tried in vain to defeat its extension in 1867. Probably between 120 and 130 Sylla and Adams machines were manufactured between 1853 and 1856. *Sylla and Adams Extension Case, Opponents' Proof*, Part I, p. 137; ‡H. Baldwin, Jr., to the Co., Aug. 24 and Sept. 24, 1867; ‡H. Day to the Co., Feb. 3, 1875; "Scientific American," June 15, 1915. *Statement of Account and Applicants' Testimony. In the Matter of the Application of Philo Sylla and Augustus Adams for the Extension of Letters Patent, Dated September 20, 1853* (Washington, 1867), pp. 3-4, 10.

[9] *Mann vs. Slifer, Walls & Shriner Mfg. Co.*, pp. 152-153, 158; Article by John F. Steward in "Farm Implement News," Jan. 1891; *Circuit Court of the United States in and for the Northern District of Illinois, Charles W. Marsh, William W. Marsh, John D. Easter, Elijah H. Gammon, Ralph Emerson, and William A. Talcott vs. Cyrus H. McCormick, Leander J. McCormick and Robert H. McCormick, Doing Business as C. H. and L. J. McCormick. Complainants' Proofs* (Chicago, 1879), p. 297.

Sylla and Adams' riding binders, while the Mann Harvester had made them well acquainted with the endless apron. Their work, therefore, was so to arrange and perfect elements already known that the desired object would be achieved. This was difficult to do.

Some years later, Charles Marsh testified under oath: "We were not in the market with a successful machine, in public estimation, prior to 1866, and then quite limited." [10] How to alter the balance of the reaper so that two extra men could ride upon it; how to place these binders where they would not interfere with the reel or with one another; how a five-foot swath could be cut without overburdening them with inflowing grain, and how this grain could be delivered to them at the most convenient angle and in a form fit for binding, were some of the difficult questions that required eight years to answer satisfactorily. The construction, method of operation, and position of the Mann endless apron were changed, although its general purpose remained the same.[11] The owners of the Marsh patents in 1873 paid Henry F. Mann a large sum to induce him to drop his suit for infringement brought against them. The brothers built their first harvester in 1858 from a Mann machine supplemented by odd reaper and corn-

[10] *In the Matter of the Application of Charles W. Marsh and William W. Marsh for the Extension of Letters Patent dated August 17, 1858, and Re-issued in Two Divisions June 27th, 1865; Nos. 2014 and 2015, Abstract of Testimony Taken by Applicants* (1872), p. 3. "Chicago Weekly Democrat," Sept. 7, 1858, p. 4.

[11] *Marshs vs. McCormicks*, p. 297. See, *Marshs' Extension Case*, p. 43, for description of the binders' stand and table. *Circuit Court of the United States, Northern District of Ohio, Eastern Division. McCormick Harvesting Machine Company vs. C. Aultman & Company et al, in Equity No. 4484, and McCormick Harvesting Machine Company vs. Aultman, Miller and Company, et al, in Equity. No. 4485. Defendants' Record*, p. 448. When it was said that a Marsh harvester had a knife 5 ft. long it did not mean that it could cut that wide in heavy grain, because if it did the binders could not keep up.

sheller castings picked up about their farm.[12] Before reaching success they had mortgaged their home and aggrieved their family and friends by their costly persistence. When they exhibited one of their machines in 1860 at a field trial near Sycamore, Illinois, Philo Sylla could not hide his scorn, and McCormick's representative said that it resembled a "cross between a windmill and a threshing machine." [13]

In truth, the twelve Marsh harvesters of 1860 did not work well, and the brothers were at the end of their resources. Providence appeared in the person of Lewis and George H. Steward, farmers of Plano, Illinois, who wished to loan money at ten per cent and increase the value of their land by stimulating the growth of the village.[14] There, beside a swamp, with the Chicago, Burlington & Quincy Railroad tracks near by, was an abandoned factory, two stories high. Beginning in the autumn of 1863, this was the plant of Marsh, Steward & Company. Lewis Steward was a "positive man," who although lacking in experience, insisted upon "running the business to suit himself." Without his aid the Marsh Harvester might

[12] Agreement of Oct. 6, 1873, between H. F. Mann and Ralph Emerson, representing the Marsh pool: "Mann will drop his suits against the makers of Marsh harvesters. The pool will pay him $12,000 for a shop right, or $19,000 for a ½ interest, or $25,000 for all his patents." I have been unable to determine which choice was accepted, but probably not the last, since Mann later sought to license the McCormicks. C. W. Marsh declined to remember the sum paid to Mann, in his testimony in *Marshs vs. McCormicks,* p. 392. The McCormick Co. to H. Day, Feb. 13, 1875. Article by H. F. Mann in "Easter's Implement World," June 1893, page 7; C. W. Marsh's reply in "Farm Implement News," June 15, 1893.

[13] *Sylla and Adams' Extension Case,* p. 10. *Sylla and Adams Opponents' Proofs,* Part I, pp. 104, 109. *Marshs vs. McCormicks,* p. 304, testimony of C. W. Marsh.

[14] *Sylla and Adams, Opponents' Proofs,* Part I, p. 107. "Deering's Farm Journal" (Chicago), Jan. 1882, p. 5. *Marshs' Extension Case,* pp. 1-2. Lewis F. Miller later claimed to have made and operated a successful harvester in 1858. See, his letter to the McCormick Co., Feb. 27, 1877. L.P.C.B. No. 170, pp. 319, 566, the Co. to L. Miller, Feb. 6 and 20, 1877.

never have been launched upon its successful career, but the arrangement was not an altogether happy one. Nevertheless, about fifty machines were sold during the next two harvests, and gave satisfaction to their purchasers.[15]

The year 1866 marks the turning point in the history of the harvester. In the preceding autumn the Marshs sold for $5,000 a one-third interest in three of their patents to Champlin & Taylor of Sycamore, Illinois, and granted John D. Easter of Chicago an exclusive license at $7 a machine royalty, to build and sell in most of Illinois, part of Minnesota, and all of Indiana and Wisconsin.[16] Easter then took as his partner a retired Methodist preacher, Rev. Elijah H. Gammon. During the next two years Easter & Gammon marketed several hundreds of the harvesters manufactured for them by Emerson, Talcott & Co. of Rockford, Illinois, and Warder, Mitchell & Co., of Springfield, Ohio.[17]

After several shifts of financial alignment, unnecessary to detail here, Gammon, Easter, the Marsh firm of Plano, and the Emerson Company of Rockford, pooled their patent inter-

[15] Up to 1872, the Plano factory had built 1550 harvesters, but many of these had not been sold. *Marshs' Extension Case,* pp. 11 and 48, 24 were built in 1864; 26 in 1865, 100 in 1866, 150 in 1867. See, Deering Harvester Co. Pamphlet (1898), "Forty Harvest Seasons, 1858-1898."

[16] J. D. Easter during the Civil War period was Seymour & Morgan's Chicago agent. "Easter's Implement World," July 1893, p. 9; *Marshs' Extension Case,* p. 3. Champlin & Taylor soon transferred its interest in the patents to Emerson, Talcott & Co. of Rockford.

[17] Emerson, Talcott & Co. began manufacturing Marsh harvesters in 1866 and by the close of 1873 had made about 1100. Neither this firm, nor Warder, Mitchell & Co., which made three or four thousand Marsh harvesters between 1867 and 1870, sold its entire output to Easter & Gammon (J. D. Easter & Co.). This Co. purchased 450 in 1867; 1146 in 1868; 2078 in 1869; 1000 in 1870; 1000 in 1871, and about 700 in 1872. *Sylla and Adams, Opponents' Proofs,* Part I, pp. 110, 116, 117; *Marshs' Extension Case,* pp. 29, 45, 47; *Mann vs. Slifer, Walls & Shriner Mfg. Co.* (founded in 1866), pp. 116, 133, 159, 226. Warder, Mitchell & Co., as Warder, Bushnell & Glessner, later became one of the units of the International Harvester Co.

ests in May, 1869, and decided upon the number of harvesters that each could make and sell annually. Fearing a suit by Sylla and Adams for infringement, they agreed to stand together in their own defense and mutually to share its cost.[18] At this time the Marsh brothers turned their chief attention to the trans-Mississippi area as a selling field. To build machines for this market, they organized the Marsh Harvester Company at Sycamore, Illinois.[19] Gammon and Steward were in control of the Plano works, while Easter organized his own selling firm at Chicago. The following year, William Deering, a rich wholesale dry-goods merchant of Portland, Maine, brought his great business talent and forty thousand dollars to the aid of the Plano factory.[20] Success was now assured. Probably ten thousand Marsh harvesters were sold by the close of the 1872 harvest, when the brothers' original patent was extended.[21]

[18] Agreement of May 5, and supplementary agreement of May 18, 1869. Each party was to pay into the pool $2 for each machine sold since 1867. Gammon was to pay for 400, Easter 1100; C. W. & W. W. Marsh 300, and Emerson & Co. 75. Emerson was virtually the head of the "ring."

[19] As late as 1872, the Sycamore works was building only 150 a year. Bankrupt by 1877, it was reorganized to make binders,—particularly the Crane Wire Binder (J. H. Gordon patent) and the Whitney "Low-Down" Binder. It was again bankrupt by 1884, and then C. W. Marsh, with A. M. Leslie, became the editor of the "Farm Implement News" in Chicago. "Chicago Daily Tribune," July 1 and 8, 1884.

[20] By 1875, Gammon & Deering was making 6000 harvesters a year. In that harvest, the McCormicks made 5000. In 1877 Gammon & Deering took over the business of the bankrupt J. D. Easter which included the manufacturing interests of the Marshs in their harvester (Lewis Steward & Co. of Plano). Deering bought out Gammon, moved to Chicago in 1880, and there erected a large plant. The Plano factory was then occupied by the newly organized Plano Mfg. Co. (W. H. Jones, E. H. Gammon, and Lewis Steward). This firm removed to West Pullman, Chicago, in 1893, and nine years later was one of the five units merged into the International Harvester Co. R. L. Ardrey, "The Harvesting Machine Industry," in the "Scientific American," Supp., Dec. 20, 1902. "Easter's Implement World," June 1893, p. 3.

[21] MS. Decision of the Comm'r. of Patents, Aug. 9, 1872, on the Marshs' application for extension. *Marshs' Extension Case*, p. 29. Probably about

After 1865, the Marsh Harvester was mentioned with increasing frequency in the correspondence of the McCormick Company, although for several years it was generally referred to as a "humbug" unworthy of serious consideration.[22] Even as late as 1868 the clerks in the office assured agents that the very heavy grain of that harvest would bring the downfall of the new rival. Before the next season had come, however, experiments were under way at the factory for the purpose of constructing a harvester to drive the Marsh from the field.[23] These were unsuccessful, and the experience of five more summers was necessary before the McCormicks were convinced that the high wages paid to harvest labor, the efficient operation of the Marsh machine, and its popularity, particularly in the vast wheat areas of Nebraska and Minnesota, left them no choice but to manufacture one of their own.[24] In August, 1873, Cyrus McCormick was informed by his Chicago office:

3500 Marsh harvesters were manufactured for sale in 1872. *Marshs' vs. McCormicks,* p. 321. On Jan. 24, 1879, C. W. Marsh thought 100,000 of his harvesters in all had been made, but of this number one-third in his opinion had been manufactured illegally without his license.

[22] L.P.C.B. No. 90, p. 450, the Co. to C. B. Pinkham, Marshalltown, Ia., May 30, 1866; No. 107, p. 12, to F. G. Smyth, Madison, Wis., July 29, 1868; No. 126, p. 262, to L. Y. Hyde, St. Charles, Minn., July 29, 1868, and June 3, 1871. G. Monser, Wenona, Ill., to the Co., June 13, 1867, June 26, 1868. W. J. Hays, Decatur, Ill., to the Co., July 4, 1868.

[23] The McCormick Co. apparently never completed its harvester. L. J. to C. H. McCormick, Feb. 28, Mch. 1 and 27, 1869. These letters show that the Co. thought of taking a license under the Sylla and Adams patent, owned by C. Aultman. C. H. to L. J. McCormick, Dec. 2, 1869: "Marsh's has been in *demand . . . said to be.* This is another huge puff! Wonder if he hopes to *sell rights? What* has he patented, *not his?"*

[24] Letters to the Co. of W. F. Carr, Freeport, Ill., July 31, 1869, July 21, 1872; A. D. Wright, Cresco, Ia., June 7, 1869; F. G. Smyth, Madison, Wis., Aug. 25, 1869, and J. Edgar, Rochester, Minn., Sept. 19, 1870, and Aug. 20, 1872. Some believed that by using a harvester, between 50 cents and $1.00 an acre could be saved, including the value of 1 bus. of grain per acre. Harvest wages ranged from $2.50 to $3.00 per day although a boy to drive a machine could be had for $.75 a day. But in a letter to J. C.

The evidence accumulates that the Marsh Harvester, or that class of machine, is fast becoming the most popular machine in market. . . . Mr. L. J. is beginning to feel the pressure of these *facts,* which come to us from our *best* and *most reliable* agents, and he has had me write Baldwin to investigate what is the scope and validity of the Patents that stand in the way of manufacturing Harvesters. L. J. is strongly inclined (provided the way is open) to take hold of that machine, the Marsh Harvester, without making any experiments, and build a certain proportion of the coming year's machines of that style.[25]

Cyrus McCormick gave his consent, and thereby added harvester patents to his other worries arising from questions concerning the mower and self-rakes.[26]

By "that class of machine" in the letter quoted above, was meant the harvesters unprotected by the Marsh patents which several firms were building in response to the growing demand. The Bayliss Harvester Company of Massillon, Ohio, the Garnhart & Rice factory at Madison, Wisconsin, the Adams & French Company (Sandwich Mfg. Co.) of Sandwich, Illinois, the St. Paul Harvester Works at St. Paul, Minnesota, and two plants at Polo, Illinois, making the Elward Harvester, were the more important of these new concerns.[27] They either relied upon their own patents to withstand

Beltion, Greenwood, Miss., Sept. 22, 1875 (L.P.C.B. No. 162, p. 185), the Co. stated that a harvester could not cut as much in a day as a self-rake machine, since the riding bandsters were swamped with grain if the harvester were driven at ordinary speed.

[25] ‡W. J. Hanna to C. H. McCormick, Aug. 25, 1873; L.P.C.B. No. 145, p. 267, *idem to idem,* Sept. 10, 1873. J. Edgar to the Co., from Rochester, Minn., Aug. 16, 1873; from Storm Lake, Ia., June 13, 1873: "The Marsh has been the rage." G. D. McArthur, Winnebago City, Minn., to the Co., June 15, 1874.

[26] C. H. McCormick to W. J. Hanna, Aug. 28, 1873.

[27] The Rice Harvester was the invention of Dr. E. B. Rice of Madison. J. H. Garnhart was a St. Louis promoter to whom Rice assigned ½ of his interest in the patent in exchange for financial aid. Their factory opened in 1872. L.P.C.B. No. 145, p. 217, W. J. Hanna to W. D. Baldwin, Sept. 6, 1873; F. G. Smyth, Madison, Wis., to C. H. & L. J. McCormick, Jan. 8, 1872, and Sept. 3, 1873; D. W. Cobb, Sparta, Wis., to the Co., July 18,

an attack by the Marsh brothers, or were making under license from Mann, Sylla and Adams, or other inventors who claimed to have anticipated the chief features of the Marsh machine.

It was high time by 1873 for the courts to judge between these tangled claims of priority. Since the first Marsh patent had recently been extended, there was little doubt that suits for infringement were about to begin. Thus, whichever harvester the McCormicks should choose to build, they must be prepared to defend it in the courts as well as in the field, although in their judgment none of the patents was "worth a pinch of snuff." [28] Negotiations with Marsh, Bayliss, Garnhart, Elward, and Mann continued for over a year. The several types of machines were compared while working side by side in the field, and were studied by the experts in the factory.[29] A decision to license from Marsh was changed after the Garnhart Harvester had been more closely examined. Finally, in late October, 1874, a contract was closed with Dr. E. B. Rice, its patentee.[30]

1872. John W. Elward of Polo, Ill., patented improvements on binder stands and harvester platforms in 1870 and 1871. He was associated there with the Polo Manufacturing Company and the Polo Harvester Company. Adams & French first built harvesters in 1872, making about 300 that year. J. Edgar, Mason City, Ia., to the Co., Aug. 1, 1872.

[28] Thus in Aug., 1873, the Marshs were suing the Elward Harvester manufacturers and they, building under the Mann patent, were, in turn suing the Marshs. Mann was suing Slifer, Walls & Shriner, Emerson, Talcott & Co., and Edwin Bayliss. L.P.C.B. No. 145, pp. 7-8, 45, W. J. Hanna to W. D. Baldwin, Aug. 25, 1873; W. D. Baldwin to the Co., Aug. 27, 1873. *United States Circuit Court, in and for the Northern District of Illinois, Charles W. Marsh et als. vs. the Polo Manufacturing Company et als. In Equity . . . Complainants' Proofs* (Chicago, 1879).

[29] L.P.C.B. No. 145, pp. 124, 517, the Co. to E. C. Beardsley, Aurora, Ill., Sept. 1, 1873; to J. H. Garnhart, Sept. 23, 1873; No. 147, p. 688, to H. F. Mann, Jan. 15, 1874; No. 150, p. 755, to E. Healy, Earlville, Ia., June 3, 1874; No. 152, p. 128, to F. G. Smyth, Madison, Wis., July 1, 1874.

[30] L.P.C.B. No. 145, p. 133, the Co. to W. D. Baldwin, Sept. 2, 1873; ‡W. J. Hanna to C. H. McCormick, Sept. 2, 1873; Telegram of L. J. Mc-

McCormick well knew that he would soon be under the fire of the Marsh brothers, and he at once sought to retain the best available counsel. Because they were already suing Bayliss and the Elward Harvester folk for infringement, he endeavored to draw these firms, and several others who were threatened, into a defensive alliance.[31] Charles Colahan was sent to Shabbona Grove and Plano to question men who had known the Marsh brothers fifteen years before, and to purchase any patents which would antedate and cover their monopolies. McCormick was especially anxious to increase his protection upon the binder's stand and table of the Garnhart Harvester because those elements seemed principally to infringe.[32]

The Garnhart and Marsh elevating devices, on the other hand, were quite unlike, since the former lifted the grain between two canvas aprons moving in close proximity, while the latter employed a series of traveling, endless belts from which pins or carrier-rakes projected.[33] Whatever hope McCormick

Cormick to the Co., Oct. 16, 1874; W. D. Baldwin to the Co., July 8, 1875.

[31]‡ C. Colahan to C. H. McCormick, Oct. 29 and 31, 1874; W. D. Baldwin to C. H. McCormick, Dec. 7, 18, and 22, 1874; C. H. McCormick to H. Day, Dec. 31, 1874. L.P.C.B. No. 155, p. 1, the Co. to E. Bayliss, Massillon, O., Jan. 1, 1875; p. 17, to J. Rhodes & Son, Hastings, Minn., Jan. 2, 1875. J. Rhodes & Son to the Co., Jan. 8, 1875: Bayliss and the Elward Cos. can't coöperate against Marsh for they accuse each other of infringement.

[32] W. D. Baldwin to the Co., Sept. 12 and 14, 1874; J. S. Isett, Spruce Creek, Pa., to the Co., Aug. 24, Sept. 22, Oct. 6, and Dec. 11, 1874; L.P.C.B. No. 154, pp. 153, 812, the Co. to Dr. E. B. Rice, Madison, Wis., Sept. 28, and Nov. 7, 1874. Probably the most important of the auxiliary agreements made in this connection was with John Werner of Prairie du Lac, Wis., whose harvester was manufactured by the Patrons of Husbandry. For $1.25 per machine royalty, Werner licensed the McCormicks to use his excellent binder's stand. J. Werner to the Co., Jan. 4, Apr. 16, Nov. 29 and Dec. 30, 1875; Dec. 10, 1876; Jan. 22, and Feb. 12, 1877; L.P.C.B. No. 162a, pp. 78-80, 459, the Co. to J. Werner, Dec. 23, 1875.

[33] *Marshs' Extension Case*, 1872, p. 16. The Marsh elevator was slotted, —part stationary and part revolving. "The Iron Age," Sept. 27, 1877.

may have had that this feature of his machine was immune
from attack was rudely shaken early in 1875, when in spite of
his opposition, the Marshs obtained reissues of their patents
with their specifications sufficiently different from the originals to cover broadly all methods of elevating the cut grain
over the main wheel. Doubtless the McCormicks had been
chiefly in their thoughts, for no sooner were the reissues secured than they filed a bill of complaint against the Chicago
partners in the federal court.[34] About the same time they cir-
cularized the country-side with a leaflet stating thirty-seven
reasons why their harvester was better than the McCormicks'
and warning all farmers, under penalty, not to purchase the
infringing machine.[35] Henry F. Mann, who was disappointed
because the Chicago partners had declined to build his harvester, also brought suit, but after some months consented to
have it dismissed.[36] Apparently the Marsh pool had been seeking favorable decrees in actions against little manufacturers

[34] W. D. Baldwin to the Co., Jan. 28, and Mch. 22, 1875; C. Colahan to
C. H. McCormick, Mch. 11, 1875; ‡H. Day to the Co., Feb. 3, 1875.
The Marshs' bill of complaint was filed April 2, 1875. The McCormicks,
Bayliss, the Polo Mfg. Co., and the Polo Harvester Co., defendants in the
cases brought by the Marshs, pooled their witnesses and jointly employed
as one of their counsel, S. A. Goodwin of Chicago. Polo Mfg. Co. and
Polo Harvester Co., Polo, Ill., to the Co., May 12 and 18, 1875. L.P.C.B.
No. 157, p. 816, the Co. to L. F. King, Polo, Ill., May 13, 1875.

[35] Notice of C. H. & L. J. McCormick to all Agents, Feb. 12, 1875.
1875 Broadside of R. Ellwood & Co., agent of C. H. & L. J. McCormick
at Sycamore, Ill., entitled "The McCormick Harvester Ahead." "Numerous
scurrilous and abusive circulars have come out against us, reporting our
Harvester a failure. If so, why all this fuss and squirming by the opposition? . . . If we have infringed the Marsh Patents we can pay, and farmers
who have been raising so much hullabaloo about patents adding $60-$100
to the price of machines, should be glad to see us win against Marsh,
meaning more competition and lower prices for machinery."

[36] ‡C. H. McCormick to E. N. Dickerson, Nov. 27, 1876. H. F. Mann
to the Co., Oct. 25, 26, and Nov. 27, 1876. These letters show that the
McCormicks paid Mann $1000. For this sum he consented to withdraw his
action, provided that they kept the terms of the agreement in confidence.

who were unable to employ the best of patent lawyers in their defense, so as to help its cause against the McCormicks.

In July, 1875, Cyrus McCormick and his corps of attorneys met in lengthy conference at Taylor's Hotel, Jersey City, to frame a reply to the Marsh bill. "We unanimously concluded that we had a good and full defense. These reissues [of the Marshs] are unlawful since they aren't the same as the originals of 1858." [37] Thus Cyrus McCormick summarized the result of the discussion and correctly indicated the grounds upon which the case would ultimately be decided in his favor in October, 1883.[38] The testimony given by his experts and witnesses was so damaging that the Marsh pool did not press the action with vigor after the initial hearing.[39] Financial difficulties helped also to moderate the earlier aggressiveness of the plaintiff. Above all, the courts were coming to view with

[37] C. H. to L. J. McCormick, July 28, 1875. W. D. Baldwin to the Co., May 11 and 20, 1875; The McCormicks' answer to the Marshs' bill of complaint was filed on Aug. 2, 1875. C. H. McCormick to W. D. Baldwin, July 20, 1875. L.P.C.B. of C. H. McCormick, Nov. 1873-June 1876, p. 329, C. H. McCormick to E. N. Dickerson, Nov. 20, 1875: "Parsons is figuring with the Marshs on the matter of an arrangement to support their patents, paying a *moderate* fee to them, and stipulating to *keep up* the price of the machine—*wh. might be important.*"

[38] ‡C. A. Spring, Jr., to C. H. McCormick, Oct. 2, 1883: Judge Drummond called this morning to say that he would dismiss the Marsh suit on the ground that the plaintiffs had invalidated their patents by reissuing them. ‡M. D. Leggett to C. A. Spring, Jr., Oct. 20, 1883.

[39] ‡C. H. McCormick to H. Day, Dec. 21, 1875, and to "Dear Sir," Dec. 31, 1875: I think Marsh will be glad to compromise and save his patents. We believe we have the name of the party who invented the Marsh machine, as patented in 1858. ‡C. H. McCormick to E. N. Dickerson, Dec. 14, 1875: The taking of testimony in the Marsh case will close Feb. 15th, next. E. N. Dickerson to the Co., Mch. 1, 28, and Apr. 6, 1877. J. N. Jewett's telegram to C. H. McCormick, May 27, 1879. Parkinson & Parkinson to the Co., Oct. 20, 1882. L.P.C.B. ‡163, p. 732, the Co. to E. S. Renwick, N. Y. City, Feb. 29, 1876. Early in 1877, the St. Paul Harvester Works brought suit against the McCormicks for infringing the Elward patents. This controversy was ended in 1883 by a mutual inter-licensing agreement between the two companies.

disfavor the common practice of exercising the legal privilege of amending a patent specification, for the unlawful purpose of covering a competitor's device that was not an infringement of the original grant.[40]

No sharp line of demarcation separated the harvester period from that of the harvester-binder. In fact, there is slight justification for the view that most farmers of the decade 1868 to 1878, thought of reaping in terms of the harvester. Certainly this was not true of the East, and even in the Middle West there were many more self-rake reapers and reaper-mowers sold each year than harvesters. Several of the largest firms in the country, including the McCormicks, did not begin to manufacture them until 1875 or later, and by 1875 Walter A. Wood & Company and Gammon & Deering already were making and selling wire-binders. Neither the harvester nor the self-binder increased the speed of cutting grain. Each, however, accelerated and eased the work of binding. The harvester did not come into its own until an automatic binding device was substituted for the sheaf-makers riding upon the machine. Thereafter, it became a familiar sight in the world's grainfields.

Even before the Marsh brothers built their first implement, a few men had endeavored to construct a mechanism which would tie knots in straw, wire, or cord. If a practical knotter could be made, the chief hurdle in the path toward automatic binding would be surmounted, although the problems would still remain of compressing and sizing the gavel to be bound, and cutting the binding material after each sheaf was made.

Much talent and time were wasted by inventors for many years in endeavoring to fashion a device which would bind

[40] A fire in the Patent Office in Sept., 1877, which destroyed records and models, was also a source of much embarrassment to those who were parties to suits involving patents. Baldwin, Hopkins & Peyton to C. Colahan, June 3, 1878. Parkinson & Parkinson to the Co., Sept. 13, 1882. *Supra,* ftn. 19.

with straw. For reasons of economy and convenience, farmers usually tied their sheaves with straw, and it was, therefore, natural to have this material in mind when the problem of automatic binding was faced. But straw was short in length, uneven in size, and too brittle to stand much tension. Now and again, after 1850, the press announced that a practical straw-binder had been invented.[41] A fortune still awaits the genius who can make one operate with success under actual harvest conditions.

John E. Heath of Warren, Ohio, heads the long list of binder patentees in the United States. His non-automatic twine-binder of 1850 did not accomplish its designed purpose but it was of significance in clarifying the general problem involved.[42] Other inventors during that decade, including Edward Renwick and Peter Watson in 1853, C. A. McPhitridge in 1856, and Allen Sherwood in 1858, helped to point the way for those who followed them, although their twine- or wire-binding appliances could not be relied upon in a harvest field.[43] Henry M. and William W. Burson of Rockford, Illinois, between 1860 and 1866 advanced the quest measurably nearer the goal.[44] Their hand-operated wire and twine

[41] Letters to the McCormick Co. of D. Whiteman, Xenia, O., May 31, 1858; and E. A. Wible, Mendon, Ill., Mch. 23, 1858. Catalog of Witt, Butler & Co. of Dublin, Ind., 1861; L.P.C.B. No. 155, p. 378, the Co. to S. S. Jackman, Milton, Wis., Jan. 22, 1875; S. S. Jackman to the Co., Jan. 13, June 30 and Dec. 28, 1874; W. Wheeler to W. M. Barger, Lincoln, Neb., June 18, 1877. The Sycamore Marsh Harvester Co. manufactured a straw-binder in 1877. C. Colahan to C. H. McCormick, Nov. 28, 1878.

[42] "American Harvester Patents, 1825-1851, Specifications and Drawings," John E. Heath's patent of July 22, 1850. This shows a cut of his machine.

[43] "Kansas City Implement and Farm Journal," June, 1887. "Prairie Farmer," Sept. 8, 1859, p. 183. L.P.C.B. No. 44, p. 19, the Co. to G. D. Rollin, Glenwood, Ia., July 15, 1861. J. R. Bennett to C. H. McCormick, Jr., Feb. 9, 1884.

[44] *Marshs' Extension Case* (1872), p. 36. W. W. Burson took out six patents on binding attachments between 1860 and 1866. *McCormicks vs. Aultman, Defendants' Record,* pp. 103 ff. 449. Perhaps one thousand Burson binders were sold in the four harvests, 1862-65. W. W. Burson, between

attachments showed how a practical knot could be made mechanically. The fifty or more patents granted to them for devices connected with harvesting implements and machine-knit hosiery deserve a wider recognition. Henry Burson's appliance bound straight, light grain with wire successfully enough in a field trial at Dixon, Illinois, in 1862, to arouse McCormick's interest and to induce Emerson, Talcott & Company to manufacture one thousand of them for sale in the next harvest.[45] They did not fulfill the hope aroused, and the McCormick Company soon branded them "a swindle" and "sheer humbug."

"In process of time," wrote a clerk in the office, "something may grow out of them, and if so we shall be ready to avail ourselves of it. Many manufacturers advertise them as an accompaniment to their machines and in this way they do well as decoy ducks to get men to buy their machines. We notice some say that if the binder does not give satisfaction nothing will be asked for it—a pretty good intimation that they don't expect it will—although it answers the purpose of Selling the machines." [46]

The attention paid to the Bursons in the Middle West and to Allen Sherwood in the East at least had two immediate results of importance for the future. Jacob Behel of Rockford

1878-1890, did much to perfect the knotter, etc., for twine-binders. J. P. Alexander, "American Harvesting Machines," in "American Inventor" (Washington) VII, No. 15, pp. 8-9. *Willson & Brown vs. McCormicks,* pp. 380 ff, testimony of W. W. Burson. L.P.C.B. No. 187, p. 715, the Co. to W. W. Burson, Rockford, Ill., Feb. 3, 1879; No. 207, p. 346, C. H. McCormick, Jr., to W. W. Burson, Nov. 4, 1880; No. 208, p. 841, the Co. to W. W. Burson, Dec. 29, 1880.

[45] "Chicago Daily Tribune," July 26 and 29, 1862. "The Cultivator," Dec. 1862, p. 377. L.P.C.B. No. 55, pp. 547, 551, the Co. to W. W. Burson, Rockford, Ill., Dec. 18, 1862; to J. L. Briggs, Geneseo, Ill., Dec. 18, 1862. W. S. to C. H. McCormick, Jan. 4, 1863.

[46] L.P.C.B. No. 58, p. 789, the Co. to C. H. Loomis, Kewanee, Ill., Apr. 14, 1863; No. 60, p. 309, to O. Gable, Anamosa, Ia., May 25, 1863; No. 68, p. 766, to C. Childs, Omaha, Neb., Apr. 18, 1864.

in 1864 constructed his famous "knotting bill and turning cord-holder," and thus one long step more was taken toward the time when the first practical binder could appear.[47] Then, also, began the twenty-year discussion concerning the injury done to threshing machines, the digestive tracts of cattle, and the bolting cloths of flour-mills by pieces of binding-wire mixed with the grain. Harvesting implement manufacturers, who in a short while would vehemently defend the wire-binder against these charges, now warned farmers that wire was a menace.[48]

Although over eighty patents had been granted by 1868 for automatic binding devices, the McCormick partners with much justification derided the "new fangled, half-fledged contrivances, calculated to delude the farmers by representations of wonder-working powers no machine yet possesses." [49] Nevertheless, in that year, S. D. Carpenter was exhibiting his self-binder in the streets of Madison, Wisconsin.[50] He had found a way to compress the bundle of grain and regulate the speed of the tying apparatus. Not far away at Janesville, Sylvanus D. Locke, who had been hard at work on the problem for seven years, was about ready to seek a manufacturer for his

[47] The failure of the McCormicks to purchase Behel's "tying-bill" patent was a serious mistake because the device became standard in all twine-binders. See, *Minneapolis Harvester Works vs. McCormick Harvesting Machine Co.*, p. 165. *Mann vs. Slifer, Walls & Shriner Mfg. Co.*, p. 99, testimony of Behel. ‡C. Colahan to C. H. McCormick, Sept. 23, 1879; W. Lathrop, Rockford, Ill., to C. Colahan, Nov. 15, 1881, and to C. H. McCormick, Jr., Sept. 12, 1883.

[48] L.P.C.B. No. 104, p. 59, W. J. Hanna to C. A. Atkinson, Davenport, Ia., Apr. 1, 1868.

[49] Pamphlet of C. H. McCormick & Bros. for 1867, p. 6. L.P.C.B. No. 96, p. 623, the Co. to F. G. Smyth, Madison, Wis., Mch. 21, 1867: "The Binder won't hurt much. Your children will see a Binder at work but we doubt if you or we shall ever see a successful one"; No. 118, p. 192, to Richeson & Broderick, Maysville, Ky., Mch. 18, 1870; No. 121, p. 326, to A. J. Hood, Spring Green, Wis., Aug. 29, 1870.

[50] F. G. Smyth, Madison, Wis., to the Co., June 15 and 24, 1868. "Chicago Times," Aug. 12, 1867.

wire-binder with its gavel-sizing mechanism.[51] In the same town that summer, Charles B. Withington, a model-maker and silversmith by trade, puzzling over a way automatically to reciprocate the binding-carriage, was giving his thoughts a direction which would lead him a few years later into the employ of the McCormicks and the thick of the wire-binder patent war.[52] Hector Holmes of Minnesota also began his experiments with twine-binders in 1868. James F. Gordon, seemingly unwilling to decide whether his home was Kalamazoo, Michigan, or Rochester, New York, had just been granted his first patent, and his wire-binder was soon to be a storm center both in the court-room and in the harvest field. He and his brother, John H., were born in Scotland, and their persistence in invention was equalled only by their never-ending chase after alleged infringers of their monopolies.[53]

These were the most important of the many men who were then working on the problem. It is significant that most of them thought of a wire-binder as an attachment for a harvester rather than a reaper. In their view grain to be bound must first be elevated, and the harvester was already prepared to do that. Ten years later men were to seek a method of making sheaves in a position close to the cutting level of the machine.[54]

[51] S. D. Locke took out forty-three patents between 1865 and 1879, all relating to harvesting machinery.

[52] U. S. Patent Office, *Withington vs. Gordon, Grain-Binder Interference, Withington's Brief* (Wash. 1875), p. 8. Withington states that he built a full-sized binding machine in the Harris Reaper Works, Janesville, in 1872. That autumn he took his binder to the shops of J. S. Marsh & Co. and Slifer, Walls & Shriner at Lewisburg, Pa.

[53] MS. Report of a conference between C. H. McCormick, Jr., and D. M. Osborne in Washington in Apr., 1883. C. H. McCormick, Jr., wrote that the Gordons were as "dogged" as Scotchmen usually are "before the suns of America have thawed them out."

[54] The first "low-down" binders, as they were to be called, are associated with Chas. Whitney of Sycamore, Ill., who had been experimenting since 1869. See, *Marshs vs. McCormicks*, pp. 281 ff. *United States Circuit*

There were several reasons why wire at the outset took precedence over twine. Suitable types of either material were scarce in 1870, but wire of the proper size, price, and tensile strength was soon developed. The wish of western farmers to fence their fields, and the lack of wood for this purpose, acted as a sharp spur to the wire industry. The wire-binding mechanism did not need to be either as delicate or as complicated as that for twine. A major element of a twine-binder is the compressing arms which encircle the middle of the gavel and hold it tightly while the knotting bill is tying the cord. Less emphasis upon a special compression device was required with a wire-binder, since the tough wire largely served that purpose by being drawn taut about the sheaf. The two ends of the strand could then be twisted together and no knot was required. Twine, on the other hand, is limp and easily broken by the expanding pressure of the bundle. Only after long search and repeated experiments was it determined that manila, jute, or sisal would best serve the purpose. These came from abroad and were for some years difficult to procure in sufficient quantities and at a price low enough to tempt farmers to buy.[55]

Court of Appeals for the Sixteenth Circuit, Nos. 171 and 172, October Term, 1894. McCormick Harvesting Machine Company vs. C. Aultman & Company, et al. McCormick Harvesting Machine Company vs. Aultman, Miller & Company et al. Submitted May 22nd, 1894. Decided July 2, 1895, p. 452, testimony of C. Whitney. The Marsh-Whitney platform ("low-down") binder was designed for wire in 1880, and for twine, 1882 ff. Aultman, Miller & Co., first sold its "Buckeye Down" binders in 1883. They were a success. Walter A. Wood also had a platform-binder in 1882 but it did not work well. The McCormicks and Deerings put experimental semi-low-downs in the field in 1883, but they were not satisfactory.

[55] Deering Harvester Co., Pamphlet, "Forty Harvest Seasons, 1858-1898." W. Deering was one of the first to appreciate the value of manila twine. He made a contract with Edwin H. Fitler of Phila. in 1879 to supply it. Deering Harvester Co. Pamphlet, "The Foreign Commissioners Visit the Northwest and Learn Why Bonanza Farming Pays" (Chicago, 1894). *Appellant's Brief, United States Circuit Court of Appeals for the*

Of all the manufacturers of harvesting machinery in the United States in 1870, Walter A. Wood & Company of Hoosick Falls, New York, was doubtless the most eager to be first in the market with a practical automatic binder.[56] Seventeen years before this time, Wood opened a factory to manufacture Manny reapers and mowers. By the eve of the Civil War he had developed his own light, two-wheeled mower and self-rake, and his annual sales were as large as those of McCormick. He was careful at the beginning of his career not to jeopardize his position by participating in expensive patent lawsuits, and he agreed to pay McCormick a license fee even before the relation of that inventor's patents to the Manny machine had been determined by the courts.[57] Although few manufacturers were bolder than he in their pro-

6th Circuit, Oct. 1893. McCormicks vs. Aultman, Robert H. Parkinson, Counsel for Appellant, (Chicago, n.d.). L.P.C.B. No. 188, p. 393, the Co. to N. Long & Co., Russellville, Ky., Feb. 27, 1879.

[56] W. D. Baldwin to the Co., Aug. 11, 1874: "Emerson & Co. spent $10,000 on the automatic binder question [Burson] and gave it up in despair. Wood has probably spent $100,000 on it and is still working on it. He has bought up many patents in this class. I must therefore suggest caution. . . ."

[57] In 1853, Wood made 500 machines; in 1862, 6,425; in 1869, 23,000. His Co. had manufactured a total of 234,120 machines by 1875. On the early history of Wood, Thayer & Co., Wood, Ball & Co., and Walter A. Wood & Co., see "The Cultivator," July 1854; May, 1858, and Apr. 1859; "Genesee Farmer," July 1860, p. 229; "Iron Age," Oct. 11, 1877. Wood made his agreements to pay a royalty to C. H. McCormick on Apr. 25, 1856, and Apr. 22 and 29, 1857. In the Patent Office of the United States. In the Matter of the Application of Cyrus H. McCormick for the Extension of His Patent for an Improvement in Reaping Machines, dated Jan. 31, 1845, pp. 11-15. This shows that up to Dec. 7, 1858, Wood had paid McCormick $16,000. ‡W. A. Wood to C. H. McCormick, Jan. 11, 1865: "You are aware—as a Christian man must be—that I paid you several years ago, over fourteen thousand dollars which should be refunded to me . . . [since] your patents were not sustained by the courts. When it is paid to me, I shall be ready to go on with such intercourse with you, as becomes Christian men and respectable manufacturers of Reaping and Mowing Machines." No record has been found that this was repaid but it most probably was, in view of their later cordial relations.

duction and selling policies, he avoided litigation whenever possible. Fire caused him a heavy loss in 1860, but the Civil War soon came to increase his fortune and the popularity of his machines. When he formed a joint-stock company in 1865, he was the leading manufacturer of harvesting machinery east of the Alleghenies. Favored by his ready access to the ports of Boston and New York, his name was soon well known in the harvest fields of Europe. Cyrus McCormick's personal relationships with Wood were more cordial than with any other rival. This good feeling was no doubt promoted by the fact that Wood's focus of interest was not the Middle West.

Early in 1869 Wood placed Locke under contract to continue his experiments at the Hoosick Falls factory. As a result of this assistance, Locke was able in the harvest of 1871 to work his binder with fair success at Alton, Illinois, and at Owatonna, Minnesota.[58] Wood assumed that he controlled Locke's future and wished to join with him in opening a factory at Alton. Locke refused and sought to make an agreement with the McCormicks. A contract was actually drawn in December, 1871, but the partners were then advised that the most noteworthy features of Locke's binder were not original.[59] Negotiations abruptly ceased and the angry inventor

[58] L.P.C.B. No. 130, p. 100, the Co. to S. H. Stowers, Owatonna, Minn., Oct. 19, 1871; #S. H. Stowers to the Co., Nov. 13, 1871. #C. A. Spring, Jr., to C. H. McCormick, June 19, 1871.

[59] #S. D. Locke to C. H. McCormick, Oct. 27 and Dec. 13, 1871; Jan. 3, 1872. Locke wished $105,000 for his patents, if his binder proved to be a success. MS. contract of S. Locke with C. H. & L. J. McCormick, Dec. 1871; H. G. Miller to C. H. McCormick, Dec. 18, 1871. #Wm. Anson Wood to C. H. McCormick, Dec. 20, 1871. This disgruntled brother of Walter A. Wood had developed a good mower. He wished McCormick to manufacture it and to send him abroad to take charge of his European business. He strongly advised McCormick not to buy a license from Locke, both on the ground that the price asked was too high, and because Walter Wood had other patents which anticipated most of Locke's devices. #See his letters to C. H. McCormick of Feb. 9, July 29, Oct. 4 and 18, Dec. 15 and 31, 1872. #L.P.C.B. No. 2, 2nd ser., p. 203, C. H. McCormick to W. Anson Wood, Dec. 15, 1871.

returned to Hoosick Falls. Here he opened the brief wire-binder phase of harvester history in 1873, by selling three of his machines.[60]

In the meantime, the attitude of the McCormicks toward the new development had undergone a significant change. "We keep our eye close on all Self Binders," an agent was assured in the summer of 1871, "and when one is brought out that is a *Binder*, we shall *secure* it. We encourage everything in that line, for it is the great thing to be desired and sought for." [61] This accurately summarized their attitude. They watched Withington and the Gordon brothers as they attached their binding mechanisms to Marsh harvesters and experimented in the summers of 1871, 1872 and 1873. They were aware that two small firms at Lewisburg, Pa., gave Withington employment, and that James F. Gordon sold an interest in his patents to several Canadians operating a factory at London, Ontario.[62] Nor were they blind to the fact, as 1874 opened,

[60] As a matter of fact, Locke sold a binder to one of Wood's agents in 1871, but it was probably never used except experimentally. In 1872, Locke had two trial machines in the field. There were about 250 Wood-Locke binders marketed in 1875. W. D. Baldwin to C. H. McCormick, Mch. 11 and 14, 1875. *McCormicks vs. Aultman, Defendants' Record*, p. 449.

[61] See, letters of the Co. in L.P.C.B. No. 122, p. 374, and No. 124, p. 183, to L. F. Parker, Davenport, Ia., Nov. 18, 1870, and Jan. 7, 1871; No. 137, p. 281, to J. Edgar, Rochester, Minn., Aug. 21, 1872; No. 142, p. 485, to H. O. Goodrich, Jerseyville, Ill., June 17, 1873; No. 143, p. 612, to Chadbourne Bros., Rochester, Minn., July 2, 1873. But as late as Mch. 26, 1874, L. J. McCormick telegraphed to C. H. McCormick: "Believe wire binder is humbug." L.P.C.B. No. 149, p. 40.

[62] J. F. Gordon made his first full-sized machine in 1864 but did not patent it until May 12, 1868. It was not a success until 1871 when he attached it to a Marsh Harvester. J. H. Gordon built his first packer binder in 1873 and sold one in 1874. It was the first to use packers to bring grain into the binding receptacle and there to press it into a bundle. J. F. Gordon conveyed a ⅛th right in his patents of 1872 to E. C. Eells of London, Ontario, and a ¼th right in his 1868 patent to J. M. Currier of Ottawa in Aug. and Oct., 1872. J. H. Gordon was a licensee of his brother for Mich. and Ind., 1870 ff., and had a ¼th interest in his brother's patent of 1868 from Jan. 1872, ff. On Jan. 23, 1875, the Gordons put their patents in

that the time had at last arrived for action. In that year the big manufacturers raced for the possession of the key binder patents of the country, and at its close the McCormicks were well satisfied with their share of the prizes. The tortuous course of the negotiations need not be followed, but in the autumn they took a license from S. D. Carpenter and engaged Withington to work in their factory.[63]

They compared the merits of the Kalamazoo binder of John H. Gordon and the machine of James F. Gordon so highly praised by his Canadian spokesmen. Finally, after long deliberation, the McCormicks signed the most costly contract, as it proved to be, in their business history. They arranged for a license under the James F. Gordon patents, and made an advance royalty payment of $20,000.[64] Gordon assumed that the Chicago partners intended to build his binder, but in fact they had not decided which was the best of the several types, and the Carpenter and Withington patents apparently covered some of the most important elements of the Scotchman's

charge of a trustee who was to manage the licensing,—J. F. Gordon—10/24 interest; J. H. Gordon—5/24; and the two Canadians—9/24. W. D. Baldwin to the Co., Feb. 3, 1875. L.P.C.B. No. 163, pp. 317-319, the Co. to W. D. Baldwin, Feb. 9, 1876.

[63] *Ibid.*, No. 153, p. 439, No. 154, p. 671, the Co. to S. D. Carpenter, Aug. 11, and Oct. 29, 1874. L.P.C.B. No. 154, p. 102, R. H. to C. H. McCormick, Sept. 24, 1874. S. D. Carpenter to the Co., Nov. 20, 1875. The McCormicks purchased the Carpenter patents in 1876. They bought a one-half interest in Withington's patent in 1874 and the balance in 1876.

[64] By the contract, the McCormicks agreed to pay Gordon $80,000 for a ¼th interest in his patents (or $16 royalty per machine), if, in the judgment of a referee, Gordon managed in two years, either to procure a right under the Locke and Sherwood patents, or by that date had so changed his machine, as to avoid these monopolies. Since the McCormicks, at least by Aug., 1875, had decided to cast aside the Gordon contract, they were advised by their attorneys to buy any patents quickly, which if secured by Gordon, would antedate Locke and Sherwood. J. R. Parsons to C. H. McCormick, Aug. 19, 1875; C. Colahan to C. H. McCormick, Dec. 28, 1878, and Jan. 2, 1881. ‡C. H. McCormick to E. N. Dickerson, May 20, 1881: The Gordon contract was "badly drawn and mixed," a "very complicated affair," containing enough "matter in it for a number of lawsuits."

machine. The McCormick license was not an exclusive one, and soon the Gordon brothers, joining forces, came to terms with Gammon, Deering & Steward, D. M. Osborne & Company, Walter A. Wood, and the "Buckeye" factories.[65]

The various wire-binder claims were already in collision before the Patent Office. "Interference" after "interference" was declared. McCormick and his lawyers were busy in Washington protecting his interests and endeavoring so to issue or reissue Withington's and Carpenter's patents as to give him control of the binder field. Among the most active of the opponents of the McCormicks at the capital was Walter A. Wood. It was clear, however, that his resistance was for the purpose of coercing his rival to make an agreement for their mutual benefit.[66] Wood, through his partner and son-in-law, J. Russell Parsons, endeavored to draw the McCormicks into a patent pool.[67] He was the more eager to effect this since his Locke binder was not giving complete satisfaction, and Withington seemed certain to prove his priority of invention over

[65] ‡C. H. McCormick to C. C. Colby, Ottawa, Can., Mch. 19, 1875. D. M. Osborne & Co. for $10,000 bought shares in the J. F. and J. H. Gordon patents on Jan. 1, 1877, and purchased the ⅜th rights of the two Canadians for $20,000 in May. Wood in 1876 bought an interest in the J. F. Gordon patent of 1876, and by 1879 was a licensee of both Gordons. He was convinced that it would be well for the McCormicks and the owners of the Gordon patents to unite their forces,—that there was much money to be made from wire-binders, but only if the essential monopolies were controlled by a few manufacturers, and if "promiscuous licensing" were guarded against. Gammon, Deering & Steward worked experimental wire-binders in the harvest of 1872, and first sold a few of Gordon's patent in 1874. Deering Harvester Co. Pamphlet, 1898, "Forty Harvest Seasons, 1858-1898." W. Deering claimed that in 1875 he put the first successful wire-binder on the market. It was a J. H. Gordon "Packer Binder."

[66] L.P.C.B. No. 157, pp. 399-401, C. H. McCormick to H. Baldwin, Jr., Apr. 23, 1875. H. Baldwin to the Co., June 21, 1875. According to report, Wood had said that the country was big enough for both McCormick and himself, and they should come to terms.

[67] J. R. Parsons, by early training a civil engineer, was thirty-six years old in 1866 and had been in Wood's employ since 1852. ‡C. C. Colby, to C. H. McCormick, Nov. 30, 1874.

Locke in their interference case relating to the wire-tension mechanism.[68] McCormick, as always, hesitated to coöperate with a competitor, and suspected that his counsel, W. D. Baldwin, who strongly urged him to accept Parson's proposals, was working mainly in Wood's behalf.[69] Nevertheless, Parsons and his son, Willie, visited White Sulphur Springs, West Virginia, in September, 1875, to play croquet with McCormick while they discussed ways and means of uniting their patents.[70] The pooling agreement there made came to naught. Locke refused to have the McCormicks licensed to use his inventions. He had not forgotten his rebuff by them several years before, and Parsons was unable to gain his coöperation except upon terms so favorable to himself that McCormick would not accept.[71]

[68] W. D. Baldwin to C. H. McCormick, Dec. 22 and 31, 1874, #Mch. 8, 13, 1875, and to the Co., Jan. 2, 20, 25. Feb. 12, Mch. 18, May 14, 15, June 10 and July 8, 1875. C. H. McCormick to the Co., Aug. 3, 1875. Locke's binding mechanism was heavy and complicated and discharged the sheaves with such force that grain was shattered from the hulls. His patents were nevertheless valuable and in Feb., 1875, Wood agreed to pay him $3,000 a year and $6 per machine for an exclusive license to run for ten years from Aug. 1, 1874. G. F. Edmunds, Burlington, Vt., to S. D. Locke, May 3, 1881.

[69] Letters to the Co. from W. D. Baldwin, May 14, 1875, and from C. H. McCormick, Aug. 3, 1875. Telegram and letter from the Co. to C. H. McCormick, Aug. 1, 1875. L. J. to C. H. McCormick, Sept. 26, 1875. Memo. of C. H. McCormick, Sept. 18, 1875.

[70] C. H. McCormick to J. R. Parsons from Hot Springs, Va., Aug. 12, 1875; telegrams from C. H. to L. J. McCormick, Aug. 24 and Sept. 12, 1875; and his letter to E. N. Dickerson from Rockbridge Alum Springs, Va., Sept. 18, 1875. J. R. Parsons to the Co., Aug. 13, 1875, and to C. H. McCormick, Aug. 19, 1875. C. H. McCormick, Jr., MSS. Book "B," Nettie F. McCormick to C. H. McCormick, Jr., Sept. 21, 1875.

[71] J. R. Parsons' telegrams to C. H. McCormick, Oct. 4 and 23, 1875; L.P.C.B. No. 162, p. 255, L. J. McCormick's telegram to C. H. McCormick, Oct. 6, 1875; W. A. Wood to C. H. McCormick, Oct. 19, 1875; J. R. Parsons to C. H. McCormick, Oct. 30 and Nov. 5, 1875; Nettie F. McCormick to L. J. McCormick, Nov. 1, 1875. C. H. McCormick to J. R. Parsons, Nov. 3, 1875. In Jan., 1886, the McCormick Harv. Mach. Co. agreed to pay S. D. Locke $75,000 for all his interest in his patents.

Finally, on May 19, 1876, Wood and the McCormicks made a temporary contract, each party pledging not to act "prejudicial to the interests of the other, and [both] shall in all proper ways endeavor to continue their relations of good will and amity." Neither would sue the other on any matter connected with wire-binders, nor would either oppose the efforts of the other to secure reissues of wire-binder patents. Wood promised to do all in his power to prevent Locke from suing McCormick or from gaining reissues of his patents. This concordat was to extend until November, 1877, and thereafter until either party gave a month's notice of its intention to withdraw.[72] Both sides carried out the agreement in good faith, but it was little more than a gesture of cordiality. By 1881 its exact meaning was in dispute. Wood, who so much wished to pool his patents with the McCormicks, sought without success to buy Locke's monopolies and to induce him to withdraw his interference case against Withington. Locke's pride held him to a course of action most detrimental to his own welfare. Wood bought an interest in the Gordon patents, and Withington eventually won the interference case against Locke.[73]

While these negotiations were in progress, the McCormicks cautiously added the Withington wire-binder to their selling list. In 1878 it took the field in earnest. Soon they could speak

[72] C. H. McCormick's telegram to Nettie F. McCormick, May 13, 1876: "Telegraph tonight. Should I close with Parsons five dollars license." C. H. McCormick's telegram to Nettie F. McCormick, May 17, 1876, and her reply on May 17, 1876. H. Day to the Co., May 23, 1876. C. H. McCormick to H. Day, May 27, 1876: "L. J. doesn't think the agreement is of much value." The agreement is in the files of the Nettie F. McCormick Biog. Asso.

[73] W. D. Baldwin to the Co., June 28, 1876: "As this makes the twelfth time I think that Withington's case has been argued, and we have been successful in every instance, we have some cause for congratulation." ‡C. H. McCormick to E. N. Dickerson, Mch. 31, 1877: Wood still talks of pooling patents with us, despite Locke.

with sober truth of its "paramount superiority" over the Gordon and Locke machines. Since 1874, several Gordon-Withington interference cases had been running their slow course before the Patent Office.[74] In 1880 the Gordon brothers and Osborne, who had purchased a three-eighths interest in their patents, sought a "show-down" by bringing suit against the McCormicks for infringement. The reciprocating feature of the Withington and Gordon binders was principally at issue. By this, the binder mechanism advanced on its frame to gather up a gavel of grain from the receiver, and then bound and discharged it as it moved back to its original position.[75] The Gordons claimed that the McCormicks had not paid them the royalty agreed upon by the contract of 1874, although in fact every wire- and twine-binder sold by them had been of the Gordon type. The defendants denied that their machines infringed, and added that the Gordons had secured $20,000 under false pretenses in 1874, since they had not invented the devices embraced in their patent of 1868 under which the license had been granted.[76]

[74] L.P.C.B. No. 162a, p. 495. F. Matthews to W. D. Baldwin, Dec. 27, 1875, and No. 163, pp. 317-319, the Co. to W. D. Baldwin, Feb. 9, 1876. U. S. Pat. Office, *Withington vs. Gordon, Grain Binder Interference, Withington's Brief.* W. D. Baldwin to the Co., Jan. 7, 20, 25, Feb. 2, 3, Mch. 4, June 10 and July 8, 1875; Jan. 31, 1880; Oct. 14, 1881. F. H. Matthews to C. H. McCormick, Nov. 29, 1878. C. Colahan to C. H. McCormick, Oct. 5, 1878.

[75] L.P.C.B. No. 162, pp. 304-305, C. B. Withington to W. D. Baldwin, Oct. 2, 1875; and No. 163, p. 446, the Co. to W. D. Baldwin, Feb. 15, 1876. ‡Ross and Parker, Rochester, N. Y., to the Co., Oct. 9, 1880.

[76] There is considerable evidence to show that Gordon journeyed to Lewisburg, Pa., in early 1875, saw Withington and his reciprocating binder there, and then, returning to Rochester, built one of his own. Statements of J. P. Miller and F. A. Donachy, Lewisburg, Pa., Sept. 18, 1879. The Gordons and Osborne sued the McCormicks in both N. Y. and Chicago. The N. Y. case involved wire-binders under the 1874 contract, and the Chicago case, twine-binders. Letters to C. H. McCormick from C. Colahan, Dec. 20, 1880, June 20, 1881, and June 23, 1882; E. N. Dickerson, Aug. 29, 1881; and from G. Harding, Mch. 3, 1882. W. D. Baldwin to the Co.,

Even the invincible Harding, whom the McCormicks retained as their chief counsel, was unable to carry this case through to a successful conclusion. Conference after conference between the litigants failed to bring a compromise until late in 1884. At that time the Gordons released the McCormicks from their contract of ten years before and guaranteed them against any future suit under their patents. The McCormicks agreed, in turn, to pay $225,000, which was equivalent to a $6.00 royalty on each of the binders they had hitherto made.[77] Well knowing that if settlement were by check, his rivals would photograph it for use in their advertisements, Cyrus McCormick, Jr., one afternoon after banking hours, presented the astonished Osborne with a quarter of a million dollars in small bills.[78] If the elder McCormick had lived to see the end of this most expensive lawsuit of his career, he would have enjoyed the embarrassment of his rival. His widow wrote to her son:

I am glad it is closed. . . . We will now close the leaves of this book and turn to a *new one*. I should have stood firm at Utica for $200,000 and told Butler not to yield. We would have been just $25,000 better off—I feel it—sure. This has depressed me when calls for noble effort have come to us. But, I do accept this as *past,* and I now turn to the future with stout heart and courage that we shall make it up by being liberated from these fetters of lawsuits to turn our thoughts to the economy of our manufacturing

Jan. 13, 29, and Mch. 8, 1880. C. H. McCormick to E. N. Dickerson, ‡Nov. 19, 1880 and June 8, 1881.

[77] "Chicago Daily News," Sept. 13, 1884. "Daily Union and Advertiser" (Rochester, N. Y.), Nov. 24, 1884. ‡Agreement of Nov. 20, 1884, between the McCormick Harv. Mach. Co. and James F. and John H. Gordon of Rochester and D. M. Osborne of Auburn, N. Y. The "release and shop right" therein granted did not include the Gordon patents on the "low-down" and "semi-low-down" binders. ‡C. H. McCormick, Jr., to C. H. McCormick, Nov. 26, 1883. ‡P. Arnold to the Co., Apr. 15, 1884.

[78] MS. notes of C. H. McCormick, Jr., for his son. This was on Nov. 20, 1884. To pay in cash, rather than by check, was preferred by C. H. McCormick, Jr., since a photograph of the latter would show his signature.

and shipping, and to the extension of our sales—and to be ingenious in our workshops in utilizing men's labor—especially in finding new ground to sell in.[79]

The Gordon affair forms part of the last chapter in the history of the wire-binder in the United States. Long before it was over, twine was the chief subject of discussion in harvest field and factory office. The wire-binder gained no strong foothold in the East, and even in the wheat belt of the upper Mississippi Valley its period of supremacy was limited to about four harvests.[80] Frowned upon by cattle-owners, threshing crews, and millers, it could not survive the appearance of a perfected twine-binder and cheap twine. The use of automatic binders did not much reduce harvesting expense when compared with the harvester, but farmers liked to keep in step with their most progressive neighbors; they were pressed to buy by expert salesmen, and preferred to be independent of a large extra labor-force at harvest time.[81]

One or two small firms were making and selling a few cord-binders even when wire-binders were first introduced.[82] Several

[79] C. H. McCormick, Jr., MSS. Book "B," Nettie F. McCormick to C. H. McCormick, Jr., Nov. (?), 1884.

[80] These were the harvests from 1877 to 1880. See, *McCormicks vs. Aultman, Defendants' Record,* p. 449.

[81] R. L. Ardrey, "The Harvesting Machine Industry," in "Scientific American," Dec. 20, 1902. For a study of the comparative costs of harvesting wheat with reaper, self-rake, harvester, binder, etc., see Leo Rogin, "The Introduction of Farm Machinery In Its Relation to the Productivity of Labor in the Agriculture of the United States During the Nineteenth Century" (Berkeley, Cal., 1931), pp. 125 ff. C. Colahan to C. H. McCormick, Jr., July 4, 1882: "Automatic Binders are popular in all wheat districts East, and . . . the desire of the Farmer to escape the expense and arbitrary dictation of harvest help, is as general this year as it was West in 1879." *Post,* p. 608.

[82] E.g., the Fassett twine binder. W. R. Baker to C. H. McCormick, from Rochester, Minn., Aug. 16, 1875; L.P.C.B. No. 173, p. 674, the Co. to C. B. Withington, July 21, 1887: Fassett is anxious for us to license and says his machine is now complete. See also, M. A. Keller, Littlestown, Pa., to C. H. McCormick, Feb. 28, 1877, and F. H. Matthews to C. H. McCormick,

in Wisconsin and Minnesota sought to exploit the inventions of John F. Appleby, and two at Rockford, Illinois, similarly revolved about Marquis L. Gorham until his premature death in 1876.[83] Appleby first worked upon his famous twine-binder in 1858 when he was only eighteen years of age. His experiments were interrupted by service in the Civil War, and at its close he turned his attention for almost a decade to wire-binders. In exchange for financial aid, he gave an interest in his patents to Dr. Edwin D. Bishop of Mazomanie, Wisconsin, and contracted with Parker & Stone of Beloit to manufacture his machines.[84] Here he lived from 1870 to 1875, continuing his experiments in the machine-shop of this firm. The significance of his work was not then apparent, and the McCormick brothers, to their subsequent regret, refused Appleby's request in 1873 that they make his machine on their "own terms." This was his wire-binder, but it included, at least in primitive form, the tying device which a few years later made Appleby's name well known wherever twine-binders were used.[85] In the

July 8, 1876. Manufacturers, like the Whiteleys, who were early in the field with twine-binders, did their best to arouse the fears of farmers about the danger of wire. F. H. Matthews to C. H. McCormick, Feb. 12, 1879.

[83] The Gorham binder was made in 1874 ff. by Norman C. Thompson, and by Clark & Utter, both of Rockford. *McCormicks vs. Aultman, Defendants' Record,* pp. 148-152, 162 ff. Thompson apparently sold no Gorham machines until 1876, and then only one or two. He made fifty in both 1878 and 1879 and sold most of them.

[84] *McCormicks vs. Aultman, Defendants' Record,* pp. 100-101, 256-260. Appleby was granted about thirty patents in all. Deering & Company Pamphlet, "The Foreign Commissioners Visit the Northwest and Learn Why Bonanza Farming Pays" (Chicago, 1894), p. 3. *Minneapolis Harvester Works vs McCormick Harv. Mach. Co.,* p. 57, testimony of E. D. Bishop. After Dec., 1875, Bishop gave up his medical practice, and devoted all of his time to the Appleby binder until his retirement in Oct., 1883.

[85] E. D. Bishop, to the McCormick Co., Aug. 20, 1873. Some experts believe that Appleby's knot-tying device was the invention of Jacob Behel, and that he deserves remembrance chiefly because he was the first successfully to coördinate the Behel knotter, the Gorham sizer, and the Marsh Harvester. *Supra,* pp. 538-539, and *post,* p. 560.

summer of 1874 Appleby and Bishop went to Rockford to see Gorham's twine-binder at work in the harvest. Around this visit chiefly centers the controversy, even yet unsettled, concerning the invention of Appleby's automatic bundle-sizer and knotter. Should Gorham have the credit? The sizing mechanisms patented by the two inventors were very similar in form. There is little doubt that Appleby turned again from wire to twine after his Rockford trip and quickly perfected his machine.[86] Gorham's patent was issued in 1875, but Appleby, due to "interferences" declared, was unable to secure his until 1878 and 1879. To harvesting machinery manufacturers of fifty years ago, the priority issue between these men was more than an academic question. Hundreds of thousands of dollars hung upon the answer.

The first Appleby twine-binder was made at Beloit in 1875. Some of its imperfections were corrected in the four made by Parker & Stone for the following harvest.[87] Thereupon, Appleby also engaged the Milwaukee Harvesting Machine Com-

[86] No Appleby wire-binder was ever sold. *McCormicks vs. Aultman, Defendants' Record*, pp. 29, 46, 60-61, 68, 75, 100-101, 107, 234-235, 266-267, and 283, testimony of Appleby. He began to work on a full-sized machine in Parker & Stone's shops in Feb., 1875. It did not operate well in that harvest. Stone showed one in 1876 to men from N. C. Thompson's shop at Rockford, where Gorham was employed. J. Werner, Jr., Prairie du Lac., Wis., to the Co., Apr. 16, 1875. By means of reciprocating packers, the grain was straightened wisp by wisp and compacted into a rude gavel. It was then carried along to the binding receptacle. While the knot was being tied a vertical rack descended and shut off the inflowing grain until the tying was done. Gorham had the idea of starting the binding mechanism to work by applying just enough pressure on the slowly yielding compression. After the gavel was tied, the binding receptacle opened automatically and dropped the bundle to the ground. His most important patent was dated Feb. 9, 1875.

[87] Beloit was a center of reaper manufacturing at least as early as 1850, when Israel Love made fifty Fountain machines there. During the rest of the decade, Love & Orton, Love & Stone, Parker & Love, Love, Otis & Co., D. S. Warner & Co., and Parker & Stone made a few hundred machines (E. B. Forbush) under license yearly. Parker & Stone apparently began to manufacture in 1857, and became Parker & Dennett in late 1878. Parker & Stone made 115 Appleby's in 1878.

pany (Blanchard & Arnold) to build his implement, but this firm was able to turn out only four in 1877, and about one hundred in 1878.[88] Appleby later claimed that by the close of the summer of 1877, his knotter could be relied upon in every respect, and that the Rockford builders of the Gorham binder carefully studied it when it was exhibited that autumn at the Janesville and Freeport fairs.[89] However that may be, Cyrus McCormick sent Colahan to Beloit in November to have a look. His report was the capital blunder of his ten years of service. "In my own mind I do not see any new or original feature of invention that could be sustained in view of prior Patents. . . . It would not be of any value whatever to you . . . if you owned all of these Patents, and I will so report at Chicago verbally." [90] Thus the McCormicks lost their second opportunity to align with Appleby, and in 1878 he gave Gammon & Deering of Plano an exclusive license to build for the Illinois market at $5 a machine royalty.[91] Soon, George Esterly & Son, Hoover, Gamble & Allen of Miamisburg, Ohio, and the Minneapolis Harvester Works, were also his licensees.[92] Be-

[88] The Milwaukee Harvester Co. was said to have greatly improved the original heavy Appleby binder and to have eliminated 91 pieces. In fact it claimed to have made the first successful one in 1875 for the 1876 harvest. In 1902 it was one of the five firms that merged to form the International Harvester Co. *McCormicks vs. Aultman, Defendants' Record,* p. 236, testimony of J. F. Appleby.

[89] *Ibid.,* p. 238.

[90] C. Colahan, Beloit, Wis., to C. H. McCormick, Dec. 1, 1877.

[91] Deering Harvester Co. Pamphlet, 1898, "Forty Harvest Seasons, 1858-1898." The Appleby-Deering contract was made Nov. 29, 1878, but a preliminary arrangement was agreed upon earlier in the year. Its first Appleby binders took the field in 1879. There were seventy-five in all.

[92] *McCormicks vs. Aultman, Defendants' Record,* pp. 254-255. The Hoover Co., making "Excelsior" machines, took license in 1878, Esterly in 1879 and the Minneapolis Harv. Works in early 1880. *Minn. Harv. Works vs. McC. Harv. Mach. Co.,* p. 198. From the time Appleby came to work for the Minneapolis Harvester Works in Feb., 1880, it had exclusive right to all his new inventions. This was supposed to give it a big advantage over the other Appleby licensees. Esterly & Son made about thirty Applebys for 1880.

tween four and five thousand Appleby machines were sold in the harvest of 1880, although it was generally admitted that they did not give as good service as those binding with wire.[93]

The McCormick Company did not lead in this development, and its delay in entering the race was due in large measure to the lack of harmony between the partners. Leander and his son Robert Hall hesitated to prepare for the shift from wire to twine.[94] As early as 1877, the senior partner and his wife realized that the hue and cry raised against the wire-binder spelled its ultimate doom, a view confirmed late in the same year by Colahan's warning that it was high time to be up and doing.[95] But the two brothers could not reach an agreement upon any policy, and the long absence of Mr. and Mrs. Cyrus McCormick in Europe after July, 1878, caused further delay. Due, however, to their repeated and urgent letters from Paris, the officials of the company who attended a meeting at the works in late December decided to purchase twine-binder patents.

Six months later Cyrus McCormick, Jr., finished his course at Princeton College.[96] Even in 1875, when only sixteen years

[93] On each of these, Appleby received a royalty fee of $5. Probably less than two hundred had been sold in 1878. The 1880 harvest was the first in which twine-binders were quite extensively used, and in that season W. A. Wood found purchasers for about 4600 of his own manufacture. D. M. Osborne & Co. began making Appleby binders in 1882. During the same season C. Aultman & Co. sold about 6500. #C. Colahan to C. H. McCormick, Aug. 26 and Sept. 25, 1880; W. R. Baker to the McCormick Co., Sept. 11, 1880; *Minn. Harv. Works vs. McC. Harv. Mach. Co.*, pp. 73, 130, 139; *McCs. vs. Aultman, Defendants' Record*, p. 448.

[94] C. Colahan to C. H. McCormick, Nov. 29, Dec. 4, 19, and 28, 1878; Feb. #4, 8, 9, and 10, 1879.

[95] *Idem* to *idem*, Dec. 8, 1877; Oct. 4, Nov. 18 and Dec. 28, 1878; April 12, 1879. L.P.C.B. No. 170, p. 776, the Co. to M. A. Keller, Littlestown, Pa., Mch. 5, 1877; C. H. McCormick, Aix la Chapelle, to F. H. Matthews, Aug. 23, 1878: "I don't think we need fear anything from twine binding for another year to come, at least, although it has been tried over here and the knot found to be fast."

[96] *McCs. vs. Aultman, Defendants' Record*, p. 542. According to C. H. McCormick, Jr.'s testimony here, he entered the business as Asst. to the

of age, he had occasionally written business letters dictated by his father, and in 1877 and 1878 he accompanied the wire-binder in Europe.[97] Reapers and mowers were subjects of daily discussion in his home and held a deep interest for him. He followed his own preference when he entered his father's business. The twine-binder question was the first study of his career.[98]

Under his leadership, the company made up for lost time before the close of 1880. In January of the preceding year, Colahan complained to Cyrus McCormick that the firm had spent "less than $500 on cord binder patents."[99] Although this was true, it left a somewhat wrong impression. Several of the monopolies controlled by the company, covering the reciprocating feature of the wire-binder, were equally applicable to a twine machine. Thus also, the firm had bought in 1877 a one-half interest in the valuable George H. Spaulding (Rockford) patent of May 31, 1870, on a device automatically to size the gavels bound by either twine or wire.[100] But

President in the autumn of 1879. He had attended the meeting at the works on Dec. 30, 1878, referred to in the text. C. Colahan to C. H. McCormick, Dec. 30, 1878: "I am very happy to inform you that your letter and cable enabled me to overcome the opposition . . . and shall proceed at once, to establish your manufactory in a Cord Binder."

[97] C. H. McCormick, Jr., for C. H. McCormick, to the Co., Aug. 3, 1875.

[98] *Minn. Harv. Works vs. McC. Harv. Mach. Co.*, pp. 191, 230, the testimony of C. H. McCormick, Jr.; letters to C. H. McCormick, from #F. H. Matthews, Feb. 12, 1879, #W. J. Hanna, Aug. 24, 1880, C. Colahan, Aug. 24, 1880 and Sept. 21, 1881. L.P.C.B. No. 193, p. 102, the Co. to E. C. Beardsley, Minneapolis, Aug. 26, 1879; they were then anxious to examine a St. Paul string-binder and a Travis string-binder. L.P.C.B. No. 186, pp. 488, 497, the Co. to S. L. Beardsley, Kalamazoo, Mich., Dec. 19, 1878.

[99] C. Colahan to C. H. McCormick, Jan. 26, 1879.

[100] Letters to C. H. McCormick from F. H. Matthews, Sept. 29, 1876, #C. Colahan, July 25, 1881, and #C. H. McCormick, Jr., July 21, 1881. L.P.C.B. #171, p. 432, the Co. to Baldwin, Hopkins & Peyton, Apr. 9, 1877. G. H. Spaulding, Rockford, Ill., to the Co., July 13, 1875, May 23 and Oct. 30, 1877. He said he had tried his new harvester and it worked splendidly. Apparently, the McCormicks did not pay more than $2500 for their ½ interest in this patent. See, testimony of C. H. McCormick, Jr., in *McCs.*

purchasing began in earnest in 1879, and soon thereafter even the critical Colahan admitted that his employer was as amply fortified with cord-binder patents as any other manufacturer. Among these, apparently the most value was the one covering the improved compressor, cord-holder, and knotter of Charles Jewell of Monmouth, Illinois.[101] Not every patent sought was obtained, and of this number the McCormicks probably most regretted that Walter A. Wood "outsmarted" them in 1879 and secured the twine-binder invention of Hector A. Holmes and his son of Owatonna, Minnesota.[102]

While this eager search was in progress, Charles B. Withington, Ole O. Storle, and E. W. Jenkins were each building a twine-binder in the McCormick shops, and the factory office was endeavoring to determine what type of cord would give

vs. Aultman, Defendants' Record, p. 553. Spaulding entered Deering's employ in Apr., 1882, and worked for him five years.

[101] C. Colahan to C. H. McCormick, ‡Aug. 26, 1880, and Jan. 19, 1881: "My preparation of your cord binder interests has been worth $50,000 to you. I make you more money than all your lawyers and inventors. I paid $1280 for the Jewell patent." The "interference" between Jewell's and Appleby's swinging cord-holder (so as to give and take up the slack of the cord, and thus prevent breakage) was filed by the McCormicks on Apr. 23, 1880. Because Jewell was dead, the McCormicks lost their best witness. The decision went against Jewell's claim. The McCormicks' appeal was also lost on the ground that Jewell's device had broken in the harvest of 1879 and hence had not been "reduced to practice" before Appleby's. United States Patent Office. John F. Appleby, Assignor to the Minneapolis Harvester Works, vs. Charles Jewell, Assignor to the McCormick Harvesting Machine Company. Interference. Brief in Behalf of Jewell and Assignee. Parkinson & Parkinson for Jewell's Assignees. (Cincinnati, n.d.), pp. 1-30. United States Patent Office. John F. Appleby, Assignor to the Minneapolis Harvester Works, vs. Charles Jewell, Assignor to the McCormick Harvesting Machine Co. Interference. Brief in Behalf of Jewell's Assignee, Appellant. Parkinson & Parkinson, Counsel for Appellant. (No place or date of pub. shown.)

[102] The Hector A. and Watson M. Holmes' patent was dated Dec. 3, 1878. McCs. vs. Aultman, Defendants' Record, p. 55. Of approximately 50,000 binder sales in 1885, 5/6ths were of the Appleby type (including McCormicks') and the rest were the Holmes, made solely by Walter A. Wood. The Holmes differed only in details from Appleby's.

the best service. In the spring of 1880, as soon as the green grain in Texas was tall enough, these experimental machines were sent there accompanied by expert mechanics.[103] They were worked gradually northward until the last wheat was cut in Canada. Cyrus McCormick, Jr., followed them through the grain in the Red River Valley of the North, recording their virtues and faults in his note-book, and writing long reports almost daily to his father and to the Chicago office. Twine of varying ply and materials was thoroughly tested and an effort was made to give each implement a severe trial in tangled and down grain.[104]

Harvest on the "bonanza" farms about Fargo resolved itself into an open-air convention of inventors and manufacturers. Here on August 13th, Cyrus McCormick, Jr., first met Appleby, who said that he was bound by a "five year contract with the Minneapolis Co. but . . . perhaps he could arrange to put his "Knot tyer" on our present Binder." [105] McCormick was the more willing to negotiate with Appleby because the Storle, Withington, and Jenkins' machines were not measuring up to standard, and the Chicago firm was in a quandary to decide what was best to do for the following year. Its agents were clamoring for a twine-binder, and painting doleful word-pictures of the situation if the McCormicks continued to rely upon wire in 1881. Of the three experimental machines, the "Storle" was doing the best work, and yet if several thousands of these were manufactured, and the company later

103 L.P.C.B. No. 200, p. 505, telegram of the Co. to D. B. Heller, Dallas, Tex., Apr. 13, 1880, and No. 202, pp. 220, 541, the Co. to C. B. Withington, Dallas, Tex., May 28, 1880, and to R. Newton, June 7, 1880. C. H. Mc-Cormick, Jr., to C. H. McCormick, Aug. 18 and 26, 1880.

104 C. H. McCormick, Jr., Centralia, Ill., to C. H. McCormick, June 16 and July 28, 1880.

105 Letters to C. H. McCormick from C. H. McCormick, Jr., July 31 and Aug. 13, 1880; ‡C. Colahan, July 29, and Aug. 26, 1880. Minn. Harv. Works vs. McC. Harv. Mach. Co., pp. 16, 107, 110.

found a binder that they liked better, they would be saddled for years to come with the necessity of keeping "Storle" repairs and "extras" on hand.[106]

In late September, Appleby and Bishop came to the Chicago Exposition and resumed with the McCormicks the conversation begun at Fargo.[107] Although Appleby's customary fee was $5.00 a machine, he was willing to license the Chicago firm at $3.75. While Colahan at this time was visiting the fair at St. Louis, he saw a Gorham twine-binder manufactured by Thompson of Rockford.[108] He was at once struck by its resemblance to Appleby's. Because Gorham's machine was simpler in construction, Colahan believed that it would be cheaper to build and less likely to get out of order. Following his advice, the McCormicks in early November took a license under the several Gorham patents at $2.50 a machine.[109] Four days earlier they closed with Appleby at $3.50, and since this inventor admitted that there were grounds for Gorham's claims of priority, the McCormicks were allowed to reserve two-thirds of the royalties due, until the courts should reach

[106] L.P.C.B. No. 204, the Co. to C. H. McCormick, Jr., Aug. 2, 1880. C. H. McCormick, Jr., to the Co., Aug. 9, 10, 12, 1880. The Co. to C. H. McCormick, ‡July 28, 31, Aug. 1, Sept. 7, 9, 13, and 15, 1880, and to C. H. McCormick, Jr., Aug. 9, 16, 18, and ‡Sept. 11, 1880.

[107] *Minn. Harv. Works vs. McC. Harv. Mach. Co.*, pp. 141, 237. ‡C. Colahan to C. H. McCormick, Sept. 20, 21, 24, 25, 28, and 29, 1880. ‡C. A. Spring, Jr., to C. H. McCormick, Jr., Sept. 20 and 25, 1880, and to C. H. McCormick, Sept. 27 and 30, 1880. C. H. McCormick, Jr., MSS. Book "B," Nettie F. McCormick to C. H. McCormick, Jr., Oct. 22, 1880.

[108] N. C. Thompson & Co. started business in 1859, making Manny machines. ‡C. Colahan in a letter to C. H. McCormick, on Nov. 5, 1880, described Thompson as "a shrewd, experienced business man, formerly a Banker in Georgia, & a capitalist." ‡Colahan's telegram and letter to C. H. McCormick, Oct. 7, 1880, and to C. H. McCormick, Jr., Oct. 9, 1880.

[109] ‡C. Colahan to C. H. McCormick, Oct. 27 and Nov. 13, 1880. ‡C. H. McCormick, Jr.'s telegram to C. H. McCormick, Oct. 28, 1880 and ‡letter of Oct. 29, 1880. ‡The Co. to C. H. McCormick, Nov. 2, 11, 13, 1880. L.P.C.B. No. 207, p. 575, the Co.'s telegram to N. C. Thompson, Nov. 13, 1880. ‡C. H. McCormick, Jr., to C. A. Spring, Jr., Nov. 16, 1880.

a final decision as to the validity of his patents.[110] Certainly there was reason for Appleby's caution, in view of the fact that in 1879 the Patent Office had declared that his automatic sizing device was anticipated by Gorham.[111] Fifteen years later Judge Taft of the United States Circuit Court of Appeals delivered an opinion in which he said: "The Gorham binder was . . . the first one in the history of the art which successfully bound grain in the field with twine automatically. . . . In it is the modern twine binder, modified only by the mechanical and economical skill of the manufacturer and the tributary inventive faculty of a mere improver [Appleby]. . . . These circumstances [i.e. Appleby's visit to Gorham in 1874] tend strongly to show that Appleby took Gorham's idea as developed in his patented and operative machine. . . . Part for part, element for element, function for function, the Appleby machine parallels that of Gorham." [112] If weight should be given to court decisions, Gorham deserves more credit than Appleby for the invention of a practical twine-binder.

[110] *Circuit Court of the United States in and for the Northern District of Ohio, Eastern Division. McCormick Harvesting Machine Co. vs. C. Aultman & Co. In Equity, No. 4484 and vs. Aultman, Miller & Co. In Equity, No. 4485. Complainant's Paper Exhibits*, pp. 80-81. This gives the McCormicks-Appleby contract of Nov. 3, 1880 (accepted Nov. 9). "The peculiar feature of invention in controversy [with Gorham] relates particularly to the automatic feeding device in connection with the automatic trip in sizing or regulating the dimensions of the bundle by said Appleby." *Minn. Harv. Works vs. McC. Harv. Mach. Co.*, pp. 16 ff., 112, 114, 120, 239-241, testimony of C. H. McCormick, Jr. The only right which Appleby thought he perhaps could not convey, was the tripping mechanism, seemingly covered by earlier Gorham patents. Letters to C. H. McCormick from ‡C. Colahan, Nov. 5, 1880, ‡C. A. Spring, Jr., Nov. 6, 7, 9, and 10, 1880 and a ‡telegram from C. H. McCormick, Jr., Nov. 3, 1880. Telegram of C. H. McCormick to C. H. McCormick, Jr., Nov. 3, 1880. L.P.C.B. No. 207, p. 460, the Co. to J. F. Appleby, Minneapolis, Nov. 9, 1880. C. H. McCormick to C. A. Spring, Jr., Nov. 8, 12, 15, 1880.

[111] *McCs. vs. Aultman, Complainant's Paper Exhibits*, p. 155. ‡C. Colahan to C. H. McCormick, Nov. 12, 1880.

[112] *McCs. vs. Aultman, Defendant's Record*, p. 374. *McCs. vs. C. Aultman & Co. et al. Decision*, pp. 16-17, 19. *Scientific American*, June 5, 1915, p. 514.

Dr. Bishop now began his three years of service with the McCormicks in order to give them the benefit of his experience in the making of Appleby binders.[113] But the more they studied the Gorham patents, the more convinced they were that these grants could be used to compel every twine-binder firm to pay a royalty.[114] The McCormicks were in a position to bargain because, as has already been indicated, they then owned some of the most valuable patents in the country. Surely Thompson of Rockford would be happy to unite with the big Chicago firm for the purpose of forcing every other manufacturer to come to terms.[115] William N. Whiteley's effort at this time to induce the Gorham heirs to grant him a license was the only serious obstacle to be overcome before an agreement could be reached.[116] In late October, 1881, Thompson and the Gorham heirs, represented by their attorney William Lathrop, sold the McCormicks a shop right, under their patents, for $15,000. These monopolies, together with the Pascal and Newel Whitney (Osage, Ia.) patent of Oct. 6, 1874, the Greenhut patent, and the fifty per cent interest in the Spaulding patent, owned by the McCormicks, were pooled.[117] It was agreed that licenses should be granted to

[113] Bishop was employed in the first instance chiefly because Appleby was unable to furnish the McCormicks with a perfect set of patterns. See, *Minn. Harv. Works vs. McC. Harv. Mach. Co.*, p. 242. C. H. McCormick's telegram to C. A. Spring, Jr., Nov. 17, 1880. L.P.C.B. No. 242, p. 322, the Co. to E. D. Bishop, May 10, 1884; #E. K. Butler to C. H. McCormick, Jr., Oct. 8, 1883; Letters to C. H. McCormick from #C. Colahan, Nov. 11, 1880, C. A. Spring, Jr., Oct. 8, and from the Co., Nov. 15, 1880. #J. F. Appleby to the Co., Nov. 12, 1880. #C. A. Spring, Jr., to C. H. McCormick, Jr., Nov. 26, 1881.

[114] #C. Colahan, to C. H. McCormick, Nov. 11, 1880.

[115] #C. Colahan to N. C. Thompson, Nov. 11, 1880.

[116] #C. Colahan to C. H. McCormick, Nov. 9, 1880, and Oct. 25, 1881. #N. C. Thompson to C. Colahan, Oct. 20, 1881.

[117] The J. B. Greenhut (Peoria) binder patent of Sept. 8, 1868, extended in 1881, covered a vibrating arm, elastic compressor, and cord knotter. #J. B. Greenhut, Peoria, to the Co., Sept. 13, 1880: "You only gave me $300 when I sold my patent to Colahan and I want more before I aid you to secure its reissue." As a matter of fact, the price paid Greenhut in Oct.

other manufacturers of twine-binders at not more than $10 royalty a machine. Those who refused to pay should be sued for infringement. Each of the three parties was to share equally in the proceeds of the pool. The Gorham heirs, however, were to have preferential treatment, since the first $100,000 in profits should be entirely given to them, and only thereafter should Thompson and the McCormicks divide the further returns between themselves equally until they, too, had $100,000.

The pool at once pressed its demands energetically upon every concern making twine-binders in the country. Its emissary was most often Charles Colahan, who now received part of his yearly salary from the associates.[118] There was need to collect quickly, for the progress of invention was so rapid that within a few years at most, manufacturers would perfect devices whereby they could avoid infringing any of the patents in the pool. For this reason it seemed advisable to demand so moderate a sum as a royalty or for a shop right that any company would probably choose to pay it rather than submit to the expensive hazard of an almost interminable lawsuit.[119]

The fact that Osborne owned a half-interest in the Spaulding patent was a source of embarrassment to the members of the pool, and particularly to the McCormicks.[120] Their right

1880 was $350. See, #C. A. Spring, Jr., to C. H. McCormick, Jr., Oct. 7, 1880. #C. H. McCormick, Jr., to C. H. McCormick, Oct. 24, 1881. The Whitney patent on a cord holder also had been purchased for $350. See, #C. Colahan to C. H. McCormick, Nov. 1, 1880. W. R. Baker to C. Colahan, Mch. 13, 1882. "Chicago Times," Mch. 24, 1882.

[118] After May, 1882, ⅓ of Colahan's salary of $4,000 a year was paid by the McCormick Harv. Mach. Co. and ⅔ by the pool. This arrangement continued until his release on Feb. 9, 1884. Thereafter he worked against the McCormicks.

[119] #C. H. McCormick, Jr., to C. H. McCormick, Aug. 25, 1882.

[120] Osborne, however, was handicapped by the fact that he had not taken a license under the Appleby patents, and he feared a suit by their owners. He apparently relied for protection upon the primitive patent of Allen Sherwood of Auburn, N. Y. However, in 1883, Osborne bought a shop

to demand a moiety of the profits was based partly upon their share in this patent, although a valid license under it could probably not be granted without Osborne's consent. If Osborne should sell his half or issue licenses under it to other manufacturers, the purpose of the pool would be partly thwarted. Osborne realized his strategic position, and was the more ready to worry the McCormicks since he was suing them at this time for infringing the Gordon wire-binder patents. He demanded the right to enter the pool on equal terms with the other members. When this was refused he threatened to sell his interest in the Spaulding patent to Wood, Deering, or Whiteley.[121]

By the close of 1881, it was evident that the big manufacturers would not tamely pay upon demand. Appleby was defiant.[122] Eighteen makers of twine-binders were his licensees, right from the Appleby's. By that time he had been making twine-binders for three years.

[121] For some time, Osborne had wished to pool patents with the McCormicks. See, C. Colahan to C. H. McCormick, ‡Oct. 7, 1880; ‡June 28, Dec. ‡16, ‡19, ‡20, 28, 1881; July 22, 1882. D. M. Osborne to the Co., Sept. 17, 1881, to N. C. Thompson, Nov. 21, 1881, to C. H. McCormick, ‡Dec. 24, 1881; N. C. Thompson to D. M. Osborne, Nov. 23, 1881; ‡C. H. McCormick, Jr., to C. Colahan, Dec. 2, 1881, and to C. H. McCormick, Dec. 14 and 17, 1881; Telegrams of C. H. McCormick, Jr., to C. H. McCormick, Dec. 14, 15, and 16, 1881. See also, ftn. ‡100, supra.

[122] Apparently, the McCormick Co. paid Appleby $6,000 when the contract of 1880 was made. See, ‡C. H. McCormick, Jr., to C. A. Spring, Jr., Nov. 15, 1880. In Oct. 1881, Appleby asked McCormick to give $50,000 for a shop right. C. Colahan to C. H. McCormick, Oct. 13 and Nov. 10, 1881; and to C. H. McCormick, Jr., Nov. 10, and ‡Nov. 25, 1881. On May 30, 1882, this question was finally determined and Appleby was paid $35,000 cash for a shop right "in full for all dues and demands which have or may accrue under the license of Nov. 3, 1880, during the entire term for which said patents have been granted." McCs. vs. Aultman, Complainant's Paper Exhibits, p. 81. "St. Paul Pioneer Press," Feb. 24, 1882, article headed "There Will Be War, Sure." Circular Letter of J. F. Appleby, May 1, 1882, in which he refers to the "old worn out trick tried many times before." ‡C. H. McCormick, Jr., to C. H. McCormick, May 31, 1882. L.P.C.B. No. 223, pp. 349-352, the Co. to R. Newton, Louisville, Ky., May 1, 1882.

and if his patents were not ample to protect them, they would in all likelihood fall back upon him for reimbursement. When asked by a reporter whether he feared the outcome of a suit for infringement of the Gorham patents, he was alleged to have replied: "Not a particle in the courts of earth, and I feel even more secure if it is ever appealed to the Court of Heaven." [123]

This was partly bluff, no doubt, but he knew that his licensees, including some of the largest firms in the land, would not give up without a fight. Only tall, lean, William N. Whiteley, in his cap and farmer's boots, was ready to surrender and buy a shop right from the pool for his huge "Champion" Works in Ohio. He signed notes for $75,000 in May, but quickly regretted that he had yielded when he heard the rising storm of protest against the "Ring." [124] By October he was in the forefront of the opposition and announced that he would not honor his pledge because he had been misled into the belief that the pool patents were valid.[125]

When the McCormick-Gorham associates found that they

[123] "St. Paul Pioneer Press," Feb. 25, 1882. "Minneapolis Tribune," Mch. 25, 1882. Both papers call the pool's course "a game of bluff." W. Lathrop to C. H. McCormick, May 29, 1882. Circular Letter of Minneapolis Harvester Works, Mch. 31, 1882, to "Our Agents and Customers." ‡Circular of Hoover & Co., Reaper, Mower, and Binder Works at Miamisburg, O., Apr. 10, 1882: "Campaign canards that really do not merit any notice from us."

[124] On Oct. 12, 1881, Appleby, Bishop, and Parker & Stone sold out all their interest in the Appleby patents to Whiteley, Fassler & Kelly. See, ‡McCormick Harv. Co. Circular to their Gen'l. Agents, Feb. 28, 1882; Baldwin, Hopkins & Peyton to the Co., June 13, 1882. G. Harding to C. H. McCormick, Apr. 29, 1882. "Elgin Advocate" (Elgin), June 10, 1882. W. Lathrop to C. H. McCormick, May 2, 8 and 29, 1882, and to W. N. Whiteley, May 26, 1882. ‡C. H. McCormick, Jr., to C. H. McCormick, May 23, 29, 1882.

[125] W. Lathrop to C. H. McCormick, Oct. 30 and Nov. 20, 1882. ‡C. H. McCormick, Jr., to C. H. McCormick, Nov. 2, 1882. H. M. Gorham to Whiteley, Fassler & Kelly, Nov. 20, 1882. G. Harding to C. H. McCormick, Jr., Dec. 14, 1882, and to C. H. McCormick, Jan. 20, 1883.

were to have no easy task in bringing their competitors to heel, they engaged the services of George Harding, one of the ablest patent lawyers of his day.[126] They followed his advice and avoided starting suit in Ohio or Michigan where the judges of the United States Circuit Court were believed to be unfriendly to complainants in patent infringement cases. Whiteley and the "Buckeye" folk thereby gained immunity for a time. On Harding's recommendation, the pool began action against Deering and the Minneapolis Harvester Company in the spring of 1882, and for good measure it also filed bills of complaint against Esterly and the St. Paul Harvester Works.[127]

Now that the pool evidently meant business, matters moved rapidly to a show-down. The Appleby licensees, under Deering's and Whiteley's leadership, held several conferences in Chicago in the early autmn of 1882 to determine upon a joint course of action.[128] Several expedients were tried. The most dangerous, and one which barely failed to bring down the pool with a crash, was an offer made to Mrs. Gorham of $100,000

[126] C. H. McCormick to C. H. McCormick, Jr., N. Y., Dec. 21, 1881. G. Harding to C. H. McCormick, Apr. 8, 1882.

[127] Circular Letter of Wm. Deering, Chicago, to his Agents and Customers, Apr. 10, 1882: "I should not consider the suit of sufficient importance to mention to you, only that it has been made the occasion by a well-known concern for a *Buncombe Advertising Dodge*. . . . Any machine that requires this class of advertising must be in sad need of substantial merits to commend it. . . . I was the first to put a successful twine binder in the field and I will not be scared out." J. G. Parkinson to C. Colahan, May 18, 1882. "Chicago Daily Tribune," June 6, 1882. W. Lathrop to C. Colahan, Jan. 8, 1882. G. Harding to C. H. McCormick, Mch. 3, and Apr. 8, 1882. L.P.C.B. No. 221, pp. 853-854, the Co. to A. E. Mayer, Columbus, O., Mch. 20, 1882, and No. 222, pp. 86-88, to Knapp, Burrell & Co., Portland, Ore., Mch. 24, 1882. These letters show that the McCormicks were seeking all possible advertising value from the suits.

[128] ‡C. H. McCormick, Jr., to C. H. McCormick, July 27 and Sept. 8, 1882. G. Esterly & Son to the Co., Sept. 7, 1882. ‡C. Colahan to C. H. McCormick, Oct. 9, 1882. Telegram of C. Colahan to C. H. McCormick, Jr., Oct. 5, 1882. W. Lathrop to C. Colahan, Sept. 28, and Oct. 12, 1882.

for all her rights in her husband's patents.[129] This good lady, without business experience and "tormented out of all peace of mind" by lawsuits brought in her name and by manufacturers invading the peace of her home to talk about matters she did not understand, was anxious to be rid of it all.[130] Cyrus McCormick, Jr., hurried to Rockford. With great difficulty, and $10,000, he persuaded her to remain loyal and to convey her husband's patents to William Lathrop. Thereby she was relieved of all annoyance, except to endorse for deposit the checks which soon flowed in as her share in the profits of the pool.[131]

Baffled in their effort to split the pool in this way, several of the larger manufacturers tried in late 1882 to unite and buy all of the patents which threatened their safety. The sum most often mentioned was $160,000, but the McCormick-Lathrop-Thompson League would not accept it.[132] Then Whiteley, who had recently purchased a large interest in the Appleby patents, and Osborne, with his share in the Spaulding and Gordon monopolies, tried in vain to gain admittance to the pool. The lure of profits in business outweighed any obligation to stand firm against a common enemy.[133] This was

[129] "Deering's Farm Journal," May, 1897, p. 3. *McCs. vs. Aultman, Defendants' Record,* pp. 51-52. The story as here told, ten or fifteen years after the event, varies somewhat from the account in the text based upon contemporary letters. *McCs. vs. Aultman, Complainant's Paper Exhibits,* pp. 46-48. W. Lathrop to C. H. McCormick, May 31, 1882. C. Colahan's telegram to C. H. McCormick, Jr., Nov. 13, 1882. ‡C. Colahan to C. H. McCormick, Oct. 18 and 27, 1882.

[130] W. Lathrop to C. H. McCormick, May 2, 1882, and to C. Colahan, Nov. 14, 1882.

[131] *McCs. vs. Aultman, Complainant's Paper Exhibits,* pp. 44-46, 58-63. W. Lathrop to C. H. McCormick, Jr., Nov. 1 and 18, 1882. ‡C. H. McCormick, Jr., to C. H. McCormick, Nov. 2, 1882.

[132] W. Lathrop to C. H. McCormick, Jr., Jan. 18 and 19, 1883. N. C. Thompson to C. H. McCormick, Jr., Jan. 24, 1883.

[133] W. Lathrop to C. H. McCormick, Jr., Mch. 6 and 20, 1883, and D. M. Osborne to him on Oct. 22, 1883. ‡C. H. McCormick, Jr., to C. H.

in May, 1883, when the little makers of Appleby binders had already for some months past been aware that their bigger brothers were not interested in their welfare. Thus, in the preceding autumn, Hoover & Company and the Marsh brothers passed under the yoke of the pool, each buying a shop right for about $15,000.[134]

William Deering capitulated in May, 1883, and paid $26,000.[135] His surrender was good evidence that the fight was lost, and by the close of the year a dozen other firms had made their submission for sums ranging between $5,000 and $15,000.[136] Mrs. Gorham's $100,000 had been paid and Thompson and McCormick were receiving their first dividends from the pool. Before 1884 ended, however, Thompson was bankrupt and about a year later he sold all of his patents and interests in the pool to the McCormicks.[137]

McCormick, Apr. 7, 19 and 26, 1883, and #C. Colahan to him, Apr. 17, 26 and 30, 1883.

[134] W. Lathrop to C. Colahan, Oct. 19, 1882. #C. Colahan to C. H. McCormick, Oct. 27, 1882, and #C. H. McCormick, Jr., to him, Oct. 26 and 28, 1882. W. Lathrop's telegram to C. Colahan, Nov. 14, 1882. L.P.C.B. No. 227, p. 795, the Co. to C. H. McCormick, Jr., Sept. 27, 1882, and No. 228, pp. 61-62, E. K. Butler to him, Oct. 4, 1882.

[135] C. Colahan to C. H. McCormick, July 22, 1882. W. Lathrop to C. Colahan, Sept. 26, 1882, and Mch. 14, 1883. #C. H. McCormick, Jr., to C. H. McCormick, May 5 and 11, 1883. W. Lathrop to C. H. McCormick, Jr., May 14, 1883.

[136] #C. H. McCormick, Jr., to C. H. McCormick, May 9 and 12, 1883. *McCs. vs. Aultman, Defendants' Record,* pp. 539-540. Gibbs & Sterrett, Corry, Pa., $5 license; Van Brunt & Son, Horicon, Wis., $5 license; Sandwich Mfg. Co., $12,000; Whiteley, Fassler & Kelly, $42,500; Esterly & Son, $15,000; Deering & Co., $26,000; Plano Mfg. Co., $14,500; Johnston Harvester Co., $5,000; Dorsey Mfg. Co., $7,250; Dennett Harv. Mach. Co., $13,000; Minneapolis Harv. Works, $15,000; St. Paul Harvester Works, $6,000; D. S. Morgan & Co., $5,000 (or $25,000?); J. F. Seiberling, $8,600; Winona Harv. Works, $9,000. "Chicago Times," July 28, 1883.

[137] *McCs. vs. Aultman, Defendants' Record,* pp. 558-559, C. H. McCormick, Jr., testified that Mrs. Gorham received a total of $105,000 from the pool, and N. C. Thompson about $60,000 or $65,000. W. Lathrop to C. H. McCormick, Jr., Oct. 10, Nov. 5, 7, 23, Dec. 15, 1883, and Sept. 13,

These agreements with Deering and the others were made the more promptly because the pool reduced its initial demands. Their resolve to do so was most probably hastened by a letter of Nettie F. McCormick to her eldest son. Her advice on this occasion well illustrates her good business sense and the close attention with which she followed the work of the Harvester Company: "Lack of promptness in moving," she wrote, "or lack of *deciding* while the iron is hot may lose us the expected profits of the pool. Dragging along loses everything in such a business where the best chance of bringing the parties to terms is while they are under the impression of their peril in not coming to terms. . . . Delay is loss. Strike while the iron is hot. And in the pool cases make more moderate demands than we have made but *settle quick*. That is the secret. Settle while they are in the mood for settling." [138]

By January, 1884, Whiteley, Aultman, Wood, and Osborne were the only four manufacturers of note who stubbornly refused to do homage. Whiteley acknowledged the error of his ways in February and paid $42,500.[139] Costly lawsuits were

1884. Up to Sept., 1884, Thompson had received $25,800 from the pool and the McCormicks $45,281.25. Both Lathrop and Thompson conveyed their rights in the pool to the McCormicks on Sept. 14, 1885.

[138] C. H. McCormick, Jr., MSS., Nettie F. McCormick to C. H. McCormick, Jr., Mch. 21, 1883. See also, her letter of Apr. 11, 1883, to E. K. Butler urging (ordering) him to interest himself in the pool. The aged Cyrus McCormick largely left the management of pool matters to his son.

[139] W. Lathrop to C. H. McCormick, Jr., Dec. 5, 1883, and Feb. 4, 1884. Whiteley, Fassler & Kelly's telegram to C. H. McCormick, Jr., Mch. 6, 1884. C. H. McCormick, Jr., to P. Arnold, Oct. 13, 1883. "Implement Age," Apr. 1, 1898; W. Lathrop to C. Aultman & Co., Canton, O., Aug. 19, 1885; C. H. McCormick, Jr., to R. H. Parkinson, Cin., O., Aug. 13, 1885, and to W. Lathrop, Aug. 17, 1885. Circular of D. M. Osborne & Co., Apr. 24, 1882: We are not liable to the Gorham Pool since we don't make Appleby binders. *Supra,* ftn. 120, ‡C. H. McCormick, Jr., to C. H. McCormick, Nov. 26, 1883; W. Lathrop to the Co., Mch. 8, 1884; D. M. Osborne to C. H. McCormick, Jr., Feb. 14 and 25, 1885; to W. Lathrop, June 17, and Aug. 13, 1885, and to C. H. McCormick, Jr., Dec. 17 and 31, 1885. Circular Letter to Agents of Walter A. Wood & Co., Mch. 31, 1882.

necessary in order to coerce the others and before they were ended, the elder McCormick had passed from the scene. Osborne settled for $22,500 on March 18, 1886, Walter A. Wood four months later for $10,000, and Aultman in 1898 for about $23,000. The McCormick Company's total profit from its participation in the pool appears to have been about $75,000.

The winners and losers in this thirty-year patent war be-ᐟ tween makers of harvesting machinery are difficult to distinguish. Certainly the little builders were merely pawns in the struggle. The "giants" in the business had, with hardly an exception, opened their factories during the decade before the Civil War, and save for Deering, no small manufacturer of 1870 was of much greater consequence by 1885.[140] The ten or a dozen producers who controlled the rather small annual supply of reapers and mowers in 1860, were equally masters of an output ten times as large twenty-five years later.

These few outstanding manufacturers often talked of price-fixing agreements, but apparently no suggestion to unite into one great trust was ever made.[141] The International Harvester

It is interesting to note that on Aug. 25, 1882, C. H. McCormick, Jr., wrote his father that Wood had been asked $100,000 for a shop right under the pool patents. Wood told Colahan he would pay whatever Whiteley paid. ‡C. Colahan to C. H. McCormick, Aug 24, 1882; ‡C. H. McCormick, Jr., to C. H. McCormick, Sept. 14, 1883. W. Lathrop to C. H. McCormick, Jr., June 8, 1885; J. G. Parkinson to C. H. McCormick, Jr., Mch. 31, Nov. 11, and Dec. 19, 1885. Wood offered $5,000, W. A. Wood to the Co., June 10, 1885. "Federal Reporter," Vol. LVIII, pp. 773-784; LXIX, pp. 371-405; "U. S. Supreme Court Reports," Vol. CLXIX, pp. 606-612.

[140] Possibly William Anson Wood, a brother of Walter Wood, was an exception. At his Youngstown, O., factory between 1874 and 1881, William Wood claimed to have made 40,000 machines. See, a pamphlet entitled "The Farm Supply Industry of Chicago" (Chicago, 1882).

[141] The only merger of much significance during the period was in 1874, when the Cayuga Chief Manufacturing Co. of Auburn (Cyrenus Wheeler) consolidated with D. M. Osborne & Co. of the same city. "Farm Implement News," IX, part 2 (1888), p. 15. Rival companies occasionally co-

Company was still in the future. Each producer placed much stress upon his independence of action, and unrestrained competition was the order of the day. When, now and again, an autumn conference resulted in a mutual resolve not to sell below a certain price in the following harvest, simply one more pledge was made to be broken as soon as the new year came and the embattled agents began skirmishing among the farmers for their patronage.

Patent pools stand alone as examples of joint efforts extending over considerable periods of time and yielding a large monetary return to their members. These were coöperative, however, in only a limited sense. They did not align the manufacturers in solid front against the farmers or the suppliers of factory raw materials. Being effective weapons in a civil war and not against an outside foe, they excellently illustrate the bitterness of competition within a single industry. It is significant that in every instance they drew under one management patents relating only to a single type of machine. General patent pools were suggested but never formed.

Lawsuits, patents, and pools move together through the history of the industry between 1855 and 1885. If balances were struck between damages and royalties paid, and damages and royalties received by a big manufacturer during this period, whether the result were a profit or a loss, it would probably be quite small in amount. Invention was so active that an alert manufacturer, who had been forced to buy a license from a rival, could usually find an overlooked patent and strike back blow for blow. Hundreds of infringement suits were commenced but most of them were compromised at some stage of their slow course toward the Supreme Court. Patent lawyers were found more frequently around a conference table than in a court-room. The caprice of judges and

operated in purchasing binder-wire, e.g., Wood and the McCormicks in 1877. *Post,* p. 620.

Patent Office officials on matters relating to patents was notorious, and more equitable decisions could often be arrived at by negotiations between the litigants.

This presumes, however, that the resources of the manufacturers in conflict were about equal. The "little man," unable to engage expert attorneys, had small show against a giant who bullied him. Nor did he have the capital to purchase the key patents covering his output. He was, therefore, obliged to pay royalty to his big competitor and enter the selling field under a severe handicap. Because types of implements were changing so rapidly, he was periodically faced with the alternative of making expensive alterations in factory machinery or going out of business.[142] Unless he were exceptionally fortunate, his future and his present were one—to earn a modest living by supplying the locality in the immediate neighborhood of his plant. In this small circle, at least, he could undersell any competitor who was obliged to pay heavy freights.[143]

Although inventors were responsible for the great progress made in the method of harvesting grain, most of them were as obscure as the small factory-owners. Cyrus McCormick alone reached the summit both as an inventor and as a manufacturer,[144] but the inventive period of his life closed ten years before his plant was notable for its size. After 1855 almost all of the outstanding inventors were either not engaged in making machines for sale or were among the minor builders. The factory of the Marsh brothers was always small, and they

142 Ardrey, "The Harvesting Machine Industry," in "Scientific American," Supp., Dec. 20, 1902.

143 L.P.C.B. No. 238, p. 689, the Co. to A. W. Lukens, N. Y., Nov. 30, 1883. "I consider the outlook for *all small* Harvesting Machine Manufacturers as very risky, too many machines are being built, and the prices are sure to be cut so that no living profit will be left."

144 Cyrenus Wheeler and Samuel Johnston were also inventors, but their contributions were important rather than epoch-making.

were in serious financial straits by 1884. John F. Appleby, who was never a manufacturer, retired to Santa Cruz, California, before the decade of the 1880's was over.[145] Lewis F. Miller, of hinged-bar mower fame, was one of the "Buckeye" group in Ohio, but he was crowded out of the public eye by his partner Cornelius Aultman, the money master of the firm. The patentee and the owner of the patent were now rarely identical. In this generation, the possession of a patent was more often an evidence of a full purse than of an ingenious brain.

[145] In 1874 Appleby did organize the Appleby Reaper Works at Mazomanie, Wis., to make self-rakes, but it was short-lived. Appleby died in 1917.

CHAPTER XIV

GRASSHOPPERS, GRANGERS, AND THE GROWTH OF THE INDUSTRY 1873-1879

IN the summer of 1874 the office of the McCormick Company requested the agent at Kankakee, Illinois, to "capture some Chinch Bugs, put them in a small bottle of spirits and ship them to us by express so that we may have lifelike specimens of our worst competitors always with us."[1] Year after year these pests curtailed the sale of harvesting machinery in one district or another of the Old Northwest, Missouri, and Kansas, but the writer of the lines above would have done well to have reserved his superlative for the grasshoppers, or Rocky Mountain locusts, as they were sometimes called.[2]

These "winged devils" seldom ventured east of the Mississippi River, but they annually worked a more or less widespread devastation throughout the broad belt of country from

[1] L.P.C.B. No. 152, p. 671, the Co. to J. H. Shaffer, Kankakee, Ill., July 14, 1874.

[2] The chinch-bugs were particularly numerous in the harvests of 1874 and 1877. Letters to the Co. from F. G. Smyth, Madison, Wis., July 18, 1873, and Aug. 10, 1874; Frank Craycroft, Sedalia and Kansas City, Mo., June 26 and July 1, 1874: I have lost 200 sales because of chinch bugs, I. N. Van Hoesen, Lawrence, Kas., July 7 and Sept. 1, 1874: "I could have trebled the number of my sales, but for the chinch bugs"; J. H. Osborne, Mattoon, Ill., June 23, 1874: "A great many farmers have ploughed ditches and have been dragging logs in them to keep the [chinch] bugs out of their corn"; D. H. Smith, Sparta, Wis., June 26, 1876, May 30, June 6, 13, 27, 1877, May 7 and 22, 1878; W. Westerman, Dubuque, Ia., June 4 and 12, 1877. Tonney Bros. & Durland, Flora, Ill., to G. A. Willey, June 19, 1874: "Chinch bugs have ruined my fine prospects."

Texas north to Minnesota and the Dakotas, and as far west as the irrigated valleys of Colorado and Utah.[3] In the wake of their raids corn-fields resembled a stand of stark green poles, and the stalks of small grain, shorn of their heads, were left valueless except for fodder and bedding.[4]

The "hopper horror" was the more intense because the menace always threatened but often did not come.[5] In some years, as in 1867 and 1868, and between 1873 and 1876, the plague was particularly severe. But even in those harvests when the grain-fields of many tiers of counties were stripped bare, farmers living but a short distance away, tense with fear that their turn would come on the morrow, were left [6] immune. Day after day, while their wheat was in the milk, the grain-growers of western Iowa or southern Minnesota watched countless millions of grasshoppers in flight, making clouds "like an April snowstorm extending from 200 yards from the ground, *up as far as the eye can reach.*" [7] The

[3] Letters to the Co. of D. N. Barnhill, Jefferson, Texas, Apr. 5, Dec. 4 and 12, 1867, and Apr. 10, 1868; J. H. Robinson, Austin, Texas, Jan. 29, 1868; H. C. Addis, Omaha, May 12, 1875; J. L. Lowell & Co., Salt Lake City, Apr. 9, May 1 and Aug. 29, 1877; H. L. Lathrop, Omaha, Aug. 28, 1877.

[4] Letters to the Co. of H. C. Addis, Omaha, Neb., June 3, 1875, and W. N. Spring, Sioux City, Ia., July 31, 1876.

[5] L.P.C.B. No. 191, p. 9, the Co. to W. N. Spring, Le Mars, Ia., May 28, 1879.

[6] W. H. Sibley, Des Moines, Ia., to the Co., June 29, 1868: "Farmers are sitting up nights watching for the grasshoppers and grumbling because they don't come. Say anything about their buying a machine & they say 'grasshoppers.' I am tired & sick of hearing them grumble." J. F. Montgomery, Fairmont, Neb., Apr. 24, 1877: "The Hopper Wail broke out at Hastings on Saturday." L.P.C.B. No. 152, p. 673, the Co. to Hall & Brewster, Mankato, Minn., July 14, 1874. D. W. Pratt, Wisner, Neb., to the Co., May 27, 1875.

[7] W. N. Spring, Sioux City, Ia., to the Co., June 5, 1873, July 9, 1874, and Aug. 17, 1876. In the last letter, written from Le Mars, Ia., he said that grasshoppers were flying by in such numbers as to darken the sun and that their wings made a noise like a whirlwind. H. C. Addis, Lincoln, Neb., June 16 and 17, 1875: "Men all over the State wild with excitement

chances were good that this impending fate would not fall, sufficiently so, in fact, to encourage farmers year after year to plant their fields and trust that Providence would provide winds strong enough to keep the scourge from making its descent.[8] Little wonder that under these conditions agents wrote to the McCormicks of "delirious," "panic-stricken" homesteaders, with "grasshoppers on the brain." [9] It was enough to take "the sand right out of us all." [10]

Days in mid-week were set aside for fasting and prayer when "every business house was closed and every one went to church—even the saloons closed down." Men talked of the plagues of the Book of *Exodus* and wondered wherein they had sinned by breaking the soil of a new and otherwise fair country.[11] The grasshoppers, and probably the mosquito, were the only insects which delayed the advance of the agricultural frontier during the course of United States history. Some homesteaders gave up in despair and retraced their way east-

and anxiety, everything at a stand still. No man can tell what is best. In three or four days the whole story will be told."

[8] Letters to the Co. of G. B. Franklin, Jackson, Minn., Oct. 5 and 21, 1874; G. H. Brewster, Mankato, Minn., May 3, 1875, and B. H. Goulding, Kearney Junction, Neb., June 9, 1875. W. N. Spring, Yankton, to Co., Apr. 17, 1877: "Hoppers are hatching by the millions on the sunny side of the bluffs. Nothing but the interposition of Divine power can save this afflicted country."

[9] Letters to the Co. of W. F. Carr, White Cloud, Kas., Mch. 30, 1867, and W. N. Spring, Sioux City, Ia., June 24, 1874. L.P.C.B. No. 107, p. 210, the Co. to J. W. Van Hoesen, Manhattan, Kas., Aug. 12, 1868.

[10] S. Jones, Vermilion, D. T., to the Co., July 31, 1876.

[11] G. H. Brewster, Mankato, Minn., to the Co., Apr. 27, 1877: The day after the folk of Mankato prayed for Divine aid, the weather turned very cold, with snow, and killed all the 'hoppers that had hatched up to that time. E. P. Dorval, Caledonia, Minn., to the Co., May 8, 1877. J. B. Cooke, Carroll City, Ia., June 5, 1877: "Do you suppose that if some black Moses should rise up and undertake to cross the blacks into Canada through Lake Erie and Hayes should lead up his Southern Battalions and they should be swallowed up in the waves . . . that the grasshopper plague would end?"

ward.[12] Others with more courage, or perhaps because they had no better place to go, stayed to fight the pest.[13] Communities offered bounties of as much as twenty cents a quart for the insects, and a boy with a net could sometimes collect four or five bushels a day.[14] Straw, hay, or manure, mixed with sulphur, were burned, but it seemed that the smoke only stunned the sturdy beasts and they soon revived after the fires were out.[15] When a field lying fallow appeared to sway in the sun because of the teeming life which covered it, men sprayed it with kerosene or dragged over it a piece of sheet-iron covered with coal-tar. "Hopper-dozing" machines were invented, some consisting of a push-scoop backed by revolving rollers to crush the insects as they slid down between them.[16]

Nature also aided the farmer. Blackbirds, turkeys and prairie chickens grew fat.[17] From one neighborhood came the word that an army of toads was devouring the grasshoppers.

[12] Letters to the Co. of J. Edgar, Owatonna, Minn., June 5, 1874, and Feb. 20, 1875; G. Freudenreich, Alexandria, Minn., July 11, 1876 and June 4, 1877. L.P.C.B. No. 155, p. 596, the Co. to W. F. Callaway, Columbus, Neb., Feb. 5, 1875.

[13] G. H. Brewster, Mankato, Minn. to the Co., Mch. 31, 1877. To paraphrase: My noteholders are homesteaders. They lack titles to their lands and so have no taxes to pay. They have little choice but to stay where they are since they would lose their homes if they left, and would not be permitted to seat another steading. If they had received their titles four years ago, their holdings would be mortgaged and they would now be swamped. I am trying to get them to prove their titles so that they can give me a mortgage as security for the payment of their reaper notes. But most of them prefer not to have title to their land since they would then have to pay taxes on it. They tell me they wish to be free from taxes until the 'hoppers leave. Some, with the permission of the govt., have deserted their holdings to work elsewhere until the plague disappears. They will be back.

[14] G. H. Brewster, Mankato, Minn., to the Co., June 1 and 18, 1875.

[15] E. Hooper, Grand Island, Neb., to the Co., Aug. 8, 1875.

[16] Letters to the Co. of G. A. Freudenreich, Sauk Centre, Minn., May 22, 1877; A. Burlingame, Algona, Ia., June 3, 1877; G. H. Brewster, Mankato, Minn., May 25, 1877; J. J. Rhodes, Litchfield, Minn., May 29, 1877; J. B. Cooke, Carroll City, Ia., and W. N. Spring, Sioux City, Ia., June 5, 1877.

[17] W. N. Nichols, Beatrice, Neb., Apr. 28 and May 8, 1877.

There was general agreement that a "little red parasite" destroyed many eggs, and "a maggot" often killed the insects even while in flight.[18] A late warm autumn might hatch the eggs in the ground or so mature them that the winter's cold could be relied upon to do the rest.[19] A February thaw followed by a hard freeze and a cold, wet spring in 1877 was given the credit for the respite vouchsafed from the plague in that harvest and for several years thereafter.[20] Farmers suffered "an all winter nightmare" when they knew that their land harbored innumerable grasshopper eggs.[21] Even if the baby insects were killed by a belated cold snap in the spring there was always the danger that a migrating swarm would descend from the sky as soon as summer came. In fact a neighborhood usually feared a "foreign invasion" more than its own crop of grasshoppers because these often left when about six weeks old, or as soon as their wings were large enough to carry them aloft in a strong breeze.[22] The voracious appetites of the old fellows were most to be dreaded.

This "hoppersition" was ruinous to many homesteaders and exceedingly costly to all manufacturers of harvesting machinery. It frayed the nerves of farmers and agents, and led to the cancellation of orders for reapers and mowers, the refusal to

[18] Letters to the Co. of W. N. Spring, Sioux City, Ia., July 16, 1874, Aug. 28, 1876, June 27, and July 5, 1877; G. H. Brewster, Mankato, Minn., Aug. 19, 1876, and May 14, 1877.

[19] Letters to the Co., of H. Lepin, Hastings, Neb., Mch. 30, 1875 and W. N. Spring, Sioux City, Ia., Aug. 16, 1876.

[20] Letters to the Co. of J. Collins, Council Bluffs, Ia., Dec. 16, 1876; G. H. Brewster, Mankato, Minn., Mch. 31 and Apr. 27, 1877; J. F. Montgomery, Hastings, Neb., Apr. 29, 1877; F. Craycroft, Sedalia, Mo., May 25, 1877 and I. N. Van Hoesen, Lawrence, Kas., May 19, 1877.

[21] G. H. Brewster, Mankato, Minn., to the Co., Apr. 26, 1876.

[22] *Idem* to *idem,* Mch. 31, 1877. If grasshoppers destroyed the growing grain in the spring, farmers would plow it under and plant corn. Letters to the Co. of H. C. Addis, Omaha, June 9, 1875, and E. A. McNair, Dallas, Texas, Mch. 22 and May 3, 1877. L.P.C.B. No. 156, p. 862, the Co. to G. H. Brewster, Apr. 7, 1875.

deliver machines to those whose stripped fields were good evidence that they would have no money, and heavy losses because destitute farmers were unable to pay for implements purchased in earlier harvests.[23] Judging from the correspondence of the McCormick firm, the districts about Sioux City, Iowa, and Owatonna, Minnesota, suffered the most severely from these insects between 1868 and 1878.[24] The local newspaper minimized the effects of the scourge,[25] as did those of Chicago when a cholera epidemic swept through the city, but the letters of agents and farmers tell pitiable tales of hundreds of families seeking charity, with insufficient grain to make bread or seed their land for the next harvest. The McCormicks sent money for salesmen to distribute in small sums to the needy, and they perforce extended the time for the payment of reaper notes until a crop could be made.[26] "Not only farming but all branches of business hangs upon the legs of the grasshoppers," wrote the agent at Omaha in 1868.[27] This

[23] Letters to the Co. of W. H. Sibley, Des Moines, Ia., May 25 and June 3, 1868; Clark & Plummer, Plattsmouth, Neb., June 2, 1868; H. C. Addis, Omaha, Neb., May 27, 31, 1873, June 15 and 17, 1875; F. B. Taylor & Co., Frankfort, Kas., Aug. 4, 1874; W. N. Spring, Sioux City, Ia., July 16, 1874: "I must say I am getting somewhat disgusted with this country! No fault of the land etc *but* these cursed pests!!" E. Hooper, Grand Island, Neb., to the Co., Mch. 12, 1875: Because of the grasshoppers, our lawyers refuse to accept cases involving suits against farmers for debts. L.P.C.B. No. 159, p. 145, the Co. to W. D. Nichols, Beatrice, Neb., June 19, 1875. Some farmers doubtless used grasshoppers as a pretext for not paying their bills.

[24] G. H. Brewster, Windom, Minn., to the Co., Mch. 27, 1877: "Everyone of the counties in my territory has been 'grasshoppered' for four years."

[25] Letters to the Co. of H. R. Gould, Omaha, Aug. 18, 1876, and W. N. Spring, Sioux City, Ia., June 22, 1877. ‡C. A. Spring, Jr., to C. H. McCormick, Oct. 10, 1866.

[26] Letters to the Co. of J. Edgar, Owatonna, Minn., June 5, and Sept. 29, 1874; C. S. Burch, Alexis, Neb., Aug. 6, 1874; W. Van Eps, Sioux Falls, Mch. 1, 16, and May 24, 1875. L.P.C.B. No. 156, p. 248, the Co. to W. Van Eps, Sioux Falls, D. Terr., Mch. 6, 1875.

[27] Letters to the Co. of H. C. Addis, Omaha, Neb., May 20, 1868; D. W. Pratt, Wisner, Neb., June 15, 1875, and Hawley & Burks, Lincoln, Neb., Aug. 26, and Sept. 4, 1876.

terse statement accurately summarizes the condition of many other communities along the 95th meridian during the dozen years immediately following the Civil War.[28]

Some discovered an element of humor in the situation, while others felt that the grasshoppers were a blessing in disguise. They invaded homes and places of business, made pavements slippery with their crushed bodies, and turned some women from long, wide skirts and bustles to overalls with each leg tied tightly at the bottom.[29] They were defended on the score that they made farmers thrifty, drove the weak-kneed from the land, encouraged the raising of stock and induced crop diversification.[30] To the McCormicks, however, the grasshoppers of the plains and the chinch-bugs of the prairies were unmitigated evils.

The ravages of these insects, as well as the other adverse circumstances mentioned in an earlier chapter, prompted the distressed farmers of the central West to organize for their own protection. The Noble Order of the Patrons of Husbandry, more often known as the Grange, came opportunely to furnish a convenient medium for the expression of their discontent.[31] "Acts of God" in the form of bad weather or armies of grasshoppers could not be fought effectively, but the rail-

[28] I. N. Van Hoesen, Lawrence, Kas., to the Co., May 17, 1875: "But you can mark down one thing. If we are ravaged by the Grass Hoppers this year, Kansas as a State, Kansas securities, Kansas merchants, Kansas farmers, and Kansas McCormick Reaper agents both general & sub are all everlastingly gone up & will be everlastingly insolvent."

[29] W. N. Spring to the Co., Aug. 9, 1876.

[30] Letters to the Co. of W. H. Sibley, Grove City, Ia., May 25, and Sept. 13, 1868; H. C. Addis, Grand Island, Neb., Mch. 17, 1875; G. H. Brewster, Mankato, Minn., Mch. 24, 1876; W. N. Spring, Sioux City, Ia., Apr. 29, 1876.

[31] Letters to the Co. of J. Rhodes, Hastings, Minn., Apr. 8, 1867, and D. W. Cobb, Lexington, Ky., June 1, 1868. During the period of acute agrarian discontent in the early 1870's, the Noble Order of the Patrons of Husbandry was not the only organization used by the farmers, but because the Grangers were the most widespread and aggressive, their name has been customarily used to designate the entire movement.

roads with their high freight and grain warehouse charges, and the manufacturers of agricultural implements who were believed to be rolling in wealth extorted from the farmers, were tangible foes who might be humbled.[32] Since, as a rule, only one railroad served the town to which a farmer brought his grain for shipment and since competing lines sometimes pooled their traffic and made mutual agreements about rates, they were in his eyes a capitalistic monopoly of the worst type. Agricultural machinery manufacturers were also engaged in bitter competition, but unlike the railroads they were unable to unite. To sell their output they often sharply lowered their prices at harvest-time. Although this practice worked to the advantage of the purchaser of a reaper, it also indicated to him how large a reduction could be made without doing away with a considerable profit on each sale.[33] This rivalry gave rise to many lawsuits, and the published testimony seemed to leave no doubt that C. H. McCormick & Bro. and other firms were paying fabulous dividends annually on their invested capital.[34] Railroads and reaper manufacturers were essential to the

[32] J. Edgar, Rochester, Minn., to the Co., Nov. 17, 1870: "The Railroad has been grading [grain] so sharply & driving off competition in such a manner, that farmers can get no proper price for their wheat, & are either holding or drawing [it] to any other points they can reach."

[33] L.P.C.B. No. 140, pp. 719-720, the Co. to J. Edgar, Rochester, Minn., Apr. 9, 1873: "We are sure that any marked reduction . . . would only confirm them [farmers] in their half drawn conclusions that all Reaper Makers were Extortionists and Monopolists of the worst type."

[34] For the inaccuracy of this belief, see *supra*, p. 475. Letters to the Co. of W. J. Hayes, Bloomington, Ill., May 24, 1873; F. Craycroft, Chillicothe, Mo., July 25, 1873; P. Mohan, St. Louis, Nov. 14, 1873. G. W. Russell, Woodstock, Ill., Jan. 15, 1874; A. S. Johnston, Three Rivers, Mich., Mch. 25, 1874; C. Hertel, Jr., Freeburgh, Ill., Apr. 6, 1874; T. E. Alderman & Son, Nevada, Ia., June 17, 1874, and M. J. Mead, Orleans, Ind., July 13, 1874. When the Grangers of Iowa began to make the Werner Harvester they sold it for $140, or for about $40 less than the McCormick Harvester. L.P.C.B. No. 144, pp. 340-341, the Co. to F. Craycroft, Chillicothe, Mo., July 28, 1873; No. 166, to Gove & Son, Linn., Mo., May 31, 1876.

grain-grower, and his fight to force both to do his will was an acknowledgment of his dependence upon them.

The McCormicks occupied a somewhat unique position in this contest. Because they were one of the largest makers of harvesting implements, and had been pioneers in the industry, many farmers thought only of them when reapers and mowers were mentioned, and erroneously believed that they dominated the field. Low prices of grain, extravagant freight charges, and all the ills deemed to flow from organized capital were epitomized by Chicago, because as a center of rail and lake transportation it had gradually drawn to itself most of the grain of the central West. There the hated stock-brokers and middlemen grew rich at the farmers' expense and there, too, was the McCormick factory. This firm charged more for its machines than its competitors and gave its agents lower commissions. It required its clients to pay all freight charges, and unlike several of its chief rivals, it declined to wholesale its output to its representatives.[35] Since the salesmen of other reaper and mower factories habitually concentrated their efforts against the McCormick machines, it was natural for them to unite in attempting to direct the wrath of the Grangers toward the Chicago partnership.[36]

The Grangers proposed to buy machinery in car-load lots at low cash prices direct from the manufacturers without the intermediation of agents.[37] In this way they would abolish the

[35] ‡W. J. Hanna to O. E. Rundell, Wykoff, Minn., Apr. 2, 1873. F. Craycroft, Chillicothe, Mo., to the Co., Apr. 24, 1873. G. A. Willey, Belleville, Ill., to the Co., Feb. 27, 1874.

[36] Letters to the Co. of E. W. Brooks, Red Wing, Minn., Apr. 1, 1873: "When they [Grangers] talk of monopolists they end by saying 'and especially the McCormick.'" J. Edgar, Storm Lake, Ia., June 13 and Aug. 16, 1873; P. Mohan, Mexico, Mo., July 22, 1873. L.P.C.B. No. 150, p. 454, the Co. to E. W. Brooks, Red Wing, Minn., May 26, 1874.

[37] Letters to the Co. of J. Edgar, Cedar Falls, Ia., June 18, 1872; N. Peirce, Riceville, Ia., Jan. 9, 1872; G. Monser, Wenona, Ill., Mch. 12, 1872; J. S. Denman, State Agt., P. of H., Southern Minn., Winona, Minn., June

"vicious credit system," save for themselves the cost of the salesmen's commissions, and give their favor exclusively to the one maker of a particular type of implement who most liberally conceded to their wishes. If machinery manufacturers declined to do without agents, Granger societies were ready to act in that capacity and charge nothing for their services. They would, to be sure, sell only to their own members, but this would induce all farmers to join their ranks and secure the benefits of coöperative buying.[38] They might also try coöperative manufacturing in order both to secure implements at a low cost and to demonstrate the truth of their charges that the McCormicks and others were making exorbitant profits.

When in 1870 the McCormick factory office first heard of the Grangers it greeted their ambitious program with amused scorn. Although there is "no law to prevent people making fools of themselves," wrote a clerk, there is an immutable "law of supply and demand" which will continue, in spite of the farmers, to fix machine prices at a level fair to all concerned.[39] The Grangers could not be laughed out of existence, but almost three years passed after this hasty judgment was delivered, before the increasing hard times had so multiplied the number of societies that they became an object of real concern to the McCormicks. By then the partners had invested

18 and 27, 1873; W. E. Bledsoe, Sec. of Caverna Grange, Horse Cave, Ky., Apr. 25, 1874.

[38] Letters to the Co. of H. Robinson, Sec. of La Prairie Farmers' Club, Hallock, Ill., Mch. 4, 1873; J. A. Freeman, Sec. and Genl. Agt., Eastern Ia. Central Asso. of P. of H., Round Grove, Ia., Mch. 9, 1873; J. A. Creighton, Fairfield, Ill., May 26, 1873. Granger purchasing agents, representing all of the clubs in one locality, were especially numerous in 1874. There is humor in the assurance so often given by the Granges, with their many members, that they would keep secret whatever concession in prices the McCormicks would make to them.

[39] L.P.C.B. No. 118, 636, W. J. Hanna to E. W. Brooks, Red Wing, Minn., Mch. 24, 1870.

too much money in their new plant to regard with indifference a widespread movement designed virtually to boycott any manufacturer who did not meet its demands. Cyrus McCormick, furthermore, was ambitious for political office and headed the Democratic organization in Illinois. Although the Granges were not officially in politics, their members were, and both Republicans and Democrats realized that victory would be won in the important by-elections of 1874 by the major party which captured the farmers' votes.[40] This was an added reason why the factory office should treat the Grangers with respect.

But political considerations had rarely been permitted by Cyrus McCormick to injure his business, and neither he nor his chief subordinates believed that the Granger movement could long survive. In their view, it would most likely become "the prey of demagogic politicians" and, if so, it would split into discordant factions and become powerless. Certainly the time was not yet at hand to scrap long-established business

[40] *Supra*, p. 334. C. H. McCormick to the Editor of "Springfield Journal" (Springfield, Ill.), May 7, 1873. In this letter, soon published, C. H. McCormick offended some of his agents by saying that "it is . . . obviously the right of every farmer or set of farmers, to employ [their own] agents to *purchase* for them," and that the McCormick Co. would be happy to sell to them or to the farmers directly "from our City Office." The clerks of this office made haste to assure their agents that in every instance where this practice was followed, they would receive their usual commission. "Chicago Times," Apr. 25, and May 16, 1873. J. S. Buck, Princeton, Ill., to the Co., June 13, 1873. Dr. S. G. Rogers, a Granger of Chicago, endeavored to interest C. H. McCormick in a scheme to colonize the poor of the city on homesteads in Kansas and found a town there to be called McCormick. C. H. McCormick was then to establish a residence in the state and be elected U. S. Senator by its legislature. Perhaps money would be needed to influence votes in the assembly but "what is expenses to you. . . . Caldwell *bought* up the *whole* Legislature for $100,000 but Ingalls the present Senator's expenses was only $11,000. . . . You may be *President* next term." S. G. Rogers to C. H. McCormick, Aug. 30, Sept. 7, 8, 10, 15, 1873. C. H. McCormick to S. G. Rogers, Sept. 10, 23, 1873. In the latter of these letters, McCormick declined to have any part in the scheme: "Poor people would have a very hard time in Kansas, as I learn from friends there."

methods, discharge the carefully chosen force of agents, and throw the firm upon the mercy of the farmers. Rather than do that, the partners would close their factory and look elsewhere for their income.[41]

Their determination to concede as little as possible to the Grangers was stiffened by the counsel of their general agents. They obviously were not qualified to give an unbiased opinion, but they were in essential agreement as to the policy which should be followed by their employer. In their judgment many of the leaders of the movement were interested only in gaining personal advantage, while the rank and file were mostly the least substantial men of the country-side.[42] The solid German and Scandinavian farmers, following the advice of their pastors, rarely joined. During the long cold winter of 1872-1873 "farmers had nothing to do but talk over their wrongs. They grew cross, morose and sour and almost revolutionary. I think as soon as the weather gets thoroughly settled so they can go to work again . . . everything will resume its usual quiet."[43] According to the agents, the Grangers might embarrass the

[41] L.P.C.B. No. 140, pp. 541-42, the Co. to M. T. Grattan, Preston, Minn., Apr. 1, 1873; pp. 595-96, to E. W. Brooks, Red Wing, Minn., Apr. 3, 1873; p. 644, to J. A. Mills, Argos, Ind., Apr. 5, 1873; No. 141, p. 274, to A. Perry & Co., Farmington, Ia., May 1, 1873: "A rise of a few cents a bushel in grain would knock the bottom out of the whole concern at once." G. A. Willey, Belleville, Ill., to the Co., Jan. 24, 1874.

[42] Letters to the Co. of W. J. Hays, Bloomington, Ill., May 21, 1873; A. Perry & Co., Farmington, Ia., May 20, 1873; E. W. Brooks, Red Wing, Minn., Apr. 1, 1873: "The Master of the State Grange . . . bought a reaper of us in 1866 and hasn't yet finished paying for it. So I don't believe any organization under his lead will succeed in breaking up monopolies very fast." In Brooks's letters of Jan. 19, 1874, and Apr. 3, 1875, he stated that the "Grand Lecturer" of the P. of H. for the U. S. was T. A. Thompson who failed as a farmer here and took seven years to settle for a McCormick reaper. In fact, because of interest charges, he finally paid $342.10 for it. See also, letters to the Co. of J. H. Shaffer, Kankakee, Ill., Jan. 15, 1874, and D. H. Smith, Sparta, Wis., Jan. 17, 1874.

[43] Letters to the Co. of J. S. Buck, Princeton, Ill., Apr. 23, 1873, and W. J. Hays, Bloomington, Ill., Mch. 13, 1873.

trade by delaying their orders for machines until the last moment before harvest, but if no reduction of price were forthcoming they would be obliged to buy anyway rather than see their crops go unharvested. "Resolutions don't cut wheat." [44] As to their wish to purchase in car-load lots for cash from only one manufacturer, that was patently absurd because they had no ready money and "not even 3" farmers could agree among themselves upon the one make of implement that all should buy. Perhaps it would be well "to call their bluff" and offer a lower cash rate to any group which would engage to purchase five or more machines. [45] Farmers were as individualistic as the manufacturers. They could never coöperate for long and if they attempted to make implements for themselves, they would quickly learn that they had neither the business experience to run a factory, nor the mechanical skill to turn out an efficient reaper or mower. The Grangers, said the salesmen, confused cheapness and economy. [46] They doubtless would favor the lowest-priced machine, and to meet this demand the McCormicks should resume the production of an inexpensive dropper or the "Old Reliable." [47]

If the firm discriminated between its customers and gave

[44] Letters to the Co. of M. T. Grattan, Wykoff, Minn., June 26, 1873; Thompson & Young, Elkader, Ia., June 18, 1873; S. Newman, Independence, Ia., June 9, 1873. The generally good crops of 1873 injured the Grangers since they had to have machines to cut their grain. M. T. Grattan, Preston, Minn., June 2, 1873: "As Harvest nears they forget their rhodomontade, come down from the skies, and see that they have harvests to cut, which will not come down for resolutions."

[45] Letters to the Co. of J. Edgar, Rochester, Minn., Apr. 5, 1873; J. H. Shaffer, Kankakee, Ill., Jan. 15, 1874; E. C. Beardsley, Aurora, Ill., Jan. 13, 1874; E. K. Butler, Sterling, Ill., Jan. 19, 1874, and of A. D. Wright, Austin, Minn., Jan. 24, 1874.

[46] W. J. Hays, Bloomington, Ill., to the Co., July 13, 1873; J. H. Shaffer, Kankakee, Ill., to the Co., Jan. 16, 1874.

[47] ‡W. J. Hanna to C. H. McCormick, Aug. 30, 1873. Letters to the Co. of Armstrong, Nixon & Co., Kokomo, Ind., Sept. 1, 1873; F. Craycroft, Sedalia, Mo., Jan. 17, 1874; E. H. Brooks, Red Wing, Minn., Mch. 20, 1874.

lower rates to Grangers than to others, it would ruin the business. "No club shall club us." [48] The agents urged the McCormicks to be courteous in their replies to letters from the Grangers, but otherwise to ignore them, since the movement would collapse within a very short time. It will be interesting, they concluded, to appoint a few members of the Grangers as our sub-agents and watch to see whether they will pass on their commissions to their clients.[49] This summarizes the attitude of the McCormick agents toward the movement.

In its correspondence and in an article upon the subject in the May, 1873, number of "The Farmers' Advance," the factory followed this advice very closely. It reminded the Grangers that their salesmen were employees and not middlemen and that they were as necessary to the firm as clerks were to the owner of a store.[50] Most of the general agents were working for a salary, rather than commissions, and the cost to the farmer was the same whether they sold one or a hundred machines.[51] As long as grain-growers had no ready cash to pay for implements, salesmen were indispensable since the home office obviously could not know the financial standing of each of the ten thousand men who annually sought to buy a machine. "Would you, a farmer, sell a horse on credit to the first stranger who came along?" [52] A farmer's note did

[48] Letters to the Co. of W. J. Hays, Decatur, Ill., Apr. 14, 1873, and of P. Mohan, St. Louis, Mch. 29, 1873.

[49] Letters to the Co. of F. Craycroft, Chillicothe, Mo., Jan. 9, Feb. 9, Apr. 5, 1874; I. A. Sea.er, Quincy, Ill., Feb. 28, 1874; F. P. Bartlett, Chariton, Ia., Apr. 18, 1874; S. L. Beardsley, St. Joseph, Mich., Jan. 19, 1875. L.P.C.B. No. 150, pp. 571-72, the Co. to A. M. Hamilton, Keswick Depot, Va., May 29, 1874.

[50] "The Farmers' Grange Movement" in "The Farmers' Advance," May, 1873. L.P.C.B. No. 132, p. 144, the Co. to P. Hillebrandt, Durant, Ia., Feb. 12, 1872.

[51] L.P.C.B. No. 134, p. 613, the Co. to N. H. Beals, Shell Rock, Ia., June 5, 1872.

[52] "The Farmers' Advance," May, 1873. L.P.C.B. No. 140, p. 344, the Co. to W. Jackson, Gooding's Grove, Ill., Mch. 15, 1873.

not become more valuable because its signer was a Granger. Common sense made clear that the owner of a business must be allowed to choose his own employees.

The McCormicks announced that they would not reduce their charge for an implement sold on credit, but to any group, Granger or otherwise, which would pay spot-cash for five or more machines, they would abate $5 per machine from their announced cash price.[53] They hastened to point out, however, that where a club ordered from the factory less than a car-load lot, the higher freight on a small shipment would probably more than equal the reduction of $5.00.[54] They were willing, as always, to sell directly to a farmer without the intervention of an agent, but whenever this was done they would pay the usual commission to the salesman whose territory included the home of the purchaser.[55] Their long-established principle of "one price for all" would be maintained.[56] The Grangers deserved the good wishes of every one as long as they kept out of politics and did not attempt to achieve the impossible, "such as regulating other people's business." [57] The Chicago firm bade them Godspeed in their fight against the monopolist, but asked them to bear in mind that manufacturers of harvesting machinery did not deserve this title. In this industry the intense competition was the best guarantee

[53] *Ibid.*, No. 132, p. 702, the Co. to G. Monser, Wenona, Ill., Mch. 16, 1872. The Co. might also give a reduction on the time price to a group of five or more purchasers, if each one would endorse the notes of the other four: "a thing we are pretty sure they won't do." *Ibid.*, No. 140, pp. 541-42, the Co. to M. T. Grattan, Preston, Minn., Apr. 1, 1873.

[54] *Ibid.*, No. 140, p. 240, the Co. to J. A. Freeman, Round Grove, Ia., Mch. 10, 1873.

[55] L.P.C.B. No. 142, pp. 449-450, the Co. to E. Johnston, Shell Rock, Ia., June 16, 1873; No. 143, p. 443, the Co. to J. Rhodes & Son, Hastings, Minn., July 8, 1873.

[56] *Ibid.*, No. 140, p. 215, the Co. to H. Robinson, Hallock, Ill., Mch. 7, 1873, No. 149, p. 47, the Co. to A. S. Johnstone, Three Rivers, Mich., Mch. 27, 1874.

[57] "The Farmers' Advance," May, 1873.

of a fair price. "No set of resolutions will induce the farmer to sell below market price. And the same is true in our business as well." [58]

This stand brought cold comfort to the Grangers. Enough of them transferred their patronage to implement-makers who were more amenable to their pressure to cause considerable embarrassment to the McCormick agents in some districts. Nevertheless, the new factory was not ready for operation until so late in the winter of 1872-1873 that it was unable to make sufficient mowers to meet the demand. The McCormicks' total sale of machines in 1873 was larger than in any preceding year. The builders of the Wood, Marsh, "Climax," and "Buckeye" implements were especially friendly to the Grangers, but while they reduced prices they also increased the commissions of their agents.[59] To hold some of their best salesmen the McCormicks were forced to follow suit.

The hard times which led to the formation of Granger societies demanding the abolition of all agents, increased the manufacturers' dependence upon them because the financial status of a would-be purchaser of a machine required more careful probing than in days of prosperity. The high cost of labor induced Grangers to favor the use of harvesters, but they were more complicated than self-rake reapers, and field

[58] L.P.C.B. No. 140, pp. 541-542, the Co. to M. T. Grattan, Preston, Minn., Apr. 1, 1873. A. H. Hirsch, "Efforts of the Grange in the Middle West to Control the Price of Farm Machinery," in "The Mississippi Valley Historical Review," XV, No. 4 (Mch. 1929), pp. 473-496.

[59] Letters to the Co. of J. S. Buck, Princeton, Ill., June 13, 1873; P. Mohan, St. Louis, Sept. 10, 1873; F. Craycroft, Sedalia, Mo., and Girard, Kan., Jan. 17, 23, and Mch. 5, 1874; D. H. Smith, Sparta, Wis., Feb. 26, 1874; J. A. Miller, Argos, Ind., Mch. 31, 1874; W. L. P. Wiard, Louisville, Ky., June 7, 1875, and June 7, 1876; and of O. M. Carter, Ashland, Neb., Sept. 1, 1873: "You pay your agents $20 per sale, the 'Buckeye' firm $30 and it collects its own notes, Elward and Marsh $45, Haines and Manny $50." L.P.C.B. No. 148, p. 252, the Co. to W. N. Spring, Sioux City, Ia., Feb. 11, 1874.

experts were indispensable to teach farmers how to operate them. Thus, the very conditions which aroused the wrath of grain-growers against the agency system compelled the manufacturer to lay more stress upon it than ever before.[60] By driving many small builders of harvesting machinery into bankruptcy, the depression period, contrary to the will of the Grangers, left a few big firms in complete control of the industry.[61]

The McCormick firm would have sold more machines in 1873 and 1874 if there had been no Granger organizations, but as it was they enjoyed the best seasons of their history up to that time.[62] Grasshoppers caused them more loss than the Grangers. The firm slightly lowered its prices each year between 1872 and 1875, but it is by no means clear that the

[60] L.P.C.B. No. 149, p. 150, the Co. to Bischof, Zimmerer & Stevenson, Seward, Neb., Apr. 3, 1874. *Ibid.*, No. 151, p. 22, telegram of the Co. to G. A. Willey, Belleville, Ill., June 8, 1874. It was at this time that Louis Frank began his long career as an expert both in the harvest fields of the United States and Europe. He was a personal attendant of C. H. McCormick for considerable periods between 1878 and 1884, and lived to write his reminiscences in manuscript in 1931. E. K. Butler, who had been an agent, was another of these early harvester experts. He was later (1888-1898) to hold the position of Secretary of the McCormick Harvesting Machine Company.

[61] "Arguments Before the Committee on Patents of the House of Representatives, in February and March 1878, on House Bill No. 1612 to Amend the Laws Relating to Patents" (Washington 1878), pp. 55-63.

[62] L.P.C.B. No. 146, pp. 621-623, the Co. to J. Edgar, Rochester, Minn., Dec. 2, 1873; No. 147, pp. 690-691, to G. Russell, Woodstock, Ill., Jan. 17, 1874. Agents in 1873 found that the Grangers, unable to compel manufacturers to lower prices, declined to buy machines since they believed their organization would be stronger by the next summer and they could then gain what they desired. Letters to the Co. of A. Perry & Co., Farmington, Ia., July 10, 1873; G. Monser, Wenona, Ill., Apr. 25, 1873; W. J. Hays, Bloomington, Ill., June 4, 1873; I. A. Seaver, Quincy, Ill., July 12, 1873; F. Craycroft, Chillicothe, Mo., July 25, 1873; H. C. Addis, Omaha, Neb., May 9 and Aug. 7, 1873: "The Grangers do us no harm in western Ia. but they do in Neb. where the movement is new, and the farmers are in their first flush of enthusiasm about it." J. H. Shaffer, Kankakee, Ill., Jan. 31, 1874; G. W. Russell, Woodstock, Ill., Apr. 28, 1874.

farmer societies forced this reduction.[63] The cost of raw materials was dropping rapidly and the expense of manufacturing an "Advance" machine in 1875 was over thirty-five per cent less than in 1873. In other words, at the close of the Grangers' period of greatest activity the McCormicks were making a larger profit from the sale of each machine than before the agitation for lower prices commenced.[64] If all the Grangers in the Union had been able simultaneously to exert their full force against a recalcitrant manufacturer they might have gained what they desired. The immense size of the country's grain area was one of the chief handicaps to their success. Whenever they were able to embarrass a firm in one or two states during a harvest season, it could, nevertheless, enjoy a profitable year by disposing of its output in regions where they were weak.[65]

This is not to discount the Grangers' capacity for annoyance. Where farmers gained control of the state assemblies they raised the taxes on unsold reapers in the charge of agents,[66] and both by laws and by intimidating the courts they

[63] The credit price of an "Advance" in 1873 was $200; in 1874, $195, and in 1875, $170. The manufacturing cost of "The Advance" in 1873 was about $107; in 1874, about $84.50, and in 1875 about $69. #F. H. Matthews to C. H. McCormick, Sept. 22, 1874, and Sept. 10, 1875. One concession made by the McCormick Co. in 1874 was to permit a farmer to buy "The Advance" as a reaper alone, and return the mowing parts of the machine to the factory. The reaper part was sold at $170 on credit, or $160 cash.

[64] L.P.C.B. No. 145, pp. 204-207, C. A. Spring, Jr., to C. H. McCormick, Sept. 6, 1873. #F. H. Matthews to N. F. McCormick, Sept. 9, 1874. He judged that due to lower cost of materials, the Co. would save $100,000 more in 1875.

[65] The Grangers of Ill. and Ia. alone bothered the McCormick Co. in 1872. Those of Minn. and Neb. were the most troublesome in 1873. In 1874 the movement was at its peak, but the clubs in the border states claimed most of the attention of the McCormick office. Thereafter they were of little importance in so far as the McCormicks were concerned, although they are occasionally mentioned in the correspondence as late as 1879.

[66] L.P.C.B. No. 141, pp. 829, 833, 846, the Co. to N. M. Lester, Eddyville, Ia., to W. J. Van Hoesen, Macomb, Ill., and to W. J. Hays, Bloomington,

made it more difficult for creditors to distrain upon the property of their debtors. In former hard-time periods, however, similar legislation had been enacted and it may be doubted whether the Granger societies were solely, or even mainly, responsible for the relief acts of the early 'seventies.[67] In some localities, and particularly in Wisconsin, they urged all farmers not to purchase machinery made outside of their state.[68] In Illinois, Iowa, Missouri, Wisconsin, and Nebraska, they endeavored, with ill sucess, to manufacture harvesting implements. Some of the leading Grangers, in fact, refused to patronize these concerns and bought of the McCormick agents in direct violation of their own principles.[69] The farmers'

Ill., May 28, 1873: "When taxation is inevitable the best that can be done is to be on good terms with the assessors and take measures to have the Sums only *nominal*."

[67] W. J. Hays, Bloomington, Ill., to the Co., Feb. 2, 1874. M. T. Grattan, Preston, Minn., Nov. 8, 1877: "Our weak kneed elective judiciary either did not, or else were afraid to bring the repudiating Grangers about their ears by an obnoxious opinion on the exemption law." J. Edgar, Waseca, Minn., to the Co., Feb. 14, Mch. 28, and Aug. 20, 1873. The laws of Minn. exempt 80 acres (Ia.—40 acres) of land, its improvements, and some stock from seizure for debt. A homestead, by U. S. law, is exempt from seizure until the patent is secured. L.P.C.B. No. 146, pp. 113-114, the Co. to J. Edgar, Rochester, Minn., Oct. 29, 1873: "The Federal Courts have decided that a creditor cannot distrain on a homestead for debt if it were incurred prior to time that full title to the land was secured. This will hurt us."

[68] Letters to the Co. of W. P. Dewey, Lancaster, Wis., Feb. 18, 1872; F. G. Smith, Madison, Wis., Jan. 26, 1874, and of D. H. Smith, Sparta, Wis., Feb. 6, 1874.

[69] L.P.C.B. No. 147, pp. 690-91, the Co. to G. W. Russell, Woodstock, Ill., Jan. 17, 1874: "Some Grangers in Iowa are starting a Reaper factory . . . and we are glad of it for then they will see for themselves what it costs to build machines & run a factory." E. Printeney, Frankfort, Kas., to Co., Jan. 20, 1874. E. W. Brooks, Red Wing, Minn., to Co., Jan. 19, 1874: "A reaper factory has been started to make Hubbard R-M'S and to wholesale them for cash, presumably to Grangers." E. K. Butler, Stirling, Ill., to Co., Jan. 19, 1874: "The Lyndon Grange of this county is preparing to swindle its members by organizing a stock company to manufacture mowers." H. C. Addis, Omaha, to Co., Jan. 27, Feb. 16, 1874, and Mch. 1, 1875: "At Fremont, Neb., the Grangers built 150 implements in 1874 and

party in Minnesota nominated one of McCormick's leading salesmen for the state legislature.[70] Josiah A. Noonan, who for many years before the Civil War had been the postmaster of Milwaukee, came to Chicago in 1873 and with the aid of a loan from Cyrus McCormick established a Granger paper called the "Industrial Age." When Noonan was unable to repay his debt, the inventor was indulgent and the "Industrial Age" remained his stout champion. In the spring of 1875 the inventor offered Dudley W. Adams, the Master of the National Grange, "ample and convenient quarters in some of my buildings . . . on terms advantageous to you" as a center for the activities of the Patrons of Husbandry throughout the United States.[71] Adams's reply, if any, to this shrewd offer, has been lost.

The ineffectiveness of the Grangers' efforts to make the manufacturers of farm implements bend to their will was also due to their early absorption in the problem of regulating

propose to make 300 for 1875. These machines resemble the Haines Header." F. Craycroft, Sedalia, Mo., to Co., July 29, 1874: "The Grangers have a machine shop at Boonville." M. T. Grattan, Preston, Minn., to Co., June 2, 1873: "I have just sold a reaper at full price to Major Foster the Grand Mogul of the Grangers in Fillmore Co." W. J. Van Hoesen, Macomb, Ill., to Co., June 28, 1873: "I sold a machine at full price to the 'Chief Marshall' of the Grangers in this county." W. Ray, Danville, Ill., to Co., July 1, 1873: "Please sell me a mower at a low figure, and in return I, as the business agent of the farmers' clubs in Vermilion Cy., will use my influence in your behalf."

[70] E. H. Brooks, Red Wing, Minn., Oct. 8, 1874, to the Co. He declined to run.

[71] Letters to C. H. McCormick of #A. C. Dodge, June 28, 1873, #S. T. K. Prime, Dwight, Ill., Feb. 25, 1874, #D. E. Bradley, Sept. 24, 1874, and of #J. A. Noonan, Milwaukee, July 21, 1873, Apr. 22 and Sept. 24, 1874, and Feb. 26, 1875. Noonan had written an editorial in the "La Crosse (Wis.) Democrat" in C. H. McCormick's behalf. See also, #S. M. Allen, Sec., Ill. State Farmers' Asso., Kewanee, Ill. to J. A. Noonan, Dec. 3, 1873: "I am doing all that I can to help your paper." #L.P.C.B. of C. H. McCormick, Nov. 1873-June 1876, p. 279, C. H. McCormick to D. W. Adams, Waukon, Ia., Mch. 8, 1875. "Chicago Times," Mch. 3, 1875 and Dec. 19, 1878. Noonan was bankrupt by 1878.

railroad and grain warehouse charges. The office of the Mc-
Cormick factory realized from the beginning of the movement
that it might help itself by sympathizing with the farmers in
their opposition to exorbitant and discriminatory freight
rates.[72] Here the manufacturer and the grain-grower stood on
common ground, for the Chicago firm had for many years
been hampered by the high costs of transportation in its efforts to develop markets far distant from its factory.[73] Rebates on shipments were first granted to the McCormicks in
1876, or too late to gain their support in the fight of the railroads with the farmers. Except for delivery to points along
the Mississippi River, the company no longer relied upon in-
land waterways,[74] but the railroads, although they handled
freight more quickly and carefully than river- and canal-boats,
were a never-ending source of aggravation on account of their
erratic tariffs and the "public-be-damned" attitude of their
officials.

The McCormicks also saw eye to eye with the Grangers on
other issues. The farmer resented the wide difference in the
sales value of a bushel of wheat in his barn and in Chicago
or New York. He believed that if there were a near-by flour-
mill to buy his grain he would receive a higher price for it.
A home market of this kind would make him independent of
railroads and middlemen, stimulate the growth of towns, bring

[72] L.P.C.B. No. 140, p. 440, Co. to W. J. Hays, Bloomington, Ill., Mch.
21, 1873; No. 147, p. 563, to F. Craycroft, Chillicothe, Mo., Jan. 10, 1874:
"The question of the Grangers does not seem to us half so important as it
was a year ago." E. C. Beardsley, Aurora, Ill., to the Co., Jan. 13, 1874.

[73] *Ibid.*, No. 86, p. 820, Co. to Genl. Fght. Agt., Chicago & Alton RR.,
Jan. 9, 1866; No. 86, p. 853, to C. M. Gray, Fght. Agt., Michigan Southern
RR., Jan. 10, 1866.

[74] *Post*, p. 714. L.P.C.B. No. 90, p. 548, and No. 98, p. 343, Co. to D. W.
Fairbank, Concord, Ill., June 2, 1866, and May 10, 1867: "Canal boats are
about as antiquated as hand Rakers & we think as little of one as the
other." J. Rhodes & Son, Hastings, Minn., Mch. 12, 1873: "Won't you ship
us via Mississippi River this spring when the water is high so that we
won't have to haul machines forty-five miles in wagons from Winona?"

capital to his neighborhood, relieve the money stringency, and permit him to buy manufactured goods at a lower cost.[75] With this desire, the McCormicks were in full accord. The prosperity of the grain-grower meant their own well being, and any means of promoting it, so as to allow the farmer to pay his debts and buy new machinery, naturally enlisted their support. When a Granger advocated lower tariffs for the purpose of increasing the foreign market for grain and reducing the price of clothing and household furnishings, the Chicago partners could again give a hearty acquiescence.[76] They had no fear of the rivalry of foreign-made reapers and mowers, and a revenue tariff squared both with their political views and their wish to lessen the cost of the iron and steel needed in their factory. They assured the Grangers that if Congress could be persuaded to reduce the import duties, the price of agricultural machinery would certainly fall. Cyrus McCormick was also ready to meet the Grangers half-way on their soft money program, since he believed that an immediate resumption of specie payments was neither necessary nor desirable.

Agrarian leaders who talked of the benefits of a local market to compete with the produce merchants of the big cities, were aware that all of the grain pouring out of the central West each year could not be used by the people of the United States. Sale abroad of a large portion of each crop was necessary, but a Mississippi Valley farmer would be happier if his grain could move overseas without going through Atlantic ports. Any diversion of route and economic realignment which would emancipate him from the middlemen, railroad magnates, and money lords of the East were keenly desired. This

[75] C. C. Royce, Ashton, Ill., to the Co., Aug. 22, 1872.

[76] L.P.C.B. No. 140, pp. 545-546, Co. to P. Mohan, St. Louis, Mo., Apr. 1, 1873: "We believe that the Society will run into a political complexion, and bring about an era of Free Trade, and in that way reduce the prices of machinery by affording us material at low prices."

wish naturally suggested a reëstablishment of the prewar alliance between the Gulf States and the Middle West. Although the sharp issues of war and reconstruction prevented the political unity of the Great Valley, at least New Orleans and Mobile, rather than New York and Philadelphia, might well be the outports for his grain. Here excellent water transportation would serve to keep freight charges on the Illinois Central and other north-south railroad lines at reasonable figures. What could be more natural than for the agrarian societies of West and South to stand shoulder to shoulder against the industrial and capitalistic East?

Cyrus McCormick was an enthusiastic supporter of this plan. In both the religious and political fields he was working at this time to unite the North and the South. The rewelding of the economic bond was equally in harmony with his purpose. This was statesmanship, although his large investment in the Southern Railway Association, formed to control a long stretch of the railroad link between Chicago and the Gulf, should probably be borne in mind. During his stay in England he made the acquaintance of many of the leading manufacturers and bankers there and he knew that they were ready to sell goods to, or invest money in, the United States, if some means could be found to furnish them with trustworthy information concerning the financial standing of those who might wish to deal with them. The Gulf States had looked to England for capital and a cotton market since the early nineteenth century, and she could perhaps be made the instrument to free the Middle West from its bondage to the East.

Patriotism, politics, and business considerations joined to engage Cyrus McCormick's support of the Mississippi Valley Society of London, organized at this time to make this dream come true. William T. Cordner, sent to England by Missouri in 1872 to advertise the resources of his state, apparently was the first to suggest its formation.[77] The association called itself an international chamber of commerce and its general objects were to promote direct trade between Europe and the Mississippi Valley, to encourage immigration there, and to invite the investment of capital in companies chartered to develop the resources of the South and West. Each state was urged to send an exhibit of its minerals, manufactures, and agricultural products to the home office of the society on the Strand in London.[78] Manufacturers of Great Britain were asked to display their goods at state fairs in the Great Valley.[79] As Sir Edwin Pearson, Chairman of its Executive Committee, wrote:

Capitalists must be taught the fact that your valley is the source from which a large part of the breadstuffs and provisions have to be drawn to support our working population, and that your cotton fields form the real basis of one of our most important industries. They must also be taught that your valley constitutes one of the most important outlets for our manufactures, and that the employment of English capital and labour is assisting in your development, and the establishment of direct trade exchanges is an efficient

[77] "Prospectus" of the Mississippi Valley Society (no date or place of publication shown, but probably London, 1873). The North Atlantic Forwarding & Express Company, formed at this time, aroused McCormick's interest, although he finally decided not to invest in it. It was designed to establish agencies so that *"the producer in the West and the purchaser in Europe shall be brought together without the intervention of men in the seaboard cities of the United States."* This quotation is from a letter of its vice-pres., ‡D. Webb, to C. H. McCormick, Apr. 27, 1874. See also, *supra,* pp. 156-157.

[78] Pamphlet entitled "Direct Trade Between Great Britain and the Mississippi Valley, United States" (London, 1874). The special aim of the society was declared to be "to fix attention upon the Valley of the Mississippi as the *great coming* market; the world's new theatre of production and consumption." E. W. Norfolk to T. Wright, May 16 and Aug. 18, 1874; O. F. Davis, Land Commr., Union Pacific R.R., Omaha, to C. H. McCormick, Dec. 11, 1873; ‡C. R. Griffing, Cincinnati, to C. H. McCormick, June 4, 1874. By 1874 the legal name of the association was The International Chamber of Commerce and Mississippi Valley Society.

[79] E. W. Norfolk to T. Wright, Aug. 14, 1874.

way of cheapening the necessaries of life here and of extending an already important market for our own productions. . . . Our main obstacle here is to combat the utter ignorance which prevails respecting the extent, character, and resources of your wonderful valley.[80]

Chapters of the society appeared between 1873 and 1875 in many of the cities of the South and Middle West. The newspapers of the valley gave it much favorable publicity.[81] Generals P. T. Beauregard and J. B. Hood, Jacob Thompson, James B. Eads and Charles P. Chouteau were among its more prominent members.[82] Jefferson Davis when in London in 1874 inquired at its home office concerning the practicability of establishing a steamship service between Europe and the southern seaboard with steel vessels of light enough draft to carry passengers and freight directly to the ports of the Mississippi Valley. When he returned to England two years later in the interest of this enterprise he was the president of the American branch of the society.[83] The Chicago chapter was formed in the autumn of 1873 with Cyrus McCormick at its

[80] E. Pearson, London, to J. H. Oglesby, New Orleans, May 2, 1874.

[81] "New Orleans Price Current," Feb. 21, 1874; "New Orleans Times," Mch. 4, 1874; "New Orleans Picayune," Feb. 22, and Mch. 14, 1874: This city should share the vast annual wealth that comes to New York as a result of the fact that 700 ships and 270,000 immigrants enter her port. Our lands are so rich that "if they are tickled with a hoe [they] will laugh with a harvest." Capital alone is needed to develop them and restore to Louisiana her pre-war prosperity. "New Orleans Republican," Mch. 19, 1874: "Let England colonize the Mississippi Valley with her capital and cultivators. Let her pay for their products in her goods. She will make more out of the Mississippi Valley than she makes out of Australia. . . . And the free navigation and agricultural development of the Mississippi Valley will make England thank God that Packenham (sic) was pickled and sent home in a cask, from before New Orleans, instead of bringing Louisiana under the policy of Canning and Castlereagh." C. R. Griffing to D. Cameron, Apr. 3, 1875.

[82] R. W. Fort, Mobile, Ala., to C. H. McCormick, Mch. 24, 1874.

[83] C. R. Griffing to C. H. McCormick, June 4, 1874. E. W. Norfolk, London to T. Wright, May 21, 1874. "Lynchburg Virginian," Nov. 2, 1875.

head and with its office next to his own in the McCormick Block. Helped by the endorsement of the Chicago Board of Trade, it soon had about thirty-five members including L. Z. Leiter, Paul Cornell, R. T. Crane, John Crerar and J. F. Armour.[84]

In accordance with the original plan, a visiting delegation of English business men made a tour of the Mississippi Valley in the autumn of 1874. John Crossley, a prominent manufacturer of carpets, member of Parliament, and president of the society in London, was its leader. He and his party were entertained at a banquet in Chicago in October, and they received an equally gratifying welcome in other cities.[85]

This early enthusiasm, however, quickly disappeared. The American members were for the most part busy men of affairs who found no time to comply with the insistent requests of the London office for American newspapers, maps, trade statistics, and information about the financial responsibility of companies who sought to sell their securities in England.[86] There was dissatisfaction from the outset because the by-laws required that a large percentage of the $25 annual dues should

[84] E. W. Norfolk to T. Wright, July 17, Sept. 3, 1873, Jan. 22 and Feb. 10, 1874. ‡T. Wright to C. H. McCormick, Nov. 17, 1873. C. H. McCormick to C. R. Griffing, Oct. 9, 1874. "Chicago Daily Tribune," Nov. 14 and 19, 1873. "Chicago Times," Nov. 14, 19, 27, 1873. Balance-sheet of the society for the period Oct. 26 to Dec. 29, 1874. "Code of By Laws of the Chicago Branch of the International Chamber of Commerce and Mississippi Valley Society, Adopted Nov. 5, 1874." Since Sir John S. Gibbons, who as Lord Mayor of London at the time of the Chicago Fire had been active in raising funds to relieve the sufferers from that disaster, was on the council of the society, it was believed that Chicago business men would wish to join it.

[85] ‡J. Crossley, New York, to C. H. McCormick, Nov. 18, 1874. Circular letter of C. R. Griffing, Jan. 20, 1875, to the members of the Miss. Valley Soc. of Chicago. Chicago was heralded as "the future London of America." "Chicago Times," Oct. 15, 1874.

[86] E. W. Norfolk, London, to C. H. McCormick, June 1, 1875, and to D. Cameron, July 8, 1875. C. R. Griffing, London, to D. Cameron, Aug. 5, 1875.

be sent to London to pay the expenses incurred in advertising the resources of the Mississippi Valley in Europe.[87] Although President Grant was reported to have been "very favorably impressed with any movement which promises to bring large capital for long term loans or permanent investment," Congress did not reduce the tariff rates and English manufacturers could hardly expand their markets in the Mississippi Valley until this was done.[88] The society had hoped to counteract in England the adverse effect of the Panic of 1873 upon the reputation of American securities, but this was much too difficult a task to carry out by a few months of work.[89] Cyrus McCormick soon lost interest in an enterprise which could show so little actual accomplishment, and by the spring of 1875 his assistant informed him that: "The Miss. V. Society owes $58.22 up to May 1st, and I thought it was possible that the furniture might be attached for unpaid debts." [90]

Although several objectives of the Mississippi Valley Society were the same as those sought by the Grangers, they neither endorsed it nor expressed approval of the part played

[87] T. D. Worrall, London, to T. Wright, Chicago, Oct. 24, 1874. D. Cameron, Chicago to E. W. Norfolk, Feb. 10, 1875. E. W. Norfolk to T. Wright, Aug. 6, 1874, and to D. Cameron, Mch. 20, 1875.

[88] R. M. Woods, Springfield, Ill., to C. H. McCormick, Oct. 15, 1874.

[89] C. H. McCormick to J. Crossley, London, Dec. 22, 1874. In its "Prospectus" the Society proposed to "discourage and frown down all disreputable undertakings, worthless investments and wild cat schemes, which to a certain extent during the past few years have brought all American enterprises into discredit."

[90] ‡C. A. Spring, Jr., to C. H. McCormick, May 25, 1875. The society in Chicago apparently gained a half-dozen new members during the summer, but it is almost unmentioned in McCormick's correspondence after 1875. In fact, on May 21, R. S. McCormick wrote to C. H. McCormick that "he had not been able to dispose of the desk, carpet, etc." of the society. On Aug. 24, 1875, the London office issued new regulations granting the American branches more autonomy. The New Orleans branch was made the head of all the chapters in America and it was to serve as a clearing house for all information sent to, or coming from, England. ‡C. H. McCormick to Jefferson Davis, Mch. 29, 1876.

by Cyrus McCormick in its formation. The membership of
the society and its platform, however, make clear that some
of the grievances of the Grangers were not peculiarly their
own. Since the agrarian movement was dramatic and widespread, it tends to obscure the dissatisfaction of other economic groups in the Mississippi Valley at this time, because
of the dominance of the East.

Between 1872 and 1875 the McCormick Company, in spite
of the Grangers and hard times, almost doubled the number
of its annual sales.[91] The winter of 1872-1873 was unusually
severe in Minnesota and Iowa. Snow blocked the roads for
weeks at a time. Many families were destitute, and several
hundred people, as well as thousands of cattle, died of cold or
starvation.[92] Spring was backward, but except in the "grasshoppered" districts of the central West, crops in 1873 were
large.[93] Grain commanded a fair price until the financial panic
of the autumn temporarily broke the market. During the last
three months of the year money was almost unobtainable in
the country districts and several banks failed which had been
used as collectors by McCormicks' agents.[94] The few farmers

[91] The McCormick Co. sold about 6,875 machines in 1872 and 13,031 in
1875.

[92] M. T. Grattan, Preston, Minn., to the Co., Jan. 14, 15, 1873. Grattan
calls it "Minnesota's coldest winter." He speaks of people freezing to death.
J. Rhodes & Son, Hastings, Minn., Jan. 15, 1873: "One hundred lives lost
in this neighborhood from the cold."

[93] ‡W. J. Hanna to C. H. McCormick, Sept. 10, 1873. L.P.C.B. No. 139,
p. 542, the Co. to F. G. Smyth, Madison, Wis., Jan. 27, 1873; No. 140,
p. 376, the Co. to P. Mohan, St. Louis, Mch. 18, 1873; No. 142, p. 25, the
Co. to A. E. Crossett, Ackley, Ia., June 2, 1873.

[94] Letters to the Co. of F. Craycroft, Chillicothe, Mo., Dec. 18, 1873;
A. M. Hamilton, Keswick, Va., Oct. 4, 1873; Hall & Brewster, Mankato,
Minn., Sept. 23, 1873. J. H. Shaffer, Kankakee, Ill., Sept. 29 and Oct. 3,
1873; H. G. Grattan, Waukon, Ia., Oct. 17, 1873; and J. Edgar, Rochester,
Minn., Oct. 20, 1873; L.P.C.B. No. 145, p. 805, the Co. to All Agents,
Oct. 14, 1873; No. 146, p. 14, the Co. to H. G. Grattan, Waukon, Ia.,
Oct. 22, 1873. McCormick's agents often used lawyers, banks, or merchants

who were willing to sell their wheat at the prevailing price declined to pay their debts because they hoped that their little hoard of money would allow them in the next harvest to purchase farm implements for cash at very low figures. Most grain-growers, however, refused to move their crops to market until late spring, since it was then that wheat usually commanded the highest price of the year.[95] As a result, much grain spoiled in the stack or so deteriorated in quality that its owners were obliged to sell it in May for less than it would have brought the preceding autumn. There was more spring threshing than ever before.[96]

Uncheered by signs of better times and with more and more Granger societies being founded,[97] the McCormicks in the winter of 1873-1874 arranged with J. F. Seiberling of Akron, Ohio, to make a few of his inexpensive droppers for sale to small farmers who could not afford to spend nearly two hun-

to collect for them. Of these, the merchants were too often primarily concerned to collect their own debts from farmers, and this was also true of the sub-agents themselves who were not infrequently storekeepers. On the other hand, A. Perry & Co. of Farmington, Ia., wrote to the Co. on Jan. 22, 1873, that the storekeepers of his town complained that the farmers paid the implement dealers first. Banks, on the whole, were the most satisfactory collectors, except on the frontier where they were often unsafe.

[95] Letters to the Co. of J. Edgar, Mankato, Minn., Jan. 20, and Mch. 3, 1873; C. E. Shaffer, St. Peter, Minn., Apr. 3, 1873; W. F. Cowhan, Jackson, Mich., Nov. 10, 1873; E. W. Brooks, Red Wing, Minn., Nov. 6, 1873, and D. H. Smith, Sparta, Wis., June 11, 1874.

[96] A. D. Wright, Cresco, Ia., to the Co., Jan. 21 and Sept. 26, 1873. For this reason, many farmers wished McCormick to alter the due-date of his reaper notes from Dec. 1st to June 1st. E. W. Brooks, Red Wing, Minn., to the Co., Nov. 10, 1873.

[97] L.P.C.B. No. 146, p. 288, the Co. to A. Perry & Co., Farmington, Ia., Nov. 8, 1873: "All that we require is for every one owing us to help us to the extent of their ability. We don't want to increase the number of Widows & Orphans and Starving Children . . . but what we have a right to expect is that those *fully* able to pay us will do so. . . . It is much easier for our debtors to sustain us than for us to sustain them." In the spring of 1874 the Co. deemed the collection question to be so serious that it sent a letter directly from its office to each man who was overdue in his payments.

dred dollars for "The Advance" reaper-mower.[98] They also revived the "Old Reliable" combined machine, improved it in detail, and called it the "New Reliable." [99] Armed with these inexpensive implements, and reducing the cash price of "The Advance" somewhat below the 1873 figure, they felt well prepared to hold their own against their rivals.

Although competition had always been keen, the correspondence of 1874 and the years immediately following portrays a state of war hitherto unexampled in its intensity. Letters from the office to the agents are filled with admonitions to have "spunk," "grit," and "sand," to "spit on your fists," "make it hot for them," and "to keep on top of the heap." These "pep talks," as they would be called to-day, were not without result.[100] The precise methods to be used to defeat the opposition were left for the individual salesman's own ingenuity and conscience to determine. The report of one traveling representative on the failure of a Minnesota agent, suggested the best qualifications for success:

Edgar appears to have trouble all over his Dist. and I can't understand it as the agts. elsewhere are getting along. The only reason I can assign is that he has too many *church men* for agts. I believe in religion & temperance but it ain't worth a "cuss" to run the Reaper trade on in Minnesota: it requires cheek &

[98] J. F. Seiberling, Akron, O., to the Co., Jan. 25, 1874. Seiberling states that each of the 44 shops making his dropper pays him $5.00 royalty a machine. The McCormick Co. finally persuaded him to reduce his fee to $3.75, and it thus gained a slight advantage over other manufacturers of droppers. It continued to pay him a royalty until 1878. L.P.C.B. No. 148, pp. 392-93, the Co. to J. F. Seiberling, Feb. 21, 1874. Droppers were especially well liked by farmers in Ky., Tenn., Mo. and Utah.

[99] L.P.C.B. No. 147, p. 628, the Co. to H. G. Grattan, Waukon, Ia., Jan. 14, 1874. The McCormick Co. built 1000 of the "New Reliables" for 1874. These were one-wheeled, self-rake, combined machines but their divider and reel caused much complaint, and they were never made again. See, W. Westerman, Dubuque, Ia., to the Co., Apr. 26, 1875.

[100] L.P.C.B. No. 150, 151, 152, 159, 160, 161 (May to August, 1874 and 1875), *passim*.

muscle and I am sorry to say some "evasions" from the truth to successfully sell McCormick Harvesters with the opposition we have up here. You have got to fight the Devil with fire and it is no use trying to fool him on sweetened water. . . . The whole Harvester fraternity are bucking against our Machine.[101]

Minnesota was doubtless the hottest spot on the entire battle-front, for there the enmities aroused by the skirmishing to the southward in June and July reached a climax. There, too, since the selling season was almost over, each manufacturer endeavored to unload his surplus machines at sacrifice prices, and to test out as secretly as possible the value of new devices which might be incorporated in the implements to be built during the winter.

One objective of the conflict of 1874, so far as the McCormicks were concerned, was to determine whether they could hold their position in the forefront of the industry without yielding to the growing demand of the farmers for a harvester.[102] Even early in the season it was apparent what the answer would be. The crops suffered from drought and the dry upstanding grain greatly favored the success of both headers and harvesters.[103] By early July the McCormicks were bending every effort to dispose of their entire stock of combined machines, since any surplus would be most difficult to sell in 1875 when they hoped to have their own harvester and an improved "Advance" in the field.[104] They raised commis-

[101] G. A. Willey, Rochester, Minn., to the Co., Aug. 8, 1875.

[102] The Marsh Harvester had also injured McCormick's business in 1873. J. Edgar, Rochester, Minn., to the Co., July 28 and Aug. 16, 1873, and June 16, 1874. *Supra,* Chap. XIII, pp. 530-532.

[103] G. D. McArthur, Winnebago City, Minn., to the Co., June 15, 1874: "All of my German trade that I have held for years are buying the Marsh Harvester." H. C. Addis, Omaha, to the Co., July 11, 1874. L.P.C.B. No. 150, p. 637, the Co. to A. T. Averill, Cedar Rapids, Ia., May 30, 1874; No. 151, p. 516, to J. Edgar, Rochester, Minn., June 21, 1874.

[104] *Ibid.,* No. 153, p. 88, the Co. to E. W. Brooks, Hudson, Wis., July 22, 1874. About a dozen "New Advance" were made for experimental purposes in this harvest. It had a "single-frame" rather than "double-frame" and was

sions $5 to $10 with the understanding that agents would pass on this amount as a rebate to the purchaser. Other manufacturers were also making a pretense of maintaining prices by employing this subterfuge.[105] The Chicago firm cleared a net profit of $276,000 by selling over a thousand more machines than ever before.[106]

The summer of 1875, with its incessant rain and heavy, lodged grain, contrasted sharply with the conditions of the preceding harvest. The weather could hardly have been more unfavorable for the introduction of the McCormick Harvester. Farmers turned again to cradles or self-rake reapers and McCormick's supply of "The Advance" was sold out before the end of May.[107] The competition with Marsh was so keen that Cyrus McCormick must have been reminded of his early rivalry with Obed Hussey.[108] For the first time in

manufactured under license from J. A. Saxton of Canton, O. The Mc-Cormick Co. also had 'a new "single-frame" mower (the "Prize Mower"), which required the payment of a $2.50 royalty fee to Saxton. These "single-frame" machines were considerably lighter than their predecessors.

[105] G. Monser, Wenona, Ill., to the Co., Aug. 10, 1874, and W. L. Wiard, Louisville, Ky., Apr. 1, 1875. L.P.C.B. No. 156, p. 741, the Co. to E. W. Brooks, Red Wing, Minn., Mch. 31, 1875. Private circular of J. Edgar, Rochester, Minn., to his sub-agents, July 7, 1874.

[106] Nevertheless, at the close of the harvest they had a surplus of 4500 machines. #F. H. Matthews to C. H. McCormick, Sept. 22, 1874. The McCormick Co. sold 8445 machines in 1874 and of this number 482 were droppers. Only 660 droppers were sold in 1875. The droppers were also "single-frame" and on each one sold the Co. was obliged to pay Saxton a royalty of $2.50 as well as the $3.75 to Seiberling.

[107] Letters to the Co. of H. J. Prier, Indianapolis, Ind., May 1, 1875; T. H. Ritter, Bellefontaine, O., May 4, 1875; F. Craycroft, Sedalia, Mo., Aug. 3, 1875; D. W. Pratt, Wisner, Neb., Sept. 5, 1875, and of G. D. McArthur, Winnebago, Minn., Sept. 9, 1875. L.P.C.B. No. 161 (Aug., 1875), passim; No. 158, pp. 708-709, the Co. to W. N. Spring, Sioux City, Ia., June 9, 1875; No. 160, pp. 856-857, the Co. to F. P. Bartlett, Chariton, Ia., Aug. 2, 1875. Heavy rains came late in Minn. and Neb. and damaged much grain in the shock.

[108] With each of its harvesters the McCormick Co. furnished a bundle-carrier and an awning to protect the binders from the sun. Ibid., No. 157, p. 805, the Co. to Johann & Bro., Port Washington, Wis., May 11, 1875.

many years the company encouraged its agents to enter field trials with other makes of harvesters. The tide of battle veered back and forth as the summer advanced. By its close, however, the McCormicks were confident that theirs was the victory.[109] Their altered Garnhart Harvester needed much improvement in detail, but it had no serious defects and "you can blow it as hard as you like and the machine will back you up." [110]

The Texas trade was reopened for the first time since 1869, and over four hundred machines were sold there before the close of the harvest. Thereafter, more and more farmers each year were added to the list of McCormick clients in the Lone Star State.[111] New agents were appointed in Utah, the first sale was made in Nevada, and the McCormicks followed the frontier into the Dakotas and the rich Republican River Valley of Nebraska.[112] In spite of the rainy harvest and the dis-

In this month the McCormicks priced their harvester at $175 cash, while the Marsh Harvester sold for $165. In July it was said that Marsh sold as low as $140 and $150, and the McCormicks dropped their price in the next month. *Ibid.*, No. 158, p. 554, the Co. to T. H. Ritter, Columbus, O., June 4, 1875.

[109] L.P.C.B. No. 159, p. 76, the Co. to M. T. Grattan, Austin, Minn., June 16, 1875; p. 69, the Co. to J. Edgar, Rochester, Minn., June 16, 1875; p. 266, telegram to C. H. McCormick, June 23, 1875. S. L. Beardsley, Buchanan, Mich., to the Co., June 28, 1875.

[110] *Ibid.*, No. 159, pp. 438, 705, the Co. to J. A. Shaffer, Kankakee, June 28, 1875, and to J. Edgar, Rochester, Minn., July 6, 1875.

[111] E. A. McNair, Dallas, to the Co., Feb. 2, 27, Mch. 26, Apr. 30, July 9, Sept. 15, 1875. In the letter of Mch. 26, the agent informed the Co. that the Grange purchasing agent had adopted the McCormick machines. "I find assuming a sort of high toned Bank of England kind of respectability takes mighty well and separates us from the clap-trap carpetbag class of machine men who have been over running this country." Texas will soon be the banner McCormick state. L.P.C.B. No. 159, p. 388, the Co. to E. A. McNair, June 26, 1875. By 1878 the McCormick Co. had also appointed a general agent at Austin. In 1883 the Co. sold about 1000 machines in Texas.

[112] The country south of the Platte River in Nebraska was a much better selling territory than that to the north. Spare parts were particularly in

appointment because only 3,500 of their 5,000 harvesters found purchasers, it was a most successful year. Over thirteen thousand sales were made and a net profit of about a half-million dollars was shown when the accounts were balanced in August.[113] The Grangers were no longer troublesome and the depredations of the grasshoppers were less widespread than for several years in the past. Apparently the worst of the hard times was over.[114]

The seven lean years in the central West between 1869 and 1875 were succeeded by eight harvests when times were considerably brighter for the farmers, and very prosperous for the McCormicks both at home and abroad. Although an improvement in the general business situation was apparent in demand in this region, since farmers could get no hard wood to make their own repairs. *Ibid.*, No. 140, p. 480, the Co. to W. N. Spring, Sioux City, Ia., Mch. 25, 1873: "We look forward to the time when the vast country northwest of Yankton shall be our main territory for the sale of Reapers." No. 151, p. 157, the Co. to B. F. Gorsuch, Carson City, Neb., June 11, 1874. The Zion's Cooperative Asso. at Salt Lake, which McCormick had used as an agent for several years, was virtually bankrupt by the opening of 1874. About five hundred machines were sold in Utah in 1873, but very few of them were McCormicks'. The "Champion" was the most popular. D. W. Pratt to the Co., from Wisner, Neb., Apr. 7, 13, 29, 1875 and from Salt Lake City, Dec. 24, 1875, Jan. 7, 1876: "There are 800-100 harvesting machines sold each year in this Terr. and it is mostly a cash trade. I have picked out J. W. Lowell & Co. as your agent." H. C. Addis to the Co., Feb. 1, 4, 19, 1874. *Post,* ftn. 138.

[113] L.P.C.B. No. 160, p. 300, the Co. to J. Edgar, Rochester, Minn., July 17, 1875. F. H. Matthews to C. H. McCormick, Aug. 3, 11, Sept. 20, Oct. 4, 21, 1875. The unusually large corn crop of 1875 aided McCormicks' collections.

[114] In "Van Nostrand's Electric Engineering Magazine" (N. Y.) IV (1871), p. 544, it was estimated that about 125,000 harvesting machines were made each year in the U. S. "Arguments Before the Committee on Patents of the House of Representatives, in February and March, 1878, on House Bill 1612, to Amend the Laws Relating to Patents" (Washington, 1878), pp. 5-7, 40, 55-63. Here it is stated that in 1875 about 159,410 harvesting machines were made for sale. Of these, 2,500 were manufactured in New England, 63,225 in N. Y., 47,850 in Ohio, 23,650 in Ill. On the other hand, "The Iron Age" (N. Y.), Oct. 11, 1877, reported that about 100,000 harvesting machines were made annually in the U.S. Probably this figure for 1877 should be twice as large.

1875, two years more went by before money began to flow freely toward the factory office from purchasers who in many instances had bought their machines five or six years before.[115] The partners no longer had to borrow in order to pay current expenses, and the new plant which was thought so big when it was completed in 1873 was already taxed to capacity to meet the demand. The per machine cost of manufacturing annually decreased between 1875 and 1880,[116] and the profits steadily mounted until early in the next decade when the gain from the business of two harvest seasons almost equalled the entire capitalization of the company.[117]

Because of low prices and unfavorable weather, land-owners in the diversified farming belt of the central West did not

[115] As an example of the continuance of the "hard times" through 1876, see G. A. Freudenreich, Alexandria, Minn., to the Co., Nov. 5, 1876. In the Sauk Centre district, foreclosures were then taking place at the rate of two or three daily, and Freudenreich had seen a team, harness, and wagon sell for $.57. See also, letters to the Co. of W. N. Spring, Sioux City, Ia., Oct. 24, 1876, W. H. Bowman, Farmington, Ia., Oct. 31, 1876, L. H. Shepard, Burnett, Wis., Sept. 10, 1876, and J. H. Shaffer, Kankakee, Ill., Sept. 1, 1876. For letters to the Co. of the autumn of 1877 showing that farmers in many sections had money for the first time in almost a decade, see E. W. Brooks, Winona, Minn., Sept. 27, G. H. Brewster, Mankato, Minn., Sept. 1, and F. Craycroft, Sedalia, Mo., Sept. 14. F. H. Matthews to C. H. McCormick, Sept. 21, 1877. In 1877, $1,118,510.23 was sent in by agents; in 1878, $1,597,757.54, and in 1879 up to Oct. 22,—$1,347,387.37. See, #"Memo. Comparing Cash Receipts from Agents, Oct. 22, 1879."

[116] The per machine cost of manufacturing in 1876 was $62.61; in 1877, $55.02; in 1878, $38.77, in $1879, $38.25, in 1880, $41.21, and in 1881, $44.28. Of this, the labor cost in 1879 was $14.82, 1880, $15.07, 1881, $17.39. Factory materials were lower in price in the fall of 1877 than at any time since 1860. L.P.C.B. No. 174, p. 729, F. H. Matthews to C. H. McCormick, Oct. 2, 1877. In the autumn of 1878, iron and steel were at still lower levels. See, *Idem* to *idem*, Aug. 26, 1878. In Sept., 1879, however, they had considerably advanced over the figure of the autumn before. #C. A. Spring, Jr., to C. H. McCormick, Sept. 20, 1879. L.P.C.B. No. 195, p. 260, the Co. to B. Holbrook, Bloomington, Ill., Oct. 25, 1879

[117] The approximate net profit of the firm in 1877 was $325,000, in 1878, $618,000, in 1879, $475,000, in 1880, $1,192,733, and in 1881, $1,232,781. C. H. McCormick to H. Day, Feb. 13, 1882. #C. A. Spring, Jr., to C. H. McCormick, Oct. 1, 1881.

seed as much wheat as usual in the autumn of 1875. The open winter, followed by a rainy spring and summer, damaged the small grain in this section of the Mississippi Valley. Rust also took a heavy toll.[118] North of Kansas, however, the wheat crop was excellent, although some farmers succumbed to "Black Hills fever" and ran away from their debts.[119] Here, in these new wheat lands, grain-growers insisted upon using harvester-binders. These cost about $125 more than the harvester, which but a year or two before had been considered the ideal machine for cutting wheat, but farmers were eager to be freed from "the necessity of having a house full of hired help, many of them the worst kind of tramps."[120] Compared with a harvester, an automatic binder saved an average of a bushel of grain per acre, and the labor of two men. By the close of the summer of 1876 each of McCormick's forty general agents was displaying a wire-binder, the successful product of two seasons of experimentation in many harvest fields between Texas and Canada.[121]

[118] L.P.C.B. No. 167, p. 60, the Co. to C. H. McCormick, N. Y., July 6, 1876; No. 168, p. 633, to J. J. Rhodes, Hastings, Minn., Oct. 28, 1876. Letters to the Co. in 1876 of J. S. Buck, Princeton, Ill., Jan. 31, G. Reynolds, Litchfield, Ill., Apr. 3, C. L. Granger, Effingham, Ill., Apr. 21, G. A. Willey, Belleville, Ill., May 14, F. Craycroft, Sedalia, Mo., June 18, July 5, 14, 15, Sept. 2, and of W. Westerman, Dubuque, Ia., July 5. Many farmers in Kas. had experimented with flax for several years but were now said to be returning to corn and the small grains. F. Craycroft, Columbus, Kas., to the Co., Apr. 18, 1877.

[119] W. N. Spring, Sioux City, Ia., to the Co., Mch. 27, July 11, 1876, and Apr. 7, 1877: "The fools are not all dead yet." F. J. Montgomery, Hastings, Neb., to the Co., July 16 and Aug. 1, 1876. The first McCormick agent in the Black Hills region was appointed in 1881, but the Co. was unrepresented there by 1883. The McCormicks sold 10,029 machines in 1876 and had 7,735 left over.

[120] Letters to the Co. of E. W. Brooks, Red Wing, Minn., Mch. 17, 1876, J. J. Rhodes, Hastings, Minn., Apr. 12, 1876, I. N. Van Hoesen, Lawrence, Kas., May 26, 1876, and of G. W. Brewster, Mankato, Minn., June 7, 1876.

[121] L.P.C.B. No. 162a, p. 98, the Co. to S. L. Beardsley, Buchanan, Mich., Dec. 1, 1875, No. 167, p. 823, to E. A. McNair, Dallas, Texas, Aug. 15, 1876. The McCormick Co. made about 25 binders of the Withington type in

The Centennial Exposition of 1876 at Philadelphia afforded an opportunity to show the new harvester-binder to the farmers of the eastern states.[122] They came in large numbers to view the machine, but they did not respond with many orders. All things considered, the Great Fair was a disappointment to Cyrus McCormick, notwithstanding the fact that it was an important landmark in the development of his foreign market.[123] Agricultural Hall, where he was allotted an inadequate space for his exhibit, had a leaky, tar-covered roof which was whitewashed on its underside. Bits of lime scaled off and fell down on his display, and when the weather grew

1875 for experimental purposes. Except for some wire breakage they did excellent work. In that harvest neither the Gordon nor Locke (Wood) type of binder performed well. In 1876, R. Hall McCormick, with expert mechanics from the factory, worked the binder through the harvest from Texas to Canada. As a result of the field tests in Texas an improved tucker was added in June, and thereafter the Withington binder defeated the Locke and Gordon in almost every field contest where they were worked side by side. The McCormicks sold sixteen binders that year and a thousand in 1877, although all of their harvesters were so made that binders could be added to them later. It was generally acknowledged to be the best on the market but it was not perfect, occasionally breaking wire or tying too loose bundles. A total of about 1500 wire-binders were sold in the U. S. in 1876, 3500 in 1877, and 15,000 in 1878.

[122] The McCormick Co. also exhibited an improved "Advance" and a mower. L.P.C.B. No. 165, p. 63, the Co. to C. B. Withington, Phila., Apr. 17, 1876. The eastern trade did not perceptibly increase as a result of the Fair although for the first time since before the Civil War an agent was appointed in N. J. in the autumn of 1878, and one in central N. Y. in the spring of 1879. E. K. Butler, from Washington, D. C., to the Co., May 11, 1878. He believed that the Co. could sell many machines on the east coast if it were willing to forego freight charges. As a matter of fact, about 100 machines every year were sold by the McCormicks in Pa.

[123] *Supra*, p. 445. Mrs. McCormick visited the Centennial for about ten days in late Sept., staying at the Transcontinental Hotel: "full of the worst kind of *malarious* odors, but I have an outside room and keep windows up day and night. . . . If there should remain one wheat drill or sewing machine or lace shawl or oil painting or even a *peruvian mummy* not seen by me, I should not count it any great loss, having seen so much that is·delightful and improving." C. H. McCormick, Jr., MSS. Book "B," N. F. McCormick to C. H. McCormick, Jr., Sept. 30, 1876.

warm the tar seeped through and dropped to the floor.[124] Although his machines were of fine workmanship, they were not as appealing to the eye as the gold, silver, and rosewood mower exhibited by Andrew Whiteley. Steam was not available before mid-June and until that time Charles Colahan, who represented McCormick, operated the binding mechanism with a crank, laboriously tying about three thousand sheaves of straw with wire.[125]

For reasons of economy, the Finance Committee revoked its early promise to give $5,000 in prizes to the victors in the harvesting machinery field contests. Instead of money, identic bronze medals were prepared, with all distinctions between the merits of the winners confined to the report of the Bureau of Awards. The arena was the farm of C. S. Vandegrift near Eddington, Pennsylvania, and Colahan leased fourteen acres of grain near by as a testing ground where his employer's machines could be groomed for the race.[126] "The Advance" reaper-mower, however, reached the field at the last moment and was improperly "set up" when it entered the trial. Both the grass and grain to be cut were crushed down by rollers so as to compel the rival machines to overcome the most difficult of field conditions. The contest was won by the "Champion" entries.[127]

[124] Letters to the Co. of C. H. McCormick, Oct. 29, 1875, and of C. B. Withington, from Philadelphia, Apr. 18, 19, 21, 26, 27, 1876. L.P.C.B. No. 162, pp. 424, 686, 732, and No. 163, p. 74, letters of the Co. to B. Landreth, Philadelphia, between Oct. 14, 1875 and Jan. 25, 1876.

[125] C. Colahan to C. H. McCormick, May #21, 24, 25, and June 10, 1876.

[126] C. Colahan to C. H. McCormick, June #1, 3, 5, 6, 9, and July 14, 1876. L.P.C.B. No. 166, pp. 84, 255, Co. to C. Colahan, June 1 and 8, 1876. E. H. Knight, Philadelphia, to Co., Sept. 25, 1876.

[127] C. Colahan to C. H. McCormick, June 28 and #July 22, 1876. L.P.C.B. No. 166, p. 609, Co. to C. Colahan, June 22, 1876. "Chicago Times," July 11, 1876. "Frank Leslie's Illustrated Newspaper" (New York), July 22, 1876, p. 321. McCormick received two bronze medals and the accompanying certificates of award for his exhibit. See, The United States Centennial Commission to C. H. McCormick, Oct. 27, 1877.

In the same year the McCormick, made a fresh start on the Pacific Coast.[128] The Farmers' Co-operative Union of San José and Stockton was one of their principal representatives in California, while in Oregon and Washington Territory, as in Texas, Granger societies were often employed as their agents. Farmers in the far Northwest rarely suffered from a poor harvest and the general agent with his office at Portland or Salem, Oregon, gradually built up a profitable market for Chicago-made machines in his large sales territory. Reapers and mowers were freighted long distances to farmers living in the Rogue River Valley of southern Oregon.[129]

Agricultural conditions in California were so unlike those of the central West that McCormicks' traveling agents there

[128] L. P. C. B. No. 163, pp. 49, 333, the Co. to P. Mohan, San Francisco, Jan. 24, 1876. P. Mohan to the Co., Dec. 21, 1875, Jan. 11, and Feb. 11, 1876. He estimated that in 1875 three thousand reapers and mowers from the East entered the port of San Francisco for sale in Cal., Ore., and Wash. Terr. Most of these bore the stamp of the "Buckeye," "Champion" and "Wood" firms. The McCormick harvester-binder was not sent to the West Coast until 1878, or two years after it was first sold in the Middle West.

[129] L.P.C.B. No. 166, pp. 344, 849, the Co. to P. Mohan, June 12 and July 30, 1876. The McCormicks sold 144 machines on the West Coast in 1876. Of these about fifty were purchased by farmers in Ore. and Wash. Terr. J. A. Miller, Portland, Ore., to P. Mohan, Apr. 19, Aug. 6, 1876; June 18, and Sept. 6, 1877. P. Mohan to the Co., July 15, 1876. L. W. S. Downs, Portland, Ore., to the Co., Dec. 8, 1876. Downs claimed that for 36 years the wheat crop of Oregon had not failed, and that the wheat commanded 5¢ a bushel higher price in the English market than any other. Due to the big immigration and more favorable climate, Oregon in his opinion would soon grow more wheat than California. He said it had the highest yield per acre of any state in the U. S. L.P.C.B. No. 169, p. 825, No. 170, p. 587, the Co. to T. B. Wait, Salem, Ore., Jan. 12, and Feb. 21, 1877. Letters to the Co. of Knapp, Burrell & Co., Portland, Ore., Aug. 25, 1877, and of Cunningham & Co., Salem, Ore., Nov. 3, 1877. The McCormick Co. continued to ship machines to Ore. by way of Cape Horn, allowing about four months from N. Y. for the trip. Surplus machines in Utah were sometimes sent overland to the Oregon market. Railroad rates on machines from Chicago to Sacramento in Apr., 1878, were 5¢ a pound. J. H. Shields, Roseburg, Ore., June 18 and Aug. 5, 1878. About 115 McCormick harvester-binders were sold in Ore. in 1878.

felt that they were in a foreign land. Both in California and northern Utah wheat was often very heavy, so much so in fact that harvesters were impractical because the riding gavel-makers could not tie sheaves fast enough to keep the loose grain from spilling from the binders' table as the machine moved ahead. The harvest season in California was usually so dry that ripe grain could be left standing for days without being cut, although there was danger that the wind would shell out the kernels.[130] Wooden wheels warped in the hot sun, and unless provided with lugs, they failed to grip the hard-packed soil firmly enough to operate the gears and cogs of a machine.[131] Both California and some sections of Oregon and Washington were admirably adapted to the use of a header. Although large wheat ranches were a striking characteristic of California at this time, there were many small farmers who could not afford, and did not need, this big expensive imple-ment.[132] Manufacturers of reapers and binders encouraged the quite general feeling that the use of headers resulted in weedy fields, since they cut only the tops of the grain stalks and left the shorter tares to ripen and drop their seeds.[133]

Many California farmers, however, were exasperated by purchasing machines from eastern manufacturers who aban-doned the field after a year or two, leaving their clients unable to secure spare parts. The McCormick firm was obliged to

[130] P. Mohan to the Co., Aug. 22, Oct. 26, and Nov. 7, 1876.

[131] Farmers' Union, San José, Cal., to the Co., June 8, 1878.

[132] B. F. Luce, San Francisco, to the Co., June 22 and Oct. 7, 1875. In 1874 there were over 2,000,000 acres under wheat in central Cal. Dr. Glenn of the San Joaquin Valley had a farm of 27,000 acres.

[133] Letters to the Co. of P. Mohan, July 6, 1876, Farmers' Coöp. Union, Stockton, Cal., Sept. 26 and Oct. 12, 1876 (this "Union" asked the Mc-Cormick Co. not to confuse it with the Grangers), L. W. S. Downs, Port-land, Ore., Nov. 21, 1876, T. B. Wait, Salem, Ore., Jan. 26, 1877, and of E. E. Ames, Mch. 15, and May 31, 1878: "Your harvester-binders are mak-ing converts of those who hitherto have used headers." J. H. Shields, Port-land, Ore., June 22, 1878: "The binder is driving the header out of Oregon." L.P.C.B., No. 177, p. 629, the Co. to E. E. Ames, Feb. 15, 1878.

assure a business house of Sacramento, which it wished as its agent, that it was determined to make California a permanent part of its sales territory.[134] Nevertheless, trade there was never large or very remunerative. Several poor crop years in the 1870's because of drought were partly to blame, but high freight charges and unwillingness to manufacture headers were probably more important.[135] McCormicks' general agent complained that California was "the hardest country I've ever seen to get a foothold in." [136] The popularity of the header could not be undermined, and in the 1880's more and more Californians used a combine that not only snipped off the heads of their wheat but threshed and bagged it as well.[137]

Thanks to John W. Lowell & Co. of Salt Lake City, a considerable market for mowers and droppers was developed in northern Utah, and this energetic agency was soon wagoning machines six hundred miles northward for sale in eastern

[134] E. E. Ames, Sacramento, to the Co., Dec. 14, 1876, and Mch. 14, 31, 1877. *Ibid.*, No. 169, pp. 791, 820, the Co. to E. E. Ames, Jan. 11, and to H. E. Hills, San José, Cal., Jan. 12, 1877.

[135] Letters to the Co. of J. A. Miller, San Francisco, Jan. 3, 1877; E. E. Ames, May 11, and Sept. 22, 1877. Drouth in 1877 ruined business, and the harvest of 1876 was also below average. Farmers in 1878 were too poor to buy. Farmers' Union, San José, Cal., to the Co., May 16, 1878. Not until 1879 did the McCormick Co. appoint a permanent general agent for Cal., and as late as 1882 the firm complained that its business in that state did not pay. It was selling 250-300 machines a year there by 1884. L.P.C.B. No. 188, p. 52, the Co. to E. E. Ames, Sacramento, Feb. 11, 1879, and No. 222, p. 606 to N. E. Barnes, San Francisco, Apr. 10, 1882. #J. D. Hooker, San Francisco, Cal., to C. H. McCormick, Jr., Aug. 17 and 21, 1883.

[136] McCormicks' traveling representative also found Cal. a most expensive country to work in, both because of the large amount of advertisement necessary, and the long distances which had to be traveled. P. Mohan, San Francisco, to the Co., Apr. 29, 1876.

[137] As early as 1876 one correspondent claimed that Cal. wheat was gradually being displaced by orchards, vineyards, and cotton. J. A. Miller, San Francisco, to the Co., Dec. 16, 1876. Nebraska farmers were also buying many headers at this time. E. S. Hawley & Co., Nebraska City, Neb., to the Co., June 28, 1876.

Montana.[138] In like manner, the general agent at Omaha extended the scope of his operations to eastern Colorado and found about a hundred purchasers each year in the vicinity of Denver, Greeley and Boulder.[139]

Helped by their new wire-binder, the fine weather, excellent crops, and rising grain prices, the McCormick factory was overburdened with orders in 1877. The emergence of farmers from the long period of depression was reflected in their good spirits and their willingness to buy expensive automatic binders.[140] Land values were rising and homesteaders who had

[138] Letters to the Co. of D. W. Pratt, Feb. 23, 27, Mch. 26, Apr. 16, June 11, Aug. 19, Sept. 11, 13, and Dec. 10, 1876. He found Utah a safe place in which to sell, since the farmers owned their land and were there to stay. About fifty McCormick machines were sold there in 1876, and twice that number in 1877. The first sales in Mont. were in 1878 and the first agent was there in the winter of 1879-80. Letters to the Co. of J. W. Lowell & Co., Salt Lake City, Mch. 1, Aug. 29, 1877, Mch. 19, 1878, and of C. H. Smyth, Salt Lake City, June 25, 1878; L.P.C.B. No. 168, p. 107, the Co. to D. W. Pratt, Salt Lake City, Sept. 4, 1876.

[139] *Ibid.*, No. 165, p. 513, the Co. to H. R. Gould, Omaha, May 11, 1876. Here the agent was directed not to bestow much attention upon Colo. because it was too far away. McCormick Co. sold 80 harvesters and 6 mowers there in 1877 and about 100 in 1878. H. R. Gould, Omaha, to the Co., June 30, 1877: "It is terrible work to bind by hand in Colo. where the straw is so hard they have to lay some in their irrigation ditches to soften so they can use it for bands. So they particularly need automatic binders." Wm. Billing, Denver, Colo., to the Co., Dec. 23, 27, 1877, Jan. 9, 20, Feb. 19, 1878: "Farms look poor around here but it will be a paradise as soon as irrigation comes." He had been apptd. genl. agent. Hitherto the business had been managed from Omaha.

[140] Letters to the Co. in 1877 of J. A. Seaver, Quincy, Ill., May 28, E. A. McNair, Dallas, Texas, May 23, G. A. Freudenreich, Brainerd, Minn., May 29, T. H. Ritter, Columbus, O., May 21, W. F. Cowhan, Jackson, Mich., May 8, O. T. Grattan, Decorah, Ia., Apr. 24, F. Craycroft, Sedalia, Mo., Mch. 15, I. N. Van Hoesen, Lawrence, Kan., Mch. 22, J. F. Montgomery, Hastings, Neb., Mch. 18, and A. M. Hamilton, Staunton, Va., May 18. L.P.C.B. No. 164, p. 421, Co. to W. R. B. Smyth, Freeport, Ill., Mch. 22, 1876: "The cash price of a harvester-binder is $300, and the credit price, $330. A binder alone sells for $125 cash or $140 on credit terms." Small grain in the central belt of the Middle West was so fine in 1877 that farmers from Ohio to Kansas were lamenting that they had not seeded

abandoned their holdings because of the grasshoppers were returning to resume the work of improvement in earnest. The rush of settlers to begin farming along the Northern Pacific and St. Paul & Pacific Railroads meant a greatly enlarged acreage of spring wheat and a corresponding increase in the market for agricultural machinery.[141]

Late in July, 1877, when the final shipments of the season were ready to leave for Minnesota, the McCormick Company and many other manufacturing concerns in Chicago and elsewhere were rudely shaken out of their complacency by a widespread railroad strike, the most serious labor disturbance in United States history up to that time.[142] Fearing the destruction of their property, double shifts of watchmen were maintained at the plant, which was about to close for the taking of the annual inventory. According to Mrs. McCormick, the strikers were mostly "chronic malcontents" and " 'won't work' people" who in the face of a superior force of troops and police would "submit this time, hoping to *organize* better *next time.*"[143] She sensed, however, that this unrest had a deep significance for the propertied interests of the country. When, in the following spring, Chicagoans were nervous because of

more of it. Some Minnesota and western Iowa farmers still complained of grasshoppers. The McCormick Co. sold 10,354 machines.

[141] The harvest season of 1877, as well as all others between 1875 and 1879, was very rainy throughout broad areas of the central West. Letters to the Co. from G. A. Freudenreich, Alexandria, Minn., and Fargo, Dak. Terr., May 29, June 25, Nov. 19, 30, and Dec. 6, 1877, G. H. Brewster, Mankato, Minn., Oct. 29, 1877, and A. B. Montgomery, Princeton, Mo., Dec. 14, 1877.

[142] Telegrams of C. H. McCormick to the Co., July 25, 1877, and of L. J. McCormick to F. H. Matthews, July 27, 1877. C. A. Spring, Jr., to C. H. McCormick, July 26 and 28, 1877. L.P.C.B. No. 173, pp. 717, 745, Co. to M. T. Grattan, Preston, Minn., July 25, 1877, and to E. W. Brooks, Red Wing, Minn., July 27, 1877; No. 173, pp. 669, 724, telegrams of Co. to L. J. McCormick, July 20 and 26, 1877.

[143] C. H. McCormick, Jr., MSS. Book "B," N.F. to C. H. McCormick, Jr., July 24, 1877. "Chicago Times," July 26, 1877. The strikers seemed to be particularly determined to compel McCormicks' employees to quit work.

a "communist scare," she sent a press clipping about it to her eldest son, then in Princeton College, warning him that it was "the muttering of a coming storm." "I wish you would pass it [the clipping] to some of the young men," she added, "who, from their position, will probably be called upon to meet these questions in the future. *All* young men will have to deal with them—but some will have a *controlling* position." [144] Prophetic words, in view of the part that her son would be called upon to play in the historic strike at the McCormick Works eight years later!

As early as 1868 the prevention of social unrest had been advanced by a Chicago pastor as one important reason why Cyrus McCormick should contribute to the support of a church mission among the foreign population. "If you were not a Christian," the request ran, "I would urge this matter as a judicious investment to be more than repaid by the enhanced value of property in a city where peace and order are best secured by the restraints of religion." [145] The inventor sent $500, but six years later he consented to become an honorary member of the First Regiment, Illinois National Guard, which was believed to be "a matter of necessity for the welfare of Chicago." [146] Not long thereafter, he aided in the purchase of uniforms and equipment for the Second Regiment. This unit had "won great credit for its action during the . . . disturbances [of the summer of 1877] and can equally be relied on in the future." [147] The Church was property's first line of defense, and if that failed, then powder and shot could be used as a last resort.

[144] *Ibid.*, Book "E," N. F. McCormick to C. H. McCormick, Jr., May 6, 1878.

[145] ‡D. C. Marquis, Chicago, to C. H. McCormick, Mch. 25, 1868.

[146] Committee on Honorary Members, 1st Regt., Ill. Natl. Guard to C. H. McCormick, Oct. 9, 1874. "Chicago Daily Tribune," July 27, 1874, May 9, and 11, 1876.

[147] W. J. Onahan, Chicago, to C. H. McCormick, Aug. 30, 1877.

In the spring of 1878, Marshall Field, C. P. Kellogg, Edson Keith, R. T. Crane, and others of the most respected men of the city, answered the communist agitation by forming a Citizens' Association for their mutual protection.[148] The business interests of Chicago were classified according to kind, and as secretly as possible were apportioned quotas of money to raise for the purchase of a battery of six guns and equipment for the Sixth Regiment and two hundred cavalrymen.[149] Cyrus McCormick joined the association in 1879 and was advised by Charles A. Spring, Jr., to help liberally to keep the regiments up to full strength, since they were "of vital importance . . . for our preservation." [150]

[148] The communists were said to be organizing military companies. "Chicago Daily Tribune," Apr. 25, 26, 27, 28, May 6, 27, June 2, 15, 17, 27, 1878. Chicago was in financial difficulty at this time, and the school-teachers were paid in scrip. The letter of June 3, 1878, written to C. H. McCormick by Susan Prince, Principal of the Pickard School, might well have been penned fifty-five years later when the teachers were in a similar predicament. "Some of the teachers of this school are not able to *cash* their *scrip* and are in need of money for *board* and *other* necessaries. Thinking *you may* be able to take some of it for taxes, I dare to address you. It is *humiliating* —begging the *favor;* but a *horror* of *running into debt drives* us to it. We have worked faithfully for what was *promised* us; and *regret* our *misfortune,* being in a city that considers it *right* to meet its *obligations* in *such* a way."

[149] J. W. Oakley, Chicago, to McCormick Co., May 27 and June 1, 1878: "Thirty or Forty Citizens of the City have had during the last 2 Weeks several private meetings to ascertain by means best at hand what danger if any was to be anticipated the coming summer from the communistic element in the city. A committee . . . reported . . . after taking some time to investigate the matter, [that] in their judgment [there] was a good deal cause of alarm & recommended the purchase of arms & guns, etc. . . . I think it most important that our subscriptions are kept strictly private & do not purpose that any one except the contributors shall know *who* contribute unless they tell it themselves." The Citizens' Association also had as its program "the consolidation of the three Towns comprised in the city limits, . . . the total suppression of the stenches, the consideration of plans for water supply, sewerage and main drainage, . . . the abatement of the smoke nuisance, the better regulation of the bridges, and the street pavements."

[150] ‡C. A. Spring, Jr., to C. H. McCormick, Nov. 15, 1879. A. L. Bell, Chicago, to C. H. McCormick, Jr., Jan. 25, 1886, Bell asked McCormick to

The McCormicks had much at stake and every year's business added to their wealth. Counting the harvester-binder as two implements, they sold over eighteen thousand machines in 1878, and their net profits were well above $600,000. Never had there been such a season before.[151] The early spring and favorable prices encouraged the farmers of the central belt of the Middle West to devote more land than usual to the small grains. Crops were excellent everywhere except in California.[152] Although D. M. Osborne and the "Buckeye" companies of Ohio were now in the field with many wire-binders, the McCormick agents took orders for almost two thousand more of these machines than the factory could supply. Angry farmers and salesmen that summer made life exciting for the clerks in the Chicago office,[153] and at its close Cyrus McCor-

contribute $100 to aid in recruiting the 1st Regt. up to 800 men. "We give our time to the work of the regiment & believe that the time is not far distant when Chicago will need us for the protection of lives & property." McCormick declined. This is interesting in view of the strike at the McCormick Works a few months later, culminating in the Haymarket Riot in early May.

[151] L.P.C.B. No. 180, p. 374, Co. to H. R. Gould, Omaha, May 16, 1878: "The facts of the case are that we are driven to death here at the factory; are running 22 hours out of the 24, shipping out ten carloads a day, and are still 150 carloads behind our orders." The Co. sold a total of 18,401 machines in 1878, including 6,084 binders. W. J. Hanna to C. H. McCormick, Sept. 7, 1878; F. H. Matthews to N. F. McCormick, Oct. 9, 1878, and to C. H. McCormick, Feb. 21, 1879.

[152] Letters to the Co. in 1878 of G. H. Brewster, Mankato, Minn., Feb. 6, W. N. Spring, Sioux City, Ia., Jan. 18, Mch. 14, 23, May 28, F. Craycroft, New Madrid, Mo., Feb. 11, W. W. Hamilton, Casey, Ill., Mch. 2, T. H. Ritter, Columbus, O., Mch. 2, S. L. Beardsley, Kalamazoo, Mich., Mch. 11, H. S. Shields, Louisville, Ky., Mch. 19, and L. P. Gillette, Lincoln, Neb., Mch. 23.

[153] Letters to the Co. in 1878 of W. Billing, Denver, Colo., June 15, 24, 25, D. W. Pratt, Belleville, Ill., June 13, W. F. Cowhan, Jackson, Mich., June 19, and E. W. Brooks, Red Wing, Minn., June 22. H. M. Griffin wrote from Hastings, Neb., June 24: "Our agents are terribly disappointed after working so hard." G. A. Freudenreich of St. Cloud, Minn., on June 4, believed that the exhaustion of the supply was "the most destructive bombshell that has ever struck our cause." H. S. Shields of Louisville, Ky., wrote

mick cabled from France that he had won the highest award of the Paris Exposition.[154] Nothing more was needed to make it a memorable year.

The next season was scarcely less remunerative, although farmers complained once again of hard times. The company introduced its new iron-mower with great success and made ready to replace its old standby, "The Advance," by a new two-wheeled reaper-mower with a controllable self-rake.[155] Price slashing by competitors led the McCormicks for the first time in their business history to give a ten- or twenty-dollar credit for the old machine of any farmer who would purchase a new one. By this desperate expedient they held their own in the bitter trade war, and helped also by the fair harvest, they sold almost as many implements as in the preceding year.[156]

on May 25 that he was "swamped" with orders, while G. H. Brewster of Mankato, Minn., angrily made plain that after the long hard times "agents are now entitled to all the machines they can sell." See also, W. J. Hanna to A. Hinton, Castalia, N. C., Aug. 9, 1878.

[154] C. Colahan to C. H. McCormick, Aug. 14, 1878. L.P.C.B. No. 183, p. 815, Co. to F. Craycroft, Sedalia, Mo., Sept. 10, 1878: "Victories have been *thundering all round the sky!* The McCormicks never had such brilliant prospects."

[155] *Supra*, p. 403. Agents, as early as 1877, pressed the McCormick Co. to build a light iron-mower. See, H. R. Gould, Omaha, to Co., Feb. 26, 1877; H. S. Shields, Louisville, Ky., to Co., Feb. 18, 1878. In 1877, also, the Co. for the first time realized that it was seriously handicapped by not having a controllable rake on "The Advance." See, F. H. Matthews to C. H. McCormick, Sept. 2, Oct. 1, 8, and Nov. 29, 1877, Nettie F. McCormick to Co., Oct. 10, 1877, F. Craycroft, Sedalia, Mo., to Co., June 3, 1878, and D. H. Smith, Sparta, Wis., to Co., Feb. 5, 1878. Unexpectedly, the demand for "The Advance" revived in 1879, and the Co. was unable to meet the demand both for it and the iron-mower. The call for binders was not as heavy as had been anticipated.

[156] L.P.C.B. No. 191, pp. 433-434, Co. to E. K. Butler, Sedalia, Mo., June 11, 1879. Although competition in 1879 was particularly keen, superlatives would not be amiss in a description of the price-cutting tactics of any other harvest in the 1870's. For example, J. P. Whedon with obvious exaggeration wrote to the Co. from Sparta, Wis., on June 27, 1877: "Rival agents are trading machines for anything—Postage Stamps—Sauer Kraut—

Scarcity of wire had perhaps delayed the coming of the automatic binder, and in the summer of 1877 the McCormicks had been obliged to curtail their sales because they could not buy enough to meet their needs.[157] Wire, to be serviceable for tying gavels of grain, had to be of the right size, tough, pliable, inexpensive, and evenly spooled.[158] Annealed steel wire, averaging fifteen pounds to a spool, was found most satisfactory, and in 1876 there were only two mills in the country prepared to furnish it in amounts sufficient to supply the demands of the manufacturers of binders. These were the Cleveland Rolling Mill Company and the Washburn & Moen Manufacturing Company of Worcester, Massachusetts.[159] In the autumn of 1877, Wood and McCormick, who together dominated the wire-binder field, estimated that they could together sell about two thousand tons in the next harvest.[160] They joined force and "bull-dozed" the Cleveland firm into reducing its price to eight cents a pound, or considerably below its original offer. By their agreement the wire was to be

Hogs—Cats, Chickens, Mules, Spavined Horses and everything else." L.P.C.B. No. 190, p. 808, Co. to S. L. Beardsley, Kalamazoo, Mich., May 26, 1879: "It is always well to keep a cut [in price] quiet as long as you can as by so doing you can get some orders before the opposition find it out."

[157] L.P.C.B. No. 173, p. 256, Co. to Washburn & Moen Mfg. Co., Worcester, Mass., June 30, 1877.

[158] L.P.C.B. No. 172, p. 230, Co. to J. D. Allen, Le Roy, Minn., May 18, 1877; No. 174, p. 808, F. H. Matthews to C. H. McCormick, Oct. 8, 1877.

[159] Ibid., No. 174, F. H. Matthews to C. H. McCormick, Oct. 2, 1877. Cooper, Hewitt & Co. of Trenton, N. J., was selling wire by 1878.

[160] Ibid., No. 173, pp. 165-166, F. H. Matthews to C. H. McCormick, June 26, 1877: "Everything is going along with a perfect rush,—more so than I have ever seen it. . . . The Binders are doing splendidly but require close attention. . . . Nobody is doing anything with Binders but Wood & ourselves & we are beating Wood everywhere." See also, his letter to C. H. McCormick of July 13, 1877, and his letter in L.P.C.B. No. 173, p. 470, to E. W. Brooks, Red Wing, Minn., on July 11, 1877, in which he writes: "This harvest has demonstrated that we have . . . the only successful Binder in the field & the enthusiasm of the farmers over its working is something entirely unparalleled in the history of the business." By 1878 Osborne was also a serious competitor in the wire-binder field.

retailed to farmers for eleven or twelve cents a pound, and the mill was obliged to pledge that it would not sell to other parties.[161] There was considerable justification for this monopoly. The mechanism of a wire-binder, no matter how perfectly it was constructed, would not operate unless the wire were exactly adapted to it. The manufacturers, for the sake of the success of their machines, as well as for profit, felt obliged to control the wire supplied to their purchasers.[162] In order to secure so favorable a contract from the Cleveland Rolling Mills Company, McCormick and Wood guaranteed to pay cash for their wire. McCormick's bill was over $250,000. The farmers wished to buy it on credit terms, but although they were allowed to do so in many cases, the manufacturers' outlay for the wire was so large that every effort was made to sell it for cash.[163] In some instances it was wholesaled by the firm

[161] J. R. Parsons, Hoosick Falls, N. Y., to Co., Sept. 14, 1877, and to C. H. McCormick, Oct. 16 and Nov. 29, 1877; telegram of C. H. McCormick, to McCormick Co., Oct. 8, 1877. Nettie F. McCormick to F. H. Matthews, Oct. 6 and 10, 1877, F. H. Matthews to C. H. McCormick, Oct. 17 and Nov. 28, 1877, and (L.P.C.B. No. 175, p. 38) to L. J. McCormick, Oct. 16, 1877; W. A. Wood to C. H. McCormick, Dec. 7, 1877. The several efforts made by manufacturers of harvesting machinery between 1875 and 1880 to coöperate to keep up prices, failed. Aultman, Miller & Co., and particularly D. M. Osborne, were leaders in seeking to reach an agreement. Manufacturers were usually asked to pledge that they would adhere to their list prices. Promises to do so were broken, often because they could not control their agents.

[162] L.P.C.B. No. 186, p. 17, the Co. to G. W. Allen, Auburn, N. Y., Dec. 3, 1878: "We are going to discharge our St. Louis agent because he has bought wire from a rolling mill, and not from us." Ibid., pp. 163, 312, the Co. to Cleveland Rolling Mill Co., Dec. 6, 1878. Catalog for 1879 of D. M. Osborne & Co., Auburn, N. Y.

[163] The total amount of wire purchased by the McCormicks for the 1878 harvest was 1430 tons. The 3500 tons used in 1879 cost them a cash outlay of over $625,000. G. H. Brewster, Mankato, Minn., to the Co., Mch. 6, 1878. L.P.C.B. No. 185, pp. 92-93, the Co. to G. A. Freudenreich, St. Cloud, Minn., Oct. 30, 1878. The McCormick Co., whenever possible, sold wire to its own agents for cash. See, Ibid., No. 187, p. 403, the Co. to D. B. Heller,

to the agents and they were permitted to make a small profit by selling it to farmers. Even though so many tons of binding material were contracted for in 1878, crops ripened two weeks earlier than usual and Minnesota agents and farmers frantically called for wire when it did not reach them fast enough to meet the needs of the harvest.[164] The agent at Red Wing, among the most trusted of all McCormicks' field force, came to Chicago to tell his sad story that "would [make you] cry till a bucket wouldn't hold the tears." [165] He was sent on to Cleveland to do what he could to rush the wire forward from the mill. The cost to the McCormicks of shipping the heavy spools by express to Minnesota and Dakota that summer was about $25,000.[166] And yet the "St. Paul Pioneer Press" hotly attacked the Chicago firm for obliging the farmers of Minnesota to wait for their supply.[167]

Even before wire-binders had become of any significance in the harvests of America, men had pointed out that if they were used they would be dangerous to stock and injurious to threshing and milling machinery.[168] Little pieces of wire

Dallas, Texas, Jan. 21, 1879, and F. H. Matthews to C. H. McCormick, Jan. 27, 1879. With the advent of binders, inability to sell out the season's supply was a more serious matter than ever before, because it meant that much wire, representing a considerable amount of money, would also have to be carried over.

[164] *Ibid.*, No. 180, pp. 247, 361, the Co. to Cleveland Rolling Mill Co., Cleveland, May 11, 15, 1878, and No. 182, p. 148, to Washburn & Moen Mfg. Co., Worcester, Mass., July 4, 1878.

[165] E. W. Brooks, Red Wing, Minn., to the Co., June 29, 1878; F. H. Matthews to C. H. McCormick, Aug. 3, 1878, and W. J. Hanna to C. H. McCormick, Aug. 10, 1878. L.P.C.B. No. 182, pp. 80, 797, the Co. to E. W. Brooks, July 2 and 29, 1878, and No. 183, p. 146, to F. M. Thornton, Benson, Minn., Aug. 5, 1878.

[166] W. J. Hanna to C. H. McCormick, Aug. 21, 1878.

[167] "St. Paul Pioneer Press," July 28, 1878.

[168] *Supra*, Chap. XIII, p. 539. Farmers who had witnessed the field trials of McCormicks' wire-binders of 1875 were asked to make written statements denying that grain, so bound, injured either stock or threshing machines. L.P.C.B. No. 164, p. 175, the Co. to J. Edgar, Rochester, Minn.,

would be eaten by cattle with the straw or would tear the
bolting cloths and damage the brushes and stones of flour
mills. In so far as the millers were concerned, this forecast was
true, but there were few well-authenticated stories of cows
dying because they swallowed bits of metal.[169] It so happened
that several firms were making cord-binders as soon as wire-
binders in any number were placed upon the market.[170] These
builders of twine-binders were located either in Wisconsin or
near the great wheat-fields of Minnesota. Here at St. Paul
and Minneapolis were some of the largest flour-milling companies in the land. It was probably more than a coincidence
that the first vigorous protest against wire-binders came from
Minneapolis millers, living near the factories of twine-binder
firms who wished to sell, but dared not as yet to guarantee their
output.[171] In short, sales propaganda partially accounts for
the embarrassment of the McCormicks, Wood, Osborne, and
Gammon & Deering in the winter of 1878-1879. The "Cham-

Mch. 13, 1876. W. N. Spring, Sioux City, Ia., to the Co., Sept. 6, 1876.
J. Beggs, McGregor, Ia., to the Co., June 16, 1877.

[169] L.P.C.B. No. 173, p. 693, the Co. to W. VanEps, Sioux Falls, D.T.,
July 23, 1877; No. 188, p. 213, to D. H. Smith, Sparta, Wis., Feb. 18, 1879:
"It is rather singular that with 20,000 wire binders in use, this should be the
only case [of a cow dying from eating wire] . . . that we have heard of,
but such is the fact. . . . We suppose however that hereafter whenever a
cow or an ox dies for any cause its death will be attributed to the Wire
Binder, especially if the owner has a note to pay." No. 188, p. 393, to
C. Long & Co., Russellville, Ky., Feb. 27, 1879; No. 194, p. 54, to R. Newton, Austin, Texas, Sept. 20, 1879. The McCormick Co., in its confidential
correspondence, admitted that there was wire in wheat. *Ibid.*, No. 186, p. 678,
the Co. to W. A. Wood, Hoosick Falls, N. Y., Dec. 26, 1878: "There is no
doubt that there was wire in wheat this yr. probably always will be. . . .
We must face it."

[170] R. Newton, Austin, Texas, to the Co., June 1, 1878. This agent speaks
of tests being made in Texas of twine-binders manufactured at Beloit, Wis.

[171] Letters of the Co. in L.P.C.Bs. No. 184, p. 609, to D. W. Pratt, St.
Louis, Oct. 14, 1878; No. 185, pp. 528, 555, to F. M. Thornton, Benson,
Minn., Nov. 18, 1878, and to Fuller, Johnson & Co., Madison, Wis., Nov. 19,
1878; No. 186, p. 17, to G. W. Allen, Auburn, N. Y., Dec. 3, 1878. C. Colahan to C. H. McCormick, Nov. 18, 1878.

pion" concerns in Ohio, also preparing to build twine-binders, joined in the hue and cry against these firms for making machines which were dangerous alike to man and beast.[172] The millers of the Twin Cities resolved that they would pay ten cents less per bushel for wheat that was cut by wire-binders than for wheat bound by hand or automatically with twine. That a miller could tell when he bought a car-load of wheat what particular type of harvesting implement had cut the straw from which the grain had been threshed, was highly improbable.[173] At least some owners of threshing machines which moved through the country-side each autumn and winter, endorsed the attack of the millers against wire-binders.[174]

The offending firms at once decided to coöperate and start a backfire against this "libelous and slanderous" campaign of whispers, innuendoes, and forthright attacks upon a machine in which they and thousands of grain-growers had invested much money.[175] Because threshing crews ordinarily cut the bands around the sheaves with butcher-knives or hatchets, it was not strange that pieces of wire became mixed with the grain.[176] The McCormicks and other makers of wire-binders

[172] L.P.C.B. No. 186, p. 678, the Co. to W. A. Wood, Hoosick Falls, Dec. 26, 1878. F. H. Matthews to C. H. McCormick, Feb. 12, 1879.

[173] L.P.C.B. No. 186, p. 650, the Co. to N. Long & Co., Russellville, Ky., Dec. 26, 1878.

[174] F. A. Hodge, Independence, Ia., to I. N. VanHoesen, Aug. 15, 1877.

[175] Letters of the Co. in L.P.C.Bs. No. 184, pp. 638-639, to D. M. Osborne & Co., Auburn, N. Y., and to W. A. Wood, Oct. 16, 1878; No. 185, p. 503, to D. W. Pratt, St. Louis, Mo., Nov. 16, 1878. This agent was urged to procure statements from prominent millers in his district to the effect that wire did not injure their machinery. "This course will commit the millers to us before they are tampered with"; No. 186, pp. 251, 256, 417, to W. A. Wood and to Gammon & Deering, Dec. 11, 1878, and to D. M. Osborne & Co., Dec. 16, 1878; No. 186, pp. 339-385 (Dec., 1878) to many agents asking them to get affidavits from millers and farmers concerning the harmlessness of wire-binders. F. H. Matthews to C. H. McCormick, Nov. 29, 1878.

[176] L.P.C.B. No. 168, p. 56, the Co. to J. F. Utley, Sterling, Ill., Aug. 29, 1876.

soon provided *gratis,* or sold for a small price, "wire-retaining" nippers which cut the wire and held it until it was removed.[177] Where it was then flung by the busy workman obviously determined whether these nippers were much of an improvement over the knife or hatchet. While doing their utmost to overcome the prejudice against wire, the McCormicks and their competitors shrewdly let down an anchor to windward by experimenting with twine-binders, and racing for control of the basic patents covering these machines.[178] For many years in Europe, horseshoe magnets had been placed in the grain-spouts of flour-mills in order to remove metallic objects such as tacks and overall buttons. The McCormick Company sent magnets made by the Western Electric Manufacturing Company of Chicago to their agents for trial in the flour-mills of their districts.[179] One of the largest millers of St. Louis testified to their value, but the Illinois Millers' State Association, after a lively session, recommended that the use of wire-binders should be discontinued.[180] A reversal of opin-

[177] Letters to the Co. of S. L. Beardsley, Kalamazoo, Mich., July 21, 1877, and L. P. Gillette, Lincoln, Neb., Sept. 24, 1877. F. H. Matthews to C. H. McCormick, July 17, 1877. L.P.C.B. No. 179, pp. 128-129, the Co. to T. Cunningham & Co., Salem, Ore., Apr. 12, 1878, and No. 189, p. 519, to Waite, Burnell, Huggins & Co., London, England, Apr. 11, 1879.

[178] *Ibid.,* No. 173, p. 674, the Co. to C. B. Withington, July 21, 1877.

[179] Letters of the Co. in *Ibid.,* No. 187, p. 618, to H. S. Shields, Louisville, Ky., Jan. 28, 1879; No. 188, pp. 141, 232, 297, to E. W. Brooks, Red Wing, Minn., Feb. 14, 18 and 21, 1879; pp. 233, 238, to N. Long & Co., Russellville, Ky., Feb. 18, 1879; p. 621 to H. A. VanCampen, Cannon Falls, Minn., Mch. 10, 1879; and No. 189, p. 195, to Moline Plow Co., Kansas City, Mo., Mch. 28, 1879. Printed letter, entitled "Wire in Wheat," dated Chicago, Jan. 31, 1879, and addressed by D. Ransom, Osborne's agent there, "To Millers and Mill Furnishers."

[180] This was the Yaeger Milling Co. of St. Louis. It should be noted that the grain received by millers in the southern farming belt of the Middle West, in contrast with the grain of Minn., was not usually cut by wire-binders. To counteract the resolution of the Minneapolis Millers' Asso., the McCormick Co. secured from E. F. Archibald, who owned four flour-mills in Minn., a statement that wire did not injure milling machinery. The

ion was now sought from the millers of Minneapolis and St. Paul, but although they endorsed the use of magnets in their meeting of February, 1879, they declined to admit that this device would wholly protect their machinery against damage.[181] The agitation against wire-binders, however, subsided by harvest-time and the McCormicks and other firms found no trouble in selling all that they could build.

The dangers attending the use of the wire-binder were far overshadowed in importance by the saving in labor and the gain in comfort brought by the machine to the farmer with many acres under grain.[182] Ways to remove wire from wheat, satisfactory to all concerned, would surely have been found if the need to do so had persisted. The speedy collapse of the wire-binder boom after 1879 was not caused by the protests of millers and stock-raisers, but resulted from the opportune appearance of an equally effective mechanism which made bands from harmless cord. The ingenuity of Gorham and

"Chicago Daily Tribune," Dec. 5, 1878; "Leffel's Illustrated Milling and Mechanical News" (Springfield, O.), Mch., 1879; "Prairie Farmer," Feb. 8, 1879; "Western Rural" (Chicago), Feb. 15, 1879.

[181] L.P.C.B. No. 188, p. 312, Co. to E. W. Brooks, Red Wing, Minn., Feb. 22, 1879. F. H. Matthews to C. H. McCormick., Feb. 12, 1879. The McCormick Co., Wood, Osborne, and Gammon & Deering sent a man to Minneapolis and St. Paul to show the millers there how readily wire could be removed by the use of magnets. See, L.P.C.B. No. 188, p. 173, Co. to D. M. Osborne & Co., Feb. 15, 1879. "The Farmers' Advance," May, 1879; "The Minneapolis Tribune," Feb. 19, 1879; "The American Miller," Mch. 1, 1879; "St. Paul Pioneer Press," Feb. 23, 1879.

[182] "The Iron Age," Oct. 11, 1877. Here it was doubted whether wire-binders would ever come into general use except in regions of large-scale farming and where labor was high in price. In the opinion of the writer, it was more economical to use a Marsh Harvester than a wire-binder, as long as the daily wage of a harvest hand was not more than $2.40 (and it was usually considerably more in the Mississippi Valley). L.P.C.B. No. 188, p. 393, Co. to N. Long & Co., Russellville, Ky., Feb. 27, 1879; No. 189, p. 163, to Ames & Humphrey, Russell, Kan., Mch. 26, 1879: "The fact is that the Wire Binders are a necessity for handling grain. Farmers will have them in spite of all millers can say and if your mill will not buy their wheat the time will come when you will have to quit grinding."

Appleby, rather than an occasional dead cow or injured mill-stone, was the primary factor making for progress in the art of harvesting grain at this time.

The prosperity of the McCormick Company did not prevent the discord between the two brothers from reaching a climax during these years. In 1873 the senior partner consented with much reluctance to admit Robert Hall McCormick to the firm. The young man was self-confident and aggressive, and soon determined to concentrate his attention upon patents, the most complicated of subjects and one which required cautious handling even by the expert. He was expected to be the understudy of his father in the superintendence of the factory, but he found the outside work more congenial to his tastes, and Leander J. McCormick was not the one to say him nay. Cyrus McCormick, however, engaged Charles Colahan in May, 1874, to assist the company in matters relating to lawsuits and patents. Colahan thought of himself as an efficiency expert on most matters connected with the operation of a factory, and like Hall McCormick was impetuous and quick of temper.[183] Colahan could find his way about in the patent maze with considerable ease, but he was an employee without authority of his own. Hall McCormick, backed by his father, had abundant power. That he quickly came into conflict with the omniscient Colahan was not to the young man's discredit, for none could work with him without friction. Whether Hall served the good of the firm on each of the several occasions when he gave public vent to his dislike for Colahan is another question. At one time Colahan, who was not known in Washington to be an employee of McCormick, was collecting in-

[183] *Supra,* Chap. X, ftn. 71, C. Colahan to C. H. McCormick, June 14, 30, and Dec. 5, 1877. He mentioned the lack of "system, order, & discipline" at the factory, and added that the situation there had not improved since his report of similar tenor a year before. See also, his letters to C. H. McCormick of Mch. 30, May 23, Nov. 28 and 29, 1878, in which he criticized the laxness of control by the central office over its agents.

formation at the Patent Office for use in lawsuits. Hall Mc-
Cormick berated him in the presence of the commissioner for
being there contrary to his orders.[184] On another occasion
the young man discharged him, but Colahan, probably with
many embellishments, laid his troubles before Cyrus McCormick and was reinstated.[185]

Hall McCormick and his father retained the ownership of
several patents which, according to Cyrus McCormick's interpretation of the articles of partnership, should have been assigned to the firm.[186] The young man was not content to be a
partner in name only. Either due to ill fortune, poor judgment, or deliberate choice, on several occasions when he
tried to spread his wings he ran counter to the wishes of the
elder McCormick. Probably it was inevitable that trouble
should arise, since Cyrus McCormick, who controlled seventy-
five per cent of the capital of the enterprise, had the indomitable will to have his way upon any matter which came before
him for decision. And he was not of a mind to be checkmated
by a youth who had reached his majority long after the Mc-
Cormick name had become a household word wherever harvesting machinery was used.

[184] *Idem* to *idem*, Apr. 21, 1877.
[185] *Idem* to *idem*, Feb. #4, #8, #10, 15, 25, Mch. 6, 1879. #C. A. Spring, Jr.,
to C. H. McCormick, Feb. 7, 1879. C. H. McCormick, Jr., to N. F. Mc-
Cormick, Feb. 10 and 14, 1879. Unable to secure permission from L. J. and
R. H. McCormick to buy certain patents which he believed to be important,
Colahan purchased them on his own account, and later sold them to the firm
for $6900. #C. A. Spring, Jr., to C. H. McCormick, Oct. 29 and Dec. 17,
1879.
[186] Letters to C. H. McCormick from C. Colahan, Apr. 21, 1877, Dec. 4
and 28, 1878, F. H. Matthews, Aug. 28, 1877, and from H. Day, Feb. 23,
27, 1878. C. H. McCormick, Jr., MSS. Book "B," N. F. McCormick to
C. H. McCormick, Jr., Mch. 8, 1878. C. H. to L. J. McCormick, June 17,
1878. Colahan believed that L. J. McCormick resisted his wish to begin immediate preparations for the manufacture of twine-binders because he
(L. J. McCormick) realized that the patents held in his own name would
thereby be rendered worthless. See also, F. H. Matthews to C. H. Mc-
Cormick, Feb. 12, 1879.

Hall McCormick, unfortunately for his cause, was not highly regarded by several men on the office staff, and they did not always present him in his best light to their senior employer. F. H. Matthews, the manager of the office, was in a most difficult situation with Leander McCormick at his elbow and Cyrus usually out of the city. Matthews was caught between the millstones. To preserve a semblance of harmony he swung his favor back and forth between the partners, and as a result finally lost the confidence of both. Finding it impossible to maintain a high morale in the factory office, he gave up trying to do so, was at his desk but a few hours each day, and frequently absented himself altogether.[187] William John Hanna, who had penitently returned to the employ of the firm early in 1878, was a devoted follower of Cyrus McCormick.[188] Since he had worked for the company for twenty-five years, he resented the orders of men whom he had tutored a few years before in the ways of the business. He early began the practice of sending long reports to his absent chief, detailing the lamentable situation in the factory office and commenting with a caustic pen about Matthews, Leander, and Hall.[189] Charles Colahan also wrote frequently to Cyrus McCormick

[187] W. J. Hanna to C. H. McCormick, Sept. 3, 7, 1878. F. H. Matthews to N. F. McCormick, Oct. 9, 1878: "A divided house cannot stand." I must leave if "this jarring" continues as it has for two or three years past. C. Colahan to C. H. McCormick, Dec. 28, 1878, Feb. 10, and Mch. 6, 1879; #C. H. McCormick, Jr., to N. F. McCormick, June 27, 1879. From his letters to H. Day on Aug. 25 and Sept. 2, 1876, it is apparent that C. H. McCormick even then realized the need for a change of office personnel and policy.

[188] In Apr., 1878, Hanna was reëngaged by the McCormick Co. for $2,000 a year. Since leaving its employ he had been a partner in a commission house which failed. By 1879, however, he was a director of the McCormick Harv. Mach. Co., although his salary was still less than $3,000 a year.

[189] Letters to C. H. McCormick of C. A. Spring, Jr., #July 13 and Aug. 15, 1878, and of W. J. Hanna, Aug. 21, and Nov. 27, 1878: "I write this way in obedience to my promise to keep my eyes open and to watch your interests closely."

in the same vein, and even Matthews, as the time drew near for the inventor to return from France, veered over entirely to his support.[190]

This atmosphere of mutual distrust was the more tense because of the controversy arising over the invention of the Mc-Cormick reaper. Within the family, and most probably unknown to the outside world, Leander McCormick claimed that his brother was glorying in the renown as an inventor that their father, Robert, justly deserved. On his long annual visits to the Valley of Virginia, Leander collected statements from old residents there to substantiate his accusation. The evidence in support of each side of this question has been presented at length in earlier chapters of this biography, where the conclusion is reached that Cyrus McCormick's title to fame as the inventor of the first practical reaper is secure.[191] Probably Leander did not wish to make an irreconcilable breach between himself and his brother, but if that were his purpose, he could not have selected a more certain method of achieving it.

Several years after Hall McCormick was admitted to the firm he became a partner in a Chicago commission house, and also manufactured threshing machines and traction engines. These digressions from a task demanding all of his time and thought to do well, annoyed Cyrus McCormick, although both he and his wife hoped that their nephew would find his outside interests so engrossing that he would leave the harvester business severely alone. They did not relish, however, the use of the McCormick name to advertise and give prestige to implements over which they had no control.[192]

190 F. H. Matthews to C. H. McCormick, Jan. 3, 1879: "I will be very glad when Cyrus, Jr., comes to take part in the business. He is a fine business man and true gentleman." See also, his letters to C. H. McCormick of Mch. 14, 27 and Apr. 5, 1879.

191 "Hutchinson," I, Chaps. IV and V.

192 This was the commission business of McCormick, Beebe & Co., organized in 1877. W. J. Hanna to C. H. McCormick, Aug. 21, 1878.

In short, Hall McCormick was at the heart of the controversy between the brothers in the 1870's. As soon as Cyrus' eldest son finished at Princeton College in 1879 he would be ready to enter the firm. Whether he should hold a more responsible position and have a larger financial interest than his cousin were most delicate questions to answer. After Spring's resignation in 1873 the wishes of the inventor had not been given a consideration proportionate to his large stake in the enterprise. With much delay the manager of the factory office publicized the honors and the awards conferred upon him in France in 1878, although they were well calculated to help the sale of McCormick implements.[193] He was highly displeased by his brother's insistence that he pay more than the cost of construction for those machines shipped overseas which had done so much to give prestige to the McCormick name.[194] Because of these circumstances it was imperative in the view of Cyrus McCormick that his son should be enabled to voice his will by giving him an influential position in the firm. Leander was not opposed to making his nephew a partner, but he refused to agree that he should have a higher place than his own son. Cyrus McCormick, however, was so angered by Hall's course that he early in the controversy made clear that he would decline to sign a new partnership contract unless the young man were dropped from the firm.[195] This was unthink-

Pamphlet, "The McCormick Thresher, Farm Engines, Traction [Self-Propelling] Engines, Manufactured Especially for Foreign Trade. R. H. McCormick, Chicago, Illinois, 1878." Testimonials in this pamphlet suggest that R. H. McCormick had sold his first machines in 1876. F. H. Matthews to C. H. McCormick, Aug. 28, 1877. #L.P.C.B. of C. H. McCormick, Nov. 1873-June 1876, p. 412, C. H. McCormick to H. Day, Apr. 25, 1876. Here the inventor complained that Hall McCormick failed to reach the factory in the morning at the opening bell.

[193] W. J. Hanna to C. H. McCormick, Sept. 3, 7, and Nov. 27, 1878; #C. H. McCormick, Jr., to N. F. McCormick, Jan. 13, 1879.

[194] F. H. Matthews to C. H. McCormick, June 15, 1878.

[195] C. H. McCormick to H. Day, Apr. 23, 1878. See, however, C. H. McCormick to J. N. Jewett, July 11, 1879, for a modification of this position.

able to Leander, who had come more and more to rely upon his son's judgment in business matters. If Hall were forced out, he would leave also. Thus there was deadlock by the autumn of 1878.[196]

At this time Cyrus McCormick, seriously ill in France and harried by problems arising from his European business, was at a disadvantage in negotiations with his brother. Each wrote to the other through the medium of a lawyer. Henry Day of New York and Charles A. Spring, Jr., who once again was the inventor's mainstay in Chicago, were also actively seeking to find some formula whereby the partners could be brought to common ground.[197] Cyrus now offered to accept his nephew as a partner if he would agree to stay away from the factory and its office.[198] When this was declined he proposed "to sell all property and patents to highest bidder." That he should have seriously suggested such a way out probably is less an expression of his considered purpose than of his extreme weakness and feeling of discouragement resulting from the painful operations whereby the carbuncle on his neck was re-

[196] L. J. McCormick to J. N. Jewett, Aug. 16, 1878. In this letter L. J. McCormick wished to know for what sum his brother would sell out his interest in the firm. Jewett was C. H. McCormick's lawyer. H. Day to C. H. McCormick, Apr. 3, and 17, 1878, and J. N. Jewett to N. F. McCormick, Nov. 29, 1878. In a ‡letter of Feb. 2, 1879, to his mother, C. H. McCormick, Jr., stated he had been told that L. J. McCormick would hold out for his son's retention as long as there remained a chance of gaining his point, but if bad came to worst, he would yield rather than abandon so profitable a business. On ‡Jan. 29, 1879, C. A. Spring, Jr., wrote in the same vein to C. H. McCormick.

[197] ‡*Idem* to *idem,* from Aix-la-Chapelle, Aug. 29, 1878: "Papa is still at work on his letter to L. J. I persuaded him to expunge some expressions calculated only to arouse ire and not in direct answer to his complaints."

[198] C. H. McCormick's cable to "McCormick," Oct. 7, 1878. C. H. McCormick, Jr., MSS., Book "A," N. F. McCormick to C. H. McCormick, Jr., Oct. 1, 1878. Mrs. McCormick writes that she has persuaded her husband to offer the European business to the firm. She thought this might please L. J. McCormick. ‡W. C. Goudy to J. N. Jewett, July 8, 1879.

moved.[199] For the next nine months, however, the subject of the withdrawal from the business of either Cyrus or Leander was often discussed. Neither would agree to pay the other's price, although in view of the sum for which Leander sold his share in the enterprise about ten years later, Cyrus would have made an excellent bargain if he had accepted his brother's demand in 1879. Leander could not buy out Cyrus's interest since he did not have enough money and he already owed his elder brother $150,000.[200]

[199] C. H. McCormick, Jr., MSS., Book "A," Nettie F. McCormick to C. H. McCormick, Jr., Nov. 15, 1878, and Book "B," Feb. 22, 1879. Mrs. McCormick hoped that L. J. McCormick did not know of the serious nature of her husband's illness. "We could not *stand* so *strongly* if *anyone else knew he was not entirely well.*" Her letter to her eldest son on Jan.(?), 1879, makes clear that neither she nor her husband was eager to invest the large additional sum of money in the factory that would be required if L. J. McCormick withdrew.

[200] ‡Letters of J. N. Jewett to W. C. Goudy, July 3, 23, and 24, 1879; to C. H. McCormick, July 7, 1879; and to H. Day, July 19, 1879. ‡W. C. Goudy to J. N. Jewett, July 23, 1879. ‡H. Day to C. H. McCormick, July 26 and 31, 1879. In July 1879, L. J. and R. H. McCormick proposed to sell out their ¼th interest in the factory, its land, binder patents, etc. for $650,000. This offer did not include the factory raw materials and the machines already manufactured or partly manufactured. C. H. McCormick declined to accept, but replied that he would sell his ¾th interest for three times the above amount, and would include in his offer *all* of the patents. L. J. and R. H. McCormick refused, since, as ‡W. C. Goudy wrote to J. N. Jewett on July 24, 1879: "It is not the fault of my clients that they have less money than yours." L. J. and R. H. McCormick then offered to transfer title to their property, listed above, with the exception of their interest in the patents, for $200,000. If C. H. McCormick declined (as he did), then L. J. and R. H. McCormick were willing to enter a new partnership with him. The question of whether Leander, after withdrawal, should be allowed to license or to manufacture under the patents of the firm, was at the heart of the discussion. The debt of $150,000 was a continued subject of friction between the brothers, because of the many questions arising concerning security, interest rate, and time of repayment. See, F. H. Matthews to C. H. McCormick, Aug. 21, 1876. ‡Memo. of C. H. McCormick, Jr., Aug. 5, 1879. "C. H. McC. agrees that L. J. McC. may use two basic mower patents of the firm in his own factory, provided he will not begin to manufacture until the $150,000 debt is paid and will not take any of the best men from

Who should have the "controlling voice in the business" was another basic question in the long controversy.[201] In all routine matters, the senior partner was willing to allow his brother and nephew a free hand in managing the factory, but since his financial stake in the firm was much larger than theirs, he insisted that he should have the final word if a disagreement arose over some important problem connected with the plant. In the office of the company his will must be law at all times.[202] L. J. McCormick's attorney replied that this proposal might be worthy of serious consideration if the inventor intended to give his daily, personal attention to the affairs of the concern. If it were accepted, however, and the senior partner wielded his authority "through hired employees and his inexperienced son [then] . . . Mr. L. J. McCormick and his son would naturally cease to give any personal attention to the business and would do so because they would be powerless in determining any question presented."[203] This was an interesting prediction in view of the situation nine months later.[204]

While these futile negotiations were in progress, Leander and his son let it be known that they were planning to establish a harvesting machinery factory of their own. Perhaps this news was designed only to lead Cyrus McCormick to

the McC. works." In other words, the inventor feared that his brother would fail as an independent manufacturer and would therefore be unable to repay his loan.

201 ‡J. N. Jewett to W. C. Goudy, July 3 and 8, 1879, and his reply of ‡July 10, 1879. A typewritten MS. entitled "Copy of Correspondence About Partnership Matters Leading to the Formation of the Corporation of the McCormick Harvesting Machine Company," p. 4, C. H. McCormick to J. N. Jewett, July 7(?), 1879.
202 Ibid., pp. 6-10, 12, J. N. Jewett to W. C. Goudy, July 9, 1879, and C. H. McCormick's written comments on this letter. C. H. McCormick to J. N. Jewett, July 11, 1879.
203 Ibid., pp. 7, 11, W. C. Goudy to J. N. Jewett, July 8 and 10, 1879.
204 Post, p. 638.

accede to their wishes, but they at least asked a foreman at the plant to enter their employ in case their hope were realized.[205] Mrs. McCormick believed that their worst enemy could not wish a more cruel punishment for them, since in her opinion they could not succeed as independent manufacturers.[206] Although Cyrus McCormick, Jr., and Spring agreed with her, the news of their intention made it imperative that she and her husband should return from Europe at the earliest moment possible.[207] The discord between the partners was now known to all, and the citizens of Urbana, Ohio, invited Leander and his son to locate their factory in that town.[208] Perhaps, however, they would decide at the last moment that the business in Chicago was too profitable to be abandoned.

In the summer of 1879, after Cyrus McCormick returned from Europe, Henry Day came to Chicago in the rôle of peacemaker. When the inventor would yield no further than to have Robert Hall as assistant superintendent of manufacturing provided "he would do all required of him and give his best services to the work," Day advised Leander to ac-

[205] ‡C. H. McCormick, Jr., to N. F. McCormick, Feb. 2, 1879. ‡G. B. Averill to C. H. McCormick, July 17, 1879. Averill was a foreman in the factory. In this letter he states that he is resigning in order to go with L. J. McCormick.

[206] C. H. McCormick, Jr., MSS. Book "B," Nettie F. McCormick to C. H. McCormick, Jr., May 5, 1879.

[207] C. H. McCormick, Jr., MSS. Book "B," *idem* to *idem*, Feb. 22, 1879: "Our irons are burning in Chicago." C. A. Spring, Jr., wrote to C. H. McCormick on Feb. 27, 1879, advising him that his interests at Chicago needed his attention far more than those in Europe. C. H. McCormick, Jr., MSS. Book "B," N. F. McCormick to C. H. McCormick, Jr., Mch. 26, 1879: "Go home we *must*—and that *immediately!* There is not a *week* to *lose*—from all we hear. They are trying to get different men in our employ now to promise to go with them into a new business! Say nothing of our coming, as it may make them more active, but we are coming in *April* certainly." As a matter of fact, Mr. and Mrs. McCormick did not reach the U. S. until late May.

[208] L.P.C.B. No. 193, p. 73, L. J. McCormick (by W. J. Hanna) to E. G. Wiley, Cashier, 3rd Natl. Bank, Urbana, O., Aug. 25, 1879.

cept.[209] For another week the conversations continued almost without a pause.[210] Finally, on August 11, 1879, the general structure of the McCormick Harvesting Machine Company was agreed upon. The inventor should own three-quarters, and Leander and Hall, together, one-quarter of the stock in this new concern. Leander was guaranteed the right to choose two of the six directors, and the personnel of the board should not be changed unless the holders of at least four-fifths of the stock consented.[211] The capital of the company, divided into shares of $100 each, was to be $2,500,000. Of this total, C. H. McCormick should own 18,700 shares, his brother 6,248 shares, C. H. McCormick, Jr., 48 shares, and R. H. McCormick, L. Hamilton McCormick, C. A. Spring, Jr., and W. J. Hanna, one share each.[212] This arrangement was to last for at least five years, and during that period Cyrus McCormick was to be the president. Leander, the vice-president and super-intendent of the manufacturing department, was obligated to "give reasonable attention to his said office of Superintendent . . . but temporary absence shall not vacate the office, or deprive him of his salary." If his son so desired, and was willing to "give his best services," he could be assistant-super-

[209] ‡H. Day to C. H. McCormick, July 31, 1879. ‡Memo. of C. H. McCormick, Jr., Aug. 7, 1879.

[210] ‡Memo. of C. H. McCormick, Jr., Aug. 10, 1879: "A day of rest comes upon us most gratefully at this time when troubles, perplexities and business cares are engrossing our time and thought during the whole week from early Monday morning till late Saturday night, but we leave them all then and enjoy a repose of mind & body on this the Lord's day. This after-noon father began to talk of some of his old recollections and alluded to his father's connexion with the Reaping Machine. I took a few notes of what he said."

[211] ‡Articles of agreement to date from Aug. 1, 1879, but made on Aug. 11, 1879. The new firm bought all the property of the partnership, except the reaper notes due, for $1,250,000.

[212] ‡C. A. Spring, Jr., to C. H. McCormick, Sept. 9, 1879. The directors were all the stock-holders except L. H. McCormick. ‡Subscription Paper for Capital Stock in McCormick Harv. Machine Co., dated Aug. 13, 1879.

intendent of the factory. He decided to accept. Leander cove-
nanted to pay his debt of $150,000 to his brother within five
years.[213]

Each brother wished his son to be the secretary of the company, but Cyrus McCormick, Jr., advised his father to agree
to a compromise whereby J. P. Whedon of the factory office
should have this position. Cyrus, Jr., was content to serve in
the office and field at a small salary until "some active experience in the business" would entitle him to step in "the Secretaryship with more merit." [214] Against the wish of Leander,
C. A. Spring, Jr., was named the general superintendent of
the company.[215]

The arrangement was an unhappy one almost from the outset. Cyrus McCormick, Jr., quickly proved his worth and was
accorded a prominence in the affairs of the concern out of all
proportion to his meager salary and small holding of stock.[216]
The title to certain patents was still in dispute, since the inventor believed that the spirit of the articles of association

[213] ‡Articles of Agreement, made Aug. 11, 1879, and to date from Aug. 1.
[214] ‡C. H. McCormick, Jr., to C. H. McCormick, Aug. 29, 1879, and
‡J. N. Jewett to him on Aug. 30, 1879. Jewett believed that if C. H. Mc-
Cormick would yield on the subject of the secretaryship, it would be "an
important matter of conciliation." The duties of the office were unimportant,
and "by and by you can have your way without any ill will or unjust
criticism."
[215] ‡H. Day to C. H. McCormick, July 28, 1879. As early as June, 1879,
F. H. Matthews had been offered a good position by Ayres Sons' Iron
Works of Youngstown, O. He asked $15,000 of the McCormick Co. and
"full control of all," if he were to stay with it. C. H. McCormick, Jr.,
advised against paying him so much, and Matthews left. ‡C. H. McCormick,
Jr., to N. F. McCormick, June 27, 1879. ‡C. A. Spring, Jr., to C. H. Mc-
Cormick, Oct. 3, 1879.
[216] Until late Aug., at least, the outlook for peace seemed bright. H. Day
to C. H. McCormick, Aug. 29, 1879: I know that R. Hall McC. is very
anxious that all causes of difference should be buried. ‡C. A. Spring, Jr.,
to C. H. McCormick, Aug 30, 1879: R. Hall McC. is now ready to do anything for the sake of harmony. ‡C. Colahan to C. H. McCormick, Aug. 24,
1880.

obliged his brother and nephew to assign them to the firm, while they, on the contrary, could find no stipulation to this effect in the bond.[217] Rumor persisted that they planned to open their own factory after a year or two. Tempers were frayed and things were said which left deep wounds even after apologies were duly offered and accepted. The controversy outwardly still turned about the interpretation of lawyers' phrases in business documents, but it had become an irrepressible conflict between kinsmen of divergent personalities.[218]

Leander and Hall believed that there was "a conspiracy" to ignore them on the part of those in the office and several of the leading men at the plant. In their opinion, their authority at the works was being undermined because orders were sent direct by the clerks to the foremen. For this reason, so it was said, they stayed away from the plant for long periods and showed little interest in the business.[219] The eight hundred workmen at the factory seriously needed closer supervision.

On February 16, 1880, Cyrus McCormick submitted to the board of directors a written statement concerning the management of the plant, and the non-assignment to the firm of several patents held by his brother and nephew. They, in turn, prepared a pamphlet designating most of his "complaints or

[217] C. H. to R. H. McCormick, July 1, 1880. At the meeting of the Bd. of Directors on Feb. 11, 1880, L. J. and R. H. McCormick declined to assign the title to these patents to the firm. See, "Typewritten Copy of Matters Expunged from pp. 16-42 of the Record of the Directors' Meetings of the McCormick Harv. Mach. Co."

[218] ‡J. N. Jewett to C. H. McCormick, Aug. 30, 1879: "Hall cannot set up any manufacturing by himself and his father is too conservative and cautious a man to risk his fortune upon any such venture." Spring, however, was not so confident. C. A. Spring, Jr., to C. H. McCormick, ‡Sept. 6, Nov. 1, 1879, ‡Oct. 13 and 15, 1880. J. P. Whedon to C. H. McCormick, Aug. 20, 1880. A memo. of C. H. McCormick, dated Aug. 11, 1883, shows that he was offended by the oft-repeated statement of his brother that he had "built up the business."

[219] J. P. Whedon to C. H. McCormick, Oct. 1, 7, Nov. 15, 1879, and ‡C. A. Spring, Jr., to him on Oct. 2, 7, 18, 21, Nov. 1, 10 and 11, 1879. R. H. McCormick to Board of Directors of McCormick Harv. Mach. Co., Apr. 6, 1880.

charges" as "paltry" and "of a personal nature" unsuited for presentation to the directors of the company. They alleged that C. H. McCormick was using these matters "as a pretext to import old grievances into this new corporation and force one or both of us to withdraw." [220] Accompanying this printed reply when it was laid before the directors at their meeting of April 6, were a letter from Hall McCormick resigning his position as assistant superintendent of manufacturing, and another from Leander J., stating that he had "decided upon a temporary absence from the duties of my office . . . for a period of six months or thereabouts," in order to sail for Europe in mid-April.[221]

When the board reassembled about one week later, its president answered this pamphlet in a communication twenty-three typed pages in length. He refused to modify "the facts" that he had submitted in February, and denied that they were "personal" in nature or that it was his purpose to render their "positions . . . intolerable and oblige them to withdraw." He supported his stand by one statement signed by the clerks in the office and another drawn up by prominent employees of the factory. After referring to the resignation of Hall McCormick, he closed his letter by writing: "I now propose that the position of Superintendent of the manufacturing department, occupied by L. J. McCormick, be declared vacated." [222] The

[220] Printed pamphlet, without title, date, or name of author, in the form of a communication (obviously from L. J. and R. H. McCormick) to the Bd. of Directors of the McCormick Harv. Mach. Co., p. 1.

[221] "Secretary's Record, The McCormick Harvesting Machine Company," pp. 18-19, L. J. McCormick to the Bd. of Directors, Apr. 6, 1880, and R. H. McCormick to *idem*, Apr. 6, 1880. After stating that his influence at the factory had been destroyed because the office ignored him and gave orders directly to the workmen, Hall McCormick concluded: "I consider these things a violation of the contract by which I hold my office, and self-respect will no longer allow me to fill the same, which I hereby resign." L. J. McCormick to L. J. Boeck, Mch. 19, 1880.

[222] C. H. McCormick to the Bd. of Directors of the McCormick Harv. Mach. Co., Apr. 14, 1880. L.P.C.B. No. 200, p. 513, C. A. Spring, Jr., to F. H. Matthews, Apr. 13, 1880: "We have a Directors' meeting tomorrow

directors adopted this motion and also spread upon their minutes a resolution censuring Leander and his son.[223] The inventor determined that they should never again direct the production department of the firm. Cyrus McCormick, Jr., at once took charge of the patent business which his cousin had heretofore managed.[224]

Leander contended that he had been forced out of his position contrary to the terms of the articles of association and that he was then, and always has been, ready to perform his duties with due diligence. Although his brother argued that he had broken the articles because an eight months' absence was not a "temporary" one, Leander laid claim to his full salary until the five-year period of the contract ended in August, 1884.[225] As directors, he and his son opposed the enlargement of the works, an increase of the capitalization of the company, and pressed for a declaration of dividends from

and expect a lively time." "Secretary's Record, The McCormick Harv. Mach. Co.," p. 20. L. J. and R. H. McCormick were not present at this meeting.

[223] "Typewritten Copy of Matters Expunged from pp. 16-42 of the Record of the Directors' Meetings of the McCormick Harv. Mach. Co." Undated pencil draft, in the hand of J. P. Whedon, Secy., of the reasons for the resolution of censure.

[224] J. P. Whedon to C. H. McCormick, Aug. 7, 1880. #C. A. Spring, Jr., to C. H. McCormick, Aug. 1, 1880: R. Hall McC. attended the stockholders' meeting today. I took pains to make him feel that he can get any information about the business that he desires. C. H. McCormick to H. Day, Dec. 27 and 30, 1880.

[225] L. J. McCormick returned from Europe near the close of Nov. 1880. #C. A. Spring, Jr., to C. H. McCormick, Oct. 12, 1880. H. Day to C. H. McCormick, Nov. 30 and Dec. 22, 1880. Day hoped that C. H. McCormick would not be "so harsh" as to force L. J. McCormick out of all control of a business in which he owned a quarter interest. #L.P.C.B. No. 5, 1st ser., C. H. McCormick to H. Day, Dec. 4, 1880, and Jan. 6, 1881. *Idem* to *idem*, Jan. 5, 1881. #C. H. McCormick, Jr., to C. H. McCormick, July 16, 22, Aug. 1, 2, and 24, 1881. #L. J. McCormick to the McCormick Harv. Mach. Co., undated, but most probably written either in July, 1881, or Aug., 1882. See, #C. H. McCormick, Jr., to C. H. McCormick, Aug. 15, 1882.

Cyrus H. McCormick
From a photograph by Max Platz, Chicago, about 1885

the large annual profits.[226] They insisted that the resolution of censure should be expunged and that Cyrus should pay the wholesale, rather than the cost price, of the two or three hundred machines built by the firm for his foreign sales in 1878 and 1879.[227] In the autumn of 1885, Leander published the statements he had been collecting in the Valley of Virginia to show that his brother had not invented the famous first McCormick reaper of 1831.[228]

After long negotiation, marked by much acrimony, Cyrus agreed to give the firm about $60,000 for the machines supplied for the European market. This sum was much larger than the implements in question had cost to make, and the inventor's payment of it marked an abandonment of his long-held position.[229] In 1886 a salary adjustment was made with

[226] "Secretary's Record, McCormick Harv. Mach. Co.," pp. 31, 33, and 59. R. P. Ranney, Cleveland, O., to C. H. McCormick, Jr., Feb. 1, 1883. C. H. McCormick to Bd. of Directors, McCormick Harv. Mach. Co., June 9, 1883. C. H. McCormick urged without success that the capital stock should be increased "to enable its business to be conducted safely and properly." Possibly there was also in his mind a desire to enlarge thereby his degree of control. He was stopped, however, by Art. V of the "By-Laws" which declared that the annual "net profits . . . shall not be expended to increase the capital stock without the consent of Cyrus H. McCormick and Leander J. McCormick, while they or either of them are Directors."

[227] H. Day to C. H. McCormick, Dec. 14, 1881, and May 9, 1882; C. H. McCormick, Jr., to H. Day, Dec. 16, 1881; Written Statement of C. H. McCormick to C. H. McCormick, Jr., and W. J. Hanna, Mch. 14, 1882.

[228] "Hutchinson," I, Chap. V. N. F. McCormick to C. H. McCormick, Jr., Sept. 16, 1885: We must not notice their pamphlet in regard to the invention of the reaper. "It is a dead issue they are raising."

[229] This settlement was on Nov. 18, 1882. It embraced 245 machines, plus extras and wire. C. H. McCormick believed that he had three very good reasons for paying only the cost of production for these machines, viz., (a) he had made no money for himself in the foreign business, (b) it had greatly increased the sales and prestige of McCormick implements at home, (c) between 1864 and 1878 he had paid only cost price for the foreign supply. MS. entitled "C. H. McCormick's Acct. with C. H. & L. J. McCormick, Nov. 18, 1882." ‡H. Day, to C. H. McCormick, July 29, 1879: L. J. McCormick is willing that you should pay only the cost price for the 1878

Leander [230] and the offending resolution, as well as other entries in the minute-book of the board of directors displeasing to him, were deleted on the ground that they dealt with "matters . . . of a personal nature not effecting the business of the company and . . . therefore not material to be preserved." [231] The balance of advantage in these several "compromises" rested with Leander and his son. Mrs. McCormick and Cyrus, Jr., had yielded much for the sake of peace. [232] In 1890 the interest of Leander and Hall in the business was purchased for about $3,250,000. Thus ended forever their connection with the McCormick Harvesting Machine Company. [233]

machines since they were sent to Europe as an experiment, but he claims that those taken there in 1879 were "made for the trade" and hence the firm is entitled to a profit on them. Letters to C. H. McCormick of J. P. Whedon, Sept. 24, 1879, ‡C. H. McCormick, Jr., Dec. 16, 1881, and H. Day, May 9, 1882. Written statement of C. H. McCormick, Mch. 14, 1882. C. H. McCormick to H. Day, May 5, 1882.

[230] C. H. McCormick, Jr., MSS. Book "B," N. F. McCormick to C. H. McCormick, Jr., Dec. 6, 1884, and July 14, 1885. C. H. McCormick, Jr., to N. F. McCormick, July 11, 13, 17, Aug. 8, and Sept. 19, 1885. C. A. Spring, Jr., to N. F. McCormick, Mch. 10, 1885. C. H. McCormick, Jr., to L. J. McCormick, Nov. 20, 1885. L. J. McCormick to C. H. McCormick, Jr., Nov. 21, 1885. He acknowledges receipt of a check for $26,666.66.

[231] "Secretary's Record, The McC. Harv. Mach. Co.," p. 95. R. H. McCormick to C. H. McCormick, Jr., Sept. 11, 19, Oct. 12, Nov. 2, 1885. C. H. McCormick, Jr., to R. H. McCormick, Oct. 30, 1885. It took many weeks to reach an agreement upon the form that this expunging resolution should take. Hall, speaking for his father, insisted that it should "state that the charges were made without cause." Hall, however, agreed that it should not "cast any reflection" upon C. H. McCormick. But how do the first without also doing the second? The resolution, as adopted, admitted that the matters deleted had been of a personal nature and hence were out of place in the record book of the directors. C. H. McCormick had emphasized that his statement of Feb. 16, 1880, had not been of a personal nature.

[232] N. F. McCormick to C. H. McCormick, Jr., Sept. 16, 1885: "We have always wanted to live in peace and harmony—and we can if we are wise, I feel."

[233] C. H. McCormick, Jr., to L. J. McCormick, Dec. 16, 1889. On Jan. 10, 1890, L. J. McCormick resigned as vice-pres. and director, and R. H. McCormick as director of the company. See pp. 117-118 of the "Secretary's Record, McC. Harv. Mach. Co."

CHAPTER XV

A WORLD MARKET COMES AT LAST, 1876-1885

O NE of the most powerful allies of the American manufacturer of harvesting machinery in his search for a
world market was the upward trend of labor costs in Europe
as more and more peasants each year moved from their holdings to the western hemisphere, Australia, and New Zealand.[1]
With the exception of Norway and Sweden, emigration was
heaviest from the British Isles and those countries on the Continent where the most small grains were grown.

Paradoxically, implement-makers increased their sales
abroad by finding more purchasers at home. The use of harvesting machinery helped to enlarge the total grain yield of
the United States, while at the same time it lowered the cost
of production per acre when compared with the more primitive
methods which it superseded. In some measure because of this,
American wheat could undersell the Russian and Danube Valley crops in Europe. Hard times resulted there on the many
farms that still relied upon expensive hand labor at harvest

[1] Remarks by European observers about the shortage of farm labor, and
its effect upon the use of agricultural machinery, occur with increasing
frequency after 1870. For example, see, "Exposition Universelle de Vienne
en 1873. France Commission Supérieure, Rapports" (Paris, 1875) I, 104;
"United States Consular Reports. Reports from the Consuls of the United
States on the Commerce, Manufactures, etc., of their Consular Districts"
No. 33, September 1883, (Washington 1883), p. 500, "The labor market in
all districts [in Denmark] has been more restricted than in former years.
This is mainly due to the large flow of emigration which took place last
year from all Scandinavian countries to the United States, as also to the
extra labor called for from the construction of new railways in Jutland and
the island of Fyen."

time. Peasants had the options of buying machinery, becoming the lease-holders or hired men of landowners who could afford to purchase it, moving to the towns to work in the mills, or going to the country with which they were unable longer to compete.[2] If they moved to the Argentine, New Zealand, Australia, Canada or the United States, they settled for the most part in areas adapted to wheat culture. They had to have machinery and it made little difference to Cyrus McCormick whether they were in America or the Antipodes when they bought it. His agents would be there to supply them. Each reaper used by a new-comer in the United States helped to increase the exportable surplus of grain, and hence impelled more immigrants to come from Europe to America. The manufacturers of harvesting implements were thus in a happy situation, since apparently the more machines they sold, the more they could sell in the future.

The following excerpts from the "United States Consular Reports" for 1883 tell the story: "This stupendous international grain trade of the late years . . . has been the means of bringing the agricultural interests in many countries [in Europe] under a serious crisis, owing to the severe competition to which they have had to submit from all quarters of the globe." "These millions of quarters of wheat and maize

[2] *Ibid.*, p. 444: "When I asked why the young people [of Birmingham, Eng.] did not emigrate instead of going into a trade [nail-making] already overcrowded, he laughed at me and asked how long I thought it would take to save enough from his earnings (6s. a week) to pay the expenses of emigrating." "Farmers' Advance," Jan. 1882, p. 4. #"The American Settler" (London), Apr. 30, 1881, p. 32, "That emigration is the solution of the difficulties which surround our farming population is obvious." ‡Pamphlet by Olive Logan, "The American Abroad" (no date or place of publication shown) pp. 12-13, "The overwhelming competition of the Western States with the farmers of Great Britain, forcing upon them for a number of years past the necessity of overworking and exhausting the soil, is compelling large numbers of that thrifty and well-to-do class to throw up their farms, and either turn their attention to other businesses, for which they are generally unfitted, or emigrate."

are thrown upon the European markets, and . . . produce so much anxiety amongst the agricultural interests throughout Europe." "Writers in Europe now console their readers by saying that the peak of *cheap* production in the United States has been reached, and that with exhausted soil, thronging immigrants to feed, and a greater cost of production, America's exportable surplus will now diminish. On the contrary I think the culminating point, instead of being now reached, may only be looked for in a very remote future." "Last winter, I learn, American wheat and flour were for the first time brought to the Breslau market." "There is now no longer a prejudice existing against American flour in the European markets. In fact, its superior quality has become proverbial." [3] The United States was taking the place of Russia and Hungary as the chief exporter of wheat to England, France, Italy, and the other countries of Europe which were not self-sufficing. This deluge of grain doubtless made bread cheap and banished the fear of famine in a year like 1879, when the continental harvest failed, but it also brought distress as well as aid.

Why a Russian clung to his sickle as long as he lived along the Volga, but signed an order-blank for a reaper almost as soon as he broke the sod of Manitoba, is a question admitting of no certain answer. Although he probably had more money when in his native land, McCormick's salesman there could not persuade him to buy. Perhaps the land of golden opportunity, as he believed America to be, gave him the confidence to use implements that seemed far beyond his reach in his old home. The wish to imitate his progressive neighbors so as to get ahead as rapidly as possible, probably also played its part. The high-priced land, small holdings, and cheap labor of the Continent were replaced in the New World by large homesteads and harvest hands demanding three or four dollars a day. These conditions made intensive cultivation seem less re-

[3] "U. S. Consular Reports," 1883, No. 33, pp. 495, 497, 503, 510.

munerative than to spread a minimum of labor over a maximum acreage.[4] To do this to the best advantage, farm machinery was necessary. Whatever may have been the cause, manufacturers of harvesting implements noticed that the high sales resistance of Europeans disappeared when they became "outlanders" in a temperate climate colony.

The development by the McCormicks of markets in Canada, Australia, New Zealand, and the Argentine between 1875 and 1885 illustrate these general tendencies. The press of Canada took little notice of reapers before 1845, but during the next decade firms in New York State sold a few machines there.[5] Within ten years the wheat crop of Canada quadrupled in size, and in 1854 England endeavored to allay the discontent of her lusty colony by making the Canadian Reciprocity Treaty with the United States.[6] This agreement stimulated some lines of trade between the two neighbors, and was a boon to New England shipping, but a duty of about $15 was assessed by Canada upon every reaper crossing her frontier.[7] Several manufacturers of harvesting implements, Ketchum, Seymour & Morgan, Manny, and others, evaded this tariff by arranging with Canadian factories to build their machines.

[4] *Ibid.*, p. 506. Between 1874-1881, the average wheat yield per acre in New Zealand was about 27¼ bushels; Tasmania, 18¼ bus.; Australia, 12 bus.; France, 16; Belgium, 26; Russia, 5½. The average per acre in England between 1865 and 1879 was 26½ bus. In 1882, Washington Terr., with the highest yield per acre in the United States, produced 35 bus., but the average throughout the nation probably approximated that of Australia.

[5] "The British American Cultivator" (Toronto), Dec. 1845, p. 364; Feb. 1846, p. 42; Mch. 1846, p. 84. C. McCormick also sold a few machines in Canada prior to 1854, see "Hutchinson," I, pp. 325, 355, 420, 428, 430. T. J. Paterson to C. H. McCormick, Jan. 11, 13, and Mch. 13, 1856. MS Volume, "McCormick Extension Case, Patent of 1845," testimony of Joseph Ganson.

[6] "Gardeners' Chronicle," Feb. 11, 1854, p. 90; Apr. 4, 1857, p. 243. Purchasers of land from the government in Canada were obliged to settle upon it and bring at least twelve acres under cultivation within four years.

[7] T. J. Paterson to W. S. McCormick, May 14 and June 8, 1855. Paterson hoped to make an agricultural society the consignee at London, Ontario, for in this way the duty might be avoided.

Cyrus McCormick, however, followed his fixed policy and refused to sub-license. Since the London-Toronto-Lake Simcoe district was the chief Canadian wheat area, he relied upon T. J. Paterson, his agent at Rochester, New York, to look out for his interests there. Between 1855 and 1857, over twenty-five McCormick sub-agents were appointed in Canada, but the few sales by no means justified this elaborate organization.[8] Except as a matter of pride, the inventor was not eager at this time to sell across the border unless the midwestern demand in any harvest fell short of his expectation.[9] To compete successfully with Canadian machines, he was obliged to pay the tariff himself, and much "red tape" was necessary in order to bring unsold implements back to this country. If T. J. Paterson can be believed, "The Canadians are clannish & strongly prejudicial," and "where a machine gets a right start and works up to the mark . . . it is hard to convince them any other . . . will do." [10] Helped by a head start, McCormick's rivals were strongly entrenched across the border and he could not dislodge them. In 1857 he tried the expedient of wholesaling fifty of his reapers to an Ohioan for the Canadian market, but the purchaser defrauded him of much of the price agreed upon.[11] Following this misadventure, McCormick dis-

[8] T. J. Paterson to W. S. McCormick, Feb. 18, 19, Apr. 27 and June 25, 1855; Mch. 17, 1857. McIntosh & Walton, Toronto, to C. H. McCormick, Mch. 2, 1855. L.P.C.B. No. 1, pp. 112, 375, W. S. McCormick to T. J. Paterson, Mch. 26, Apr. 23, May 9 and 19, 1856; No. 6, pp. 713-724, the Co. to J. Everhart, Massillon, O., Apr., 1857; No. 8, p. 219, W. S. McCormick to T. J. Paterson, July 28, 1857.

[9] W. S. McCormick to J. L. Wilson, Aug. 16, 1855. L.P.C.B. No. 2, p. 22, W. S. McCormick, to T. J. Paterson, May 29, 1856. T. J. Paterson to W. S. McCormick, Mch. 26, 1856.

[10] T. J. Paterson to W. S. McCormick, June 11, 1855, July,(?) 1856, and Apr. 16, 1857. Machines made in Canada were selling for $125 or $130, and the McCormick was offered there for $160. L.P.C.B. No. 8, p. 467, W. S. McCormick to T. J. Paterson, Aug. 13, 1857.

[11] J. Everhart to C. H. McCormick, Feb. 9, Apr. 7, Aug. 1, 17 and Oct. 15, 1857. L.P.C.B. No. 6, pp. 50, 178-179, 670, the Co. to J. Everhart, Apr. 3,

charged his agents in Canada and had them close out their stock of implements at bargain prices.[12] For almost twenty years after this time the Dominion was rarely mentioned in the correspondence of the factory office, and cash was demanded for the few machines that were sold there.[13] As a rule, when a request came from Canada for a reaper, the office replied that its supply was exhausted and that, because of the tariff, the writer could purchase more economically from a firm in his own country.[14]

By the late 1870's railroad building in Canada was rapidly opening to settlement large areas of land suitable for grain culture. The region about Winnipeg was soon connected by rail with ports on Lake Superior, whence the grain was carried by ship to Chicago and Buffalo.[15] McCormick's agent in central Minnesota in 1876 was eager to extend his district across the frontier, but the Chicago partners, in view of the seventeen and one-half per cent duty and the known preference of Cana-

11 and May 12, 1857. C. H. McCormick eventually was given the agent's farm in part payment of his debt. The farm was sold in Dec., 1863, for $4,000. L.P.C.B. No. 71, p. 392.

12 See, letters of the Co. in *ibid.*, No. 9, p. ?, to T. Musson, Etobicoke, Canada, Dec. 10, 1857; No. 8, p. 800, to T. J. Paterson, Sept. 18, 1857. This letter shows that McCormick, in 1857, had sold only three machines in Canada. No. 12, p. 736, to T. J. Paterson, June 24, 1858; No. 14, p. 766, to J. P. Williams, Jr., Prince Edward Dist., Canada West, Sept. 23, 1858.

13 *Ibid.*, No. 41 (May, 1861), p. 696. By this time McCormick had but two agents in Canada, and these were dropped within the next three years. No. 69, p. 62, the Co. to J. B. McCormick, Apr. 23, 1864: "High freights and duties have about played out that business [in Canada] and . . . the Canadians are a little shy of trading with Yankees, fearing they will get the worst of the bargain always."

14 *Ibid.*, No. 57, p. 726, the Co. to J. H. Ela, Rochester, Wis., Mch. 13, 1863.

15 H. A. Innis, "Industrialism and Settlement in Western Canada," in the "Report of the International Geographical Congress," July, 1928, (Cambridge, England). In 1881, Manitoba produced 3½ million bus. of wheat; as much oats, and over ½ million bus. of barley. Wheat was reported to average 28 bus. per acre. "Farmers' Advance," Mch., 1882, p. 6.

dians for binders made under their own flag, hesitated to give their permission.[16] Manufacturers in the United States were unable adequately to protect their implements in Canada, because of the law that no device could be patented there if it had been covered for over a year by the patent of another country.[17] Since many of the mechanical elements of a successful wire- or twine-binder were patented in the 1860's or early 1870's few were eligible to protection in Canada by the time United States firms were ready to exploit the Manitoba market. In short, the tariff and patent laws of Canada were well calculated to promote home industry. The McCormicks could only ineffectually protest when a factory at London, Ontario, made their wire-binder without license.[18] Since the grain of Manitoba ripened after harvest was over in the United States, American manufacturers often tested their improvements north of the border. This furnished Canadian builders an excellent opportunity to keep in touch with the progress of invention.

Thus, year after year the grain exports of Manitoba increased, but very few McCormick-made binders worked through its harvests. "The irksomeness of the tariff on agricultural machinery going into Canada," wrote a clerk in the

[16] G. Freudenreich, Alexandria and St. Cloud, Minn. to the Co., Mch. 20, and Dec. 18, 1876; Apr. 3 and 29, 1878. L.P.C.B. No. 183, p. 26, the Co. to W. N. Spring, Sioux City, Ia., July 31, 1878. Two harvester-binders were being sent to Grand Forks, Dak. Terr., for introduction to the Manitoba trade. No. 185, p. 799 and No. 189, p. 9, the Co. to G. Freudenreich, Nov. 30, 1878, and Mch. 22, 1879.

[17] A device patented in Canada had to be manufactured there within two years after the date of its patent, and thereafter it could not be imported to Canada.

[18] ‡Baldwin, Hopkins, and Peyton to the Co., Oct. 4, 1879. ‡C. A. Spring, Jr., to C. H. McCormick, Sept. 19, and Oct. 22, 1879. See, letters of the Co. in L.P.C.B. No. 195, pp. 325½; 475; No. 196, p. 157, to J. Elliott & Son, London, Ont., Oct. 29, Nov. 3, and 24, 1879; No. 210, p. 172, to D. Maxwell, Paris, Ont., Feb. 10, 1881; No. 243, p. 861; No. 244, p. 588, to Wesbrook & Fairchild, Winnipeg, June 27, and Aug. 9, 1884.

McCormick office in 1882, "is much more felt in the region where the line of separation is only imaginary. It seemed different when we had to cross the Lakes to reach Canada. It seemed then as though it really was a foreign country, but now in the district alluded to [Manitoba] they are our near neighbors.[19] This neighbor, however, continued to raise its duty on agricultural implements in spite of the pressure brought by United States manufacturers upon the State Department at Washington to intercede in their behalf.[20] But Manitoba, with its "bonanza" farms, was too tempting to be neglected. For the harvest of 1883 the McCormicks sent a large consignment of machines to an agent at Winnipeg and over six hundred were sold.[21]

At the same time, much thought was given to the advisability of scaling the tariff wall by assembling the separate pieces of their implements at a Canadian branch factory. After a long conference with his father on this matter, Cyrus McCormick, Jr., tabled the suggestion, since he believed that the Manitoba boom was too dependent upon one crop to last long and the Dominion would most likely amend her tariff legisla-

[19] *Ibid.*, No. 227, p. 735, the Co. to Deere & Co., Moline, Ill., Sept. 25, 1882. Parkinson & Parkinson, Cincinnati, to the Co., May 6, 1882.

[20] L.P.C.B. No. 232, p. 857, C. H. McCormick, Jr., to Wesbrook & Fairchild, Winnipeg, Manitoba, May 9, 1883. #C. A. Spring, Jr., to C. H. McCormick, Apr. 16, 1883: Canada has raised her tariff on reapers and mowers to 37½%, but we succeeded in running in some twenty carloads while it was still at 25%.

[21] See, letters of the Co. in L.P.C.B.; No. 228, pp. 258, 410, 655, 849; No. 229, p. 288, to Wesbrook & Fairchild, Winnipeg, Oct. 14, Nov. 6, 16, and Dec. 6, 1882; No. 223, p. 793, to Qu'Appelle Farm Syndicate, Winnipeg, May 16, 1882. Three hundred and seventy-five mowers and 590 harvester-binders were sent to Canada in 1883; No. 237, p. 36, to J. M. Power, Assiniboine Farm, Elkhorn, Manitoba, Sept. 5, 1883. #C. A. Spring, Jr., to C. H. McCormick, Jr., Sept. 29, 1883. For 1884, Wesbrook & Fairchild, the agent at Winnipeg, bought over 300 more at wholesale price from the McCormick Co., which promised not to send any other machines into that province of Canada.

tion so as to levy heavy duties upon imported machine parts.[22]
Nor would the company voluntarily permit its implements to
be made in Canada: "for we have never yet departed from
the original rule established by our President, Hon. C. H.
McCormick, many years ago, of keeping the manufacture of
our machines entirely within our own control, and we think
this course has tended largely toward building up the reputation which our name now holds so universally. . . . No matter
how much royalty you might pay, we would never feel relieved of the responsibility of machines which bore our
name." [23] Although agricultural implements made in the
United States could not be sold to advantage within Canada,
the Russian Mennonites and other Europeans who migrated
to Manitoba depended upon binders of Yankee invention to
harvest their grain.

Of the countries south of the United States, Mexico, Chile,
and the Argentine alone showed any interest in harvesting
machinery prior to 1885. A few sales had been made by
American firms in Mexico and Chile before the Civil War,
but no serious effort was made to exploit this field until the
mid-1870's.[24] By then, Wood, Osborne, and Adriance, Platt

---

[22] L.P.C.B. No. 235, pp. 93, 112, C. H. McCormick, Jr., to Wesbrook &
Fairchild, June 1 and July 6, 1883. ‡E. K. Butler to Nettie F. McCormick,
Oct. 30, 1883: "I believe that country [Manitoba] is yet too new and
business too much scattered and times too hard for us to push our business
there through salaried agents."

[23] See, letters of the Co. in L.P.C.B. No. 6, p. 365, to N. W. Brown,
Whitby, Canada, Apr. 20, 1857; No. 235, p. 433, to Wesbrook & Fairchild,
Winnipeg, Man., July 14, 1883; No. 237, p. 244, to B. Cromyn, London,
Ont., Sept. 17, 1883.

[24] "Patent Office Records, McCormick Extension Case, Patent of 1847"
(Washington, 1861), pp. 8-9. Here it is testified that J. H. Manny sold
some reapers in South America in 1857. J. A. Pitts, Buffalo, to C. H.
McCormick, Sept. 2, 1857. Pitts wished a reaper sent to his son in Chile
and it was shipped a week later. "Chicago Daily Democrat," Sept. 10,
1857. This was probably the first McCormick sale in that country. Pitts
was a builder of threshing machines and sold twenty of them in Chile

& Co., were boasting of agencies at Valparaiso, Montevideo,[25] and Buenos Ayres. The McCormicks were looking toward Mexico as a place where new devices might be tried in the early harvest and possibly a few machines sold each year for cash.[26] When the Mexican Ambassador to the United States visited Chicago in 1878 as the guest of the Manufacturers' Association, they showed him every courtesy and conducted him through their works.[27] Puebla and Chihuahua were the only states of Mexico which seemed promising, and in 1879, Father E. T. Gillow, a large landowner of San Martin in Puebla, bought four harvester-binders and three droppers.[28]

in 1858. L.P.C.B. No. 37, pp. 88, 293, the Co. to W. Granger & Co., Nov. 29 and Dec. 6, 1860. W. H. Randall, Santiago, Chile, to the Co., Sept. 2, 1867. Randall stated that grain in Chile was cut by hand, although there were ranches raising 20,000 or more bushels of wheat a year. C. H. Mc-Cormick, Jr., to McCormick Co., Jan. 10, 1885: "We should open an agency in Chile."

[25] Circular entitled "Machines à Faucher et à Moissonner de Wood, 1867." In this, Wood advertised that he made a mower with its cutter set low, particularly for the "South American market." L.P.C.B. No. 172, p. 139, the Co. to T. Drysdale, Buenos Ayres, May 11, 1877. This shows that Wood had an agent there at least as early as 1871. *Sprague & Parsons vs. Adriance & Platts,* (N. Y. 1874), pp. 658, 660. Catalog of D. M. Osborne & Co., 1879. L.P.C.B. No. 197, p. 168, the Co. to A. R. Kyte & Co., N. Y. City, Dec. 26, 1879.

[26] L.P.C.B. No. 158, p. 328, the Co. to E. M. Castillo, Dallas, Texas, May 28, 1875, and No. 184, p. 771, to Crane, Breed & Co., Cincinnati, Oct. 22, 1878. The Co. refuses to send machines to Mexico, since it hasn't been able to keep up with the home demand, which is more profitable than foreign markets. Signor Marinal, Washington, D. C., to Baldwin, Hopkins & Peyton, Mch. 29, 1877.

[27] "Chicago Daily Tribune," Sept. 4, 6, and 12, 1878. L.P.C.B. No. 183, p. 505, the Co. to C. Mason, Chicago, Aug. 26, 1878.

[28] Letters of the Co. in *ibid.,* No. 188, p. 807, and No. 189, pp. 30, 160, 174, in Mch., 1881, to Father E. T. Gillow, San Martin, Mexico. John F. Fullen, an expert, was sent to attend these machines; No. 191, p. 308, to J. W. Foster, U. S. Legation, Mexico City, June 6, 1879: "We are glad that our machines worked so well in Mexico." F. H. Matthews to C. H. McCormick, Apr. 21, 1879. C. H. McCormick attended a banquet in Chicago in honor of President Diaz in Mch., 1883.

This beginning did not lead to further orders, but in 1884 a consignee was named in Chihuahua and at least three binders were sold there.[29]

Although the McCormick Company was unable to develop a market in Peru and Chile before 1885,[30] it had sold about four hundred machines in the La Plata Valley by that year. As the result of an arrangement with Jas. E. Ward & Co., of New York City, Dumaresq Le Bas of Montevideo was appointed McCormicks' agent in 1879 and a dozen wire-binders were sent to him.[31] The trade grew slowly even after the Chicago firm dispatched an expert to assist in their introduction, prepared Spanish posters and pamphlets, and specially equipped all harvesters for that market with ox-tongues. At the end of four years of effort, Le Bas was able to sell only about fifty machines yearly. There was no regular steamship service between New York and Montevideo, and when the McCormicks' expert wished to reach Uruguay as quickly as possible he was obliged to go by way of Liverpool. Since the country to the south of the La Plata River produced more

[29] Letters of the Co. in L.P.C.B. No. 197, p. 81, to Elmendorf & Co., San Antonio, Texas, Dec. 23, 1879; No. 230, p. 417, to J. A. McDowell, Saltillo, Mexico, Jan. 20, 1883; No. 232, p. 871, to Count LaGrand, N. Y. City, May 9, 1883; No. 241, pp. 213, 240, to W. H. Hatch, Dallas, Texas, Mch. 26, 1884: "Ship two harvester-binders to A. Cordero and to V. Horcasitas of Chihuahua."

[30] Letters of the Co. in ibid., No. 172, p. 138 to J. Innes & Co., Valparaiso, May 11, 1877: "We would like to introduce wire binders in Chile"; No. 193, p. 356, to R. Ritchie, Valdura, Chile, Sept. 5, 1879: "We are sending circulars"; No. 236, p. 640, to W. R. Grace & Co., N. Y., Aug. 24, 1883, and No. 236, pp. 479, 626, 717, to W. H. Crossman & Bros., N. Y., Aug. 16, 24, and 29, 1883: "We are shipping a mower to Valparaiso."

[31] Letters of the Co. in ibid., No. 179, p. 698; No. 188, p. 47, Hughes & Ayres, N. Y. City, Apr. 30, 1878, and Feb. 11, 1879: "We are anxious to introduce machines to Argentina"; No. 182, p. 183, to Ludmann & Co., N. Y. City, July 5, 1878: "We have shipped a sample machine to Argentina"; No. 192, pp. 301, 371, to Jas. E. Ward & Co., July 28, 1879; No. 193, p. 275, to J. K. Theobald & Co., Montevideo, Sept. 4, 1879.

grain than Uruguay, an agency was opened at Buenos Ayres in 1883.[32] Thereafter, the annual sales in the valley increased.

Trade with South Africa was even less remunerative than with the Argentine. When the McCormicks heard that many substantial farmers were moving to the Cape of Good Hope from New Zealand and Australia, they appointed an agent at Malmesbury and sent him several reapers in 1882. This consignment, as well as a further shipment forwarded by way of New York and London two years later, arrived too late for the harvest.[33] Inadequate boat service between the United States and the Cape was a severe handicap to American manufacturers who wished to trade there.

Both the South American and South African markets were of minor importance when compared with the new sales territory in New Zealand and Australia.[34] This was opened as a result of the Centennial Exposition at Philadelphia in 1876. Visitors from these colonies to the Fair encouraged Walter A. Wood to send about fifty of his wire-binders to their remote home in time for the harvest of 1876-1877.[35] They,

[32] Letters of the Co. too numerous to list here, in *ibid.*, No. 197 (Dec. 1879), to No. 241 (Mch. 1884) to Jas. E. Ward & Co., and W. H. Crossman & Bros. of N. Y. City; Dumaresq Le Bas of Montevideo, and to the McCormicks' Argentina expert and representative, Lee Borrell.

[33] O. S. Gage to C. H. McCormick, from London, June 6, 1878. Gage, who was McCormick's English agent, had just sold a wire-binder to a resident of South Africa. Many letters of the Co. in L.P.C.Bs. No. 183 to No. 249 (Aug. 1878-Dec. 1882) to W. H. Crossman & Bros., New York City; H. W. Peabody & Co., Boston; Coombs, Crosby & Eddy, New York City; E. Benedict, New York City, and to Smuts & Koch, Malmesbury, Cape of Good Hope. The "Scientific American," June 10, 1882, pp. 359, 362-3, tells of C. Aultman & Co.'s (Canton, O.) sales in South Africa.

[34] L.P.C.B. No. 242, pp. 27, 292, telegram of Co. to C. H. McCormick, Jr., N. Y., Apr. 28, 1884, and letter to W. H. Crossman & Bros., May 9, 1884; No. 242, pp. 284, 384, 495; Co. to J. E. Ward & Co., May 9, 14, and 19, 1884; Co. to G. B. Averill, in No. 242, p. 444, May 17, 1884, and No. 243, p. 814, June 26, 1884.

[35] W. D. Baldwin to C. H. McCormick, July, 9, 1877. C. H. McCormick to F. H. Matthews, July 10, 1877. Everingham, Greenfield & Co., Ballarat, Australia, to Co., May 26, 1877.

however, were not the first reapers to cross the Pacific Ocean. Almost twenty-five years before, Obed Hussey had tried without success to sell a dozen implements at Melbourne.[36] At that time, the few Australians who cut their grain with machines used a header-thresher invented by John Ridley of Northumberland, then living in South Australia.[37] A McCormick implement made by Burgess & Key won a prize in Australia in 1856 and the inventor apparently shipped twenty-five Chicago-made reapers there in 1858. Of the self-rakes which he sent to Great Britain during the Civil War, one found its way to Australia and another to New Zealand.[38] Thereafter, until the Centennial Exposition, the letter-books of the Chicago partners rarely mention these countries, although their grain exports were yearly becoming of more importance in the European markets.[39]

The interest awakened by the Fair led McCormick to patent his machines in New South Wales, Victoria, and New Zealand.[40] Protection of this kind seemed especially desirable since

[36] "Hussey Extension Case, Patent of 1847," pp. 58-59.

[37] Peter T. Dondlinger, "The Book of Wheat" (N. Y. 1908), p. 91, Bennet Woodcroft, "Appendix to the Specifications of English Patents for Reaping Machines" (London, 1853), pp. 47, 107. "Mechanics' Magazine" (London), Vol. IV. (new ser.), Mch. 8, 1861, p. 164.

[38] L. J. McCormick, London, to C. H. McCormick, May 29, 1862. #J. Todd, Castlemains, Scotland, to C. H. McCormick, June 6, 1863, and Sept. 25, 1865.

[39] "Mechanics' Magazine," Mch. 8, 1861, p. 164. During the four years, 1856-1859, £600,000 worth of grain were exported from South Australia, or 5£ 4s per annum for each person living there. "New York Sun," Oct. 5, 1878. In Australia, 900,000 acres were under cultivation in 1876, and the export of wheat and flour was valued at £1,500,000. Mary A. McCormick to Nettie F. McCormick, Aug. 3, 1870: "I hear that the machines for New Zealand were shipped yesterday."

[40] Letters of the Co. in L.P.C.B. No. 169, p. 650, to A. M. Greenfield, Ballarat, Australia, Jan. 3, 1877; No. 170, p. 500, to T. Whitaker, Howlong, New South Wales, Feb. 15, 1877; No. 171, p. 790, to Stuart, Couche & Co., Melbourne, Apr. 27, 1877; No. 186, p. 70, to H. W. Peabody & Co., Boston, Dec. 3, 1878. C. Colahan to C. H. McCormick, July 28, 1876. W. D. Baldwin's telegram to Co., July 8, 1877. #C. H. McCormick to R. Mason, London, July 10, 1877. #E. A. Mason, London, Sept. 7, 1877. C. H.

the twenty per cent import duty at Melbourne, when added to the freight charges, raised the price of a foreign-made harvester-binder so high that Australians were impelled to build them in their own factories.[41] Arkell, Tufts & Co., a forwarding house of London and New York, which was pleased with the wire-binders sent by McCormick to England in 1877, asked for the New Zealand agency and an immediate shipment of fifty to Morrow, Bassett & Co., of Christchurch (Port Lyttelton). The McCormick brothers, now that Leander for the first time consented to have most of the foreign business handled as a company enterprise rather than as the private venture of Cyrus alone,[42] agreed to sell at $216, gold, f.o.b. New York, if Arkell would pay the expenses of an expert from Chicago to attend the machines after their arrival in New Zealand.[43] These terms were accepted and, excepting for the

to L. J. McCormick, Sept. 25, 1877. ‡Haseltine, Lake & Co., to C. H. McCormick, Aug. 25, 1877. Haseltine, Lake & Co., to J. S. Morgan & Co., Dec. 24, 1877. Although shipments to Australia and New Zealand were made in the name of the Co., patents were granted there to C. H. McCormick alone. See ‡L.P.C.B. of C. H. McCormick, June, 1876-Apr., 1878, pp. 134-137, C. H. & L. J. McCormick to Morrow, Bassett & Co., Apr. 7, 1878.

[41] Stuart, Couche & Co., Melbourne, to Co., Aug. 20, 1877. Everingham, Greenfield & Co., Ballarat, Australia, to Co., May 26, 1877: "The harvester-binders made by our colonial workmen are failures." The Wood binder was being built in Melbourne by "pirates" in 1878, and was underselling the McCormick by 20£. See, L.P.C.B. No. 184, p. 156, No. 186, pp. 305-6, the Co. to McLean Bros. & Rigg, Melbourne, Sept. 21, and Dec. 12, 1878. Apparently, by the autumn of 1879, the import tariff on harvesting machinery was abolished. L.P.C.B. No. 194, p. 63, the Co. to McLean Bros. & Rigg, Sept. 20, 1879.

[42] C. H. to L. J. McCormick, Sept. 25, 1877. In this, McCormick thinks of Australia primarily as a market for surplus binders.

[43] F. H. Matthews's telegram and letters to C. H. McCormick, July 7, 11, and 12, 1877. Matthews believed that a profit of $6000 could be made on the fifty binders. Mr. Morrow who had been in England, visited the McCormick factory on his way back to N. Z. C. H. McCormick, Jr., MSS. Nettie F. McCormick to C. H. McCormick, Jr., July 19, 1877; F. C. Newell, London, to the Co., July 11 and 15, 1877; Arkell, Tufts & Co.,

fact that the consignment was to be forwarded by way of England and not around Cape Horn, they are typical of the many contracts for deliveries in Australia and New Zealand made during the next eight years.[44] Company management of the overseas trade hereafter insured the continuous attention to its development which Cyrus McCormick had been unable to give; cash sales guaranteed the partners against loss; and the insistence upon the dispatch of a man qualified to set up and operate the machines in the field made certain that their reputation would not suffer because of the purchasers' inexperience. Sailing vessels over the long ocean route were used because of the prohibitive freight charges on machine shipments from Chicago to San Francisco.[45]

The principal farming section of New Zealand was in the South Island on the level land flanked by mountains and sea near Christchurch and Dunedin.[46] On these well-watered but almost treeless plains, often swept in the Christmas harvest season by sand blown before a burning northwest wind, heavy

London, and N. Y., to the Co., July 7, 11, 14, and Sept. 18, 1877; E. C. Beardsley, from R. M. SS. *Australia,* to the Co., Nov. 7 and 14, 1877.

[44] F. H. Matthews to C. H. McCormick, Feb. 21, 1879. By this date the N. Z. and Australian consignees were requesting the privilege of buying on credit terms. McCormick finally consented to allow ninety days, without interest, or 1 year at 6%. Shipments for N. Z. and Australia went through Boston rather than New York after 1881. In Boston, H. W. Peabody & Co. offered a larger choice of ships and a lower freight rate. The competition of Boston and N. Y. for this trade illustrates the lively rivalry between these ports. See, the many letters of the Co. to H. W. Peabody & Co. during 1882, in L.P.C.Bs. No. 220-224. *Ibid.,* No. 232, p. 696, the Co. to R. W. Cameron & Co., N. Y., May 2, 1883. The rate to N. Z. *via* Eng. was about $12.60 per ton of 40 cu. ft. and *via* Cape Horn, $7.00 per ton, plus 5% for primage in each instance. *Ibid.,* No. 242, p. 454, the Co. to R. W. Cameron & Co., May 17, 1884.

[45] Ibid., No. 203, p. 218, the Co. to E. P. Vining, Gen'l. Agt., U. P. R.R., Omaha, Neb., June 19, 1880.

[46] A few McCormick machines were shipped to Wellington and Auckland in the North Island. *Ibid.,* No. 190, p. 152, the Co. to R. W. Cameron & Co., N. Y., May 2, 1879.

yields of winter wheat and oats were produced.[47] Some holdings, divided into small fields by gorse hedges and sod fences, were a thousand acres or more in extent. To the eye of an Illinoian, the house and barns of a New Zealander could not compare in style and size with those in his own state, but he noted with approval that they were protected from the hot gales by tree barriers of eucalyptus, poplars, and weeping willows. Although McCormick's expert in 1877 remarked that the farmers were "the slowest-easy-go-easy-people I ever saw," he admitted that in intelligence they probably averaged higher than those living on the prairies of the Middle West.[48] Since the New Zealand wheat area was small, it could not be counted upon to absorb several thousand harvesting machines a year for long in the future.

While the boom lasted, however, it was a profitable one for the McCormicks, Osborne, and Wood. The excellent performance of the fifty binders brought the brothers an order for eight hundred more.[49] In July, 1878, over five hundred and fifty were stowed below decks in the ship *Alexander McNeill*, bound on its four or five months' passage around the Horn from New York to Port Lyttelton.[50] In this harvest also, they

[47] "United States Consular Reports," No. 33, p. 506. There were only about 55,000 farmers in N. Z. and 113,000 in Australia.

[48] E. C. Beardsley, Christchurch, N. Z., to the Co., Dec. 7 and 30, 1877; Jan. 31, 1878. A competitive trial was held in N. Z., and Osborne won. Beardsley, the expert, who had not forgotten his training in the U. S., sadly wrote: "I had canvassed the makeup of the Committee and could not find that they were susceptible of 'argument.'" The audience was in favor of the McCormick binder, but the Jury gave the palm to Osborne's.

[49] Morrow, Bassett & Co., to the Co., Jan. 3, Feb. 1, Mch. 29, 1878. Arkell, Tufts & Co. to the Co., Mch. 6, May 6, 10, and June 13, 1878. L.P.C.B. No. 178, p. 390, the Co. to Arkell, Tufts & Co., Mch. 20, 1878. No. 180, p. 817, and No. 183, pp. 450-451, to Morrow, Bassett & Co., May 30 and Aug. 21, 1878.

[50] R. W. Cameron & Co., N. Y., to the Co., June 24, 1878. L.P.C.B. No. 182, pp. 841-845, the Co. to Morrow, Bassett & Co., Christchurch, July 30, 1878; No. 187, pp. 141-142, the Co. to *ibid.*, Jan. 10, 1879. By this time, Arkell Tufts & Co., over its protest, had been shelved as exclusive agent

sent sixty-four machines to Australia and Tasmania.[51] By the close of the season, agents had been appointed in Sydney, Melbourne, and Adelaide, and McCormick binders had won eleven first prizes in trials in Australia and New Zealand. Drought, however, seriously curtailed the crop yield, the market was glutted with American machinery, and, as a result, shipments from Chicago for the 1879 season were very light.[52] In that year the twine-binders of Wood, Osborne, Deering, and Johnston brought in the Antipodes as severe a reaction against wire-binders as in the United States.[53] Not until 1881, when the McCormicks were prepared to supply the demand for the new machine, could they again meet the competition of their rivals on equal terms. All in all, between 1877 and 1884, they shipped to Australia and New Zealand about 3500 harvester-binders, together with wire, twine, some

for N. Z., and the McCormicks were dealing directly with the consignee to whom this letter is addressed. *Ibid.*, No. 197, p. 311, the Co. to Beach & Brown, N. Y., Jan. 2, 1880. #C. H. McCormick, Jr., to C. H. McCormick, Oct. 17, 1881. The McCormicks finally paid Arkell, Tufts & Co., $400 damages.

[51] F. H. Matthews to C. H. McCormick, Feb. 12 and May 30, 1879. Of the 64, 44 went to Melbourne and 20 to Sydney. All were sold in 1878. E. C. Beardsley, Christchurch, to Co., Dec. 30, 1877: "Our machines must have iron, rather than wooden, wheels in Australia because the weather is so dry." W. H. Town, Melbourne, to C. H. McCormick, Aug. 9, 1880. The McCormick agents in Australia were F. Lassetter & Co., Ltd., Sydney, and McLean Bros. & Rigg, Adelaide and Melbourne. They were also Deering's agents.

[52] Nettie F. McCormick, St. Moritz, Switzerland, to C. H. McCormick, Aug. 22, 1878. F. H. Matthews to C. H. McCormick, Feb. 12, Mch. 14, and May 30, 1879. F. C. Newell, Hobart, Tasmania, to W. N. Spring, Sioux City, Ia., Dec. 21, 1878.

[53] L.P.C.B. No. 200, p. 134, the Co. to E. C. Beardsley, Minneapolis, Mch. 30, 1880. The demand for a twine-binder had been insistent as early as 1877. See, Haseltine, Lake & Co., to J. S. Morgan & Co., Dec. 24, 1877. The McCormicks sent an experimental twine-binder to N. Z. for the harvest of 1879-80. See, L.P.C.B. No. 198, p. 298. The Co. to E. W. Brooks, Red Wing, Minn., Feb. 9, 1880. W. H. Town, Melbourne, to the Co., Aug. 9 and Oct. 4, 1880.

400 mowers, and a few reapers and droppers. This was the largest and most profitable foreign field of sale developed during the lifetime of Cyrus McCormick. Compared with Great Britain and Europe, it cost very little effort and brought a much richer return.

By 1880 the sun never set upon McCormick machines. They were working in some harvest field every day in the year. Although this was a matter of much gratification to the inventor, victories in Europe always aroused his enthusiasm more than conquests below the equator or beyond the 180th meridian. Europe was his province, and whatever success was there attained, was due to his personal endeavor.

With some misgivings, he granted the wish of Abel A. Westengaard to be his agent in the Scandinavian states.[54] Early in July, 1875, Westengaard reached Copenhagen where he planned to make his headquarters. As he walked down the gang-plank of his ship, he noticed implements on the dock from the "Champion" Works in Ohio.[55] This was a foretaste of the ill luck which pursued him during the next seven years. His failure could not be blamed upon lack of energy. He appointed over seventy agents, tacked up posters in many railroad stations and country taverns, distributed "newspapers" in Swedish sent to him from the Chicago factory, exhibited the machines at work wherever possible, and rented a fine store with big show windows in Copenhagen. The first season he sold two machines. In 1876 there was a severe drought; in 1877, the crops were drowned by the excessively wet weather,

[54] A reaper had been sold in 1874 to the brother of Westengaard, who lived in Denmark. Letters to the Co. in L.P.C.B. No. 80, p. 210 to J. T. Griffin, London, May 25, 1865; No. 134, p. 542, to T. Thompson, McGregor, Ia., June 1, 1872; No. 158, pp. 333-34, to C. H. McCormick, May 29, 1875. C. H. McCormick, Hot Springs, Ark., to the Co., June 1, 1875.

[55] Letters of the Co. to A. A. Westengaard in L.P.C.B. No. 158, p. 547, June 4, 1875; No. 159, p. 315, June 25, 1875, No. 161, p. 95, Aug. 4, 1875. A. A. Westengaard to the Co., from Leith, Scotland, June 29, 1875, and from Copenhagen, July 5 and 21, 1875.

and the years that followed brought but little improvement.[56] Westengaard was not more astonished by the difficulty of selling harvesting implements in Scandinavia than by the volume of American meat products, grain, and machinery that he saw unloaded at Copenhagen for sale in Denmark, Russia, and Germany.[57] "The United States spoil the trade here," he wrote in 1879, "because they ship such enormous quantities of corn, grain, pork, etc. over here, and make prices so low, that the farmers are not able to spare money to buy machines." The McCormick Company agreed with him and complained that "our consignment to your country has given us nothing but trouble and loss and we have decided to not re-embark on any such scheme again." [58] By 1881, seventy-four machines in all had been shipped to him, and he had sold only fifty-five. Two of the balance were sent by rail to Charkoff, Russia, and were so broken in transit that they were worthless. The remaining seventeen were lost at sea on their way from Copenhagen to Odessa.[59] After 1882, the McCormicks were content to handle the small Scandinavian trade through their London office.[60]

While Westengaard was losing his campaign, the McCor-

[56] See, the many letters from A. A. Westengaard to the Co., between 1875 and 1879, and the replies of the Co. in L.P.C.Bs. No. 162-192 (1875-1879).

[57] A. A. Westengaard to the Co., May 19 and Sept. 1, 1876, Feb. 17 and Apr. 2, 1877. Because of the heavy crop yield in Denmark, eight men were needed to follow the reaper, rather than five, as in the U. S.

[58] A. A. Westengaard, to C. H. McCormick, Apr. 26, 1879. L.P.C.B. No. 249, p. 670, the Co. to A. A. Westengaard, Jan. 23, 1883.

[59] Letters of the Co. to A. A. Westengaard, in *ibid.*, No. 203, pp. 399-400, June 26, 1880, and No. 249, pp. 267, 412, Feb. 20, and May 1, 1882. A. V. Perrin, Charkoff, to C. A. Spring, Jr., Jan. 31, 1881. *Ibid.*, No. 249, pp. 470, 557, the Co. to G. A. Freudenreich, Odessa, July 15, 1882.

[60] *Ibid.*, No. 236, p. 261, the Co. to Bryson & Dick, Hammond, Ill., Aug. 7, 1883; No. 244, p. 307, to M. Grunske, Allamont, Dak. Terr., July 29, 1884; p. 778, to H. Shultz, Woodbury, Minn., Aug. 22, 1884. Parkinson & Parkinson, Cincinnati, to the Co., Oct. 22, 1884.

mick Company was enjoying better fortune elsewhere in Europe. The stimulus to foreign sales given by the Centennial Exposition was intensified by the development at that time of successful wire-binders in the United States. The ebb and flow of McCormick's interest in the European market corresponded quite closely with the appearance in America of new types of machinery for harvesting grass or grain. He was at his best when introducing a new device, and hitherto, by a happy coincidence, on each occasion when he had something novel to offer, there had been a World's Fair either in England or France to serve his purpose. Nor was it to be otherwise in this instance. Since Paris planned to open a great Exposition in 1878, the two years before that event were spent in adapting the wire-binder to service under European harvest conditions.

As an earlier chapter has shown, McCormick had little left abroad by 1876 except the prestige of his name and a group of influential friends who were ready to help him. It was necessary to build anew on these foundation stones, but he declined to give much attention, thereafter, either to Germany or Austria-Hungary. As a first move, he engaged Rush F. Mason, a Chicagoan resident in London, who imported "American groceries, fish, and meats for English palates," to exhibit a binder at the Smithfield Cattle Show in December, 1876. This annual fair attracted buyers and dealers from far and wide, and was similar in nature and purpose to the wool markets of the cities of Germany and Russia. McCormick's entry excited much interest, and Mason, although declining the terms offered for the exclusive agency of Great Britain and the Continent, agreed to advertise the machines and to arrange for patents in England, Austria-Hungary and Germany.[61] J. S. Morgan & Co. of London consented temporarily

[61] R. F. Mason, London, to the Co., Nov. 12, 1875; July 22, and Sept. 2, 1876: #I. J. Mason, Chicago, to C. H. McCormick, Dec. 9, 1876; #R. F.

to be the financial clearing-house for the enterprise and Cyrus McCormick had the good of his foreign business in mind when he gave a "grand dinner" for Mr. Morgan at Delmonico's late in the following year.[62] Two harvester-binders were also sent to Hamburg, but J. R. McDonald & Co., now the agent of Walter A. Wood, declined to do more for their advancement than to arrange a field trial on the farm of a prominent Mecklenburg landowner.[63]

The bright hopes of 1876 were not realized in the following harvest. Cyrus McCormick, Jr., having just graduated from high school, sailed for England with Professor Francis L. Patton and Dr. William S. Plumer, who were on their way to a Presbyterian conclave at Edinburgh.[64] The young McCormick was more interested in the Liverpool trials of the Royal Agricultural Society where the new wire-binder was to com-

Mason, to C. H. McCormick, Dec. 16, 1876, Feb. 23, and Mch. 9, 1877. R. F. Mason died in England on June 30, 1877. ‡E. A. Mason to C. H. McCormick, July 18, 1877. Since July 1, 1877, a patent in Germany gave protection in all the states of the Empire. L.P.C.B. No. 169, p. 95, F. H. Matthews, for C. H. McCormick, to J. S. Morgan & Co., London, Eng., Nov. 24, 1876.

[62] C. H. McCormick, Jr., MSS. Book "B," Nettie F. McCormick, to C. H. McCormick, Jr., Nov. 10, and 14, 1877: "I think *English business* drew papa gradually into the dinner, . . . It seemed a fitting recognition of Mr. Morgan's kindness and friendship to our family. . . . Mr. Darling [the caterer] went quite beyond anything of the kind here since the time of Mr. Peabody." Mr. and Mrs. Roger Pryor, David D. Field, Cyrus Field, and Mr. and Mrs. E. H. Harriman were among the twenty-eight at the banquet.

[63] L.P.C.B. No. 173, p. 11, the Co. to J. R. McDonald & Co., June 21, 1877. J. R. McDonald to the Co., July 7, 27, and Aug. 7, 1877. ‡F. C. Newell, London, to C. H. McCormick, July 15 and 20, 1877. Telegram of the Co. to C. H. McCormick, June 20, 1877. ‡F. C. Newell, Hamburg, to C. H. McCormick, July 20, 26, 30, Aug. 5, 23, and 31, 1877. An agent for McCormick was appointed at Brahlstorf, Mecklenburg. F. H. Matthews to C. H. McCormick, June 16 and 18, 1877.

[64] C. H. McCormick, Jr., MSS. Book "B," Nettie F. McCormick to C. H. McCormick, Jr., June 11 and 17, 1877. C. H. McCormick to Brown, Shipley & Co., Liverpool, June 22, 1877.

pete against the machines of Wood and Osborne. Before he entered college that autumn he had undergone a rather severe initiation into his father's business, and according to his associates, acquitted himself admirably.[65]

Upon his arrival in England he learned that no machine could enter the Liverpool trials unless the operator—in this case F. C. Newell, an expert from Chicago—were equipped with "wire-retaining nippers" for cutting the wire that bound the sheaves, and holding it so that it would not become mixed with the straw. To his dismay, he was unable to procure shears of this type in England. Several cables were necessary before he could make those at home understand what was needed. His father, who was probably as anxious to help him do well in his first venture as to have the binder compete in the trials, seemingly tabled all other business until the nippers were secured and dispatched posthaste to London.[66] But they were of no avail. In spite of the pains taken to find a team of iron-gray color, so that it would not show perspiration, the platform of the McCormick harvester-binder was too short for the heavy English grain, the smooth-rimmed master wheel slipped in the muddy field, and the binding mechanism did not make sheaves often enough. The Wood binder, aided by a year of testing in England and J. T. Griffin's "splendid collation and unlimited champagne" for the judges, won the

[65] F. L. Patton to Nettie F. McCormick, Sept. 29, 1877. F. C. Newell, to C. H. McCormick, July 15, 1877.

[66] C. H. McCormick, Jr., MSS. Nettie F. McCormick to C. H. McCormick, Jr., July 15, 1877: "But what relevancy there is in our knowing that nippers were, or were not retained in Great Britain we cannot imagine!" *Idem* to *idem*, Aug. 3, 1877. They finally arrived too late for the trial, but, in the meantime, Newell had had several pairs specially made in England. F. C. Newell to the Co., July 17 and 20, 1877. ‡F. C. Newell to C. H. McCormick, July 11 and 18, 1877. Telegram stub-book of C. H. McCormick, for the period Aug. 6-25, 1877. The Co. to C. H. McCormick, July 31, 1877. L.P.C.B. No. 173, p. 855, the Co. to F. C. Newell, Aug. 3, 1877.

award.[67] Further trials in Germany and England only made more evident the necessity of evolving a "deep harvester" with a wider platform for the overseas trade.[68]

Nor was the Liverpool defeat the only foretaste given the young McCormick of the problems he would have to handle for himself within a few years. Rush Mason died early in the summer, and agency matters were at "sixes and sevens." [69] Because the patents taken out on the binder in England embraced more than McCormick could rightfully claim in view of the prior grants there to Wood and the Gordons, they were probably void.[70] The son conferred with business men and lawyers of London about these matters, and brought back to the United States a clear view of the situation so that his father could decide what it was best to do.

Owing to Rush Mason's death and a dispute over his bill for expenses, McCormick in the autumn of 1877 made Otis S. Gage of Chicago and London his representative in England and on the Continent. Gage, with doubtful right under his contract, soon placed the business of selling in the hands of Waite, Burnell & Co., of London and Paris.[71] Elaborate

[67] Letters of F. C. Newell to ‡C. H. McCormick, July 15 and Aug. 2, 1877; to C. H. McCormick, July 11 and 17, 1877, and to the Co., Sept. 12, 1877. ‡C. H. McCormick, Jr., to C. H. McCormick, July 13, 1877.

[68] ‡F. C. Newell to C. H. McCormick, Sept. 1, 7, and 12, 1877.

[69] ‡Rush F. Mason & Co., to C. H. McCormick, Sept. 10 and Oct. 4, 1877. ‡F. C. Newell to C. H. McCormick, Aug. 6, 1877.

[70] Robertson, Brooman & Co., London, to C. H. McCormick, Oct. 25, 1877. C. H. McCormick's cable to Robertson, Brooman & Co., Oct. 16, 1877. ‡C. H. McCormick to Haseltine, Lake & Co., London, Sept. 7, 1877. C. H. Crawford, London, to C. H. McCormick, Dec. 28, 1877. By this time, however, the Gordons' English patents had lapsed for non-payment of dues. ‡O. S. Gage, London, to C. H. McCormick, Feb. 25, 1878.

[71] O. S. Gage, to the Co., July 9, 21, and Aug. 1, 1877. Contract between O. S. Gage and C. H. McCormick, Nov. 30, 1877. J. S. Morgan & Co., London, to C. H. McCormick, Dec. 19, 1877. Waite, Burnell & Co., Paris, to C. H. McCormick, Dec. 19, 1877. L.P.C.B. No. 178, p. 209, the Co. to A. A. Westengaard, Mch. 12, 1878. O. S. Gage to C. H. McCormick, Jan. 10, Feb. 2, and Apr. 8, 1878.

preparations went forward to advertise the machines, and the factory prepared a silver-plated binder and mower for the Paris Exhibition. Besides these display machines, about forty other binders were shipped for sale and field trials in England and on the Continent.[72] The chief victories abroad in the past had been won when Cyrus McCormick was present to supervise, and he was eager in 1878 to enter the arena again. But his crowded days suggested that he should not take the time to go, and Mrs. McCormick was unwilling to leave her young children at home in the charge of maids and governesses for so long a period. For these reasons, she feared that her husband would send young Cyrus as his representative to Paris, "like a lamb among wolves to that most dangerous & gilded pathway to destruction!" [73] This course, however, was adopted by mid-May, but to the relief of both mother and son, the inventor soon decided to make the voyage.

"Dear papa," wrote Mrs. McCormick, "who has fought so many battles of the reapers, looks at the coming struggle, and quite naturally is eager to be in the midst of it. He feels that this may be his last great international fight, and he wants a fair field and no favor. I sometimes think that success will depend on his presence. There are so many unfair influences

[72] Letters of the Co. in L.P.C.B. No. 178, p. 483, to O. S. Gage, Mch. 23, 1878, sending 10,000 circulars in English, 15,000 in German, and 25,000 in French; No. 176, p. 410, to Union Brass Mfg. Co., Dec. 28, 1877; No. 178, p. 88, to W. B. Fox & Bros., N. Y., Mch. 6, 1878; No. 180, p. 155, to O. S. Gage, May 9, 1878. Chicago Nickel Plating Co., to the Co., Jan. 5, 1878. R. C. McCormick, U. S. Comm'r. Gen'l, N. Y., to C. H. McCormick, Feb. 4, 1878. These exhibition machines were shipped on the *U. S. SS. Wyoming.* Of the forty, only fifteen were "deep harvesters." Two front-cut mowers were also sent.

[73] C. H. McCormick, Jr., MSS. Nettie F. McCormick to C. H. McCormick, Jr., Mch. 14, 25, May 17 and June 5, 1878. C. H. McCormick, Jr., MSS. Book "G," Nettie F. McCormick to C. H. McCormick, n.d., but probably early June, 1878. C. H. McCormick, Jr., to C. H. McCormick, June 19, 1878: "Please don't worry about me. I shall always be conservative."

brought to bear to defeat the most meritorious performance of the machine without his vigilant eye and experienced mind." [74]

Before he could clear his desk of the most pressing business matters and sail on the SS. *Germanic* on July 20, his son was already in Europe, exhibiting the binder in Holland, and with the aid of an expert mechanic, Louis Frank, grooming the machines for the Bristol trials of the Royal Agricultural Society. Mrs. McCormick, in poor health and wishing to consult specialists in Europe, also crossed the Atlantic, taking her three small children with her, and the medals won in earlier exhibitions in England and on the Continent.[75] Cyrus McCormick arrived in England in time to accompany his son to Bristol, where their binder "walked through like a breeze and only stopped once when a clod of dirt got caught on the sickel (*sic*) bar." The Wood and Osborne binders were defeated in the two-day trial and McCormick received the gold medal.[76]

[74] C. H. McCormick, Jr., MSS. Nettie F. McCormick to C. H. McCormick, Jr., June 1 and 6, 1878. ‡C. H. McCormick, Jr., to C. H. McCormick, June 8, 1878.

[75] C. H. McCormick, Jr., MSS. Book "F," Nettie F. McCormick to C. H. McCormick, Jr., June 14, 1878, and Book "G," June 16, 1878. The son sailed on the *Baltic* June 20, and arrived at Liverpool on June 29th. "The narrow limits of the ship make it easy for people to approach you whom you would not *like at all* to know. So be careful and find out about *any*body who makes up to you. . . . If you learn fresh caution about where you leave your money when you sleep or bathe it will not be amiss." Characteristically, C. H. McCormick, Jr., on the day he reached London, went to hear Dr. Spurgeon at the Tabernacle. Mrs. McCormick, not certain that her husband would follow her, reached England early in July on the SS. *Adriatic,* accompanied by Miss H. M. Hammond, the children, and a maid. By late July the two younger children were at Ramsgate while Mrs. McCormick and her daughter Virginia were touring the Continent. See, C. H. McCormick, Jr., MSS. Book "F," letters of Nettie F. McCormick from Chaumont, Basle, Lindau, Ragatz, and St. Moritz, to C. H. McCormick, Jr., July 27, 28, 31, Aug. 5, 9, 19, 20, 23, 24, 25, 28, 30, and Sept. 2, 1878.

[76] ‡C. H. McCormick, Jr., to Nettie F. McCormick, Aug. 1, 4, and 8, 1878. "Engineering" (London), XXVI (1878), pp. 30-32. "Mercury and Daily Post" (Bristol), and "Times and Mirror" (Bristol), Aug. 6 and 7, 1878. "London Times," Aug. 9, 1878. Walter A. Wood was also present

With this victory won, the father and son went at once to Paris. Attention to matters connected with the Exhibition did not prevent them from visiting Cabanel, the artist who had once done portraits of Cyrus McCormick and his wife. "In his studio we saw on the easel portraits of Mr. Mackey [*sic*] the Californian Millionaire, who made so much money in the Big Bonanza Mine, and his wife. Mr. Mackey is having *four portraits* painted, to give to friends." [77] After ten days in Paris, they registered at the Kaiserbad Hotel at Aix la Chapelle. Here for two weeks Cyrus McCormick, Sr., took the warm sulphur baths and enjoyed the companionship of his son.

I go with a bottle to a dairy about half mile away [Cyrus, Jr., reported to his mother], and get it filled with pure milk! Delicious! Milked right into the bottle by a funnel. By nine he [father] is ready for breakfast, served in our little parlor, and . . . he is ready by 10, or half past, either to read mail, dictate letters, walk if it is fine, etc. About 1:30 we take a bare roll and glass of milk and water & then, latterly, write for an hour more, and then go and take from one and a half to two hours of billiards. This is good exercise for him, windows open, fresh air, and a seat near at hand. It . . . diverts his mind. . . . I manage it so that we play about an even game, he winning one, then I, etc.! Generally the nip and tuck games are the ones he enjoys most. . . . This is our regular routine. [78]

This period of rest was the more pleasant because of the news which came from week to week of fresh victories won

at this trial. The Johnston Harvester Co. had a twine-binder on the field but did not work it.

[77] ‡C. H. McCormick, Jr., to Nettie F. McCormick, Aug. 12, 1878. The reference is to John W. Mackay of Comstock Lode fame. Cabanel painted a portrait of Virginia McCormick later in the autumn. See, C. H. McCormick, Jr., MSS. Nettie F. McCormick to C. H. McCormick, Jr., Nov. 29, 1878.

[78] ‡C. H. McCormick, Jr., to Nettie F. McCormick, Aug. 19, 24, 29, and 30, 1878. C. H. McCormick, Jr., MSS. Book "F," Nettie F. McCormick to C. H. McCormick, Jr., Sept. 2, 1878.

by Louis Frank and the binder in England and Scotland.[79]
Most gratifying of all was the word that Cyrus McCormick
was the only exhibitor of agricultural machinery to whom the
highest prize of the Paris Exposition was awarded, and would
most probably be promoted to the rank of Officer in the Legion
of Honor. The inventor was now anxious to return to the
United States since business differences with his brother,
Leander, had reached a crisis. When the date for the distribution of medals at Paris was postponed until October 21, it
was little wonder that he exclaimed to his son, "That knocks
things into a cocked hat!"[80] McCormick and his wife were
together in Paris once again by early September and decided
to await the awards. Cyrus, Jr., returned to Princeton.[81]

The months which followed were very busy ones. McCormick informed Gage that he would not be bound by the two-

[79] ‡C. H. McCormick, Jr., to Nettie F. McCormick, Aug. 28, 1878. He
tells his mother of the medals won in field trials at Ayr, Penryth, Glasgow,
and in Dumbarton Cy., Scotland. L.P.C.B. No. 185, pp. 427, 437, the Co. to
Morrow, Bassett & Co., Nov. 14, 1878. Besides the above, there are also
listed here the successes at Bourges and Lille in France, and at Haddington,
the Northamptonshire County Show, and Lincolnshire Society Fair in
England and Scotland. Nettie F. McCormick, St. Moritz, to C. H. McCormick, Aug. 22, 1878: "The immense success already accomplished . . . I
am sure will benefit your health to a certain extent. Truly we have been
much blessed in all things." C. H. McCormick to F. H. Matthews, Aug. 23,
1878.

[80] ‡C. H. McCormick, Jr., to Nettie F. McCormick, Aug. 27, 1878, and
to Virginia McCormick, Aug. 24, 1878. Other American exhibitors receiving the Grand Prize were Tiffany & Co., Thomas Edison, Elisha Gray,
Wheeler & Wilson, Memphis Cotton Exchange, etc. Nettie F. McCormick
to C. H. McCormick, Aug. 11, 1878. E. H. Knight, Paris, to C. H. Mc-
Cormick, Aug. 29, 1878. In the field trials held in connection with the
Exhibition both McCormick and Wood won *objets d'art* (vases).

[81] ‡C. H. McCormick, Jr., to Nettie F. McCormick, Aug. 24, 30, and
Sept. 11, 1878. C. H. McCormick MSS. Book "F," Nettie F. McCormick
to C. H. McCormick, Jr., Sept. 2, 1878. C. H. McCormick, Jr., sailed for
the U. S. on Sept. 12, 1878. C. H. McCormick, Jr., *SS. Germanic,* to Nettie
F. McCormick, Sept. 13, 1878.

year contract made with Waite, Burnell & Co.[82] This company was one of the best known in Europe and McCormick wished to employ it as his agent, but, in his opinion, his interests were not adequately protected by the existing arrangements. He gave Gage reason to sue by summarily dismissing him, and Waite, Burnell & Co. insisted that the inventor must fulfill the contract which it had accepted in good faith from his agent. McCormick was hampered in his negotiations with Gage and the English firm by the situation in Chicago—not knowing whether Leander would coöperate in the manufacture of a large number of machines for the European market. With some difficulty Mrs. McCormick, who remembered only too well the Burgess & Key fiasco, restrained her husband from licensing Samuelson of Banbury, England, to manufacture for him. She finally persuaded him to offer Leander a share in whatever arrangement (with Waite, Burnell & Co.) should eventually be made, believing that the large profits in prospect would make his brother more pliable, and above all would change their residence from a business office to a home by transferring to the factory the worry and the correspondence arising from the management of foreign sales.[83] Before this happy time could come, however, the Gage-Burnell tangle had to be unsnarled, and McCormick called for advice from Judah P. Benjamin, his old friend who was now a distinguished Queen's counsel. This was in September, 1878, and for the next six weeks McCormick and his wife kept close to their rooms in the Hotel du Jardin writing business letters

[82] C. H. McCormick, Jr., MSS. Book "B," Nettie F. McCormick to C. H. McCormick, Jr., June 15, 1878. C. H. McCormick to C. H. McCormick, Jr., June 17, 1878, and to O. S. Gage, Sept. 20, 1878.

[83] C. H. McCormick, Jr., MSS. Nettie F. McCormick to C. H. McCormick, Jr., Nov. 2, 1877, and Oct. 1, 1878. C. H. McCormick to Waite, Burnell & Co., Sept. 21 and Oct. 4, 1878, and to O. S. Gage, Oct. 4, 1878. Nettie F. McCormick to C. H. McCormick, Aug. 27 and 28, 1878. ‡C. H. McCormick, Jr., to Nettie F. McCormick, Sept. 27, 1878. B. Samuelson & Co., to C. H. McCormick, Oct. 7, Dec. 8 and 14, 1878. C. H. McCormick's cable to the Co., Oct. 7, 1878.

and consulting with their solicitors.[84] A daily walk in the Garden of the Tuileries, an occasional excursion by Mrs. McCormick and her daughter Virginia to the picture galleries, or a search for tapestries, rugs and other furnishings for their new house in Chicago, were the only interruptions in their daily routine. They were "in" but not "of" Paris, as Mrs. McCormick wrote to her son.[85]

The last ten days of October, 1878, were among the most significant in the life of Cyrus McCormick. On the evening of the twentieth he was summoned to the residence of the Minister of Agriculture where he was promoted to the rank of Officer of the Legion of Honor as "a particular mark of [the] good will" of the President of the Republic.[86] Noon of the following day at the Palace of Industry was one of the red-letter moments of the inventor's career.

The vast building was filled to its utmost and the costumes were brilliant, while uniforms and orders of all kinds shone with dazzling splendor. The Prince of Wales & the Marshall led the cor-

[84] C. H. McCormick, Jr., MSS. Nettie F. McCormick to C. H. McCormick, Jr., Sept. 11, 21, and Oct. 14, 1878. J. P. Benjamin had been a U. S. Senator from La., and during the Civil War was Attorney General, Secretary of War and Secretary of State of the Confederate States. See, his letters to C. H. McCormick, dating between Sept. 22, and Dec. 26, 1878, and those of Clarkes, Rawlins, & Clarke, solicitors of London, to C. H. McCormick, between Oct. 16, and Dec. 31, 1878. C. H. McCormick to Waite, Burnell & Co., Oct. 5 and 11, 1878.

[85] C. H. McCormick, Jr., MSS. Nettie F. McCormick to C. H. McCormick, Jr., Oct. 12, 1878: "We have never been outside our room an evening since we came, and we have never taken a meal away from our own table, and yet, with the many things in the pursuit of our business here, there is hardly time enough in the twenty-four hours to do all we have to do."

[86] The French Minister of Foreign Affairs to C. H. McCormick, Oct. 21, 1878. Other Americans who received the rank of "Officer" at this time were Walter A. Wood, F. A. P. Barnard, Andrew White and W. W. Story. McCormick and Wood were the only two exhibitors at the Fair to receive it. #C. H. McCormick, Jr., to C. H. McCormick, Oct. 23, 1878. R. C. McCormick, "Our Success at Paris in 1878" in "North American Review," July, 1879, pp. 1-22. "Chicago Daily Tribune," Oct. 12, 1878.

tege [of which McCormick was a member] and all that music, & the trappings of Royalty & the éclat of an assemblage of genius . . . in every walk of life could lend, was present on this occasion. After addresses by the President Marshall & by the Minister of Agriculture, the presidents of the Groups and the Commissions of the several countries received the medals in baskets to hand to the exhibitors.[87]

Cyrus McCormick was tired that evening and a sore spot on the back of his neck made it pleasant to remove his collar and dream in his room of the events of the last twenty-four hours. His wife and two daughters attended the "grand fete at Versailles," where a "well dressed mob" of twenty-five thousand struggled for enough breathing space to view the fireworks.

When the inventor awakened the next morning, the sore spot had become a painful pimple. Several days later he was under the care of specialists and his life was despaired of. The pimple was now a malignant carbuncle. He characteristically refused an anæsthetic when the lancet and heat were applied. On November 11, after the crisis was over, Mrs. McCormick confided to her son: "He seemed shattered, as I never saw him before—trembling, high fever—could not collect his mind readily. . . . Papa is now *certainly better,* eating a partridge. . . . I am of course fatigued, with watching, lifting, poultices, dressing, feeding, etc. But thank God his life is spared." [88]

[87] C. H. McCormick, Jr., MSS. Nettie F. McCormick to C. H. McCormick, Jr., Oct. 21, 1878.
[88] C. H. McCormick, Jr., MSS. Nettie F. McCormick to C. H. McCormick, Jr., Oct. 21, and Nov. 11, 1878. Nettie F. McCormick to J. P. Benjamin, Nov. 4, 1878. C. A. Spring, Jr., to Mr. and Mrs. C. H. McCormick, Oct. 21, and Nov. 7, 15, and 26, 1878. ‡C. H. McCormick, Jr., to N. F. McCormick, Nov. 11 and 14, 1878. "Lexington Gazette and Citizen" (Lexington, Va.), Dec. 20, 1878. Nettie F. McCormick's cable to C. A. Spring, Jr., Nov. 5, 1878. Pencil Memo. of C. H. McCormick, written in Feb., 1884. Dr. Edward Warren, Paris, to C. H. McCormick, Jan. 14, 1879. McCormick had also suffered from a carbuncle in Dec., 1865. ‡C. A. Spring, Jr., to C. H. McCormick, Dec. 13, 1865.

The period of convalescence was very long, and Mrs. Mc-
Cormick, three children, a nurse, and day and night attendants
for the almost helpless patient, found the hotel suite rather
small. Well might she write that "these recent weeks have been
the greatest trial . . . of my life." [89] Cyrus McCormick was
accustomed to wait upon himself and the many weeks of forced
inactivity frayed his nerves. He knew that he should be up
and doing. No agreement had been reached with his English
agents and the detailed reports sent by trusted employees at
the Chicago factory were far from reassuring.[90] The season
in Paris was very rainy, and if Mrs. McCormick's wish had
been followed the invalid would have been taken to the Riviera.
He required her presence as never before. His imperious will
still asserted itself on small matters relating to the family
routine, but on business questions during that winter, his wife
made his decisions. He reasoned as clearly as ever, but he was
unable to point his thoughts toward a conclusion.[91] He sat in
thought hour after hour "with a band running from the back
of the armchair around his forehead as a support." [92] By
Christmas Day he was still weak, but for the first time since
late October the letters of his wife to Cyrus, Jr., begin to

[89] C. H. McCormick, Jr., MSS. Nettie F. McCormick to C. H. McCormick, Jr., Nov. 15, 20, 29, and Dec. 9, 1878.

[90] Letters to C. H. McCormick from W. J. Hanna, Nov. 27, 1878, C.
Colahan, Dec. 30, 1878, and F. H. Matthews, Jan. 27, 1879.

[91] C. H. McCormick, Jr., MSS. Nettie F. McCormick to C. H. McCormick, Jr., Nov. 15, 29, Dec. 2, and 9, 1878; Jan. 6, 11, Feb. 28, Apr. 15,
22, and 28, 1879. In this last letter, Mrs. McCormick tells of her efforts to
have her two daughters tutored in French and drawing. "This worried
him [C. H. McCormick] a good deal for he said, 'I need all the spare
time of all in the house. I have weighty things on hand—more responsibility than I can carry & these things *ought not to be!* What signifies a
week or two of these lessons'. . . . I cannot wonder at papa's feeling, so
harassed is he by the troubled situation of business at home." As soon as
"he commenced to feel himself," he consented to tutors in history and
French for the children.

[92] C. H. McCormick, Jr., MSS. Book "B," Nettie F. McCormick to C.
H. McCormick, Jr., Jan. (?), 1879.

regain much of their usual buoyancy. "Papa walks all over the room. This has been a *gay day* for the children and a contented day for us." [93]

The McCormicks stayed in Paris until mid-April, 1879. The inventor's feebleness made it advisable to do so, but they would probably have moved earlier in the year to London so as to negotiate with their English agents more conveniently, if their solicitors had not warned them that Gage would bring suit as soon as they landed on British soil. This threat was removed by April and on the fourteenth of the following month the wearisome dispute was brought to a close.[94] Terms of settlement for the forty-one harvester-binders sold in 1878 were agreed upon, and Waite, Burnell, Huggins & Co., consented to act as agent for McCormick in Great Britain and Europe for two years, and buy not over two hundred machines for the 1879 harvest at £45 each, delivered in Liverpool. It also promised to pay Gage the commissions rightfully his due. This release of McCormick from any obligation to Gage was at least a technical admission that the inventor had been within his rights when he dismissed him. McCormick guaranteed that he would not manufacture machines in Great Britain during the life of the contract.

The day after this contract was signed McCormick and his family sailed on the *SS. Germanic* for New York. As he boarded the steamer he was handed a letter notifying him of his election as a corresponding member of the Department of

[93] C. H. McCormick, Jr., MSS. Book "B," *idem* to *idem*, Dec. 25, 1878, and Jan. 1, 1879. On Jan. 1, 1879, McCormick left his apartment for the first time since October 23rd. It was April before he was able to feed and dress himself or to get up from his chair alone. Even then he needed a cane or an arm to support him when he walked.

[94] C. H. McCormick to Clarkes, Rawlins & Clarke, Jan. 8, 1879. See, the many letters of these solicitors to C. H. McCormick in late 1878 and early 1879. C. H. McCormick to F. H. Matthews, May 1, 1879. C. H. McCormick, Jr., MSS. Book "B," Nettie F. McCormick to C. H. McCormick, Jr., Feb. 10, 22, Mch. 13 and 20, 1879.

Mrs. Cyrus Hall McCormick
From a portrait by G. P. A. Healy, 1860

Rural Economy, Academy of Sciences, Institute of France, in recognition of the fact that he had "done more than any other living man for the cause of agriculture in the world." While at sea, he acknowledged this outstanding tribute by writing: "I am more deeply touched by this unanimous election . . . than by any previous honor of my life." [95] Another ambition of his life was realized almost as soon as he reached New York, when his eldest son finished his course at Princeton and began his long career in the industry created by his father.

During his two summers abroad, Cyrus McCormick, Jr., had come to share his parents' enthusiasm for the foreign branch of the business, but he was determined that if it should continue to be carried on his father's private account, the correspondence relating to it should be handled by the factory office. The overseas market should be developed with consistent vigor or not at all.[96] By this time, consignments of machines could be more conveniently sent to Europe than heretofore, because shipping firms had established branch offices in Chicago and routed goods on through bills of lading to their destination, thus making it unnecessary for a manufacturer to employ a forwarding house in New York or Boston.[97] A McCormick binder could be laid down in Liverpool for about $17 freight.

Crops in Europe in 1879 were exceptionally light, and

[95] M. Dumas and M. Bertrand, Perpetual Secretaries of the Academy of Sciences, Institute of France, to C. H. McCormick, May 12, 1879. C. H. McCormick's reply is dated May 16. "New York Herald," June 9 and 10, 1879. "Chicago Daily Tribune," June 27, 1879.

[96] C. H. McCormick, Jr., also supported his mother in her insistence that machines for the foreign market should be made at Chicago, and not by a licensee abroad. #C. H. McCormick, Jr., Bristol, Eng., to Nettie F. McCormick, Aug. 4, 1878. Nettie F. McCormick, St. Moritz, to C. H. McCormick, Aug. 27, 1878. C. H. McCormick, Jr., Bristol, to C. H. McCormick, July 8, 1878: The English and foreign trade should be made a regular department like any other branch of the business.

[97] F. H. Matthews to C. H. McCormick, May 30, 1879.

Waite, Burnell & Co. was unable to pay for the two hundred machines sent to them by the date stipulated in the contract.[98] Lankester & Company of London thereupon began its twenty years of service as McCormick's agent for Great Britain, and by 1882 had also been entrusted with the supervision of sales in most of Western Europe.[99] Among its several correspondents in France was Albaret & Cie., which for so long a time had been promoting McCormick's interest there.[100] A French house in Algiers found a few purchasers for mowers and binders in North Africa, in spite of the low price of harvest labor. The fate of the display cards prepared in Chicago for that trade illustrates the strange quirks which characterized the foreign

[98] The Co. to Waite, Burnell & Co., Paris, Aug. 14, 1879. Waite, Burnell & Co. to the Co., July 9, 1879, and ‡to C. H. McCormick, July 22; Sept. 16, 18, and 23, 1879; Jan. 20, 1880. ‡File of Clarkes, Rawlins & Clarke in 1879. ‡C. H. McCormick to Clarkes, Rawlins & Clarke, London, Sept. 8, 1879: "Waite, Burnell & Co. made no concessions last winter, and I will not make any to them." As a matter of fact, he did extend their notes, ‡C. H. McCormick to Waite, Burnell & Co., Sept. 9, 1879. Of the 200, the company sold 35 in France and 48 in Great Britain. Thirteen first prizes and two second prizes were won in France during the harvest. ‡J. Davies, London, to C. H. McCormick, Oct. 11, 1879. Pawle, Fearon & Coldham, London, to C. H. McCormick, Jan. 22, 1880.

[99] C. H. McCormick terminated his business relations with the London house of Waite, Burnell & Co., on July 1, 1880, and fortunately lost no money by its collapse. Lankester had been an employee of this firm until its failure, and then reorganized it as his own. He was not McCormick's exclusive agent in Great Britain until 1881. McCormick continued to use the Paris house of Waite, Burnell & Co. as his agent until it also fell in 1882. G. C. Clough, London, to C. H. McCormick, Jan. 9, 1880. L.P.C.B. of C. H. McCormick, Nov., 1880, to May, 1881, pp. 56-59, C. H. McCormick to Samuelson & Co., Banbury, April 22, 1880. See, printed letter of Lankester & Co., Dec. 1, 1880, and L.P.C.B. No. 249, p. 85, the Co. to Lankester & Co., Oct. 12, 1881.

[100] ‡Waite, Burnell & Co., London, to C. H. McCormick, Aug. 8, 1879. Albaret et Cie., Liancourt, France, to the Co., July 22, 1879. Letters of the Co. in L.P.C.B. No. 249, pp. 294, 610, 659, to F. Lankester & Co., Nov. 27, 1882, Jan. 5, 1883, and to A. Albaret, Feb. 28, 1882; p. 781 to Roche Papillon, Chartres, Mch. 26, 1883; No. 231, p. 787, to E. Benedict, Mch. 28, 1883. In 1881 the price of a McCormick harvester-binder, f.o.b. Havre, was £43, but few were sold in France.

business. "We put your posters on the walls at the agricultural fair at Blidah," wrote the agent to McCormick. "Placards upon white paper are particularly forbidden, that color being exclusively reserved for everything belonging to the Government, and that is official. I had to paint the four corners of these bills red, before using them." [101]

Of all the awards to McCormick after 1878, none brought him so much satisfaction and was better calculated to win attention in the United States, than the first prize which he gained after a four-day trial before the Royal Agricultural Society at Derby, England, in 1881.[102] This association was generally conceded to be the world's "highest tribunal in agricultural affairs." [103] Manufacturers eagerly sought the stamp of its approval in every contest held under its patronage. In 1880 McCormick was at a disadvantage in Great Britain because his twine-binder was not ready for sale, and many stock-raisers complained that their cattle were injured by wire in grain.[104] In the following summer, several of his new twine

[101] ‡DeFranquefort, Algiers, to the Co., July 11, 1884. Letters of the Co. in L.P.C.B. No. 220, p. 831, to E. Benedict, Feb. 13, 1882; No. 222, p. 598, to *ibid.,* Apr. 8, 1882; No. 249, pp. 389, 541, 567, to Waite, Burnell & Co., Apr. 19, 1882, and to G. A. Freudenreich, Marseilles, Oct. 6 and 21, 1882. Jules Thiollier & Co. was agent in 1883, and DeFranquefort in 1884. Prior to 1883, the Algerian trade had been handled by the agent for France. No. 249, pp. 591, 757, to Jules Thiollier & Co., Nov. 14, 1882, and Mch. 5, 1883. ‡C. A. Spring, Jr., to C. H. McCormick, Jr., Mch. 24, 1883. Inquiries from Egypt also were made at this time but it is doubtful whether any sales were made there. L.P.C.B. No. 239, pp. 588, 645, the Co. to Markt & Co., N. Y. City, Jan. 10, 1884.

[102] Coming in the 50th Anniversary year of his invention of the reaper, it was particularly pleasing to him.

[103] C. H. McCormick, Jr., to McCormick Co., Aug. 11, 1881.

[104] Waite, Burnell & Co. to the Co., Jan. 28 and Feb. 27, 1879. L.P.C.B. No. 188, p. 478, the Co. to Waite, Burnell & Co., Mch. 4, 1879. P. Lankester, London, to C. H. McCormick, July 22, 1880. G. S. Clough to C. H. McCormick, July 31, 1880. In late 1880, McCormick had shipped a combined reaper-mower and an iron-mower to London for exhibition at the Smithfield Show, held annually in December.

machines were aboard the *SS. Britannic,* on their way to the trial at Derby in August.[105] The steamer ran aground off the coast of Ireland and her holds filled with water. For almost three weeks the binders rusted under the sea. In the meantime, an unusually hot summer so forwarded the British harvest that the date of the contest was advanced to late July. Certainly Walter A. Wood, whose machines were already in England, was not unhappy to learn of this change, and the McCormicks believed that he, as much as the sun, was responsible for their dilemma. Cyrus McCormick, Jr., cabled the society and secured a postponement of the trial for one week. He rushed several more binders by express to New York, but with no great hope that they could reach Liverpool in time to compete.[106]

Two weeks before the contest, the *SS. Britannic* was floated and towed into port. When W. H. Town and Louis Frank, the experts of McCormick in England, paid £10 salvage money and recovered the submerged binders, they found the bearings and pinions rusted together in an immovable mass, and the timbers water-logged and warped. Working day and night during the few hours remaining, they had one of the machines ready to enter the rain-drenched field when the trumpet sounded.[107] "Old Rusty," as the crowd promptly dubbed it, cut the lodged grain more quickly and tied better sheaves than any of its seven rivals. Wood's binder did not place. Statis-

[105] L.P.C.B. No. 214, p. 844. The machines left Chicago on June 16. ‡L.P.C.B. of C. H. McCormick, Nov. 1880-May 1881, pp. 487-489, C. H. McCormick to R. C. Ransome, Ipswich, Eng., May 4, 1881. After requesting Ransome to make arrangements for the entry of the twine-binders at the Derby, C. H. McCormick characteristically added: "Let me say to you, my dear friend, that now as heretofore, I take my aim for the bull's eye!"

[106] ‡W. H. Town, London, to the Co., July 23, 1881. C. H. McCormick, Jr.'s, telegram to C. H. McCormick, July 23, 1881.

[107] L.P.C.B. No. 216, pp. 692, 783, the Co. to C. H. McCormick, Jr., Fargo, Aug. 8 and 11, 1881. C. H. McCormick to J. S. Cothran, Sept. 22, 1881.

tics of the long and grueling trial leave no doubt that the best machine won, but the cheers of the spectators were probably the more lusty because of the grit and good sportsmanship displayed by its attendants.[108]

The victories won by McCormick in France in 1878 had not been promptly publicized by the factory office, but now that Cyrus, Jr., was there, the leading newspapers of the United States and the agents of the firm as far distant as New Zealand, were immediately apprised of the Derby award.[109] Young McCormick, who was in the Red River Valley harvest fields when the joyful news was flashed to him, hastened to assure his father that "nothing short of these boundless prairies would be able to hold me" from coming to offer congratulations in person. He was not where "the Wood Binder twineth," as he wrote, but he would see to it that every thing possible should be done to make "a big thing of what *really* is a big thing." [110] Wood should now pay heavily for

[108] "Engineering," XXXII (1881), 194-195. #Louis Frank, Trentham Hall, Staffordshire, to C. H. McCormick, Aug. 20, 1881: "It was rather a sad sight to see Woods returning four flat car loads of machines the next day without an Honorourable Mention. They had been jeering at me when I came on the field at first and telling me that I was not a goeing [*sic*] to get on as well as I did at Marmont and Bristol. I told them that a still tounge [*sic*] made a wise head, and I would tell better at the close of the trial." Frank was starting four machines for the Duke of Sutherland. "Chicago Daily Tribune," Aug. 12, 1881.

[109] C. H. McCormick, Jr., to E. K. Butler, Aug. 11, 1881. E. K. Butler to C. H. McCormick, Jr., Aug. 13, 1881. McCormick Harv. Mach. Co. Catalog for 1882, p. 10. "Daily Argus" (Fargo) Aug. 12 and 21, 1881. #MS. article by C. H. McCormick, Jr., dated Aug., 1881. L.P.C.B. No. 249, pp. 120, 182, the Co. to Albaret et Cie., Oct. 24 and Dec. 19, 1881.

[110] C. H. McCormick, Jr., to the Co., Aug. 11 and 15, 1881; to C. H. McCormick, Aug. 11 and 12, 1881, and to W. H. Town, Aug. 12, 1881: Get two or three copies of all notices published in English papers. These victories are "matters of history" and "we desire to have our records very full on all these subjects." C. H. McCormick, Jr., MSS. Nettie F. McCormick to C. H. McCormick, Jr., Aug. 13, 1881: "It ought to tell upon our business immensely. It ought in order to repay us for our great outlay & trouble in it."

broadcasting a distorted account of the Paris awards three years before.

During the last few years of Cyrus McCormick's life, a larger business was done with Russia than with any other foreign land except New Zealand. The period of readjustment necessitated by the freeing of the serfs was over, and many Russian landowners were alive to the fact that their wheat was declining in importance in European markets because of increasing importations from the United States and the colonies of Great Britain.[111] Johnston, Wood, Osborne and several English firms were profiting by the sale of harvesting machinery in Russia,[112] but McCormick had kept aloof since his unsuccessful attempt in the early 1860's. Occasionally a reaper or mower was sold there by his English representatives, and in 1879, on his recommendation, Waite, Burnell & Co. sent a wire-binder to Alexis V. Perrin for exhibition in Russia.[113]

Perrin, who spoke eight languages, was born in Russia and had been an immigration agent on the Continent for the Chicago & Northwestern Railroad. He was one of the few McCormick agents who stands out from his interminable letters as a unique personality. He brought the best of references to his new employer, Bayard Taylor's and E. W. Stoughton's among the rest. Although he had an exaggerated opinion of his own

[111] The Russian wheat crop of 1878 was estimated at 214,500,000 bus. and that of the U. S. at 422,000,000 bus. #U. S. Treasury Dept., Bureau of Statistics, to W. D. Baldwin, Oct. 22, 1879. #Baldwin, Hopkins & Peyton to C. H. McCormick, Oct. 24, 1879.

[112] G. A. Freudenreich, Odessa, to the Co., Sept. 27, 1880: Wood has been established in Russia for almost twenty years, and introduced his binder here in 1874. Osborne has had an agency here for at least five years, and brought in his binder three years ago. A. V. Perrin, Charkoff, to Nettie F. McCormick, Oct. 21, 1880, and #to C. H. McCormick, May 7, 1881.

[113] L.P.C.B. No. 183, p. 63, the Co. to O. S. Gage, Aug. 1, 1878. #A. V. Perrin to Nettie F. McCormick, Nov. 11, 1881. In this, Perrin briefly sketches his early life.

ability, and wrote in Napoleonic phrase of his achievements
and his hopes, he spoke truthfully when he described himself
as a "stirring young man." [114] The United States consul at
Odessa admitted that Perrin was "the most energetic and indefatigable" person he had ever known, but added that he was
also "a steam engine without a governor." This was his chief
fault. If he could have tolerated a superior to direct his tireless will to do, he would have been one of the ablest of
McCormick's helpers. Perrin and Colahan were of the same
type, and the inventor liked them both. He defended Perrin
long after the men of the factory office were agreed that he
should seek employment elsewhere.[115]

In the autumn of 1879, having come to an agreement with
McCormick, Perrin began his campaign in his characteristic
"large way" by opening offices in Charkoff and Moscow, and
appointing agents far and wide both in Russia and Roumania.[116] Handicapped by the peasants' complete ignorance of
machinery, he endeavored by means of a lecture-tour to persuade every agricultural society in Russia to establish a school
where a selected number of laborers from each estate could
be taught to operate and care for harvesting implements. In
lengthy cablegrams he kept Chicago informed of his progress.[117] The home office was alarmed by his extravagant

[114] ‡A. V. Perrin to C. H. McCormick, n.d., but probably early Sept.,
1879.
[115] ‡C. H. McCormick, Jr., to C. H. McCormick, Aug. 4, 1881.
[116] Perrin "made a special journey from Russia to Chicago" in the late
summer of 1879 to see C. H. McCormick, and as a result of this visit he
signed a contract in Oct. to work for $1500 a year and $200 a month
expenses. A new contract at the same salary was made on Dec. 1, 1880.
‡C. A. Spring, Jr., to C. H. McCormick, Sept. 10, Oct. 4, and Nov. 7,
1879. L.P.C.B. No. 194, p. 492, C. A. Spring, Jr., to A. V. Perrin, Oct. 3,
1879. No. 195, p. 604, the Co. to C. H. McCormick, Nov. 7, 1879. ‡A. V.
Perrin to C. H. McCormick, Oct. 17 and 26, 1879. ‡C. H. McCormick,
Jr., to Drexel, Morgan & Co., N. Y., Oct. 21, 1879.
[117] A. V. Perrin, Charkoff, to C. H. McCormick, Dec. 19, 1879, and
from Moscow, May 26, 1880.

course, and before the winter was over sent George A. Freudenreich, a Minnesota agent of Swiss birth, to hold him in check.[118] Friction between the two men was inevitable, but the Minnesotan soon shared the enthusiasm of his unmanageable associate for Russia as a potentially rich sales territory— a "golden elephant" in Perrin's quaint phrase.[119]

Southern Russia, and especially the German settlements there, held out the most encouragement. Freudenreich made Odessa his headquarters and the port of entry for almost all of the machines ordered from Chicago. Reapers and mowers were his chief stock in trade. The clergy encouraged the Russian peasants to persist in their primitive farming methods, and the harvester-binder was too startling an innovation to carry a wide appeal.[120] Successive failures of the grain crop in the Volga Valley were turning its landowners to a larger emphasis upon stock-raising, and this trend helped to widen the market for mowers.[121] The district about Kazan on the middle Volga was particularly cordial toward harvesting implements, and when Perrin exhibited a wire-binder at the Fair there in August, 1880, "schools were dismissed and a holiday declared for the trial. Mine did so well that several bouquets of flowers in the shape of sheaves bound with our wire were

[118] ‡C. A. Spring, Jr., to C. H. McCormick, Oct. 18, 1879. ‡J. P. Whedon to C. H. McCormick, Jr., Nov. 28, 1879, L.P.C.B. No. 195, p. 623; No. 196, p. 195, telegrams of C. A. Spring, Jr., to C. H. McCormick, Nov. 8, and 25, 1879; No. 197, p. 610, the Co. to the Imperial and Royal Consulate Gen'l of Russia, N. Y., Jan. 15, 1880; No. 198, p. 84, C. H. McCormick, Jr., to Drexel, Morgan & Co., Jan. 31, 1880.

[119] ‡A. V. Perrin, Taganrog, to C. H. McCormick, Aug. 18, 1880, Feb. 19, Mch. 1, and 25, 1881. L.P.C.B. No. 200, p. 118, the Co. to E. C. Beardsley, Minneapolis, Minn., Mch. 29, 1880. ‡C. H. McCormick to A. V. Perrin, Dec. 24, 1880.

[120] G. A. Freudenreich, Charkoff and Odessa, to the Co., Sept. 22 and Oct. 6, 1880. A. V. Perrin, Lemberg, Austria, to the Co., Oct. 8, 1880: "The Russian gov't. has aided us by removing the duties on wire and implements."

[121] A V. Perrin, Charkoff, to C. H. McCormick, Jr., Mch. 5, 1881.

presented to me, and one large one inscribed from the ladies
. . . was put on the machine. The sheaves from the 1½ acre
lot were all carried away as souvenirs." [122]

Drought and a plague of beetles hampered sales in 1880,[123]
but the next year purchasers were found for three hundred and
fifty mowers, as well as one hundred and fifty binders and
reapers. Implements were exhibited and advertising circulars
distributed as far east as the Ural Mountains, but it was 1884
before trade in the lower Volga provinces and the Caucasus
region was energetically developed. A total of between fifteen
hundred and two thousand McCormick machines was sold in
Russia between 1880 and 1884, and of these almost two-
thirds were mowers.[124]

[122] A. V. Perrin, Kazan, to the Co., Aug. 4, 1880.
[123] A. V. Perrin, Odessa, to the Co., Aug. 18, 1880. G. A. Freudenreich,
Odessa, to the Co., Aug. 18 and 19, 1880. In 1880 the *Hindoo* of the
Wilson Line, on its way to Russia, sank with 21 McCormick machines
aboard. L.P.C.B. No. 199, pp. 138, 269, 563, the Co. to Sanderson & Son,
N. Y. C., Mch. 4, 1880. Sales were light (195 machines) in 1882 because
of the failure of the grass crop in southern Russia, but there was a decided
"pick up" during the next two harvests. Freudenreich emphasized that,
except in the Caucasus, a good crop could not be depended upon as in the
U. S., but that the gov't. was encouraging reforestation in order to make
droughts less likely to occur.
[124] ‡G. A. Freudenreich, Odessa, to the Co., Aug. 3, 1881. The McCormick twine-binder won first prize in 1881 in a field contest under the
auspices of the Royal Agricultural Society of St. Petersburg. L.P.C.B.
No. 249, p. 531, the Co. to G. A. Freudenreich, Sept. 30, 1882. In 1882,
McCormick sent one of these machines to the Imperial Agr'l. Museum in
that city. A. V. Perrin, Odessa, to C. H. McCormick, July 26, 27, 1880;
May 14, 16, 20, June 9, 14, 20, July 3, 1881, and ‡Apr. 4 and 13, 1881. G.
A. Freudenreich, Moscow, to C. H. McCormick, Sept. 2, 1880. ‡C. A.
Spring, Jr., to C. H. McCormick, Oct. 4, 9, 18, 28, and 29, 1880: "We have
put about $20,000 already in the Russian business, not counting the value
of the machines shipped there." Freudenreich sold only 19 harvester-binders
and 39 mowers, for a total of $9,657.75. From 1882 to 1883 the Co. dis-
couraged attempts by their Russian agents to spread their trade over too
much territory. This conservative policy was probably the result of a conference with the U. S. consul at Odessa who visited Chicago in Aug.
1881.

In the summer of 1881, Perrin was obliged to flee from Russia to escape arrest by the police. He was in the United States by mid-September asking Cyrus McCormick to request the State Department at Washington to intercede in his behalf. The inventor wished to help him, but Cyrus McCormick, Jr., with the unanimous support of Freudenreich and the staff of the factory office, persuaded his father that the company could well dispense with his services. Perrin doubted it, and was certain that the Russian market would collapse without his aid.[125] When he returned to Europe in late 1881 to look for a new field of endeavor, he fired a parting shot at young McCormick. "I give you my last signal from this shore. I advise you not to compel me to turn hostile toward you, . . . Remember that if I am not treated well, I am capable of turning into a hiena [sic]." [126] Perhaps that was his fate.

[125] ‡A. V. Perrin, London, to C. H. McCormick, Jr., Dec. 26, 1881, and from Bucharest and Lemberg, to C. H. McCormick, Aug. 6, 11, 13, and 17, 1881; from Chicago, Nov. 9, 1881. L.P.C.B. No. 249, pp. 8, 75, the Co. to G. A. Freudenreich, Odessa, Aug. 3 and Sept. 21, 1881. E. K. Butler's telegram to C. H. McCormick, Aug. 23, 1881. C. H. McCormick, Jr., to C. H. McCormick, Aug. 26 and Sept. 5, 1881, ‡Sept. 14, 16 and 17, 1881. G. A. Freudenreich to the Co., Feb. 5, Mch. 1, 6, 1881, and ‡Aug. 3, 1881: "Perrin was tipped off by the Chief of Police at Charkoff that the police were after him on account of his former expatriation, so he skipped over the border to Roumania." ‡W. Hoffman, U. S. Chargé des Affaires, St. Petersburg, to G. A. Freudenreich, Aug. 9, 1881. C. H. McCormick, MSS. Book "B," Nettie F. McCormick to C. H. McCormick, Jr., Sept. 13, 1881. ‡E. K. Butler to C. H. McCormick, Aug. 22, 1881, L.P.C.B. No. 217, p. 643, the Co. to I. N. Van Hoesen, Lawrence, Kansas, Sept. 20, 1881. Perrin was going to Kansas to see if he could sell machines to Russian Mennonites. He soon returned.

[126] ‡A. V. Perrin to C. H. McCormick, Nov. 17, 1881, and from Quarantine, N. Y., Nov. 7 (doubtless should be Dec. 7), 1881. L.P.C.B. No. 249, p. 170, the Co.'s cable to Maszewski, Odessa, Dec. 13, 1881. A. V. Perrin to J. Maszewski, Oct. 4, 1881. ‡E. K. Butler to C. H. McCormick, Jr., Nov. 5, 7, and 16, 1881. L.P.C.B. No. 219, p. 491, telegram of C. H. McCormick, Jr., to C. H. McCormick, Dec. 14, 1881. The McCormicks loaned Perrin money so that he could pay his passage, and gave him a letter of recommendation to Percy Lankester of London. Until the summer of 1884, Perrin occasionally wrote to either C. H. McCormick

Cyrus McCormick used two types of agents in the foreign field. Some, like Griffin and Perrin, worked for a salary and commissions, and were not unlike the canvassers of the factory at home. The more usual practice, however, was to sell machines for cash or on short-term credit to an overseas firm which would be guaranteed the exclusive right to market them within its own country. The maximum retail price which it might charge was often stipulated, but it sometimes bought implements at so low a wholesale rate that it could afford to sell them for a sum little if any higher than in the United States. In many instances, McCormick was unable to offer foreign consignees as favorable terms as his rivals, because of his uncertainty concerning the price which the Chicago partnership would charge him for his machines. As a rule, McCormick was undersold by his competitors abroad.

All in all, he probably marketed about twelve thousand machines outside of the United States during his lifetime.[127] In so far as England and Europe, exclusive of Russia, were concerned, his margin of profit was very small. He would probably have abandoned this troublesome trade at an early date if its value had been gauged solely by the yearly cash balances.[128] In some seasons his sales in France were fewer in number than the prizes awarded him there.

or C. H. McCormick, Jr., in a vein similar to that of the quotation in the text. He apparently found employment with an English firm. ‡A. V. Perrin, Rouen, Apr. 6, 1882, and from Copenhagen, Aug. (?), 1882, to C. H. McCormick. In the N. F. McCormick Biog. Asso. files is a folder containing twenty-one letters written by Perrin to Mrs. McCormick between Sept., 1879, and July, 1884.

[127] In making this estimate a harvester and binder are counted as one machine. Of the 12,000, approximately 4,500 were sold in England and Western Europe, 1,800 in Russia, 4,000 in Australia and N. Z., 1,000 in Canada, 400 in the Argentine, and 300 in other countries.

[128] Waite, Burnell & Co., Paris, to C. H. McCormick, July 27, and Aug. 6, 1881. C. H. McCormick, Jr., MSS. Book "B," Nettie F. McCormick to C. H. McCormick, Jr., Oct. 11, 1883: "We sell so little in Europe it doesn't matter much whether we are protected by patents there or not."

The emphasis given to the western European market reflected in a measure the provincialism of America. The midwestern farmer felt a strong attraction for a machine that won medals from royal agricultural societies or which was used on the estates of kings and emperors. For some reason, the belief was current that the juries at foreign field trials were less susceptible than those in the States to the pre-contest wiles of competitors, and therefore rendered decisions based solely upon the merits of the implements. After reading the letters of the "jockeys" who rode these machines at the races, the validity of this assumption may well be questioned. In no instance on either side of the Atlantic, so far as the available records show, was money paid to a juror to win his favor, but every expedient short of bribery with cash was employed. Western Europe was the expensive business playground of the magnates of the industry in the United States. Their victories abroad were extremely flattering to their pride, and had an advertising value at home many times larger than the heavy cost involved.

Probably one of the most gratifying results to Cyrus McCormick of his thirty-five years of effort to place his machines in foreign harvest fields was the realization by 1880 that his name stood for business integrity and financial security the world around. His signature was known and honored by the chief banking houses of Great Britain and Europe, and the scrupulous care with which he carried out the letter of his agreements contributed its share to overcome the distrust abroad of a people whose states had in some instances repudiated their debts. When the International Harvester Company, about twenty years later, began to develop the foreign market for American harvesting implements as never before, it found that the McCormick name furnished a sure foundation upon which to build.

CHAPTER XVI

BUSINESS EXPANSION AND REFORM, 1879-1884

THE launching of the McCormick Harvesting Machinery Company, attended by the return of Charles A. Spring, Jr., as the general manager, the beginning of Cyrus McCormick, Jr's., long association with the enterprise, and the early withdrawal of Leander McCormick and his son from the superintendence of machine-building, signified that the inventor for the first time in twenty years had complete control of his own business. Because his days of foreign travel and active participation in politics were over, the seminary and his reaper industry in Chicago could henceforth receive more of his attention. As he was always unwilling to license other manufacturers to make his machines, so he also preferred whenever possible to do without partners. Excepting for a few years during the 1850's, his wish to act alone in business had never been gratified. Between 1879 and 1884, however, since he owned a majority of the stock of his company, he could at last have his own way. His eldest son and Spring would ever make it their study to do as he wished.

Early in 1879 when Cyrus McCormick, Jr., was completing his course at Princeton College, he received a long, confidential letter of advice from William J. Hanna.

"Be *ready* to hear, *but* . . . *do your own thinking,*" Hanna cautioned. "Be careful to keep all at a respectful distance, until you satisfy yourself by observation as to how matters stand. . . . The place is ripe for you . . . [and] the position is one anyone might covet—the most extensive business of the

687

kind in the world. . . . I rejoice that this business . . . is about to take new life and fresh impetus in the person of one who bears the full name and character of him who founded it so long ago." [1]

There was need for reform. With but slight exaggeration, Hanna complained that the firm "practically has no head— every man in the office seems to do what is right in his own eyes—makes his own hours, and goes home when he pleases without leave. . . . A general laxity prevails, and that laxity extends to the agents likewise. They are allowed far too much freedom, and feel quite independent of the *apparent* government of the office." [2] With equal justification, the factory might also have been included in this indictment. The young McCormick faced a difficult task when his days as a student ended. He resolved to master his father's business by working in each of its several departments.

In pursuit of his goal, he held a roving commission for several years. Whatever authority he exercised was not due to any office assigned him by vote of the directors, but to the fact that his father spoke through his voice, and because his keen perception of the proper policy to adopt quickly gained him the respect of his associates. His willingness to assume responsibility and to work hard surprised and somewhat annoyed Charles Colahan, who saw his own preëminence in patent matters threatened by a youth whose precise and clear-cut descriptions of complicated mechanical devices early won the praise of the firm's attorneys. [3] While in his early twenties

[1] W. J. Hanna to C. H. McCormick, Jr., Apr. 8, 1879.
[2] *Idem* to *idem*, Apr. 8, 1879.
[3] C. C. Copeland to C. H. McCormick, Aug. 27, 1882: "Robt. Parkinson [a lawyer] told me that your son can describe the points of a new machine better than any man who writes him with the exception of one . . . old inventor, and that he—Cyrus—will carry your business—harvester—to a pinnacle that will surprise everyone." ‡C. H. McCormick, Jr., to C. H. McCormick, Apr. 6, 1883.

he was the leading spirit in the McCormick-Gorham patent pool, which collected tribute from most of the binder-makers of the land.[4] His energy and enthusiasm seemed to be exhaustless. A morning at his desk or in conference with lawyers was sometimes followed by work until midnight at the works, studying the processes of manufacturing, and seeking to discover how better machines could be made at a smaller cost of labor, time and materials. Although he left the plant late in the evening, he was frequently back at its gate before seven in the morning, greeting the old employees by name and making them feel that he was interested in their problems.[5]

In August of each year his address was Fargo, Dakota Territory, where he probably heeded his mother's advice "to put a cabbage leaf in his hat" for protection from the sun, and experimented with wire- and twine-binders on the "bonanza" farms of the Red River Valley. Everywhere he was "known and spoken of as the son of the 'great reaper man'! It makes me feel keenly the tremendous responsibility of the position in which you have put me, and to fill it creditably and according to your wishes is my constant aim & care."[6] In 1881 Colahan reported to the inventor that his son was "carrying the 'whole load.'" By then, C. A. Spring, Jr., believed that the factory was "in better working trim than it has ever been before since my connexion with the business."[7]

Nothing so pleased Cyrus McCormick during his lifetime as

[4] *Supra*, pp. 561 ff.
[5] L.P.C.B. No. 210, p. 709, the Co. to J. Heywood, Indianapolis, Ind., Mch. 3, 1881; No. 245, p. 704, the Co. to Detroit Blower Co., Detroit, Mich., Oct. 11, 1884.
[6] ‡C. H. McCormick, Jr., to C. H. McCormick, Sept. 2, 1882.
[7] ‡C. Colahan to C. H. McCormick, Sept. 13, 1881, and C. A. Spring, Jr., to him on Sept. 26, 1881. L.P.C.B. No. 208, p. 290, C. A. Spring, Jr., to J. F. Fullen, London, Ont., Dec. 8, 1880: "Mr. C. H. McCormick, Jr., looks after the factory more than anyone else." On Sept. 7, 1881, C. H. McCormick, Jr., was appointed superintendent of the works, and G. B. Averill, asst. sup't.

the success of his eldest son. Although he might chide him for "wasting" a day in summer by shooting wild pigeons in Wisconsin, he not unlikely would call him to Richfield Springs from Chicago during the rush season, doubtless for the purpose of talking business, but even more to gratify his longing to see his namesake who was keeping the McCormick banner in the van.[8] So closely did they work in harmony, that it is impossible today to distinguish the decisions of the father from those of the son. It would appear, however, that the inventor and his wife did little more than outline the general course to be followed.

Although the annual profits and number of sales were never so large as between 1880 and 1884, the new and persistent emphasis of the company was upon greater economy and efficiency of operation by all of its departments.[9] Since the cost of factory raw materials was rising, and competition was forcing down the price of machines, the total of these many little savings with the trebling in the annual sales, accounts for the big increase of profits. The many letters criticizing salesmen for paying too much for office desks, carpets, and harness, nevertheless strike a somewhat incongruous note in a year when the net return amounted to almost half of the firm's capital.[10]

Economy was the rule in large matters as well as small. Thus in August, 1881, when a portion of the central building

8 C. H. McCormick to C. H. McCormick, Jr., from Eureka Springs, Ark., May 20, 1882. ‡C. H. McCormick, Jr., to C. H. McCormick, May 23, 1882.

9 C. H. McCormick, Jr., MSS. Book "B," Nettie F. McCormick to C. H. McCormick, Jr., Oct. 18, 1881.

10 L.P.C.B. No. 184, p. 807, the Co. to D. W. Pratt, St. Louis, Oct. 24, 1878; No. 228, p. 298, to W. H. Town, Kansas City, Mo., Oct. 17, 1882. In 1880 the profit of the firm was $1,192,733.83 on about 22,000 sales, as compared with $722,326.91 in 1879 on 18,700 sales. ‡C. A. Spring, Jr., to C. H. McCormick, Oct. 5, 1880, and Oct. 1, 1881. In 1881 the profit was $1,232,781.15 on 30,793 sales.

of the factory was destroyed by fire, Mrs. McCormick wrote to E. K. Butler of the office staff: "Let this rebuilding go on, but let it be done in the most *economical* manner, buying your brick where you can most cheaply & using our tug, I suppose, to bring material. Building in Chicago has such a boom this autumn that it may be difficult to get bricklayers, but . . . you can make many a young man who *wants work* but never handled a trowel feel that he can lay brick. . . . There must be a *first time,* & this is the time to begin with many a young man." [11]

As a result of this misfortune, which without the aid of the Chicago Fire Department might have occasioned a heavier loss than the Fire of 1871, the company organized its own fire-fighting force. Thereafter, the watchmen, accompanied by their savage dogs, continued to make their hourly rounds, but they were no longer relied upon to fight a blaze without expert supervision. [12]

Savings were also effected by the use of new appliances in the office and factory. Here, too, the hand of Cyrus McCormick, Jr., was apparent. His course of study at college had been classical rather than practical in its emphasis, but his lack of formal business training at least enabled him to come to his task with an open mind, unfettered by the practices of the past and ready to adopt whatever methods seemed best calculated to effect the ends desired. Twenty-five years before, the two or three clerks in the office, in order to keep busy ten hours a day, were obliged to spend part of their time in the factory packing machines for shipment or tacking canvas aprons on the back rails of the hand-rake reapers. [13] Now,

[11] Nettie F. McCormick to E. K. Butler, Aug. 29, 1881. This fire caused a loss of about $25,000. "Chicago Times," Aug. 27 and 28, 1881.

[12] L.P.C.B. No. 219, p. 639, the Co. to J. Rood, Chicago, Dec. 20, 1881; No. 228, pp. 467, 561, to R. Newton, Louisville, Ky., Oct. 27, and Nov. 1, 1882. *Supra,* p. 516.

[13] "The Farmers' Advance," Mch., 1882.

sixteen men were hard pressed to answer the correspondence. Cyrus McCormick still insisted that they should be at their desks at seven o'clock every morning, although he found it necessary to extend a few minutes of grace to the older members of the staff.[14] Between 1873 and 1879, while the office was at the factory, this early starting hour was most difficult to observe, and the partners provided a twelve-seated omnibus to carry the clerks from the business district to the works.[15] But after the office was moved to the McCormick Block at the corner of Dearborn and Randolph streets, there was no excuse for tardiness. The able Charles A. Spring, Jr., who on several occasions gained what he wanted by threatening to resign, refused to be at his desk by seven o'clock. Thereupon, he was allowed to choose his own hours for work and was assigned a private office "on the pleasant side" of the building.[16]

Liaison between the down-town headquarters of the company and the factory was maintained by telegraph and telephone, and by an express-wagon drawn by a "stylish pair of mules." For long-distance calls, as to Milwaukee, the telephone was often so unsatisfactory that the speaker gave up trying to make himself understood and took refuge in a telegram.[17]

[14] ‡C. A. Spring, Jr., to C. H. McCormick, Aug. 30, Sept. 6, and 8, 1879. L.P.C.B. No. 230, p. 472, the Co. to A. W. Nichols, Lawtey, Fla., Jan. 23, 1883.

[15] In 1882, this omnibus was sold to a purchaser in Colorado. *Ibid.*, No. 222, p. 162, No. 225, p. 107, Co. to E. W. Brooks, Red Wing, Minn., Mch. 28, 1882, and to W. Billing, Denver, Colo., June 22, 1882. The office was moved back to the city in late August, 1879.

[16] This was in the autumn of 1881. ‡C. A. Spring, Jr., to C. H. McCormick, Feb. 1, 1881, C. H. McCormick, Jr., MSS. Book "B," Nettie F. McCormick to C. H. McCormick, Jr., Oct. 18, and 19, 1881.

[17] ‡C. A. Spring, Jr., to C. H. McCormick, Oct. 13 and Nov. 28, 1879. Letters of the Co. in L.P.C.Bs. No. 213, p. 746, to G. W. Fulton, Mgr., Western Union Telegraph Co., Chicago, May 12, 1881; No. 225, p. 394, to E. C. Keller, Mattoon, Ill., July 3, 1882; No. 232, p. 271, to F. Craycroft, Sedalia, Mo., Apr. 13, 1883, and No. 234, p. 287, to C. B. Field,

With the advent of the typewriter and calligraph in the office in 1882, came the first "lady" stenographer, accompanied by all of the little readjustments of routine and changes in "atmosphere" entailed by her presence. Men eagerly sought employment as typists, but women were as competent and charged less for their services.[18]

Even before the first typewriter was purchased, the half-dozen principal men of the staff no longer penned their own letters but dictated them to a copyist clerk, skilled in shorthand. He wrote them out with a fair hand, took off a letter-press copy for the files, and signed the originals with a rubber name-stamp. A communication which reached a finished form in this way was marked "Phonographic Letter," the 1880 equivalent of "Dictated But Not Read." [19] The company encouraged its more important general agents to perform their duties with greater economy and comfort by furnishing them with safes, coal-stoves, horses, enclosed buggies for winter

Milwaukee, Wis., June 19, 1883. ‡C. H. McCormick, Jr., N. Y. City, to C. H. McCormick, Apr. 6, 1883: *"On their wire* [Postal Telegraph Co.] I talked thru *telephone* to *Chicago!* Mr. Geo. Pullman and some of his friends was (*sic*) at the other end."

[18] The first woman employee of the McCormick Co. was Miss Jennie A. Wells of Bloomington, Ill., who began work as a typist in Aug., 1882. By 1885, a Miss Bancroft had also been added to the office force. The pay of a stenographer and shorthand-writer was about $1000 a year. *Ibid.*, No. 223, p. 461, No. 226, p. 871, C. H. McCormick, Jr., to Miss Hattie K. Perry, Indianapolis, May 5, and Aug. 12, 1882; No. 224, p. 245, C. Colahan to Remington & Son, Ilion, N. Y., May 29, 1882; No. 227, p. 1, C. H. McCormick, Jr., to Miss J. A. Wells, Aug. 14, 1882; No. 228, p. 459, to J. G. Cross, Bloomington, Ill., Oct. 26, 1882, and No. 240, p. 435, to J. L. Martin, Quincy, Ill., Feb. 21, 1884. The McCormick Co. mailed its first typewritten letter on June 7, 1882 (*Ibid.*, No. 224, p. 512). It had received its first one from the Rochester Agrl. Works of Rochester, N. Y., in the autumn of 1874. The McCormicks hesitated to adopt the machine because of the difficulty experienced in making a retained copy of the correspondence written on it.

[19] *Ibid.*, No. 179, p. 211, the Co. to Cleveland Rolling Mill Co., Cleveland, O., Apr. 16, 1878. This is the first to bear the stamp, "Phonographic Letter."

travel, stationery, electric pens, heliographs, hectographs, type-writers, and calligraphs. Some were also allowed clerk hire.[20] The competition between rival manufacturers for the services of expert salesmen was so keen that any McCormick representative could count upon considerate treatment if he proved his worth.

With much hesitation, Cyrus McCormick, Jr., tried out a few electric lights at the factory in 1882, generating the power from the main engine. Although over one hundred were in use there a year later, they were still experimental because it was a matter for argument whether the brilliant illumination was worth the extra cost, when compared with gas.[21] The verdict was finally in favor of electricity, probably because the company could produce its own current, and the increasing pressure annually for a larger output of machines made night work imperative during six months of the year.

A score of horses and mules, "with plenty of heft," were used to pull freight cars around the twenty-acre factory yard. Employees in 1883 invited Cyrus McCormick, Jr., to "send a dective [sic] . . . among us & find the feeling of the men" toward a foreman who was said to treat them as cruelly as he

[20] Ibid., No. 179, p. 281; No. 203, p. 570; No. 230, p. 885; No. 233, p. 599; No. 240, pp. 130, 203; and No. 245, p. 415, the Co. to M. T. Grattan, Preston, Minn., Apr. 18, 1878, June 30, 1880, J. B. Heywood, Indianapolis, Feb. 16, 1883, D. H. Smith, Sparta, Wis., June 1, 1883. W. H. Town, Kansas City, Feb. 5, 1884, E. C. Beardsley, Minneapolis, Feb. 9, 1884, and to W. R. Smyth, Mankato, Sept. 24, 1884. As a method of duplicating letters, the electric pen was being superseded by the heliograph in 1879. See, Ibid., No. 195, p. 804, the Co. to H. R. Gould, Omaha, Neb., Nov. 15, 1879.
[21] Ibid., No. 223, p. 720, No. 234, p. 489, the Co. to G. B. Averill, May 13, 1882, and to Whitman & Barnes Mfg. Co., Syracuse, N. Y., June 22, 1883. ‡C. H. McCormick, Jr., to C. H. McCormick, June 1, 1882, and May 2, 1883. C. H. McCormick, Jr., opposed the construction of elevated railways in Chicago on streets fronting his father's properties. "Chicago Times," Aug. 5, 1883.

did the animals.[22] The offending boss was dismissed. McCormick, by then the factory superintendent, was always ready to listen to the complaints of his workmen. The labor situation in Chicago, however, offered no encouragement to employees who were striving for higher pay and shorter hours. Expert mechanics might secure a raise, but there were too many job-seekers at the factory gate every morning for McCormick to bend to the will of discontented, unskilled laborers.[23] Factory foremen received between $2,200 and $2,500 a year; carpenters about $3.25 a day; blacksmiths and iron-finishers from $2.00 to $2.50; drill men $1.75; ordinary laborers $1.25, and boys, $1.00[24] Moulders, casting-makers, and twine-binder men were paid by the piece. Youths between twelve and fifteen years of age tended the bolt and nut-making machines. Yearly contracts were drawn for the skilled mechanics to sign, but the agreement could be broken by either party if a month's notice were given. Membership in unions was tolerated but the McCormicks insisted upon maintaining an "open shop." [25]

Mrs. McCormick's outlook upon the growing tension between capital and labor is well shown by her letter to her son at the time of the strike at the factory in the spring of 1885.

[22] "Many Employees" to "Mr. McCormick," Jan. 1, 1883. L.P.C.B. No. 230, pp. 218, 583, the Co. to G. W. Kennedy, Sibley, Ill., Jan. 11, 1883, and to J. L. Martin, Quincy, Ill., Jan. 29, 1883; No. 238, p. 14, to C. H. Wiltshire, Baldwin, Ill., Oct. 18, 1883.

[23] *Ibid.*, No. 216, p. 858, the Co. to J. M. Akers, Byron, Minn., Aug. 17, 1881; No. 245, p. 559, to W. E. Byrns, Adams, Ind., Oct. 11, 1884; No. 246, p. 844, to H. R. Gould, Omaha, Neb., Dec. 22, 1884.

[24] C. H. McCormick to John McCormick, New York, Mch. 22, 1882.

[25] L.P.C.B. No. 218, p. 451, No. 227, pp. 7, 631, the Co. to J. Swope, Uniontown, Ky., Oct. 27, 1881, to R. Newton, Louisville, Ky., Aug. 14, 1882, and to H. A. Young, Red Wing, Minn., Sept. 18, 1882. Foundry clerks received $2 a day and the operators of wood-working machines, $1.75. ‡C. A. Spring, Jr., to C. H. McCormick, Sept. 12, and Nov. 10, 1879. J. B. Taylor, Iron Moulders' Union, Chicago, to C. H. McCormick, Nov. 6, 1876, and the Co.'s reply on Nov. 21, in L.P.C.B. No. 169, p. 54.

This strike is a sad experience to us all [she wrote], a *new* experience to us all. Our men have always felt a kind of loyalty to our interests, and attachment to us as employers, but this strike shows a change in their attitude, whether with reason or not. . . . I would like to get at the bottom of this matter. I would like to know exactly the facts. . . .

Humanitarian reasons alone would lead us to wish to deal fairly with our working men and to pay the price their work is worth, not getting a dollar's worth of work for fifty cents . . . to do *justly* does not mean to make hasty concessions under compulsion. It would be a very grave mistake to yield to the demand made when the yielding would seem like submitting to the dictation of our workmen. This would never do, because we should soon have the fresh trouble on our hands of a new demand for another increase of wages.

. . . Concession on both sides, I think, is the right way. Capital and labor must both make concessions. . . . It is very evident that as a class, *those who win strikes are not much better satisfied than those who lose.*[26]

The number of employees at the works varied between seven hundred in the early autumn and over twice as many during the busy season when day- and night-shifts were used.[27] Most of them worked ten hours a day and the long-continued agitation throughout the country to reduce this stint to eight had, as yet, been largely without result. The firm did not attempt to patronize its employees or to supervise their time when they were not at the factory. Their homes were so scattered that a night-school at the plant was impracticable. The company took pride in pointing out that working conditions were comfortable because the plant was heated with steam, adequately lighted and ventilated, and provided with all modern sanitary conveniences.[28] Good water was available in every

[26] C. H. McCormick, Jr., MSS. Book "B," Nettie F. McCormick to C. H. McCormick, Jr., Apr. 12, 1885.

[27] By 1884, eighteen hundred were employed at the factory when the rush was at its maximum.

[28] For a good description of the routine of the foundry, see, L.P.C.B. No. 245, p. 326, the Co. to J. Wilson & Son, N. Y., Sept. 17, 1884.

shop, and in summer a "hygienic drink" was supplied for all. Cleanliness was strictly enforced. In the wood-working department the air was purified by a suction system which drew the sawdust through pipes to the furnaces.[29]

The men were paid each Tuesday in cash. They received to the nearest dollar their due up through the preceding Friday, and the balance was carried on the books until the next pay-day.[30] The company closed its factory for a quarter of a day in April, 1883, with the hope that its force would use the opportunity to vote against Carter Harrison who was seeking reëlection as Mayor of Chicago, but this is the sole example of an attempt to marshal the workmen for political purposes.[31] Although the McCormicks were Democrats, the majority sentiment in the factory office was decidedly Republican. The clerks did not hesitate in 1884 to voice their opinion that Cleveland's victory would result in a business depression.[32]

Because the boarding-house and cottages erected near the factory by the McCormicks in 1872 were not large enough, most of their employees lived several miles away in the city, and trusted that the early-morning accommodation train would allow them to reach the factory gate by seven o'clock. The firm divided its work-day into quarters, and if a laborer were tardy he was docked two and one half hours pay. For this

[29] MS. in Room 400, 606 S. Michigan Ave., Chicago, unsigned and undated, but probably written in late 1884 or early 1885.

[30] L.P.C.B. No. 211, p. 2, the Co. to Parlin & Orendorff Co., Canton, Ill., Jan. 13, 1881.

[31] ‡E. K. Butler to C. H. McCormick, Jr., Apr. 4, 1883. Harrison was reëlected. C. H. McCormick, Jr., took active part in the efforts of the reform party to defeat him.

[32] L.P.C.B. No. 243, p. 428, E. K. Butler to C. L. Granger, Ft. Dodge, Ia., June 16, 1884; No. 246, p. 291, the Co. to H. R. Gould, Omaha, Nov. 14, 1884: "The result of the late election discourages us in making an investment at the present time, believing most thoroughly that the prices of everything in the way of manufactured goods will go lower and business be extremely dull for the next year or two at best."

reason McCormick, together with the owners of the near-by Chicago Malleable Iron Works, called the attention of the railroad company to the loss suffered by the workmen whenever the train ran behind its schedule.[33] If the horse-car were used in preference to the railroad, a walk of over a mile was necessary to bridge the distance between the factory and the end of the line. Passenger-transportation by water was apparently not thought of and, in fact, any boat drawing over ten feet could not reach the McCormick wharf.[34]

Between 1880 and 1885 the factory was enlarged almost every year. New buildings were erected to afford cover for completed implements until the time for their shipment arrived. These warehouses, several stories high, were equipped with elevators so that the machines could be shunted from storage to freight car with a minimum of effort.[35] To secure lighter and more durable implements the trend in construction was from wood to iron and steel. Much new machinery was installed to enable this shift to be made. Nevertheless, ten million feet of ash, hickory, oak, and poplar were needed each season, and the company for the first time turned from Indiana and Michigan to southern lumbermen for its supply. By 1885 negotiations were in train for the purchase of timber tracts and sawmills in Missouri and Arkansas.[36] The Mc-Cormicks employed their own lumber inspectors, and their

---

[33] *Ibid.*, No. 229, p. 672, the Co. to Supt. P. C. & St. L. R.R., Logansport, Ind., Dec. 21, 1882; No. 211, p. 2, to Parlin & Orendorff Co., Canton, Ill., Jan. 13, 1881.

[34] *Ibid.*, No. 212, p. 535, C. A. Spring, Jr., to Cleveland Rolling Mills, Cleveland, O., Mch. 30, 1881.

[35] By 1885, the capacity of the two fireproof storage houses at the factory was twenty-five thousand machines. A freight car of ordinary size held eleven harvester-binders or thirty-two mowers. A 6 ft. McCormick harvester-binder weighed about 1575 lbs. *Supra,* Chap. XII, ftn. 77.

[36] *Ibid.*, No. 230, p. 286, the Co. to Moline Lumber Co., Moline, Ill., Jan. 13, 1883; No. 246, pp. 764, 849, to R. T. Thomas, Kansas City, Mo., Dec. 17, 1884, and to E. R. Lentz, Poplar Bluff, Mo., Dec. 22, 1884.

dock was often piled high with "culls" awaiting removal by the sawmill owner who had hoped that the defects in his plank would not be noticed.

Two examples will serve to illustrate the many changes made by the new régime at the works in its efforts to attain greater systematization and efficiency of operation. Hitherto, over fifty gallons of oil had been used each week by the lathe-men. Now the company put all iron filings and shavings in a covered metal basin, revolved it rapidly by steam, and in a few moments the oil, separated by centrifugal force from the iron, dripped into a tank below the container, ready for reuse.[37] By 1879, Cyrus McCormick was able to know not only the cost of building one of his machines, but also the portions of this sum which were chargeable to labor, materials, and "running expenses," including light, heat, insurance, etc. Because the timekeeper recorded in his book on each of his hourly rounds the class of work each man was doing, and the rate of pay prescribed for that service, it was possible for the office to determine both the labor cost of an entire implement and of any one of its parts. Thus, in 1879, $14.82 of the $38.25 cost of a machine was paid out in wages, while $13.99 of the $41.78 average three years later was chargeable to the same expense.[38] Since labor was $3.00 higher per machine in 1881 than in 1882, and wages remained constant, it is probable that the installation of new machinery and more efficient management were responsible for some of the saving effected. These improvements, as well as the enlarged plant, made it possible to complete 55,000 implements in 1884 with less confusion

[37] "The Iron Monger" (London), Nov. 17, 1883, p. 703.
[38] ‡C. A. Spring, Jr., to C. H. McCormick, Jr., Oct. 5, 1880, Sept. 27, 1881, and Sept. 18, 1882. Supra., Chap. XIV, ftn. 116. Prices of materials rose quite rapidly after 1879. Between that date and 1882, white-ash plank advanced from $24 to $29 per M, and pig-iron from $20 to $26 per ton. The average cost of building a machine in 1872 had been $121.52.

than had attended the building of 20,000 only four years before.[39]

By 1880, all parts of the McCormick machines with the exception of the sickles and knives were made at the factory. A year later the firm considered the advisability of manufacturing its own malleable iron, but decided that this material was too conveniently supplied by the neighboring Chicago Malleable Iron Works to warrant a change.[40] When the factory was humming at full speed, about seventy-five tons of iron were needed a day. To make castings of the proper degree of toughness, a blend of three varieties of pig-iron was used, while machine parts subjected to heavy strains were fashioned from Norway iron.[41] In 1883, the company advertised that its workmen, with the aid of "twelve acres of machinery," handled annually about fifteen thousand tons of iron and malleable castings, eighteen miles of wrought-iron pipe, one hundred and thirty-one miles of chain, 241,000 yards of canvas, and 48,000 gallons of linseed-oil, turpentine, varnish, and lard oil. Steel from Birmingham and Sheffield, England, had been supplanted in favor by the output of Pittsburgh mills, deemed to be of equal quality.[42]

Aided by good harvests, fair grain prices, a rapid expansion of transportation lines, and a rush of settlers to wheatlands offered for sale by the national government and the railroads, the McCormick Harvesting Machine Company and its leading competitors enjoyed an unexampled prosperity between 1879 and 1884.[43] Although it is true to say that the McCor-

[39] ‡C. A. Spring, Jr., to C. H. McCormick, Mch. 30, 1883.

[40] L.P.C.B. No. 210, p. 266, letter of the Co. of Feb. 15, 1881. The sickles were usually made by Whitman & Miles Mfg. Co. (Whitman & Barnes) of Akron, Ohio.

[41] "The Farmers' Advance," May, 1880.

[42] McCormick Harvesting Machine Co. Catalog for 1883, p. 6.

[43] The McCormicks sold an average of about 15,000 machines a year in the late 1870's; 31,793 in 1881, 46,683 in 1882, 48,020 in 1883 and 54,841 in 1884. In its Catalog for 1884, the Walter A. Wood Mowing and Reaping

mick Company trebled its annual sales during these six years, the statement conveys a somewhat erroneous impression. The automatic binder was useless without the harvester to which it was attached, but they were two separate implements and were always so counted in arriving at a season's sales total.[44] In like manner, the cost of production per machine will seem to have been reduced by a surprising amount between 1875 and 1884, unless it is borne in mind that the automatic binder, although a masterpiece of delicate workmanship, was smaller in size and much less expensive to build than either a reaper, mower, or harvester. For this reason, the average cost of production in a year when fifteen thousand twine-binders were constructed, naturally was less than it had been a decade before when they were unknown.

The coming of the automatic-binder age also necessitated a change in the character of the other machines produced by makers of harvesting implements. Since the binder was attached to a harvester, rather than to the combined reaper-mower, a demand at once arose for a single mower. To meet this need, the McCormicks built a light iron grass-cutter, and

Machine Co. claimed that during its lifetime of about thirty years it had made nearly a half-million machines. Over ¼th of this total had been produced between 1881 and 1883. Forty-five thousand were manufactured in 1883. In "The Buckeye" (Canton, O.), for Sept., 1882, p. 4, it is asserted that the several "Buckeye" factories made 55,000 implements in 1882. In 1880 there were about 1940 agricultural machinery (of all kinds) factories in the U. S., representing a capital investment of over $62,000,000 (as compared with $17,500,000 in 1860) and employing about 50,000 people. One item of their output was 1,244,264 scythes. According to the "American Inventor" (Cincinnati), Nov., 1884, p. 403, about 175,000 grain- and grass-harvesting machines were annually sold in the U. S. This is probably too low.

[44] The Co. was in fact reluctant to sell a binder as a separate machine, because if it did so, it was usually left with a plain harvester, difficult to dispose of by itself. The binding mechanism, aside from the packer and decks, would as a rule outwear the harvester to which it was attached. See, E. D. Bishop, Longmont, Colo., to the Co., Aug. 11, 1881, and L.P.C.B. No. 242, p. 861, the Co. to H. R. Gould, Omaha, Neb., June 4, 1884.

by 1884 were selling about twenty thousand of them a year.[45] For small farmers who devoted most of their land to grain but did not grow enough to warrant the purchase of a harvester-binder, a light single-reaper, known as "The Daisy," was produced.[46] Except for its self-rake, this implement was in most respects similar to the McCormick machine of 1831, a remarkable tribute to the permanent worth of that invention. Stock-raisers and border-state farmers who cut much hay and little grain each season were accommodated with an improved dropper, first placed on the market in 1880.[47] A few header attachments were built for sale in farming areas where the wheat was sometimes too short to be reached by the reel of the harvester-binder. Whether big headers, propelled from the rear, should be manufactured for the West Coast and the dry-weather trade of Colorado, Kansas and Nebraska, was a question often discussed but always answered in the negative.[48]

Long-sustained but unsuccessful efforts were made during this period to devise a "low down" machine which would make sheaves automatically without first elevating the cut grain.[49]

[45] In 1883, the McCormick Co. also introduced a wide, centre-draft mower for the first time. The 200 made for that harvest did not work well, but the implement was improved during the winter at the factory. *Ibid.,* No. 235, the Co. to S. B. Tinkham, Chariton, Ia., July 23, 1883.

[46] ‡C. A. Spring, Jr., to C. H. McCormick, Nov. 15, 1879. Its selling price was $125, or about one-half the cost of a harvester-binder. It was made largely according to the design of H. E. Pridmore, a skilled mechanic who had recently entered the employ of the Co. "The Farmers' Advance," Jan., 1883, p. 3.

[47] C. Colahan to C. H. McCormick, Dec. 19, 1878; F. H. Matthews to C. H. McCormick, Jan. 27, 1879.

[48] The selling price of the header attachment for harvesters was $20. See, L.P.C.B. No. 203, p. 751, the Co. to W. Billing, Denver, Colo., July 6, 1880; No. 228, p. 409, to S. B. Tinkham, Chariton, Ia., Oct. 24, 1882; No. 230, p. 527, to N. E. Barnes, San Francisco, Cal., Jan. 26, 1883.

[49] *Supra,* Chap. XIII, ftn. 54. After three years of unsuccessful attempts to build a practical platform binder, the McCormick Co. wrote in Dec., 1884: "We . . . have about abandoned all hopes of anyone ever succeeding in operating a platform Binder successfully." In 1884 it built 150 ex-

Equally baffling was the problem of inventing an attachment whereby a wire-binder could be transmuted into a twine-binder. In other words, many a farmer who owned a wire-binder saw twine gain the ascendency while his machine was still in good condition. He could not gratify his desire to keep up with the times unless he were willing to pay about $125 for a new binding apparatus, in most respects identical in form to the one that he had bought but a few years before. Although his conclusion was a mistaken one, it was natural for him to believe that the manufacturers of harvesting machinery had made no serious effort to find a simple and inexpensive way whereby his binder could use twine instead of wire.[50]

If a harvester-binder and a "Daisy" reaper, each with a knife five feet in length, worked for a day side by side through a field of ripe grain, one would cut as much as the other. For this reason it has often been pointed out that McCormick's machine of 1831 reaped as many acres, although at a greater labor cost, as the improved implement of fifty or one hundred years later. This is true, but harvester-binders were often made "wide," with a knife seven or eight feet long. Drawn by three or four horses and equipped with an equalizer so that each animal would pull the same weight, this machine could reap between eighteen and twenty acres a day, or over half as much again as the implement of 1831. Thus, by 1880 Mc-Cormick was manufacturing "wide" harvester-binders for the

perimental all-steel harvesters, "the greatest step forward we have made for years." These were about 200 pounds lighter than the regular harvesters. L.P.C.B. No. 244, p. 843, the Co. to B. Craycroft, Chillicothe, Mo., Aug. 26, 1844.

[50] *Ibid.*, No. 199, p. 674, the Co. to R. Newton, Louisville, Ky., Mch. 19, 1880; No. 209, p. 1, to M. Sheehan, Fargo, Dec. 30, 1880; No. 223, p. 831, to S. W. Chapman, Elgin, Ill., May 17, 1882. Wire-binder purchasers were the more aggrieved because the Co. in 1880, when it had no twine-binder to meet the swelling demand, had promised customers that it would soon be in a position to supply twine attachments to those who bought wire-binders.

Minnesota-Dakota market, and "deep" machines, leaving a very short stubble, for the grain-growers of England.[51]

Improvement of the agency system went hand in hand with the reforms effected at the factory and in the office. Shortly after the Civil War, the company endeavored to place the entire supervision of its local salesmen in the charge of the forty or fifty general agents. This decentralization of control was carried so far that by 1876 even the names of the local canvassers were unknown to the Chicago headquarters.[52] Gradually, thereafter, a method was devised whereby the busy clerks in the home office, without much additional burden, could keep close watch over the thousand and more district salesmen. Rules were formulated for their guidance, and frequent checkups, through traveling representatives, were made to see that the general agents were requiring their enforcement.[53] Care was taken not to prescribe too rigid a code of regulations, since selling conditions in the "cash area" from Ohio to eastern Kansas were quite unlike those in the "credit belt" of Minnesota, the Dakotas, and Nebraska. Here to the north and west of Chicago was a new, one-crop country where

[51] In 1876, the Co. claimed that a 6 ft. knife-bar would be impractical since the binding mechanism could not work fast enough to take care of the grain, but in 1878 the McCormicks began making them, as well as the regular 5 ft. harvesters. The knife-bar was lengthened with an eye to the rich "bonanza" farmer trade in the Valley of the Red River of the North. *Ibid.*, No. 233, p. 636, the Co. to J. A. Peck, Butte, Montana, June 4, 1883. Here it is said that a 6 ft. harv.-binder, operated by 3 horses working abreast, would regularly cut 15 acres of grain a day, but that many farmers with level land averaged 20 acres. In Feb., 1881, the credit price of a 5 ft. harv.-binder was $290, and of a 6 ft., $300. By Oct., 1882, the price of a McCormick 5 ft. harv.-binder had fallen to $260, of a 6 ft., $270, and of a 7½ ft., $280, 10% off in each case for cash.

[52] *Ibid.*, No. 166, p. 78, the Co. to R. S. and W. G. McCormick, Chicago, May 31, 1876.

[53] W. J. Hanna to C. H. McCormick, Jr., Apr. 8, 1879. L.P.C.B. No. 199 (Mch. 1880) *passim*, letters to the general agents. The Co., as a rule, refused to reply to letters from local salesmen. They were turned over for answer to the general agent in charge of the writer's district.

exemption laws and the solvency of every prospective buyer had to be studied with special diligence.[54] To remove the temptation to sell to improvident farmers who could never pay, agents in this region worked for a salary rather than for commissions.

The task of selling was now quite usually separated from the business of collecting. If an agent's salary were over $1,200 he was obliged to post a bond for $7,500 or more when he began work.[55] He signed several contracts stipulating his duties and obligations in selling machines, spare parts, and twine or wire.[56] He pledged that he would not handle the binding material or the harvesting implements of any other manufacturer. A collector, whether a bank, lawyer, merchant, traveling agent or district salesman, received either a salary or a percentage of the money taken in.[57] He was expected to send cash to the Chicago office by draft, check, or express as soon as possible, but if for any reason he opened an agency account at a local bank, it must be in the name of the McCormick Company and subject to its order.[58] In this way, the firm hoped to

[54] *Ibid.*, No. 200, p. 310, No. 201, p. 770, the Co. to M. Sheehan, Fargo, Apr. 5, and May 20, 1880. In a letter (No. 202, p. 770) to L. P. Gillette, Lincoln, Neb., June 12, 1880, a Co. clerk stated with considerable exaggeration that the lower central west trade was 75% cash. No. 212 (Apr. 1881), pp. 492, 496: We want to do away with so many credit transactions gradually working our sales in N. West up to a higher grade, even if we do reduce the number of our sales. #C. Colahan to C. H. McCormick, Aug. 9, 1881.

[55] L.P.C.B. No. 202, p. 222-224, the Co. to M. T. Grattan, Preston, Minn., May 28, 1880.

[56] *Ibid.*, No. 237, p. 471, the Co. to F. Windeier, Chicago, Sept. 29, 1883. No. 242, p. 96, to E. C. Beardsley, Minneapolis, May 1, 1884: "The general agent for your district must post a bond of from $12,000 to $15,000." The agent's commission on the sale of a machine was usually from 15 to 20%, on repairs, 20%, and on twine and wire, 10%. The commission on credit sales was usually 2 or 3% lower than on transactions for cash.

[57] *Ibid.*, No. 222, p. 106, the Co. to G. S. Robinson, Sycamore, Ill., Mch. 25, 1882.

[58] *Ibid.*, No. 240, p. 302, the Co. to 1st National Bank, Peoria, Ill., Feb. 15, 1884.

avoid complications in case of his insolvency or death. Each item of expense above $5 had to be supported by a voucher.[59]

With one exception, the general agents were on a salary basis by 1880, and they were obliged annually to bring their books to Chicago for audit. They had no more important task than to keep in touch at all times with the financial condition of their sub-agents.[60] A salesman forfeited a part of his commission if he sold a machine to a farmer who was unable to complete payments on it. After a general agent appointed as many salesmen as were needed to cover his territory adequately, he sent a list of their names to the home office with pertinent data concerning each. The district of a local agent was made small enough so that he would not need to divide his commissions with assistants. Otherwise he would doubtless be unwilling to split his percentage with a farmer in order to clinch a sale.[61]

To urge this rather surprising reason as a justification for a small agency district, suggests that the McCormicks had been forced to depart far from their old sales methods in order to meet the intense pressure of competition. No longer could they boast of "A Fixed Price and One Price to All." They now published a price list in the spring, and then wrote to their general agents that each type of implement must net them at Chicago a sum often considerably less than the amount announced. This meant that if a salesman were unable to sell machines because of under-cutting by rivals, he could put a farmer in good humor by offering him an implement for less

[59] Ibid., No. 245, p. 308, the Co. to M. Sheehan, Fargo, Sept. 16, 1884.

[60] The exception was John W. Lowell of Salt Lake City. See, "Tullidge's Quarterly Magazine" (Salt Lake City), Vol. II, No. 2 (July, 1882), pp. 289-296. L.P.C.B. No. 228, pp. 61-62, E. K. Butler to C. H. McCormick, Jr., Oct. 4, 1882.

[61] Ibid., No. 188, p. 195, the Co. to C. B. Pinkham, Marshalltown, Ia., Feb. 17, 1879; No. 211, p. 61, to W. M. Baker, Baltimore, Md., Feb. 19, 1881.

than the sum advertised on the show-bills.[62] To combine portions from two letters written to general agents during the week of June 1, 1883:

We do not think it advisable for you to any longer attempt to control the prices of machines sold by your agents, beyond the fact that they must account to you for so much, all they get over that is their profits and for which they must do the work. There is no use for us to attempt to disguise the fact that we have been imitated by others until there are other good machines in the market and that farmers cannot be bull-dozed or led to pay $25 to $50 more for our machines than they will for others; notwithstanding *we* know they are worth more and can get a *little* more. . . . We do not believe it is necessary or best to tell *all* your agents they may sell at a minimum price. We do admit that in a moral light it would be just and [a] much pleasanter way to do business but in the machine business nowadays we are all forced to do many unpleasant things; in short, be what might be termed a little "tricky"; therefore you will see that our desire is for you to meet such cases when you believe that we would make money by it.[63]

These concessions were granted for the purpose of holding competent agents in the employ of the company, as well as to sell more machines. If salesmen on a commission basis were not allowed to cut prices, they could find few purchasers unless they were willing to pass on a part of their own percentage to the buyers.[64] The firm sometimes attempted to maintain its

[62] *Ibid.*, No. 222, pp. 420-421, the Co. to F. Craycroft, Sedalia, Mo., Apr. 3, 1882; No. 230, pp. 586, 654, to J. J. Wogan, Lincoln, Neb., Jan. 30, 1883 and to J. Esterly & Son, White Water, Wis., Feb. 5, 1883; No. 233, p. 350, to W. Baker, Baltimore, May 24, 1883. In 1883, the announced price of a McCormick 5 ft. harvester-binder was $260. General agents were advised, however, that should their best local salesmen refuse to work if the price were kept at so high a figure, they might sell for less, provided only that a machine sold on credit terms must net the firm $225 cash.

[63] L.P.C.B. No. 233, pp. 501, 665, E. K. Butler to G. J. Wilmot, St. Joseph, Mo., May 30 and to W. N. Spring, Le Mars, Ia., June 5, 1883.

[64] The McCormick Co. in 1882 stood firm upon its announced prices in spite of discontented agents and reductions by the opposition. In the autumn,

list prices by promising its agent a bonus in addition to his regular commission on each sale. It was understood, of course, that this extra compensation would be given to the grain-grower who bought a machine.[65] Thus a McCormick harvester-binder cost a farmer some $50 or $75 less in 1884 than in 1880, but it is impossible to be more definite since its price varied in a single season in proportion to the amount of competition in particular sales districts. Money prizes were occasionally offered to salesmen if they would dispose of more than a certain number of machines and keep the cost of selling and collecting below twenty-six per cent of the sales price of the implement. Thirty per cent was the usual percentage which had to be allowed for these services.[66] Agents were given the option of selling wire and twine for a ten per cent commission, or of buying it for cash from the McCormicks for fourteen per cent below the retail price. The company's net profit from its trade in these binding materials was always small when compared either with its large outlay of money for them or with its gain from the sale of machines.[67]

In the early 1880's there was less emphasis than ever before

however, it urged its general agents to hold the best local salesmen in their employ by assuring them that there would be a liberal reduction in 1883. *Ibid.*, No. 227, p. 880, No. 228, p. 203, the Co. to E. C. Beardsley, Minneapolis, Oct. 2, and to J. B. Heywood, Indianapolis, Oct. 11, 1882; No. 231, pp. 795, 853, to G. J. Wilmot, St. Joseph, Mo., Mch. 28, 1883, and to Dennett Harv. Mach. Co., Milwaukee, Wis., Mch. 30, 1883.

[65] *Ibid.*, No. 233, p. 500, the Co. to W. Westerman, St. Cloud, Minn., May 30, 1883.

[66] *Ibid.*, No. 196, p. 231, No. 239, p. 570, the Co. to B. Holbrook, Nov. 21, 1879, and to N. B. Fulmer, Red Wing, Minn., Jan. 9, 1884. *Post,* ftn. 136.

[67] *Ibid.*, No. 197, p. 240, No. 246, p. 528, the Co. to S. L. Beardsley, Kalamazoo, Mich., Dec. 29, 1879, and to C. L. Wicker, Chicago, Dec. 1, 1884. ‡C. A. Spring, Jr., to C. H. McCormick, Mch. 30, 1883. The McCormick Co.'s net profit on its investment of $1,250,000 in wire and twine in 1882 was $130,000, the largest up to that time. L.P.C.B. No. 226, p. 169, the Co. to W. M. Baker, Baltimore, Md., July 18, 1882; No. 209, p. 730, to D. W. Pratt, St. Louis, Mo., Jan. 29, 1881.

upon the utility of farm canvassing during the winter months. Northwestern grain-growers refused to order machines until they were reasonably certain that there would be no grasshoppers.[68] For this reason the demand in any locality was always uncertain until the eve of harvest, and the firm was obliged to build warehouses at such central points as St. Cloud, Minnesota, and Fargo, Dakota Territory, in order to house machines shipped from Chicago in anticipation of sales that might never materialize.[69] These were boom years, however, and a shortage of implements was far more to be feared than an over-supply. An agent no longer had to seek farmers. He could sit at his desk and they would come to him, eager to buy. In each of the five years between 1880 and 1884, the company completely sold out its stock of most kinds of machines, in several instances even before the harvest season was well advanced.[70] Local agents, who usually were salesmen of other agricultural implements as well, wished to receive their quota of McCormick mowers and harvesters as soon as the rush for seeders, drills, and plows had made a vacant space in their stores, and after the tax assessor had made his annual spring visitation.[71] For a few weeks farmers would be too busy to come to town, but as soon as their land was seeded, they were ready to consider the merits of the rival makes of harvesting

[68] G. A. Freudenreich, McCauleyville, Minn., to the Co., Apr. 18, 1877. The deep snows of the winter and the "mud embargo" of the spring often prevented energetic agents from canvassing as much as they desired.

[69] A warehouse was built at St. Cloud in 1880, and one at Fargo a year later.

[70] L.P.C.B. No. 204, p. 192, the Co. to G. H. Brewster, Mankato, Minn., July 15, 1880; No. 214 (June 1881), pp. 614, 618; No. 215 (July, 1881), p. 724; No. 235 (July, 1883), p. 408. #C. A. Spring, Jr., to C. H. McCormick, July 29, 1882: "Never, in all my experience have we had such a good crop everywhere."

[71] Ibid., No. 220, p. 497, the Co. to D. H. Smith, Sparta, Wis., Jan. 25, 1882; No. 221, p. 185, to D. W. Pratt, St. Louis, Mo., Feb. 21, 1882; No. 240, p. 161, to Elizabethport Steam Cordage Co., N. Y., Feb. 7, 1884.

implements. Then was the time to have the new models on display and to parade them through the streets with a band at the head of the column. A dealer's store was often quite like a club, where farmers gathered near the stove to play cards, checkers or dominoes, within eye-shot of the consignment of attractively painted machines, just in from Chicago.[72]

Although McCormick's sub-agents might complain of too high prices, too small commissions, unfilled orders, and of excessive attention given to the brisk cash trade of the winter wheat belt when the Northwest was clamoring for machines, they rarely resigned and had never been more prosperous. They were now receiving as much for making a sale, as for a sale and collection ten years before. A harvester-binder was almost twice as costly as a reaper and hence the *ad valorem* commission was correspondingly higher. Furthermore, every binder placed in a farmer's hands meant that the agent would collect a small fee for several years by selling the wire or twine necessary to operate it. Granted that the McCormick Company met the terms offered by its competitors, less hard work was necessary in order to sell machines than at any earlier period, and the business of many local agents increased with every succeeding harvest. "It is the 'old, old story' repeated again this year," wrote W. J. Hanna in June, 1881, "that our works with all their increased facilities do not seem able to keep up with the demand." [73]

[72] "The Farmers' Advance," May, 1882. L.P.C.B. No. 236, pp. 27-28, the Co. to Moore & Bell, Longmont, Colo., July 30, 1883: "Could we only get farmers to make up their minds within a reasonable time as to what machine they would purchase, one-half of the difficulties of distributing machines for sale would be at an end."

[73] *Ibid.*, No. 214, p. 684, the Co. to E. W. Brooks, Red Wing, Minn., June 10, 1881; No. 216, p. 93, No. 218, p. 375, C. H. McCormick, Jr., to F. Baumann, Chicago, July 13 and Oct. 24, 1881. In the autumn of 1881, the foundry was enlarged, and an engine-house, boiler-house, and a three-story warehouse repair-shop building (90 ft. by 44 ft.) were erected. ‡C. H. McCormick, Jr., to C. H. McCormick, July 21, 1881. "The Farmers' Advance," Jan., 1882.

Every salesman was urged to caution his clients to observe the three basic rules for the care of a harvesting machine, to keep it oiled, to sharpen its knife frequently, and to protect it from the weather when not in use.[74] The company hesitated to put such a complicated mechanism as a binder in a farmer's hands until it had taught its field force how to operate and repair it. Local salesmen with the aid of the general agent were obliged to fix broken machines and to rejuvenate with paint those that remained unsold from an earlier harvest. The home office of the company insisted that the factory "should not be made a graveyard for broken-down or imperfect machines." [75] "Our rule . . . is that every general shall take care of his own wounded and bury his own dead." If bad came to worst, agents could sell old implements at auction or dismantle them and dispose of the pieces as spare parts.[76]

With the harvester-binder age came the field experts who somewhat relieved the pressure hitherto brought upon the local salesman to repair machines in his district. These experts, one hundred and forty in number by 1883, were sent out from Chicago during the harvest to set up implements and instruct farmers in their use. They were under the orders of the general agent in whose territory they were working, but their progress northward with the ripening grain was directed by telegram from the home office. The company was much embarrassed for a few days during the height of the season in 1883 when contact with this field force was broken by a telegraphers' strike. The experts received a wage of from $60 to $75 a

[74] "Champion Machine Company (Springfield, O.,) Agents' Hand Book," 1882, p. 2.

[75] L.P.C.B. No. 226, p. 865, the Co. to D. W. Pratt, St. Louis, Mo., Aug. 12, 1882.

[76] Ibid., No. 227, p. 701, the Co. to J. B. Heywood, Indianapolis, Sept. 22, 1882: "Commissions will be too easily earned, if every machine slid through the agent's hands, and gave him no further trouble in any shape." No. 231, p. 509, to D. W. Pratt, St. Louis, Mo., Mch. 14, 1883; No. 239, p. 498, to J. C. Mickle, San Francisco, Cal., Jan. 4, 1884.

The company was unenthusiastic about this annual "nuisance," and at least on one occasion tried unsuccessfully to secure pledges from other manufacturers not to exhibit. The salesmen, on the other hand, were always insistent that the firm should be represented, and as a rule it obligingly yielded.[82] Against its better judgment, it entered several local harvester-binder field trials in 1882 and 1883. The decisions handed down by the judges of these contests served only to confirm the company in its long-held opinion that they were useless both as an advertising device and as an impartial test of the relative worth of the rival machines.[83]

During the Civil War, and for ten years thereafter, the company, wishing to be free of all bother concerning freights and their collection, allowed each general agent to arrange for machine shipments with the railroads serving his territory. By 1876, however, whenever the pool agreements were broken, it was possible to secure large rebates from competing lines if the matter were handled by the central office of the firm.[84] Over their protest, the agents relinquished the privilege of making their own bargains with the roads. They were now required to send to the company every spring a list of the number of car-loads of implements they wished delivered to

[82] *Ibid.*, No. 227, p. 549, the Co. to E. H. Everett, Kalamazoo, Mich., Sept. 13, 1882.

[83] Telegram and letter of C. H. McCormick, Jr., to the Co. from Lexington, Ky., June 20, 1883. L.P.C.B. No. 234, p. 374, C. H. McCormick, Jr., to E. C. Beardsley, Minneapolis, June 21, 1883; No. 238, p. 733, the Co. to R. Newton, Louisville, Ky., Dec. 3, 1883.

[84] *Supra*, Chap. XII, ftn. 77. When it was rumored that a pool was to be formed, the Co., realizing that higher rates were in the offing, rushed their shipments forward with all speed. *Ibid.*, No. 163, p. 297, the Co. to E. A. McNair, Dallas, Texas, Feb. 8, 1876; No. 189 (Apr. 1879), pp. 586 ff., telegrams of the Co. to genl. agents; No. 199, p. 335, the Co. to W. Billing, Denver, Colo., Mch. 11, 1880; No. 202, p. 317, to H. R. Gould, Omaha, Neb., June 1, 1880; No. 225, p. 471, to H. N. Johnston, Brockport, N. Y., July 5, 1882; No. 240, p. 420, to W. S. Krebs, Albert Lea, Minn., Feb. 20, 1884.

each station in their district.[85] When two railroads served a single town, the firm played one against another and secured the largest rebate possible.[86] If it could gain lower rates than those granted to a competitor, so much the better.[87] The amount of the rebate was highly confidential, although it was sufficiently definite for the company to send out a bill for it to the road in question at the close of the shipping season.[88] It sometimes amounted to twenty per cent or twenty-five per cent of the published car-load rate and was occasionally as high as fifty per cent on the mileage tickets used by binder experts.[89] Whether the rebate should be kept by the company, given to the agents, or passed on to the purchasers of machines, was never certainly decided. Practice varied, de-

[85] *Ibid.*, No. 173, p. 316, the Co. to G. W. Brewster, Mankato, Minn., July 3, 1877. Because of complaints by agents, the Co. decided in 1881 to allow them once again to make their own freight contracts if they so desired. It did not work successfully. No. 210, p. 289, to M. Sheehan, Fargo, Feb. 16, 1881: "Go ahead and make best contracts you can or let your locals do it! After one year's experience we incline to think no general agent will care to have a hand in it, and we propose in 1882 to step in and make freight contracts on best terms we can to every point." No. 218, p. 235, to W. M. Baker, Baltimore, Md., Oct. 18, 1881.

[86] *Ibid.*, No. 210, p. 570; No. 218, p. 479; No. 242, p. 169, the Co. to E. W. Brooks, Red Wing, Minn., Feb. 26, 1881, to E. C. Beardsley, Minneapolis, Oct. 29, 1881, to B. Craycroft, Chillicothe, Mo., Apr. 5, 1884.

[87] *Ibid.*, No. 164, p. 590, the Co. to E. A. McNair, Dallas, Texas, Mch. 29, 1876.

[88] Rebates were not collectable until six or nine months after the shipments had been made. *Ibid.*, No. 190, p. 249, the Co. to Keystone Mfg. Co., Kansas City, Mo., May 6, 1879; No. 200, p. 306; No. 240, p. 633, to Genl. Fght. Agt., C. B. & Q. R.R., Chicago, Apr. 5, 1880, and Mch. 3, 1884; No. 202, p. 241, to S. W. Chapman, Elgin, Ill., May 29, 1880.

[89] This was given by the Chicago & NW. R.R. to the McCormick Co. on mileage tickets in 1880. This road allowed only a 33⅓% rebate to other manufacturers. See, *Ibid.*, No. 202, p. 219, the Co. to J. P. Watson, Marshall, Minn., May 27, 1880. The rebate on a C. B. & Q. R.R., 1000-mile ticket in Apr., 1880, was ⅓rd of the $30 price. *Ibid.*, No. 200, p. 724; No. 210, p. 165, the Co. to E. W. Brooks, Red Wing, Minn., Feb. 10, 1881; No. 240, p. 583, to W. R. Smyth, Mankato, Minn., Mch. 1, 1884; No. 242, p. 175, to Northern Pacific R.R., St. Paul, Minn., May 5, 1884.

pending upon the extent of the competition in a particular sales district, or the demand for implements during the harvest-season.[90]

Roads facing heavy competition, such as the Chicago & Northwestern, Wabash, Illinois Central, and Chicago, Burlington & Quincy, were generous in granting rebates, while others, and especially the Grand Trunk, the Michigan Central, and the Union Pacific were difficult to deal with and were held in low esteem by the factory office.[91] Using coöperation and coercion, the farmers of some states during the Granger period had been enabled to lower railroad rates by law. At the time when this legislation was enacted, the manufacturers of agricultural machinery were receiving few, if any, concessions from the transportation lines. But now, in spite of these reduced tariffs, the McCormick Company, by promising a railroad all of its shipments, or by threatening to boycott it if no favors were extended, secured considerably lower rates than were paid by the farmers who had gained their victories after so much strenuous and noisy effort.[92]

Railroads fixed the maximum weight of a car-load of machines at twenty thousand pounds. If this total were exceeded,

[90] *Ibid.*, No. 209, p. 630, the Co. to F. Craycroft, Sedalia, Mo., Jan. 26, 1881: "Now, as we see it, no consignee has any claim on us for *rebates.*" No. 221, pp. 210, 325, to M. Sheehan, Fargo, D. Terr., Feb. 22, 27, 1882; No. 232, p. 134, to W. S. Krebs, Albert Lea, Minn., Apr. 6, 1883: "We turn all our rebates over to the agents in the districts concerned"; No. 242, p. 366, to R. B. Swift, St. Louis, Mo., May 13, 1884: "We would like to save the rebates for ourselves."

[91] *Ibid.*, No. 210, p. 823, the Co. to W. P. Utley, Mason City, Ia., Mch. 8, 1881; No. 231, p. 469, to E. H. Everett, Kalamazoo, Mich., Mch. 13, 1883; p. 561, to E. C. Beardsley, Minneapolis, Mch. 16, 1883; No. 234, pp. 411, 871, to W. F. Cowhan, Jackson, Mich., June 22 and July 3, 1883; No. 238, p. 455, to J. P. Scranton & Co., Detroit, Mich., Nov. 15, 1883; No. 240, p. 249, to W. Westerman, St. Cloud, Minn., Feb. 13, 1884; No. 243, p. 359, to J. J. Wogan, Lincoln, Neb., June 14, 1884.

[92] L.P.C.B. No. 221, p. 240, the Co. to J. B. Heywood, Indianapolis, Ind., Feb. 23, 1882.

an additional freight charge was levied. In the early 1880's the roads began the practice of announcing rates on agricultural machinery at so much per one hundred pounds.[93] Twine and wire for several years were not in the same tariff classification as implements. Until this annoyance was removed, the McCormicks billed their twine as "rope." Although the gunnysacks obviously contained balls of cord, the railroads would have assessed a higher rate if they had been correctly labelled.[94]

The principal sales territory for harvester-binders moved quite rapidly north and west of Chicago during the decade following 1875. Kansas grew the most wheat in 1879, but Minnesota was then the banner McCormick state. Its farmers bought almost fifty-five hundred of his machines that season, or nearly as many as the total output of the factory a dozen years before.[95] With every succeeding harvest, more and more reapers and mowers also found purchasers in the diversified farming belt to the southward. By 1883, fifteen thousand iron-mowers were insufficient to supply the de-

[93] *Ibid.,* No. 210, p. 293, the Co. to E. W. Brooks, Red Wing, Minn., Feb. 16, 1881; No. 221, p. 255, to C. B. Pinkham, Marshalltown, Ia., Feb. 23, 1882; No. 224, p. 39, to G. E. Monk, Milwaukee, Wis., May 20, 1882: "Every car that leaves Chicago is weighed by a Weighing Association on behalf of all the Railroads in Chicago. These weigh-masters are not in the employ of any special Road."

[94] *Ibid.,* No. 211 (Feb. 1881), p. 106. In the same manner, if repair parts and wire were billed as "castings," the freight rate on them was lower than if they were designated by their own name. By 1882, the McCormick Co. had induced many railroads to place binder-twine and wire in the same freight classification. In 1884, most railroads running out of Chicago agreed to place machines, wire, and twine in the same class. This was not true of the eastern lines, see, No. 241, p. 742, the Co. to M. Sheehan, Fargo, D. Terr., Apr. 21, 1884.

[95] "The Daily Inter Ocean," Sept. 12, 1879; "The Minneapolis Tribune," Sept. 3, 1880; "The Farmers' Advance," May, 1879, Jan., 1881, and Mch., 1882. McCormick's first sale in Minnesota was to Major A. M. Fridley in 1854. In 1877, the McCormicks sold 2200 in that state. F. H. Matthews to C. H. McCormick, Aug. 13, 1877.

mand,[96] and this central area absorbed so many machines that the agents in the north country were annually under-supplied.

The increase of McCormick's business in Minnesota was in a measure due to the opening of the Red River Valley of the North, the most sensational development in the history of wheat culture between 1875 and 1880. Stretching from Breckinridge to Winnipeg and for about thirty miles west into Dakota Territory, rich bottom-lands untouched by a plow as late as 1869 were producing eight million bushels of wheat ten years later. Many homesteaders and a few "bonanza" farmers thronged to the valley as soon as the Northern Pacific, and St. Paul & Pacific railroads were ready to carry their grain to the docks at Duluth or to the millers of the Twin Cities.[97]

New-comers broke the tough sod in June, allowed it to lie fallow all summer, cross-plowed and harrowed it again in the autumn, and by the next spring were ready to seed it with eighty or one hundred pounds of wheat to the acre. The preparation of an acre of land cost about five dollars and it would produce from twenty to twenty-five bushels or wheat, or at least half as much again as the per acre average of the United States.[98] The Red River Valley farmer was assured of a fair profit on his investment if the price of wheat held above seventy-five cents a bushel and if drought and grasshoppers continued to pass him by.

Oliver Dalrymple, a large landowner of Minnesota, was one of the first "bonanza" farmers to settle near Fargo. As a manager of property owned by others, his twelve hundred acres

[96] The McCormick Co. sold 6,000 iron-mowers in 1880, 9,000 in 1881, and 15,000 in 1882. They were among the most satisfactory implements that the firm ever built.

[97] "The Farmers' Advance," May, 1880, and Jan., 1881.

[98] "U.S. Consular Reports for 1883," No. 3, p. 453. Here it is said that it cost an average of $14 to cultivate, reap, thresh, haul to market, etc., the wheat raised on an acre of land in the U.S.

of wheat in 1876 expanded to twenty thousand acres by 1879. By then he was one of the biggest grain-growers east of the Rockies. "Frank Leslie's Illustrated Newspaper" of New York City published a double-page picture of the 1878 harvest on one of Dalrymple's farms, where four hundred men and eighty wire-binders, working in brigades of about twenty-five each, were employed to cut the grain.[99] A single swath was over a mile long, and a harvester-binder might travel forty miles in the course of its day's work without turning many corners.[100] The land under Dalrymple's supervision was divided into two-thousand-acre farms, each with its own foreman, laborers, buildings, and bookkeeping, and with contact maintained by telephone between the several units. In this "coming country of the Northwest" there were many other big wheat ranches by 1880, owned by individuals or syndicates.[101] Their existence depended upon machinery, and if they marked the beginning of a tendency which would some day become the norm in American agricultural economy, the fate of the small farmer was sealed. Nevertheless, in much the same manner as the little landowners of the South looked to the masters of the big plantations for guidance, the homesteaders of the Red River Valley gave their favor to the machine manufacturers patronized by Dalrymple, the Sharon Land Co., J. P. Watson,

[99] "Frank Leslie's Illustrated Newspaper," Oct. 19, 1878. Dalrymple estimated that he needed one harvester-binder for every 250 acres of wheat. "The Farmers' Advance," May, 1882. O. Dalrymple managed the Red River properties of G. W. Cass, E. P. Cheyney, and the Grandin brothers.

[100] C. H. McCormick, Jr., to C. H. McCormick, Aug. 16, 1880. Here, McCormick, Jr., tells his father that five McCormick binders between 4 A. M. and 8 P. M. cut 133 acres on the Stickney-Smith farm. Each machine traveled forty miles, going eight times around a five-mile piece of grain. W. R. Baker, to Nettie F. McCormick, Aug. 11, 1880.

[101] G. A. Freudenreich, McCauleyville, Minn., to Co., Apr. 18, 1877. In 1880 there were 82 farms in the Red River Valley of over 1000 acres each. By 1890 there were 323 of this size. See, Harold E. Briggs, "Early Bonanza Farming in the Red River Valley," in "Agricultural History" (Washington, D. C.), Jan., 1932, pp. 26 ff.

or G. W. Barnes & Co. of Glyndon.[102] For this reason, and because the three months' rush of each selling-season climaxed in the valley, McCormick and his competitors were keen rivals for their trade. Their estates were the August rendezvous of manufacturers who wished to try out new machines. Here Cyrus McCormick, Jr., gained his first field experience and often dined with Oliver Dalrymple. Since harvester-binders and the Red River Valley went hand in hand, he looked upon both as peculiarly his province.[103]

Compared with Walter A. Wood and Company, the McCormicks were slow in winning the "bonanza" farmers to their standard. They made their first sales in the valley in 1874. Two years later they displayed a wire-binder on the Dalrymple estate, but its proprietor bought over one hundred machines from Walter A. Wood during the next three harvests. For a decade after 1879, however, the Chicago firm held first place in Dalrymple's favor.[104] Although Wood, Osborne and other manufacturers early appointed agents along the Red River, it tried for a time to develop trade there through its repre-

[102] G. A. Freudenreich, St. Cloud, Minn., to the Co., Apr. 3 and 10, 1878.
[103] *Supra,* Chap. XIII, p. 558. C. H. McCormick, Jr., to C. H. McCormick, Aug. 16, 1880. C. H. McCormick, Jr., MSS. Nettie F. McCormick to C. H. McCormick, Jr., July 30, and Aug. 13, 20, 1880: "Where would the *twine binder* have been *but for you,* my child. Echo answers No where." "The Daily Argus" (Fargo and Moorhead), Aug. 11, 1881. In Room 400, 606 S. Michigan Ave., is a L.P.C.B. of C. H. McCormick, Jr., containing the letters of Aug., 1881, written by him from the Red River Valley while testing twine-binders. L.P.C.B. No. 223, p. 811, C. H. McCormick, Jr., to M. Sheehan, Fargo, May 16, 1882.
[104] W. R. Baker, Hastings, Minn., to the Co., Aug. 10, 1876. O. Dalrymple purchased 10 Wood binders in 1876, 31 in 1877, 35 in 1878, and 30 in 1879. In 1878 he also bought 3 McCormick binders, in 1879, 11, and in 1880, 35 more. About ten years later he transferred most of his patronage from McCormick to the Deering Co. McC. Harv. Mach. Co. Catalog, 1880, letter of O. Dalrymple, St. Paul, Minn., to McCormick Co., Mch. 31, 1880. See also, his letter to the Co. of Nov. 30, 1880. "The Minneapolis Tribune," May 15, 1881; ‡C. Colahan to C. H. McCormick, Aug. 11, 12, 1881; E. C. Beardsley, Fargo, to C. H. McCormick, Jr., Aug. 19, 1881.

sentative at St. Cloud, Minnesota, a hundred miles away.[105] Nor were the McCormicks among the first to build a warehouse at Fargo to provide cover for implements which otherwise would be deposited in the mud or dust along the tracks of the Northern Pacific.[106] From the outset, the binder-builders offered the big farmers liberal discounts for cash purchases of car-load lots of machines. Until about 1880, the McCormicks declined to withhold from an agent his regular percentage of the sales price when one of these aristocrats of the agricultural world sent his order direct to Chicago.[107] Thereafter, however, the commission was deducted from the cash price of a machine, and the McCormicks were thus enabled to meet the terms offered by their rivals. The McCormick salesmen, deprived of their premium, took consolation from the thought that the small grain-grower would imitate the choice of his big neighbor.[108] By 1880, in fact, it was said that one-half of the wheat of the Red River Valley was cut by McCormick machines.[109]

[105] Letters of G. A. Freudenreich, Alexandria, Minn., to the Co., June 25, Aug. 6, 16, Sept. 3, Nov. 19, 30, 1877. The first resident McCormick agent in the valley was appointed in Nov., 1877.

[106] The McCormick Co. leased a lot at Fargo for five years in 1877, but took no steps to build upon it until the autumn of 1881. By that time the Osborne, Wood, and Deering Cos. already had warehouses there. In 1882, the McCormicks were obliged to enlarge their original building. L.P.C.B. No. 214, p. 178; No. 217, pp. 14, 15, 178, letters and telegrams of C. H. McCormick, Jr., to M. Sheehan, Fargo, May 25, Aug. 24, 29, 1881; No. 218, pp. 481-483, E. K. Butler to C. H. McCormick, Jr., Oct. 29, 1881; No. 228, pp. 273, 387, to W. Westerman, St. Cloud, Minn., Oct. 16, 1882.

[107] Ibid., No. 189, p. 522, the Co. to G. Freudenreich, St. Cloud, Minn., Apr. 11, 1879.

[108] In 1881, the Co. offered car-load lots of 6 ft. harv.-binders to big farmers for $220, and in 1884, 7½ ft. ones for $160. These were cash prices, included delivery at Fargo, and in each case no commission was to be given to the agent. Ibid., No. 212, p. 717; No. 242, p. 788, the Co. to M. Sheehan, Fargo, Apr. 7, 1881, and May 31, 1884.

[109] E. C. Beardsley, Minneapolis, to the Co., Aug. 15, 1880. In 1877, of an estimated 425 sold along the route of the Northern Pacific in the Red River

In the preceding autumn agents everywhere, and especially those in Minnesota, urged the McCormicks to have a twine-binder ready for sale by the next summer. The men in the Chicago office, knowing that the firm was not yet prepared to abandon wire, attempted to divert the attention of the field force to the new front-cut, light iron-mower, the new front-cut dropper, and above all to the iron frame, combined machine with a controllable rake, known as the "Imperial." [110] As for the twine-binder, "We do not hear that any of the Gas Companies have closed their works because Mr. Edison is at work inventing an Electric light. . . . The crop of 1880 *must be saved with Wire Binders.*" [111] They were so certain that they could sell as many of these machines as they could make, in spite of the clamor for twine, that they were running their factory twenty-two hours out of the twenty-four. They planned, however, to experiment with the twine-binder during the harvest, but their agents were instructed to say that there was none yet on the market which could do as good work as McCormicks' wire-binder. [112] "When the 'first prize blue ribbon' cord Binder appears," however, "just put on your spectacles & see if you don't find the name of *'McCormick'* on

Valley, 82 were McCormicks'. In 1881, the McCormick Co. sold about 700 there. G. Freudenreich, Alexandria, Minn., to the Co., Sept. 3, 1877.

[110] *Supra,* Chap. X, p. 403. McC. Harv. Mach. Co. Catalog for 1880. The iron-mower was first sold in 1879. The Co. built only 2000 Imperials in 1880, and the demand for them was so great that agents were much dissatisfied because of their small quotas. But the Imperials of 1880 and 1881 did not perform satisfactorily in farmers' hands. In 1882, however, they operated so well that they would harvest flax, the most difficult of all crops to cut. See, #C. Colahan to C. H. McCormick, July 27, and 31, 1880, and Aug. 6, 1881; E. C. Beardsley, Minneapolis, to C. H. McCormick, Jr., Sept. 8, 1880.

[111] L.P.C.B. No. 200 (Mch. 1880), pp. 216, 217; No. 201, p. 633, the Co. to R. Newton, Louisville, Ky., May 15, 1880.

[112] *Ibid.,* No. 199, p. 703, the Co. to G. T. Wilmot, Emporia, Kansas, Mch. 20, 1880.

Harvest on a "Bonanza" Farm in Dakota Territory

Twenty eight-foot-cut McCormick harvesters and binders, cutting and binding a crop of 3,700 acres (from the catalog of the McCormick Harvesting Machine Company, 1884)

it!" [113] The twine-binders of Wood and Osborne were the two most feared that season, although the McCormicks professed that each was experimenting at the farmers' expense and that neither had a practical machine.[114] They urged that wire was cheaper than twine and that no cord-binder yet invented could tie sheaves as tightly as wire could do.[115]

In other words, the company endeavored through their agents to quiet the rising demand for twine-binders until they were ready to take advantage of it. To a degree they were successful, since their stock of binders was exhausted before the harvest was fairly started,[116] but the twine mania would not down and the machines of Wood and Osborne did good work. By mid-July, the office confidentially admitted that it must fall in line before the next harvest arrived.[117] This decision was

[113] *Ibid.*, No. 196, p. 129, the Co. to E. W. Brooks, Red Wing, Minn., Nov. 21, 1879; No. 198, p. 334, to D. W. Pratt, St. Louis, Mo., Feb. 10, 1880; No. 199, p. 364, to R. Newton, Louisville, Ky., Mch. 11, 1880.

[114] *Ibid.*, No. 199, p. 496, the Co. to D. W. Pratt, East St. Louis, Ill., Mch. 16, 1880; No. 202, p. 45, to E. W. Brooks, Red Wing, Minn., June 6, 1880: "Twine Binders have demonstrated their complete worthlessness all through the South."

[115] *Ibid.*, No. 202, p. 56, the Co. to O. H. Simpson & Co., Boston, May 25, 1880: "Twine must not cost farmers over 18¢ a lb., if it is to compete with wire"; No. 202, pp. 108-109, to E. W. Brooks, Red Wing, Minn., May 26, 1880. ‡C. A. Spring, Jr., to C. H. McCormick, Jr., Oct. 5, 1880, and to ‡C. H. McCormick, Oct. 5, 1880. The wire needed to bind an acre of grain cost between forty and fifty cents, as a rule.

[116] *Ibid.*, No. 201, p. 412, the Co. to E. W. Brooks, Red Wing, Minn., May 8, 1880; p. 563, to D. B. Heller, Dallas, Texas, May 12, 1880; No. 202, p. 738, to M. T. Grattan Preston, Minn., June 11, 1880: "The recoil from string to wire demand, is something we were not prepared to meet, and there is wailing and gnashing of teeth among the poor dupes who believed all that Osborne & others promised. There never was a greater boom for Wire Binders than just now, and when hereafter some one does make a good Twine Binder, the people will be afraid of it for some time."

[117] ‡C. A. Spring, Jr., to C. H. McCormick, July 26, 1880. L.P.C.B. No. 205, p. 106, W. J. Hanna to C. H. McCormick, Jr., Aug. 9, 1880: "The Gen'l Agts., Local Agents and the farming public generally seem alike infected with a perfect mania for Twine Binders, and prophesy all sorts of evil, if we do not this Fall show our hands in this matter."

made with great reluctance because the McCormick wire-binder had no peer of its kind, and to discard it before perfecting an equally good twine machine spelled disaster.[118] Due to the unsatisfactory results of its season-long experiments in the field with cord-tying mechanisms devised by its own experts, the firm was obliged, as has already been mentioned, to take license under the patents of Gorham and Appleby.[119] By the next May the McCormicks had added their own improvements to the twine-binder and were ready to match it against any on the market.[120]

It cuts your wheat and binds it good,
And leaves behind the "Marsh" and "Wood,"
Although they've done the best they could,
"The McCormick's Still Ahead." [121]

[118] *Ibid.*, No. 205, pp. 273-274, W. J. Hanna to C. H. McCormick, Jr., Aug. 16, 1880; p. 304, to R. Newton, Louisville, Ky., Aug. 18, 1880: "It won't do for us to rush pell-mell into this Twine business all at once with none of our agents instructed in its use or management. We must go slow if we would go sure, and by every means in our power we must aim to maintain the paramount supremacy of our Wire Binder."

[119] *Supra,* Chap. XIII, p. 559. "Chatfield (Minn.) Democrat," Aug. 7, 1880; "Fargo (Dak. Terr.) Daily Argus," Aug. 25, 1880. L.P.C.B. No. 200, p. 505, telegram of Co. to D. B. Heller, Dallas, Texas, Apr. 13, 1880; No. 202, p. 541, the Co. to R. Newton, Louisville, Ky., June 7, 1880: "We are confident we have the best knot tier, but our compression mechanism is unsatisfactory." Letters to C. H. McCormick from ‡C. Colahan, Aug. 4, 1880, ‡C. A. Spring, Jr., Aug. 1, 1880, and from C. H. McCormick, Jr., Aug. 16, 1880: "We have been too inattentive of our competitors' machines heretofore, and look at them only when we find we are falling behind." Apparently the poor performance of McCormick's eight experimental twine-binders in the late summer of 1880 was due more to their careless construction than to any fault in mechanical principle.

[120] The McCormick Co. instructed its agents to call its machine the McCormick twine-binder, not the "Appleby." L.P.C.B. No. 220, p. 732, the Co. to W. J. Van Hoesen, Macomb, Ill., Feb. 7, 1882; No. 221, p. 532, to W. Varcoe, Mineral Point, Wis., Mch. 7, 1882. Hitherto, it had called its binder an "Appleby." See, *ibid.*, No. 210, p. 324, to R. Newton, Louisville, Ky., Feb. 17, 1881, and No. 215, pp. 189-190, to S. B. Town, Quincy, Ill., June 22, 1881.

[121] Poster of the McCormick Harv. Mach. Co., June 1, 1882.

Even in the harvest of 1881 they preferred to push the wire-binder more strongly than twine, but before the season was over, although they cleared out almost their entire stock, they were convinced that its day was done.[122] Thereafter, they gave up its manufacture altogether and by 1883 were ready to sell the few still on hand for almost any price that a farmer would offer.[123] Thus an excellent machine was virtually obsolete four years after it had pleased grain-growers more than any harvesting implement built by the firm up to that time. No better illustration can be cited of the rapid progress of invention in the agricultural machinery industry.

Manila was found to be the most satisfactory material to use for twine. Not only was it somewhat cheaper than hemp, but it was lighter, more even in quality, and better resisted heat and dampness.[124] With a tensile strength of from sixty

[122] The McCormick Co. in this harvest tried to keep the price of twine at a high figure so as to induce farmers to favor wire-binders. Agents were ordered to sell a twine-binder to a purchaser, only if he would not buy a wire-binder. The latter was warranted to be the best on the market, while the former was guaranteed to be as good as any make of twine-binder, but not as good as the wire-binder. The McCormicks sold about 3000 wire-binders and 5500 twine-binders. Their supply of the former was exhausted by June 1, 1881. L.P.C.B. No. 207, pp. 504-06; No. 208, p. 202; No. 209, p. 715; No. 210, p. 828, and No. 213, p. 518, the Co. to M. Sheehan, Fargo, Nov. 10, 1880, E. W. Brooks, Red Wing, Minn., Dec. 6, 1880, J. E. Ward & Co., N. Y., Jan. 29, 1881, F. Craycroft, Sedalia, Mo., Mch. 8, 1881, and to H. R. Gould, Omaha, Neb., May 4, 1881.

[123] Ibid., No. 230, p. 138, the Co. to G. J. Wilmot, St. Joseph, Mo., Jan. 8, 1883, No. 231, p. 18, to N. B. Fulmer, Red Wing, Minn., Feb. 17, 1883. Efforts to dispose of the 200 or 300 remaining wire-binders in the 1883 harvest were not wholly successful, and the Co. doubted whether it could ever sell the balance. Of course, wire had to be carried in stock for about a decade after the manufacture of wire-binders ceased in 1881. The Co. sold 2420 tons of wire in 1883, as compared with 3400 tons in 1880.

[124] Supra, Chap. XIII, ftn. 55. Ibid., No. 205, p. 714, telegram to C. A. Spring, Jr., to W. R. Baker, Sept. 3, 1880; No. 208, p. 22, the Co. to Kentucky River Mills, Frankfort, Ky., Nov. 29, 1880; No. 223, p. 77, to E. H. Everett, Kalamazoo, Mich., Apr. 21, 1882. By 1883, hemp twine had been improved, but because it deteriorated rapidly it had to be used in the same year that it was manufactured.

to seventy-five pounds, it averaged about thirty feet to a pound. It was spooled in four-pound balls and a dozen of these were baled in gunny-sacking for shipment. In 1880 the Mc-Cormicks purchased it from the Elizabethport (N. J.) Steam Cordage Company for fourteen cents a pound and the freight charge to Chicago. They retailed it for eighteen cents a pound, and because they lost the interest on the large sum they had to pay to the manufacturer upon delivery, their margin of profit from its sale was small.[125] Since half manila, half sisal twine could be sold to the farmers at about two cents a pound cheaper than pure manila, it was preferred by them.[126] Consequently the McCormicks were forced to shift to this type in 1883, although they insisted that because manila averaged considerably more feet to the pound it was in reality cheaper than the mixed variety.[127] By 1882 cordage companies had advanced their price to fifteen cents per pound, and Wood, Deering, and the McCormicks agreed to charge farmers twenty cents, or seventeen cents cash. It was generally estimated that

---

[125] *Ibid.*, No. 212, p. 830, the Co. to Elizabethport Steam Cordage Co., Apr. 13, 1881, and No. 213, pp. 345, 362, telegram and letter to it, Apr. 27, 28, 1881. Contracts for twine for 1881 show that it was bought for about 14¢ a lb. The retail price to farmers was 18¢ plus freight from Chicago; No. 207, pp. 690, 736, the Co. to John Boute's Sons, Cincinnati, O., Nov. 20, 1880, and to Elizabethport Steam Cordage Co., N. Y., Nov. 22, 1880. McCormick Co. Catalog for 1881. For 1881, the balls were packed in boxes, rather than bales, but farmers protested against the cost of, and the freight charge on, the boxes. The Co. thenceforward used bales. They cost 36¢ and the farmers were expected to pay for them.

[126] ‡C. A. Spring, Jr., to C. H. McCormick, July 31, 1880. The Deering Co. used single ply manila in 1880, averaging 600 ft. to the lb.; the Mc-Cormicks' 3-ply manila, averaging 800 ft. to the lb., and mixed sisal and manila, 625 ft. The Wood Co. also used manila. Warder, Bushnell, & Glessner Co's. Catalog for 1881 stated that with the "Champion" twine-binder any cord strong enough could be used; "thin or thick, even or knotty, dry string or tarred rope." This was most probably "just talk."

[127] L.P.C.B. No. 221, p. 120, the Co. to Elizabethport Steam Cordage Co., Feb. 20, 1882; p. 417, to E. C. Beardsley, Minneapolis, Mch. 2, 1882; No. 226, p. 349, to Pearson Cordage Co., Boston, July 22, 1882; No. 229, p. 378, to H. S. Burrell, N. Y., Dec. 11, 1882.

wire as a binding material was about five cents per acre cheaper than twine.[128]

Bits of wire had been swallowed by cattle to their injury, and now farmers grumbled because crickets, mice, and grasshoppers ate the twine. For this problem the manufacturer had no solution, but at least the millers ceased their complaints. The twine was steeped in oil, and because much of this evaporated, a ball would often not weigh four pounds when it reached the purchaser.[129] Therefore he had still another reason to protest. "This is a rather knotty question to solve," wrote a clerk in the Chicago office in 1882, "and the only remedy we could suggest at the present time is to adopt Jay Gould's plan, i.e., water your stock. If you put a few pails of water on it before it is weighed, we thing it will hold out." [130] After making tests at the factory, however, it was discovered that three quarts of oil to twelve balls of twine, rather than a gallon or more as hitherto used, would be sufficient to keep the cord pliable and tough.[131] Judging from silence of the records, this change removed all difficulties.

[128] In making its season's purchase of binding material, the McCormick Co. estimated 400 lbs. of wire for each wire-binder and 200 lbs. of twine for each twine-binder. However, they sold 166 lbs. of twine for each twine-binder in 1882, and 141 in 1883. Estimates of the comparative need per acre of wire and twine vary, but the proportion was usually given as 1½ lbs. of twine to 2½ lbs. of wire. The price of wire tended downward between 1880 and 1884 and twine cost about twice as much a lb. as wire. For example, in 1882 the McCormicks sold wire for 10½¢ a lb. and twine for 20¢.

[129] L.P.C.B. No. 221, p. 448, the Co. to S. Sunday, Franklin Grove, Ill., Mch. 3, 1882; No. 224, pp. 444-445, to S. B. Town, Bloomington, Ill., June 5, 1882; No. 235, p. 504, to W. N. Baker, Baltimore, July 16, 1883. In 1881 the cordage manufacturers placed each ball of twine in a paper-bag to prevent the oil from evaporating, but the farmers complained that the bag was weighed with the twine and they had to pay for it.

[130] Ibid., No. 225, E. K. Butler to E. C. Beardsley, Minneapolis, Minn., July 3, 1882.

[131] Ibid., No. 228, pp. 91, 412, the Co. to Elizabethport Steam Cordage Co., N. Y., Oct. 6 and 25, 1882; p. 190, to A. E. Mayer, Columbus, O., Oct. 11, 1882; No. 238, p. 108, to M. Sheehan, Fargo, Oct. 24, 1883: "Most manufacturers put 3 gals. of oil on a bale of twine. We only allow 3 quarts to be used on this amount."

The McCormicks sold about 48,000 machines in 1883.[132] They announced in their advertisements that if these implements, with the teams which drew them, were each allowed a space of twenty-five feet, they would make a parade two hundred and twenty-seven miles long: "the grandest army of all the ages, and bound on the grandest mission—peace." They dispensed enough wire and twine each season to encircle the earth over thirty-five times, long enough, in fact, to keep a locomotive going ahead day and night at twenty miles an hour for over five years to travel the distance from one end to the other.[133] To complete this large number of implements, the factory was obliged to finish over two hundred every working day for nine months, and shipments had to begin early in the new year, both because the space at the plant was too small to accommodate them, and in order to avoid the freight congestion which always occurred in the late spring.[134]

In 1883, there were approximately seventy-seven thousand twine-binders made in the United States by about twenty-five

[132] Of the 46,660 machines sold by the McCormick Co. in 1882, 14,000 were twine-binders. Deering made almost as many for that harvest, Wood, 8000, and Osborne, 5,000. *Ibid.*, No. 227, p. 237, the Co. to E. H. Everett, Kalamazoo, Mich., Aug. 28, 1882: "When we look back and see that we have made and shipped out nearly forty-eight thousand complete machines, it almost staggers us, even."

[133] "The Interior," Dec. 14, 1882, p. 4: "The Farm Implement and Country Hardware Trade," Apr. 30, 1884, p. 2.

[134] ♯C. A. Spring, Jr., to C. H. McCormick, Jr., Nov. 14, 1881. L.P.C.B. No. 204, pp. 24, 515, the Co. to F. H. Matthews, Youngstown, O., July 10, 1880, and to F. Craycroft, Sedalia, Mo., July 24, 1880; No. 212, p. 580, to E. W. Brooks, Red Wing, Minn., Apr. 1, 1881; No. 213, p. 186, to A. E. Mayer, Columbus, O., Apr. 22, 1881; No. 213, p. 641, to R. Newton, Louisville, Ky., May 7, 1881. Due to a switchmen's strike in Chicago for wages of $3 a day, "We have stacks and stacks of machs. of all kinds and don't know what to do with them. . . . Neither men nor companies will give in and we and the public suffer." The strike began May 1 and ended May 17th, when the workmen yielded. *Ibid.*, ♯216, p. 635, the Co. to G. Brewster, Mankato, Minn., Aug. 4, 1881: "We are disgusted with all railroads. Freight congestion will never be relieved until they double track their roads."

firms.[135] Of this total, McCormick and Deering sold nearly thirty thousand, and if to this number is added the output of three or four other large manufacturers, the unimportance of three-fourths of these factories to the industry as a whole is at once made clear. Although the demand for binders showed no sign of abating, the price-cutting war between these firms had made it possible for a farmer to purchase a machine for about $75 less in 1883 than in 1880.[136] Several leading manufacturers, and particularly D. M. Osborne, believed that the producers of harvesting implements were foolishly throwing away a glorious opportunity to make larger profits. Since they could reach an understanding about the price for which twine should be sold,[137] why could they not fix the retail price of binders, or perhaps go so far as to pool all their patents?[138] This had

[135] #C. Colahan to C. H. McCormick, May 18, 1883. The McCormicks sold 15,000 twine-binders in 1883 and about 18,000 in 1884.

[136] A 6 ft. harv.-binder sold for $300 in 1880 and for as low as $200 or $210 in 1883 and 1884, although $230 was the more usual price. #C. H. McCormick, Jr., to C. H. McCormick, Oct. 21, 1882: We must reduce prices next year, although the opposition will doubtless sell for $10 or $15 less than any figure we set.

[137] On twine-price agreements, see, L.P.C.B. No. 218, p. 663, the Co. to G. Esterly & Son, White Water, Wis., Nov. 7, 1881; No. 219, p. 656, to S. B. Town, Bloomington, Ill., Dec. 20, 1881; No. 229, p. 77, to D. M. Osborne, Auburn, N. Y., Nov. 22, 1882.

[138] Ibid., No. 228, pp. 510, 797, the Co. to J. F. Utley, Sterling, Ill., Oct. 30, 1882, and to G. Esterly & Son, White Water, Wis., Nov. 14, 1882. A convention of binder manufacturers met at Cleveland in Nov., and at Chicago in Jan., 1883. W. J. Hanna represented the McCormick Co. at Cleveland. There a schedule of prices was drawn up, or at least the manufacturers agreed upon the minimum sum that each sale must net them after paying the commission of the agent. Ibid., No. 232, p. 627, No. 233, p. 772, the Co. to Warder, Bushnell and Glessner, Apr. 30 and June 7, 1883; No. 246, p. 286, to Esterly Harvesting Mach. Co., White Water, Wis., Nov. 7, 1884: "There was a time when farmers would go to fairs and take special pains to see Self-Binding Harvesters, as they were a new thing, but those days are past. . . . They go [now] as a rule to have a good time . . . and . . . are more interested in the trotting matches which are the great feature of the fairs." #C. Colahan to C. H. McCormick, Aug. 22, 27, 1883.

been an unattainable objective for twenty years, but in the autumn of 1883 it was sought after with unusual vigor.

Meetings were held in Chicago and at Niagara Falls in August and September.[139] Cyrus McCormick, Jr., was one of a committee of five to frame resolutions for consideration by the general meeting. In his opinion there was no use to set prices unless each manufacturer were limited in the number of implements that he could build.[140] Informal agreements of previous years had come to naught because the output of machines of a single type had exceeded the demand for them, and in consequence each maker fought with all of his rivals to clear out his own stock. To assign quotas, however, required first of all that an estimate should be made of the country-wide demand for binders in 1884. This was naturally most difficult to do, but when 65,000 were decided upon, it was found that the total number of binders that all the builders wished to turn out was 105,000. In other words, no manufacturer was ready to limit his output to the number assigned him on the schedule.[141]

Granted, however, that further discussion of this matter would lead to a compromise acceptable to all, there was the still more difficult problem of devising a method of compelling a recalcitrant producer to abide by his pledge. The only suggestion seriously advanced was that the binder manufacturers

[139] L.P.C.B. No. 236, pp. 194, 460, the Co. to G. Esterly, White Water, Wis., Aug. 4, 15, 1883. C. H. McCormick, Jr., to C. H. McCormick, Aug. 11, 1883. The makers wished to fix the price of a 6 ft. H.B. @ $240, 5% off for cash.

[140] ‡C. H. McCormick, Jr., to C. H. McCormick, Aug. 25, 29, 1883; ‡D. M. Osborne to C. H. McCormick, Jr., Aug. 29, 1883. C. H. McCormick wished to have the committee meet with him at Richfield Springs, N. Y., but Osborne declined. ‡C. H. McCormick's telegram to C. H. McCormick, Jr., Sept. 5, 1883.

[141] ‡C. H. McCormick, Jr., to C. H. McCormick, Sept. 13, 1883. L.P.C.B. No. 237, p. 70, C. H. McCormick, Jr., to D. M. Osborne, Sept. 7, 1883. If the schedule had gone into effect, the McCormick Co. would have been obliged to curtail its binder output from about 15,000 to 10,000.

should form an association and appoint a commissioner with power to investigate charges, assess damages for violations of the agreement, and render decisions from which there should be no appeal. But could this official's impartiality be relied upon, and would he be able during the rush of a harvest-season to force a manufacturer to do his will in time to prevent serious losses to other producers who were obeying the rules? [142] Prices of binders were tentatively agreed upon, and it was decided that no commission of over twenty per cent should be given to an agent. This arrangement, however, could hardly be satisfactory, since the big "Champion" firms did not pay agency commissions but wholesaled their machines to their salesmen and cared not a whit what they charged the farmer.[143]

In view of all these difficult questions, Cyrus McCormick, Jr., refused to sign the completed treaty, and the effort to cooperate therefore failed.[144] The Niagara meeting dissolved after adopting the meaningless resolution that the binder-makers would keep up prices in 1884, although no definite figures were stipulated. McCormick's action was doubtless conditioned in large degree by the opposition of his parents to the proposed plan.[145] Mrs. McCormick reminded him that har-

[142] ‡C. H. McCormick, Jr., to C. H. McCormick, Sept. 8, 1883, and to Nettie F. McCormick, Sept. 10, 1883.

[143] ‡E. K. Butler, to C. H. McCormick, Jr., Sept. 17, 1883.

[144] L.P.C.B. No. 237, p. 571, C. H. McCormick (by C. H. McCormick, Jr.), to D. M. Osborne, Sept. 19, 1883; No. 238, p. 16, the Co. to G. Esterly & Son, White Water, Wis., Oct. 18, 1883: "Our recent experience in conventions has satisfied us that we were not a success in managing other people's business." In 1884, particularly, trouble was caused by agents persuading farmers to buy from them at lower rates, after they had already given their orders to rival salesmen. Ibid., No. 242, p. 827, the Co. to W. Billing, Denver, Colo., June 3, 1884.

[145] C. H. McCormick, Jr., MSS. Book "B," Nettie F. McCormick to C. H. McCormick, Jr., Aug. 20, 1883, and Sept. 11, 1883; L.P.C.B. No. 237, p. 201, the Co. to J. B. Heywood, Indianapolis, Ind., Sept. 14, 1883; No. 246, p. 457, to W. Westerman, St. Cloud, Minn., Nov. 25, 1884. Nettie F. Mc-

vesting machinery builders were probably no more able to carry out contracts of this nature than were the railroad men who broke the many they made. "I know that when I feel the question is dropped by us . . . I have peace of mind," she continued, "and when the question is agitated as to bringing in outside people—Reaper people or anyone else—I am troubled and have anxious hours." [146]

During these years, while the McCormick Company was enlarging its plant, reforming its mode of operations in office, factory, and field, and changing the character of its implements to include the newest types of harvesting machinery, it also manifested for the first time a keen interest in its history. Willingness to face forward and to discard outmoded machines and business practices was necessary for survival in a bitterly competitive industry. But to look backward was also a key to success. The past furnished inspiration, and its study revealed mistakes which could be avoided in the future. More than material considerations, however, underlay the determination of Cyrus McCormick, Jr., to outdistance all competitors and to know more intimately the story of his father's early career. "McCormick" stood for harvesting machinery the world over, and the name brought responsibility as well as distinction to those who bore it. Particularly was this true in the case of the namesake and eldest son of the founder. The mantle of authority had fallen upon his shoulders. Duty and family pride required that the name and the business should not suffer under his leadership.

Unlike his father, Cyrus McCormick, Jr., kept a diary, both as an aid to his memory and because he believed that he was participating in events of more than passing importance. The

Cormick to E. K. Butler, Sept. 11, 1883. A meeting of binder manufacturers held in Chicago in Nov., 1884, was equally futile.

[146] C. H. McCormick, Jr., MSS., Book "B," Nettie F. McCormick to C. H. McCormick, Jr., Aug. 23 and Sept. 6, 1883.

contrast between the old and the new fascinated him, and stories about the early days of the reaper added to the appeal of the periodical newspaper published by the firm. The advanced age of several men who had been long in McCormick's employ gave warning that they should write down their memories of the past before it was too late. At a time when harvesters and automatic binders, unassociated in their origin with the McCormick name, were becoming standard in the grain-fields everywhere, it was well to let the world know that these new implements were based upon the pioneer work of Cyrus McCormick.[147] Questions raised by his brother and others concerning the true story of the invention of the reaper could also be best answered from historical data. World's fairs, magazine articles, and mechanical dictionaries, like the one compiled by Edward H. Knight, were making the people of the United States aware of their contributions to, and dependence upon, applied science. McCormick had promoted the development of both agriculture and manufacturing which together comprised much of the economic life of America. His reaper had played an important part in the agricultural revolution and he had laid the foundation and kept in the forefront of a large industry. He desired the recognition that was his due, and history could furnish the proof of his merit.

Because machine designs changed so rapidly and farmers sometimes worked their reapers for twenty years or more, the factory as early as 1859 had "a little museum," containing duplicates of every type of implement that it had manufactured. Helped by these, the clerks could identify at once the size and shape of the spare part ordered by the owner of an old machine. Although the purpose of this collection was emi-

[147] C. H. McCormick to G. S. Bowen, May 23, 1878: "The leading plans of the self binding part of these machines were invented by others, while they have been brought to the present state of practical utility, economy & adaptation to public wants in my works & by their operation in the field by men engaged with me in my business."

nently a practical one, its destruction by the Fire of 1871 was later regretted by Cyrus McCormick, Jr., chiefly because of its historical significance. He began a search for old implements, newspaper and magazine articles, posters, pamphlets, and handbills, pertinent to the early days of the industry.[148] The care with which his father and mother had preserved copies of much of their correspondence, and seemingly filed away every printed and written document that came to their desks, was a most valuable foundation of materials to build upon.

Cyrus McCormick's interest in his early career increased as the years advanced. By 1880 he liked to sit in his easy-chair and recall the days at "Walnut Grove," and his travels far and wide throughout the Middle States and the Northwest, spreading the gospel of his reaper. Occasionally, when the mood for reminiscence was strong upon him, he wrote briefly of his youth or talked while his eldest son took notes on what he said. "Walnut Grove" in the Valley of Virginia was acquired in 1882 as a memorial to be cherished by the family forever. Still there, were the brick house that had been home to Cyrus McCormick for almost twenty-five years, the workshop with some of the same tools he had used to fashion the first reaper, and the fields where he had convinced doubting neighbors that the age-long search for a way to cut grain by horse-power was at last ended. He now had its five hundred acres of rolling land carefully surveyed, drained, and fenced. A new barn

---

[148] L.P.C.B. No. 233, p. 118, 355, the Co. to J. Zook, Unionville, Ia., May 15, 1883, and to S. A. Cockayne, Moundsville, W. Va., May 24, 1883; No. 236, pp. 841, 842, to H. O. Goodrich, Jerseyville, Ill., Sept. 4, 1883, and to A. E. Mayer, Columbus, O., Sept. 4, 1883; No. 237, p. 506, to E. Brammall, Benton Harbor, Mich., Oct. 1, 1883; No. 238, pp. 52, 793; No. 241, p. 608, to A. E. Mayer, Columbus, O., Oct. 22, Dec. 6, 1883, and Apr. 16, 1884; No. 245, p. 164, to the Editor, "Magazine of American History," New York, N. Y., Sept. 5, 1884; No. 246, pp. 479, 505, 518, to R. Newton, Louisville, Ky., Nov. 26 and 29, 1884, and to P. R. Frear, Germantown, Pa., Nov. 28, 1884.

was erected and the house was repaired and partially refurnished. It was hoped that the tenant would make the property pay its own way, and would reflect in his work upon it some of the affection with which it was regarded by its owner.[149]

The fiftieth anniversary of the invention of the reaper quickened the desire of the family and the firm to reconstruct the story of the formative period. A poster at this time, portraying the first trial of the McCormick machine, illustrates the pride of the company in its past. Another depicted a reaper on the field of Gettysburg with the contending armies surging about it. It aroused only a mild protest from one southern agent and symbolized the close of the Reconstruction Period.[150] A half-century of business life in young America conferred a title of respectability which upstart manufacturers could only envy. These lithographs were designed to impress this fact upon all who saw them. To some they were also a reminder that Cyrus McCormick was growing old.

[149] W. T. Rush, Staunton, Va., to C. A. Spring, Jr., July 20, 1882; J. D. McGuffin, Steele's Tavern, Va., to C. A. Spring, Jr., Aug. 8, 1882; ‡C. H. McCormick, Jr., to C. H. McCormick, Oct. 28, 1882; R. S. McCormick, St. Louis, Mo., to C. H. McCormick, Nov. 5 and 11, 1882. "Walnut Grove" was the property of R. S. and W. G. McCormick, who had inherited it from their father, Wm. S. McCormick. The home farm contained 518 acres and was valued at $30 or $35 an acre. R. S. McCormick owed C. H. McCormick a large sum of money and released "Walnut Grove" to him in Nov., 1882, in return for a reduction of this debt by the amount of $17,064.

[150] These were the showbills of 1883 and 1884.

CHAPTER XVII

CYRUS McCORMICK AT HOME

ALTHOUGH business was life to Cyrus McCormick, and he was unhappy only when illness kept him from being up and doing, he often remarked that his ceaseless activity denied him the enjoyment of a real home.[1] Even in his old age, after a house altogether to his liking had been built in Chicago, his search for better health compelled him to be away from the city a large part of each year. During the half-century following his first long absence from "Walnut Grove" in 1831 as a salesman of his father's hemp-breaks, he traveled many thousands of miles, but there is no record of a journey made for pleasure alone.[2] In his opinion, a vacation meant a change of place for work, and not an opportunity to rest.

Even his wedding trip in 1858 was a roundabout excursion from Chicago to Washington where important patent issues were pending. There, in the Maynard House, he first lived with his bride, and his apartment was an office as much as a home.[3] Mrs. McCormick was soon taking the air in her carriage on

[1] Letters of C. H. McCormick to T. J. Massie, Aug. 6, 1866, H. Chrisman, Apr. 27, 1877, D. L. Moody, Feb. 23, 1881, and to Mrs. Massie, May 4, 1869: "I suppose there are few men in the Country so much pressed in their business matters as I have been for some time."

[2] "Hutchinson," I, pp. 38-41.

[3] MS. Recollections of Sarah Kearney, a servant of the McCormicks in Washington. They lived also at Brown's Hotel there for awhile. At this time, Mr. and Mrs. McCormick owned a cottage and a lot on the Potomac at Point Lookout, Md. These were sold in Oct., 1870, for $50. ‡L.P.C.B. No. 1, 2nd ser., p 298, C. H. McCormick to H. G. Faut, Oct. 21 and 27, 1870.

736

pleasant afternoons with the wife of the Commissioner of Patents.[4] Thus she was introduced to her husband's affairs and found them fascinating. Thereafter, amid the daily whirl of patents, reapers, and real estate, she frequently expressed a longing for settled domestic life, but she was always unable, and perhaps unwilling, to banish business from her fireside.[5]

By 1874 she was the mother of five children, and two others had died in their infancy. Although nurses and governesses assisted in their upbringing she usually shared a portion of each day with them. Friends warned her that the double strain of business and home duties would undermine her health,[6] but it may be doubted whether her increasing deafness after 1868 or her need for eye-glasses a decade later could be charged to her strenuous routine.[7] Unlike her husband, she knew how to

[4] C. H. McCormick to W. S. McCormick, Apr. 24, 1858.

[5] C. H. McCormick, Jr., MSS. Book "B," Nettie F. McCormick to C. H. McCormick, Jr., July 18 and 26, 1871: "I am helping him [C. H. Mc-Cormick] constantly and he thinks he could not get on in his business without me." *Ibid.*, N. F. McCormick to C. H. McCormick, Jr., July 11 (probably a mistake for Dec. 11), 1877: "Then I come home and find a visitor to dinner . . . and three people on business . . . a telegram from papa that needs attention, a letter on business to send to Mr. Matthews . . . then a few clothes to send away to persons who need them now if they need them at all, and then some attention to the children." *Ibid.*, N. F. McCormick to C. H. McCormick, Jr., July 29, 1877: "Well, I am accustomed to plans being upset, or rather to have *no plans.*" N. F. to C. H. McCormick, Aug. 28, 1878: "The habits of business, always, and at all times & in all places, leaves [*sic*] little room for any family life, such as I see it in well regulated families; or for good sleeping, or eating in quiet—or with any regularity as to the family having any regard for meeting each other at any regular times around the family board."

[6] Mary A. to Nettie F. McCormick, Aug. 3, 1870, Sept. 3, and Oct. 2, 1877. The children of Mr. and Mrs. McCormick, besides those already mentioned in this narrative, were, Anita, b. July 4, 1866; Alice, b. May 15, 1870, and d. Jan. 25, 1871; Harold Fowler, b. May 2, 1872; and Stanley Robert, b. Nov. 2, 1874.

[7] C. H. McCormick, Jr., MSS. Book "B," N. F. McCormick to C. H. McCormick, Jr., Sept. 11, 1878. J. M. McCue, Afton, Va., to J. D. Davidson, Apr. 8, 1881. In this letter McCue called Mrs. McCormick "quite deaf." Shortly thereafter she purchased an ear-phone, and her hearing somewhat

relax, and she found rest in good books, works of art, the theater, and European travel. He was nearly twenty-five years her senior, but she was to outlive him by almost forty years.

Inability to manage his varied interests effectively from a single center chiefly explains why McCormick was so long denied a home. Chicago was an ideal location for his factory, but his financial affairs focused in New York and his legal business in Washington. After his brothers were entrusted with the active control of manufacturing the inventor spent much of his time in the two eastern cities and in the promotion of his market abroad. Two residences awaited him in the 'sixties whenever he wished to live in Chicago. On the north side of the city he also owned a half-block of land which he refused to sell in spite of the heavy taxes, seemingly hoping that the day would eventually come when he could build there the home of his dreams. This big lot on Rush Street was flanked on one side by the residence of Isaac N. Arnold, able supporter of Lincoln and member of Congress. The friendship of McCormick and Arnold was sometimes strained when the congressman's cow and horse grazed on the inventor's grass, or when boys disturbed the exclusive neighborhood by making merry on the vacant lot with marbles or ball.[8] To be rid of this nuisance McCormick fringed his common with elms and cotton-woods and enclosed it with a board-fence. After the improved during the next year. See, C. H. McCormick, Jr., MSS. Book "D," Memoir of N. F. McCormick by Dr. J. G. McClure. ‡C. H. Mc-Cormick, Jr., to N. F. McCormick, Mch. 12, 1883. ‡C. H. McCormick to Dr. S. B. Hartnett, St. Louis, May 10, 1883, and Dr. Hartnett's replies of May 12 and 20. He diagnosed Mrs. McCormick's ear trouble as "chronic aural catarrh." Apparently her hearing was largely restored by 1885. See, C. H. McCormick, Jr., MSS. Book "B," Helen B. Potts to N. F. Mc-Cormick, May 24, 1885.

[8] L. J. to C. H. McCormick, May 30, 1865; C. A. Spring, Jr., to C. H. McCormick, June 23 and 29, 1866, ‡Apr. 9 and 29, 1867, ‡May 19, 1869, and ‡Apr. 12, 1871. L.P.C.B. No. 97, p. 657, No. 98, p. 479, C. A. Spring, Jr., to I. N. Arnold, Apr. 20, and May 14, 1867; No. 103, p. 666, to J. R. Leesbey, Mch. 21, 1868; No. 119, p. 840, to C. H. McCormick, May 13, 1870.

Great Fire of 1871 destroyed these improvements he had it refenced, since near-by residents complained anew that the place was frequented on Sundays by "hoodlums from the 'sands.' " By then the property was valued at over $65,000.[9]

In his manner of living the Cyrus McCormick of the mid-1850's, who received business men in his hotel bedroom and bargained with them while he shaved,[10] was a far cry from the Chevalier of the Legion of Honor a dozen years later established in his richly furnished residence on lower Fifth Avenue, New York, with a ménage that cost him about $25,-000 annually.[11] Here Horace Greeley often dropped in before breakfast to talk of the affairs of the day. Samuel J. Tilden, Horace White, Cyrus Field, J. Gordon Bennett, S. L. M. Barlow, Roger Pryor, and others of the great or near-great who lived about Gramercy Park knew his drawing-room well. Old friends from Virginia or their children, eager to see the metropolis, enjoyed his hospitality for weeks at a time. Maids, coachmen, governesses, cooks, and valets did his bidding, and not far from his door was his rented stable of seven stalls with ample room for his landau and sleigh.[12] A late-afternoon drive

[9] Letters to C. H. of L. J. McCormick, Mch. 16, 1871; I. N. Arnold, Jan. 6, 11, Apr. 8, and May 8, 1873, and of H. W. King, June 3, 1873. H. W. King to C. A. Spring, Jr., June 11, 1873. L.P.C.B. No. 142, p. 409, C. A. Spring, Jr., to H. W. King, June 14, 1873.

[10] MS. vol., *McCormick Extension Case, Patent of 1845*, testimony of Daniel S. Warner of Beloit, Wis., relating to his call upon McCormick at the Tremont House, Chicago, in 1857. At that time the inventor was clean-shaven but from 1859 until the end of his life he had a full beard.

[11] This estimate is based upon material in account-books and letters in the Nettie F. McCormick Biog. Asso. files.

[12] C. H. McCormick to C. A. Spring, Jr., Apr. 5, 1867, and to S. L. M. Barlow, June 15, 1867. Cyrus H. McCormick to the author, Dec. 10, 1931. A letter of A. M. Hoyt to C. H. McCormick, on Feb. 7, 1867, reveals that Hoyt was gratifying the wish of the inventor to meet Genl. W. T. Sherman. McCormick and Genl. P. H. Sheridan were friends when the latter lived in Chicago in the late 1870's. On Nov. 13, 1879, McCormick helped to welcome Genl. Grant to Chicago. J. D. Davidson to C. H. McCormick, June 6, 1868. ‡C. H. McCormick to R. Pryor, Nov. 11, 1881; G. W. Webb

with Mrs. McCormick in Central Park and dinner at Delmonico's were usual items on his daily calendar of appointments. The Chicago Fire of 1871 brought this New York chapter of his life to an abrupt close.[13]

Mr. and Mrs. McCormick for the next three years were too much occupied with the work of reconstruction in the burned city to give thought to a home for themselves.[14] By 1874 the inconveniences of life in a hotel or in a rented house poorly arranged for the needs of a large family led her to wait no longer upon her husband's initiative. She asked architects to submit plans for a residence to be erected on the Rush Street property.[15] The inventor refused to be hurried, however, maintaining that the choice of a " 'first class,' elegant mansion house needs much thought." Two more years went by before ground was broken for the new home.[16] Thereafter Mr. and Mrs. McCormick, who were often in the East or

to C. H. McCormick, Jr., Dec. 14, 17, 1881; Virginia McCormick to C. H. McCormick, Jr., Dec. 19, 1881.

[13] C. H. McCormick, Jr., MSS. Letter Book "B," Nettie F. McCormick to C. H. McCormick, Jr., July 13, 18, 1871. When business obliged the inventor and his wife to stay in the city during the summer they frequently visited their friends, John C. Lord and Henry Day at Morristown, N. J. The N. Y. residence was sold to S. R. Roe, Highland Falls, N. Y., for $42,500 in 1879, or for but little over half the purchase price of 1866. The decline in value was largely due to "the exodus up town." #E. Ludlow & Co., N. Y. City to C. H. McCormick, Aug. 11, 1879. There are many letters of H. Day to C. H. McCormick in regard to the renting of this house, 1871-78, in the files of the N. F. McCormick Biog. Asso.

[14] Following the fire, Mr. and Mrs. McCormick lived at the St. Caroline's Court Hotel, Chicago, until late 1872. Thereafter for three years they were at 62 N. Sheldon St. From 1875 to 1879 their home was at 363 Superior St.

[15] Nettie F. McCormick to C. Vaux, Mch. 25, 1874; #F. and E. Baumann, Chicago, to C. H. McCormick, Apr. 3, 1874.

[16] C. H. McCormick to C. Vaux, Feb. 25, 1875; Nettie F. McCormick to C. Vaux, Apr. 16, 1874; C. Vaux to N. F. McCormick, Apr. 2, 20, 1874, #Jan. 2, 27, 1875, and to #C. H. McCormick, Mch. 23, 1875. The "Chicago Times," Feb. 21, 1875, p. 2, announced that C. H. McCormick would build a home on his Rush Street lot.

abroad, endeavored by telegraph or cable to direct the smallest details of the construction work. Their eldest son, then seventeen years of age, visited the site each day after his high school classes were over, and kept his parents informed of the progress made by the workmen.[17] Mrs. McCormick's knowledge of practical matters and her assiduous attention to minutiæ are well illustrated by her insistence that broken glass should be mixed with the mortar, and tin cuttings packed around the foundation walls of the stable, in order to keep out the rats. Nothing was too small to escape her notice. By her directions stone guards were set to protect each side of the stable entrance from carriage wheels, the bath-tubs were made of a certain depth, and a small leak in the roof of the tower which capped the new home was repaired in the manner that she prescribed.[18]

Several last-minute alterations in the plans and the difficulty of making decisions upon questions of detail while they were in France, delayed the completion of the residence until early 1879.[19] Although it was then ready for occupancy, several more years went by before Mrs. McCormick was satisfied with the grading and landscaping of the broad lawn, the curve

[17] C. H. McCormick, Jr., to C. H. McCormick, Sept. 18 and 24, 1876. C. H. McCormick, Jr., MSS. Book "B," Nettie F. McCormick to C. H. McCormick, Jr., Sept. 17, 1876. The architects, Cudell & Blumenthal of Chicago, were selected in Mch., 1877, after plans submitted by Olmsted & Vaux of N. Y. had been rejected.

[18] C. H. McCormick, Jr., MSS. Book "B," Nettie F. McCormick to C. H. McCormick, Jr., July 24, Oct. 29, and July 11 (probably a mistake for Dec. 11), 1877; Book "F," N. F. McCormick to C. H. McCormick, Jr., Sept. 2, 1878. N. F. McCormick to the McCormick Co., Oct. 10, 1877. C. A. Spring, Jr., to C. H. McCormick, Aug. 12, 1878. During the mild winter of 1877-78, Mrs. McCormick customarily spent an hour or more each day at the building site.

[19] C. A. Spring, Jr., to C. H. McCormick, Dec. 10, 1878. At this time furniture was moved from 363 Superior St. to the new home. The McCormicks were in France. See also, Spring's letter to C. H. McCormick of Jan. 17, 1879.

of the driveway and the furnishings of the many rooms between the billiard salon in the basement and the music conservatory on the top floor.[20] The total cost was about $175,-
000.[21] If a visitor from the South may be believed, even the
horses, pony, and cow in the barn were surrounded with more
luxury than the state of Virginia could provide for its governor.[22]

Mr. and Mrs. McCormick's hopes of over twenty years
were completely realized in their new home.[23] Their pleasure
was the more keen because of the favorable attention given to
it by the press of Chicago and New York. To have it called
"the chief of the many private residences which have made
Chicago noted as a city where not only solidity and wealth but
genuine taste in art prevails," went far to repay their large
expenditures of time, thought, and money.[24] The architect
found his inspiration in the period of the late Renaissance. If
the exterior aspect of the house does not conform with the
æsthetic standards of to-day, its dignified simplicity at least
has far more appeal than the castellated and gingerbread struc-

[20] C. H. McCormick, Jr., to C. H. McCormick, July 27, 1883; C. H.
McCormick to C. H. McCormick, Jr., July 29, 1883.

[21] C. A. Spring, Jr., to N. F. McCormick, May 30, 1879, and to C. H.
McCormick, Jr., Sept. 11, 1880. When a new home had first been a subject
of discussion, Mrs. McCormick hoped that it would not cost over $75,000.
She then had in mind a two-story brownstone house with a mansard roof.
N. F. McCormick to C. Vaux, Mch. 25, 1874.

[22] J. M. McCue, Afton, Va., to J. D. Davidson, Apr. 8, 1881. The interior
of the barn has been remodeled. Part of it to-day is used as a private garage
and the remainder is the library of the McCormick Historical Association.
A picture of the residence appeared in the "Daily Graphic" (N. Y.), of
Feb. 5, 1883, p. 663.

[23] ‡C. H. McCormick, Jr., to Nettie F. McCormick, June 27, 1879:
"I never saw Papa more pleased." ‡C. H. McCormick, Jr., to N. F. Mc-
Cormick, Dec. 30, 1878, and Jan. 13, 1879. To combine sentences from each
letter: "The woodwork of the new house is simply magnificent, undoubtedly
the finest thing of the kind in the city. . . . Our new House is the grandest
sight I ever saw. I like the Music Room best and the Dining Room next."

[24] "Chicago Daily Tribune," Jan. 1, 1880.

tures which have too often survived from this decade of American life. The matched pair of zinc lions, *couchant,* which the venerable Dr. Plumer searched for in the East at the behest of his friends, have disappeared from the front lawn; [25] the Lake Superior brownstone is badly weathered, but the straight lines, sharp angles, and impressive strength of the building still reflect the character of the inventor.[26]

The "social dedication of the new family residence" was delayed until May, 1880, when Mr. and Mrs. McCormick gave a "Soirée Musicale et Dansante" in honor of their eldest son upon his twenty-first birthday. At this "most notable and elegant society event of the season," the three hundred guests were entertained by a concert of instrumental and vocal music. After playing familiar selections from the compositions of German masters, the orchestra introduced Chicagoans to Goldmark's "Die Ländliche Hochzeit." A Maennerchor sang Scottish ballads, but the voice and charm of Miss Fanny Kellogg were rewarded with the more applause.

Following the recital, the guests were taken by the hydraulic elevator from the conservatory to the first floor of the residence. Here the furnishings surpassed in costliness any hitherto seen in Chicago. The main hall was frescoed after the manner of one of the castles of King Henry IV of France, and the walls of the large dining-room were hung with tapestries dating from his reign. On the ceiling were painted in intricate design the Cross of the Legion of Honor, a reaper,

25 W. S. Plumer, N. Y., to C. H. McCormick, June 5, 1877. In this he wrote that he could get a pair of iron lions, *couchant,* for $140 cash, or zinc ones (right, male, and left, female) *couchant,* for $264.

26 The old home is now the residence of Mr. Harold F. McCormick. Its number is 675 Rush St., although in 1880 it was #135. C. H. McCormick described the building material used as "Lake Superior red sandstone" in a letter to Messrs. Herter & Co., of N. Y., on Mch. 10, 1877. See, #L.P.C.B. of C. H. McCormick, June, 1876-Apr., 1878, p. 46. The stone was furnished by a "Col. Brownell" of Marquette, Mich. See, "Chicago Times," Aug. 6, 1876.

sheaves of grain, bee-hives, and the names of Pomona, Flora, Ceres, and Diana.[27] The furniture of the drawing-room across the hall was of Louis XVI style and its ceiling was done in oils to represent the sky, flowers, and birds. The woodwork throughout the house was especially admired, the rooms being variously finished in walnut, ebony, satinwood, bird's-eye maple, rosewood, and mahogany. If the younger children had not been asleep, the guests might have been shown on an upper floor the school-room and the nursery with "Walter Crane drawings of Mother Goose subjects" on its walls, and the tiles of its fireplace depicting stories from the Bible. The reporters of this "most recherché event" also noted that the residence was heated by steam, that there were vault rooms for the safe-keeping of silver and linens, a telephone cubicle, and an electric burglar-alarm on each of the ground-floor windows.[28]

The emphasis given to music on this occasion, and the profusion of flowers in the wide hall and on the banquet-table, were more revealing expressions of Cyrus McCormick's personality than the deep carpets, the frescoes, and the richly

[27] The McCormick coat-of-arms appeared in a shield over the mantel above the fireplace in the dining-room. #L. Marcotte to C. H. McCormick, May 21, 1878. L. Marcotte, of N. Y. and Paris, had charge of the interior-decorating of both the McCormick residence and the home of Marshall Field. An ink sketch by C. H. McCormick, Jr., of the McCormick arms will be found in #L.P.C.B. of C. H. McCormick, Nov., 1880-May, 1881, p. 88.

[28] This account of the entertainment has been drawn from "The Daily Inter Ocean" and "The Daily Telegraph," both of Chicago, May 25, 1880. The "Telegraph" added, "The toilets of the ladies were something magnificent, and, consequently, far above the intelligence of the male reporter, so the 'Telegraph's' representative, feeling that it would be utter desecration on his part to attempt a description of them, wisely forbore." As an illustration of C. H. McCormick's habit of deliberating long before making a decision, he wrote at least eighteen letters in 1877 asking the advice of prominent Chicagoans who used steam-heat in their homes, before he concluded to install it in his own residence. Electricity as an illuminant probably superseded gas in his home in 1882. See, #Northwestern Electric and Gas-Lighting Co. to C. H. McCormick, Mch. 20, 1882.

Cyrus Hall McCormick's Residence at 675 Rush Street, Chicago

From a photograph by P. B. Greene, Chicago

bound sets of the classics on the shelves of his large library.[29] Although he liked material comforts, *objets d'art* and the classics were concessions to his station in society and evidences of his willingness to conform to the standards of life set by the substantial rich of his generation. He did not surround himself with them in the hope that outsiders would believe that they were essential to his happiness. Mrs. McCormick could appreciate and enjoy them, and it was always his study to give her pleasure. He continued to confine his reading to the Bible, religious magazines, and the newspapers.

Music and flowers, however, had been his delight since boyhood. He had been the precentor of the little Presbyterian meeting-house near "Walnut Grove," and the voice of Miss Nettie Fowler, so it is said, first drew his attention to her as she sang in the choir of a Chicago church. Hymns and folk-songs were his special favorites but he enjoyed instrumental music as well, particularly if it were played on a violin. He learned to bow a fiddle at an early age, and although he used it but little in his later life, he desired to have it always near at hand. Wherever he lived for any considerable period of time, there must be flowers, preferably the old-fashioned varieties to remind him of his mother's garden in the Valley of Virginia.

Thus he was not without sentiment, although he detested sentimentality about any subject.[30] He loved small children and liked to talk to them after lifting them to his knee. "Jo" Anderson, who had been his slave and boyhood companion,

---

[29] In a letter to C. Vaux on Mch. 25, 1874, Mrs. McCormick wrote that the new residence required a large library in order to accommodate the many books of the family. On Apr. 7, 1879, however, she told her eldest son (C. H. McCormick, Jr., MSS. Book "B") to buy whatever volumes he needed for his work at Princeton, and added, "During all these years we have not had many."

[30] C. H. McCormick, Jr., MSS. Book "B," N. F. McCormick to C. H. Cormick, Jr., Oct. 6, 1877.

was assured of a "God bless you" and a gift of money whenever he wrote to "Dear Master" of his wants.[31] Pressure of business and not a feeling of superiority kept him from corresponding with old friends in Virginia. Whenever they talked with him after the Civil War they found him cordial and democratic,[32] but any one who presumed that a chance acquaintanceship in the early days warranted a request for a loan was courteously refused. He was never a "hail-fellow, well met," and he seldom made a social call. Casual acquaintances complained that his manner was cold, imperious, and calculated to inspire awe. Doubtless it was, and even among his close kinsfolk he had his favorites.[33] A fortunate few of his many nieces and nephews could count upon his help when they were in financial trouble, although he sometimes accompanied it with a lecture about sound business practices. His immediate family and his few intimate friends found him good company, able both to enjoy a joke and to laugh heartily.[34] This side of his nature was rarely reflected in his corre-

[31] Mary A. Chapman to N. F. McCormick, Dec. 22, 1870. C. H. McCormick to "Jo" Anderson, Greenville, Va., Jan. 19, 1870, June 16, 1882, and Dec. 21, 1883. "Jo" Anderson to C. H. McCormick, Aug. 13, Nov. 17 and 28, 1879. ‡L.P.C.B. Nov. 1880-May, 1881, p. 3, C. H. McCormick to W. R. Selleck, Nov. 16, 1880.

[32] "Lexington (Va.) Gazette and Citizen," Oct. 8, 1875. C. H. McCormick to J. D. Davidson, Jan. 27, 1881. C. H. McCormick to Mrs. M. V. M. Ligon, Massie's Mills, Va., Feb. 3, 1881: "It makes me feel old and lonesome to note how many of my old Virginia friends are passing on."

[33] See, ‡C. H. McCormick to T. J. Massie, Aug. 6, 1866 and to L. J. McCormick, Apr. 25 and May 6, 1870; Mary Adams to C. H. McCormick, Aug. 9, 1866; ‡C. A. Spring, Jr., to C. H. McCormick, Aug. 9, 1866; N. F. McCormick to C. A. Spring, Jr., June (?), 1869. Letters to N. F. McCormick of Mary C. Shields, Aug. 10, 1870, Henrietta McCormick, Sept. 2, 1870, and Mary A. Chapman, Jan. 9, 1871. ‡L.P.C.B. of C. H. McCormick, Nov., 1873-June, 1876, pp. 42-47, C. H. McCormick to H. Adams, Mch. 18, 1874, and his letter in ‡L.P.C.B. Nov., 1880-May, 1881, pp. 86-87, to Mrs. Amanda Adams.

[34] ‡A. S. Garnett, M.D., to C. H. McCormick, Sept. 6, 1883: "I hope soon to see you on my trip east and enjoy the pleasure of a long chat and

spondence. In controversy his favorite weapon was a bludgeon, not a rapier; his style was heavy and discursive, and the bits of humor which rarely slipped from his pen were barbed. He was not eloquent, but his words carried weight because he was always in earnest.

He was proud of his success and jealous of the honors he had received.[35] If his title of inventor were attacked, his frank statement of his services to agriculture often left the impression that he was inordinately vain. His reaper was one of the dearest interests of his life. He asked justice for himself as he expected to render it to others. The danger of being thought conceited was a minor consideration when he was called upon to defend the very foundation upon which he had built his career for half a century.[36]

Some of his attitudes could hardly be called democratic, although the meaning of this much-abused term is ever in doubt. He was eager for the attention of royalty and members of the nobility when he was abroad.[37] Advantage to his business was always an important consideration when he sought these contacts. He wished one of his daughters presented at the Court of Queen Victoria, and he was proud of his family crest.[38] He and Mrs. McCormick had their portraits painted

a good hearty laugh. There are few people of the present generation who know how to laugh—it seems with the majority to be a hybrid affair that has nothing characteristic. They laugh as if they were afraid of doing something wrong."

[35] ‡L.P.C.B. of C. H. McCormick, Nov., 1880, to May, 1881, pp. 73-74, 142-144, 164, C. H. McCormick to Gov. R. C. McCormick, N. Y., Dec. 22, 1880, and to E. H. Knight, Washington, D. C., Jan. 22, and Feb. 1, 1881.

[36] Memo. of a conversation between C. H. McCormick, W. J. Hanna, and C. H. McCormick, Jr., on Mch. 14, 1882.

[37] W. Hoffman, U. S. Legation, Paris, to C. H. McCormick, Jan. 6, 1868.

[38] J. Welsh, Envoy Extraordinary and U. S. Minister to England, London, to C. H. McCormick, May 8, 1879; P. Lankester, London, to C. H. McCormick, Oct. 30, 1883. Lankester was sending a copy of the McCormick coat-of-arms, properly colored, at a cost of £210.

by several of the best-known artists of their time [39] and he occasionally loaned these pictures for exhibition in museums of art.[40] Even• as a youth he was set apart from his fellows by his careful attire. By 1860 he patronized the best tailors in New York and London, and his scrupulous neatness of dress was a subject of favorable remark by his associates. His Calvinism, when combined with his rapid rise from debt and obscurity to world reputation and a mansion on Fifth Avenue, confirmed him in the belief that the Lord was on his side. Outstanding success, a will to power, the necessity of protecting himself from impostors, and his determination to have all fair-minded men acknowledge the rightfulness of his course, served to temper his democracy.

Success to him did not mean the accumulation of money.

[39] A full-length portrait of Mrs. McCormick was painted by G. P. A. Healy in 1860. See *supra,* p. 8 and the "Chicago Daily News" of Feb. 23, 1935. Erastus D. Palmer of Albany made a marble bust of her in 1866, which he considered "my best" of a woman up to that time. Alexandre Cabanel did separate portraits of Mr. and Mrs. McCormick in 1867. Sir John Watson Gordon of London, just before his death in 1864, finished a portrait of Mr. McCormick. G. P. A. Healy did portraits of him in 1881 and 1883. See, Receipt of Healy for $1250, Jan. 1, 1861; Letters to C. H. McCormick of H. E. Watson, May 29, June 2, 14, 24, 1864; ♯E. D. Palmer, Oct. 4, 1866; ♯S. P. Avery, Dec. 22, 1866; N. F. McCormick, Dec. 5, 1881; G. P. A. Healy, Jan. 16, 1882. Virginia McCormick to C. H. McCormick, Jr., Dec. 16, 1881; C. H. McCormick to C. H. McCormick, Jr., Dec. 21, 1881.

[40] "Chicago Daily Tribune," Dec. 27, 1860, and Jan. 1, 1861. The bust of Mrs. McCormick and the Watson portrait of Mr. McCormick were exhibited at the National Academy of Design in the autumn of 1866, and the inventor was made a life Fellow of this institution in the following year. D. Huntington to A. H. Ritchie, Mch. 30, 1866. ♯T. A. Richards to C. H. McCormick, May 28, 1867. In the parlor of the McCormick residence at 40 Fifth Ave. in 1867 were ten oil paintings, and two bronzes, "Lorelei" and "Boy Holding His Foot." The subjects of his engravings were most miscellaneous in character, e.g., "A Methodist Church Conference," "The Yacht, America," "Niagara Falls," "Nathan Hale," and "The Death of Webster." He frequently purchased paintings for his home, and in 1871 contributed $1000 to help establish the Metropolitan Museum of Art in New York City. "Chicago Times," Aug. 20, 1876, and Jan. 13, 1884.

In the many hundreds of his letters, profits are given a subordinate place among the objectives of a season's business. The focus of his endeavor was always the victory to be gained over competitors, knotty mechanical problems and other obstacles. He gloried in a fight, neither asked nor gave quarter, and as an earlier biographer has written, liked to follow "the line of most resistance." [41] In so far as the records show, he did not know the meaning of discouragement. A defeat was merely an indication that he must vary his method of attack. Although he occasionally expressed a longing for calm seas, he was never willing to seek a safe harbor while a storm was raging. His victories sometimes meant large financial gain, but they were chiefly gratifying to him because they kept him in the lead of his industry. To start with nothing and build a fortune of $10,000,000 was doubtless good evidence of material success, but others of his generation who were penniless in their youth amassed a far larger amount during their lifetime.[42] His invention was worth much more to the world than the gold that came to him from the sale of his reaper.

McCormick was far more careful of his small expenses than of his large ones. In his view, money was not meant to be wasted upon little things, and he sometimes carried this rule to lengths that irritated his subordinates to the point of revolt.[43] Thus he once criticized C. A. Spring, Jr., for writing

[41] H. Casson, "Cyrus McCormick, His Life and Work (Chicago, 1909)," p. 141.

[42] According to his yearly financial balance-sheets, his wealth, in round numbers, rose as follows: $4,000,000 in 1866; $5,500,000 in 1869; $7,000,000 in 1876; $8,840,000 in 1881; and about $10,000,000 in 1884.

[43] Undated MS. "Reminiscences of C. H. McCormick," by Judge M. F. Tuley. "I have known him to haggle over a 5 cent mistake in a bill and half an hour afterwards contribute five to ten thousand dollars toward expenditures [of the Democratic Party]." #L.P.C.B. of McCormick & Funkhauser, p. 68, C. H. McCormick to C. W. Allen, Supt. of Dorn M. & M. Co., Oct. 19, 1869: "I *can't understand* how you shd. have to pay Eight Dollars a day for four days for a horse & buggy as you suggest. In any ordinary time a *one horse* buggy wd. be supposed sufficient to carry you."

him on such heavy correspondence paper that the letter needed an extra stamp. A few weeks later he took him to task for using a superfluous word in a telegram.[44] McCormick was quick of temper and when in an explosive mood he harshly censured petty mistakes. Secretaries did not remain long in his employ, and the "turn-over" of his body-servants was surprisingly large. When his employer was angry, Spring knew that his cue was to retort in kind. McCormick disliked a cringer or a flatterer but if the victim of his wrath defended himself manfully, reconciliation with mutual expressions of regret was soon effected. Terse telegrams were his hobby, and he not infrequently underlined the redundant words in those that came to him.[45]

To question the accuracy of bills was almost a habit. His insistence upon a reduction in the amount claimed and his

[44] ‡L.P.C.B. No. 1, 2nd ser., p. 125, C. H. McCormick to C. A. Spring, Jr., June 11, 1870; C. A. Spring, Jr., to C. H. McCormick, ‡June 15, July ‡23, and 28, 1870, and Jan. 1, 1872. In his letter of July 23, Spring wrote: "You might come and take charge of it [your business] yourself, but in that case you would have considerable to learn and it would take time." Judging from the letter of Jan. 1, 1872, McCormick had charged Spring before the office force with endeavoring to injure his business. Spring demanded either proof or apology. See also, L. J. to C. H. McCormick, Sept. 3, 1870. *Supra,* Chap. X, ftn. 45.

[45] MS. "Recollections of My Father," by Harold F. McCormick, written in Mch., 1909, and cited hereafter as H. F. McCormick, "Recollections." ‡L.P.C.B. of C. H. McCormick, Nov., 1880-May, 1881, pp. 47, 49, C. H. McCormick to Dun, Wyman & Co., N. Y., Dec. 7, 1880. In regard to an unsatisfactory negro house-servant, McCormick wrote: "I found that he had nothing better than the manners of a negro plantation, and I told him that I required proper and courteous language from my servants, which embraced the proper use of the word *sir* as found in genteel families and as he would find throughout my household, from my friends and clerks as well as my servants." C. H. McCormick, Jr., MSS. Book "B," N. F. McCormick to C. H. McCormick, Jr., Mch. 22, 1883; ‡L.P.C.B. No. 1, 2nd ser., p. 209, C. H. McCormick to C. A. Spring, Jr., July 28, 1870: "Mrs. McC. *has said* to me that I might better pay for some words more when telegraphing in a hurry, than take time to shorten." ‡L.P.C.B. No. 1, 2nd ser., p. 88, *idem* to *idem,* May 13, 1870.

refusal to settle until an accommodation was made, saved him a considerable sum of money during his lifetime. This characteristic was doubtless due in part to his determination not to be imposed upon because of his wealth. He persuaded Potter Palmer of the Palmer House in Chicago to furnish him meals at less than the regular price, but when he protested the fee asked by the surgeons in Paris who had removed his carbuncle, he was curtly reminded that he owed his life to their skill.[46] Sharply contrasting with his inclination to haggle over small sums, was his willingness to donate thousands of dollars for the support of benevolences or religious enterprises in which he was interested.

In like manner he was chary of the minutes of his day. Both Mrs. McCormick and he thought of time as a tangible something that was sinful to waste. She urged her children to write down how long it took them to brush their teeth and put on their clothes in the morning so that they would be reminded of their slowness in reaching the breakfast-table.[47] The hours were too short to accomplish all that the inventor planned to do, and he worked harder than any of his subordinates. Decisions were made after long deliberation, and were then executed rapidly and relentlessly. He was not brilliant in the sense that the proper course of action flashed upon him by inspiration, but his mind was a tireless engine apparently never at rest unless he slept.[48]

[46] P. Palmer to C. H. McCormick, Aug. 6, 1876: "The price that we agreed upon for dinners I wish confined to yourself only for the reason that seventy-five cents does not pay me the actual cost of dinners." The letterhead of the hotel affirmed that it was the "Only Fire Proof House in the United States." E. Warren, M.D., Paris, to C. H. McCormick, Jan. 14, 1879. ‡L.P.C.B. of C. H. McCormick, Nov., 1873-June, 1876, p. 405, C. H. McCormick to L. D. Bulkley, M.D., Apr. 4, 1876.

[47] C. H. McCormick, Jr., MSS. Book "B," N. F. McCormick to C. H. McCormick, Jr., Sept. 6, 1869.

[48] C. Bentley, "Cyrus Hall McCormick" (Chicago, 1915), pp. 21-25.

Dawn often found him at his desk, deep in thought or busy with important correspondence. Because he was at his best in these early hours when the house was quiet, he reserved them for his hardest problems. Mrs. McCormick read the Scriptures shortly after seven o'clock each morning and he often joined her in her devotions before going down to the morning meal. He scorned to be taken to his office in a carriage since his liking for a brisk walk after breakfast overbalanced his desire to save time.[49] A long day at his desk, in a court-room, or in conference with his lawyers at a hotel, was sometimes followed by work until midnight at his home. This was life for Cyrus McCormick, and he would not have had it otherwise.[50]

Although he was a man of powerful physique, his ability to toil ceaselessly for so many years was probably due in large measure to his refusal to worry about his losses or to become unduly elated about his victories. Calm followed quickly the many little outbursts when "burned rascal" and "confounded fool" exhausted his stock of expletives and left him silent. As a rule he was not impulsive, and except when angry he rarely voiced an opinion that did not rest upon reason rather than emotion. He was poised in the midst of excitement and was at his best when his associates believed that defeat was

[49] C. H. McCormick to T. B. Taylor, May 6, 1867. When her son was in Princeton, Mrs. McCormick hoped that he would read his Bible at 8:15 each morning so they would be both engaged in their devotions at the same time. C. H. McCormick, Jr., MSS. Book "B," N. F. McCormick to C. H. McCormick, Jr., June 5, 1878.

[50] Penciled memoir written by C. H. McCormick in Feb., 1884: "I would have been dead long ago if I had given up business. My vitality this winter is better than last." Cyrus H. McCormick, "In the Days of the Elder McCormick," in the "Harvester World," Mch., 1925. C. H. McCormick, Jr., MSS. Book "C," pp. 459-460, N. F. McCormick to C. H. McCormick, Jr., undated, but probably 1874: "Poor papa would be benefitted here, but his existence depends upon being with the living, moving, vital world. He would not care to read and the time would hang heavily on his hands."

certain.[51] His erect carriage and aggressive stride betokened self-confidence. When publicly criticized he replied sharply and moved ahead along the course that he had determined upon. Popularity and applause were dear to him, but he believed that the sacrifice of his own convictions was too high a price to pay for acclaim.[52]

McCormick worked methodically as well as persistently, although by the late 1870's his eldest son often urged him to employ regularly a private secretary so that he would no longer need to be reminded by his wife of the many things that he should do.[53] As the inventor preferred to play a lone hand in business and rarely agreed with his partners, so he also found that Mrs. McCormick or some other member of his family was the only companion in his study with whom he could be completely happy. It was his practice to take a scrap of paper, usually the back of an envelope, and jot down the items of business which needed his attention. These ranged in importance from having his shoes resoled to engaging counsel for an important lawsuit.[54] He often filled the bottom of these memoranda with verses from the Bible or with lines from hymns, repeated over and over, indicating perhaps the subject which was uppermost in his subconscious mind. Before answering important letters he dissected them upon separate sheets of paper, noting down all the points requiring his con-

[51] C. H. to W. S. McCormick, Apr. 24, 1858. MS. Sketch of C. H. McCormick, entitled "A Busy Life," written in 1885 by W. J. Hanna. H. F. McCormick, "Recollections."

[52] Letter of C. H. McCormick in "Chicago Times" of July 5, 1866.

[53] C. H. McCormick, Jr., Bristol, Eng., to C. H. McCormick, July 8, 1878: You would "save thousands or at least hundreds of dollars to have a secretary whose only business was to answer your letters at once and keep before you matters of importance which have to be attended to *before a certain day!* Many of these must necessarily slip from your mind from their very number, and surely Mamma can't remember them all, and *attend to them too,* besides looking after all the multitude of her other cares." Nettie F. McCormick, St. Moritz, to C. H. McCormick, Aug. 25, 1878.

[54] As an example, see his memo. of July 7, 1875.

sideration. These analyses, as well as his replies, afford excellent examples of his ability to find the heart of a matter. It was this quality of mind, and his fertility of suggestion after studying a problem, which led the best patent lawyers in the land to submit their briefs to him for criticism before presenting them in court.[55]

His stress upon the value of time and his loss of interest in a project after its administration had been reduced to a routine were somewhat contradicted by his occasional attention to details when he believed that otherwise he might be cheated. Thus, in 1860 he employed a man and his wife as his coachman and cook. He wrote out a long contract for their signature and after advancing them money to help pay their fare to Chicago he required the husband to deposit his gold watch as a pledge of good faith.[56] Twelve years later McCormick was pressed almost beyond endurance with duties connected with the presidential campaign, the seminary, and the rebuilding of his burned properties in Chicago. Nevertheless, among his papers for that year is a very long specification in his handwriting giving detailed directions to a contractor who had been engaged to keep water-tight the roof of one of his business blocks.[57] He early learned the value of putting all business propositions in writing. Even in dealing with his own kinsfolk formal correspondence was the rule.

"Indomitable perseverance in a business properly *understood* almost insures ultimate success." [58] In this maxim McCormick squeezed over forty years of experience and gave first place to that trait of character which so deeply impressed all who knew him. The memoirs of his friends leave some

[55] E. N. Dickerson to C. H. McCormick, May 10, 1875.

[56] ♯Agreement of C. H. McCormick with Patrick Gaven and wife, Sept. 15, 1860. This document is formally witnessed.

[57] Agreement between C. H. McCormick and the U. S. Pipe Protecting and Roofing Co., Aug. 19, 1872.

[58] C. H. McCormick to H. B. Tomlin, Feb. 9, 1877.

doubt whether his "bluff, outspoken ruggedness" or his "cordiality, good humor, and courtliness" deserve the more stress, but they all agree that he had in fullest measure "indomitable perseverance" and a "bull dog tenacity." [59]

The story of the Presbyterian Seminary in Chicago has amply illustrated his refusal to admit defeat when issues of the first importance to him were at stake. He was equally pertinacious about small matters if they involved a principle or infringed his rights. In this connection a somewhat petty but aggravating mishap during the Civil War is one of the most revealing episodes of his entire career. Mrs. McCormick and he, with their two young children, a cousin, and two servants, were returning to Chicago from Washington in March, 1862.[60] After stopping for a few days in Philadelphia, they went on the evening of the eleventh with their nine trunks to the Pennsylvania Central station to take the express for the West. Because it was nearly train-time when they reached the terminal, McCormick left his luggage to be checked before he purchased the tickets. While he was at the wicket paying for the fares the other members of the party boarded the train and the trunks were weighed and loaded into the baggage-car. Upon his return he was told that there was an excess charge on his luggage of $8.70. Since it had been carried without fee from Washington to Philadelphia, he considered the demand unjust and declined to pay. He insisted that the trunks should be put back upon the platform but they were buried beneath other baggage and the station officials refused to delay the departure of the train. Thereupon he hurried his companions from their seats and all returned to their hotel.

Early the next morning McCormick called upon J. Edgar Thomson, the president of the railroad. After hearing the

[59] "Chicago Daily News," May 16, 1884. Undated MS. "Reminiscences of C. H. McCormick," by Judge M. F. Tuley.

[60] ‡J. Skirving, Germantown, Pa., to C. H. McCormick, Mch. 19, 1862.

story Thomson telegraphed to have the baggage held at Pittsburgh and gave the inventor a note of identification so that he could get it there. As it turned out, the order went unheeded and the trunks were carried through to Chicago, where they were placed with other unclaimed articles in the baggage-room. Although it was early spring, lightning struck the station during the night and it was completely destroyed by fire. Four of the nine trunks were saved, and of the five which were burned, all except one belonged to Mr. and Mrs. McCormick. They estimated their loss at about $5,500, including diamonds and other jewelry of much sentimental value given by the inventor to his wife shortly before their marriage.[61] She immediately prepared a list of the burned articles, but the Pennsylvania Central showed no inclination to settle without a lawsuit. The inventor's attitude toward the war made it unlikely that his claim would find favor at that time with either judge or jury. Whether the railroad could be held responsible for an "Act of God" was highly doubtful, unless weight were given to the fact that the baggage-man at Philadelphia had wrongly entrained the luggage before the tickets were presented to him, and had refused to restore it to McCormick upon demand. Had not the railroad thereby appropriated his property against his will? The inventor thought that it had done so, but he decided to wait until peace was restored before putting the matter in the charge of his lawyers.

[61] The facts here given have been drawn from the testimony in the case, printed in *Court of Appeals, State of New York. Cyrus Hall McCormick, Plaintiff and Respondent against the Pennsylvania Central Railroad Company, Defendant and Appellant, Case on Appeal* (N. Y., 1879), pp. 2-105. On pp. 7-14 are listed the items of personal property lost by Mr. and Mrs. McCormick in the fire. This list includes a Hudson Bay sable muff, a diamond necklace, two diamond brooches, one diamond ring, one diamond bracelet, a gentleman's diamond brooch, cameo sleeve-buttons, black frock-coat, silk-velvet vest, embroidered slippers, camel's hair India shawl, silk mantilla with bertha of Guipure lace, a fine point-lace set, a plaid stone-colored grenadine, infants' clothes of Irish poplin trimmed with velvet, an Allen's patent pistol, opera glasses, six photographs by Brady, two French grammars, and two packages of letters.

When, in the summer of 1865 the time seemed ripe for action, witnesses of the episode in the Philadelphia station were almost impossible to find. Not until two years later was a summons served upon the railroad, and it was 1869 before the case first came up for trial in a court of New York State.[62] In their desperate search for evidence, McCormick's lawyers had been finally obliged to employ secretly the detective agency that was customarily used by the railroad itself.[63] Mrs. Mc-Cormick had her first experience as a witness and she confessed that she was "a little nervous . . . having to testify in a large room full of people." [64]

On this occasion McCormick won a judgment for over $10,600. The defendant appealed the case and after losing again in the Supreme Court, gained from the Court of Appeals an order for a new trial in the Circuit Court.[65] By agreement between the parties to the action, the issue was here retried without a jury and in December, 1877, a judgment for McCormick was entered for over $16,000. Once again the railroad company carried the case to a higher tribunal.[66] The Supreme

[62] ‡H. Baldwin, Jr., to C. H. McCormick, July 24, 1865, and Mch. 20, 1867; ‡C. A. Spring, Jr., to C. H. McCormick, Apr. 1, 1869.

[63] C. H. McCormick to C. A. Spring, Jr., undated but late in Mch., 1869. ‡W. D. Baldwin to C. H. McCormick, May 8, 1869; ‡H. Baldwin, Jr., to C. H. McCormick, May 13, 1869: "Please be careful to cut off the printed heads from the Detective reports I sent you. . . . Do not omit this. The headings might be seen by the Co.'s counsel."

[64] Nettie F. McCormick to C. A. Spring, Jr., May 11, 1869. C. H. Mc-Cormick to C. A. Spring, Jr., May 17, 1869.

[65] At this time the railroad offered to settle for $3,000. McCormick refused. L.P.C.B. No. 132, p. 678, C. H. McCormick to D. D. Lord, Mch. 15, 1872. ‡D. D. Lord to C. H. McCormick, Feb. 14, 1871, May 3, and 25, 1872, and Feb. 28, 1873. ‡L.P.C.B. of C. H. McCormick, Nov., 1873-June, 1876, p. 343, C. H. McCormick to H. Day, Dec. 21, 1875: "I want my RR. case pushed."

[66] ‡L.P.C.B. of C. H. McCormick, June, 1876-Apr., 1878, pp. 43, 82, 89, C. H. McCormick to E. W. Stoughton, N. Y., Mch. 6, May 17, June 2, 1877: "The presidential election has held up my RR. case. Please get it brought to trial quickly now." But Stoughton was busy with the famous Emma Mine Case and there was further delay. Nettie F. to C. H. &

Court sustained the inventor but the Court of Appeals in March, 1880, reversed the judgment and ordered a new trial. The matter was threshed over anew in the Circuit Court, and the inventor was awarded damages of six cents.[67]

Refusing to yield, McCormick instructed his counsel to reargue his cause before the Supreme Court. This ruled that he had not received his due from his nominal victory and ordered a new trial in the Circuit Court. Here a jury decided in fifteen minutes that he was entitled to damages of over $13,000. The Supreme Court affirmed the judgment.[68] When McCormick learned that the railroad intended to appeal once more to the highest court which had hitherto failed to appreciate the justice of his claim, he determined to reinforce his staff of Democratic lawyers with a prominent Republican.[69] Roscoe Conkling was the choice and in April, 1885, the tribunal of last resort unanimously awarded damages of over $18,000 to the

L. J. McCormick, Oct. 10, 1877. C. H. McCormick, Jr., MSS. Book "B," N. F. McCormick to C. H. McCormick, Jr., Jan. 14, 1878: "The lawyer for Penn R.R. in Baggage case has appealed again!! Much to our surprise! Too bad! But he will lose it again!" ‡L.P.C.B. of C. H. McCormick, June, 1876-Apr., 1878, p. 132, C. H. McCormick to D. D. Lord, N. Y., Mch. 29, 1878. H. H. Finley, Washington, D. C., to C. H. McCormick, Dec. 27, 1877.

[67] ‡Letters of Beach & Brown, N. Y., to C. H. McCormick, Sept. 2, Oct. 14, 1879, Mch. 30, June 14, and Nov. 9, 1880. Telegram of C. H. McCormick to C. H. McCormick, Jr., Nov. 2, 1880. ‡L.P.C.B. of C. H. McCormick, Nov., 1880-May, 1881, pp. 93, 490, C. H. McCormick to Beach & Brown, N. Y., Dec. 31, 1880, and to C. H. McCormick, Jr., May 5, 1881.

[68] ‡Ibid., May 10, 1881-Jan. 14, 1882, pp. 198-199, 223, C. H. McCormick to E. W. Stoughton, Dec. 22, 1881, and to Beach & Brown, Jan. 5, 1882. ‡Letters of Beach & Brown to C. H. McCormick, May 18, 20, Oct. 28 and Dec. 22, 1881; Jan. 9, Mch. 20, May 12, 22, 1882; May 22, June 1, 1883. Telegram of G. Harding to C. H. McCormick, May 12, 1882. ‡C. H. McCormick, Jr., to C. H. McCormick, May 15, 1882. The "Chicago Daily Tribune," May 13, 1882.

[69] ‡Beach & Brown to C. H. McCormick, June 20 and 28, 1883. ‡W. A. Beach to C. H. McCormick, Jan. 17, 1884, and his telegram to McCormick of Jan. 21, 1884. Telegram of R. Conkling to C. H. McCormick, Jr., Jan. 21, 1884.

inventor.[70] The railroad thereupon acknowledged defeat but McCormick had not lived to enjoy his victory. Eighteen years of counsel fees cost more than the amount awarded to his heirs, but the expense would have been immaterial to him when compared with the satisfaction he would have derived from making clear that he was right.[71]

Although he liberally contributed to the support of colleges and seminaries, he believed that the school of practical experience afforded the most valuable training for youth. His children were instructed by governesses, tutors, and in private academies. Only his eldest son was a graduate of a city high school.[72] With much difficulty Mrs. McCormick persuaded her husband to allow Cyrus, Jr., to enroll at Princeton for a special course of study. The youth demonstrated his talent for business during his summer abroad in 1877, and his father, feeling so strongly the need of an assistant, at once discovered reasons why he should not attend college. The boy already knew enough to enable him to succeed as a manufacturer; his health might be impaired by too much study, and only fifty per cent of the alumni of the University of Virginia had distin-

[70] "Cyrus H. McCormick, Respondent v. The Pennsylvania Central Railroad Company, Appellant," in *Reports of Cases Decided in the Court of Appeals of the State of New York* (H. E. Sickels, State Reporter), XCIX (Albany, 1885), pp. 65-74. "New York Commercial Advertiser," Apr. 29, 1885. "The Mail and Express" (N. Y.), Apr. 29, 1885; "Chicago Evening Journal," Apr. 29, 1885; "Chicago Daily News," Apr. 30, 1885; "Chicago Daily Tribune," Apr. 30, 1885. This extensive publicity cost only $100. #A. C. Brown to C. H. McCormick, Jr., Apr. 14, 16, 29, 30, May 6, 11, and Oct. 6, 1885. In his letter of Apr. 29, he wrote: "You will see (by reading the opinion) that your father's course from first to last is approved and vindicated by our Court of last resort. The Mgr. of the Asso. Press says that we can't get any such lengthy article as we want, without paying advertising rates."

[71] Conkling's fee alone was $1500. R. Conkling to C. H. McCormick, Jr., May 23 and June 5, 1885.

[72] From 1875 to 1877, while living at 363 Superior St., C. H. McCormick, Jr., walked more than a mile each morning to the high school at the corner of Halsted and Madison Strs.

guished themselves after graduation. In this vein he wrote to President McCosh [73] but Mrs. McCormick intervened in behalf of her son and he arrived on the campus shortly after the autumn term opened. She felt that her husband was secretly gratified because she had won her point, since friends congratulated him upon sacrificing his own interests for the sake of his children. She was delighted at her success and wrote to her son: "Don't think anything *too hard* for me for I am *very skillful,* you know!" [74] High grades received in his courses and his selection to be one of the Glee Club quartette also flattered his father's pride,[75] but in the following summer Mrs. McCormick was obliged again to use much persuasion before the youth was released from reaper duty so that he could return to college for another year.[76]

As a father the inventor was a not unusual blend of austerity and indulgence. He was fifty when Cyrus, Jr., was born, and thereafter for the rest of his life there was always at least one child in his home under twelve years of age.[77] If he were ill, in conference, or occupied with a business problem, the romping of his children annoyed him, but usually he wel-

[73] C. H. McCormick to Rev. J. McCosh, Princeton, N. J., undated but probably written in the late summer of 1877. McCormick suggested that his son might work in the factory or its office from 7 A.M. until noon, and then devote each afternoon to study. ‡L.P.C.B. No. 4, 2nd ser., p. 26, Nettie F. McCormick to J. McCosh, Sept. 25, 1877.

[74] C. H. McCormick, Jr., MSS. Book "B," Nettie F. McCormick to C. H. McCormick, Jr., Oct. 1 and 2, 1877.

[75] C. H. McCormick, MSS. Book "G," N. F. McCormick to C. H. McCormick, Jr., Oct. 6, 1879. In June, 1877, C. H. McCormick was elected an honorary member of the Clio Society of Princeton. G. S. Munson to C. H. McCormick, June 16, 1877.

[76] N. F. to C. H. McCormick, Aug. 20, 22, 25, 1878: "You should have help, my dear husband, and can have help less costly to Cyrus's future— me for instance." C. H. McCormick, Jr., MSS. Book "B," N. F. McCormick, St. Moritz, to C. H. McCormick, Jr., Aug. 23, 1878.

[77] ‡C. H. McCormick to T. J. Massie, Aug. 6, 1866, and to "Jo" Anderson, Jan. 19, 1870.

comed them to his chair or simulated astonishment when they sprang upon him from their favorite hiding-places about the home.[78] He willingly resigned their upbringing to the capable charge of his wife. They agreed, however, that the children should be taught, sternly if necessary, the meaning of duty and the value of money.[79] Nothing should be left undone to prepare them to move easily within their own circle of society, but they must never deserve the title "idle rich." For every privilege that wealth conferred there was a corresponding obligation. Goodness meant personal uprightness, religious faith, and aid to those who were less fortunate. As Mrs. McCormick wrote to her eldest son in 1878: "There is *no* expense necessary for your comfort and education and advancing your position or interests that we would not readily incur. *All we have* is our children's, while they do credit to us."[80]

Her letters tell of velocipedes, kittens, squirrels, a parrot, mocking-birds, canaries, a pony, a stamp collection, stereopticons, croquet and lawn-tennis. One son had his packing-box cave in the basement and whistled no end while he played with his five kittens. If his wish were granted, he soon traded these animals for two tame squirrels. Whatever may have been the nature of the business deal by which they were acquired, "Zip" and "Zoe" were soon racing about the house, until one met an untimely death by falling into an open register.[81] McCormick

[78] H. F. McCormick, "Recollections."

[79] ‡L.P.C.B. of C. H. McCormick, Nov. 1873-June, 1876, p. 412, C. H. McCormick to H. Day, N. Y., Apr. 25, 1876: "It is at least well & safe that they [children] be trained in youthful or early life as if they were dependent upon their own labor & efforts for their success afterwards, . . . and so I am endeavoring to train my own children—by example as well as precept, and so I told Hall [McCormick] that my son or myself, as the case might be, would be at the Works at the hour of commencing business if our positions respectively called for it."

[80] C. H. McCormick, Jr., MSS. Book "B," Nettie F. McCormick to C. H. McCormick, Jr., Mch. 8, 1878.

[81] H. F. McCormick, "Recollections." ‡C. H. McCormick, Jr., to C. H. McCormick, Sept. 4, 1882, and Aug. 2, 1883. C. H. to C. H. McCormick,

liked to play croquet with his children and on one occasion, at least, took several of them to a horse-race.[82] As they grew older he pitted his skill against theirs at billiards and made certain that his sons learned to ride horseback. Mrs. McCormick and he liked a spirited, well-matched team that could do a mile in fast time on Lake Shore Drive. "Napoleon," "Billy," "Princeton," "Belle," "Jimmy," "Hector," "Achilles," or "Chub," the pony, rarely go unmentioned in the family correspondence of the 1870's.[83]

Cyrus McCormick was of imposing presence, bringing with him, according to his friends, an atmosphere of greatness when he entered a room. He was about six feet tall and weighed slightly more than two hundred pounds. His erect carriage, ruddy complexion, heavy eyebrows, full gray beard, and black hair made him a noteworthy figure in any assemblage.[84] By the early 1870's, however, his splendid physique

Jr., Aug. 5, 1883. C. H. McCormick, Jr., MSS. Book "B," N. F. McCormick to C. H. McCormick, Jr., Sept. 6, 1869, and May 22, 1878.

[82] C. H. McCormick, Jr., MSS. Book "B," N. F. McCormick to C. H. McCormick, Jr., July 30, 1880. ‡Virginia to H. F. McCormick, July 19, 1883; C. H. McCormick to C. H. McCormick, Jr., July 21, 1883. When he was a young man C. H. McCormick occasionally went hunting. He seems never to have derived keen enjoyment from the sport and most probably gave it up altogether soon after settling in Chicago in 1847. Spring's letter of ‡May 1, 1871, telling of his slaughter of one thousand wild pigeons in a day and a half at Portage City, Wis., awakened no desire in his employer to dust off his shot-gun.

[83] ‡C. H. McCormick from N. Y. to J. Milligan, Dec. 13, 1881: "I should be in Chicago exercising around my billiard table." His first billiard table was purchased at least as early as Dec., 1866. L.P.C.B. No. 24, pp. 141-142, C. H. McCormick to F. O. Rogers, Niles, Mich., Oct. 17, 1859; Letters of C. A. Spring, Jr., to C. H. McCormick, July 20, Nov. ‡8, ‡12, 1866. ‡H. D. Turner to C. H. McCormick, Oct. 4, 1870; L.P.C.B. No. 147, pp. 60-61, W. J. Hanna to C. S. Dole, Crystal Lake, Ill., Dec. 18, 1873. C. H. McCormick to Mr. Willetts, July 7, 1875; C. H. McCormick, Jr., MSS. Book "B," N. F. McCormick to C. H. McCormick, Jr., Mch. 27, 1878; Book "E," N. F. McCormick to C. H. McCormick, Jr., May 8, 1878, and Sept. 6, 1879.

[84] G. W. Webb to C. H. McCormick, Jr., Dec. 10, 1881. At this time C. H. McCormick weighed 209 lbs. In a ‡letter to S. A. Darrach on Aug. 27,

was beginning to rebel against the heavy strain that he had compelled it to bear for so many years. Too little exercise and too much food and work were largely to blame. He enjoyed the table, eating generous servings of meat and desserts, and drinking several glasses both of milk and water with every meal.[85] Rare roast-beef and cherry pie were highly esteemed for dinner, while his breakfast almost invariably centered about a large bowl of mush and milk.[86] The eating of this cereal was almost a ritual. After grace was said and the napkin was fastened by an elastic band about his neck, he would take a spoonful of steaming mush and dip it into a bowl of cold milk. Long practice had schooled him to make the two come out even so that the last bit of cereal was moistened by the last drops of milk. Visitors, however, were not so expert and at least one was embarrassed by McCormick's courteous insistence that he should have some more mush, or some more milk, as a surplus of the one indicated a need for the other.[87]

In 1845, while McCormick was stopping in Cincinnati, he was first bothered by eczema. Thereafter, for the rest of his life he was unable to do more than keep the infection localized.[88] It was particularly annoying in summer, and by the eve of the Civil War he regularly sought relief during the hot season at mineral springs in Vermont or New York. Internal and external applications of sulphurated and carbonated water seemed to help. A supply of Vichy, Congress, Bethesda Spring, or Missisquoi bottled water was kept in his home throughout the year. Because he believed that its use promoted general well-being, he insisted that his wife and children should

---

1883, C. H. McCormick stated that he weighed 215 lbs., and that the distance from the floor to his armpits was fifty-seven inches. "In winter clothing," he was fifty-four inches around his waist. R. H. Parkinson to C. H. McCormick, Jr., May 22, June 13, 1884.
[85] ‡C. H. McCormick, Jr., to N. F. McCormick, Mch. 17, 1879.
[86] ‡*Idem* to *idem,* Mch. 9, 1883.
[87] H. F. McCormick, "Recollections."
[88] C. H. McCormick to C. H. McCormick, Jr., May 30, 1882.

share it with him.[89] Shortly after his return from Europe in 1864 he complained of rheumatism. The following year he was confined to his home with a carbuncle and a "protracted visitation of boils." [90] Severe colds, sore throat, and rheumatic pains recurred with increasing frequency as time went on. In 1870 he wrote that his throat had been sore "more or less for 2 years" and five years later a doctor, after a careful examination, informed him that he had "a mild chronic catarrhal condition . . . but nothing like true Bright's disease. You probably can not be completely cured." [91] This catalog of infirmities will leave the wrong impression if it is presumed that McCormick was ill during most of the decade following the close of the war. He was usually driving ahead as vigorously as ever, although the state of his health was a topic given increasing attention in his correspondence.[92] In 1874 he spent some weeks at the mineral springs at Waukesha, Wisconsin, and at the Dansville Health Institution in New York State. May and June of the next year found him at Hot Springs, Arkansas, enjoying the waters with Joseph Medill. Temporarily he was much benefited.[93] A niece who accompanied him found it: "a horribly forlorn place—the people enough to strike terror to the stoutest heart—the animals have the appearance of dug-up

[89] ‡C. H. McCormick, Manchester, Vt., to T. J. Massie, Aug. 6, 1866; to J. C. Derby, Sept. 24, 1866; to J. D. Davidson, Mch. 18, 1867, Apr. 6, 1868, and Apr. 27, 1869; to C. Adams, July 30, 1868; to T. P. Wright, Nov. 30, 1868. ‡C. A. Spring, Jr., to C. H. McCormick, Aug. 12, 1869; L. D. Bulkley, M.D., N. Y., to C. H. McCormick, Jan. 24, 1876. ‡Telegram of C. H. McCormick, to Caswell, Hazard & Co., Aug. 13, 1883.

[90] ‡C. A. Spring, Jr., to C. H. McCormick, Dec. 13, 1865; C. H. McCormick to ?, Jan. 2, 1866, and to R. W. Forbes, Jan. 19, 1866.

[91] J. N. Danforth, M.D., Chicago, to C. H. McCormick, Dec. 27, 1875.

[92] C. H. McCormick to J. D. Davidson, Mch. 18, 1867: "Friends tell me that my appearance has not changed in twenty years" but I know they do not speak seriously. Two folders in the files of N. F. McCormick Biog. Asso. contain 48 letters of doctors, medical diagnoses, etc., relating to C. H. McCormick between 1867 and 1883.

[93] C. H. McCormick to H. Day, May 15, 1875.

skeletons—the pigs' noses are sharpened to knife-blade fineness from rooting about stones &c. But the visitors don't cultivate the herd I have mentioned, so are not contaminated." [94] By autumn the inventor turned to the spas of his native state for help. Old friends gave him a most gratifying reception but he carried his rheumatism back to the North.[95]

Of the many mineral springs Mr. and Mrs. McCormick visited during these years, those at Richfield in Otsego County, New York, were their favorite. Here in a beautiful country, fifteen miles from the nearest railroad, were a large hotel and health-giving waters. A stay at this spot was usually included in their summer itinerary. Because they wearied of the "same inane dancing at night, [and the] same inane company on [the] piazzas," they occasionally rented a cottage so that they could be by themselves.[96] In 1871 McCormick purchased a half-dozen acres of land on a hilltop near the village.[97] The site was entirely undeveloped, a grazing place for cattle and sheep, and scarred with the burrows of many ground-hogs. But the view was a magnificent one and McCormick hoped soon to enjoy it from the veranda of a summer-home. The Chicago Fire intervened to thwart his plan.[98] Shrubbery, flowers, and an orchard were planted, however, and a caretaker worked on

[94] Amanda Shields to Nettie F. McCormick, May 28, 1875: "He [C. H. McCormick] thinks me giddy to go on horseback rides."

[95] ♯L.P.C.B. of C. H. McCormick, Nov. 1873-June, 1876, p. 361, C. H. McCormick to L. D. Bulkley, M.D., Jan. 17, 1876: "At night I have my feet and legs massaged after standing in cold water awhile. My skin affection seems to be better." On Apr. 4, 1876 (ibid., p. 405), he wrote to him that the latter had not improved.

[96] C. H. McCormick, Jr., MSS. Book "B," N. F. McCormick to C. H. McCormick, Jr., July 29, 1877, and July 27, 1880; to ?, Aug. (?), 1869.

[97] ♯Sales Agreement, Jan. 27, 1871, between H. W. Ford et al and C. H. McCormick. The price was $600 an acre.

[98] L. J. McCormick wrote his brother on Apr. 15, 1871, that he believed it to be a mistake to build a home so far from Chicago. ♯L.P.C.B. of C. H. McCormick, Nov., 1873-June, 1876, p. 49, C. H. McCormick to Dr. J. M. Stevenson, Apr. 1, 1874.

the property annually during the spring and summer months.[99] Several years later the proposed residence was once more a subject of earnest discussion, but it was 1882 before the completed structure was ready for occupancy.[100] In remembrance of the village in northern New York where Mrs. McCormick had lived before her marriage, the new home was named Clayton Lodge,[101] The inventor spent many weeks there in 1882 and 1883, happy after so long a time to be back upon the land, enjoying his roses, and supervising the draining and landscaping of his little estate.[102] The location held the more attraction for him because Richfield was the summer rendezvous of many prominent Presbyterians. His porch was almost daily the scene of an informal conference on matters of importance to his denomination.[103]

[99] C. H. McCormick to H. W. Ford, Utica, N. Y., May 19, 1871; ‡H. M. Johnson, Richfield Springs, N. Y., to C. H. McCormick, May 26, 1871; ‡C. Vaux, N. Y., to C. H. McCormick, July 18, 1871; L.P.C.B. No. 133, pp. 89, 211, C. H. McCormick to G. Hayward, Richfield Springs, N. Y., Mch. 31 and Apr. 6, 1872; ‡G. Hayward to C. H. McCormick, Mch. 25, Apr. 2, 14, and May 5, 1872; J. E. Dolphin, Richfield Springs, to C. H. McCormick, Nov. 8, 1877.

[100] *Idem* to *idem*, June 5 and Nov. 6, 1879, May 3 and June 19, 1880; ‡L.P.C.B. of C. H. McCormick, Nov., 1873-June, 1876, p. 299, C. H. McCormick to C. Vaux, Mch. 24, 1875; ‡H. M. Johnson to C. H. McCormick, Sept. 8, 1879. Although C. H. McCormick was improving his Richfield Springs property at this time, he was still (both in 1875 and 1879) undecided whether to sell it or to build a summer-home there. Construction was started in the autumn of 1880.

[101] McKim, Mead & White were the architects and Frederick Olmsted supervised the landscaping. Letters to C. H. McCormick of ‡C. H. McCormick, Jr., May 8, 1881; ‡H. M. DeLong, June 29, July 11 and 29, 1881; ‡McKim, Mead & White, Mch. 30, 1882, and ‡R. Wickham, July 7, 1882. C. H. McCormick, Jr., MSS. Book "B," N. F. McCormick to C. H. McCormick, Jr., Nov. 26, 1884.

[102] C. H. McCormick, Jr., MSS. Book "B," Nettie F. McCormick to C. H. McCormick, Jr., Oct. 28, 1883: "You ought to realize as I told you that the whole matter [of the Gorham Pool] rests on *your* shoulders, as Papa here is thinking only of getting a ditch dug and laying the pipe." H. F. McCormick, "Recollections."

[103] The Christian School of Philosophy, a Presbyterian summer-school, met at Richfield Springs. C. H. McCormick to C. H. McCormick, Jr.,

Several years before this time Mrs. McCormick first called her husband "dear aged father" in her letters to her son.[104] As early as 1875 rheumatism sometimes made it hard for him to walk, and massages of his limbs became a customary part of his morning and evening routine.[105] His dependence upon his wife increased and he was lonesome and ill at ease if she were not with him. By 1878 his doctor wished him to hold in rigid check his desire for meats, fish, and coffee, but there is no indication that he followed the advice.[106] The ordeal in Paris that autumn and winter left him physically broken and unable for weeks afterwards to handle his affairs with his customary acumen. His body never completely recovered from this severe shock. Thereafter he was an invalid, unable to walk without the aid of a cane or a crutch, and sometimes too feeble to leave his bed or wheeled-chair.[107] Although his mental vigor returned, he was usually content to rely upon Mrs. McCormick and their eldest son to carry out, and often to make, decisions relating to his business.[108] Occasionally he showed no interest in the problems brought before him for discussion,

Aug. 28, 1883. C. H. McCormick paid the debt of the Richfield Springs Presbyterian Church in Aug., 1883.

[104] C. H. McCormick, Jr., MSS. Book "B," Nettie F. McCormick to C. H. McCormick, Jr., June 6, 1878. In a letter to him on Mch. 29 of this year, she wrote: "Papa has had the usual March cold prostration although I have given him quinine."

[105] Letters to C. H. McCormick of E. N. Dickerson, Apr. 26, 1875, and of H. Day, Apr. 28, 1875; C. H. McCormick, Jr., MSS. Book "E," Nettie F. McCormick to C. H. McCormick, Jr., May 6, 1878.

[106] C. H. McCormick, Jr., MSS. Book "B," Nettie F. McCormick to C. H. McCormick, Jr., Feb. 28, 1879; ‡C. H. McCormick, Jr., to Nettie F. McCormick, Aug. 12, 1878.

[107] Supra, pp. 672 ff. ‡C. H. McCormick, Jr., to Nettie F. McCormick, June 27, 1879.

[108] C. H. McCormick, Jr., MSS. Book "B," Nettie F. McCormick to C. H. McCormick, Jr., Apr. 15 and 28, 1879, and Aug. 22, 1882; C. H. McCormick to W. W. Snow, Aug. 9, 1883.; ‡E. K. Butler to C. H. Mc-Cormick, Jr., Nov. 27, 1883; C. H. McCormick, Jr., MSS. Book "B," Nettie F. McCormick to C. H. McCormick, Jr., Dec. 4, 1883: "Read Father's letters carefully. They have meaning and he is not deceived."

and dozed at the table with his meal untouched before him. At such times old age had the upper hand, but as a rule he was eager to keep informed about the world outside his home.[109] Friends noticed that he had mellowed and was more ready than ever before to extend aid to those in need or to advise with the many who came to his door asking the benefit of his experience.[110] McCormick had often compared life to a battle, and now that evening was falling he fought for six years to keep within the light.

Every medical expedient known in his day was tried with the hope of relieving the rheumatism in his right hip and knee. Besides mineral-water baths, massages, and the prescriptions of the best doctors in the country, he submitted to electrical treatments, the Swedish Movement cure, and the Electric Homeopathic Italian System of Medicine. He never lost faith that his health would return, and he liked physicians to tell him of his "wonderful constitution" and "extraordinary pulse." [111]

In May, 1882, he was taken to Seligman, Missouri, in a private car furnished by the Illinois Central Railroad. From there a stage carried him eighteen miles over rough roads to Eureka Springs, Arkansas. Upon his arrival he proudly wrote home that he was not "a whit the worse from the jostling and tossing effect upon my joints," and he gave proof of his fine spirits by persuading the stage-driver to reduce his charge for the trip from $21 to $15.[112] The resort proved to be "an

[109] Virginia McCormick to C. H. McCormick, Jr., Dec. 19, 1881.
[110] "The Interior," Aug. 7, 1884.
[111] ‡C. A. Spring, Jr., to C. H. McCormick, Jr., Oct. 7, 1881. C. H. McCormick, Jr., MSS. Book "B," N. F. McCormick to C. H. McCormick, Jr., Oct. 16, 1881. C. H. McCormick to N. F. McCormick, May 13, 1882. The Swedish Movement Cure was administered by Dr. Leonard Lundgren of Chicago in the autumn of 1882. See also, C. H. McCormick to J. Medill, Jan. 24, 1883.
[112] C. H. McCormick to C. H. McCormick, Jr., May 13, 1882. Letters to C. H. McCormick of W. S. Davis, Seligman, Mo., dating between May 17 and 28, 1882.

awfully rough place" and the food poor in quality and insufficient in amount. By good fortune he met a Mrs. Bredell at the hotel, a Presbyterian lady from St. Louis who had raised $100 for her church "by the making of mince meat." "So you see," wrote the inventor to his son, "she is one of our sort and very much of a lady etc. etc." He joined with her to purchase delicacies from St. Louis, and asked his wife to send him his favorite recipe for coffee.[113] Senator B. H. Hill of Georgia had a room on the third floor of the hotel and McCormick's was on the first. The senator would limp down one flight of steps while the inventor was pulling himself up the other in order that they might talk together on the second-floor veranda. Their friendship and the piano-playing of Hill's daughter helped to while away the time.[114] McCormick chafed, however, at the lonesomeness, the dearth of news, and the increasing heat. Five weeks of treatments and mineral baths brought him but slight relief, although when he left he arranged for Eureka water to be sent him regularly to Richfield Springs.[115]

In March of the next year his eldest son accompanied him in a private car furnished without charge by the Wabash, St. Louis & Pacific Railroad, to Hot Springs, Arkansas.[116] There at the Arlington Hotel the food was adequate although the Chicago home was asked to send him fifty pounds of yellow corn-meal for mush.[117] The McCormick of an earlier day flashes out from his note sent early one morning to the steward of the inn: "Ordered oatmeal with sweet milk—sent

[113] Telegram and letter of C. H. McCormick to C. H. McCormick, Jr., May 15, 1882. C. H. to N. F. McCormick, June 7, 1882.

[114] C. H. McCormick to C. H. McCormick, Jr., June 5, 1882.

[115] Letters of C. H. McCormick to C. H. McCormick, Jr., May 21, 23, 25, 1882, C. H. McCormick, Jr., MSS. Book "B," N. F. McCormick to C. H. McCormick, Jr., July 23, 1882.

[116] J. C. Gault to C. H. McCormick, Jr., Mch. 7, 1883. ‡Letter and telegram of C. H. McCormick, Jr., to N. F. McCormick, Mch. 12, 1883.

[117]‡C. H. McCormick, Jr., to N. F. McCormick, Mch. 14 and 15, 1883.

to me corn mush. Waited then & received cracked wheat—had ordered balance of breakfast in 20 mins. from first order, & finally this breakfast was brought to me about ½hr. after the time it was to be here, thus losing ½hr. of my time in waiting." [118]

Mrs. McCormick joined her husband at Hot Springs soon after her son was obliged to leave.[119] For all the benefit gained by his eleven weeks' stay, he might better have remained at his home in Chicago or Richfield. He believed that the summer and autumn at Clayton Lodge improved his health, but his feebleness increased and he could no longer write except with great difficulty.[120] Nevertheless, he entertained the faculty and students of the seminary at his Chicago residence in early February, 1884, and two months later welcomed two hundred and fifty guests who came at his invitation to greet President McCosh of Princeton College.[121] On April 30 he wired his son, who was then in New York City, to call upon Samuel J. Tilden with the hope that he would reconsider his decision not to be a candidate for the presidential nomination of his party. Except for several notes prepared by others for his signature and relating to his personal affairs, this telegram was McCormick's last communication.

That evening he suddenly weakened and was carried to his bed. He rallied four days later and hope for his recovery revived. His will to live mustered to his support his small reserve of strength, but it was insufficient. Old age, and not any one disease, struck him down. The relapse came on May 7, but his

---

[118] ‡C. H. McCormick to the Steward, Arlington Hotel, Apr. 29, 1883.

[119] N. F. McCormick to C. H. McCormick, Jr., Apr. 30, 1883.

[120] C. H. McCormick to Jas. McCormick, May 18, 1883, and to G. Pick, June 4, 1883; to "Dear Cousin," Sept. 7, 1883: "I hope I am getting the better of my rheumatism in my joints by increased strength in them while thankful the pain is slight." S. C. P. Miller, Princeton, N. J., to C. H. McCormick, Mch. 31, 1884.

[121] "Chicago Daily Tribune," Apr. 10, 1884, pp. 4, 7.

physicians refused to admit until the eleventh that he had lost his last fight. Gathering his family around his bedside early that morning, he led them in prayer and sang with them several old hymns of the church. Whispering, "It's all right. It's all right. I only want Heaven," he lapsed into unconsciousness. These were his last words. The end came at seven o'clock on the morning of the thirteenth of May.[122] Two days later a long cortège moved slowly from the home on Rush Street to Graceland Cemetery.[123]

Much was said and written at that time in honor of the inventor, but no words were more eloquent or fitting than the sheaf of ripe wheat and the floral reaper with its main wheel missing which stood beside his casket as a tribute from the workmen of his factory. In these was symbolized his outstanding service to his own and to later generations. Wherever in the annual harvest season men use machines to reap grain, there Cyrus Hall McCormick has his most enduring monument.

[122] The "Daily Inter Ocean," and the "Chicago Daily Tribune" of May 14, 1884. "The Interior," Aug. 7, 1884.

[123] "Chicago Evening Journal," May 15, 1884; "Chicago Daily News," May 16, 1884. Dr. Herrick Johnson and other Presbyterian clergymen conducted the funeral service. Among the honorary pall-bearers were Joseph Medill, C. A. Spring, Jr., Judge Drummond, Judge M. Skinner, Judge M. Tuley, W. C. Gray, and Dr. Isham. C. H. McCormick's will was signed and sealed on July 15, 1881. He bequeathed his Chicago and Richfield Springs residences to his widow. All his other property was left in trust to her and C. H. McCormick, Jr., who were also the executors. Nothing should be sold for five years. At the end of that time one-fifth of his estate should go to his widow, and the balance should be equally divided between his children when each reached the age of twenty-five. "Chicago Daily Tribune," May 20 and July 25, 1884.

BIBLIOGRAPHICAL GUIDE

The full title of each source given below will be found by referring to the designated page and foot-note of the text. Works infrequently cited in the biography are not included in this list.

	PAGE	FOOT-NOTE
"Agronomische Zeitung,"	416	26
"American Farmer,"	371	19
Ardrey, "The Harvesting Machine Industry,"	571	142
Aultman vs. Holley and Fittz,	78	40
"Bell's Weekly Messenger,"	422	45
Boyle,	65	1
Brown and Bartlett Extension Case,	375	27
"Daily Illinois State Journal,"	324	58
"Daily Illinois State Register,"	318	35
"Daily Inter Ocean,"	38	1
Dorsey Extension Case,	392	82
"Easter's Implement World,"	524	6
"Engineering,"	407	4
"Farm Implement News,"	370	14
"Farmer and Gardener,"	426	58
"Farmer's Magazine,"	406	3
"Frank Leslie's Illustrated Newspaper,"	399	97
"Gardeners' Chronicle,"	406	2
"Genesee Farmer,"	98	110
"Hutchinson," I,	43	13
"Iron,"	445	113
"Journal de l'Agriculture Pratique,"	415	23
Knight, "American Mechanical Dictionary,"	524	7
"Landwirtschaftliche Zeitung,"	409	8
"Lexington Gazette,"	100	3

INDEX

Adams, Augustus (*See,* Sylla, Philo, and Adams, Augustus)
Adams, Hugh, C. H. McC. & Co. and, 75, 107, 124; death of, 124; debt to McC. of, 103; home of, 104
Adriance, John P., Hinged-bar Pool and, 373ff; lawsuits of, 376n; mfrs. who licensed, 372, 375n, 394n, 398; machines made by, 368n, 372; patents of, 372, 373; South American sales of, 651
Agents, Civil War and, 83-85, 87, 89; freight rates and, 471, 714-715; Grangers and, 583-586, 588-589, 591; honesty of, 76, 87, 451, 453n, 511, 648; number of, 118, 124, 608, 704, 713; sales methods of, 76, 362, 426n, 460, 469-471, 476n, 488-492, 510, 602-603, 605n, 704-711, 731n; terms of appt. of, 87, 470, 486n, 488n, 583n, 586, 588, 604, 621n, 627n, 693-694, 704-712, 721; supervision by factory office of, 690, 704-712, 714; types of McC's foreign, 685
Albaret et Cie., McC's machines and, 424, 430, 432, 440, 446, 676
Algeria, McC's machines in, 415, 676
American Colonization Society, McC's aid to, 284
American Exchange in Europe, Ltd., McC's relations with, 157, 158
American Sunday School Union, McC's aid to, 298
American Tract Society, McC's aid to, 299
Anderson, "Jo," McC. and, 4, 282, 745
Appleby, John F., binders of, 552-555, 558ff, 627; Gorham *vs.*, 552,

553, 559-561; later career of, 571-572; licensees of, 554, 559ff, 724; McC. and, 552, 554, 557n, 558ff, 724; McC.-Gorham Pool and, 561ff
Argentina, harvesting machinery in, 651, 652n, 653-654, 685; immigration to, 644
Arizona, McC's mines in, 190-195
Atkins, Jearum, self-rake of, 393n, 394, 397n, 405
Atlantic & Pacific Telegraph Company, McC. and, 156
Aultman, Cornelius, "Buckeye" machines and, 371-373, 378n, 386-388, 452, 493, 541n, 546, 554, 588, 618, 701n; Chicago Fire and, 503n; Hinged-bar Pool and, 373ff; license from McC. of, 377; McC. sued by, 386-390, 569, 572; McC.-Gorham Pool and, 565, 568, 569; Self-Rake Pool and, 397n, 398n, 400; mentioned, 530n, 572, 588
Australia, farmers in, 658n; grain exports of, 655n; immigration to, 643, 644, 646n; McC's machines in, 654-660, 685n
Austria-Hungary, agrl. conditions in, 406, 427-428, 643, 645; McC's machines in, 416, 422, 427-428, 440, 443n, 444-445, 662; Vienna Exposition in, 419n

Baldwin, Henry, Jr., and Wm. D., relations of McC. with, 365n, 380-382, 384, 385n, 386n, 387-389, 390n, 400, 402n, 431, 531, 542n, 547, 548n, 757n
Ball, Ephraim, mower of, 371-373, 375n, 387, 414, 503n
Barlow, S. L. M., relations of McC. with, 158n, 167n, 168, 313, 739

777